▲ INDIVIDUAL INCOME TAX FORMULA

Income (broadly conceived)	$XX,XXX
Less: Exclusions	(X,XXX)
Gross income	$XX,XXX
Less: Deductions for adjusted gross income	(X,XXX)
Adjusted gross income	$XX,XXX
Less: Deductions from adjusted gross income—	
The greater of—	
The total itemized deductions	
or standard deduction	(X,XXX)
Personal and dependency exemptions	(X,XXX)
Taxable income	$XX,XXX

▲ BASIC STANDARD DEDUCTION AMOUNTS

	Standard Deduction Amount	
Filing Status	1996	1995
Single	$4,000	$3,900
Married, filing jointly	6,700	6,550
Surviving spouse	6,700	6,550
Head of household	5,900	5,750
Married, filing separately	3,350	3,275

▲ AMOUNT OF EACH ADDITIONAL STANDARD DEDUCTION FOR AGE & BLINDNESS

	Standard Deduction Amount	
Filing Status	1996	1995
Single	$1,000	$ 950
Married, filing jointly	800	750
Surviving spouse	800	750
Head of household	1,000	950
Married, filing separately	800	750

▲ PERSONAL AND DEPENDENCY EXEMPTION AMOUNT

1996:	$2,550
1995:	$2,500

CONCEPTS IN FEDERAL TAXATION

1997
EDITION

CONCEPTS IN FEDERAL TAXATION

1997
EDITION

KEVIN E. MURPHY
Oklahoma State University

CONTRIBUTING AUTHORS:

RICK L. CROSSER
Weber State University

MARK HIGGINS
University of Rhode Island

WEST PUBLISHING COMPANY
Minneapolis/St. Paul　　New York　　Los Angeles　　San Francisco

Copyediting: Polly Kummel
Composition: Parkwood Composition, Inc.
Index: Terry Casey
Part and Chapter opening art: Randy Miyake, Miyake Illustration.
Communication icon: Merry Sawdey/Shade Tree Designs
Production, prepress, printing, and binding: West Publishing Company.

WEST'S COMMITMENT TO THE ENVIRONMENT

In 1906, West Publishing Company began recycling materials left over from the production of books. This began a tradition of efficient and responsible use of resources. Today, 100% of our legal bound volumes are printed on acid-free, recycled paper consisting of 50% new paper pulp and 50% paper that has undergone a de-inking process. We also use vegetable-based inks to print all of our books. West recycles nearly 22,650,000 pounds of scrap paper annually—the equivalent of 187,500 trees. Since the 1960s, West has devised ways to capture and recycle waste inks, solvents, oils, and vapors created in the printing process. We also recycle plastics of all kinds, wood, glass, corrugated cardboard, and batteries and have eliminated the use of polystyrene book packaging. We at West are proud of the longevity and the scope of our commitment to the environment.

 PRINTED ON 10% POST CONSUMER RECYCLED PAPER  Printed with **Printwise** Environmentally Advanced Water Washable Ink

APPENDIX D

Statements on Responsibilities in Tax Practice are published for the guidance of members of the Institute and do not constitute enforceable standards. The statements have been approved by at least two-thirds of the members of the Responsibilities in Tax Practice Committee and the Tax Executive Committee. Statements containing recommended standards of responsibilities that are more restrictive than those established by the Internal Revenue Code, the Treasury Department, or the Institute's Code of Professional Conduct depend for their authority on the general acceptability of the opinions expressed. These statements are not intended to be retroactive.

*Copyright © 1994 by the
American Institute of Certified Public Accountants, Inc.
1211 Avenue of the Americas, New York, N.Y. 10036-8775
Reprinted with permission.*

Library of Congress Cataloging-in-Publication Data

Murphy, Kevin E.
    Concepts in federal taxation, 1997 edition / Kevin E. Murphy.
       p.   cm.
    Includes index.
    ISBN 0-314-07366-3 (hard) ISSN 1081-1338
    1. Taxation—Law and legislation—United States. I. Title.
KF6289.M87   1997a
343.7304—dc20
[347.3034]

                                                                              95-47062
                                                                                CIP

▲ BRIEF TABLE OF CONTENTS ▲

Preface *xxiii*

Introduction   xxix

▲ PART I
CONCEPTUAL FOUNDATIONS OF THE TAX LAW   1

CHAPTER 1   Federal Income Taxation—An Overview   2

CHAPTER 2   Income Tax Concepts   48

▲ PART II
GROSS INCOME   89

CHAPTER 3   Income Sources   90

CHAPTER 4   Income Exclusions   141

▲ PART III
DEDUCTIONS   183

CHAPTER 5   Introduction to Business Expenses   184

CHAPTER 6   Business Expenses   231

CHAPTER 7   Losses—Deductions and Limitations   277

▲ PART IV
INCOME TAX ENTITIES   325

CHAPTER 8   Taxation of Individuals   326

CHAPTER 9   Other Tax Entities   383

▲ PART V
PROPERTY TRANSACTIONS   433

CHAPTER 10   Acquisitions of Property   434

CHAPTER 11   Cost Recovery on Property: Depreciation,
             Depletion, and Amortization   481

APPENDIX TO CHAPTER 11
        MACRS Class Lives and
        MACRS Depreciation Schedules 527

CHAPTER 12 Property Dispositions 542

CHAPTER 13 Nonrecognition Transactions 589

APPENDIX TO CHAPTER 13
        Selected SIC Product Classes 621

▲ PART VI
TAX CONSIDERATIONS 635

CHAPTER 14 Other Factors Affecting Tax Liability 636

CHAPTER 15 Tax Research 684

APPENDIX A Tax Rate Schedules and Tax Tables A-1

APPENDIX B Tax Return Problem B-1

APPENDIX C Tax Forms C-1

APPENDIX D Statements on Responsibilities in Tax Practice D-1

GLOSSARY G-1
INDEX I-1

▲ TABLE OF CONTENTS ▲

Preface   xxiii

▲ INTRODUCTION   xxix
Why Study Federal Income Taxation   xxix
Significance of Tax Costs   xxx
Conservation of Wealth   xxxii
Taxes Influence Routine Decisions   xxxiii
Self-Protection   xxxiii

PART I
CONCEPTUAL FOUNDATIONS OF THE TAX LAW   1

▲ **CHAPTER 1**   Federal Income Taxation—An Overview   2
Introduction   3
Definition and Evaluation of a Tax   3
Definition of a Tax   3
Standards for Evaluating a Tax   5
Tax Rates and Structures   7
   Tax Rate Definitions   7
   Tax Rate Structures   8
Major Types of U.S. Taxes   11
Income Taxes   11
Employment Taxes   12
   Social Security Taxes   13
   Unemployment Taxes   14
Sales Tax   15
Property Taxes   15
Other Taxes   16
   Excise Taxes   16
   Wealth Transfer Taxes   16
Sources of Federal Income Tax Law   18
Federal Income Tax Terminology   19
Income   19
Deductions   21
Income Tax Rates   21
Tax Prepayments   23
Tax Credits   24
Filing Returns   24
Individual Income Tax Calculation   25
Deductions for Adjusted Gross Income   26
Deductions from Adjusted Gross Income   27
Personal and Dependency Exemptions   29

Tax Planning   29

   Mechanics of Tax Planning   29

      Timing Income and Deductions   30

      Income Shifting   33

   Tax Evasion and Tax Avoidance   34

Ethical Considerations in Tax Practice   35

Summary   38

Key Terms   38

Primary Tax Law Sources   39

Discussion Questions   40

Problems   41

Discussion Cases   46

Tax Planning Case   47

Ethics Discussion Case   47

▲ **CHAPTER 2**   Income Tax Concepts   48

Introduction   49

General Concepts   50

   Ability-to-Pay Concept   50

   Administrative Convenience Concept   51

   Arm's-Length Transaction Concept   52

   Pay-as-You-Go Concept   53

Accounting Concepts   54

   Entity Concept   54

      Assignment-of-Income Doctrine   57

   Annual Accounting Period Concept   58

      Accounting Method   58

      Tax Benefit Rule   59

      Substance-over-Form Doctrine   60

Income Concepts   61

   All-Inclusive Income Concept   61

   Legislative Grace Concept   62

   Capital Recovery Concept   63

   Realization Concept   63

      Claim-of-Right Doctrine   64

      Constructive Receipt Doctrine   65

      Comparing Claim of Right and Constructive Receipt   66

   Wherewithal-to-Pay Concept   67

Deduction Concepts   68

   Legislative Grace Concept   68

   Business Purpose Concept   68

   Capital Recovery Concept   71

Summary   73

Key Terms   74

Primary Tax Law Sources   74

Discussion Questions   76

Problems   77

Discussion Case   87

Tax Planning Case   87

Ethics Discussion Case   88

PART II
GROSS INCOME   89

▲ **CHAPTER 3**   Income Sources   90

Concept Review   91

Introduction   91

What Constitutes Income   92

  Income Is Derived from Labor and Capital   93

  Income as an Increase in Wealth   94

  What Constitutes Income: Current View   95

Common Income Sources   96

  Earned Income   96

  Unearned Income   98

  Rental and Royalty Income   98

  Annuities   99

  Calculation of Gain/Loss on Sale of Investments   101

  Income from Conduit Entities   102

  Transfers from Others   102

  Prizes and Awards   103

  Unemployment Compensation   103

  Social Security Benefits   103

  Alimony Received   107

  Imputed Income   108

  Below Market-Rate Loans   109

  Payment of Expenses by Others   113

  Bargain Purchases   113

Capital Gains and Losses—An Introduction   114

  Capital Gain-and-Loss Netting Procedure   115

  Tax Treatment of Capital Gains   117

  Tax Treatment of Capital Losses   117

  Capital Gains and Losses of Conduit Entities   118

Effect of Accounting Method   119

  Cash Method   119

  Exceptions Applicable to the Cash Method   120

  Accrual Method   121

  Exceptions Applicable to the Accrual Method   122

  Hybrid Method   123

  Exceptions Applicable to All Methods   123

  Installment Sales   123

  Long-Term Construction Contracts   124

Summary   124

Key Terms 126

Primary Tax Law Sources 126

Discussion Questions 128

Problems 129

Discussion Cases 139

Tax Planning Case 140

Ethics Discussion Case 140

▲ **CHAPTER 4**   Income Exclusions   141

Concept Review 142

Introduction 142

Donative Items 143

Gifts 144

Inheritances 145

Life Insurance Proceeds 145

Scholarships 147

Certain Death Benefits 148

Employment-Related Exclusions 148

Foreign Earned Income 149

Payments Made on Behalf of an Employee 149

Payments to Qualified Pension Plans 150

Group Term Life Insurance 151

Health and Accident Insurance Premiums 152

Meals and Lodging Provided by the Employer 153

General Fringe Benefits 154

Other Benefits Paid by an Employer 155

Employer Benefit Plans 155

Returns of Human Capital 157

Workers' Compensation 157

Damage Payments for Personal Injury or Sickness 158

Payments from Health and Accident Policies 159

Investment-Related Exclusions 160

Municipal Bond Interest 160

Stock Dividends 162

Discharge of Indebtedness 162

Improvements by a Lessee 165

Summary 165

Key Terms 167

Primary Tax Law Sources 167

Discussion Questions 169

Problems 170

Integrative Problems 178

Discussion Case 180

Tax Planning Case 181

Ethics Discussion Case 181

PART III
DEDUCTIONS 183

▲ **CHAPTER 5** Introduction to Business Expenses 184

Concept Review 185

Introduction 185

Reporting Deductions 188

Conduit Entity Reporting 189

Classification of Deductions 191

Profit-Motivated Expenditures 191

Trade or Business or Production-of-Income Expenses? 192

Trade or Business Expenses 193

Expenses for the Production of Income 194

Rental Activity 195

Personal Expenditures 197

Mixed Business and Personal Expenditures 197

Mixed-Use Assets 197

Mixed-Use Expenditures 198

Tests for Deductibility 199

Ordinary, Necessary, and Reasonable in Amount 199

Ordinary Expense 199

Necessary Expense 200

Reasonable in Amount 201

Not a Personal Expense 201

Not a Capital Expenditure 202

Repair-and-Maintenance Expense 204

Start-up Costs 204

Not Frustrate Public Policy 205

Expenses of an Illegal Business 206

Lobbying Expenses and Other Political Activities 206

Not Related to Tax-Exempt Income 207

Expenditure Must Be for Taxpayer's Benefit 208

Timing of Deductions—Effect of Accounting Method 208

Cash Method 209

Accrual Method 211

Related Party Accrued Expenses 215

Financial and Taxable Income Differences 215

Summary 217

Key Terms 218

Primary Tax Law Sources 218

Discussion Questions 220

Problems 221

Comprehensive Problem 228

Discussion Cases 229

Tax Planning Case 230

Ethics Discussion Case 230

▲ **CHAPTER 6**   Business Expenses   231

Concept Review   232

Introduction   232

Business Expenses   233

Entertainment, Auto, Travel, Gift, and Education Expenses   233

Meals and Entertainment   233

Auto Expenses   237

Travel Expenses   239

Business Gifts   241

Substantiation Requirements   242

Education Expenses   242

Compensation of Employees   243

Bad Debts   245

Other Business Expenses   247

Legal Fees   251

Limited Mixed-Use Expenses   251

Hobby Expenses   252

Vacation Home Expenses   254

Home Office Expenses   256

Summary   258

Key Terms   259

Primary Tax Law Sources   259

Discussion Questions   260

Problems   261

Integrative Problem   272

Discussion Cases   274

Tax Planning Case   275

Ethics Discussion Case   275

▲ **CHAPTER 7**   Losses—Deductions and Limitations   277

Concept Review   278

Introduction   278

Annual Losses   280

Net Operating Losses   281

Tax-Shelter Losses: An Overview   283

The At-Risk Rules   285

Passive Activity Losses   287

Passive Activity Definition   287

Types of Income   290

Taxpayers Subject to the Limits   291

General Rule for Passive Activities   292

Dispositions of Passive Activities   292

Exceptions for Rental Real Estate   295

Transaction Losses   298

Trade or Business Losses   299
   Business Casualty and Theft Losses   299
Investment-Related Losses   303
   Capital Losses   303
   Specially Treated Investment Losses   304
   Personal Use Losses   307
Summary   309
Key Terms   310
Primary Tax Law Sources   311
Discussion Questions   312
Problems   313
Comprehensive Problem   321
Discussion Cases   322
Tax Planning Case   322
Ethics Discussion Case   323

PART IV
INCOME TAX ENTITIES   325

▲ **CHAPTER 8**   Taxation of Individuals   326
Concept Review   327
Introduction   327
Personal and Dependency Exemptions   328
Dependency Requirements   329
   Gross Income Test   329
   Support Test   329
   Relationship or Member of Household Test   330
   Citizen or Residency Test   330
   Joint Return Test   331
Filing Status   331
Married, Filing Jointly   331
Married, Filing Separately   332
Single   332
Head of Household   333
Deductions for Adjusted Gross Income   334
Reimbursed Employee Business Expenses   335
   Accountable Reimbursement Plans   335
   Nonaccountable Reimbursement Plans   336
Deductions for Self-Employed Taxpayers   338
Retirement Plan Contribution Deductions   339
   Individual Retirement Accounts   340
Moving Expenses   341

Deductions from Adjusted Gross Income   342

Standard Deduction   342

Itemized Deductions   343

Medical Expenses   344

Taxes   346

Interest Expense   347

Charitable Contributions   350

Miscellaneous Itemized Deductions   352

**Itemized Deductions and Exemptions—Reductions
by High-Income Taxpayers   354**

Exemption and Standard Deduction Restrictions on Dependents   355

Calculating Tax Liability   356

Tax on Unearned Income of a Minor Child   357

Filing Requirements   358

Summary   358

Key Terms   359

Primary Tax Law Sources   359

Discussion Questions   360

Problems   362

Integrative Problems   370

Discussion Cases   375

Tax Planning Case   375

Ethics Discussion Case   376

APPENDIX TO CHAPTER 8
Comprehensive Tax Return Illustration   377

▲ **CHAPTER 9**   Other Tax Entities   383

Concept Review   384

Introduction   384

Corporations   385

Income Tax Considerations   386

Tax Rate Differentials   386

Personal Service Corporations   389

Owner-Employee Status   389

Special Rules for Corporations   391

Dividends-Received Deduction   392

Passive Activity Losses   393

Capital Loss Limitations   394

Charitable Contribution Limitations   395

Organizational Costs   397

Calculation of Taxable Income   397

Accounting Periods and Methods   398

Distributions to Shareholders   399

Multiple Corporations   400

Controlled Groups   400

Fiduciaries   402

Estates   402

Trusts   402

Income Taxation of Fiduciaries   403

Charitable Contributions   404

Accounting Periods   404

Exemption Amounts   404

Income Tax Calculation   404

Conduit Entities   405

Accounting Periods   406

Accounting Methods   407

Basis in Partnerships and S Corporations   407

Sole Proprietorships   409

Partnerships   410

Legal Characteristics   410

Partners Are Not Employees   411

Basis of Partnership Interest   412

Partnership Distributions   413

Partnership Terminations   413

Limited Liability Companies (LLCs)   414

Limited Liability Partnerships (LLPs)   414

S Corporations   415

Qualification Requirements   415

Revocation of the S Election   416

Change from C Corporation to S Corporation   416

Employee Status of Stockholders   416

Distributions and Basis Adjustments   417

Uses of Entities   417

Income Splitting   417

Summary   420

Key Terms   421

Primary Tax Law Sources   421

Discussion Questions   423

Problems   425

Discussion Cases   430

Tax Planning Cases   430

Ethics Discussion Case   431

PART V
PROPERTY TRANSACTIONS   433

▲ **CHAPTER 10**   Acquisitions of Property   434

Concept Review   435

Introduction   435

Classes of Property   436

The Property Investment Cycle   437

Adjusted Basis   438

Increases in Basis   439

Decreases in Basis   440

Basis in Conduit Entities   442

Property Dispositions   444

Initial Basis   445

Purchase of Assets   445

Determining the Amount Invested   445

Basis of a Bargain Purchase   447

Purchase of Multiple Assets   447

Purchase of a Business   448

Purchase of the Assets of a Business   448

Purchase of Corporate Stock   450

Constructed Assets   451

Specially Valued Property Acquisitions   451

Basis of Property Acquired by Gift   452

General Rule for Gift Basis   452

Split Basis Rule for Loss Property   453

Special Sales Price Basis   454

Holding Period   454

Basis of Property Acquired by Inheritance   454

Primary Valuation Date   455

Alternate Valuation Date   455

Distribution Date   456

Other Considerations   456

Property Acquired from a Spouse   457

Personal Use Property Converted to Business Use   458

General Rule for Basis   459

Split Basis Rule   459

Basis in Securities   460

Stock Dividends   461

Taxable Stock Dividends   462

Transfers of Assets to a Controlled Corporation   462

Wash Sale Stock Basis   463

Summary   464

Key Terms   467

Primary Tax Law Sources   467

Discussion Questions   468

Problems   469

Integrative Problem   478

Discussion Cases   479

Tax Planning Case   480

Ethics Discussion Case   480

▲ **CHAPTER 11**   Cost Recovery on Property:
                     Depreciation, Depletion, and Amortization   481

Concept Review   482

Introduction   482

Capital Recovery from Depreciation or Cost Recovery   484

Section 179 Election to Expense Assets   486

Qualified Taxpayers   486

Qualified Property   486

Limitations on Deduction   487

  Annual Deduction Limit   487

  Annual Investment Limit   489

  Active Trade or Business Income Limit   489

Modified Accelerated Cost Recovery (MACRS)   490

Property Subject to MACRS   491

Basis Subject to Cost Recovery   492

MACRS Recovery Period   492

MACRS Conventions   495

  Mid-quarter Convention   498

Depreciation Method Alternatives   499

Using MACRS Percentage Tables   501

MACRS Straight-line Election   503

Alternative Depreciation System (ADS)   504

Limitations on Listed Property   505

Listed Property in General   505

  Limitation on Passenger Autos   506

  Adequate Record Keeping   507

Depletion   507

Depletion Methods   508

Cost Depletion   508

Percentage Depletion   509

Intangible Assets   510

Summary   512

Key Terms   514

Primary Tax Law Sources   514

Discussion Questions   515

Problems   516

Integrative Problems   523

Discussion Cases   525

Tax Planning Cases   525

Ethics Discussion Case   526

APPENDIX TO CHAPTER 11
MACRS Class Lives and
MACRS Depreciation Schedules   527

▲ **CHAPTER 12**   Property Dispositions   542

Concept Review   543

Introduction   543

Realized Gain or Loss   545

Amount Realized   546

Effect of Debt Assumptions   548

Character of Gain or Loss   549

Capital Gains and Losses   549

Capital Asset Definition   550

Long-Term versus Short-Term Classification   550

Capital Gain-and-Loss Netting Procedure   551

Capital Gain Exclusion on Qualified Small Business Stock   555

Capital Gains and Losses—Planning Strategies   556

Net Capital Gain Position   556

Net Capital Loss Position   557

Short Sales   557

Worthless Securities   557

Basis of Securities Sold   559

Section 1231 Gains and Losses   560

Definition of Section 1231 Property   561

Section 1231 Netting Procedure   561

Dispositions of Rental Activities   565

Depreciation Recapture   565

Section 1245 Recapture Rule   567

Section 1250 Recapture Rule   567

Installment Sales of Depreciable Assets   569

Section 1245 and Section 1250 Properties   570

Summary   571

Key Terms   573

Primary Tax Law Sources   573

Discussion Questions   573

Problems   575

Integrative Problem   584

Comprehensive Problems   585

Discussion Cases   586

Tax Planning Cases   587

Ethics Discussion Case   588

▲ **CHAPTER 13**   Nonrecognition Transactions   589

Concept Review   590

Introduction   590

Rationale for Nonrecognition   591

Commonalities of Nonrecognition Transactions   591

Like-Kind Exchanges   596

Exchange Requirement   596

Like-Kind Property Requirements   598

Effect of Boot   601
  Receipt of Boot   601
Related Party Exchanges   605
Carryover of Tax Attributes   606
Involuntary Conversions   607
Treatment of Involuntary Conversion Gains and Losses   607
Qualified Replacement Property   609
Sale of a Principal Residence   610
Principal Residence   610
Replacement Period   611
Deferral of Gain   612
Sale of a Principal Residence—Taxpayers Older Than 55   614
Gain Exclusion Requirements   614
One-Time Exclusion of Gain   615
Interaction of Deferral and Exclusion Provisions   616
Summary   617
Key Terms   618
Primary Tax Law Sources   618
Discussion Questions   619
Problems   620
Comprehensive Problem   627
Discussion Cases   627
Tax Planning Cases   628
Ethics Discussion Case   629

APPENDIX TO CHAPTER 13
Selected SIC Product Classes   621

PART VI
TAX CONSIDERATIONS   635

▲ **CHAPTER 14**   Other Factors Affecting Tax Liability   636
Concept Review   637
Introduction   637
Accounting Periods   637
Limitations on Choice of Taxable Year   639
  Partnership Limitations   639
  S Corporation Limitations   641
Accounting Methods   642
Restrictions on Use of the Cash Method   643
Long-Term Construction Contracts   644
  The Lookback Method   645

Taxpayers Exempt from Percentage-of-Completed-Contract Method 647

Accounting for Inventories 647

Determining Inventory Cost 648

Inventory Flow Assumptions 650

Electing LIFO 651

Income Tax Credits 652

Business Tax Credits 652

Investment Tax Credit 652

Foreign Tax Credit 652

Research and Experimental Credit 654

Rehabilitation Tax Credit 655

Individual Tax Credits 656

Earned Income Credit 657

Child and Dependent Care Credit 658

The Alternative Minimum Tax 660

Basic AMT Computation 661

AMT Adjustments 663

AMT Preferences 667

AMT Exemptions 668

AMT Tax Credits 668

Tax Planning and the AMT 670

Key Terms 671

Primary Tax Law Sources 671

Discussion Questions 672

Problems 674

Discussion Cases 682

Tax Planning Case 682

Ethics Discussion Case 683

▲ **CHAPTER 15** Tax Research 684

Introduction 685

Primary Sources of Federal Income Tax Law 685

Legislative Sources 685

The U.S. Constitution 685

Internal Revenue Code of 1986 687

Tax Treaties 691

Administrative Sources 691

Treasury Regulations 691

Revenue Rulings and Procedures 692

Acquiescence and Nonacquiescence 692

Other Pronouncements 693

Judicial Sources 693

Trial Courts 694

Appellate Courts 695

Supreme Court 695

Citations to Primary Authorities   695
   Committee Reports   695
   Code and Regulations   696
   Other IRS Pronouncements   697
   Court Decisions   697

Secondary Sources of Federal Income Tax Law   698
Tax Services   698
Citators   699
Tax Periodicals   700
Computer-Assisted Tax Research   700

Tax Research   701
Tax Compliance versus Tax Planning   701
Step 1: Establish the Facts and Determine the Issues   701
Step 2: Locate the Relevant Authorities   702
Step 3: Assess the Importance of the Authorities   702
   Code and Regulations   702
   Pronouncements   703
   Court Decisions   703
Step 4: Reach Conclusions, Make Recommendations,
   and Communicate the Results   704

Comprehensive Research Example   704
Step 1: Establish the Facts and Determine the Issues   704
Step 2: Locate the Relevant Authorities   704
Step 3: Assess the Importance of the Authorities   705
   The Code   705
   Regulations   706
   Court Decision   707
Step 4: Reach Conclusions, Make Recommendations,
   and Communicate the Results   707

The Audit and Appeal Process within the IRS   707
Tax Return Selection Processes   708
Types of Examinations   708
Settlement Procedures   709
Administrative Appeals   709

Summary   710
Key Terms   710
Primary Tax Law Sources   711
Discussion Questions   711
Research Problems   713
Income Problems   713
Deduction Problems   714
Loss Problems   717
Property Problems   718
Accounting Methods/Procedure Problems   720

▲ **APPENDIX A**   Tax Rate Schedules and Tax Tables   A-1

▲ **APPENDIX B**   Tax Return Problem   B-1

▲ **APPENDIX C**   Tax Forms   C-1

▲ **APPENDIX D**   Statements on Responsibilities
in Tax Practice   D-1

Glossary   G-1
Index   I-1

Concepts in Federal Taxation is designed for use in an introductory tax course. The textbook provides a conceptual approach that is new to teaching introductory tax materials. The book is sufficiently rigorous for those students who will go on to specialize in the area of taxes but is unlikely to intimidate those who plan to pursue other areas of accounting and business.

The 1997 edition has been revised to make it easier to implement the teaching objectives of the Accounting Education Change Commission. The writing assignment icon has been replaced by a communications icon. The communications problems instruct the student to perform a specific task, such as writing a letter to a client or drafting a memorandum to a supervisor explaining the tax effects. To avoid clutter in the text, the problems designed to enhance critical thinking are highlighted as such in the solutions manual. The problem sets have been expanded and altered to provide more choices of problems. This edition adds 20 percent new problems and modifies 30 percent of the existing problems. In addition, Appendix B is a new tax return problem, and all integrative and comprehensive problems have been replaced or modified. The in-depth discussion of the Accelerated Cost Recovery System in Chapter 11 has been eliminated and the chapter revised to enhance the understanding of the Modified Accelerated Cost Recovery System. The new electronic study guide, *Tax Tutor*, will allow instructors to use class time more efficiently.

As the 1997 edition went to press, Congress was considering legislation that would affect material in the text. If such legislation is enacted, a supplement explaining the changes and how they affect tax law and filing procedures will be distributed free of charge with the text. The supplement will include new problems that correspond to the changes. The supplement may also be obtained from the Murphy Concepts section on West Publishing Company's World Wide Web home page (http://www.westpub.com/Educate).

The Conceptual Approach

This textbook evolved as a solution to a problem that has frustrated academicians for many years in teaching the first tax course at the undergraduate level. The problem is what I refer to as the "technical approach." The technical approach treats income tax in such great depth that the first-time tax student has difficulty understanding the myriad rules, exceptions to the general rule, and exceptions to the exceptions. As a result, students tend to view the first tax course as a long string of unrelated topics that they must memorize in order to pass the course. The premise of the conceptual approach is that what is important at the introductory level is that students gain a conceptual view of income tax law and be able to relate the concepts to basic aspects of everyday economic life. In the long run, all students taking the course will benefit from gaining more general knowledge than an introductory tax course usually provides.

Chapter 2 develops the conceptual framework and uses it to explain the operation of the tax system in general. Each subsequent chapter begins with a brief review of the concepts used in that chapter's discussion. Students are encouraged to return to Chapter 2 and to review the concepts whenever they are uncertain about the application of a particular concept. Each chapter presents the tax law in terms of the appropriate concepts.

The approach of this textbook is consistent with the way real learning takes place. Real learning is the ability to store information in long-term memory (called *propositions*). As new information arrives in short-term memory, it combines with stored propositions to form new propositions. It is this linkage of prior memory with new information that is the key to learning. Providing the conceptual framework up front creates in long-term memory basic propositions about income tax law. The brief review of these propositions at the beginning of each chapter further stimulates the memory. As new information is introduced in the chapter, it combines with the stored concepts—which makes it easier to learn the material. In addition, using each chapter's material to link the concepts highlights the integrative nature of tax law and dispels the notion that tax law is a subject that can be mastered only through memorization.

Chapter Pedagogy

The decision to use the conceptual approach in this textbook was based on the desire to make the text more "student friendly" by providing many examples that use familiar situations. The literature of cognitive psychology tells us that extensive elaborations lead to greater recall. Elaboration is the process of adding something to new information to make it more meaningful. The examples in this book are elaborations designed to add substance to the tax law being discussed, which is why this book has many more examples than other textbooks. The examples are presented in a question-and-discussion format that fully explains the question being asked.

The textbook also takes a different approach to footnotes. Rather than interrupt the text with extensive footnoting of specific subsections or paragraphs of the Internal Revenue Code, the primary tax law sources appear at the end of each chapter with explanatory notations. This approach uses more references to Treasury regulations, Revenue rulings, and court cases than usually appear in an introductory tax book. This allows the student who wishes to explore a topic further to find the primary tax law sources, which are more explanatory than the Internal Revenue Code.

End-of-Chapter Material

Problems.   Many end-of-chapter problems do not call for mathematical solutions. Rather, they require the student to explain the appropriate treatment, based on the concepts. The problems are a valuable learning tool that encourages students to apply the concepts in order to arrive at a solution. More traditional problems are also provided; all can be solved by reference to the examples in the chapter and they address every aspect of the chapter. The problems take advantage of the richness and vastness of income tax to show students how the concepts apply in practice. In most cases, two or more problems are provided for each aspect. This allows the instructor to choose problems of varying levels of difficulty, based on the instructor's desired level of emphasis for each topic.

Other Features.   In addition to discussion questions and problems covering the material in each chapter, various other material is provided. *Tax planning cases* require students to use the materials in the chapter to devise an optimal tax plan for the facts given. *Discussion cases* are used to stimulate thinking about issues raised in the chapter. *Ethics discussion cases* provide ethical dilemmas related to the chapter material that the student must resolve according to the Statements on Responsibilities in Tax Practice of the American Institute of Certified Accountants

(AICPA). Chapter 1 includes a discussion of the ethical considerations in tax practice, particularly with regard to the AICPA's Statements. The complete set of AICPA statements appears in Appendix D. All case material can be used to emphasize communication in the tax curriculum. As a further aid to those who wish to integrate communication assignments in their courses, problems that are amenable to such use have been designated with a communications icon (see margin). The instructor's manual (discussed later) provides specific suggestions on use of the various materials to emphasize communication and group work in the introductory tax course. *Comprehensive problems* cover a number of issues discussed within the chapter. *Integrative problems* require the student to bring together material learned in previous chapters and combine it with information in the current chapter. Integrative problem 70 in Chapter 4 provides the information necessary to calculate the gross income of a married couple. Integrative problem 82 in Chapter 8 follows up by providing the information necessary to complete the tax return for the married couple. This approach allows the student to do a fairly complex tax return in two stages, spreading the work out over the semester rather than preparing it for a single due date. This two-stage tax return problem has been recast in the instructor's manual with the appropriate tax-reporting documents for those who would like to assign a tax return problem but find the problem in Appendix B unsuited to their needs.

The tax return problem in Appendix B is presented in three phases, which correspond to the organization of the text. Each phase presents some information in actual tax documents that a taxpayer might receive from commonplace third-party sources. Upon working through Appendix B, the student will have completed a fairly complex tax return. The problem can be worked with tax preparation software or manually. This approach familiarizes students with tax reporting and tax compliance forms and relates to the material as it is being covered, rather than in one burst at the end of the semester.

Organization

The entire textbook can be covered in one semester, although some instructors will find it convenient to skip selected chapters. For example, Chapter 15 discusses the basic aspects of tax research. This chapter can be omitted by those who would like to spend more time on other aspects of the course. Instructors who have their students engage in tax research during the first tax course will want to use Chapter 15 early in the course.

By its very nature, the introductory tax course contains much material that relates almost solely to individual taxpayers. I have tried to deemphasize the individual aspects of taxation and focus on transactions common to all tax entities. In this regard, the mechanics of the individual tax calculation are not discussed in depth until Chapter 8. Chapter 1 introduces the individual tax formula and briefly discusses the for versus from adjusted gross income distinction that is unique to individuals. This allows the text to focus more on the overall scheme of taxation—what is income, what is a deduction, and so on—with individual tax return preparation a secondary issue. Further, itemized deductions are not accorded the traditional in-depth treatment. Again, the focus is on the more common itemized deductions, and elaborate technical detail is omitted for the more unusual items.

The text is organized into five parts, each of which contains chapters of related materials. The flow of the material is designed to lead the student into the calculation of taxable income and the problems associated with various aspects of the calculation.

Part I introduces the student to the conceptual foundations of tax law. Chapter 1 provides an overview of the tax system, briefly discusses other types of taxes, outlines the general income tax calculation, discusses the nature of tax planning, and introduces ethical considerations of tax practice. Chapter 2 develops the conceptual foundation of the income tax system, using a framework that discusses and illustrates the underlying concepts.

Part II addresses the calculation of gross income. Chapter 3 classifies various sources of income and explains the common problems encountered within each income classification. Its overview of property transactions differentiates the taxation of capital gains and losses from other sources of income. Accounting methods that affect the recognition of income are introduced at the end of the chapter. Chapter 4 classifies allowable exclusions from income according to the purpose of the exclusion and discusses the problems commonly encountered with exclusions in each category.

Part III discusses the deductions that are allowed in computing taxable income. Chapter 5 provides an overview of the general criteria necessary to obtain a tax deduction. The chapter concludes with a discussion of the effect of a taxpayer's accounting method on the timing of deductions. Chapter 6 addresses specific business expense deductions that are subject to special rules and/or limitations. Deductions for losses are covered in Chapter 7. Annual losses are distinguished from transaction losses, and the limitations on the deductibility of the two types of losses are discussed. This includes the treatment of net operating losses, the at-risk rules, passive losses, capital losses, and casualty and theft losses.

Part IV provides an overview of the taxation of various types of income tax entities. The unique features of the individual income tax calculation and deductions of individual taxpayers are discussed in Chapter 8. Chapter 9 introduces the general tax treatment of other types of income tax entities, including corporations, estates, trusts, partnerships, limited liability entities, and S corporations.

Part V covers property transactions. The property investment cycle is introduced in Chapter 10, and common acquisition problems are discussed. Chapter 11 provides the allowable deductions for property expenditures. This includes the MACRS depreciation system, depletion deductions, and allowable amortization deductions. Dispositions of property are discussed in Chapter 12. The calculation of the gain or loss from a disposition of property is explained, and the classification of gains and losses from property is discussed. Chapter 13 covers the common nonrecognition situations related to property dispositions, including exchanges, involuntary conversions, and sales of a principal residence.

Part VI considers other aspects of the income tax law. Chapter 14 provides an overview of other items that affect tax liability. Accounting periods and methods are discussed in more detail in this chapter. The chapter also discusses the general operation of the alternative minimum tax and tax credits. Chapter 15 provides the mechanics of tax research. As mentioned earlier, instructors wishing to introduce their students to tax research will want to introduce this chapter early in the course.

Supplementary Materials

Materials have been specifically developed to aid the instructor in teaching this new approach to the introductory course. This includes an instructor's manual, a solutions manual, transparency masters, a test bank, a reader, and *Tax Tutor*. In addition, other West supplementary materials are available to adopters.

Instructor's Manual. The *Instructor's Manual* includes suggested syllabi for a one-semester course and a two-quarter course. Syllabi of several adopters of the 1996 edition are provided so that users can see how other instructors are using the material in their courses. In addition, the materials include suggestions for incorporating communication and group assignments in the income tax curriculum. Each chapter begins with an overview of the chapter and specific teaching tips related to the chapter. Each chapter also presents specific ideas for communication and group assignments in that chapter. This is followed by a set of lecture notes for the chapter. The lecture notes are designed to assist the instructor in organizing classroom activities and include suggestions for incorporating material from the problems in the instructor's lecture. Each chapter also features an annotated bibliography on selected topics from each chapter for instructors who wish to have their students explore additional aspects of these topics. The instructor's manual is available on floppy disk to allow instructors to easily edit the material for their specific classroom needs.

Solutions Manual.   The *Solutions Manual* provides in-depth discussions of the solutions to the end-of-chapter material. The actual text of each discussion question and problem are reproduced with the solution. This makes it easier for instructors to integrate the problem material in their lecture notes. A chart at the beginning of each chapter cross references problems in the 1996 edition with their counterparts in the 1997 edition. The chart notes any change made to the problem in the 1997 edition. A second chart lists all problems in the 1997 edition and describes the topic of each problem. To assist instructors in developing their problem assignments, both charts are coded to flag problems developed for specific purposes. Critical thinking, communications skills, and comprehensive and integrative problems are all designated in the charts.

Transparency Masters.   A separate set of *Transparency Masters* provides overheads of solutions to all problems and cases for use in the classroom.

Test Bank.   The *Test Bank* that accompanies this book includes a variety of testing approaches. The material is designed to help instructors fashion exams that are consistent with a conceptual teaching approach. This includes matching questions, multiple choice questions, short answer questions, and comprehensive problems. Part of the package accompanying this book is *WESTEST*™ 3.1, software for producing tests and examinations.

Reader.   *Insights: Readings in Federal Taxation,* 1997 Edition, provides articles from leading tax and popular journals that instructors can use to enhance students' appreciation of the importance of taxation. There are several articles for each chapter. The articles present additional background and interesting applications of the chapter material to real situations. This item is for sale at a nominal charge.

Tax Tutorial.   The *Tax Tutor,* developed by John Price of the University of North Texas, is an electronic study guide customized for *Concepts in Federal Taxation.* The *Tax Tutor* reviews each major topic in the chapter and asks students to complete the related interactive self-study questions. Students who answer the questions incorrectly are prompted to review the related material and redo the problem. When the student has completed all the work, the program administers a chapter exam. The software is flexible, allowing instructors to use the *Tax Tutor* however they deem most appropriate. It can function solely as a suggested study tool, or the instructor can compile the exam results and use them in the course grading scheme. This item is for sale at a nominal charge.

Other Supplementary Materials.   In addition to the materials developed specifically for this textbook, the following West Publishing products are available:

- *West® CD-ROM Federal Tax Library*™ (Compact Disc with Read-Only Memory). The library provides a complete desktop tax research library. Qualified adopters receive one subscription to the complete *Federal Tax Library* through August 31, 1996.

- *WESTLAW®.* WESTLAW is a computer-assisted tax and legal research service that provides access to hundreds of valuable information sources, including the Dow Jones News/Retrieval Database. Qualified adopters receive six free hours of WESTLAW during unrestricted hours (restricted hours are 12:30 P.M. to 5:00 P.M. EST).

- *Tax Legislation Update.* If necessary, a supplement covering new tax legislation affecting the text will be distributed free of charge to adopters.

- *World Wide Web Site Access.* Adopters will have access to the Murphy Concepts section of West Publishing Company's home page on the World Wide Web (http://www.westpub.com/Educate). Supplements for new tax legislation and other information updating the book and supplements will be available for downloading and printing.

- *TurboTax®.* The tax preparation software by Chipsoft, Inc., is a best-selling tax preparation software package. *TurboTax* can be used to solve the comprehensive problems and the problems in Appendix B. The *TurboTax* package, available for student purchase, includes disks bound with a workbook by Sam Hicks. *MacIntax®* and *TurboTax® for Windows®* are also available.

Acknowledgments

The completion of this project required the help of many individuals. I am deeply indebted to my colleague, John Wilguess, who provided valuable insight and overview throughout. Will Yancey, Texas Christian University, Bobbie C. Martindale, Dallas Baptist University, Martha L. Wartick, University of Missouri at St. Louis, and Rick Walter, University of Louisville, have made significant suggestions for improving the text and related materials. Joseph P. Matoney, University of Rhode Island, assisted in the design of the tax return problem. Doug Laufer, Weber State University, assisted in the preparation of the instructor's manual and the test bank. James Young, George Mason University, generously provided advance information on the 1997 inflation adjustments.

The following reviewers provided valuable suggestions about the revisions for the 1997 edition: Rick Walter, University of Louisville; David S. Hulse, University of Kentucky; John Price, University of North Texas; Will Yancey, Texas Christian University; Jamie T. Doran, Muhlenberg College; Kathy Krawczyk, North Carolina State University; and Betsy Willis, Baylor University.

Secretarial assistance was provided by Lois Pazienza, Cherry Brown, Saundra Manzer, Linda Wheeler, and Beverly Dunham.

I would like to thank the copyeditor, Polly Kummel, for her outstanding work on this project. Lastly, the authors would like to thank all the talented individuals at West Publishing who have helped us with this project (especially Rick Leyh, Brent Gordon, Jayne Lindesmith, and John Tuvey).

Suggestions

Concepts in Federal Taxation will be revised annually. I encourage all adopters to participate in the continuing development of the book by providing comments and/or suggestions for improving the textbook and supplementary materials. Please address these comments to me at Oklahoma State University or to Rick Leyh, Editor, West Educational Publishing Company, 1515 Capital of Texas Highway South, Suite 402, Austin, Texas 78746.

Kevin E. Murphy

▲ INTRODUCTION ▲

If you are beginning the study of the federal income tax law and plan to become a tax attorney or accountant, why you are taking this course is obvious. But if you want to become a management accountant or auditor, why should you study federal income taxation? Don't accountants rely on tax specialists to do tax research and prepare tax returns? Better yet, why should a business executive, an attorney, a physician, or a farmer take a tax course? They too can, and often do, have professional tax advisers to take care of their tax problems. The heart of the answer lies in the fact that most economic transactions have an income tax effect.

The income tax law influences personal decisions of individuals. The decision to buy a house instead of renting one may depend on the after-tax cost of the alternatives. Although the payment of rent reimburses the owner of the dwelling for mortgage interest and property tax, a tenant cannot deduct the cost of renting a home. However, a homeowner can save income tax by deducting home mortgage interest and property tax and perhaps reduce the after-tax cost of buying relative to renting.

WHY STUDY FEDERAL INCOME TAXATION

▲ **EXAMPLE 1** Zola lives in an apartment she rents for $700 per month. She is considering purchasing a house, which will require an initial cash outlay of $5,000 and monthly payments of $850. Although none of the $5,000 initial down payment is deductible, $800 of the monthly payment is deductible as interest expense. Assuming that Zola earns 6% on her investments and is in the 28% tax rate bracket, what is the after-tax monthly cost of purchasing the house?

Discussion: Assuming that Zola itemizes her deductions, the $800 interest payment will be deductible. Her taxable income will be reduced by $800 per month, resulting in tax savings of $224 ($800 × 28%). This leaves her with a net after-tax house payment of $626. However, she will lose interest income on the $5,000 investment of $25 per month [$5,000 × (6% × 1/12)]. She will not have to pay any tax on the lost interest, resulting in an after-tax interest loss of $18 [$25 − ($25 × 28%)]. Her net after-tax monthly cost of purchasing the house is $644 ($626 + $18). Because this is less than her rent of $700, Zola will come out ahead by $56 per month by purchasing the house.

This analysis of Zola's investment in a house considers only the tax aspects of the investment. Clearly, other factors influence the decision to purchase a house—potential appreciation in value, the intangible value of owning your own home, and so on. The point is that the tax consequences are one objective factor to consider when making various decisions, but they are rarely the sole and/or controlling factor.

Other personal decisions are often influenced by tax savings. For example, a taxpayer may decide to accelerate or defer charitable donations or elective medical treatment to claim the deductions in the year that results in the most significant tax savings. Even child-care decisions may be based on the availability of tax savings in the form of a child-care tax credit.

▲ **EXAMPLE 2** On January 1 of each year, Steve gives $2,000 to his church. For 1996, Steve's income is more than double its usual amount because of a one-time gain from a sale of stock. In a typical year, Steve is in the 28% tax rate bracket. Because of his increased income in 1996, Steve estimates that he will be in the 36% tax rate bracket, but his income will return to normal in 1997. What steps might Steve take to reduce his tax bill?

Discussion: Instead of waiting until January 1, 1997, to make his regular $2,000 donation, which will reduce his tax by $560 ($2,000 × 28%), Steve could pay the contribution in 1996. By taking the deduction in 1996 when he is in the 36% tax rate bracket, Steve saves $720 ($2,000 × 36%) in tax. By accelerating his $2,000 charitable contribution by a few days, he saves an extra $160 in tax ($720 − $560).

From these examples, you can see that income taxes can and do have an influence on routine decisions. However, the cost of the income tax is more than just the outlay for the tax liability. A knowledge of the income tax laws enables taxpayers to make decisions that can reduce these other costs. By being familiar with the tax laws, an individual can enter into transactions that will provide the best tax result for both the taxpayer and the taxpayer's family. By minimizing the income tax burden, taxpayers conserve wealth that can be put to other uses. Last, taxpayers are responsible for reporting their correct taxable income to the government. Knowing the tax laws protects against audits by the IRS that could result in additional tax owed and penalties for improper reporting of the tax liability.

Significance of Tax Costs

Keeping records and filling out forms to comply with the tax law can consume a substantial amount of time. Table I–1 presents the IRS's estimates of the time involved in record keeping, learning about the tax law, preparing a return, and assembling the various commonly filed tax forms. As you can see, the IRS estimates that completing and filing the basic tax return form (Form 1040) requires more than 11 hours on average. When you consider that many taxpayers file a

▲ **Table I–1**

ESTIMATED TAX RETURN
PREPARATION TIME,
INTERNAL REVENUE
SERVICE—1995

SOURCE: Internal Revenue Service,
Form 1040 Instructions, 1995.

Estimated Preparation Time

The time needed to complete and file the following forms will vary depending on individual circumstances. The estimated average times are			
Form	**Record Keeping**	**Learning About the Law or the Form**	**Preparing the Form**	**Copying, Assembling, and Sending the Form to the IRS**
Form 1040	3 hr., 8 min.	2 hr., 54 min.	4 hr., 43 min.	53 min.
Sch. A (1040)	2 hr., 32 min.	26 min.	1 hr., 10 min.	27 min.
Sch. B (1040)	33 min.	8 min.	17 min.	20 min.
Sch. C (1040)	6 hr., 26 min.	1 hr., 10 min.	2 hr., 5 min.	35 min.
Sch. C-EZ (1040)	46 min.	4 min.	18 min.	20 min.
Sch. D (1040)	51 min.	42 min.	1 hr., 1 min.	41 min.
Sch. E (1040)	2 hr., 52 min.	1 hr., 7 min.	1 hr., 16 min.	35 min.
Sch. EIC (1040)		2 min.	4 min.	5 min.
Sch. F (1040):				
Cash Method	4 hr., 2 min.	35 min.	1 hr., 14 min.	20 min.
Accrual Method	4 hr., 22 min.	25 min.	1 hr., 19 min.	20 min.
Sch. R (1040)	20 min.	15 min.	22 min.	35 min.
Sch. SE (1040):				
Short	20 min.	13 min.	11 min.	14 min.
Long	26 min.	22 min.	34 min.	20 min.

multitude of forms and schedules to detail their tax affairs, the time involved in complying with the tax law is quite substantial.

Tax compliance also may cost a taxpayer money. Taxpayers must weigh the cost of the time and investment needed to prepare their own tax returns, the out-of-pocket cost of hiring a tax preparer to prepare the return, and the risk of additional time and monetary costs for any errors. Thus, taxpayers need to choose whether to save money and spend the time to prepare their own tax returns or to pay to have someone else help to determine the proper amount of income tax.

When deciding whether to prepare their own returns, taxpayers should be aware that the amount of income tax shown on the return may contain errors or differences of opinion that may be found in an IRS audit. These differences of opinion can result from a taxpayer's or the tax preparer's lack of familiarity with the tax law and how it applies to the taxpayer. Similarly, the IRS agent performing the audit may not fully understand the law as it applies to a particular situation. In addition to clerical mistakes, tax return errors can be the result of inadequate communication between a taxpayer and tax preparer. A tax audit may reveal that the taxpayer either is entitled to a refund or owes more tax. If you are entitled to a refund, you have lost the use of the money while it was held by the U.S. Treasury. If you have to pay more tax, you will probably have to pay extra costs in the form of penalties and interest on the tax you owe. An audit of your return will require an additional investment of your personal time and quite likely additional out-of-pocket costs for professional tax advice. In addition, many taxpayers are intimidated when facing an income tax audit.

As your involvement in professional activities increases, taxes and the costs of compliance grow in importance. If you are like most taxpayers, you will want to pay the least tax required by the law. You will also want to spend as little time and money as possible to satisfy the compliance requirements. As Table I–2 shows, in 1970 an average taxpayer worked approximately 116 days to pay federal, state, and local taxes. By 1995, the time a person had to work to pay taxes had increased by 8.6 percent, to 126 days. In 1995, a taxpayer worked about one-third (34.5 percent) of the year to pay taxes. Figure I–1 divides an eight-hour work day into the minutes necessary to pay typical expenses. An average person worked 1 hour and 49 minutes each day to pay federal taxes and 57 minutes a day to pay state and local taxes during 1995. Thus, 2 hours and 46 minutes of each working day are devoted to the payment of taxes. The time worked to pay taxes is almost the same as the time worked to pay for household, food and tobacco, and health care

▲ Table I–2

TAX FREEDOM DAY

Tax Year	Freedom Day	Number of Days	Increase in Days	% of Year
1950	April 3	93		25.5
1960	April 16*	107	13	29.3
1970	April 26	116	10	31.8
1980	May 1*	122	6	33.3
1991	May 3	123	-0-	33.7
1992	May 2*	123	-0-	33.6
1993	May 3	123	-0-	33.7
1994	May 5	125	2	34.2
1995	May 6	126	1	34.5

*Leap year caused Tax Freedom Day to appear one day early.
SOURCE: Tax Foundation, *Tax Features*, May 1995, p. 1.

▲ **Figure I–1**

TAX BITE IN THE
EIGHT-HOUR DAY

SOURCE: Tax Foundation, *Tax Features*, May 1995, p. 3.

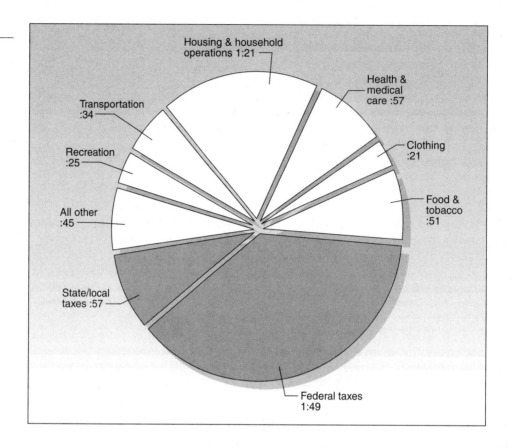

costs, 3 hours and 9 minutes. As Table I–2 and Figure I–1 demonstrate, the amounts paid for taxes represent major expenditures for the typical taxpayer.

Conservation of Wealth

An understanding of basic tax concepts and planning can often help conserve wealth by reducing taxes. To reduce taxes, you need to be able to recognize potential planning situations and problems. Because you know your financial affairs better than anyone else, you are in the best position to spot potential tax-saving opportunities. You should never wait for your tax adviser to find new ways to save you taxes. Although a competent tax adviser will know about tax-planning techniques and current tax developments, you will be more familiar than an adviser is with your financial affairs and objectives. A tax adviser is best used in the same way you use other professionals. When you visit your physician, you usually describe the symptom that brought you to the office to help the doctor identify the proper treatment. When you visit your attorney for a legal problem, you take along the information necessary to help the lawyer identify the legal issues. In both instances, you evaluate information and decide when you need professional assistance. Likewise, you will need to evaluate information, based on your understanding of the tax laws, to determine when you need to consult a professional tax adviser.

▲ **EXAMPLE 3**   Gwen, 19, is a full-time student at State University. Her parents pay all her expenses, which total $12,000 a year. Gwen does not have any other source of support, and she does not pay any income tax. Gwen's father, Marty, owns a substantial portfolio of stock that earns $12,000 in income each year. Marty is in the 31% tax rate bracket.

Discussion: A tax plan could save Marty money by transferring ownership of the stock portfolio to Gwen, who is in a lower tax bracket. Marty pays $3,720 ($12,000 × 31%) in tax on the investment income. The amount of income left after paying tax is $8,280 ($12,000 − $3,720).

If Marty gave the stock portfolio to Gwen as a gift (which is not subject to income tax), Gwen would be taxable on the income at a lower tax rate than her father. Assuming the $12,000 in investment income is taxed at 15%, Gwen's tax on the income would be $1,800. The family could save $1,920 ($3,720 − $1,800) in tax by shifting the income to Gwen. The amount of income left after paying tax is increased to $10,200 ($12,000 − $1,800).

Taxes Influence Routine Decisions

An auditor, management accountant, attorney, physician, or a farmer may never prepare a business tax return. Yet, they need a general understanding of the tax effects of their daily business decisions. For example, an auditor might find that an improperly recorded transaction results in an undisclosed tax liability or refund. A managerial accountant may need to consider the tax effects of buying or selling plant assets or acquiring a new business. To provide reliable advice to clients, lawyers often need a general understanding of how the tax laws apply to different types of entities. A doctor may need a general understanding of fringe-benefit plans that can be set up to keep highly qualified nurses and medical technicians as employees. A farmer can benefit from familiarity with the complex rules that govern reporting of income from farm production and the deduction of farm expenses. Individuals can also benefit from a knowledge of the tax laws in their everyday decisions.

▲ **EXAMPLE 4**   Isaac wants to buy a new car. During a special promotion, the dealer will finance the purchase with a 6% loan. Isaac knows that he can obtain a home equity loan from his bank at 8% interest. If Isaac is in the 28% tax bracket, which loan should he use to finance his new car?

Discussion: Interest paid on personal loans is not deductible. However, interest paid on a home equity loan is deductible. If Isaac itemizes his deductions, the interest on the home equity loan is deductible. This makes the real after-tax cost of the home equity loan 5.76% [8% − (8% × 28%)]. Therefore, the home equity loan actually offers a lower after-tax cost than the dealer loan.

However, note that if Isaac does not itemize deductions (i.e., he uses the standard deduction), he receives no benefit from the deduction for home equity loan interest. In this case, the dealer loan would have a lower after-tax cost, because neither loan would produce deductible interest.

Self-Protection

Another reason for being aware of the federal income tax law is self-protection. Perhaps you have heard others say that all they have to do is give a list of income and deduction items to their tax return preparer. When they get the completed tax return back and pay the tax due, their responsibility for complying with the tax law is finished. If any mistakes are made, it is the preparer's problem. This assumption is erroneous and can lead to disaster.

Taxpayers are fully liable for additional tax, interest, and penalties due because of an error on their tax return. If a person paid to prepare a return misinterprets the information and/or makes a mistake that results in an underpayment of tax, the taxpayer will have to pay any additional amounts owed to the government. Whether the preparer will reimburse the taxpayer for the penalties and interest depends on the agreement with the preparer. Legal recourse against the preparer is available in certain circumstances, but the cost of obtaining reimbursement (e.g., legal fees, court costs) from the preparer may be prohibitive. For your own protection, you should always examine the completed return. Before you sign and file the return, thoroughly review it with your preparer and be sure you understand any entries that do not seem to be correct. Again, a knowledge of the tax law can help you catch errors or other misrepresentations made by a tax preparer before the return is filed.

▲ **EXAMPLE 5**   Raul gave his tax return preparer a list of income and deduction items to be reported on his tax return. The income items totaled $50,000, and the deduction items totaled $14,000. When the preparer put the information on the return, he omitted $10,000 of the income and reported only $40,000 ($50,000 − $10,000) in income. In addition, the preparer included a $2,000 deduction twice so that total deductions were reported as $16,000. As a result, Raul understated his taxable income by $12,000 ($36,000 correct taxable income − $24,000 reported taxable income).

Discussion: If the IRS detects the errors on the return, Raul will have to pay the IRS the additional tax due on the $12,000 understatement plus penalties and interest. Depending on their agreement for preparing the return, Raul may or may not recover part of his costs from the preparer. If the preparer does not agree to reimburse Raul for his mistakes, Raul may take legal action to obtain the amount due from the preparer. However, this can be a costly process and may not be worth the additional tax and penalties and interest due.

Clearly, all taxpayers can benefit from a basic knowledge of the tax law. Although the federal income tax is only one of many taxes that government bodies use to raise revenue, it is by far the most important in terms of revenue produced and the number of taxpayers affected. Therefore, this book focuses on federal income tax law.

Federal income tax law is a complex array of statutory, administrative, and judicial authorities. Because of its ability to affect taxpayers' decisions, lawmakers frequently make changes in the tax law to achieve economic, social, and/or political objectives. This causes the tax law to be in constant evolution. Professional tax advisers spend a significant portion of their time maintaining their knowledge of this changing body of law. Fortunately, many aspects of the tax law have remained stable over time. The approach used in this book is to provide a conceptual framework for analyzing how particular transactions should be treated for federal income tax purposes. The book then presents the general operation of the tax law and explains it in terms of the basic concepts. Throughout the book, the focus of the discussion is on those aspects of the federal income tax that have remained stable over time. A knowledge of the basic operation of the tax law will enhance your ability to make the best decisions for your individual situation.

CONCEPTUAL FOUNDATIONS OF THE TAX LAW

CHAPTER 1
FEDERAL INCOME TAXATION—AN OVERVIEW

CHAPTER 2
INCOME TAX CONCEPTS

Federal Income Taxation— An Overview

▲ CHAPTER LEARNING OBJECTIVES

■ Discuss what constitutes a tax and the various types of tax rate structures that may be used to calculate a tax.

■ Introduce the major types of taxes in the United States.

■ Identify the primary sources of federal income tax law.

■ Define *taxable income* and other commonly used tax terms.

■ Introduce the calculation of taxable income for individual taxpayers and the unique personal deductions allowed to individuals.

■ Develop a framework for tax planning and discuss the effect of marginal tax rates and the time value of money on tax planning.

■ Make the distinction between tax avoidance and tax evasion.

■ Introduce ethical considerations related to tax practice.

We have all heard the adage, "There's nothing certain but death and taxes." However, equating death and taxes is hardly a fair characterization of taxation. It is often stated that taxes are the price we pay for a civilized society. An early decision of the U.S. Supreme Court described a tax as "an extraction for the support of the government." Regardless of your personal view of taxation, society as we know it could not function without some system of taxation. People constantly demand that the government provide them with various services, such as defense, roads, schools, unemployment benefits, medical care, and environmental protection. The cost of providing the services that the citizens of the United States demand is principally taxation. People are introduced to taxation at an early age. Remember the candy bar that had a price sticker of 25 cents yet its actual cost was 27 cents? The tax collector is all around us. Upon receiving their first paycheck, many are surprised that the $100 they earned resulted in a check of only $80 after taxes were deducted. The point is that taxes are a fact of life. Learning to deal with taxes, and perhaps using them to your advantage, is an essential element of success in today's world.

The federal income tax is a sophisticated and complex array of laws that imposes a tax on the income of individuals, corporations, estates, and trusts. Current tax law has developed over a period of more than 80 years through a dynamic process involving political, economic, and social forces. At this very minute, Congress is considering various changes in the tax law; the Internal Revenue Service (IRS) and the courts are issuing new interpretations of current tax law, and professional tax advisers are working to obtain the meaning of all these changes.

The purpose of this book is to provide an introduction to the basic operation of the federal income tax system. However, before looking at some of the specifics, it is helpful to have a broad understanding of taxes and how the federal income tax fits into the overall scheme of revenue production. Toward this end, this chapter briefly discusses what constitutes a tax, how taxes are structured, and the major types of taxes in the United States before considering the federal income tax. Next, the primary sources of tax law authority are introduced. These sources provide the basis for calculating the tax and the unique terminology of federal income taxation. This chapter also introduces the tax calculation for individuals, the discussion of which serves as a reference for discussion in succeeding chapters. The next section of the chapter provides a framework for tax planning and a discussion of tax avoidance and tax evasion.

Because ethics has become an important issue in the accounting profession in recent years, the chapter concludes with a brief discussion of the ethical considerations related to tax practice. The discussion provides the background that will help you detect ethical issues that you will face if you go on to practice in the tax area.

Because this is a tax text, one starting point is to define what is meant by the term *tax*. Particular types of taxes and tax rules are often criticized as being loopholes, unfair, or creating an excessive burden on a particular group of taxpayers. The discussion that follows presents the four criteria commonly used to evaluate these criticisms. In addition, three different types of tax rate structure are presented as an aid in evaluating whether a particular tax is "good" or "bad."

Definition of a Tax

What is a tax? The Internal Revenue Service defines a tax as "an enforced contribution, exacted pursuant to legislative authority in the exercise of the taxing power, and imposed and collected for the purpose of raising revenue to be used for public or governmental purposes. Taxes are not payments for some special privilege granted or service rendered and are, therefore, distinguishable from various other charges imposed for particular purposes under particular powers or functions of government."[1]

A tax could be viewed as an involuntary contribution required by law to finance the functions of government. The amount of the contribution extracted from the taxpayer is unrelated to any privilege, benefit, or service received from the government agency imposing the tax. According to the IRS definition, a tax has the following characteristics:

1. The payment to the governmental authority is required by law.

2. The payment is required pursuant to the legislative power to tax.

3. The purpose of requiring the payment is to provide revenue to be used for public or governmental purposes.

4. Special benefits, services, or privileges are not received as a result of making the payment. The payment is not a fine or penalty that is imposed under other powers of government.

Although the IRS definition states that the payment of a tax does not provide the taxpayer with directly measurable benefits, the taxpayer does benefit from, among other things, military security, a legal system, and a relatively stable political, economic, and social environment. Payments to a government agency that relate to the receipt of a specific benefit—in privileges or services—are not considered taxes; they are payments for value received or are the result of a regulatory measure imposed by the government agency.

> ▲ **EXAMPLE 1**   Keith lives in Randal County. Randal County enacted a law setting a 1% property tax to provide money for county schools. The 1% tax applies to all property owners in Randal County. All school children in the county will benefit from the tax, even if their parents do not own property or pay the tax. Is the 1% property tax a tax according to the definition?
>
> *Discussion:*   The property tax is a tax. The tax is a required payment to a government unit. The payment is imposed by a property tax law. The purpose of the payment is to finance public schools. The tax is levied without regard to whether the taxpayer receives a benefit from paying the tax.
>
> ▲ **EXAMPLE 2**   Assume that in example 1 the tax is imposed on a limited group of property owners to finance the construction of new sewer lines to their properties. Is the 1% tax a tax as defined by the IRS?
>
> *Discussion:*   Each payer of the tax receives a direct benefit—a new sewer line. Therefore, the 1% tax payment is considered a payment to the government unit to reimburse it for improvements to the taxpayer's property. The taxpayers would treat the payment as an investment in their property and not as a tax. The 1% tax in this case is a special assessment for local benefits. An assessment differs from a tax in that an assessment is levied only on specific groups of taxpayers who receive the benefit of the assessment.

Certain payments that look like a tax are not considered a tax under the IRS definition. For example, an annual licensing fee paid to a state to engage in a specific occupation such as medicine, law, or accounting is not a tax, because it is a regulatory measure that provides a direct benefit to the payer of the fee. A fee paid for driving on a toll road, the quarter deposited in a parking meter, and payments to a city for water and sewer services are payments for value received and are not taxes according to the IRS's definition. Fines for violating public laws and penalties on tax returns are not taxes. Fines and penalties are generally imposed to discourage behavior that is harmful to the public interest and not to raise revenue to finance government operations.

Standards for Evaluating a Tax

In *The Wealth of Nations*, Adam Smith identified four basic requirements for a good tax system. Although other criteria can be used to evaluate a tax, Smith's four points are generally accepted as valid and provide a basis for discussion of the primary issues regarding taxes. These requirements are equality, certainty, convenience, and economy. Although Smith clearly stated the maxims, taxpayers have different opinions as to whether the federal income tax strictly satisfies the four requirements.

1. **Equality**—A tax should be based on the taxpayer's *ability to pay*. The payment of a tax in proportion to the taxpayer's level of income results in an equitable distribution of the cost of supporting the government.

The concept of equality requires consideration of both horizontal and vertical equity. **Horizontal equity** exists when two similarly situated taxpayers are taxed the same. **Vertical equity** exists when taxpayers with different situations are taxed differently but fairly in relation to each taxpayer's ability to pay the tax. This means that those taxpayers who have the greatest ability to pay the tax should pay the greatest proportion of the tax. These equity concepts are reflected to a great extent in the federal income tax. Certain low-income individuals pay no tax. As a person's taxable income level increases, the tax rate increases from 15 percent to 28 percent to 31 percent to 36 percent to 39.6 percent.

▲ **EXAMPLE 3**   Tom and Jerry each earn $15,000 a year and pay $1,500 in tax.

Discussion: The two taxpayers pay the same amount of tax on the same amount of income. Because they are treated the same, based on the facts given, horizontal equity exists.

Discussion: A slight change of facts provides a different result. If Tom is married and supports his wife and 5 children and Jerry is single with no one else to support, the tax appears unfair and not horizontally equitable. The lack of horizontal equity exists because the taxpayers' situations are no longer the same, yet they pay the same amount of tax on the same income.

▲ **EXAMPLE 4**   Assume that because of the size of his family Tom (example 3) pays $500 in taxes. Jerry still pays $1,500.

Discussion: In this situation, vertical equity is considered to be present. Because he presumably has a greater ability to pay tax, Jerry pays a larger amount of tax than Tom—Jerry's income, although equal to Tom's, supports fewer people.

Some taxpayers consider inequitable the tax law provisions that treat similar income and deductions differently. For example, a person investing in bonds issued by a city does not have to pay tax on the interest income. In contrast, interest income earned on an investment in corporate bonds is taxed. People who operate proprietorships may deduct the cost of providing their employees with group term life insurance but may not deduct the cost of their own group insurance premium. If the proprietor incorporates, the cost of the insurance for both the shareholder-employee (owner) and employees can be deducted. Thus, the perception of equality often depends on the taxpayer's personal viewpoint. Because the concepts of equity are highly subjective, a tax rule considered equitable by one taxpayer is often considered unfair by a taxpayer who derives no benefit. Often, when evaluating the equality of a tax provision, taxpayers do not consider—or are not aware of—the economic, social, and administrative reasons for what may seem to be an inequity in the tax law.

▲ **EXAMPLE 5**   Karen is a single mother who earns $10,000 a year. Jane and her husband Ben earn $75,000 a year. Karen and Jane each pay Neighborhood Day Care $2,000 per year for taking care of 1 child while they work. Because the payment is for qualified child care, Karen is entitled to a $600 reduction in her income tax because of her low income level. Because of their high income level, Jane and Ben receive only a $400 reduction in their income tax. Who is more likely to view this treatment as being inequitable?

Discussion: Jane and Ben may view the tax rule as unfair, because Karen receives a larger reduction in tax for the same amount of payment for day care. However, there is increasing emphasis on tax relief for families. Congress has decided that it is important that children be adequately cared for while parents are at work. Thus, Karen's family is given a larger tax break to help provide child care. Without the larger tax reduction, Karen might not be able to afford to pay child-care costs. The difference in treatment could also be based on the ability to pay child-care costs. In addition, the difference in treatment depicts a situation of vertical equity. Because Jane and Ben have higher incomes, vertical equity requires that they pay a higher tax (through receiving a smaller tax credit).

2. **Certainty**—A taxpayer should know when and how a tax is to be paid. In addition, the taxpayer should be able to determine the amount of tax to be paid.

Certainty in the tax law is necessary for tax planning. An individual's federal income tax return is due on the fifteenth day of the fourth month (usually April 15) after the close of the tax year. A corporation's return is due on the fifteenth day of the third month after the close of its tax year.[2] The balance of tax due with the return is usually paid by check to the IRS. However, determining the amount of tax due may not be so simple. When planning an investment that will extend over several tax years, the ability to predict with some degree of certainty how the results of the investment will be taxed is important to the investment decision. Frequent changes in the tax law create uncertainty for the tax planner. In its 1990 *Annual Report*, the IRS stated that the Internal Revenue Code had been changed more than 100 times since 1980. In addition to these legislative amendments to the tax law, the IRS and the courts issue a constant stream of decisions and interpretations on tax issues, which results in a tax law that is in a continual state of refinement. However, for the average individual taxpayer, who has wages subject to withholding, receives some interest income, owns a home, pays state and local taxes, and perhaps donates to a church or other charities, there is little complexity and a great deal of certainty in the tax law despite the numerous changes to the tax system.

3. **Convenience**—A tax should be levied at the time it is most likely to be convenient for the taxpayer to make the payment. The most convenient time for taxpayers to make the payment is as they receive income and have the money available to pay the tax.

Most taxpayers would argue that it is not convenient to keep records, determine the amount of tax due, and fill out complex forms. However, certain aspects of the income tax law make it more convenient than it might be otherwise. Based on the **pay-as-you-go concept,** taxes are paid as close to the time the income is earned as is reasonable. The pay-as-you-go system results in the collection of the tax when the taxpayer has the money to pay the tax. This tax payment system applies to all taxpayers, including the self-employed and those who earn their income from investing activities. This system is discussed in more detail later in this chapter.

The federal income tax is based on self-assessment and voluntary compliance with the tax law. Taxpayers determine in privacy the amount of their income, deductions, and tax due. The tax calculated by the taxpayer is considered correct unless the IRS detects an error and corrects it or selects the return for an audit. The federal income tax system relies on the honesty and integrity of taxpayers in determining their tax payments. This system of self-assessment and voluntary compliance promotes convenience for taxpayers.

> 4. **Economy**—A tax should have minimum compliance and administrative costs. The costs of compliance and administration should be kept at a minimum so that the amount that goes to the U.S. Treasury is as large as possible.

The IRS operates on a budget of about one half of 1 percent of the total taxes collected. However, the IRS's budget does not reflect the full cost of administering the tax law. A taxpayer's personal cost of compliance can be substantial. Taxpayers often need to maintain accounting records for tax reporting in addition to those that are necessary for business decisions. A corporation, for example, might use different depreciation methods and asset lives for financial reporting and for income tax. The taxpayer's personal cost also includes fees paid to attorneys, accountants, and other tax advisers for tax-planning, compliance, and litigation services.

Tax Rates and Structures

Tax rates are often referred to as a *marginal rate, an average rate,* or an *effective rate.* In addition, a tax rate structure is frequently described as being *proportional, regressive,* or *progressive.* Because a tax rate structure indicates how the average tax rate varies with changes in its tax base, examining a rate's structure helps in understanding and evaluating the effect of a tax.

To compute a tax it is necessary to know the tax base and the applicable tax rate. The tax is then computed by multiplying the tax base by the tax rate:

$$\text{Tax} = \text{Tax base} \times \text{Tax rate}$$

A **tax base** is the value that is subject to tax. The tax base for the federal income tax is called **taxable income.** Other common tax bases include the dollar amount of a purchase subject to sales tax, the dollars of an employee's wages subject to payroll tax, and the assessed value of property subject to property tax.

Tax Rate Definitions.   When working with the federal income tax, different measures of the rate of tax paid from one year to the next are often compared in order to evaluate the effectiveness of tax planning and to help make decisions about future transactions. Three different rates are commonly used for these comparisons:

- The marginal tax rate
- The average tax rate
- The effective tax rate

The **marginal tax rate** is the rate of tax that will be paid on the next dollar of income or the rate of tax that will be saved by the next dollar of deduction. The marginal tax rate is used in tax planning to determine the effect of reporting additional income or deductions during a tax year. One objective of tax planning is to minimize the marginal rate and to keep the marginal rate relatively constant from one year to the next. The marginal tax rates for an individual taxpayer are 15 percent, 28 percent, 31 percent, 36 percent, and 39.6 percent.[3] If you know a person's taxable income (the tax base), you can find the marginal tax rate by looking it up in the tax rate schedules in Appendix A.

▲ **EXAMPLE 6** Don has an asset he could sell this year at a $10,000 profit, which would increase his marginal tax rate from 15% to 28%. If he waits until next year to sell the asset, he is sure his other income will be less and the $10,000 gain will be taxed at 15%. Should Don sell the asset this year or wait until next year?

Discussion: By waiting until next year to sell the asset, Don's tax savings on the sale are $1,300 [$10,000 × (28% − 15%)]. In addition, he will postpone the payment of the tax interest free for a year (a time value of money savings). Assuming that he can sell the asset early in the next year and does not need the proceeds from the sale before next year, he should wait until next year to sell the asset to take advantage of the lower marginal tax rate and the time value of money savings on the tax to be paid on the gain.

The **average tax rate** is the total federal income tax divided by taxable income (the tax base). This is the average rate of tax on each dollar of income that is taxable. The **effective tax rate** is the total federal income tax divided by the tax-payer's economic income (taxable income plus nontaxable income). Economic income is a broader base; it includes all the taxpayer's income, whether it is subject to tax or not. The effective tax rate is the average rate of tax on income from all taxable and nontaxable sources.

▲ **EXAMPLE 7** Assume that in example 6 Don sells the asset in 1996 and reports taxable income of $40,000. Also, Don collects $50,000 on a life insurance policy that is not taxable income. Don's tax on $40,000 is $8,080 (using the tax rate schedules in Appendix A). In addition, the only difference between Don's economic income and his taxable income is proceeds from the life insurance policy. What are Don's marginal, average, and effective tax rates?

Discussion: Based on the facts given, Don's marginal tax rate is 28% (from the tax rate schedules). His average tax rate is 20.2% ($8,080 ÷ $40,000). The effective tax rate on his economic income of $90,000 ($40,000 in taxable income + $50,000 in nontaxable income) is 8.98% ($8,080 ÷ $90,000) and is much less than both the marginal and average tax rates.

Tax Rate Structures.   Tax rate structures are described as being proportional, regressive, or progressive. The structures explain how the tax rates vary with a change in the amount subject to the tax (the tax base).

PROPORTIONAL RATE STRUCTURE.   A **proportional rate structure** is defined as a tax for which the average tax rate remains the same as the tax base increases. This rate structure is also referred to as a *flat tax*. If you charted a proportional tax rate structure on a graph, it would look like the first chart in Figure 1–1.

If a tax rate is proportional, the marginal tax rate and the average tax rate are the same at all levels of the tax base. As the tax base increases, the total tax paid will increase at a constant rate. Examples of proportional taxes are sales taxes, real estate and personal property taxes, and certain excise taxes, such as the tax on

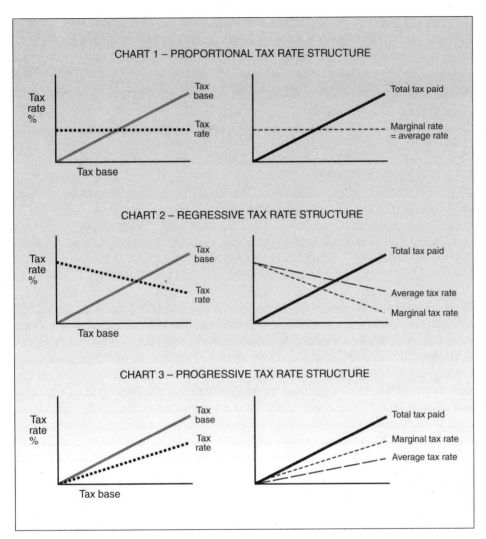

gasoline. The sales tax is a fixed percentage of the amount purchased, property tax is a constant rate multiplied by the assessed value of the property, and the gas tax is a constant rate per gallon purchased.

▲ **EXAMPLE 8**   Betsy bought a new suit for $350. The sales tax at 7% totaled $24.50. Steve bought a new lawn tractor for $3,500. At 7%, the sales tax he paid came to $245. Is the sales tax proportional?

Discussion: Betsy's and Steve's marginal tax rate is 7%. In addition, Betsy's average tax rate is 7% ($24.50 ÷ $350), the same as Steve's (7% = $245 ÷ $3,500). The sales tax is proportional, because the marginal and average tax rates are equal at all levels of the tax base (the selling price).

REGRESSIVE RATE STRUCTURE.   A **regressive rate structure** is defined as a tax in which the average tax rate decreases as the tax base increases. On a graph, a regressive tax rate structure would look like chart 2 in Figure 1–1.

If a tax rate structure is regressive, the marginal tax rate will be less than the average tax rate as the tax base increases. Note that although the average tax rate and the marginal tax rate both decrease as the tax base increases, the total tax paid will increase. As a result, a person with a low tax base will pay a higher average and a higher marginal rate of tax than will a person with a high tax base. The person with the high tax base will still pay more dollars in total tax. Although a pure regressive tax rate structure (as defined earlier) does not exist in the United States, example 9 illustrates a regressive tax.

▲ **EXAMPLE 9**   Each year, Alan purchases $4,000-worth of egg rolls and Tranh purchases $17,000-worth of egg rolls. A tax is levied according to the dollar value of egg rolls purchased per the following tax schedule:

Tax Rate Schedule		Alan		Tranh	
Base	Rate	Purchases	Tax	Purchases	Tax
$-0- < $5,001	10%	$4,000	$400	$ 5,000	$ 500
$5,001 < $10,001	7%			5,000	350
More than $10,000	5%			7,000	350
Totals		$4,000	$400	$17,000	$1,200
Marginal tax rate			10%		5.0%
Average tax rate			10%		7.1%

Discussion: This tax rate schedule is regressive. The average tax rate applicable to Alan (10%) is greater than the average tax rate for Tranh (7.1%), even though Tranh's tax base is higher. Note that Tranh pays more total tax ($1,200) than Alan ($400).

If a different base is used to evaluate the tax rate structure, the same tax that may be viewed as proportional by one taxpayer may be considered regressive by another taxpayer. For example, using total wages as the tax base for evaluation, a person who spends part of her wages for items subject to sales tax would pay a lower average rate of tax than the person who spends all of his wages on taxable items.

▲ **EXAMPLE 10**   Judy earns $25,000 a year and spends it all on items subject to sales tax. Guillermo earns $30,000 a year and is able to save $5,000 of his earnings. He spends the remaining $25,000 on purchases subject to sales tax. If the sales tax rate is 10% of purchase price, is it a regressive tax?

Discussion: Judy and Guillermo pay the same total sales tax ($2,500). Thus, the tax is proportional when evaluated by using purchases as the tax base. However, Guillermo's average tax rate based on wages [8.3% = ($2,500 ÷ $30,000)] is less than Judy's [10% = ($2,500 ÷ $25,000)]. Thus, the sales tax is regressive when using wages to evaluate the tax.

Although property taxes are a proportional tax according to these definitions, an investor in property subject to property taxes might consider the effect of the tax on investments regressive compared to investments in stocks and bonds, which are not subject to property taxes. Similarly, low-income wage earners who pay Social Security tax on all their wages may consider this tax regressive compared to a person whose wages exceed the amount subject to the tax.

PROGRESSIVE RATE STRUCTURE.   A **progressive rate structure** is defined as a tax in which the average tax rate increases as the tax base increases. On a graph, a progressive tax rate structure would look like chart 3 in Figure 1–1.

If a tax rate structure is progressive, the marginal tax rate will be higher than the average tax rate as the tax base increases. The average tax rate, the marginal tax rate, and total tax all increase with increases in the tax base. A person with a low tax base will pay both lower average and marginal rates of tax than will a person with a high tax base.

The progressive tax rate structure reflects the embedding in the federal income tax rates of Adam Smith's equality criterion. Recall that according to this criterion, taxpayers should pay tax according to their ability to pay the tax. The use of progressive rate structures, wherein higher taxable income levels pay higher marginal tax rates, promotes equality.

▲ **EXAMPLE 11**   Doug reports $16,000 a year in taxable income from wages he earns watering the greens at the Hot Water Golf Course. Shawana earns $28,000 in annual taxable income as a first grade teacher.

Discussion: Doug's and Shawana's 1996 income taxes using the single taxpayer rates are as follows:

	Doug's Tax (income: $16,000)	Shawana's Tax (income: $28,000)
Tax on income below $24,000 @ 15%	$2,400	$3,600
Tax on income above $24,000 @ 28%	-0-	1,120
Total tax	$2,400	$4,720
Marginal tax rate	15%	28%
Average tax rate	15%	17%

Discussion: As a result of Shawana's larger tax base and the progressive tax rates, her marginal and average tax rates are higher than Doug's. Thus, the tax rate structure of the federal income tax promotes equality among taxpayers.

MAJOR TYPES OF U.S. TAXES

The federal, state, and local governments use a variety of taxes to fund their operations. Figure 1–2 depicts tax revenues generated by federal, state, and local government bodies by source for 1995. An examination of the sources of tax revenue shows that the bulk of the federal government's revenues is derived from the income tax and social insurance taxes. State and local governments also receive a substantial portion of their revenues from a tax on income, with the sales tax and the propery tax also providing significant revenue. In terms of overall taxes collected in the United States, the federal income tax produces almost as much revenue as all other forms of state and local taxes combined. The amount of Social Security tax collected by the federal government is the largest source of government revenue, nearly surpassing the total revenue intake of all state and local governments combined. Although this text covers the basic operation of the federal income tax, it is helpful to have a basic understanding of the other taxes levied by governments. As will be seen throughout the text, many taxes affect and interact with the rules for the federal income tax. Each major type of tax is discussed briefly in turn. Do not be concerned with the mechanics of the taxes at this point. Focus only on their general nature.

Income Taxes

The federal government levies a tax on the income of individuals, corporations, estates, and trusts. Most states also tax the income of these taxpayers, and a few local governments also impose an income tax on those who work or live within their boundaries. The income tax is levied on a *net* number—taxable income. In its simplest form, taxable income is the difference between the total income of a

▲ **Figure 1–2**

1995 GOVERNMENT
REVENUES BY SOURCE
(ESTIMATED IN BILLIONS)

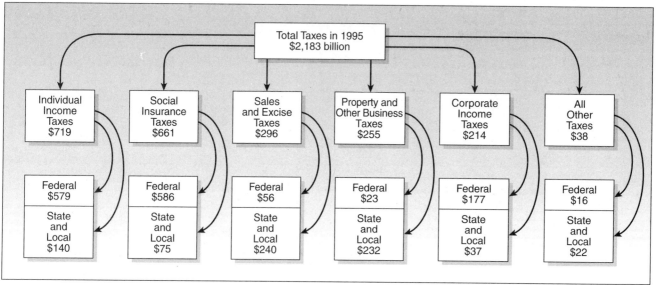

SOURCE: Tax Foundation, Inc.,
estimates based on National Income
and Product Account definitions.
Figures may not add because of
rounding.

taxpayer and the deductions allowed that taxpayer. Thus, the study of income taxation is really the study of what must be reported as income and what is allowed as a deduction from that income to arrive at taxable income.

Each of the three government units that impose an income tax has its own set of rules for determining what is included in income and what is deductible from income to arrive at taxable income. However, because most state and local governments begin their taxable income calculation in relation to the federal income tax computation, an understanding of the federal income tax rules is essential for calculating most income taxes. This book makes no attempt to cover the myriad state and local income tax rules.

Income taxes are determined on an annual basis. However, the United States uses a pay-as-you-go collection system under which taxpayers pay an estimate of their tax as they earn their income. Employers must withhold income taxes from wages and salaries of their employees and remit them on a timely basis to the appropriate government body.[4] When taxpayers file their tax returns, these prepaid amounts are credited against their actual tax bill, resulting in either a refund of taxes, if the prepaid amount is greater than the actual tax, or an additional tax due, if the prepaid amount is deficient.[5] Self-employed taxpayers and those with other sources of income that are not subject to withholding (e.g., dividend and interest income) must make quarterly estimated tax payments that are applied against their tax bills upon filing of the return.[6]

Employment Taxes

All employees and their employers pay taxes on the wages earned by employees. Employees pay **Social Security taxes** that are matched by their employers.[7] Self-employed individuals pay the equivalent of both halves of the Social Security tax by paying the **self-employment tax**.[8] In addition to the Social Security tax, employers pay unemployment compensation taxes to both the federal and state government.

Social Security Taxes.   Under the Federal Insurance Contribution Act (FICA), a tax is levied on wages and salaries earned. The Social Security system was originally designed to provide retirement benefits to all individuals who contributed to the system. This function has been expanded to include many other social programs, such as medical insurance, disability benefits, and survivor's benefits. The result of this expansion of coverage has been a great increase in the amount of Social Security taxes paid by workers and employers. It should be stressed that the Social Security system is not a "funded" system. Current payments into the system are used to pay current benefits; technically, any excess is placed in a fund. However, the federal government often borrows against this "fund" to pay general government expenses. Thus, there is no absolute guarantee that the amounts paid by current taxpayers will actually be available to them when they are eligible to receive their benefits.

The Social Security tax is imposed on employees and self-employed individuals. Employers are required to match employees' payments into the system.[9] Because a self-employed person is both an employee and an employer, the self-employment tax rate is twice the employee tax, resulting in an equivalent payment of tax by employee/employer and the self-employed.[10] The tax on employees and employers is a constant percentage of wages up to a maximum wage base. Both the percentage and the maximum wage base have been raised over time. As Table 1–1 shows, the tax has two components. In 1996, a tax of 6.2 percent is levied on the first $62,700 of wages for Old Age, Survivors, and Disability Insurance (OASDI). A tax of 1.45 percent on all wages pays for Medical Health Insurance (MHI). Note that before 1994, the MHI portion was subject to a maximum wage base. This established a maximum amount of Social Security tax that any taxpayer would pay. However, the abolition of the maximum MHI wage base for tax years after 1993 effectively eliminated the ceiling on Social Security tax.

Year	OASDI[1]	MHI[2]	Total	Maximum Wage Base	Maximum Tax Paid
1992	6.20		6.20	$ 55,500	$3,441
		1.45	1.45	$130,200	$1,888
			7.65		$5,329
1993	6.20		6.20	$ 57,600	$3,571
		1.45	1.45	$135,000	$1,958
			7.65		$5,529
1994	6.20		6.20	$ 60,600	$3,757
		1.45	1.45	Wages earned	No maximum
			7.65		
1995	6.20		6.20	$ 61,200	$3,794
		1.45	1.45	Wages earned	No maximum
			7.65		
1996	6.20		6.20	$ 62,700	$3,887
		1.45	1.45	Wages earned	No maximum
			7.65		

▲ **Table 1–1**

SOCIAL SECURITY TAX RATES FOR EMPLOYEES AND EMPLOYERS

[1]Old Age, Survivors, and Disability Insurance
[2]Medical Health Insurance

▲ **EXAMPLE 12**   Jenny earned $2,000 during February 1996 in her job as a carpenter for Acme Construction Co. How much Social Security tax must be paid by Jenny and Acme on her February earnings?

Discussion: Jenny must pay 6.2% (OASDI) and 1.45% (MHI) on the first $62,700 of income earned in 1996. Thus, Jenny must pay $153 [($2,000 × 6.2%) + ($2,000 × 1.45%)] in Social Security taxes on her wages. Acme must match the $153 in Social Security taxes Jenny paid on the wages.

▲ **EXAMPLE 13**   Chandra earned $85,000 as the administrator of the Local Accounting Program in 1996. How much Social Security tax does Chandra pay in 1996?

Discussion: Chandra pays the maximum OASDI of $3,887 (6.2% × $62,700) and $1,233 (1.45% × $85,000) of MHI for a total Social Security payment of $5,120. Her employer is required to pay the same amount on Chandra's behalf.

As with income taxes, Social Security taxes are withheld from the employee's pay by employers and remitted to the federal government with the employer's Social Security payment and other federal tax withholdings.

▲ **EXAMPLE 14**   Assume that in example 12 Acme also withheld $312 in federal income tax and $87 in state income tax from Jenny's February earnings. What is Jenny's actual take-home pay for February?

Discussion: Jenny's February take-home pay is $1,448 after withholding for income tax and Social Security. Out of her earnings of $2,000, $153 is withheld for payment of Social Security tax, $312 for federal income tax, and $87 for state income tax. Acme must pay these taxes to the appropriate government unit on a timely basis. Acme will also remit its $153 in Social Security taxes on Jenny's wages when it makes Jenny's payments.

Self-employed individuals pay a tax equal to the sum of the employee's and employer's payments. Thus in 1996, self-employment income is subject to a tax of 12.4 percent (6.2% × 2) on the first $62,700 of income for OASDI and 2.9 percent (1.45% × 2) on all self-employment income for MHI. Because employees are not taxed on the Social Security contribution made on their behalf by their employers, self-employed taxpayers are allowed to deduct one-half of their self-employment tax as a business expense to equalize the tax treatments of employees and the self-employed.

▲ **EXAMPLE 15**   Assume that in example 13 Chandra's $85,000 in earnings constitute self-employment income rather than wages as an employee. How much self-employment tax must Chandra pay on her self-employment income?

Discussion: Chandra pays $7,775 (12.4% × $62,700) of OASDI and $2,465 (2.9% × $85,000) of MHI, for a total self-employment tax of $10,240. Note that this is equal to the total tax paid by Chandra and her employer ($5,120 × 2) in example 13. Because Chandra is self-employed, she must pay the equivalent of the employee's and employer's tax.

Unemployment Taxes.   Employers must also pay state and federal unemployment taxes on wages paid to employees to fund unemployment benefits. The Federal Unemployment Tax (FUTA) is 6.2 percent of the first $7,000 in wages paid to each employee. Unemployment taxes do not have to be paid for employees who earn less than $1,500 per calendar quarter and certain classes of agricultural workers. Because each state also levies an unemployment tax, employers are allowed a credit of up to 5.4 percent for the state unemployment taxes they pay. Thus, the minimum FUTA tax rate is 0.8 percent (6.2% − 5.4%).

Sales Tax

Most state and local governments raise significant amounts of revenue from a sales tax. A sales tax is based on a flat percentage of the selling price of a product or service. In contrast to income and employment taxes, which are based on the income of taxpayers, a sales tax is based on a taxpayer's consumption of goods and services. The business that sells the goods or services subject to the tax collects the tax for the government. However, the tax is still paid by the taxpayer purchasing the goods or services. Each government unit that imposes a sales tax determines which goods and/or services are subject to the tax. Thus, not all goods and services are subject to a sales tax. For example, medical services are typically exempted from the tax. Other items that are often exempted from the sales tax are food, farm equipment, and sales to tax-exempt organizations.

Property Taxes

A tax on the value of property owned by taxpayers is called a *property tax.* In general, **real property** is land and any structures that are permanently attached to land, such as buildings. All other types of property are referred to as **personal property.** Because real property is immobile and difficult to conceal from tax assessors, local governments such as cities, counties, and school districts prefer it as a revenue source.

Property taxes are referred to as **ad valorem taxes,** because they are based on the value of the property being taxed. However, most property taxes are not based on the true fair market value of the property. Rather, the assessed value of the property is used to determine the tax. The *assessed value* of property varies widely but is typically 50 to 75 percent of the estimated market value of the property. Market values are determined by the designated assessment authority (e.g., the county assessor) based on various factors such as recent comparable sales, replacement cost per square foot, and other local market conditions. The assessed value is then computed as the predetermined percentage of the assessor's valuation.

> ▲ **EXAMPLE 16**   Maria Corporation owns a piece of land that it purchased for $6,000 in 1992. During the current year, the county tax assessor determines that the fair market value of the land is $8,000. In the county in which the land is located, assessed values are 50% of the fair market value. What is the assessed value of Maria Corporation's land?
>
> *Discussion:*   Maria Corporation's assessed value is $4,000 ($8,000 × 50%). Note that the local authority can increase or decrease property taxes on the land by varying the percentage of fair market value that is subject to tax. Thus, if the county raised the percentage to 75%, the corporation would pay property tax based on an assessed value of $6,000 ($8,000 × 75%).

Taxes on personal property are not as common as real property taxes. The mobility and ease of concealment of personal property make the collection of a personal property tax administratively difficult. However, many local governments continue to selectively impose personal property taxes on types of property that are easier to track. Because of the relatively small number of establishments, property taxes on business property are still widely used. In addition, automobiles and boats are often assessed a personal property tax as part of their annual licensing fee.

▲ **EXAMPLE 17**   Oklahoma imposes an annual tag fee on automobiles. The licensing fee is $18. A personal property tax is also levied, based on the initial selling price of the automobile and its age. During 1996, Darla paid a $94 tag fee on her automobile. How much of the fee is a personal property tax?

Discussion: Darla's personal property tax on the automobile is $76 ($94 − $18). The $18 licensing fee is not a tax.

Other Taxes

Income taxes, employment taxes, sales taxes, and property taxes are the primary revenue producers for the various forms of government. However, businesses and individuals pay a number of other taxes. The most important of these are excise taxes and wealth transfer taxes. In addition, state and local governments impose taxes on certain occupations (e.g., liquor dealers) and franchise taxes for the privilege of doing business within their jurisdiction.

Excise Taxes.   Excise taxes are imposed on various products and services. The federal government imposes excise taxes on a vast array of products and some services. Many states also levy excise taxes on the same products and services. An excise tax differs from a sales tax in that it is not based on the sales value of the product. Rather, an excise tax is typically imposed on a quantity, such as a gallon of gasoline or a pack of cigarettes. Some products subject to excise taxes include

Alcohol	Guns
Coal	Shells
Diesel fuels	Telephone services
Fishing equipment	Tires
Gasoline	Tobacco

In addition to these excise taxes, in 1990 Congress added a 10-percent luxury tax on certain items. The 10-percent luxury tax applied to the purchase price of automobiles, boats, airplanes, jewelry, and furs that exceeded a set price for the items. Congress repealed the luxury tax on all items except automobiles, effective for 1993. In 1995, the tax on automobiles is imposed on the purchase price in excess of $32,000.

Wealth Transfer Taxes.   Transfers of wealth between taxpayers are taxed by the federal gift tax and the federal estate tax. Most states also impose taxes on the value of an estate. These taxes are essentially a tax on the right to transfer property to another. **Gift taxes** are paid by the donor of property—the person making the gift. The person who receives the gift, the donee, is not subject to either the gift tax or income tax on the gift. The **estate tax** is paid by the administrator (called the *executor*) of a deceased taxpayer's estate from the assets of the estate. Both the gift tax and the estate tax are based on the fair market value of the property being transferred. In addition, there are numerous exclusions from both taxes, the effect of which is to tax only relatively large gifts and estates. Although gift and estate taxes are vaguely familiar to many people, they are relatively minor revenue producers. However, a basic understanding of the operation of the two taxes will aid in understanding some of the income tax issues related to gifts and estates that are discussed later in the text.

FEDERAL GIFT TAX.   A gift tax is imposed on the fair market value of gifts made between individuals.[11] Neither the donor nor the donee is subject to income tax on gifts. The donor of the gift property is responsible for reporting and paying the gift tax. The gift tax has several exclusions, the most basic of which is an annual exclusion of $10,000 per donee.[12] Under this provision, taxpayers can give as many individuals as they wish as much as $10,000 a year each and pay no gift tax. A married couple can use this exclusion to make tax-free gifts of up to $20,000 per person per year. Taxpayers are also allowed to make unlimited gifts to their spouses and to charities without payment of gift tax.

▲ **EXAMPLE 18**   Ansel and Hannah gave their daughter a new car for graduation. The car cost $18,000. Is the gift subject to the gift tax?

Discussion: Ansel and Hannah each are entitled to give $10,000 to any person each year. Therefore, they may make gifts of up to $20,000 to an individual without incurring any gift tax. Because the fair market value of the car is less than $20,000, it is not subject to gift tax.

▲ **EXAMPLE 19**   On their 25th wedding anniversary, Ansel gave Hannah a diamond ring that cost $30,000. Is the gift subject to the gift tax?

Discussion: Gifts to a spouse are not subject to gift tax, regardless of the value transferred. Therefore, the ring is not subject to the gift tax.

As these examples illustrate, the most common forms of gifts, such as those for birthdays, graduations, weddings, and anniversaries are not subject to the gift tax. However, when a gift is made that is not totally excludable under one of these provisions, the taxpayer may use the unified donative-transfers credit to avoid payment of the gift tax.[13] The **unified donative-transfers credit** allows a lifetime credit of $192,800 against gift and estate taxes. The credit is equivalent to being able to exclude $600,000 in property from the gift and/or the estate tax.

FEDERAL ESTATE TAX.   The estate tax is levied on the fair market value of the assets a taxpayer owned at death.[14] The executor of the estate is responsible for valuing the assets of the estate, administering the assets before their distribution to the heirs, paying the estate taxes, and distributing the assets to the estate's beneficiaries. As with the gift tax, several exclusions and the unified donative-transfers credit serve to limit taxation of estates to those estates that are fairly substantial.[15] The fair market value of the estate's assets is reduced by funeral and administrative costs, debts owed by the taxpayer, amounts bequeathed to charities, and the marital deduction for property passing to the surviving spouse. The marital deduction is unlimited—all amounts that pass to a surviving spouse are exempt from the estate tax. Judicious use of the marital deduction and the donative-transfers credit allow the value of most estates to go untaxed at the death of the first spouse. Because the unified donative-transfers credit is a cumulative lifetime amount that applies to both gifts and property passing through the estate, careful planning is required in order to minimize the lifetime tax on gifts and property held at death. Suffice it to say that the gift and estate tax provisions can be quite complex. Taxpayers with substantial assets should seek competent professional advice in planning their estates to minimize the liability for these taxes.

Although the transfer of property from an estate to the heirs of the decedent has no income tax effect, the estate itself is subject to income tax while it holds the assets of the decedent. The executor of the estate must file an income tax return that reports the income and the deductions related to the assets of the decedent for the period between the date of death and the final distribution of the estate's assets. The taxable income calculation of an estate is discussed in Chapter 9.

SOURCES OF FEDERAL INCOME TAX LAW

This text contains a general discussion of the federal income tax and by itself should not be considered a substitute for the original sources of the tax law. Before making a final decision about a tax issue, you should review the appropriate original source of the tax rule on which you are going to rely. Thus, it is important to be aware of the legislative, administrative, and judicial sources of tax law. These sources are frequently referred to as *primary sources* of tax law. The discussion that follows briefly outlines the primary sources. A more detailed discussion of the primary authorities is contained in Chapter 15, Tax Research. The remainder of this text generally will not make specific references to sources of tax law. Instead, this book makes generic reference to "tax law" in order to simplify the discussion.

The end of each chapter includes a list of applicable sources keyed to footnote numbers in the chapter and a brief summary of each source. For those who wish to read the primary sources, they are available in most university and public libraries. Briefly, our citations follow common tax practice, with deference to *The Bluebook: A Uniform System of Citation* (Harvard Law Review Association) and the *Chicago Manual of Style* (University of Chicago Press). For example, *Sec. 61* refers to Section 61 of the Internal Revenue Code of 1986 as amended. *Reg. Sec. 1.61-2* refers to the second Treasury regulation issued that interprets Section 61. *Helvering v. Gregory*, 69 F.2d 809 (2d Cir. 1934), is a citation to a 1934 court case that was decided by the U.S. Court of Appeals for the Second Circuit. The case is located in volume 69 of the *Federal Reporter* case series, beginning at page 809. A complete explanation of all citations and how to locate the primary sources can be found in Chapter 15.

The federal income tax law dates to 1913 and has been amended, revised, and reworked numerous times since. The current statutory source of federal income tax law is the **Internal Revenue Code of 1986,** as amended (referred to as the *Code*). The tax law is laid out in the Code by section number. Thus, the basic reference to a particular tax law provision is to the section of the Code in which the law is stated. Often, particular tax treatments are referred to by their Code section number. For example, Section 179 allows a taxpayer to elect to deduct up to $17,500 of the cost of qualifying depreciable property in the year of acquisition (rather than depreciating it over its tax life). Tax practitioners refer to this election as the *Section 179 election*. Therefore, when appropriate, references to Code sections will include the popular terminology associated with that section.

The Internal Revenue Service is the branch of the Treasury Department that is responsible for interpreting and administering the tax law. The Treasury provides overall interpretive guidance on the Code by issuing **Treasury regulations.**[16] Regulations undergo an intensive review and public comment process before they are issued. Because of this intensive review, interpretations of regulations generally carry considerable authority, sometimes approaching that of the Code.

In fulfilling its administrative function, the IRS issues revenue rulings, revenue procedures, and a variety of other pronouncements that provide guidance on the interpretation of the Code. Because the IRS issues several hundred rulings each year, they do not undergo the extensive review process accorded regulations. As such, they are given less weight as an authority than a Treasury regulation.

In addition to providing interpretive guidance, the IRS has responsibility for ensuring taxpayers' compliance with the tax law. During 1994, the IRS processed 207 million tax returns, provided tax preparation assistance to 65.3 million taxpayers, and audited 1.08 percent of the individual tax returns filed by individual taxpayers in 1993. When audited by the IRS, taxpayers are allowed to present their reasoning for the items in question on their return. As might be expected, disputes often arise between taxpayers and the IRS concerning its interpretations and enforcement of the tax law. Most disputes are resolved through the IRS appeals process. However, taxpayers who are dissatisfied with the result of the appeals process are entitled to take their disputes to court for settlement.

Court decisions establish precedent in the interpretation of the tax law. Taxpayers and the IRS are generally bound by the interpretation of a court on a particular issue. However, the loser of an initial court case may choose to appeal the decision to a U.S. Circuit Court of Appeals. A loss at the appellate level may be further appealed to the U.S. Supreme Court. However, the Supreme Court limits its review of tax cases to those of major importance (e.g., a constitutional issue) or to resolving conflicting decisions in the appellate courts. A Supreme Court decision is not subject to review—it is the final interpretation of the law. Only Congress can override an interpretation of the Supreme Court by amending the Code section in question.

Tax information is also published in a variety of secondary sources. These sources include tax reference services, professional tax journals, tax newsletters, and textbooks. Secondary sources are useful when researching an issue, and they often are helpful for understanding the primary sources. However, you should exercise care when using secondary sources, because their interpretations are not authoritative.

FEDERAL INCOME TAX TERMINOLOGY

Individuals, corporations, and certain estates and trusts are subject to tax on their federal taxable income. Federal taxable income is defined by the tax law and differs from both financial accounting and economic measures of income. The general computational framework for determining the taxable income of all taxpayers is shown in Exhibit 1–1. Both the terms used in the computations and the order of the computational framework are prescribed in the tax law.

Income

The term *income* is used in several different ways. Therefore, always be sure you understand the context in which the term is used. As broadly defined, income includes both taxable and nontaxable types of income. This definition includes all income that belongs to the taxpayer. *Gross income* is a more restrictive term. As

▲ **Exhibit 1–1**

INCOME TAX COMPUTATIONAL FRAMEWORK

	Income "Broadly Defined" (includes income from all sources)
Minus:	Excluded income
Equals:	Gross income
Minus:	Deductions and exemptions
Equals:	Taxable income
×	Tax rate (schedule of rates)
Equals:	Income tax
Minus:	Tax prepayments
	Tax credits
Equals:	Tax (refund) due with return

Exhibit 1–1 shows, **gross income** is income broadly defined minus income items that are excluded from taxation.[17] Items of gross income are included in the computation of taxable income. Generally, gross income is the starting point for reporting income items on a tax return. Chapter 3 discusses the most commonly encountered gross income items.

A fundamental rule to observe in regard to income is that an item is included in gross income unless it is specifically excluded by the tax law. **Exclusions** represent increases in a taxpayer's wealth and recoveries of the taxpayer's capital investment that Congress has decided should not be subject to income tax. Thus, income exclusions are not counted as gross income. Common income exclusions include inheritances, gifts, and interest on certain municipal bonds. Exclusions are discussed in Chapter 4.

Although not an explicit part of the income tax computation, deferrals of income and deductions are also found in the tax law. A **deferral** is an item that does not affect the current period's taxable income but will affect taxable income in some future tax year. Thus, a deferral is like an exclusion in that it does not have a current tax effect. However, it differs in that an exclusion is *never* subject to tax, whereas a deferral *will* be subject to tax at some point in the future.

Taxable income is a net number and is the tax base. Taxable income is determined by subtracting deductions and exemptions from gross income. Taxable income is the tax base that is multiplied by the applicable tax rate schedule to compute the federal income tax. Taxable income is usually different from financial accounting income computed by using generally accepted accounting principles.

The differences between financial accounting income and taxable income generally arise because taxable income is computed according to the rules prescribed by the tax law. Tax accounting rules are not based on generally accepted accounting principles (GAAP). GAAP are concerned with determining the "true income" for an annual period. The income tax is geared to producing and collecting tax revenues and providing incentives for particular economic and social transactions. An important difference between the two objectives is that the income tax system attempts to collect the tax on income in the period during which the taxpayer has the resources to pay the tax. Under GAAP, having the resources to pay taxes is of no concern. As a result, specific income and deduction items may be accelerated, deferred, or permanently excluded from the current year's taxable income computation versus the GAAP treatment. For example, prepaid rental income may be amortized over the lease period for financial reporting but must be reported in full in the year it is collected for tax reporting. Another example is the treatment of depreciable property. For tax purposes, assets must be depreciated by using a statutorily determined recovery period, without regard for its actual useful life. For financial reporting, the same asset is depreciated over its useful life. These are but two examples of income and deduction items that are different for financial and taxable income and that will be discussed throughout the text.

Income is also referred to as *ordinary income*. **Ordinary income** is the recurring income earned by a taxpayer for a tax year.[18] It is the common type of income that people and businesses expect to earn. Ordinary income typically includes business profits, rent from property, interest on investments, dividend income, and wages. Ordinary income is subject to tax using regular tax rates and computations explained in later chapters. That is, ordinary income receives no special treatment under the tax laws.

Income also results from gains. A **gain** is the difference between the selling price of an asset and its tax cost and is the result of disposing of the asset.[19] Usually, a gain will be the result of a sale of a single asset. Most gains produce ordinary income. However, gains on the sale of certain types of assets receive special treatment in the determination of taxable income and the tax liability. These gains are called *capital gains* and result from the sale of a capital asset.

Deductions

Deductions are amounts that the tax law specifically allows as subtractions from gross income. Deductions are a matter of legislative grace. The concept of legislative grace gives us a basic rule to follow in order to determine items that qualify for deduction. The rule is that an item may not be deducted unless the tax law specifically permits it. Deductions are characterized as *expenses*, *losses*, and *exemptions*.

An **expense** is a current period expenditure that is incurred in order to earn income. Deductions for expenses are limited to those incurred in a trade or business,[20] in an income-producing activity (investment activity),[21] and certain specifically allowed personal expenses of individuals. Trade or business expenses and income-producing expenses must be ordinary, necessary, and reasonable in amount in order to be deductible. Allowable personal expenses are deductible as itemized deductions and are subject to strict limitations.

The term **loss** refers to two distinctly different types of events. A loss occurs when an asset is disposed of for a selling price that is less than its tax cost. This type of loss is referred to as a **transaction loss** and represents a loss of capital invested in the asset. In later chapters, it will be necessary to apply limits to the amount of a loss that can be deducted in a tax year. To apply the limits, losses are characterized as personal, business, or capital. These limits deny deductions for most personal losses, place a cap on the amount of capital losses that may be deducted in the year of the loss, and allow business losses to be fully deducted as incurred.

The second type of loss is an annual loss. An **annual loss** results from an excess of allowable deductions for a tax year over the reported income for the year. The treatment of the annual loss depends on the activity in which the loss is incurred. Chapter 7 discusses the limitations on and treatment of all losses, transaction and annual.

Individuals, trusts, and estates may subtract predetermined amounts called **exemptions** to determine their taxable income. The exemption deduction for individuals is, in effect, Congress's recognition that people need a minimum amount of income to provide for their basic living expenses. Thus, this minimum amount of income is deducted as an exemption and is not subject to tax. The deduction for individual exemptions is reduced for high-income taxpayers. Apparently, the reduction is Congress's way of saying that these taxpayers have enough income to support themselves and that the ability-to-pay concept should prevail. Because the minimum basic costs of living increase each year due to inflation, the exemption amounts are indexed to inflation and increase each year to reflect the increased costs individuals incur.

Income Tax Rates

The 1996 tax rate schedules for two classes of individual taxpayers and corporations are reproduced in Table 1–2.[22] A full set of tax rates for individuals, corporations, estates, and trusts for 1995 and 1996 is reproduced in Appendix A. The income tax is calculated by multiplying taxable income by the applicable tax rates. Each year, the IRS publishes new tax rate schedules that are adjusted for cost-of-

▲ Table 1–2

1996 TAX RATE
SCHEDULES

| Single Taxpayers | | | |
If taxable income is over	But not over	The tax is	Of the amount over
$ -0-	$ 24,000	..................15%	$ -0-
24,000	58,150	$ 3,600.00 + 28%	24,000
58,150	121,300	13,162.00 + 31%	58,150
121,300	263,750	32,738.50 + 36%	121,300
263,750	....	84,020.50 + 39.6%	263,750

| Married Taxpayers Filing Jointly and Surviving Spouse | | | |
If taxable income is over	But not over	The tax is	Of the amount over
$ -0-	$ 40,100	..................15%	$ -0-
40,100	96,900	$ 6,015.00 + 28%	40,100
96,900	147,700	21,919.00 + 31%	96,900
147,700	263,750	37,667.00 + 36%	147,700
263,750	....	79,445.00 + 39.6%	263,750

| Corporate Tax Rate Schedule | | | |
If taxable income is over	But not over	The tax is	Of the amount over
$ -0-	$ 50,000	..................15%	$ -0-
50,000	75,000	$ 7,500 + 25%	50,000
75,000	100,000	13,750 + 34%	75,000
100,000	335,000	22,250 + 39%	100,000
335,000	10,000,000	113,900 + 34%	335,000
10,000,000	15,000,000	3,400,000 + 35%	10,000,000
15,000,000	18,333,333	5,150,000 + 38%	15,000,000
18,333,333	....	6,416,667 + 35%	18,333,333

living increases. Adjusting the tax rate schedules for changes in the cost of living helps to minimize a hidden tax that results from inflation.

Assume the following information (shown in Exhibit 1–2): A single taxpayer's taxable income in 1995 was $56,000. The rate of inflation in 1995 was 2.84 percent, and the taxpayer was able to keep up with inflation by increasing her income. Her taxable income goes up by $1,590 to $57,590 ($56,000 × 1.0284%) in 1996. At this point, the taxpayer is no better or worse off in 1996 than in 1995. Her income increase merely kept up with the rate of inflation. The top panel of Exhibit 1–2 shows that failure to adjust the 1996 tax rates for the 2.84 percent inflation rate results in $476 in additional tax. The increased tax is attributable to two sources. First, the increased income results in an additional $445 (28% × $1,590) in tax, even if the marginal rate stays the same from the first to the second year. Second, the problem worsens when the inflated income pushes the taxpayer into a higher marginal tax bracket (tax bracket creep) causing an additional $31 in tax [(31% − 28%) × ($57,590 − $56,550)]. Thus, the taxpayer is worse off, because she pays $476 more tax on the same deflated income when tax rates are not adjusted for inflation. The net result is an increase of after-tax income of only $1,114 ($1,590 − $476), which is less than the rate of inflation.

The bottom panel of Exhibit 1–2 calculates the tax using the actual 1996 rates, which are adjusted for the 2.84 percent inflation rate. The tax on a 1996 taxable

	Tax Year	
	1995	1996
Taxable income	$56,000	$56,000
Increase in taxable income due to 2.84% inflation	-0-	1,590
Inflation-adjusted taxable income	$56,000	$57,590
Tax using 1995 single taxpayer rates:		
Tax on base amount	$ 3,503	$12,799
Excess taxed at marginal rate		
28%	9,142	
31%		322
Total tax	$12,645	$13,121
Additional tax resulting from inflation		$ 476

Tax on $57,590 at 1996 tax rates	
Tax on $24,000	$ 3,600
Tax on income in excess of $24,000	
($57,590 − $24,000) × 28%	9,405
Tax at 1996 rates	$13,005
1995 After-tax income ($56,000 − $12,645)	$43,355
1995 Inflation rate adjustment	× 1.0284
1996 Real after-tax income	$44,586
Actual 1996 after-tax income ($57,590 − $13,005)	$44,585 *

*The $1 difference is due to rounding in the calculation of the inflation-adjusted amounts.

▲ **Exhibit 1–2**

THE HIDDEN
INFLATION TAX

income of $57,590 is $13,005. This is a reduction of $116 ($13,121 − $13,005) over the tax calculated using 1995 rates on the same income. The adjustment for inflation in the tax rate brackets leaves the taxpayer with the same inflation-adjusted after-tax income in 1996 [($56,000 − $12,645) × 1.0284% = $44,586 = ($57,590 − $13,005)] that the taxpayer had in 1995. Thus, the adjustment of the tax brackets for inflation each year ensures that taxpayers whose income merely keeps pace with inflation will not realize a decrease in real after-tax income.

Tax Prepayments

The pay-as-you-go system requires the payment of tax as the income is earned and when the taxpayer has the resources available to pay the tax. Tax prepayments are subtracted from the income tax liability to determine whether the taxpayer has underpaid and owes additional tax with the return (tax due) or is entitled to a refund of overpaid taxes (refund due). Employees prepay taxes on wages through payroll-tax withholding. Other types of income, such as pensions and some gambling winnings, are also subject to the withholding of tax by the payer. The employer or other person withholding the tax pays the tax withheld to the IRS, to be credited to the taxpayer's account with the government.

Self-employed people and taxpayers with income not subject to withholding (trade or business income, interest income, dividend income, gains from sales of assets, etc.) are required to make quarterly payments of their current-year estimated tax payments. An individual usually makes quarterly payments on April 15, June 15, and September 15 of the tax year and on January 15 of the next year. This corresponds to the fifteenth day of the fourth, sixth, and ninth months of the tax year and the fifteenth day of the first month of the following year. A corporation makes its estimated tax payments on the fifteenth day of the fourth, sixth, ninth, and twelfth months of its tax year. Estates and trusts follow the estimated tax schedule used by individuals. Estimated tax payments, like withheld amounts, are subtracted as credits for the prepayment of tax.

Tax Credits

A **tax credit** is a direct reduction in the income tax liability. In effect, tax credits are treated like tax prepayments. As Exhibit 1–1 shows, a credit is not deducted to arrive at taxable income but is instead subtracted directly from the tax due. Thus, a tax credit is more valuable than a deduction of an equal amount, because the credit yields a larger reduction in the total tax due. Tax credits are often used as incentives to encourage taxpayers to enter into specific types of transactions that Congress feels will further some public purpose.

If a taxpayer's marginal tax rate is 31 percent, a $5,000 tax deduction has the same value as a $1,550 tax credit ($5,000 × 31%). Likewise, a $1,000 tax credit has the same value as a $3,226 deduction if the marginal rate is 31 percent ($1,000 ÷ 31%).

▲ **EXAMPLE 20**   Ron and Martha, whose marginal tax rate is 31%, paid $1,000 for child care.

Discussion: If the expenditure is treated as a credit, the tax they owe for the year will be reduced by the full $1,000. If the expenditure is treated as a deduction, their tax would be reduced by $310 ($1,000 × 31% marginal rate). Treatment of the expenditure as a credit would save them $690 more than treatment as a deduction.

Filing Returns

In general, all income tax entities must file an annual tax return (see Chapter 8 for individual filing requirements). Returns for individuals, estates, trusts, and partnerships must be filed on or before the fifteenth day of the fourth month following the close of the entity's tax year (April 15 for calendar-year taxpayers). Corporate tax returns are due on or before the fifteenth day of the third month following the close of a corporation's tax year (March 15 for calendar-year corporate taxpayers). Taxpayers who cannot complete and file their returns by the regular due date can apply for extensions for filing the return. Individuals are granted an automatic four-month extension by applying for the extension by the due date of the return. Corporations are allowed an automatic six-month extension; partnerships and trusts can automatically extend their filing date by three months. Filing an extension does not extend the time for paying the tax. Applications for automatic extensions must show and include payment of the estimated amount due with the final return.

▲ **EXAMPLE 21**   Thelma procrastinates about preparing her tax return and determines that she cannot complete the return by April 15. She has withholdings and estimated tax payments totaling $8,600 and estimates that her total tax liability for the year will be $8,950. What must Thelma do to extend the date for filing her return?

Discussion: Thelma can extend the period for filing her return to August 15 (four months from April 15) by filing the application for automatic extension by April 15. This only grants Thelma permission to delay the filing of the return. She must pay the $350 ($8,950 − $8,600) estimated tax she owes when she applies for the extension.

Taxpayers and the government can correct errors on returns within a limited time period called the **statute of limitations.** Generally, once the statute of limitations has expired, corrections cannot be made. The general statute of limitations is three years from the due date of the return, not including extensions. The three-year statute of limitations has several exceptions, the most important of which deal with fraudulently prepared returns. The statute of limitations runs for six years when a taxpayer omits gross income in excess of 25 percent of the gross income reported on the return. The government can bring charges of criminal fraud against a taxpayer at any time. That is, neither the three-year nor the six-year statute of limitations protects a taxpayer who willfully defrauds the government.

The government corrects errors on taxpayers' returns through its audit process (discussed in Chapter 15). Taxpayers correct errors on prior year returns by filing amended returns. Amended returns are not used to adjust returns for previous years (see discussion of the tax benefit rule in Chapter 2). An amended return should be filed only when a taxpayer finds that an item of income that should have been included in gross income was omitted in the original filing or if the taxpayer improperly included an item of income in income in a prior year. Taxpayers also should file amended returns if they find that they failed to take an allowable deduction or if they find that they took an improper deduction on an earlier return.

▲ **EXAMPLE 22**   Geraldo Corporation incurred a net operating loss in 1995, its first year of operation. Because the controller knew that Geraldo was going to suffer a loss, he took no deductions for depreciation for 1995. Geraldo's independent auditor came upon the error in 1996 and advised Geraldo that it must take all allowable deductions in the proper year. Should Geraldo file an amended return for 1995?

Discussion: Because the depreciation was not treated properly on the 1995 tax return, Geraldo should file an amended return that takes the proper depreciation deduction for 1995.

▲ **EXAMPLE 23**   Walstad Corporation is an accrual basis taxpayer. In 1995, Walstad determined that one of its customers with an accounts receivable balance of $40,000 was in bankruptcy. After conferring with the customer's lawyers, Walstad determined that it would be able to collect only $15,000 of the account and deducted the $25,000 uncollectible amount as a bad debt expense. In 1996, the customer's bankruptcy was settled, and Walstad received $10,000 as a final settlement of the account it had written off. Should Walstad file an amended return for 1995 and correct the bad debt deduction?

Discussion: The actual bad debt is $30,000 ($40,000 − $10,000). The $25,000 bad debt deduction that Walstad took in 1995 was an estimate of the amount of the bad debt. Therefore, the deduction was not incorrect at the time the return was filed. Walstad should deduct the additional $5,000 ($30,000 − $25,000) of actual bad debt in 1996 to adjust the estimate. Amended returns are not filed to adjust estimates on prior year returns. Adjustments to estimates are made on the return for the year in which the actual amount of the deduction becomes known.

INDIVIDUAL INCOME TAX CALCULATION

The general tax calculation presented in Exhibit 1–1 applies to all taxpayers. However, the tax law modifies this calculation for individuals in order to take into account the unique characteristics of individual taxpayers.

The calculation of an individual's taxable income is outlined in Exhibit 1–3. Note that the general flow remains the same—deductions are subtracted from gross income to arrive at taxable income. Gross income is determined under the

	All sources of income (broadly defined)		$ XXX
Minus:	Exclusions from income		(XXX)
Equals:	Gross income		$ XXX
Minus:	Deductions *for* adjusted gross income		
	Trade or business expenses		
	Rental and royalty expenses		
	Other specifically allowable deductions		(XXX)
Equals:	**ADJUSTED GROSS INCOME**		$ XXX
Minus:	Deductions *from* adjusted gross income		
	Personal deductions: the greater of		
	1. itemized deductions (allowable personal expenses and certain other allowable deductions)		
	OR		
	2. individual standard deduction		(XXX)
Minus:	Personal and dependency exemptions		(XXX)
Equals:	Taxable income		$ XXX

general tax formula. The distinguishing feature of the individual taxable income calculation is that deductions are broken into two classes—deductions for adjusted gross income and deductions from adjusted gross income. This dichotomy of deductions results in an intermediate income number called the **adjusted gross income (AGI).**[23] As will become clear in the discussion that follows, this is a very important income number, because it is used to provide limitations on the deductions from adjusted gross income of an individual taxpayer. Deductions are discussed in more detail in later chapters. However, at this point a general knowledge of the computational form and allowable deductions of individuals is necessary. Both types of deductions are discussed in turn.

Deductions for Adjusted Gross Income

Individuals are always allowed to deduct the qualified expenses they incur as **deductions for adjusted gross income.** In contrast to deductions from adjusted gross income, deductions in this class are not subject to reduction based on the income of the taxpayer. That is, once the allowable amount of an expenditure in this category has been determined, it is not subject to further reduction based on the income of the taxpayer. The allowable deductions for adjusted gross income are generally those that are incurred in a trade or business of the taxpayer or that are related to the earning of other forms of income. In addition, several other specifically allowed items are deductible for adjusted gross income. Deductions for adjusted gross income include

Trade or business expenses

Rental and royalty expenses

Capital loss deduction

Alimony paid

Contributions to individual retirement accounts (IRAs)

Moving expenses

Reimbursed employee business expenses

One-half of self-employment taxes paid

A percentage of self-employed medical insurance premiums

Although these expenditures are not limited by the income of the taxpayer, other limitations in the tax law may serve to reduce the current period's tax deduction. For example, the allowable deductions for rental properties may be limited by either the vacation home rules or the passive activity loss rules. Losses on the sale of capital assets are deductible but are first netted against capital gains. If the result is a net capital loss, the current year's deduction is limited to a maximum of $3,000.[24] These losses and other limits are covered in the chapters on deductions and losses. The important point to remember for now is that once the allowable amount of a deduction for adjusted gross income has been determined, it is not subject to further reduction. In addition, there is no preset minimum allowable amount of deductions for adjusted gross income.

Deductions from Adjusted Gross Income

Individuals are allowed to deduct certain personal expenditures and other specified nonpersonal expenditures as **deductions from adjusted gross income.** These deductions are commonly referred to as **itemized deductions.** Note in Exhibit 1–3 that individuals deduct the greater of their allowable itemized deductions or the standard deduction.[25] The **standard deduction** is an amount that Congress allows all taxpayers to deduct, regardless of their actual qualifying itemized deduction expenditures. Thus, taxpayers itemize their deductions only if their total allowable itemized deductions exceed the standard deduction. For 1996, the standard deduction for a single individual is $4,000 and $6,700 for a married couple.

> ▲ **EXAMPLE 24**   Festus is a single taxpayer with total allowable itemized deductions of $1,800 in 1996. What is Festus's allowable deduction from adjusted gross income?
>
> *Discussion:*   Festus deducts the larger of his $1,800 in itemized deductions or the $4,000 standard deduction for a single individual. In this case, Festus deducts the $4,000 standard deduction.
>
> ▲ **EXAMPLE 25**   Assume that in example 24 Festus's total allowable itemized deductions are $6,700 in 1996. What is his allowable deduction from adjusted gross income?
>
> *Discussion:*   Festus would deduct the $6,700 in actual itemized deductions because it exceeds his $4,000 standard deduction.

As these examples illustrate, just because a particular expenditure is allowed as an itemized deduction does not necessarily mean that a taxpayer incurring the expense will actually deduct it. Itemized deductions reduce taxable income only when a taxpayer's total itemized deductions exceed the allowable standard deduction.

In addition to providing all taxpayers with some minimum amount of deduction, the standard deduction eliminates the need for every taxpayer to list every qualifying personal expenditure. This makes it easier for taxpayers with small amounts of qualifying expenditures to comply with the tax law and relieves the government from having to verify millions of deductions that would have been claimed as a result of itemizing. Thus, the standard deduction is an important tool that the government uses to promote income tax law compliance by removing the burden of record keeping and reporting for relatively small amounts of deductible items.

In the deduction classification scheme, specifically allowed personal expenditures are classified as itemized deductions.[26] In addition to personal expenditures, investment expenses and certain other employment-related expenses are deductible as itemized deductions. Many allowable itemized deductions are subject to an income limitation. That is, the amount of the qualifying expenditure must be reduced by a percentage of the taxpayer's adjusted gross income to determine the actual deduction. The effect of using this type of income limitation is to disallow deductions for amounts that are small in relation to the taxpayer's income.

▲ **EXAMPLE 26**   Qualifying medical expenses are deductible to the extent that they exceed 7.5% of a taxpayer's adjusted gross income. During the current year, Li has an adjusted gross income of $40,000 and incurred $4,200 in qualified medical expenses. What is Li's itemized deduction for medical expense?

Discussion: Li must reduce the $4,200 of qualified medical expenses by $3,000 ($40,000 × 7.5%), resulting in deductible medical expenses of $1,200.

Note that the effect of the limitation is to allow larger deductions for taxpayers with smaller incomes. Another taxpayer incurring the same $4,200 in expenses and who had an adjusted gross income of only $25,000 would be allowed to deduct $2,325 [$4,200 − ($25,000 × 7.5% = $1,875)] of the medical expenses.

The following list is intended to acquaint you with the categories of itemized deductions available to individuals. At this point, you should note the types of personal expenses that are allowed as a deduction. Do not be concerned about the detailed deduction requirements and limitations. These issues are explained in more detail in Chapter 8.

MEDICAL EXPENSES—Unreimbursed medical expenses are deductible to the extent that they exceed 7.5 percent of adjusted gross income. Medical expenses include the cost of medical insurance, physicians, hospitals, glasses and contact lenses, and a multitude of other items. Because of the AGI limit, many taxpayers benefit from these deductions only when there is a major illness in the family.[27]

TAXES—State, local, and foreign income taxes, real estate taxes, and state and local personal property taxes may be deducted.[28]

INTEREST—An individual's deduction for personal interest expense is limited to the following:[29]

■ Home mortgage interest related to the acquisition of a home or to a home equity loan

■ Investment interest expense

CHARITABLE CONTRIBUTIONS—Gifts to qualified charitable organizations may be deducted. Generally, the deductible contribution may not exceed 50 percent of the taxpayer's adjusted gross income.[30]

PERSONAL CASUALTY AND THEFT LOSSES—Deductions are allowed for losses of property from casualty or theft, subject to two limitations. Because of the limitations, most taxpayers must have a large total loss for the year to get a deduction for a personal casualty or theft loss.[31]

MISCELLANEOUS ITEMIZED DEDUCTIONS—This is a broad category of deductions that includes most expenses related to the production of investment income. The following list of miscellaneous deductions illustrates the types of items deducted in this category:

- Business expenses of an employee not reimbursed by an employer
- Investment-related expenses
- Expenses related to tax return preparation, planning, and examination

Generally, the deduction allowed for miscellaneous itemized deductions must be reduced by 2 percent of the taxpayer's adjusted gross income.[32]

Personal and Dependency Exemptions

Individuals are allowed to deduct a predetermined amount for each qualifying exemption.[33] In 1996, individuals deduct $2,550 for each qualifying personal and dependency exemption. The intention is to exempt from tax a minimum amount of income that is used to support the taxpayer and those who are dependent on that taxpayer. Because support costs increase with inflation, the exemption amounts are increased each year to account for the prior year's inflation. **Personal exemptions** are allowed for the taxpayer and the taxpayer's spouse. **Dependency exemptions** are granted for individuals who are dependent on the taxpayer for support. Although there are five technical tests (discussed in Chapter 8) that must be met to qualify as a dependent, the underlying reasoning is that the dependent must rely on the taxpayer for basic living costs. Thus, children of a taxpayer and other relatives, such as parents and grandchildren who live with the taxpayer, are the most common dependents.

> ▲ **EXAMPLE 27**   John and Nancy are married and have 3 small children who live with them and depend on them for their support. What is John and Nancy's 1996 exemption deduction?
>
> *Discussion:*   John and Nancy are entitled to 2 personal exemptions and 3 dependency exemptions. Their deduction is $12,750 ($2,550 × 5 exemptions).

TAX PLANNING

The objective of tax planning is to maximize after-tax wealth. An effective tax plan results in a reduction of taxes for the planning period. Because a planning period may be two or more years, focusing on reducing tax for one year without considering any offsetting effects for other years can lead to excessive tax payments. The traditional planning technique of deferring income and accelerating deductions may not always be the best tax plan. The traditional technique considers only the time value of money savings that can be obtained from delaying tax payments on income or receiving tax savings from deductions sooner. Although the time value of money must always be considered, changes in marginal tax rates from one year to the next can have effects that offset the time value of money. Thus in many cases, changes in both the marginal tax rate and the time value of money must be considered when developing a tax plan. The mechanics of tax planning demonstrate basic techniques that can be used to help make tax-planning decisions. The planning discussion concludes by pointing out that tax avoidance is acceptable but tax evasion is not.

Mechanics of Tax Planning

The mechanics of tax planning focus on the issues of timing and income shifting. The timing question to be answered is when income and deductions should be claimed to save the most *real tax*. To make decisions involving timing, it is necessary to compare the tax effects of changes in marginal tax rates and the time value of money. To make the optimal choice among different alternatives, it is necessary to do the calculations to determine the *real* after-tax cost of each alternative. Income shifting involves moving income among related taxpayers to achieve the lowest marginal taxes (and lowest total tax) on the entire income of the related taxpayers. Shifting is commonly done by transferring income-producing property between family members and by using corporations that taxpayers control to shift income into the lowest marginal tax rates.

Timing Income and Deductions.   A taxpayer's marginal tax rate and the time value of money must be considered in tax planning. The traditional technique of deferring income and accelerating deductions relies solely on the time value of money savings from delaying the tax payment or receiving the tax deduction savings earlier. For example, a taxpayer who expects to be in a 28-percent marginal tax bracket for the next several years might be indifferent about reporting $1,000 in extra income in 1996 or 1997. Regardless of which year the income is reported, the taxpayer pays $280 in tax and keeps $720 ($1,000 − $280) in after-tax income. When the present value of the tax payment is considered (see Table 1–3 for present values factors), it becomes clear that choice of years does make a difference. If the taxpayer's applicable interest rate is 10 percent and the marginal rate is expected to remain the same, deferring payment of the tax until 1997 results in an interest-free loan. The present value of the tax savings is $25:

Tax paid in 1997	$280
10% present value factor	× 0.909
Present value of tax paid in 1997	$255
Present value of tax paid in 1996	280
Real tax savings by deferring income	$ 25

If the marginal rate is expected to decrease to 15 percent in 1997, the taxpayer has a greater incentive to defer the income. By deferring the income to 1997, the taxpayer receives the benefit of an interest-free loan for one year plus the benefit of the lower marginal tax rate. Deferring the income to 1997, would result in a real tax benefit of $144:

Tax paid in 1997 ($1,000 × 15%)	$150
10% present value factor	× 0.909
Present value of tax paid in 1997	$136
Present value of tax paid in 1996	280
Real tax savings by deferring income	$144

Table 1–3 shows how much $1 to be paid at a future date is worth today at the discount rate indicated.

If the taxpayer expects the marginal tax rate to increase to 31 percent next year, the income should be reported in 1996. Deferring the income to 1997 would have a real tax cost of $2:

Tax paid in 1997 ($1,000 × 31%)	$310
10% present value factor	× 0.909
Present value of tax paid in 1997	$282
Present value of tax paid in 1996	280
Real tax cost of deferring income	$ 2

The same approach can be used to determine the best timing for a deduction. However, keep in mind that deductions are the opposite of income—they reduce

Present Value of a Single Payment							
Year	5%	6%	7%	8%	9%	10%	12%
1	0.952	0.943	0.935	0.926	0.917	0.909	0.893
2	0.907	0.890	0.873	0.857	0.842	0.826	0.797
3	0.864	0.840	0.816	0.794	0.722	0.751	0.712
4	0.823	0.792	0.793	0.735	0.708	0.683	0.636
5	0.784	0.747	0.713	0.681	0.650	0.621	0.567
6	0.746	0.705	0.666	0.630	0.596	0.564	0.507
7	0.711	0.665	0.623	0.583	0.547	0.513	0.452
8	0.677	0.627	0.582	0.540	0.502	0.467	0.404
9	0.645	0.592	0.544	0.500	0.460	0.424	0.361
10	0.614	0.558	0.508	0.463	0.422	0.386	0.322

▲ Table 1–3

PRESENT VALUE TABLES

taxes paid. Therefore, the optimal choice for deductions is to maximize the real after-tax reduction in taxes paid. In many situations, it may be necessary to compare the offsetting effects of income and deduction items.

▲ **EXAMPLE 28**   Ann Corporation owes a $2,000 expense that may be paid and deducted on the cash basis of accounting in either 1996 or 1997. The applicable interest rate is 10%. In which year should Ann Corporation take the deduction if its 1996 marginal tax rate is 25%?

Discussion: The optimal year for taking the deduction depends on Ann Corporation's expected marginal tax rate in 1997. The following schedule calculates the real tax savings (real tax cost) of deducting the expenses in 1996 as compared to deferring the deduction until 1997 at different assumed marginal tax rates:

	Assumed 1997 Marginal Tax Rates		
	15%	25%	34%
Tax saved by 1997 deduction	$ 300	$ 500	$ 680
Present value @ 10%	× 0.909	× 0.909	× 0.909
Present value of tax savings	$ 273	$ 455	$ 618
Less: Tax savings of deduction in 1996 @ 25% marginal tax rate	(500)	(500)	(500)
Deduction in 1996 will result in:			
Tax savings	$(227)	$ (45)	
Tax cost			$ 118

Discussion: Ann Corporation should claim the deduction in 1996 if it expects the marginal tax rate to remain at 25% or decrease to 15%. If the corporation expects its marginal rate to increase to 34%, it should defer the deduction to 1997 to save $118.

▲ **EXAMPLE 29**   Lanny's marginal tax rate for 1996 is 28%. Lanny has $20,000 in income and $10,000 in deductions that could be reported in 1996 or deferred to 1997. Lanny expects his 1997 marginal tax rate to be 31% and the applicable interest rate to be 10%. When should the items be reported if both the income and deductions must be reported in the same year?

Discussion: The result of reporting both the income and the deductions in 1996 as compared to 1997 is as follows:

	1996	1997
Increase in income	$ 20,000	$ 20,000
Less: Increase in deductions	(10,000)	(10,000)
Net increase in taxable income	$ 10,000	$ 10,000
Marginal tax rate	× 28%	× 31%
Tax on net increase in income	$ 2,800	$ 3,100
Present value factor		× 0.909
Present value of tax in 1996	$ 2,800	$ 2,818

Discussion: Lanny should report the items in 1996 to save $18 in real tax cost.

▲ **EXAMPLE 30**   If Lanny could report the income or deductions separately, when should the income and the deductions be reported to maximize the tax savings?

Discussion: The tax cost of reporting each item must be considered separately and the total result compared to reporting both items in 1996 (which was previously determined to be the optimal same-year reporting).

Income

| | Report income in | |
	1996	1997
Increase in taxable income	$20,000	$20,000
Marginal tax rate	× 28%	× 31%
Increase in tax	$ 5,600	$ 6,200
Present value factor		× 0.909
Present value of tax in 1996	$ 5,600	$ 5,636
Net tax savings from reporting in 1996	36	

Deductions

| | Report deductions in | |
	1996	1997
Decrease in taxable income	$10,000	$10,000
Marginal tax rate	× 28%	× 31%
Tax savings from deduction	$ 2,800	$ 3,100
Present value factor		× 0.909
Present value of tax savings	$ 2,800	$ 2,818
Net tax savings from reporting in 1997	18	

Discussion: If Lanny reports the $20,000 of income in 1996, he has a real tax savings of $36. Deferring the reporting of the $10,000 in deductions until 1997 results in a real tax savings of $18. Thus, by reporting each item separately in the period that is optimal, he saves $54. This compares to a savings of $18 when both income and deductions are reported in the same tax year.

In summary, there are four general rules of thumb to follow when planning the timing of income and deductions; two are based on time value of money propositions, and two are based on marginal tax rate considerations:

Time Value of Money

1. Defer recognition of income.
2. Accelerate recognition of deductions.

Type of Item	Marginal Tax Rate		
	Increasing	Decreasing	Unchanged
Income	Calculate	Defer	Defer
Deduction	Calculate	Accelerate	Accelerate

▲ **Table 1–4**

SUMMARY OF TAX-PLANNING RULES

Marginal Tax Rate

　　3. Put income into the year with the lowest expected marginal tax rate.

　　4. Put deductions into the year with highest expected marginal tax rate.

These general rules of thumb can be used in most situations. However, if there is a conflict between the time value rule and the marginal tax rate rule, the only way to determine the optimal strategy is to calculate the real tax cost of each. Table 1–4 summarizes the rules of thumb and indicates when calculation of the real tax cost is necessary.

Income Shifting.　　Income shifting is a method commonly used to reduce taxes. The basic idea behind income shifting is to split a single stream of income between two or more taxpayers to lower the total tax paid. The total tax paid is lower because of the progressive tax rate structure. For example, if a taxpayer in the 31-percent marginal tax rate bracket can shift $1,000 in income to another taxpayer who is in the 15-percent marginal tax rate bracket, $160 [$1,000 × (31% − 15%)] of tax will be saved on the $1,000 in income. Obviously, taxpayers shifting income will want the income to go to taxpayers whom they want to benefit, such as children or grandchildren.

▲ **EXAMPLE 31**　　A married taxpayer has $100,000 in taxable income in 1996. The taxpayer has 2 children who have no taxable income. What are the tax savings if the taxpayer can legally shift $10,000 in income to each of her children?

Discussion:　　The taxpayer saves $2,693 in tax by shifting $10,000 in taxable income to each child. Using the rates for married taxpayers, the tax on $100,000 in taxable income is $22,880:

$$\$21,919 \; + \; 31\% \; (\$100,000 \; - \; \$96,900) \; = \; \$22,880$$

By splitting the income into 3 streams, the taxpayer pays tax on $80,000, and each child pays tax (at single taxpayer rates) on $10,000. This results in a tax of $20,187:

Tax on $80,000 for a Married Couple

$$\$6,015 \; + \; 28\% \; (\$80,000 \; - \; \$40,100) \; = \; \$17,187$$

Tax on $10,000 for a Single Person

$$\$10,000 \; \times \; 15\% \; = \; \$1,500 \; \times \; 2 \; = \; \underline{\quad 3,000}$$

$$\text{Total tax paid} \qquad \underline{\$20,187}$$

The result of the income shift to the children is a reduction in the total tax paid on the $100,000 in taxable income of $2,693 ($22,880 − $20,187).

It should be noted that numerous provisions in the tax law make it difficult to get the full advantage of income shifting. For example, merely directing some of your income to be paid to your children will not shift the income for tax purposes. In order to shift income to family members, you will generally need to transfer ownership of income-producing property to the children in order to shift the income from the property. Unless the parents are willing to give up ownership of income-producing property, income shifting to children is difficult to achieve. Even if a valid transfer of property ownership is made, if the child is younger than 14, provisions exist to take away much of the marginal rate advantage of such a shift.

Another popular income-shifting technique used by owners of a business is to incorporate the business and split income between themselves and the corporation. A review of the corporate tax rates (see Table 1–2) shows that the first $50,000 in taxable income of a corporation is taxed at 15 percent. The owners can split the income by paying themselves salaries, which are deductible by the corporation, and reduce the corporation's taxable income to the lower tax brackets.

▲ EXAMPLE 32   Assume that the $100,000 in taxable income in example 31 comes from a business owned by the taxpayer. If the taxpayer incorporates the business and pays herself a salary of $50,000, what is the tax savings?

Discussion: Splitting the income between the taxpayer and a corporation results in a tax savings of $6,593. The taxpayer pays tax on $50,000, and the corporation pays tax on $50,000 ($100,000 income − $50,000 salary). This results in a tax of $16,287:

Tax on $50,000 for a Married Couple

$$\$6,015 + 28\% \, (\$50,000 - \$40,100) = \$8,787$$

Tax on $50,000 for a Corporation

$$\$50,000 \times 15\% = \underline{7,500}$$

$$\text{Total tax paid} \qquad \underline{\underline{\$16,287}}$$

Before incorporation, the tax paid by the married couple was $22,880. The incorporation and split of the income saves $6,593 ($22,880 − $16,287) in tax.

Numerous other income-shifting techniques can be used by owners of a business. These include shifting income by employing children and using fringe-benefit packages to get tax-subsidized health care. It should be noted that careful planning is required in order to gain the optimal tax advantage from such shifting plans. The tax law contains many provisions that are designed to block blatant shifting schemes that lack economic substance. These provisions are discussed throughout the remainder of the text as they apply to the study of income and deductions.

Tax Evasion and Tax Avoidance

Taxpayers do not have to pay more income tax than is required by the tax law. In fact, taxpayers may plan transactions to make their tax bills as low as possible. In this regard, Judge Learned Hand stated: "[A] transaction, otherwise within an exception of the tax law, does not lose its immunity, because it is actuated by a desire to avoid, or, if one choose, to evade, taxation. Any one may so arrange his affairs that his taxes shall be as low as possible; he is not bound to choose that pattern which will best pay the Treasury; there is not even a patriotic duty to increase one's taxes."[34]

Tax evasion occurs when a taxpayer uses fraudulent methods or deceptive behavior to hide the actual tax liability. Tax evasion usually involves three elements:

- Willfulness on the part of the taxpayer

- An underpayment of tax
- An affirmative act by the taxpayer to evade the tax

Tax evasion often involves rearranging the facts about a transaction in order to receive a tax benefit. An intentional misrepresentation of facts on a tax return to avoid paying tax is not acceptable taxpayer behavior. Tax evasion is illegal and is subject to substantial penalties. Note that unintentional mathematical or clerical errors on the return are not generally considered tax evasion.

Tax planning uses tax avoidance methods. **Tax avoidance** is the use of legal methods allowed by the tax law to minimize a tax liability. Tax avoidance generally involves planning an intended transaction to obtain a specific tax treatment. Further, tax avoidance is based on disclosure of relevant facts concerning the tax treatment of a transaction.

▲ **EXAMPLE 33**   Ted, an accountant, uses the cash method of accounting. To avoid reporting additional income in 1996, he does not send his December bills to clients until January 2, 1997.

Discussion: The income was properly reported when collected in 1997. Under the cash method of accounting, Ted properly reported income when his clients paid him. Ted's activity involved permissible tax avoidance.

▲ **EXAMPLE 34**   Ken, a painter, spent all the cash he received for his art work. He deposited payments he received by check to his business bank account. When he filed his tax return, he intentionally did not report the cash receipts as income.

Discussion: Ken is engaged in tax evasion. Ken's method of reducing his tax is illegal, and he is subject to substantial penalties.

At this point, you are probably wondering, "How will the IRS ever know?" Most people are aware that it is almost impossible for the government to track every cash receipt of income. In fact, the probability that the IRS will detect underreporting of cash income is quite low. This has led many taxpayers to play the "audit lottery," omitting cash income or overstating deductions, because they know that they probably will not be caught. The IRS estimates that this behavior results in a loss of nearly $100 billion per year in tax revenue. This loss must be made up through higher taxes on wage earners and honest taxpayers. It is clear that if taxpayers were more honest in their reporting of income and deductions, everyone's taxes could be lowered. There is no clear-cut, cost-efficient solution to the evasion problem. However, as future professionals and taxpayers, you should recognize your obligations to your profession and the country when it comes to tax evasion situations. Only through education and ethical taxpayer behavior will the tax evasion problem be resolved. Keep in mind that avoiding detection by the IRS does not somehow magically transform a fraudulent act into allowable behavior. The idea that something is not illegal unless one is caught is an idea that should have died ages ago.

ETHICAL CONSIDERATIONS IN TAX PRACTICE

The field of tax practice is virtually unregulated—anyone who wishes to can prepare tax returns for a fee. However, anyone who prepares tax returns for monetary considerations, or who is licensed to practice in the tax-related professions, is subject to various rules and codes of professional conduct. For example, the Internal Revenue Code contains provisions (see Exhibit 1–4 for a list of preparer penalties) that impose civil and criminal penalties on tax return preparers for various improprieties.

▲ **Exhibit 1–4**

I.R.C. Violations with Penalties for Tax Return Preparers

Understatement of taxpayer's liability due to unrealistic positions

Understatement of taxpayer's liability due to willful or reckless conduct

Failure to furnish a copy of a return to the taxpayer

Failure to sign a return

Failure to furnish identifying information

Failure to retain a copy or a list of returns prepared

Failure to file correct information returns

Negotiation of tax refund check

Improper disclosure or use of information on taxpayer's return

Organizing (or assisting in doing so) or promoting and making or furnishing statements with respect to abusive tax shelters

Aiding and abetting an understatement of tax liability

Aiding or assisting in the preparation of a false return

All tax practitioners are subject to the provisions of *IRS Circular 230*, "Regulations Governing the Practice of Attorneys, Certified Public Accountants, Enrolled Agents, and Enrolled Actuaries Before the Internal Revenue Service." Tax attorneys are subject to the ethical code of conduct adopted by the state(s) in which they are licensed to practice. Certified Public Accountants (CPAs) who are members of the American Institute of Certified Public Accountants (AICPA) are governed by the institute's Code of Professional Conduct. The AICPA's Statements on Responsibilities in Tax Practice provide eight advisory guidelines for CPAs who prepare tax returns. Although tax practitioners who are not members of the AICPA are not bound by the Code of Professional Conduct and the Statements on Responsibilities in Tax Practice, the rules and guidelines contained in them provide useful guidance for all return preparers.

The AICPA Code of Professional Conduct is a set of rules that set enforceable ethical standards for members of the institute. The standards are broad and apply to all professional services that a CPA may render, including tax advice and tax return preparation. For example,

1. Rule 102 requires CPAs to perform professional services with objectivity and integrity; they should avoid any conflict of interest. CPAs should neither knowingly misrepresent facts nor subordinate their judgment to that of others in rendering professional advice.

2. Rule 202 requires compliance with all standards that have been promulgated by certain bodies designated by the AICPA's governing council.

3. Rule 301 states that CPAs will not disclose confidential client data without the specific consent of the client, except under certain specified conditions.

The eight Statements on Responsibilities in Tax Practice (SRTP) provide guidance on what constitutes appropriate standards of tax practice. The statements are intended to supplement, not replace, the Code of Professional Conduct. Because they specifically address the problems inherent in tax practice, each statement is briefly described here. The full text of the SRTP is reproduced in Appendix D.

SRTP No. 1: *Tax Return Positions.* CPAs should not recommend that a position be taken on a return unless they believe that, if the position is challenged, it is likely to be sustained, which is known as the *realistic possibility standard.* CPAs should not prepare a return or sign as preparer of a return if they know that the return takes a position that could not be recommended because it does not meet the realistic possibility standard. However, a CPA may recommend any return position that is not frivolous, so long as the position is adequately disclosed on the return. SRTP Interpretation No. 1-1 (reproduced in Appendix D) contains the AICPA interpretation of the realistic possibility standard.

SRTP No. 2: *Answers to Questions on Returns.* A CPA should make a reasonable effort to obtain from the client and provide appropriate answers to all questions on a tax return before signing as preparer. Where reasonable grounds exist for omission of an answer, no explanation for the omission is required, and the CPA may sign the return unless the omission would cause the return to be considered incomplete.

SRTP No. 3: *Procedural Aspects of Preparing Returns.* A CPA may in good faith rely upon, without verification, information furnished by the client or third parties. Reasonable inquiries should be made if the information furnished appears to be incorrect, incomplete, or inconsistent. The CPA should make use of previous years' returns whenever possible in order to avoid omissions. In addition, the CPA may appropriately use information from the tax return of another client if the information would not violate the confidentiality of the CPA-client relationship and is relevant to and necessary for proper preparation of the return.

SRTP No. 4: *Use of Estimates.* A CPA may prepare returns using estimates provided by the taxpayer if it is impracticable to obtain exact data and the estimates are reasonable, given the facts and circumstances.

SRTP No. 5: *Departure from Previous Position.* If a CPA follows the standards in SRTP No. 1, the result of an administrative proceeding or court decision with respect to a prior return of the taxpayer does not bind the CPA as to how the item should be treated in a subsequent year's return.

SRTP No. 6: *Knowledge of Error: Return Preparation.* A CPA who becomes aware of an error in a previous year's return—or of the client's failure to file a required return—should promptly inform the client and recommend measures to be taken to correct the error. The CPA may not inform the IRS of the error except when required to do so by law. If the client does not correct the error, the CPA should consider whether to continue the professional relationship and must take reasonable steps to ensure that the error is not repeated if the relationship is continued.

SRTP No. 7: *Knowledge of Error: Administrative Proceedings.* When a CPA becomes aware of an error in a return that is the subject of an administrative proceeding, the CPA should promptly inform the client of the error and recommend measures to be taken. The CPA should request the client's consent to disclose the error to the IRS but should not disclose the error without consent unless required to do so by law. If the client refuses disclosure, the CPA should consider whether to withdraw from representing the client in the administrative proceeding and whether to continue a professional relationship with the client.

SRTP No. 8: *Form and Content of Advice to Clients.* A CPA should use judgment to ensure that advice given to a client reflects professional competence and appropriately serves the client's needs. For all tax advice given to a client, the CPA should adhere to the standards of SRTP No. 1, pertaining to tax return positions. A CPA may choose to notify a client when subsequent developments affect advice previously given on significant tax matters but is under no strict obligation to do so.

SUMMARY

Taxes are a fact of everyday life. Taxes are levied on income, products, property holdings, and transfers of wealth. The federal income tax is the largest revenue producer of all the taxes currently in use in the United States. Therefore, a solid understanding of the basic rules of the income tax system is essential to maximize your after-tax income.

The term *tax* has been defined, and concepts have been examined that will help you reach your own conclusions about whether a tax is "good" or "bad." Keep these evaluations in mind as you continue through the text and as you read articles on proposed tax legislation.

The income tax law is a complex body of constantly changing information that is issued by legislative, administrative, and judicial sources. When evaluating a particular tax rule, it may be necessary to consult resources in all three areas.

Tax terms used in income tax computation have been defined in this chapter. Subsequent chapters explain the terms and build on the basic information. When you encounter a new term in later chapters, do not hesitate to refer to this chapter to see how the new term fits into the computational framework.

The study of federal income taxation will help you evaluate how business and personal financial decisions influence the amount of income tax you will have to pay. Awareness of basic income tax concepts will help you recognize opportunities to minimize compliance costs, save taxes, avoid IRS penalties, and make more informed business decisions.

The practical approach to tax planning discussed in this chapter does not require you to be a tax specialist to become an effective tax planner. In later chapters, you will be asked to solve tax-planning problems that require you to make decisions about when an item of income or deduction should be reported. When solving these problems, you will need to consider the effects of changes in the marginal tax rate and the time value of money.

Finally, always be aware of the difference between tax evasion and tax avoidance. Avoid tax evasion—it is illegal. Tax avoidance is legal and is expected of taxpayers.

KEY TERMS

adjusted gross income (AGI) (p. 26)
ad valorem tax (p. 15)
annual loss (p. 21)
average tax rate (p. 8)
certainty (p. 6)
convenience (p. 6)
deduction (p. 21)

deductions for adjusted gross income (p. 26)
deductions from adjusted gross income (p. 27)
deferral (p. 20)
dependency exemption (p. 29)
economy (p. 7)
effective tax rate (p. 8)

equality (p. 5)
estate tax (p. 16)
exclusion (p. 20)
exemption (p. 21)
expense (p. 21)
gain (p. 20)
gift tax (p. 16)
gross income (p. 20)

horizontal equity (p. 5)
Internal Revenue Code of 1986
   (p. 18)
itemized deduction (p. 27)
loss (p. 21)
marginal tax rate (p. 8)
ordinary income (p. 20)
pay-as-you-go concept (p. 7)
personal exemption (p. 29)
personal property (p. 15)

progressive rate structure (p. 10)
proportional rate structure
   (p. 8)
real property (p. 15)
regressive rate structure (p. 9)
self-employment tax (p. 12)
Social Security taxes (p. 12)
standard deduction (p. 27)
statute of limitations (p. 24)
taxable income (p. 7)

tax avoidance (p. 35)
tax base (p. 7)
tax credit (p. 24)
tax evasion (p. 34)
transaction loss (p. 21)
Treasury regulation (p. 18)
unified donative-transfers credit
   (p. 17)
vertical equity (p. 5)

PRIMARY TAX LAW SOURCES

[1] Rev. Rul. 77-29.

[2] Sec. 6072—Specifies the general rules for due dates of tax returns.

[3] Sec. 1—Imposes a tax on the taxable income of different classes of individual taxpayers; provides tax rates by class of taxpayer and requires adjustment of rate schedules each year for inflation; limits the tax rate on net long-term capital gains to 28%.

[4] Sec. 3402—Requires employers to withhold estimates of taxes on wages and salaries paid to employees.

[5] Sec. 31—Provides that amounts withheld as tax from salaries and wages are allowed as credits against that year's tax liability.

[6] Sec. 6654—Provides that all individuals must pay estimated taxes when their tax liability is expected to be greater than $500; imposes a penalty for not paying the proper amount of estimated tax.

[7] Sec. 3101—Imposes the Social Security tax on employees; provides rates of tax to be paid.

[8] Sec. 1402—Defines *self-employment income* and provides for the tax to be paid on base amounts as specified in the Social Security Act for each tax year.

[9] Sec. 3111—Imposes the Social Security tax on employers for wages paid to employees.

[10] Sec. 1401—Provides the tax rates for self-employment taxes.

[11] Sec. 2501—Imposes a gift tax on transfers of property by gift.

[12] Sec. 2503—Allows exclusion from gift tax of gifts up to $10,000.

[13] Sec. 2505—Allows unified credit against taxable gifts.

[14] Sec. 2001—Imposes a tax on the assets of an estate. Provides tax rates on estate assets and for unlimited marital exclusion.

[15] Sec. 2010—Provides for unified tax credit against tax liability of an estate.

[16] Sec. 7801—Directs the secretary of the Treasury to issue the regulations necessary to implement and interpret the tax law.

[17] Sec. 61—Provides the general definition of *gross income* as all income from whatever source derived.

[18] Sec. 64—Defines *ordinary income* as income that does not result from the sale or exchange of property that is not a capital asset or an asset described in Sec. 1231.

[19] Sec. 1001—Prescribes the calculation of gains and losses for dispositions of property; defines *amount realized* for purposes of determining gain or loss for dispositions.

[20] Sec. 162—Allows the deduction of all ordinary and necessary expenses incurred in a trade or business of the taxpayer.

[21] Sec. 212—Allows the deduction of all ordinary and necessary expenses incurred in a production-of-income activity of the taxpayer.

[22] Sec. 11—Imposes an income tax on corporations and provides the applicable tax rate schedules.

[23] Sec. 62—Defines *adjusted gross income* for individual taxpayers and specifies the deductions allowed as deductions for adjusted gross income.

[24] Sec. 1211—Sets forth the limit on deductions of capital losses of corporations and individuals.

[25] Sec. 63—Defines *taxable income*. Allows individual taxpayers to deduct the greater of their allowable itemized deductions or the standard deduction. Standard deduction amounts are specified and are required to be adjusted annually for inflation.

[26] Sec. 211—Generally allows specific personal expenditures as itemized deductions of individuals.

[27] Sec. 213—Allows the deduction of medical expenses as an itemized deduction for individual taxpayers; defines *medical expenses* and prescribes limitations on the amount of the deduction.

[28] Sec. 164—Specifies the allowable deductions for taxes.

[29] Sec. 163—Specifies the allowable deductions for interest.

[30] Sec. 170—Allows the deduction of contributions to qualified charitable organizations.

[31] Sec. 165—Specifies the allowable deductions for losses.

[32] Sec. 67—Limits the allowable deduction for miscellaneous itemized deductions to the excess of 2% of adjusted gross income.

[33] Sec. 151—Allows an exemption deduction for the taxpayer, the taxpayer's spouse, and for each qualifying dependent.

[34] Helvering v. Gregory, 69 F.2d 809 at 810 (2d Cir. 1934).

DISCUSSION QUESTIONS

1. Briefly state Adam Smith's four requirements for a good tax system.

2. Based on the discussion in the chapter, evaluate how well each of these taxes meets Adam Smith's four requirements:
   a. Income tax
   b. Employment taxes

3. Based solely on the definitions in the chapter, is the Social Security tax a proportional, regressive, or progressive tax? Explain, and state how the tax might be viewed differently.

4. Based solely on the definitions in the chapter, is the sales tax a proportional, regressive, or progressive tax? Explain, and state how the tax might be viewed differently.

5. As stated in the text, the federal income tax is the largest revenue-producing tax currently in use in the United States. Why do you think that the income tax produces more revenue than any other tax?

6. How are federal, state, and local income taxes collected by the government? Consider the cases of an employee and a self-employed taxpayer.

7. How is a sales tax different from an excise tax?

8. Who is responsible for collecting sales and excise taxes? Who actually pays the tax?

9. Why is a tax on real property used more often than a tax on personal property?

10. The gift tax is supposed to tax the transfer of wealth from one taxpayer to another. However, the payment of gift tax on a transfer of property is relatively rare. Why is gift tax not paid on most gifts?

11. The estate tax is a tax on the value of property transferred at death. Why is payment of the estate tax not a common event?

12. What is the basis for valuing assets transferred by gift and at death?

13. Who is responsible for reporting and paying gift taxes? estate taxes?

14. Identify three primary sources of tax law.

15. Explain why the following statement is not necessarily true: "If the IRS disagrees, I'll take my case all the way to the Supreme Court."

16. What is the federal income tax base?

17. What is an exclusion?

18. How is a deferral different from an exclusion?

19. How is gross income different from income?

20. What are the three basic tests that an expense must satisfy in order to be deductible?

21. What is the difference between an expense and a loss?

22. How is a transaction loss different from an annual loss?

23. How does the legislative grace concept help identify amounts that qualify for deduction?

24. What is the purpose of the exemption deduction?

25. Based on the example in Exhibit 1–2, explain how inflation can have two effects that result in a hidden tax.

26. Explain the pay-as-you-go system.

27. What is a tax credit?

28. How is a tax credit different from a tax deduction?

29. If you were in the 31% marginal tax bracket and you could choose either a $1,000 tax credit or a $2,500 tax deduction, which would give you the most tax saving? Why?

30. What is the statute of limitations, and what role does it play in the filing of tax returns?

31. How is the calculation of taxable income for an individual different from the calculation of a corporation's taxable income?

32. How do deductions for adjusted gross and deductions from adjusted gross income of an individual differ?

33. What is the purpose of the standard deduction for individuals?

34. Randy is studying finance at State University. To complete the finance major, he has to take a basic income tax course. Because Randy does not intend to be a tax expert, he considers the course a waste of his time. Explain to Randy how he can benefit from the tax course.

35. Evaluate the following statement: "The goal of good tax planning is to pay the minimum amount of tax."

36. It has often been said that only the rich can benefit from professional tax planning. Based on the information presented in this chapter, why is this statement at least partially true?

PROBLEMS

37. State whether each of the following payments is a tax. Explain your answers.
   a. A $5 fee paid to the city to license the family pet.
   b. The Department of Motor Vehicles charges $295 for a current auto license tag for your car. The fee is made up of two parts: a $15 basic fee for all registered autos and a fee ($280) determined by the current value of the auto.
   c. Postage of $3.75 to mail a package to San Jose.
   d. The city put in sewer lines and assessed each property owner $6,000 for his or her share of the cost.
   e. Bella withdrew $12,000 from her individual retirement account (IRA). In addition to paying the regular income tax on the withdrawal, she had to pay an additional 10% ($1,200) early distribution penalty to the IRS. The penalty is imposed to discourage withdrawal of funds before retirement.

38. Explain why each of the following payments does or does not meet the IRS's definition of a tax:

    a. Jack is a licensed beautician. He pays the state $45 each year to renew his license to practice as a beautician.

    b. Polly Corporation pays state income taxes of $40,000 on its $500,000 of taxable income.

    c. Winona pays $15 annually for a safety inspection of her automobile that is required by the state.

    d. The Judd Partnership owns land that is valued by the county assessor at $30,000. Based on this valuation, the partnership pays county property taxes of $800.

    e. Andrea fails to file her income tax return on time. She files the return late, and the IRS assesses her $25 for the late filing and $5 for interest on the tax due from the due date of the return until the filing date.

39. Susan is single with a gross income of $80,000 and a taxable income of $60,000. In calculating taxable income, she properly excluded $4,000 of tax-exempt interest income. Using the tax rate schedules in the chapter, calculate Susan's

    a. Total tax   **c.** Average tax rate

    b. Marginal tax rate   **d.** Effective tax rate

40. A taxpayer has $80,000 of taxable income for the current year. Determine the total tax, the marginal tax rate, and the average tax rate if the taxpayer is a

    a. Single individual

    b. Married couple

    c. Corporation

41. Rory earns $54,000 per year as a college professor. Latesia is a marketing executive with a salary of $100,000. With respect to the Social Security tax, what are Rory's and Latesia's

    a. Total taxes?   **c.** Average tax rates?

    b. Marginal tax rates?   **d.** Effective tax rates?

42. For each of the following, explain whether the rate structure is progressive, proportional, or regressive:

    a. Plain County imposes a 4% sales tax on retail sales within the county. The sales tax does not apply to services, medical goods and supplies, and groceries.

    b. The licensing fee for an automobile consists of two parts, a flat fee of $30 on all automobiles and a variable fee based on the weight of the vehicle per the following schedule:

Vehicle Weight (in pounds)	Tax
0 to 1,500	$ 45
1,501 to 3,000	$ 85
3,001 to 4,500	$120
4,501 and above	$150

    c. The city of Thomasville bases its dog licensing fee on the weight of the dog per the following schedule:

Weight (in pounds)	Tax Rate
0 to 40	$ 2 + 50% of weight
41 to 80	$22 + 40% of weight in excess of 40 lbs.
81 and above	$36 + 30% of weight in excess of 80 lbs.

43. The country of Boodang is the leading producer of sausage. Boodang imposes three different taxes on its citizens and companies. The taxes are designed to encourage production of sausage and discourage its consumption. Each tax applies as follows:

- Income tax—Rates apply to each taxpayer's total income:

$ -0- -$ 50,000	5% of total income
$ 50,000–$200,000	$2,500 + 10% of income in excess of $ 50,000
$200,000–$500,000	$17,500 + 20% of income in excess of $200,000
$500,000 or more	40% of all income

In calculating total income, sausage workers are allowed to deduct 25% of their salary. Companies that produce sausage are allowed to deduct 50% of their sales. No other deductions are allowed.

- Sausage tax—All sausage purchases are subject to a 100% of purchase price tax. Citizens who consume less than 10 pounds of sausage per year are given a 50% rebate of the sausage tax they paid.
- Property tax—Taxes are based on the distance of a taxpayer's residence from state-owned sausage shops per the following schedule:

0–2 miles	$15,000 per mile
2 miles–5 miles	$ 5,000 per mile
5 miles or more	$ 2,000 per mile

Given the definitions in the chapter, are Boodang's taxes progressive, proportional, or regressive? Evaluate and discuss each tax and the aspect(s) of the tax that you considered in making your evaluation.

44. Joe Bob is an employee of Rollo Corporation, and he receives a salary of $7,500 per month. How much Social Security tax will be withheld from Joe Bob's salary in
a. March?
b. November?

45. Return to the facts of problem 44. Assume that each month Joe Bob has $2,100 in federal income tax and $900 in state income tax withheld from his salary. What is Joe Bob's take home pay in
a. March?
b. November?

46. Smalltime Corporation has 2 employees. During the current year, Perry earns $55,000 and Trahn earns $90,000. How much Social Security tax does Smalltime have to pay on the salaries earned by Perry and Trahn?

47. Eric is a self-employed financial consultant. During the current year, Eric's self-employment income is $70,000. What is Eric's self-employment tax?

48. Darrell is an employee of Whitney's. During the current year, Darrell's salary is $80,000. Whitney's self-employment income is also $80,000. Calculate the Social Security and self-employment taxes paid by Darrell and Whitney. Write a letter to Whitney in which you state how much she will have to pay in Social Security and self-employment taxes and why she owes those amounts.

49. Classify the following items as ordinary income, a gain, or an exclusion:
a. The gross revenues of $160,000 and deductible expenses of $65,000 of an individual's consulting business
b. Interest received on a checking account
c. Sale for $8,000 of Kummel Corporation stock that cost $3,000
d. Receipt of $1,000 as a graduation present from grandfather
e. Royalty income from an interest in a gold mine.

50. Explain why each of the following expenditures is or is not deductible.
    a. Alfredo, Inc., pays $300,000 in salaries to employees. The $300,000 is deductible.
    b. Winona sells furniture at a garage sale for $200. She paid $800 for the furniture. The $600 loss is not deductible.
    c. Rangoon Corporation sells office equipment for $2,300. The tax cost of the equipment was $3,200. Rangoon can deduct the $900 loss on the sale of the equipment.
    d. Inga owns an apartment complex. During the current year, the apartments are painted at a cost of $4,000. Inga can deduct the $4,000 painting cost.
    e. Mark paints his personal residence at a cost of $600. The painting cost is not deductible.

51. Classify each of the following transactions as a deductible expense, a nondeductible expense, or a loss:
    a. Nira sells for $4,300 stock that cost $6,000.
    b. Chiro Medical, Inc., pays $2,200 for subscriptions to popular magazines that it places in its waiting room.
    c. Lawrence pays $200 for subscriptions to fly-fishing magazines.
    d. The Mendota Partnership pays $200,000 to install an elevator in one of its rental properties.
    e. Sterling Corporation pays $6,000 for lawn maintenance at its headquarters.

52. Based on the following information, what are the taxable income and tax liability for a single individual?

Total income	$86,000
Excludable income	1,200
Deductions for adjusted gross income	1,800
Deductions from adjusted gross income	6,000

53. Based on the facts in problem 52, calculate the taxable income and the tax liability for a married couple.

54. Reba's 1996 income tax calculation is as follows:

Gross income	$120,000
Deductions for adjusted gross income	(3,000)
Adjusted gross income	$117,000
Deductions from adjusted gross income:	
Standard deduction	(4,000)
(Total itemized deductions are $2,000)	
Personal exemption	(2,550)
Taxable income	$110,450

Before filing her return, Reba finds an $8,000 deduction that she omitted from these calculations. Although the item is clearly deductible, she is unsure whether she should deduct it for or from adjusted gross income. Reba doesn't think that it matters where she deducts the item, because her taxable income will decrease by $8,000 regardless of how the item is deducted. Is Reba correct? Calculate her taxable income both ways. Write a letter to Reba in which you explain any difference in her taxable income arising from whether the $8,000 is deducted for or from adjusted gross income.

55. Since graduating from college, Mabel has used the firm of R&P to prepare her tax returns. Each January, Mabel receives a summary information sheet, which she fills out and sends to R&P along with the appropriate documentation. Because she has always received a refund, Mabel feels that R&P is giving her good tax advice. Write a letter to Mabel in which you explain why she may not be getting good tax advice from R&P.

56. Michiko and Saul are planning to attend the same university next year. The university estimates tuition, books, fees, and living costs to be $9,000 per year. Michiko's father has agreed to give her the $9,000 she needs to attend the university. Saul has obtained a job at the university that will pay him $11,000 per year. After discussing their respective arrangements, Michiko figures that Saul will be better off than she will. What, if anything, is wrong with Michiko's thinking?

57. Ruby has an opportunity to earn a $5,000 bonus. She can receive the bonus in either 1996 or 1997. When she receives the bonus, she intends to invest it in a certificate of deposit (CD). What additional information does she need in order to decide whether to take the bonus in 1996 or 1997?

58. Art is in the 31% marginal tax bracket for 1996. He owes a $10,000 bill for business expenses. Because he reports taxable income on a cash basis, he can deduct the $10,000 in either 1996 or 1997, depending on when he makes the payment. He can pay the bill at any time before January 31, 1997, without incurring the normal 8% interest charge. If he expects to be in a 36% marginal tax bracket for 1997, should he pay the bill and claim the deduction in 1996 or 1997?

59. Elki would like to invest $100,000 in tax-exempt securities. He now has the money invested in a certificate of deposit that pays 5.75% annually. What rate of interest would the tax-exempt security have to pay to result in a greater return on Elki's investment than the certificate of deposit? Work the problem, assuming that Elki's marginal tax rate is 15%, 28%, 31%, and 39.6%.

60. Talisa and Curan are married and have 3 dependent children. They estimate their 1996 taxable income will be $148,000. They would like to lower their overall tax liability on the income. Talisa owns $30,000 face value of 10% taxable bonds. Curan thinks that they can save some taxes either by transferring ownership of the bonds to their children or by selling the bonds and reinvesting in tax-exempt bonds. Which of the following strategies provides the highest after-tax return?

    a. The ownership of the bonds is legally transferred to their children. Each child will receive $10,000 face value of the bonds.

    b. The bonds are selling for $62,000. Talisa purchased them for $58,000. If they sell the bonds, they will reinvest the proceeds in tax-exempt municipal bonds yielding 4%.

61. For each of the following situations, state whether the taxpayer's action is tax evasion or tax avoidance:

    a. Tom knows that farm rent received in cash or farm produce is income subject to tax. To avoid showing a cash receipt on his records, he rented 50 acres for his choice of 5 steers to be raised by the tenant. He used 2 of the steers for food for his family and gave 3 to relatives. Because he did not sell the livestock, he did not report taxable income.

    b. Betty applied for and received a Social Security number for Kate, her pet cat. Surprised by how easy it was to get a Social Security number, she decided to claim a dependent exemption on her tax return for Kate. Other than being a cat, Kate met all the tests for a dependent.

    c. Glen has put money in savings accounts in 50 different banks. Glen knows a bank is not required to report to the IRS interest it pays him that totals less than $10. Because the banks do not report the payments to the IRS, Glen does not show the interest he received as taxable income. Although Glen's accountant has told him all interest he receives is taxable, Glen insists that the IRS will never know the difference.

    d. Bob and Sue entered a contract to sell their home at a $25,000 gain in 1995. To avoid reporting the gain in 1995, they closed the sale and delivered possession of the home to the buyers on January 2, 1996.

    e. Asha's taxable income for 1996 puts her in the 31% marginal tax bracket. Asha has decided to purchase new equipment for her business some time during 1997. A special election allows Asha to treat $17,500 of the cost of the equipment as a current period expense. Because she expects to be in a lower tax bracket next year, Asha buys and begins using $17,500-worth of the equipment during December 1996. She claims a $17,500 expense deduction under the special election for 1996.

62. In each of the following situations, explain why the taxpayer's action is or is not tax evasion:

  a. Jamal owns an electrical appliance repair service. When a client pays him in cash, he gives the cash to his daughter Tasha. Jamal does not report the cash he gave to Tasha in his business income. Tasha has no other income, and the amount of cash that she receives from Jamal is small enough that she is not required to file a tax return.

  b. Roberta and Dudley are married. Roberta usually prepares their tax return. However, in 1995 she was in the hospital and unable to prepare the return, so Dudley did it. In preparing their 1996 return, Roberta notices that Dudley included $2,000 of tax-exempt municipal bond interest in their 1995 gross income. To correct this mistake, Roberta takes a $2,000 deduction on the 1996 return.

  c. In 1996, Hearthome Corporation receives notice that the IRS is auditing the corporation's 1994 return. In preparing for the audit, Hearthome's controller, Monique, finds a mistake in the total for the 1994 depreciation schedule that resulted in a $5,000 overstatement of depreciation expense.

  d. In the process of preparing his 1996 return, Will becomes unsure of the treatment of a deduction item. He researches the issue and can find no concrete tax law authority pertaining to the particular item. Will calls his buddy Dan, an accounting professor, for advice. Dan tells Will that if the law is unclear, he should treat the deduction in the most advantageous manner. Accordingly, Will deducts the full amount of the item, rather than capitalizing and amortizing it over 5 years.

  e. Sonja is a freelance book editor. Most companies for which she works pay her by check. In working out the terms of a job for a new client, the client agrees to pay her by giving her a new computer valued at $3,600. In preparing her tax return, Sonja notes that the client failed to report to the IRS the value of the computer as income for Sonja. Aware that her chances of getting caught are small, Sonja does not include the $3,600 value of the computer in her gross income.

DISCUSSION CASES

63. A value-added tax has been the subject of much debate in recent years as a tax to use to help reduce the deficit. Various forms of value-added taxes are used throughout Europe, Canada, and in many other countries. To acquaint yourself with the basic operation of a value-added tax, read the following article:

Peter Chin and Joel G. Siegel, "What the Value Added Tax Is All About," *TAXES—The Tax Magazine*, January 1989, pp. 3–13.

After reading the article consider the following circumstances:

Joe is married and has 2 children. Joe, a brain surgeon, earns about $300,000 annually from his medical practice and averages about $250,000 in investment income. Jane, Joe's wife, spends most of her time doing volunteer work for charitable organizations. Tom is also married and has 5 children. Tom earns $20,000 per year working as a maintenance man for Joe.

While Joe was working late one night, he and Tom had a serious disagreement about two new tax bills recently introduced to help reduce the deficit. The first bill would levy a 10% value-added tax on all goods and services. A second bill introduced at the same time would add an additional 10% tax to each of the five current tax rate brackets (i.e., 15% would become 25%, 28% would become 38%, 31% would become 41%, 36% would become 46%, and 39.6% would become 49.6%.

Joe is concerned that the imposition of a value-added tax would mean that fewer people could afford medical treatment. Both his patients and his practice would suffer from the tax. Tom strongly disagrees with Joe. He thinks that Joe does not want to pay his fair share of taxes. Tom charges that Joe can afford to hire tax accountants to help him avoid paying higher income taxes, even with the higher tax rates. By enacting a value-added tax, Tom believes that high-income taxpayers like Joe will have to pay up. He thinks it is the only fair way to raise taxes to bring down the deficit.

After several hours of arguing, neither could convince the other that he was wrong. Joe finally ended the discussion by saying that he would get an independent person knowledgeable in tax law to decide who is right.

REQUIRED: You work for the firm that prepares Joe's tax return and advises him on managing his finances. The tax partner of your firm asks you to prepare a memorandum discussing the merits and the deficiencies of the two proposals as they apply to Joe and Tom. In your memorandum, you are directed to specifically consider the following and provide a response:

a. What is a value-added tax, and how does it work?

b. Evaluate the rate structures of the two proposed taxes. Are they proportional, progressive, or regressive?

c. What, if anything, is wrong with Tom's and/or Joe's point of view? Be sure to explain this part in depth.

64. Norman and Vanessa are married and have 2 dependent children. This is a summary of their 1995 tax return:

Adjusted gross income	$55,050
Deductions from adjusted gross income:	
Standard deduction	(6,550)
Exemptions ($2,500 × 4)	(10,000)
Taxable income	$ 38,500
Tax liability	$ 5,775

a. Assuming that Norman and Vanessa's 1996 adjusted gross income will increase at the 2.84% rate of inflation and that the standard deduction and exemption amounts do not change, calculate their 1996 taxable income. Calculate the tax liability on this income using the 1995 tax rate schedules (Appendix A).

b. Calculate Norman and Vanessa's projected 1996 taxable income and tax liability, assuming that their adjusted gross income will increase by 2.84% and that all other inflation adjustments are made. Compare these calculations with those in part a, and explain how the inflation adjustments preserve Norman and Vanessa's after-tax income.

65. Bonnie is married and has 1 child. She owns Bonnie's Rib Joint, which produces a taxable income of approximately $120,000 per year.

a. Assume that Bonnie's taxable income is $40,000 without considering the income from the rib joint. How much tax will she pay on the $120,000 of income from the rib joint?

b. You work for the firm that prepares Bonnie's tax return. Bonnie has asked the partner for whom you work to advise her on how she might lower her taxes. The partner has assigned you this task. Draft a memorandum to the partner that contains at least two options Bonnie could use to lower her taxes. For each option, explain the calculations that support the tax savings from your recommendation.

TAX PLANNING CASE

66. Return to the facts of problem 61. Assume that you are the CPA in charge of preparing the tax return for each of the taxpayers in the problem. Based on the Statements on Responsibilities in Tax Practice (Appendix D), explain what you should do in each case. Your discussion should indicate which, if any, of the eight statements is applicable and your obligations with regard to each applicable statement. If the facts are not sufficient to determine whether a statement applies to a situation, discuss the circumstances in which the statement would apply.

ETHICS DISCUSSION CASE

Income Tax Concepts

▲ Chapter Learning Objectives

■ Discuss the operation of the U.S. income tax as a system and how concepts, constructs, and doctrines provide overall guidance in the tax treatment of items that affect taxable income.

■ Identify the general concepts that underlie the tax system and explain how the concepts affect taxation.

■ Explain the effect of accounting concepts, how such concepts provide guidance in determining when an item of income should be included in gross income, and when an expense item is deductible.

■ Describe income concepts and explain how they aid in determining which items constitute gross income for tax purposes.

■ Discuss deduction concepts and how such concepts affect what may be deducted for income tax purposes.

The federal income tax is based on a system of rules and regulations that deter- **INTRODUCTION**
mine the treatment of various items of income and expense. The key point to be
made is that federal income taxation is based on a *system*. As such, it shares the
characteristics of any type of system. We are all familiar with systems; our society
is organized by systems of rules. Some systems are natural and afford us little
leeway in abiding by them. For example, gravity is part of the environmental
system in which we live and a force that cannot be overcome without great difficulty. Because of our knowledge of and experience with the concept of gravity,
we have learned that we must be aware of its effects on our behavior. For example,
because of the effect of gravity you cannot walk off a cliff without suffering grave
consequences.

Most of the legal and social systems we deal with every day are artificial. That
is, people make rules and prescribe actions to enforce them. In these systems,
detailed rules are developed for general concepts. For example, all states have
testing requirements that must be met in order to get a driver's license. A person
who moves from one state to another generally has no problem passing the test
in the new state, because the general concepts involved in driving an automobile
do not change from location to location.

Artificial systems are distinguished from natural systems by exceptions to the
general rules of the system. These exceptions are necessary in order to meet specific needs. Returning to our driving example, we know that most states permit
you to make a right turn at a red light after making a complete stop (i.e., the
general rule). However, traffic experts have determined that some intersections
are so hazardous that the general rule cannot be followed. The result is an exception to the law—we cannot make a right turn on red after a complete stop at some
intersections. How do we identify those instances in which we may not make a
right turn on red? Simple—the rules provide that an appropriately labeled sign
be posted to alert us to the exception.

As with all artificial systems, the federal income tax system has been developed around general concepts that guide us in its application to various types of
transactions. There are, of course, exceptions that do not follow from the application of the general concepts. These exceptions generally stem from the desire to
use the tax system to promote some social, economic, or political goal. For example, the income tax law provides an exclusion from income for employer-
provided health insurance policies. This payment of the employee's expenses by
the employer could be taxed. However, in order to encourage employers to provide health-care coverage for their employees (a social goal), Congress has excluded such payments from the employee's income. Another example of an
exception involves losses on the sale of stocks. Net loss deductions on the sale of
stocks by individuals are limited to $3,000 per year. However, to encourage in-
vestment in small companies (an economic goal), a special provision in the tax
law allows the deduction of up to $50,000 in losses from an investment in the
stock of a new company. The only effective way to learn the exceptions in the tax
law is through experience and study. That is, there are no explicit "no right turn
on red" signs in the tax law. The major exceptions to the general concepts of
taxation are presented in this book, but the focus is on developing the ability to
determine the treatment of transactions by applying the general concepts of
taxation.

This chapter groups income tax concepts by their major function(s) within the
income tax system. The four major groupings for discussion purposes are *general
concepts*, *accounting concepts*, *income concepts*, and *deduction concepts*. Throughout
the remaining chapters, the text constantly refers to these concepts to help explain

the tax treatments being presented. You must understand these concepts, so we suggest that you return to this chapter and review the applicable concepts before you begin reading a new chapter. To help you, each chapter begins with a summary of the concepts applicable to the chapter's material.

Before beginning the discussion of the concepts, it is necessary to introduce a bit of terminology used throughout the remainder of the book. A **concept** is a broad principle that provides guidance on the income tax treatment of transactions. Because a specific concept covers many transactions, concepts are broad. A **construct** is a mechanism that has been developed to implement a concept. A **doctrine** is a construct that has been developed by the courts. Thus, constructs and doctrines are the interpretive devices necessary to apply a concept. When this book refers to a concept, the text includes all its related constructs and doctrines. An example of a concept is the annual accounting period concept; it requires all income tax entities to report their results on an annual basis. In order to properly identify the income of each annual period, each entity must select an accounting method. In this example, *annual accounting period* is the concept, and *accounting method* is the construct necessary to implement the concept. Thus, when we talk about the annual accounting period concept, the construct accounting method is implicitly a part of the concept.

This chapter introduces and discusses the fundamental concepts of income taxation. The discussion of each concept includes the fundamental constructs and doctrines necessary to begin the study of income taxation.

GENERAL CONCEPTS

General concepts provide guidance on the overall operation and implementation of the income tax system. As such, these concepts apply to almost every aspect of the system, be it an accounting issue, an income issue, or a deduction issue.

Ability-to-Pay Concept

A fundamental concept underlying the income tax structure is the **ability-to-pay concept.** This concept states that the tax levied on a taxpayer should be based on the amount that the taxpayer can afford to pay. The first result of this concept is that the income tax base is a *net* income number (i.e., income minus deductions and losses) rather than a gross figure such as total income received. Therefore, the tax base recognizes different deduction levels incurred by taxpayers as well as different levels of income.

▲ **EXAMPLE 1**   Jerry and Jody each have a total income of $65,000. Jerry's allowable deductions are $20,000, and Jody's allowable deductions are $35,000.

Discussion: Although Jerry and Jody have identical total incomes, Jerry's allowable deductions are $15,000 less than Jody's. Thus, Jerry has a greater ability to pay taxes than does Jody. Allowing deductions in the income tax base recognizes taxpayers' varying abilities to pay.

The example of Jerry and Jody illustrates that the notions of *income* and *deduction* are fundamental constructs that are used to implement one aspect of the ability-to-pay concept. Losses and tax credits also reduce the amount of tax due and are related to a taxpayer's ability to pay tax. These constructs were defined and discussed in Chapter 1, and we will not elaborate further at this juncture. However, we would note that the study of income taxation is essentially the study of what comprises these constructs. It is important to remember that these constructs are really the basic elements of the system.

A second aspect of the ability-to-pay concept is the use of a progressive tax rate structure. Recall that a progressive tax is one in which higher levels of the tax base are subjected to increasingly higher tax rates. Individuals with large taxable incomes pay a higher marginal tax rate than do individuals with small taxable incomes. Thus, both the tax base—taxable income—and the tax rate applied to the base are determined by the taxpayer's ability to pay tax. It should be noted that the ability-to-pay concept is undermined by provisions that exclude certain types of income from the tax base. That is, to the extent that a taxpayer has income that is not subject to tax because of an allowable exclusion, the taxpayer is being taxed at less than her or his ability to pay.

▲ **EXAMPLE 2**   Dewitt and Gloria are a retired couple with a taxable income of $32,000. The primary source of their taxable income is Gloria's pension and taxable dividends and interest. In addition, Dewitt and Gloria own municipal bonds that pay annual interest of $14,000 that is not included in their taxable income. What is the effect of the exclusion of the bond interest on the ability-to-pay concept?

Discussion: Because the $14,000 in interest income from the bonds is available to pay Dewitt and Gloria's taxes, the exclusion of the interest from the tax base allows them to pay less tax than they could afford to pay. This effect is somewhat mitigated by the lower interest rates found on tax-exempt bonds versus taxable bonds. That is, by investing in municipal bonds, Dewitt and Gloria have accepted a lower interest rate than they could have obtained by investing in taxable bonds. Thus, they have paid some implicit tax (although nothing goes to the federal government) on the bonds by accepting the lower tax-exempt bond rate.

Administrative Convenience Concept

Throughout the discussion of the income tax a particular item often is not treated consistently with the basic concept applicable to the situation. Many of these treatments result from the **administrative convenience concept.** This concept states that items may be omitted from the tax base whenever the cost of implementing a concept exceeds the benefit of using it. The cost is generally the time and effort for taxpayers to accumulate the information necessary to implement the concept as well as the cost to the government of ensuring compliance with the concept. The benefit received from implementation is generally the amount of tax that would be collected. Thus, many items that meet the definition of *income* are not taxed, because the costs of collecting the information necessary to ensure compliance are greater than the tax produced by the income.

▲ **EXAMPLE 3**   Bravo Co. provides a break room for its employees. Free coffee is provided to the employees in the break room at a cost to Bravo of 10 cents per cup. Leroy is an employee of Bravo Co. who drinks 3 cups of coffee in the break room on an average day. Is Leroy taxed on the free coffee he receives from Bravo Co.?

Discussion: Under general concepts of income recognition (discussed later in this chapter and in depth in Chapter 3), Leroy is in receipt of income when he drinks the free coffee provided by his employer. This is, in effect, a form of compensation Bravo provides to its employees. However, the cost of each employee's tracking his or her consumption of coffee, as well as the cost of the government's ensuring that all employees include the cost of their free coffee in their income, exceeds the additional tax that would be collected. Thus, under the administrative convenience concept, Leroy is not taxed on the free coffee.

Another aspect of this concept relates to deductions for individuals. The tax law allows individuals to take deductions for certain personal expenditures (e.g., medical expenses, charitable contributions). However, many individuals incur only small amounts of these allowable personal deductions. In these situations, the tax law allows a taxpayer to take a standard deduction in lieu of accumulating the information necessary to deduct the actual allowable deductions. This treatment saves taxpayers' time in accumulating and reporting deduction information and the government's time in ensuring the accuracy of the information reported (i.e., the standard deduction does not need to be audited).

> ▲ **EXAMPLE 4**   Tara believes that she probably does not have a significant amount of allowable personal deductions in 1996. Even if she searches her records, she figures it's unlikely she can document more than $4,000, the 1996 standard deduction for a single taxpayer.
>
> *Discussion:*   Tara may elect to deduct the $4,000 standard deduction. This relieves her of having to document her small amount of allowable personal deductions, and the government incurs no costs to ensure that her deductions are correct. When taxpayers' allowable personal deductions are close to the amount of their allowable standard deduction, it is more convenient for them to deduct the allowable standard deduction than spend a lot of time trying to document deductions that may provide very little tax savings.

Arm's-Length Transaction Concept

In seeking to pay the minimum amount of tax, taxpayers often structure transactions that may not reflect economic reality. In many such cases, the transaction is not given any tax effect, because the transaction is deemed not to conform with the **arm's-length transaction concept.** An arm's-length transaction is one in which all parties to the transaction have bargained in good faith and for their individual benefit, not for the benefit of the transaction group. Transactions that are not made at arm's length are generally not given any tax effect or are not given the intended tax effect.

> ▲ **EXAMPLE 5**   Bo is the sole shareholder of Shoe Co. Bo owns a shoe-stretching machine for which he paid $15,000 and that is worth $18,000. Bo sells the machine to Shoe Co. for $5,000. Can Bo deduct the loss on the sale of the machine to Shoe Co.?
>
> *Discussion:*   Because Bo was, in effect, negotiating with himself when he sold the machine to Shoe Co., the transaction was not made at arm's length, and Bo will not be allowed to deduct the loss on the sale. NOTE: Bo can deal at arm's length with Shoe Co. However, the tax law assumes that related parties (defined subsequently) do not transact at arm's length. One effect of this assumption is that losses on sales to related parties are always disallowed, even if the transaction is made at arm's length and the price reflects fair market value.

As example 5 shows, transactions that are not made at arm's length generally involve an element of self-dealing. The tax law has formally incorporated the notion of self-dealing through a set of **related party provisions.**[1] Some of the more common related party relationships (depicted in Figure 2–1) are

1. Individuals and their families. Family members include a spouse, brothers, sisters, lineal descendants (children, grandchildren), and ancestors (parents, grandparents).
2. Individuals and a corporation if the individual owns more than 50 percent of the stock of the corporation.
3. A corporation and a partnership if the same person owns more than 50 percent of both the corporation and the partnership.

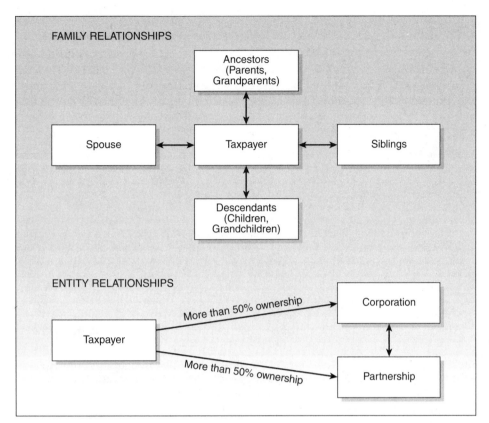

Note that all these relationships have the potential for self-dealing, either because of family relationships or a substantial ownership interest in an entity. The more-than-50-percent test for corporations and partnerships is based on the level of ownership necessary to control the actions of these entities. In example 5, Bo and Shoe Co. are related parties, because Bo owns more than 50 percent of Shoe Co. and effectively controls Shoe Co.'s actions. Thus, when Bo deals with Shoe Company, he really deals with himself. In trying to circumvent the related party rules, individuals might attempt to reduce their direct ownership in a corporation or a partnership by distributing ownership among family members, other corporations, or partnerships that they control. This effort is stymied by the **constructive ownership rules,** which state the relationships within which an individual is deemed to indirectly own an interest actually owned by another person or entity. These rules can be complex and are beyond the scope of this text.

Pay-as-You-Go Concept

The U.S. income tax system is one in which voluntary compliance is essential to the operation of the system. Most taxpayers comply with the requirement that they file a return each year and pay the tax due on their taxable income. However, the payment of the entire tax bill at the end of the year could be unduly burdensome for those taxpayers who do not have the foresight to save money for the payment of the tax or who do not have the ability to adequately estimate the amount of the tax they owe. To alleviate situations in which taxpayers are faced with a huge tax bill at the end of the year, the **pay-as-you-go concept** requires taxpayers to pay tax as they generate income. This concept is implemented through withholding and estimated tax payment requirements. The withholding provisions require employers to withhold amounts from each employee's paycheck to pay the tax on the income in that check. The withheld amounts are remitted to the government, and taxpayers receive credit on their tax returns for the tax paid through withholding. This minimizes the probability of a taxpayer facing a huge tax bill at the end of the year. Note that the taxpayer might pay too much tax through this process. In such cases, the government simply refunds the excess tax that has been paid.

> ▲ **EXAMPLE 6**   Giovanna is a machinist who works for Adilia Co. During the current year, Giovanna earned $32,500 and had $3,450 federal income tax withheld from her paycheck. In filing her return, Giovanna's actual tax was determined to be $3,675. How much tax must Giovanna pay when she files her return for the current year?
>
> *Discussion:*   Although Giovanna's actual tax is $3,675, she has already paid in $3,450 through withholding. Therefore, she has to pay only $225 ($3,675 − $3,450) when she files her current year's return. NOTE: The withholding provisions ease for Giovanna the burden of having to come up with the full $3,675 when she files her tax return. By having Giovanna pay as she goes (her employer withholds tax payments), the tax system encourages voluntary compliance; it spreads the burden of taxes over the period of time during which the income is being earned.

Although salaries paid by employers constitute a large percentage of the income taxed in the United States, it is by no means the only source of income for individual taxpayers. That is, taxpayers often earn income independent of any employee-employer relationship. Many people are their own bosses (i.e., self-employed), others earn income from investments such as savings accounts, dividends from stock, and sales of assets, and retired individuals collect pensions, Social Security benefits, and income from investments. To ensure that such taxpayers have the means to pay the tax due on these various sources of income, all individual taxpayers are required to make quarterly estimated tax payments—to meet the estimated tax payment requirements—when their estimated tax due for the year is at least $500.[2] Corporations also must file quarterly estimated tax payments. Thus, taxpayers who have significant amounts of income that are not subject to withholding by employers are also required to adhere to the pay-as-you-go concept. Failure to make the required estimated tax payments will result in a penalty for underpayment of estimated taxes.

ACCOUNTING CONCEPTS

Accounting concepts guide the proper accounting for and recording of transactions that affect the tax liability of taxpayers. In order to determine the treatment of a transaction, we must first identify the appropriate taxpaying unit. Next, we must ascertain the rationale that controls its tax treatment in order to record it. Finally, the transaction must be reported in the correct tax period. These ideas appear to be rather simplistic and part of basic bookkeeping. That is partly true. However, without these basic accounting concepts, the tax system could not function in an orderly and efficient manner. Perhaps even more important, without these concepts taxpayers could manipulate their affairs so as to avoid paying taxes for many years.

Entity Concept

The most basic accounting concept is the entity concept. According to the **entity concept,** each tax unit must keep separate records and report the results of its operations separate and apart from other tax units. The tax law requires that all tax units be classified as one of two basic entity types: taxable and conduit. The characteristics and unique features of each of the taxable and conduit entities are discussed in detail in Chapters 8 and 9.

Taxable entities are those that are liable for the payment of tax. That is, taxable entities must pay a tax based on their taxable income. The four entities responsible for the payment of income tax are individuals; regular, or C corporations; estates; and some trusts.

Conduit entities are nontaxable reporting entities. A conduit entity is one in which the tax attributes (income, deductions, losses, credits) of the entity flow through the entity to the owner(s) of the entity for tax purposes. The entities record transactions undertaken by the entity and report the results to the government. However, these entities pay no tax on the results of their operations. Rather, the tax characteristics (i.e., the income, deductions, losses, tax credits, etc.) of the operating results are passed through the conduit entity and are taxed to its owners. NOTE: All conduit entities are owned by one or more taxable entities. Two types of conduit entities authorized by the tax law are partnerships and subchapter S corporations.[3,4] Hereafter, any reference to a corporation means a taxable C corporation. Conduit corporations are referred to as *S corporations*.

Trusts are a mixture of taxable and conduit entities. A trust is an arrangement in which a trustee manages assets for the benefit of another, referred to as the *beneficiary*. The trust reports the results of its operations to the government (a conduit characteristic). Any income distributed by the trust to the beneficiary is taxable to the beneficiary. However, the trust must pay income tax on any income that is earned but not distributed to the beneficiary (a taxable entity characteristic). Thus, trusts are both taxable and conduit entities in that they are taxed on income that is retained and are not taxed on income that is distributed. The calculation of the taxable income of a trust is discussed in Chapter 9.

To illustrate the relationship between the two basic types of entities, consider a 100-percent owner of a corporation. The corporation is recognized as an entity separate from its owner for purposes of recording transactions. That is, the owner cannot commingle personal transactions with those of the corporation for tax purposes. All income, deductions, losses, and credits attributable to the operation of the business are identified and recorded on the books of the corporation. The summarized results of these transactions are then reported on the corporation's tax return, and a tax is paid on the corporate taxable income. The owner of the corporation only includes as income on an individual tax return any salary or dividends she or he receives from the corporation. However, a different result is obtained if the corporation is organized as an S corporation. As a conduit entity, the S corporation still identifies and records on its books only those items that are attributable to the operation of the corporation. The summarized results of the transactions are reported to the government, but the S corporation pays no tax on its income. Rather, the income of the S corporation is reported on the tax return of the owner, along with the owner's other items of income and deductions, and a tax is paid based on the owner's taxable income.

▲ **EXAMPLE 7**   Martina and Fran each own 50% of the stock of Card Corporation. During the current year, Card Corporation had a taxable income of $80,000 and paid a total of $20,000 in dividends. What are the tax effects of Card Corporation's income and dividend distributions?

Discussion: As a separate and distinct taxable entity, Card Corporation must pay the tax on its $80,000 in taxable income. Martina and Fran each must include the $10,000 in dividends she received from Card Corporation in her calculation of taxable income. Note that the dividends are being taxed twice—once when included as income by the corporation and again when distributed to the shareholders.

▲ **EXAMPLE 8** Assume the same facts as in example 7, except that Card Corporation is an S corporation. What are the tax effects of Card Corporation's income and dividend distributions?

Discussion: An S corporation is a conduit entity. Therefore, the $80,000 in taxable income flows through to the owners and is included on their tax returns. Card Corporation pays no income tax. Martina and Fran each must include $40,000 in income on her individual tax return. Because the $80,000 is being taxed to the owners, the dividends paid are not taxed again to the owners. Rather, the dividends are considered a repayment of their investment that reduces the amount invested in the stock of the corporation.

The distinction between entities becomes blurred when a business is owned as a sole proprietorship. Although not technically a conduit entity, the sole proprietorship does not pay tax on its income. The books of the sole proprietorship are kept separate and distinct from the personal transactions of the owner. However, the income tax attributes of the business are reported on the owner's return, in much the same manner as a conduit entity.

▲ **EXAMPLE 9** Karina is a machinist for Silver Marine Co. At nights and on weekends, Karina repairs washing machines and dryers. During the current year, Karina's income from her repair business was $10,000, and she incurred $3,500 in expenses to produce this income. She also earned a salary of $30,000 from Silver Marine Co. and had $400 in interest income from a savings account. How should Karina treat these items on her tax return?

Discussion: Karina's repair business is a sole proprietorship, which is similar to a conduit entity. In accounting for the repair business, she must keep the results of the repair business separate from her other taxable transactions. The business income of $10,000 and business expenses of $3,500 result in an income of $6,500 from the repair business. The $6,500 in business income is then added to her salary and interest income on her individual return, and Karina pays tax on the sum of all her income.

The result for our sole proprietor appears to be much ado about nothing. However, two important aspects of this entity treatment prevent income manipulation. First, by not allowing the commingling of business and personal transactions, owners cannot turn nondeductible personal items into deductible business expenses. The classic example of this separation is interest expense. As we shall see in Chapter 5, all interest paid on debt incurred in a trade or business (i.e., the sole proprietorship) is fully deductible, whereas interest paid on debt used for personal purposes (other than qualified home mortgage interest) is not deductible. The entity concept requires the owner to identify these two types of interest for each entity and deduct them according to the rules for each entity. Without such a split, business owners would effectively be allowed to deduct all their interest, and basic wage earners would get no deduction for interest on their personal debts. This treatment would result in an inequity most taxpayers would not tolerate.

▲ **EXAMPLE 10** In example 9, assume that Karina owns a van that she uses on repair calls. Karina also drives the van to work at Silver Marine and for various other personal purposes such as trips to the store, taking the kids to school, and so on. How should Karina account for the van and its operating costs?

Discussion: For tax purposes, the van is viewed as two distinct assets. One asset is used in her repair business, whereas the other asset is used as a personal vehicle. Karina must keep records that adequately document the use of the van in her repair business. She can deduct the costs incurred in using the van in her repair business. The costs incurred for her personal use of the van are not deductible. This separation of business and personal use is required by the entity concept.

The second major aspect of the reporting of a conduit entity's income on the return of the owner of the entity is that conduit entities are not useful in income-shifting strategies. This results from the progressive nature of the federal income tax. Recall that in a progressive tax rate structure, the higher your taxable income is, the greater your marginal tax rate becomes. If each conduit entity paid tax on its separate income, taxpayers would be able to arrange their affairs into a multitude of conduit entities, all of which are taxed at the lowest marginal income tax rate. Under such circumstances, the income tax would effectively become a flat tax at the lowest tax rate instead of the progressive rate desired. By passing the income through to the owners of the conduit entity, income shifting by using such entities is not an effective tax-planning strategy. As an aside, it should be noted that the tax laws' requirement that taxable entities aggregate results from all their income-producing activities also contains a positive element. That is, if the conduit entity posts a loss from its operations, the taxable entity or entities that own the conduit are generally allowed to use this loss to offset income from other sources.

▲ **EXAMPLE 11**   Assume the same facts as in example 9, except that Karina's repair income was $8,000 and her expenses for producing this income were $11,000. How should Karina treat this on her tax return?

Discussion: The loss from the repair business flows through to Karina's individual return. The $3,000 loss is deductible on Karina's individual tax return, reducing the tax she would have paid on her other income.

Assignment-of-Income Doctrine.

One corollary of the entity concept is the judicially developed **assignment-of-income doctrine**.[5] According to this doctrine, all income earned from services provided by an entity are to be taxed to that entity, and income from property is to be taxed to the entity that owns the property. Merely directing payment of income (i.e., assigning income) that has been earned by one entity to another, although legal, does not relieve the owner of the income from paying tax. Thus, it is not possible to avoid the payment of tax on wages earned by simply having them paid to someone else. Although you may legally assign the right to receive income to another, the income tax is imposed on the person who earns the income.

▲ **EXAMPLE 12**   Sharon owns a landscaping business. Sharon has a two-year-old son, Jeffrey. To provide funds for Jeffrey's college education, Sharon has every tenth customer make her or his check payable to Jeffrey. Sharon deposits the checks in a savings account in Jeffrey's name. Is Sharon taxed on the amounts paid to Jeffrey?

Discussion: Under the assignment-of-income doctrine, Sharon cannot escape taxation on the income from her labor by directing the payments to Jeffrey. Sharon is taxed on all income earned by the landscaping business, regardless of who receives payment for the services.

Similarly, the owner of a building cannot escape taxation on the income from the building by having the rents paid to another entity. The only legal way for the building owner to pass the taxability of the income to the other entity is to legally transfer ownership of the building to that entity.

▲ **EXAMPLE 13**   Andrea owns a house that she rents out to college students attending State University. Her grandson Andy is a college student who goes to school at State University. To help Andy with his college expenses, Andrea has her tenants pay the rent to Andy. Is Andrea taxed on the rental income?

Discussion: Because Andrea is the owner of the rental property, she is taxed on all rents, whether she or Andy receives the payments. Under the assignment-of-income doctrine, the owner of property is taxed on the income of the property, regardless of who actually receives the income.

Discussion: In order for Andrea to avoid payment of tax on the rental income, she would have to make a valid gift of the house to Andy. This would make Andy the owner of the property and thus taxable on the rental income. Andy would pay no income tax on the receipt of the gift property. Andrea may or may not have to pay a gift tax on such a transfer.

Annual Accounting Period Concept

The second accounting concept is that of an annual accounting period. The **annual accounting period concept** states that all entities must report the results of their operations on an annual basis and that each taxable year is to stand on its own, apart from other tax years.[6] The most basic result of this concept is that all entities must choose an annual accounting period for reporting their results to the government. The two basic types of accounting periods are calendar years, which end on December 31, and fiscal years, which can end on the last day of any other month the taxpayer chooses. Although all entities are allowed to choose their accounting period, most individuals elect to be calendar-year taxpayers. This book assumes the taxpayer is using the calendar year unless otherwise noted. The election of a fiscal year carries some important restrictions, the most important of which are discussed in Chapter 14.

Accounting Method.   An important outgrowth of the annual accounting period requirement is that each taxpayer must select an **accounting method** to determine the year(s) in which taxable transactions are to be reported.[7] The two basic allowable methods are the **cash basis of accounting** and the **accrual basis of accounting.** Taxpayers using the cash basis are taxed on income as it is received and take deductions as they are paid. In contrast, accrual basis taxpayers report their income as it is earned and take deductions as they are incurred, without regard to the actual receipt or payment of cash. At this point, a simple example will illustrate the basic differences between the two methods of accounting.

▲ **EXAMPLE 14**   Steen, Inc., is in the carpet-cleaning business. In December 1996, Steen cleans Gary's business office and bills him $200. Gary pays Steen in January 1997.

Discussion: Assume that both Steen, Inc., and Gary are cash basis taxpayers. Although Steen earns the $200 during 1996, it is not taxed on the $200 until payment is received in 1997. Similarly, Gary takes the deduction for the carpet-cleaning expense in 1997 when he makes the payment.

▲ **EXAMPLE 15**   Assume that in example 14 both Steen, Inc., and Gary are accrual basis taxpayers.

Discussion: Steen must include the $200 in the year in which it was earned, 1996, and Gary takes his deduction in the year the carpet-cleaning expense is incurred, 1996.

Discussion: Assume that Steen, Inc., is on the cash basis and Gary is on the accrual basis of accounting. Steen does not include the $200 in income until it is received in 1997. Gary deducts the carpet-cleaning expense in the year incurred, 1996.

Note that the use of the cash method is a violation of generally accepted accounting principles (GAAP), which require books to be kept using the accrual method. The accrual method used for tax purposes is generally the same as that used in financial accounting under GAAP. However, various limitations and exceptions apply to the application of each method. The most important of these are discussed as they apply to income recognition in Chapter 3 and to deductions in Chapter 5. Some additional special accounting methods are covered in Chapter 14.

Tax Benefit Rule.   The requirement that each tax year stand on its own, apart from other tax years, leads to some problems when circumstances arise in which one transaction could affect more than one year. This has led to development of the **tax benefit rule.** Under this rule, any deduction taken in a prior year that is recovered in a subsequent year is reported as income in the year it is recovered, to the extent that a tax benefit is received from the deduction.[8] The tax benefit received means the amount by which taxable income was actually reduced by the deduction recovered. Consider the following examples:

▲ **EXAMPLE 16**   Rayson Corporation is an accrual basis taxpayer selling widgets for cash and on account. Late in 1994, Rayson sells $500-worth of widgets on account to Tom. In 1995, before any payment is made to Rayson, Tom is sentenced to 20 years in prison for embezzlement. How should the corporation account for this series of events?

Discussion: Because Rayson Corporation is on the accrual basis, it includes the $500 sale to Tom as income in the year of the sale, 1994. The tax law does not generally allow taxpayers to use the allowance method of accounting for bad debts, so Rayson must wait until it determines that Tom's debt is worthless to take a bad debt deduction. Going to jail for 20 years is enough evidence that Tom won't repay the debt, so Rayson should take a bad debt deduction of $500 in 1995. The recognition of the bad debt in 1995 stems from the requirement that the events of each tax year stand alone. Rayson Corporation does not go back to amend the income reported in 1994.

▲ **EXAMPLE 17**   While Tom is in prison, his aunt dies and leaves him a considerable inheritance. He had always felt badly about not paying Rayson Corporation for the widgets, so in 1996 he sends Rayson a check for the $500. How should Rayson account for the $500?

Discussion: Because Rayson Corporation took a deduction for Tom's bad debt in 1995, the tax benefit rule requires it to include the $500 in its 1996 income. Note again that there is no attempt to adjust the prior year's income. The events of each tax year stand apart from each other under the annual accounting period concept.

As these examples demonstrate, the tax benefit rule has its most common applications in situations in which an annual accounting period and an accounting method interact. It is necessary to put accrual basis and cash basis taxpayers in the same position after accounting for all years involved. In example 16, if Rayson Corporation had been a cash basis taxpayer, it would have recognized no income from the initial sale to Tom, because it never received payment. However, when Rayson received the $500 payment in 1996, it would have been included in income under the cash basis. Thus, over the three-year period, both a cash basis and an accrual basis taxpayer would have recognized income of $500 from the transactions in examples 16 and 17.

Substance-over-Form Doctrine.   The accounting concepts, constructs, and doctrines presented to this point require that all transactions be traced to and recorded by the entity responsible for that transaction in accordance with the method of accounting selected by that entity. Occasionally, the basis for recording the transaction is not clear. That is, taxpayers attempting to avoid taxation sometimes carefully sculpt transactions that are unrealistic in the ordinary sense.

▲ **EXAMPLE 18**   Bill is the sole proprietor of Bill's Sub Shop. In order to lower his tax on the income from the sub shop, Bill "employs" his 3-year-old daughter as a janitor at a salary of $200 per week. Is Bill's employment of his daughter unrealistic?

Discussion: Because it is unlikely that a 3-year-old could perform such services, Bill's characterization of his daughter as an employee is unrealistic.

Although the courts have consistently held that taxpayers are under no legal obligation to pay more tax than the law prescribes (i.e., tax avoidance is a legal activity), the courts have also said that transactions must bear some semblance to reality. This judicially created concept is referred to as the **substance-over-form doctrine.** The doctrine states that the taxability of a transaction is determined by the reality of the transaction, rather than some (perhaps contrived) appearance.[9] This is generally interpreted to mean that a transaction is to be taken at its face value only when it has some business or economic purpose other than the avoidance of tax.

▲ **EXAMPLE 19**   In example 18, should Bill be allowed to deduct the salary paid to his daughter?

Discussion: Because the payment of the salary to the daughter is unrealistic under the circumstances, Bill would not be allowed a deduction for the salary paid to her. This arrangement lacks economic substance and is solely for the purpose of tax avoidance. Thus, the form of the arrangement (daughter as an employee) is ignored, and the tax treatment is based on the substance of the transaction (a gift to his daughter, which is not deductible).

When might substance over form apply? This is a difficult and subjective question that has no hard-and-fast answers that apply in every situation. However, a few factors should alert us to the possibility of this doctrine's being invoked by the IRS. The major element to look for is whether the transaction has economic substance. Most legitimate business transactions are made at arm's length between two parties, neither of which stand to benefit by mutual manipulation of the transaction. Consider the following examples:

▲ **EXAMPLE 20**   Selma is the president and chief executive officer of Megainternational Corporation. Megainternational is a large, publicly held corporation that operates in more than 50 countries around the world. During the current year, Selma receives a salary of $1,000,000 and a bonus of $2,000,000. The bonus is based on a percentage of Megainternational's profits. Can Megainternational deduct the $3,000,000 salary and bonus paid to Selma?

Discussion: Megainternational can deduct the entire $3,000,000 in salary and bonus paid to Selma. The salary-and-bonus contract was negotiated at arm's length between Selma and Megainternational. Because Megainternational is a publicly held corporation, Selma is not able to exert undue influence over her contract, and the salary and bonus paid to her would be typical of such a position.

▲ **EXAMPLE 21**   Eugene is the president and chief executive officer of Florence Dunes Co. Florence is a closely held corporation that is wholly owned by Eugene and his wife

Dahlia. Florence pays Eugene a salary of $300,000 during the current year and a bonus of $200,000. The bonus is paid even though Florence has only $250,000 in income. Although Florence has been in business for more than 10 years, it has never paid a dividend. Can Florence deduct the $500,000 in salary and bonus it pays to Eugene?

Discussion: Because Florence is wholly owned by Eugene and Dahlia, salary payments to the owners are subject to extra scrutiny. All deductions are subject to the requirement that they be reasonable under the facts and circumstances. In Eugene's case, the first question is whether the $300,000 salary is reasonable when compared with the salaries paid by other, comparable companies to executives who do not control the corporation. Any portion of the salary that is unreasonable is considered a dividend paid to the owner. Dividends are not deductible expenses of a corporation.

Eugene's bonus payment is suspicious under the circumstances. Because Florence has never paid a dividend, the payment of such a large bonus relative to the income of the corporation to a 100-percent owner appears to be more in the nature of a dividend distribution. Thus, although the *form* of the payment is a salary bonus, the *substance* of the payment is that of a dividend distribution under the facts presented. It is unlikely that the bonus can be deducted as a salary payment by Florence.

In many situations, the tax law itself specifies that certain transaction forms be treated according to their underlying substance. For example, in the area of alimony and child support, the tax law specifies that the amount of an alimony payment that varies according to some contingency related to a child is treated as a child support payment. This distinction is critical, because alimony is taxable to the receiver and deductible by the payer, whereas child support payments have no effect on the taxable income of either party.[10]

▲ **EXAMPLE 22**   Dick and Jane divorce in the current year. They have 2 children who are in Jane's custody throughout the year. The divorce decree specifies that Jane will receive $100 per month per child for child support and $2,000 per month as alimony. However, the alimony will be reduced by $600 per month per child when the child reaches age 18, marries, or if the child dies. How much of the $2,000 payment is alimony, and how much is child support?

Discussion: Because the alimony is reduced when an event related to the children occurs, the tax law treats the reduction in alimony related to the contingency as child support. That is, the agreed-upon alimony will ultimately be reduced by $1,200 per month, at which time Jane will receive only $800. The $800 is considered the true alimony payment to Jane, and the remaining $1,200 is child support for income tax purposes. From the $2,200 Jane receives each month, $1,400 [$1,200 + (2 × $100)] is child support, and $800 is alimony.

Income concepts determine what constitutes taxable income, explain why one type of income is taxed differently than other income, and establish the period in which income is to be reported.

INCOME CONCEPTS

All-Inclusive Income Concept

The broadest income concept is the **all-inclusive income concept.** Under this concept, all income received is considered taxable unless some specific provision can be found in the tax law that excludes the item in question from taxation. Income can be received in any form: cash, property, services, and so on. Thus, the tax law always starts with the proposition that anything of value received is taxable.[11]

Many situations dealing with income recognition are covered in Chapter 3, so we are using only one example here to illustrate the pervasive nature of this concept.

▲ **EXAMPLE 23**   Felicia is a tax accountant with Oil Rich Co. Alice is a plumber. Both are cash basis taxpayers. Felicia had a problem with her plumbing that Alice fixed. The normal charge for this service would have been $300. However, Alice agreed to waive her fee in exchange for some tax advice from Felicia relating to her business. Do either Felicia or Alice have taxable income from this agreement?

Discussion: Both Felicia and Alice have income from rendering services, Alice from the plumbing repair and Felicia from the provision of tax advice. Although income was never reduced to cash by either party, both received something of value in exchange for their services. Alice should report the $300 as income when she receives the promised tax advice. Felicia should report $300 of income when Alice fixes her plumbing.

We noted earlier that certain items of income are not subject to tax. How do we know which items are taxable and which are not? As with all exceptions to the general concepts, only study and experience in working with the tax laws provide answers. Chapter 4 discusses some major income items that are excluded from taxation.

Legislative Grace Concept

Exclusions are based on the **legislative grace concept.** This concept states that any tax relief provided to taxpayers is the result of specific acts of Congress that must be applied and interpreted strictly. Note that relief from taxes on income received can take several forms. Income can be either permanently excluded from tax, or it may be deferred for taxation in a future period (resulting in a time value of money savings). *Legislative grace* means that only Congress can grant an exclusion from income, and the exclusion must be taken in its narrowest sense. An example illustrates these two related notions.

▲ **EXAMPLE 24**   Jorge receives 200 shares of MNO Corporation common stock as a gift from his grandfather. At the date of the gift, the shares have a fair market value of $20,000. During the current year, Jorge receives dividends totaling $2,000 on the stock. Recall that the tax law excludes the value of a gift from the gross income of the recipient. What are the tax effects for Jorge of the gift from his grandfather?

Discussion: The receipt of the stock as a gift from the grandfather is specifically excluded from Jorge's income by the tax law. However, the exclusion applies only to the value of the gift received and does not exclude from tax any subsequent income Jorge receives on the gift property.[12] Therefore, Jorge is taxed on the $2,000 in dividends received on the stock.

One other form of tax relief that Congress has provided is special treatment for certain types of income. Most income received and allowable losses incurred by taxpayers are simply added to (deducted from, in the case of losses) the income tax return of the taxpayer and taxed according to the taxpayer's marginal tax rate. In tax jargon, this is referred to as *ordinary income (loss)*. Congress has created a special class of income treatment for gains and losses arising from the sale of capital assets. A **capital asset** is generally defined as any asset that is *not* a receivable, inventory, real or depreciable property used in a trade or business, and certain intangible assets, such as copyrights.[13] Thus, capital assets primarily consist of stocks, bonds, and other investment-related assets. In addition, all personal use assets (home, furniture, clothing, automobile, etc.) of individual taxpayers are capital assets.

The gains and losses from the sale of capital assets, known as **capital gains** and **capital losses,** must be separated from other gains and losses and aggregated through a prescribed netting procedure before they enter into the taxpayer's income calculation. Net long-term capital gains are currently given preferential treatment through a cap on the tax rate that must be paid on this type of income. Currently, the maximum tax rate paid on net long-term capital gains is 28 percent, versus the top marginal tax rate of 39.6 percent for individual taxpayers. If the netting procedure results in a net capital loss for the year, only $3,000 of the net capital loss can be deducted from an individual's tax return per year.[14] Chapter 3 provides an overview of capital gains, and Chapter 12 covers capital gains and losses in more detail. For now, just remember that capital gains and losses are treated differently than all other types of income and losses.

Capital Recovery Concept

Once it has been determined that an item of taxable income has been received, the next logical step is to determine the amount of the income that belongs in the calculation of taxable income. In most cases, this is straightforward. However, sales of investment and/or business assets require more guidance. The **capital recovery concept** states that no income is taxed until all capital previously invested in the asset is recovered.[15] That is, on any asset purchased, all investment in that asset must be recorded in order to determine the amount of profit (or loss) made upon disposition of the asset. The amount invested in an asset is referred to as its **basis.**[16]

▲ **EXAMPLE 25**   Earl purchases 100 shares of ABC Co.'s common stock at a total cost of $1,000. When he sells the stock, one lot of 50 shares is sold for $600 and the other 50 shares are sold for $300. What are the tax effects of these sales?

Discussion: Because there are 2 separate sales of the stock at different prices, each sale must be considered separately. Each 50-share lot has a basis of $500 (half the $1,000 purchase price). The lot sold for $600 results in a $100 ($600 − $500) taxable gain. That is, Earl has recovered $100 more than he had invested in the 50 shares.

The 50 shares sold for $300 result in a loss of $200 ($300 − $500). Note that a loss is nothing more than invested capital that has not been recovered. Because of the capital recovery concept, we recognize gains only when the recovery from the disposition of an asset is greater than the amount invested in the asset. A loss results when all the capital invested in an asset is not recovered upon its disposition.

Realization Concept

A crucial question regarding income items is when to recognize the income (i.e., in which accounting period it should be taxed). In this regard, the taxpayer's accounting method resolves many of the problems. However, some general concepts provide additional guidance. The most basic recognition concept is the **realization concept.** This concept states that no income is recognized for tax purposes (i.e., is included in taxable income) until it has been realized by the taxpayer. In most cases, realization occurs when an arm's-length transaction takes place: Goods are sold, services are rendered, and so on. Mere changes in value without the advent of a realization event—in which the taxpayer receives the change in value—do not result in a taxable recognition.[17]

▲ **EXAMPLE 26**   Assume that in example 25 Earl purchases the 100 shares of ABC common stock on July 2, 1996. On December 31, 1996, the 100 shares have a fair market value of $1,200. The first lot of 50 shares is sold on February 5, 1997. As of December 31, 1997, the remaining 50 shares have a fair market value of $400. What is Earl's recognized income from the stock in 1996? in 1997?

Discussion: Although the shares gain $200 in value as of December 31, 1996, Earl still holds the shares and has not realized the increase in value. Therefore, the change in value does not result in a recognition of income in 1996. He realizes the $100 gain from the sale of the first 50 shares in 1997 and reports it in that year. The loss in value of $100 as of December 31, 1997, has not been realized, so Earl cannot deduct this loss in value until he realizes it through sale.

Claim-of-Right Doctrine.

To aid in determining when a realization has occurred, the **claim-of-right doctrine** states that a realization occurs whenever an amount is received without restriction as to its disposition.[18] An item is received without restriction when the receiver has no definitive obligation to repay the amount received. Income received under a claim of right is reported in the year of receipt. If income is realized under a claim of right and a repayment of part or all of the receipt occurs in a later year, it is accounted for as a deduction in the year of repayment because of the annual accounting period concept. When a taxpayer receives amounts, but their use is restricted in some substantial manner, those amounts are not realized until the restriction is removed.

▲ **EXAMPLE 27**   Sadie, a landlord and a cash basis taxpayer, enters into a 1-year lease agreement with Bob, as tenant, on December 1, 1996. The lease agreement calls for a monthly rent of $500, with payment of first and last months' rents upon signing. In addition, Bob is required to pay a $100 cleaning deposit that is to be returned at the end of the lease if the property is returned in good condition. What are tax effects for Sadie of receiving the $1,100?

Discussion: The first and last months' rents are taxable when received. Sadie is on the cash basis and has an unrestricted right to the use of the rent payments. However, she must return the cleaning deposit at the end of the lease if Bob abides by its terms. Because of this restriction, Sadie does not have a claim of right to the cleaning deposit when she receives it, and it is not taxed at that time. If Sadie keeps all or a part of the deposit at the end of the lease, it is included in her income at that time.

▲ **EXAMPLE 28**   Assume that in example 27 Sadie sells the building in 1997 before the end of the lease term. Because of the sale, Sadie returns the last month's rent prepayment to Bob. How should Sadie account for the repayment of the last month's rent?

Discussion: Because Sadie had previously included the last month's rent in her 1996 income, she is allowed to deduct the repayment in 1997. NOTE: The mere possibility that a repayment might be required does not negate Sadie's unrestricted use of the rent prepayment when she receives it.

Note that the claim-of-right doctrine applies when something of value has been received by the taxpayer. The question to be answered in such cases is whether the receipt has resulted in a realization of income. If the taxpayer has a clear obligation to repay the amount received, the taxpayer does *not* have a claim of right to the amount and is not taxable on the receipt. However, if there is no clear and definitive obligation to repay, the taxpayer is deemed to have received income.

▲ **EXAMPLE 29**   Herbert Corporation borrowed $10,000 from Local Bank to purchase a stamping machine. Herbert will repay the $10,000 by making monthly payments with interest at 14% over the next 6 years. Does Herbert Corporation have income from the receipt of the $10,000 it borrowed from Local Bank?

Discussion: Because Herbert Corporation is obligated to repay the $10,000 loan, it does not have a claim of right and is not required to recognize the $10,000 as income.

Constructive Receipt Doctrine.   Accrual basis taxpayers recognize income when it has been earned, whereas a cash basis taxpayer recognizes income when it is received. Whether a receipt has occurred is not critical for accrual basis taxpayers. However, a major question for cash basis taxpayers is when is income received? That is, is income received only when it has been physically received in the form of cash? The all-inclusive income concept tells us that income can be received in any form—cash, property, or services. Thus, it is not necessary for a cash basis taxpayer to reduce the income to cash to be in receipt of income. A more fundamental problem is what constitutes a receipt. Based on the **constructive receipt doctrine,** cash basis taxpayers are deemed to be in receipt of income when it is credited to their accounts or otherwise made unconditionally available to the taxpayers.[19] For example, interest income is taxed on the day it is credited to a savings account, regardless of when the taxpayer actually withdraws it. That is, the interest income is available for use by the taxpayer when it is credited to the account and is taxed at that time. Physical possession of the interest income is not required for it to be taxed. Note that this is not a problem for an accrual basis taxpayer—the interest income would be taxed in the period in which the income was earned, regardless of when the actual payment was received. Once income has been made unconditionally available, taxpayers cannot turn their back on the income and thus select the year for taxation.[20] To be considered unconditionally available, the taxpayer must be aware that the income is available for use.

▲ **EXAMPLE 30**   At the December 12, 1996, meeting of the board of directors of Gould Co., the board awards bonuses to all officers in the amount of 5% of their annual compensation. The bonuses are to be paid in December. Samantha, the controller of Gould Co., requests that her bonus not be paid until January 1997. In what year is Samantha taxed on the bonus?

Discussion: Because the board made the bonus unconditionally available to Samantha in December, she is in constructive receipt of the bonus in 1996 and is taxed as if she received the bonus in that year.

However, income is *not* constructively received if the taxpayer's control of its receipt is subject to substantial limitations or restrictions.

▲ **EXAMPLE 31**   Aardvark Corporation mails its annual dividend checks to shareholders on December 31, 1996. Alana receives her dividend check on January 4, 1997. In what year is the dividend taxable to Alana?

Discussion: Because Alana does not have any control over the dividend check and does not have unrestricted use of the check until she receives it on January 4, 1997, she is taxed on the dividend in 1997. Although she knows that the check is coming, it is not available for use as of December 31, 1996.

▲ **EXAMPLE 32**   Assume that Aardvark Corporation policy is to mail its annual dividend checks to shareholders so that the checks arrive on or before December 31 of each year. Alana has been a shareholder of Aardvark for 5 years. Alana's dividend check arrives in her mailbox on December 31, 1996. However, Alana is out of town to visit relatives for the holiday and does not return until January 4, 1997, at which time she deposits the check in her checking account. In what year is the dividend taxable to Alana?

Discussion: Because the dividend is made annually, Alana is aware that the check is coming. She is taxed on the dividend in 1996, because it is available to her on December 31 and she knew that the check was coming.

▲ **EXAMPLE 33**   Paul is selected the outstanding player in the Super Bowl on December 31, 1964. He is awarded a car worth $10,000, which he picks up 3 days later at the dealer that supplied the car. When is Paul taxed on the award?

Discussion: As long as Paul could not have picked up the car under any condition on December 31, it is not made unconditionally available to him until the first date on which he can pick it up. Therefore, he is taxed on the value of the car in 1965.[21]

These are just a few applications of the constructive receipt doctrine. More detail on different types of restrictions and conditions is covered in the discussion of income sources in Chapter 3. At this point, the important point to remember is that cash basis taxpayers do not have to actually receive cash to trigger income recognition; the only requirement is that the income be unconditionally within their control.

▲ **Figure 2–2**

CONSTRUCTIVE RECEIPT AND CLAIM OF RIGHT

Comparing Claim of Right and Constructive Receipt. One of the most difficult problems encountered by beginning tax students is determining when the claim-of-right and constructive receipt doctrines apply. Figure 2–2 presents a time

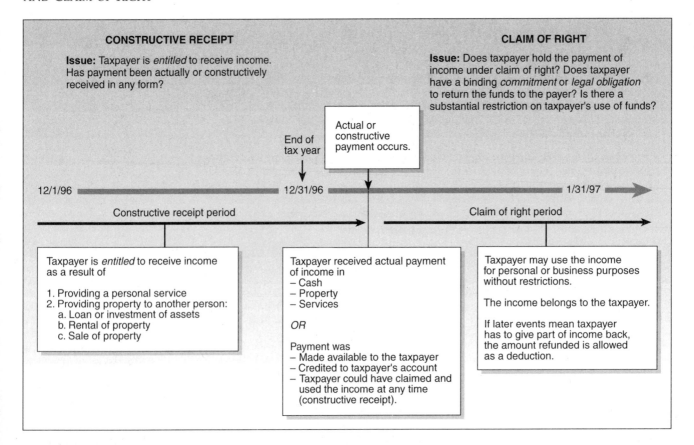

line that differentiates the two doctrines. In Figure 2–2, note that the constructive receipt doctrine applies when an item of income has not yet been physically received by the taxpayer. The question to be answered in determining whether the item is currently taxable is whether the taxpayer has the income within his or her control. This is in contrast to the claim-of-right doctrine where an amount has been received. The question in this case is whether the amount received is currently taxable.

Wherewithal-to-Pay Concept

The income tax system is philosophically based on the ability-to-pay concept. Features such as progressive tax rates and taxation based on the net income of a taxpayer are derived from the concept that the amount of tax paid should be in relationship to the ability of the taxpayer to pay the tax. Ability to pay the tax in the current tax year is also important for income-recognition purposes. To distinguish general ability-to-pay principles and income-recognition applications, we use the **wherewithal-to-pay concept.** This concept states that income should be recognized and a tax paid on the income when the taxpayer has the resources to pay the tax. Although this would generally require that the transaction in question provide cash to pay the tax, the receipt of other asset forms and relief from debts are considered forms of receipt with which tax can be paid.[22] NOTE: The concept applies equally to both cash and accrual basis taxpayers.

The wherewithal-to-pay concept provides the rationale for the deferral of recognition on several types of realized gains.

> ▲ **EXAMPLE 34**   Mike exchanges a computer with a basis of $600 that he uses in his dental practice for a new computer. The new computer cost $3,000, but Mike is given a trade-in value of $1,000 for his old computer and has to pay only $2,000 out of pocket for the new computer. Has Mike realized a gain from the exchange? If so, is the gain available to pay tax?
>
> *Discussion:*   An exchange does constitute a realization. Mike has disposed of the computer in an arm's-length transaction and converted its value toward the purchase of the new computer. The substance of the transaction is a sale of the old computer for $1,000 and the purchase of the new computer for $3,000.
>
> Although Mike has realized a gain of $400 ($1,000 - $600) on the exchange, all the gain has been reinvested in the purchase of the new computer, and none of the $1,000 he received for his old computer is available to pay the tax on the $400 gain.

Mike's computer transaction is an example of a like-kind exchange. Because Mike exchanged business property that is of like kind (in this case, one computer for another computer), the tax law allows him to defer recognition of the gain until he disposes of the new computer in a transaction that gives him cash (or other assets) with which to pay the tax. Like-kind exchanges and other types of transactions in which gains are deferred under the wherewithal-to-pay concept are discussed in Chapter 13.

Another important application of this concept is the acceleration of income recognition by accrual basis taxpayers on advance receipts for goods and services. In general, accrual basis taxpayers recognize income in the tax year in which the income is earned, without regard to when cash payment is actually received. However, when an accrual basis taxpayer receives an advance payment for goods and services, the IRS takes the position that the taxpayer is in the best position to pay the tax in the period in which the cash is received rather than when it is earned.[23]

▲ **EXAMPLE 35**   Return to the facts of example 27. Assume that Sadie, the landlord, is an accrual basis taxpayer. She receives the first and last months' rent on the 1-year lease in December 1996. In which year(s) should the $1,000 first and last months' rent receipts be taxed?

Discussion: Under the accrual method of accounting used in financial accounting, Sadie is deemed to have earned only the December rent in 1996; the $500 advance receipt for the last month's rent is not recognized until it is earned in 1997.

Application of the wherewithal-to-pay concept would cause the entire $1,000 received in December to be taxed in 1996. That is, the $500 advance receipt for the last month's rent that will not be earned until next year is available for Sadie to use to pay her taxes and should be taxed at the time she receives it.

The income concepts discussed here apply to income-recognition problems. No attempt has been made to cover every situation in which these concepts might apply. Rather, throughout the remaining chapters these concepts serve as the basis for discussing the treatment of income items.

DEDUCTION CONCEPTS

The federal income tax is based on the general proposition that taxpayers will pay tax according to their ability to pay. This results in the tax being assessed on the income net of the costs of producing that income. The tax law provides for this through the allowance of deductions (and losses) in computing a taxpayer's taxable income. The fundamental questions that need to be answered in regard to deductions are what types of expenditures are deductible, how much is deductible, and when the deduction can be taken. Deduction concepts provide the basis for resolving these issues.

Legislative Grace Concept

The most fundamental deduction concept is that of legislative grace. Applied to deductions, this concept means that deductions are allowed only as a result of a specific act of Congress and that any relief granted in the form of a deduction must be strictly interpreted. In contrast to the all-inclusive income approach to the recognition of income—where we assume that everything is taxable unless we can find a provision exempting an item from tax—deductions must be approached with the philosophy that nothing is deductible unless a provision in the tax law allows the deduction.

Business Purpose Concept

The allowance of deductions is governed by the **business purpose concept.**[24] This concept means that a deduction is allowed only for an expenditure that is made for some business or economic purpose that exceeds any tax avoidance motive. This concept has been interpreted to mean that the expenditure was made in connection with a profit-seeking activity.[25] Note that a transaction may be entered into for a profit and for the additional profit from the tax savings associated with the deductibility of the expenditures related to the transaction. Two general types of expense deductions in the tax law embody this profit motive requirement: expenses incurred in a trade or business and those related to the production of income (investment activity).[26,27] These two general types of expenses are commonly referred to as **trade or business expenses** and **investment expenses.**

A third category of expenses that is specifically disallowed (with a few specific exceptions) are those expenses that are personal in nature, known as **personal**

expenses.[28] As stated in Chapter 1, the tax law does allow individuals to deduct certain personal expenditures from adjusted gross income. The list of deductible personal expenses includes medical expenses, home mortgage interest, income and property taxes, personal casualty losses, and charitable contributions. Recall that these expenses are deductible only if they exceed the taxpayer's allowable standard deduction amount. In addition, many of the expenses are limited to a percentage in excess of the individual's adjusted gross income.

In order to determine the tax treatment of any expenditure, the motive behind the transaction must be determined. Based on the motive—profit or personal purposes—it is categorized in one of these general classes:

1. Trade or business expenses

2. Investment expenses

3. Personal expenses

Distinguishing a personal expenditure (category 3) from a profit-motivated activity (i.e., categories 1 and 2) is generally a fairly easy task.

▲ **EXAMPLE 36**   Peter pays $1,000 for a new couch for his home. Is this a personal expenditure?

Discussion: As long as the couch is not used in Peter's trade or business or is not held as an investment by Peter, its use is personal and no deduction would be allowed for the purchase of the couch.

▲ **EXAMPLE 37**   Peter purchases a couch for the reception area of his optometry practice. What is the proper treatment of the couch?

Discussion: Because providing a place for clients to sit while they wait is something that businesses normally do, the couch is properly classified as related to his trade or business of optometry. Peter can therefore take the deductions allowed for the couch.

A more difficult task is distinguishing a trade or business activity from an investment activity. This is covered in depth in Chapter 5, but consider the following examples:

▲ **EXAMPLE 38**   Roger owns Gould Trucking Co. The physical layout of the company includes an office building, a parking lot for his trucks, and a maintenance shop. During the current year, Roger purchases the house next door to his trucking company and rents it out to individuals unrelated to the trucking company. Is the house an investment activity or part of his trucking business?

Discussion: Because Roger purchased the house to produce rents, which is an investment activity unrelated to his trucking business, it is considered an investment activity. He must account for the house and any related expenses under the rules for investments, not as part of his trade or business of trucking.

▲ **EXAMPLE 39**   Assume that instead of renting the house out, Roger allows his drivers to stay in the house during rest periods between trucking runs. How should the house be treated?

Discussion: In this case, the use of the house is related to his trucking business. Therefore, the house is considered a trade or business asset and is accounted for under the rules for trade or business assets.

Once the general category to which an expenditure belongs has been determined, the tax law provides specific rules regarding deductibility for each category. For example, business expenses are generally limited only by the reasonableness (i.e., what a prudent businessperson would pay in the same circumstances) of their amount, whereas deductions for investment expenses of individuals are often subject to a limitation based on the income of that taxpayer. Losses incurred in a trade or business are fully deductible, but losses from the sale of personal use assets (automobile, furniture, clothing, personal residence, etc.) are generally not deductible. These are just a few general examples of the importance of distinguishing the activity in which an expenditure has been incurred. Chapters 5 through 7 discuss the specifics of differences in deductions and losses in the three classes of expenditures. For now, consider the following treatments of the sale of an automobile:

▲ **EXAMPLE 40**   Jill owns an automobile that has a basis of $8,000. She sells the automobile for $5,000. How much of the $3,000 loss can Jill deduct on her tax return?

Discussion: The deductibility of the loss depends on the use of the automobile. If Jill uses the automobile in a business, the loss would be fully deductible. However, if the use of the automobile was purely personal, no loss on the sale would be allowed.

▲ **EXAMPLE 41**   Assume that Jill sells the automobile for $9,000, resulting in a $1,000 gain. Is the gain taxable in all cases?

Discussion: Yes, the gain would be taxed even if it were used for purely personal purposes. Remember that the all-inclusive income concept requires that all income be taxed unless specifically excluded by the tax law. There is no exclusion in the tax law for income from the sale of personal use assets.

Although the tax law provides a general disallowance of deductions for personal expenditures of individuals, some specific deductions are allowed for personal expenditures. Based on the ability-to-pay concept, the tax law allows individuals to take personal and dependency exemption deductions. That is, each individual is allowed to deduct a predetermined amount for herself or himself and for each person who is dependent on that person for their living expenses. This deduction recognizes that a basic cost of living must be paid in order to live and that this money is not available for the payment of taxes.

Certain personal expenditures, referred to as *itemized deductions*, for medical care, charitable contributions, home mortgage interest, casualty losses, and other miscellaneous types of personal expenses are also allowed as deductions.[29] As with exemptions, these are items that Congress feels are necessary living expenditures that are not available for the payment of tax. In order to create some equity for taxpayers of different means and for administrative convenience, a minimum deduction for these types of expenditures (itemized deductions) is allowed to all individual taxpayers through the provision of a standard deduction.

▲ **EXAMPLE 42**   Mary and Tom are both single taxpayers. Mary makes a salary of $50,000 and Tom makes $20,000. Mary has total allowable itemized deductions of $8,000 for 1996. Tom's total allowable itemized deductions are $2,000. The standard deduction for a single taxpayer in 1996 is $4,000, and the personal exemption deduction amount is $2,550. Given these facts, what are Mary's and Tom's total allowable deductions for 1996?

Discussion: Each is entitled to the $2,550 personal exemption deduction. Because Mary's itemized deductions exceed the standard deduction, she is allowed to deduct her actual $8,000 in expenditures, for a total deduction of $10,550. Tom's itemized deductions are less than the minimum allowable standard deduction, so he is allowed to deduct the $4,000 standard deduction in lieu of his $2,000 in actual expenditures, for a total deduction of $6,550.

The allowance of a standard deduction is unique to individual taxpayers. Individuals, estates, and trusts are allowed to take exemption deductions. The constructs of exemptions and standard deduction amounts do not apply to other tax entities, which may take only those deductions that are based on the business purpose concept in connection with a profit-motivated activity.

Capital Recovery Concept

After establishing the category of an expenditure, the next question to be answered is how much of the expenditure can be deducted. In general, the amount of a deduction can never exceed its cost. This is derived from the capital recovery concept discussed earlier. Under this concept, no income is realized until the amount invested has been recovered. The amount of investment in an asset is referred to as the asset's *basis*. Thus, the amount invested in an item, its cost, is the maximum amount that can be deducted in determining taxable income.

▲ **EXAMPLE 43**   Wojo's Warblers, Inc., sells miniature porcelain birds. Wojo's purchased a shipment of the birds several months ago at a per-unit cost of $45. Wojo's recently sold the entire shipment for $65 per unit. It will cost $50 per unit to replace the birds sold. How much income does Wojo's, Inc., have from the sale of each bird?

Discussion: Although it will cost Wojo's $50 to replace each porcelain bird, its income calculation is based on the amount actually invested in each bird. Therefore, the per-bird profit is $20 ($65 − $45).

The year(s) in which expenditures may be deducted is generally determined by the taxpayer's accounting method. However, even cash basis taxpayers cannot deduct capital expenditures in total in the period in which they are paid.[30] The main characteristic of a **capital expenditure** is that its usefulness extends substantially beyond the end of the tax year in which the expenditure is made.[31] The classic example of a capital expenditure is the purchase of a long-lived asset such as a building.

▲ **EXAMPLE 44**   In 1996, Amy Corporation, a cash basis taxpayer, purchases a computer to use in its consulting business. Amy pays $15,000 for the computer, which it expects to be able to use in its business for at least 5 years. When can Amy Corporation deduct the $15,000 investment in the computer?

Discussion: Because the use of the computer extends beyond the end of 1996, Amy cannot deduct the entire $15,000 in 1996, even though it is on the cash basis. Amy Corporation must capitalize the $15,000 cost and deduct it over its tax life through depreciation deductions. Specific rules for depreciating property for tax purposes are covered in Chapter 11.

In example 44, the computer would have an original basis equal to its cost, $15,000. As depreciation deductions are taken on the computer, the investment is being recovered against current period income. Therefore, the basis must be reduced whenever part of the investment is recovered through a tax deduction. To understand why basis is reduced for recoveries, consider the following example:

▲ **EXAMPLE 45**   Amy Corporation takes depreciation on its computer at $3,000 per year. At the end of 5 years, when total depreciation taken amounted to $15,000, it sells the computer for $5,000. What is Amy Corporation's gain (loss) on the sale of the computer?

Discussion: Amy Corporation's gain is $5,000. When the computer is sold, it has no capital investment remaining in the computer, because it has deducted the entire $15,000 cost against income during the 5 years it used the computer.

Note that if basis was not reduced for the depreciation deductions taken, Amy Corporation would have a loss of $10,000 ($5,000 − $15,000) on the sale. Allowing the corporation to deduct a $10,000 loss and $15,000 of depreciation would result in a total deduction of $25,000. This would be a violation of the capital recovery concept, which limits deductions to the amount invested in an asset.

Similarly, any additional capital expenditures pertaining to the computer would be added to the computer's basis for recovery over the remaining tax life. Because the amount of capital invested in a long-lived asset varies throughout its tax life because of these adjustments to basis, the investment in an asset is more appropriately referred to as its *adjusted basis*.[32] An asset's **adjusted basis** is the amount of unrecovered investment in the asset after considering increases and decreases in the original amount invested in the asset.[33]

For any given expenditure, a deduction for the expenditure can take place at three points in time:

- In the period paid or incurred
- Over the useful life of the expenditure
- Upon disposition of the asset created by the expenditure

When the benefit of expenditures does not extend beyond the end of the current tax year, the expenditures are deducted in the year in which they are incurred (accrual basis) or paid (cash basis). These are the normal, recurring expenditures commonly made to produce the income being generated. Examples of currently deductible expenditures include salaries, rental payments, supplies, bank charges, and utilities.

Expenditures that benefit more than the current tax year must be capitalized. If the asset created by the expenditure is depreciable in nature, its cost is recovered by depreciation deductions over its useful tax life.[34] Long-lived assets that do not depreciate are recovered through amortization over the useful life of the asset. In order to be depreciable or amortizable, the asset must have a determinable life or period of usefulness to which the cost can be attributed.

▲ **EXAMPLE 46**   Joe, a cash basis taxpayer, prepays the rent on his business building for 3 years on July 1, 1996. The monthly rental is $1,000, resulting in a $36,000 pre-payment. How much rent can Joe deduct in 1996 through 1999?

Discussion: Although Joe uses the cash method of accounting, the rent prepayment benefits tax years 1996, 1997, 1998, and 1999 and must be capitalized and amortized according to the number of rental months in each year. In 1996, the building is rented for 6 months, resulting in a $6,000 deduction. In 1997 and 1998, Joe can deduct 12 months of rent, $12,000, with the remaining $6,000 deductible in 1999.

Assets such as land and common stock that do not have determinable lives are neither depreciable nor amortizable. Capital recovery on this type of asset does not take place until there is a disposition of the asset.

▲ **EXAMPLE 47**   The Stephanie Partnership purchases some land in 1992 for $20,000. The land is held until 1996, when it is sold for $30,000. What deductions can the partnership take on the land and when can it take them?

Discussion: Land is not a depreciable asset, because it has no determinable life, so no capital recovery deductions are allowed until the land is sold. In 1996, Stephanie recognizes a gain of $10,000 from the sale of the land. That is, the $20,000 basis is deducted from the $30,000 selling price.

It is possible for capital recovery to occur at more than one point in time for any given asset.

▲ **EXAMPLE 48**   Raul purchases a heavy-duty truck for use in his construction business in 1994 at a cost of $30,000. He uses the truck until 1996, when it is sold for $6,000. How much can Raul deduct in 1994, 1995, and 1996 for use of the truck, and what is his gain or loss on the sale of the truck?

Discussion: The heavy-duty truck is eligible for a special-election-to-expense (the Section 179 election to expense, discussed in Chapter 11) deduction of $17,500 in the year of purchase, 1994.[35] In addition, the remaining $12,500 of cost can be depreciated over 5 years for tax purposes. Under the rules for straight-line depreciation (discussed in Chapter 11), Raul is allowed a depreciation deduction of $1,250 in 1994, $2,500 in 1995, and $1,250 in 1996. This leaves him an adjusted basis of $7,500 at the date of the sale and a loss on the sale of $1,500:

Calculation of Adjusted Basis

Original basis	$ 30,000
Less: Amounts recovered (deducted) against income	
First year election to expense	(17,500)
Depreciation	
1994	(1,250)
1995	(2,500)
1996	(1,250)
Total recovered through deductions against income	$(22,500)
Adjusted basis at date of sale	$ 7,500

Calculation of Loss on Sale

Selling price	$ 6,000
Less: adjusted basis	(7,500)
Loss on sale	$ (1,500)

Discussion: In this example, Raul recovers his $30,000 investment in the truck as follows: (1) $17,500 in the year of purchase through the election to expense, (2) $5,000 in depreciation during the period he uses the truck, and (3) $7,500 recovered against the $6,000 selling price when the truck is sold.

These deduction concepts are applicable to all deduction situations. As with the other concepts presented, this chapter does not attempt to cover all applications of the deduction concepts. Throughout the remaining chapters, the discussion of deductions is presented with reference to the applicable deduction concepts.

The federal income tax is based on a system of rules and regulations. These rules and regulations are based on general concepts that can be used to determine the income tax treatment of most transactions. As with all systems devised by human beings, the federal income tax system contains exceptions to the treatments prescribed by the system's concepts. Throughout the remaining chapters, the treatment of various transactions is developed by reference to the applicable concepts. In order to deal with the federal income tax system effectively, knowledge of the

SUMMARY

▲ **Table 2–1**

INCOME TAX CONCEPTS
WITH RELATED
CONSTRUCTS AND
DOCTRINES

General Concepts	Income Concepts	Accounting Concepts	Deduction Concepts
Ability to Pay Income, exclusions, deductions, losses, tax credits Progressive rate structure **Administrative Convenience** Standard deduction **Arm's-Length Transaction** Related party Constructive ownership **Pay as You Go** Withholding Estimated tax payments	**All-Inclusive Income** **Legislative Grace** Capital asset— Capital gains and losses **Capital Recovery** Basis **Realization** Claim of right Constructive receipt **Wherewithal to Pay**	**Entity** Taxable/Conduit Assignment of income **Annual Accounting Period** Accounting method Tax benefit rule Substance over form	**Legislative Grace** **Business Purpose** **Capital Recovery** Basis Capital expenditure

concepts on which it is based is essential. This chapter has presented the basic tax concepts and categorized them according to their use within the tax system: general, accounting, income, and deduction concepts. For reference purposes, each category is summarized in Table 2–1.

KEY TERMS

ability-to-pay concept (p. 50)
accounting method (p. 58)
accrual basis of accounting
  (p. 58)
adjusted basis (p. 72)
administrative convenience
  concept (p. 51)
all-inclusive income concept
  (p. 61)
annual accounting period concept
  (p. 58)
arm's-length transaction concept
  (p. 52)
assignment-of-income doctrine
  (p. 57)
basis (p. 63)

business purpose concept (p. 68)
capital asset (p. 62)
capital expenditure (p. 71)
capital gains (p. 63)
capital losses (p. 63)
capital recovery concept (p. 63)
cash basis of accounting (p. 58)
claim-of-right doctrine (p. 64)
concept (p. 50)
conduit entity (p. 55)
construct (p. 50)
constructive ownership rules
  (p. 53)
constructive receipt doctrine
  (p. 65)

doctrine (p. 50)
entity concept (p. 54)
investment expense (p. 68)
legislative grace concept (p. 62)
pay-as-you-go concept (p. 53)
personal expense (p. 68)
realization concept (p. 63)
related party provisions (p. 52)
substance-over-form doctrine
  (p. 60)
taxable entity (p. 55)
tax benefit rule (p. 59)
trade or business expense (p. 68)
wherewithal-to-pay concept
  (p. 67)

PRIMARY TAX LAW SOURCES

[1] Sec. 267—Defines related parties and provides limits on deductibility of certain transactions between related parties.

[2] Sec. 6654—Provides that all individuals must pay estimated taxes when their tax liability is expected to be greater than

$500; imposes a penalty for not paying the proper amount of estimated tax.

[3] Sec. 701—Provides that partners, not the partnership, are responsible for payment of tax on the income of the partnership.

[4] Sec. 1336—Prescribes the taxation of income by S corporations.

[5] Lucas v. Earl, 281 U.S. 111 (1930)—Established the assignment-of-income doctrine in holding that salaries and fees earned by the taxpayer but paid to his wife under a valid agreement were still income to the taxpayer who earned the income.

[6] Burnet v. Sanford & Brooks Co., 282 U.S. 359 (1931)—Held that the transactions of each tax year should stand separate and apart from transactions of other tax years.

[7] Sec. 446—Sets general rules for methods of accounting, including the allowance of the cash and accrual methods; requires that the method selected by a taxpayer clearly reflect income.

[8] Sec. 111—Establishes the tax benefit rule.

[9] U.S. v. Phellis, 257 U.S. 156 (1921)—Made the first application of the substance-over-form doctrine; held that the substance of a transaction should be considered and the form of a transaction can be disregarded in applying the provisions of the tax law.

[10] Sec. 71—States that alimony received is taxable; defines *alimony*.

[11] Sec. 61—Provides the general definition of *gross income* as all income from whatever source derived.

[12] Willcuts v. Bunn, 282 U.S. 216 (1931)—Determined that gain on the sale of tax-exempt securities is taxable income.

[13] Sec. 1221—Defines *capital assets*.

[14] Sec. 1211—Sets forth the limit on deductions of capital losses of corporations and individuals.

[15] Sec. 1001—Prescribes the calculation of gains and losses on dispositions of property; defines *amount realized* for purposes of determining gain or loss on dispositions.

[16] Sec. 1012—Defines *basis of property*: The general rule for the initial basis of a property is its cost.

[17] Eisner v. Macomber, 252 U.S. 189 (1920)—In holding that a stock dividend did not constitute gross income, determined that increases in value that have not been realized are not subject to tax.

[18] North American Oil Consol. v. Burnet, 286 U.S. 417 (1932)—Established the claim-of-right doctrine in holding that an amount received under the clear control of the taxpayer was income even if some portion of the amount received might have to be repaid in the future.

[19] Reg. Sec. 1.446-1—Requires all items that constitute gross income be included in gross income in the tax year in which the item is actually or constructively received.

[20] Hamilton National Bank of Chattanooga v. CIR, 29 B.T.A. 63 (1933)—Held that "a taxpayer may not deliberately turn his back upon income and thus select the year for which he will report it."

[21] Hornung v. CIR, 47 T.C. 428 (1967)—Held that the value of an automobile received by a football player as most valuable player in championship game was not included in income until the player had actual possession made available to him.

[22] Reg. Sec. 1.61-1—States that income can be realized in any form, including cash, services, and property received.

[23] Reg. Sec. 1.61-8—States that advance receipts of rents are included in gross income in the year of receipt, regardless of the taxpayer's accounting method.

[24] Helvering v. Gregory, 293 U.S. 465 (1935)—Originated the business purpose concept; held that the transaction in question had no business purpose, therefore the applicable tax law did not apply.

[25] CIR v. Transport Trading & Terminal Corp., 176 F.2d 510 (2d Cir. 1949)—Expanded the application of the business purpose concept enunciated in *Helvering v. Gregory* to include any tax law provisions pertaining to commercial transactions.

[26] Sec. 162—Allows the deduction of all ordinary and necessary expenses incurred in a trade or business of the taxpayer.

[27] Sec. 212—Allows the deduction of all ordinary and necessary expenses incurred in a production-of-income activity of the taxpayer.

[28] Sec. 262—Sets the general rule for the disallowance of deductions for personal expenditures by individuals.

[29] Sec. 211—Generally allows specific personal expenditures as itemized deductions of individuals.

[30] Sec. 263—Provides the general rule that disallows current period deductions for capital expenditures.

[31] Reg. Sec. 1.461-1—Specifies that expenditures that create an asset with a life expectancy that extends substantially beyond the end of the tax year must be capitalized.

[32] Sec. 1011—Provides general rules for determining the adjusted basis of property.

[33] Sec. 1016—Provides the general rules for adjustments to basis of property for capital expenditures and recoveries of capital subsequent to purchase.

[34] Sec. 167—Allows a depreciation deduction for property subject to exhaustion and wear and tear on property used in a trade or business or held for the production of income.

[35] Sec. 179—Provides an election to expense of up to $17,500 of the cost of depreciable tangible personal property in the year of purchase for tax years after 1992.

DISCUSSION QUESTIONS

1. This chapter compared the operation of the income tax system to the operation of other systems we have devised to govern our everyday lives. Choose an example of a system you deal with in your everyday life, and explain part of its operation in terms of concepts, constructs, and exceptions to the general concepts and constructs.

2. The chapter stated that the ability-to-pay concept is fundamental to the operation of the income tax system. What is the ability-to-pay concept, and what are the two basic aspects of the income tax system that are derived from the concept? What might the tax system be like without this concept?

3. What is an arm's-length transaction? What is its significance to income taxation?

4. Explain how the related party construct and the arm's-length transaction concept interact.

5. Why is the pay-as-you-go concept important to the successful operation of the income tax system? What other types of taxes are based on this concept?

6. What is the difference between a taxable entity and a conduit entity?

7. Why is the tax benefit rule necessary? That is, which concept drives the need for this construct? Explain.

8. What are the two basic methods of accounting that may be used by taxpayers? How do the two basic methods differ?

9. What is the effect of the capital recovery concept on income recognition?

10. Chapter 1 discussed how gross income is equal to all income received, less exclusions. Which concepts form the basis for this calculation of gross income? Explain.

11. What is capital gain income? How is it different from ordinary income?

12. Why does the doctrine of constructive receipt apply only to cash basis taxpayers?

13. How is the wherewithal-to-pay concept different from the ability-to-pay concept?

14. Explain how the business purpose concept provides the basis for determining which expenses are deductible.

15. What is a capital expenditure?

16. The legislative grace concept is both an income concept and a deduction concept. Explain how the application of the concept differs for income items and deduction items.

17. The capital recovery concept is both an income concept and a deduction concept. Explain how the application of the concept differs for income items and deduction items.

PROBLEMS

18. Which of the following are based on an ability to pay? Explain.
    a. State Y collects a sales tax of 5% on all purchases of goods and services.
    b. State X collects a sales tax of 5% on all purchases of goods and services but gives low-income families a tax credit for sales taxes.
    c. Students at State University are given free parking in designated lots. Faculty and staff must pay $125 per year for parking at State University.
    d. Barton City charges all customers a flat monthly rate of $10 for garbage pickup.

19. Which of the following are based on an ability to pay? Explain.
    a. Local County assesses property taxes at the rate of 1% of assessed value.
    b. The University library allows all students, faculty, and staff to check out books free of charge. Students who do not return books by the due date are fined $1 for each day the book is late. Staff members are fined 50 cents for each day a book is late. Faculty members are not fined when they return books late.
    c. The country of Lacyland assesses an income tax based on the following schedule:

Taxable Income	Income Tax
$ -0- to $20,000	20% of taxable income
$20,001 to $60,000	$ 4,000 + 15% of taxable income in excess of $20,000
$60,001 and above	$10,000 + 10% of taxable income in excess of $60,000

    d. State Z imposes a 10-cent per gallon tax on gasoline but gives low-income taxpayers a tax credit for gasoline taxes paid.

20. Sheila, a single taxpayer, is a retired computer executive with a taxable income of $40,000 in the current year. Sheila receives approximately $30,000 per year in tax-exempt municipal bond interest. Adam and Tanya are married and have no children. Adam and Tanya's $40,000 taxable income is comprised solely of wages they earn from their jobs. Calculate and compare the amount of tax Sheila pays versus Adam and Tanya's tax. How well does the ability-to-pay concept work in this situation?

21. Andrew and Barbara each receive a salary of $80,000. Neither Andrew nor Barbara has any other source of income. During the current year, Barbara paid $800 more in tax than Andrew. What might explain why Barbara paid more tax than Andrew when they both have the same income?

22. Which of the following are related parties:
    a. Nina and her brother Julius? Yes
    b. Nina and the Porta Bella Partnership? Nina owns a one-third interest in the partnership. Two of Nina's friends own the remaining partnership interest. No · less than 50%
    c. Nina and her aunt Louise? No
    d. Nina and Camp Corporation? Nina owns 70% of Camp Corporation. Three unrelated parties own 10% each. Yes
    e. Nina and her grandson Monte? Yes

23. In each of the following cases, determine whether Inez is a related party:
    a. Inez owns 500 shares of XYZ Corporation's common stock. XYZ has 50,000 shares of common stock outstanding.
    b. Inez owns a 40% interest in the Tetra Partnership. The other 60% interest is owned by 3 of Inez's friends.
    c. Inez owns 40% of the stock in Alabaster Co. Her husband Bruce owns 30% and her brother-in-law Michael owns the remaining 30%.
    d. Inez is a 100% owner of Nancy Corporation.

24. Junior bought some stock several years ago for $6,000. He is thinking of selling the stock and has 2 offers. His broker told him he could sell the stock for $6,600 and he would have to pay a $900 commission, for a net realization of $5,700. His sister Bonnie offered to pay Junior $5,700 with no commissions paid on the transaction. What is the potential problem with the sale of the stock to Bonnie? Write a letter to Junior in which you explain the likely tax result if he sells the stock to Bonnie.

25. Doiko Corporation owns 90% of the stock in Nall, Inc. Trebor owns 40% of the stock of Doiko. Trebor's sister owns the remaining 60% of Doiko. During the current year, Trebor purchased land from Nall for $43,000. Nall had purchased the land for $62,000. Based on the income tax concepts, what are the likely tax effects of Trebor's purchase of the land?

26. Ed runs an auto repair business out of the garage attached to his personal residence. How should Ed account for each of the following items?
    a. Cash received from repair services, $28,000.
    b. Interest paid on his home mortgage, $7,300.
    c. Power jack hoist purchased at a cost of $12,000.
    d. Electricity bills, $3,600 (Ed does not have separate electricity service to the garage).
    e. Checks received from customers that were returned by bank, $1,600. The bank charged Ed's account $35 for processing the bad checks.
    f. Telephone bill for phone in the garage, $420 (Ed has a separately listed phone in his house).
    g. Advertising in the local newspaper, $800.
    h. Interest paid on home furniture loan, $600.

27. Jie owns a lawn mower repair business. Her repair shop is in a building she constructed on the lot on which her personal residence is located. How should Jie account for each of the following?
    a. Interest paid on her home mortgage, $9,200. Interest of $4,000 is paid on a separate loan that she used to construct the repair shop.
    b. Property taxes, $1,800.
    c. Insurance on all buildings and furnishings, $1,700.
    d. Electricity bills, $3,800. (Jie is not billed separately for electricity service to her repair shop).
    e. Cost of remodeling the kitchen, $3,200.
    f. Telephone bills, $970. Jie uses one telephone number for her residence and her business. The cost of having an extra line to the shop is $30 per month. The $970 includes a charge of $250 for an ad in the business section of the telephone directory.
    g. Cost of operating her van for one year, $7,800. Jie uses the van in her repair business and for personal use.

28. Henrietta is the president and sole shareholder of Clutter Corporation. In 1993, Henrietta transferred ownership of her personal residence to the corporation. As part of the transfer, Clutter Corporation assumed Henrietta's mortgage on the house. At the same time, she and the corporation entered a lease agreement that allows Henrietta to lease the property for as long as she wants at an amount approximating the monthly mortgage payments on the house. During the current year, Clutter paints the house at a cost of $5,000, makes other repairs totaling $3,000, and adds an entertainment room at a cost of $30,000. Current-year property taxes and interest paid by Clutter on the house are $1,400 and $18,000, respectively. Henrietta paid $18,000 in rent to Clutter. Write a memorandum to the controller of the Clutter Corporation in which you discuss the potential tax ramifications of this arrangement for Henrietta and Clutter Corporation.

29. Aiko, Lani, and Charlie own the 3-Star Partnership, sharing profits and losses 25:40:35. During the current year, 3-Star has total gross income of $320,000 and total allowable deductions of $220,000. How should each of the following taxpayers account for 3-Star's results? Explain.
    a. 3-Star Partnership
    b. Aiko
    c. Lani
    d. Charlie

30. Alicia owns 40% of the common stock of Dahl Co. During the current year, Dahl reported a taxable income of $80,000 and paid $20,000 in cash dividends. What are the income tax effects for Alicia of her investment in Dahl Co. if Dahl is organized as
    a. A corporation?
    b. An S corporation?

31. Binh owns several businesses. The total income generated by all his businesses puts him in the highest marginal tax bracket. Seeking to lower the overall tax on his business income, Binh is thinking of creating two S corporations and putting half his business interests in each. Will this arrangement lower his overall tax? Write a letter to Binh in which you explain the tax effects of organizing his businesses as two separate S corporations. In your letter suggest an alternative plan that might lower his tax.

32. Christie purchases a one-third interest in the Corporate Capital Partnership (CCP) in 1995 for $35,000. During 1995, CCP earns an income of $45,000, and Christie withdraws $5,000 in cash from the partnership. In 1996, CCP suffers a loss of $30,000, and Christie withdraws $12,000.
    a. What are the tax consequences for Christie of this investment in 1995 and 1996?

33. Elroy is a self-employed electrician. Whenever a customer pays him in cash, he gives the cash to his son, Errol. Because he does not actually have use of the cash, Elroy thinks that he should not be taxed on the amounts he gives to Errol. What are the tax effects of this arrangement? Explain.

34. Milton is an inventor who has also written several successful mystery novels. Because he didn't really need the income from the novels, Milton wrote the novels under an assumed name and had the royalties from the novels paid to Hammer Corporation. When Milton incorporated Hammer, he gave all the stock to his three sons. The sons are employed by the corporation. The salaries paid to the sons are approximately equal to the royalties earned each year from the novels. Analyze the tax results of this arrangement.

35. Esmeralda is an attorney. Before 1996, she is employed by the law firm of Ellis and Morgan (E&M). Esmeralda is not a partner in E&M; her compensation consists of a fixed salary and a percentage of any fees generated by clients she brings or refers to the firm. In January 1996, she becomes a partner in the law firm of Thomas, Gooch, and Frankel (TGF). As a partner, Esmeralda agrees to turn over to TGF any income from the practice of law from the date of her admittance to the practice. In leaving E&M, it is agreed that she will continue to receive her percentage of fees from clients she referred to E&M during her employment there. In return, Esmeralda agrees that, upon request, she will consult E&M attorneys regarding those clients. During 1996, she consults with 2 of her former E&M clients and receives $12,000 from E&M per their agreement. The $12,000 consists of $10,000 as a percentage of fees for client referrals after she left E&M and $2,000 as a percentage for work done before she left E&M. Esmeralda turns the $12,000 over to TGF per her partnership agreement. Is Esmeralda taxed on the $12,000 she receives from E&M? Explain.

36. For each of the following situations, determine the proper year for recognition of the income or deduction if the taxpayer is (1) a cash basis taxpayer and (2) an accrual basis taxpayer:
    a. Harry does some legal work for Janet in December 1996. Janet pays Harry's bill in January 1997.
    b. Ruben sells land to Mark on July 1, 1995, for $30,000. The terms of the sale call for Mark to pay Ruben $10,000 on July 1, 1995, and $10,000 on July 1 of 1996 and 1997.
    c. Acme Hardware Co. purchases new counters for the store on October 4, 1996, at a cost of $6,500. The counters have an estimated useful life of 20 years, but the tax life is 7 years.
    d. Odakota pays his employee, Sally, $13,480 in salary up to December 22, 1996. As of December 31, Odakota owes Sally $390 for the period of December 22 through December 31. The $390 is to be paid on the next pay date, which is January 5, 1997.
    e. Judy purchases office supplies costing $800 on December 28, 1996. Judy pays for the office supplies on January 28, 1997.

37. For each of the following situations, determine the proper year for recognition of the income or deduction if the taxpayer is (1) a cash basis taxpayer and (2) an accrual basis taxpayer:
    a. Helen fixes Mark's plumbing in November 1996. Mark receives the bill in December 1996 but does not pay Helen until January 1997.
    b. The Outback Brewing Co. purchases a new delivery van on October 30, 1996. The purchase is financed with a note that will be paid off over 3 years. Outback expects to use the van for 3 years, but the tax life of the van is 5 years.
    c. Morbid Marble Mortuaries, Inc., sells a headstone to Lorissa for $6,000. The terms of the sale call for Lorissa to pay $3,000 in the year of sale and $1,000 in each of the succeeding 3 years.
    d. Maury's Computer Consultants, Inc., performs work for Janis in 1995. Maury's bills Janis in 1995, but no payment is received. In 1996, Janis files for bankruptcy, and Maury's determines that it will be able to collect nothing on her account.

38. Tim has state income taxes of $3,800 withheld from his salary during 1995. On his 1995 federal income tax return, Tim properly deducts the $3,800 as state taxes paid. Upon filing his 1995 state income tax return, he determines that his actual state income tax for 1995 is only $3,000, and the state sends him an $800 refund. What are the tax consequences of the refund? Explain in terms of the concepts presented in the chapter. How would your answer change if Tim's actual state income tax is $4,100 and he has to pay $300 with his state return?

39. Jamal Corporation is an accrual basis taxpayer. In 1995, Jamal writes off a $400 account receivable from a customer who has died. In 1996, the former customer's estate sends Jamal a check for $250. What are the tax effects of the receipt of the $250 in 1996? Explain. How would your answer be different if Jamal Corporation is a cash basis taxpayer?

40. Jerry and his wife Joanie own a successful concrete company that is organized as a corporation. Jerry spends all his time running the company, whereas Joanie has a full-time job as a legal secretary. The corporation pays Joanie a salary of $45,000 a year as vice president. Write a letter to Jerry and Joanie in which you explain any tax problem(s) they may have as a result of this arrangement.

41. The Prevetti Partnership is engaged in the purchase and management of apartment complexes. The partnership entered into an agreement with Parsnip Development Co. on July 1 of the current year to purchase the Perry Apartments. The sales agreement stated the purchase price of $5,000,000. It also provided for "other payments to seller," composed of a $500,000 payment for a covenant not to compete, $50,000 for the seller's management advice during the period of ownership transition, and a financing fee of $100,000. In addition, the seller is to receive the first $400,000 of the rent collected by Prevetti. The purchase was completed on August 5. Monthly rentals on the property are $90,000. Prevetti paid Parsnip the first $400,000 of rent it collected per the purchase agreement. How much rental income does the Prevetti Partnership have for the current year? Explain.

42. For each of the following tax treatments, determine the concept, construct, or doctrine that provides the rationale for the treatment:
   a. Lester purchases some stock for a total cost of $2,500. On December 31, 1995, the stock is worth $2,800. In August 1996, he sells the stock to his brother Rufus for $2,000. Lester has no income from the stock in 1995, and he is not allowed to deduct the $500 loss on the sale of the stock to Rufus in 1996.
   b. Kerry is an employee of Ross Co. During the year, Ross withholds federal income taxes of $3,500 from her salary. Her tax liability for the year is only $3,200, so she receives a refund of $300.
   c. Catherine is a city government employee. She often uses the city's photocopier to make personal photocopies and has her secretary type an occasional personal letter. The value of these services for the current year is approximately $55 but is not included in Catherine's gross income.
   d. Dante's allowable personal deductions are only $2,800 this year, so he deducts the standard deduction of $4,000 in computing his taxable income.

43. For each of the following tax treatments, determine the concept, construct, or doctrine that provides the rationale for the treatment:
   a. During 1996, Trafalger Corporation pays $475,000 in estimated tax payments. Trafalger determines its actual tax liability for 1996 is $490,000, so it pays only $15,000 with its 1996 tax return.
   b. The Parsnip Partnership is an accrual basis taxpayer. During 1995, Parsnip deducted as a bad debt expense a $5,000 account receivable that it determined it could not collect. In 1996, Parsnip receives a $1,000 payment on the account. Parsnip must include the $1,000 in its 1996 gross income.
   c. Kuri sells land for $30,000; its cost was $20,000. Under the sales agreement, the buyer is to pay Kuri's son $10,000 of the sales price. Kuri must recognize a gain of $10,000 on the sale.
   d. Jevon owns 20% of the stock of Cowdery, Inc., an S corporation. During the current year, Cowdery reports an income of $45,000 and pays no dividends. Jevon must include $9,000 in gross income.

44. EAL Corporation purchases a delivery truck costing $33,000 for use in its floral business in 1993. It deducts $3,300 in depreciation on the truck in 1993, $6,600 in 1994, $6,600 in 1995, and $3,300 in 1996. It sells the truck in 1996 for $22,000. What is its gain (loss) on the sale of the delivery truck?

45. George purchases stock in Dodo Corporation in 1993 at a cost of $40,000. In 1996, he sells the stock for $26,000. What is the effect of the sale of stock on George's 1996 taxable income? Assume that George sells no other assets in 1996.

46. Chelsea, who is single, purchases land for investment purposes in 1992 at a cost of $43,000. In 1996, she sells the land for $57,000. Chelsea's taxable income without considering the land sale is $70,000. What is the effect of the sale of the land on her 1996 taxable income, and what is her 1996 tax liability? Would your answer change if Chelsea were married?

47. Determine whether the taxpayer in each of the following situations has realized income. Explain why there has or has not been a realization, and determine the amount of income to be reported.
    a. Ward owns 300 shares of Montezuma common stock. During the current year, Montezuma splits the stock 2 for 1. As a result of the split, Ward receives an additional 300 shares of stock.
    b. Shannon is the sole shareholder of Bubbles, Inc., a corporation. During the current year, Bubbles has taxable income of $80,000.
    c. Bob's Balloon Flights owes Kona Bank $100,000. Bob's is having cash-flow problems because of a decline in tourism and cannot make full payment on its loan from Kona. Rather than foreclose on the loan, Kona reduces the debt to $60,000 so that Bob's can stay in business.
    d. Alfredo runs a ballet studio. He charges customers $50 per month for lessons. Alternatively, customers can pay a lump sum of $480 for 1 year of lessons. During the current year, Alfredo receives $11,000 in monthly payments and $18,000 in 1-year prepayments.

48. Determine whether the taxpayer in each of the following situations has realized income. Explain why there has or has not been a realization, and determine the amount of income to be reported:
    a. Ramrod Development Co. purchases land costing $230,000. Ramrod subdivides the land into 100 lots, incurring legal fees of $20,000. It also spends $50,000 to install utility and sewer connections to each lot. The lots are priced to sell at $50,000 each, but none has sold as of the end of the year.
    b. Eugene is a computer consultant. Rashid is an accounting professor. Rashid needs help installing some new software on his home computer. Eugene offers to install the software if Rashid will help him set up the books for a new company he is forming. Eugene installs the software in December. Rashid sets up the books in February.
    c. Sasha is an employee of Chasteen Hair Products. Chasteen provides all employees with free medical coverage. During the current year, the cost of Sasha's coverage is $1,900.
    d. In November, Ira wins an all-expense-paid trip for two to the Super Bowl in January. Ira plans to take his best friend to the game. The estimated value of the trip is $4,300.

49. Ayah signs a contract to write a book for East Publishing Co. in 1996. Under the terms of the contract, she receives a $5,000 advance against future royalty payments upon signing the contract. The contract stipulates that if Ayah does not write a suitable book or if the royalties from the book are insufficient to cover the advance, she must repay any portion not earned. Does Ayah have any income from the receipt of the royalty advance? Explain in terms of the income tax concepts presented in the chapter.

50. Determine whether the taxpayer in each of the following situations has a claim of right to the income received:
    a. Trigger, Inc., receives a $5,000 stud fee for services rendered by one of its prized horses. Under its standard contract, Trigger will return the fee if a live foal is not born.
    b. Orville works as a salesman for Brewster Co. He receives a travel allowance of $1,000 at the beginning of each quarter. At the end of each quarter, he must make a full accounting of his travel expenses and reimburse Brewster for any of the $1,000 not spent on approved travel.
    c. Assume that in part b, Orville is not required to account for his actual travel expenses for Brewster and is not required to return unused portions of the travel advance.
    d. Arco Architecture, Inc., receives $10,000 from a client for work done by a subcontractor on the client's project. Arco, in turn, pays $10,000 to the subcontractor.

51. Determine whether the taxpayer in each of the following situations has a claim of right to the income received:

 a. Sulley's Spa Spot sells hot tubs that have a 2-year warranty. The warranty provides for the replacement of all parts and the cost of labor to replace the parts. In addition, Sulley's may replace the hot tub in lieu of repairing it. During the current year, Sulley's hot tub sales total $250,000. Sulley's estimates that 10% of all hot tubs sold will require warranty work.

 b. In 1994, Retro Fit Construction Co. purchased equipment by borrowing $100,000 from Fifth State Bank. After paying off $30,000 of the loan, Retro has financial problems in 1996 and cannot afford to make its regular payment. Rather than have Retro default on the loan, Fifth State Bank agrees to reduce the debt to $50,000.

 c. Larry's Lawncare Service provides lawn mowing and fertilization services to residential customers. Customers can pay by the month, or they can purchase a one-season contract for $1,000. The contracts obligate Larry's to provide the necessary mowing and fertilization from April through October. In September, Larry's has a "pre-season" sale that allows current customers to purchase next season's contract for $800. Fourteen customers buy the discounted contract in September.

 d. Alexander Associates does some computer consulting for Bertman, Inc., in September. Bertman pays Alexander's $3,000 bill for the work in October 1996. In late November, Bertman's computer system crashes and Bertman sues Alexander, seeking reimbursement in the amount of $3,000. The lawsuit is scheduled for court in March 1997.

52. Consider the following two situations. Although they are similar, their treatments are exactly opposite. Identify the concept underlying both treatments, and explain why the concept treats the two situations differently.

 a. Sam is an employee of Dunbar Co. The company regularly mails salary checks to employees to arrive on or before the last day of each month. Sam's regular paycheck arrives at his house on December 31, 1996, but Sam is away on a ski trip and does not return until January 2, 1997. Sam deposits the check in his bank account the following day. The check is included in Sam's 1996 income.

 b. Percy is an employee of Daly Co. In November 1996, Percy's position is eliminated in a "streamlining" of company costs. As part of the cost reduction program, Percy is entitled to severance pay; however, his boss tells him that it will be 3 or 4 months before the severance payments are made. The check arrives by mail on December 31, 1996, while Percy is away on a ski trip. He returns on January 2, 1997, and deposits the check in his bank account the following day. The severance pay check is not taxable until 1997.

53. Determine whether the taxpayer in each of the following situations is in constructive receipt of income. If not, explain when the income will be constructively received.

 a. Morton earns a salary of $5,000 per month from Shipley Co. In December, Morton is notified that Shipley is unable to meet its December payroll obligation until sometime in January.

 b. Constancia works as an agent for Wesellum Realty. During 1996, Constancia borrows $10,000 from Wesellum. Wesellum deducts amounts against the loan from Constancia's commission checks. Constancia actually receives $17,000 in commissions during 1996, and an additional $5,000 in commissions is applied against her loan.

 c. Mikhail is the president of Boris Manufacturing, Inc. His employment contract entitles him to a bonus each year based on that year's profitability. The bonus is not payable until February 15 of the following year. In December 1996, he receives a $25,000 advance on his 1996 bonus. The following February, the actual amount of the bonus is determined to be $40,000, and Mikhail receives the remaining $15,000 on February 15, 1997.

54. Using the income concepts presented in this chapter, discuss whether the taxpayer has realized income in each of the following situations:

a. Adco Corporation pays the health insurance premiums for all its employees. Adrian is an employee of Adco. Health insurance premiums Adco pays for Adrian cost $1,150 for the current year.

b. The Sung Partnership buys a parcel of unimproved land for $32,000. Sung spends an additional $22,000 to put in roads and sewerage and to grade the property for subdividing. The property is subdivided into 15 lots and offered for sale at $10,000 per lot.

c. Doctors and nurses at Valley View Hospital are allowed to eat free of charge in the hospital cafeteria during their shifts. Sue, a doctor, eats meals valued at $1,900 during the current year.

d. Wayman wins the golf championship at his country club. In addition to a handsome trophy, he receives merchandise worth $500 for winning the tournament.

e. Rock signs a contract to play football for the Rangers. In addition to a salary of $1,000,000 per year for 5 years, Rock is to receive a signing bonus of $5,000,000 to be paid 10 years from the date the contract was signed.

55. Elmo Corporation leases land to Valerie for $1,000 per month under a 30-year lease. The terms of the lease provide that any improvements to the land made by Valerie revert to Elmo upon termination of the lease. Valerie constructs a building on the property at a cost of $12,000. At the end of the lease, the fair market value of the land is $60,000, and the fair market value of the building is $30,000. Elmo Corporation sells the property 2 years later for $105,000.

a. List three points at which Elmo Corporation might recognize income from the improvements made by Valerie.

b. According to the income concepts presented in the chapter, when should Elmo Corporation recognize income from the lease? Explain.

c. Would your answer to part b be different if the lease provides that any improvements made by Valerie can be deducted from the rental payment made to Elmo Corporation?

56. For each tax treatment described, determine the applicable income tax concept(s), and explain how it forms the basis for the treatment:

a. Jackson owned some coupon bonds with detachable interest coupons. He detached coupons worth $5,000 and gave them to his son to buy a car. Jackson is taxed on the $5,000 of interest, even though he never actually received the interest.

b. Joan's barn on her ranch was destroyed by a tornado. The barn had an adjusted basis of $24,000. Joan received insurance proceeds of $35,000 and built a new barn costing $40,000. Joan does not have to recognize the gain realized on the barn in the current period.

c. Elvis borrowed $30,000 from University Credit Union to purchase a new X car. He is not taxed on the receipt of the $30,000.

d. Kelley lost the diamond ring she received from her husband Ian. The ring had a basis of $2,000, and she received $3,000 from her insurance company. Kelley used the money to pay off some medical bills. Kelley must recognize a $1,000 gain on the loss of her diamond.

57. Seymour is a salesman who travels extensively to see clients. In the current year, Seymour buys a new car costing $24,000. Seymour uses the car primarily to travel to see clients during the week. On weekends, he uses the car to run personal errands. What is the tax problem Seymour faces regarding the new car? Explain.

58. Arnold is a college professor specializing in robotics. During the current year, he attends a meeting on robotics in San Diego. Because of the desirable location of the meeting, he takes along his wife Hortense and their 2 children. The meeting lasts for 3 days, but Arnold and his family stay for 2 weeks. What tax problem is posed by this situation? Explain in terms of the concepts presented in the chapter.

59. For each of the following situations, determine the deduction concepts involved, and explain how they form the basis for the tax treatment described:

   a. Individuals are allowed to deduct medical expenses.

   b. Happy Burgers, Inc., owns a chain of drive-in restaurants in California. Seeking to expand its operations, Happy spent $90,000 investigating locations in Oregon. Happy decided that expanding into Oregon was not a wise move at the time, but it is allowed to deduct the $90,000.

   c. Lage's Licorice Co. suffers a fire in one of its warehouses. Equipment that cost $40,000 and that had been depreciated $15,000 is destroyed. The equipment, which cost $50,000 to replace, is uninsured. Lage is allowed to deduct a loss of $25,000 on the equipment.

   d. While Ray is out to dinner one night, someone breaks into his personal car. The thief steals his stereo and his golf clubs. The fair market value of the items stolen is $300. Because he has a $500 deductible on his insurance policy, he receives no reimbursement from his auto insurance. To make matters worse, no tax deduction for his loss is allowed.

60. For each of the following situations, determine the deduction concepts involved, and explain how they form the basis for the tax treatment described:

   a. Jamie sells her personal residence at a loss of $9,000. Jamie is not allowed a deduction for the loss.

   b. Jamie sells a building used in her business at a loss of $9,000. Jamie is allowed to deduct a $9,000 loss on the sale of the building.

   c. Last year, Gardner Corporation purchased equipment costing $10,000. The equipment was eligible for a special expense election, and Gardner deducted the $10,000 cost in the year of purchase. Gardner is not allowed a depreciation deduction on the equipment in the current year.

   d. The Orlando Jams Partnership borrows $500,000 to use as working capital. During the current year, the partnership pays $45,000 in interest on the loan and repays $100,000 of the loan principal. Orlando can deduct the $45,000 interest payment but cannot deduct the repayment of the loan principal.

61. Sidney lives in Hayes, Kansas. He owns some land in Cotulla, Texas, that he inherited from his father several years ago. The land is unimproved and has never produced income. On January 26, 1996, Sidney receives a statement of delinquent taxes on the property for 1993, 1994, and 1995 for $120. On February 10, 1996, Sidney and his wife Ellen start to drive to Cotulla; they arrive on February 20 and pay the taxes on the same day. The cost of the trip for Sidney and Ellen is $450. Sidney and Ellen would like to deduct the cost of the trip. Write a letter to Sidney and Helen in which you explain what they can deduct.

62. Doris purchases a ski cabin in Montana during the current year. Doris hires a real estate management company to rent out the cabin on a daily basis. The real estate management company tells Doris to expect an average of 70 rental days per year. Doris intends to use the cabin for her vacation 3 weeks during the year. What tax problem is posed by the ski cabin? Explain.

63. Explain why the legal fees paid in the following three situations are treated differently for income tax purposes:

   a. Jim pays $10,000 in legal fees in obtaining a divorce. None of the $10,000 is deductible.

   b. Camella invents and patents a device that shells nuts. When she learns that another company is selling copies of her device, she pays an attorney $10,000 to enforce her patent. The $10,000 is fully deductible.

   c. Melody pays $10,000 in legal fees for advice relating to various investments she owns. Only $6,000 of the fees is deductible.

64. Explain why the loss resulting from the sale of a computer in the following three situations is treated differently for income tax purposes:
   a. Monica sells her personal computer at a loss of $1,300. None of the loss is deductible.
   b. Omar sells a computer used in his carpeting business at a loss of $4,300. The loss is fully deductible.
   c. Jerry sells his computer at a loss of $3,800. Jerry used the computer to keep track of his investment portfolio. Only $3,000 of the loss is deductible.

65. A truck owned by Duster Demolition Services is involved in an accident. The truck originally cost $30,000, and $10,000 of depreciation had been taken on the truck as of the date of the accident. The cost of repairing the truck is $3,000, for which the insurance company reimburses Duster $2,000.
   a. How much of a loss, if any, is Duster entitled to deduct as a result of the accident?
   b. What is the adjusted basis of the truck after the accident?

66. Determine the proper treatment of each of the following expenditures:
   a. Zoe purchases land costing $8,000. During the current year, she pays $2,000 to have utilities and sewer lines installed on the property. Zoe also pays $600 in interest on the loan used to obtain the land and $300 in property taxes on the land.
   b. On August 2, Carruth Corporation pays $11,000 for a 2-year fire insurance policy on its manufacturing facility.
   c. The Freeborn Partnership purchases a rental property costing $125,000. Before it rents out the building, Freeborn repaints it at a cost of $2,000 and spends $1,200 on other minor repairs. After the property is rented, a pipe bursts, requiring $2,000 in repairs.
   d. Aqua Robotics, Inc., purchases and pays for supplies costing $1,400 on December 26. As of December 31, the company has not used $1,200-worth of the supplies.

67. Determine the taxpayer's adjusted basis in each of the following situations. If any changes are made in the original basis of the asset, explain why they are necessary.
   a. Simone purchases 300 shares of Wilguess, Inc., stock in 1994 for $6,300. In 1994 and 1995, Wilguess pays cash dividends of $2 per share. In 1996, Wilguess pays a 40% stock dividend (nontaxable), and Simone receives an additional 120 shares of stock.
   b. Symbol Corporation purchases a building in 1993 at a cost of $240,000. Annual maintenance costs on the building are $80,000. In 1995, Symbol adds a wing to the building at a cost of $60,000. In 1996, the building is painted at a cost of $25,000. Symbol deducts $4,800 in depreciation in 1993, $7,300 in 1994, and $8,100 in 1995 and 1996.
   c. Lorissa purchases land as an investment in 1994 for $33,000. Property taxes on the property are $400 per year. In 1995, Lorissa is assessed $2,000 by the county assessor for her share of a sidewalk that the county builds adjacent to the land. Lorissa pays the assessment in 1996.
   d. The Barton Brothers Partnership purchases a computer in 1994 for $8,000. The partnership elects to deduct the entire cost of the computer in 1994. In 1996, Barton Brothers spends $300 to repair the computer.

68. Wiggins, Inc., is a manufacturer of fire extinguishers. The fire extinguishers come with a 2-year warranty. Wiggins engineers estimate that approximately 2% of the extinguishers will be defective and require payment under the warranty. Discuss the propriety of allowing Wiggins a deduction in the current year if
   a. Wiggins is a cash basis taxpayer.
   b. Wiggins is an accrual basis taxpayer.

69. The controller of Newform Oil Co. has come to you for advice. Newform recently cleared a forested area and began drilling an oil well on the site. The well is a gusher, and Newform's geologists estimate that it will produce for at least 10 years. Environmental restoration laws will require Newform to completely reforest and restore the oil well site when the well is taken out of production. An engineering firm hired by Newform estimates that the cost of complying with the environmental requirements will be $8,000,000. For financial accounting purposes, Newform intends to amortize the estimated cost over the 10-year expected life. In addition, it plans to put $500,000 per year into an account that should provide the $8,000,000 necessary to perform the restoration.

   The controller would like your advice on the deductibility of the costs of restoration. That is, when can Newform deduct the costs and how much can it deduct? Based on the concepts discussed in this chapter, write a memorandum to the controller detailing what you think is the proper treatment of the restoration costs for tax purposes.

DISCUSSION CASE

70. Biko owns a snowmobile manufacturing business, and Miles owns a mountain bike manufacturing business. Because each business is seasonal, their manufacturing plants are idle during their respective off-seasons. Biko and Miles have decided to consolidate their businesses as one operation. In so doing, they expect to increase their sales by 15% and cut their costs by 30%. Biko and Miles own their businesses as sole proprietors and provide the following summary of their 1995 taxable incomes:

TAX PLANNING CASE

	Biko	Miles
Business income		
Sales	$ 600,000	$ 450,000
Cost of goods sold	(400,000)	(300,000)
Other expenses	(100,000)	(75,000)
Business taxable income	$ 100,000	$ 75,000
Other taxable income		
(net of allowable deductions)	20,000	35,000
1995 taxable income	$ 120,000	$ 110,000

Biko and Miles don't know what type of entity they should use for their combined business. They would like to know the tax implications of forming a partnership versus a corporation. Under either form, Biko will own 55% of the business and Miles will own 45%. They each require $60,000 from the business and would like to increase that by $5,000 per year.

   Based on the information provided, do a three-year projection of the income of the business and the total taxes for a partnership and for a corporation. In doing the projections, assume that after the initial 30% decrease in total costs, their annual costs will increase in proportion to sales. Also, assume that their nonbusiness taxable income remains unchanged. Use the 1996 tax rate schedules to compute the tax for each year of the analysis.

**ETHICS
DISCUSSION CASE**

71. You are a CPA who has been preparing tax returns for Sign, Seal, and Deliver, a mid-size CPA firm, for the last 5 years. During the current year, you are assigned the individual return of a new client, Guadalupe Piaz. Guadalupe has completed and returned the tax return questionnaire that the firm sent to her.

In reviewing the questionnaire, you notice that Guadalupe has included an entry for $10,000 in cash dividends received from Quinn Corporation. However, there is no supporting documentation for the dividend payment in the information Guadalupe provided.

What concerns you is that until this year you had prepared the tax return for Quinn Corporation (it was reassigned to another firm member when you were promoted late last year). You know that Quinn Corporation was organized as an S corporation during the years that you prepared the return. During that period, Quinn was equally owned by 3 shareholders and Guadalupe was not among them. In addition, the corporation was highly profitable, averaging approximately $6,000,000 per year in taxable income. Given this information, what are your obligations under the Statements on Responsibilities in Tax Practice (Appendix D)? Write a memorandum to your supervisor explaining your concerns and what actions, if any, you will need to take before you can prepare Guadalupe's return.

GROSS INCOME

CHAPTER 3
INCOME SOURCES

CHAPTER 4
INCOME EXCLUSIONS

Income Sources

▲ CHAPTER LEARNING OBJECTIVES

■ Discuss the historical development of what constitutes gross income and how it affects the current view of gross income.

■ Distinguish earned income from unearned income, and discuss the tax problems associated with each type of income.

■ Identify sources of income that result from transfers from others and discuss the tax rules for each type of income.

■ Discuss imputed income and identify the common sources of such income and their tax treatments.

■ Provide an overview of the tax treatment of capital gain income.

■ Describe the primary accounting methods used for tax purposes and how income is recognized under each method: the cash method, the accrual method, and the hybrid method.

■ Discuss the exceptions to the general rules of income recognition for each of the accounting methods.

▲ CONCEPT REVIEW ▲

Ability to pay   A tax should be based on the amount that the taxpayer can afford to pay, relative to other taxpayers.

Administrative convenience   Those items for which the cost of compliance would exceed the revenue generated are not taxed.

All-inclusive income   All income received is taxable unless a specific provision can be found in the tax law that either excludes the income from taxation or defers its recognition to a future tax year.

Annual accounting period   All entities must report the results of their operations on an annual basis (the tax year). Each tax year stands on its own, apart from other tax years.

Arm's-length transaction   A transaction in which all parties to the transaction have bargained in good faith and for their individual benefit, not for the benefit of the transaction group.

Assignment of income   The tax entity that owns the income produced is responsible for the tax on the income, regardless of which entity actually receives the income.

Capital recovery   No income is realized until the taxpayer receives more than the amount invested to produce the income. The amount invested in an asset represents the maximum amount recoverable.

Claim of right   A realization occurs whenever an amount is received without any restriction as to its disposition.

Constructive receipt   Income is deemed to be received when it is made unconditionally available to the taxpayer.

Legislative grace   Any tax relief provided is the result of a specific act of Congress that must be strictly applied and interpreted. All income received is taxable unless a specific provision can be found in the tax law that excludes the income from taxation. Deductions must be approached with the philosophy that nothing is deductible unless a provision in the tax law allows the deduction.

Realization   No income (or loss) is recognized until it has been realized. A realization involves a change in the form and/or the substance of a taxpayer's property rights that results from an arm's-length transaction.

Related party   Family members, corporations that are owned by family members, and certain other relationships between entities in which the power to control the substance of a transaction is evidenced through majority ownership.

Tax benefit rule   Any deduction taken in a prior year that is recovered in a subsequent year is income in the year of recovery, to the extent that a tax benefit was received from the deduction.

Wherewithal to pay   Income is recognized in the period in which the taxpayer has the means to pay the tax on the income.

INTRODUCTION

The first step in calculating the taxable income for any tax entity is determining its gross income. Gross income equals all income received, less exclusions from income. Therefore, all items of income realized during the period under consideration must first be identified. Next, the income items are analyzed and segregated into those that are taxable and those that are excluded from taxation. Finally, the proper tax year for recognition of the income items must be determined. The purpose of this chapter is to introduce the basis for identifying income sources and to discuss those sources that present particular problems. In addition, a brief overview of the tax treatment of capital gains and losses is presented. The chapter also considers the effect of an entity's accounting method on the recognition of income and exceptions to the general methods of accounting. Exclusions from income tax are discussed in Chapter 4.

WHAT CONSTITUTES INCOME

The all-inclusive income concept provides the basis for calculating gross income. Under this concept, any income received is assumed to be taxable unless some provision in the tax law allows its exclusion. This concept is the basis of the Internal Revenue Code's definition of *gross income*:

> SECTION 61 GROSS INCOME DEFINED
>
> (a) General Definition.—Except as otherwise provided in this subtitle, gross income means all income from whatever source derived, including (but not limited to) the following items:
>
> (1) Compensation for services, including fees, commissions and similar items;
> (2) Gross income derived from business;
> (3) Gains derived from dealings in property;
> (4) Interest;
> (5) Rents;
> (6) Royalties;
> (7) Dividends;
> (8) Alimony and separate maintenance payments;
> (9) Annuities;
> (10) Income from life insurance and endowment contracts;
> (11) Pensions;
> (12) Income from discharge of indebtedness;
> (13) Distributive share of partnership gross income;
> (14) Income in respect of a decedent; and
> (15) Income from an interest in an estate or trust.

The phrase "all income from whatever source derived" is the statutory equivalent of the all-inclusive income concept's requirement that any income received is initially considered taxable. This phrase has been part of the income tax law since the Sixteenth Amendment to the Constitution empowered Congress in 1913 to "lay and collect taxes on *incomes, from whatever source derived*" [emphasis added]. In Section 61 of the Code, the phrase "except as otherwise provided" allows for items to be excluded from gross income, provided that the specific exclusion is found within the Internal Revenue Code.

The realization concept requires that income be realized before it is included in gross income. However, nothing in the definition of gross income in the Internal Revenue Code requires that income be *realized* before it is *recognized*. Although absent from the Internal Revenue Code, the realization concept was developed primarily by the courts in response to cases requiring an interpretation of the statutory definition of *income*. As a result, the concept has been adopted by the Internal Revenue Service in the regulation that interprets the definition of gross income:

> (a) General Definition. Gross income means all income from whatever source derived unless excluded by law. Gross income includes income *realized* in any form, whether in money, property, or services. Income may be *realized*, therefore, in the form of services, meals, accommodations, stock, or other property, as well as in cash.[1]

Thus, a better working definition would be that gross income includes all income realized from whatever source derived, unless specifically excluded.

At first glance, the statutory and administrative definitions of income appear to be quite simplistic and straightforward. However, a linguist would no doubt be bothered by the circular nature of the definition: Gross income means all income. In fact, no definition of the term *income* exists in the Internal Revenue Code. Thus, the threshold question of whether a particular item is or is not income is not answered by these definitions of gross income. Perhaps wisely, Congress has never seen fit to attempt to define the term *income*. Do you think that drafters of tax legislation in 1913 could have foreseen the complexities of business in the 1990s and been able to draft a precise definition of income to cover such items as incentive stock options and gains from currency translations? By not providing a precise definition, what constitutes income evolves with changes in society. In this regard, the courts have played a major role in guiding taxpayers on the treatment of various transactions in which it is not clear whether the statutory definition of income has been met.

Income Is Derived from Labor and Capital

In 1920, the U.S. Supreme Court considered the first case addressing the concept of income. In determining that specific provisions in the tax law that included stock dividends as taxable income were unconstitutional, the Supreme Court said, "Income may be defined as the gain derived from capital, from labor, or from both combined, provided it be understood to include profit gained through sale or conversion of capital assets."[2]

This initial attempt at defining income implies that income could be generated from only two sources: capital and labor. The Court also emphasized the necessity of a realization as a precondition to the existence of income:

> Here we have the essential matter: *not* a gain *accruing* to capital, not a *growth or increment of value in* the investment; but a gain, a profit, something of exchangeable value *proceeding from* the property, *severed from* the capital however invested or employed, and *coming in*, being *"derived"*—that is, *received* or *drawn by* the recipient (the taxpayer) for his *separate* use, benefit and disposal; *that* is income derived from property. Nothing else answers the description. [Court's emphasis][3]

In fact, a vast majority of items we commonly think of as income fit nicely into this definition: wages, income from a sole proprietorship (income from labor), interest, dividends, rental income, and royalty income (income from capital). However, this definition did not contemplate sources of income that were not returns from labor or capital, such as windfalls. Consider the following examples:

▲ **EXAMPLE 1**   Lee is playing golf one day and hits an enormous hook into the woods. While searching for his ball, Lee finds a tattered sack full of $100 bills. The police are never able to locate the owner, and Lee is allowed to keep the money, which totals $50,000. Does Lee have income from finding this money?

Discussion: Given the Supreme Court's definition, it would seem that such a windfall would not be considered as "derived from capital, from labor, or from both combined." However, it would appear that such a "treasure trove," as it is referred to in income tax jargon, would fit the statutory definition of "income from whatever source derived." In fact, the courts have said that such treasure troves do constitute income.[4]

▲ **EXAMPLE 2**   Johnson, Inc. leases a lot and a building to Wenona Corporation under a 99-year lease that permits Wenona to remodel the building at its own cost. The lease provides that all improvements are Johnson's property upon termination of the lease. Twenty years after remodeling the original building, Wenona defaults on the lease payment, and Johnson repossesses the property. The net increase in the value of the property from the remodeling of the building is $50,000. Does Johnson, Inc., have taxable income when it retakes possession of the building?

Discussion: On similar facts, in 1940 the Supreme Court held that Johnson, Inc. was taxable on the increase in the value of the property attributable to the remodeling of the building at the time it repossessed the property.[5]

Although the Court's decision on the facts in example 2 would appear to fit the notion of income "derived from capital," it does not square with the requirement that income be realized by "severing" it from the capital investment and that it be *"received* or *drawn* by the recipient (the taxpayer) for his *separate* use, benefit and disposal." In addressing this issue, the Court said:

> While it is true that economic gain is not always taxable as income, it is settled that the realization of gain need not be in cash derived from the sale of an asset. Gain may occur as a result of exchange of property, payment of the taxpayer's indebtedness, relief from a liability, or other profit realized from the completion of a transaction. The fact that the gain is a portion of the value of property received by the taxpayer in the transaction does not negative its realization.[6]

This decision severely weakened the earlier realization requirement by suggesting that any definitive event could be properly considered a realization of income. At this point, there was no requirement that the income be severed from the capital and available for use by the taxpayer. However, in reaction to this decision, in 1942 Congress adopted a provision that excluded from gross income such increases in the value of property upon termination of a lease, to the extent that the lessee's improvements did not constitute a payment in lieu of rent.[7] This exclusion is discussed in Chapter 4.

Income as an Increase in Wealth

As can be seen from the discussion of court cases that define income, the courts increasingly diluted the original judicial requirement that income be derived from capital or labor and that recognition of the income required a realization. In 1955, the Supreme Court closed the circle on its original definition in a case involving the taxability of punitive damages awarded in an antitrust action. In finding that such windfall profits were taxable income, the Court did not even attempt to reconcile its decision with the earlier "gain derived from capital or labor" requirement. Rather, the Court relegated this concept to minor status in determining that *any* increase in the wealth of the taxpayer that has been realized is subject to income tax:

> But it [income derived from capital or labor] was not meant to provide a touchstone to all future gross income questions. . . . Here we have instances of *undeniable accessions to wealth, clearly realized* and over which the taxpayers have *complete dominion.* The mere fact that the payments were extracted from the wrongdoers as punishment for unlawful conduct cannot detract from their character as taxable income to the recipients . . . We find no . . . evidence of intent to exempt these payments. [emphasis added][8]

Thus, the Court adopted a much broader concept of income, "undeniable accessions to wealth," as its interpretation of "income from whatever source derived." The notion of income as an increase in wealth is not new or, for that matter, surprising. Economists have long argued that the true measure of income is the change in wealth for the period under consideration. Using the economist's definition of income, all gains received during the period, whether realized or not, are considered income. Where the tax law deviates from the economists' notion of income is in the requirement that the increase in wealth be "clearly realized." Note also that the tax law definition of income not only requires a realization but also that the taxpayer have "complete dominion" over the realized income. The requirement of complete dominion means that the taxpayer must have a claim of right to the income. Recall that the claim of right doctrine says that any amount received without restriction as to its disposition is income in the period received.

What Constitutes Income: Current View

Given this brief historical account of how the concept of income developed, what is considered income today? Although the courts continue to consider the issue, no significant developments have occurred since the Supreme Court determined that any increase in wealth that has been realized constitutes income. Thus, it is safe to say that the first requirement is that the taxpayer experiences an increase in wealth. An increase in wealth can be through an increase in net worth or through consumption.

▲ **EXAMPLE 3**   Tran purchases 100 shares of XYZ Co. stock during 1996 at a cost of $2,000. As of December 31, 1996, the shares of stock are worth $2,500. Does Tran experience an increase in wealth during 1996 as a result of this stock purchase?

Discussion: Tran's wealth increases during 1996 as a result of the stock purchase. Her net worth increases by $500 over what it was before she purchased the stock.

▲ **EXAMPLE 4**   Cara's car needs new spark plugs. She calls Local Service Station and learns that it will cost $50 to get the job done. Rather than pay the $50, Cara purchases the spark plugs for $15 and installs them herself. Has Cara's wealth increased as a result of installing the spark plugs herself?

Discussion: Cara's wealth has increased by the $35 she saved by doing the job herself. Through consumption of the labor and overhead involved in the $50 charged by Local, her net worth has increased by the $35 she saved.

Although an increase in wealth is a necessary condition for the recognition of income, it alone is not sufficient to trigger taxation. Before an increase in wealth becomes taxable (i.e., is recognized income), it must also be realized. As stated previously, realization is not an explicit statutory requirement for the recognition of income; however, over the years the concept has become so basic to the structure of the tax system that the general premise of the requirement is simply not challenged. What typically is challenged by taxpayers is what constitutes a realization. A reasonable working definition contains the following two elements:

- A change in form and/or substance of the taxpayer's property (or property rights)
- The involvement of a second party in the income process

The most common forms of income realization involve the receipt of something of value (cash, stock, services) for a service rendered or the sale, exchange, or lease of a property.

▲ **EXAMPLE 5**   Return to the facts of example 3. Does Tran realize any income from her dealings in XYZ Co.'s stock?

Discussion: Although Tran's wealth increases through the increase in the value of the stock, she has not realized that wealth through sale, exchange, or other disposition of the stock. That is, the form of her property (stock) has not been changed through a transaction with another party.

▲ **EXAMPLE 6**   Return to the facts of example 4. Has Cara realized the increase in wealth she obtained by repairing the car herself?

Discussion: Cara has had a change in the form of her property through the repairs but because no second party was involved, she would not be considered to have a realization of income.

In general, any increase in wealth that has been realized by a taxpayer must be recognized (i.e., included in gross income) for tax purposes in the period in which the realization occurs. However, this general rule has several exceptions. As previously stated, some income realizations are excluded by law and therefore are never recognized for tax purposes. The tax laws also provide for deferral of gains on certain types of property transactions in which the wherewithal to pay tax from the transaction is lacking. The recognition of gains from this class of transactions is deferred to a future period when a transaction occurs that provides the cash to pay the tax.

> ▲ **EXAMPLE 7**   Duc's business automobile, which had an adjusted basis of $2,000, was destroyed in a tornado. Duc received a check for $6,000 from his insurance company. Duc used the $6,000 as a down payment on a new business automobile costing $30,000. Has Duc realized a gain from the destruction of his old automobile? If so, must he recognize the gain in the period of the trade-in?
>
> *Discussion:*   Duc has realized a gain of $4,000 ($6,000 in insurance proceeds − the adjusted basis of $2,000) on the destruction of his automobile. He realized a gain because he received something of value, $6,000 in cash, for his old automobile in a transaction with another party.
>
> Duc will not have to recognize the gain (include the gain in gross income) on the destruction of his automobile in the current period. When the entire proceeds from the casualty are reinvested in a qualifying replacement asset, the tax law allows the deferral of gains from casualties on business property that has been replaced. In this case, Duc reinvested the entire $6,000 he received for his old automobile and has no cash remaining to pay the tax on the gain.
>
> Although Duc does not have to pay tax on the gain in the current period, he will pay tax on the gain when he disposes of the new business automobile in a taxable transaction. Chapter 13 discusses the rules for deferrals of gains and the mechanics of the calculations to ensure that the tax is eventually paid on the gain.

COMMON INCOME SOURCES

This chapter discusses four categories of income sources to provide a framework for working with income sources. The first two categories are based on the Supreme Court's early definition of income as being derived from labor, which is referred to as *earned income*, and income derived from capital, referred to as *unearned income*. The third category consists of transfers from others. The fourth category considers taxable sources of imputed income.

Earned Income

The most common form of income for individuals is compensation paid for their services. That is, individuals provide their labor for the production of goods and services. In return for their labor, they are compensated by the entity for which they are performing the work. Providing labor for compensation produces **earned income**. All amounts paid by an employer to or on behalf of an employee are taxable unless specifically excluded by law. In addition, income generated from the operation of a business is considered earned by the owner. Income from illegal activities (gambling, drugs, extortion, etc.) is also considered earned and subject to tax.[9] The most common forms of earned income are

1. Wages, salaries, tips, bonuses and commissions
2. Income from the active conduct of a trade or business

3.   Income from the rendering of services

4.   Income from the performance of illegal activities

The taxability of earned income sources is undisputed. However, two problems often arise with this type of income. The first problem stems from a desire to take advantage of the progressive nature of the tax rate schedules by transferring income earned by a high marginal tax rate payer to a family member who is in a lower tax bracket. These attempts are foiled by the assignment-of-income doctrine, which requires the entity earning the income to pay the tax on the income, regardless of who actually receives the income.

> ▲ **EXAMPLE 8**   Thelma has a successful carpet-cleaning business. In order to lower her taxes, she instructs every fifth client to make the check out to Thelma's son. Her son is a college student who does not work and uses the checks received from Thelma's business to pay for his college expenses.
>
> *Discussion:*   Because the payments made to the son were earned by Thelma, she must include the payments in her taxable income. Therefore, this scheme results in no tax savings to Thelma. NOTE: There are legal ways for Thelma to transfer taxability of the income earned from her carpet-cleaning business to her son. The simplest method would be to employ her son in the business and pay him a reasonable salary for his labor. This would lower Thelma's taxable income through a deduction for compensation and transfer the income to her son for taxation at a lower marginal tax rate.

Taxpayers may also attempt to transfer income to establish a basis for taking business deductions.

> ▲ **EXAMPLE 9**   Michael has a computer in a separate room of his house that he uses to perform work related to his employment as an engineer for Ajax Corporation as well as for personal purposes. Because he is not considered to be in a trade or business, the tax law does not allow a deduction for either the office or the computer. Michael's wife Daniela does the bookkeeping and payroll work for several small businesses. In order to establish a trade or business for himself, Michael has the payments for Daniela's bookkeeping services made out to him.
>
> *Discussion:*   No marginal tax rate savings result from the transfer of income from Daniela to Michael, because Michael and Daniela commingle their respective incomes on their joint tax return. The tax benefit to be derived from such a scheme would be the additional deductions Michael could take for the office and the computer, if he can establish their use in the business of bookkeeping. However, under the assignment-of-income doctrine, Daniela would still be deemed to have earned the payments for her services, and Michael could not claim the checks he receives as income he earned in a trade or business. Thus, he could not take any deductions for the office or the computer.

The second concern with earned income is what constitutes a receipt of income. Typically, earned types of income are received in cash. However, if receipts of cash were the sole source of earned income, clever taxpayers could arrange their affairs to receive significant amounts of their income in other forms, thus avoiding tax. To counter such tax avoidance schemes, a **cash-equivalent approach** is used to measure receipts of income. Under this approach, the receipt of anything with a fair market value will trigger recognition of income. Thus, income can be realized in the form of property, services, meals, lodging, stock, and so on.

> ▲ **EXAMPLE 10**   Betty agreed to clean Shiro's house once a week, in return for which Shiro agreed to mow Betty's lawn once a week. Betty usually charges $20 to clean a house, which is what Shiro charges to mow a lawn. Do Betty and/or Shiro have taxable income from this arrangement?

Discussion: Yes, both have income of $20 per week from this arrangement. Each receives something of value in return for her or his services. Therefore, they are taxed as if they had paid each other cash.

Under the constructive receipt doctrine, a cash basis taxpayer does not have income until there is an actual or constructive receipt of the income earned. Therefore, a cash basis taxpayer who sells merchandise or performs services on general account does not recognize income until the account is paid with something of value. However, if the customer of such a taxpayer gives the taxpayer a promissory note for the amount due, the fair market value of the note is considered a receipt of property and is taxable when received.

▲ **EXAMPLE 11**   Farnsworth, a cash basis taxpayer, puts a new roof on EM Corporation's warehouse in late November and bills it $3,000. EM pays the bill in January. When is Farnsworth taxable on the $3,000 roofing job?

Discussion: Because Farnsworth does not receive something of value until January, the $3,000 is not included in his taxable income until that time.

▲ **EXAMPLE 12**   Assume that in example 11 EM Corporation gives Farnsworth a valid note payable for $3,000 when it completes the roofing job in November. Farnsworth does not discount the note, although local banks typically discount such personal notes by 30%. EM pays the note in full in January. How does this affect Farnsworth's recognition of income?

Discussion: Because Farnsworth could have converted the note to cash upon receipt, the amount of cash he could have received from discounting the note, its fair market value, is taxable upon receipt. Therefore, $2,100 [$3,000 − (30% × $3,000)] is taxable in the year Farnsworth receives the note. The remaining $900 is taxable when he receives full payment on the note the following January.

Unearned Income

The **unearned income** category of income includes the earnings from investments and gains from the sale, exchange, or other disposition of investment assets. The distinguishing feature of this type of income is that it constitutes a return on an investment and producing the income does not require any labor by the owner of the investment. The most common forms of unearned income are

1. Interest income
2. Dividend income
3. Income from rental and royalty-producing activities
4. Income from annuities
5. Income from conduit entities
6. Gains from the sale of investments producing any of the five forms of unearned income

As with earned sources of income, the inclusion of unearned types of income in the tax base is not controversial. However, a few practical difficulties do arise.

Rental and Royalty Income.   The first problem deals with the definition of *rental and royalty income.* Technically, the tax law defines these two types of income as gross income from the property, less the related expenses to produce the income.

▲ **EXAMPLE 13**   Ali Corporation owns an apartment building and rents the units. During 1996, Ali receives total rents of $15,000 and incurs costs of $13,000 related to the apartments. What is Ali Corporation's rental income for 1996?

Discussion: Ali Corporation has rental income of $2,000 ($15,000 − $13,000).

▲ **EXAMPLE 14**   Assume that because utility and maintenance costs are higher than expected, Ali's total expenses related to the apartments are $18,000 in 1996. What is Ali's rental income for 1996?

Discussion: Ali Corporation does not have any rental income in 1996. Rather, it has a rental loss of $3,000, the deduction of which is subject to the rules for deducting losses, discussed in Chapter 7.

Annuities.   The second item to consider is the taxation of annuities. An **annuity** is a string of equal payments received over equal time periods for a determinable period. The purchase of annuity contracts has become increasingly popular in recent years as a way to guarantee income during a taxpayer's retirement years. A typical annuity is illustrated in the top panel of Exhibit 3–1. In the typical annuity situation, an individual pays a certain sum now, in return for which the seller of the annuity promises to make set payments for a period of time in the future. The payments are calculated to provide the purchaser with a predetermined rate of return on the investment. The problem with these arrangements is determining how much of each payment is a return *of* the original capital investment and how much is a return *on* the investment. Recall that the capital recovery concept exempts returns of capital from taxation; only returns on capital are taxable sources of income.

▲ **EXAMPLE 15**   Susan, 40, purchases an annuity contract for $25,000. Under the contract, when Susan reaches 62, she is to receive $5,000 per year until she dies. Actuarial tables indicate that Susan is expected to live until she is 77. How much income will Susan earn in total from this investment?

Discussion: Because we do not know precisely how long Susan will live, it must be assumed that she will live until she is 77, the average life expectancy. Under this assumption, she will receive payments totaling $75,000 ($5,000 × 15) from the contract, resulting in a total profit of $50,000 ($75,000 − $25,000).

In example 15, the major tax problem is determining when to recognize the $50,000 in earnings from her investment. Although it is clear that she will not

---

General Operation of an Annuity		▲ **Exhibit 3–1**
Current Investment Future Receipts		ANNUITIES

General Operation of an Annuity

Current Investment   Future Receipts

($$$) $ $ $ $ $ $

Annuity Exclusion Ratio

$$\frac{\text{Cost of the contract}}{\text{Expected return on the contract}} = \text{Exclusion ratio}$$

Where

Expected return = Contract payment × Expected number of payments

Amount of each payment excluded = Contract payment × Exclusion ratio

Amount of each payment taxable = Contract payment − Amount excluded

▲ **Exhibit 3–1**

ANNUITIES

realize any income until she begins receiving payments on the contract, taxation once the payments begin is more controversial. A strict application of the capital recovery concept would exempt the first $25,000 as a repayment of capital investment. However, the tax law views the amounts paid out under the contract as being partly a return *of* her original capital investment (excluded) and partly a return *on* her capital investment (taxable income).[10] The general formula for determining the amount of each payment that is a return of capital and therefore excluded from income, called the **annuity exclusion ratio,** is shown in the lower panel of Exhibit 3–1.

The taxable and excluded portions of any annuity payment can easily be determined by using the annuity formulas in Exhibit 3–1.

▲ **EXAMPLE 16**   How much of each $5,000 payment that Susan receives from the annuity contract is taxable?

Discussion: The exclusion ratio on the contract is $25,000 ÷ $75,000 = 1/3. Therefore, one-third of each $5,000 payment, $1,667, is not taxable, because it is considered a return of her $25,000 investment. The remaining $3,333 is taxed as a return on capital.

To make the annuity calculations, you must assume that a fixed number of payments is to be made under the contract. For payments that continue until the death of the taxpayer, the number of payments is determined by the life expectancy of the annuitant at the date the annuity commences. However, life expectancies are merely averages. As such, few people die at their average life expectancy: Some people die before the average, whereas others outlive their life expectancies. Therefore, in most cases adjustments are required to ensure that proper capital recovery of the annuity investment is made.

▲ **EXAMPLE 17**   Assume that Susan lives for 20 years and receives payments totaling $100,000 under the annuity contract. How is Susan taxed on these payments?

Discussion: Because we do not know how long Susan will live when the payments start, we figure the annual exclusion and income as in example 16. That is, she will exclude $1,667 per year.

After she receives the 15th payment (i.e., the expected number of payments used in the exclusion calculation), Susan will have excluded her entire $25,000 investment ($1,667 × 15 = $25,000). At that time, her capital investment will have been fully recovered. Therefore, payments 16 through 20 will be fully taxable.

Note that during the 20 years of payments, Susan will recognize $75,000 ($100,000 received − the $25,000 investment) in income.

Years 1–15:	$50,000 ($3,333 × 15)
Years 16–20:	$25,000 ($5,000 × 5)

What happens when an annuity owner dies before her life expectancy? In this case, her capital recovery is incomplete; she has not fully recovered her capital investment through an exclusion. To allow full recovery of capital in this situation, the tax law permits a deduction in the year of death for the unrecovered portion of the annuity investment.

▲ **EXAMPLE 18**   Assume that Susan dies in the 10th year of the annuity contract. How would this be treated on her year-10 tax return?

Discussion: The $5,000 received in year 10 would be reported as all other annuity payments were reported: $3,333 would be taxable, and $1,667 would be excluded.

After 10 years, Susan would have excluded a total of $16,670 ($1,667 × 10 years) of her $25,000 investment. The remaining $8,330 ($25,000 − $16,670) of her original investment, which was not recovered, is deductible on her year-10 tax return. There-fore, over the 10-year period she will have recovered her $25,000 capital investment through $16,670 of excluded income and a deduction of $8,330 in the year of death.

Note the effect of the annual accounting period concept on the reporting of annuities. This concept requires not only an annual reporting of income but also embodies the notion that the events of each tax year are to stand apart from each other. Thus, we do not go back and adjust the annuity calculations on prior years' returns when we know the true number of payments. Rather, we apply the capital recovery concept as it applies to the individual year in question.

As a final note on annuities, the exclusion ratio is used when the taxpayer receives amounts that represent both a return of investment in the contract and a return on the investment in the contract. Many pension plans are structured so that amounts paid into the plan by the employee and the employer are excluded from current taxation. Such plans are called *qualified plans* and allow the deferral of tax on payments into the plan and earnings on the plan's assets until they are withdrawn. As such, the taxpayer has no previously taxed capital investment in the plan. Therefore, all amounts paid from the plan are subject to tax.

▲ **EXAMPLE 19**   Agatha worked for Crystal Co. for more than 30 years. As part of her employment contract, Crystal matched contributions Agatha made to a qualified plan. None of the payments to the plan or the earnings on the plan investment was subject to tax. Over the years, Agatha accumulated $420,000 in her pension plan. At retirement, she will receive $850 per month from the plan. How much of the monthly payment is subject to tax?

Discussion: Because the $420,000 in the pension plan is income that has not been taxed, the full amount of each payment is subject to tax. Agatha must include all payments she receives from the plan in her gross income in the year she receives the payments.

Calculation of Gain/Loss on Sale of Investments.

Another aspect related to unearned income is the calculation of gains (losses) from sales, exchanges, or other dispositions of investment property. Again, this is not a particularly per-plexing problem. However, you should keep in mind what constitutes a gain. A gain is the result of a realization in excess of capital investment.[11] The amount of unrecovered capital investment in a property is its adjusted basis.[12] More formally,

	Proceeds from sale of property
Less:	Selling expenses
Equals:	Amount realized from sale of property
Less:	Adjusted basis of property sold
Equals:	Gain (loss) on sale

▲ **EXAMPLE 20**   The Alima Partnership buys a rental property in 1994 for $70,000. In 1996, after deducting depreciation of $5,000, Alima sells the rental property for $90,000 and pays a $6,000 commission on the sale. What is Alima's gain (loss) on the sale of the rental property?

Discussion: The Alima Partnership realizes $84,000 ($90,000 − the $6,000 commis-sion) from the sale. Because Alima has already recovered $5,000 of its investment through depreciation deductions, the adjusted basis for the rental property is $65,000 ($70,000 − $5,000). This results in a gain of $19,000 ($84,000 − $65,000).

Note that property dispositions can also result in losses. A loss results when a property is disposed of at less than its adjusted basis. That is, a loss represents incomplete capital recovery.

▲ **EXAMPLE 21**   Assume that in example 20 the Alima Partnership is able to sell its rental property for only $60,000 and pays a $3,000 commission on the sale. What is Alima's gain (loss) on the sale of the rental property?

Discussion: In this case, the Alima Partnership realizes only $57,000 ($60,000 − $3,000) on the sale, resulting in a loss on the sale of $8,000 ($57,000 − $65,000). Note that the $8,000 loss represents Alima's unrecovered investment in the rental property. Allowing Alima to deduct the $8,000 loss fully recovers its original $70,000 investment:

Capital deducted as depreciation	$ 5,000
Capital deducted against sales price	57,000
Capital deducted as a loss	8,000
Total amount invested	$70,000

Income from Conduit Entities.   The last consideration related to unearned forms of income is the recognition of income from conduit entities (primarily S corporations and partnerships). Recall that a conduit entity is not taxed on its income; rather, the income from the conduit flows to the owner(s) of the entity for taxation. Thus, taxpayers who own investments in such entities must recognize their share of the conduit's income on their tax return.[13] Conversely, distributions from a conduit entity are not taxed; they are merely a return of capital investment in the entity.

▲ **EXAMPLE 22**   Ansel owns a 20% interest in Forrest, Inc. Forrest is organized as an S corporation and has a taxable income of $80,000 in the current year. Forrest also distributes $20,000 in dividends. What amount of income must Ansel recognize from his ownership in Forrest, Inc.?

Discussion: Ansel must recognize his proportionate share of Forrest's income, $16,000 (20% × $80,000). Because he is taxed on his share of Forrest's income, the $4,000 in dividends (20% × $20,000) received is not taxed; it is considered a return of his investment, which reduces the basis of his investment in Forrest.

▲ **EXAMPLE 23**   Assume that in example 22 Forrest, Inc., is a corporation. What amount of income must Ansel recognize from his ownership in Forrest, Inc.?

Discussion: As a corporation, Forrest is taxed on the $80,000 in income it earned; it does not flow to the owners. Ansel is taxed on the $4,000 in dividends he receives from Forrest.

Transfers from Others

As the discussion of what constitutes income indicated, not all income is the result of labor or capital. Tax entities, particularly individuals, sometimes receive amounts that are neither earned nor unearned, yet they constitute realizations of increases in wealth and as such are taxable to the recipient. In this area, there are four common sources of taxable transfer income:

- Prizes and awards
- Unemployment compensation
- Social Security benefits
- Alimony received

Prizes and Awards.   With two exceptions, any prizes or awards received are taxable to the recipient.[14] One way to avoid tax on the receipt of a prize or award is to immediately transfer the prize or award to a government or other qualified charitable organization such as a church, school, charity, and so on. This exclusion is available only for certain awards, such as those for literary, scientific, and charitable achievements for which the taxpayer did not take action to obtain the award and for which no future services must be performed as a condition of receiving the award. Thus, winnings on game shows cannot be excluded, even if they are immediately transferred to a local charity, because the contestant voluntarily entered the contest.

> ▲ **EXAMPLE 24**   Letisha received the outstanding teacher award at State University. The award included a cash prize of $5,000. Is the $5,000 taxable to Letisha?
>
> *Discussion:*   If Letisha keeps the $5,000, she will have to include it in her gross income. However, if she was chosen from among all teachers at State University and the award does not require her to perform a specific future service, she can avoid taxation by transferring the check to a government body or charitable organization.

The second class of awards that may be excluded is employee achievement awards that are paid in the form of property and are based on length of service or on safety achievements. The maximum dollar exclusion for such awards is $400 per employee per year. However, if the award comes from a qualified plan, the individual limit is raised to $1,600. A qualified plan is a formal written plan or program to award all employees who qualify under the plan's requirements. The plan must not discriminate in favor of highly compensated employees.

> ▲ **EXAMPLE 25**   At her retirement party, Tova received a Rolex watch worth $1,200 in recognition of her 30 years of service to her employer. Is the receipt of the watch taxable to Tova? If so, how much income must she recognize?
>
> *Discussion:*   Because the watch is an award of property that was given in recognition of length of service, at least $400 of the $1,200 fair market value of the watch may be excluded. If Tova's watch was given as part of a qualified plan, she may exclude the entire $1,200 from her taxable income, because it is worth less than the $1,600 limit for such plans.

Unemployment Compensation.   Amounts received from state unemployment compensation plans are considered substitutes for earned income and are always taxable to the recipient.[15] Unemployment compensation is designed to aid individuals who become unemployed until they can find new employment. A similar type of benefit paid by states to individuals is workers' compensation. Workers' compensation is paid to employees who are injured on the job and cannot continue to work as a result of their injuries. A specific exclusion from income is provided for workers' compensation payments and is discussed in Chapter 4.

Social Security Benefits.   Before 1983, Social Security benefits were excluded from taxation. The exclusion was evidently based on administrative convenience because the tax law contained no specific exclusion for such payments. This made some sense, because the payments made by an employee into the fund are not exempt from tax. However, the matching portion paid by the employer is not taxable to the employee. Thus, under the capital recovery concept, it could be said that half of each payment received from Social Security represented a return of the taxpayer's investment and was therefore excluded, much like the annuities discussed earlier. However, when Congress decided to begin taxing Social Security benefits in 1984, politicians were concerned about taxing those whose main source of income came from Social Security. That is, Congress questioned the ability of lower-income taxpayers to pay the tax. To negate this possibility, Congress used a lesser-of formula to determine the amount of Social Security to include in gross income; the formula allows lower-income taxpayers to escape taxation on Social Security benefits.[16] Calculation of the taxable portion of Social Security benefits before 1994 is presented in Exhibit 3–2.

Although the second formula seems unduly complex, modified adjusted gross income serves as a "floor" value under which no Social Security benefits are taxed. Note that as long as the taxpayer's modified adjusted gross income is less than the base amount, none of the Social Security benefits is subject to tax. Thus, people with relatively modest incomes are not taxed on Social Security benefits.

Recall from Chapter 1 that adjusted gross income (AGI) is defined as gross income less deductions for adjusted gross income. Deductions allowable for AGI include trade or business expenses, rental and royalty expenses, reimbursed employee business expenses, payments into pension accounts (IRAs), and certain other business- and investment-related expenses. As such, adjusted gross income provides a measure of the individual's ability to pay tax. In the second formula, the two major additions to AGI, for the foreign earned income exclusion and tax-exempt interest (both exclusions are discussed in Chapter 4), are there to ensure that individuals with large, untaxed economic incomes pay some tax on Social Security benefits.

▲ **EXAMPLE 26**   Judith is a single individual who receives $4,000 in Social Security benefits during 1993. Her adjusted gross income before considering the taxability of the Social Security benefits is $10,000. How much of the $4,000 is taxable?

Discussion: None of the $4,000 is included in Judith's gross income, because her modified adjusted gross income falls below the $25,000 floor value for taxation of unmarried taxpayers. Per the formulas in Exhibit 3–2, Judith includes in income the *lesser* of

$$1/2(\$4,000) = \$2,000$$
$$\text{OR}$$
$$1/2(\$10,000 + \$2,000 - \$25,000) < 0$$

▲ **EXAMPLE 27**   Jack and Bettina received the following income during 1993:

Retirement pay	$23,000
Tax-exempt bond interest	$10,000
Social Security benefits	$ 6,000

How much of the $6,000 must be included in their gross income?

▲ **Exhibit 3–2**

CALCULATION OF TAXABLE PORTION OF SOCIAL SECURITY BENEFITS RECEIVED BEFORE 1994

The taxable portion of Social Security is equal to the lesser of

　　1. one-half of the Social Security benefits received during the year

OR

　　2. one-half of the amount by which modified adjusted gross income exceeds the base amount

Where

　　Modified adjusted gross income = Adjusted gross income + one-half the Social Security benefits received during the year + any foreign earned income exclusion + any tax-exempt interest

And

　　Base amount = $25,000 for an unmarried individual
　　　　　　　　$32,000 for a married couple, filing jointly
　　　　　　　　$ -0- for all others

Discussion: Social Security benefits of $2,000 are taxable per the following formulas:

The lesser of

$$1/2(\$6,000) = \$3,000$$

OR

$$1/2(\$23,000 + \$3,000 + \$10,000 - \$32,000) = 1/2(\$36,000 - \$32,000) = \$2,000$$

Note that if Jack and Bettina were not required to include their tax-exempt interest in the Social Security benefits calculation, their income ($26,000) would have fallen below the base amount for a married couple ($32,000) and no part of their benefits would have been taxed. Thus, the adjustment for tax-exempt interest has made a portion of their benefits taxable in accord with Congress's intent: to apply the tax to individuals with large economic incomes.

▲ **EXAMPLE 28**   Ruth is a retired executive whose adjusted gross income for 1993 is $80,000. In addition, Ruth receives $5,000 in Social Security benefits. How much of the $5,000 must be included in Ruth's gross income?

Discussion: Ruth must include $2,500 in her gross income per the following formula:

The lesser of

$$1/2(\$5,000) = \$2,500$$

OR

$$1/2(\$80,000 + \$2,500 - \$25,000) = \$28,750$$

Example 28 illustrates how, once a taxpayer's modified adjusted gross income reaches the level at which formula 2 exceeds one-half of the Social Security benefits, the maximum amount of Social Security subject to tax is one-half of the benefits received, no matter how much the taxpayer's income increases. Thus, formula 1 establishes a "ceiling" value for the taxation of Social Security benefits received before 1994.

For tax years after 1993, a second-tier inclusion rule applies to higher-income taxpayers. The second tier applies to unmarried individuals with modified adjusted gross incomes greater than $34,000 and married couples filing joint returns with modified adjusted gross incomes exceeding $44,000. The rules discussed earlier (the 50% formula) remain in effect for taxpayers with modified adjusted gross incomes that are less than these amounts.

For tax years after 1993, taxpayers with modified adjusted gross incomes above the threshold levels of $34,000 and $44,000 have to make an additional computation to determine the amount of Social Security benefits that they must include in gross income. As outlined in Exhibit 3–3, the new second-tier rule increases the taxable portions in the original Social Security formulas from 50 percent to 85 percent. In addition, formula 2 is increased by the amount of Social Security included under the 50-percent formula or a fixed amount ($4,500 for single individuals, $6,000 for married taxpayers filing joint returns), whichever is less. This change in formula 2 requires taxpayers subject to the second-tier rules to calculate the amount of Social Security they would have included in their gross income under the 50-percent formula.

▲ **EXAMPLE 29**   Assume the same facts as in example 26, except that the tax year is 1996. How much of the $4,000 in Social Security benefits is included in Judith's gross income?

Discussion: None of the $4,000 is included in Judith's gross income, because her modified adjusted gross income is below the $25,000 floor value for unmarried individuals. Note that the new second-tier rule does not apply to Judith, and her Social Security benefits will not be subject to tax.

▲ **Exhibit 3–3**

CALCULATION OF SECOND
TIER FOR INCLUSION OF
SOCIAL SECURITY
BENEFITS RECEIVED AFTER
1993

The taxable portion of Social Security is equal to the lesser of

1. 85% of the Social Security benefits received during the year

OR

2. The sum of
   a. 85% of the amount by which modified adjusted gross income exceeds the base amount

   PLUS

   b. The smaller of
      the amount of Social Security benefits included in gross income under the 50%
      formula
      OR
      $4,500 for an unmarried individual
      $6,000 for a married couple filing jointly

Where

Modified adjusted gross income = Adjusted gross income +
one-half of the Social Security benefits received during the year +
any foreign earned income exclusion + any tax-exempt interest

And

Base amount $34,000 for an unmarried individual
$44,000 for a married couple filing jointly
$ -0- for all others

▲ **EXAMPLE 30**   Assume the same facts as in example 27, except that the tax year is 1996. How much of the $6,000 in Social Security benefits received by Jack and Bettina is included in their gross income?

Discussion: Jack and Bettina's modified adjusted gross income is $36,000 ($23,000 + $3,000 + $10,000). Because their modified adjusted gross income is less than $44,000, Jack and Bettina's Social Security benefits are taxed under the 50% formula. They include $2,000 in Social Security benefits in their gross income.

▲ **EXAMPLE 31**   Dieter and Luann are a married couple whose adjusted gross income is $42,000. In addition, they received $10,000 in Social Security benefits. How much of the $10,000 must be included in Dieter and Luann's gross income?

Discussion: Dieter and Luann's modified adjusted gross income is $47,000 [$42,000 + $5,000 (1/2 × $10,000)]. Because their modified adjusted gross income exceeds the $44,000 base amount, they are subject to the second-tier rule. Under the 50% formula, their taxable Social Security is $5,000:

The lesser of

$$1/2(\$10,000) = \$5,000$$
$$\text{OR}$$
$$1/2(\$47,000 - \$32,000) = \$7,500$$

Under the second-tier rule, Dieter and Luann must include $7,550 of the Social Security benefits in gross income:

The lesser of

1. 85% × $10,000 =	$8,500
OR	
2. The sum of	
a. 85% × ($47,000 − $44,000) =	$2,550
b. the smaller of	
$5,000 (amount included under the 50% formula)	
OR	
$6,000	5,000
Equals	$7,550

▲ **EXAMPLE 32**   Camilla is a single individual whose adjusted gross income is $33,000. In addition, she receives $6,000 in Social Security benefits and has tax-exempt municipal bond interest income of $2,000. How much of the $6,000 must be included in Camilla's gross income?

Discussion: Camilla's modified adjusted gross income is $38,000 [$33,000 + $3,000 (1/2 × $6,000) + $2,000], and she is subject to the second-tier rule. Under the 50% formula, her taxable Social Security is $3,000:

The lesser of

$$1/2(\$6,000) = \$3,000$$
OR
$$1/2\ (\$38,000 - \$25,000) = \$6,500$$

Under the second-tier inclusion rule, Camilla must include $5,100 of the Social Security benefits in gross income:

The lesser of
1.   85% × $6,000 = $5,100
OR
2.   The sum of
    a.   85% × ($38,000 − $34,000) = $3,400
    b.   the smaller of
        $3,000 (amount taxable under the 50% formula)
    OR
        $4,500   <u>3,000</u>
Equals $6,400

Example 32 illustrates how the modification of formula 2 invokes the new ceiling of 85 percent of Social Security benefits received sooner than under the 50 percent formula. That is, if she had not had to add to formula 2 the $3,000 of Social Security included under the 50-percent formula, Camilla would have had to include only $3,400 of Social Security benefits in her gross income.

Alimony Received.   In divorce situations, one spouse often makes payments to a former spouse. These payments may be to provide for the support of children (called **child support payments**), they may be simply a sharing of income between the two parties (called **alimony**), or they may constitute a division of marital property **(property settlement).** Child support payments are not taxable to the recipient, regardless of how the recipient actually spends the money.[17] However, payments that are a sharing of current income (alimony) are taxable to the recipient and deductible for adjusted gross income by the payer. That is, alimony is an allowable transfer of income from one former spouse to another. In order to be considered alimony, all the following conditions must be met:

1.   The payment must be in cash

2.   The payment must be in a written agreement (either a separation or divorce agreement)

3.   The written agreement does not specify that the payments are for some other purpose (i.e., child support)

4.   The payer and the payee cannot be members of the same household at the time of the payment

5.   There is no liability to make payments for any period after the death of the payee.[18]

These requirements are intended to ensure that both parties to the agreement concur on the amount of alimony being paid. One controversial tax aspect of divorce involves property settlements. Payments and transfers pursuant to property settlements between spouses do not have any income tax consequences.

▲ **EXAMPLE 33**   Walt and Janice were divorced during the current year. As part of the divorce settlement, Walt paid Janice $100,000 for her interest in their home (the home had a fair market value of $200,000) and agreed to pay Janice $12,000 per year in alimony. The home had an adjusted basis to Walt and Janice of $120,000. What are the tax effects of the payments Walt makes to Janice?

Discussion: The $100,000 payment to Janice is not a taxable disposition by Janice, and no deduction is allowed to Walt, because it is a property settlement payment. The $12,000 per year of alimony is included in Janice's gross income and is deductible for adjusted gross income by Walt.

This treatment of property settlements may tempt the spouse making a property settlement to try to disguise the settlement as deductible alimony payments. A complex set of "recapture" rules has been designed to stop this so-called front loading of property settlements disguised as alimony payments during the first three years of separation. The recapture rules require the spouse making the alimony payment (and taking the alimony-paid deduction) to include in income the excess deductions taken when the property settlement has been disguised as alimony. The spouse receiving the disguised payments is allowed a deduction to offset the overstated alimony. These recapture rules have removed the incentive to disguise property settlements as alimony.

▲ **EXAMPLE 34**   In example 33, assume that instead of specifying the $100,000 as a property settlement in their divorce decree, Walt agreed to pay Janice alimony of $112,000 in the first year and $12,000 per year for every year after the first year. What are the tax effects of the payments Walt makes to Janice?

Discussion: The large payment in the first year relative to the other years (front loading) will trigger the alimony recapture rules. The net effect of the recapture rules will be to treat the additional $100,000 in the first year as a property settlement. That is, the net tax treatment is identical to that in example 33.

The final problem in the alimony area is the attempt to disguise child support payments as alimony. To counter this problem, the tax law requires that any reductions in alimony payments that are the result of a contingency related to a child are classified as child support payments.[19]

▲ **EXAMPLE 35**   Ben and Diane were divorced in the current year. As part of their divorce agreement, Ben is to pay Diane alimony of $500 per month until their son reaches age 18, at which time the payments will be reduced to $200 per month. What are the tax effects of the payments Ben makes to Diane?

Discussion: Because the payments are to be reduced to $200 when their child reaches age 18 (a contingency related to a child), only $200 per month of all payments made are considered alimony. The remaining $300 is a nondeductible child support payment.

Imputed Income

Two major sources of income that are untaxed under current law are the goods and services produced by individuals for personal consumption and individuals' use of their personal residence and other durable goods. To understand why these items constitute income under the principles described earlier in the chapter, consider the following example:

> ▲ **EXAMPLE 36**   Jana has a garden in which she grows tomatoes for her personal consumption. The full cost of producing the tomatoes amounts to $40. At current prices, it would have cost $100 to purchase the tomatoes. Does Jana have income from growing and consuming her tomatoes?
>
> *Discussion:*   Although Jana's wealth has increased by $60 from growing and consuming her own tomatoes rather than purchasing them, she does not have to recognize the $60 as income. The key factor in the nonrecognition of the income is that the $60 increase in wealth was not realized in an arm's-length transaction with another party. Note that if Jana had sold the tomatoes for $100 and used the money for other purposes, she clearly would have realized the income, and the $60 increase in wealth would be subject to tax.

This example of income from in-kind consumption is but one of many types of **imputed income** from which taxpayers profit on a daily basis but is not subject to taxation. The primary reason that these kinds of income are not taxed is that there is no realization of the income. In addition, even if in-kind consumption were considered a realization, such income would not be taxed, because it would be administratively inconvenient: Imagine the nightmare of having to keep track of all the tasks you perform for yourself rather than hire someone else to do the work! How could the government audit this type of income?

Although the vast majority of imputed income is not taxed, the tax law does identify several specific items of imputed income that must be taxed. The three most common forms of imputed income subject to tax are

- Below market-rate loans
- Payment of expenses by others
- Bargain purchases

Below Market-Rate Loans.   Before 1984, a common tax-planning technique that taxpayers used to shift income from high marginal tax rate taxpayers to low marginal tax rate taxpayers was the use of an interest-free loan, called a **below market-rate loan.** The savings that could have been realized from such a plan are illustrated in the following example:

> ▲ **EXAMPLE 37**   Binh, who is in the 36% marginal tax rate bracket, lent his son Chee $50,000 interest free. Chee, who is a 15% marginal tax rate payer, put the money in a savings account earning 10%. How much tax does the family save through this arrangement?
>
> *Discussion:*   If Binh invested the $50,000 at the same earnings rate, the tax savings would be $1,050. That is the difference between the tax Binh would have paid on the $5,000 in interest, $1,800 ($5,000 $\times$ 36%), and the tax paid by Chee on the $5,000 in interest, $750 ($5,000 $\times$ 15%).

In 1984, Congress curtailed some advantages of interest-free loans by enacting provisions that consider such loans as consisting of two transactions: a normal interest-bearing loan (at the current federal rate of interest) and an exchange of cash between the lender and the borrower to pay the interest on the loan. The imputed exchange of cash is the amount of cash necessary for the borrower to pay the lender the interest on the loan. A conventional interest-bearing loan and an interest-free loan are compared in Figure 3–1.

▲ Figure 3–1

IMPUTED INTEREST RULES

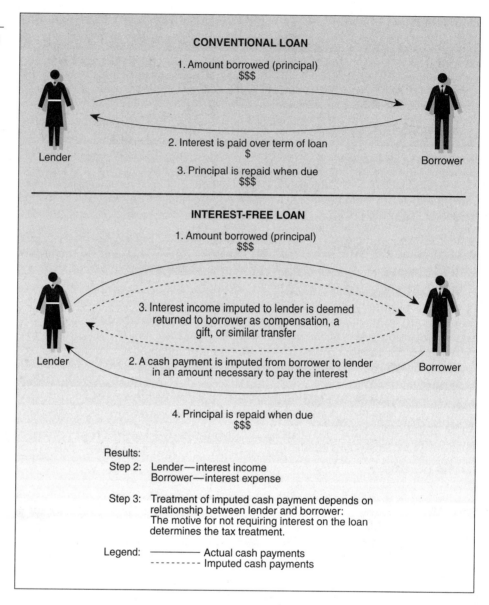

Under the imputed interest rules,[20] the lender is deemed to have interest income at the federal rate of interest, whereas the borrower is deemed to have made a payment (first imputed cash payment) of the interest (step 2 at the bottom of Figure 3–1). The imputed payment of cash (second imputed cash payment) from the lender to the borrower (step 3 at the bottom of Figure 3–1) may also produce income taxable income to the borrower, depending on the type of loan.

The three basic types of loans are

■ Gift loans

■ Employment-related loans

■ Corporation/shareholder loans

A gift loan is one made between family members. The imputed cash exchange on these loans is considered a gift from the lender to the borrower and is not subject to tax (the exclusion for gifts is covered in Chapter 4).

▲ **EXAMPLE 38**   What is the tax treatment of the loan Binh made to Chee in example 37 if the federal rate of interest is 8%?

Discussion: The first step in accounting for an interest-free loan is to determine the amount of imputed interest on the loan using the applicable federal rate of interest. In this case, the amount of imputed interest is $4,000 ($50,000 × 8%). This is the amount of interest income the lender is deemed to have earned (and the borrower is deemed to have paid) from the making of the loan. In this case, interest income of $4,000 is imputed to Binh, and interest expense of $4,000 is imputed to Chee. Binh therefore includes $4,000 of interest in his gross income. Chee has interest expense of $4,000, the deductibility of which depends on how he uses the money (interest deductions are discussed in Chapter 5). NOTE: Because this is a gift loan of less than $100,000, the amount of interest imputed may be less than the $4,000 federal rate. See examples 41–43.

The second step is to give effect to the motive for the nonpayment of interest on the loan. This is done by assuming that the lender gave the borrower the cash with which to pay the interest imputed on the loan in the first step. This imputed payment of cash is then taxed as any payment of cash would be taxed. In this case, Binh is deemed to have made a gift to his son of the $4,000 in interest. The receipt of the gift is not taxable to Chee, nor is it deductible by Binh.

When a loan is made to an employee by an employer, the imputed exchange of cash in the second step is deemed to be compensation paid to the employee and thus is taxable to the employee and deductible by the employer.

▲ **EXAMPLE 39**   In the previous example, assume that Binh lent the $50,000 to Celine, an employee of his roofing business. What is the tax treatment of the loan?

Discussion: As in the gift loan, Binh is assumed to have received (and Celine is assumed to have paid) interest income of $4,000. The imputed payment of cash for the interest is considered a payment for compensation. Therefore, Binh is deemed to have paid Celine $4,000 in compensation, which is taxable to Celine and deductible by Binh.

Note that the net effect of this arrangement for Binh is zero. That is, he has an increase in his income of $4,000 because of the imputation to him of the interest income on the loan, which is counterbalanced by the compensation payment deduction of $4,000. Whether the same is true for Celine depends on whether she can deduct the interest expense imputed on the loan. For example, if Celine used the $50,000 for a purely personal purpose such as the payment of a personal debt, the interest would not be deductible. In that case, the net effect for Celine would be an increase in taxable income of the $4,000 in imputed compensation.

When an interest-free loan is made to a shareholder of a corporation, the imputed exchange of cash is deemed to be a dividend paid to the shareholder and thus is taxable to the shareholder. A corporation is not allowed a deduction for dividends paid to shareholders.

▲ **EXAMPLE 40**   In example 39, assume that Celine is a shareholder of Binh's roofing business, which is organized as a corporation. The loan is made from the corporation to Celine. What is the tax treatment of the loan?

Discussion: The $4,000 in interest is imputed to the corporation and Celine, as in the previous example. The $4,000 imputed exchange of cash to pay the interest is deemed a dividend paid to Celine and is taxable to her as dividend income. Binh's corporation is deemed to have paid a dividend of $4,000, which is not deductible by the corporation.

A summary of the treatments of the second imputed cash payment for the three types of loans is presented in Table 3–1.

EXCEPTIONS TO IMPUTED INTEREST RULES.   There are two exceptions to the rules for interest-free loans. First, any loan of $10,000 or less is exempted from the imputed interest rules. This exception is for administrative convenience; it would be very costly to keep track of all small loans that people make to friends and relatives. Therefore, a small amount of income can still be shifted through the use of $10,000 interest-free loans.

The second exception is for gift loans of $100,000 or less. On such loans, the imputed interest on the loan cannot exceed the borrower's net investment income (investment income less the costs of producing the income) for the year. Further, if the borrower's net investment income for the year does not exceed $1,000, the imputed interest is deemed to be zero; the loan has no tax effect. Therefore, gift loans that do not produce much income for the borrower or that are used for in-kind consumption by the borrower escape the imputed interest rules.

▲ **EXAMPLE 41**   Allegra lent her daughter Elena $50,000, which she used to purchase a new house. The loan was interest-free, the federal rate of interest was 8%, and Elena had $600 in investment income for the year. What are the tax consequences of the loan?

Discussion: Because this was a gift loan of less than $100,000, the imputed interest is limited to Elena's net investment income for the year. However, because Elena's investment income is less than $1,000, no interest is imputed on the loan. Therefore, the loan has no income tax effects for either Allegra or Elena.

▲ **Table 3–1**

TREATMENT OF SECOND
IMPUTED CASH PAYMENT

Type of Loan	Lender	Borrower
Gift loans	Imputed payment is a gift made to the borrower—*no income tax effect.*	Imputed payment is a gift received from the lender—*no income tax effect.*
Employment-related loans	Imputed payment is compensation paid to the borrower—*lender gets a deduction for compensation paid.*	Imputed payment is compensation received by the borrower—*borrower has compensation income.*
Shareholder loans		
1. Loan to a shareholder	1. Imputed payment is a dividend paid to the borrower—*lender gets no deduction for dividends paid.*	1. Imputed payment is a dividend received from the lender—*borrower has dividend income.*
2. Loan to the corporation	2. Imputed payment is a contribution to corporate capital—*no deduction allowed to lender (added to basis in stock).*	2. Imputed payment is receipt of contributed capital—*no income imputed to the borrower.*

▲ **EXAMPLE 42**   Assume the same facts as in example 41, except that Elena's investment income was $2,500.

Discussion: In this case, interest on the gift loan would be imputed at $2,500, Elena's investment income. Allegra would have interest income of $2,500, and Elena would have interest expense of $2,500.

▲ **EXAMPLE 43**   Assume the same facts as in example 41, except that Elena's investment income was $6,000.

Discussion: In this case, interest at the federal rate of $4,000 ($50,000 $\times$ 8%) is less than Elena's investment income of $6,000. Therefore, interest of $4,000 is imputed on the loan. That is, none of the special exceptions for gift loans is applicable. NOTE: Interest is never imputed at a rate greater than the applicable federal interest rate.

Payment of Expenses by Others.   Whenever one taxpayer pays another taxpayer's expenses, the taxpayer who received the benefit of the payment has realized an increase in wealth and is taxed on the payment, unless the payment constituted a valid gift (gifts are excluded from income).[21] The more common situations involve payments of expenses of an employee by an employer, taxes of the lessor paid by the lessee of property, and the payment of the personal expenses of the principal shareholder of a closely held corporation (a closely held corporation is one in which five or fewer shareholders own more than 50 percent of the stock of the corporation).

▲ **EXAMPLE 44**   Ramona is the president of DEF, Inc. Ramona's employment contract states that DEF is to pay Ramona a salary of $100,000 and the federal income tax due on the salary. In the current year, the tax on Ramona's DEF salary totals $27,000, which is paid by DEF. What is Ramona's gross income from DEF?

Discussion: The payment of the $27,000 of tax on Ramona's salary is considered compensation income paid to Ramona. Therefore, her gross income from DEF is $127,000.

▲ **EXAMPLE 45**   Joe lost his job this year. Because he was having trouble paying all his bills, his grandfather agreed to pay Joe's home mortgage until he could find a new job. His grandfather made payments on Joe's mortgage totaling $10,000 during the current year. What are the tax effects of the payment of Joe's mortgage by his grandfather?

Discussion: The payment of the mortgage is not meant to be compensation from grandfather to Joe; rather, it is in the nature of a gift from grandfather to Joe to help him through his tough economic times. Therefore, the payments are not taxable to Joe (gifts are excluded from income).

These two examples illustrate the key consideration in determining whether the payment of an expense by another is taxable: intent to compensate. That is, when payments are made on behalf of another in an employment or other business-related context, they are generally taxable. Payments made on behalf of family members that are unrelated to employment or other business matters are generally considered nontaxable gifts.

Bargain Purchases.   Ordinarily, when taxpayers astutely purchase property for less than it is worth, they are not taxed immediately on the increased wealth resulting from the purchase. Any such gain will be reflected when the property is sold. However, a true **bargain purchase** is taxable to the buyer. Such a purchase occurs when the difference between the purchase price and the fair market value represents an effort by the seller to confer an economic advantage to the buyer.[22] That is, the purchase price does not result from an arm's-length transaction. As such, bargain purchases are typically found in employer/employee purchases and other instances in which the seller perceives some ultimate advantage in selling the property to a particular taxpayer at less than fair market value.

▲ **EXAMPLE 46**   Sterling is an employee of Shelf Road Development Co. The company recently subdivided some property and offered lots for sale at a price of $50,000. Shelf sells Sterling a lot for $20,000. How much gross income does Sterling have from the purchase of property?

Discussion: The difference between the $50,000 fair market value and the $20,000 purchase price—$30,000—is taxable to Sterling as compensation. The purchase price, an attempt to compensate Sterling, is not the result of an arm's-length bargain.

▲ **EXAMPLE 47**   Karolina wants to purchase a new Bugatti roadster. She knows that such cars usually sell for about $50,000. However, she finds a dealer who is having financial difficulties and is able to purchase a Bugatti for only $40,000. Does Karolina have gross income from the purchase of the Bugatti?

Discussion: Because the dealer gains no long-term benefit from selling the car to Karolina for $40,000, her astute purchase is not considered a bargain purchase for tax purposes. Further, the purchase price is the result of an arm's-length transaction. Therefore, she is not taxed on the $10,000 below market-value purchase.

CAPITAL GAINS AND LOSSES—AN INTRODUCTION

Whenever a property is sold, exchanged, or otherwise disposed of, a realization occurs, and the entity owning the property must calculate the gain (loss) resulting from the disposition of the property. The income tax provisions governing property transactions are an important part of the income tax system. Chapters 10 through 13 discuss in detail various aspects of income tax accounting for the acquisition, use, and disposition of property. However, because of their importance in the income tax system, we briefly discuss capital gains and losses at this point.

A capital gain or a capital loss results from the sale or other disposition of a capital asset. As discussed in Chapter 2, a **capital asset** is any asset that is not a receivable, an item of inventory, depreciable property used in a trade or business, or real property used in a trade or business.[23] Thus, the most common capital assets are investment assets (stocks, bonds, rental property held for investment) and assets used for personal use purposes (home, furniture, clothing, personal automobile, etc.) by individuals.

Since 1921, the tax law has provided some form of preferential tax treatment for capital gains. For example, until 1987, individuals were allowed to deduct 60 percent of any net long-term capital gains. This meant that only 40 percent of net long-term capital gains was subject to tax. During most of this time, the top marginal tax rate was 50 percent, resulting in a maximum tax rate on long-term capital gains of 20 percent (50% × 40%). Although the 60-percent capital gains deduction was repealed in 1986, all the mechanisms for accounting for capital gains and other limitations were left in place. Therefore, although the tax savings may not be as great as they once were, accounting for capital gains and losses remains an important aspect of our tax system. The basic aspects of accounting for capital gains and losses are discussed in the sections that follow. More detailed analysis is provided in Chapter 12.

Capital Gain-and-Loss Netting Procedure

The income tax law determines the treatment of capital gains and losses on an annual basis. That is, all capital gains and losses occurring during a tax year are aggregated through a prescribed netting procedure to determine the net effect of all capital asset transactions for the year.[24] The special tax treatments (if any are applicable) are applied only to the net results for the year, not to individual transactions.

Exhibit 3–4 outlines the procedure for determining the net long-term capital gains or losses for the year. The first step requires segregation of the year's gains into long-term and short-term gains and losses. Whether a gain (loss) is short term or long term depends on its holding period. As the phrase indicates, the **holding period** is how long the taxpayer owned the asset that was sold. Assets held for more than one year produce **long-term capital gains** and **long-term capital losses**. Assets held for one year or less produce **short-term capital gains** and **short-term capital losses**.[25] The distinction is important, because preferential treatment is accorded only to net *long-term* capital gains.

The second step in the netting procedure is to reduce the gains and losses for the year into one net long-term position (either a gain or a loss) and one net short-term position (either a gain or a loss). At this stage, all capital gains and losses for the year have been reduced to two numbers—one for the effect of long-term gains and losses and another for short-term gains and losses.

▲ **EXAMPLE 48**   Astrid had the following capital gains and losses for the current year:

Long-term capital gain	$13,000
Long-term capital loss	($ 4,000)
Short-term capital gain	$ 8,000
Short-term capital loss	($10,000)

What are Astrid's net long-term and net short-term capital gain (loss) positions for the year?

Discussion: Astrid has a net long-term capital gain of $9,000 and a net short-term capital loss of $2,000 for the current year:

Long-term Gain/Loss Netting	
Long-term capital gain	$13,000
Long-term capital loss	(4,000)
Net long-term capital gain	$ 9,000

Short-term Gain/Loss Netting	
Short-term capital gain	$ 8,000
Short-term capital loss	(10,000)
Net short-term capital loss	$(2,000)

After the capital gain-and-loss transactions for the year have been reduced to a long-term and a short-term position for the year, the next step is to reduce the capital gain position for the year to either a gain or a loss on capital asset transactions for the year. Thus, if the short- and long-term positions are opposite (one is a gain and one is a loss), the two positions must be netted together to determine whether a gain or a loss has resulted from the taxpayer's capital asset transactions for the year.

▲ **Exhibit 3–4**

CAPITAL GAIN-AND-LOSS
NETTING PROCEDURE

Step 1	Segregate all capital gains and losses occurring during the year into short-term gains and losses and long-term gains and losses.
Step 2	Combine all long-term gains and losses to determine a net long-term position for the year. Combine all short-term gains and losses to determine a net short-term position for the year.

Long-term gains	$XXX	
Long-term losses	(XXX)	
Net long-term gain (loss)		$XXX or $(XXX)
Short-term gains	$XXX	
Short-term losses	(XXX)	
Net short-term gain (loss)		$XXX or $(XXX)

Step 3	If the positions determined in step 2 are opposite (i.e., one is a gain and one is a loss), net the two positions together to obtain either a gain or a loss position for the year.
	If the positions determined in step 2 are the same (i.e., either both are gains or both are losses), no further netting is necessary.
Step 4	Capital gain-and-loss treatments (individuals)

Short-term capital gain—no special treatment
Long-term capital gain—taxed at a maximum rate of 28%

Capital losses—Individuals may deduct only $3,000 in net capital losses per year. Any excess loss is carried forward to the next year's capital gain-and-loss netting. In determining the $3,000 deduction, short-term capital losses are deducted before long-term losses.

▲ **EXAMPLE 49** Return to the facts of example 48. What is Astrid's net capital gain or loss for the year?

Discussion: Astrid has a net long-term capital gain of $7,000 for the year. Because the first netting resulted in a long-term capital gain and a short-term capital loss, one more netting is necessary to determine Astrid's net capital gain position for the year:

Net long-term capital gain	$9,000
Net short-term capital loss	(2,000)
Net long-term capital gain	$7,000

Note that the effect of the netting procedure is to summarize all of Astrid's capital gains and losses for the year in a net gain position. This is the purpose of the procedure—to reduce all capital gains and losses occurring during the year into either a net gain or a net loss position.

If the first netting produces short- and long-term positions that are the same (both are gains or both are losses), the taxpayer's gain or loss position for the year is known and no further netting is necessary.

▲ **EXAMPLE 50** Milton had the following capital gains and losses for the current year:

Long-term capital gain	$3,000
Long-term capital loss	($1,000)
Short-term capital gain	$6,000
Short-term capital loss	($2,000)

What is Milton's net capital gain (loss) position for the current year?

Discussion: The first netting results in a net long-term capital gain of $2,000 and a net short-term capital gain of $4,000:

Long-term Gain/Loss Netting	
Long-term capital gain	$3,000
Long-term capital loss	(1,000)
Net long-term capital gain	$2,000

Short-term Gain/Loss Netting	
Short-term capital gain	$6,000
Short-term capital loss	(2,000)
Net short-term capital gain	$4,000

Because both the long- and short-term positions are gains, it is clear that Milton has a gain in his capital asset transactions for the year. Therefore, no further netting is necessary. He will report a long-term capital gain of $2,000 and a short-term capital gain of $4,000 on his current year's tax return.

After the net capital gain (loss) position for the year has been determined, each of the four types of gains and losses is subject to special rules in the calculation of taxable income. These rules are outlined in step 4 of Exhibit 3–4 and discussed in the next section. One thing you should note is that the tax treatments are applied to the net gain (loss) for the entire tax year, not for individual gains and losses occurring during the year.

Tax Treatment of Capital Gains

The only current tax relief is for **net long-term capital gains** of individuals. Net short-term capital gains receive no tax relief and are merely added to gross income. Net long-term capital gains are also added to gross income. However, the tax law provides that net long-term capital gains cannot be taxed at a marginal tax rate greater than 28 percent. This provision provides tax savings only to taxpayers whose marginal tax rate is greater than 28%. Taxpayers in the 15- and 28-percent brackets receive no benefit from having net long-term capital gains.

▲ **EXAMPLE 51**   Assume that in example 50 Milton is a single individual with taxable income of $80,000, not including capital gains. What is the tax on his net capital gains?

Discussion: Milton would pay a tax of $560 ($2,000 × 28%) on his net long-term capital gain and a tax of $1,240 ($4,000 × 31%) on his net short-term capital gain. In 1996, single individuals began paying a 31% marginal tax rate at a taxable income of $58,150. Because Milton's taxable income is greater than this amount, his marginal tax rate is 31%. The short-term capital gain is added to his gross income and taxed at his marginal tax rate. The net long-term capital gain is taxed at the 28% capital gain rate, not his actual marginal tax rate. Milton saves $60 [$2,000 × (31% − 28%)] because of the provision limiting capital gains to 28%.

Tax Treatment of Capital Losses

Net capital losses of individuals are deductible up to an annual limit of $3,000.[26] Capital losses are deductible as a deduction *for* adjusted gross income. Any capital loss in excess of the $3,000 limit is carried forward to the next year and is used in the next year's capital gain-and-loss netting.[27]

▲ **EXAMPLE 52**   Chalmer has a net long-term capital gain of $6,000 and a net short-term capital loss of $17,000 in the current year. What is the effect of Chalmer's capital asset transactions on his taxable income?

Discussion: Because the long- and short-term positions are opposite, they are netted together, resulting in a net short-term capital loss of $11,000 ($6,000 − $17,000). Chalmer can deduct $3,000 of the loss as a deduction for adjusted gross income in the current year. The remaining $8,000 loss is carried forward to next year as a short-term capital loss and used in next year's capital gain-and-loss netting.

When an individual has both a net short-term capital loss and a net long-term capital loss in the same year, the short-term loss must be used toward the $3,000 annual limit before any long-term loss is deducted.[28]

▲ **EXAMPLE 53**   During the current year, Zerenda has a $2,000 net short-term capital loss and a $5,000 net long-term capital loss. What is the effect of Zerenda's capital asset transactions on her taxable income?

Discussion: Because the long- and short-term positions are both losses, no netting is necessary. Zerenda deducts $3,000 of the total loss as a deduction for adjusted gross income. The $3,000 loss deduction is composed of the $2,000 short-term loss and $1,000 of the long-term loss. The remaining $4,000 ($5,000 − $1,000) of the long-term loss is carried forward to the next year as a long-term capital loss and used in next year's capital gain-and-loss netting.

One thing to remember when dealing with personal use assets (which are capital assets) is that gains on the sale of personal use assets are taxable under the all-inclusive income concept. However, losses on personal use assets are disallowed. Therefore, if a personal use asset is sold at a gain, the gain is a capital gain and subject to the rules for capital gains. A loss on the sale of a personal use asset is not deductible and does not enter into the capital gain netting procedure.

▲ **EXAMPLE 54**   Morgan sells for $3,400 a diamond necklace she purchased in 1980 at a cost of $2,000. Larry sells his personal truck, for which he paid $12,000, for $5,000. What are the effects of the sales on Morgan's and Larry's incomes?

Discussion: Morgan has a long-term capital gain of $1,400 ($3,400 − $2,000) from the sale of her necklace. The $1,400 gain must be combined with her other capital gains and losses in the capital gain-and-loss netting procedure. Larry's loss of $7,000 ($5,000 − $12,000) on the sale of his truck is a nondeductible personal use loss. Therefore, the loss has no effect on his taxable income.

Capital Gains and Losses of Conduit Entities

All items of income—gains, losses, deductions, and credits—of a conduit entity flow through the entity and are reported directly by the owners of the conduit. However, many items realized at the conduit level receive special treatment on the owners' tax returns. To provide owners with the information necessary to prepare their returns properly, a conduit entity is required to report each owner's share of the "ordinary" taxable income or loss separately from those items that receive special treatment.[29] The ordinary taxable income or loss is the income that results from income, gains, losses, and deductions that receive no special treatment. Because capital gains and losses are aggregated in the netting process on an owner's return, they must be allocated to each owner.

▲ **EXAMPLE 55**   Parnell and Isis are equal partners in the Steiner Partnership. Steiner has total income of $70,000, consisting of the following items in the current year:

Gross income from sales	$120,000
Trade or business expenses	90,000
Ordinary income	$ 30,000

Long-term gain on investment property	50,000
Short-term loss on Webto stock	(10,000)
Total income	$ 70,000

How do Steiner's results affect Parnell and Isis?

Discussion: As equal partners, Parnell and Isis share the partnership items equally. Each reports $15,000 (50% × $30,000) in ordinary income from the partnership. In addition, each will have a long-term capital gain of $25,000 and a short-term capital loss of $5,000 that each must include in his or her capital gain-and-loss netting.

▲ **EXAMPLE 56**   Assume that in addition to the items reported to her in example 55, Isis has the following income items:

Salary from Webto Corporation	$64,000
Dividend income	4,000
Long-term capital loss	(14,000)

What is Isis's adjusted gross income?

Discussion: Isis's adjusted gross income is $89,000:

Salary from Webto Corporation	$64,000
Dividend income	4,000
Ordinary income from Steiner Partnership	15,000
Net long-term capital gain ($25,000 − $14,000 − $5,000)	6,000
Adjusted gross income	$89,000

Note that if the Steiner Partnership were not required to report its capital gains and losses separately, Isis's adjusted gross income would be $100,000 [(1/2 × $70,000) + $64,000 + $4,000 − $3,000] because of the limitation on capital loss deductions. Because capital gains and losses are reported separately from the partnership's ordinary income, Isis's $14,000 long-term capital loss is deducted against the $25,000 long-term capital gain from the partnership and is not subject to the capital loss limitations.

EFFECT OF ACCOUNTING METHOD

Once an income item has been identified as taxable, the tax year for recognition must be determined. In general, the taxpayer's accounting method dictates the proper period for inclusion. The two basic accounting methods allowed for tax purposes are the cash method and the accrual method.[30] We will discuss each method and its general income-recognition criteria in turn. Within each of the two basic accounting methods are exceptions to the treatments prescribed by the methods. These exceptions are generally designed to either discourage tax avoidance schemes or are based on the wherewithal-to-pay concept, which states that income should be taxed when the taxpayer has the means to pay the tax. More detailed accounting methods requirements are covered in Chapter 14.

Cash Method

Taxpayers using this method of accounting recognize income when it is actually or *constructively* received. Recall that reduction to cash is not necessary to trigger income recognition because of the cash-equivalent approach to income recognition under the cash method of accounting. All that is required is that something with a fair market value (property, services, etc.) be received. Under the constructive receipt doctrine, income is received when it is made unconditionally available to the taxpayer and is subject to the taxpayer's complete control.

Because of its simplicity (a checkbook is all the record keeping that is required), most individuals use the cash method. In addition, this method gives taxpayers a somewhat limited ability to determine the year of taxation by accelerating or deferring cash receipts.

▲ **EXAMPLE 57**   Harold is a cash basis taxpayer who repairs and maintains air conditioners and heating units in his spare time. The current year has been a good one for Harold, and he expects to be in the top marginal tax bracket. Next year, he plans to expand his business with a resulting increase in expenses and a drop in his marginal tax rate. What can Harold do to lower his tax bill?

Discussion: To lower his taxes, Harold should defer receipt of some of his repair and maintenance income until next year, when his marginal tax rate will be lower. This can be accomplished by delaying billings to customers until next year or by easing any credit terms he extends to customers.

Because of this ability to determine the year of taxation using the cash method, several restrictions are placed on the use of the method by certain types of taxpayers. These restrictions are discussed more fully in Chapter 14. The most basic restriction on the use of the cash method is that taxpayers who sell inventories must account for sales, purchases, and inventories using the accrual basis.[31]

Exceptions Applicable to the Cash Method.   The major income-recognition exception for cash basis taxpayers is for investments in **original issue discount (OID) securities**. An OID security is a debt instrument that has interest payable at maturity rather than throughout the life of the debt. Before the OID rules were codified, cash basis taxpayers could defer interest income by purchasing OID instruments.

▲ **EXAMPLE 58**   First Financial, Inc., loaned Heywood $10,000 on an interest-only basis, with interest payable annually at 10% for 3 years. Under the agreement, Heywood paid $1,000 in interest at the end of each year for 3 years. The $10,000 loan balance was repaid at the end of the third year. How much income does First Financial recognize each year?

Discussion: This is a conventional debt situation wherein interest is received throughout the term of the loan and is recognized accordingly. The $1,000 in interest received each year would be included in First Financial's gross income.

▲ **EXAMPLE 59**   As an alternative, First Financial could lend the money on a discount basis. As an OID debt, the face amount of the debt would be $13,310, payable at the end of 3 years, and Heywood would still receive the $10,000 at the inception of the loan. If First Financial is a cash basis taxpayer, how would it recognize the interest under the general rules for the cash method?

Discussion: Under the cash method, First Financial would recognize no income until it receives payment at the end of the third year. At that time, First Financial would recognize the difference between the amount received at maturity and the amount Heywood actually received as income, $3,310 ($13,310 − $10,000). Note that First Financial receives slightly more interest under this arrangement, because interest is being earned on the annual interest payment that is not being made throughout the 3 years.

Current tax law requires that all OID securities with a maturity of more than one year be accounted for on the accrual basis, using the effective interest method.[32] The intent of this provision is to discourage cash basis investors from deferring income using OID instruments.

▲ **EXAMPLE 60**   What is the proper income recognition for First Financial in example 59?

Discussion: Because the loan is made on an OID basis and has a term of more than one year, First Financial must recognize the interest annually, using the effective interest method. Under this method, the book value of the debt is increased each year for the prior year's interest, which was accrued but not paid. Interest is calculated as the product of the book value outstanding throughout the year and the rate of interest charged on the loan.

Year 1	$10,000 \times 10\% =$	$1,000
Year 2	$(\$10,000 + \$1,000) \times 10\% =$	$1,100
Year 3	$(\$10,000 + \$1,000 + 1,100) \times 10\% =$	$1,210
Total income recognized =		$3,310

Series E and EE **savings bonds** issued by the U.S. government are OID securities that are exempt from the OID rules.[33] Taxpayers purchasing these bonds are not required to amortize interest income during the life of the bonds, although they may elect to amortize all such bonds they hold currently. If such an election is made, they must amortize interest on any bonds they purchase in the future.

▲ **EXAMPLE 61**   Henry purchased for $650 a Series EE savings bond with a face value of $1,000 in the current year. The savings bond matures in 10 years and was priced to yield a 6% annual return. How should Henry account for the interest income related to the savings bond?

Discussion: Because Series EE savings bonds are exempted from the OID rules, Henry will not have to recognize interest on the bond until he cashes in the bond. If Henry cashes in the bond at maturity, he will receive the $1,000 face value of the bond. At that time, he would recognize $350 ($1,000 − $650) in interest income. NOTE: Henry may elect to amortize the interest earned on the bond each year, using the effective interest method. However, if he makes this election, any other Series EE bonds he owns, as well as any others he may purchase in the future, must also be amortized. That is, you must use the same accounting method for all such bonds.

Accrual Method

Taxpayers using this method recognize income when it is *earned*, regardless of the actual period of receipt. Income is considered earned when (1) all events have occurred that fix the right to receive the income, and (2) the amount of income earned can be determined with reasonable accuracy.[34] In the majority of cases, these recognition criteria parallel the recognition rules for financial accounting. Some significant differences between the two are discussed later.

Two important aspects of the accrual method should be noted at this point. First, the checkbook approach commonly used by cash basis taxpayers is not sufficient to account for the many accruals and deferrals of income required by the accrual method. Thus, this is a more costly method. Second, accrual basis taxpayers have little control over the timing of their income, because the earning of the income, not the receipt of payment, is the critical recognition event.

▲ **EXAMPLE 62**   Assume the same facts as in example 57, except that Harold has elected to be an accrual basis taxpayer.

Discussion: Harold must recognize the income from the performance of his repair and maintenance services in the year in which they are performed, not when he receives payment for them. Therefore, he has little ability to control the timing of his income recognition to take advantage of marginal rate differences between tax years.

Exceptions Applicable to the Accrual Method.   The receipt of prepaid income by accrual basis taxpayers is generally taxable in the tax year in which payment is received (under the wherewithal-to-pay concept). Thus, advance receipts of rent, interest, royalties, payments for goods, and payments for services are taxable when the cash payment is received, even for accrual basis taxpayers.[35]

There are two exceptions to the general rule for prepayments received for goods and services. For service prepayments, the accrual method may still be used if the services will be performed before the end of the tax year following the year of receipt.[36] This is referred to as the **one-year rule for services.**

▲ **EXAMPLE 63**   On July 1, 1996, Toy's Termite Service, Inc., receives $1,200 on a one-year service contract. Under the contract, Toy's is to perform pest control once per month. Assuming that Toy's uses the accrual method of accounting, when should the $1,200 be recognized for tax purposes?

Discussion: The services are to be performed before December 31, 1997 (the end of the tax year following the year of receipt). Therefore, under the one-year rule for services, Toy's may use the accrual method to recognize income from the contract. Six months of services are to be performed in 1996 and 1997, resulting in the recognition of $600 in income in each year. NOTE: If Toy's uses the cash method of accounting, the entire $1,200 is taxable in the year of receipt. The one-year rule is an exception for accrual basis taxpayers.

▲ **EXAMPLE 64**   Assume the same facts as in example 63, except that the $1,200 advance receipt is for a two-year service contract. When should Toy's recognize the income from the contract?

Discussion: Because the contract continues past December 31, 1997 (the end of the tax year following the year of receipt), the one-year rule for services does not apply. Toy's must recognize the entire $1,200 in 1996. NOTE: A one-year prepayment contract always meets the one-year rule requirement, but a two-year prepayment contract never meets the one-year rule requirement.

It should be noted that the one-year rule applies only to advance receipts for services. Advance receipts for rents and interest are never deferred under the one-year rule for services; they are always taxable in the year of receipt.

The second exception to the general rule for prepayments is for prepaid receipts received for goods. In order to use the accrual method to account for advance receipts for goods, the prepayment must be less than the cost of the goods and the prepayment must be deferred for financial accounting purposes.[37]

▲ **EXAMPLE 65**   Anne wants to buy a new car, but none of the dealers in her area has the exact car she wants. Local Car Sales, Inc., agrees to order the car she wants from the factory. The agreed-upon price for the car is $17,500, and Anne agrees to give Local a $500 deposit on the order, the balance to be paid upon delivery. Local receives the deposit on December 27, 1996. The car arrives the following February, and Anne pays Local the $17,000 balance due on the car. How should Local Car Sales, Inc., account for the $500 deposit received in 1996?

Discussion: Assuming that the $500 deposit is less than the cost of the car to Local, Local may defer recognition of the deposit until 1997, provided that it also defers recognition for financial accounting purposes.

Hybrid Method

The **hybrid method of accounting** allows the taxpayer to account for sales of merchandise and the related cost of goods sold on the accrual basis and all other items of income and expense on the cash basis. Thus, the hybrid method is a mixture of the accrual and cash methods. This method is most commonly used by taxpayers who have inventories and therefore must use the accrual method to account for sales and the cost of goods sold from inventories. Such taxpayers must still use the cash method to account for other revenues and must use the cash method for all other expenses.

▲ **EXAMPLE 66**   Sunshine is a cash basis taxpayer who repairs and maintains hot tubs in her spare time. She also sells hot tubs. How must Sunshine account for sales of the hot tubs?

Discussion: Sunshine must use the accrual method to account for sales and calculate cost of goods sold for the hot tubs. However, she may elect to use the hybrid method of accounting, which would allow her to use the cash method for her service income and for all other expenses.

Exceptions Applicable to All Methods

Certain taxpayers must use two major income-recognition methods, regardless of their accounting methods. These methods relate to installment sales of property and accounting for long-term construction contracts.

Installment Sales.   An **installment sale** occurs whenever property is sold and at least one payment is received in a tax year subsequent to the year of sale. Taxpayers who are not dealers in the particular type of property but who make casual sales of property must recognize income from the sale by using the installment method, unless they elect to recognize the entire gain in the year of the sale.[38] The installment method is based on the wherewithal-to-pay concept and recognizes income proportionally as the selling price is received.[39]

▲ **EXAMPLE 67**   Lene purchases a tract of land in 1992 at a cost of $20,000 as a speculative investment. In 1996, she sells the land for $50,000. The terms of the sale require the buyer to pay Lene $10,000 in 1996, $20,000 in 1997, and $20,000 in 1998 with interest at 8% on the outstanding balance. How much income must Lene recognize in 1996 through 1998?

Discussion: Because Lene is not a dealer in property, she must use the installment method, unless she elects to recognize the entire $30,000 ($10,000 + $20,000 + $20,000 − $20,000) gain in 1996. Under the installment method, the gain is recognized proportionately as the $50,000 selling price is received.

1996	$10,000 × ($30,000 ÷ $50,000) = $ 6,000
1997 & 1998	$20,000 × ($30,000 ÷ $50,000) = $12,000

In addition, Lene has interest income of $3,200 ($40,000 × 8%) on the outstanding balance in 1997 and $1,600 ($20,000 × 8%) in 1998.

The use of the installment method by other taxpayers (i.e., dealers in property generally cannot use the installment sales method) has been severely restricted in recent years.

Long-Term Construction Contracts.   Taxpayers in the construction industry typically undertake projects that span a number of years. In the past, the income recognition on contracts spanning more than one tax year could be deferred until the completion of the contract. Although this method is still allowable in greatly restricted circumstances (see Chapter 14), most long-term construction contracts must be accounted for by using the **percentage-of-completed contract method.**[40] As the name of the method implies, income is recognized according to the amount of work completed on the contract each year. The work completed must be based on costs incurred during the year in relation to the estimated total costs of the project.

▲ **EXAMPLE 68**   Acme Construction Corporation enters into a contract in 1996 to construct a bridge for Garden City. The contract price for the bridge is $10,000,000, and Acme estimates its total cost of building the bridge to be $8,000,000. In 1996, Acme's actual costs were $2,000,000. How much gross income from the contract must Acme report in 1996?

Discussion: Using the percentage-of-completion method, Acme reports gross income from the contract of $2,500,000 in 1996.

$$\text{Work completed} = (\$2,000,000 \div \$8,000,000) = 25\%$$
$$\text{Gross income} = 25\% \times \$10,000,000 = \$2,500,000$$

To ensure that contractors do not manipulate their income by inaccurately estimating contract costs, a look-back rule is applied at the completion of the contract, and interest is charged on any deficient income reporting. This rule and other aspects of the method are discussed more fully in Chapter 14.

SUMMARY

This chapter focused on the determination of taxable income sources. In general, a taxpayer is in receipt of income when an increase in wealth is realized. Realization requires a change in the form or substance of a taxpayer's property or property rights and the involvement of a second party in an arm's-length transaction.

The four primary sources of income are earned income (income from labor), unearned income (income from investments), transfers from others (increases in wealth that are not the result of either labor or investment), and imputed income (increases in wealth realized because another party confers an economic advantage). Within each of these categories are various problems of realization and recognition. In most instances, application of the income tax concepts provides a solution to the problem. In other cases, the treatment is prescribed by law and must be learned through study and experience. To aid you in reviewing these sources of income, Table 3–2 classifies the income items discussed in this chapter and summarizes the major problems within each category of income.

Capital gains and losses are subject to special reporting rules. All capital gains and losses for a tax year are segregated from other forms of income and subjected to the capital gain-and-loss netting procedure. The purpose of the capital gain-and-loss netting procedure is to reduce a taxpayer's capital gain and loss trans-

	Income Sources	**Major Problems**
Earned Income	Wages and salaries Tips, commissions, bonuses Income from sole proprietorship—either the active conduct of a trade or business or the rendering of services Income from illegal activities—gambling, drug dealing, racketeering, etc.	Assignment of income What is a receipt?
Unearned Income	Income from investments—interest, dividends, rental income, royalty income, income from annuities, gains (losses) from the sale of investments Income from investment in conduit entities	Definition of income from rents and royalties Capital recovery on annuities Calculation of gain (loss) Income from conduit entity
Transfers from Others	Prizes and awards Unemployment compensation Social Security benefits Alimony received	Exception for prizes and awards given to charity Exception for employee awards for length of service or safety Calculation of taxable portion of Social Security benefits Front loading of alimony payments to disguise a property settlement Child support payments disguised as alimony
Imputed Income	Below market-rate loans Payment of expense by others Bargain purchases	Exceptions for below-market rate loans Gift vs. compensation for payment of expenses by others Compensatory nature of bargain purchase

▲ **Table 3–2**

INCOME SOURCES BY CLASS OF INCOME

actions for the tax year to a net figure that represents the gain or loss for the year. Net long-term capital gains of individuals are taxed at a maximum rate of 28 percent. Up to $3,000 of net capital losses of individuals are deductible for adjusted gross income. Any excess losses are carried forward to the next year's netting.

The period in which an item of income is recognized is determined by the taxpayer's method of accounting. The two basic accounting methods are the cash method and the accrual method, although some taxpayers may use a combination of the two methods called the *hybrid method*. Exceptions to the general recognition rules exist for certain installment sales and long-term construction contracts. Other specific recognition exceptions exist for both the cash and the accrual methods.

KEY TERMS

alimony (p. 107)
annuity (p. 99)
annuity exclusion ratio (p. 100)
bargain purchase (p. 113)
below market-rate loan (p. 109)
capital asset (p. 114)
cash-equivalent approach (p. 97)
child support payment (p. 107)
earned income (p. 96)
holding period (p. 115)
hybrid method of accounting
     (p. 123)

imputed income (p. 109)
installment sale (p. 123)
long-term capital gain (p. 115)
long-term capital loss (p. 115)
net long-term capital gain (p. 117)
net capital losses (p. 117)
one-year rule for services (p. 122)
original issue discount security
     (OID) (p. 120)
percentage-of-completed contract
     method (p. 124)

property settlement (p. 107)
savings bond (U.S. government-
     issued) (p. 121)
short-term capital gain (p. 115)
short-term capital loss (p. 115)
unearned income (p. 98)

PRIMARY TAX LAW SOURCES

[1] Reg. Sec. 1.61-1—States that income can be realized in any form, including cash, services, and property received.

[2] Eisner v. Macomber, 252 U.S. 189 at 207 (1920)—In holding that a stock dividend did not constitute gross income, determined that income is derived from labor and capital.

[3] Eisner v. Macomber at 207.

[4] Cesarini v. Comm., 428 F.2d 812 (6th Cir. 1970)—In determining that cash found in a purchased piano was included in gross income, established that "treasure troves" constitute gross income.

[5] Helvering v. Bruun, 309 U.S. 461 (1940)—Held that a landlord realized gain on the forfeiture of a leasehold for the nonpayment of rent and that the increase in the value of the property was taxable even though the gain was not severed from the property. (Subsequently overturned by enactment of Sec. 109).

[6] Helvering v. Bruun at 469.

[7] Sec. 109—States that gross income does not result from increases in the value of a property at the termination of a lease.

[8] Glenshaw Glass v. Comm., 348 U.S. 426 at 430–431 (1955)—Determined that income consists of undeniable accessions to wealth that are completely controlled by the taxpayer.

[9] Reg. Sec. 1.61-14—States that income from illegal activities is included in gross income.

[10] Sec. 72—Describes the general rules for the taxation of annuities and presents the

formula for determining the amount of each payment that is taxable.

[11] Sec. 1001—Prescribes the calculation of gains and losses on dispositions of property; defines *amount realized* for purposes of determining gain or loss on dispositions.

[12] Sec. 1016—Provides the general rules for adjustments to basis of property for capital expenditures and recoveries of capital subsequent to purchase.

[13] Reg. Sec. 1.61-13—States that a partner's share of the partnership's income is included in the gross income of the partner.

[14] Sec. 74—States that prizes and awards are taxable; details situations under which a qualified prize or award may be excluded from income.

[15] Sec. 85—States that unemployment compensation payments received are taxable.

[16] Sec. 86—States that Social Security payments received are taxable for high-income taxpayers; provides the formula for determining the taxable portion of Social Security payments.

[17] Reg. Sec. 1.71-1—States that child support payments are not taxable.

[18] Sec. 71—States that alimony received is taxable; defines *alimony* and presents the required recapture for front loading of alimony payments.

[19] Reg. Sec. 1.71-IT—Discusses what constitutes a contingency related to a child.

[20] Sec. 7872—Prescribes the treatment of below market-rate (interest-free) loans and

the exceptions to the below market-rate rules.

[21] Old Colony Trust Co. v. CIR, 279 U.S. 716 (1929)—Determined that the payment of a corporate officer's state and federal taxes by the corporation constituted gross income to the officer; established that payment of another's expense in an employment-related setting is compensation that is included in gross income.

[22] CIR v. Smith, 324 U.S. 695 (1945)—Held that selling stock to an employee at less than its fair market value constituted compensation received by the employee; established that a "bargain purchase" in an employment-related setting is included in gross income.

[23] Sec. 1221—Defines *capital assets*.

[24] Sec. 1222—Defines *short-term and long-term capital gains and losses*; prescribes the netting procedure used for capital gains and losses.

[25] Sec. 1223—Defines *holding period* for purposes of determining short-term and long-term classification of capital gains and losses.

[26] Sec. 1211—Sets forth the limit on deductions of capital losses of corporations and individuals.

[27] Sec. 1212—Allows the carryforward of disallowed capital losses by individuals.

[28] Reg. Sec. 1.1211-1—Requires the deduction of short-term capital losses before long-term capital losses in determining the current year's capital loss deduction.

[29] Sec. 703—Requires a partnership to state separately the items of income, gain, losses, deductions, and credits provided in Sec. 702 in computing its taxable income. Sec. 702 requires partners to separately account for their share of capital gains and losses, gains and losses on the sale of certain types of business property, charitable contributions, foreign taxes, and other items as prescribed by the secretary of the Treasury. Sec. 1366 contains similar provisions for S corporations.

[30] Sec. 446—States general rules for methods of accounting, including the allowance of the cash and accrual methods.

[31] Reg. Sec. 1.446-1—Requires the use of the accrual method for sales and cost of goods sold for sales of inventories; allows accounting of other income and expenses with the cash basis (the hybrid method is an acceptable accounting method).

[32] Sec. 1273—Prescribes the methods for determining the amount of original issue discount to include in gross income.

[33] Sec. 1272—Provides for the inclusion of original issue discount on debt instruments in gross income. Allows the exclusion of U.S. savings bonds from the OID rules.

[34] Sec. 451—Sets forth general rules for taxable year of inclusion of gross income items.

[35] Reg. Sec. 1.61-8—States that gross income includes rental and royalty income and that advance receipts of rent are included in gross income in the year of receipt, regardless of the taxpayer's accounting method.

[36] Rev. Proc. 71-21—Prescribes the conditions under which an accrual basis taxpayer may defer an advance receipt for services (one-year rule for services).

[37] Reg. Sec. 1.451-5—Specifies the conditions under which an accrual basis taxpayer can defer recognition of income from an advance receipt for goods.

[38] Sec. 453—Prescribes the required treatment of installment sales of property.

[39] Temp. Reg. Sec. 15a.453-1—Provides the calculations for determining the amount of income to be recognized under the installment method of accounting.

[40] Sec. 460—Requires the use of the percentage-of-completed-contract method of accounting for long-term construction contracts.

DISCUSSION QUESTIONS

1. How is the definition of *income* for income tax purposes different from the definition used by economists to measure income?

2. One of Adam Smith's four criteria for evaluating a tax is certainty. Does the income tax definition of *gross income* promote certainty in the U.S. tax system? Explain.

3. What is the difference between realized income and recognized income?

4. Buford purchased a new automobile in March for $23,000. In April, Buford receives a $500 rebate check from the manufacturer. The rebate was paid to all customers who purchased one of the manufacturer's automobiles in March. Should Buford include the $500 rebate in his gross income? Explain.

5. During her vacation, Janita found a gold bar from a sunken ship while she was scuba diving off the coast of Texas. Is Janita taxed on her find? If so, when is she taxed, and how much should she include in her income?

6. What is a cash equivalent? How does a cash equivalent affect the reporting of income?

7. What type of income does a sole proprietor of a business receive?

8. What is the difference between earned income and unearned income?

9. How is the gross income from a rental property or a royalty property determined?

10. Explain how the capital recovery concept applies to the taxation of annuities. Consider both purchased annuities and pension payments in your answer.

11. Explain the difference in determining the amount of income recognized from a conduit entity versus a taxable entity.

12. What effect does an asset's adjusted basis have in determining the gain or loss realized upon its sale?

13. This chapter noted that returns on investment are taxable, whereas returns of investment are not taxable. What is the conceptual basis for this treatment? Cite examples of each type of return, and explain why they are or are not taxable.

14. Prizes and awards are generally taxable. Under what conditions is the receipt of a prize or award not taxable?

15. Are Social Security benefits taxable? Explain.

16. How is the taxation of an alimony payment different from the taxation of a child support payment?

17. What incentive does a taxpayer have to disguise a property settlement as an alimony payment?

18. Does the tax treatment of below market-rate loans violate any income tax concepts? If so, how? Explain.

19. Evaluate the following statement:

    Whenever another person pays an expense for you, you are in receipt of taxable income.

20. What is a bargain purchase?

21. How is capital gain income treated differently from other forms of income?

22. What is the purpose of the capital gain-and-loss netting procedure?

23. Are all losses realized on the sale of capital assets deductible?

24. Why is it important that a conduit entity separate the reporting of its capital gains and losses from its report of other forms of income?

25. Detail any significant differences in the recognition of income using the cash method and using the accrual method of accounting.

26. Explain the hybrid method of accounting.

27. How does the wherewithal-to-pay concept affect the tax treatment of prepaid income?

28. Under what circumstances can the following taxpayers defer recognition of prepaid income beyond the year of receipt?
    a. A cash basis taxpayer
    b. An accrual basis taxpayer

29. What is an installment sale?

30. How is the degree of completion of a long-term construction contract determined?

PROBLEMS

31. Mitch travels extensively in his job as an executive vice president of Arthur Consulting Co. During the current year, Mitch used frequent flier miles that he had obtained during his business travel to take his family on a vacation to Europe. The normal airfare for the trip would have been $6,000.
    a. Discuss whether Mitch has realized income from the use of the frequent flier miles for personal purposes.
    b. Do you think that Mitch will have to recognize any income from the use of the frequent flier miles? Explain.

32. Two Sisters is a partnership that owns and operates a farm. During the current year, the partnership raised and harvested hay at a cost of $50,000. It then traded half the hay for quarter horse breeding stock—young horses worth $40,000. Two Sisters fed the remainder of the hay to the horses, which were worth $60,000 at the end of the year. How much income does the partnership have from these transactions during the current year?

33. Darcy borrowed $4,000 in 1993 from her employer to purchase a new computer. She repays $1,000 of the loan plus 6% interest on the unpaid balance in 1993, 1994, and 1995. After closing a big deal in 1996, she receives the original loan agreement stamped "paid in full" across the face. Does Darcy have any income from the cancellation of the loan in 1996? Explain.

34. Heidi sells her carpet-cleaning business to Elki. As part of the sales agreement, Elki pays Heidi $3,000 for her agreement not to open another carpet-cleaning business in the area for three years. Is Heidi taxed on the $3,000? Explain.

35. How much gross income does each of the following taxpayers have for the current year?
    a. Doris owns a retail sporting goods store. During the current year, her total revenues were $450,000 and she incurred $390,000 in expenses. She employs her six-year-old son as a consultant. The $12,000 consulting fee paid to her son is included in the $390,000 expense figure.
    b. Mike tends bar at a local night spot. During the current year, he received $8,000 in salary and made $11,000 in tips. In addition, he took bets for a local bookmaker who paid him $3,000.

36. In each of the following cases, determine who is taxed on the income:
    a. For $200, Lee purchased an old car that was badly in need of repair. Lee worked on the car for 3 months and spent $300 on parts to restore the car. Lee's son Jason needed $2,000 to pay his college tuition. Lee gave the car to Jason, who sold it for $2,000 and used the money to pay his tuition.
    b. Erica loaned a friend $20,000. The terms of the loan require the payment of $2,000 in interest each year to Erica's daughter. At the end of 4 years, the $20,000 loan principal is to be repaid to Erica. Erica's daughter will use the $2,000 to pay her college tuition.

37. Determine whether Frank or Debra, his daughter, is taxable on the income in each of the following situations:
   a. Frank owns 8% bonds with a face value of $12,000 that pay interest annually on December 31. On April 1, Frank makes a valid gift of the bonds to Debra.
   b. Several years ago, Frank wrote a book for which he still receives royalty payments. On July 1, Frank directs the publisher of the book to pay all future royalties to Debra.
   c. Frank owns U.S. Series E savings bonds with a face value $10,000 that he had purchased many years ago for $4,000. On November 25, 1996, Frank makes a valid gift of the bonds to Debra. The bonds mature on December 31, 1996, and Debra receives the $10,000 face value of the bonds at that time.
   d. Frank owns 100 shares of ABC common stock. On April 15, ABC declares a $5 per share cash dividend payable to shareholders of record as of May 1. On April 20, Frank makes a valid gift of the shares to Debra. Debra receives the $500 dividend in May.

38. In each of the following cases, determine who is taxed on the income:
   a. Camille owns several rental properties that produce $3,000 in rental income each month. Because of the age of the properties, Camille is concerned about her potential liability from accidents on the property. On June 1, she forms the CAM Rental Corporation and tranfers ownership of the rental properties to the corporation. The tenants continue to pay Camille the monthly rent, which she deposits in her personal checking account.
   b. Jimbob owns royalty interests in several oil wells. On March 1, Jimbob instructs the payers of the royalties to pay half of each royalty payment to his son Joebob.
   c. Assume the same facts as in part b, except that on March 1 Jimbob gifts a half interest in each royalty contract to Joebob.

39. Determine whether any income must be recognized in each of the following situations, as well as who must report income, how much that taxpayer should report, and when that taxpayer will report the income:
   a. Patz Corporation owns a gourmet restaurant. The restaurant needs to remodel its kitchen but is short of cash. Dennis owns Tucky's Accessories, a restaurant supply store. The manager of Patz makes a deal with Dennis to have Tucky's do the kitchen remodeling, in exchange for which Patz will cater Tucky's company picnic. Tucky's does the remodeling and Patz caters the picnic. It costs Patz $800 to cater the picnic, a job for which it would have charged $1,500.
   b. Geraldo is a sales manager who enjoys collecting antique guns. Geraldo attends various shows around the country at which collectors and dealers sell and trade guns. During the current year, Geraldo sells 3 guns for a total of $6,200 (the cost of the guns to Geraldo was $4,000) and purchases 2 guns at a total cost of $2,400. In addition, he exchanges a gun for which he had paid $700 for another gun worth $800.

40. You have been assigned to prepare the tax return for a new client, Thuy Griswold. Her husband Jerry died during the current year, and Thuy came to your firm for assistance, because Jerry had always done their taxes. Thuy has provided you with last year's return. After reviewing the return, only one item is unclear to you. Jerry reported $550 of income from an annuity purchased from New Bradenton Life Insurance. Write a letter to Thuy requesting the information you will need to determine the tax treatment of the annuity.

41. Several years ago, Minnie purchased an annuity for $102,000. The annuity is to pay Minnie $20,000 per year for life after she reaches age 65. Minnie turns 65 in 1996, at which time her life expectancy is 17 years.
   a. How should Minnie treat the $20,000 payment she receives in 1996?
   b. Shortly after receiving her payment for the year 2002, Minnie is killed in an automobile accident. How does the executor of Minnie's estate account for the annuity on her return for the year 2002?
   c. Assume that the accident does not occur until 2017. How does the executor of Minnie's estate account for the annuity on her 2017 return?

42. Duc has been employed by Longbow Corporation for 25 years. During that time, he purchased an annuity at a cost of $50 per month ($15,000 total cost). The annuity will pay him $200 per month for 10 years after he reaches age 65. Duc turns 65 this April and receives 8 payments on the contract.

    a. How much income does Duc have from the contract in the current year?

    b. Assume that the contract allows Duc a choice—$200 a month for 10 years or $175 per month for life after reaching age 65. Assuming that Duc's life expectancy is 12 years, how much income would he recognize in the current year if he elects the second option?

    c. Assume that Duc dies on April 2 at age 75 (in the ninth year that he receives payment). How does the executor of his estate account for the contract if Duc elected to receive $175 per month?

    d. Assume that Duc dies on April 2 at age 80 and he elected to receive $175 per month. How does the executor of his estate account for the contract in the year of his death?

43. Hank retires this year after working 30 years for Local Co. Per the terms of his employment contract, Hank is to receive a pension of $600 per month for the rest of his life. During the current year, he receives 7 pension payments from Local. At the time of his retirement, his life expectancy is 15 years.

    a. How much taxable income does Hank have if his employer's plan was noncontributory (i.e., Local Co. paid the entire cost of the plan; Hank made no contributions to the plan)?

    b. How would your answer change if Hank had contributed $27,000 to the pension plan? Assume that the $27,000 had been included in Hank's income (i.e., he has already paid tax on the $27,000).

    c. What if Hank had contributed $27,000 to the plan and none of the $27,000 was taxed (i.e., the tax law allows certain pension contributions to go untaxed during the contribution period)?

44. Ratliff Development Corporation purchases a tract of land in 1995 at a cost of $120,000 and subdivides the land into 30 building lots. The cost of subdividing is $6,000. In 1995, Ratliff installs roads and utilities at a cost of $36,000 and pays property taxes totaling $2,000 in 1995 and 1996. Interest paid on the loan used to purchase the land is $10,000 in 1995 and $6,000 in 1996. In 1996, Ratliff sells 10 lots for a total of $350,000. What is the corporation's gain (loss) on the sale of the lots?

45. The Rosco Partnership purchases a rental property in 1991 at a cost of $120,000. From 1991 through 1996, Rosco deducts $14,000 in depreciation on the rental. The partnership sells the rental property in 1996 for $138,000 and pays $7,000 in expenses related to the sale. What is Rosco's gain (loss) on the sale of the rental property?

46. Reddy owns some common stock with a market value of $15,000. The stock currently pays a cash dividend of $1,200 per year (an 8% annual yield). Reddy is considering selling the stock, which she purchased 13 years ago for $5,000, and using the proceeds to purchase stock in another company with a 10% annual dividend yield. If Reddy's goal is to maximize future dividends on her common stock investments, should she make the sale and purchase the new shares? Assume that Reddy is in a 28% marginal tax rate bracket.

47. How much income should the taxpayer recognize in each of the following situations? Explain.

  a. Julius owns a 25% interest in the Flyer Co., which is organized as a partnership. During the current year, Julius is paid $14,000 by Flyer as a distribution of earnings. Flyer's taxable income for the year (calculated without any payments made to partners) is $40,000.

  b. Felix owns 1,000 shares of Furr Co., which is a publicly traded corporation. Furr has 1,000,000 shares of stock outstanding during the current year. Furr has a net income of $2,500,000 and pays out a $2 per share dividend during the current year.

  c. Andrea is the sole proprietor of Andrea's Art Shop. During the current year, Andrea's has total revenue of $160,000 and total expenses of $115,000. Andrea draws a monthly salary of $2,500 from the shop that is not included in the $115,000 in expenses.

  d. Maryanne owns 60% of the stock of Sterling Safe Co., an S corporation. During the current year, Sterling has a taxable income of $200,000 and pays out dividends of $100,000 to its shareholders.

  e. Assume the same facts as in part d, except that Sterling incurs a loss of $40,000 during the current year.

48. DeWitt is the president of Weaver Co. and owns 20% of the common stock of the company. During the current year, DeWitt is paid a salary of $160,000 and receives a $20,000 bonus. Weaver has taxable income of $450,000 and pays cash dividends of $150,000. How much gross income does DeWitt have if

  a. Weaver is a corporation?

  b. Weaver is an S corporation?

49. Pablo wins a new automobile on a television game show. The car has a listed sticker price of $32,500. How much income does Pablo have from the receipt of the car? Explain.

50. Determine the amount of income that must be recognized in each of the following cases:

  a. Ramona is a production supervisor for White Co. During the current year, Ramona's division had no accidents, and White rewarded that safety achievement with a $200 cash award to each employee in the division.

  b. Lenny retires from the Brice Co. this year. At his retirement reception, the company gives him a set of golf clubs valued at $600 in appreciation for his years of loyal service.

  c. Fatima is named Humanitarian of the Year by Local City for her volunteer service. She receives a plaque and an all-expense paid trip to Washington, D.C., where she will meet the president. The value of the trip is $1,400.

  d. Sook is a college professor specializing in computer chip development. During the current year, he publishes a paper that explains the design of a revolutionary new chip. Softmicro, Inc., awards him $10,000 for the best breakthrough idea of the year. Sook uses the money to purchase a computer workstation to use in his research.

51. Has the taxpayer in each of the following situations received taxable income? If so, when should the income be recognized? Explain.

   a. Charlotte is a lawyer who specializes in drafting wills. Charlotte wants to give her husband a new gazebo for Christmas. In November, she makes a deal with Joe, a local handyman, to build a gazebo. In return, Charlotte is to draft a last will and testament for Joe's father. The gazebo normally would cost $3,000, which is approximately what Charlotte would charge for drafting the will. Joe builds the gazebo in time for Christmas. Charlotte drafts the will and delivers it to Joe the following January.

   b. Ed buys 500 shares of Northstar stock in January 1995 for $4,000. On December 31, 1995, the shares are worth $4,600. In March 1996, Ed sells the shares for $4,500.

   c. Dayo is the director of marketing for Obo, Inc. In December, the board of directors of Obo votes to give Dayo a $10,000 bonus for her excellent work throughout the year. The check is ordered and written on December 15 but is misplaced in the mail room and is not delivered to Dayo until January 5.

   d. John is unemployed. During the current year, he receives $4,000 in unemployment benefits. Because the unemployment is not enough to live on, John sells drugs to support himself. His total revenue for the year is $120,000. The cost of the drugs is $60,000.

52. Elwood had to retire early because of a job-related injury. During the current year, he receives $13,000 in Social Security benefits. In addition, he receives $4,000 in cash dividends on stocks that he owns and $8,500 in interest on tax-exempt bonds. Assuming that Elwood is single, what is his gross income if

   a. He receives no other sources of income?

   b. He also receives $9,000 in unemployment compensation?

   c. He sells some land he owned for $80,000? He paid $50,000 for the land.

53. Hermano and Rosetta are a retired couple who receive $16,000 in Social Security benefits during the current year. They also receive $10,000 in interest on their savings account and taxable pension payments of $28,000. What is their gross income if

   a. They receive no other sources of income?

   b. They receive $12,000 in interest from tax-exempt bonds they own?

54. Upon returning from lunch, you find the following message on your voice mail:

> This is Jarrett Ogilvie. I'm not one of your clients, but I need some advice. I received a statement in the mail from the Social Security Administration reporting the eighty-five hundred dollars I received from them last year. It says that a portion of my Social Security may be taxable. Last year was the first year I ever received Social Security and I'm confused. I thought Social Security wasn't taxable. Could you call me and explain this?

What facts will you need from Jarrett to determine what portion, if any, of the $8,500 of Social Security benefits are taxable? In your answer, explain how different facts may lead to different taxable amounts.

55. Albert and Patricia are divorced during the current year. As part of their divorce agreement, Patricia agrees to pay Albert alimony of $85,000 in the current year and $5,000 per year in subsequent years. What tax problem is presented by this agreement? What will be the ultimate tax treatment of the alimony payments?

56. Will and Janine are divorced during the current year. Will is to have custody of their two children and will receive their house as part of the divorce settlement. The house, which Will and Janine bought for $60,000, is worth $90,000. Janine is to receive one of their automobiles, for which they paid $21,000 and is now worth $9,000. Will will get the other automobile, which cost $6,000 and is worth $2,000. Janine is to pay Will alimony of $400 per month. However, the alimony payment is to be reduced by $100 per month as each child reaches age 18 or if a child should die or marry before reaching age 18. What are the tax effects of the divorce settlement for Will and Janine?

57. Simon and Sherry are divorced during the current year. As part of their property settlement, Simon gives Sherry 25% of the stock in his 100% owned corporation, Hobday, Inc. The stock has a fair market value of $80,000. Rather than pay Sherry alimony, Simon agrees to make Sherry a vice president of Hobday with an annual salary of $70,000. In her position, Sherry has no responsibilities and no involvement in the company. What are the tax implications of this arrangement? Explain.

58. Which of the following interest-free loans are subject to the imputed interest rules?
    a. Alamor Corporation loans Sandy, an employee, $8,000. The loan is to be repaid over 4 years. Sandy uses the proceeds to buy a used automobile. She has $1,100 in investment income during the current year.
    b. Trinh loans her son Jimmy $80,000. The loan is to be repaid over 20 years. Jimmy uses the loan to purchase a cabin in the mountains. He has $300 in investment income during the current year.
    c. Abdula Corporation loans Augie, an employee, $80,000. The loan is to be repaid over 20 years. Augie uses the loan to purchase a new house. He has $300 in investment income during the current year.
    d. Isabel owns 10% of Marcos Corporation. Isabel loans Marcos $20,000 to use for working capital. The loan is to be repaid over 5 years. Marcos has no investment income during the currrent year.
    e. Stuart loans his sister Sima $120,000. The loan is to be repaid over 20 years. Sima uses the loan to purchase a new home. She has no investment income during the current year.

59. Laura made the following interest-free loans during the current year. Discuss the income tax implications of each loan for both Laura and the borrower. In all cases, the applicable federal interest rate is 8%.
    a. On April 15, Laura loaned $20,000 to her brother Hyun to pay his income taxes. Hyun is financially insolvent and has no sources of investment income.
    b. On March 1, Laura loaned $15,000 to her secretary George. George used the money as a down payment on a new house.
    c. On July 1, Laura loaned her father $200,000. Her father used the money to buy a franchise to open a yogurt store. He made $5,000 on the yogurt store during the current year.
    d. On January 1, Laura loaned $50,000 to Lotta, Inc. Laura is the sole shareholder of Lotta, Inc., which is organized as a corporation.

60. On January 1, Wilton loaned Andy $80,000. The loan is to be repaid in 5 years with no interest charged. The applicable federal rate is 6%. Discuss the treatment of the loan for both Wilton and Andy in each of the following independent situations:
    a. Andy is Wilton's son, and he used the loan to purchase a new home. Andy had no sources of investment income during the year.
    b. Andy is Wilton's son, and he used the loan to purchase some investment property. Andy's net income from all investments for the year was $3,000.
    c. Assume the same facts as in part b, except that Andy is an employee of Wilton's.
    d. Assume the same facts as in part b, except that Andy is a shareholder in Wilton's corporation, which made the loan to Andy.

61. Determine whether the following taxpayers have taxable income from the payment of their expenses:
    a. Julia's mother, Henrietta, was short of cash when it came time to pay her property taxes. Julia paid Henrietta's property taxes of $350.
    b. Kurt fell sleep at the wheel one night and crashed his car into a telephone pole. Repairs to the car cost $600. Kurt wasn't covered by insurance and didn't have the cash to pay the repair shop. Because he needed his car in his job as a salesman, his employer paid the repair bill.
    c. Leonard leased a building from the PLC Partnership for $800 per month. The lease agreement required Leonard to pay the property taxes of $1,100 on the building.
    d. On July 1, Gino bought some land from Harco Corporation for $14,000. As part of the sales agreement, Gino agreed to pay the property taxes of $700 for the year. Harco had paid $10,000 for the land.

62. Randy worked during the summer for Yardco Yard Service. Randy was paid $3,400 in cash compensation by Yardco. In addition to the cash payments, Yardco gave Randy a truck worth $800 and agreed to pay Randy's college tuition of $1,300 as part of his compensation package. How much gross income does Randy have from this arrangement?

63. Aziza is the sole owner of Azi's Fast Pizza. During the current year, Azi's replaces its fleet of delivery vehicles. Aziza's son purchases one of the old vehicles for $500, its tax basis to Azi's. Similar vehicles are sold for $4,000. What tax problem is posed by this situation? Explain who, if anyone, should report income from the transaction.

64. Determine whether the taxpayer has income that is subject to taxation in each of the following situations:
    a. Capital Motor Co. is going out of business. As a result, June is able to purchase a car for $13,000; its original sticker price was $22,000.
    b. Chuck is the sole owner of Ransom, Inc., a corporation. Chuck purchases a machine from Ransom for $8,000. Ransom had paid $44,000 for the machine, which was worth $30,000 at the time of the sale to Chuck.
    c. Gerry is an elementary school teacher. She receives the Teacher of the Month Award for the month of February. As part of the award, she gets to drive a new car supplied by a local dealer for a month. The rental value of the car is $350 per month.
    d. Payne has worked for Stewart Co. for the last 25 years. On the 25th anniversary of his employment with Stewart, he receives a set of golf clubs worth $900 as a reward for his years of loyal service to the company.
    e. Anna entered a sweepstakes contest that was advertised on the back of a cereal box. She was recently informed that she has won $20,000 in the contest. The prize will be paid out in 10 annual installments of $2,000. She receives her first check this year.
    f. Terry buys an antique vase at an estate auction for $780. Upon returning home, she accidentally drops the vase and finds that a $100 bill had been taped inside it.

65. Pedro purchases 50 shares of Piper Co. stock on February 19, 1994, at a cost of $4,300. Pedro sells the 50 shares on July 2, 1996, for $8,200. On March 14, 1996, Pedro purchases 100 shares of Troxel stock for $9,700. He sells the Troxel shares on December 18, 1996, for $6,600. What is the effect of the stock sales on Pedro's 1996 income?

66. Jawan has the following capital gains and losses for 1996:

Short-term capital gain	$ 500
Short-term capital loss	2,000
Long-term capital gain	6,000
Long-term capital loss	10,000

What is the effect of the capital gains and losses on Jawan's 1996 income?

67. Refer to problem 66. In 1997, Jawan has the following capital gains and losses:

Short-term capital gain	$3,200
Long-term capital gain	7,300
Long-term capital loss	6,000

What is the effect of the capital gains and losses on his 1997 income?

68. Clark and Jill are married and have an eight-year-old daughter. During the current year, they sell land for $135,000. They had purchased the land as an investment three years ago for $85,000. Their other income and deduction items for the current year are

Jill's salary	$96,000
Clark's salary	67,000
Interest and dividend income	6,000
Short-term loss on sale of White, Inc., stock	(13,000)
Deductions for adjusted gross income	4,500
Total itemized deductions	18,500

Calculate Clark and Jill's taxable income and income tax liability for the current year. Do they obtain any tax relief on the sale of the land?

69. Ozzello Property Management is organized as a partnership. The owners, Lorenzo, Erwin, and Michelle, share profits and losses 20:30:50. Ozzello has the following results for the current year:

Management fees	$230,000
Long-term gain on sale of investments	22,000
Short-term loss on sale of investments	(4,000)
Salaries paid to employees	67,000
Office rent	43,000
Office expenses	19,000

Determine each partner's share of Ozzello's taxable income for the current year.

70. Ramona owns 20% of the stock of Miller, Inc. Miller reports the following items for the current year:

Sales	$3,400,000
Gain on sale of stock held for 2 years	250,000
Cost of goods sold	1,800,000
Operating expenses	900,000
Dividends paid to stockholders	180,000

What are the effects on Ramona's taxable income if Miller, Inc., is organized as
a. A corporation?
b. An S corporation?

71. Chloe and Emma start a new business, Cement Sidewalks and Accessories (CSA), during the current year. CSA is organized as a partnership. Chloe and Emma come to your firm for advice on the tax consequences of their business. Your supervisor gives you the following information, as prepared by Chloe and Emma for their first year of operation:

Sales	$190,000
Cost of materials	(90,000)
Labor costs	(80,000)
Other expenses	(40,000)
Loss on sale of stock	(12,000)
Cash withdrawals by partners	(60,000)
Loss	$(92,000)

Prepare a memo for your supervisor explaining the ramifications of CSA's first-year results for Chloe's and Emma's tax liabilities.

72. Caine opens a consulting business after leaving his previous employer in September. During the remainder of 1996, he records the following:

	Amount Earned	Cash Received	Liability Incurred	Cash Paid
Consulting revenue	$35,000	$25,000		
Supplies, utilities, etc.			$14,000	$12,000
Wages of secretary			5,600	5,000
Equipment purchased			15,000	6,000

The allowable depreciation on the equipment for tax purposes is $3,000.
   a. What is Caine's taxable income if he elects the cash method of accounting?
   b. What is Caine's taxable income if he elects the accrual method of accounting?
   c. Which method would you recommend that he elect? Why?

73. Bonnie opens a computer sales and repair service during 1996. Her records show the following for 1996:

	Sales Made	Cash Received	Liability Incurred	Cash Paid
Repair revenue	$21,000	$17,500		
Computer sales	18,000	11,500		
Computer purchases			$45,000	$20,000
Employee wages			13,000	12,000
Supplies, utilities, etc.			7,000	6,500

Bonnie has computers on hand on December 31 that cost $36,000 and have a retail selling price of $49,000.

   Bonnie needs help figuring her taxable income for 1996. Is more than one income figure possible for 1996? If so, explain why, and compute taxable income under the various methods.

74. Arlene is a lawyer. She began the current year with $8,000 in accounts receivable from customers. During the year, she billed customers $180,000 in fees and received $140,000 in payments on account. During the year, she wrote off $12,000 of the receivables as being uncollectable, leaving her a year-end receivable balance of $36,000. What is Arlene's gross income if
   a. She uses the cash basis of accounting?
   b. She uses the accrual basis of accounting?

75. Determine how much interest income Later Federal Loan Co., a cash basis taxpayer, must recognize on each of the following loans in 1996:
   a. A $10,000, 8.5%, 6-month loan made on October 1, 1996. The principal and interest are due on April 1, 1997.
   b. A $10,000, 6-month loan, discounted at 8% on October 1, 1996. Later gives the borrower $9,615, and the borrower must repay the $10,000 face amount on April 1, 1997.
   c. A $10,000, 2-year loan, discounted at 6% on October 1, 1996. Later gives the borrower $8,900; the $10,000 face amount is to be repaid on October 1, 1998.

76. In January 1996, Conan, a cash basis taxpayer, purchases for $4,000 a Series EE savings bond with a maturity value of $4,800 (a 6% annual yield). At the same time, he also purchases for $5,000 a 3-year bank certificate of deposit with a maturity value of $6,650 (a 10% annual yield). Both securities mature in 1998. Must Conan recognize any income in 1996? How much income must Conan recognize in 1998?

77. Lorene, Inc., owns an apartment complex. The terms of Lorene's lease agreement require new tenants to pay the first and last month's rent as well as a cleaning deposit at the inception of the lease. The cleaning deposit is returned when tenants move out and leave their apartment in good condition. If the apartment is not in good condition, Lorene hires a cleaning company and uses the tenant's deposit to pay the cleaning bill, with any excess deposit returned.

   During 1996, Lorene receives monthly rents totaling $38,000, last month's rent deposits from new tenants of $14,000, and security deposits of $7,000. Lorene keeps $5,000 in cleaning deposits to pay the cleaning company bill on apartments that are not left in good shape (the $5,000 is the actual cost that is paid in cash to the cleaning company) and returns $4,000 in deposits. Lorene's expenses (other than the cleaning costs) related to the rental property are $28,000. What is Lorene, Inc.'s 1996 gross income from the rental property if Lorene is a cash basis taxpayer? an accrual basis taxpayer?

78. The A.B. Partnership constructed a commercial building at a cost of $320,000. A.B. rented the building to Harko Storage Co.. Harko signed a 20-year lease that required Harko to pay $33,000 per year in rent. In addition, Harko was required under the lease to pay A.B.'s annual property taxes on the building. The property taxes were estimated at $5,500 per year. The terms of the lease also stipulated that any permanent improvements to the building would remain A.B.'s, and Harko would not be reimbursed for any such expenditures. Harko installed carpeting, fixtures, and other improvements costing $30,000. How much income must the A.B. Partnership recognize from the lease in the first year? the last year?

79. Determine the proper year(s) for reporting the income in each of the following cases:
   a. Lagoon Inc., an accrual basis taxpayer, owns an amusement park. The park is open April through September. In October, Lagoon begins selling discounted season passes for the upcoming season. By the end of the year, Lagoon has received $40,000 from the advance sale of the discounted passes.
   b. Arnie sells and repairs televisions. In December of the current year, a customer special-ordered a television set that retails for $2,600 (Arnie's cost is $1,300). Arnie required the customer to prepay $1,500 as a condition of placing the order.
   c. Quick Systems, Inc., an accrual basis taxpayer, leases out computer equipment. During December, Quick receives $22,000 from customers as advance rent for January.
   d. Trinh is a service representative for Harrington Corporation. Trinh and Harrington are cash basis taxpayers. In addition to her salary, Trinh receives a bonus equal to 5% of all receipts collected from her customers during the year. On December 30, a customer gives her a $5,000 check payable to Harrington for Trinh's work during the current year. Trinh returns to her office on January 3 and promptly gives the check to the company's controller.

80. How much income would an accrual basis taxpayer report in 1996 in each of the following situations?
   a. Toby's Termite Services, Inc., provides monthly pest control on a contract basis. Toby sells a 1-year contract for $600 and a 2-year contract for $1,100. In October, Toby sells 10 one-year contracts and 5 two-year contracts.
   b. John's Tractor Sales receives a $150 deposit from a customer for a new tractor that the customer orders in December. The tractor arrives the following February, at which time the customer pays the remaining $9,800 of the agreed-upon sales price.
   c. A customer of First Financial Lending sends First Financial two $600 checks in December in payment of December and January interest on a loan.
   d. First Financial Lending receives interest payments totaling $8,400 in January 1997 in payment of December 1996 interest on loans.

81. Daryl purchases some land in 1992 at a cost of $60,000. In 1996, he sells the land for $100,000.
   a. How much gain (loss) does Daryl realize on the sale of the land?
   b. Assume that the sales contract on the land calls for the buyer to pay Daryl $40,000 at the time of sale and $15,000 per year for the next 4 years with interest on the unpaid balance at 8%. How much income must Daryl recognize in 1996? in 1997?

82. In 1993, Patricia purchases a rental property as an investment at a cost of $66,000. From 1993 through 1996, she takes $6,000 in depreciation on the property. In 1996, she sells the property for $50,000.
    a. How much gain (loss) does Patricia realize on the sale of the rental property?
    b. Assume that the sales contract on the rental property calls for the buyer to pay Patricia $10,000 per year for 5 years with interest on the unpaid balance at 10%. How much income (loss) must Patricia recognize in 1996?

83. Assume the same facts as in problem 82, except that Patricia sells the rental property for $80,000, payable at $20,000 per year for 4 years with interest on the unpaid balance at 10%. How much income (loss) must Patricia recognize in 1996?

    Assume that in addition to the sale of the rental property, Patricia sells other capital assets that result in a loss of $26,000. What would you recommend that Patricia do regarding the gain on the sale of the rental property?

84. WCM Builders enters into a contract to build a shopping mall in 1996 for $4,000,000. Completion of the mall is expected to take 2 years and cost WCM $3,000,000. Upon signing the contract, WCM receives $500,000. During 1996, WCM incurs costs of $1,200,000 and receives a $1,000,000 progress payment. WCM's forewoman estimates that the job is 50% complete at the end of 1996. How much income must WCM recognize in 1996 from work done on the mall?

85. Quapaw Construction Co. entered into an agreement with Paine County to resurface 30 miles of highway. The contract was for $600,000. Quapaw estimated its total cost of the project to be $450,000. During the current year, Quapaw completed 12 miles of resurfacing, incurred $150,000 in actual costs, and received $300,000 in advance payments on the project. How much income will Quapaw have to recognize during the current year?

DISCUSSION CASES

86. Yung is the sole owner of Southern Hills Insurance Agency. Yung's primary business is the sale of fire and casualty policies. He has recently expanded his business by selling life insurance policies. Under his agreement with Heart Life Insurance Co., he receives a basic commission on each policy he sells. The basic commission is equal to the cost of the insurance minus the first year's premium. Under the agreement, Yung collects the cost of the insurance policy and remits the first-year premium to the company. He is also entitled to an override commission, which is paid on subsequent years' premiums. To build up his life insurance business, Yung enters into separate contracts with clients in which he agrees to act as an insurance consultant for a fee that is equal to the first-year premium. The client pays Yung the fee, which he remits to Heart Life. This contract effectively waives Yung's basic commission and offers the insurance at a discounted price, a practice that is illegal under state law. During the current year, Yung sold policies that had a cost of $50,000 and first-year premiums of $18,000 (which were remitted to Heart Life). He also received $11,000 in override commissions from policies sold in previous years. How much income must Yung report from the life insurance policies in the current year? Explain.

87. Kerry is employed as a ticket vendor at an off-track betting parlor in New York. No credit is extended to customers, and employees are not allowed to bet on races. Kerry is a compulsive gambler and occasionally places bets without paying for them. In the past, she has always managed to cover her bets without being detected by her employer. Earlier this year, Kerry ran up $80,000 in bets that she did not pay for and won only $33,000. She was unable to cover this large loss and turned herself in to her employer. Kerry was convicted of grand larceny and sentenced to five years of probation, required to perform 200 hours of community service, and pay a $500 fine. Her employer was liable to the racetrack for the bets she made and obtained a judgment against her for the $47,000 shortfall it had to pay because of her indiscretions. How much, if any, gross income must Kerry recognize from her illegal betting?

88. Nick and Jolene are married. Nick is 61 and retired in 1994 from his job with Amalgamated Co. Jolene is 56 and works part time as a special education teacher. Nick and Jolene have a substantial amount of investment savings and would like to reorganize it to achieve the best after-tax return on their investments. They give you the following list of projected cash receipts for 1996:

Jolene's salary	$13,000
Nick's pension—fully taxable	11,000
Interest income	4,000
Dividend income	4,000
Social Security benefits	7,000
Farmer's Fund annuity	6,000

In addition, Nick tells you that he owns a duplex that he rents out. The duplex rents for 1996 are $18,000, and Nick estimates expenses of $22,000 related to the duplex. The annuity was purchased 18 years ago for $20,000. The annuity pays $500 per month for 10 years.

Nick and Jolene's investments consist of the following:

6-month certificates of deposit (CD) 2,000 + 2,000 = 4000	$100,000
1,000 shares of Lardee's common stock (current market value = $7 per share, projected 1996 dividend = $1 per share)—cost	10,000
2,000 shares of Corb Co. common stock Div income 1,000 (current market value = $40 per share, projected 1996 dividend = $1.50 per share)—cost Div income 3,000	20,000

1. Assuming that Nick and Jolene have total allowable itemized deductions of $7,300 in 1996 and that they have no dependents, determine their 1996 taxable income and tax liability based on the projections they gave you.

2. The 6-month CDs consist of two separate $50,000 certificates, both of which yield 4% interest. One CD matures on January 3, 1996. Nick's banker tells him that he can renew the CD for one year at 4%. Nick's stockbroker tells him that he can purchase tax-exempt bonds with a yield of 3%. Nick would like you to determine whether the tax-exempt bonds provide him a better after-tax return than the CD.   p-261

3. Jolene is concerned that they are not getting the best return on their Corb Co. stock. When they purchased the stock in 1985, the $1 per share dividend at that time was yielding 10% before taxes. However, the rise in market value has far out-paced the dividend growth, and they are yielding only 3.75%, based on the current market value. Jolene thinks they should sell the stock and either purchase the 3% tax-exempt securities or the 4% CD, if it would be a better deal from an income tax viewpoint. Calculate the tax effect on their 1996 income of selling the shares, and determine whether they should sell the shares and invest the after-tax proceeds in tax-exempt securities or the 4% CD. Do this calculation after you have determined the best option regarding the CD that matures in January.

89. The Gallery is an indoor recreational facility. It employs 95 minimum-wage employees and 7 management-level staffers. During the past month, all employees participated in a promotion to enhance sales by distributing discount coupons to potential customers. The employee who had the most coupons redeemed was to receive a $150 credit toward the purchase of a mountain bike. The general manager won the coupon promotion. After accepting the $150 credit, he instructed the controller, Aretha, not to include the $150 on his pay stub or on his Form W-2. Aretha is a CPA and a member of the AICPA. You prepare the tax return for the gallery. Aretha has advised you of the situation regarding the general manager; she is concerned about the effect on her career of following the general manager's instructions. Prepare a letter to Aretha explaining the potential ramifications effects of following the general manager's instructions and what actions, if any, she should take to avoid adverse career effects.

Income Exclusions

▲ CHAPTER LEARNING OBJECTIVES

■ Discuss the requirements for the exclusion of an item of income.

■ Explain the rationale for excluding items from gross income.

■ Identify the allowable exclusions for donative items of income: gifts, inheritances, life insurance proceeds, scholarships, and certain death benefits.

■ Describe the effect of employment-related exclusions on the after-tax compensation of employees.

■ Discuss the nontaxable fringe benefits that a business may provide to its employees.

■ Identify payments that represent returns of human capital and are excluded from income as capital recoveries: workers' compensation, damage payments for personal injuries, and medical expense reimbursement payments.

■ Discuss the exclusions from income allowed for investment-related items: municipal bond interest, stock dividends, discharge of indebtedness, and improvements by a lessee.

▲ CONCEPT REVIEW ▲

Administrative convenience   Those items for which the cost of compliance would exceed the revenue generated are not taxed.

All-inclusive income   All income received is taxable unless a specific provision can be found in the tax law that either excludes the income from taxation or defers its recognition to a future tax year.

Basis   This is the amount of unrecovered investment in an asset. As amounts are expended and/or recovered relative to an asset over time, the basis is adjusted in consideration of such changes. The **adjusted basis** of an asset is the original basis, plus or minus the changes in the amount of unrecovered investment.

Capital recovery   No income is realized until the taxpayer receives more than the amount invested to produce the income. The amount invested in an asset represents the maximum amount recoverable.

Claim of right   A realization occurs whenever an amount is received without any restriction as to its disposition.

Legislative grace   Any tax relief provided is the result of a specific act of Congress that must be strictly applied and interpreted. All income received is taxable unless a specific provision can be found in the tax law that excludes the income from taxation. Deductions must be approached with the philosophy that nothing is deductible unless a provision in the tax law allows the deduction.

Realization   No income (or loss) is recognized until it has been realized. A realization involves a change in the form and/or the substance of a taxpayer's property rights that results from an arm's-length transaction.

Substance over form   Transactions are to be taxed according to their true intention rather than some form that may have been contrived.

Tax benefit rule   Any deduction taken in a prior year that is recovered in a subsequent year is income in the year of recovery, to the extent that a tax benefit was received from the deduction.

Wherewithal-to-pay   Income is recognized in the period in which the taxpayer has the means to pay the tax on the income.

INTRODUCTION

After identifying all the sources of income received during an accounting period, the next step in calculating taxable income is determining which, if any, of the income sources do not have to be included in the current period's gross income. This step requires identification of income items that are subject to exclusion or deferral. The all-inclusive income concept considers taxable any income received unless a specific provision can be found that exempts the item from taxation. Under the legislative grace concept, only Congress can provide such tax relief. In addition, tax relief provisions are strictly applied and interpreted, thereby explicitly limiting the scope of any tax relief provision to that which Congress intended.

Congress has chosen to exempt certain items that meet the definition of *gross income* for several reasons. Some of the relief provisions are designed as equity measures that relieve the item from double taxation. Other provisions are meant as incentives for taxpayers to engage in the activity. Most incentive provisions have as their goal some social objective, such as encouraging firms to provide medical coverage for their employees. As the provisions are introduced, the chapter states the rationale for providing the relief.

This chapter discusses the most common exclusions found in the tax law. Because they represent exceptions to the general concepts of income recognition, exclusions are an area of the tax law that can be mastered only through exposure and study. The more you encounter and work with these items, the more familiar they will become. In addition, this chapter introduces several common deferral provisions. Recall from Chapter 1 that the difference between an exclusion and a deferral of income is that an exclusion is permanent—it is never subject to taxation.

On the other hand, a deferral is not taxed in the current period but will be taxed in some future period(s). Most deferrals are a result of the wherewithal-to-pay concept and are not taxed currently, because the transaction has not produced the cash with which to pay the tax.

Exhibit 4–1 lists the titles of the Internal Revenue Code sections that allow the various exclusions. As you can see from the list, the number of exclusions and the topics they cover is formidable. The discussion in this chapter focuses on those exclusions that have the widest application. To provide a frame of reference for your study of exclusions, they are grouped into four categories: donative items, employment-related exclusions, returns of human capital, and investment-related exclusions.

DONATIVE ITEMS

Items in this category are receipts of wealth that the receiver has not earned and for which no future services are to be rendered as a result of the transfer, nor are they the result of an investment. Because they represent realized increases in

▲ **Exhibit 4–1**

INCOME EXCLUSIONS BY INTERNAL REVENUE CODE SECTION

Sec. 101	Certain death benefits
Sec. 102	Gifts and inheritances
Sec. 103	Interest on state and local bonds
Sec. 104	Compensation for injuries or sickness
Sec. 105	Amounts received under accident and health plans
Sec. 106	Contributions by employer to accident and health plans
Sec. 107	Rental value of parsonages
Sec. 108	Income from discharge of indebtedness
Sec. 109	Improvements by lessee on lessor's property
Sec. 111	Recovery of tax benefit items
Sec. 112	Certain combat pay of members of the armed forces
Sec. 115	Income of states, municipalities, etc.
Sec. 117	Qualified scholarships
Sec. 118	Contributions to the capital of a corporation
Sec. 119	Meals or lodging furnished for the convenience of the employer
Sec. 120	Amounts received under group legal services plans
Sec. 121	One-time exclusion of gain from sale of principal residence by individual who has attained age 55
Sec. 122	Certain reduced uniformed services retirement pay
Sec. 123	Amounts received under insurance contracts for certain living expenses
Sec. 125	Cafeteria plans
Sec. 126	Certain cost-sharing payments
Sec. 127	Educational assistance programs
Sec. 129	Dependent care assistance programs
Sec. 130	Certain personal injury liability assignments
Sec. 131	Certain foster care payments
Sec. 132	Certain fringe benefits
Sec. 133	Interest on certain loans used to acquire employer securities
Sec. 134	Certain military benefits
Sec. 135	Income from United States savings bond used to pay higher education tuition and fees
Sec. 136	Energy conservation subsidies provided by public utilities

wealth, items in this class fit the definition of *income*. However, Congress has determined that such items should not be taxed either for equity or incentive reasons. Donative items include gifts and inheritances, life insurance proceeds, scholarships, and certain death benefits.

Gifts

The value of property acquired by **gift** has been excluded from income taxation since 1913. Gifts received are not subject to income taxation;[1] however, the donor (person making the gift) is subject to the gift tax rules on the making of a gift. Thus, the exclusion of gifts from income tax is an equity measure that prevents a double tax on a gift. However, neither Congress nor the Treasury has ever attempted to provide a strict definition of what constitutes a gift. The most authoritative definition was developed by the U.S. Supreme Court in 1960:

> A gift in the statutory sense, . . . proceeds from a detached and disinterested generosity, . . . out of affection, respect, admiration, charity, or like impulses, . . . And in this regard, the most critical consideration, as the Court was agreed in the leading case here, is the transferor's "intention." . . . What controls is the intention with which payment, however voluntary, has been made.[2]

In the majority of situations, the intention to make a gift is clear. People make gifts to friends and relatives all the time "out of affection, respect, admiration, charity, or like impulses" with no expectation of any consideration in return.

▲ **EXAMPLE 1**   Odom gives his daughter Althea a new car worth $18,000 when she graduates from college. Does Althea have taxable income from the receipt of the car?

Discussion: It is unlikely that Odom is attempting to compensate his daughter; he gave her the car out of affection and respect for her accomplishments, and it therefore constitutes an excludable gift.

Recall that the legislative grace concept requires a strict application and interpretation of the exclusion for gifts. Thus, only the receipt of a gift is a nontaxable event; any subsequent earnings from property received as a gift are subject to taxation. Subsequent earnings may be in the form of income flows from the property (interest, dividends, rents, royalties, etc.) or gains from the sale of the property.

▲ **EXAMPLE 2**   For Christmas, Zane's uncle Bob gives him 100 shares of ABC Co. stock that has a fair market value of $200. Sometime later, Zane receives a cash dividend of $50 on the stock. Does Zane have any taxable income from the stock?

Discussion: The receipt of the stock is a gift, the value of which is excluded from Zane's income. However, the exclusion applies only to the receipt of the gift; any subsequent earnings on the gift property are subject to tax. Thus, Zane must include the $50 dividend in his taxable income. NOTE: If the dividend had already been declared when Bob made the gift, Bob would have been taxed on the dividend under the assignment-of-income doctrine. Under such circumstances, the cash dividend would have been an additional gift.

The major problem with gifts involves gifts made in a business setting. Per the standard outlined, the donor's intent in making the gift is controlling. That is, if the gift was meant to be compensation for past, present, or future services, the gift is not really a gift but is taxable as compensation.

▲ **EXAMPLE 3** Over the years, Albert has provided Phillip with the names of many potential customers. Albert has never asked Phillip for anything but his friendship in return. In 1996, Phillip has a particularly good year and decides to give Albert a new automobile worth $20,000 for being such a good friend through the years. Does Albert have income from the receipt of the automobile?

Discussion: On similar facts, in 1960 the Supreme Court held that the automobile did not constitute a gift, although both parties testified that nothing was owed between the two and that the automobile was meant to be a present. The Court felt that the nature of their past relationship indicated that the automobile was either compensation for past customer leads or an inducement to Albert to continue providing such information in the future.

As example 3 illustrates, gifts between individuals who also engage in business with one another are always suspect. In most cases, such "gifts" have some compensatory element to them and as such do not meet the income tax definition of a gift. Note that the treatment of business gifts is an application of the substance-over-form doctrine, which taxes transactions according to their true intention rather than their technical form.

Inheritances

As with gifts, the value of property received by **inheritance** has been excluded from taxation since 1913. The rationale for exclusion also follows that for a gift—property held in an estate is subject to an estate tax; thus, the income tax exclusion for inheritances avoids a double taxation of the property of a deceased taxpayer. There are no particular problems in this area. Remember, the legislative grace concept requires that exclusions be strictly applied. In the case of inherited property, the exclusion is limited to the value of property received. Any subsequent earnings from the inherited property are not excludable.[3]

▲ **EXAMPLE 4** Elinor receives 100 shares of Pleasing Pools common stock worth $6,000 from the estate of her uncle Frank. She subsequently receives dividends totaling $200 on the stock. What are the tax effects for Elinor of receiving the stock?

Discussion: Elinor is not taxed on the $6,000 value of the stock received from the inheritance. However, she is taxed on the income received from the stock subsequent to its receipt and must include the $200 dividend in her gross income.

▲ **EXAMPLE 5** Elinor holds the stock she received from her uncle's estate for two years, at which time she sells it for $8,500. Does Elinor have a taxable gain from the sale of the stock?

Discussion: Elinor is taxed on the gain from the sale of the stock. Her taxable gain is $2,500 ($8,500 − $6,000). Note that the $6,000 fair market value of the stock received from the estate becomes Elinor's basis. Because the value of the inheritance (in this case $6,000) must never be taxed, it is permanently excluded from income. Therefore, under the capital recovery concept, Elinor does not have income unless she receives more than $6,000 for the stock upon disposition.

Life Insurance Proceeds

Payments from life insurance upon the death of the insured are generally excluded from income tax,[4] although **life insurance proceeds** may be included in the decedent's gross estate and subject to the estate tax. Life insurance proceeds resemble inheritances, which are excluded from taxation. Thus, the exclusion of life insurance proceeds provides equity with other forms of inherited property.

▲ **EXAMPLE 6**   Alice's husband Ralph dies this year. Ralph has a $200,000 life insurance policy that names Alice as the beneficiary. Alice invests the $200,000 in a certificate of deposit that earns 6% annually. What are the tax effects of the receipt of the $200,000 for Alice?

Discussion: The receipt of the $200,000 face value of the policy is excludable under the provision for receipt of life insurance proceeds. However, the subsequent earnings on the proceeds, $12,000 per year, are subject to tax.

The life insurance proceeds exclusion applies to such payments even if the payments are received in installments, although any earnings included in the installment payments are taxable.

▲ **EXAMPLE 7**   Assume the same facts as in example 6, except that Alice elects to take the proceeds in installments of $32,000 per year for 10 years. What are the tax consequences of the receipt of the annual installments?

Discussion: The $200,000 face value of the policy is excludable. However, Alice will receive a total of $320,000 under the installment plan. Thus, she must recognize the $120,000 ($320,000 − $200,000) in earnings as they are received. The payments are in the form of an annuity, so the annuity formula described in Chapter 3 is used to determine the taxable portion of each payment:

Annuity Exclusion Formula

$$\text{Amount excluded} = \frac{\text{Cost of contract}}{\text{Expected return}} \times \text{Payment received}$$

$$\text{Amount excluded} = \frac{\$200,000}{\$320,000} \times \$32,000 = \$20,000$$

$$\text{Taxable amount} = \$32,000 - \$20,000 = \$12,000$$

Note that this treatment is consistent with the treatment in example 6. In both cases, Alice invests the $200,000 proceeds at a 6% annual return. In example 7, the fact that she makes the investment with the insurance company does not provide her with any tax relief. It is taxed as any investment of the proceeds would be taxed.

An exception to the exclusion for life insurance proceeds is made for amounts paid to the owner of a policy that was obtained for a consideration (i.e., purchased). That is, if a taxpayer purchases or otherwise obtains for some valuable consideration a policy on the life of another, the receipt of the insurance proceeds is considered the realization of an investment.

▲ **EXAMPLE 8**   Athena owned a life insurance policy on herself that had a face value of $50,000. During a financial crisis, she assigned the proceeds of the policy to Helena for $10,000. Helena subsequently paid premiums on the policy totaling $20,000 before Athena died. What is the tax effect of Helena's receipt of the $50,000 life insurance proceeds?

Discussion: Because Helena purchased the policy for a consideration, she is taxable on the receipt of the $50,000. Under the capital recovery concept, she is allowed to recover her $30,000 investment in the policy before she recognizes any income. Therefore, she has a realized and recognized gain of $20,000 on the receipt of the life insurance proceeds.

This exception to the life insurance exclusion provisions does not apply to policies owned by partners or partnerships in which the insured is a partner or a corporation in which the insured is an officer or a shareholder. Payments on such contracts are excluded, because they are deemed to be for legitimate business purposes rather than for speculative gain. This type of life insurance is usually used to fund buy-out agreements on the death of a partner or a key employee and are necessary to ensure continuation of the business in most cases.

▲ **EXAMPLE 9**   Nina and Chen are partners in a consulting business. The business has been highly profitable, and each has a considerable equity interest in the partnership. When they realize that paying off each other's estate in the event of death would drain the business of all its resources, the partnership purchases life insurance payable to the partnership for $500,000 on both Nina and Chen. After several years, Chen dies in an automobile accident, and the partnership receives the $500,000. At that time, Chen's equity in the partnership is $400,000, which is paid to his estate. Is the partnership in receipt of taxable income?

Discussion: Because the partnership is the owner of the policy that was taken out for legitimate business reasons (to ensure continuity of the business), the $500,000 received by the partnership is excluded from taxation. Note that this is the case even though only $400,000 was required to settle Chen's account. The $100,000 windfall for the partnership remains tax free.

Scholarships

A college student who is a candidate for a degree may exclude the value of a **scholarship,** provided that the award does not require the student to perform any future services such as teaching, grading papers, or tutoring.[5] That is, the scholarship must be gratuitous in nature and not merely a form of compensation for past, present, or future services.

▲ **EXAMPLE 10**   Diane received a $1,000 scholarship to the College of Agriculture. The college gives such scholarships annually to students in the top 10% of their class. There are no other criteria or obligations for the receipt of the scholarship. Is the scholarship eligible for exclusion?

Discussion: Because the scholarship is based solely on merit and does not require Diane to provide any services to the college, it is eligible for the exclusion for scholarships.

▲ **EXAMPLE 11**   Peggy received a graduate assistant scholarship from the School of Accounting to aid her in her graduate studies. As part of the scholarship, which pays $300 per month, she is to work for an accounting professor for 10 hours per week, grading papers and assisting the professor in her duties. Is the scholarship eligible for exclusion?

Discussion: Because Peggy is required to perform services in return for her scholarship, the $300 per month that she receives is not eligible for exclusion as a scholarship.

The amount of the exclusion is limited to the direct costs of the student's college education. Direct costs consist of the student's tuition, fees, books, supplies, and other equipment required for the student's course of instruction.[6] Amounts received in excess of the direct costs of the education are taxable. This puts students receiving scholarships on an equal footing with nonstudents regarding personal living expenses. That is, individuals are not allowed to deduct personal living expenses. Therefore, students who receive amounts for personal living expenses must include such amounts in income in order to provide equity with nonstudents, who are effectively taxed on income they spend for personal living expenses. Thus, scholarships that are specified as being for the payment of a student's room and board are fully taxable.

▲ **EXAMPLE 12**   Henrietta receives a scholarship for $10,000 to attend Local University. The cost of her tuition, books, fees, and supplies total $9,000 for the year. How much of the $10,000 scholarship is taxable?

Discussion: Henrietta may exclude only the $9,000 she spent on the direct costs of her college education. The remaining $1,000 is included in her gross income.

Certain Death Benefits

When an employee dies, the employer often makes payments to surviving dependents to help them out financially while they adjust to life without the income of the deceased. As such, the payments may constitute an excludable gift. However, it is often difficult to determine whether such payments meet the income tax definition of a gift. In order to eliminate some of the uncertainty surrounding **death benefit payments,** the tax law allows one $5,000 exclusion for death benefits paid to a deceased employee's beneficiaries. In order to qualify for this exclusion, the payment must be made solely because of death and cannot represent payment for services performed before the employee died.[7] If more than $5,000 is paid to more than one beneficiary, the $5,000 exclusion must be taken pro rata among the beneficiaries.[8] That is, the total amount of excludable death benefit payments cannot exceed $5,000.

▲ **EXAMPLE 13**   Shiro is an agent for All Farmers Insurance Co. until his death. Shortly after his death, All Farmers pays his widow Yoko $2,000 in commissions he earned before he died and $5,000 as a death benefit. In addition, each of his 2 children is paid $2,500 in death benefits. How much of the $12,000 ($2,000 + $5,000 + $2,500 + $2,500) paid as a result of Shiro's death may be excluded from income of the beneficiaries?

Discussion: The $2,000 in commissions was earned by Shiro before he died and is not a payment made because of his death. Therefore, the $2,000 is not eligible for exclusion. The $5,000 death benefit exclusion must be allocated pro rata among the 3 beneficiaries. Yoko will exclude $2,500, and each of their children will exclude $1,250:

$$\text{Total death benefits paid} = \$5,000 + \$2,500 + \$2,500 = \$10,000$$

Pro Rata Allocation of $5,000 Exclusion

Wife	($5,000 ÷ $10,000) × $5,000 = $2,500
Each child	($2,500 ÷ $10,000) × $5,000 = $1,250

Yoko is taxed on the remaining $2,500 of the payment she receives, and each child is taxed on the remaining $1,250 of the payment that each receives. NOTE: The total amount excluded cannot exceed $5,000, regardless of how much is paid out or to how many beneficiaries the payments are made.

EMPLOYMENT-RELATED EXCLUSIONS

The largest class of exclusions is certain payments made to or on behalf of an employee by an employer. This category of exclusions is costly in terms of the tax revenue lost to the government, because these payments are deductible by the employer and yield no tax revenue because of the exclusion from income granted the employee. These relief provisions are intended to provide equity in cases of double taxation and act as incentives to employers and employees to engage in the specified activity.

Foreign Earned Income

U.S. citizens are subject to tax on all income they receive, regardless of the source. Thus, taxes are levied on worldwide income. To provide relief from double taxation for U.S. citizens working in foreign countries, the tax law allows individuals two options. First, taxpayers may include the **foreign earned income** in their taxable income, calculate the U.S. tax on the income, and take a tax credit for any foreign taxes paid.[9] The amount of the allowable tax credit is the lesser of (1) the actual foreign taxes paid, or (2) the U.S. tax that would have been paid on the foreign earned income. Under the second option, individuals may exclude up to $70,000 in foreign earned income for each full year they work in a foreign country.[10] In order to take advantage of these options, an individual must be either a bonafide resident of the foreign country or must be present in the foreign country for 330 days in any 12 consecutive months. Selection of the most tax-advantageous option will depend on the amount of income earned abroad as well as the relative marginal tax rates between the foreign country and the United States. Thus, in order to select the optimal choice in a given situation, both options must be calculated to determine which option results in the lower net tax payable.

> ▲ **EXAMPLE 14**   Rollie works on a drilling rig in South America during all of the current year. He earns $80,000 from this job and pays $20,000 in tax to the appropriate South American government. Should he elect the tax credit or the exclusion option? Assume that he has sufficient other income from U.S. sources to make him a 31% marginal tax rate payer.
>
> *Discussion:*   Rollie should elect the option that minimizes the amount of U.S. tax paid on the foreign income. Under the tax credit option, the gross tax on the $80,000 would be $24,800 (31% × $80,000), and he would receive a tax credit for the $20,000 of foreign tax paid, resulting in a net U.S. tax of $4,800 ($24,800 − $20,000). Under the exclusion option, he pays no tax on $70,000 of excluded income. The remaining $10,000 of income not eligible for exclusion produces a tax of $3,100 (31% × $10,000). Therefore, the exclusion option results in a tax savings of $1,700 ($4,800 − $3,100).

Payments Made on Behalf of an Employee

Recall from the discussion of income sources in Chapter 3 that when one person pays the expenses of another in an employment setting, the person whose expenses were paid generally has taxable income. However, the tax law does exempt from taxation the payment of the following employee expenses by an employer:

- Payments to qualified pension plans
- Group term life insurance
- Health and accident insurance premiums
- Meals and lodging provided by the employer

The favorable tax treatment accorded these items has encouraged employers to provide more and more of an employee's compensation in the form of excludable fringe benefits. This is quite advantageous to the employee, as the following example illustrates:

▲ **EXAMPLE 15**   Lacy Corporation offers its employees various fringe-benefit package options. Under one of Lacy's options, the employee may participate in the company's accident and health insurance plan or may take the cost of the plan, $1,200 per year, in cash.

Discussion: As discussed later, health and accident insurance premiums paid by an employer on behalf of an employee are excludable from income. Assuming that an employee would ordinarily purchase such insurance, selection of this option effectively increases that person's after-tax compensation from Lacy Corporation by $1,200. An employee who elects to take the $1,200 in cash will be taxed on the receipt of cash. Assuming a 28% marginal tax rate, an employee taking the cash option would have only $864 [$1,200 − (28% × $1,200)] to purchase insurance after paying the tax. In most cases, the employee could not purchase a comparable insurance plan for this amount and would be worse off by electing the cash option.

This example illustrates the tremendous advantage of employer-provided benefits. Employees get benefits at no tax cost that they would otherwise purchase. This use of before-tax compensation can greatly increase the employee's effective pay rate. If the benefit is clear for the employee, what is the incentive for the employer to provide these tax-free benefits? The employer realizes a tax savings from a deduction for the payment of the tax-free benefit as an ordinary and necessary business expense, but it would get the same deduction for any form of compensation paid to the employee. The key for the employer is that the market for employees demands that each employee be paid a certain wage. Thus, the employer will pay the same price for labor, whether the payment is totally in cash or a combination of cash and tax-free benefits. Thus, it makes sense for firms to increase their effective compensation to employees by providing the tax-free benefits: $1,000 in cash compensation is not worth as much after taxes as the same $1,000 in compensation paid in the form of tax-free benefits. In this way, employers are able to increase their employees' real after-tax compensation without an increase in cash outflow. In addition, the tax-free fringe benefits are generally not subject to payroll taxes (e.g., Social Security, unemployment tax), reducing the cost of compensation for the employer.

Although some qualifications for exclusion are quite complex, the discussion that follows is designed to provide an overview of the tax-free benefits that an employer can provide to an employee. Therefore, most of the complexities involved in the exclusions are omitted.

Payments to Qualified Pension Plans.   The income tax law provides many different ways for individuals to provide for their retirement on a tax-deferred basis. Individuals who are not covered by an employer-provided pension plan can set up an individual retirement account (IRA) and deduct contributions made to the account for adjusted gross income.[11] Self-employed individuals are allowed to establish either an IRA or what is referred to as a *Keogh plan* and deduct amounts paid into the plan for adjusted gross income.[12] In addition to the tax deductions allowed for payments into such plans, any earnings on the assets in the plans are not subject to tax as the income is earned. Rather, the retirement plan is taxed when amounts are drawn from the plan. Thus, retirement plans defer current income until the taxpayer retires. The operation of IRAs and the deduction limits are discussed in Chapter 8.

Many companies provide pension plans for their employees. Several allowable variations of such plans permit employers and employees to make payments into the plans and receive the same tax treatment as IRA and Keogh plans. Such plans are referred to as **qualified pension plans.**[13] Payments made by an employer to an employee's account in a qualified pension plan are not taxable in the period in which the payments are made. The tax on such payments is deferred until the employee actually withdraws the payments from the plan.[14] As such, this is not a true exclusion on which a tax is never paid but a deferral of income-recognition to a future period. An added benefit of a qualified pension plan is that the *earnings* on amounts paid into such plans are not taxed until they are withdrawn by the employee. The deferral of income through pension plan payments is mentioned in this chapter because of the growing popularity of employer-sponsored pension plans as an employee fringe benefit.

> ▲ **EXAMPLE 16**   Linda is an employee of Ross Co. Ross has a qualified pension plan for its employees under which it contributes 5% of each employee's salary to the plan each year. Linda's salary for the current year is $30,000, resulting in a pension plan payment of $1,500. How is Linda taxed on the $1,500?
>
> *Discussion:*   Because Ross Co.'s plan is qualified, the $1,500 payment is not taxed to Linda in the current period. When Linda withdraws the $1,500 from the plan (either at retirement or when she leaves the company), she will be taxed on amounts paid into the plan by Ross as well as any earnings on the amounts in her pension plan.

In addition to the deferral of amounts paid into qualified pension plans by employers, employees may defer taxation of any amounts that they pay into such plans until they withdraw amounts from the plan.

> ▲ **EXAMPLE 17**   Assume that in example 16 Ross Co.'s pension plan allows employees to contribute up to 5% of their annual earnings to the plan. What is the tax effect to Linda if she contributes the maximum allowed under the plan?
>
> *Discussion:*   Linda can contribute a maximum of $1,500 of her $30,000 salary. Because Linda is not taxed on the contribution now, her gross salary from Ross Co. is reduced to $28,500 ($30,000 − $1,500) by the contribution to the plan. As with the employer's contribution, Linda will be taxed on her contribution when she withdraws it from the plan.

What is the benefit derived from payments to pension plans? First, by deferring tax on payments to the plan until a future period, a time value of money savings is effected on the tax being deferred. A second benefit is that the earnings in the plan accumulate tax free, allowing a larger buildup of funds at retirement than if the earnings were taxed as they were earned. Last, employees often have less income when they retire, resulting in a tax on the deferred income at a lower marginal tax rate.

Group Term Life Insurance.   One of the most popular employee benefits is the exclusion of the premiums paid by an employer on the first $50,000 face amount of **group term life insurance.** This exclusion is available only for term insurance that is provided to a group of employees on a nondiscriminatory basis.[15] Payments made on whole life policies, term insurance purchased for individuals (not a group policy), or plans that discriminate in favor of highly compensated individuals are not eligible for exclusion. The intention of this provision is to encourage employers to provide life insurance to all their employees so that their families have a cushion if the employee dies while still working (a social goal). If an employee's qualified group term policy has a face value greater than $50,000, the premiums paid on the coverage in excess of $50,000 are taxable to the employee. That is, only the premiums paid on $50,000 of group term life insurance are excludable from the employee's income. The IRS provides tables that calculate the income from premiums paid in excess of the $50,000 exclusion.[16] This table is reproduced in Table 4–1. Note that the premium cost is related to the employee's age and is stated per $1,000 of coverage.

▲ **EXAMPLE 18**   Jim is an employee of Panko Builders with an annual salary of $40,000. Panko provides group term life insurance to all its employees at twice their annual salaries. Jim's $80,000 of group term life insurance cost Panko $400 during the current year. How much taxable income does Jim receive from the provision of the life insurance if he is 33?

Discussion: Jim is allowed to exclude the premiums paid on the first $50,000 of the group term life insurance. The premiums paid on the $30,000 of excess coverage must be included in his gross income as compensation from Panko. Using Table 4–1, the amount of the premiums taxed to Jim is $32 (rounded):

Cost per $1,000 of coverage for 33-year-old	$1.08
Coverage in excess of $50,000	× 30
Gross income from excess coverage	$ 32

▲ **EXAMPLE 19**   Assume that Panko also provides $100,000 of whole life insurance to all management-level employees. Jim is in a management-level position. The cost of his $100,000 policy to Panko was $1,800. How much taxable income does Jim receive from the provision of the whole life insurance?

Discussion: There is no exclusion for the provision of whole life insurance to employees. Therefore, Jim must include the $1,800 cost of the policy in his gross income as compensation from Panko.

Health and Accident Insurance Premiums.   Premiums paid by an employer to purchase **health and accident insurance** coverage for employees (and their dependents) are excluded from the employee's income.[17] The exclusion also applies to companies that choose to "self-insure" by making payments to a fund that is used to pay employees' medical expenses. However, if **a self-insured medical plan** discriminates in favor of highly compensated employees, the amounts paid for medical expenses of highly compensated employees covered by the plan are included in the individual's taxable income.

▲ **Table 4–1**

GROSS INCOME FROM GROUP TERM LIFE INSURANCE IN EXCESS OF $50,000

	Includable Income per $1,000	
Employee's Age	**Monthly**	**Annually**
Under 30	$ .08	$ .96
30 to 34	.09	1.08
35 to 39	.11	1.32
40 to 44	.17	2.04
45 to 49	.29	3.48
50 to 54	.48	5.76
55 to 59	.75	9.00
60 to 64	1.17	14.04
65 to 69	2.10	25.20
70 and older	3.76	45.12

▲ **EXAMPLE 20**   Rory is an employee of Royce Co. Royce provides health and accident insurance for all its employees. During the current year, Royce pays $1,300 for each employee for coverage under the plan. Does Rory have taxable income from the payment of the premiums?

Discussion: The $1,300 is not taxable to Rory, because it is a payment for a health and accident insurance plan premium that is not discriminatory.

▲ **EXAMPLE 21**   Cory is a senior vice president of Discriminator Corporation. The corporation has a self-insured health and accident plan that covers only executive officers of the corporation. Discriminator makes monthly payments to a fund that is used to reimburse the executives for any medical expenses they incur. During the current year, Cory incurs $3,700 in medical expenses, all of which are reimbursed by the plan. Does Cory have taxable income from the payment of her medical expenses by the plan?

Discussion: Because the plan discriminates in favor of highly compensated employees (only executive officers are covered), all payments from the plan are taxable to Cory. Thus, Cory must include the $3,700 reimbursement in her gross income.

Note that the exclusion is allowed only for the premiums paid by an employer for the purchase of health and accident insurance on a nondiscriminatory basis. The taxation of payments made to the employee from such plans is discussed in the section on returns of human capital.

Meals and Lodging Provided by the Employer.   The value of meals provided to an employee free of charge may be excluded from the employee's income if the meals are provided on the employer's business premises and the provision of the meals is "for the convenience of the employer."[18] Note that the exclusion is for the **meals provided by the employer;** cash meal allowances are generally taxable, because they are not meals provided by the employer.[19] To satisfy the convenience-of-the-employer requirement, the provision of the meals must have a substantial noncompensatory business purpose.

▲ **EXAMPLE 22**   Hilda waits tables at Jiffy Fast Foods. To encourage employees to stay on the premises during their food breaks, Jiffy allows employees to eat one free meal per shift. Is Hilda taxable on the value of the meals she receives from Jiffy's?

Discussion: Because the provision of the meals serves a business purpose (keeping employees close at hand during their meal breaks), the value of the meals is excluded from Hilda's income. Note that this is the case even if Hilda eats her free meal before or after her shift starts.

▲ **EXAMPLE 23**   Blue Trucking Co. gives all its drivers meal vouchers that are honored at various truck stops on the company's trucking routes. The drivers pay for their meals with the vouchers, which are then billed to Blue Trucking Co. Brian is a driver for Blue; he consumed meals costing a total of $3,900 during the current year. Can Brian exclude the value of the meals provided by Blue?

Discussion: Because the meals were not provided on Blue's business premises, they are taxable as compensation to Brian. Brian must include the $3,900-worth of meals in his gross income.

In order to exclude the value of **employer-provided lodging,** the lodging must meet an additional requirement: The acceptance of the lodging must be a condition of employment. That is, the employee has no choice but to live in the employer-provided housing.

▲ **EXAMPLE 24**   Rona is an employee of Arctic Pipeline Co. Because the construction site of a new pipeline is in a remote area, all employees are required to live in temporary quarters erected at the construction site by Arctic. The cost of the lodging to Arctic is estimated at $7,200 per employee per year. Does Rona have taxable income from the provision of the lodging?

Discussion: Because the lodging on the employer's business premises (the job site) is for the convenience of the employer (employees can work more hours if they don't have to make a long commute), and is required as a condition of employment, it is not taxable to the employee. Therefore, Rona may exclude the $7,200 of employer-provided housing from her gross income.

General Fringe Benefits.   The tax law also allows the exclusion of four general types of employment-related fringe benefits:

- No additional cost services
- Employee discounts
- Working-condition fringes
- De minimis fringe benefits[20]

No additional cost services and **employee discounts** must be made available to employees on a nondiscriminatory basis and must also be in the same line of business in which the employee works. For example, a hotel chain may allow hotel employees to stay free at any of its hotels on a space-available basis with no tax consequences to the employee. However, if the hotel chain also allows free hotel rooms to employees of its rental car business, the fair market value of the hotel room is taxable to the employee. Reciprocal agreements between companies in the same line of business are allowed.

▲ **EXAMPLE 25**   Marshall is an employee of Deloitte Airlines. Deloitte and Arthur Air have a reciprocal agreement under which their employees may fly free of charge on each other's airlines on a space-available basis. Marshall used the agreement to take 2 free flights on Arthur Air that would have cost him $880 if he had paid the regular fare. Is Marshall taxed on the value of the free flights?

Discussion: Because Marshall is an airline employee and the free flights are available to all employees, he is allowed to exclude the value of any flights on either Deloitte or Arthur as a no additional cost service. Therefore, the free flights are not taxable to Marshall.

▲ **EXAMPLE 26**   Assume that Deloitte also owns a finance company. Employees of the finance company are allowed to take free flights only on Deloitte Airlines on a space-available basis. Janelle is a financial analyst with Deloitte's finance company. She took 2 free flights on Deloitte that would have cost $1,060 if she had paid the regular fare. Is Janelle taxed on the value of the free flights?

Discussion: Because Janelle does not work in the same line of business as the free service, she is not allowed to exclude the value of the free flights. She must include the $1,060 value of the flights in her gross income.

In order to exclude employee discounts, the discount must be made available to all employees on a nondiscriminatory basis and the goods and/or services provided must be in the same line of business. Note that the exclusion for discounts would ordinarily constitute a bargain purchase. The distinguishing feature between a valid employee discount and a taxable bargain purchase is that employee discounts must be made available to all employees in order to be excluded.

Bargain purchases are essentially employee discounts that are made available only to select employees. The excludable discount on goods is limited to the gross profit percentage on the goods purchased (i.e., employees can't buy goods below the employer's cost tax free). Excludable service discounts are limited to 20 percent. Any employee discount on services in excess of 20 percent is taxable to the employee (the first 20 percent of the discount is excludable).

▲ **EXAMPLE 27**   All-City Hardware allows all its employees to buy its products at a 25% discount. All-City marks up all its products by a minimum of 100% of its cost. Arnold is a store employee who bought various tools that normally retail for $200 (cost to All-City of $100) for $150 during the current year. Is Arnold taxed on the $50 discount?

Discussion: Because the discount is available to all employees and the discount does not exceed All-City's gross profit percentage (100% markup on cost equals a gross profit percentage of 50%), the discount is excludable from Arnold's gross income.

▲ **EXAMPLE 28**   In addition to the tools, Arnold buys a used delivery truck from All-City. The truck is worth $8,000, but All-City sells the truck to Arnold for $5,000, because he has been such a good employee through the years. Is Arnold taxed on the $3,000 discount?

Discussion: Because the discount on the truck is not available to all employees, Arnold is taxed on the $3,000 as a bargain purchase.

A **working-condition fringe benefit** is any item provided to the employee that would have been deductible by the employee as an employee business expense if the employee had paid for the item. This class of fringe benefits includes dues to professional organizations, professional journals, uniforms, and so on.[21] Although not normally deductible as an employee business expense, the payment of parking by an employer is designated as a working-condition fringe benefit. Since 1993, Congress has limited the amount of employer-provided parking that is excludable from income. The limit is $165 per month for 1996 and was $160 in 1995. In contrast to discounts on goods and services, working-condition fringes can be given on a discriminatory basis. For example, a company can provide free parking only to officers of the company, and the fringe benefit will remain tax free—up to the $165 per month maximum exclusion.

De minimis fringes are those items that are too small to permit a reasonable accounting.[22] This would include such items as personal use of the office photocopier and free coffee in the employees' break room. Also included in this category would be employee parties and small holiday gifts, such as a Christmas ham. This exclusion is based on administrative convenience—the cost of accumulating the information necessary to tax such items would exceed the revenue derived from taxing the items.

Other Benefits Paid by an Employer.   Several other employer-paid fringe benefits are also excludable from income. An employee may exclude up to $5,000 per year of employer-provided **child and dependent care services**.[23] The value of the use of an **employer's athletic facility** may also be excluded, provided that the facility is on the employer's premises and substantially all use of the facility is by employees and their families. In addition, up to $5,250 in payments made for such costs as tuition and books is excludable if the payments are made from a nondiscriminatory **educational assistance program**.[24]

Employer Benefit Plans

As the number of tax-free benefit options proliferated in the late 1970s and early 1980s, employers began to realize that they could not afford to offer all benefits to all employees. Further, every employee did not derive the maximum benefit from every type of benefit. For example, single individuals with no dependents receive no benefit from employer-provided child and dependent care. In response to this situation, firms developed cafeteria plans. In a **cafeteria plan,** a menu of tax-free benefits is offered at the employer's cost. The rules for cafeteria plans allow employers to offer any benefit that is specifically excluded by the tax law in their plans.[25] Each employee is allowed to choose a certain dollar amount of benefits from the menu or may choose to take the cash cost of the benefit. That is, employees who do not want to take all their allowable dollar amount in tax-free benefits are allowed to take the cash equivalent of the benefits. Employees who choose the tax-free benefits are not taxed on the value of the benefit; however, those who elect to receive cash are taxed on the amount of cash received. In order to receive this favorable treatment, the employer must make the benefits of the plan available to all employees on a nondiscriminatory basis. All benefits received from a plan that discriminates in favor of highly compensated employees are included in gross income.

> ▲ **EXAMPLE 29**   Theodore is the chief financial officer of CEO Corporation. CEO has a cafeteria plan that allows all employees to select from a menu of tax-free benefits a total of 5% of their annual compensation. Theodore's annual salary is $100,000, allowing him to select $5,000 in benefits from the plan. Under the plan, he selected $50,000-worth of group term life insurance and health and accident insurance at a cost to the company of $4,000. He took the remaining $1,000 of allowable benefits in cash. What are the tax consequences to Theodore of the cafeteria plan?
>
> *Discussion:*   The plan is nondiscriminatory, because it covers all employees and allows benefits in proportion to their salaries. Therefore, Theodore can exclude the value of the tax-free benefits (group term life insurance and health insurance) he selected. He must include in his gross income the $1,000 of benefits he took in cash.

Another type of plan that has gained popularity is the **flexible benefits, or salary reduction, plan.**[26] With this type of plan, the employee has an annual amount withheld from his or her salary that is used to pay medical care expenses or child-care costs. As the costs are incurred, the employer reimburses the employee from the account. Amounts paid into the account by the employee are not included in the employee's gross income, thus the term *salary reduction plan*. These plans allow employees to pay for medical costs and child care with before-tax dollars rather than after-tax dollars.

> ▲ **EXAMPLE 30**   Bale Corporation has a flexible benefits plan that allows employees to have amounts withheld from their salaries to pay for unreimbursed medical costs and child-care costs. Melchior is an employee of Bale whose annual salary is $45,000. Melchior has Bale withhold $8,000 under the plan to pay for health and accident insurance, dental costs, eyeglasses, and so on for his dependents. During the year, Melchior incurs $9,500 in such costs, and Bale reimburses him the $8,000 that had been withheld. What is the tax effect on Melchior of the flexible benefits plan?
>
> *Discussion:*   Melchior's salary is reduced by the $8,000 he paid into the plan, leaving him with a gross income of $37,000. He is not taxed on the amounts he is paid for reimbursements from the plan ($8,000 in this case).
>   Note that Melchior has been able to pay for $8,000 of his costs with before-tax dollars. Without such a plan, Melchior still would have spent the $8,000, but the income would have been subject to tax. Therefore, he would have had to make more than $8,000 before taxes to have $8,000 after taxes to pay for these expenses.

One final note on this type of plan: The regulations governing these plans do not allow the company to return unused payments to the employee. The employee makes an annual election of the amount she or he wants put into the plan. Any amounts put into a flexible benefits or salary reduction plan that are not spent during the year are retained by the plan and are not available to the employee in subsequent years. That is, the employee loses any payments that are not reimbursed during the plan year.

▲ **EXAMPLE 31**   Assume that in example 30 Melchior spent only $7,500 of the $8,000 he paid in during the year. What is the effect on Melchior?

Discussion: Melchior is still allowed to exclude the $8,000 he paid into the plan, reducing his gross income to $37,000. However, the plan would keep the $500 he paid in but did not spend. It would not be available for Melchior to use to pay his expenses in the next plan year.

Individuals often receive payments that are intended either to reimburse them for the costs of injuries or to compensate them for injuries in such a way as to "make them whole." Such payments are not deemed to increase wealth; rather, they are viewed as a return of human capital lost because of injury or sickness. As such, they are treated as a capital recovery that is not subject to tax. However, payments that are meant to replace lost income do not constitute returns of human capital and are generally taxable. Various types of payments received as compensation for injury or sickness are excluded from gross income. The list of excluded payments includes

RETURNS OF HUMAN CAPITAL

- Workers' compensation payments received as compensation for personal injury or sickness
- Damage payments received on account of personal injury or sickness
- Payments received for personal injuries or sickness that are paid from health and accident policies purchased by the taxpayer
- Payments received from employer-provided health and accident insurance if the payments
  1. Are made for the permanent loss or loss of use of a member or function of the body, or for permanent disfigurement of the body; or
  2. Are based on the nature of the injury and are computed without reference to the period of time the employee is absent from the workplace; or
  3. Are payments received to reimburse the taxpayer for expenses incurred for medical care.

Workers' Compensation

Payments from a state **workers' compensation** fund are excluded from taxation. These payments are made to workers who become unable to work as a result of a work-related injury. Although the payments are somewhat of a substitute for earned income, Congress has provided relief from taxation for such payments, because they are related to an injury suffered on the job and help taxpayers through the period they are recovering from their injuries. As such, they help to restore the human capital of the individual. Note that this is not true for unemployment compensation benefits. Unemployment compensation is meant to be a substitute for income and is therefore subject to tax.

Damage Payments for Personal Injury or Sickness

Damage payments for personal injury or sickness are excluded from taxation.[27] The courts have interpreted **personal injury** to include any personal wrong committed against the taxpayer, such as libel, slander, breach of promise to marry, invasion of privacy, assault, and battery. The exclusion also applies to loss-of-income payments that result from the personal injury.[28]

▲ **EXAMPLE 32**   Rose was hit by an automobile while riding her bicycle to work. Although she was not hospitalized, her injuries prevented her from working for two weeks. The insurance company of the driver of the automobile paid Rose $2,000 for her pain and suffering and reimbursed her $650 for the wages she lost when she was unable to work. How much of the $2,650 Rose received is included in her gross income?

Discussion: None of the $2,650 is taxable. The $2,000 payment for pain and suffering is an excludable damage payment. In addition, because the loss-of-income payment is related to the personal injury, it is excluded from income.

▲ **EXAMPLE 33**   Elliot works as a corner grocer. A feature on the local news about organized crime portrayed Elliot as having links to organized crime. Elliot was outraged, the allegation was false, and he sued the television station for libel and slander. The court awarded Elliot $5,000 for the public humiliation he suffered and $60,000 for loss of his business reputation. How much of the $65,000 is included in Elliot's gross income?

Discussion: The $5,000 payment for his public humiliation is a personal injury and therefore excluded from gross income. Although the $60,000 payment for loss of business reputation is based on estimated lost income, the courts have held that such payments are for a personal injury and thus are excludable.[29]

The treatment of other payments made in connection with a personal injury is more controversial and has resulted in much litigation. In addition to payments for pain and suffering (which are excluded as damages), the courts often award **punitive damages** and/or **loss-of-income damages** in personal injury actions. Damage payments made to replace lost income are generally taxable as a replacement of taxable income unless they are related to a personal injury. Punitive damages are meant to punish the offender in a personal injury case for gross negligence or the intentional infliction of harm to the other party. Punitive damages are included in gross income unless they are the result of a claim for physical injury or physical sickness.[30]

▲ **EXAMPLE 34**   Assume that in example 32 Rose had sued the driver of the automobile. In addition to the payments for pain and suffering, the courts awarded her $10,000 in punitive damages for the gross negligence exhibited by the driver. Are the punitive damages included in Rose's gross income?

Discussion: Because the punitive damages relate to a physical injury, they are excluded from Rose's gross income.

▲ **EXAMPLE 35**   Assume that in example 33 the court found that the television station intentionally harmed Elliot, and he was awarded $30,000 in punitive damages. Are the punitive damages included in Elliot's gross income?

Discussion: Because the punitive damages do not result from a physical injury or physical sickness, they are included in Elliot's gross income.

Payments from Health and Accident Policies

Health and accident insurance policies may be provided by an employer to an employee, or they may be purchased separately by the taxpayer. In either case, payments for medical expenses from such policies are excluded, because they make the taxpayer whole.[31]

An important distinction between employer- and taxpayer-purchased policies is that all health and accident insurance payments from policies purchased by an individual taxpayer are excluded from taxation. The exclusion for payments from employer-provided policies is limited to those for medical care, loss of body parts, or payments made for specific types of injuries. Thus, amounts received as **disability payments** (sick pay or wage-continuation plans) from an employer-provided health and accident plan would be included in gross income. However, the same payments made from a plan purchased by the individual taxpayer would be excluded from gross income. The disparity in treatment is apparently an additional incentive Congress has provided to individuals to purchase adequate health insurance. Figure 4–1 summarizes the tax treatment of payments received from health and accident policies.

▲ **EXAMPLE 36** Sean was involved in an automobile accident in which he sustained severe injuries. The costs of his medical care totaled $8,000. His employer-sponsored plan paid $6,400 of the medical costs and $2,200 in sick pay. In addition, a policy that he had purchased separately paid the remaining $1,600 of his medical costs and an

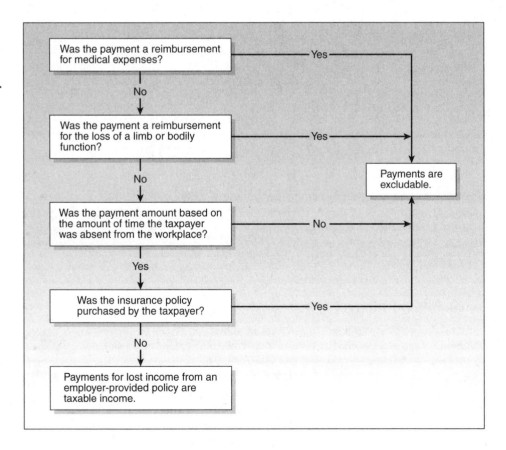

▲ **Figure 4–1**

TAXABILITY OF PAYMENTS
RECEIVED FROM HEALTH
AND ACCIDENT POLICIES

additional $1,000 for income lost while he was unable to work. What are the tax consequences of the receipt of the payments from the two plans?

Discussion: The $8,000 in reimbursed medical care expenses is excludable. The $6,400 payment from his employer-provided plan was for medical expenses and is excludable. The remaining $1,600 of medical expense payments came from a plan that Sean purchased and is also excludable. The $1,000 lost-income payment from his personal plan is also excludable, because Sean purchased the policy. However, the $2,200 in sick pay from his employer's plan is not excludable and must be included in his gross income. Payments for loss of income are excluded only if the payment comes from a policy that the taxpayer purchased. All other payments for loss of income are included in gross income.

A problem sometimes arises with reimbursements for medical care when an individual takes an allowable medical deduction for unreimbursed medical expenses in one tax year and then is reimbursed for those expenses in a subsequent year. Individuals are allowed to deduct unreimbursed medical expenses but only to the extent that they exceed 7.5 percent of the individual's adjusted gross income (the specifics of this deduction are covered in Chapter 8). Under the tax benefit rule, any reimbursed amount that was deducted in a prior year must be included in taxable income in the year of the reimbursement, to the extent that a tax benefit was received from the deduction.

▲ **EXAMPLE 37** Jo is seriously injured in a ski accident late in 1995. The cost of her medical care, which she pays in cash, is $5,000. Because she believes that her insurance company will not reimburse her for these costs, she correctly includes the $5,000 in medical costs as a deduction on her 1995 tax return, which she files in February 1996. Because of the limitations on medical deductions, her actual medical deduction is for only $1,000 of the $5,000. In May 1996, her insurance company reimburses her for $4,500 of the medical costs. What is the proper treatment of the $4,500 reimbursement?

Discussion: Because the medical costs she deducts on her 1995 return are reimbursed in 1996, Jo must include the reimbursement in her 1996 gross income to the extent she receives a tax benefit from the deduction. In this case, her actual deduction is only $1,000 because of the medical deduction limitations. Therefore, she includes only the amount deducted on her 1995 tax return, $1,000, in her 1996 gross income.

INVESTMENT-RELATED EXCLUSIONS

Several exclusions in the income tax law provide relief from taxation on certain investment-related transactions. These include exclusions from income for certain municipal bond interest and the receipt of a stock dividend. Other provisions allow deferral of income in certain discharge-of-indebtedness situations and for improvements made by a lessee of property.

Municipal Bond Interest

In general, interest income is fully taxable when received by a taxpayer. Thus, interest on savings accounts and from investments in corporate bonds is included in gross income. However, the tax law provides an exclusion from interest earned on bonds issued by state and local governments (cities, counties, state agencies such as turnpike authorities) of the United States as well as those of U.S. possessions (Guam, Puerto Rico),[32] called **municipal bond interest.** Note that the exclusion from tax does not include interest on U.S. government obligations such as

Treasury bills, nor does it apply to interest received on foreign government obligations.

▲ **EXAMPLE 38** During the current year, Jorge received the following interest payments:

General Motors bonds	$ 350
Province of Ontario bonds	220
State of Oklahoma bonds	330
Puerto Rico Port Authority bonds	100
Total interest received	$1,000

How much of the $1,000 in interest is taxable to Jorge?

Discussion: Only interest on the debt obligations of state and local governments of the United States and its possessions is excluded from gross income. This would include the interest Jorge received on the state of Oklahoma bonds and the Puerto Rico bonds, a total of $430. The interest on the General Motors bonds and the Ontario bonds is fully taxable. Thus, Jorge has taxable interest income of $570.

Municipal bond interest is excluded because it allows municipalities to raise money for projects at lower interest rates than comparable taxable bonds.

▲ **EXAMPLE 39** ALF Corporation is considering investing in some bonds. ALF's broker has told the company that it can buy City of Nashville tax-exempt bonds at a yield of 6%. Assuming that ALF is in the 34% tax bracket, what would a fully taxable bond of the same risk have to yield to provide an equivalent return?

Discussion: Because tax will have to be paid on the taxable bond, it will have to have a higher before-tax yield to provide the same 6% after-tax return on the City of Nashville bonds. To find the after-tax equivalent return, equate the 6% return to the after-tax return, X, and solve:

$$0.06 = X - 0.34X$$
$$0.06 = X(1 - 0.34)$$
$$0.06 = X(0.66)$$
$$0.06 \div 0.66 = X$$
$$0.0909 = X$$

Therefore, any taxable bond with a pretax yield greater than 9.09% will provide ALF with a higher after-tax return than the Nashville bonds.

Proof: Assume that ALF invests $1,000 in the City of Nashville bonds yielding 6% and another $1,000 in Togoto, Inc., bonds yielding 10%. Which bond investment has the greater after-tax return?

Discussion: The Togoto, Inc., bonds have a greater after-tax return. This is shown by computing the after-tax income from each $1,000 investment:

City of Nashville interest ($1,000 × 6%)	$ 60
Income tax	(-0-)
After-tax income	$ 60
Togoto, Inc., interest ($1,000 × 10%)	$100
Income tax ($100 × 34%)	(34)
After-tax income	$ 66

Stock Dividends

The Supreme Court ruled in 1920 that the receipt of a **stock dividend** does not constitute a realization of income.[33] That is, a dividend paid in stock of the same company (either a stock dividend or a stock split) is merely "slicing the pie" into smaller ownership units, with no resulting increase in shareholder wealth. The value of a shareholder's interest does not change; it is merely spread over more ownership units.

▲ **EXAMPLE 40**   Imelda owns 100,000 shares of Smith common stock, for which she paid $1,200,000 several years ago. During the current year, when Smith had a total of 1,000,000 shares outstanding, Smith declared and distributed a 20% stock dividend. Imelda received 20,000 new shares (of the 200,000 total dividend issued) from the dividend. What are the tax consequences for Imelda from the receipt of the dividend?

Discussion: Imelda's wealth has not increased from the receipt of the shares. Before the dividend, she owned 10% (100,000 ÷ 1,000,000) of Smith. After the dividend, she still owns 10% (120,000 ÷ 1,200,000). Therefore, she has not realized an increase of wealth from the dividend and is not taxed on the value of the 20,000 shares received. NOTE: Imelda's original 100,000 shares had a basis of $12 per share ($1,200,000 ÷ 100,000). She now owns 120,000 shares with a total basis of $1,200,000. Thus, her basis per share is now $10 ($1,200,000 ÷ 120,000).

▲ **EXAMPLE 41**   After making the stock dividend, Smith paid a cash dividend of $2 per share on the 1,200,000 shares outstanding. Imelda received $240,000 from the dividend. What are the tax effects of the dividend for Imelda?

Discussion: The exclusion from tax is only for the shares of stock received from a stock dividend. Any subsequent cash dividends received on the stock are fully taxable. Imelda must include the $240,000 cash dividend in her gross income.

However, if the receiver of the stock dividend has the option to receive cash in lieu of stock, the dividend is taxed as if the cash option had been selected.[34] In this case, the shares of stock are deemed to have a cash equivalent and thus are taxable.

▲ **EXAMPLE 42**   Opubco, Inc., a public utility, declares a 10% stock dividend when its stock is selling for $50 per share. Stockholders have the option of receiving $5 cash per share in lieu of the stock. Ginny owns 1,000 shares of Opubco stock. She elects to take the 100 additional shares of Opubco stock. What is the tax effect of the receipt of the stock dividend for Ginny?

Discussion: Because Ginny could have received cash instead of the shares of stock, she is taxed on the fair market value of the shares received, resulting in taxable income of $5,000 (100 × $50). Her basis in the 100 shares she actually received is the taxable income reported, $5,000.

Discharge of Indebtedness

Under the general principles of income recognition, the borrowing of money is not a taxable event, because the borrower is under an obligation to repay the loan. Similarly, the repayment of the loan principal does not generate taxable income. However, if a lender forgives all or a portion of the debt of the borrower, the borrower realizes an increase in wealth from the reduction of the liability. That is, the borrower who is relieved of a debt has obtained a claim of right to the amount of debt forgiven. This increase in wealth, known as a **discharge of indebtedness,** is generally taxable to the borrower.

▲ **EXAMPLE 43**   Leonard borrowed $17,000 from his employer to purchase a new car. Several years later, when Leonard had paid the debt down to $3,000, his employer told Leonard he no longer owed the debt as a bonus for Leonard's hard work and devotion to the company. Is Leonard taxed on the forgiveness of the $3,000 owed on the loan?

Discussion: Leonard is taxed on the $3,000. His wealth has increased as a result of the extinguishment of the liability, and he now has obtained a claim of right to the $3,000, because he is no longer under any obligation to repay.

The tax law provides an exception to the general rule of taxability of a discharge of indebtedness when the borrower is insolvent (liabilities exceed assets), both before and after the forgiveness of the debt.[35] This exception includes any debt reductions as a result of a bankruptcy proceeding.

▲ **EXAMPLE 44**   Because of a slump in the real estate market, Koka Properties, Inc., was having trouble paying its debts. The value of Koka's assets was $400,000, and its liabilities were $600,000. In order to help Koka restore stability, its bank forgave a $100,000 line of credit loan it had made to Koka several years earlier. What are the tax effects of the $100,000 forgiveness of debt?

Discussion: Because Koka is still insolvent ($400,000 − $500,000) after the debt reduction, it does not have to recognize the $100,000 forgiveness as income.

However, if the discharge makes the debtor solvent, the debtor must recognize income to the extent that the debtor is solvent after the debt reduction. That is, if the taxpayer has a positive net worth after the forgiveness of debt, he or she is deemed to have the wherewithal to pay, up to the amount of the solvency.

▲ **EXAMPLE 45**   In example 44, what would the tax effects be if Koka's bank line of credit, which was forgiven, had been $250,000?

Discussion: The tax law provides that income from the discharge of indebtedness is excluded only if the borrower is insolvent after the discharge. Therefore, income must be recognized to the extent that the borrower is solvent after the debt reduction. Applying this to Koka, its net worth after the discharge is $50,000 ($400,000 − $350,000), which must be included in its gross income.

When a taxpayer is allowed to exclude discharge of indebtedness income because of insolvency, any tax attributes the taxpayer has in relation to the debt must be reduced by the amount of the exclusion. Tax attributes that must be reduced include net operating loss carryforwards, capital loss carryforwards, and the basis of property purchased with the debt.

A second exception to the taxability of debt discharges applies to taxpayers who have been negatively affected by depressed real estate markets. Taxpayers other than corporations can elect to exclude from income some cancellation of "qualified real property business indebtedness." **Qualified real property business indebtedness** is debt incurred or assumed in connection with real property used in a trade or business that is secured by that real property. Only debt incurred before 1993 qualifies for the exclusion, unless it is incurred to refinance previously incurred qualified debt or is qualified acquisition debt. Qualified acquisition debt is debt incurred to acquire, construct, or substantially improve real property that is secured by such debt.

The amount of the exclusion for qualified real property debt is the lesser of (1) the property's adjusted basis or (2) the excess of the principal amount of the debt immediately before the discharge over the fair market value of the property that secures the debt. Note that part 2 of the exclusion formula effectively restricts application of this relief provision to those situations in which the amount of debt on the property is greater than the property's fair market value. The adjusted basis of the property must be reduced by any amounts excluded under this provision.

▲ **EXAMPLE 46**   In 1991, the Felicia Partnership purchased a building that now has a fair market value of $120,000; Felicia uses the building, secured by a mortgage of $160,000, in its insurance business. Felicia negotiates a reduction in the mortgage debt to $100,000. If the partnership's adjusted basis in the building is $70,000, how much of the $60,000 debt reduction must Felicia include in its gross income?

Discussion: The debt is qualified real property business indebtedness, because the debt is secured by real property that the partnership uses in its insurance business. Felicia may exclude $40,000 of the $60,000 debt reduction:

The lesser of
1. $70,000 (adjusted basis)
OR
2. $40,000 ($160,000 indebtedness before the discharge − $120,000 fair market value of the building)

Felicia must include $20,000 ($60,000 − $40,000) of the discharged debt in gross income. The adjusted basis of the building is reduced by the $40,000 of excluded discharge of indebtedness income, leaving an adjusted basis after the discharge of $30,000 ($70,000 − $40,000). Note that the basis reduction will reduce the amount of Felicia's subsequent depreciation deductions on the building. This ultimately results in Felicia's recognizing the debt discharge through higher taxable incomes in the future as a result of the smaller depreciation deductions.

▲ **EXAMPLE 47**   Assume the same facts as in example 46, except that Felicia's adjusted basis in the building is $25,000.

Discussion: In this case, Felicia's exclusion is limited to its $25,000 adjusted basis:

The lesser of
1. $25,000
OR
2. $40,000

Felicia will have to include $35,000 ($60,000 − $25,000) of the debt discharge in gross income. The adjusted basis in the building is reduced to zero ($25,000 - $25,000).

If the qualified property is secured by more than one qualified real property indebtedness, the fair market value of the property must be reduced by the outstanding principal amount of the other indebtedness in calculating the amount of the exclusion.

▲ **EXAMPLE 48**   Heinrich owns a building with a fair market value of $200,000 that he has used in his floral design business since 1989. The building is secured by two mortgages: The first mortgage is for $150,000, and the second mortgage is for $80,000. The lender on the first mortgage agrees to reduce the debt to $100,000. If Heinrich's adjusted basis in the building is $140,000, how much of the $50,000 discharge of indebtedness income must Heinrich include in his gross income?

Discussion: The debt is qualified real property business indebtedness. In calculating the amount of the exclusion, the $200,000 fair market value must be reduced by the $80,000 second mortgage to a net fair market value of $120,000. Heinrich can exclude $30,000 of the debt discharge:

The lesser of
1. $140,000 (his adjusted basis)
OR
2. $30,000 ($150,000 indebtedness before the discharge − $120,000 net fair market value of the building).

Heinrich must include $20,000 ($50,000 − $30,000) of the debt discharge in his gross income. The adjusted basis of the building is reduced to $110,000 ($140,000 − $30,000).

Improvements by a Lessee

The tax law provides that a property owner does not have income when a lessee makes improvements to the owner's property or when such improvements revert to the property owner at the termination of the lease.[36] This allows the property owner to defer the gain in the value of the property from the improvements until the property is sold, at which time the owner will have the wherewithal to pay the tax on the increased value from the **improvements by a lessee.**

▲ **EXAMPLE 49**   Natasha leased a building from Rudy Corporation under a 10-year lease that provided that any improvements made by Natasha would revert to Rudy at the expiration of the lease. Natasha added a wing to the building at a cost of $40,000. When the lease ended, the new wing increased the value of the property by $75,000. Does Rudy Corporation have any income from the addition of the new wing by Natasha?

Discussion: Rudy will not be taxed on the increased value of the property until it sells or otherwise disposes of the property in a taxable transaction. At that time, the $75,000 increase in value will be reflected in any gain from the property's disposition.

The exclusion from income for improvements by a lessee does not apply when the improvements are made in lieu of rent. When that is the case, the lessee is paying the rent in the form of the improvement rather than in cash. Under the cash-equivalent approach to income recognition, the value of such improvements is included in income.[37]

▲ **EXAMPLE 50**   Andrea leased a building from Petros for $2,000 per month. The bathroom was in need of repair, so Petros agreed to reduce Andrea's rent by the cost of repairing the bathroom. Andrea paid $1,800 to have the bathroom repaired and paid Petros only $200 for the next month's rent. What are the tax effects to Petros of the payment of the repairs by Andrea?

Discussion: Because the repair improvement was made in lieu of a rental payment, the $1,800 is considered a rental payment received by Petros. It is not excludable as an improvement by a lessee.
    Although Petros recognizes income from the repairs, he is allowed a deduction for the repair cost as an ordinary and necessary expense. The net effect of this situation for Petros is no increase in his income. This effect follows from the substance of the transaction: If Andrea had paid Petros the $2,000 monthly rent and Petros then reimbursed Andrea for the repairs, Petros would include the repairs in income through the rent payment and deduct the repair expense payment.

SUMMARY

All income received by a taxpayer is taxable unless specifically excluded by the tax law. Excludable forms of income must be identified in order to determine a taxpayer's gross income. Exclusions from income are a result of the legislative grace concept. Under this concept, only Congress can provide relief from tax. Any relief provided must be strictly applied and interpreted. As applied to exclusions, this means that a specific provision must be found in the tax law before an income item can be excluded from taxation. Exclusions from income are usually meant to avoid double taxation or to provide incentive for taxpayers to enter into a tax-favored transaction. Often, amounts are excluded from taxation based on the

▲ **Table 4–2**

INCOME EXCLUSIONS BY CATEGORY

	Exclusions	Major Problems
Donative Items	Gifts Inheritances Life insurance proceeds Scholarships Death benefits	What is a gift? No exclusion for future earnings on amounts excluded for gifts, inheritances, life insurance proceeds Only direct costs of education excludable for scholarships

Employment-related Exclusions	Foreign earned income
	Employer-provided benefits
	  Pension plan payments
	  Group term life insurance
	  Health/accident insurance
	  Meals and lodging
	  No additional cost services
	  Employee discounts
	  Working-condition fringes
	  De minimis fringes
	  Child care
	  Athletic facilities
	  Educational assistance
	Employee benefit plans
	  Cafeteria plans
	  Flexible benefits/salary reduction plans
		Nondiscrimination requirement for most benefits
		Each benefit has specific requirements and/or limitations

Returns of Human Capital	Workers' compensation Damages for personal injury Payments from employee-purchased health/accident plan Payments from employer-provided health/accident insurance for medical expenses	Payments for lost income—wage continuation/disability payments Payments for punitive damages Tax benefit rule for medical expenses reimbursed in a year subsequent to deduction
Investment-related Exclusions	Municipal bond interest Stock dividends Discharge of indebtedness—insolvent debtor Discharge of indebtedness—qualified real property business indebtedness Improvements by a lessee	Taxability of gain on disposition of tax-exempt securities/nontaxable dividend shares Cash option on stock dividend Insolvent debtors who become solvent after discharge of debt Improvements made in lieu of rent

wherewithal-to-pay concept, under which amounts are taxed when the means are available to pay the tax.

This chapter identified and discussed four general classes of exclusions: donative items, employment-related exclusions, returns of human capital, and investment-related exclusions. Because all these exclusion items represent departures from the general concepts of income recognition, there is no hard-and-fast method for learning the various types of exclusions. To aid you in your study of exclusions, Table 4–2 summarizes by category the exclusions discussed in this chapter and points out the major problems involved within each category. At the completion of this chapter, you should be able to compute the gross income for most common situations faced by taxpayers.

KEY TERMS

cafeteria plan (p. 156)
child and dependent care services (p. 155)
damage payments (p. 158)
death benefit payment (p. 148)
de minimis fringe benefit (p. 155)
disability payment (p. 159)
discharge of indebtedness (p. 162)
educational assistance program (p. 155)
employee discount (p. 154)
employer-provided lodging (p. 153)
employer's athletic facility (p. 155)
flexible benefits plan (p. 156)

foreign earned income (p. 149)
gift (p. 144)
group term life insurance (p. 151)
health and accident insurance (p. 152)
improvements by a lessee (p. 165)
inheritance (p. 145)
life insurance proceeds (p. 145)
loss-of-income damages (p. 158)
meals provided by employer (p. 153)
municipal bond interest (p. 160)
no additional cost services (p. 154)

personal injury (p. 158)
punitive damages (p. 158)
qualified pension plan (p. 151)
qualified real property business indebtedness (p. 163)
salary reduction plan (p. 156)
scholarship (p. 147)
self-insured medical plan (p. 152)
stock dividend (p. 162)
workers' compensation (p. 157)
working-condition fringe benefit (p. 155)

[1] Sec. 102—States that the value of property received by gift or inheritance is excluded from gross income.

[2] Comm. v. Duberstein, 363 U.S. 278 at 283 (1960)—Held that a Cadillac received by a taxpayer from a businessman to whom he occasionally gave names of potential customers was not a tax-free gift.

[3] Reg. Sec. 1.102-1—States that property received by gift or inheritance is not subject to income tax, but income earned on such property subsequent to receipt is not excluded.

[4] Sec. 101—States that life insurance payments and $5,000 in death-benefit payments paid are excluded from gross income.

[5] Sec. 117—States that qualified scholarships are excluded from gross income and the amount of the exclusion is limited to qualified tuition and related expenses.

[6] Prop. Reg. Sec. 1.117-6—Defines *scholarships* and discusses the types of expenditures that are excludable as direct education costs.

[7] Rev. Rul. 62-102—Assumes that voluntary payments made by an employer to a deceased employee's family are compensation for past services.

[8] Reg. Sec. 1.101-2—Explains the allocation of the $5,000 per employee death-benefit exclusion among beneficiaries.

[9] Sec. 901—Allows a tax credit for foreign taxes paid on earned income.

[10] Sec. 911—Allows the exclusion of up to $70,000 of foreign earned income from gross income in lieu of the tax credit provided by Section 901.

[11] Sec. 219—Allows a deduction for adjusted gross income for up to $2,000 in contributions to qualified retirement accounts.

PRIMARY TAX LAW SOURCES

[12] Sec. 401—Allows self-employed individuals to establish retirement accounts that allow deductions for contributions comparable to those provided by employer-sponsored pension plans.

[13] Sec. 401—Prescribes the requirements for a qualified employer-provided retirement plan.

[14] Sec. 402—Prescribes the tax treatment of qualified employer-provided pension plans.

[15] Reg. Sec. 1.79-4T—Discusses the nondiscrimination rules as they apply to the provision of group term life insurance to employees.

[16] Reg. Sec. 1.79-3—Specifies the taxability of premiums paid on group term life insurance in excess of $50,000.

[17] Sec. 106—States that gross income does not include payments for health and accident insurance coverage by an employer for an employee.

[18] Sec. 119—Provides an exclusion from gross income for meals and lodging provided by an employer to an employee.

[19] Reg. Sec. 1.119-1—Defines terms for purposes of the exclusion for meals and lodging provided by an employer.

[20] Sec. 132—Excludes no-additional-cost services, qualified employee discounts, working-condition fringes, and de minimis fringe benefits from gross income; also provides that employer-provided parking and on-premises athletic facilities are excludable fringe benefits.

[21] Reg. Sec. 1.132-5—Discusses working-condition fringes and gives examples of qualifying working-condition fringe benefits.

[22] Reg. Sec. 1.132-6—Discusses de minimis fringe benefits and provides examples of such benefits.

[23] Sec. 129—Excludes up to $5,000 per year for employer-provided dependent care.

[24] Sec. 127—Excludes up to $5,250 in reimbursements to an employee from an employer's qualified educational assistance plan. This exclusion expired on December 31, 1994. However, this provision has expired before and been retroactively rein-stated by later legislation. Legislation pending when this book went to press will retroactively reinstate the exclusion for payments made after December 31, 1994. Therefore, we have left the exclusion in the text because it is likely that Congress will renew it.

[25] Sec. 125—Provides an exclusion for benefits selected under a cafeteria plan; defines a *cafeteria plan* and describes the types of benefits the plan may offer.

[26] Prop. Reg. Sec. 1.125-1—Provides information about cafeteria plans in a question-and-answer format; question 7 answers questions relating to what constitutes a flexible benefits (salary reduction) plan.

[27] Sec. 104—States that amounts received for workers' compensation and damages for personal injuries are excluded from gross income.

[28] Rev. Rul. 85-97—Allows the exclusion of loss-of-income payments resulting from a personal injury.

[29] Roemer, Jr. v. Comm., 716 F.2d 693 (6th Cir. 1983)—Held that damages paid for injury to professional reputation are excludable as payments for personal injury. The IRS said in Revenue Ruling 85-143 that it would not follow *Roemer* and would continue to tax such damage payments. However, in *Threlkeld v. Comm.*, 848 F.2d 81 (6th Cir. 1988), the court rejected the IRS's position in Revenue Ruling 85–143.

[30] Glenshaw Glass v. Comm., 348 U.S. 426 (1955)—Held that punitive damage payments constitute gross income and are not excludable. Sec. 104 excludes punitive damage payments that are the result of a physical injury or physical sickness.

[31] Sec. 105—States that payments for medical expenses from an employer-provided plan are excluded from gross income.

[32] Sec. 103—States that interest received on state or local government bonds is excluded from gross income.

[33] Eisner v. Macomber, 252 U.S. 189 (1920)—Held that a stock dividend did not constitute gross income.

[34] Sec. 305—States that stock dividends with a cash option are taxable.

[35] Sec. 108—Provides an exclusion from gross income for the discharge of indebtedness of an insolvent taxpayer and for discharges of indebtedness on qualified real property indebtedness.

[36] Sec. 109—States that the value of improvements made to a lessor's property

by a lessee are not income to the lessor at the termination of the lease.

[37] Reg. Sec. 1.109-1—States that improvements made by a lessee to a lessor's property that are in lieu of rental payments are included in gross income as income from rents.

DISCUSSION QUESTIONS

1. What are the two reasons most commonly advanced for excluding items from income? Give examples of each, and explain how they accomplish the purpose of the exclusion.

2. What is the difference between an exclusion of income and a deferral of income?

3. How can gifts be used to lower the overall tax paid by a family?

4. Why are life insurance proceeds excluded from the gross income of the beneficiary of the policy?

5. Are all scholarships excluded from tax? Explain the circumstances under which a scholarship would not be excluded from gross income.

6. What is the purpose of the death benefit exclusion?

7. What tax relief is provided to U.S. citizens who earn income in a foreign country and pay taxes in that country?

8. How do employees benefit from payments made into a qualified pension plan on their behalf?

9. Distinguish group term life insurance from whole life insurance.

10. What is the difference in the tax treatment of a medical insurance plan that is purchased from a third-party insurer and a self-insured medical reimbursement plan?

11. What is the difference between a qualified employee discount and a bargain purchase by an employee?

12. What is the difference between a cafeteria plan and a flexible benefits (salary reduction) plan?

13. Why are workers' compensation payments treated differently than unemployment compensation payments for tax purposes?

14. What is a personal injury for purposes of excluding damage payments received?

15. Are punitive damages taxable? Explain.

16. Are payments for loss of income taxable? Explain.

17. Discuss the difference in the tax treatment of payments received from an employer-provided health and accident insurance policy and a health and accident insurance policy purchased by the taxpayer.

18. What is the purpose of excluding municipal bond interest from gross income?

19. Are all stock dividends received excluded from gross income?

20. In 1995, Bud borrows $20,000 from a friend. Before Bud can repay any of the loan, the friend dies. His friend's last will and testament provides that any amounts owed to him are to be forgiven upon his death. Does Bud have gross income from the forgiveness of debt?

PROBLEMS

21. Throughout the textbook, it has been stated that tax relief can come in several forms. Assuming that the taxpayer in question is in a 31% marginal tax rate bracket and the time value of money is 6%, determine the tax value of the following forms of relief:
    a. A $2,000 item of income that is excluded from income
    b. A $2,000 expenditure that is deductible in computing taxable income
    c. A $2,000 expenditure that is eligible for a 10% tax credit
    d. A $2,000 item of income that is deferred for five years (assume no change in the marginal tax rate)

22. A tornado did extensive damage in the community in which Bodine Co. had its primary manufacturing facilities. Bodine gave $1,000 to each household that suffered damage from the tornado to help residents while repairs were being made. Some (but not all) payments were made to Bodine employees. What are the tax consequences of the receipt of the $1,000 by Bodine employees? Explain.

23. On May 1, Raisa received a $1,000, 6% bond of Altomba Corporation as a graduation present from her aunt Lenia. The bond pays interest semiannually, on June 30 and December 31. What are the tax effects of this transfer for Raisa and Lenia for the current year?

24. During the current year, Alexis gives her daughter Tabatha stocks worth $100,000 on the condition that she pay her son Rory the first $6,000 in dividends on the stock each year. Discuss the taxability of this arrangement in each of the following cases:
    a. The stocks pay total dividends of $8,000. Tabatha pays Rory $6,000 under the agreement.
    b. The stocks pay total dividends of $4,500. Tabatha pays Rory $4,500 under the agreement.

25. Herman inherits stock with a fair market value of $80,000 from his grandfather on March 1. On May 1, Herman sells half of the stock at a gain of $5,000 and invests the $45,000 proceeds in Jordan County school bonds. The bonds' annual interest rate is 6%, which is paid semiannually on July 31 and January 31. On October 15, Herman receives a $2,000 dividend on the remaining shares of stock. How much gross income does Herman have from these transactions?

26. Fatima inherits a rental property with a fair market value of $90,000 from her aunt on April 30. On May 15, the executor of the estate sends her a check for $8,000. A letter accompanying the check states that the $8,000 comes from the rent received on the property since her aunt's death. Fatima receives $5,600 in rent on the property during the remainder of the year and she pays allowable expenses of $4,200 on the property. How much gross income does Fatima have from these transactions?

27. Binh met Anika 10 years ago at a cocktail party. Anika was a wealthy investor with extensive holdings in the oil and gas industry. Binh was a real estate agent earning about $35,000 a year. Several months after they met, Binh proposed marriage and Anika accepted. Just before the wedding, Anika told Binh that she had a "mental hangup" about marriage, and Binh agreed to live with her without benefit of matrimony. In return, Anika promised to leave Binh her entire estate. In the ensuing years, they had an intimate marriagelike relationship, attending social, business, and family functions together. Anika died in 1994. No will was found immediately. A few months after Anika's death, her sister found a one-page paper signed by Anika. The paper left Anika's entire estate to her brothers and sisters and named her sister as executor of the estate. Binh sued Anika's estate and won a judgment of $2,000,000 for sevices rendered to Anika during their relationship. The estate appealed the decision, which was affirmed as to liability but reversed and remanded for a new trial on the amount of the judgment. Binh and the estate subsequently worked out an agreement in which the estate paid Binh $1,200,000 in settlement of his claim. Can Binh exclude the $1,200,000 payment as an inheritance? Discuss, and explain why you think the payment is (or is not) an excludable inheritance.

28. Allison dies during the current year. She is covered by a $500,000 life insurance policy payable to her husband Bob. Bob elects to receive the policy proceeds in 10 annual installments of $64,000. Write a letter to Bob explaining the tax consequences of the receipt of each installment.

29. Earl is a student at Aggie Tech. He receives a $5,000 general scholarship for his outstanding grades in previous years. Earl is also a residence hall assistant, for which he receives free room and board worth $6,000 per year. Earl's annual costs for tuition, books, and supplies are $8,000. Does Earl have any taxable income from the scholarship or the free room and board?

30. Assume the same facts as in problem 29, except that Earl is not a residence hall assistant and his general scholarship is for
   a. $5,000
   b. $10,000

31. Fawn receives a $2,500 scholarship to State University. Discuss the taxability of the scholarship under each of the following assumptions:
   a. The scholarship is paid from a general scholarship fund and is awarded to students with high academic potential. Recipients are not required to perform any services to receive the scholarship.
   b. The scholarship is paid by the finance department. Recipients are required to work 10 hours per week for a professor designated by the department.

32. Determine whether the taxpayers in each of the following situations have realized taxable income:
   a. Alexander inherited a tract of land from his uncle who died during the current year. A friend of Alexander's who is a petroleum engineer told him he thought there might be oil on the land. Alexander had the land surveyed, and an oil deposit worth an estimated $5,000,000 was discovered on the property.
   b. Mickey was given two tickets to the World Series by a friend. Mickey sold the tickets for $500 apiece.
   c. Hannah is the purchasing agent for Slim Diet Centers. Harold, a salesman who does considerable business with Hannah, gave her a set of golf clubs worth $750. Harold told Hannah that he was giving her the clubs to show his appreciation for being such a good friend throughout their business dealings.
   d. Melanie's father died during the current year. Melanie was the beneficiary of a $200,000 life insurance policy on her father's life. She received the proceeds on August 1 and immediately invested in a bank certificate of deposit with a 9% annual earnings rate.

33. Armando, a manager for Petros Pizza Pies (PPP), dies in an accident on July 12. PPP pays his wife Penelope $600 in salary that had accrued before Armando died. Armando was covered by a $90,000 group term life insurance policy, which is also paid to Penelope. In addition, the board of directors of PPP authorizes payment of $6,000 to Penelope and $4,000 to their child in recognition of Armando's years of loyal service and contributions to the success of the company. What are the tax consequences of the payments to Penelope and her child?

34. Lucinda is a welder for Big Auto Co., Inc. Lucinda dies in an automobile accident on March 14 of this year. Big Auto has a company policy of paying $4,000 to the spouse of any employee who dies. In addition to the $4,000 payment, Big Auto pays Harvey, Lucinda's husband, $1,800 in salary and $1,300 in vacation pay Lucinda had earned before her death. Harvey also collects $90,000 from a group term life insurance policy Big Auto provided as part of Lucinda's compensation package. Lucinda had contributed to a qualified employer-sponsored pension plan. Big Auto had matched Lucinda's contributions to the plan. The plan allows the beneficiary of an employee who dies before payments begin to take the plan balance as an annuity or in a lump sum. Harvey elects to take the $210,000 plan balance in a lump sum. Write a letter to Harvey explaining the tax consequences of each payment he receives.

35. Joan is a single individual who works for Big Petroleum, Inc. During all of 1996, Joan is stationed in West Africa. She pays West African taxes of $20,000 on her Big Petroleum salary of $90,000. Her taxable income without considering her salary from Big is $30,000. How should Joan treat the salary she receives from Big Petroleum on her 1996 U.S. tax return?

36. Assume that in problem 35 Joan pays $23,000 in West African taxes. Would your answer change? Explain.

37. Boris is a systems specialist with a public accounting firm. He is single. During all of 1996, Boris is on temporary assignment in London. He pays $25,000 in British income tax on his $105,000 salary. Boris knows little about taxes and seeks your advice on the taxability of the salary he earns while in London. Write Boris a memorandum explaining the tax treatment of his London salary. Assume that Boris has no other income sources and that he does not itemize deductions.

38. Ariel works for Sander Corporation for 30 years. Sander has a pension plan in which it matches employee contributions by up to 5% of the employee's salary. Ariel retires during the current year. Her pension plan contains payments and earnings of $300,000, half of which are attributable to payments made by Ariel and half attributable to payments made by Sander. Under the plan, Ariel is to receive $2,000 per month until she dies (her estimated life expectancy is 20 years). What is the tax treatment of each $2,000 payment under each of the following assumptions?
   a. The plan is a qualified pension plan. Therefore, no tax has been paid on any of the contributions or earnings in the plan.
   b. The plan is not a qualified plan. Therefore, Ariel has paid tax on all contributions and earnings in the plan.

39. Erwin works for Close Corporation for 24 years. Close has a qualified, noncontributory pension plan that pays employees with more than 5 years of service $75 per month per year when they reach age 65. Erwin turns 65 in February of this year and retires in June. Payments from Close's plan begin in July. In preparing for his retirement, Erwin had purchased an annuity 15 years ago for $18,000. The annuity pays $150 per month for life beginning at age 65. Erwin begins receiving the annuity payments in March, at which time his life expectancy is 15 years. How much gross income does Erwin have from the receipt of the payments from Close and the annuity in the current year?

40. Leyh's Outdoor Adventures, Inc., would like to begin providing life insurance coverage for its employees. Three employees are officers; each earns $100,000 per year. The other three employees each earn $40,000 per year. Ricardo, president of Leyh's, comes to you for advice on how to provide the coverage. He provides three alternatives, each of which will cost Leyh's $15,000 per year (an average of $2,500 per employee):
Option 1—Give each employee $2,500 to purchase coverage.
Option 2—Buy a group term life insurance policy under which each employee would be covered for an amount equal to twice her or his annual salary.
Option 3—Buy a whole life insurance policy under which each employee would receive $100,000-worth of coverage.
   Ricardo asks you to evaluate these options and advise him on the tax consequences of each. Write a letter to Ricardo explaining the tax effects of each option. Include your recommendation of the option that provides the greatest overall tax benefits.

41. Bear Co. provides all its employees with a $10,000 group term life insurance policy. Elk Co. does not provide any life insurance but pays $10,000 to survivors of employees who die. Jackie, an employee of Bear Co., dies during the current year. Rosetta, an employee of Elk Co., dies during the current year. Jackie and Rosetta are sisters-in-law. Write a letter to their husbands, Bo and Carl, explaining the tax effects of the $10,000 payments they receive.

42. Horace is an employee of Ace Electric Co. Ace provides all employees with group term life insurance equal to twice their annual salary. How much gross income does Horace have under each of the following assumptions?
    a. Horace is 26 and earns $18,000 per year.
    b. Horace is 26 and earns $38,000 per year.
    c. Horace is 63 and earns $38,000 per year.
    d. Horace is 46 and earns $80,000 per year.

43. Abe is an employee of Haddock, Inc. Haddock provides basic health and accident insurance to all its employees through a contract with Minor Accident Insurance Co. Because the Minor policy does not cover 100% of medical costs, Haddock provides all executive officers with a self-insured plan to pay any medical costs not covered by Minor's policy. Abe is eligible for both plans. During the current year, premiums on the Minor policy for Abe were $1,450. Abe also received reimbursements from the self-insured plan of $1,900.
    a. What are the tax consequences for Abe of the payments made by Haddock?
    b. What difference would it make if all employees were covered under both plans?

44. Faldo, Inc., provides medical coverage to employees through a self-insured plan. Nick, the president of Faldo, receives $3,400 in medical expense reimbursements from the plan during the current year. Discuss the tax consequences to Nick under the following circumstances:
    a. All employees are fully covered by the plan.
    b. All employees are covered by the plan. However, only Faldo's executive officers are fully reimbursed for all expenses. All other employees are limited to a maximum reimbursement of $1,000.

45. Adam works during the summer as a fire watcher for the Oregon forest service. As such he spends three weeks in the woods in a forest service watchtower and then gets a week off. Because of the remoteness of the location, groceries are flown in by helicopter to Adam each week. Does Adam have any taxable income from this arrangement? Explain.

46. Don is the production manager for Corporate Manufacturing Facilities (CMF). CMF works three production shifts per day. Because Don is so integral to CMF's operations, CMF requires Don to live in housing that CMF owns so that he can be available for any emergencies that arise throughout the day. The housing is located four blocks from the CMF plant. Is Don taxed on the value of the housing? Explain.

47. Determine whether the taxpayer has received taxable income in each of the following situations. Explain why any amount(s) may be excluded:
    a. Jim is an employee of Fast Tax Prep, Inc. All employees of Fast Tax are eligible for a 30% discount on the preparation of their income tax return. Jim's tax return preparation would normally have cost $500, but he paid only $350 because of the discount.
    b. Mabel is a lawyer for a large law firm, Winken, Blinken, and Nod. Winken pays Mabel's annual licensing renewal fee of $500 and her $200 annual dues to the American Lawyers' Association. Mabel also takes advantage of Winken's educational assistance plan and receives payment for the $7,000 cost of taking two night school courses in consumer law.
    c. Lori Co. runs a nursery near its offices. Employees are allowed to leave their children in the nursery free of charge during working hours. Nonemployees may also use the facility at a cost of $200 per month per child. Dolph is an employee of Lori with two children. Both children stay at Lori's facility while Dolph is at work.
    d. At the sporting goods store where Melissa works, her employer allows all employees to purchase goods at a 30% discount. Melissa purchases for $700 camping and fishing supplies that retail for $1,000. The goods had cost her employer $600.

48. Courtney is an employee of Hawkins Co. An average of three times a week she works out during her lunch hour at a health club provided by Hawkins. Discuss the taxability of Hawkins's provision of the health club in the following situations:

   a. The health club is owned by Hawkins and is located on its business premises. All employees and their dependents are allowed to use the facility. The cost of joining a comparable facility is $60 per month.

   b. The health club is located in Hawkins's office building, but is owned by Manzer Fitness World. Hawkins pays the $60 per month health club dues.

   c. Hawkins is in the health club business. The health club is used primarily by customers, although several employees, including Courtney, use the health club.

49. Dow, 42, is a manager for Winter Co. In addition to his $45,000 salary, Dow receives the following benefits from Winter during the current year:

   ■ Winter pays all its employees' health and accident insurance. Premiums paid by Winter for Dow's health insurance are $1,800.

   ■ Winter provides all employees with group term life insurance at twice their annual salary. Premiums on Dow's $90,000 of coverage are $900.

   ■ Winter has a flexible benefits plan in which employees may participate to pay any costs not reimbursed by their health insurance. Dow has $2,000 withheld from his salary under the plan. His actual unreimbursed medical costs are $2,320. Winter pays Dow the $2,000 paid into the plan during the year.

   ■ All management-level Winter employees are entitled to employer-provided parking. The cost of Dow's parking in a downtown garage is $2,400 for the year.

   ■ Winter pays Dow's $150 monthly membership fee in a health club located in the building in which Dow works. Dow uses the club during his lunch time and on weekends.

   REQUIRED: Compute Dow's gross income for the current year.

50. Becky, 45, is a senior vice president for South Publishing Co. During the current year, Becky's salary is $150,000 and she receives a $20,000 bonus before the end of the year. South matches employee contributions to its qualified pension plan up to 10% of an employee's annual salary before bonuses. Becky contributes the maximum to the plan. Becky also receives the following benefits from South during the year:

   ■ South has a cafeteria plan that allows all employees to select tax-free benefits or the cash equivalent on 6% of their annual salary before any bonus or pension plan payments. Becky uses the plan to purchase health and accident insurance for her daughter at a cost of $1,800, group term life insurance coverage of $200,000 at a cost of $1,200, and child care at a cost of $4,000. She takes the remaining $2,000 in cash.

   ■ All executive officers' medical expenses are covered by a self-insured medical reimbursement plan. Becky is fully reimbursed for her $800 in medical expenses.

   ■ South pays the employee's share of Social Security taxes on all executive employees' regular salaries.

   ■ Executive officers are provided with covered parking at company headquarters. All other employees must pay for their own parking. Becky's free parking is worth $3,600 this year.

   ■ Becky belongs to several professional organizations. South pays Becky's dues of $900 to these organizations. In addition, South pays the dues for all executive officers at one social club. South pays Becky's $3,000 country club membership.

   ■ The executive officers eat lunch in a private dining room at company headquarters. The purpose of the dining room is to encourage the officers to interact in an informal setting. They often discuss business but are not required to follow an agenda. The value of the meals Becky ate in the dining room this year is estimated at $2,500.

   REQUIRED: Compute Becky's gross income from South Publishing for the current year.

51. Jill, 43, is an employee of Primus University. Jill's annual salary is $44,000. Primus provides all employees with health and accident insurance (Jill's policy cost $1,800) and group term life insurance at twice their annual salary rounded up to the nearest $10,000 ($90,000 of coverage for Jill). In addition, Primus pays the first $1,000 of each employee's Social Security contribution. Primus has a qualified pension and a flexible benefits plan. Jill has $4,000 of her salary withheld and paid (and Primus matched the payment) into the pension plan. She also elects to have $1,300 of her salary paid into the flexible benefits plan. Because her medical costs are lower than expected, Jill gets back only $1,250 of the $1,300 she paid into the plan. What is Jill's gross income for the current year?

52. Samantha is an employee of Strong Co. Strong provides medical insurance for all its employees. The cost of Samantha's policy for the current year is $2,600. Because Strong's medical insurance has a $300 deductible and pays only 80% of most medical expenses, it also offers employees a flexible benefits plan to pay any unreimbursed expenses. During the current year, Samantha has $100 per month paid into the flexible benefits plan. Samantha has $1,300 in medical expenses and $600 in dental expenses. The medical insurance policy pays $800 of the medical expenses. Samantha is reimbursed for the remainder of her expenses from the flexible benefits plan. Discuss the effect of Strong's provision of the medical insurance and flexible benefits plans on her gross income and the taxability of the payments that Samantha received under the plans.

53. Determine the taxability of the damages received in each of the following situations:
    a. Helio Corporation sues Wrongo Corporation, charging that Wrongo made false statements about one of Helio's products. Helio claims that the statements injured its business reputation with its customers. The court awards Helio $2,000,000 in damages.
    b. Lien is injured when a ski lift she is riding on comes loose and crashes to the ground. Lien sues the ski resort and receives $12,000 in full payment of her medical expenses, $4,000 for pain and suffering, and $6,500 for income lost while she recovers from the accident. The company that manufactured the ski lift also pays Lien $50,000 in punitive damages.
    c. A major broadcasting company reports that Dr. Henry Mueller was engaged in Medicare fraud. The doctor is incensed and sues the company for libel. The court rules that the report was made with reckless disregard for the truth and awards Mueller $20,000 for the humiliation he suffered because of the allegation, $200,000 for loss of his business reputation, and $150,000 in punitive damages.

54. May was injured when a forklift tipped over on her while she was moving stock in the company warehouse. Because of her injuries, she could not work for 3 weeks. Her employer paid her $400, which was half her normal wages for the 3-week period. She also received $600 in workers' compensation for the injury. May is required to include the $400 she received from her employer in her gross income but excludes the $600 workers' compensation payment. Discuss why the payments are taxed differently.

55. How much income does each taxpayer recognize in each of the following situations?
    a. Toko was injured in an automobile accident. Toko sued the driver of the other car and received $4,000 for his pain and suffering, $2,000 in lost wages while he recuperated from his injuries, and $8,000 in punitive damages.
    b. A national magazine identified Michael as an individual who consistently cheated on his taxes. As a tax preparer, Michael was incensed about the charges, sued the magazine, and won when the court ruled that the charges were false and that he was not a public figure. The court awarded Michael $10,000 for the humiliation he suffered from the libel, $80,000 for loss of his business reputation, and $100,000 in punitive damages.

56. Bill was severely injured when he was hit by a car one morning while he was out jogging. He spent 1 month in the hospital and missed 3 months of work because of the injuries he sustained in the accident. Total medical costs were $70,000. Bill received the following payments as a result of the accident:
- His employer-provided accident insurance reimbursed him for $55,000 of the medical costs and provided him with $4,000 in sick pay while he was out of work.
- A private medical insurance policy purchased by Bill paid him $15,000 for medical costs.
- His employer gave Bill $3,000 to help him get through his rehabilitation period.
- A separate disability policy that Bill had purchased paid him $6,000.

How much gross income does Bill have as a result of the payments received for the accident?

57. Determine the tax treatment of the payments received in each of the following cases:
   a. Anastasia is covered by her employer's medical insurance policy. During the current year, the policy reimburses her for $960 of the $1,200 of medical costs she incurred.
   b. Alfredo, who is self-employed, is injured in a snowmobile accident. The insurance he purchased covers $3,200 of the $3,900 in medical costs related to the accident. It also pays him $2,000 to cover the income he loses during his recuperation.
   c. Libby is injured when a company truck backs over her at a warehouse. The company pays her $2,200 in medical expenses from its self-insured medical reimbursement plan (all employees are covered by the plan). During her recuperation, the company pays her normal $1,300 salary. In addition, she receives $600 from an insurance policy the company purchased to cover its liability to injured employees.
   d. Shortly after beginning work for El Dorado Corporation, Manny is injured when a lathe he is operating breaks his leg. Because he has not worked for the company long enough to qualify for employee medical insurance coverage, the company pays his $800 medical bill.

58. Determine Rona's gross income from the following items she receives during the current year:

Interest on savings account	$400
Dividends on Microsoft stock	200
Interest on Guam development bonds	300
Dividend on live insurance policy	100
(the company is a mutual life insurance company and the dividend is a return of part of the premiums she paid on the policy)	

In addition, Rona owns 500 shares of Cochran Corporation common stock. Cochran has a dividend reinvestment plan through which stockholders can receive a stock dividend equal to 5% of their holdings in lieu of a cash dividend of equal value. Rona takes the 25 shares of stock, which are worth $3 per share.

59. Horatio owns Utah general purpose bonds with a face value of $50,000 that he purchased last year for $52,000. During the current year, Horatio receives $2,400 in interest on the bonds. In December, Horatio sells the bonds for $48,000. What is the effect of the bond transactions on Horatio's gross income for the current year?

60. Determine the amount of gross income Elbert must recognize in each of the following situations:
   a. In October, Elbert sells City of Norfolk bonds with a face value of $4,000 for $6,500. Elbert had purchased the bonds 2 years ago for $3,900. Elbert had received $250 in interest on the bonds before he sold them.
   b. Elbert owns 500 shares of Tortoise, Inc., common stock for which he had paid $5,000 several years ago. Tortoise declares and distributes a 10% stock dividend during the current year. On December 31, Tortoise common stock is selling for $15 per share.
   c. In December, Elbert sells City of Quebec bonds with a face value of $7,000 for $6,800. Elbert had purchased the bonds in January for $7,100. Elbert received $1,900 in interest on the bonds before he sold them.

61. Maysa is considering making an investment in municipal bonds yielding 4%. What would the yield on a taxable bond have to be to provide a higher after-tax return than the municipal bond if Maysa is in a 31% marginal tax rate bracket?

62. Vito is having financial difficulties during the current year. Among other debts, he owes More Bank $200,000. Rather than lend Vito more money to help him out, More Bank agrees to reduce his debt to $175,000.

   a. How much gross income must Vito recognize if his assets total $300,000 and his liabilities are $260,000 before the forgiveness of debt?

   b. Assume the same facts as in part a, except that Vito's liabilities are $400,000 before the forgiveness of debt.

   c. Assume the same facts as in part a, except that Vito's total liabilities are $315,000 before the forgiveness of debt.

63. Orts Block and Tackle Shop is experiencing cash flow problems during the current year. Among other debts, Orts owes Cowdrey State Bank $80,000. After negotiations, Cowdrey agrees to reduce Orts's debt to $50,000 with a 1% increase in the interest rate on the $50,000 debt. How much income does Orts have from the debt reduction under the following circumstances?

   a. Orts is a sole proprietorship owned by A.J. A.J.'s total assets are $180,000 and his total liabilities are $200,000 before the debt reduction.

   b. Assume the same facts as in part a. The Cowdrey debt was incurred to purchase a storage building with a current fair market value of $40,000. The building cost $120,000 when it was purchased in 1991 and has an adjusted basis of $90,000.

   c. Assume the same facts as in part b, except that Orts is organized as a corporation.

64. Helena has assets of $130,000 and liabilities of $160,000. One of Helena's debts is for $120,000. Discuss the tax consequences of the reduction of this debt in each of the following circumstances:

   a. The debt was incurred by Helena for medical school expenses. She borrowed $120,000 from her grandfather, who agreed to reduce the debt to $80,000, because Helena had done so well in school.

   b. The debt was incurred to purchase property used in Helena's business. In order to help Helena back on her feet, the bank that loaned her the money agreed to reduce the debt to $80,000.

   c. The debt was incurred to purchase equipment used in Helena's business. The debt is owed to the manufacturer of the equipment. Because the equipment did not perform as advertised by the manufacturer, the manufacturer agreed to reduce the debt to $80,000.

65. Determine the amount of income that must be recognized in each discharge of indebtedness situation that follows. Assume in all cases that the related debt was incurred before 1993.

   a. Noreen owns a building with a fair market value of $80,000 that she uses in her construction business. The building is secured by a debt of $110,000 and has an adjusted basis of $20,000. The lender reduces the debt to $85,000.

   b. Armando owns a building with a fair market value of $300,000 that he uses in his business. The building is secured by a debt of $400,000 and has an adjusted basis of $250,000. The lender reduces the debt to $340,000.

   c. Lane owns a building with a fair market value of $60,000 that she uses in her consulting business. The building has an adjusted basis of $35,000 and is secured by 2 debts: The first is a mortgage of $50,000, and the second is a mortgage of $40,000. The lender of the second mortgage agrees to reduce the mortgage to $25,000.

   d. Newton purchased a warehouse to use in his wholesaling business in 1988 at a cost of $240,000. The warehouse is currently worth $220,000 and has an adjusted basis of $210,000. Newton's business has been experiencing financial difficulties, and his bank agrees to reduce the $200,000 debt on the warehouse to $165,000 to help him out.

66. Determine the amount that should be included in the taxpayer's gross income in each of the following situations:

    a. Tim is selected as the outstanding business professor at State University and is given a cash award of $1,000.

    b. Sarah is awarded the Nobel Prize in economics. She assigns the $1,000,000 award to her university department to establish a scholarship fund for economics students.

    c. Salina is an apartment manager, for which she is paid $6,000 per year. The owner of the apartments offers her the option of a $300 per month living allowance or the use of one apartment rent free. Salina chooses to live in the apartment, which normally rents for $400 per month.

    d. Tom is injured in an accident at work that causes him to miss several months of work. During the time he isn't working, he receives $800 from workers' compensation and $1,300 from a disability plan paid for by his employer.

    e. Terry, an employee of Green University, has an annual salary of $45,000. Green has a qualified pension plan into which all employees contribute 5% of their annual salaries. Green matches the employee's contribution.

67. Connors Partnership owns a building that it has rented out to Corner Grocery Store for the last 10 years. Corner goes out of business and returns the property to Connors. Corner had made improvements to the store costing $30,000 during the 10-year lease period. The partnership had paid $60,000 for the building, which is now worth $200,000. Does Connors have any gross income from the ending of the lease? Discuss when Connors will recognize any income from the building.

68. Jonas owns a building that he leases to Dipper, Inc., for $5,000 per month. The owner of Dipper has been complaining about the condition of the restrooms and has proposed making improvements that will cost $24,000. Dipper's owner is willing to pay to have the improvements made if Jonas will reduce the monthly rent on the building to $4,000 for one year. Write a letter to Jonas explaining the tax effects for Jonas of the proposal by Dipper's owner.

INTEGRATIVE PROBLEMS

69. Edna, 63, is a widow and works for Rhododendron Corporation. Her annual salary at Rhododendron is $40,000. Rhododendron provides the following benefits to all employees:

    ■ Medical insurance—The cost of Edna's policy is $1,800. She incurs $950 in valid medical expenses and is reimbursed for $560 of the expenses by the company policy.

    ■ Group term life insurance—Each employee is provided with $80,000-worth of coverage under the policy.

    ■ Qualified pension plan—Rhododendron matches employee contributions up to $1,500. Edna contributes 5% of her salary to the plan.

    Edna has the following other items that may affect her current-year taxes:

    a. She receives $100 per month from an annuity she purchased from Florence General Life Assurance Co. The annuity cost $9,720. Edna is to receive the annuity for life. When she began receiving the payments at age 60, her life expectancy was 18 years.

    b. She receives a $400 refund of last year's state income taxes during the current year. Last year, her itemized deductions totaled $5,600. In the current year, Edna's itemized deductions are $3,800.

    c. She has a separate medical policy she purchased to cover costs that her employer-provided policy does not cover. She pays $1,400 for the policy, which reimburses her for $350 of her medical expenses.

    d. She owns 5% Puerto Rico bonds with a face value of $40,000. The bonds pay interest annually on December 20.

    e. She sells stock she owned for $18,000 on July 1. She had paid $14,000 for the stock three years earlier. Edna invests the proceeds from the sale of the stock in a money-market savings account that pays 5% interest.

f. Her brother dies and leaves her the farm that had been owned by their father (her brother had inherited the farm). The farm is valued at $160,000. Edna leases the farm to a local farmer and receives $9,000 in rents during the current year.

g. On April 1, she gives $5,000 of Kao Corporation bonds she owns to her granddaughter. The bonds pay annual interest of 6% on December 31.

h. She receives a watch worth $900 from Rhododendron for her 20 years of loyal service to the company. Rhododendron does not routinely give out length-of-service awards.

i. She sells land that she had held as an investment for $15,000 on October 1. She had paid $24,000 for the land 2 years earlier. Edna invests the proceeds in State of Oregon bonds that pay 4% interest annually on December 31.

REQUIRED: Compute Edna's gross income, adjusted gross income, taxable income, and her income tax liability. Edna has no dependents.

70. Carmin Kovach is single and has 2 children from her previous marriage. Anika, 9, lives with Carmin. Julius, 11, lives with his father, Ray. Carmin pays alimony of $300 per month to Ray. The payments are to continue until Julius reaches age 18, when they will be reduced to $100.

Carmin is 32 and employed as a nuclear engineer with Atom Systems Consultants, Inc. (ASCI). Her annual salary is $80,000, and ASCI has an extensive fringe benefits program for its employees.

ASCI has a qualified pension plan that covers all employees. Under the plan, ASCI matches any contribution to the plan up to 10% of the employee's annual salary. Carmin makes the maximum allowable contribution of $8,000, and it is matched by ASCI.

ASCI provides medical coverage to all employees (no dependent coverage is provided). Carmin's medical coverage costs ASCI $2,100 during the current year. She receives $450 in reimbursements for her medical costs. ASCI also provides employees with a flexible benefits plan. Carmin pays $3,000 into the plan. She uses $1,800 to purchase medical coverage for Anika. Her medical, dental, and optometry costs not covered by insurance total $1,600; the flexible benefits plan reimburses her $1,200 for these costs.

ASCI also provides employees with group term life insurance of twice their annual salary, up to a maximum coverage of $150,000. Carmin's group term life insurance premiums cost $400. Because of the sensitive and sometimes dangerous nature of her work, ASCI also provides Carmin with a $300,000 whole life insurance policy. The whole life insurance policy costs $650.

Taking advantage of ASCI's educational assistance program, Carmin enrolls in two night classes in advanced nuclear physics at a local college. ASCI pays her tuition, fees, books, and other course-related costs of $7,000.

Carmin also receives certain other fringe benefits not available to all employees. She receives free parking in the company's security garage that would normally cost $200 per month. In addition, ASCI pays the $1,000 cost of her nuclear engineer's license and $600 per year in professional association dues and professional magazine subscriptions. ASCI also pays Carmin's $900 dues to a health club that is located in the same building as her office.

Carmin routinely enters sweepstakes contests. This year, she is notified that she has won $10,000 in a breakfast cereal promotion. The prize is to be paid equally over 10 years. She receives the first payment on December 28, although she doesn't deposit the check in her checking account until January 3.

In January, Carmin's father dies. Social Security pays her $400 as a survivor's benefit. She also receives stock valued at $18,000 and her father's house, which has a value of $85,000, as her share of her father's estate.

Carmin rents her father's house on August 1. The monthly rent is $700, and the lease agreement is for one year. The lease requires the tenant to pay the first and last months' rent and a $500 security deposit. The security deposit is to be returned at the end of the lease if the property is in good condition. On August 1, Carmin receives $1,900 from the tenant per the terms of the lease agreement. In November, the plumbing freezes and several lines burst. The tenant has the repairs made and pays the $600 bill.

In December, he reduces his rental payment to $100 to compensate for the plumbing repairs. Carmin pays other deductible costs for the rental that total $4,200. The allowable depreciation on the rental house is $1,020.

Carmin owns several other investments. She receives the following amounts (all in cash) from the stocks and bonds she owns:

General Dynamics common stock	$ 300
City of Toronto bonds	400
State of Nebraska bonds	600
New Jersey economic development bonds	200
Grubstake Mining Development common stock	3,000

Carmin owns 2,000 shares of Grubstake Mining Development common stock. Grubstake is organized as an S corporation and has 100,000 shares outstanding. Grubstake reports taxable income of $400,000 during the current year.

Carmin slips on a wet spot in front of a computer store during the current year. She breaks her ankle and is unable to work for 2 weeks. She incurs $1,300 in medical costs, all of which are paid by the owner of the store. The store also gives her $500 for pain and suffering resulting from the injury. ASCI continues to pay her salary during the 2 weeks she misses because of the accident. ASCI's plan also pays her $400 in disability pay for the time she is unable to work.

REQUIRED: Calculate Carmin's adjusted gross income on her 1996 tax return. Then do one (or both) of the following, according to your professor's instructions:

a. Include a brief explanation of how you determined each item that affected adjusted gross income and any items you excluded from gross income. Your solution to the problem should contain a list of each item included in adjusted gross income and its amount, with the explanations attached.

b. Write a letter to Carmin explaining how you determined each item that affected adjusted gross income and any items you excluded from gross income. You should include a list of each item included in adjusted gross income and its amount.

DISCUSSION CASE

71. Germaine, 22, is a single individual with no dependents; she recently graduated from college. She has job offers from two firms. Germaine likes both companies equally well and has decided to base her decision on which company offers more. Details of each job offer are as follows:

Company A—Annual salary of $30,000, employer-provided health and accident insurance (employer cost: $2,100), group term life insurance coverage at twice the annual salary (premiums for $60,000-worth of coverage are $450), employer-provided day-care facility (employer's cost per dependent is $150 per month), and company-provided parking ($900 per year).

Company B—Annual salary of $32,000, a cafeteria plan under which employees can choose benefits of up to 10% of annual salary or take the cash equivalent. In addition, the company has a flexible benefits plan in which employees may participate by setting aside up to 10% of annual salary per year for payment of unreimbursed medical expenses.

Germain has come to you for advice. Write a letter to Germaine explaining the tax effects of the two job offers and the income she can expect from each offer. Assume that she has no other income sources and that she itemizes deductions.

e wants to invest $10,000. His options are

Gibraltar Corporation bonds with an annual interest rate of 8%.

State of Hawaii bonds with an annual interest rate of 5%.

Series EE savings bonds; a $10,000 investment will pay $14,300 in 5 years.

ume that Zane is a 28% marginal tax rate payer, the time value of money is 6%, Zane intends to hold any amounts invested for 5 years. Which option will provide greatest after-tax return? Would your answer change if Zane's marginal tax rate is 36%?

73. You are a CPA working for a local firm and have been assigned the 1996 tax return of Bobby Crosser. In going over the data that Bobby provided to the firm, you are surprised to see that Bobby has reported no dividend income or gains from the sale of stock. You recently prepared the 1996 gift tax return of Bobby's aunt Esther. In that return, Esther had reported a gift of stock to Bobby on January 6, 1996. The stock had a fair market value of $50,000, and Esther's basis (which became Bobby's basis) in the stock was $5,000. What are your obligations under the Statements on Responsibilities in Tax Practice? In your discussion, state which standard(s) may be applicable to this situation and what might result from applying the standard(s).

DEHUCTIONS

CHAPTER 5
INTRODUCTION TO BUSINESS EXPENSES

CHAPTER 6
BUSINESS EXPENSES

CHAPTER 7
LOSSES—DEDUCTIONS AND LIMITATIONS

Introduction to Business Expenses

▲ CHAPTER LEARNING OBJECTIVES

■ Introduce the reporting of allowable deductions by individuals, corporations, and conduit entities.

■ Describe the classification of expenditures as those that are related to a taxpayer's trade or business, those for the production of income, and those for personal expenditures.

■ Discuss the criteria for distinguishing a trade or business from a production-of-income activity.

■ Describe mixed-purpose assets and mixed-use expenditures and discuss the tax treatment of such assets and expenditures.

■ Explain the ordinary, necessary, and reasonable requirements for the deduction of trade or business and production-of-income expenses.

■ Discuss the general classes of expenditures for which a deduction is not allowed.

■ Explain the general rules for deducting expenses under the cash and the accrual methods of accounting and the specific requirements for related party accrued expenses.

▲ **CONCEPT REVIEW** ▲

Ability to pay   A tax should be based on the amount that the taxpayer can afford to pay, relative to other taxpayers.

Accounting method   A taxpayer must adopt an accounting method that clearly reflects income.

Administrative convenience   Those items for which the cost of compliance would exceed the revenue generated are not taxed.

Annual accounting period   All entities report the results of their transactions on an annual basis (the tax year). Each tax year stands on its own, apart from other tax years.

Arm's-length transaction   A transaction in which all parties to the transaction have bargained in good faith and for their individual benefit, not for the benefit of the transaction group.

Basis   This is the amount of unrecovered investment in an asset. As amounts are expended and/or recovered relative to an asset over time, the basis is adjusted in consideration of such changes. The **adjusted basis** of an asset is the original basis, plus or minus the changes in the amount of unrecovered investment.

Business purpose   To be deductible, an expenditure or a loss must have a business or other economic purpose that exceeds any tax avoidance motive. The primary motive for the transaction must be to make a profit.

Capital recovery   No income is realized until the taxpayer receives more than the amount invested to produce the income. The amount invested in an asset represents the maximum amount recoverable.

Entity   All items of income, deduction, and so on are traced to the tax unit responsible for the item.

Legislative grace   Any tax relief provided is the result of a specific act of Congress that must be strictly applied and interpreted. All income received is taxable unless a specific provision can be found in the tax law that excludes the income from taxation. Deductions must be approached with the philosophy that nothing is deductible unless a provision in the tax law allows the deduction.

Related party   Family members and corporations that are owned by family members are considered related parties, as are certain other relationships between entities in which the power to control the substance of a transaction is evidenced through majority ownership.

Tax benefit rule   Any deduction taken in a prior year that is recovered in a subsequent year is income in the year of recovery, to the extent that a tax benefit was received from the deduction.

Wherewithal to pay   Income is recognized in the period in which the taxpayer has the means to pay the tax on the income.

Chapter 1 pointed out that deductible expenditures are grouped into three broad categories. These categories are business expenses, losses, and other itemized deductions. This chapter focuses on the general requirements for deducting business expenses. Specific business-expense deductions are the topic of Chapter 6, deductions for losses are discussed in Chapter 7, and itemized deductions that are specific to individual taxpayers are fully discussed in Chapter 8.

INTRODUCTION

Tax **deductions** are a matter of legislative grace. As a result, two restrictions immediately apply to deductions. First, only deductions allowed by the tax law may be subtracted to compute taxable income. The deduction provisions are part of Congress's approach to implementing the ability-to-pay concept. By allowing deductions, Congress is, in effect, recognizing the inequity that could result from imposing a tax on gross income rather than taxable income. Therefore, Congress allows deductions for the costs of earning income and certain other expenditures. Second, a deduction is allowed for an item only if all the requirements for the deduction are satisfied. Because deductions are intended to provide relief from tax, the deduction rules are strictly interpreted and applied. Thus, a deduction is not allowed merely because a taxpayer thinks it is fair or equitable to use the expenditure to reduce income.

▲ **EXAMPLE 1**   Joan earns $25,000 in wages as a county property tax assessor. John owns and operates his own business selling Slippery Oil. John's Slippery Oil sales were $60,000, the cost of the oil sold was $25,000, and he had other business expenses of $10,000.

Discussion: Joan should report $25,000 in wages as gross income. Because the tax law allows a deduction for the cost of sales and business expenses, John has a gross income of $35,000 ($60,000 − $25,000) and will report $25,000 in taxable income from his business ($35,000 − $10,000). After recovering his expenses, John will pay tax on his increase in wealth according to the ability-to-pay concept. Compared with Joan's tax treatment, it would be inequitable to tax John on his gross income and deny him a deduction to recover the amounts he invested to earn a profit.

▲ **EXAMPLE 2**   Randy and Cindy are both practicing CPAs, specializing in tax. Randy has enrolled in law school so he can take tax courses. Randy has no intention of getting a law degree. Cindy has enrolled in a master's program in tax to improve her skills as a tax accountant. Eventually, Cindy hopes to earn the master's degree.

Discussion: Both Randy and Cindy have incurred expenses to improve or maintain their skills as practicing tax accountants. However, Randy cannot deduct his expenses. Educational expenses that qualify a person for a new profession (the practice of law) are not deductible. Cindy's expenses can be deducted, because they relate to her job and do not qualify her for a new profession.[1] Although treating Randy differently than Cindy seems unfair, Randy did not satisfy all the requirements of the tax law to claim an educational expense deduction.

To deduct a **business expense,** the expenditure must have a business purpose that is unrelated to its tax effect. Under the business purpose concept, there must be a business purpose for the expenditure that exceeds any tax-avoidance motive. Failure to establish a business purpose for the expense can result in the loss of the deduction. In most instances, a business purpose can be established by showing that the expense was related to a profit-motivated transaction. When the taxpayer has both business and personal reasons for an expenditure, the taxpayer risks losing the deduction. For these expenditures, the taxpayer will need to show that the business purpose was the primary or dominant motive for the transaction.

▲ **EXAMPLE 3**   Zoltan is a physician who has not seen his sister for more than 10 years, because she lives in Kenya. Zoltan would like to visit his sister and write a book about his experiences. He has never written a book. Because his trip has a business purpose—to write a book—Zoltan intends to deduct the full cost of his trip as a business deduction. Has Zoltan met the dominant motive requirement for deducting the cost of the trip?

Discussion: Because Zoltan has several motives for making the trip, he will have to prove that the dominant motive is a business purpose. Based on the facts, it would appear that Zoltan is not entitled to a deduction, because the primary purpose of his trip is a personal reason (to visit his sister). Because Zoltan has no experience in writing travel books, he would have a hard time proving that writing the book is his dominant motive.

Gross income has been defined to include only the excess of an individual's capital investment. As a result, the expenditure or consumption of capital to earn income results in a tax deduction. The capital recovery concept limits the amount of a deduction to the amount of the expenditure or the taxpayer's investment in an asset. As a result of this concept, the deduction for an item may not exceed the taxpayer's cost. For example, the payment of a $500 business expense would be limited to a $500 deduction. In this chapter, basis is used to identify the amount that can be deducted under the capital recovery concept. *Basis* is a technical term that was introduced as a construct in Chapter 2 and is discussed in detail in Chapter 10. For discussion purposes, think of basis as the cost of an asset or the dollar amount of a specific expenditure. Thus, basis represents the maximum amount of an expenditure that can be deducted as a recovery of capital.

The accounting concepts discussed in Chapter 2 influence the tax treatment of deductions. Although a deduction of basis is allowed under the capital recovery concept, the entity concept requires the taxpayer claiming the deduction to own the capital being deducted as a recovery. Thus, the entity concept prevents one taxpayer from deducting another taxpayer's expenditures.

▲ **EXAMPLE 4**   Miranda is a public accountant and is required by state law to have a license to practice public accounting. When the state license renewal fee came due, Miranda was short of money and could not renew her license. Miranda's mother paid the license renewal fee for her so she could continue working as a public accountant. Can Miranda deduct the fee as a business expense?

Discussion: The license renewal fee is Miranda's business expense, and only she can deduct the payment of the fee. Because Miranda did not pay the license renewal fee, she is not allowed a deduction for the business expense. Because the license renewal fee is not Miranda's mother's expense, her mother cannot deduct the payment of the expense. Based on these facts, neither Miranda nor her mother can deduct the payment of the license renewal fee.

Note that the bad tax result here could have been avoided if Miranda's mother had either gifted or made a valid loan to Miranda of the money necessary to pay the licensing fee and Miranda had made the payment from her own funds.

The annual accounting period concept requires the taxpayer to use an acceptable accounting method to determine the year in which a deduction should be reported. Once an accounting method is adopted, it should be used as the basis for the systematic and consistent allocation of expenses to the proper tax years. Failure to claim an expense in the correct year can result in loss of the deduction. If an expenditure, such as utilities and office supplies, benefits only one tax year, it is allowed as a deduction in the year benefited. When an expenditure provides benefits for more than one accounting period, the expenditure is usually allocated, based on the annual accounting period concept, to the proper tax years by using an acceptable accounting method. Examples of expenses that may need to be allocated are prepaid rent, prepaid interest, and prepaid insurance as well as depreciation on buildings and equipment. If the expenditure has an indefinite life, it is normally not deducted until the accounting period in which the asset is disposed of, abandoned, or proved to have lost its value. Thus, assets such as securities and land that do not have definite useful lives are not subject to amortization or depreciation for tax purposes.

As deductions are more closely examined in the rest of this chapter, the concepts discussed in Chapter 2 will be related to the specific rules and requirements for a deduction. The discussion and examples throughout this chapter consider deduction issues from the points of view of individuals, corporations, and conduit entities (partnerships and S corporations). Situations in which a tax rule applies only to individual taxpayers will be pointed out.

REPORTING DEDUCTIONS

The phrases **deductions for adjusted gross income** and **deductions from adjusted gross income** identify where in the tax computation an individual taxpayer deducts an allowable expense. Because all of a corporation's expenses are related to a business purpose, it is not necessary to use these two phrases when discussing its deductions; a corporation does not have personal expenses similar to those of an individual, which are deducted from adjusted gross income. Thus, the term **adjusted gross income** is unique to the individual tax computation.

Chapter 1 introduced an income tax computational framework as an overview of the federal income tax computation. At this point, we expand the framework for computing an individual's income tax (see Exhibit 5–1) to illustrate how individuals deduct various expenses. This chapter discusses the distinctions among *trade or business*, *production of income*, and *personal expenses*. Note in Exhibit 5–1 that trade or business expenses are deducted *for* adjusted gross income, whereas production-of-income expenses are subtracted as a deduction *from* adjusted gross income.[2] Recall that amounts deducted for adjusted gross income are always deductible, but deductions from adjusted gross income are subject to various limitations.

Trade or business expenses, expenses related to the production of rent and royalty income, losses on sales of property used in a trade or business, and capital losses (limited to $3,000) are deducted from gross income to compute adjusted gross income. As a result of legislative grace, these deductions receive more favorable treatment than deductions from adjusted gross income. Unless the passive

▲ **Exhibit 5–1**

INDIVIDUAL INCOME TAX COMPUTATIONAL FRAMEWORK

Income "broadly defined"
(includes income from all sources)
Minus: Excluded sources of income
Equals: Gross income
Minus: Deductions for adjusted gross income
　　　Trade or business expenses
　　　Rent and royalty expenses
　　　Trade or business losses
　　　Capital loss deduction ($3,000 maximum)
　　　Other specifically allowable deductions
Equals: Adjusted gross income
Minus: Deductions from adjusted gross income
　　　The greater of:
　　　　1. Standard deduction
　　　　or
　　　　2. Allowable itemized deductions:
　　　　　Deductible personal expenditures
　　　　　　Medical expenses
　　　　　　Home mortgage interest/investment interest
　　　　　　Property taxes/state income taxes
　　　　　　Charitable contributions
　　　　　　Personal casualty losses
　　　　Other miscellaneous itemized deductions
　　　　　Investment expenses for the production of income
　　　　　Expenses related to tax return preparation and compliance
　　　　　Unreimbursed employee business expenses
　　Minus: Personal and dependency exemptions
　　Equals: Taxable income

activity rules discussed in Chapter 7 apply, trade or business expenses and losses and rent expenses deducted for adjusted gross income are fully allowed as deductions to compute taxable income.

The allowable deduction from adjusted gross income is the greater of the taxpayer's standard deduction amount or allowable itemized deductions.[3] **Itemized deductions** consist of allowable personal expenditures[4] and miscellaneous itemized deductions. Most itemized deductions are subject to income limitations. For example, investment expenses are deductible as miscellaneous itemized deductions. However, miscellaneous itemized deductions must be reduced by 2 percent of adjusted gross income in calculating the amount of the total expense that can be deducted.[5] In addition, total itemized deductions are reduced for high-income taxpayers. As a result, deductions from adjusted gross income receive less favorable treatment than deductions for adjusted gross income. Except for rent and royalty expenses deducted for adjusted gross income and investment interest, all expenses for the production of income are deductible as miscellaneous itemized deductions, subject to the 2 percent of adjusted gross income limitation. The computation of allowable personal itemized deductions and the applicable limitations are discussed in Chapter 8. If the taxpayer uses the predetermined standard deduction, all tax benefits available from an itemized deduction for investment expenses are lost.

▲ **EXAMPLE 5**   Jennifer owns a dress shop. During the current year, she incurred $43,000 in valid expenses related to the dress shop. In addition, Jennifer incurred $6,000 in expenses related to production-of-income activities. If Jennifer's adjusted gross income is $83,000 without considering either of these expenses, how much expense can she deduct?

Discussion: Trade or business expenses are deductions for adjusted gross income. The $43,000 in trade or business expenses reduces her adjusted gross income to $40,000 ($83,000 − $43,000). Production-of-income expenses are deductible as miscellaneous itemized deductions, subject to the 2% of adjusted gross income limitation. Therefore, Jennifer is allowed to deduct only $5,200 [$6,000 − ($40,000 × 2%)] of the production-of-income expenses.

Note another advantage of the deductions for adjusted gross income: By reducing adjusted gross income, the amount of any deduction from adjusted gross income that is subject to a limitation increases. In this case, the $43,000 in business expenses allowed Jennifer an extra $860 ($43,000 × 2%) deduction of her production-of-income expenses. Thus, correct classification of a deduction as for adjusted gross income versus from adjusted gross income is critical in the calculation of an individual's taxable income.

Conduit Entity Reporting

Conduit entities (partnerships and S corporations) are not subject to tax. Rather, the taxable income from the conduit flows through to each owner, and each is taxed on his or her individual tax return. As discussed in Chapter 3, the conduit entity reports some items separately to the partner or shareholder, because certain income items (such as capital gains) are subject to special tax rules; they are not included in the calculation of a conduit entity's ordinary taxable income or loss.[6] Certain deductions also are subject to special tax rules—typically limitations on the amount that can be deducted by the owners—and must be reported separately. For example, investment expenses of individuals are miscellaneous itemized deductions that must be reduced by 2 percent of adjusted gross income. Therefore, as with some income items, not all deductions of a conduit are used in calculating ordinary taxable income or loss.

▲ **EXAMPLE 6**   The Hackett Group (HG), a partnership, operates a management consulting firm; it consists of three equal partners, Mark, Nancy, and Ahmed. HG's taxable income for the year is $255,000, consisting of the following:

Sales revenues	$1,500,000
Short-term capital gain	27,000
Trade and business expenses	(1,260,000)
Investment expenses	(12,000)
Taxable income	$ 255,000

How must the Hackett Group report its results to Mark, Nancy, and Ahmed for tax purposes?

Discussion: Because the Hackett Group must report each partner's share of short-term capital gain and investment expenses, the Hackett Group cannot divide the partnership's taxable income of $255,000 equally and report ordinary taxable income of $85,000 ($255,000 ÷ 3) to each partner. Rather, the Hackett Group uses only the partnership's sales revenue and business expenses to calculate the ordinary taxable income for each partner. As a result, each partner's share of the ordinary taxable income is $80,000 [($1,500,000 − $1,260,000 = $240,000) ÷ 3]. The Hackett Group must report to each partner $9,000 ($27,000 ÷ 3) of short-term capital gain and $4,000 ($12,000 ÷ 3) of investment expenses.

Because investment expenses must be reduced by 2 percent of adjusted gross income, investment expenses are not included in calculating the conduit's ordinary taxable income or loss. Otherwise, each partner would be able to deduct the full amount of the investment expenses.

▲ **EXAMPLE 7**   Assume the same facts as in example 6. Ahmed is single; his adjusted gross income for the year is $25,000, and his total itemized deductions are $12,000 (before considering the information in example 6). What is the effect on Ahmed's taxable income of stating the investment expenses separately?

Discussion: If the Hackett Group did not report both investment income and expenses separately, Ahmed's ordinary taxable income from the Hackett Group would be $85,000 ($255,000 ÷ 3). He would have an adjusted gross income of $110,000 ($25,000 + $85,000), itemized deductions of $12,000, and taxable income of $95,450 ($110,000 − $12,000 − $2,550).

Because the capital gains and investment expenses receive special tax treatment, HG must report these items separately. Ahmed's share of the ordinary income is $80,000, and his adjusted gross income is $114,000 ($25,000 + $80,000 + $9,000). The $4,000 of investment expenses is a miscellaneous itemized deduction, which is reduced by 2% of adjusted gross income.

Investment expenses	$4,000
Limitation: 2% × $114,000	(2,280)
Investment expense deduction	$1,720

Ahmed's itemized deductions total $13,720 ($12,000 + $1,720), and his taxable income is $97,730 ($114,000 − $13,720 − $2,550). Because HG reports these items separately, Ahmed's taxable income increases by $2,280 ($97,730 − $95,450).

In essence, the owner and not the conduit entity is subject to tax. The conduit is viewed as only a form of organization, the income and deductions from which flow through to each owner. This ensures that income and deductions of a conduit are treated similarly to income and deductions incurred by an individual taxpayer.

As example 7 illustrates, it is important that a conduit entity report separately any deduction that receives special tax treatment. The following is a list of commonly incurred deductions that a conduit entity must report separately:

- Charitable contributions
- Investment interest expense
- Investment expenses
- Section 179 expense
- Nondeductible expenses

CLASSIFICATION OF DEDUCTIONS

Proper application of the ability-to-pay and legislative grace concepts requires the separation of expenditures that qualify for deduction from those that are not allowed by the tax law. The basic test to be applied to obtain the initial classification of expenditures is whether the expenditure is related to a profit-motivated transaction or is motivated by personal needs and wants. Thus, expenditures are initially classified as profit-motivated or personal expenditures. Figure 5–1 illustrates this classification scheme.

Profit-Motivated Expenditures

As discussed in Chapter 1, a taxpayer may legitimately plan transactions to avoid the payment of tax. Because business profits reflect tax costs and savings, the tax effect of a transaction is an important planning consideration. A legitimate business reason for entering a transaction is to save taxes. However, the tax law prohibits deductions that are motivated solely by the expected tax benefits (savings). To be deductible, the business purpose concept requires an expenditure to have a bonafide business reason other than tax avoidance. If the sole purpose of a transaction is tax savings, it will not be allowed as a deduction.

The courts maintain that the presence of a business purpose does not always require that a transaction be recognized. Where objective evidence indicates no potential for economic profit apart from tax savings, a transaction can be disregarded.[7] Thus, to be deductible, the dominant motive for incurring a business expense must be to earn a profit that is independent of any tax savings. Therefore,

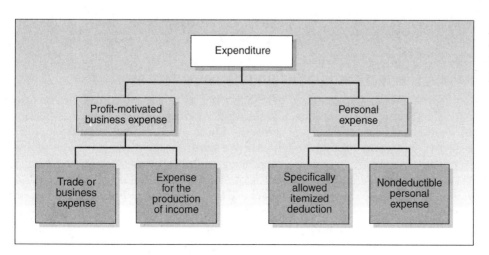

▲ **Figure 5–1**

CLASSIFICATION OF DEDUCTIONS OF AN INDIVIDUAL

only expenses that satisfy the requirement that profit be the **dominant motive** are classified as business expenses.

> ▲ **EXAMPLE 8**   Harry's son Junior wants to open a motorcycle dealership. Because Junior is short of funds, Harry purchases a building for the dealership and leases it to Junior. No lease is signed, but Harry tells Junior not to worry about paying rent until the dealership begins to show a profit. In addition, Harry agrees not to sell the building without Junior's approval. Is Harry's dominant motive in acquiring the building to obtain a profit?
>
> *Discussion:*   On the facts presented, Harry's dominant motive in acquiring the building is to help his son get his business established. Because there is no formal rental agreement and Harry will not sell the building without Junior's approval, the purchase of the building and the payment of costs related to the building are in the nature of a gift. Harry is not attempting to profit from either rental payments or potential appreciation in the value of the business. Therefore, any expenditures Harry makes regarding the building would not be classified as business expenses. As personal expenses, only those personal expenses specifically allowed by the tax law (interest, property taxes) would be deductible.

Recall from Chapter 2 that the business purpose concept means that the taxpayer's dominant motive for an expenditure is to earn an economic benefit (profit) before considering the effects of tax savings. Thus, profit-motivated expenses, or expenses related to a business purpose, are deductible as business expenses. Throughout the remainder of this text, reference to a *business expense* means that the expenditure satisfies the dominant profit-motive requirement.

Based on the legislative grace concept, business expenses are grouped into two main categories:

- Trade or business expenses
- Expenses for the production of income

Both classifications apply to individuals and certain conduit entities (partnerships, S corporations, etc.). However, production-of-income expenses do not apply to corporations. A corporation's expenses are always classified as trade or business expenses, regardless of the underlying business purpose. The deductions allowed under these two provisions of the tax law are the types of expenses that you would expect to find on a typical income statement. For example, on an income statement you would expect to find employee wages, depreciation expense, advertising, and similar items subtracted from income to determine net income. Thus, you are already familiar with several types of expenses that are allowed as business deductions.

Trade or Business or Production-of-Income Expenses?

Because business expenses are classified either as related to a trade or business or for the production of income, it is necessary to look at these two classifications more closely. Although many of the same kinds of expenses can be deducted in these two categories, the tax result can be significantly different. As explained later, classification of an activity as either a trade or business or for the production of income depends on the facts related to the particular activity. No single definition applies to all situations. Because both types of activities must be profit motivated, a trade or business will most likely be identified by the extent of the taxpayer's involvement and whether the intent is to earn a living from the activity.

Trade or Business Expenses.   If a taxpayer's activities qualify as a trade or business, the related expenses are fully deductible. As you can see from the following excerpt from the tax law, **trade or business expenses** is broadly defined:

> SEC. 162. TRADE OR BUSINESS EXPENSES.
>
> (A) IN GENERAL—There shall be allowed as a deduction all the ordinary and necessary expenses paid or incurred during the taxable year in carrying on any trade or business, including—
>
> (1) a reasonable allowance for salaries or other compensation for personal services actually rendered;
>
> (2) traveling expenses (including amounts expended for meals and lodging other than amounts that are lavish or extravagant under the circumstances) while away from home in the pursuit of a trade or business; and
>
> (3) rentals or other payments required to be made as a condition to the continued use or possession, for purposes of the trade or business, of property to which the taxpayer has not taken or is not taking title or in which he has no equity.

A taxpayer may deduct "all the ordinary and necessary expenses" of operating a "trade or business." But what is a trade or business? The Internal Revenue Code contains at least 50 references to a trade or business without defining the meaning of the phrase. The Treasury regulations are similarly silent on the definition of a trade or business. Therefore, the task has been left to the courts to resolve. One interpretation observed for many years was that taxpayers who held themselves out as engaged in the selling of goods or services were engaged in a trade or business. Although noting that a person selling goods and services would usually be engaged in a trade or business, in 1987 the Supreme Court rejected these activities as the single appropriate test for a trade or business. Instead, the Court took a broader view of what constituted a trade or business.

The Court has stated that to be engaged in a trade or business a taxpayer must meet the following requirements:

■ Profit motivation—The primary purpose for engaging in the activity must be to earn income or a profit.

■ Continuous and regular activity—There must be continuity and regularity in the taxpayer's involvement in the activity.

■ Livelihood, not a hobby—The activity must not be sporadic, a hobby, or an amusement diversion.[8]

The Court went on to say that whether an activity meets these tests must be determined by examining the facts in each case. In this regard, the Court noted that taxpayers meeting the prior "holding out as a seller of goods and services" test would normally meet the requirements for being engaged in a trade or business.

As a general rule, an employee is usually engaged in the trade or business of rendering services to the employer. The most common problem encountered in delineating a trade or business activity from a production-of-income activity involves dealings in securities. A person who transacts in securities may be an active investor, an active trader, or a dealer in securities. Unlike active traders and dealers, active investors are not considered to be in a trade or business.

An **active investor** is a person who continuously, regularly, and extensively manages her or his own portfolio with a view toward long-term appreciation in the portfolio's value and not short-term profit. Unlike a trader, an active investor purchases an investment with the intent to hold it for the long term and is less influenced by daily changes in market prices. An active investor's income is earned from interest, dividends, and gains from long-term holdings of securities. An active investor is never deemed to be engaged in a trade or business. Accordingly, the investor's activities are related to the production of income, and the investment expenses are deductible only as miscellaneous itemized deductions.

An **active trader** earns a livelihood buying and selling securities for personal profit. The active trader neither buys and sells for customers nor provides services to others that warrant fees or commissions. The main source of an active trader's income is from selling securities for more than they cost in order to make a profit. The securities are typically held for a short time before they are sold. The active trader does not intend to hold investments for a long time to collect income from interest, dividends, and long-term gains from appreciation of these investments but tries to capture the short-term swings in the market. Thus, an active trader may be distinguished from the active investor by the nature of the investing activities and the source of income. If the trader's activities are frequent and substantial, the trader will be deemed to be engaged in a trade or business. As such, the active trader's expenses will be deductible for adjusted gross income.

Distinguishing a trader from an active investor is often quite difficult. The determination of whether a taxpayer should be classified as a trader or an active investor is best left to a tax expert.

A **securities dealer** purchases a security expecting to realize a profit from selling it to a customer for a fee or commission. Dealers do not normally look to an increase in market prices to provide a profit. The dealer acts as an agent who performs the services of a wholesaler or retailer in bringing together a buyer and a seller. Dealers have customers with whom they deal in order to earn a profit. Dealers are deemed to be engaged in a trade or business.

Expenses for the Production of Income.   If the taxpayer's business activity fails to qualify as a trade or business, expenses related to the production of income may still be deductible under Section 212 of the Internal Revenue Code. Although the formal tax term for these deductions is *nonbusiness expenses*, we will refer to these items as **investment expenses**, consistent with the terminology used by most taxpayers. The tax law provides a broad definition of **production-of-income expenses** that an individual taxpayer can deduct:

SEC. 212. EXPENSES FOR THE PRODUCTION OF INCOME.
In the case of an individual there shall be allowed as a deduction all the ordinary and necessary expenses paid or incurred during the taxable year—
(1) for the production or collection of income;
(2) for the management, conservation, or maintenance of property held for the production of income, or
(3) in connection with the determination, collection, or refund of any tax.

The objectives of Section 212 are to tax the net profits of income-motivated transactions and to allow individuals a deduction for costs related to compliance with the tax law. However, expenses deducted under this provision receive less favorable treatment than trade or business expenses. Generally, expenses related to earning rent and royalty income are treated the same (as deductions for adjusted gross income), whether they are considered to be for the production of income or trade or business expenses. However, as shown in Exhibit 5–1, other investment and tax-related expenses allowed by Section 212 are deducted from adjusted gross income as "other miscellaneous itemized deductions." In addition, total itemized deductions are often subject to special adjustments (discussed in Chapter 8) that reduce the amount allowed as a deduction for computing taxable income.

▲ **EXAMPLE 9**   Grady owns a large portfolio of stocks, bonds, and other securities. What is the treatment of Grady's securities activities in each of the following cases?

Case A

Grady spends all his time managing his portfolio. He continuously trades securities to obtain a profit from short-term price increases. Grady rarely holds a security for the dividend or interest income it may produce or for long-term appreciation in value. Grady has no other job and receives the bulk of his income from his securities dealings.

Case B

Grady is employed as a chemist for Dough Co. He spends an average of five hours per week studying investment materials and making investment decisions. Grady primarily invests in securities for their dividend and interest income and long-term appreciation potential. Because his portfolio is quite extensive, more than half of his income comes from his security investments.

Discussion: In case A, Grady's activities constitute a trade or business. His primary motive is profit, he engages in the activity on a continual and regular basis, and his securities activities are his livelihood. Grady's business expenses would be deductible for adjusted gross income. In addition, gains and losses from his securities dealings would be considered gains and losses from a trade or business.

In case B, Grady's security dealings are a production-of-income activity. He receives a substantial portion of his income from his securities, but it is not his livelihood, nor does he engage in the activity with the continuity and regularity of a trade or business. Therefore, Grady's expenses are deductible as miscellaneous itemized deductions. In addition, gains and losses Grady incurs from selling the securities are capital gains and losses.

To be deductible, investment expenses must bear a reasonable and proximate (close) relationship to the earning of taxable income. That is, the expenses must have a business purpose. Deductible investment expenses may relate to income earned in a prior year, the current year, or to be earned in a future year. In addition, the expenses may relate to a single transaction, such as the sale of a security, as well as to recurring transactions, such as the collection of interest or dividends. For example, the cost of a safe deposit box used to store stocks and bonds is an investment expense. The securities stored in the box may have paid interest and dividends in a prior year but not the current year. On the other hand, they may be paying income in the current year but may not have paid interest and dividends in prior years. Alternatively, they may never have paid interest or dividends, but they are being held for sale when their market value increases. Regardless of which situation applies, the safe deposit box rent is deductible. Other deductible expenses related to investing might include employee wages, depreciation, advertising, advisory fees, office rent, and subscriptions to financial publications.

Rental Activity

Depending on the extent of the taxpayer's activities related to renting out real estate, the activity could be deemed either a trade or business or an investment activity. For many years, the mere rental of a single piece of improved real estate was considered a trade or business, whereas the rental of unimproved real estate was subject to an "all the facts and circumstances" test to determine the classification of the rental activity.[9] Improved real estate is land that has a building or other capital improvement built on it. Unimproved real estate is raw land without a building or other structure on it. In recent years, several courts have begun to apply a facts-and-circumstances test to both improved and unimproved real estate to determine whether rental property is a trade or business or investment asset. The courts have looked to the scope of the rental activities and the extent of the taxpayer's involvement with the rental operations to classify the property.

For example, the U.S. Tax Court considered whether a rental activity was a trade or business for purposes of the home office deduction.[10] The court indicated that, as a matter of law, a rental activity is not automatically a trade or business. Classification as a trade or business depends on the facts related to the taxpayer's activities. In examining the facts, the Tax Court looked at the scope of ownership and management activities in classifying a rental activity as a trade or business instead of an investment activity. The IRS has stated that rental property must produce income from an active trade or business, as opposed to passive income that would be earned on a portfolio investment (stocks and bonds), to qualify as property used in a trade or business.

▲ **EXAMPLE 10**   Frank agreed to lease land located in downtown Chicago to Sleepytime Motels for 99 years. Under the lease, Sleepytime had the right to construct a motel on the land. Sleepytime is responsible for all expenses, claims, and liabilities related to the property. In the event of default on the lease, Frank has the right to assume ownership of the building and possession of the property. Is Frank's rental activity a trade or business or a production-of-income activity?

Discussion: Because Frank is not actively involved in the management of the property, the income earned is similar to the income that would be earned by an investor in stocks and bonds. Thus, the lease described would not constitute a trade or business. Frank's rental activity would be considered a production-of-income activity.

▲ **EXAMPLE 11**   Yolanda owns two rental properties. She obtains tenants for the properties, makes repairs when necessary, provides maintenance of the properties, pays expenses related to the properties, and is subject to claims and liabilities arising from the rental properties. Is Yolanda's rental activity a trade or business or a production-of-income activity?

Discussion: Because Yolanda actively manages the two properties, pays expenses related to the properties, and is liable for claims on the properties, she would be deemed to be engaged in a trade or business.

Note in Exhibit 5–1 that rental expenses are deductible for adjusted gross income. This is true whether the rental activity is classified as a trade or business or for the production of income. Therefore, the proper classification of rental deductions is not an issue in preparing a taxpayer's return. However, when the taxpayer decides to sell the property, the classification becomes important. Disposal of rental property at a gain results in similar tax treatment whether the property is classified as a trade or business or an investment asset. However, if the rental property is disposed of at a loss, the full amount of the loss can be deducted in the year of the sale only if the property is used in a trade or business (Exhibit 5–1). Investment property sold at a loss is classified as a capital loss. Although net capital losses are also deducted for adjusted gross income, a capital loss may be limited to a $3,000 deduction each year until it is fully used. Because of the limitation on capital losses, classification of rental real estate as an investment asset is usually less desirable than classification as a trade or business asset when the property is sold at a loss.

▲ **EXAMPLE 12**   Frank sells the property in example 10 at a $10,000 loss during 1996. How much of the loss can Frank deduct?

Discussion: Because Frank's rental activity is a production-of-income activity, the $10,000 is a capital loss. The $10,000 loss would be included in the 1996 capital gain-and-loss netting. If Frank had no other capital gains and losses during 1996, he could deduct only $3,000 of the loss in 1996, with the remaining $7,000 of loss carried forward to 1997.

▲ **EXAMPLE 13**   Assume that Yolanda sells one of her rental properties in example 11 at a $10,000 loss during 1996. How much of the loss can Yolanda deduct?

Discussion: Because Yolanda's rental activities constitute a trade or business, the $10,000 loss on the sale of the rental property is deducted in full in 1996 as a trade or business loss.

The trade or business versus investment characterization of rental real estate is also important if the taxpayer wants to claim deductions or credits, such as home office expenses, that are available only to a trade or business activity.

Personal Expenditures

An individual's personal expenditures are also grouped into two categories. The two categories are allowable personal itemized deductions and nondeductible personal expenses. In contrast to expenditures for a business purpose in which all ordinary and necessary expenses are deductible, the tax law severely limits deductions for personal expenditures. As shown in Exhibit 5–1, those personal expenses that are allowed are deductible from adjusted gross income. In addition, most personal itemized deductions are subject to a limit based on the taxpayer's adjusted gross income. A major problem in determining an individual's personal itemized deductions is that many assets and expenses are used for both business and personal purposes. Proper accounting for such assets and expenses requires segregation of the business portion from the personal portion.

Mixed Business and Personal Expenditures

These categories of expenditures, *mixed-use assets* and *mixed-use expenditures*, present special problems for individual taxpayers. A person's expenses related to mixed-use assets and mixed-use expenditures must be analyzed and allocated between profit-motivated and personal expenditures. To the extent an expense is related to a profit-motivated transaction, it is treated as a business expense. Unless the personal expenditure qualifies as an itemized deduction, it is not deductible.

Mixed-Use Assets.   A **mixed-use asset** is an asset that is used both to earn income and for personal purposes. For tax purposes, the single asset is effectively treated as two separate assets. One is a business asset, and the other is a personal use asset. For example, a taxpayer may own one car that he uses to travel for his business and to provide local transportation for his family. To deny a deduction for the business use of the car would violate both the ability-to-pay and capital recovery concepts. Because the income earned using the car is taxable, a deduction is allowed for the expense related to the business use of the car. The cost of using the car to provide local transportation for the family is a personal expense that is not deductible. Thus, an expense that is related to using a mixed-use asset must be reasonably allocated between business and personal use. The portion of the expense reasonably allocated to business use is treated the same as other expenses that are related to the profit-motivated activity. An expense allocated to personal use cannot be deducted unless it qualifies as a specifically allowed itemized deduction.

▲ **EXAMPLE 14**   Aaron purchases a computer in 1995 at a cost of $8,000. Aaron uses the computer in his dry-cleaning business and for personal purposes after work and on weekends. During 1995, Aaron's records indicate that 75% of the computer's use is for business purposes and 25% for personal purposes. How should Aaron treat the computer for tax purposes?

Discussion: Aaron must treat the computer as 2 separate assets for tax purposes. For purposes of computing depreciation on the computer, only $6,000 ($8,000 × 75%) of the cost can be depreciated for tax purposes. The remaining $2,000 of cost is considered a personal use asset. Depreciation is not allowed on personal use assets.

▲ **EXAMPLE 15**   Aaron sells the computer in 1997 for $4,000. His business use remains at 75% for 1996 and 1997. Aaron properly deducts $2,400 in depreciation on the computer for 1995 through 1997. What is Aaron's taxable gain or loss on the sale of the computer?

Discussion: Aaron must treat the sale of the computer as the sale of 2 assets—one a business asset and one a personal asset. The $4,000 sales price and the $8,000 purchase price must be allocated between business and personal use:

		Business	Personal
Selling price—$4,000 × 75%		$3,000	
$4,000 × 25%			$1,000
Less: Adjusted basis			
Original cost—$8,000 × 75%	$6,000		
$8,000 × 25%			(2,000)
Less: Depreciation	(2,400)	(3,600)	
Loss on sale		$ 600	$1,000

The $600 loss on the business portion of the computer is deductible as a business loss. However, the $1,000 loss on the personal use portion is a nondeductible personal use loss.

Mixed-Use Expenditures.   Mixed-use expenditures are also subject to special treatment. **Mixed-use expenditures** are expenses that are incurred for both profit and personal reasons. As with mixed-use assets, these expenditures must be allocated between business and personal use and deducted according to the rules for each use. In addition, certain types of mixed-use expenditures (e.g., hobby and vacation home expenses, which are discussed in Chapter 6), are subject to special rules designed to prevent taxpayer abuse by disallowing all or part of an otherwise deductible expenditure.

▲ **EXAMPLE 16**   Pam traveled to San Diego for 4 days primarily for business reasons. Her air fare cost $800, and she incurred expenses of $200 a day for lodging and incidentals. Because Pam had never been to San Diego, she stayed 2 extra days to visit the zoo and to tour the city. How much of her costs can be deducted as a business expense?

Discussion: Pam has incurred mixed-use expenditures. The expense relates to a business trip and a personal vacation. Because the primary motive (as evidenced by spending more days on business than for personal purposes) for making the trip was to conduct business, Pam can deduct the full $800 air fare. She can also deduct $200 for each day she was in San Diego to conduct business. Pam cannot deduct any part of the $200 per day for lodging and incidentals for the 2 extra days she stayed for personal reasons.

In classifying expenditures, only expenses that have a business purpose are treated as deductible trade or business and investment expenses. In addition to having a business purpose, these expenses must also be

TESTS FOR DEDUCTIBILITY

- Ordinary
- Necessary
- Reasonable in amount

Note that all three requirements must be met in order to deduct a trade or business or an investment expense. Deductible trade or business and investment expenses may *not* be any of the following:

- A personal expense
- A capital expenditure
- A payment that frustrates public policy
- An expense related to tax-exempt income
- Another person's expense

The discussion that follows examines each requirement for determining deductible business and investment expenses.

Ordinary, Necessary, and Reasonable in Amount

Trade or business and investment-related activities are allowed a deduction for the ordinary and necessary expenses of earning income. In addition, the tax law provides that a trade or business can deduct reasonable salaries. According to the IRS and the courts, an expense must be reasonable in amount to be ordinary and necessary.[11] Thus, the portion of an expense that is not reasonable in amount will not be deductible because it is not ordinary or necessary. Because of their importance in identifying deductible business expenses, these terms need further consideration.

Ordinary Expense.   An expenditure must qualify as an ordinary expense to be deductible. The term *ordinary* is generally interpreted to have two meanings. First, the expense must be of a kind commonly incurred in the particular income-earning activity.[12] Thus, the expense may be said to be customary or usual in the activity. An **ordinary expense** is one that is normal, common, and accepted under the circumstances of the business community. In addition, although the expense must be common to the income-earning activity, it does not have to be a regularly recurring item for the taxpayer.

> ▲ **EXAMPLE 17**   Kara owned and operated a pet shop. One day, a customer was bitten by a snake. Although the accident was the customer's fault, he filed a law suit against Kara for $25,000. After Kara paid her lawyer $2,500 to defend her, the customer dropped the suit. Are the legal fees an ordinary expense for Kara?

Discussion: Lawsuits by customers are a common occurrence in today's business environment. The cost of defending the business against the disgruntled customer is a normal cost of doing business, although it is not a recurring expense. The legal fees would satisfy the ordinary test.

▲ **EXAMPLE 18**   The Russo Co., which raises hogs, entered into a contract with the local feed mill to buy hog feed. Under the terms of the agreement, Russo agreed to purchase a quantity of grain and pay for the grain in advance. The mill agreed to deliver the feed as needed and to charge the deliveries against Russo's advance payment at the lower of the market price on delivery or a maximum price agreed to in the contract. Is the advance payment of the hog feed an ordinary expense?

Discussion: The payment for the grain qualifies as an ordinary expense. The advance purchase of the grain for feeding livestock is the normal way farmers conduct their business. By ensuring that the grain is available, Russo can better plan the scope of its farm operations for the coming months.

As these examples illustrate, an ordinary expense may or may not be a frequently occurring item. Also, the determination of what is usual or customary depends on the nature of the taxpayer's business. A typical expense for a pet shop (bird seed) is not a typical expense for an auto mechanic (repair parts).

The second meaning of *ordinary* is that the expenditure is an expense that is assignable to the current accounting period. A capital expenditure that provides future benefits cannot be deducted now.[13] Capital expenditures that benefit more than one tax year should be allocated by means of a depreciation, depletion, or amortization deduction to the accounting periods receiving benefit from the use of the asset.

▲ **EXAMPLE 19**   Gustav Brothers, a partnership, buys a $20,000 machine in the current year to use in its business. The machine has a 7-year tax life. When can the partnership deduct the cost of the machine?

Discussion: The machine is to be used to earn income during several tax years. As a result, the cost of the machine must be capitalized and allocated to the years benefited by the use of the machine. The deductions allowed for depreciation are discussed in Chapter 11.

Necessary Expense.   An expense must also be necessary to be deductible. The courts have defined a **necessary expense** as one that is "appropriate and helpful" to the taxpayer's income activity.[14] An expense will be considered necessary if a reasonable and prudent businessperson would incur the expense in a similar situation. It is important to note that the term *necessary* does not mean that the expense must be essential to the continued existence of the income activity in order to be deductible. In most cases, the courts have tended to accept the taxpayer's judgment of the business necessity of the expenditure rather than attempt to determine the commercial value of the expenditure.

▲ **EXAMPLE 20**   A tax lawyer purchased a large red, white, and blue flag with the numerals 1040 for his yacht. While using his yacht, many people inquired about the flag, and the tax attorney obtained a few customers as a result of such contact. Can the lawyer deduct the cost of operating his yacht as a promotional expense?

Discussion: On similar facts, the Tax Court determined that operating the yacht was not the ordinary method of promoting the taxpayer's business. Further, the court determined that the expenses of the yacht were so personal in nature that it could not be necessary in the common sense of the word.

▲ **EXAMPLE 21**   Buster, Inc., is a women's clothing store in Fashion City. One day a year, the company pays $500 to publish a full-page advertisement in the town newspaper to announce its annual clothing sale. Is the cost of the advertisement deductible?

Discussion: The $500 paid for the sale advertisement is deductible. The expense satisfies both the ordinary and necessary tests. It is customary for clothing retailers to advertise their merchandise. In addition, the advertisement is helpful to the business, because it both promotes the store to the public and attracts the attention of the company's customers and provides them with an incentive to shop at the store—to take advantage of the sale prices.

Reasonable in Amount.   An expense must also be reasonable in amount to be deductible. An expense does not satisfy the ordinary and necessary tests unless it is reasonable in amount. The reasonableness test most often becomes an issue in transactions involving related parties. When unrelated parties are dealing at arm's length in their own best interests, the result of the negotiations will normally be a fair market value. However, related parties have incentives to shift income by charging prices higher or lower than what would be paid in an arm's-length transaction, so these costs would not constitute **reasonable expenses.**

▲ **EXAMPLE 22**   Tara operates a shoe store in a building she rents from her father for $1,000 per month. Comparable store space is readily available for rent at $400 per month. Is the rental payment reasonable?

Discussion: Tara will be allowed a $400 rent expense deduction unless she can establish that the location or other unique features of her father's building justify a higher rent than other, comparable store space. Unless Tara can prove otherwise, the $600 excess payment will be considered a nondeductible payment to her father (a gift).

▲ **EXAMPLE 23**   Roy pays Sally $100 per week to clean his medical office. When Sally became ill, he hired his daughter, Janice, to fill in and keep the office tidy. Roy paid Janice $300 a week. How much of the $300 payment is reasonable?

Discussion: Of the $300 per week paid Janice, he will be allowed to deduct only $100, because that was the amount he was paying Sally. Unless Roy can prove otherwise, Janice's $300 weekly salary will be considered excessive, because he would normally pay $100 a week for the same services.

NOTE: In each of these examples, the apparently unreasonable compensation was paid to a related party. It is unlikely that the taxpayers in these examples would have paid the same amounts had the transactions been with an unrelated party.

Not a Personal Expense

The tax law specifically disallows a deduction for personal, living, and family expenses.[15] Because deductions are a matter of legislative grace, this rule eliminates deductions for expenditures that do not have a business purpose, such as

- Premiums the insured taxpayer pays on life insurance.
- Insurance premiums paid on the taxpayer's home and personal property.
- Expenses of maintaining a home such as rent, utilities, and maintenance.
- Losses from disposing of property held for personal, living, or family purposes.
- The cost of transportation, meals, or lodging unless they are related to a trade or business, the production of income, charitable contributions, or medical expenses; the personal cost of commuting to work and back is not deductible.

- Legal fees and costs related to obtaining a divorce; the portion of the attorney's fee paid to obtain alimony or other taxable income is allowed as a deduction for the production of income.

- The costs of obtaining an education to meet the minimum requirements of the taxpayer's trade or business or that are part of a program that would qualify the taxpayer to enter a new business or profession.

Frequently, an expense will be incurred for both business and personal reasons. Does the business purpose automatically qualify the expense for deduction? According to the IRS and the courts, the answer is no. To be deductible, the expense must bear a proximate relationship to the income-producing activity.[16] In addition, the primary or dominant motivation for incurring the expense must be the business purpose. A significant business motivation is not enough.

▲ **EXAMPLE 24**   Atman and Sarita are good friends. Atman also supplies Sarita with artwork that she sells to customers in her interior decorating business. Atman took Sarita to dinner at the Greyhouse. During the meal, they discussed business, and Sarita agreed to buy several pieces of art. Atman paid for the meal. Is the cost of the meal a business expense or a personal expense?

Discussion: If Atman took Sarita to dinner just to spend time with a friend, the fact that the conversation drifted to business does not result in a business deduction for the meal. Because the dominant motive for the expense is personal, the expense is not deductible.

If Atman took Sarita to dinner so he would be able to discuss his artwork and to solicit an order for paintings and the event centered around a business discussion, Atman could deduct the cost of the meal as a business expense, because the dominant motive was a business purpose.

▲ **EXAMPLE 25**   Bud and Gloria operate a hot tub manufacturing business. In June, they attended a three-day trade show in Paris and obtained a large number of orders for their hot tubs. In June, they also sent their 13-year-old son Dave to Cannes for three weeks to visit a friend who is a lawyer. The lawyer's son lived with Bud and Gloria while in the United States as an exchange student. The lawyer also represents their biggest customer in France. The lawyer's son and Dave have developed a friendship over the years. Is the cost of the trips deductible as a business expense, or is it a personal expense?

Discussion: The cost of Bud's and Gloria's attending the trade show is a deductible business expense because the primary motive for the trip was a business purpose. Dave's trip is primarily personal and not deductible. The motivation for Dave's trip was to create goodwill with the lawyer who is associated with a customer. Dave's trip is unrelated to the active conduct of the hot tub business.

Not a Capital Expenditure

A **capital expenditure** that results in an asset that benefits future accounting periods is not allowed as a current deduction, because the useful life extends beyond the end of the tax year.[17] Capital expenditures include the cost of acquiring land, buildings, machinery and equipment, furniture and fixtures, the cost of perfecting or defending title to property, and purchased goodwill. Amounts paid for freight and installation charges related to getting an asset to the taxpayer's location and set up are included in the asset's basis. If the taxpayer constructs an asset for his or her own business, the property's basis includes both the direct and indirect costs of production. If an asset has a useful life that extends substantially beyond the end of the tax year of the expenditure, its immediate deduction is generally not allowed.

▲ **EXAMPLE 26**   Paula bought Colleen's advertising agency. As part of the purchase price, Paula paid Colleen $12,000 not to open another advertising agency in the area for 3 years. Can Paula deduct the $12,000 as a current business expense?

Discussion: The $12,000 payment (known as *a covenant not to compete*) will benefit Paula's business for 3 years by not having Colleen as a competitor during that period. Thus, the benefit of the payment extends substantially beyond the end of the tax year and must be capitalized and amortized as an intangible asset.

The capital recovery and the accounting period concepts require deduction of an asset's basis through depreciation, amortization, depletion, or as a reduction in the amount realized on the asset's disposition. For example, assets with a limited life, such as buildings and equipment, are subject to a depreciation expense deduction. The cost of assets with an indefinite useful life, such as land, are permanently capitalized until the asset's disposition. Based on the administrative convenience concept, tools that wear out and are thrown away within one year can be deducted in the year of purchase. Contrary to the general rule, by legislative grace Congress permits taxpayers to take a current deduction for certain long-lived assets. For example, a taxpayer can elect to expense certain

- Research and experimentation expenditures
- Soil and water conservation expenditures
- Certain depreciable business assets
- Expenditures by farmers for fertilizer
- Several other specific capital expenditures

The commission paid on the acquisition of a security is not a current deduction. When a commission is paid on the purchase of a security, it is considered part of the cost of buying the asset and is added to the security's basis. When the security is sold, the basis is deducted from the sale price as a capital recovery. The commission paid on the sale of a security is a reduction in the amount realized on the sale.

▲ **EXAMPLE 27**   Connie purchased 100 shares of Calvinator Corporation stock for $100 per share. She also paid a commission on the purchase of $400. What is the basis of the 100 shares of stock?

Discussion: The basis of the stock is the cost of obtaining the stock. Because the commission is part of the cost of acquiring the stock, it is added to basis; commissions are not current period expenses. Therefore, the cost of the 100 shares of stock is $10,400 [(100 × $100) + $400].

▲ **EXAMPLE 28**   Connie sold the 100 shares of stock purchased in example 27 for $130 per share. She paid a commission of $600 on the sale. What is Connie's gain (loss) on the sale of the stock?

Discussion: Connie has a gain of $2,000 on the sale. The $600 commission is a reduction of the amount realized on the sale; it is not a current period expense:

Selling price (100 × $130)	$13,000
Less: Commissions	(600)
Amount realized from sale	$12,400
Less: Basis of shares sold	(10,400)
Gain on sale	$ 2,000

Repair-and-Maintenance Expense.   The difference between a capital expenditure that results in an asset and a **repair-and-maintenance expense** is important. Repair-and-maintenance expenses are allowed as a deduction in the current accounting period.[18] Repairs include repainting an office, fixing a leaking water or gas line, patching a roof, and replacing a broken glass in a window. These expenses generally include the costs of keeping business assets in normal operating condition. Unlike improvements and replacements, repairs do not appreciably extend an asset's useful life or materially add to its value. **Improvements,** such as rewiring or putting a new roof on a building, should be capitalized, because they either extend useful life or add to the value of the property. A **replacement,** such as a major overhaul of a machine, that extends the life of an asset should also be capitalized. In addition, expenditures made as part of a plan to recondition, improve, or alter an asset (called *betterments*) should be capitalized as assets, although individual expenditures considered separately might qualify as repairs.[19] The costs of improvements, replacements, and betterments should be deducted in the accounting periods benefited by their use, based on an acceptable depreciation or amortization method.

Start-up Costs.   Capital expenditures can also include start-up costs. **Start-up costs** are related to investigating and creating a new active trade or business. The start-up costs to be capitalized are the expenses incurred before the new business begins its activities. Start-up costs could include

- Surveys and analyses of markets, facilities, and labor force
- Travel to develop the business and locate potential customers and suppliers
- Advertising the new business
- Salaries to train employees
- Salaries for executives and consultants
- Various other expenses such as legal and accounting fees

The items included as capitalized start-up costs must be similar to expenses that would be deductible in expanding an existing business.

If the taxpayer begins the new business, she or he can elect to amortize the start-up costs over a period of 60 months or longer.[20] The amortization deduction is allowed starting in the month the new business begins its operations. If the taxpayer does not elect to amortize the start-up costs, the costs become locked in and can be deducted only upon disposition of the business. If the taxpayer does not enter the new business, expenses related to investigating the new business are not deductible.[21] The transaction is given this treatment because the taxpayer's motivation is deemed to be primarily personal before a new business is begun. A taxpayer's efforts to investigate a business do not establish a business purpose for the expenditures.

It is important to note that a taxpayer operating an existing trade or business can claim a current deduction for the cost of investigating, expanding, or establishing new locations for the same line of business. The investigation costs are considered an ordinary and necessary expense of the existing trade or business and therefore fully deductible when incurred. However, an existing business entering an unrelated trade or business is subject to the same capitalization rules as a new business.[22] If the unrelated business is not acquired, the investigation expenses become nondeductible.

▲ **EXAMPLE 29**   Jason has operated Main Street Cafe for 15 years. He would like to branch out by opening another cafe in a nearby city. Can Jason deduct the costs of investigating the feasibility of opening the second cafe?

Discussion: Whether Jason decides to expand his business and open a second cafe or not, he can deduct the costs of investigating a location for a second cafe as a current deduction. Because the expenses are related to opening a business that is related to Jason's existing business, they are allowed as a current deduction, no matter what he decides.

▲ **EXAMPLE 30**   What would happen if Jason, in example 29, investigated opening a retail store selling speed boats?

Discussion: The retail speed boat store would be a new business, because it is unrelated to his cafe business. If Jason decided not to enter the retail boat business, he could not deduct any investigation expenses. The expenses would be considered non-deductible personal expenses. If Jason acquires the retail store, he would have to capitalize the investigation expenses and amortize them over 60 months, starting with the month the new business started.

The costs of organizing a corporation or partnership must also be capitalized. Organization costs are those costs incurred to organize a corporation or a partnership. Such costs include legal, accounting, filing, and other fees and costs incidental to the start-up of a corporation or a partnership. They are similar to start-up costs in that they are incurred before the entity is actually legally organized. As such, they are subject to the same election, to amortize the expenditures over a period of 60 months or more, as for start-up costs.[23]

Not Frustrate Public Policy

In a long series of cases before 1970, the courts disallowed deductions (usually for fines and penalties) for expenditures that the courts thought were frustrating public policy by encouraging unlawful conduct.[24] The courts' rationale in these cases was that it was neither ordinary nor necessary to violate the law. In 1969, Congress preempted the court battles by amending Section 162 to disallow certain categories of payments. The following payments are explicitly stated in the tax law as nondeductible expenditures:

- Direct or indirect illegal bribes or kickbacks to government officials and employees, including payments to federal, state, local, and foreign government officials and employees as well as officials and employees of a government agency

- Direct or indirect payments to any person of an amount that constitute an illegal bribe, kickback, or other illegal payment under federal or state law (if the state law is generally enforced)

- Bribes, kickbacks, or rebates by a provider of services, supplier, physician, or other persons who furnish items or services under Medicare or Medicaid

- Fines, penalties, or similar payments to a governmental unit for the violation of any law

- Certain damage payments for violation of the antitrust laws

   ▲ **EXAMPLE 31**   Rapid Trucking Co. incurred several weight overload fines. Although Rapid took reasonable precautions to avoid violating the overall weight limit, loads that shifted during transit resulted in violations of the axle-weight limit. Can Rapid deduct the overload fines?

Discussion: Even if Rapid Trucking Co. had exercised all due care and incurred the overweight fines without willful intent, the fines would not be allowed as a deduction. A deduction for fines is specifically disallowed as being in violation of public policy.

▲ **EXAMPLE 32**   Chitsa is a tax return preparer. She forgot to sign tax returns she prepared for her clients. As a result, she was fined $50 for each unsigned return. Can Chitsa deduct the fines as a cost of doing business?

Discussion: The tax law requires a return preparer to sign each return prepared for a fee. A $50 penalty is assessed for each return not properly signed. The penalties paid by Chitsa are not deductible as an expense related to her tax return preparation business.

Expenses of an Illegal Business.

Although the tax law specifically denies a deduction for the listed expenditures on the basis that they are illegal payments, a taxpayer can deduct the legal ordinary and necessary expenses related to carrying on an illegal trade or business.[25]

▲ **EXAMPLE 33**   Bert is engaged in the business of illegally trafficking in liquor, gambling, and betting on horse races. The business is operated out of the Overflow Club. Under state law, the activities are illegal. What expenses may Bert deduct against his illegal income?

Discussion: Bert's income from the illegal activities is taxable under the all-inclusive income concept. The payment of fines for breaking the law and bribes paid to protect the business from raids and arrests by state and county law officers are not deductible. However, legitimate expenses incurred in the illegitimate business are deductible. Among the allowable expenses would be rent, utilities, and employee wages.

A special provision in the tax law denies all deductions other than cost of goods sold for individuals engaged in the illegal trafficking of controlled substances (drugs).[26]

Lobbying Expenses and Other Political Activities.

Relying on the ordinary and necessary requirement for deducting business expenses, in 1918 the Treasury Department promulgated regulations that denied deductions for expenditures for the promotion or defeat of legislation, and political contributions. With minor changes in language, these restrictions have been retained. The denial of such deductions has been upheld by the courts on the grounds that money was an "insidious influence" on politics.

Contributions to political campaigns and expenditures to influence public opinion about legislation, a referendum, or how to vote in an election are not deductible. This denial of deductions extends to advertising in a political party's convention program, admission to political fund-raising dinners, and events such as an inaugural ball, parades, and concerts.

▲ **EXAMPLE 34**   The accounting firm of Williams, Daniels, and Thomas contributed $100 to a political campaign fund. The objective of the group managing the fund is to defeat a senator who has proposed legislation that would be unfavorable to CPAs and to support candidates who favor CPAs' positions. Can the firm deduct the $100 payment?

Discussion: The firm's political contribution is not allowed as a deduction because the fund supports the election of a candidate and attempts to influence public opinion concerning the suitability of the senator to hold office.

LOBBYING EXPENSES.   Before passage of the Omnibus Budget Reconciliation Act (OBRA) of 1993, costs incurred for lobbying in favor of or against legislation of direct interest to the taxpayer's trade or business were deductible. Under this exception to the general rule disallowing political expenditures, the taxpayer was allowed to deduct the cost of traveling, preparing testimony, and communicating the taxpayer's view directly to legislators or the legislative body. The taxpayer was also permitted to deduct membership dues paid to lobbying organizations. For tax years after 1993, OBRA disallows a deduction for expenses incurred in connection with influencing federal or state legislation or for expenses associated with attempting to influence officials in the federal executive branch. As a result, **lobbying expenses,** including dues to lobbying organizations, are no longer deductible.[27] The new rules do not apply to attempts to influence a local legislative body (i.e., town council) or to the cost associated with monitoring federal or state legislation, unless the taxpayer then attempts to influence the same or similar legislation. In addition, under the administrative convenience concept, the law allows taxpayers who incur a *de minimis* amount of in-house lobbying expenses (less than $2,000 during the year) to deduct these expenses. In-house expenditures are expenditures for lobbying (e.g., costs of labor and materials) but do not include payments to professional lobbyists, dues, or other similar payments that are allocable to lobbying. If a taxpayer's total in-house lobbying expenditures exceed $2,000, no deduction is allowed for any of the in-house expenditures.

▲ **EXAMPLE 35**   Kathleen, a Realtor, testified before a state legislative committee, giving her thoughts on the effect of the new building code requirements on housing starts. She incurred $2,500 in costs to prepare her testimony and to travel to and stay in the state capital. Are these expenses deductible?

Discussion: Because the purpose of the expenses was to influence the legislative process, these expenses are not deductible. They are not deductible under the de minimis rule because the total expenditure exceeds $2,000. However, if Kathleen had gone to the legislative meetings only to listen and to monitor the legislation—as opposed to presenting her views—her expenses would have been deductible.

Not Related to Tax-Exempt Income

Expenses incurred to earn tax-exempt income are not allowed as a deduction.[28] Allowing the deduction of these expenses would violate the ability-to-pay concept by giving the taxpayer the double benefit of excluding income while deducting the related expenses. Frequently, taxpayers have to allocate investment expenses to both taxable and tax-exempt income. When making the allocation, expenses directly related to a class of income are allocated to that income. Expenses indirectly related to more than one class of income are allocated among the various classes of income by using a reasonable accounting method. One reasonable method of allocating indirect expenses is by total investment income.

▲ **EXAMPLE 36**   Clemons incurred $5,000 in investment expenses related to earning $3,000 in interest on taxable bonds and $3,600 in interest on tax-exempt bonds. The expenses are not directly allocable to either class of income. How much of the $5,000 in investment expenses can Clemons deduct as a production-of-income expense?

Discussion: Clemons can deduct only the portion of the expenses that is incurred to produce taxable income. The portion attributable to the production of tax-exempt income is not deductible. The investment expenses are allocated to the classes of interest income as follows:

Bonds	Total Investment Income	% of Total Income	Investment Expenses
Taxable interest income	$3,000	45.5%	$2,273
Tax-exempt interest income	3,600	54.5	2,727
Totals	$6,600	100.0%	$5,000

Clemons is allowed a deduction for the expenses related to the taxable bonds ($2,273). The investment expenses related to tax-exempt bonds ($2,727) are not deductible.

Expenditure Must Be for Taxpayer's Benefit

To be deductible, an expenditure must be for the taxpayer's benefit or be a payment of the taxpayer's obligation. A payment of another person's obligation does not result in a tax deduction for either person. The person making the payment cannot deduct an expense that is not related to her or his business, because the payment lacks a business purpose.[29] The person for whom the debt is paid is not entitled to another entity's deduction for a capital recovery.

▲ **EXAMPLE 37**   Marty's mother, Mary, owed $5,000 in back property taxes. To help Mary out of financial difficulty, Marty paid the property taxes. Can either Marty or Mary take a deduction for the property taxes paid by Marty?

Discussion: Although property taxes are allowed as a personal itemized deduction, Marty may not claim a deduction for payment of his mother's obligation. The property taxes were not Marty's obligation, and Marty did not benefit from the use of the property subject to the taxes. Mary may not deduct the payment of taxes, because she did not pay the expense.

In order to make sure that a deduction is allowed for the taxes, Marty could have made a gift of the $5,000 to Mary and had her pay the taxes directly.

An exception to the disallowance of the payment of another's expenses is made in the case of medical expenses of a dependent. All medical expenses paid on behalf of a taxpayer's dependent are deductible by the taxpayer, subject to the limitations on medical expense deductions.

TIMING OF DEDUCTIONS— EFFECT OF ACCOUNTING METHOD

The annual accounting period concept requires taxpayers to determine the expenses that can be deducted for each tax year. To assign expenses to the correct year, the tax law requires the taxpayer to adopt an accounting method that clearly reflects income. **Accounting method** refers to the overall method used to compute income and deductions belonging to the tax year. *Accounting method* also refers to the method used to compute the amount of particular income or deduction items. For example, the taxpayer may determine net income for a business using either the cash or the accrual method. In addition, to calculate the deduction for automobile expenses, the taxpayer must elect to use either the actual cost method or the standard rate method (discussed in Chapter 6).

If the taxpayer adopts a method of accounting that does not fairly reflect income (such as accrual method for expense and the cash method for income), the IRS can designate the method to be used by the taxpayer.[30] The accounting method adopted by the taxpayer is important, because it controls the timing of a deduction. Deduction of an expense in the wrong accounting period is not allowed.

▲ **EXAMPLE 38**   Craig pays $100 for supplies on December 28, 1996. His taxable income for 1996 is the lowest it has ever been, and he does not need more deductions for the year. Although he uses the cash method of accounting and normally expenses supplies when he buys them, he decides to save the $100 deduction until 1997. He reasons that his actions are proper, because he has not used the supplies. When should Craig deduct the cost of the supplies?

Discussion: Given his accounting method, Craig must deduct the expenses in 1996. He must use a method of accounting that fairly reflects income and apply that method on a consistent basis. As a cash basis taxpayer, Craig must deduct the $100 supplies expense in 1996. Under the cash method, he cannot take the deduction in 1997.

Cash Method

A cash basis taxpayer may claim a deduction in the year an expense is paid. The basic question to be answered then is when does payment occur? If a check is honored when it is taken to the bank for deposit, an expense is generally considered paid on the date the taxpayer gives or mails the check to the creditor. If the check is not honored when presented for payment, the timing of the deduction is not clear. Depending on the facts that caused the check to be dishonored, the deduction could be delayed until the check is made good. If the check was intended as payment of the debt but was not honored because of clerical errors, the deduction should be allowed when the check was mailed if it is promptly paid. If the taxpayer did not have the funds to pay the check and intended for the check to be a promise to pay in the future (i.e., a note), the deduction should be allowed in the year the check (note) is paid.

▲ **EXAMPLE 39**   On December 31, 1996, Elvira, a cash basis taxpayer, mails a $500 check to her attorney to pay for legal fees related to her business. The attorney receives the check on January 2 and deposits it in her account. When can Elvira deduct the legal fees?

Discussion: If the check is honored by the bank when it is presented for payment, Elvira can claim the deduction when she mailed it—in 1996—although the check was not cashed until 1997.

If the check bounces because Elvira does not have sufficient funds for the check to clear, the deduction is not allowed until sufficient funds are deposited and the check clears or Elvira makes some other form of payment to the lawyer.

When a property or service is used to pay an expense, payment occurs when the taxpayer gives the property or renders the service to the creditor. If property or services are used to pay an expense, the amount deductible is generally the fair market value of the property or services given the creditor. However, a cash basis taxpayer will have to recognize the fair market value of services used to pay an expense as income and then deduct the expense incurred in providing the service. When the fair market value of an asset is more or less than its basis, the transfer of property will result in a realized gain or loss.

▲ **EXAMPLE 40**   Sandra has worked out an agreement with a local radio station for advertising. The radio station will run 30-second commercials in exchange for interior decorating services offered by her business. During the current year, she provides enough interior decorating services to compensate the radio station for $2,500-worth of advertising. Her expenses related to performing the services total $1,200. How should Sandra treat this arrangement?

Discussion: Sandra should deduct $2,500 in advertising expense and report $2,500 in service sales related to the advertising contract. Her $1,200 in expenses related to doing the work for the radio station are deductible as normal business expenses.

Payment of an expense by charging it to a credit card is treated as payment on the date the transaction is charged to the card.[31] It does not matter when the taxpayer pays the credit card company. If a taxpayer gives his or her own note payable to a creditor, or the creditor charges an item on an open account, the expense is not considered paid until the note or open account is paid off. On the other hand, a taxpayer may go to the bank and borrow money, give the bank a note for the loan, and then use the money to pay expenses. Expenses paid with borrowed money are allowed as a deduction regardless of when the loan is repaid.

▲ **EXAMPLE 41**   Laval owes $3,000 in expenses that are tax deductible. However, he does not have the cash to write a check. How can Laval obtain a current deduction for the expenses?

Discussion: If Laval charges the expenses to a credit card, he is deemed to have paid the expense on the date of the charge and can take a deduction on the charge date. He can pay the credit card balance when he has the money.

If the expenses are not payable by credit card, Laval could borrow the money from a friend or a bank and give them his note. He could use the cash to pay the expense and claim a deduction on the payment date. He could repay the note when he has the funds.

If Laval pays the expense by giving a note directly to the creditor, the expense is not deductible until the note is paid.

A cash basis taxpayer may deduct prepaid expenses in the year paid if the prepayment does not create an asset that extends substantially beyond the end of the year of payment. Thus, the late 1996 purchase of office supplies to be used in January 1997 can be deducted when the supplier is paid in 1996. However, the IRS has said that if $1,000 in business insurance is prepaid for one year on July 1, 1996, the expense must be allocated by charging $500 to 1996 and $500 to 1997. The courts differ with the IRS on this issue. The courts have held that a prepayment of an expense that will be used up before the end of the tax year following the year of prepayment can be deducted when paid.[32] That is, such prepayments are deemed not to extend substantially beyond the end of the tax year. This is referred to as the **one-year rule for prepaid expenses.** In order to qualify a prepaid expense under the one-year rule, the taxpayer must show that the payment is required by the creditor and that the payment does not distort income.

▲ **EXAMPLE 42**   Woody rents his office building. According to his 15-year lease, he is required to pay the $12,000 rent in advance on August 1 for the period September 1 through August 31. Woody has complied with the lease terms for the last 3 years. Can Woody deduct the $12,000 in the year it is paid?

Discussion: Woody can deduct the $12,000 annual rent when paid. Because the terms of the lease require the prepayment, the deduction will not distort income, and because it is used up before the end of the tax year following the year of prepayment, he will not need to amortize the expense. Note that a prepayment that extended beyond 1 year (e.g., a 2-year rent prepayment) would have to be allocated to the periods benefited by the expense.

Prepaid taxes are deductible in the year paid, even if the prepayment results in a refund in a later year. Under the tax benefit rule, the tax refund is reported as income.

▲ **EXAMPLE 43**   Plain County assesses property taxes annually on December 1. The taxes are not due and payable until March 1. Hortense always pays her property taxes before December 31. When can Hortense deduct the tax payments?

Discussion: Although Hortense is not under a legal obligation to pay the taxes until March 1, the taxes are deductible when paid in December under the one-year rule.

▲ **EXAMPLE 44**   Charles has $2,200 in state income taxes withheld from his paycheck during 1996. How much of the $2,200 can Charles deduct in 1996?

Discussion: State income taxes are deductible as a personal itemized deduction. Assuming that Charles itemizes his deductions on his 1996 tax return, he can deduct the $2,200 in state income taxes paid during 1996.

▲ **EXAMPLE 45**   Assume that after deducting the $2,200 in state income taxes Charles files his state tax return and receives a refund of $300. How should Charles treat the $300 refund?

Discussion: Under the tax benefit rule, the $300 refund is a recovery of an expense deducted in a prior year. Therefore, Charles must include the $300 in his gross income in the year of receipt, 1997. NOTE: The $300 is not a reduction of 1997 state taxes paid. Also, if Charles does not itemize his deductions in 1996, the refund in 1997 is not included in his gross income, because he receives no tax benefit from the state income tax deduction.

Prepaid interest is not generally deductible under the one-year rule. The tax law effectively requires all interest to be accounted for with the accrual method.[33] In essence, prepaid interest is payment for the use of money over time. As a result, it is allocated to the periods in which the money is used. The only exception to this rule is the payment of "points" on a loan used to purchase or construct a principal residence. The treatment of points is discussed further in Chapter 8.

▲ **EXAMPLE 46**   On April 1, 1996, Tasi borrows $10,000 from his bank. The $10,000, 10%-interest, 1-year note is due on March 31, 1997. In order to increase his expenses for 1996, Tasi prepays the $1,000 in interest on the note on December 31, 1996. How much of the $1,000 of prepaid interest is deductible in 1996?

Discussion: Because interest expense is a charge for the use of money over a period of time, Tasi must allocate the prepaid interest to the time period in which the money is used. Tasi may deduct only the interest related to the period of April 1 through December 31, 1996, $750 [$1,000 $\times$ (9 $\div$ 12)] in 1996. The remaining $250 in prepaid interest is not allowed as a deduction until it accrues in 1997.

Accrual Method

An accrual basis taxpayer may deduct expenses in the year in which two tests are met. The first test is called the *all-events test*. The **all-events test** is met when all the events have occurred that determine that a liability exists and the amount of the liability can be determined with reasonable accuracy.

▲ **EXAMPLE 47**   Hunter manufactures and sells electronic components for radar. The electronic components are fully warranted against defects for a period of 3 years from the date of sale. Based on experience, Hunter knows that 5% of the components will be returned under the terms of the warranty. Hunter estimates that warranty costs related to 1996 sales at $15,000. Does Hunter satisfy the all-events test with regard to the $15,000 of estimated warranty expense?

Discussion: Although Hunter can reasonably anticipate $15,000 in warranty costs for 1996, the liability does not satisfy the all-events test. Because the actual payee and the nature of the claim are unknown, the amount of the warranty expense must be estimated. Thus, the warranty liability is not fixed, and it is not determinable with reasonable accuracy. None of the estimated warranty expenses is allowed as a tax deduction until the parts are actually returned and the warranty obligation becomes certain. NOTE: This treatment differs from financial accounting. In financial accounting, reasonable estimates of expenses are sufficient to fix the liability for the expense. Tax accounting differs in the requirement that the payee be known before an amount is considered fixed.[34]

The second test requires economic performance to have occurred with regard to the liability. Economic performance occurs when services or property are provided to the taxpayer or when the taxpayer uses property. Table 5–1 summarizes when economic performance is considered to have occurred for several commonly accrued expenses. For example, interest accrues with the passage of time, and compensation of employees accrues as workers perform services. Only when the all-events test and the **economic performance test** have been met can an expense be accrued and deducted for tax purposes.

▲ **EXAMPLE 48**   Assume in example 47 that in 1997 customers return defective components sold in 1995 and 1996. It costs Hunter $4,000 to replace the defective parts. When can Hunter deduct the $4,000?

Discussion: When the defective components are returned and they are replaced or the sale price is refunded, Hunter has satisfied the all-events test and economic performance has occurred. Hunter may deduct the $4,000 in warranty expenses in 1997.

▲ **Table 5–1**

SUMMARY OF ECONOMIC PERFORMANCE TESTS

Source of Expense	When Economic Performance Occurs
Taxpayer is to receive property or services from others.	As taxpayer receives property or services.
Taxpayer is to use property owned by others.	As property is used by taxpayer.
Taxpayer is to provide property or services to others.	As taxpayer provides property or services to others.
Taxpayer owes interest expense.	With passage of time, as taxpayer uses money borrowed.
Taxpayer owes compensation to employees.	As employees render services.
Taxpayer owes vacation pay to employees.	When paid by taxpayer, or when accrued if paid within 2½ months after close of year.
Payments required under ■ Workers' compensation laws. ■ Payment of liability for tort.	As payments are made by taxpayer.
Payments for accrued recurring items ■ Sales commissions. ■ Shipping costs.	When paid by taxpayer if immaterial *or* for a material item if it is treated the same for financial purposes.
Prepaid items ■ Insurance. ■ Warranty contracts. ■ Service contracts.	When paid only if immaterial *and* service is provided in a reasonable time after close of year.

The purpose of the economic performance test is to disallow a current deduction for costs that will not have to be paid in the near future. This contrasts with financial accounting for such costs, where an accrual is necessary in order to properly match expenses to the revenues being generated. In working with the income tax accrual method, you should keep in mind that matching expenses to revenues is not a general criterion that must always be satisfied. Rather, income tax accounting is designed to effect the ability-to-pay and wherewithal-to-pay concepts that assess the tax according to the amount available in the current period to pay taxes.

▲ **EXAMPLE 49**   Big Oil Co. enters into an offshore oil- and gas-drilling lease in 1996. In 1997, Big installs a platform and commences drilling. The terms of the lease obligate Big to remove its offshore platform and well fixtures upon abandonment of the well or termination of the lease. Based on past experience, Big estimates that the well will be productive for 10 years, at which time it will cost $2,000,000 to remove the platform and fixtures. When can Big deduct the cost of removing the platform and fixtures for financial accounting purposes? for income tax purposes?

Discussion: Proper matching of expenses to revenues for financial accounting purposes requires Big to accrue a portion of the estimated cost of removing the platform and fixtures over the life of the well. Therefore, Big would expense $200,000 ($2,000,000 ÷ 10 years) per year beginning in 1997. For income tax purposes, the cost of removing the platform and fixtures is not deductible until economic performance of the liability occurs. Thus, Big will not be able to deduct any of the costs until it begins removal and incurs costs related to the removal.

▲ **EXAMPLE 50**   Janson Corporation runs charter aircraft services. In 1996, Janson enters into a lease agreement with Dana Airlines to lease one of its aircraft for the next 4 years. The lease obligates Janson to pay Dana a base rental of $500,000 per year. In addition, Janson must pay $25 to a repair escrow account for each hour flown. The amounts in the escrow account are to be used by Dana to make necessary repairs to the aircraft. At the end of the lease, any amount remaining in the escrow account is to be returned to Janson. In 1996, the aircraft flies 1,000 hours, and Janson pays $25,000 into the escrow account. Repairs to the plane in 1997 cost $20,000. In 1998, $20,000 is released from the escrow account to pay Dana for the repairs. When can Janson deduct the costs associated with the lease?

Discussion: Janson can deduct the $500,000 rental payment each year, because both the all-events and economic performance tests are met as Janson uses the plane. However, the $25,000 paid into the escrow account for repairs is not deductible until economic performance occurs. Economic performance occurs when the repair service is rendered. Janson must wait until the repairs are made in 1997 to deduct the $20,000. Note that under financial accounting rules the amounts paid into the escrow fund would be deducted as they are paid as a cost of using the plane that year.

An exception to the economic performance test permits a taxpayer to take a current deduction for an item even if economic performance has not yet occurred. This is known as the *recurring item exception.* Use of this exception requires all of the following:

■ That the all-events test is met without regard to economic performance.

■ That economic performance occurs within the shorter of
   a. $8^{1}/_{2}$ months after the close of the year.
   b. A reasonable time after the close of the year.

■ That the taxpayer consistently treats the item as incurred in the year the all-events test is met.

■ That the expense either is not material or the accrual of the expense results in a better matching of income and expense than accruing the expense in the year in which economic performance occurs.[35]

Congress intended this exception to apply primarily to accrued expenses—those expenses that have not yet been paid but that meet the all-events test and will be paid within a reasonable time after the close of the year.

▲ **EXAMPLE 51**   Arturo has a commission agreement with his sales force. Under the agreement, he is to pay his salespeople a percentage of their net sales for 1996. Because of accounting requirements, he pays the salespeople their commissions in February 1997. When can Arturo deduct the commissions?

Discussion: Under the matching exception, Arturo can deduct the accrued commissions in 1996. Although economic performance (payment of commissions) does not occur until 1997, deducting the payment in 1996 results in a better match of sales income and commission expense.

Prepaid expenses qualify under the recurring item exception only if the expense is not material. A material prepaid expense (e.g., insurance) cannot qualify for the recurring item exception, because deducting the total amount of the expense in the current period does not result in a better match of the expense with income. If an item is considered material for financial accounting purposes, it is treated as material for tax purposes. However, if an item is immaterial for financial purposes, it is not necessarily immaterial for tax purposes. For an item to qualify as immaterial for tax purposes, the actual amount of the item *and* its relationship to other items of income and expense for the entity must be immaterial.

▲ **EXAMPLE 52**   Robin enters into a 1-year maintenance contract on July 1, 1996, by paying $12,000. The cost of the maintenance contract is a large expense relative to the total expenses of her business. For financial reporting, the expense is prorated, $6,000 to 1996 and $6,000 to 1997. When can Robin deduct the $12,000 cost of the maintenance contract?

Discussion: Robin should deduct $6,000 in 1996 and $6,000 in 1997. Robin does not qualify for the recurring item exception because the item is material. She does not qualify under the matching criteria because taking a current deduction for the expense does not result in a better match of the expense with income.

▲ **EXAMPLE 53**   Robin enters into a 1-year maintenance contract on July 1, 1996, by paying $12,000. The cost of the contract is a minor expense relative to the total expenses of her business for both financial and tax purposes. For financial reporting, the expense is prorated, $6,000 to 1996 and $6,000 to 1997. When can Robin deduct the $12,000 cost of the maintenance contract?

Discussion: Robin can deduct $12,000 in 1996. Robin qualifies for the recurring item exception because the item is immaterial. NOTE: Robin's prorating the expense for financial purposes does not affect her tax treatment.

▲ **EXAMPLE 54**   Claudio begins carrying a new line of clothing in his men's shop in 1996. He pays $5,000 for advertising the introduction of the new line in 1996. Claudio does not expect to have to run the advertising campaign in the future. When can he deduct the cost of the advertising?

Discussion: Under the matching exception, Claudio should deduct $5,000 for advertising in 1996. According to the IRS, expenses such as advertising, which cannot be practically associated with income of a particular period, should be assigned to the period in which the costs are incurred. The matching requirement is satisfied if the taxpayer reports the advertising expense in the same accounting period for both financial and tax reporting.

Related Party Accrued Expenses

The tax law limits the timing of the deduction of accrued expenses payable to a related cash basis taxpayer. **Related parties** are members of an individual's family and business entities in which the person directly or constructively owns more than a 50-percent interest. The arm's-length transaction and business purpose concepts require that related party transactions be scrutinized closely to discourage unwarranted tax avoidance. The ownership of a controlling interest in a business entity permits the taxpayer to exert significant control over the timing of transactions between the business and the taxpayer. The objective of the related party limitations is to defer accrued expenses from transactions that lack economic substance. For example, an accrual basis corporation and a cash basis related party could time a transaction to permit a deduction for the corporation in one year with the income reported by the related party in a later year. Thus, the taxpayers would receive benefit from the interest-free use of the deferred tax payment (the benefit is the interest related to the present value of the deferred tax).

▲ **EXAMPLE 55**   Kool Corporation, an accrual basis taxpayer, accrues a $10,000 bonus payable to Ivan for its year ending December 31, 1996. Kool pays the bonus to Ivan on February 28, 1997. Ivan owns 90% of Kool Corporation. Ivan reports his income on the cash basis. What tax savings might Ivan realize from the accrual?

Discussion: Assuming a 31% marginal tax rate and an 8% interest rate (the present value factor for one year would be 0.926), Ivan could save $229 by structuring the transaction to accelerate the deduction while deferring the income. The tax savings are solely the result of the timing of the transaction [($10,000 × 31%) − ($10,000 × 31% × 0.926)]. However, the related party rules discussed next prevent this result.

The related party rules prevent the abuse in example 55 by requiring an accrual basis taxpayer to use a cash method of accounting for expenses that are paid to a cash basis related party. If an accrual basis taxpayer accrues an expense payable to a cash basis related party, the expense is not deductible until it is paid in cash and included in the related cash basis taxpayer's gross income.[36] Thus, the tax law requires a matching of the deduction with the related reporting of income to avoid potential tax avoidance. If both parties are accrual basis taxpayers, the problem does not arise. The accrual accounting method would result in the transaction being recognized by the related parties at the same date.

▲ **EXAMPLE 56**   What is the proper treatment of the bonus in example 55?

Discussion: Kool Corporation may not deduct the accrued bonus for tax purposes until the cash is paid to Ivan and included in his taxable income. Thus, Ivan reports the $10,000 bonus as income in 1997 when it is received, and Kool Corporation deducts the expense in 1997. The related party rules require both parties to recognize the transaction on the same date.

If Ivan and Kool Corporation are both accrual basis taxpayers, they would both accrue the transaction for the year ended December 31, 1996, regardless of when the cash was paid. Ivan would report income, and Kool would claim a deduction for the expense in 1996.

Financial and Taxable Income Differences

Financial accounting rules place a strong emphasis on the matching of expenses to the income generated during the period. In addition, conservatism dictates that expenses and losses be recognized for financial accounting purposes before they are actually incurred. As a result, financial accounting promotes the use of reasonable estimates of the expenses incurred to earn income. However, tax accounting rules emphasize objectivity in measuring taxable income to be sure the proper tax is collected each year. The tax law's objectivity is essential to protecting revenue collection. Because of the time value of money, deduction of an expense too early would reduce the time value of tax collections. Deducting an expense in the wrong year to receive the benefit of a higher marginal tax rate will also reduce tax collections. Thus, the timing of deductions is a critical issue.

The all-events and economic performance tests create temporary differences between financial (book) and taxable income. For example, the tax law generally requires the use of the specific charge-off method (discussed in Chapter 6) for computing a bad debt deduction. Financial accounting requires the use of the allowance method, which uses a reasonable estimate of the current year's bad debt deduction to be charged against income.

▲ **EXAMPLE 57**   For financial reporting, Press Corporation estimates its bad debt expense to be 2% of credit sales. For 1996, Press records $500,000 in credit sales and $10,000 (2% × $500,000) in bad debt expense. However, a review of individual accounts receivable indicates that on the specific charge-off method, actual bad debts for 1996 total $6,000. How much can Press deduct for bad debts for tax purposes?

Discussion: Although the allowance method is used to estimate bad debt expense for financial reporting, the specific charge-off method must be used for tax reporting. As a result, Press should deduct $10,000 in bad debt expense for financial income reporting and $6,000 in bad debt expense for tax income. The difference in the book and tax deductions results in a $4,000 temporary difference.

For financial accounting, vacation pay accrues as it is earned by the employees. The economic performance requirement allows vacation pay as a deduction when paid or when accrued if payment occurs within $2^1/_2$ months after the close of the year. Similar rules apply to allowances for warranties. Warranty repair allowances are estimated and deducted as sales are made for financial accounting, but tax accounting allows a deduction only when the taxpayer performs warranty services.

Other tax laws, which are discussed in this and later chapters in the text, also create differences between book and taxable income. These differences are temporary differences in some instances and permanent differences in others. For example, capital expenditures benefiting future tax years are not currently deductible. However, the tax law makes several exceptions to this requirement to promote economic and social objectives. Chapter 11 discusses a special provision that allows a business to expense $17,500 of the cost of new equipment in the year it is purchased. For a small business, these expenditures could be a significant drain on working capital. Allowing an immediate tax deduction for the expenditure takes into account two concepts: The immediate tax reduction recognizes that an investment in capital expenditures may reduce the taxpayer's wherewithal to pay, and the election to expense assets adds administrative convenience by eliminating the need to make annual depreciation calculations and keep detailed records for small investments in business assets.

Other temporary differences are caused by the tax law calculation of depreciation. For example, current tax depreciation rules ignore an asset's salvage value and compute depreciation over a predefined statutory life instead of the asset's useful life. These tax rules have the effect of allowing deductions for tax purposes before they are allowed for book income. Because the capital recovery concept limits the total depreciation deduction to the investment in the asset for both book and tax purposes, the difference is in the timing of deductions.

The tax laws also create permanent differences between book and taxable income. Provisions that disallow 50 percent of the cost of business meals and entertainment, limit the deduction of business gifts to $25 per donee, deny a deduction for excessive compensation paid to employees, and the federal income tax expense are examples of expenses that do not reduce taxable income but are deducted for financial reporting. As a result, these expenses create permanent differences between book and taxable income. On the other hand, the tax law allows deductions that are not recognized as expenses for financial reporting.

As discussed in Chapter 1, the personal and dependency exemptions and the standard deduction are tax accounting constructs. These constructs make the tax rate structure more progressive and enhance administrative convenience, which makes the tax law easier to enforce. The use of exemptions and standard deductions is foreign to financial reporting. Further, the tax law allows a percentage depletion deduction for certain natural resources. Percentage depletion is a tax deduction based on a percentage of income from the mineral source. The deduction is allowed even if the taxpayer has fully recovered the capital invested in the asset. This deduction violates both the capital recovery concept and financial reporting's cost depletion rules. However, Congress, in its exercise of legislative grace, has decided that it is desirable to violate the concept to provide tax incentives to promote the economic objective of developing natural resources. In doing so, the tax law has again introduced permanent differences between book and taxable income.

SUMMARY

Tax deductions are a matter of legislative grace. Therefore, expenses incurred in a trade or business or for the production of income that have a business purpose are allowed as deductions. Personal expenditures are not deductible unless they are specifically allowed itemized deductions. A conduit entity is not taxed. Rather, deductions flow through to each owner and are treated similarly to deductions incurred by an individual taxpayer. Mixed-use expenditures and expenses related to using mixed-use assets must be analyzed to determine the business deductions allowed for such expenditures.

An activity will generally be considered a trade or business if it is profit motivated and the taxpayer is regularly and continuously involved in the activity to earn a livelihood. A profit-motivated activity that does not satisfy the continuous and regular involvement or the livelihood requirement will usually be considered an income-producing activity. Trade or business expenses receive preferential treatment compared to expenses for the production of income in the individual income tax calculation. Trade or business expenses and losses, rent and royalty expenses, and capital losses (subject to the $3,000 annual limitation) of individuals are deducted for adjusted gross income. As a result, they are fully deductible unless the passive activity loss limitations apply. Expenses for the production of income are generally deductions from adjusted gross income (itemized deductions). Because they are treated as miscellaneous itemized deductions, expenses for the production of income will generally be subject to an income limitation.

To be deductible, a business expense must be ordinary, necessary, and reasonable in amount. A deductible expense may not be

- A personal living expense
- A capital expenditure
- An expenditure that frustrates a public policy
- Related to earning tax-exempt income
- An expenditure for another person's benefit

The year in which a deduction is taken is determined by the taxpayer's accounting method. A cash basis taxpayer may deduct expenses when paid. An accrual basis taxpayer may deduct expenses when the all-events test is met and economic performance has occurred. Both cash and accrual basis taxpayers generally must allocate prepaid expenses and capital expenditures to the accounting period benefiting from the use of the asset. Accrued expenses owed to a related cash basis taxpayer are not allowed as a deduction until the item is paid and included in the cash basis taxpayer's income. Temporary and permanent differences between financial reporting income and taxable income arise from the tax law's emphasis on the accounting period concept and objectivity in measuring and reporting allowable deductions.

KEY TERMS

accounting method (p. 208)
active investor (p. 193)
active trader (p. 194)
adjusted gross income (p. 188)
all-events test (p. 211)
business expense (p. 186)
capital expenditure (p. 202)
conduit entity (p. 189)
deductions (p. 185)
deductions for adjusted gross income (p. 188)
deductions from adjusted gross income (p. 188)

dominant motive (p. 192)
economic performance test (p. 212)
improvements (p. 204)
investment expense (p. 194)
itemized deduction (p. 189)
lobbying expense (p. 207)
mixed-use asset (p. 197)
mixed-use expenditure (p. 198)
necessary expense (p. 200)
one-year rule for prepaid expenses (p. 210)

ordinary expense (p. 199)
production-of-income expense (p. 194)
reasonable expense (p. 201)
related party (p. 215)
repair-and-maintenance expense (p. 204)
replacement (p. 204)
securities dealer (p. 194)
start-up costs (p. 204)
trade or business expense (p. 193)

PRIMARY TAX LAW SOURCES

[1] Reg. Sec. 1.162-5—Allows the deduction of education expenses that maintain or improve skills required in the taxpayer's employment or that meet the express requirements of the taxpayer's employer or applicable laws in order to retain employment.

[2] Sec. 62—Defines *adjusted gross income* for individual taxpayers and specifies the deductions allowed as deductions for adjusted gross income.

[3] Sec. 63—Defines *taxable income*; allows individual taxpayers to deduct the greater of their allowable itemized deductions or the standard deduction. Standard deduction amounts are specified and are required to be adjusted annually for inflation.

[4] Sec. 211—Generally allows specific personal expenditures as itemized deductions of individuals.

[5] Reg. Sec. 1.212-1—Requires investment-related expenses of individuals to be de-

ducted as miscellaneous itemized deductions, subject to the 2% of adjusted gross income reduction rule.

[6] Sec. 703(a)—Requires that the taxable income of a partnership be computed in a manner similar to an individual's. However, certain deductions are not allowed, and the items listed in Sec. 702(a)(1) through 702(a)(7) must be reported separately. Likewise, Sec. 1363(b) requires that the taxable income of an S corporation be computed in a manner similar to an individual's. Also, certain deductions are not allowed [Sec. 703(a)], and the items listed in Sec. 1366(a) must be reported separately.

[7] Knetsch v. U.S., 348 F.2d 932 (Cl. Ct. 1965)—Disallowed deductions from an investment in which the sole anticipated gain was the tax savings from the investment.

[8] Comm. v. Groetzinger, 480 U.S. 23 (1987)—Provides the current criteria for

determining what constitutes a trade or business.

[9] Hazard v. Comm., 7 T.C. 372 (1946)—Held that the rental of a single parcel of improved property constituted a trade or business.

[10] Curphrey v. Comm., 73 T.C. 766 (1980)—Held that the ownership and rental of real property does not automatically constitute a trade or business, that the ultimate determination is based on the facts and circumstances of each taxpayer, and that the scope of ownership and management activities is an important consideration.

[11] Comm. v. Lincoln Electric Co., 176 F.2d 815 (6th Cir. 1949)—Held that the reasonableness of a payment is an element to consider in determining whether the payment is ordinary and necessary.

[12] Deputy v. DuPont, 308 U.S. 488 (1940)—Held that an ordinary expense is one that is normal, usual, or customary in the particular business of the taxpayer.

[13] Comm. v. Tellier, 383 U.S. 687 (1966)—Held that the term *ordinary* distinguishes those expenditures that are currently deductible from those that are capital in nature.

[14] Welch v. Helvering, 290 U.S. 111 (1933)—Defines what constitutes an ordinary and necessary expense.

[15] Sec. 262—Provides the general rule for the disallowance of deductions for personal expenditures by individuals.

[16] U.S. v. Gilmore, 372 U.S. 39 (1963)—Held that the origin of an expense determines its deductibility.

[17] Sec. 263—Provides the general rule that disallows current period deductions for capital expenditures.

[18] Reg. Sec. 1.162-4—Allows the deduction as an ordinary and necessary business expense of incidental repairs that do not add to the value of the property or that do not appreciably prolong the life of the property.

[19] Reg. Sec. 1.263(a)-1—Defines the characteristics of a capital expenditure.

[20] Sec. 195—Provides the rules for amortization of start-up costs of a new business.

[21] Rev. Rul. 72-254—States that the expenses related to a general search for a new business are not deductible.

[22] The Colorado Springs National Bank v. U.S., 505 F.2d 1185 (10th Cir. 1974)—Held that the deductibility of the costs of investigating a new business depends on whether the business being investigated is in the same or a similar line of business in which the taxpayer is already engaged.

[23] Sec. 248—Allows a corporation to amortize over 60 months the costs of organizing the corporation. For partnerships, similar rules are found in Sec. 709.

[24] Hoover Motor Express Co. Inc. v. U.S., 356 U.S. 38 (1958)—Held that payments contrary to public policy are not ordinary and necessary.

[25] Max Cohen v. Comm., 176 F.2d 394 (10th Cir. 1949)—Held that expenses related to an illegal business are deductible as ordinary and necessary business expenses.

[26] Sec. 280E—Specifically disallows the deduction of business expenses of drug dealers (cost of goods sold is not a business expense).

[27] Sec. 162(e)—Disallows the deduction for certain lobbying and political expenditures.

[28] Sec. 265—Disallows the deduction of expenditures related to the production of tax-exempt income.

[29] Reg. Sec. 1.162-1—Disallows deductions for expenses that are not related to a taxpayer's own trade or business or production-of-income activities.

[30] Sec. 446—Provides the general rules for methods of accounting, including what constitutes a permissible method.

[31] Rev. Rul. 73-39—States that an expense of a cash basis taxpayer is deductible in the year in which it is charged to a credit card, not the year in which the credit card payment is made.

[32] Martin J. Zaninovich v. Comm., 616 F.2d 429 (9th Cir. 1980)—Allowed the deduction of prepaid expenses by a cash basis taxpayer when the expense would expire before the end of the tax year following the year of the payment and the payment was required. This is the one-

year rule for prepaid expenses by cash basis taxpayers.

[33] Sec. 461—Provides the general rules for determining the year in which a deduction may be taken, provides the criteria for the all-events and economic performance tests, disallows the current deduction of prepaid interest.

[34] Hughes Properties Inc. v. U.S., 106 S. Ct. 2092 (1986)—Held that a liability must be fixed and determinable in that the payee is known before an expense can be accrued.

[35] Reg. Sec. 1.461-4—Explains the economic performance test and the application of the exception for recurring items.

[36] Sec. 267—Defines related parties and disallows accrual of deductions to a cash basis–related party.

DISCUSSION QUESTIONS

1. All allowable deductions of individual taxpayers are classified as either for adjusted gross income or from adjusted gross income. Why are deductions for adjusted gross income usually more advantageous than deductions from adjusted gross income?

2. Why does the computation of adjusted gross income apply only to individual taxpayers and not to other tax entities such as corporations?

3. What is the fundamental requirement that must be satisfied in order to deduct a business expense?

4. What are the two primary categories of business expense? Why is it necessary to classify business expenses in these two categories?

5. Why must a conduit entity report certain deductions separately?

6. What is the effect on a partner's individual tax return if a partnership does not report separately the partner's pro rata share of investment expenses and instead includes these expenses in determining the partnership's ordinary taxable income?

7. The rules for deducting business expenses assure that virtually all expenses related to a trade or business or a production-of-income activity are deductible at some time during the life of the activity. However, few personal expenditures are deductible. Why is there such a difference in treatment of the expenses?

8. Discuss how well the rules for deducting expenses implement the ability-to-pay concept.

9. How are mixed-use expenditures and expenses related to mixed-use assets treated for tax reporting?

10. What is a trade or business?

11. What is an activity for the production of income?

12. Why is it important to distinguish a trade or business activity from a production-of-income activity?

13. Sam owns a 30-unit apartment complex. How would you decide whether the apartment complex represents a trade or business or an investing activity for Sam? What difference would the classification make for tax reporting?

14. What requirements must be met in order to deduct a trade or business expense? an expense related to the production of income?

15. When are capital expenditures deductible?

16. How do you distinguish a currently deductible expenditure from a capital expenditure? Give examples of each type of expenditure.

17. Why are start-up costs related to the investigation of a business opportunity treated differently depending on the current trade or business of the taxpayer?

18. Explain the rationale for not allowing a deduction for political and lobbying expenditures.

19. Explain why the income tax concepts support a deduction for some expenses of an illegal business.

20. Why are expenses related to the production of tax-exempt income not deductible?

21. What is/are the criterion (criteria) for the deduction of an expense by a cash basis taxpayer?

22. What constitutes the payment of an expense by a cash basis taxpayer?

23. What are the criteria for the current deduction of a prepaid expense by a cash basis taxpayer?

24. What tests must be met in order for an accrual basis taxpayer to deduct an expense?

25. What is the general purpose of the economic performance test?

26. Alexandra is a veterinarian who is an employee of Fast Vet Services. Susan is a self-employed veterinarian. During the current year, Alexandra and Susan have the same amounts of income and deductions. Why might a deductible expense paid by Susan have an effect on her taxable income different from the payment of the same expense by Alexandra?

PROBLEMS

27. Discuss how an individual would deduct each of the following expenditures. If more than one treatment is possible, discuss the circumstances under which each type of deduction would be obtained:
    a. Amos purchased 500 shares of Lietzke stock for $50 per share. Amos also paid $1,200 in commissions on the purchase.
    b. Dandy owns an optical store. She paid $2,000 in medical insurance premiums on her employees and $1,400 on a medical policy covering her and her family.
    c. Oscar is a finance professor at State University. He purchased professional journals costing $400 that he uses to keep current on the latest developments in finance.
    d. Gerry is a nurse. He paid $350 for nursing uniforms.
    e. Edgar owns a rental property. His rental income for the year was $13,000, and his allowable expenses were $9,000.

28. Determine how each of the following expenses would be deducted for tax purposes. If the expense is not deductible, explain why not.
    a. Chander paid $500 in interest on a loan he used to purchase equipment he used in his retail business.
    b. Peter paid $500 in interest on a loan he used to purchase 1,000 shares of Pickled Pepper stock.
    c. Portia paid $500 in interest on a loan she used to purchase her personal automobile.
    d. Jordan's primary source of income is from his wholesale warehousing business. During the current year, he paid $8,000 in state income taxes.
    e. Alphonse is a professional golfer who likes to race cars in his spare time. He spent $60,000 on various expenses related to racing cars during the current year.
    f. Barry is an insurance agent. He bought a golf cart and had his insurance company logo put on the golf cart to attract customers while he played golf.

29. Andy, Azim, and Ashwin operate the Triple-A Steak House, a popular restaurant and bar. The three, who have been friends since childhood, are equal partners in the establishment. For the year, Triple-A reports the following:

Sales revenues	$ 680,000
Short-term capital gains	7,000
Short-term capital losses	(14,000)
Trade and business expenses	(420,000)
Investment expenses	(4,000)
Taxable income	$ 249,000

How must the Triple-A Steak House report its results to each of the partners for tax purposes?

30. Carol, Careen, and Cathy own and operate Computer Hardware and Essentials, an S corporation. Carol owns 60%, Careen owns 25%, and Cathy owns 15%. For the year, the store reports the following:

Sales revenue	$690,000
Long-term capital gains	10,000
Trade and business expenses	(420,000)
Charitable contributions	(3,000)
Non-deductible expenses	(8,000)
Short-term capital losses	(17,000)
Taxable income	$252,000

How must Computer Hardware and Essentials report its results to its three shareholders for tax purposes?

31. Louise receives a $15,000 annual fee for serving as trustee of her mother's trust. Being a trustee is a new experience for her. She estimates that it takes her 30 hours a week to stay abreast of the bookkeeping, correspondence, and trust management functions. The trust's assets are primarily stocks, bonds, money market funds, land rentals, and oil royalties. Because Louise is independently wealthy, she would not have consented to serve as trustee for anyone other than her mother. Louise says she is lucky she doesn't have a regular job—she would be unable to keep up. She intends to continue serving as trustee as long as her mother lives. Write a letter to Louise explaining whether she is engaged in the trade or business of being a trustee.

32. Fernando is a retired auto mechanic. Since retiring four years ago, he has made stained glass windows. Because he has only occasional sales, Fernando treats this activity as a hobby. A friend of Fernando's recommends him to a local merchant who is renovating her office and needs someone to make and install 15 new windows. The job takes Fernando a month to complete and he is paid $3,000. In preparing his tax return, Fernando is unsure whether the $3,000 he receives is subject to self-employment tax. The instructions accompanying his federal income tax return indicate that a payment is subject to self-employment tax only if an individual is engaged in a trade or business. Is Fernando considered to be engaged in a trade or business?

33. Marilyn began performing as a professional entertainer when she was 4. She has performed with several well-known entertainers. During 1995, she performs a total of about 3 weeks. In 1996, she works full time for nearly the entire year at a clerical job. During 1996, she withdraws from the entertainers' union and does not have either a manager or agent. She auditions for several jobs and rehearsed with one group but cannot find work as an entertainer. She incurs expenses for theater and movie tickets, hair styling, makeup, wigs, costumes, and other expenses common to entertainers. Is Marilyn engaged in the trade or business of being a professional entertainer? Explain why or why not.

34. Max owns an office building that he rents for $750 a month. Under the terms of the lease, the tenant is responsible for paying all property taxes and costs related to the building's operation and maintenance. The only cost to Max in relation to the lease is an annual legal fee for renewing the lease. Is Max engaged in the trade or business of renting real estate? How would you classify his deduction for the attorney's fee?

35. Don was a senior vice president of a bank until its officials found he had embezzled more than $1,000,000. Don had set up fictitious checking accounts and deposited the funds into the accounts. He then created fictitious loans to himself. The embezzled money was used for personal purposes and to keep the fictitious loan payments current. Thus, he created fictitious loans to make payments on prior fictitious loans. Don worked hard to keep the loans current so he would not be detected. Because of a tax audit, he is seeking your advice. If his embezzlement activity is a trade or business, he claims he should be able to deduct as an ordinary and necessary expense the payments on the loans to keep his actions secret. What advice would you give Don concerning his business and deductions? Explain.

36. Angela owns a duplex. She rents out one unit and lives in the other unit. During the current year, she paid $6,400 in interest on the loan she used to buy the duplex, $800 in property taxes on the duplex, and $1,500 in dues to the duplex association that maintains the grounds and the swimming pool. How much of each expenditure can she deduct, and how would she deduct it?

37. Mika owns a single-family rental dwelling that she rents out for $625 a month for the entire year. Mika lives 12 miles from the rental house and makes 2 trips each month to inspect the house and to collect rent. In connection with the rental property, she incurs the following expenses for the current year:

Mortgage interest		$2,800
Taxes		740
Repairs and maintenance		
Replace dishwasher – *Capital Expenditure*	$480	
Paint interior of the dwelling	700	
Clean carpets	140	
Remove dead tree	275	
Spray for roaches	160	1,755
Advertising in local newspaper		60
Business gift (fruit basket & wine		
given to tenant)		50
Depreciation		2,450

A tenant moves into the house on January 2. Because the tenant goes to Mika's church and is having financial difficulty, Mika pays the cost of renting a moving truck ($190) and hires two people ($200) to help the tenant move. How should Mika report the income and deductions on her income tax return?

38. Hamid owns and lives in a duplex. He rents the other unit to an unrelated married couple for $875 per month. During the current year, he incurs the following expenses related to the duplex:

Mortgage interest		$8,200
Property taxes		950
Utilities		1,650
Repairs		
Paint exterior of duplex	$1,400	
Fix plumbing in rental unit	280	
Shampoo carpet in both units	220	
Fix dishwasher in Hamid's unit	90	1,990
Homeowners association fee		450
Insurance		750
Special property tax assessment to		
pave sidewalks		2,300
Depreciation (both units)		3,800

How should Hamid treat the expenditures related to the duplex? Explain.

39. In 1996, RayeAnn acquires a car for $12,000. She uses the car in her advertising business and for personal purposes. Her records indicate the car is used 65% for business and that her total annual operating expenses, including depreciation, are $2,900.
  a. How should RayeAnn treat the operating costs of the car for tax purposes?
  b. In 1999, RayeAnn sells the car for $6,000. Her business use for 1997 through 1999 remains at 65%, and she properly deducted $4,680 in depreciation. What is her taxable gain or loss from the sale of the car?

40. Harry and Sydney each inherited 50% of the stock in their father's corporation when he died. Harry had been working for their father and wanted to retain control of the business. Sydney was not really interested in the family business and wanted to sell her stock to outsiders. In order to retain control of the corporation, Harry made Sydney a vice president of the corporation with an annual salary of $200,000. The only requirements of the position were that Sydney not sell her stock and that she allow Harry to run the business. Can the corporation deduct the $200,000 salary it pays to Sydney?

41. Discuss whether the following expenditures meet the ordinary, necessary, and reasonable requirements:
   a. Sadie owns 5 shares of Megaconglomerate stock. She spent $4,000 to attend the annual shareholders' meeting.
   b. Sam runs a successful medical practice. Because he has a substantial investment portfolio, he spent $3,000 to attend a seminar on investing strategies.
   c. Alana is a self-employed tax attorney. She spent $5,000 to attend the American Institute of Certified Public Accountants' annual conference on income tax developments.
   d. Kevin owns a large ranching operation. Kevin is deeply religious and feels it is important that his employees have access to religious counseling. He hired an ordained minister to live on the ranch and be available to counsel his employees on any religious problems they might have.

42. Discuss whether the following expenditures meet the ordinary, necessary, and reasonable requirements:
   a. The Brisbane Corporation is being sued in connection with allegations that it produced a faulty product. Brisbane has hired an expert witness to testify that the product was not faulty. The expert's standard fee is $200 per day plus expenses. Brisbane has agreed to pay her standard fee plus expenses and a bonus of $5,000 if the company wins the lawsuit.
   b. Shannon is a professor who teaches film study at Burwood College. Her annual salary is $45,000. She maintains an extensive library of films and books at her home. During the year, she spends $15,000 on new material for her library. Most of the material is available at the university library.
   c. Francis operates a video store and rents the building from his aunt Shirley who acquired the building last year. Francis pays the previous owner $600 a month in rent. When Francis's lease expires, his aunt increases the rent to $750. Rent for a comparable building in the area is $850.
   d. Max owns a dairy farm in Wisconsin. During the year, he makes 10 phone calls to his sister Ruby, who is an accountant. The calls, which total $150, are for financial and business advice. Ruby prepares Max's business and personal tax returns.

43. Big Star Auto regularly advertises on local television. The owner of Big Star pays her 6-year-old grandson $250 for each television commercial in which he appears for Big Star. During the current year, the grandson appeared in 100 commercials. Big Star wants to deduct the full $25,000 as a business expense. The grandson will report the $25,000 as income. Can Big Star Auto deduct the advertising fee paid to the owner's grandson? Explain.

44. For each of the following situations, discuss whether the expense is currently deductible or must be capitalized:
   a. The Mickleham Hotel installs a $125,000 sprinkler system to comply with recently enacted fire regulations.
   b. The Healesville Corporation pays a real estate commission of $35,000 in acquiring its new office building.
   c. The Doverson Co. pays $25,000 to repave its parking lot.
   d. The Watsonia Co. pays $56,000 to add an air-conditioning system to its warehouse. The company had agreed to air condition the warehouse as part of a three-year labor agreement with its employees.
   e. Hua pays $600 to repair the walls and ceiling of his rental property after his tenant moves out.

45. Leonard owns an apartment complex. During the current year, he paid $14,000 to have all the apartments painted and recarpeted. Gena purchased an apartment complex during the current year. Before she could rent out the apartments, she paid $14,000 to have the apartments painted and recarpeted. Discuss the tax treatment of the $14,000 expenditures by Leonard and Gena.

46. In auditing the Philbin Corporation's repair expense account, Sara found a $28,000 entry. Because the amount was so large, she obtained the supporting documentation. The invoice listed the Fradin Roofing Co. as providing the service. The description of the work performed by the company was not attached to the invoice. However, a notation on the check listed "office roof." What factors does Sara need to consider in determining whether the Philbin Corporation can deduct the expense?

47. Elmo was laid off from his job during the current year. He decided to start his own business and spent $5,000 investigating various types of businesses and their potential locations. In August, he opened up a bicycle repair shop. Discuss the proper treatment of the $5,000 he spent before starting the business.

   What would be the proper treatment of the expenses for Elmo's investigation if he decided not to open a new business?

48. Two brothers spent $4,500 on travel, surveys, and financial forecasts to investigate the possibility of opening a bagel shop in the city. Because their suburban bagel shop has been so successful, the brothers would like to expand their operations. What is the proper treatment of their expenditures if

   a. They open a bagel shop in the city?

   b. They decide not to open a bagel shop in the city?

   c. Answer a and b assuming they are investigating opening a computer store in the city and they operate a bagel shop in the suburbs.

49. What is the proper tax treatment for each of the following expenses?

   a. All apartment house construction in Sandy Beach must comply with local and state building codes. To ensure that these codes are observed, Rex, a city building inspector, regularly visits construction sites. Shoddy Construction deposits $20,000 in a fund to provide a scholarship for Rex's son to attend college. The payment is in appreciation for Rex's help in getting around a building code violation.

   b. Rachel operates a pharmacy. She pays a 10% commission on all Medicare and Medicaid business and a 5% commission on all other business sent her way by the Last Stop Nursing Home.

   c. Kelly is a registered nurse. She receives a $1,750 per month salary working for a local clinic. Because Kelly is five minutes late to work two days in a row, the clinic fines her $25. Thus, her salary for the current month is $1,725.

50. What is the proper tax treatment for each of the following expenses?

   a. Bernilyn, a commercial real estate broker, is late for a meeting with her boss when she is stopped and ticketed $150 for speeding. She is using a company car when she receives the ticket.

   b. Russell is an employee of the Dinsmore Corporation, a small plumbing repair business. Russell learns that his boss Simon, the sole owner of the business, was arrested twenty years ago for burglary. Because Simon needs access to homes and businesses to do his work, he pays Russell $100 per month for his silence.

   c. Anastasia owns a travel agency. The daughter of the president of her largest corporate client is getting married, and Anastasia insists on paying for her bridal shower at a local restaurant.

   d. The San Martin Construction Co. pays local union officers $20,000. The payments are made to ensure that San Martin continues to receive future construction contracts. The payments are standard practice in the area.

51. Are the following payments deductible?
    a. A contribution to a fund to finance Honest Abe's campaign for mayor.
    b. A contribution to the Hardcore Gamblers' Association to fund efforts to persuade the public to vote in favor of parimutuel betting on licensed turtle races.
    c. Joyce, who is in the import-export business, sends an employee to Washington, D.C., to monitor current legislation. The expenses for the one-week trip are $1,500.
    d. Assume the same facts as in part c, except that the expenses total $2,200.
    e. Ruth, a small business owner, incurs $1,800 in travel, lodging, and meal expenses to testify in Washington, D.C., on the effect on small business of new environmental regulations.

52. Marcus is the vice president of human resources for Griffin Industries. He spent one week testifying before Congress about the effect of health-care legislation on small business. The cost of his trip was $2,750. Can Griffin Industries deduct the cost of Marcus's trip?

53. For the current year, Rufus paid an adviser $1,200 to help him manage his investments. The adviser's fee is not directly related to any particular investment owned by Rufus. Rufus owns $30,000-worth of City of Chicago bonds that pay him $2,250 in interest and $20,000-worth of Ford Motor Co. bonds that pay him $1,800 in interest each year. What is the proper tax treatment for the investment advice?

54. Tracy and Brenda are equal partners in Crescent Home Furniture, which is organized as an S corporation. For the year, the company reported sales revenue of $205,000 and business expenses of $135,000. Crescent also earned $8,000 in taxable interest and dividend income and $2,500 in tax-exempt interest on its investments. The investment portfolio consists of $32,000 in tax-exempt securities and $48,000 in taxable securities. Not included in the business expenses is a $1,500 fee Crescent paid for investment advice. As the staff accountant in charge of taxes for Crescent Home Furniture, write a memo to Judy, the accounting manager, explaining how the company must report its results to Tracy and Brenda.

55. Determine the current tax deduction allowed in each of the following situations:
    a. Doug, John's son, bought a new car that is titled in Doug's name. John paid for Doug's auto license tag. The tag cost $220: $40 for registration plus $180 in property taxes based on the value of the auto. Doug qualifies as John's dependent for tax purposes. Doug uses the auto for personal transportation.
    b. Elvis owns Ace Auto Repair. Elvis's head mechanic was arrested for drunken driving. Because Elvis needed the mechanic back at work as soon as possible, Elvis paid the $500 bail to get the mechanic out of jail. To keep him out of jail, he paid $450 in attorney's fees and the $500 fine the court imposed on the mechanic.

56. The Adelaide Advertising Agency, a cash basis taxpayer, bills its clients for services it renders and any out of pocket expenses it pays to third parties on behalf of its clients. For example, in creating a television commercial for a client, Adelaide charges the client for its staff time in creating the commercial and the third-party costs of filming and editing the commercial. During the year, Adelaide bills its clients $2,674,000. Of this amount, $674,000 is for expenses it pays to third parties. On December 31, the accounts receivable ledger shows a balance due to Adelaide of $256,000, $67,000 of which is for third-party expenses. How much of the third-party expenses can Adelaide deduct during the current year?

57. Chin borrowed $25,000 on a 2-year loan from State Bank to purchase business equipment. Under the terms of the loan, State Bank deducted the $4,500 in interest on the loan and gave Chin the $20,500 net proceeds. Chin will repay State Bank $25,000 in 2 years. When can Chin deduct the $4,500 in interest if he is a cash basis taxpayer? Would your answer be different if Chin were an accrual basis taxpayer?

58. Pope Corporation pays $50,000 per year for hurricane insurance. Reorder Corporation has determined that it suffers only $150,000 in hurricane damage every 5 years. Reorder self-insures for hurricanes by depositing $30,000 each year in a hurricane damage fund. Discuss the deductibility of the hurricane insurance payments by Pope and Reorder.

59. Appliance Sales Corporation sells all types of appliances. In addition, it offers purchasers of its appliances the option of purchasing repair contracts. During the current year, Appliance estimates that repairs totaling $10,800 will be made under the contracts sold during the current year. Actual repair costs were $7,500 related to last year's contracts and $1,450 on contracts sold during the contract year. How much repair cost can Appliance deduct during the current year?

60. Gonzo Co. is an accrual basis taxpayer. Gonzo provides medical insurance for its employees through a self-insured reimbursement plan. Gonzo pays $150 per month per employee into the plan fund. The fund is then used to reimburse employees' medical expenses. During the current year, Gonzo paid $90,000 into the fund and paid medical reimbursement claims totaling $78,300. How much can Gonzo deduct for the provision of employee medical coverage? Discuss.

61. Damon's Lawn and Garden Supply, an accrual basis taxpayer, is the exclusive dealer for Tru-Cut lawn mowers. In 1996, Damon's enters into an agreement by which it will pay the Dash Corporation, the manufacturer of Tru-Cut, an additional $15 per lawn mower. In exchange, the Dash Corporation agrees to provide advertising and promotion to Damon's for a 2-year period. Damon's purchased and paid for 200 lawn mowers in 1996 and 350 lawn mowers in 1997. The Dash Corporation paid $2,750 for advertising and promotion in 1996 and $5,500 in 1997. How much of the amount paid to the Dash Corporation for advertising and promotion can Damon's deduct in 1996? in 1997?

62. Joy incurs the following expenses in her business. When can she deduct the expenses if she uses the accrual method of accounting? the cash method?
    a. Joy rents an office building for $850 a month. Because of a cash-flow problem, she is unable to pay the rent for November and December 1996. On January 5, 1997, Joy pays the $2,550 rent due for November, December, and January.
    b. Joy borrows $75,000 on a 1-year note on October 1, 1996. To get the loan, she has to prepay $7,125 in interest.
    c. Joy owes employees accrued wages totaling $28,000 as of December 31, 1996. The accrued wages are paid in the regular payroll on January 5, 1997.
    d. Joy purchases $1,600-worth of supplies from a local vender. The supplies are delivered on January 29, 1996. The supplies are fully used up on December 30, 1996. Because of unusual circumstances, a bill for the supplies arrives from the vendor on January 10, 1997, and is promptly paid.
    e. While at a trade convention, Joy purchases some pens and paperweights to send out as gifts to her clients. She charges the $650 cost to her credit card in December 1996. She pays the credit card bill in January 1997.

63. The Parr Corporation incurred the following expenses. When can it deduct the expenses if it uses the accrual method of accounting? the cash method?
    a. The Parr Corporation mailed a check for $7,500 to the United Way on December 26, 1996. The company's canceled check shows that the United Way did not deposit the check until January 16, 1997.
    b. For 1996, the Parr Corporation estimates its warranty expense to be 2% of sales. The company's sales for 1996 were $2,100,000. The actual warranty costs paid in 1996 were $40,000.
    c. On August 1, 1996, the Parr Corporation borrowed $250,000 on a 1-year note. Because the company is experiencing a cash-flow problem, the bank agreed to allow Parr to pay the interest when the note matures. In exchange, the interest rate on the note is 10%—3% above the current market rate.
    d. The Parr Corporation advertises on radio and in the newspaper. During the year, the company was billed $18,000 for advertising. The beginning balance in the advertising payable account on January 1, 1996, was $3,000, and the ending balance on December 31, 1996, was $4,200.
    e. On August 1, 1996, the Parr Corporation pays $2,200 for a 1-year fire insurance policy for the period August 1, 1996, through July 31, 1997. Parr's insurance company requires the 1-year prepayment, which the company makes every year.

64. Kai, a cash basis taxpayer, is a 75% owner and president of the Finnigan Fish Market. Finnigan, an S corporation, uses the accrual method of accounting. On December 28, 1996, Finnigan accrues a bonus of $40,000 to Kai. The bonus is payable on February 1, 1997. When is the bonus deductible? How would your answer change if Finnigan is a cash basis taxpayer?

65. Lonnie owns 100% of Quality Co.'s common stock. Lonnie, the president of Quality, is a cash basis taxpayer. Quality is short of cash as of December 31, 1996, the close of its tax year. As a result, it is necessary to accrue a $50,000 bonus payable to Lonnie. As soon as the cash becomes available on January 15, 1997, Quality pays Lonnie the bonus in cash. When is the bonus deductible for the accrual basis corporation? How would your answer change if Lonnie is an accrual basis taxpayer?

66. During the year, the Li Real Estate Co. sold 225 homes, a record number. In appreciation of this accomplishment, the company gave each seller a wall clock that had a retail value of $95. What is the company's deduction for financial accounting purposes? for tax purposes?

COMPREHENSIVE PROBLEM

67. Carol is a single mother who owns a wholesale auto parts distributorship. The business is organized as a sole proprietorship. Her business has advanced, and she can no longer devote the time necessary to do her own tax return. Because she always has prepared her own return, Carol is familiar with most tax rules applicable to her business and personal affairs. However, she has come to you for advice with respect to a number of items she paid during the current year. You are to determine whether she can take a deduction for the expenditures in the current year.

   a. Carol purchased a small building on March 2 to use as a warehouse for her auto parts inventory. To purchase the building, she borrowed $150,000 on a 30-year loan and paid $25,000 in additional cash. Carol also incurred $2,400 in legal and other fees to purchase the building. The bank charged her $3,750 in points (prepaid interest) to obtain the loan. After acquiring the building, Carol spent an additional $15,000 to renovate it for use as a warehouse. The $15,000 included $5,000 for painting.

   b. Carol had her office building painted at a cost of $10,000 and paid $8,000 to have it landscaped. Carol paid for the building renovation in part a and the office building work by borrowing $50,000 on April 1 at 7% interest (see part f for details of the interest payments).

   c. On May 1, Carol prepaid a 1-year fire insurance policy on her 2 buildings. The policy cost $1,800, and the insurer required the prepayment. On July 1, Carol prepaid a $4,500, 2-year maintenance contract on the buildings.

   d. Carol started a self-insured medical reimbursement plan for her employees this year. Based on actuarial assumptions, she deposited $12,000 in a fund to pay employees' medical expenses. Actual payments from the fund totaled $10,600.

   e. Carol purchased a new automobile costing $28,000. She can document that her business use of the automobile came to 80% and that her out-of-pocket operating costs totaled $3,100.

   f. Carol paid the following interest on business-related loans:

Warehouse	$11,600
Office building	3,700
Renovation loan	1,500

   The renovation loan was for $50,000. Because she spent only $33,000 renovating the new building and painting and landscaping the old building, she used the additional $17,000 to purchase City of Seattle bonds with a yield of 6%.

g. Carol became active in politics and contributed $900 to the presidential campaign of an independent candidate. Carol made the contribution because she believed that, if elected, the candidate would institute policies beneficial to her business. The candidate lost the election and immediately started a grassroots lobbying organization. The purpose of the organization is to keep track of elected officials' campaign promises and report to the public when they vote contrary to their stated campaign promises. Carol paid $750 in dues to join the lobbying organization.

h. Carol's oldest son began college during the current year. She paid her son's tuition and living expenses, a total of $12,500, out of the company's checking account. During the summer, her son worked for the business and Carol paid him $3,300, the same amount she paid other college students working during the summer. Because she consults her son from time to time on the operation of the business, she thinks that at least some of the $12,500 should be deductible.

i. Carol has always itemized her deductions. This year, her mother and father retired and could no longer afford the mortgage interest and property taxes on their home. Rather than have them sell the house, Carol made the payments for them. They received a statement from their bank indicating that a total of $7,850 in mortgage interest and taxes were paid in the current year. Carol knows that mortgage interest and property taxes are deductible as itemized deductions and would like to add them to her personal interest and property tax payments.

j. Because of the success of her business, Carol has received many offers to invest in various business ventures. One offer was to establish a chain of nursing homes in Florida. Carol spent two weeks in Florida evaluating the prospects of the proposed venture and incurred costs of $2,800. After careful consideration, she decided the venture was too risky and decided not to expand into the health-care business.

DISCUSSION CASES

68. JR came by the other day to talk about one of his acquaintances. It seems the fellow is engaged in criminal activities. Being good at giving advice, JR told the fellow to be sure to report all his income from his criminal activities on his tax return to keep the IRS off his back. If he fails to file properly, he risks being sent to prison for tax evasion. JR also told his friend that he could not deduct any expenses, because his activities violate both state and federal laws. JR knew a lot about the fellow's activities and how much money the guy was making. The friend had even bought a $50,000 car just like JR's. Was JR's advice good? Why? Why not?

69. Malloy Industries manufactures air conditioners. The machines used to manufacture the air conditioners usually are insulated with asbestos. Because of health risks associated with asbestos, the Occupational Safety and Health Administration (OSHA) lowered the permissible level of asbestos fibers in the air. In addition, employers who have asbestos-insulated buildings or machines are required to monitor the amount of asbestos fibers in the air to ensure that they do not exceed the permissible level. Malloy Industries, a leader in providing its employees with a safe and healthy work environment, decided to remove the asbestos insulation from its 45 machines and replace it with another insulation material. The company determined that it would be less expensive to remove the asbestos insulation from its machines than to monitor asbestos levels on a daily basis. The company has found that the replacement material is 10% less efficient than the asbestos insulation. Should Malloy Industries capitalize or deduct the expense of replacing the asbestos insulation? Write a memo to the director of finances for Malloy Industries explaining the proper tax treatment of the cost of replacing the asbestos insulation.

TAX PLANNING CASE

70. Rosita's grandmother dies in November 1995 and leaves her an investment portfolio worth $180,000. In January 1996, when Rosita receives ownership of the investments, the portfolio consists of $112,000 in tax-exempt securities and $68,000 in taxable securities. Her grandmother's accountant estimated that the tax-exempt securities would earn $8,175 in interest and the taxable securities would pay $7,140 in dividends in 1996. The management expenses were estimated at $2,100. Rosita is single, has no other investments, and earns $42,000 as an engineer. She expects that her itemized deductions, not including the management expenses, will include state income taxes of $2,800, real estate taxes of $1,600, and home mortgage interest of $4,000.

   a. What is Rosita's projected taxable income for 1996?

   b. Assume that Rosita switches $40,000 from tax-exempt securities to taxable securities and the rate of return on both portfolios remains the same. All the other information would remain unchanged, except that state income taxes would increase by $500. What is the effect on her taxable income of changing her investment strategy?

   c. Write Rosita a letter in which you explain whether she should switch $40,000 in her portfolio from tax-exempt securities to taxable securities.

ETHICS DISCUSSION CASE

71. Dan owns a successful sports bar in downtown Providence. The state is considering legislation that would restrict the sale of alcohol in restaurants and bars on Saturdays and Sundays until after 7 P.M. The association of Providence restaurant owners is thinking about hiring a lobbyist to fight the legislation. The lobbyist has told the association that the lobbying effort would cost each owner $6,000. Dan's accountant has informed him that under the new tax law, his $6,000 contribution would not be deductible for tax purposes. Dan has told his 30 employees, most of whom are students at a local college, that if the legislation passes, he will have to lay off employees. In addition, he told them that most local restaurant owners cannot afford to pay a lobbyist $6,000 to fight the legislation, because it is not tax deductible. Ann, one of Dan's employees and an accounting major, suggests that Dan pay each employee an extra $200 dollars in salary (30 × $200 = $6,000) and that they forward the payments to the lobbyist. That way, Ann reasons, the cost will be deductible as salary expense. Dan tells his accountant about Ann's idea, and his accountant thinks it is great. In fact, he is so impressed with the idea that he has offered Ann a job when she graduates next spring. Do you think Ann's idea is a legal way to deduct the lobbying expenses? What ethical standards has Dan's accountant violated? (Refer to the Statements on Responsibilities in Tax Practice.)

Business Expenses

▲ CHAPTER LEARNING OBJECTIVES

■ Discuss the tax treatment of those business expenses that have the potential for significant abuse because of the personal nature of the expenditures: meals and entertainment, automobile expenses, travel expenses, and business gifts.

■ Consider the tax treatment of other business expenses that have specific deduction requirements: education expenses, employee compensation, and bad debts.

■ Discuss the criteria for deducting other business expenses and indicate when such expenses may have to be capitalized rather than deducted as a current period expense: insurance, taxes, and legal fees.

■ Explain the potential for abuse and the consequent tax treatment of three mixed-use expenditure situations: hobby expenses, vacation home expenses, and home office expenses.

▲ CONCEPT REVIEW ▲

Ability to pay   A tax should be based on the amount that the taxpayer can afford to pay, relative to other taxpayers.

Accounting method   A taxpayer must adopt an accounting method that clearly reflects income.

Administrative convenience   Those items for which the cost of compliance would exceed the revenue generated are not taxed.

Annual accounting period   All entities report the results of their transactions on an annual basis (the tax year). Each tax year stands on its own, apart from other tax years.

Arm's-length transaction   A transaction in which all parties to the transaction have bargained in good faith and for their individual benefit, not for the benefit of the transaction group.

Assignment of income   The tax entity that owns the income produced is responsible for the tax on the income, regardless of which entity actually receives the income.

Basis   This is the amount of unrecovered investment in an asset. As amounts are expended and/or recovered relative to an asset over time, the basis is adjusted in consideration of such changes. The **adjusted basis** of an asset is the original basis, plus or minus the changes in the amount of unrecovered investment.

Business purpose   To be deductible, an expenditure or a loss must have a business or other economic purpose that exceeds any tax avoidance motive. The primary motive for the transaction must be to make a profit.

Capital recovery   No income is realized until the taxpayer receives more than the amount invested to produce the income. The amount invested in an asset represents the maximum amount recoverable.

Entity   All items of income, deduction, and so on are traced to the tax unit responsible for the item.

Legislative grace   Any tax relief provided is the result of a specific act of Congress that must be strictly applied and interpreted. All income received is taxable unless a specific provision can be found in the tax law that excludes the income from taxation. Deductions must be approached with the philosophy that nothing is deductible unless a provision in the tax law allows the deduction.

Related party   Family members and corporations that are owned by family members are considered related parties, as are certain other relationships between entities in which the power to control the substance of a transaction is evidenced through majority ownership.

Substance-over-form doctrine   Transactions are to be taxed according to their true intention rather than some form that may have been contrived.

Tax benefit rule   Any deduction taken in a prior year that is recovered in a subsequent year is income in the year of recovery, to the extent that a tax benefit was received from the deduction.

INTRODUCTION

To deduct a business expense, the expenditure must have a bonafide business purpose. This means that you initially must classify individuals' expenses as either profit motivated or personally motivated. The profit-motivated expenses are then further classified as related to either a trade or business or to the production of income. This further classification is necessary, because trade or business expenses are deducted for adjusted gross income, whereas production-of-income expenses (i.e., investment expenses) are deducted from adjusted gross income for individual taxpayers. An individual's production-of-income expenses (other than rental and royalty expenses, which are deducted for adjusted gross income) generally are treated as miscellaneous itemized deductions. Itemized deductions are limited according to an individual's adjusted gross income and are discussed in Chapter 8. Because corporations are always considered to be in a trade or business and have no personal transactions, they do not compute adjusted gross income and the classification difference is not important.

This chapter introduces and explains specific business and mixed-use expenses. Many other expenses may be deducted on a tax return. Because of space limitations, it is necessary to confine the discussion here to expenses that are common to many different types of businesses. However, the concepts discussed in Chapter 2 provide a foundation for identifying most other deductible expenses.

In addition to determining that an expense has a business purpose and is ordinary, necessary, and reasonable in amount, you may want to review the other tests discussed in Chapter 5 as you continue to read this chapter. One is that a deductible expense may not be a personal living expense. However, taxpayers often incur expenses for both profit and personal reasons. These expenses are called *mixed-use expenses*. Hobby, vacation home, and home office expenses are mixed-use expenses, which are discussed here, along with the limitations on their deduction.

BUSINESS EXPENSES

The discussion that follows focuses on deductible business expenses. Most common expenditures made in a trade or business, such as utility payments, wage payments, supplies, and rental payments, are not subject to any specific rules. However, certain types of expenses have both a business and a potential personal aspect to them. This can lead to abuse by taxpayers who attempt to convert nondeductible personal expenditures into deductible business expenses. The tax law contains specific rules to follow in those areas that have the most potential for abuse. The first category of deductions to be considered is entertainment, auto, travel, gift, and education expenses. As you read about these expenses, note the special requirements for the deduction, the types of expenses that qualify, the 50-percent limitation, and the records that are required. In the discussion of employee compensation, notice the adverse effects of excessive salary payments.

In addition, various types of deductions have special rules. The tax law makes a distinction between business and nonbusiness bad debts. As a result, the treatments of business and nonbusiness bad debts are significantly different for tax purposes. The discussion of other business expenses points out several instances in which an expenditure either is not deductible or must be treated as a capital expenditure.

Entertainment, Auto, Travel, Gift, and Education Expenses

Entertainment, auto, travel, gift, and education expenses are particularly troublesome for many taxpayers. Although the expenses are incurred for a business purpose, they often involve an element of personal benefit or enjoyment. As a result, these deductions are subject to significant restrictions and limitations. To be deductible, the expense must satisfy specific requirements and be properly documented. Even if the expense qualifies and the taxpayer keeps good records, only the business portion of the expense is allowed as a deduction. Because these deductions are a matter of legislative grace and the taxpayer receives personal benefit from the expense, the IRS closely monitors compliance with the requirements. The tax law in this area is sometimes very detailed and quite complex. The intent of the following discussion is to familiarize you with the basic requirements for deducting these expenses.

Meals and Entertainment.   A taxpayer may deduct 50 percent of the costs of meals and entertainment incurred for a business purpose.[1] The meal or entertainment expense must be an ordinary and necessary expense of the business and not be lavish or extravagant under the circumstances. In addition, to be deductible,

meal and entertainment expenses must be either directly related to or associated with the active conduct of an activity for which the taxpayer has a business purpose.

A meal or entertainment expense is **directly related** to the active conduct of the taxpayer's business if it meets all four of the following conditions:

- There is more than a general expectation of deriving income or a business benefit from the meal or entertainment.

- A bonafide business activity takes place during the meal or entertainment.

- The principal reason for providing the meal or entertainment is to conduct business.

- The expenses are related to the taxpayer and people involved in the business activity.[2]

▲ **EXAMPLE 1**   George is a funeral director in Saline City. While attending a convention of funeral directors in Orlando, he rented a hospitality room for one evening and provided snacks and beverages. Use of the hospitality room gave him the opportunity to meet with other funeral directors and major suppliers of funeral products to discuss business. Can George deduct the cost of the hospitality room and the snacks and beverages as a business expense?

Discussion: The entertainment clearly took place in a business setting and was for a direct business purpose. George can deduct 50% of his entertainment expense related to the hospitality room.

▲ **EXAMPLE 2**   Claudia opened a new medical clinic. To publicize the clinic, she held a grand opening and invited community leaders and businesspeople to attend. At the open house, she served food and beverages. Can Claudia deduct the cost of the grand opening as a business expense?

Discussion: There is a clear business purpose for the entertainment expense. Because there was no meaningful personal or social relationship between Claudia and the people she entertained, 50% of the expense is allowed as a deduction.

If a meal or entertainment expense is not deductible under the "directly related" test, the expense may be allowed as a deduction under the "associated with" test. A meal or entertainment expense is **associated with** the active conduct of the taxpayer's business if it meets both of the following conditions:

- There is a clear business purpose for the meal or entertainment.

- The meal or entertainment directly precedes or follows a substantial and bonafide business discussion.

▲ **EXAMPLE 3**   Jane owns and operates a business that makes bridal gowns and accessories. She invited 20 of her best customers to her plant for a business meeting. The business meeting and a tour of her plant took most of the day. She had lunch for her customers catered at the plant so she could show them her new products. To conclude the day, Jane took her husband, customers, and their spouses to dinner. Is the cost of the dinner a deductible associated with entertainment expense?

Discussion: The cost of the lunches for her customers qualifies as an expense directly related to doing business. The amount spent for the dinner qualifies as an expense "associated with" business, because the dinner directly followed the substantial business discussion. The cost of the entertainment of the spouses also qualifies, because there is a clear business purpose for their presence. If they were not there, the customer might not be either. It is appropriate for Jane's husband to attend, because the

customers had their spouses present. Thus, Jane can deduct 50% of the meal and entertainment expense.

The cost of a meal includes the amount spent for food, beverage, tax, and tips.
Entertainment expenses include amounts spent at night clubs, theater, and sporting events. The deduction for tickets is limited to the face value of the ticket. The
fee for leasing a luxury skybox at more than one sporting event is not deductible.
However, the tickets for the skybox are deductible—but only an amount equal to
the highest-priced nonluxury box seat for the event is deductible.

▲ **EXAMPLE 4**   Randall wanted to entertain a client after a valid business meeting by
taking her to a basketball game. However, the game was sold out. He was able to
locate an associate who would sell him tickets for $50 each. The face amount printed
on the ticket was $15. How much of the cost can Randall deduct?

Discussion: Randall can deduct the $15 face amount of each ticket. The $35 ($50 −
$15) excess purchase price is not deductible. Randall's limited deduction is $15 (2 ×
$15 × 50%).

▲ **EXAMPLE 5**   Marisa is a partner in an advertising firm. The firm leases an 8-seat
skybox at a baseball stadium for $162,000 a season ($2,000 per game). The price includes 8 tickets to each game. After a presentation to a potential client, Marisa and 2
other partners of the firm entertained 5 representatives of the prospective client at the
firm's skybox. The fair market value of the most expensive nonluxury seat at the stadium is $40. The company spent $150 on food and drinks. How much of the entertainment costs can the firm deduct?

Discussion: The cost of entertaining is deductible, because it followed a business
meeting. Although no portion of the skybox fee is deductible, the firm can deduct $235
as entertainment expense. The firm can deduct $75 ($150 × 50%) for food and drinks
and $160 for the tickets ([8 × $40 = $320] × 50%). NOTE: If the firm had entertained
only 6 individuals (and used 6 tickets), it would be allowed to deduct the cost of all 8
tickets.

The cost of membership dues for business, social, athletic, and luncheon
clubs is not deductible as an entertainment expense.[3] Although the dues at these
facilities are not deductible, the cost of meals, assuming there is a valid business
purpose, remains deductible, subject to the 50-percent limitation.

▲ **EXAMPLE 6**   Kapil is a member of the Chariho Athletic Club. He estimates that he
spends 75% of his time at the club entertaining clients. For the year, he paid dues
of $1,800 and incurred food and beverage charges of $2,200. Kapil can document
that $1,550 of the charges were for entertaining clients and followed a bonafide
business discussion. The remaining $650 in charges are personal. What amount of
the expenses at the Chariho Athletic Club can Kapil deduct as an entertainment
expense?

Discussion: Although 75% of Kapil's time is spent entertaining clients, no portion of
the dues is deductible. Kapil can deduct $775 ($1,550 × 50%) of the food and beverage
charges. The $650 in personal charges is not deductible.

As a general rule, the meal and entertainment expenses of people whose presence is necessary to conduct the business activity are deductible. The expenses of
other people can be deducted if their presence serves a clear business purpose. If
entertainment expenses are incurred for business and personal reasons, only the
expenses that have a business purpose are deductible. Thus, expenses of social
guests are nondeductible personal expenses. In addition, the tax law requires the

taxpayer or an employee of the taxpayer to be present when meals and beverages are served in order for the cost to be deductible.

▲ **EXAMPLE 7**   Tom gave a party for his clients. Tom, 6 clients, and 3 social guests were present. The party cost Tom $1,000 for food, beverages, and entertainment. How much of the $1,000 can Tom deduct as a business expense?

Discussion: Because Tom was present when the food and beverages were served, the business portion of the cost is a qualified expense. The expense for Tom and his 6 clients may be deducted because the expenditure had a business purpose. The expense related to the social guests is personal and not deductible. Tom's allowable entertainment costs are $700 [(7 ÷ 10) × $1,000]. Tom's deduction is limited to $350 ($700 × 50%).

As a further limitation, reciprocal entertaining by business associates is not permitted. Reciprocal entertaining occurs when people in a group take turns entertaining each other to attempt to make the expense tax deductible. That entertainment is treated according to its social substance rather than its business form (substance-over-form doctrine).

▲ **EXAMPLE 8**   Vanessa is an audit partner in a public accounting firm. Once a month, Vanessa has dinner with two of her college roommates who are audit partners in other firms. The three alternate picking up the check. Although the conversation often begins with personal issues, inevitably the majority of the discussion is business. Joan has saved the receipts, totaling $275, from the dinners. Do the dinners qualify as valid entertainment expenses?

Discussion: The dinners fail both the directly related test (no expectation of future profits) and the associated with test (no valid business purpose). The predominant motive for the dinner is personal. Joan can deduct no portion of the $275 as entertainment expense. In essence, the three are engaging in reciprocal entertaining.

Several exceptions to the 50-percent limitation allow a business to deduct the full cost of meals and entertainment. These exceptions also are exempt from the directly related and associated with tests for the deductibility of meals and entertainment. The more common situations in which a business expense for meals and entertainment is fully deductible are

- Expenses treated as compensation to an employee and subject to income tax withholding. This arises when the employer has a nonaccountable plan for reimbursing employees' expenses. This type of plan is discussed in Chapter 8.

- Expenses incurred while performing services for another person and that other person reimburses the expenses when the taxpayer specifically accounts for them. Note that the person who reimburses the expense is subject to the 50-percent limit.

- Recreational, social, or similar expenses primarily for the benefit of employees. The value of the entertainment is not income to employees under the de minimis fringe-benefit rule discussed in Chapter 4.

- Expenses for goods, services, and facilities that are taxable income to a recipient who is not an employee because the meal or entertainment expense represents a payment of compensation for services or a prize or an award.

- Expenses for goods, services, and facilities made available to the general public.

▲ **EXAMPLE 9**   Rubin Corporation provides the food, beverages, and entertainment for a Fourth of July picnic for its employees and their families. This is an annual event that Rubin believes benefits its employees and the company. This year, the picnic cost $5,000. How much of the $5,000 in meals and entertainment cost can Rubin deduct?

Discussion: Rubin Corporation can deduct the full $5,000, because the expense was for the recreational and social benefit of its employees. The expense is not subject to the 50% limitation. The value of the party is excluded from the employees' income under the de minimis fringe-benefit rule discussed in Chapter 4.

Auto Expenses.   A taxpayer can choose one of two methods for computing a deduction for using an auto for business purposes. These methods are the standard mileage rate method and the actual cost method. Although the standard mileage rate method is the easier way to calculate the **auto expense,** it often results in a smaller deduction. On the other hand, the actual cost method may yield a larger deduction, but it requires more record keeping. The cost of commuting from home to work and back is considered a personal expense. Neither the use of a car phone to contact customers while driving to and from work nor putting advertising on the car makes commuting deductible. As Figure 6–1 illustrates, a taxpayer's mileage or cost of travel is considered business related if the travel is

- Out of town
- From the taxpayer's home to his or her temporary workplace
- From the taxpayer's regular workplace to a temporary workplace
- From the taxpayer's regular workplace (or temporary workplace) to a second job[4]

However, the mileage between the taxpayer's second job and home is considered personal. On days when a taxpayer does not work at his or her regular job, the travel to and from the second job is considered commuting.

▲ **EXAMPLE 10**   On a typical day Carla drives 10 miles round trip between home and her office. In addition, she drives 75 miles to meet customers and to take care of other business needs. How many of the 85 miles she drives each day count as business-related miles?

Discussion: Carla can deduct the cost of driving the 75 business miles. The cost of transportation to work and back home is personal and not deductible.

▲ **Figure 6–1**

BUSINESS-RELATED
TRAVEL

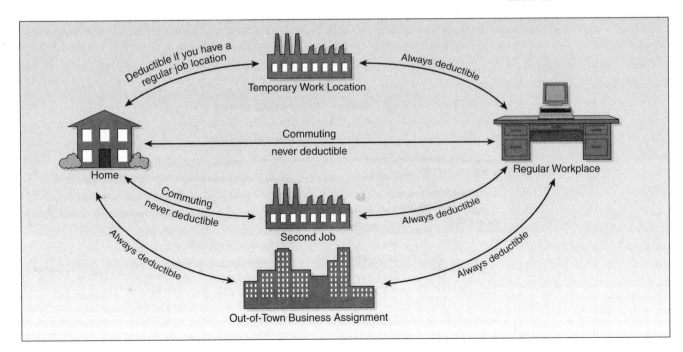

▲ **EXAMPLE 11**   Brendan works weekdays as a nurse at a local hospital. The hospital is 14 miles from his home. He also works as a waiter at a restaurant 2 nights during the week and on weekends. The week nights he works at the restaurant, he leaves directly from the hospital. The restaurant is 6 miles from the hospital and 8 miles from his home. What portion of Brendan's travel is considered business related?

Discussion: The 14 miles (28 miles round trip) from Brendan's home to the hospital are commuting and considered personal. The 6 miles from the hospital to the restaurant are business, and the 8 miles from the restaurant to his home are personal. The mileage to and from the restaurant on the weekend is considered personal, because Brendan did not work at his regular job. NOTE: If during the week, Brendan went home before going to the restaurant, his business miles would be limited to his normal travel distance (6 miles).

Regardless of which method the taxpayer chooses, the deduction can be disallowed for failure to keep records that support the date and amount of an expense that is deducted, the mileage allocations, and the business purpose for the expense.

STANDARD MILEAGE RATE METHOD.   To use the **standard mileage rate method,** which is based on administrative convenience, a taxpayer simply deducts 31 cents (30 cents in 1995) for each business mile the car was driven.[5] The standard mileage rate is an estimate of the cost of operating a car (gas, oil, repairs, insurance, depreciation, etc.). Because these costs change over time, the standard rate is adjusted each year. In addition to the standard mileage rate, the taxpayer can deduct direct out-of-pocket expenses that are unrelated to the operating costs of the car. These include the business portion of parking, tolls, interest, and property taxes. The property taxes must be based on the car's value. Interest and property taxes are deductible only if the individual is self-employed. The standard mileage rate method is subject to several limitations and requirements that should be considered before it is used. For example, the standard mileage rate method may not be used by a business that operates more than one vehicle in the business at the same time.

▲ **EXAMPLE 12**   José purchased a new car this year and drove it 10,000 miles for business purposes and 3,000 miles for personal use. What is José's deduction for the business use of the car if he elects to use the standard mileage rate method?

Discussion: José can deduct $3,100 (10,000 × 31 cents) in auto expense based on his business mileage under the standard mileage rate method. No deduction is allowed for the personal use of the car. If he paid any parking fees or tolls out of pocket while on business, these expenses are also deductible.

ACTUAL COST METHOD.   The actual cost method is a more flexible way to compute the auto expense deduction and often results in a larger tax savings. Using the **actual cost method,** a taxpayer can deduct depreciation, gas and oil, repairs, insurance, license, and other expenses of driving the car. As with the standard mileage rate, the taxpayer can deduct the business portion of the nonoperating costs of the car. If the car is used for both business and personal purposes, the expenses must be allocated according to the miles driven for each purpose. Only mileage driven for a business purpose results in a tax deduction. If the actual cost method is used, it is important to keep mileage records to support the allocation of expenses between business and personal use. The depreciation deduction under the actual cost method is subject to significant limitations, which are discussed in Chapter 11. The actual depreciation deduction is limited to statutory caps based on when the car was acquired. For example, if a car was bought in 1995 and used 100 percent for business, the maximum depreciation deduction for 1995 is $3,060.[6] This limit changes each year of the car's depreciation life.

▲ **EXAMPLE 13**   Nancy uses her car in her business of selling real estate. In 1996, she buys a new car and drives it 18,700 miles for business and 3,800 miles for commuting to and from the office and for other personal use. Depreciation, insurance, license, gas, repairs, and other operating expenses total $7,200. She can document that she paid $125 in tolls and parking while on business, and the interest expense on her car loan is $250. What is her deduction using the standard mileage rate method and the actual cost method?

Discussion: If Nancy chooses to use the standard rate method, her car expense deduction is equal to 31 cents for each business-related mile driven plus any tolls and parking:

Standard rate deduction (18,700 miles × 31 cents) =	$5,797
Tolls and parking (100% business)	125
Interest on car loan [(18,700 ÷ 22,500 = 83%) × $250]	208
Total deduction for business use of car	$6,130

Because the tolls and parking were incurred while on business, they do not have to be allocated. The interest expense is based on the ratio of business-related miles to total miles.

Discussion: If Nancy chooses to use the actual cost method, her car expense deduction is determined by allocating the costs of operating the car between business and personal use:

Actual operating expenses	$7,200
Business use percentage (18,700 ÷ 22,500)	× 83%
Business portion of operating expenses	$5,976
Tolls and parking (100% business)	125
Interest on car loan (83% × $250)	208
Total deduction for business use of car	$6,309

Tolls and parking incurred while on business do not have to be allocated. The interest expense is allocated according to the business use percentage. If Nancy is willing to keep the records necessary to support the actual cost method, she can obtain a larger car expense deduction than under the standard mileage rate method.

Travel Expenses.   A taxpayer can deduct travel expenses incurred while pursuing a business purpose. **Travel expenses** include transportation, lodging, 50 percent of the cost of meals, and incidental expenses. Incidental expenses are items such as local transportation, telephone calls, laundry, and similar expenses that are necessary while traveling. For an expense to qualify as travel, the taxpayer must be away from her or his tax home overnight. A **tax home** is the general area in which the taxpayer conducts her or his principal business activity. To be *away overnight* means a period that is long enough to require the taxpayer to rest. Overnight is substantially longer than a normal workday and can be less than 24 hours. A one-day business trip usually will not satisfy the overnight test.

▲ **EXAMPLE 14**   Theresa, a CPA, went to Houston for 10 days. The business purpose for making the trip was to audit a client's accounting records. The airplane ticket cost $195, the hotel cost $85 a night, and she spent $40 a day on meals and $15 a day for incidentals. She did not spend any time sightseeing or visiting friends. What is Theresa's deductible travel expense?

Discussion: All of Theresa's travel expenses are allowed as a deduction because they are related to business. However, she is still subject to the 50% limit on meals and entertainment costs. She can deduct:

Transportation	$ 195
Lodging (10 days × $85)	850
Meals [(10 days × $40) × 50%]	200
Incidentals (10 days × $15)	150
Total deductible travel expense	$1,395

If the primary purpose of the travel is personal, incidental business activity will not change the nature of the trip. The taxpayer cannot deduct any transportation costs if the purpose of the trip is primarily personal. However, lodging, 50 percent of meals, and incidental expenses directly related to conducting business while on a personal trip may be deducted. The primary purpose of a trip is determined by the facts and circumstances in each case. The time devoted to business activity compared to the time spent on personal activities is an important factor. If more than 50 percent of the total time is related to personal activities, the primary purpose generally is deemed personal.[7]

▲ **EXAMPLE 15**   Using the facts in example 14, assume that Theresa spent 6 days visiting family in Houston and 4 days auditing her client's records. What is Theresa's deductible travel expense?

Discussion: Because 60% (6 of 10 total days) of Theresa's time on the trip was related to personal activities, none of the transportation expense is deductible. She can deduct the other expenses to the extent related to business activities:

Transportation	$ -0-
Lodging (4 days × $85)	340
Meals [(4 days × $40) × 50%]	80
Incidentals (4 days × $15)	60
Total deductible travel expense	$480

If the primary reason for the trip is a business purpose (more than 50 percent of the trip is spent on business activities) and the taxpayer spends some time for personal activities, the tax result will be different. The cost of transportation is fully deductible, but a deduction for lodging, meals, and incidental expenses related to personal activities is not allowed.

▲ **EXAMPLE 16**   Using the facts in example 14, assume that Theresa spent 3 days visiting family in Houston and 7 days auditing her client's records. What is Theresa's deductible travel expense?

Discussion: Because more than 50% of Theresa's time on the trip was related to business activities, she can deduct all the transportation expense. She can also deduct the other expenses to the extent they related to business activities:

Transportation	$ 195
Lodging (7 days × $85)	595
Meals [(7 days × $40) × 50%]	140
Incidentals (7 days × $15)	105
Total deductible travel expense	$1,035

Expenses incurred by a spouse or a family member who accompanies the taxpayer on the trip are not allowed as a deduction, unless there is a bonafide business purpose for the person's presence and the spouse is an employee of the taxpayer. An additional limitation is imposed on travel to attend a convention, seminar, or other meeting that qualifies as related to the production of income. Expenses for attending investment-related meetings are not deductible, unless it can be shown the meeting is related to the taxpayer's trade or business.

▲ **EXAMPLE 17**   Raul is a physician who invests in real estate partnerships. He traveled from Dallas to Tulsa to attend a seminar on tax laws affecting real estate investments. Can Raul deduct the cost of attending the seminar?

Discussion: Raul is an investor in real estate partnerships, and the travel is related to the production of income. Because the travel is not related to his medical practice (trade or business), the travel expenses are not deductible.

▲ **EXAMPLE 18**   Assume that in example 17 Raul is a tax attorney who represents clients who invest in real estate partnerships. Can Raul deduct the cost of attending the seminar?

Discussion: Because the seminar is related to his trade or business as a tax attorney, Raul may deduct the allowable costs of attending the seminar as an expense incurred in his trade or business.

▲ **EXAMPLE 19**   Yusef is a self-employed insurance agent. He and his wife Ruby traveled to Washington to attend an insurance conference. Ruby is an executive secretary for Rhody Corporation. She spent her time in Washington attending the sessions, taking notes, and setting up meetings for Yusef. Can Yusef deduct the cost of attending the seminar for both of them?

Discussion: Ruby's presence at the conference serves a useful business purpose, but because she is not Yusef's employee, the expenses related to Ruby's travel are not deductible. If the hotel rate is the same for single or double occupancy, no part of the lodging would be disallowed. But if different rates apply, Yusef can deduct only the cost of single occupancy (Yusef's). All allowable costs Yusef incurred for his attendance at the conference are deductible (subject to the 50% meal and entertainment limitation), because the seminar relates to his trade or business.

Business Gifts.   A taxpayer can deduct up to $25 per year per donee for gifts to business customers. **Business gifts** are not subject to the 50-percent limitation that applies to meals and entertainment expenses. To apply the $25 limitation, direct and indirect gifts given to a person must be counted. An indirect gift is one made to a related party, such as a taxpayer's spouse or child.

▲ **EXAMPLE 20**   Sam operates a retail store. To show his appreciation for the business of his 5 best customers, he sent candy to their spouses at their home. The candy cost Sam $45 for each box. How much of the cost of the candy can Sam deduct as a business gift?

Discussion: The gift of the candy to the spouse is an indirect gift to the customer. The $20 cost per box in excess of the annual donee limit is not deductible. Sam's deduction is limited to $125 (5 gifts at $25 each).

▲ **EXAMPLE 21**   Assume that Sam also sent each of his 5 best customers custom-made desk clocks that cost $85 each. How much of the cost of the clocks is deductible as a business gift?

Discussion: Because the annual limit of $25 per donee applies to both direct and indirect gifts, none of the cost of the clocks may be deducted as a business gift. The $25 limitation was exceeded on the gift to the spouse. Therefore, Sam is over the limit on his 5 best customers.

The amount subject to the annual limit does not include incidental expenses that do not add value to the gift, such as gift wrapping, engraving, or delivering the item to the customer. An item that could be considered either a gift or an entertainment expense is generally considered entertainment and is subject to the 50-percent limitation.

Substantiation Requirements.   Entertainment, auto, travel, and gift expenses are subject to strict documentation requirements. The tax law requires the taxpayer to keep records that will show

- The amount of the expense
- The time and place of travel or entertainment, or date and description of a gift
- The business purpose of the travel, entertainment or gift
- The business relationship to the person entertained or receiving the gift[8]

These are **substantiation requirements** and failure to keep the records necessary to meet them can result in loss of the deduction.

Education Expenses.   Because education is viewed as a personal capital expenditure, individuals are not allowed to deduct education expenses. However, the tax law does allow a taxpayer to deduct education expenses if the **education expense** meets either of the following requirements:

- The education is a requirement—either by law or the taxpayer's employer—for the taxpayer's continued employment.
- The education maintains or improves the skills required in the taxpayer's trade or business.[9]

A taxpayer who is not reimbursed for an education expense can deduct the expense as a miscellaneous itemized deduction. Remember that miscellaneous itemized deductions must be reduced by 2 percent of adjusted gross income. A taxpayer who is self-employed can deduct the cost of education expenses as an ordinary and necessary business expense. The effect is that the deduction for education expenses is *for* adjusted gross income.

> ▲ **EXAMPLE 22**   Juan is a lawyer for a local law firm. State law requires that he attend 40 hours of continuing education each year, at least 6 hours of which must be on ethics. Juan attended 4 seminars (8 hours each) on estate taxes and an 8-hour seminar on ethics. All tuition for the 4 seminars came to $1,200; the ethics seminar cost $250. Can Juan deduct the cost of the continuing education seminars?
>
> *Discussion:*   The cost of all the continuing education seminars is deductible as a miscellaneous itemized deduction. The 32 hours on estate taxes qualify, because the courses either maintain or improve his skills. The cost of the ethics seminar is deductible, because it is required by state law.
>
> ▲ **EXAMPLE 23**   Phoebe has a bachelor's degree in engineering from Local University and is employed as an engineer with Koza Construction. She is enrolled in an advanced thermal dynamics course at Local U. The cost of the course is $600. Can Phoebe deduct the cost of the course as an education expense?
>
> *Discussion:*   Phoebe can deduct the $600 as a miscellaneous itemized deduction. The course qualifies as a deductible education expense, because it improves her engineering skills.

Meeting one of the requirements for deducting an education expense does not guarantee that the education expense is deductible. If the education is necessary to meet the minimum educational requirements of the taxpayer's job, the cost is not deductible. Also, if the education qualifies the taxpayer for a new trade or business, the expense is not deductible.[10]

> ▲ **EXAMPLE 24**   Linda is a biology instructor at Wakefield College. She is considered a temporary faculty member and her contract is renewed annually. The college requires that all permanent faculty members have a graduate degree and will renew Linda's

contract only if she begins work toward her master's. Linda has enrolled at Kingston University to pursue a master's degree in biology. Can Linda deduct the cost of her master's degree as an education expense?

Discussion: The cost of Linda's master's degree is not deductible. A master's in biology is the minimum requirement Linda needs to become a permanent faculty member at Wakefield College.

▲ **EXAMPLE 25** Horace is a full-time student in computer science at State University. He works part time as a programmer for a software developer. His employer has promised him a full-time job after he graduates. Can Horace deduct the cost of his college courses as an education expense?

Discussion: The cost of Horace's college courses is not deductible. Although Horace's college courses are related to his job, he is not considered to be engaged in a trade or business, because he is working only part time. In essence, the college degree provides Horace with the qualifications needed to enter a new trade or business.

A final limitation to note here is that travel that is in itself educational is not allowed as a deduction. For example, an art teacher who travels to New York City and Washington, D.C., to tour art galleries cannot deduct the cost of the travel even though it directly relates to teaching art. In contrast, if the teacher is an expert in a particular type of art and has to travel to Paris to verify the authenticity of an art object, the cost of the trip can be deducted.

In many cases, employers reimburse employees' education expenses. As discussed in Chapter 4, an employee can exclude from income up to $5,250 of education expenses reimbursed from a qualified educational assistance plan.

Compensation of Employees

The tax law provides for the deduction of reasonable salaries, wages, bonuses, and other compensation paid to employees. Thus, employee compensation is subject to two basic tests for deductibility. First, the payments must be for services actually performed by the employee. Second, the total payment for services of the employee must be reasonable in amount.[11] The determination of whether total compensation is excessive is made for each employee. When the compensation paid to an employee is found to be excessive, only a reasonable salary deduction is allowed. Whether compensation paid an employee is reasonable is decided by considering several factors, including

- Employee's duties, responsibilities, and pay history
- Volume and complexity of the business
- Time required to do the work
- Ability and accomplishments of the employee
- General cost of living and the company pay policy
- Relationship of the compensation, the gross and net income of the business, and dividends paid to shareholders[12]

Whether the remuneration is **reasonable compensation** is usually a problem when the payment is made to a **related party.** Thus, reasonable compensation issues generally arise in connection with a closely held business. In addition, the business purpose of the payment may be questioned. Lack of a business purpose will result in disallowance of the total compensation paid the person.

▲ **EXAMPLE 26** Tina is the sole shareholder of Staple Manufacturing Corporation. Tina is the president of the corporation and pays herself $200,000 a year. Her son, who is operations officer, is paid $50,000 a year. Her son seldom visits the plant, because he is a full-time student at State University. The next highest-paid employee, the general manager, is unrelated to Tina and is paid $50,000 a year. During an audit, the IRS determined that based on comparable salaries in the area, a reasonable salary for Tina should be $90,000. Based on an examination of employee records, the IRS decided that Tina's son was not an employee. The salary paid Tina's son was a sham (an assignment of income from Tina). How much of the payments to Tina and her son are deductible by Staple?

Discussion: The $110,000 ($200,000 − $90,000) excess salary paid Tina would not be a deductible expense of the corporation. The excess salary paid Tina would be taxed as a dividend payment. The salary paid to her son would be disallowed as a deduction for the corporation, because it lacks a business purpose. Under the assignment-of-income doctrine, the payment of the son's salary would be taxed as dividend income to Tina. Then, Tina would be deemed to have made a gift to her son in the amount of the salary payments. The gift received by the son is excluded from his income and is not deductible by Tina.

The tax law limits to $1,000,000 the amount a publicly traded corporation can deduct as compensation expense.[13] However, the $1,000,000 limitation applies only to a covered employee. A *covered employee* is defined as the chief executive officer (CEO) and the four officers with the highest compensations, other than the CEO, whose remuneration is required to be reported under the Securities Act of 1934. In determining a covered employee's compensation, all remuneration paid to the individual in cash or property is considered compensation. Exempted from consideration as compensation are

- Commission payments
- Qualified plan contributions (e.g., pension)
- Remuneration paid under a written binding agreement that was in effect before February 17, 1993
- Excludable employee fringe benefits (as discussed in Chapter 4)
- Performance-based compensation

For remuneration to qualify under the performance-based compensation exception, four requirements must be met. First, the payment must be made solely for the attainment of specific performance goals. The performance goal (except for stock options or stock appreciation rights) must be determined by an objective formula or standard. In essence, the formula cannot be subjective. Second, the performance goals must be established by a compensation committee consisting solely of two or more outside directors. An individual is considered an outside director if that person is not a current employee of the corporation. In addition, an individual who was previously an officer of the corporation cannot be considered an outside director. Third, the performance standards must be disclosed to and approved by the shareholders of the corporation. Fourth, the compensation committee, as described previously, must certify that the performance standards were attained before the compensation is paid.

▲ **EXAMPLE 27** Pamela is the fourth-highest-paid officer of the Vanger Corporation. Her salary for 1996 is $750,000. She also receives a bonus of $300,000 based on the performance of Vanger Corporation's stock. The bonus paid to Pamela is based solely on the performance of the corporation's stock. The standards for the bonus have been set by the outside directors, and they have certified that the performance goal was attained. The performance standards were also approved by the stockholders. Can the Vanger Corporation deduct all her compensation ($1,050,000)?

Discussion: The corporation is entitled to a deduction for the entire $1,050,000, because the $300,000 qualifies as performance-based compensation. If one of the four requirements had not been met (e.g., the performance-based standards were not approved by the shareholders), the compensation deduction would be limited to $1,000,000.

▲ **EXAMPLE 28**   Tomás is the tenth-highest-paid officer of the Mescow Corporation. His salary for 1996 is $650,000. He also receives a bonus of $400,000 based on his years of service and the performance of Mescow Corporation's stock. The standards for the bonus have been set by the outside directors, and they have certified that the requirement for earning the bonus has been attained. The performance standards have been approved by the stockholders. Can the Mescow Corporation deduct all compensation paid to Tomás ($1,050,000)?

Discussion: The corporation is entitled to a deduction for the entire $1,050,000, even though one of the four requirements (compensation is not solely based on performance) of the performance-based exception is not met. The entire compensation is deductible, because Tomás is not a covered employee. Only the CEO and the four highest-paid officers other than the CEO are covered employees.

Bad Debts

The tax law permits a capital recovery deduction for the taxpayer's basis in business and investment bad debts.[14] To be deductible, the bad debt must be related to a transaction that had a business purpose. To determine how to report the deduction, the bad debt must first be identified as a business or a nonbusiness (investment) bad debt. If the debt arose from a transaction in the taxpayer's trade or business, the bad debt is allowed as a business deduction as a **business bad debt.** Other bad debts that are not related to the taxpayer's trade or business are considered **nonbusiness bad debts.** The use of the loan proceeds by the borrower does not affect the classification as business or nonbusiness. The distinction between the two classifications is important. A business bad debt is deductible just like any other business expense. A nonbusiness bad debt cannot be deducted if the debt was voluntarily forgiven or the forgiveness of the debt was intended as a gift. In addition, nonbusiness bad debts are deducted as a short-term capital loss. The important implication of the **capital loss** treatment is that the deduction may be limited to $3,000 each year until the loss is fully used.

▲ **EXAMPLE 29**   Do-Rite, Inc., owes Kelly $10,000 for goods it purchased from Kelly on account. Because of financial difficulty, Do-Rite cannot repay the debt when it comes due in 1996. Kelly wants to deduct the $10,000 as a loss. How should she report the bad debt on her tax return?

Discussion: An account receivable from the sale of merchandise to Do-Rite is related to Kelly's trade or business. Therefore, Kelly can deduct the $10,000 bad debt as a 1996 business expense.

▲ **EXAMPLE 30**   Assume in example 29 that Do-Rite owes Kelly the $10,000 because the owner of Do-Rite is a friend of Kelly's and Kelly made the company a temporary loan to help it through a cash-flow shortage. Kelly does not do any business with Do-Rite. How should Kelly report the bad debt on her tax return?

Discussion: Because the loan is not related to Kelly's trade or business, the debt is a nonbusiness debt. Assuming Kelly does not have other capital gains or losses to report, she is permitted a $3,000 capital loss deduction in 1996, 1997, and 1998. The remaining $1,000 is deductible in 1999.

If Kelly forgave the $10,000 due from Do-Rite because the company is owned by her uncle and she wanted to do him a favor, the forgiveness would very likely be considered a gift to her uncle and not allowed as a bad debt deduction.

The amount deductible as a bad debt is limited to the taxpayer's basis in the receivable. As a result, the taxpayer's accounting method is an important factor in determining the amount deductible. If the receivable represents income owed to the taxpayer, the income must have been reported as taxable income before the taxpayer has a basis for claiming a deduction. Because of the basis limitation, a cash basis taxpayer normally will not claim a bad debt expense deduction for accounts receivable. Because a cash basis taxpayer does not report income until cash is collected, there is no tax basis in the receivable to deduct. However, an accrual basis taxpayer reports taxable income as it is earned, regardless of when the cash is received, and has a tax basis for deducting an uncollectible account.

▲ **EXAMPLE 31**   Sylvia operates a successful consulting practice. During January 1996, she performs $5,000 in services for clients who still owe her as of December 31, 1997. She reviews her client files and determines that $3,000 in receivables is uncollectible. How much of a deduction is Sylvia allowed if she uses the accrual basis of accounting?

Discussion: Using the accrual method of accounting, Sylvia would report $5,000 in income from the receivables in 1996. Because the income is reported on the accrual basis as it is earned, she has a $5,000 basis for the accounts receivable. In 1997, she can take a $3,000 bad debt deduction for the uncollectible accounts. The net result is that Sylvia's taxable income from these accounts is $2,000 for the 2-year period.

▲ **EXAMPLE 32**   Assume the same facts as in example 31, except that Sylvia uses the cash basis of accounting.

Discussion: Using the cash method of accounting, Sylvia has no reported income from the receivables, because they have not been collected. Therefore, she has no basis in the receivables and is not allowed a deduction. She reports $2,000 in taxable income when she receives cash from the collectible accounts. Note that this treatment gives Sylvia the same $2,000 in income that would have been reported on the accrual basis.

The tax law permits a bad debt deduction using the **specific charge-off method.** Based on this accounting method, a business bad debt can be written off in the accounting period in which the facts known to the taxpayer indicate the account is fully or partially uncollectible.[15] If an account is partially written off in one year and later becomes fully uncollectible, the remaining balance of the account can be written off as a bad debt. A receivable may be uncollectible for several reasons. For example, the debtor may go out of business or become bankrupt, or the collateral securing the loan may be destroyed or become worthless, indicating collection of the account is unlikely. If an account is fully or partially written off and the amount of the write-off is later recovered, under the tax benefit rule the recovered amount is reported as income in the year of collection.

▲ **EXAMPLE 33**   Raquel Corporation owns and operates a furniture store. Because it has inventory, Raquel uses the accrual method of accounting. At the end of 1996, its accounts receivable total $75,000. Based on a review of the individual accounts, Raquel identifies $2,500-worth of accounts as uncollectible. For financial accounting purposes, Raquel's accountant estimates that $4,500 of its 1996 sales ultimately are uncollectible. How much can Raquel Corporation deduct on its 1996 tax return for bad debts?

Discussion: Using the specific charge-off method, Raquel Corporation may deduct only the $2,500 in bad debts identified as uncollectible. The allowance method of accounting for bad debts, which is used for financial reporting, is not generally allowed for tax purposes.

▲ **EXAMPLE 34**   Assume that in 1997, Raquel in example 33 collects $1,000 of the accounts receivable it has written off as a bad debt expense in 1996. What is the effect on Raquel's 1997 income from the collection of the bad debt?

Discussion: Based on the tax benefit rule, the recovery of the $1,000 in bad debts deducted in 1996 must be reported as income when the accounts receivable are collected in 1997.

Nonbusiness bad debts often result from loans to family and friends. To claim a bad debt deduction for these loans, the taxpayer may have to prove that the failure to collect the loan was not motivated by the intent to make a gift. Thus, the benefit of the bad debt deduction may depend on whether the taxpayer can prove that the loan was the result of a bonafide arm's-length transaction.

▲ **EXAMPLE 35**   Wenona lent her uncle $15,000 to pay hospital and medical bills. Because the loan was to her uncle, she did not intend to charge any interest on the loan nor did she require him to sign a note. Her uncle promised to pay her back as soon as possible. Wenona's uncle died without repaying her. Can Wenona deduct the loan to her uncle as a nonbusiness bad debt?

Discussion: Although her uncle defaulted on his debt, Wenona would most likely be denied a nonbusiness bad debt deduction. There is no evidence that a bonafide arm's-length loan was made to the uncle. None of the elements found in a bonafide loan is present in this situation: no note as evidence of the debt, no collateral for the loan, no provision for interest on the loan, no payment or due date, and no collection efforts on Wenona's part. Wenona would have to prove that her intent was not to make a gift to her uncle in order to get a nonbusiness bad debt deduction.

Like business bad debts, nonbusiness bad debts are accounted for using the specific charge-off method. Unlike a business bad debt, a deduction is not allowed for partial worthlessness of a nonbusiness bad debt. The nonbusiness bad debt can be deducted only when the taxpayer finally settles the loan for less than its basis.[16]

▲ **EXAMPLE 36**   Karen owes Maria $5,000. The loan is related to Maria's business. In 1996, Karen files for bankruptcy. Maria talks to Karen's lawyers and determines that only 40% of the debt is collectible. In 1997, Maria receives $1,500 from the bankruptcy proceeding in full payment of the debt. How much of the bad debt can Maria deduct in 1996 and 1997?

Discussion: Because the debt is a business bad debt, a deduction is allowed for partial worthlessness. Maria can deduct $3,000 ($5,000 × 60%), the amount estimated as uncollectible, in 1996. When the debt is finally settled in 1997, Maria can deduct the remaining $500 ($2,000 − $1,500) of the debt that she will not collect.

Note that if Maria had received $2,800 from the bankruptcy proceeding, she would have had gross income of $800 ($2,800 − $2,000) under the tax benefit rule.

▲ **EXAMPLE 37**   Assume that the loan in example 36 was a bonafide nonbusiness bad debt. How much of the bad debt can Maria deduct in 1996 and 1997?

Discussion: A deduction is not allowed for the partial worthlessness of a nonbusiness bad debt. Maria must wait until 1997 when she knows the amount of the bad debt in order to take a deduction. At that time, Maria has a short-term capital loss of $3,500 ($5,000 − $1,500). If Maria has no other capital gains and losses in 1997, she may deduct only $3,000 of the short-term capital loss in 1997, with the remainder carried forward to 1998.

Table 6–1 summarizes the rules for deductibility of bad debts.

Other Business Expenses

Rent paid for the use of business property, business insurance, payroll taxes on employee compensation paid by the employer, property taxes on business

▲ **Table 6–1**

BAD DEBT DEDUCTIONS

	Business Bad Debts	**Nonbusiness Bad Debts**
What is deductible?	Any debt related to the taxpayer's trade or business.	Any bonafide debt that is not related to the taxpayer's trade or business.
Amount of deduction	Bad debt deductions are limited to the taxpayer's basis in the debt.	Bad debt deductions are limited to the taxpayer's basis in the debt.
When is it deductible?	Deductible in the year of partial or total worthlessness.	Deductible when the exact amount of the worthlessness becomes known.
How is it deductible?	Ordinary business expense.	Short-term capital loss.

property, interest on business indebtedness, utilities, dues to professional and business organizations, subscriptions to trade publications, supplies, and similar expenses incurred for a business purpose are allowed as a deduction. As you read the discussion of the deductions for insurance, taxes, and legal fees, pay close attention to the situations in which the expenditure is either disallowed as a deduction or required to be capitalized as an asset.

Insurance Expense.   Premiums paid for insurance to protect a taxpayer's business from loss, called *insurance expense*, are deductible. The types of insurance premiums that qualify for deduction include the following:

- Fire, theft, and other casualty insurance, and liability insurance.
- Employees' group medical and group term life insurance, and workers' compensation insurance.
- Employee performance and fidelity bonds to protect against losses caused by employees.
- Business interruption and overhead insurance to reimburse the business for lost profits and overhead from casualty or other unexpected event. However, premiums on an individual's disability income policy cannot be deducted.

> ▲ **EXAMPLE 38**   On July 1, 1996, Sook pays a $6,000 premium for a 3-year fire and casualty insurance policy on his business buildings and equipment. How much of the premium can Sook deduct in 1996?
>
> *Discussion:* Payment of the premium in advance results in a prepaid expense that benefits tax years 1996, 1997, 1998, and 1999. Regardless of Sook's accounting method, the $6,000 basis in the policy must be allocated to the periods benefited by the prepaid expense. The allocation results in a $1,000 insurance expense deduction for 1996 [$6,000 $\times$ (6 $\div$ 36 months)].

Except for qualified group term life insurance, life insurance premiums generally are not deductible. To qualify for deduction, life insurance premiums must be viewed as additional compensation to the insured person. If the payer of the insurance premiums benefits directly or indirectly when the policy pays off on the insured's death, the premium cannot be deducted.[17] Thus, insurance premiums on the life of the owner of a business, an officer of a corporation, an employee, or other person who has a financial interest in the taxpayer's business are not deductible unless they are treated as payment of compensation to the insured person. In addition, an entity other than the payer of the life insurance premiums must be the beneficiary of the policy in order for the premium to be deductible.

▲ **EXAMPLE 39**   Radon Corporation pays a $5,000 premium on a whole life insurance policy on the life of Luke. Luke is a key employee in the company. If Luke died, the company would suffer a tremendous loss. If the corporation is the beneficiary of the policy, how much of the premium can Radon deduct?

Discussion: Because Radon benefits directly or indirectly from the policy proceeds when Luke dies, the premium is not deductible. But recall from Chapter 4 that life insurance proceeds received upon the death of the insured are excluded from gross income.

▲ **EXAMPLE 40**   Assume that Luke, in example 39, is unrelated to Radon Corporation and its owners. Also, Luke's wife is the beneficiary of the life insurance policy. How much of the insurance premium can Radon deduct?

Discussion: Because Radon is not a direct or indirect beneficiary of the policy, the $5,000 premium is allowed as a deduction for additional compensation paid to Luke. Luke will have to report the $5,000 premium paid by the corporation as income. His wife can exclude the proceeds of the policy from her income when Luke dies.

Taxes.   A taxpayer is allowed a deduction for the payment of certain taxes incurred in a trade or business.[18] Some taxes are not allowed as a deduction, and others must be added to the basis of property owned by the taxpayer. Common types of deductible taxes include the following:

- State, local, and foreign real estate taxes
- State and local ad valorem personal property taxes (an ad valorem tax is based on the property's value)
- State, local, and foreign income taxes
- Payroll taxes imposed on an employer (including the employer's share of the Social Security tax and unemployment taxes)
- Sales taxes, excise taxes, fuel taxes, franchise taxes, and other miscellaneous taxes[19]

Federal income tax and gift and estate taxes are not allowed as deductions in computing federal taxable income.[20] In addition, the taxes listed are deductible *only* when they are incurred in a trade or business. The itemized deduction allowed for taxes (discussed in Chapter 8) is far more restrictive than the deductions allowed for businesses.

▲ **EXAMPLE 41**   Leslie Corporation pays the following taxes during the current year:

Federal income tax	$50,000
State and local income taxes	15,000
State and local real estate and	
personal property tax	2,000
State and local sales taxes	7,000

What is Leslie's deduction for taxes paid?

Discussion: Except for the federal income tax, Leslie may deduct all the taxes listed. Leslie's deduction for taxes paid is $24,000. The $50,000 federal income tax is never allowed as a deduction.

Sales taxes are deductible if they are paid for supplies and other items that are not capital expenditures. If the sales tax is related to the purchase of a long-lived asset, the tax must be added to the asset's basis. The sales tax is then deducted as a capital recovery through depreciation of the asset's basis.

▲ **EXAMPLE 42**   Leslie Corporation purchases a new microcomputer for use in its office. The microcomputer costs $8,000 and is subject to a 10% sales tax. What is Leslie's deduction for the $800 in sales tax paid on the microcomputer?

Discussion: Because the sales tax is related to the purchase of a depreciable asset, the $800 in tax is not currently deductible. The sales tax is added to the microcomputer's basis as part of the cost of acquiring the asset. A deduction is allowed for depreciation of the microcomputer's $8,800 tax basis.

If real estate is purchased or sold during the year, real estate taxes must be allocated between the buyer and the seller. The tax is allocated according to the number of days each owned the property during the period of time to which the tax relates (the property tax year).[21]

▲ **EXAMPLE 43**   Leslie Corporation sells land and a building on October 1, 1996. The property tax for the 1996 property tax year (a calendar year) is $3,600. Leslie pays its share of the property tax on the date the sale closes. What is Leslie's 1996 deduction for real estate taxes on the land and building?

Discussion: Leslie may deduct the property taxes for the period it owned the land and building. Leslie's deduction would be $2,700—the taxes related to the period January 1 through September 30, 1996 [$3,600 × (9 ÷ 12)]. The buyer should deduct the property tax for the remainder of the property tax calendar year because that entity was the owner of the property.

▲ **EXAMPLE 44**   Assume that in example 43, the sales price of the building is $86,000. As part of the sales agreement, the buyer agrees to pay Leslie's share of the property taxes for 1996. Is Leslie allowed a deduction for property taxes on the building in 1996?

Discussion: The payment of another's expense in a business setting is considered income for the entity for which the expense is being paid. Therefore, the payment of Leslie's $2,700 share of the property taxes must be included as part of the sales price of the building. Leslie is deemed to have received $88,700 for the building and to have paid $2,700 in property taxes. Each party to a real estate transaction must always recognize its share of the property taxes, regardless of which party actually pays the tax.

When real estate taxes are related to **assessments for local benefits,** such as sidewalks, streets, sewers, and other improvements, the tax payment is not deductible. The tax imposed for local benefits is deemed to increase the value of the taxpayer's property and is considered a capital expenditure. As a result, the tax is added to the improved asset's basis. However, under the capital recovery concept, the taxpayer will recover the tax through depreciation, amortization, or upon its disposition.

▲ **EXAMPLE 45**   The town of Guthrie imposes a special real estate tax assessment to put in new streets. Leslie Corporation has to pay $15,000 as its share of the new streets in front of its warehouse. What is Leslie's deduction for the $15,000 special property tax assessment it pays in 1996?

Discussion: The special assessment for installing streets is deemed to increase the value of Leslie's property. As a result, the special assessment is added to Leslie's basis in the land. Thus, the $15,000 tax payment is not currently deductible. When Leslie disposes of the property, the capital recovery concept permits the capitalized tax to be deducted against the amount received on the sale of the property.

Legal Fees.   Legal expenses are allowed as a deduction if they have a business purpose. To determine whether **legal fees** are deductible, look to the origin of the expense. If the legal fee originates in a profit-motivated activity or qualifies as a specifically allowed itemized deduction, it is deductible. If the expense originates from a personal transaction, such as a divorce or the preparation of a will, the expense is not deductible.

▲ **EXAMPLE 46**   Salvadore is being sued by a client who fell in his store and hurt himself. Salvadore has spent $5,000 in legal fees to defend his business against his customer's claims. Can Salvadore deduct the legal fees?

Discussion: The legal fees originated in Salvadore's business. Because the fees are an ordinary and necessary expense of doing business, Salvadore may deduct the $5,000 in legal expenses.

▲ **EXAMPLE 47**   Elissa, Salvadore's wife, has filed for divorce and has asked for a large property settlement. The only way Salvadore can pay Elissa the amount she is seeking is to sell his business. Salvadore has paid $6,000 in legal fees related to the divorce. Can he deduct his legal fees?

Discussion: Salvadore may not deduct the personal legal fees. The legal expenses did not arise from the conduct of his business. The fact that he may have to sell his business merely reflects the results of the legal claim that arose from a personal relationship.[22]

▲ **EXAMPLE 48**   Salvadore has been having a bad year. In August, he received a letter from the IRS stating that he owed an additional $34,000 in income taxes. Salvadore paid his attorney $12,000 to settle the case with the IRS. Can he deduct the attorney's fees?

Discussion: Salvadore will be able to deduct the attorney's fees, because they were incurred in relation to the collection of a tax. The tax law allows the deduction of any costs related to the collection of the tax. To the extent the amount in dispute relates to his business, he may deduct the attorney's fees as an ordinary and necessary business expense. However, any portion that relates to other types of income or deductions is only allowed as a miscellaneous itemized deduction.

In addition to the disallowance of personal legal fees, certain legal fees may have to be capitalized as part of an asset's basis. For example, legal fees related to establishing ownership of property, defending title to property, or otherwise related to the acquisition or improvement of an asset are not deductible. These costs must be added to the affected asset's basis. However, the taxpayer can deduct legal fees paid to protect an existing business, its reputation, and goodwill.

LIMITED MIXED-USE EXPENSES

As indicated in Chapter 5, **mixed-use expenses** and expenses related to using **mixed-use assets** must be analyzed and allocated between business and personal expenses. The discussion that follows examines the three areas that Congress has determined have the greatest potential for abuse: hobby, vacation home, and home office expenses. The common thread among all three activities is that they are entered into by individuals who have an incentive to attempt to convert personal expenditures within the activity to deductible business expenses. Thus, detailed rules have been written to prevent this from happening. The legislative grace, ability-to-pay, business purpose, and capital recovery concepts all apply to these deductions and indicate that these expenses should be allowed to the extent they were incurred to earn income. As these topics are discussed, note the similarities in the calculation of the deductions and how the income from the mixed activity provides a limit on the amount deductible. The common denominator among all three mixed-use activities is that business expenses in excess of income earned in a hobby, vacation home, or home office activity are not deductible, because they lack a business purpose.

Hobby Expenses

A taxpayer may engage in an income-earning activity primarily for personal reasons that prevents its qualification as a trade or business or an investment activity. The activity may be carried on mainly for recreation and personal enjoyment, with profitability a secondary concern. In tax law jargon, this type of activity is referred to as a **hobby,** because it lacks a business purpose. However, the legislative grace, ability-to-pay, and capital recovery concepts all indicate that hobby income should be taxed only to the extent it exceeds the related expenses.

The hobby rules apply when a taxpayer has income and expenses in an activity without a predominant profit motive. The tax law considers nine factors in determining whether an activity that earns income is profit motivated and should be treated as a business or is subject to the hobby rules. These factors are

- Whether the taxpayer carries on the activity in a businesslike manner
- Expertise of the taxpayer or the taxpayer's reliance on advice of experts
- Time and effort the taxpayer spends to carry on the activity
- Expectation that the assets used in the activity will appreciate in value
- Taxpayer's success in similar activities
- Taxpayer's history of income or losses in the activity
- Amount of occasional profits, if any
- Taxpayer's financial status
- Elements of personal pleasure or recreation in the activity[23]

The courts consider and weigh all these factors in determining whether a taxpayer's activity constitutes a hobby. An activity's classification as a hobby is based on all the facts and circumstances presented by the taxpayer. Thus, the classification is subjective and is not determined by a single factor or by the presence of more factors indicating a hobby than a profit objective. The courts also will consider other factors relevant to the taxpayer's situation that may indicate a profit motive. In many situations, the determination of whether an activity is a hobby is best left to a tax expert.

A taxpayer's deductible hobby expenses cannot exceed the gross income from the hobby.[24] The expenses in excess of income are referred to as **hobby losses.** Hobby losses are not deductible. Hobby deductions must be computed in a specific order. First the deductions are grouped into three classes:

1. Expenses that could be deducted as either business expenses or itemized deductions (e.g., home mortgage interest and property taxes)
2. Expenses related to the hobby that would be deductible if the hobby had qualified as a business (e.g., supplies, utilities, repairs, auto expenses)
3. Depreciation on assets used to carry on the hobby activity

Category 1 expenses are deducted from hobby income first. If any income remains, category 2 expenses are deducted. Category 3 can then be deducted to the extent that any income remains after deducting categories 1 and 2. In addition, hobby expenses in categories 2 and 3 must be reported as miscellaneous itemized deductions. Recall that miscellaneous itemized deductions (discussed in depth in Chapter 8) are subject to a 2 percent of adjusted gross income limitation. Because hobby expenses are classified as miscellaneous itemized deductions, a taxpayer might not be allowed a deduction for part or all of the hobby expenses. Thus, the benefit of hobby deductions is limited in two ways: The expenses are allowed only to the extent of hobby income, and the actual amount deductible is limited as an itemized deduction. If a taxpayer uses the standard deduction instead of listing the actual itemized deductions, all benefit from the hobby deduction is lost.

▲ **EXAMPLE 49**   Barclay is a physician. As a hobby, Barclay operates a farm where she raises exotic animals. During the year, Barclay has gross income of $18,000 from the farm and pays the following expenses:

Property taxes on the farm	$ 6,000
Labor, feed, and veterinary costs	10,000
Depreciation on farm building and equipment	4,000

How much of the $20,000 that Barclay incurs as expenses can be deducted?

Discussion: Barclay's deductions are limited to the $18,000 from the farm for the year. Her deductible expenses are determined as follows:

Gross income	$18,000
Less: Category 1 expenses that would be allowed as either personal or business deductions (e.g., itemized property tax).	(6,000)
Balance of income	$12,000
Less: Category 2 expenses of operating the farm that would be deductible in a trade or business (e.g., labor, feed, vet).	(10,000)
Balance of income	$ 2,000
Less: Depreciation expense. The $4,000 expense for this category cannot exceed the balance of income before the deduction.	(2,000)
Balance of income	$ -0-

Barclay should report $18,000 in gross income. She can deduct $6,000 in taxes as an itemized deduction and $12,000 as miscellaneous itemized deductions. She cannot deduct as a hobby expense the $2,000 in depreciation deductions in excess of income, a sum that is referred to as the *nondeductible hobby loss.*

Discussion: On the surface, it appears that Barclay's hobby has no effect on her income. However, $12,000 in hobby expenses is subject to the 2% of adjusted gross income limitation for miscellaneous itemized deductions. For example, if Barclay's adjusted gross income were $100,000 and she had no other miscellaneous itemized deductions, her deduction for hobby expenses would be limited to $16,000 ($10,000 + $6,000):

Total allowable miscellaneous itemized deductions	$12,000
Less: 2% of AGI ($100,000 × 2%)	(2,000)
Miscellaneous hobby expense deductions	$10,000
Property taxes	6,000
Total hobby expense deduction	$16,000

Therefore, although hobby expenses technically are limited to hobby income, the net effect is that Barclay reports $2,000 in income ($18,000 - $16,000) from the hobby.

Vacation Home Expenses

A **vacation home** can be a house, apartment, condominium, mobile home, boat, or similar property. A taxpayer who owns a vacation home that is used for family vacations and then rented to unrelated people during the remainder of the year is subject to special rules. The deductibility of vacation home rental expenses depends on the rental income and the extent of the taxpayer's personal use of the home.

Table 6–2 summarizes the treatment of vacation home expenses.[25] As the table shows, if the taxpayer rents out the vacation home for a minimal period during the year (14 days or fewer), the dwelling is not considered to have been used for a business purpose and is treated as a personal residence. For administrative convenience, the rental income is not reported and rent expenses are not deducted. As discussed in Chapter 8, home mortgage interest and property taxes on the property can be deducted as a personal itemized deduction.

▲ **EXAMPLE 50**   Amber owns a summer cabin that she and her family use for personal purposes from May through August of each year. In August, Expando Corporation pays Amber $1,000 to rent her cabin for 5 days. Amber's expenses related to the cabin include $5,000 in taxes and interest and $2,000 in utilities and maintenance for the year. What is the proper treatment of the summer cabin income and expense?

Discussion: Because the cabin is rented for 14 days or fewer, Amber does not have to report the $1,000 received from Expando Corporation as rental income. The cabin is considered a personal residence, and Amber may not deduct any rental expense related to the rental use of the vacation home by Expando. Amber can deduct the property taxes and interest as personal itemized deductions.

If the home is rented for more than 14 days and used for personal use for a minimal length of time (the greater of 14 days or 10 percent of the days rented), the property is treated the same as investment rental property. Expenses allocable to personal use of the dwelling are not deductible. Expenses related to rental use that have a business purpose are deducted just as they would be for any other profit-motivated transaction.

As the second row of Table 6–2 shows, using the vacation home for more than 14 days as rental property and using it for more than 14 days as a personal vacation home limits the deduction for expenses to the amount of the rental income.

▲ **Table 6–2**

SUMMARY OF VACATION HOME USE TESTS

Rent Period	Personal Use Period	Tax Result
14 days or fewer	Remainder of year.	A personal residence. Do not report income and do not deduct rent expenses.
More than 14 days	More than 14 days, or more than 10% of the number of days rented at a fair rental price, whichever is longer.	A vacation home. Report rental income and allocate rental expenses using specified priority. Expenses are limited to gross rent income. A loss cannot be deducted.
More than 14 days	14 days or fewer, or 10% or less of the number of days rented at a fair rental price, whichever is longer.	A rental property. Report like any other rental property. Expenses must be allocated between rental and personal use.

Expenses that have a business purpose are deducted in the same order as for hobby expenses. But unlike a hobby loss, vacation home expenses in excess of current income can be carried forward indefinitely for use in a later year in which there is enough rent income to offset them.

The allocation of vacation home expenses between personal use and rental use is a controversial issue. The IRS requires that the taxpayer allocate vacation home expenses between personal and rental by using the ratio of personal days to total days of use (sum of personal days and rental days).[26] However, the courts have allowed interest expense and real estate taxes to be allocated over 365 days instead of the actual number of days the home was used for personal and rental use.[27] The court's allocation of interest expense and property tax seems more reasonable than the IRS's method, because these expenses are more closely related to a period of time than to actual use. In addition, this method allocates less interest and property taxes to the rental property, leaving more to deduct as a personal itemized deduction. This generally results in the allowance of a greater overall deduction on the vacation home. Other expenses, such as utilities and maintenance, are more closely related to use and should be allocated to actual days of use. The courts' allocation of interest and taxes, which generally results in a larger deduction for the taxpayer, continues to be opposed by the IRS. Therefore, the method of allocating vacation home expenses should be chosen after consulting with a tax expert.

▲ **EXAMPLE 51**   Latoya owns a cabin that she uses for 20 days for her family's vacation during the current year. The cabin is rented to others for 40 days, for which she receives gross rental income of $5,500. Her total expenses of maintaining the cabin are

Interest and property taxes	$6,000
Utilities, insurance, and repairs	1,500
Depreciation expense	4,500

What are Latoya's allowable deductions on the cabin?

Discussion: Because Latoya used the property for personal use for more than 14 days, the total deductions allocable to the rental are limited to rent income. The first step is to allocate the expenses to rental use and personal use. Latoya has the option of using the IRS method of allocating all expenses based on the total days of use, which yields the following allocation:

	Total Cost	Rent Use Ratio	Amount Allocated to	
			Rental Use	Personal Use
Interest and property taxes	$6,000	40/60	$4,000	$2,000
Utilities, insurance, repairs	1,500	40/60	1,000	500
Depreciation expense	4,500	40/60	3,000	1,500

Latoya's deductions for the rental are limited to the $5,500 in gross rental income. Further, the $5,500 in deductions must be taken from the expenses in the same order as deductions for hobby expenses:

Gross rental income	$5,500
Less: Deductions that are allowable as either itemized	
deductions or as rental expenses (interest and property	
taxes).	(4,000)
Balance of income	$1,500
Less: Deductions that are allowable only as a rental expense	
(utilities, insurance, repairs).	(1,000)
Balance of income	$ 500
Less: Depreciation. Limited to the balance of income after	
other expenses.	(500)
Balance of income	$ -0-

The $2,500 ($3,000 − $500) in depreciation that was disallowed because of the income limitation is carried into future years for deduction if there is enough rental income to absorb the expense. In addition, Latoya can deduct the $2,000 of personal interest and property taxes as a personal itemized deduction. Assuming that Latoya itemizes deductions, the net effect of the cabin on her income is a reduction of $2,000 because of the deductions for personal itemized interest and property taxes.

Latoya may elect to allocate interest and property taxes according to the number of days in the year, rather than days of total use, per the court's method. All other expenses would still be allocated according to days of total use. This would result in a larger total deduction by allocating less interest and property taxes against the rental income and more to Latoya's itemized deductions. The allocation of the $6,000 in interest and property taxes under this allocation choice would be

	Total Cost	Rent Use Ratio	Amount Allocated to	
			Rental Use	Personal Use
Interest and property taxes	$6,000	40/365	$660	$5,340

Latoya's allowable rental deductions are still limited to the $5,500 in gross rental income:

Gross rental income	$5,500
Less: Interest and property taxes	(660)
Balance of income	$4,840
Less: Utilities, insurance, repairs	(1,000)
Balance of income	$3,840
Less: Depreciation	(3,000)
Net rental income	$ 840

Although Latoya has $840 in net rental income under this allocation method, her itemized deduction for interest and property taxes increases to $5,340. Assuming that Latoya itemizes deductions, the effect of using the court's allocation method for interest and taxes is to reduce her taxable income by $4,500 ($5,340 − $840). This compares with the $2,000 reduction in taxable income using the IRS allocation method.

Home Office Expenses

A taxpayer who operates a trade or business from home can claim a deduction for expenses related to its business use. Expenses such as mortgage interest, real property taxes, insurance, utilities, repairs, and depreciation can be allocated on a reasonable basis to the area of the home used for a business purpose. This deduction is commonly referred to as the **home office deduction.** To claim a deduction, strict tests must be satisfied.

A specific part of the home must be used exclusively for carrying on a trade or business. A taxpayer who does not have another business location can deduct the cost of using an area in the home for storing inventory on a regular basis. If a room is used for a trade or business and is also used for investing or personal activities, the exclusive use test is not met and no deduction for home office expenses is allowed.

The home office area must also be regularly used as the principal place to conduct a trade or business belonging to the taxpayer or as a place to meet or deal with patients, clients, or customers in the normal course of the trade or business.[28] If the portion of the home used for business is a separate structure, the taxpayer needs only to show that it was used in connection with a trade or business. If these tests are met, the taxpayer can deduct expenses related to using part of the home for business.

Employees who use an office in their home to conduct business for their employer must meet an additional test. Employee use must be "for the convenience of the employer" and "required as a condition of employment" before any deductions for a home office may be taken.[29] Because most employee use of a home office is for the convenience of the employee (i.e., people work at home because they want to, not because they are required to), most typical employee situations will not result in a deduction for home office expenses.

▲ **EXAMPLE 52**   Reginald is an engineer for Arclight Petroleum Co. Rather than work late at the office, Reginald often takes home Arclight work, which he works on in an office in his home. Reginald prefers to bring work home so that he can have dinner with his family and not have to return to his office late at night or on weekends. Can Reginald deduct any of the costs of maintaining the home office?

Discussion: Because Reginald's use of the office is related to his employment with Arclight, he must prove that the use of the home office is for Arclight's convenience and that it is required as a condition of his employment. Under the facts as given, Reginald's use is for his convenience, not Arclight's. Thus, the deduction would not be allowed. In addition, it is doubtful that Arclight requires Reginald to maintain an office in his home in order to maintain employment, which is also required for deductibility.

Expenses of maintaining the home are allocated between the home office and the areas used as a residence. The expenses may be allocated on the basis of the number of rooms or on the basis of square footage of floor space in the home. The method chosen should reasonably reflect the area used as an office. The home office deduction follows the same computational pattern as the hobby and vacation home deductions discussed earlier. However, the income limitation is based on income earned from the home office activity after deducting all other business expenses that are unrelated to the use of the home office. If the home office deductions exceed the income limitation, the excess may be carried forward and used to reduce income in a later year.

▲ **EXAMPLE 53**   Kendall uses 1 room in her home as the primary location for her business. Her home has 6 rooms and is 2,500 square feet. The office area is 300 square feet or 12% of the total area. For the current year, she had $15,000 in mortgage interest and real estate taxes and $8,000 in insurance, repairs, and maintenance related to her home. Kendall determined that depreciation on the house for the current year would be $4,000. Kendall had $21,000 in income and $17,800 in other business expenses. What is Kendall's allowable home office deduction for the current year?

Discussion: Kendall's home office deduction cannot exceed her income from the home office activity after deducting all other business expenses that are unrelated to the home office. Thus, her maximum home office deduction is $3,200 ($21,000 − $17,800). The amounts that Kendall can deduct for her home office are

Income limitation on home office expenses ($21,000 − $17,800)		$3,200
1. Deduct expenses otherwise allowed as a deduction under other tax rules:		
Interest and taxes ($15,000 × 12%)		(1,800)
Balance of income		$1,400
2. Deduct office expenses not otherwise allowed as a deduction:		
Insurance, repairs, and other expenses ($8,000 × 12%)		(960)
Balance of income		$ 440
3. Deduct depreciation on office portion of residence:		
Current-year depreciation	$4,000	
Business percentage	× .12	
Depreciation on office	$ 480	
Deduction limited to balance of income		(440)
Balance of income		$ -0-

The $40 ($480 − $440) in depreciation that was not allowed as a deduction in the current year because of the income limitation can be carried forward to next year.

You must be cognitive of two important points concerning the operation of a business from home. First, the expenses of operating the business that are not related to the home office are allowed as a deduction, even if the home office expense is disallowed because of the income limitation. Second, in order to deduct telephone expenses relating to a home office, the taxpayer must have a separate phone line for the business. If the taxpayer has only one phone, the basic phone charge cannot be deducted; only long distance business-related phone calls are allowed as a deduction.

▲ **EXAMPLE 54**   Alvin operates his business from home. His sales for the year total $50,000. He incurs $55,000 in travel expense, employee wages, depreciation on equipment, and other expenses unrelated to his home office. The residence expenses allocated to the home office using the approach illustrated total $2,000. What are Alvin's allowable deductions?

Discussion: Alvin's deductible loss from his business before considering a home office deduction is $5,000 ($50,000 − $55,000). He cannot deduct any of his home office expense in the current year because of the income limitations. However, the $2,000 in home office expenses can be carried to next year and deducted if he has enough income.

SUMMARY

Meal and entertainment expenses are allowed as business deductions if the expenses are ordinary, necessary, reasonable in amount, and directly related to or associated with the active conduct of the taxpayer's business activity. However, only 50 percent of the meal and entertainment expenses is normally deductible. Auto expense deductions can be based on the actual cost of using a car for business or by using a standard mileage rate method. Regardless of which method is used, the taxpayer must keep detailed records documenting the business use of the car. If the primary reason for making an out-of-town trip is a business purpose, the travel expenses for transportation, 50 percent of meals, lodging, and incidental expenses can be deducted. When time on the trip is devoted to vacation or personal activities, the amount of the deduction may be limited. A deduction is allowed for up to $25 per donee each year for business gifts. Proper documentation is necessary to be sure that an entertainment, auto, travel, or gift expense will be allowed as a deduction.

Education expenses can be deducted if the expense either is required by the employer as a condition of employment or maintains or improves the skills required in the taxpayer's trade or business. The tax law allows a deduction for reasonable compensation to employees. Unless certain exceptions are met, the deduction for compensation paid to a covered employee of a publicly traded corporation is limited to $1,000,000. Covered employees are the CEO and the next four highest-paid officers of the corporation.

Business and nonbusiness bad debts are deductible only if there is a valid business purpose. Nonbusiness bad debts that are in fact gifts are not deductible. The bad debt deduction is determined using the specific charge-off method. Deductions for insurance, taxes, and legal fees are subject to special rules that limit the deduction or, in some instances, require capitalization of the expenditure as an asset.

The deduction for hobby, vacation home, and home office expenses is limited to the amount of income earned from the activity. If these mixed-use expenses exceed the related income, the excess expenses are not allowed as a deduction from other sources of income such as wages, dividends, and interest. Taxpayers claiming deductions for a hobby, vacation home, or home office must observe strict requirements to be able to deduct the expenses.

KEY TERMS

actual cost method (p. 238)
assessment for local benefits
    (p. 250)
associated with (p. 234)
auto expense (p. 237)
business bad debt (p. 245)
business gift (p. 241)
capital loss (p. 245)
directly related (p. 234)
education expense (p. 242)

hobby (p. 252)
hobby loss (p. 252)
home office deduction (p. 256)
legal fees (p. 251)
meal and entertainment expense
    (p. 234)
mixed-use asset (p. 251)
mixed-use expense (p. 251)
nonbusiness bad debt (p. 245)
reasonable compensation (p. 243)

related party (p. 243)
specific charge-off method
    (p. 246)
standard mileage rate method
    (p. 238)
substantiation requirements
    (p. 242)
tax home (p. 239)
travel expenses (p. 239)
vacation home (p. 254)

PRIMARY TAX LAW SOURCES

[1] Sec. 274—Provides the limitations on deductions for meals and entertainment, and business gifts; requires that deductions for such items be substantiated by adequate records.

[2] Reg. Sec. 1.274-2—Explains the general rules for meal and entertainment deductions; defines expenditures *directly related* and *associated with* business for purposes of determining the deductibility of entertainment costs.

[3] Sec. 274(a)(3)—Disallows deductions for club dues organized for business, pleasure, recreation, or social purposes.

[4] Rev. Rul. 94-47—Further explains Rev. Rul. 90-23, which provides examples of allowable deductions for a taxpayer's daily transportation expenses.

[5] Rev. Proc. 95-54—Sets the 1996 standard mileage rate for determining automobile expenses at 31 cents per mile.

[6] Rev. Proc. 95-9—Provides the maximum yearly depreciation deductions on automobiles purchased in 1995.

[7] Reg. Sec. 1.162-2—Allows deduction for travel expenses; provides treatment of business travel mixed with personal activities.

[8] Reg. Sec. 1.274-5T—Provides the substantiation rules that must be followed in deducting meals, entertainment, and travel expenses.

[9] Reg. Sec. 1.162-5(a)—Sets forth the types of educational expenses that are deductible.

[10] Reg. Sec. 1.162-5(b)—Sets forth the types of educational expenses that are not deductible.

[11] Reg. Sec. 1.162-7—Sets forth guidelines for deductions of compensation paid for personal services.

[12] Internal Revenue Service Manual 4233, Sec. 232—Provides the factors that the IRS considers in determining whether compensation is reasonable.

[13] Sec. 162(m)—Sets forth the rules for deducting compensation in excess of $1,000,000.

[14] Sec. 166—Specifies the allowable deductions for bad debts.

[15] Reg. Sec. 1.166-3—Allows a deduction for partial worthlessness of a business bad debt.

[16] Reg. Sec. 1.166-5—Defines *nonbusiness bad debt* and specifies the treatment as a short-term capital loss in the year the debt becomes worthless.

[17] Sec. 264—Disallows a deduction for life insurance premiums paid on any employee when the taxpayer making the payments is the beneficiary of the policy.

[18] Sec. 164—Specifies the allowable deductions for taxes.

[19] Reg. Sec. 1.164-1—Specifies the types of taxes that are deductible as trade or business expenses.

[20] Reg. Sec. 1.164-2—Denies deductions for certain types of taxes.

[21] Reg. Sec. 1.164-6—Requires the apportionment of the deduction for real property taxes between the buyer and the seller of real property based on the number of days each party owned the property during the year.

[22] U.S. v. Gilmore 83 S. Ct. 623 (1963)—Held that the deductibility of legal expenses depends on whether the claim arises in connection with the taxpayer's business activities. The consequences of the transaction, in this case the sale of the business, are not a factor.

[23] Reg. Sec. 1.183-2—Sets forth the criteria for determining when an activity constitutes a hobby.

[24] Sec. 183—Limits the deductions allowed for hobbies.

[25] Sec. 280A—Limits the allowable deductions on home offices and vacation homes; defines requirements for home office expense deduction and what constitutes a vacation home.

[26] Prop. Reg. Sec. 1.280A-3—Requires that all expenses related to a vacation home be allocated between rental use and personal use on the basis of the number of days of total use of the vacation home.

[27] Bolton v. Comm., 694 F.2d 596 (9th Cir. 1982)—Affirmed the Tax Court's holding that the proper allocation of interest and taxes on a vacation home is based on the number of days in the year, rather than the number of days of total use.

[28] Comm. v. Soliman, 113 S. Ct. 701 (1993)—Held that for purposes of determining what constitutes a principal place of business for purposes of the home office deduction, the home office must be the focal point of the taxpayer's business.

[29] Sec. 280A—See footnote 25.

DISCUSSION QUESTIONS

1. Most expenditures that have a business purpose and meet the ordinary, necessary, and reasonable requirements are deductible. However, specific rules must be adhered to in determining the deductibility of many expenses that meet this test. Why are these specific rules necessary?

2. What requirements must be met in order for meal and entertainment expenses to be deductible?

3. How does an entertainment expense directly related to business differ from an entertainment expense associated with business?

4. What problems does the taxpayer who uses an automobile for both business and personal purposes encounter? What option(s) does the taxpayer have regarding the automobile expense deduction?

5. What records are necessary to properly document travel, entertainment, and gift expenses?

6. Under what circumstances are business gifts deductible?

7. When are educational expenses deductible? not deductible?

8. Is it possible that an education expense incurred by one taxpayer is deductible, whereas the same expense incurred by another taxpayer is not deductible? Explain.

9. Is all compensation paid to an employee deductible? Discuss the circumstances in which employee compensation cannot be deducted.

10. Explain the difference in the tax treatment of business and nonbusiness bad debts.

11. What accounting method must be used to account for bad debts that result from the sale of merchandise or the provision of services?

12. Explain how the tax benefit rule may apply to bad debt deductions.

13. Are all reasonable compensation payments made to a related party deductible? When are the payments deductible?

14. What requirements must be met in order to deduct life insurance premiums paid on an employee's policy?

15. Are sales taxes deductible? Explain.

16. Are all legal fees paid by a taxpayer deductible? Explain.

17. Explain the rationale for the treatment of deductions related to hobbies, vacation homes, and home offices.

18. What is/are the requirement(s) for determining whether a residence used for personal purposes is a vacation home or a true rental property?

19. Under what circumstances can a taxpayer deduct the costs of a home office?

20. How is the income limitation for home offices different from that for hobbies and vacation homes?

21. Discuss the reporting of deductions related to a hobby versus deductions related to a vacation home or a home office. State any potential negative tax effects from the reporting requirements.

PROBLEMS

22. After a business meeting, Tray took his client to dinner. Dinner cost $65, including $5 in sales tax and a $10 tip. The cab fare to and from the restaurant cost another $25. How much may Tray deduct as an entertainment expense?

23. Marjorie is an accountant and Alana is an attorney. They have been business acquaintances for about 10 years. They meet every Friday at 6 P.M. at a local tavern to socialize. As always happens with attorneys and accountants, they discuss what is happening in their offices. They take turns paying the bar tab, which averages $30 for each meeting. Because Marjorie has kept the receipts for the nights she paid, she would like to claim a deduction for her $600 in expenses. How much may Marjorie deduct as an entertainment expense?

24. Malina is a manager for Mail Order Co. While on a business trip to Chicago, she entertained several sales representatives of a client of Mail Order Co. The total cost of the entertainment expense was $750. When she returned home, Malina gave Mail Order Co. receipts and other information to specifically account for the entertainment expense. Mail Order reimbursed Malina for the $750 she spent on entertainment. How much can Malina deduct? what about Mail Order?

25. For each of the following situations, explain whether a deduction should be allowed for entertainment expenses:
    a. Gayle, a dentist, invites 50 of her best patients to her daughter's wedding reception. The cost of the reception related to the presence of her patients is $5,000.
    b. Stan is one of 5 shift supervisors responsible for 100 employees at Label House, Inc. Stan regularly meets with the other shift supervisors at the plant. In addition, Stan makes it a practice to go to lunch at least once a week with each of the other 4 shift supervisors in order to network. During the current year, Stan pays $1,500 for his and the other supervisors' lunches. Stan's job description does not require him to entertain the other supervisors.
    c. Jan is a real estate broker who holds an open house for a different client each Sunday afternoon. During the open house, Jan provides cookies and soft drinks for whoever visits the house. Jan pays $2,000 for open house entertainment.
    d. Felicia is vice president of sales for Drivitt, Inc. She invites the company's major clients and some of her coworkers from Drivitt to her annual Super Bowl party. Most guests attend with their spouses. The party is held in a separate room at a local sports bar and costs her $1,500.

26. Enrique owns a real estate business in Hugoville. He is an avid football fan and rents a skybox at County Stadium to see the Hugoville Hurricanes. The cost of the skybox for 8 games is $40,000, including 10 tickets to each game. The most expensive nonluxury box seat is $75. After closing a real estate deal, Enrique invites 9 business associates to watch the Monday night game in his skybox. Food and drinks cost $430. What amount can Enrique deduct as entertainment expense?

27. You have just been hired as a tax accountant by a local public accounting firm. One partner is impressed by your writing skills and asks you to write a one-page memo to a client describing the general rules on the deductibility of meals and entertainment. The client also needs to know under what circumstances the cost of its skybox (with 10 tickets) at Optus Park is deductible.

28. Pablo is a computer sales representative and spends only 2 days a month in the office. His office is 25 miles from home. Pablo spends 3 nights a month traveling to his out-of-town clients.
    a. What portion of Pablo's travel is considered business?
    b. During the year, Pablo keeps the following record of his travel:

	Miles
Home to office	600
Office to home	600
Home to local clients to home	12,400
Home to out of town clients to home	3,200

    The company reimburses Pablo for all of his lodging, meals, and entertainment while he is on the road. If he uses the standard mileage rate, what amount can he deduct as a business expense?

29. Julianita is a sales representative for a food distributor and spends only 1 day of the week in the office. Her office is 15 miles from home. She also has a part-time job as a bartender. Typically, she works 2 nights during the week and 1 night on the weekend. The restaurant where she works is 8 miles from her office and 12 miles from her home.
    a. What portion(s) of Julianita's travel is considered business?
    b. During the year, Julianita keeps the following record of her travel:

	Miles
Home to office	750
Office to home	375
Office to restaurant	200
Restaurant to home	1,800
Home to restaurant	600
Home to clients to home	8,500
Clients to restaurant	1,875

    If she uses the standard mileage rate, what amount can she deduct as a business expense?

30. Cassandra owns her own business and drives her van 18,000 miles a year for business and 2,000 miles a year for commuting and personal use. Cassandra purchases a new van in 1996 and wants to claim the largest tax deduction possible for business use. Cassandra's total auto expenses for 1996 are as follows:

Gas, oil, and maintenance	$3,250
Insurance	750
Interest on car loan	2,100
Depreciation	3,060
License	400
Parking fees and tolls	380

    Determine Cassandra's 1996 deduction for business use of the van.

31. Mario owns his own business and drives his car 14,000 miles a year for business and 6,000 miles a year for commuting and personal use. He wants to claim the largest tax deduction possible for business use of his car. His total auto expenses for 1996 are as follows:

Gas, oil, and maintenance	$2,200
Insurance	500
Interest on car loan	650
Depreciation	3,060
License	300
Parking fees and tolls	180

Determine Mario's 1996 deduction for business use of his car.

32. Prudy is a recent college graduate who has taken a position with a real estate brokerage firm. Initially, Prudy will be selling both residential and commercial property. She is thinking about buying a new car at a cost of $14,500. However, the salesperson is trying to sell her a car that costs $18,000. He has assured her that because she is now self-employed, the entire cost of the car is tax deductible. Prudy has come to you, her tax accountant, for advice about the purchase of the car. She tells you she expects that 65% of her driving will be for business purposes. She asks you to write her a letter specifying whether she can deduct the entire cost of the car, which expenses she needs to keep track of, and how these expenses are used in computing the business deduction for her car.

33. Juanita traveled to San Francisco for 6 days. The following facts are related to the trip:

Round trip airfare	$800
Hotel daily rate	
for single or double occupancy	140
Meals—$70 per day	70
Incidentals—$30 per day	30

a. If she spent 4 days on business and 2 days sightseeing, what amount may she deduct as travel expense?

b. If she spent 2 days on business and 4 days sightseeing, what amount may she deduct as travel expense?

c. Juanita spent 5 days on business and 1 day sightseeing; her husband Jorge accompanied her on the trip. Jorge went sightseeing every day and attended business receptions with Juanita at night. Assume that Jorge's expenses are identical to Juanita's. What amount may Juanita and Jorge deduct as travel expense?

34. Chai is self-employed and travels to New Orleans for a business conference. The following facts are related to the trip:

Round trip airfare	$420
Hotel daily rate for single	135
Conference registration fee	160
Meals—$62 per day	62
Incidentals—$22 per day	22

a. If Chai spends 5 days at the conference and 2 days sightseeing, what amount may he deduct as travel expense?

b. If he spends 3 days at the conference and 4 days sightseeing, what amount may he deduct as travel expense?

c. Next year, Chai would like his wife Li, who does not work, to go with him to the conference. Li's expenses would be similar to Chai's, except that the room rate for double occupancy is $150. Li would probably attend one or two sessions and the receptions at night. What portion of her expenses can they deduct?

35. Olga has to travel to Philadelphia for 2 days on business. Olga enjoys history and is planning to visit the Liberty Bell and other historic sites in the city. If time permits, she would like to make a side trip to nearby Gettysburg. A friend of Olga's tells her, "The best part of traveling on business is that once the business is over, you can sightsee all you want and the cost is tax deductible." Olga, who is self-employed, has scheduled her trip for the Labor Day weekend so that she can spend 3 days sightseeing. Write a letter to Olga in which you explain whether her friend's advice is correct.

36. Karl, a dentist, owns three rental properties. In January, he attends a 3-day conference in Phoenix entitled, "How to Build a Real Estate Empire with DEPCO Property." The following facts are related to the trip:

Airfare	$575
Hotel daily rate	100
Meals—$60 per day	60
Incidentals—$25 per day	25
Entertainment	180

What amount may he deduct as travel expense?

37. Floyd owns an antique shop. During the year, Floyd and his wife Amanda, who works as a real estate broker, attend a 2-day antique show in Boston. The following facts are related to the trip:

Train per person	$ 95
Hotel daily rate—double occupancy*	105
Meals—$40 per day per person	40
Incidentals—$18 per day per person	18

*The hotel rate for double occupancy is $20 more than the single occupancy rate.

What amount can Floyd and Amanda deduct as travel expense? Explain.

38. Bob has 6 employees in his men's clothing store. Every year at Christmas, he gives the employees a party. At the party, he gives each employee a cash gift based on the number of years the employee has worked at the store. This year, the party costs $480, and the gifts total $1,500. How much can Bob deduct as entertainment and gift expense?

39. Cameron is a salesperson for Local Feed Co. During the current year, Cameron gave Hank, his biggest customer, a gold watch for Christmas. The watch cost $700. Cameron gave Hank the watch because he wanted to maintain a good relationship with him. How much of the $700 is deductible by Cameron? What are the tax effects for Hank?

40. For each of the following situations determine whether the expenses are deductible as an education expense:

a. Dorothy owns a real estate business. She is enrolled in a 1-year weekend MBA program that meets in a city three hours away. She takes a train to and from the city. A one-year weekend pass for the train is $800. The fee for the MBA program, including lodging, meals, books, and tuition, is $25,000.

b. Forest is employed as a production manager for a printing company. He is enrolled in a night course ($350) at the local college. The course is not required by his employer but does improve his job skills.

c. Elise is a recent graduate of law school and has been hired by a local firm. The firm expects Elise to pass the bar exam on her first try. To help her prepare for the bar exam, she is taking a law review course that costs $1,500.

d. Simon is the managing partner of an accounting firm and is required to attend 30 hours of continuing education every year. State law requires that 5 hours be in ethics training. The cost of the 5-hour ethics course is $400; the remaining 25 hours of continuing education cost $1,800.

e. Assume the same facts as in part d, except that state law does not require 5 hours of continuing education in ethics.

41. Felix and Ismael were college roommates. Five years after they graduate, Ismael is a tax manager in a large public accounting firm, and Felix is still in his first job as an engineer for a construction company. Felix is not sure whether he wants to stay in engineering or change careers. Either way, he knows he will need to take some courses at the local university. While reading the Sunday paper, Felix notices an ad for the university: "Enroll now: The cost of post-baccalaureate courses is tax deductible!!" The small print advises, "Consult your tax adviser about the deductibility of each course."

    Felix calls Ismael the next day. After Felix explains that he may decide to pursue a new career, Ismael says someone on his staff will send Felix a letter detailing the tax deductibility of education expenses. You are Ismael's staff accountant; he asks you to write the letter to Felix.

42. Pat is a professor of German. During the summer, she spent two months in Germany studying local culture and perfecting her German. The cost of the summer included $2,000 for airfare, $4,000 for lodging, $1,800 for meals, and $900 for incidental expenses. How much of the travel costs can Pat deduct? Explain.

43. For each of the following situations, determine the amount that is deductible as compensation expense:
    a. Molly is the leading salesperson and third-highest-paid employee of Riveredge Corporation. She is not an officer of the company. Riveredge is a publicly traded corporation and during the year pays Molly a salary of $225,000, a bonus of $175,000, and sales commissions of $700,000. The company has no formal performance-based compensation agreement.
    b. Alejandro is the eighth-highest-paid officer of the publicly traded Mermer Corporation. The company pays him a salary of $300,000, a bonus of $650,000, and makes mortgage payments of $80,000 on his behalf. The bonus he receives is based on the stock price of the company and subjective evaluations from his peers. The performance goals were established by the compensation committee and were approved by the shareholders of the corporation. Before the company pays the bonus, the compensation committee certifies that Alejandro has attained the performance goals.
    c. Assume the same facts as in part b, except that Alejandro is the chief executive officer of Mermer Corporation.
    d. Cory is the fourth-highest-paid officer of the closely held Mast Corporation, which has assets of $14,000,000. The company pays Cory a salary of $800,000 and a bonus of $300,000. The payments are typical of a company in the industry with comparable assets.
    e. Evita is the eighth-highest-paid officer of the Acworth Co. Her salary for the year is $800,000, and she receives a bonus during the year of $400,000. The bonus is based on a complex set of formulas that factor in stock price, peer evaluations, subordinates' evaluations, and number of years with the company. The plan has been in effect since January 1, 1992.
    f. Assume the same facts as in part e, except that Evita is the second-highest-paid officer.

44. Yolanda is the third-highest-paid officer of the Dewit Corporation. Her salary is $675,000. She also receives a bonus of $420,000 based on the performance of Dewit Corporation's stock. The bonus paid to Yolanda is based solely on the performance of the corporation's stock. The standards for the bonus have been set by the outside directors and have been approved by the stockholders. Before the company pays the bonus, the outside board of directors fails to certify that the performance standards have been attained. Can the Dewit Corporation deduct her entire compensation ($1,095,000)?

45. Howard loaned $7,000 to Bud 2 years ago. The terms of the loan called for Bud to pay annual interest at 8%, with the principal amount due in 3 years. Until this year, Bud had been making the required interest payments. When he didn't receive this year's payment, Howard called Bud and found out that Bud had filed for bankruptcy. Bud's accountant estimated that only 40% of his debts would be paid after the bankruptcy proceeding. No payments were received. In the next year, Howard received $2,500 in full satisfaction of the debt under the bankruptcy proceeding. What deductions are allowed to Howard, assuming that the debt was
   a. Related to Howard's business?
   b. Unrelated to Howard's business?
   c. How would your answer to parts a and b change if Howard received $2,900 in satisfaction of the debt in the next year?

46. In 1996, Grace, Inc., has total sales of $350,000. Based on total sales, the corporation estimates that its bad debts for the year are 3% of sales. As a result, the corporation deducts $10,500 in bad debts for financial accounting purposes. At the end of 1996, the controller reviews the accounts receivable ledger to identify uncollectible accounts. She determines that $3,100 in accounts receivable cannot be collected. In addition, the accountant's analysis shows that the corporation has recovered $800 in accounts receivable written off as a bad debt for tax purposes in 1995. How should this information be reported for tax purposes?

47. UCI's financial accounting records show the following transactions in the allowance for bad debts account:

Date	Description	Debits	Credits
1/01/96	Beginning balance		20,000
7/08/96	Recovery of accounts receivable written off as uncollectible in 1995		2,000
12/31/96	Accounts specifically identified as uncollectible and written off	7,000	
12/31/96	1996 addition to account based on 1996 credit sales	____	4,000
12/31/96	Ending balance		19,000

   a. If UCI's bad debts arise from the sale of merchandise, how should the transactions in the allowance for bad debts account be reported for tax purposes?
   b. If UCI uses the cash method of accounting and the bad debts expense arose from the sale of architectural services, how would your answer to the first part change?

48. Susan loaned $2,000 to her minister a year ago. The loan is not evidenced by a note and does not bear interest. The minister has moved out of town without paying her back. She doesn't want to embarrass him by asking him to repay the loan. She would rather deduct the bad debt. How much can Susan deduct for the bad debt? Explain.

49. In addition to being an employee of Rock Hard Roofing Material, Lou owns 10% of the company's common stock. Rock Hard falls on hard times in 1995. To forestall bankruptcy, Rock Hard's employees and shareholders loan the company $1,000,000. Lou's share of the total loan is $50,000—$25,000 related to her position as an employee and $25,000 related to her ownership of stock. In early 1996, creditors force Rock Hard into bankruptcy. Lou loses her entire $50,000.
   a. Is Lou's loss related to a trade or business or an investment?
   b. Can Lou deduct her loss as a bad debt expense?

50. KOM pays the following insurance premiums during 1996:
Auto accident and liability insurance:

  Paid 1/1/96 Coverage period 1/1/96–12/31/96　　　　$3,500

  Fire, storm, and other casualty insurance:

  Paid 4/1/96 Coverage period 4/1/96–3/31/98　　　　$4,800

  Business liability insurance:

  Paid 5/1/96 Coverage period 5/1/96–4/30/97　　　　$5,000

 a. If KOM uses the accrual method of accounting, what is the amount of the 1996 insurance expense deduction?
 b. If KOM uses the cash method of accounting, what is the amount of the 1996 insurance expense deduction?

51. For each of the following situations, state whether the expense related to the transaction can be deducted as an insurance expense:
 a. Baker Co. pays the insurance premium to provide each of its employees with a $50,000 whole life insurance policy. Baker and the insurance company consider the employee the owner of the policy. As owner of the policy, the covered employee designates the beneficiary of the life insurance proceeds in the event of the employee's death. The cost for each employee's policy is $2,000 per year.
 b. Baker Co. has a nondiscriminatory self-insured medical reimbursement plan for the benefit of its employees. Once a month, Baker transfers $1,000 in cash from its general bank account to a special medical reimbursement checking account. The transfer is based on the premium an insurance company would demand to provide the same benefits to the employees.
 c. The employees of Baker Co. handle large sums of cash that are received in the mail. To protect against loss, Baker pays a $500 annual insurance premium for an employees' fidelity bond.
 d. Baker Co. is owned by Ross. Baker pays a $1,500 annual premium for a sickness and disability income continuation insurance policy on Ross. The purpose of the policy is to provide Ross with $3,500 per month of income if he is unable to work for Baker because he is sick or disabled.

52. State whether the following taxes are allowed as a current deduction for taxes paid by a business:
 a. Sales tax on the purchase of a desk
 b. State and local income, real estate, and personal property taxes
 c. Federal income, estate, and gift taxes
 d. An employer's payment to the IRS of federal income and Social Security taxes withheld from an employee's wages

53. Martin receives the following tax bills, related to a rental dwelling, from the county treasurer:

 Special assessment for installing sidewalks and streets　　　$12,000

 Real property tax on dwelling for the 1/1–12/31/1996
  property tax year, due on 10/1/96　　　　$　900

 On June 1, 1996, Martin sells the dwelling for $60,000. Martin's basis in the dwelling at the date of sale is $24,000. Martin's basis in the dwelling does not reflect the property tax bills. As part of the sale contract, the buyer agrees to pay the real property taxes when they come due on October 1, 1996, but Martin has to pay the special assessment before the sale closes. What is the proper tax treatment of the tax payments?

54. The Kimpton Corporation pays the following taxes during 1996:

Federal taxes withheld from employees	$42,000
State taxes withheld from employees	12,000
Social Security withheld from employees	8,500
Kimpton's share of Social Security taxes	8,500
Federal income tax paid in 1996 with 1995 tax return	4,200
Federal income tax paid in 1996	14,500
Real estate taxes	9,300
State income taxes paid in 1996	6,340
State income taxes paid in 1996 with 1995 return	2,560
Sales tax on capital acquisitions	5,780
Sales tax on supplies	8,120

Also, the county treasurer notifies Kimpton that it is being assessed a special real estate tax of $50,000 for upgrading the sidewalks and sewer connections in the area. The special tax is payable in 5 yearly installments of $10,000. What amount can Kimpton deduct for taxes paid in 1996?

55. Can Joe Corporation deduct the following expenses related to its business?
   a. Legal fee paid ($40,000) to acquire a competing chain of stores
   b. Legal fee paid ($12,000) to determine whether it should become an S corporation
   c. Legal fee paid ($5,000) to defend the company's president in a lawsuit filed by a disgruntled customer
   d. Legal fee paid ($500) to defend title to a vacant lot Joe is holding for construction of a storage building for use in its business
   e. Legal fee paid.($2,500) to defend against damages suffered by a customer who was injured when he fell in the company's store

56. As a hobby, Jane creates and sells oil paintings. During the current year, her sales total $7,000. How is the tax treatment of her hobby different from the treatment of a trade or business, if
   a. Her business expenses total $4,500?
   b. Her business expenses total $12,000?
   c. Assume that Jane itemizes her deductions and that she has an adjusted gross income of $38,000 before considering the effect of the hobby. Discuss the actual amount of the deduction Jane would receive in parts a and b.

57. Candy raises canaries as a hobby. Candy uses one room in her home, the bird room, for the birds. Because the birds are loose and fly around the bird room, the room cannot be used for family activities. During the year, her gross sales are $1,300. However, she has to give $60 back to a customer whose bird died within 30 days of purchase. She incurs the following expenses:

Bird seed	$305
Supplies	250
Fertilized eggs	140
Depreciation on bird room	200
Interest and property tax allocated to bird room	380
Loss on birds that died before they were sold (retail sales price)	90
State license for business	50

What is the proper tax treatment of these items? How would your answer change if her gross sales are $2,100?

58. Sharon is single and a data-processing manager for the phone company. In her spare time, she collects baseball cards. Sharon goes to card shows, subscribes to numerous magazines on baseball card collecting, and spends hours on the Baseball Home Page on the Internet. She has collected cards for the past 5 years. For 3 years, she lost money and she had a profit for 2 years. Overall, her baseball card trading has shown a slight profit. Sharon rents a two-bedroom apartment for $500 and uses one bedroom for her baseball card collecting. She bought a computer last year; 60% of its use is for personal activities and 40% for baseball card collecting. She spends approximately 15 hours a week on her collection and keeps meticulous records. For the current year, Sharon has the following income and expenses:

Sales of cards	$4,560
Cost of cards sold	1,600
Cost of new cards acquired	1,350
Registration and booth fees	800
Transportation to card shows	600
Meals attending shows	200
Cost of magazines	325
Cost of Internet connection	240
Cost of dedicated phone line for modem	260
Depreciation on computer (unallocated)	160

   a. What is the proper tax treatment of these items if Sharon is engaged in a trade or business?

   b. What is the proper tax treatment of these items if she is engaged in a hobby?

   c. What factors (e.g., facts, aspects) of Sharon's card-collecting activity indicate that it is a hobby? a trade or business?

59. Lee and Sally own a winter retreat in Harlingen, Texas, that qualifies as their second home. This year they spent 40 days in their cabin. Because of its ideal location, it is easy to rent at $120 a day and was rented for 80 days this year. The total upkeep costs of the cabin for the year were as follows:

Home mortgage interest	$9,000
Real and personal property taxes	1,200
Insurance	750
Utilities	600
Repairs and maintenance	1,000
Depreciation (unallocated)	2,500

   a. What is the proper treatment of this information on Lee and Sally's tax return, using the courts' allocation method?

   b. What is the proper treatment of this information on Lee and Sally's tax return, using the IRS allocation method?

60. Mel and Helen own a beachfront home in Myrtle Beach, S.C. During the year, they rented the house for 5 weeks (35 days) at $800 per week and used the house for personal purposes 65 days. The costs of maintaining the house for the year were

Home mortgage interest	$13,000
Real property taxes	4,500
Insurance	650
Utilities	1,000
Repairs and maintenance	480
Depreciation (unallocated)	3,500

   a. What is the proper tax treatment of this information on their tax return?

   b. What is the proper tax treatment if Helen and Mel rented the house for only 2 weeks (14 days)?

61. Teresa owns a condominium in Florida. During the current year, she incurs the following expenses related to the property:

Mortgage interest	$11,000
Property taxes	1,000
Utilities	900
Maintenance fees	1,300
Repairs	800
Depreciation	6,000

Assuming that Teresa wants to take the largest deductions allowable on the condominium, determine the amount of her deductions in each of the following cases:

Case	Rental Income	Rental Days	Personal Use Days
A	$13,000	365	0 *Rental*
B	4,000	60	10 *Rental*
C	4,000	60	20 *Vacation*
D	500 *not reported*	10	40 *Personal Residence*
E	11,000	280 × 15% = 22 → *meet rental test*	20 *Rental*

62. Conrad purchases a condominium in Aspen, Colorado. Because of his hectic work schedule, Conrad is unsure how much he will be able to use the condo over the next few years. A friend of his, who has a condo in Aspen, tells him that the condominium is both a great investment and an excellent tax shelter. Conrad's friend has been able to rent his condominium for $1,000 per week. Conrad expects to incur the following expenses related to the condominium:

Home mortgage interest	$16,000
Real property taxes	5,500
Insurance	825
Utilities	2,150
Condominium fee	2,400
Maintenance	300
Depreciation (unallocated)	6,500

Conrad is somewhat hesitant to rent his new condo out for the entire year, just in case he can sneak away from work for a few days. Therefore, he wants to explore all his options. Write a letter to Conrad explaining the different tax treatment of his condominium expenses depending on how much (i.e., the number of days) he uses it.

63. Ray, 83, is a used car dealer. He lives in a rural community and operates the business out of his home. One room in his 6-room home is used exclusively for his business office. He parks the cars in his front yard, and when customers come along, they sit on the front porch and negotiate a sale price. The income statement for Ray's auto business is as follows:

Sales		$ 110,000
Cost of cars sold		(78,000)
Gross profit		$ 32,000
Interest expense on cars	$4,200	
Property tax on cars	700	
Gas, oil, repairs	1,200	
Loan fees	3,200	
Depreciation on equipment	1,800	(11,100)
Net profit		$ 20,900

If Ray's home were rental property, the annual depreciation would be $2,900. The utilities and upkeep on the home cost Ray $6,400 for the year. Ray's mortgage interest for the year is $2,400. When asked about the loan fees, Ray bitterly responded that Jim, the bank loan officer, charged him 10% of his gross profit on cars financed through the bank. Ray said, "The money is under the table, and if I don't shell out the cash, Jim won't loan the money to my customers to buy my cars. Everybody goes to Jim—he's got the cash."

Write a letter to Ray explaining the proper treatment of this information on his tax return.

64. Hromas uses a separate room in his personal residence as an office. The room is 500 square feet of the total 2,000 square feet in the house. During the current year, Hromas incurs the following household expenses:

Mortgage interest		$12,000
Property taxes		1,400
Insurance		450
Utilities		
Gas and electric	$2,100	
Cable TV	280	
Phone ($15 per month for an extra		
outlet in the office)	450	2,830
House cleaning		1,820
Long-distance phone calls (business related)		670
Depreciation (unallocated)		$5,600

How much of a deduction is Hromas allowed for the costs of the office in each of the following situations?

a. Hromas is an independent salesperson who uses the room exclusively to call customers who buy goods from him. During the current year, his sales total $83,000, cost of goods sold is $33,000, and he incurs other valid business expenses unrelated to the office of $25,000.

b. Hromas is an employee of Ace Computer Co. He uses the office primarily when he has to bring work home at nights and on weekends. He occasionally uses the office to pay personal bills and to study the stock market so he can make personal investments. His salary at Ace is $80,000 per year. He is not paid extra for the time he spends working at home.

65. Charlotte owns a custom publishing business. She uses 600 square feet of her home (2,100 square feet) as an office and for storage. All her business has come from tele-marketing (telephone sales), direct mailings, or referrals. In her first year of operation, she has revenues of $46,000, cost of goods sold of $25,000, and other business expenses of $17,000. The total expenses related to her home are

Home mortgage interest	$7,200
Real property taxes	1,800
Insurance	350
Utilities	900
Repairs and maintenance	550
House cleaning	800
Depreciation (unallocated)	4,500

a. What amount can Charlotte deduct for her home office?
b. Would your answer in part a change if Charlotte solicited her business through direct contact (door to door)? Explain.

INTEGRATIVE PROBLEM

66. Rufus and Rhonda are a married couple with 2 dependent children. Rufus, 46, is an executive with Plowshare Corporation. Rhonda, 39, is a self-employed attorney.

Rufus receives an annual salary of $70,000. He participates in Plowshare's qualified pension plan by contributing 4% of his annual salary, which is matched by Plowshare. Rufus also receives group term life insurance at twice his annual salary. The cost to Plowshare of the coverage is $2,100. All employees are covered by a medical insurance policy (cost of Rufus's policy is $2,300). Rufus also participates in the company's flexible benefits plan by paying $175 per month into the plan. During the year, Rufus submits claims totaling $1,800 to the plan. An additional benefit that only top level executives such as Rufus enjoy is the payment of $3,250 in country club dues by Plowshare. Although Rufus occasionally entertains clients at the club, his primary use of the facility is personal.

Rhonda bills clients a total of $105,000 for services rendered during the current year. She receives $15,000 in payments from billings in prior years and $65,000 from current-year billings. Rhonda pays the following expenses related to her legal practice:

Office rent		$14,500
Secretary's salary		20,000
Withholdings from secretary's salary		
Federal income taxes	$2,040	
State income taxes	480	
Social Security taxes	1,530	4,050
Matching Social Security tax payment		1,530
Entertainment costs		6,550
Seminar costs		1,280
Insurance on building—two years		
prepaid on August 1		1,800
Supplies		3,700
Bar association dues		650
State licensing fee		675
Automobile costs		5,100
Business gifts		600
Salary paid to Rhonda		54,000
Salary paid to Rhonda's son		2,700

In addition to these out-of-pocket costs, Rhonda determines that $6,200 in accounts receivable from previous years' billings are uncollectible.

The entertainment costs consist of the following:

Dues to social club	$1,400
Meals while discussing cases with clients	2,400
Open house	2,750

Rhonda has records that show that she uses the club 70% of the time for entertainment directly related to business entertainment, 10% for entertainment associated with her business, and 20% for personal purposes. The open house costs consist of $2,300 for food and $450 for a jazz combo at a reception she hosted for clients when she moved into her new offices this year.

Rhonda uses her automobile extensively in her business. She keeps a log to record business miles and related costs. Her records show that she drove 9,000 business miles and 6,000 personal miles during the current year. In past years, she had always kept track of her business miles but failed to keep an accurate record of her actual costs. Accordingly, her records indicate that she has never depreciated any of the $24,000 cost of the automobile she purchased 2 years ago—she has used the standard mileage rate method.

Every year, Rhonda gives her top 8 clients a gift to thank them for their support of her practice. This year, she gives each client a marble paperweight engraved with the client's name. Each paperweight costs $65 plus $5 for engraving and $5 for gift wrapping.

The seminar costs relate to a 3-day meeting in New York on a legal topic involving her biggest client. Because of a special airline promotion, she takes along her 16-year-old son for free. However, she has to pay $210 per night for her hotel room instead of the $185 per night single rate. A summary of the seminar costs is as follows:

Airfare	$345
Lodging (3 nights @ $210 each)	630
Meals (including $95 for her son)	255
Taxi to and from the airport	50

Rhonda pays the $2,700 salary to her son for cleaning up after the open house reception. Although she could hire a service to do the job for $650, her son needs the money to buy a used motorcycle.

Rufus is hit by a car one morning while he is out jogging. The driver of the car is at fault, and his insurance company pays Rufus $7,000 for his pain and suffering and $12,000 of his $16,000 medical expenses. The remaining medical expenses are paid by Plowshare's medical insurance policy. Rufus also receives $2,300 in disability pay from the Plowshare policy for the time he misses from work recovering from the injury.

Rufus and Rhonda have the following investment-related items during the current year:

Interest on savings account	$ 950
Interest on Puerto Rico development bonds	7,100
Cash dividends on stock	4,350
Stock dividend shares (200 shares received when the market value of the stock was $35 per share)	7,000

Early in the year, Rhonda inherits 900 shares of stock from her grandmother. The total value of the shares is $27,000. Later in the year, the stock value begins to fall rapidly, and she sells the shares at a $7,000 loss.

Rufus and Rhonda own a cabin in the mountains. They use the cabin on weekends and for short holidays and rent it out whenever they can. During the current year, they use the cabin 15 days and rent it out 60 days. Details on the cabin income and expenses are as follows:

Rental income	$ 4,900
Mortgage interest	13,400
Property taxes	1,300
Utilities and maintenance	720
Depreciation (unallocated)	9,400

In addition, Rufus and Rhonda have $17,200 in other allowable itemized deductions.

REQUIRED: Based on the information provided, calculate Rufus and Rhonda's taxable income and their tax liability. For purposes of this problem, assume that Rufus and Rhonda are cash basis taxpayers and want to be as aggressive as possible in taking their allowable deductions. You are not required to calculate the self-employment tax on Rhonda's law practice income.

DISCUSSION CASES

67. Recently, President Bill Clinton and Hillary Rodham Clinton have faced questions about their personal finances. The president also has faced accusations concerning marital indiscretions. In response, the Clintons have incurred a substantial amount of legal expenses. The Clintons fear that the legal expenses from these allegations, as well as any future charges, could bankrupt them. Therefore, they have established the Presidential Legal Trust Fund. The Clintons established the trust with $2,000 and have asked the American people for contributions. Because the trust does not qualify as a charitable organization, contributions to the fund are not tax deductible. However, many tax specialists have suggested that the contributions to the Presidential Legal Trust Fund constitute taxable income for the Clintons. If the income is taxable to the Clintons, they will face an enormous tax liability unless their legal expenses are deductible. Using the concepts discussed in Chapters 5 and 6, determine whether the Clintons' legal expenses are deductible.

68. During the current year, Benjamin and Valerie Jones were notified that their 1994 tax return was being audited. The IRS commissioner has disallowed all the losses attributable to Valerie's cattle breeding and showing.

Valerie was raised on a small ranch where her family raised commercial cattle. When she was 18, she left the family ranch to attend college, where she obtained an accounting degree. Valerie is now employed as a full-time accountant by Veltkamp, Stannebein, & Bateson, a local accounting firm, and receives an annual salary of $45,000. Ben, a full-time househusband, takes care of their children, Kody and Jaycee.

In 1990, Valerie purchased 10 impregnated purebred Maine Anjou heifers, an exotic breed of cattle from France, for a total price of $16,375. Valerie entered into a contract with a local farmer to obtain pasture land for her herd. The contract requires a payment of $20 a month from April through October for each cow and calf. In the winter months, November through March, the cost of feeding each cow and calf is $1.50 per day. In February 1992, Valerie purchased a replacement bull with an exceptional pedigree for $7,500 to improve the quality of her calves.

She sells any inferior animals to the meat market, keeps her best heifers for breeding, and shows her best bull calves in livestock shows. The livestock shows provide her with the opportunity to show and sell her exotic cattle. Until 1994, Valerie had been responsible for getting the animals ready to show, which requires approximately 4 hours per day from November through January. Unfortunately, Valerie was injured while working with one of her bulls and was forced to pay someone to finish breaking and showing the bulls. During the summer months, Valerie pays someone to watch the cattle so she can spend time with her family.

In 1990 and 1991, Valerie realized losses in the amounts of $4,125 and $1,894, respectively. In 1992 and 1993, Valerie realized gains of $3,000 and $750, respectively. For 1994, Valerie realized an operating loss of $1,200 and a casualty loss of $7,500, because her new bull was struck by lightning and killed. Valerie has maintained adequate records for all tax years since she began the cattle venture.

Write a letter to Valerie explaining whether her ranching activity is a trade or business.

69. Kern and Mary's son lives in Japan and was just married. Several years ago, Kern wrote a best-selling legal text. They decided to take a trip around the world and to write a travel book, *Mary's Diary*, describing the reactions of an average American woman to places and events during the trip. They entered this venture in good faith with the intent to make a profit. Their trip lasted 3 months. While in Japan, they spent 4 days visiting their son and met his new wife and her family. They worked diligently on the book during the entire trip. When they returned home, they devoted 3 months to preparing the manuscript for publication. They want to deduct the travel and manuscript preparation costs as a business expense. What advice would you give them? Explain.

70. The Saffron Corporation is planning to adopt a new compensation package for its top 24 managers. The plan would provide each executive with a base salary of $500,000 and a compensation supplement based on rank and years of service. The maximum amount of supplemental compensation an individual can receive is $700,000.

TAX PLANNING CASE

The company will also institute a bonus system based on financial performance measures, internal performance measures, and individual reviews conducted by the compensation committee. The committee will solicit information from other senior members of management and from employees in the individual's department. The financial and internal measures used to determine the bonus will vary according to the executive's responsibilities. For example, a financial measure used to evaluate the vice president of manufacturing might be the ratio of cost of goods sold to sales, whereas an internal measure might be the percentage of defective units to total units produced. The compensation committee is to consist of the chief executive officer, the chief financial officer, Saffron's general counsel, and four outside directors. The company's public accounting firm would certify that the performance measures have been attained.

Margaret and José are two managers who would be affected by the new plan. Margaret is Saffron's director of marketing and José is the director of human resources. Margaret is an officer of the company and its third-highest-paid employee. Based on projections, her compensation would be $1,200,000 under the plan: the $500,000 base salary, a supplement salary of $575,000, imputed interest of $15,000 on a company loan to her, and a $110,000 bonus. José is not an officer but is the company's tenth-highest-paid employee. His projected compensation of $1,050,000 would consist of the $500,000 base salary, a supplemental salary of $460,000, and a $90,000 bonus.

The chairman of the board of directors would like to know the tax consequences of the proposed plan for Saffron Corporation. Using Margaret's and José's anticipated compensation under the plan, determine the deductibility of the compensation payments. If any of the amounts to be paid to Margaret or José are not fully deductible by Saffron, suggest alternative compensation schemes that would be deductible and would maintain the target level of compensation.

71. Tom is a CPA for a large regional firm. In preparing the tax return for Espresso Industries, Tom noticed that the firm had an unusually high amount of travel, meals, and entertainment expenses. Therefore, he decided to examine the supporting documentation. In doing so, Tom noticed that the business purpose for many of the meals was not provided. When Tom questioned Frank, the company controller, Frank assured him that all the meal and entertainment expenses were legitimate. After further examination, Tom found that for every business day in June, July, and August, four of the corporation's senior officers had been reimbursed for their lunch and dinner costs. Tom confronted Frank and the assistant controller, Doug, with this information. He informed Frank that his firm would not prepare the return unless the meals and entertainment that did not have a business purpose were omitted. Frank, angered by Tom's decision, told Tom to prepare the return and said that he would take it from there. The following Saturday, Tom was playing golf with Doug and asked him what Frank had meant by

ETHICS DISCUSSION CASE

his remarks. Doug told Tom that Frank would simply replace Tom's number with one that includes the entire meals and entertainment expense. Can Tom prepare the tax return, knowing that the company will change the meals and entertainment expense? If he does prepare the return, what ethical standards (refer to Statements on Responsibilities in Tax Practice), if any, has Tom violated? Assume that Tom prepares the return. If asked, should he prepare next year's return?

Losses—Deductions and Limitations

▲ CHAPTER LEARNING OBJECTIVES

- Explain the difference between an annual loss and a transaction loss.

- Introduce the relief provisions available to taxpayers who incur net operating losses.

- Discuss the general operation of a tax shelter.

- Introduce the at-risk rules and explain how they limit annual loss deductions.

- Discuss passive losses and explain the limitations on the deductibility of losses incurred in passive activities.

- Discuss the general treatments of transaction losses incurred in a trade or business, a production-of-income activity, and personal use losses.

- Explain the tax rules applicable to business casualty and theft losses.

- Describe the limitations on the deductions allowed for capital losses.

- Explain the tax rules applicable to personal casualty losses.

▲ CONCEPT REVIEW ▲

Ability to pay   A tax should be based on the amount that the taxpayer can afford to pay, relative to other taxpayers.

Administrative convenience   Those items for which the cost of compliance would exceed the revenue generated are not taxed.

Annual accounting period   All tax entities must report the results of their operations on an annual basis (the tax year). Each year stands on its own, apart from other tax years.

Basis   This is the amount of unrecovered investment in an asset. As amounts are expended and/or recovered relative to an asset over time, the basis is adjusted in consideration of such changes. The **adjusted basis** of an asset is the original basis, plus or minus the changes in the amount of unrecovered investment.

Business purpose   To be deductible, an expenditure or a loss must have a business or other economic purpose that exceeds any tax avoidance motive. The primary motive for the transaction must be to make a profit.

Capital recovery   No income is realized until the taxpayer receives more than the amount invested to produce the income. The amount invested in an asset represents the maximum amount recoverable.

Entity   All items of income, deduction, and so on are traced to the tax unit responsible for the item.

Legislative grace   Any tax relief provided is the result of a specific act of Congress that must be strictly applied and interpreted. All income received is taxable unless a specific provision can be found in the tax law that excludes the income from taxation. Deductions must be approached with the philosophy that nothing is deductible unless a provision in the tax law allows the deduction.

Realization   No income (or loss) is recognized until it has been realized. A realization involves a change in the form and/or the substance of a taxpayer's property rights that results from an arm's-length transaction.

Related party   Family members and corporations that are owned by family members are considered related parties, as are certain other relationships between entities in which the power to control the substance of a transaction is evidenced through majority ownership.

INTRODUCTION

The tax law allows the deduction of certain types of losses in the calculation of taxable income. The deductibility of losses is a matter of legislative grace and is based on the ability-to-pay concept. The reasoning behind deductions and losses is similar. In fact, many classification rules for deductions also apply to losses.

How are losses different from deductions? Deductions are the current expenditures (and amortization of capital expenditures) made for the production of current period income. Losses can result when an entity's deductions for the period exceed the income generated (i.e., a negative income for the period). This type of loss is referred to as an *annual loss*, or *activity loss*.

▲ **EXAMPLE 1**   Emma owns a restaurant. During the current year, she had gross income of $74,000 and allowable deductions related to the business of $90,000. What is Emma's income from the restaurant?

Discussion: Emma has suffered a business loss of $16,000 ($74,000 − $90,000). This loss is an annual loss created by an excess of allowable deductions over income.

Note that Emma can have more than one annual loss if she engages in multiple activities. Remember that the results of each entity must be kept separate and apart from all other entities for recording and reporting purposes. In this case, Emma would combine the allowable loss from her restaurant business with her income and deductions from her other activities on her individual tax return.

In contrast to an annual loss, a loss can also occur as a result of the disposition of an asset. An asset that is disposed of at less than its basis creates a loss that represents the taxpayer's unrecovered capital investment. This type of loss is referred to as a *transaction loss.*

> ▲ **EXAMPLE 2**   Alfred purchases 50 shares of Inventor, Inc., common stock for $5,000 in 1995. Alfred sells the 50 shares for $4,400 in 1996. What are the tax effects for Alfred of his investment in the Inventor, Inc., stock?
>
> *Discussion:*   Alfred has a loss of $600 ($4,400 − $5,000) on the sale of the stock in 1996. The loss represents Alfred's basis in the stock that was not recovered when he disposed of the stock.

Figure 7–1 outlines the general scheme for the treatment of losses. The first requirement is that a realization of the loss must have occurred. The realized loss may be either an annual loss or a transaction loss.

Under the business purpose concept, only losses that are the result of a profit-motivated transaction or venture are deductible. Thus, annual loss deductions are allowed only for activities that constitute a trade or business. Note in Figure 7–1 that an annual loss incurred in a passive activity is not generally allowed as a deduction. Thus, it is important to distinguish those activities that constitute a trade or business from those that are passive.

The tax treatment of transaction losses depends on the source of the loss. As a result, transaction losses are classified as related to a trade or business, an income-producing activity, or a personal use. Once a loss has been properly categorized, the rules for deductibility are applied by category, as with deductions. Figure 7–1 shows the general difference in treatments among the three categories of transaction losses. That is, all losses incurred in a trade or business are fully deductible. Losses incurred in an income-producing activity are subject to the capital loss limitations. Losses on personal use of property are generally disallowed. Thus, the general approach to the treatment of transaction losses is similar to the approach to deductions discussed in Chapter 5.

The purpose of this chapter is to discuss the tax treatment(s) of the most common types of losses. As with most areas of the tax law, there are exceptions

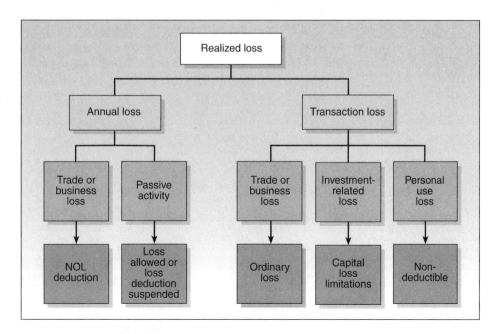

▲ **Figure 7–1**

GENERAL SCHEME FOR TREATMENT OF LOSSES

to the general treatment of losses, which are outlined in Figure 7–1. The more important of these exceptions are discussed later in the chapter.

ANNUAL LOSSES

Annual losses result from an excess of deductions over income. The only deductions allowed for annual losses are for those incurred in a trade or business. Taxpayers who have annual activities with a significant personal use element (hobbies, vacation homes, home office) are not allowed to deduct expenses in excess of income. As a result, the two primary types of annual losses are net operating losses (NOL) and passive activity losses. Figure 7–2 outlines the treatment of annual losses. When an annual loss is realized, the key question is whether the taxpayer materially participates in the operation of the business. If the taxpayer does not materially participate in the business, the passive activity loss rules apply. If the taxpayer does materially participate in the business reporting the loss, a net operating loss deduction is usually allowed. However, if the entity that owns the activity is a conduit entity, the loss flows through to the owner(s) of the entity, and the material participation test is repeated with regard to each owner's share of the loss.

▲ **Figure 7–2**

TREATMENT OF
ANNUAL LOSSES

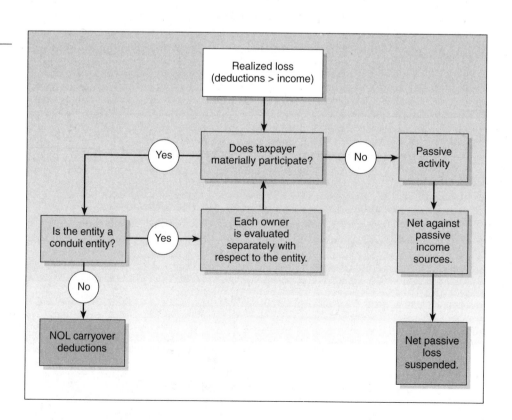

A **net operating loss (NOL)** is an annual loss incurred in a trade or business in which the taxpayer materially participates. It results from an excess of allowable deductions over income for the accounting period.

▲ **EXAMPLE 3**   Pete is the sole proprietor of Pete's Pizza Parlor. During the current year, the pizza parlor has income of $80,000 and deductions of $100,000, resulting in a net operating loss of $20,000. What is the treatment of the loss?

Discussion: Although not a true conduit entity, the loss from the Pizza Parlor flows through to the owner, Pete, and is reported on his return. Pete is allowed to deduct the $20,000 loss from the pizza parlor against his other sources of income.

What happens when a taxable entity has an NOL? Because a taxable entity (i.e., individuals and corporations) pays tax on the income it generates, it would pay no tax for the year in which an NOL occurs. Taxable entities are not allowed to pass the loss through to their owners for deduction. With no relief from this situation, taxable entities are at a distinct disadvantage.

▲ **EXAMPLE 4**   Consider the following taxable incomes (losses) for taxpayers Alicia (A) and Bernie (B), both of whom are taxable entities, for a 4-year period. The marginal tax rate for both Alicia and Bernie is 25% throughout the 4 years.

	Year 1	Year 2	Year 3	Year 4	Total
Taxpayer A	$30,000	$30,000	$30,000	$ 30,000	$120,000
Tax rate	× 25%	× 25%	× 25%	× 25%	
Tax paid	$ 7,500	$ 7,500	$ 7,500	$ 7,500	$ 30,000
Taxpayer B	$50,000	$50,000	$50,000	$(30,000)	$120,000
Tax rate	× 25%	× 25%	× 25%		
Tax paid	$12,500	$12,500	$12,500	-0-	$ 37,500
Difference in total tax paid					$ 7,500

Discussion: Although both taxpayers have the same total income over the 4-year period and the same marginal tax rate, Bernie pays $7,500 more in total tax because of the loss he suffers in year 4.

As example 4 demonstrates, the annual accounting period creates an inequity among taxpayers who suffer NOLs. If some other reporting period (i.e., every two years, every four years) had been chosen for the tax system instead of the annual accounting period, the inequity in example 4 would not have resulted.

In order to provide relief for taxpayers suffering NOLs, a carryover system allows losses incurred in one year to be deducted against income in other years. A **carryback** means that the loss may be used to reduce income in prior years. Because tax has already been paid on the prior year's income, a carryback results in a prompt refund of taxes paid. A **carryforward** means that the loss is used to offset income in future periods. In contrast to a carryback, a carryforward does not provide immediate tax savings; rather it reduces taxes to be paid on future income. An NOL may be carried back for three years. If there is not sufficient taxable income in the three-year carryback period to fully absorb the NOL, any remaining loss may be carried forward for 15 years.[1]

▲ **EXAMPLE 5**   How should Bernie, in example 4, treat the $30,000 loss in year 4?

Discussion: Bernie is allowed to carry the $30,000 loss in year 4 back to year 1 and use it to offset income. This results in a refund of tax of $7,500.

	Year 1	Year 2	Year 3	Year 4	Total
Income	$50,000	$50,000	$50,000	$(30,000)	$120,000
Less: NOL	(30,000)				
Income after NOL	$20,000				
Tax rate	× 25%				
Tax after NOL	$ 5,000				
Tax paid	12,500				
Refund due	$ 7,500				
Net tax paid after NOL	$ 5,000	$12,500	$12,500	-0-	$ 30,000

The effect of the carryback of the NOL is to equalize the taxes paid by Alicia and Bernie. After the carryback, Alicia and Bernie pay the same total tax over the 4-year period.

The carryback rules require the taxpayer to apply the loss to the earliest of the three carryback years first. If the earliest year does not have sufficient income to entirely absorb the loss, any remaining loss is carried to the second-earliest year in the carryback period. You must use the loss against all of the carryback year's income before anything can be carried forward. Thus, you cannot select one high marginal tax rate year and carry the loss back to that specific year.

▲ **EXAMPLE 6**   Assume that Bernie in example 4 had an NOL of $80,000 in year 4. What is the treatment of the NOL?

Discussion: Bernie must carry the loss back and apply it against year 1's income first. Only $50,000 of the $80,000 loss is required to eliminate the taxable income in year 1, leaving $30,000 to apply against year 2's income. Bernie receives a refund of $20,000 of the taxes paid in years 1 and 2:

	Year 1	Year 2	Year 3	Year 4
Income	$50,000	$50,000	$50,000	$(80,000)
Less: NOL	(50,000)	(30,000)		
Income after NOL	$ -0-	$20,000		
Tax rate		× 25%		
Tax after NOL	-0-	$ 5,000		
Tax paid	12,500	12,500		
Refund due	$12,500	$ 7,500		

A taxpayer may elect not to carry the loss back and instead carry the loss forward for 15 years. This may be advantageous when the prior three years' incomes were taxed at low marginal tax rates and the taxpayer anticipates higher marginal tax rates in the near future. In order to determine whether this option is optimal, the relative tax savings under each option and the effect of the time value of money (delaying receipt of tax savings on the carryforward) must be calculated.

▲ **EXAMPLE 7**   Assume that in example 6 Bernie anticipates a year 5 income of $200,000, which would put him in a 39% tax rate bracket. If the time value of money is 10%, should he elect to forgo the carryback and carry the NOL forward for deduction in year 5?

Discussion: The present values of the two options must be compared. The present value of the 3-year carryback is the $20,000 refund of taxes calculated in example 6. The carryforward option reduces year 5's taxes by $31,200 ($80,000 × 39%). Because that savings is one year in the future, the $31,200 must be discounted to the present in order to compare it with the $20,000. At a 10% time value of money, the $31,200 of year 5 taxes has a present value of $28,361 ($31,200 $\times$ .909). In this case, the marginal tax rate savings is greater than the time value of money factor, and the taxpayer is better off electing to carry the NOL forward.

Several additional problems need to be considered in regard to NOLs. First, what happens when losses from a conduit entity cause an individual taxpayer to have a negative taxable income? The tax return of an individual contains a mixture of business-related and specifically allowed personal itemized deductions and exemptions. Because an NOL can be caused only by a business loss, a negative individual taxable income does not necessarily mean that the taxpayer has an NOL from a trade or business for the year. In order to determine whether an individual does have an NOL, a complex set of adjustments is made to the negative taxable income figure. The complexity of these adjustments is beyond the scope of this textbook and is omitted from the discussion.

Related to the treatment of NOLs by individuals is a special treatment afforded to personal casualty and theft losses (discussed later in this chapter). Solely for purposes of the NOL computation of an individual, a personal casualty loss is considered a business-related loss. As a result, a personal casualty loss can create an NOL that can be carried back to prior years. This provision is designed to provide relief to individuals who suffer catastrophic personal casualty losses. Although this further complicates the calculation of an individual's NOL, the importance of the provision is that individuals who suffer large casualty losses may be entitled to additional relief (in addition to the casualty loss deduction) through the NOL provisions.

The last important aspect of NOLs is the deductibility of purchased NOL deductions. At one time, one corporation could acquire another corporation with an NOL carryforward and use the NOL to reduce the tax on its income. This created a market for corporations with unused NOLs because of the tax deductions that could be obtained from the acquisition. In many instances, the tax loss was the corporation's most valuable asset, and other firms would buy the tax loss corporation solely to obtain the tax benefits of the unused NOL. Congress responded to this selling of tax losses by enacting a provision that limits the benefits of an acquired NOL. These limitations apply when there has been a change of greater than 50 percent in the ownership of the acquired corporation. Although the mechanics of these provisions are beyond the scope of this book, it is important to be aware that you cannot always use purchased NOLs to reduce a corporation's taxable income.

TAX-SHELTER LOSSES: AN OVERVIEW

In its broadest application, the term **tax shelter** refers to any investment activity that is designed to minimize the effect of the income tax on wealth accumulation. Under this definition, an investment in tax-exempt municipal bonds would be viewed as a tax shelter. However, in tax practice, the term is generally applied to investments that produce significant tax losses as a result of the allowable deductions associated with the investment. These losses are then used to offset taxable income from other income sources. The losses from the investment "shelter" a portion (or all) of the other sources of income from taxation. The taxpayer investing in such a shelter will have to pay a tax on the investment when it is sold. However, the deduction of losses from the shelter in tax years prior to the payment of tax on the gain presents a time value of money savings opportunity.

A taxpayer is allowed to take advantage of the provisions for deductions and losses to legitimately reduce taxable income (i.e., tax avoidance is legal). In the late 1960s and early 1970s, many high-income taxpayers made substantial investments in tax shelters to reduce their income from other sources. In a typical tax shelter, the taxpayer would invest an amount in the activity. In return, the taxpayer would be allowed to deduct a share of the losses generated by the activity on her or his individual return, reducing the tax paid on other forms of income such as salaries and investment income. The amount of the deduction provided by a tax shelter could vary from three to ten times the amount invested. For a $10,000 investment, the taxpayer could take loss deductions totaling $30,000 to $100,000. During this period, the highest marginal tax rate was 50 percent. Thus, a high marginal rate taxpayer making a $10,000 investment could be guaranteed a tax savings from the investment ranging from $15,000 to $50,000. Because of this return from saving taxes, taxpayers often made investments in tax shelters that had little or no hope of long-term economic success. The tax savings provided a high enough return that success of the venture was unimportant. Many tax shelters were activities that were not economically viable investments in the absence of the tax deductions.

In 1976, Congress reacted to this perceived abuse of tax shelters with several measures, including limitations on investment interest deductions (discussed in Chapter 8) and a set of at-risk rules to limit the amount of loss deductible. However, these limitations met with limited success, because promoters of tax shelters and their clever tax advisers found ways to work around them. As a result, offerings of publicly registered tax shelters doubled in the early 1980s.

In 1986, Congress took additional action against tax shelters by severely limiting the deductions on tax shelters through enactment of the passive activity loss rules. The basic passive loss rule disallows the deduction of current period passive losses against active and portfolio income sources (salaries, trade or business income, interest, dividends). These rules are in some cases unduly complex and in other cases have hindered investment in legitimate economic investments.

In the sections that follow, the at-risk rules, which limit the amount of any deductible loss to the amount that the taxpayer has at risk in the activity, are discussed first. Then the basic operation of the passive loss rules is presented and discussed to provide an understanding of how these important limitations on losses affect investments made by taxpayers.

Before proceeding, a few basic aspects of tax shelters should be clarified. First, many tax advantages that allow such activities to generate losses are the result of a conscious effort by Congress to attract investment capital to activities with a high national priority and/or a high degree of risk. The basic intent of the generous tax laws is to provide incentive to taxpayers to engage in activities that they ordinarily would reject because of either low returns or high risk.

A limited partnership has many tax and nontax advantages that make it a preferred vehicle for tax shelters. The flow-through of the income and deductions of a partnership to the owners allows investment by many individuals who have no actual involvement in the tax shelter's business activities. In addition, it is often possible to make special allocations of income and expense items, which allow the partnership to confer many of the special tax deductions on the tax shelter's investors. A partnership also can be structured to accept investors as limited partners, so that their maximum loss from the activity is the amount of their investment in the property. Finally, a partner's tax basis in the investment includes the partner's share of its outstanding liabilities. This can significantly increase the amount of loss that can be deducted by the partners under the at-risk rules.

The At-Risk Rules

Congress enacted the at-risk rules to disallow the deduction of artificial losses generated by tax-shelter investments. The intention of the **at-risk rules** is to limit loss deductions by individuals and closely held corporations on business and investment-related activities to the amount of the taxpayer's actual economic investment. This is done by limiting the current year's loss deduction to the amount that the taxpayer has at risk in the activity.[2] The computation of the amount at risk is presented in Exhibit 7–1.

A brief review of Exhibit 7–1 clarifies what it means to "be at risk." From the computation, the at-risk amount is equal to cash or other assets that have been contributed to the activity. In addition, any debts of the activity for which the taxpayer would be responsible if the activity could not pay them are also considered to be at risk. Thus, the amount at risk in an activity is the maximum amount of personal funds (assets) that could be lost if the activity failed.

▲ **EXAMPLE 8**   Jolene purchased a business for $200,000 by investing $20,000 of her own funds and borrowing $180,000 from State Bank. Jolene is personally liable for repayment of the loan to State Bank. What is Jolene's at-risk amount in the business?

Discussion: Jolene is at risk for $200,000. If the business is not successful, she stands to lose the $20,000 in cash she invested in the business and she would be liable for payment of the $180,000 loan. Thus, she can lose a maximum of $200,000 from her investment in the business.

The amount at risk is also adjusted for the taxpayer's share of the income (loss) from the activity and reduced by withdrawals from the activity. That is, when an activity has income that is taxed to the taxpayer, the income becomes subject to loss. Similarly, losses from the activity that are deducted by the taxpayer reduce the amount that the taxpayer has to lose. Any amounts that are withdrawn from the activity by the taxpayer are no longer subject to loss and reduce the amount at risk in the activity.

▲ **EXAMPLE 9**   During the first year that Jolene operated the business she purchased in example 8, she suffered a loss of $70,000. She also withdrew $40,000 from the business for her personal use. What is Jolene's at-risk amount in the business at the end of the first year of operation?

Discussion: Jolene has a sufficient amount at risk to enable her to deduct the loss from the business. Therefore, she *must* reduce her amount at risk by the $70,000 loss.

Items That Increase Amount at Risk:	
Cash invested by the taxpayer in the activity	$XXX
Adjusted basis of property contributed to the activity	XXX
Amounts borrowed for use in the activity for which the taxpayer is personally liable	XXX
Amounts borrowed for use in the activity for which the taxpayer has pledged property not used in the activity as security	XXX
The taxpayer's share of any income produced by the activity	XXX
Items That Decrease Amount at Risk:	
The taxpayer's share of any loss produced by the activity	(XXX)
Withdrawals of assets from the activity	(XXX)
Equals: The amount at risk in the activity	$XXX

▲ **Exhibit 7–1**

COMPUTATION OF AMOUNT AT RISK

In addition, the $40,000 withdrawn from the business is no longer at risk. Thus, her amount at risk has declined to $90,000 ($200,000 − $70,000 − $40,000) at the end of the first year of operation.

In many cases, a taxpayer's amount at risk in an activity is the same as the taxpayer's adjusted basis. A main difference between a taxpayer's adjusted basis in an activity and the amount at risk in an activity occurs when basis is financed by nonrecourse debt. A **nonrecourse debt** is a liability that is secured only by the underlying property; the borrower is not personally liable for the debt.

▲ **EXAMPLE 10**   Assume that Jolene purchases $40,000-worth of equipment by borrowing from Local Bank. Local Bank made the loan with the equipment as the security for the debt. Jolene is not personally liable for the debt. How are Jolene's basis and at-risk amount affected by the purchase of the equipment?

Discussion: Jolene obtains a basis of $40,000 in the equipment. However, because she is not personally liable for the debt incurred to finance the purchase, she is not at risk with respect to the debt. That is, if her business fails, she will not be personally liable for repayment of the debt. Therefore, her at-risk amount does not increase.

A major exception to the at-risk rules is made for nonrecourse financing of real estate operations. Before 1987, the at-risk rules did not apply to real estate projects. In 1986, the at-risk rules were extended to real estate operations to a limited extent. After 1987, nonrecourse financing of real estate is considered as at risk only if the financing is made on reasonably commercial terms. In most cases, this allows shelter activities to acquire real estate with nonrecourse financing, which is considered at risk by the investors in the shelter.

▲ **EXAMPLE 11**   Assume that in example 10 Jolene had purchased a building for $40,000 with nonrecourse financing. Would the $40,000 be at risk?

Discussion: As long as the financing is made on reasonably commercial terms, the nonrecourse financing of real estate is considered at risk. Therefore, Jolene's at-risk amount will increase by the $40,000 in nonrecourse debt used to acquire the building.

▲ **EXAMPLE 12**   Ruben invested $10,000 in the Gold Partnership and received a 10% interest in the partnership. Gold used $50,000 in cash paid in by investors to purchase an apartment building that cost $1,000,000. The remaining $950,000 of the cost of the building was financed by a nonrecourse loan from State Insurance Co. The loan was made on terms comparable to other real estate loans in the area. What is Ruben's at-risk amount in the Gold Partnership?

Discussion: Ruben's at-risk amount includes the $10,000 cash contribution and his share of the nonrecourse loan. His $95,000 share of the nonrecourse loan ($950,000 × 10%) is considered at risk, because the loan was used to purchase real estate and was made on reasonably commercial terms. Thus, Ruben's at-risk amount is $105,000 ($10,000 cash investment + $95,000 share of real estate debt).

Under the at-risk rules, taxpayers cannot deduct any losses in excess of the amount they have at risk in the activity. Any current period losses that are not deductible because they exceed the taxpayer's at-risk amount are carried forward to the next year and are deductible when the taxpayer has enough at risk to allow the deduction.[3]

▲ **EXAMPLE 13**   Return to the facts of example 12. Assume that the Gold Partnership had a loss of $800,000 in the first year of operation and a loss of $600,000 in the second year. How much of the loss can Ruben deduct in each of the first 2 years?

Discussion: Ruben's share of the year 1 loss is $80,000. Because his at-risk amount is $105,000, he can deduct the full $80,000. This will reduce his at-risk amount in the partnership to $25,000 ($105,000 − $80,000). His share of the year 2 loss is $60,000. However, he can deduct only the $25,000 he has at risk. The remaining $35,000 of the loss is carried forward to succeeding years until he has enough at risk to deduct the loss.

Although the loss is deductible per the at-risk rules, the passive activity rules still apply. That is, if Ruben's investment in the partnership is considered a passive activity, the $80,000 and $25,000 in losses allowed by the at-risk rules still are subject to restrictions under the passive loss rules.

Passive Activity Losses

Although the at-risk rules provide some measure of protection against the deduction of artificial losses created by tax shelters, Congress felt that the rules still allowed too much room for abuse and promoted investment in ventures based on the tax characteristics of the investment rather than their economic potential. In 1986, Congress enacted the **passive activity loss (PAL) rules,** effective for tax years after 1986. The basic intent of these rules is to disallow the deduction of losses from passive activities against other forms of income. Thus, passive activity losses cannot generally be used to shelter other sources of income. Even the basic operation of the passive loss rules can be extremely complex. The complexity of the rules increases as a taxpayer engages in more and more passive activities.

Passive Activity Definition.   A **passive activity** is defined as the conduct of any trade or business in which the taxpayer does not materially participate.[4] In general, to be a **material participant,** the taxpayer must be involved in the operations of the activity on a regular, continuous, and substantial basis. The purpose of the material participation standard is to limit the passive loss deductions of those taxpayers investing in tax shelters who do not participate in the operation of the business in any meaningful way. However, the definition provided by Congress caused severe problems. Consider the following:

▲ **EXAMPLE 14**   Patricia worked for 20 years to build up her business. During the last 10 years, she reorganized the business and took on 2 partners to help her manage it. Patricia retired this year and no longer is involved in the day-to-day operations of the business. In retirement, she will attend 1 or 2 meetings a year to discuss general strategy with her partners. She still maintains a 1/3 interest in the partnership. Is Patricia's partnership interest a passive activity?

Discussion: Patricia no longer participates in the operation of the business in a material, substantial, and continuous manner. Therefore, under the general definition of *material participation*, her partnership interest would be considered passive.

It is doubtful that Congress intended to subject the partnership interest in example 14 to the passive loss rules. In response to numerous other instances of perceived inequities in the definition of material participation, the IRS provided seven separate tests under which a taxpayer would be considered a material participant in an activity.[5] The basic test for **material participation** is that the individual (including the individual's spouse) participates in the activity for more than 500 hours per year. The remaining six tests are based on lower levels of participation, combined with other factors about the operation of the business, that would indicate material participation and special rules to take care of situations such as that in example 14. Because the majority of taxpayers would qualify under the 500-hour standard, this book does not discuss the remaining six tests in detail.

The determination of material participation under these tests is best left to a tax professional.

Before 1994, Congress defined two particular types of activities as always being passive and two types of activities as never being passive. Rental activities and limited partnership interests were always passive. Working interests in oil and gas deposits and certain low-income housing projects were and still are active and not subject to the passive loss rules.

However, beginning in 1994, taxpayers who are involved in real property as a trade or business are permitted, if they meet certain criteria, to treat rental real estate as an active activity. The criteria for and the definition of a *real property trade or business* are discussed later in the chapter. The new law has no effect on the treatment of limited partnerships—they still are always considered a passive activity.

RENTAL ACTIVITIES.   For purposes of the passive loss rules, a rental activity is always considered a passive activity, except for certain qualifying taxpayers. A **rental activity** is defined as one in which the payment received is primarily for the use of tangible property. Rentals that include significant services are not rental activities for the passive loss rules. The IRS has provided guidelines for determining when the provision of personal services is significant and does not constitute a rental activity for passive loss purposes.[6] Some of the more common forms of this type of rental include

Hotel rooms	Hospital rooms
Car rentals	Videocassette rentals
Clothing rentals	Golf course fees
Tool rentals	Automobiles rented by dealers
Cable television rentals	while repair work is done

Although this list is not all inclusive, it illustrates the basic intent—to exclude rental activities that also provide significant services from the passive loss rules. As long as the owner(s) of such activities meet the material participation standard, the activity is not considered passive. That is, even if the activity is not considered a rental activity, each owner of the activity still must meet the material participation standard in order for the activity to be considered active.

▲ **EXAMPLE 15**   Toby is the owner of a miniature golf course. Toby and his wife Eve are actively involved in the management of the business. Each devotes an average of 40 hours per week to working at the miniature golf course and performing other business functions (record keeping, bank deposits, etc.). Is the miniature golf course a passive activity for Toby and Eve?

Discussion: The activity is not a rental activity, because it provides significant personal services. Toby and Eve participate in the operation of the activity more than 500 hours per year, making them material participants in the activity. Therefore, the activity is not a passive activity.

Note that although the activity in example 15 is not a rental activity for purposes of the passive loss rules, Toby and Eve still must meet the material participation standard in order for their business to escape classification as a passive activity.

▲ **EXAMPLE 16**   Assume that in example 15 the miniature golf course is organized as a partnership. Upon forming the business, Toby and Eve did not have the necessary capital. They got their friend Alan to invest $20,000 in the business for a 1/3 interest in the partnership. Toby and Eve run the business. Alan does not have any responsibilities for operating the business. He merely receives his annual share of the partnership's income. Is the miniature golf course a passive activity for Alan?

Discussion: Although the activity is not considered a rental activity, Alan does not materially participate in the activity. Therefore, Alan's partnership interest is considered a passive activity.

   Note that the activity remains an active business interest for Toby and Eve. That is, each taxpayer involved in the activity is evaluated separately. This is a result of the entity concept.

Given all the exceptions, what is a rental activity for purposes of the passive loss rules? The more common forms of passive activity rentals involve the rental of real property. This would include apartment buildings, rental houses, office building rentals, warehouse rentals, factory rentals, and so on. That is, these activities are all rentals of real property that include no significant provision of personal services.

▲ **EXAMPLE 17**   Both Alf and Bart are lawyers. The two decide to purchase an apartment building in 1995 at a cost of $600,000. They each provide half of the $60,000 down payment. Both are busy practicing law, so they hire Chester to manage the building. Chester has full control over all management decisions (getting tenants, collecting rent, taking care of repairs). Alf and Bart agree to split the profits evenly after paying Chester's salary of $50,000. Is the building a passive activity for Alf and Bart?

Discussion: The apartment building is a rental activity for passive loss purposes. It is a rental of tangible property with no significant services provided. Thus, it is a passive activity. This is true for both Alf and Bart.

LIMITED PARTNERSHIP INTERESTS.   A limited partnership interest is generally considered passive. In a **limited partnership,** one general partner organizes the partnership and is usually responsible for the day-to-day operation of its business. Limited partners are investors who purchase their interest to provide capital for the partnership. Limited partners generally have no responsibilities for operating the partnership. They merely invest money and receive their share of partnership income (loss). The limited partnership is the most popular tax-shelter vehicle. As a conduit entity, investors in a limited partnership are able to obtain a share of the losses of the tax shelter without any involvement in its operation. Because Congress has specified that limited partnership interests are passive, the degree of participation by a limited partner or the type of activity does not change the passive activity classification. To determine whether the general partner's interest is passive or active, evaluate the general partner's participation by using the rules for all taxpayers.

▲ **EXAMPLE 18**   Jonah purchased a limited partnership interest for $40,000. Monica is the general partner, oversees the operation of the partnership, and is responsible for its day-to-day operations. Is the activity passive for Jonah? for Monica?

Discussion: Because Jonah is a limited partner, the activity is passive for him. Monica is a general partner and must be evaluated according to the rules for all taxpayers to determine whether the activity is passive for her. She would appear to meet the material participation standard, making her interest active and not subject to the passive loss rules.

WORKING INTEREST IN OIL AND GAS.   A **working interest in an oil and gas deposit** is always considered an active business for purposes of the passive activity rules. A working interest is an outright ownership interest held by the operator of the property. As such, a working interest has unlimited liability for all debts of the operation and is responsible for the costs of operating the property. Royalty interests in the property held by individuals who are not active in its operation are not considered working interests. However, royalty interests in an oil and gas operation would not be passive. They are considered portfolio income, because they share only revenue from the deposit, not expenses from the operation of the oil and gas deposit.

> ▲ **EXAMPLE 19**   Whitney is the sole proprietor of an oil and gas drilling company. Brooke owns the mineral rights to some land on which Whitney would like to drill for oil. They enter into an agreement whereby Whitney can drill on Brooke's land; Whitney pays Brooke $2,000 for the right to drill and 1/12 of the value of any oil and gas produced from the well. Whitney is responsible for the payment of all expenses of the operation and retains the remaining value of the oil and gas produced. Is this a passive activity for either Whitney or Brooke?
>
> *Discussion:* Because Whitney is the operator of the oil and gas deposit, her interest is a working interest and is always active. Although Brooke is not at all involved in the operation of the deposit, her royalty interest would not be passive, because she does not share expenses of the operation. The royalties she receives would be portfolio income.

LOW-INCOME HOUSING PROJECTS.   Most low-income housing projects have been classified as active interests. Although such projects usually constitute rental activities (and thus are passive), Congress has exempted investment in these projects from the passive loss rules to encourage the building of low-income housing (a social goal). This allows investors to seek shelter from taxes in low-income housing projects.

Types of Income.   Under the passive activity loss rules, all income must be classified as active, passive, or portfolio income. Active and passive income result from activities considered trades or businesses. Portfolio income is income from investments. The first step is to segregate portfolio income from active (i.e., activity-based) income.

PORTFOLIO INCOME.   **Portfolio income** consists of unearned income from dividends, interest, royalties, annuities, and other assets held as investments. Portfolio income also includes income from the sale of the asset creating the portfolio income. The main characteristic of portfolio income is that such investments almost always produce positive income while the investment is held. In portfolio activities, the investor only receives income from the activity and does not share in the expenses related to the activity. Any losses on portfolio investments typically occur at the point of sale.

ACTIVE INCOME.   **Active income** is income from a trade or business in which the taxpayer materially participates. This category includes wages and salaries as well as income from a trade or business in which the taxpayer materially participates. Working interests in oil and gas deposits and certain low-income housing projects are always considered active income. As with portfolio income, this category typically produces income. However, such activities may produce losses that are not subject to the passive loss rules (the NOL rules would apply).

▲ **EXAMPLE 20**   Hai is the sole proprietor of Sno-Cone Flavors, a distributor of snow cone–making accessories. Hai has only 1 employee and works full time operating the business. During the current year, the business suffered a loss of $11,000. Is this a passive activity for Hai?

Discussion: Because Hai is a material participant in the business, it is classified as an active interest. Although the business produces a loss, the loss is not subject to the passive loss rules. The loss from the sole proprietorship flows through to Hai's individual return where it is deductible against Hai's other active and portfolio income.

▲ **EXAMPLE 21**   Willa is a mechanic at Merchant Marine Co. where she receives a salary of $30,000 per year. At nights and on weekends, Willa does repair work from her garage. For the current year, Willa's repair business showed a loss of $2,500. Are these passive activities for Willa?

Discussion: Willa's job at Merchant Marine produces active income. Assuming the repair work business is not a hobby, it also is considered active. Thus, Willa can deduct the loss from the repair work business on her individual return, reducing the tax she would have paid on her salary income.

PASSIVE INCOME.   As previously defined, *passive income* is income from a trade or business in which the taxpayer does not materially participate. Rental activities are usually passive, and limited partnership interests are always passive activities. Passive activities may produce either income or loss, but most passive activities are loss activities.

Taxpayers Subject to the Limits.   All noncorporate taxable entities (individuals, estates, trusts) are subject to the passive loss rules. Conduit entities are not directly affected by these limits, because their results are passed through and taxed to the owners. Note that in Figure 7–2 a conduit entity is usually a material participant in the operation of the business. However, the loss from the conduit flows through to the owners of the entity. Each owner must then determine whether he or she materially participates in the operation of the business in order to determine whether an NOL deduction is allowed or if his or her interest in the business is a passive activity. Thus, conduit entities must report the results of their operations to owners so that the owners may apply the applicable rules for the deduction of losses.

▲ **EXAMPLE 22**   Harnads Department Store is organized as an S corporation and is owned equally by Able, Baker, and Charlene. During the current year, Harnads had a loss from operations. How does the loss affect Harnads, Able, Baker, and Charlene?

Discussion: Harnads is a conduit entity, and the loss is passed through to Able, Baker, and Charlene. Able, Baker, and Charlene each must determine whether his or her participation in the operation of Harnads is material. If any (or all) of them do materially participate, they may deduct their share of the Harnads loss on their individual tax returns. Any who do not materially participate in the operation of Harnads are subject to the passive activity loss rules.

Two classes of corporate taxpayers are not subject to the passive loss limitations:

1. Publicly held corporations.
2. Closely held corporations, which are allowed to offset net passive losses against active income of the business. However, they cannot use passive losses to offset portfolio income.

For passive loss purposes, a corporation is a **closely held corporation** if five or fewer shareholders own 50 percent or more of the stock in the corporation during the last half of the tax year. This exception for closely held corporations provides owners of small businesses with an opportunity to avoid the passive limits by incorporating their businesses. This tax-planning mechanism is discussed and illustrated in Chapter 9.

General Rule for Passive Activities.   The purpose of the passive activity rules is to deny current loss deductions for tax-shelter activities. The general rule for implementing this intent is that passive losses may only be deducted to the extent of passive income. Under the general rule, passive losses cannot be deducted against income from portfolio or active income.

▲ **EXAMPLE 23**   Harriet has a taxable income of $100,000 in 1996 from portfolio and active income sources. In addition, she owns two passive activities. Passive activity 1 (PA1) has a net loss of $20,000 and passive activity 2 (PA2) has a net income of $2,000 in 1996. What is the effect of the two passive activities on Harriet's 1996 income?

Discussion: The $2,000 of income from PA2 is included in gross income. Under the passive activity loss rules, only $2,000 of the loss from PA1 is deductible in 1996. The net $18,000 ($20,000 − $2,000) passive loss in 1996 is not deductible against Harriet's $100,000 of taxable income from portfolio and active income sources. In essence, passive losses are only deductible up to the amount of passive income.

Any passive activity loss that is not deductible in the current year is a **suspended loss.** A suspended loss is not permanently disallowed. Suspended losses are carried forward and may be deducted against passive income in subsequent years.

▲ **EXAMPLE 24**   Assume that Harriet, in example 23, purchases passive activity 3 (PA3) in 1997. The results of the three passive activities in 1997 are as follows:

PA1	($10,000)
PA2	3,000
PA3	12,000

What is the effect of the passive activities on Harriet's 1997 taxable income?

Discussion: Harriet's net passive loss of $18,000 from 1996 is suspended and carried forward for deduction against 1997 passive income sources:

	1996	1997
PA1	$(20,000)	$(10,000)
PA2	2,000	3,000
PA3		12,000
1996 suspended loss	$(18,000) ⟶	(18,000)
1997 suspended loss		$(13,000)

As you can see, the suspension and carryforward of the 1996 net passive loss result in Harriet's being able to deduct $5,000 of the 1996 suspended loss against 1997 passive income. The $15,000 in income from PA2 and PA3 is included in Harriet's gross income. However, it would be offset by the $15,000 loss from PA1, leaving her 1997 taxable income unchanged. The $13,000 net passive loss is carried forward to 1998.

Dispositions of Passive Activities.   When a taxpayer disposes of a passive activity in a taxable transaction, any suspended loss in the activity must be accounted for. Deductions of suspended losses are allowed when passive activities are sold and when they are disposed of because the taxpayer has died.[7] However, disposition of a passive activity by gift does not result in a deduction. In each disposition case, you must calculate the amount of suspended passive loss attributable to the activity being sold in order to determine the proper deduction. In the previous examples, this was not a problem, because the taxpayer had only one activity with a loss. Thus, all suspended loss was attributable to the one activity. However, if the taxpayer owns more than one passive activity that creates losses, the total suspended loss for the period must be allocated among the loss activities in order to keep track of the amount of suspended loss attributable to each activity. The allocation of suspended losses is made on the basis of the relative loss of each activity; each loss activity is deemed to contribute proportionately to the total amount of suspended loss.

▲ **EXAMPLE 25** Continuing with Harriet's passive activities from example 24, assume that the three passive activities have the following results for 1998:

PA1	$(4,000)
PA2	2,000
PA3	(1,000)
1997 suspended loss	$(3,000)

How much of the $3,000 suspended loss is attributed to PA1? PA3?

Discussion: The $3,000 in suspended loss is allocated proportionately to the two loss activities based on their relative loss. That is, the two activities produce a total loss of $5,000 during the period. Therefore, PA1 is responsible for 4/5 ($4,000 of the total $5,000 loss), and PA3 is responsible for 1/5 ($1,000 of the total $5,000 loss). Based on this, $2,400 (4/5 × $3,000) of the suspended loss is attributed to PA1, and $600 (1/5 × $3,000) is attributed to PA3. At this point, the total suspended passive loss on PA1 is $15,400 ($13,000 from 1996 + $2,400 from 1998). PA3 has a total suspended loss of $600.

DISPOSITION BY SALE.   When an entire interest in a passive activity is sold in a taxable transaction, any suspended loss on the activity is deductible in the year of sale against portfolio and active income.

▲ **EXAMPLE 26** Return to example 25. Assume that Harriet sells PA1 on January 2, 1999, for $42,000. Her basis in PA1 is $36,000. What is the effect of the sale of PA1 on Harriet's 1999 taxable income?

Discussion: Harriet's gain of $6,000 ($42,000 − $36,000) on the sale of PA1 is included in her gross income for 1999. The suspended loss of $15,400 is deductible against active and portfolio income sources. Thus, the net effect of the sale is a reduction in her taxable income of $9,400 ($6,000 − $15,400).

From example 26, you can see that the passive activity loss rules do not permanently disallow deductions of losses. Rather, they operate as a deferral mechanism. During the period in which the passive activity is held, the entire economic loss is deductible. To see this, look at Harriet's actual losses from PA1 versus her actual loss deductions:

	1996	1997	1998	1999	Total
Actual loss	$(20,000)	$(10,000)	$(4,000)		$(34,000)
Amount deducted	$ (2,000)	$(15,000)	$(1,600)	$(15,400)	$(34,000)

One final note of caution on dispositions by sale: The gain or loss on the sale of the activity generally is a capital gain or a capital loss. Recall from Chapter 3 that gains and losses from the sale of capital assets are treated differently than other types of gains and losses. Briefly, net capital gains are taxed at a maximum rate of 28 percent, and net capital losses are limited to a deduction of $3,000 per year. Thus, in example 26, the $6,000 capital gain Harriet had on the sale of PA1 would be subject to a maximum tax rate of 28 percent.

▲ **EXAMPLE 27**   Assume the same facts as in example 26, except that Harriet sells PA1 for only $30,000, resulting in a loss of $6,000. What is the effect on Harriet's taxable income?

Discussion: Harriet still is allowed the full deduction of the $15,400 suspended loss. However, the $6,000 loss on the sale of PA1 is a capital loss and subject to the limitations on capital losses. If this is Harriet's only capital asset sale during 1999, she is allowed to deduct only $3,000 of the capital loss in 1999, with the remaining loss carried forward to the year 2000.

DISPOSITION UPON DEATH.   When a taxpayer dies while holding passive activities, the passive activities become part of the estate and subject to the estate tax. For estate tax purposes, all assets are valued at the fair market value at the date of death. Heirs who receive property from an estate take as their basis the fair market value of the property at the date of death (the estate tax valuation). The result of this valuation process is that any unrealized gain on an asset is not subject to an income tax.

▲ **EXAMPLE 28**   Felipe died and left a piece of land to his son. Felipe had paid $12,000 for the land, which was worth $23,000 at the date of his death. Upon receiving the land, Felipe's son immediately sold it for $23,000. What are the income tax consequences of the sale of the land?

Discussion: The land is valued at $23,000 for estate tax purposes. The $23,000 estate tax valuation becomes the son's basis in the land. Therefore, the son has neither gain nor loss on the sale of the land. The $9,000 in unrealized gain on the land was not subject to the income tax, because the fair market value of the land was assigned for estate tax purposes, with a corresponding increase in basis to fair market value for the son.

Because the unrealized gains on property passing through an estate escape taxation, the passive loss rules limit the amount of the deduction for suspended losses on property held at death to the amount of the suspended loss in excess of any unrealized gain on the activity. The effect of this provision is to provide the same net loss deduction the decedent taxpayer would have received had that person sold the property.

▲ **EXAMPLE 29**   Assume the same facts as in example 26, except that Harriet dies on January 2, 1999. PA1 has a fair market value of $42,000 and an adjusted basis of $36,000 as of that date. The suspended loss at that date is $15,400. How much of the suspended loss can be deducted on Harriet's 1999 income tax return?

Discussion: If Harriet had sold PA1, she would have had a gain of $6,000 on the sale, and the $15,400 in suspended loss would have been deductible. This results in a net deduction of $9,400. Because she died, the $6,000 in gain is never subject to income tax. Therefore, the suspended loss deduction is limited to the $9,400 by which she would have been able to reduce her income had the property been sold. That is, $9,400 is the amount of suspended loss in excess of the unrealized gain on PA1.

If a passive activity with a suspended loss has a basis greater than its fair market value (i.e., a loss property) at death, no deduction of the suspended loss is allowed. This is the unfortunate result of the statutory language that allows deductions only for the excess of suspended losses over unrealized gains. Under the legislative grace concept, the interpretation of the language is that because the statute is silent as to unrealized losses, no suspended loss deductions are allowed.

▲ **EXAMPLE 30**   Assume the same facts as in example 26, except that Harriet dies on January 2, 1999. PA1 has a fair market value of $30,000 and an adjusted basis of $36,000 as of that date. The suspended loss at that date is $15,400. How much of the suspended loss can be deducted on Harriet's 1999 income tax return?

Discussion: Because PA1 has an unrealized loss of $6,000 as of the date of death, there is no excess of suspended loss over unrealized gain. Therefore, no suspended loss deduction is allowed on Harriet's 1999 income tax return.

DISPOSITION BY GIFT.   When a taxpayer makes a **gift** of property to another taxpayer, there is no income tax effect for either party. The donor does not have to recognize an unrealized gain on the property, and the donee does not have income from the receipt of the gift. The donor's basis becomes the donee's basis. This is called a *carryover basis* and is necessary to ensure that any unrealized gains on the gift property do not go untaxed.

▲ **EXAMPLE 31**   John owned property with a basis of $3,000 and a fair market value of $10,000. John gave the property to his daughter Nancy as a gift. Nancy immediately sold the property for $10,000. What are the tax effects of the gift and subsequent sale?

Discussion: The receipt of the gift is not a taxable event for either John or Nancy. Nancy takes John's basis in the property. Her gain on the sale is $7,000 ($10,000 − $3,000). This treatment ensures that unrealized gains on gift property do not escape income taxation.

Because making a gift is not a taxable event for the donor, the person who receives a gift cannot take a deduction for a suspended loss. Instead, the suspended loss is added to the basis of the donee. The effect of this treatment is to recognize that the donor does not realize (or recognize) a gain on the disposition of a gift property. Because the donor does not recognize the gain, the donor cannot take an offsetting suspended loss deduction. It is carried through to the donee and remains unrealized until the donee disposes of the property.

▲ **EXAMPLE 32**   Assume that in example 31 the property John gave to Nancy was a passive activity that had a suspended loss of $20,000 at the date of the gift. What is the tax effect of the gift for John and Nancy?

Discussion: The gift has no tax effect for either party. Because John has given the unrealized gain to Nancy (i.e., John will never be taxed on the gain), he is not allowed any deductions for the suspended loss. The suspended loss becomes part of Nancy's basis in the asset, $23,000 ($3,000 + $20,000).

   This treatment prevents a taxpayer from passing suspended losses to a related taxpayer who could benefit from the suspended passive losses. Nancy is not allowed to deduct John's suspended loss against any passive income she may have. Because the suspended loss is added to the basis of the donee, the only way Nancy can benefit from the suspended loss is by selling the passive activity.

Exceptions for Rental Real Estate.   The tax law permits a taxpayer to treat rental real estate in which the taxpayer materially participates as an active activity and to use any losses to offset active and portfolio income. Before 1994, rental real estate was always considered passive and only taxpayers who met certain tests

were permitted to use losses from rental real estate activities to offset active and portfolio income. The tax law allows two exceptions, the material participation exception and the active participation exception, that permit a taxpayer to use losses from rental property to offset active and portfolio income (see Figure 7–3).

A taxpayer qualifies under the **material participation exception** if

- More than 50 percent of the taxpayer's total personal services (work) are in real property trades or businesses in which the taxpayer materially participates.
- The taxpayer performs more than 750 hours a year of service in real property trades or businesses in which the taxpayer materially participates.
- The taxpayer materially participates in the rental activity.[8]

▲ **Figure 7–3**

DETERMINING WHETHER
RENTAL PROPERTY IS
ACTIVE OR PASSIVE

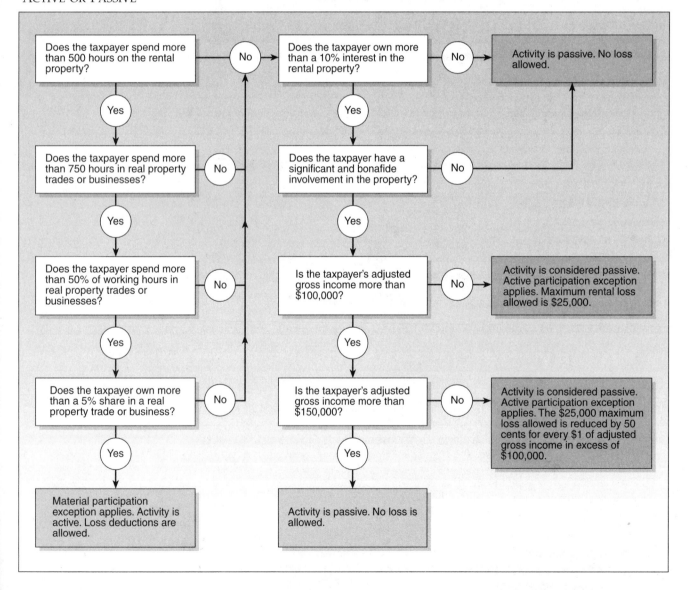

As discussed earlier in this chapter, to materially participate in an activity, the taxpayer generally must spend more than 500 hours a year working in that activity. A **real property trade or business** is any real property development, redevelopment, construction, acquisition, conversion, rental operation, management, leasing, or brokerage trade or business. In addition, an individual who is an employee of a business engaged in a real property trade or business qualifies for this exception only if the employee has an ownership interest in the business that is greater than 5 percent.

▲ **EXAMPLE 33**   Return to the facts of example 17. In 1996, Bart decides to quit practicing law and take Chester's place as the manager of the building. Bart devotes all his personal services, 2,000 hours, to managing the apartments (getting tenants, collecting rent, taking care of repairs, etc.). Alf continues to work as a lawyer. Is the apartment building a passive activity for either of them?

Discussion: In 1995, the rental activity is passive for both Alf and Bart. Under the material participation exception for rental real estate, Bart can treat the rental property as an active activity in 1996. More than 50% of his personal services are devoted to working in a real property trade or business in which he materially participates, the time he devotes to the real property trade or business is more than 750 hours, and he materially participates in the rental activity (spends more than 500 hours working in the activity). The rental property remains passive for Alf, because he fails to meet any of the tests. In fact, Alf does not even materially participate in the rental activity. NOTE: Each individual in the activity is evaluated separately, and the individual must meet all three tests to qualify a rental as an active activity.

▲ **EXAMPLE 34**   Assume the same facts as example 33, except that Alf is a real estate broker employed by a corporation in which he owns a 20% interest. He spends 1,800 hours a year as a broker and 200 hours a year helping Bart to manage the apartment building.

Discussion: Again, Bart is permitted to treat the rental activity as active only if he meets the tests described earlier. Although Alf spends more than 50% of his working hours (1,800 hours ÷ 2,000 hours) in a real property trade or business in which he materially participates and the number of hours he spends in that activity is greater than 750, he fails to materially participate in the rental real estate activity. NOTE: If Alf had spent more than 500 hours helping Bart to manage the apartment complex, he would have been able to treat the rental activity as active.

▲ **EXAMPLE 35**   Assume the same facts as example 33, except that Alf spends 525 hours as a real estate broker in a business in which he owns a 10% interest, 550 hours helping Bart to manage the apartments, and 1,200 hours practicing law.

Discussion: Although Bart continues to be entitled to consider the rental as an active activity, Alf must treat the rental property as a passive activity. Alf passes the 750-hour requirement, because he spends 1,075 hours working in a real property trade or business in which he materially participates and he materially participates in the rental activity. However, he spends less than 50% of his personal service (1,075 hours ÷ 2,275 hours) in real property trades or businesses. NOTE: If Alf spends only 1,000 hours practicing law, he passes the 50% test (1,075 hours ÷ 2,075) and thus may treat the rental activity as active.

For taxpayers who own rental real estate but who do not meet the material participation test, the tax law allows active participants in rental real estate to deduct losses as great as $25,000 per year against portfolio and active sources of income (see Figure 7–3). An **active participant** must own at least a 10-percent interest in the activity and have significant and bonafide involvement in it. *Significant and bonafide involvement* is a less stringent standard than the material participation standard discussed earlier. It requires that the individual be involved in some significant aspect of the rental (i.e., arranging financing, collecting rents, arranging for repairs and maintenance, keeping the activities records, etc.). In most cases, taxpayers eligible for this exception easily meet the significant involvement standard.

This exception, known as the **active participation exception,** is geared to individuals of more moderate means, because the $25,000 annual deduction amount is phased out when the individual's adjusted gross income exceeds $100,000. For every dollar of adjusted gross income in excess of $100,000, the taxpayer loses 50 cents of the $25,000 deduction. Thus, when adjusted gross income reaches $150,000 [($150,000 − $100,000) × $0.50 = $25,000], the deduction is no longer available.

> ▲ **EXAMPLE 36**   Rory is a mechanic who owns an apartment building that has a net rental loss of $22,000 during the current year. Rory's adjusted gross income is $120,000. If Rory owns no other passive activities, how much of the rental loss can he deduct?
>
> *Discussion:*   Because the property is rental real estate, it always is considered a passive activity unless one of the rental real estate exceptions applies. Rory owns 100% of the property, and it is assumed that he is involved in the rental in some significant way. The special deduction for rental real estate is $25,000. However, because Rory's adjusted gross income is in excess of $100,000, he must reduce the allowable deduction by $10,000 [($120,000 − $100,000) × $0.50] to $15,000. Rory can deduct $15,000 of the rental loss against his $120,000 of adjusted gross income. The remaining $7,000 is suspended and treated like any other passive loss.

Any amount not deductible in one year is suspended as a passive loss and can be deducted in a subsequent year, either against passive income or under a subsequent year's $25,000 rental real estate limit.

> ▲ **EXAMPLE 37**   Return to example 36. Assume that in the following year, Rory's rental property has a $20,000 loss and that his adjusted gross income is $90,000. How much of a rental real estate loss deduction is Rory allowed?
>
> *Discussion:*   Because his adjusted gross income is less than $100,000, there is no phase-out of the $25,000 rental real estate deduction. However, Rory's current loss of $20,000 and his suspended loss of $7,000 exceed the $25,000 rental real estate limitation. Therefore, he is able to deduct only $25,000 under the special annual deduction, and the remaining $2,000 of suspended loss is carried forward.

TRANSACTION LOSSES

A **transaction loss** results from a single disposition of property. Most transaction losses are the result of selling a property at less than its basis (i.e., incomplete capital recovery). However, other forms of disposition, such as exchanges of assets and involuntary conversions (casualties and thefts), may also produce losses.

The allowance of deductions for losses follows the same line of reasoning as for the allowance of deductions. That is, the loss must be categorized according to the activity producing the loss:

1. Trade or business losses
2. Investment-related losses
3. Personal use losses

Once categorized, the rules for deductibility of losses within each category are applied to determine the amount of deductible loss. These treatments are depicted in Figure 7–4. In general, transaction losses must have a business purpose to be deductible. Casualty losses and theft losses are the only loss deductions allowed for personal use losses.[9] If the loss is incurred in a trade or business, the taxpayer generally is allowed to take a **trade or business loss.** However, losses on sales to related parties are never allowed, regardless of their relation to a trade or business or investment activity. **Investment-related losses** involve dispositions of capital assets. Net capital loss deductions are limited for both individuals and corporations. The most important aspects of each of the three categories of transaction losses are discussed in turn.

Trade or Business Losses

In general, all transaction losses incurred in a trade or business are deductible. With one major exception, these losses are treated as ordinary losses in the period they are incurred and are deducted without limit against the income from the trade or business.[10] For an individual, a trade or business loss is deductible as a deduction for adjusted gross income.[11] An exception to this rule is for losses on exchanges of business property that must be deferred to a future period. This exception is covered in Chapter 13. The calculation of a transaction loss is straightforward—a loss results when the asset's basis is greater than the amount realized from the disposition.[12] One area that needs extra attention is the determination of the amount of loss from casualties and thefts.

Business Casualty and Theft Losses.   A **casualty** is the result of some sudden, unexpected, and/or unusual event.[13] In addition to being sudden and unexpected, actual physical damage to property must occur in order to have a **casualty loss.**[14] If there is no physical damage to property, but the property declines in value because of a sudden and unexpected event, the loss in value is not considered a casualty. The most common types of casualties include damage from fire, storms, earthquakes, and accidents. Losses that occur gradually over time do not constitute casualties. Examples of losses that are not casualties would include damage from termites, losses from insects or disease, and loss in value of land because of wind erosion.[15]

A **theft** is similar to a casualty in that it must be sudden and unexpected. A theft may occur as a result of a robbery, larceny, or an embezzlement.[16] Misplacing or losing items does not constitute a theft. The damage caused by a theft is that the entire property is lost. As such, **theft losses** are treated in the same manner as casualty losses.

When a casualty occurs, one of two things can happen. The property may be fully destroyed and have no value, or it may be partially destroyed and have some remaining value. The calculation of the amount of loss depends on whether the property was fully or partially destroyed in the casualty.[17] A theft is treated as property fully destroyed (all value lost).

BUSINESS PROPERTY FULLY DESTROYED.   When a business property is fully destroyed (or stolen), the taxpayer's entire investment in the property has been

▲ **Figure 7–4**

Treatment of
Transaction Losses

lost. The capital recovery concept allows a taxpayer to fully recover the investment in business property. The measure of a taxpayer's investment in a property is its basis. Therefore, the measure of a **business casualty loss** for fully destroyed business property is the property's basis.

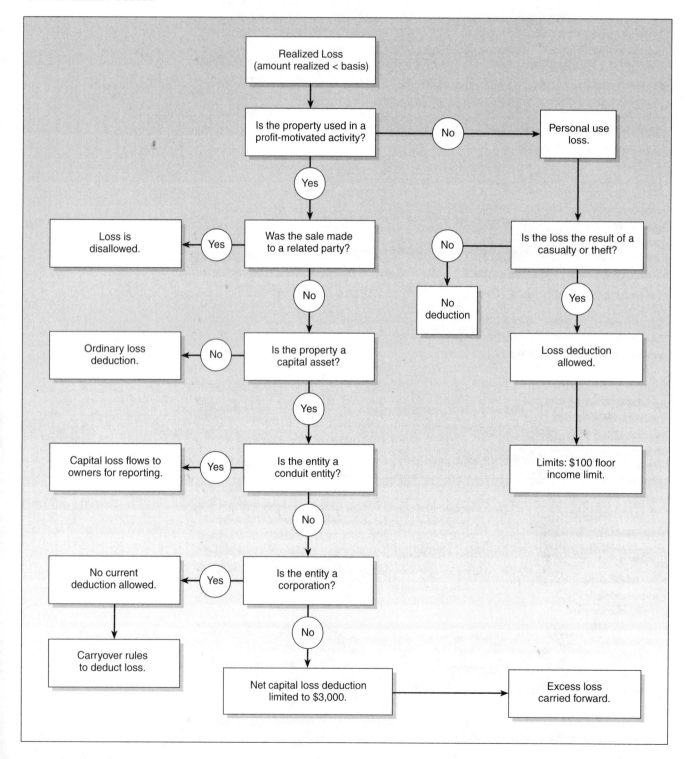

▲ **EXAMPLE 38**   A driver for Portable Phone Providers (PPP) was involved in an accident that totally destroyed one of the company's vans. The van had been purchased for $26,000, and depreciation taken to date on the van was $8,000. What is the measure of the loss on the van?

Discussion: Because the van was totally destroyed in the accident, the measure of the loss is the unrecovered investment in the van, its basis. Although the van cost $26,000, the company has recovered $8,000 of the cost through depreciation deductions. The unrecovered portion, $18,000 ($26,000 − $8,000) is the amount of the investment lost.

Most business assets are covered by insurance. Any amounts received from insurance on property subject to a casualty are a capital recovery. Thus, the amount of the loss must be reduced by any insurance proceeds received from the casualty.

▲ **EXAMPLE 39**   Assume that in example 38 PPP's van was covered by insurance and that PPP received $15,000 from the insurance company for the accident. What is PPP's casualty loss?

Discussion: PPP's loss is $3,000. Of the $18,000 of basis that was unrecovered at the date of the casualty, $15,000 was recovered from the insurance company. NOTE: When insurance proceeds are received, the loss is calculated as the difference between the amount realized (insurance proceeds) and the basis. Thus, the calculation of a casualty loss for business property fully destroyed is identical to the calculation of a loss from the sale of a property.

At this point, we should note that all casualties do not result in losses. That is, if the insurance proceeds received from a casualty exceed the adjusted basis of the property, the result of the casualty would be a **casualty gain.**

▲ **EXAMPLE 40**   Assume that in example 39 PPP received $20,000 for the destruction of its van. What is PPP's casualty gain (loss)?

Discussion: PPP has a gain of $2,000 ($20,000 − $18,000) from the casualty. PPP has recovered more than its remaining investment in the van. Therefore, under the capital recovery concept, PPP has a gain from the receipt of insurance proceeds in excess of adjusted basis.

Gains from business casualties are subject to a special election under which a casualty gain may be deferred. Because the focus of this chapter is on losses, the discussion of this election is deferred until Chapter 13.

BUSINESS PROPERTY PARTIALLY DESTROYED.   When a casualty occurs and property is not totally destroyed, an estimate of the amount lost because of the casualty must be made. The amount of the real loss from a partial destruction is the decrease in the taxpayer's wealth resulting from the casualty. This can be measured by the decline in the market value of the property that results from the casualty. The decline in the value of the property is

The fair market value of the property *before* the casualty

Less: The fair market value of the property *after* the casualty

Equals: The decline in value because of the casualty

In most cases, this is an adequate measurement of the loss the taxpayer has incurred as a result of the casualty. However, under the capital recovery concept, the maximum amount that can be recovered on any property is the amount invested in the property—its basis. Thus, a loss deduction because of a casualty can never exceed the property's basis. This leads to the following rule for measuring a loss on partially destroyed business property:

The measure of the loss is equal to the lesser of

■ The decline in the value of the property

or

■ The adjusted basis of the property

The purpose of this measurement rule is to ensure that the amount of the loss deducted does not exceed the amount of unrecovered investment in the property.

▲ **EXAMPLE 41**   This year, a hurricane damaged a warehouse used by Sugar Exporters, Inc., (SEI) in its exporting operation. SEI had paid $200,000 for the warehouse and had taken $80,000 in depreciation before the hurricane. Appraisals indicated that the warehouse was worth $300,000 before the hurricane. In its damaged state, the warehouse could be sold for only $100,000. What is the amount of loss SEI suffered on the warehouse because of the hurricane?

Discussion: The value of the warehouse declined $200,000 ($300,000 − $100,000) because of the hurricane damage. However, SEI's unrecovered investment in the warehouse is $120,000 ($200,000 − $80,000).

SEI's loss is the lesser of the decline in value because of the hurricane, $200,000, or its basis in the warehouse, $120,000. In this case, the maximum amount that SEI can recover through a loss deduction is the $120,000 basis.

As with fully destroyed business property, the calculated loss must be reduced by any insurance proceeds received because of the casualty.

▲ **EXAMPLE 42**   Assume that in example 41 SEI's warehouse was covered by insurance. SEI received $100,000 from the insurance company for the hurricane damage. What is SEI's casualty loss?

Discussion: The $120,000 loss must be reduced by the $100,000 of insurance proceeds. SEI's deductible loss is $20,000 ($120,000 − $100,000).

In many instances, the measurement of the decline in the value of a property that results from a casualty poses formidable problems. That is, by definition a casualty is the result of a sudden and unexpected event. This makes it unlikely that the taxpayer had the foresight to have the property appraised shortly before the casualty. After a property has been damaged, assessing its true condition before being damaged is often difficult. Thus, the estimate of the decline in value of the property because of the casualty is difficult to obtain. For this reason, the IRS allows the taxpayer to use the cost of repairing the property to estimate the decline in value of the property.

▲ **EXAMPLE 43**   Mammoth Co. operates ski resorts throughout the western United States. In February, an avalanche at one of its resorts damaged a ski lift. The lift had cost $450,000, and Mammoth had taken depreciation of $200,000 before the casualty. It cost $160,000 to have the lift repaired. What is the amount of Mammoth's loss because of the avalanche?

Discussion: Because of the difficulty of determining the value of the ski lift before the casualty (and after the casualty), the cost of repairing the lift can be used to estimate the decline in value because of the damage. This is a partial destruction of business property, and the amount of the loss is measured by the lesser of the decline in value, $160,000, or the basis of the ski lift, $250,000 ($450,000 − $200,000). In this case, the $160,000 cost of repairing the lift is lower than the basis and is used to measure the loss. Any insurance proceeds Mammoth received would reduce the amount of the loss that is deductible.

Investment-Related Losses

Losses on transactions related to investment activities are generally allowed as deductions. However, in contrast to trade or business losses, which are always deductible in full, the amount of the current period deduction for an investment-related loss may be limited. This occurs because investment-related assets are capital assets. A **capital asset** is defined as any asset that is not a receivable, an inventory item, depreciable or real property used in a trade or business, or certain intangible assets such as copyrights.[18] Note that the items that are not capital assets are primarily assets used in a trade or business. Thus, assets that are not used in a trade or business are capital assets. This would include both investment assets and personal use assets. There are limits on the amount of loss from the sale of capital assets that is deductible in any one tax year. In addition, the tax law provides several other significant provisions related to losses on the sale of capital assets.

Capital Losses.   When a taxpayer suffers losses on the disposition of capital assets, the tax law provides a procedure for netting these losses against any gains from capital asset dispositions during the year. As discussed in Chapter 3, the purpose of this netting procedure is to produce a single position for net capital asset transactions for the entire year. The net transaction position can be either a gain or a loss. An overview of the netting procedure was presented in Chapter 3. More specific details of the treatment of capital gains and losses are covered in Chapter 12. At this juncture, the critical aspect is the treatment of net capital losses. A **net capital loss** occurs when a taxpayer's total capital losses exceed the taxpayer's total capital gains for a tax year. The treatment of a net capital loss for an individual is different than the treatment for a corporation.[19]

NET CAPITAL LOSSES OF INDIVIDUALS.   An individual taxpayer is limited to a deduction of $3,000 in net capital losses per year. The capital loss deduction is a deduction for adjusted gross income. Any loss in excess of $3,000 is carried forward and netted against capital gains in subsequent years. Thus, the capital loss limitation is a deferral-of-loss-recognition provision, not a total loss disallowance provision.

▲ **EXAMPLE 44**   Mona has the following total capital gains and losses for 1996 and 1997. What is Mona's deductible capital loss in 1996 and 1997?

	1996	1997
Capital gains	$12,000	$17,000
Capital losses	(20,000)	(16,000)
Net	(8,000)	$1,000

Discussion: Mona has a net capital loss of $8,000 in 1996. Because of the capital loss limitations, Mona can deduct only $3,000 of this loss in 1996. The remaining $5,000 of 1996 loss is carried forward to 1997 and included in the 1997 netting:

	1996	1997
Capital gains	$12,000	$17,000
Capital losses	(20,000)	(16,000)
Net 1996 capital loss	$(8,000)	
1996 capital loss deduction	3,000	
1996 capital loss carryforward	$(5,000) ⟶	(5,000)
Net 1997 capital loss		$(4,000)
1997 capital loss deduction		3,000
1997 capital loss carryforward		$(1,000)

As you can see, the carryforward of the $5,000 capital loss from 1996 to 1997 creates a net capital loss of $4,000 in 1997. Without the carryforward, Mona would have had a $1,000 ($17,000 - $16,000) net capital gain in 1997. However, when the $5,000 of 1996 loss is carried forward and included in the 1997 netting, the result is a $4,000 loss. Per the capital loss limitations, $3,000 of the net capital loss is deductible in 1997. The remaining $1,000 of net capital loss must be carried forward and included in Mona's 1998 capital gain-and-loss netting.

NET CAPITAL LOSSES OF CORPORATIONS.   In contrast to individuals, corporations are not allowed to deduct net capital losses against noncapital gain income. Corporations can use capital losses only to offset capital gains. When a corporation incurs a net capital loss for a tax year, it is allowed to carry the net capital loss back and use it to offset any net capital gains on which it paid tax in the preceding three years. Any net capital loss that is not used in the three-year carryback period may be carried forward to offset capital gains for five years.

▲ **EXAMPLE 45**   El Fredo Corporation has the following net capital gains and losses for 1995 through 1998:

1995	1996	1997	1998
$8,000	$5,000	$7,000	$(35,000)

Assuming that El Fredo is in a 34% marginal tax rate bracket during each of these years, what is the effect of the $35,000 capital loss in 1998?

Discussion: El Fredo cannot deduct any of the $35,000 capital loss against its 1998 income. It must carry the loss back 3 years and use the loss to reduce any capital gains during that period. For El Fredo, the loss would first be applied against the $8,000 in 1995 capital gain, resulting in a $2,720 (34% × $8,000) refund of the tax paid in 1995. Applying the remaining loss against the $5,000 and $7,000 of net capital gains in 1996 and 1997, respectively, would result in refunds of $1,700 and $2,380. The 3-year carryback would use up $20,000 of the $35,000 in 1998 net capital loss. The remaining $15,000 in loss would be carried forward and used to reduce capital gains in the next 5 years.

Specially Treated Investment Losses.
Three provisions related to losses on investment assets deserve mention. Each of these provisions provides special treatment in certain transaction loss situations.

LOSSES ON SMALL BUSINESS STOCK.   In order to encourage individuals to invest in new companies, the tax law provides an exception to the $3,000 annual loss limitation on losses incurred on qualifying **small business stock.** This provision allows an individual taxpayer to deduct up to $50,000 in losses on small business stock per year. The limit is raised to $100,000 for a married couple filing a joint return.[20] Any losses on small business stock in excess of $50,000 ($100,000 for married couples) are subject to the regular capital gain-and-loss netting procedure.

▲ **EXAMPLE 46**   Linda is a single taxpayer whose only capital asset transaction for 1996 is a $70,000 capital loss on the sale of qualifying small business stock. How much of the $70,000 loss can Linda deduct in 1996?

Discussion: Linda is allowed to deduct $50,000 of the loss under the special exception for losses on small business stock. The remaining $20,000 of the loss is a capital loss subject to the annual $3,000 limitation. Thus, she can deduct an additional $3,000. This gives Linda a total loss deduction of $53,000 in 1996. The remaining $17,000 in loss must be carried forward to 1997 and deducted under the regular capital gain-and-loss netting procedure. NOTE: If Linda had been married in 1996, she and her husband could have deducted the entire $70,000 loss in 1996.

It should be stressed that the special deduction applies to losses incurred during a given tax year. Losses in excess of the allowable $50,000 ($100,000) deduction that are carried forward as a capital loss are subject to the capital loss limitation in later years, not the small business stock limitation.[21]

▲ **EXAMPLE 47**   Assume that in example 46 Linda has one capital asset transaction in 1997 that results in a $5,000 capital gain. What is Linda's 1997 capital loss deduction?

Discussion: The $17,000 in net capital loss carries forward from 1996 to be netted against the $5,000 in capital gain in 1997, resulting in a net capital loss for 1997 of $12,000. Linda cannot use the small business stock deduction on this loss, because it occurs in 1996. Therefore, only $3,000 of the $12,000 loss can be deducted in 1997. The $9,000 remaining loss must be carried forward to 1998 and included in Linda's 1998 capital gain-and-loss netting.

To qualify as small business stock, the stock must be purchased directly from the corporation at original issue. That is, the stock cannot be acquired from another individual or other taxable entity. The corporation itself must satisfy several other requirements, the most important of which is that the contributed capital of the corporation at the time the stock is issued must be less than $1 million.

LOSSES ON RELATED PARTY SALES.   In order to receive its intended income tax effect, a transaction must be entered into at arm's length. The tax law recognizes that related party transactions often lack the necessary bargaining to characterize the transactions as arm's length. The objective of the related party rules is to defer or disallow losses on transactions that are not made at arm's length. The primary provision regarding losses is that a loss on the sale of property to a **related party** is disallowed as a deduction.[22]

▲ **EXAMPLE 48**   Rasheed sold 500 shares of ABC Corporation stock to his sister Tawana for $5,000. Rasheed had paid $7,500 for the stock. Can Rasheed deduct the $2,500 loss on the sale of the stock to his sister?

Discussion: Rasheed cannot deduct the loss on the sale of the stock, because Tawana is a related party. Losses on sales of property to related parties are disallowed.

If the property subject to the related party sale disallowance is later sold to an unrelated party at a gain, the gain realized on the sale may be reduced by the amount of loss previously disallowed.[23]

▲ **EXAMPLE 49**   Assume that in example 48 Tawana later sells the shares of ABC stock to an unrelated party for $9,000. How much gain does Tawana have to recognize from the sale?

Discussion: Tawana's basis is the $5,000 she paid for the stock, giving her a gain on the sale of $4,000 ($9,000 − $5,000). Tawana is allowed to reduce her $4,000 gain by Rasheed's $2,500 disallowed loss. She has to recognize only a $1,500 ($4,000 − $2,500) gain on the sale.

The gain on a subsequent sale to an unrelated party may only be reduced to zero (no gain or loss recognized). A loss cannot be created on a subsequent sale by using the previously disallowed loss.

▲ **EXAMPLE 50**   Assume that in example 49 Tawana sells the stock to an unrelated party for $6,000. How much gain does Tawana have to recognize on the sale?

Discussion: Tawana realizes a gain of $1,000 ($6,000 − $5,000) on the sale. She may use Rasheed's $2,500 disallowed loss to reduce gain on the subsequent sale but only to zero. In this case, Tawana does not recognize any gain on the sale of the stock. However, note that the remaining $1,500 of Rasheed's previously disallowed loss is permanently lost in this case.

If the subsequent sale to an unrelated party results in a loss, the disallowed loss may not be used to increase the loss on the subsequent sale.

▲ **EXAMPLE 51**   Assume that in example 49 Tawana sells the stock to an unrelated party for $3,000. How much loss does Tawana recognize on the sale?

Discussion: The loss on the sale is $2,000 ($3,000 − $5,000). Tawana is not allowed to use Rasheed's $2,500 disallowed loss to increase the loss on the sale. Tawana is allowed to recognize only the actual $2,000 loss.

The related party disallowance rule also applies to the sale to a related party of property used in a trade or business.

▲ **EXAMPLE 52**   Catherine, the CEO of the Adtech Corporation, owns 60% of the Adtech Corporation. She sells land with a basis of $35,000 to Adtech for $31,000. Can Catherine deduct the $4,000 loss?

Discussion: Catherine cannot deduct any of the loss on the sale of the land. Because Catherine owns more than 50% of Adtech, she and Adtech are related parties. The disallowed loss of $4,000 can be used only to reduce any gain Adtech might have when it sells the land.

In summary, when property is sold at a loss to a related party, no loss is allowed. However, if the property is later sold to an unrelated party at a gain, the disallowed loss can be used to reduce the gain but not below zero (i.e., no loss allowed). Also, if the property is subsequently sold to an unrelated party at a loss, no portion of the disallowed loss from the related party sale is deductible.

The related party rules apply *only* to losses on sales to related parties. No comparable provisions restrict the reporting of gains on sales to related parties. Gains on sales to related parties are treated as any other type of gain would be treated.

WASH SALES.   A **wash sale** occurs when a security (stocks, bonds, options) is sold at a loss, and during the 30-day period before or after the loss sale date, the seller purchases substantially identical securities to replace the securities sold.[24] In a wash sale, a taxpayer's economic position with respect to the shares replaced remains unchanged. A wash sale loss lacks economic substance—in essence it is an artificial loss created for tax purposes without any change in the taxpayer's underlying economic position. The wash sale provisions recognize the substance of the transaction rather than its form (substance-over-form doctrine) by disallowing recognition of all losses on wash sales. The disallowed loss is added to the basis of the replacement shares.[25]

▲ **EXAMPLE 53**   Moses owned 400 shares of Nick Nack Corporation stock that he had purchased for $20,000 several years ago. In December of the current year, Moses sold the 400 shares for $12,000. One week later, he purchased an additional 400 shares of Nick Nack stock for $12,000. What are the tax consequences of the sale of the Nick Nack stock?

Discussion: The $8,000 loss on the sale of the 400 shares of stock is a wash sale, because Moses repurchased substantially identical shares within 30 days of the sale of the shares at a loss. The $8,000 loss is disallowed. However, the disallowance is not permanent—Moses adds the $8,000 loss to the basis of the replacement shares, giving him a basis of $20,000 in the replacement shares. Moses will be able to recover the $8,000 of disallowed loss when he disposes of the stock in a transaction that does not constitute a wash sale.

The wash sale provisions do not apply to dispositions at a gain, to securities that are sold at a loss but not replaced, or to dealers in securities.

▲ **EXAMPLE 54**   Assume that in example 53 Moses repurchased only 300 shares of the Nick Nack stock for $9,000 after the $12,000 sale. What are the tax consequences of the sale of the 400 shares of stock?

Discussion: In this case, only the 300 shares of stock that are replaced are a wash sale. The loss on the 100 shares that were not replaced, $2,000 [(100 ÷ 400) × $8,000], is recognized. The $6,000 loss on the replaced shares is subject to the wash sale disallowance and is not deductible. The basis of the 300 replacement shares is $15,000 ($9,000 + $6,000).

▲ **EXAMPLE 55**   Assume that in example 53 Moses repurchased 600 shares of the Nick Nack stock for $18,000. What are the tax consequences of the sale of the Nick Nack stock?

Discussion: The $8,000 loss on the sale of the 400 shares of stock is a wash sale, because Moses repurchased substantially identical shares within 30 days of the sale of the shares at a loss. The $8,000 loss is disallowed. However, the disallowance is not permanent—Moses adds the $8,000 loss to the basis of the replacement shares, giving him a basis of $20,000 in the 400 replacement shares. The other 200 shares that he purchased have a basis of $6,000 ($18,000 ÷ 600 = $30 × 200 = $6,000).

Personal Use Losses.   Losses on the sale or other disposition of personal use assets are generally disallowed—losses on the sale of personal use items such as autos, jewelry, furniture, and clothing have no tax effect. The only personal use loss that the tax law allows as a deduction is for losses from casualty or theft. And, under the legislative grace concept, Congress has placed several restrictions on the amount of a personal use casualty loss that may be deducted. One such restriction is that **personal casualty losses** and theft losses are only deductible as personal itemized deductions. Thus, a taxpayer must itemize in order to deduct a personal casualty or theft loss. In addition, a per occurrence and an annual limitation are imposed on personal casualty and theft losses.

MEASURING THE PERSONAL CASUALTY LOSS.   In contrast to business casualty losses, which have a measurement rule for fully destroyed property (basis) and a separate rule for partially destroyed property (the lesser of the decline in value or the basis), personal casualty and theft losses are always measured as the lesser of

■ The decline in the value of the property

or

■ The basis of the property

The effect of this measurement rule is to disallow losses in the value of property before the casualty that were attributable to everyday wear and tear from personal use. This is consistent with the general rule that losses from personal use are not deductible.

▲ EXAMPLE 56   Naomee was involved in an auto accident that totally destroyed her personal automobile. Naomee had purchased the auto several years ago for $30,000. A used car dealer told her that a comparable car could be bought today for $10,000. What is the amount of Naomee's loss on the casualty?

Discussion: The measure of the amount of loss is the lesser of the decline in value because of the casualty, $10,000, or the basis, $30,000. Thus, the amount of Naomee's loss is $10,000.

Note that the $20,000 loss in value from what Naomee paid for the auto, $30,000, and what the auto was worth before the accident, $10,000, is not a loss attributable to the casualty. The $20,000 loss in value occurred during Naomee's personal use of the auto and was not from the casualty. Thus, the loss in value from personal use is not deductible.

Discussion: If Naomee had used her car exclusively in a trade or business, the amount of loss would have been her $30,000 basis. The treatment is different because of the business purpose of the automobile. All expenses and losses incurred in a trade or business are deductible. Personal expenses and losses are generally not deductible.

LIMITATIONS ON PERSONAL CASUALTY LOSSES.   As with any casualty loss, the amount of loss must be reduced by any insurance proceeds received. In addition, you must file a claim for any insurance due in order to claim a deduction. Personal use casualty losses are also reduced by a $100 **statutory floor** per occurrence. The $100 statutory floor reduction is an element of administrative convenience. Because including $100 losses on individual returns adds cost and complexity to the tax system, the $100 floor eliminates the deduction of small personal casualty losses.

▲ EXAMPLE 57   Assume that in example 56 Naomee received $8,000 for her accident from her insurance company. What is Naomee's casualty loss?

Discussion: The $10,000 loss must be reduced by the $8,000 insurance reimbursement and the $100 statutory floor. This results in a $1,900 ($10,000 − $8,000 − $100) loss on the casualty.

The $100 statutory floor is a per occurrence limitation that is applied to each casualty or theft that occurs during the year. In addition, the tax law imposes an **annual personal casualty loss limitation** on the total of all casualty and theft losses. Total personal casualty and theft losses for the year are deductible only to the extent that they exceed 10 percent of the taxpayer's adjusted gross income.

▲ **EXAMPLE 58** Assume that in example 57 Naomee had an adjusted gross income of $15,000 in the year she sustained the loss on her personal automobile. What is Naomee's allowable itemized deduction for the casualty?

Discussion: The $1,900 loss on the automobile would be combined with any other casualty or theft losses occurring during the year. The total personal casualty and theft loss for the year is reduced by 10% of the taxpayer's adjusted gross income. In this case, Naomee's deductible loss would be $400 [$1,900 − ($15,000 × 10%)].

   Note that Naomee's loss will reduce her taxable income only if she has deductions sufficient to allow her to itemize her allowable personal deductions. If Naomee does not itemize and uses the standard deduction, she receives no tax benefit from the casualty. The 10% annual limitation also serves to eliminate many otherwise allowable personal casualty losses. For example, if Naomee's adjusted gross income had been greater than $19,000, the 10% annual limitation would have left her with no allowable casualty loss deduction.

▲ **EXAMPLE 59** Assume that in addition to the automobile casualty in example 58 Naomee had a gold ring stolen from her house during the same year. The ring had cost Naomee $1,300 and was worth $2,400 before it was stolen. Naomee's insurance reimbursed her $800 for the theft. What is Noamee's deductible personal casualty loss?

Discussion: The measure of loss on the ring is its $1,300 basis (because it is less than the $2,400 in value lost), which must be reduced by the insurance proceeds and the $100 statutory floor, resulting in a loss of $400 ($1,300 − $800 − $100). The losses on the automobile and the ring are combined for purposes of the annual 10% of adjusted gross income limitation. The total casualty and theft loss for the year, $2,300 ($400 + $1,900), is reduced by the $1,500 ($15,000 × 10%) annual limitation, resulting in a deductible loss of $800.

SUMMARY

Losses result from either an excess of deductions over income for an entire tax year (annual loss) or an excess of basis over the amount realized from a disposition of property (transaction loss). Annual losses from a trade or business in which a taxpayer materially participates are carried back 3 years and forward 15 years to offset income in the carryover period. Such losses are deductible only to the extent that the taxpayer is at risk in the activity.

   If the taxpayer does not materially participate in the operation of the trade or business generating the loss, the deduction of the loss is subject to the passive loss rules. These rules generally disallow the deduction of a net passive loss against active and portfolio income. Any loss not currently deductible is suspended and carried forward for deduction against future passive income. The material participation and active participation exceptions permit an individual to use losses from rental real estate to offset active and portfolio income. If an individual meets the material participation test, the loss from the rental property is fully deductible against active and portfolio income. If an individual meets the active participation test, the individual is allowed to deduct against active and portfolio income up to $25,000 of loss per year incurred in the rental real estate activity. When a passive activity is disposed of, any suspended loss on the activity is deductible against active and portfolio income.

   The treatment of transaction losses follows the general pattern for all deductions. Losses are classified either as personal or as related to a profit-motivated transaction or venture. The only personal use losses that are deductible are casualty and theft losses. Personal casualty and theft losses are subject to a $100 per

▲ **Exhibit 7–2**

INDIVIDUAL TAX
CALCULATION SUMMARY
TO DATE

Gross income (Chapters 3 & 4)	$XXX
Less: Deductions for adjusted gross income (AGI)	
Trade or business expenses (Chapters 5 & 6)	
Trade or business losses	
Net operating loss deductions	
Business transaction loss deductions	
Rental & royalty expenses (Chapters 5 & 6)	
Passive loss deductions	
Suspended losses freed by disposition	
Rental real estate losses	
Capital losses	(XXX)
Equals: Adjusted gross income	$XXX
Less: Deductions from adjusted gross income	
Specifically allowable personal expenditures	
(Chapter 8)	
Personal casualty and theft losses	
Production-of-income expenses (Chapters 5 & 6)	
Personal and dependency exemptions (Chapter 8)	(XXX)
Equals: Taxable income	$XXX

occurrence statutory floor limitation, and all casualty and theft losses for the year are further limited to the amount of loss in excess of 10 percent of the taxpayer's adjusted gross income.

Transaction losses that are related to a trade or business are deductible in full. Investment-related losses are subject to the capital gain-and-loss netting procedure. Net capital loss deductions of individuals are limited to $3,000 per year, with any excess capital loss carried forward for use in subsequent years. Corporations incurring net capital losses are not allowed to deduct capital losses against other forms of income. Net capital losses may be carried back three years and forward five years and used to reduce the tax on any net capital gains in the carryover years.

Several types of transaction losses are subject to special rules. Up to $50,000 ($100,000 married) in losses on qualified small business stock may be deducted as an ordinary loss. Losses on sales to related parties are specifically disallowed. If a security is sold at a loss and replaced within 30 days of the sale, the wash sale rules disallow the loss.

A summary of the reporting of losses discussed in this chapter for individuals is presented in Exhibit 7–2.

KEY TERMS

active income (p. 290)
active participant (p. 298)
active participation exception
  (p. 298)
annual loss (p. 280)
annual personal casualty loss
  limitation (p. 308)
at-risk rules (p. 285)
business casualty loss (p. 300)
capital asset (p. 303)

carryback (p. 281)
carryforward (p. 281)
casualty (p. 299)
casualty gain (p. 301)
casualty loss (p. 299)
closely held corporation (p. 292)
gift (p. 295)
investment-related loss (p. 299)
limited partnership (p. 289)
material participant (p. 287)

material participation (p. 287)
material participation exception
  (p. 296)
net capital loss (p. 303)
net operating loss (p. 281)
nonrecourse debt (p. 286)
passive activity (p. 287)
passive activity loss rules (p. 287)
personal casualty loss (p. 307)
portfolio income (p. 290)

real property trade or business (p. 297)
related party (p. 305)
rental activity (p. 288)
small business stock (p. 304)

statutory floor (p. 308)
suspended loss (p. 292)
tax shelter (p. 283)
theft (p. 299)
theft loss (p. 299)

trade or business loss (p. 299)
transaction loss (p. 298)
wash sale (p. 306)
working interest in oil and gas deposit (p. 290)

PRIMARY TAX LAW SOURCES

[1] Sec. 172—Defines a *net operating loss* and provides the rules for deducting net operating losses through a 3-year carryback and a 15-year carryforward.

[2] Sec. 465—Defines the amount at risk in an activity and limits loss deductions to the amount the taxpayer has at risk in the activity.

[3] Prop. Reg. Sec. 1.465-41—Provides examples of the application of the at-risk rules.

[4] Sec. 469—Defines *passive activities* and provides the rules for deducting passive activity losses.

[5] Reg. Sec. 1.469-5T—Provides the tests for material participation in an activity.

[6] Reg. Sec. 1.469-1T—States that suspended passive losses are carried forward to the following year, where they are treated as if they were incurred in that year; provides rules for distinguishing rental activities for purposes of the passive loss rules.

[7] Reg. Sec. 1.469-2T—Provides rules for deducting suspended losses on passive activities when the activity is disposed of in a taxable transaction.

[8] Sec. 469(c)(7)—Provides the rules for the material participation exception for rental real estate.

[9] Sec. 165—Specifies the allowable deductions for losses; limits the deductions of losses by individuals to those incurred in a trade or business, in a transaction entered into for profit, and losses resulting from storms, fires, shipwrecks, and other casualties.

[10] Sec. 65—Defines an *ordinary loss* as any loss that does not result from the sale or exchange of a capital asset.

[11] Sec. 62—Defines *adjusted gross income* for individual taxpayers and specifies the deductions allowed for adjusted gross income; allowable loss deductions include losses incurred in a trade or business, net operating losses, and capital losses.

[12] Sec. 1001—Prescribes the calculation of gains and losses on dispositions of property; defines *amount realized* for purposes of determining gain or loss on dispositions.

[13] Matheson v. Comm., 54 F.2d 537 (2d Cir. 1931)—Held that a casualty is the result of some sudden, unexpected, or unusual event.

[14] Pulvers v. Comm., 407 F.2d 838 (9th Cir. 1969)—Held that for a casualty loss to be deductible, a casualty must damage a property; mere declines in value are not deductible.

[15] Rev. Rul. 63-232—States that the loss resulting from termite damage is not a casualty loss.

[16] Reg. Sec. 1.165-8—States that a theft includes larceny, embezzlement, and robbery.

[17] Reg. Sec. 1.165-7—Provides the rules for calculating casualty losses.

[18] Sec. 1221—Defines *capital assets*.

[19] Sec. 1211—Sets forth the limit on deductions of capital losses of corporations and individuals.

[20] Sec. 1244—Defines qualified *small business stock* and allows deductions for losses of up to $50,000 ($100,000 for married, filing jointly) per year on such stock.

[21] Reg. Sec. 1.1244(b)-1—Provides the limits on the deductibility of losses on small business stock; clarifies that any loss that is carried forward to a subsequent year is not eligible for that year's special loss deduction.

[22] Sec. 267—Defines *related parties* and disallows losses on sales to related parties.

[23] Reg. Sec. 1.267(d)-1—Provides the rules for deducting disallowed losses on related party sales on subsequent sales to unrelated parties.

[24] Sec. 1091—Defines a *wash sale* and disallows current deductions for wash sale losses.

[25] Reg. Sec. 1.1091-1—States that the loss on a wash sale is disallowed on shares of stock that are actually replaced; provides basis adjustment rules for wash sale shares.

DISCUSSION QUESTIONS

1. How are deductions and losses different? How are they similar? Explain.

2. Discuss the basic differences between annual losses and transaction losses.

3. What relief is provided to a business that suffers a net operating loss?

4. What is the net operating loss carryback and carryforward period? Does a taxpayer have a choice of the years to which a net operating loss can be carried? Explain.

5. What are the characteristics of a *tax shelter*, as the term is commonly used by tax practitioners?

6. What is the amount at risk in an activity? What purpose does the amount at risk serve in regard to losses?

7. How is a taxpayer's amount at risk in an activity different from the taxpayer's basis in the same activity?

8. What is a nonrecourse debt? How is financing using nonrecourse debt different from financing using recourse debt?

9. What is the purpose of the passive loss rules?

10. Are the passive loss rules disallowance-of-loss provisions or are they loss deferral provisions? Explain.

11. When a passive loss cannot be deducted in the current year, is the deduction lost forever? Describe the general circumstances under which the loss might be deducted in the future.

12. For purposes of the passive loss rules, what is a closely held corporation? How is the tax treatment of passive losses incurred by a closely held corporation different from the tax treatment of passive losses incurred by
    a. Individuals?
    b. Corporations?

13. When a business sustains a loss from a casualty, one of two measurement rules is used to determine the amount of the loss. Why is the use of two different measurement rules necessary for determining a business casualty loss?

14. What are the limitations on the deductibility of capital losses by individuals? How do the limitations compare with those for corporations?

15. Most sales of securities at a loss result in capital losses. Under what circumstances would a loss on the sale of a security be treated as an ordinary loss?

16. Explain the rationale for allowing taxpayers to use the ordinary loss treatment for qualified small business stock when it is sold at a loss.

17. What is the purpose of the related party rules as they apply to sales of property?

18. Losses incurred on the sale of business assets are generally deductible in full in the year the loss is realized. Describe a situation in which a realized loss on the sale of a business asset is not deductible in the current year, and explain why it would not be deductible.

19. What is a wash sale? How is the treatment of a wash sale different from the treatment of other sales of securities?

20. How are the rules for deducting personal casualty and theft losses different from the rules for business casualty and theft losses? Explain the difference in treatments and the rationale for the difference.

21. Effren Corporation suffers an operating loss of $120,000 during 1997. Effren was incorporated in 1995 and had an operating loss of $40,000 in 1995 and an operating income of $90,000 in 1996. What is the treatment of the 1997 loss if
    a. Effren is a corporation?
    b. Effren is an S corporation?

22. Habiby, Inc., has the following income and expenses for 1994 through 1998. What is the amount of tax that Habiby should pay each year? Use the corporate tax rate schedules in Appendix A to compute the tax liability.

	1994	1995	1996	1997	1998
Income	$280,000	$300,000	$310,000	$ 290,000	$320,000
Expenses	(180,000)	(200,000)	(235,000)	(600,000)	(220,000)
Income	$100,000	$100,000	$ 75,000	$(310,000)	$100,000

23. Post Haste, incorporated in 1994, suffers a net operating loss of $90,000 in 1996. Post Haste had a net operating loss of $30,000 in 1994 and taxable income of $75,000 in 1995. Allison, the financial vice president of Post Haste, expects 1997 to be a banner year, with taxable income of approximately $160,000. Write a memo to Allison advising her how to treat the $90,000 loss in 1996. Post Haste normally earns 8% on its investments.

24. Marlene opened a hair salon this year. She invested $20,000 of her own money and borrowed $75,000 from her bank to finance the purchase of the assets necessary to run the business. With the $75,000, she purchased a building for $50,000 and equipment costing $25,000. What is Marlene's amount at risk in the hair salon if the $75,000 debt was secured by
    a. The business assets purchased, and Marlene is personally liable if the business assets are insufficient to satisfy the debt?
    b. The business assets purchased, and Marlene is not personally liable for payment of the debt if the business assets are insufficient to satisfy the debt?

25. Carlos opens a dry cleaning store during the year. He invests $10,000 of his own money and borrows $75,000 from a local bank. He uses $50,000 of the loan to buy a building and the remaining $25,000 for equipment. During the first year, the store has a loss of $14,000. How much of the loss can Carlos deduct if the loan from the bank is nonrecourse? How much does Carlos have at risk at the end of the first year?

26. Wayne owns 30% of Label Maker Corporation. Label Maker is organized as an S corporation. During 1996, Label Maker has a loss of $180,000. At the beginning of 1996, Wayne's at-risk amount in Label Maker is $32,000.
    a. Assuming that Wayne's investment in Label Maker is not a passive activity, what is Wayne's deductible loss in 1996?
    b. In 1997, Label Maker has a taxable income of $60,000. What is the effect on Wayne's 1997 income?

27. A taxpayer had the following income (losses) for the current year:

Active Income	Portfolio Income	Passive Income
$15,000	$25,000	$(30,000)

What is the taxpayers taxable income (loss) if
    a. The taxpayer is a publicly held corporation?
    b. The taxpayer is a closely held corporation?
    c. The taxpayer is an individual and the passive income was not from a rental activity?
    d. The taxpayer is an individual and the passive income was the result of a rental activity for which the taxpayer meets the material participation test?
    e. The taxpayer is an individual and the passive income was the result of a rental activity for which the taxpayer fails to meet the material participation test but meets the active participation test?

28. Which of the following would be a passive activity? Explain.
   a. Irving owns a 1/3 interest in a partnership. The main asset of the partnership is a working interest in an oil and gas deposit. Irving's only involvement in the business is that of providing capital to finance the operation of the partnership.
   b. Muriel rents skates at the boardwalk of Atlantic City. She has no employees and runs the entire business herself.
   c. Jack owns 20% of a building that was built as low-income housing. Jack's only involvement in the activity is to provide part of the initial capital to fund the project. He has no involvement in renting the housing units.
   d. Frida owns a 15-unit apartment building. She spends 800 hours a year—all of her working hours—managing the apartment building.
   e. Assume the same facts as in part d, except that Frida spends only 600 hours a year managing the apartment building.

29. Which of the following are passive activities?
   a. Marvin owns a 1/5 share in a limited partnership. The limited partnership's sole asset is a resort hotel.
   b. Marcie owns a royalty interest in an oil and gas operation.
   c. Neil owns an 18-hole semiprivate golf course. He is a certified professional golfer and serves as the club pro. He provides lessons and is involved in the daily management of the business.
   d. Assume the same facts as in part c, except that Neil plays on the professional tour. When on break from the tour, he mingles with the members and conducts golf clinics. The club is managed by his brother and sister.
   e. Laura owns a commercial office building. She spends more than 500 hours a year managing the building. She also spends 1,700 hours working in her own real estate development firm.
   f. Assume the same facts as e, except that Laura hires a full-time manager for the commercial office building. She spends only 75 hours meeting with the manager and reviewing the operations.

30. Sidney and Gertrude own 40% of Bearcave Bookstore, an S corporation. The remaining 60% is owned by their son Boris. Sidney and Gertrude do not participate in operating or managing the store, and they invested $20,000 in the business when it opened in 1993. The bookstore reported the following net income (loss) for the years 1993 through 1996:

1993	1994	1995	1996
$(28,000)	$(16,000)	$(10,000)	$8,000

   a. How much do Sidney and Gertrude have at risk in Bearcave at the end of each year (1993–1996)?
   b. What amount can they recognize as income or loss from Bearcave for each year (1993–1996)?
   c. Assume that Sidney and Gertrude do materially participate in Bearcave for each year (1993–1996). What amount can they recognize as income or loss from Bearcave for each year (1993–1996)?

31. Jordan and her brother Jason agree to purchase a hardware store from a local bank, which acquired it through foreclosure. Because the bank would like to sell the business, Jordan and Jason are able to buy it for only $140,000. Jordan will invest $28,000 and own 70% of the business, and Jason will invest $12,000 and own the remaining 30%. The bank is financing the remaining $100,000 with a nonrecourse loan secured by the building ($40,000), inventory ($45,000), and equipment ($15,000). Although Jordan and Jason believe that the store will prove to be an excellent investment within a few years, they expect losses of $30,000, $21,000, and $6,000 in the first three years of operation. They anticipate turning a profit of $16,000 in the fourth year. Jason and Jordan are unsure whether to operate the business as a corporation or an S corporation. Both will materially participate in running the hardware store. Write a letter to Jordan and Jason discussing how the operating results of the hardware store will be taxed if they operate as a corporation versus an S corporation.

32. Janet has a taxable income of $60,000 from her salary and investment assets. She also owns 3 passive activities that have the following income (loss) for the year:

Passive activity 1	$ 20,000
Passive activity 2	$(28,000)
Passive activity 3	$(12,000)

a. What is the effect of the passive activities on Janet's income? Explain.

b. How much suspended loss does Janet have in each passive activity?

33. Return to the facts of problem 32. In the next year, Janet has a taxable income from her salary and investment activities of $70,000. The results for her three passive activities are

Passive activity 1	$ 30,000
Passive activity 2	$(14,000)
Passive activity 3	$(6,000)

a. What is the effect of the passive activities on Janet's income? Explain.

b. How much suspended loss does Janet have in each passive activity?

34. Mason owns a passive activity that generates a passive loss of $14,000 in 1995, $12,000 in 1996, and income of $4,000 in 1997. In 1996, Mason purchases a second passive activity that has passive income of $6,000 in 1996 and $10,000 in 1997. Discuss the effect of Mason's passive activity investments on his taxable income in 1995, 1996, and 1997. Assume that neither passive activity involves rental real estate.

35. Return to the facts of problem 34. At the end of 1997, Mason sells for $16,000 the passive activity that generated the losses. What is the effect on Mason's taxable income if his basis in the activity sold is

a. $1,000?

b. $28,000?

36. Jeremy owns a passive activity that has a basis of $32,000 and a suspended loss of $14,000. Jeremy's taxable income from active and portfolio income is $70,000.

a. What is the effect on Jeremy's taxable income if he sells the passive activity for $40,000?

b. What is the effect on Jeremy's taxable income if he sells the passive activity for $20,000?

37. Return to the facts of problem 36. Assume that Jeremy died when the passive activity had a fair market value of $40,000. What is the effect on Jeremy's taxable income for the year he died?

38. Return to the facts of problem 36. Assume that Jeremy died when the passive activity had a fair market value of $20,000. What is the effect on Jeremy's taxable income for the year he died?

39. Return to the facts of problem 36. Assume that Jeremy gave the property to his son Felipe when the property had a fair market value of $40,000. What is the effect of the gift on Jeremy's taxable income? Felipe's taxable income?

40. Claudio owns a passive activity that has a basis of $28,000 and a fair market value of $38,000. The activity has suspended losses of $16,000. In an effort to reduce their estate, every year Claudio and his wife give their son Anthony and his wife a gift of approximately $40,000. During the year Anthony sells stock that results in a $10,000 short-term capital loss. A friend of Claudio's suggests that he give his passive activity to Anthony. The friend says that this will allow Claudio to avoid tax on the $10,000 capital gain and allow his son to offset his short-term capital loss with the $10,000 ($38,000 - $28,000) gain from the sale of the passive activity. In addition, Claudio can use the suspended loss from the passive activity to offset his other ordinary income. Write a letter to Claudio explaining the tax consequences of making the passive activity a gift to his son.

41. Masaya owns a passive activity that has a basis of $32,000 and a suspended loss of $13,000. Masaya's taxable income from active and portfolio income is $73,000.
    a. What is the effect on Masaya's taxable income if he sells the passive activity for $46,000?
    b. What is the effect on Masaya's taxable income if he sells the passive activity for $26,000?
    c. What is the effect on Masaya's taxable income if he dies this year while the fair market value of the passive activity is $40,000?
    d. What is the effect on Masaya's taxable income if he dies this year while the fair market value of the passive activity is $22,000?
    e. What is the effect on Masaya's taxable income if he gives the passive activity to his daughter Hideko when the fair market value of the passive activity is $40,000? What would the effect of this be on Hideko's taxable income?

42. Ann and Joyce each own a 50% interest in a 25-unit apartment complex. Joyce devotes 800 hours a year to managing the apartment complex and spends 1,250 hours as a self-employed photographer. Ann spends 1,500 hours a year as a real estate broker in a business in which she has a 15% ownership interest. She spends 600 hours a year helping Joyce to manage the apartment complex. In 1996, the apartment complex generates a total loss of $30,000. Joyce's adjusted gross income for 1996 is $110,000, and Ann's is $120,000. How much of the loss can Joyce deduct on her tax return? How much of the loss can Ann deduct?

43. Paul is a 50% owner of 8 rental houses. He spends 600 hours a year managing the properties. In addition, he owns a 15% interest in a construction business to which he devotes 1,800 hours a year. The rental units generate a loss of $40,000, and Paul's adjusted gross income for 1996, before considering the rental properties, is $120,000.
    a. How much of the loss can Paul deduct in 1996?
    b. Assume that Paul's ownership in the construction business is only 2%. How much of the loss can he deduct?
    c. Assume that Paul spends only 400 hours a year managing the rental properties. How much of the loss can he deduct?

44. Mort is the sole owner of rental real estate that produces a net loss of $15,000 in 1995 and $20,000 in 1996 and income of $8,000 in 1997. His adjusted gross income, before considering the rental property for the years 1995 through 1997, is $125,000, $130,000, and $80,000, respectively.
    a. What is Mort's adjusted gross income for 1995, 1996, and 1997, if he meets the material participation test?
    b. What is Mort's adjusted gross income for 1995, 1996, and 1997, if he is only an active participant in the rental activity?

45. Ivan and Olga own a duplex. They collect the rents and make repairs to the property when necessary. That is, they are only active participants in the rental property. During the current year, the duplex has gross rents of $19,000 and total allowable deductions of $39,000. What is the effect of the duplex rental on their taxable income if their adjusted gross income is
    a. $90,000?   c. $120,000?
    b. $160,000?   d. $135,000?

46. Jacqueline is a 60% owner of a rental property and has a significant role in the management of the property. During the current year, the property has a rental loss of $20,000. What is the effect of the rental property on her taxable income, if her adjusted gross income is
    a. $80,000?   c. $200,000?
    b. $130,000?   d. $110,000?

47. ABC Co. owns a chain of furniture stores. How much loss can ABC Co. deduct in each of the following cases? Explain.

    a. ABC closes a store in a depressed part of the county. Rather than move furniture to other stores, ABC sells furniture that had cost $300,000 for $200,000.

    b. A fire severely damages one store. The cost of repairing the fire damage is $175,000. ABC's basis in the store building is $400,000. ABC's insurance company reimburses ABC $140,000 for the fire damage.

    c. ABC decides to begin replacing some of its older delivery vans. It sells for $5,000 one van that had a basis of $8,000.

    d. ABC discovers that one of its buildings is infested with termites. The building is old and has been fully depreciated for tax purposes. The cost of getting rid of the termites is $12,500, none of which is covered by insurance.

    e. Someone breaks into one store by destroying the security system. Cash of $13,000 is missing from a safe. In addition, televisions that had cost $25,000 and were marked to sell for $45,000 are gone. The security system had a basis of $12,000. Because the system was outdated, a security expert estimates it was worth only $4,000 at the time it was destroyed.

48. The Goodson Co. is a chain of retail electronics stores. How much of a loss can Goodson deduct in each of the following cases? Explain.

    a. A mouse gnawed a hole in the wood of a 35-inch console television. The television normally sells for $2,050. The cost of the set is $1,780, and Goodson sold the damaged set for $1,500.

    b. The company replaced its inventory system. The old system cost $45,000 and had a basis of $16,000. The company sold the old system for $7,500. The new system cost $75,000.

    c. A flood damaged one of Goodson's retail stores. The building suffered extensive water damage. The basis of the building is $60,000, and the cost of repairing the damage is $72,000. The insurance company reimbursed Goodson $50,000.

    d. The owner of Goodson sold a complete home entertainment center (e.g., projection TV, VCR, stereo system) to his sister for $7,000. The usual sales price is $8,500. The cost of the system is $6,300.

    e. Assume the same facts as in part d, except that the owner sold the home entertainment center to his sister for $5,500.

    f. The owner of Goodson finds that the controller has embezzled $10,000 from the company. Before the owner can confront the controller, the controller leaves town and cannot be found.

    g. Upon arriving at the company's headquarters, the vice president of sales finds that someone has broken in and stolen 3 computers. The damage to the outside door is extensive. The cost of repairing the door is $1,500, and the cost of replacing the 3 computers is $9,500. The original cost of the computers totals $10,500. Goodson's basis in the computers is $5,000. The thieves also stole $350 from the petty cash fund. Goodson files a claim with its insurance company and receives a check for $4,800.

49. Gordon is the sole proprietor of Fashion Flowers & Florals (FFF). During the current year, one of FFF's delivery vans was involved in an automobile accident. The van had a basis of $6,000. What is FFF's allowable casualty loss deduction under each of the following situations?

    a. A comparable van sells for $4,000. FFF's van was totally destroyed in the accident. FFF's insurance paid $2,200 on the casualty.

    b. A comparable van sells for $8,400. FFF's van was totally destroyed in the accident. FFF's insurance paid $6,400 on the casualty.

50. Assume the same facts in problem 49. What is FFF's allowable casualty loss deduction under each of the following situations?
    a. A comparable van sells for $4,000. After the accident, the insurance adjuster estimated the van was worth $1,500. The insurance company paid FFF $1,200 on the casualty.
    b. A comparable van sells for $8,400. After the accident, the insurance adjuster estimated the value of the van at $1,500. The insurance company paid FFF $1,200 on the casualty.

51. Stella owns a taxicab company. During the year, two of her cabs are involved in accidents. One cab is totally destroyed, the other is heavily damaged. Stella is able to replace the destroyed cab with an identical model for $5,500. Stella's adjusted basis in the destroyed cab is $3,750, and the insurance company pays her $2,800. The adjusted basis of the damaged cab is $3,800. The insurance adjuster estimates that the damaged cab is worth $3,600. Although a comparable cab sells for $7,800, the insurance company gives Stella only $2,900. Write a letter to Stella explaining the amount of her deductible casualty loss.

52. Fogerty's Fresh Farm Produce was burglarized during the current year. In addition to taking $460 in cash from the safe, the burglars took 40 cases of beer that had cost $1,800 and had a retail value of $3,900. In entering the store, the burglars broke a glass door and damaged the security system. It cost $230 to replace the door and $600 to repair the security system. The security system had been completely depreciated for tax purposes. What is the company's deductible loss from the burglary if its insurance company paid out $2,400 on the insurance claim?

53. Wilbur owns a 25% interest in the Talking Horse Corporation, which is organized as an S corporation. His basis in the property is $18,000, and he does not materially participate in the business. For the year, Talking Horse reported an operating loss of $30,000 and a capital loss of $5,000. Wilbur's adjusted gross income is $65,000. Explain what effect these losses would have on Wilbur's adjusted gross income. If Wilbur materially participates in Talking Horse, explain what effect these losses would have on Wilbur's adjusted gross income.

54. During 1996, Yoko has total capital gains of $4,500 and total capital losses of $11,000. What is the effect of the capital gains and losses on Yoko's 1996 taxable income? Explain.
    a. Assume that in 1997 Yoko has total capital gains of $6,000 and total capital losses of $3,000. What is the effect of the capital gains and losses on Yoko's taxable income in 1997? Explain.
    b. How would your answer change if Yoko's total capital losses are $11,500 in 1997?

55. Goldie sells 400 shares of Bear Corporation stock for $7,500 on December 14, 1996. Goldie paid $24,000 for the stock in February 1993. Assuming that Goldie has no other capital asset transactions in 1996, what is the effect of the sale on her 1996 income?
    a. Assume that Goldie has no capital asset transactions in 1997. What is the effect of the Bear Corporation stock sale on her 1997 income?
    b. On July 2, 1998, Goldie sells 100 shares of Panda common stock for $15,000. Goldie purchased the stock on September 4, 1996, for $9,000. What is the effect of the sale on Goldie's 1998 income?

56. Labrador Corporation has total capital gains of $18,000 and total capital losses of $35,000 in 1996. Randy owns 25% of Labrador's outstanding stock. What is the effect on Labrador's and Randy's 1996 taxable incomes if
    a. Labrador is a corporation? Explain how Labrador and Randy would treat the capital gains and losses.
    b. Labrador is an S corporation? Explain how Labrador and Randy would treat the capital gains and losses.

57. Bongo Corporation is incorporated in 1994. It has no capital asset transactions in 1994. From 1995 through 1998, Bongo has the following capital gains and losses:

	1995	1996	1997	1998
Capital gains	$ 15,000	$ 8,000	$ 13,000	$25,000
Capital losses	(5,000)	(16,000)	(40,000)	(8,000)

Assuming that Bongo's marginal tax rate during each of these years is 34%, what is the effect of Bongo's capital gains and losses on the amount of tax due each year?

58. The Newcastle Corporation was incorporated in 1995. For the years 1995 through 1997, Newcastle has the following net capital gain or loss.

	1995	1996	1997
Net capital gain (loss)	$10,000	$(22,000)	$30,000

If Newcastle is in the 34% marginal tax bracket for each of these years, what effect do the net capital gains (losses) have on its tax liability for 1995, 1996, and 1997?

59. Ellen, a single individual, sold some stock she owned in ABC Co. at a loss of $70,000. Assuming that Ellen had no other dispositions of capital assets during the year, how much of the loss can she deduct?
    a. How would your answer change if the stock was qualified small business stock?
    b. Assume the same facts as in part a, except that Ellen is married.

60. Rick, a single taxpayer, owned 30,000 shares of qualifying small business stock that he had purchased for $300,000. During the current year, he sold 10,000 of the shares for $25,000. What are the tax effects for Rick from selling the shares?
    a. Assume that Rick also sold other capital assets at a gain of $12,000. What are the tax effects of Rick's capital asset transactions?
    b. Assume the same facts as in part a. In the year after selling the 10,000 shares of qualified small business stock, Rick had total capital gains of $16,000 and total capital losses of $12,000. What are the effects of Rick's capital asset transactions on his taxable income?

61. Evita sold 2 pieces of land during the current year. She had used the first piece as a parking lot for her pet store (she owns the store as a sole proprietor). The land cost Evita $40,000, and she sold the land for $30,000. The second piece was a building lot she had purchased as a speculative investment. Evita paid $40,000 for the lot and sold it for $30,000. Assume that Evita had no other dispositions during the year. Write a letter to Evita explaining the deductible loss from her two land transactions.

62. Elliot sold some stock he had purchased for $6,000 to his sister for $4,000. Several years later, his sister sold the stock for $7,000. What is the effect of the sales on Elliot and his sister?
    a. Assume that the subsequent sale by his sister was for $5,000.
    b. Assume that the subsequent sale by his sister was for $2,000.

63. Howard Co. is 100% owned by Rona. During the current year, Howard sold some land to Rona for $50,000 that had cost Howard $80,000 and that had a fair market value of $100,000. What are the tax effects of the sale for Howard Co. and Rona?

64. Darlene owns 500 shares of Sandmayor, Inc., common stock that she purchased several years ago for $20,000. During the current year, the Sandmayor stock declines in value. Darlene decides to sell the stock to realize the tax loss. On December 17, she sells the 500 shares for $12,000. Her investment adviser tells her she thinks the Sandmayor stock probably will begin to increase in value next year. On this advice, Darlene purchases 600 shares of Sandmayor common stock on January 10 of the next year for $15,000. The adviser turns out to be right—Darlene sells the 600 shares in May for $22,000. What are the effects of the sales on Darlene's taxable income in each year? Explain.

65. Ed owned 1,000 shares of Northern Co. for which he had paid $12,000 several years ago. On November 24, he purchased an additional 600 shares for $4,800. Ed sold the original 1,000 shares for $9,000 on December 14. What are the effects of the December 14 sale? Explain.

66. Shauna acquires 400 shares of Moorabin Corporation stock on April 7, 1995, for $22 per share. On July 8, 1996, she sells 200 shares for $16 per share. Three weeks later, acting on a tip from her broker, she repurchases 100 shares of Moorabin at $15 per share. The stock takes off, and she sells all 300 shares on December 3, 1996, at $38 per share. What is Shauna's taxable gain or loss from the stock transactions in 1996?

67. James owns a ski cabin in Colorado that he uses solely for family vacations. When James and his family arrived at the cabin for their regular August vacation, they discovered that the cabin had been broken into sometime in the last year. Several items were stolen, and some furniture was damaged. Here are the details of the items stolen and damaged:

	Cost	Value Before	Value After	Decline FML	Insurance Proceeds
Fishing equipment	$ 800	$ 550	$250 _300_		$ 125
Stereo	$1,500	$1,900	-0-		$1,600
Furniture	$4,000	$3,200	$700 _2500_		$1,200

In addition, it cost $225 to replace a window. The insurance company would not cover the cost of replacing the window, even though it was obvious that breaking it was how the thieves had gained entry. To guard against future break-ins, James had special locks installed on the windows at a cost of $640.

What is the amount of James's casualty (theft) loss before considering any annual limitations that may apply?

68. Ghon and Li own a home on Lake Gibran. During a heavy rainstorm, the lake overflows and floods the basement. The entire contents of the basement (rug, furniture, stereo, and so on), which is used as their family room, are destroyed. The insurance adjuster estimates that the damage to the basement and its contents is $15,400. Ghon and Li do not have flood insurance, so the insurance company will reimburse them only $2,400 for the damage. If their adjusted gross income for the year is $62,000, what is their deductible casualty loss?

69. Kevin is the sole proprietor of Murph's Golf Shop. During the current year, a hurricane hit the beach near Kevin's shop. His business building, which had a basis of $75,000, was damaged. In addition, his personal automobile for which he had paid $28,000 was damaged. Fair market values (FMV) before and after the hurricane were

Case A	FMV Before	FMV After
Building	$150,000	$100,000
Automobile	7,000	2,000

Case B		
Building	$150,000	-0-
Automobile	7,000	-0-

a. What is Kevin's gross loss in each of the above cases?

b. Assume that in case A, Kevin received $40,000 from his insurance company for the building and $2,000 for his automobile. What is his allowable loss?

c. Assume that the insurance proceeds were $150,000 and $2,000 in case B. What is the tax effect for Kevin of the casualty?

70. Jamila was involved in an auto accident during the current year that totally destroyed her car. Jamila had purchased the car two years ago for $28,000. Jamila had used the car in her business 75% of the time over the past two years. She had properly deducted $4,000 in depreciation for the business use of the car. The insurance company paid her $16,000, the fair market value of the car before it was destroyed. Assuming that Jamila had an adjusted gross income of $45,000 during the current year before considering the effect of the auto accident, what is the effect of the accident on her taxable income?

71. Andy sold the following assets during the year.

	Gain (Loss)
Personal automobile	$(15,000)
ABC stock	8,000
Personal furniture	1,000
BCCI bonds	(14,000)

What is Andy's deductible loss? Explain.

72. Faith, who is single, sells the following assets during 1996:

- 20,000 shares of qualified small business stock at a loss of $62,000. Faith bought the stock in 1991.
- 1,200 shares of Geelong Industries at a gain of $4,500. Faith bought the stock in 1994.
- An XZ10 sailboat at a loss of $3,500. Faith acquired the boat, which she used in her leisure hours, in 1990.
- A 1967 Holden Deluxe automobile at a gain of $5,000. Faith never used the car for business.
- 50 shares of Fremantle, Inc., at a gain of $1,300. Faith bought the stock in 1996 and sold it to her brother.
- 75 shares of the Fitzroy Corporation at a loss of $300. Faith bought the stock in 1993 and sold it to her sister.
  Calculate Faith's net capital gain (loss) for 1996.

73. Calzone Trucking Co. is a corporation that is 100% owned by Fred Calzone. Before he incorporated in 1994, Fred had operated the business as a sole proprietorship. The taxable income (loss) of Calzone for 1994 through 1996 is as follows:

COMPREHENSIVE PROBLEM

	1994	1995	1996
Taxable income (loss)	$22,000	$(77,000)	$28,000

The 1996 taxable income includes a net long-term capital gain of $4,000. Calzone Trucking's 1997 operating income is $56,000 before considering the following transactions:

a. A hail storm caused part of the roof of the truck barn to collapse. A truck inside the barn sustained damage from the falling debris. The truck barn had a fair market value of $62,000 before the damage and an adjusted basis of $33,000. Repairs to the roof cost $12,100, of which $7,700 was reimbursed by insurance. The truck, which had an adjusted basis of $41,000, was worth $58,000 before the damage and had a fair market value after the damage of $45,000. Calzone Trucking's insurance company paid $8,200 for the damages.

b. Another truck was totally destroyed when its brakes failed and plunged off a cliff. Fortunately, the driver was able to jump from the truck and escaped unharmed. The truck, which had an adjusted basis of $21,000, was worth $35,000 before the accident. Calzone received $16,400 from its insurance company for the destruction of the truck. In addition, the company was cited for failure to properly maintain the truck and paid a $8,900 fine to the state trucking commission.

c. Calzone sold equipment that had become obsolete for $16,200. The equipment had cost $30,000, and depreciation of $12,000 had been taken on the equipment before the sale.

d. Calzone sold stock it owned in two other companies. Retro Corporation stock, which had cost $17,000, sold for $39,200. Shares of Tread Corporation stock with a cost of $64,000 sold for $29,400. Both stocks had been purchased in 1993.

e. Fred's son wanted to start a delivery business. To help his son out, Fred sold him one of Calzone's used trucks for $6,000. The truck had a fair market value of $17,200 and an adjusted basis of $13,000 at the date of the sale.

REQUIRED: Calculate Calzone Trucking's 1997 taxable income. Indicate the amount and the effect of any carryforwards or carrybacks on Calzone Trucking's current, past, or future income.

DISCUSSION CASES

74. The enactment of the passive loss rules has generally diminished the attractiveness of tax shelters as investments. However, rental real estate continues to provide a viable tax shelter for certain taxpayers. Explain why this is true.

75. The Exeter Savings and Loan is located in a two-story building in downtown Exeter. The building has a basement in which the heating system for the bank is located. The bank also uses the basement to store records and photocopying equipment. Last fall, the Saugutuxet River overflowed and flooded the basement. The flood destroyed all the bank's records and damaged all the equipment. The building suffered no serious structural damage.

This is the second time in ten years that the basement has flooded. The state and county conducted a flood control study after the first flood but adopted no formal flood control plans. Fearful of another flood, the bank now stores all its records on the first and second floors.

The bank has claimed a casualty loss for the damaged records, equipment, and the decline in the market value of the building. The bank contends that because the basement of the building can no longer be used for storage, it is entitled to a casualty loss equal to the difference between the fair market value of the building before the casualty and the fair market value after the casualty. Write a memo to the president of Exeter Savings and Loan that discusses whether the bank can deduct as a casualty loss the building's decline in fair market value.

TAX PLANNING CASE

76. Jay is single and works as a salesperson. In 1996, he was selected the company's outstanding salesperson. In recognition of this honor, he received a $75,000 bonus. The bonus put him in the 36% tax bracket. Jay owns 2,400 shares of stock in Amtrav Corporation, which qualifies as small business stock. His broker has advised him to sell most, if not all, of his Amtrav stock. If he sells all his shares in the current year, he will recognize a $25 per share loss on the stock. Unfortunately, even if he sells all his stock, he will remain in the 36% tax bracket. He expects his marginal tax rate will drop to 28% next year, but it will be 31% and 36%, respectively, for the years after that. He does not anticipate any other capital gains or losses during the next 3 years. If Jay's goal is to minimize his taxes, develop a strategy for how many shares and in what year(s) Jay should sell his Amtrav stock. Assume that if he does not sell all his stock in the current year, his loss per share will remain constant and that the time value of money is 8%.

77. Anthony owns a 1992 Luxuro automobile that has a fair market value of $18,000. His son James, who is 19, borrows the car without his father's knowledge and totals it in 1995. James has been involved in 2 car accidents, and his father is afraid that James will not be able to get insurance. Therefore, Anthony decides not to file an insurance claim and deducts the loss on his 1995 tax return. In 1996, Anthony decides to have his friend Brigid, a local CPA, prepare his tax return. In preparing his 1996 return, Brigid reviews Anthony's 1995 return and finds that Anthony took a casualty loss on the Luxuro. Aware that Anthony has insurance, she is perplexed as to why Anthony deducted the loss. Anthony tells her of his son's fearsome driving record and his worry that his son could not get insurance. What are Brigid's responsibilities (refer to the Statements on Responsibilities in Tax Practice), if any, concerning Anthony's 1995 tax return? What effect does the issue have on Brigid's preparation of Anthony's 1996 return?

**ETHICS
DISCUSSION CASE**

INCOME TAX ENTITIES

CHAPTER 8
TAXATION OF INDIVIDUALS

CHAPTER 9
OTHER TAX ENTITIES

Taxation of Individuals

▲ CHAPTER LEARNING OBJECTIVES

■ Explain the requirements for exemption deductions for dependents.

■ Introduce the filing status of individual taxpayers and discuss the effect of filing status on the income tax paid by individuals.

■ Discuss the components of the individual income tax calculation.

■ Indicate the expenditures that are allowed as deductions for adjusted gross income and discuss those that present particular problems for individual taxpayers.

■ Introduce the deductions from adjusted gross income for specifically allowed personal expenditures, and explain the requirements for deduction and the applicable limitations.

■ Introduce the special provisions for the calculation of the tax of a dependent.

■ Provide a comprehensive example of an individual tax calculation.

▲ CONCEPT REVIEW ▲

Ability to pay   A tax should be based on the amount that a taxpayer can afford to pay, relative to other taxpayers.

Administrative convenience   Those items for which the cost of compliance would exceed the revenue generated are not taxed.

Annual accounting period   All entities must report the results of their operations on an annual basis (the tax year). Each tax year stands on its own, apart from other tax years.

Business purpose   To be deductible, an expenditure or a loss must have a business or other economic purpose that exceeds any tax avoidance motive. The primary motive for the transaction must be to make a profit.

Entity   All transactions must be traced to a single tax entity for recording and reporting by that entity.

Legislative grace   Any tax relief provided is the result of a specific act of Congress that must be strictly applied and interpreted. All income received is taxable unless a specific provision can be found in the tax law that excludes the income from taxation. Deductions must be approached with the philosophy that nothing is deductible unless a provision in the tax law allows the deduction.

Pay as you go   A tax should be collected as close as possible to the time in which the income is earned.

Tax benefit rule   Any deduction taken in a prior year that is recovered in a subsequent year is income in the year of recovery, to the extent that a tax benefit was received from the deduction.

Individuals are by far the biggest single group of taxpaying entities. During 1992, individuals filed more than 56 percent of all returns received by the IRS. These returns accounted for more than 60 percent of all income tax collected during 1992. Individuals are unique. Unlike corporations, which are formed to conduct a business, individuals engage in both business and personal transactions. As a result of this split for individuals, calculating the tax base of an individual requires consideration of deductions for both business-related expenditures and specifically allowable personal expenditures.

INTRODUCTION

   Individuals are taxable entities. Because all individuals who meet certain income requirements must file an annual tax return, they must adopt an accounting period. Although individuals may adopt a fiscal year if they keep a complete set of accounting records, most use a calendar year for convenience. Individuals must also choose an accounting method for reporting their various business and personal activities. Although individuals may use any method of accounting that clearly reflects their income (i.e., cash, accrual, hybrid), unless the individual sells inventories—which require use of the accrual (hybrid) method—most individuals choose the simpler cash method.

   This chapter discusses the unique features of calculating the tax base for individual taxpayers. Exhibit 8–1 presents the format for calculating an individual's taxable income, which generally is equal to gross income minus allowable deductions. Because deductions in general are allowed only under the business purpose concept, most personal expenditures by individuals are not deductible. A characteristic unique to individuals is that some minimal amount of personal expenditure is necessary to exist, money that is not available for paying taxes. Congress has recognized this characteristic by allowing some deductions for personal expenditures.

   A review of Exhibit 8–1 reveals that the basic taxable income calculation involves splitting deductions into two distinct classes—deductions for adjusted

▲ **Exhibit 8–1**

INDIVIDUAL INCOME TAX
CALCULATION

Gross income (all income received less exclusions)	$XXX
Less: Deductions *for* adjusted gross income	(XXX)
Equals: Adjusted gross income (AGI)	$XXX
Less: Deductions *from* adjusted gross income	
The greater of	
1. Itemized deductions	
OR	
2. Applicable standard deduction	(XXX)
Less: Personal and dependency exemptions	(XXX)
Equals: Taxable income	$XXX
Calculation of tax due (refund)	
Tax on taxable income (from rate schedule/table)	$XXX
Add: Additional taxes	XXX
Less: Tax credits	(XXX)
Equals: Net tax	$XXX
Less: Amounts withheld for payment of tax	(XXX)
Estimated tax payments	(XXX)
Equals: Tax due (refund of tax paid)	$XXX

gross income and deductions from adjusted gross income. This split creates the intermediate income figure called **adjusted gross income** (AGI). The basic difference between the two classes of deductions is that for-AGI deductions are closely related to the earning of income and most from-AGI deductions are personal expenditures. Adjusted gross income is important in determining the amount of allowable from-AGI deductions, because Congress has created limits that tie some allowable personal deductions to the adjusted gross income of the taxpayer. Individuals also receive personal exemption deductions for themselves and dependency exemption deductions for others who qualify as their dependents.

The remainder of the chapter discusses the basic allowable deductions for and from adjusted gross income of individuals, the dependency exemption deduction requirements, and limitations of deductions placed on high-income taxpayers and children younger than 14. The chapter concludes with a brief discussion of calculating the tax and filing the return. Exemptions and filing status of the taxpayer are discussed first, because they affect many of the topics discussed throughout the chapter.

PERSONAL AND DEPENDENCY EXEMPTIONS

In general, each individual taxpayer filing a tax return is allowed a **personal exemption** deduction of $2,550 in 1996 ($2,500 in 1995).[1] This is an amount that Congress has allowed all taxpayers in order to recognize such basic personal living costs as food and clothing, which are not otherwise allowed as a deduction. Like the standard deduction, the personal exemption amount is raised each year to account for inflation.

In addition to the personal exemption deduction, individuals are allowed a **dependency exemption** deduction for each qualifying dependent.

▲ **EXAMPLE 1**   Nelson and Alice are a married couple filing a joint return for 1996. They have 2 dependent sons, Peter and Rick. What is their total deduction in 1996 for personal and dependency exemptions?

Discussion: Nelson and Alice each are allowed a personal dependency deduction and a total of 2 dependency exemptions for Peter and Rick. Their total exemption deduction for 1996 is \$10,200 (4 × \$2,550). NOTE: The exemption for a spouse on a joint return is always considered a personal exemption. A spouse on a joint return is never considered a dependent; spouses are always considered taxpayers.

Dependency Requirements

In order to qualify as a **dependent,** an individual must meet five tests.[2] These tests are the gross income test; the support test; the relationship, or member of the household, test; the citizen or residency test; and the joint return test.

Gross Income Test.   The **gross income test** states that to be a dependent an individual's gross income (as defined for tax return purposes) must be less than the dependency exemption amount (\$2,550 in 1996). Note that excludable forms of income do not count in determining gross income for purposes of this test.

▲ **EXAMPLE 2**   Jerry's mother Jolene lived with him throughout all of 1996. Her only sources of income were \$300 from a savings account, \$3,500 in interest from tax-exempt municipal bonds, and \$2,600 in Social Security benefits. Does Jolene pass the gross income test for dependency?

Discussion: Although Jolene's economic income is \$6,400, her gross income for tax purposes is only \$300. Because this is less than the \$2,550 exemption amount, she passes the gross income test. NOTE: Although Jolene has passed the gross income test, she also must satisfy the other 4 requirements before Jerry can claim her as a dependent.

Two exceptions to the gross income test are provided for children of the taxpayer. The gross income test is waived for any child of the taxpayer who is either (a) younger than 19 at the end of the tax year, or (b) a full-time student younger than 24 at the end of the tax year.[3]

▲ **EXAMPLE 3**   Refer to example 1. Assume that Rick is 17 and earns \$3,500 per year bagging groceries after school. Peter is 25, a college student, and made \$4,800 working during the summer. Do Rick and Peter pass the gross income test for dependency?

Discussion: Rick passes the gross income test, because he is a child of the taxpayer and is younger than 19. Peter does not pass the test, even though he is a full-time college student, because he is older than 24 and has gross income in excess of \$2,550. NOTE: Peter does not qualify as a dependent, because he failed the gross income test. Although Rick has passed the test, he also must satisfy the other 4 tests before he can qualify as a dependent.

Support Test.   The **support test** requires that the taxpayer claiming the dependency exemption provide more than half the support of the dependent. Support is not necessarily related to the income of the dependent. This test simply requires a tallying up of amounts spent on support and determining whether the taxpayer seeking the dependency exemption has provided more than half of the entire amount spent on support.

▲ **EXAMPLE 4**   Refer to example 2. Assume that Jolene spent all of her \$6,400 in income to support herself. Jerry spent an additional \$4,500 to support Jolene. Does Jolene meet the support test?

Discussion: Jerry did not provide more than half of Jolene's total support of \$10,900 (\$6,400 + \$4,500) in 1996. Therefore, Jolene does not meet the support test and does not qualify as a dependent. NOTE: The fact that $6,100 of the income was not taxable has no bearing on the support test.

▲ **EXAMPLE 5**   Assume that in example 4 Jolene spent only $3,000 of the income she received in 1996 on her own support. She put the remaining $3,400 in a savings account. Does Jolene pass the support test?

Discussion: Jerry has provided more than half of Jolene's total support of $7,500 in 1996. Therefore, Jolene does pass the support test.

Two additional support situations are worth noting. First, in the case of two or more individuals who collectively provide more than 50 percent of the support of an individual who meets all the other tests for dependency, any member of the support group who contributes more than 10 percent of the total support may claim the dependency exemption through a multiple support agreement.[4] All members of the support group must agree in writing (the **multiple support agreement**) which person in the group is entitled to receive the exemption.

▲ **EXAMPLE 6**   Suzanne, Latifa, and Ben each provide 1/3 of the support of their brother Ozzie during 1996. Assuming that Ozzie meets all other dependency tests, who may take the dependency exemption for Ozzie in 1996?

Discussion: Although none of his siblings has individually provided more than half of Ozzie's support, as a group they have met the support test. By executing a multiple support agreement, the 3 can decide who will take the dependency exemption. NOTE: Only 1 member of the group may take the dependency exemption each year. It cannot be split among the group.

The second support situation deals with support of children of divorced parents. In this case, the custodial parent is entitled to the dependency exemption, regardless of actual support provided. In order for the noncustodial parent to obtain the dependency exemption, the custodial parent must agree in writing to give up the right to claim the exemption.

▲ **EXAMPLE 7**   Donna and Doug were divorced last year. Donna has custody of their dependent son. Doug paid $3,800 in child support payments during the current year. The cost of supporting the son during the year was $5,000. Who is entitled to the dependency exemption for the son?

Discussion: Because Donna is the custodial parent, she is entitled to the dependency exemption, regardless of the amount of support Doug paid during the year. The only way that Doug can take a dependency exemption for their son is if Donna agrees in writing that Doug can take the exemption deduction. The written agreement must be attached to Doug's return.

Relationship or Member of Household Test.   Under the **relationship, or member of household, test** a dependent must either be a relative of the taxpayer or a member of the taxpayer's household for the entire year. *Relatives* are defined as ancestors (grandfather), lineal descendants (granddaughter, son), and blood relationships such as aunt, nephew, or niece. Once a relative relationship is established, it does not change with divorce or death of a spouse. Thus, a wife's nephew continues to qualify as a relative even if the wife dies or the husband and wife divorce. Note that individuals who are not relatives meet this test if they are members of the taxpayer's household for the entire tax year.

Citizen or Residency Test.   Under the **citizen or residency test,** a dependent must be either (a) a citizen of the United States, or (b) a resident of the United

States, Canada, or Mexico. Alien children adopted by U.S. citizens and living with them in a foreign country qualify under this test.

Joint Return Test.   Dependents who are married may not file joint returns with their spouses for the exemption year in question. An exception to this test, which is known as the **joint return test,** is provided for married dependents who are not required to file a tax return (see the section on filing requirements) but file a return solely for the purpose of obtaining a refund.

A basic concept of the income tax system is that taxpayers pay tax according to their ability to pay. The measure of ability to pay is straightforward for an entity such as a corporation—gross income minus business-related deductions provides a reasonable measure of a corporate entity's ability to pay tax. Although this same measure may be appropriate for measuring the ability to pay tax on an individual's business income, it does not take into account a basic fact of life—individuals must incur some minimum level of personal expenditure just to stay alive. The income tax law takes this into account by allowing exemptions and setting tax rates. For example, by imposing a higher marginal tax rate at a lower level of income for an unmarried person than for a married couple, the unmarried person pays a higher average tax rate. Based on ability to pay, a single person with a taxable income of $30,000 can afford to pay more tax than a married couple with the same $30,000 in taxable income. The tax law recognizes this difference in ability to pay by basing exemptions, standard deductions, and average tax rates on the taxpayer's **filing status.**

> ## FILING STATUS

Individuals are classified in two groups—married and unmarried. Married taxpayers may either commingle all their income and deductions and file one return (joint return), or they may each file a separate return. Unmarried taxpayers may be classified as single or, if they qualify, as a head of household. This results in four filing statuses:

- Married, filing jointly (including a surviving spouse)
- Married, filing separately
- Single
- Head of household

Married, Filing Jointly

To qualify for the status of **married, filing jointly,** the taxpayers must be legally married as of the last day of the tax year.[5] If a spouse dies during the year, filing status is determined as of the date of death of the spouse if the survivor did not remarry during the year. Taxpayers who are divorced during the year or who are legally separated at the end of the year are not considered married for tax purposes. As originally conceived, the joint return filing status was designed to divide the combined income of a married couple in half and tax each half at the same rate as a single individual. The income-splitting benefit of a joint return has eroded through the years as Congress has made changes in the basic rate schedules. However, a married couple filing jointly may still pay less tax than a single individual at the same level of income. For example, an examination of the 1996 tax rate schedules in Appendix A shows that a single individual begins paying a 28-percent marginal tax rate at $24,000, whereas a married couple does not enter the

28-percent rate bracket until their taxable income reaches $40,100. Thus, at incomes greater than $24,000, married couples filing jointly pay less total tax than a single taxpayer with the same taxable income. The effect is to assess a lower average tax rate on the joint return.

In 1954, Congress recognized that the death of a spouse usually works a hardship on the survivor when a dependent child is still living in the home. In recognition of this hardship, a **surviving spouse** who has at least one dependent child or stepchild living at home may use the joint return tax rates to compute the tax for two tax years after the year in which the spouse died. In the year of death, the surviving spouse also files a joint return.

▲ **EXAMPLE 8**   Juan and Bonita are married and have 2 dependent children living at home. In 1996, Juan is killed in an avalanche while skiing. What is their filing status for 1996? How will Bonita file for subsequent years?

Discussion: In the year of Juan's death, Bonita files a joint return. In 1997 and 1998, Bonita files as a surviving spouse and uses the joint return tax rates if at least 1 of her 2 children remains a dependent and continues to live at home. If Bonita were to remarry, she would file either a joint return with her new spouse or file separately as a married taxpayer.

Married, Filing Separately

Although married taxpayers may file separate returns, there are very limited circumstances in which it is to a couple's advantage to choose this status. An examination of the tax rate schedules in Appendix A shows that married couples filing separately pay higher marginal tax rates at lower income levels than any other filing status category. As a result, the **married, filing separately,** status has the highest average tax rate of any income level greater than $20,050 in 1996. In addition, Congress has carefully crafted most other tax relief provisions to take away any advantage this filing status might offer. Its primary use is in situations of marital or financial disagreement in which the husband and wife cannot agree to file together and are not divorced or legally separated by year end.

Single

A **single** taxpayer is a person who is not married on the last day of the tax year and who does not have any dependents to support. Although single individuals pay more than a married couple filing jointly on the same taxable income, their taxes are less than those paid by a married couple filing separately. Some solace for the single taxpayer can be found in the so-called marriage penalty tax imposed on married taxpayers who have roughly equal incomes. This marriage penalty results from a married couple paying a higher tax on a joint return than each would have paid had they remained single.

▲ **EXAMPLE 9**   Harold and Sadie are a married couple with a taxable income of $60,000. If they had filed as single individuals, Harold's taxable income would have been $28,000 and Sadie's taxable income would have been $32,000. What is their "marriage penalty tax" for 1996?

Discussion: The marriage penalty is the difference in the tax that a married couple pays on their joint income versus what they would have paid had they been single taxpayers. For Harold and Sadie, the marriage tax is $1,027, calculated as follows:

Using 1996 Tax Rate Schedules

Tax on $60,000 for a Married Couple Filing a Joint Return

[$6,015 + 28% × ($60,000 − $40,100)] = $11,587

Tax on $28,000 for a Single Individual

[$3,600 + 28% × ($28,000 − $24,000)] = $4,720

Tax on $32,000 for a Single Individual

[$3,600 + 28% × ($32,000 − $24,000)] =   5,840   10,560

Marriage penalty tax $ 1,027

Head of Household

The head of household filing status recognizes that some single taxpayers share a characteristic of married taxpayers—the burden of extra living costs to support a relative. In order to qualify as a **head of household,** the unmarried taxpayer must pay more than half the cost of maintaining a home that is the principal residence for more than half the year for

- A qualified dependent, including children, parents, and other relatives; the taxpayer's parents do not have to live in the taxpayer's home if they meet the dependency tests

or

- An unmarried child or other direct lineal descendent (i.e., grandchild) who does not qualify as a dependent[6]

▲ **EXAMPLE 10**   Larry is legally divorced. His 4-year-old son lives with him for the entire year. Larry is entitled to a dependency deduction for his son. What is Larry's filing status?

Discussion: Because Larry is unmarried and maintains a household for a dependent child for more than half the year, he is entitled to file as a head of household.

▲ **EXAMPLE 11**   Assume that in example 10 Larry's son is unmarried, 26, and does not qualify as a dependent. If the son lives in Larry's home for the entire year, what is Larry's filing status?

Discussion: Although the son is not Larry's dependent, he is an unmarried child and lives in Larry's home for more than half the year. Therefore, Larry may file as a head of household, provided that he pays more than half the cost of maintaining the home. NOTE: If Larry's son were married, the son would have to qualify as Larry's dependent for Larry to claim head of household status.

A related relief provision allows an abandoned spouse to file as a head of household. A married person is treated as an **abandoned spouse** if a dependent child lives in the taxpayer's home for more than half the year and the taxpayer's spouse does not live in the home at any time during the last half of the year.[7] The benefit provided by this provision is that a married taxpayer is considered unmarried for the entire year.

▲ **EXAMPLE 12**   Loretta and Bob married in 1988. They have one child, Bobby, who is 7. During the current year, Loretta learned that Bob was having an affair with his secretary, Ellen. Bob and Ellen left the state together on March 3. Loretta is unaware of Bob's whereabouts, and no formal divorce proceedings have been initiated. What is Loretta's filing status for the current year?

Discussion: Because Loretta has a dependent child living with her and her husband has not lived in the home during the last 6 months of the tax year, Loretta is considered unmarried for the entire year. Therefore, she may file as a head of household.

Note that if formal divorce proceedings had begun and Loretta and Bob were legally separated, Loretta would have been considered unmarried under the general rules and she would have qualified as a head of household. The primary use of the abandoned spouse provision is in cases in which one spouse has left the household and no formal divorce proceedings have begun as of the end of the tax year.

DEDUCTIONS FOR ADJUSTED GROSS INCOME

This category of deductions generally consists of those expenditures that have a business purpose as well as certain expenditures that Congress has specifically allowed in the calculation of adjusted gross income. The allowable **deductions for adjusted gross income** are listed in Exhibit 8–2.[8]

It should be noted that expenditures in this category of deductions are *always* allowed as deductions. That is, after determining the allowable amount of each deduction, that amount is not subject to any income-level limitations and is always deductible. This is not always the case for deductions from adjusted gross income.

For reporting purposes, trade or business expenses, rent and royalty expenses, and reimbursed employee business expenses are subtracted directly from the related items of gross income. That is, the expenses are netted against their related gross income and reported as a net figure in the income tax calculation.

▲ **EXAMPLE 13**   Teresa is the sole proprietor of a carpet-cleaning business. During the current year, Teresa had gross income from the business of $93,000 and allowable expenses of $36,000. How should this information be reported on her return?

Discussion: The allowable trade or business expenses are netted separately against the gross income, resulting in trade or business income of $57,000. In calculating taxable income, the $57,000 in trade or business income is reported as gross income.

▲ **EXAMPLE 14**   Assume the same facts as in example 13, except that Teresa's allowable trade or business expenses totaled $101,000.

▲ **Exhibit 8–2**

LIST OF DEDUCTIONS ALLOWED FOR ADJUSTED GROSS INCOME

Trade or business expenses (losses)
Reimbursed employee business expenses
Capital loss deduction
Rental and royalty expenses
Alimony paid
Deduction for contributions to a retirement plan (other than an employer-provided plan)
Moving expenses
Net operating loss deduction
50% of the self-employment tax paid on business income
30% of a self-employed person's medical insurance premiums
Interest reported as income that has been repaid as a result of cashing in a certificate of deposit before its due date (early withdrawal penalty)
Certain deductions of life tenants and income beneficiaries of property
Certain required repayments of supplemental unemployment insurance benefits
Reforestation expenses
Certain portion of lump-sum distributions from pension plans subject to the special averaging convention

Discussion: In this case, the netting of expenses against income results in a loss of $8,000 ($93,000 − $101,000). Because it is a loss from a trade or business, it is deductible for adjusted gross income. Thus, the net figure of $8,000 is shown as a deduction for adjusted gross income.

The remaining items discussed in this section of the chapter appear as separate deductions on the tax return. Previous chapters discussed several of these deductions (e.g., trade or business expenses, rental and royalty expenses, capital losses). The deduction for alimony paid recognizes that the receiver of the alimony must recognize the income on his or her return and is allowed to avoid double taxation of the income.

Reimbursed Employee Business Expenses

It has long been held that an employee is engaged in a trade or business. However, not all employee business expenses are deductible for AGI as trade or business expenses. That is, the tax law allows a deduction for adjusted gross income only for those employee business expenses that are reimbursed by the employer, known as *reimbursed employee business expenses.*[9] Unreimbursed employee business expenses are included in miscellaneous itemized deductions, which are subject to a limitation of 2 percent of adjusted gross income (discussed later). Therefore, it is important to properly account for employee business expenses on the tax return. Unfortunately, Congress further complicated this distinction in 1988 when it restricted the deduction for adjusted gross income to those situations in which employees were reimbursed for their expenses under an accountable plan. Employees who receive reimbursements from a nonaccountable plan may deduct their expenses only as miscellaneous itemized deductions.[10]

Accountable Reimbursement Plans.   An **employer reimbursement plan** is an **accountable plan** if employees are required to make an adequate accounting of their expenses with their employer and to return excess reimbursements to the employer. An adequate accounting requires that the employee give the employer adequate documentation to support the expenditure being reimbursed as a valid business expense. This would include details as to time, place, and amount of the expense as well as the business purpose for the expense. Plans that reimburse employees by preset amounts for meals, lodging, and/or mileage (called *per-diem payments*) are considered accountable plans, provided that the employee is required to establish the business purpose for the payment and the per-diem amount does not exceed that paid by the federal government.

The treatment of reimbursements and expenses by the employee under an accountable plan depends upon the amount of reimbursement in relation to the actual expense. There are three scenarios:

■ Reimbursement equals actual expenses (any excess reimbursement is returned to the employer). In this case, the effect on the employee's income is a net change of zero. That is, the employee is neither in receipt of income from a reimbursement in excess of actual costs nor is the employee in a net deduction situation. No income is included in the employee's gross income, and no deductions, either for or from adjusted gross income, are allowed.

■ Reimbursement is less than actual expenses. The employee may be in a net deduction situation. The reimbursement must be included in the employee's gross income. The portion of the expenses reimbursed is deductible for adjusted gross income, thus canceling out the inclusion of the reimbursement in gross income. Actual expenses in excess of the reimbursement are deductible as miscellaneous itemized deductions, subject to the 2-percent adjusted gross income limitation. Further, any deduction taken for meals or entertainment costs is subject to the 50-percent limitation on meals and entertainment (see Chapter 6) before applying the overall 2% limitation.

■ Reimbursement is greater than actual expenses (i.e., excess reimbursement is not returned to the employer). In this case, the employee has net income, because the reimbursement is greater than actual expenses. The excess reimbursement is included in the employee's gross income.

Nonaccountable Reimbursement Plans.   If an employer reimbursement plan is a **nonaccountable plan,** the employee must include the reimbursement (if any) in gross income. No deductions for adjusted gross income are allowed. The employee can take deductions for expenses only as itemized deductions. As a matter of administrative convenience, employees (but not self-employed individuals) may choose to take deductions for meals and automobile mileage using the allowable federal per-diem rates rather than using actual costs. Any deduction for meals or entertainment is subject to the 50-percent limit on meals and entertainment before applying the overall 2-percent of adjusted gross income limitation.

For your reference, a summary of the reporting of reimbursements under the two types of plans is presented in Exhibit 8–3.

▲ **EXAMPLE 15**   Santamaria Co. requires its employees to adequately account for all reimbursed business expenses. Sarah, an account executive, submitted for reimbursement the following valid business expenses:

Transportation costs	$ 600
Meals	400
Lodging costs	800
Entertainment	200
Total costs	$2,000

What are the tax consequences if Santamaria reimburses Sarah the $2,000?

Discussion: Because there has been an adequate accounting, Sarah has no tax effects. None of the reimbursement is included in her gross income, and she is allowed no deductions for the expenses. NOTE: In this case, the employer is the taxpayer who effectively gets the deduction for the business expenses. Therefore, the employer is subject to the 50% limitation on meals and entertainment. The actual deduction for the employer is only $1,700 [$600 + $200 ($400 × 50%) + 800 + $100 ($200 × 50%)].

▲ **EXAMPLE 16**   What are the tax consequences if Santamaria reimburses Sarah for $1,500 instead of $2,000?

Discussion: In this case, Sarah is in a net deduction situation. The amount of the reimbursement, $1,500, is included in her gross income, and $1,500 of the expenses is deducted for AGI. The remaining $500 in unreimbursed expenses is deductible from AGI as a miscellaneous itemized deduction. Because Sarah is getting an actual deduction for meals and entertainment in this case, the 50% limit applies. Therefore, the individual costs must be allocated between for- and from-AGI, using the reimbursement ratio. The reimbursement ratio is the reimbursement divided by the total costs and equals 75% ($1,500 ÷ $2,000) in this case. The remaining 25% of each expense is unreimbursed. The allocation of deductions between for- and from-adjusted gross income is

	75% for AGI	25% from AGI	100% Total
Transportation costs	$ 450	$150	$ 600
Meals	300	100	400
Lodging	600	200	800
Entertainment	150	50	200
Total cost allocated	$1,500	$500	$2,000

Of the $500 in from-AGI expenses, only $50 ($100 × 50%) of the meals and $25 ($50 × 50%) of the entertainment costs are deductible, resulting in a total itemized deduction of $425 ($150 + $50 + $200 + $25). The $425 is combined with other allowable miscellaneous itemized deductions and subjected to the 2% of adjusted gross income limitation.

▲ **EXAMPLE 17**   Assume that Santamaria reimburses Sarah in the amount of $2,200 for the $2,000 in actual expenses. Although Santamaria's plan requires employees to return excess reimbursements, Sarah does not return the excess.

Discussion: In this case, because the plan is an accountable plan, Sarah is deemed to have made an adequate accounting of the $2,000 in actual expenses. The excess reimbursement, $200, must be included in her gross income.

Note that Santamaria will deduct the same amount that was allowed in example 15. The employer may deduct the $200 excess reimbursement as wages paid to Sarah.

Type of Plan	Gross Income Effect	Deduction For AGI	Deduction From AGI
Accountable Plans			
Reimbursement = Actual expenses	None	None	None
Reimbursement < Actual expenses	Full amount of reimbursement is included in gross income.	Reimbursed expenses; no 50% rule for meals and entertainment.	Unreimbursed expenses as miscellaneous itemized; 50% rule applies for meals and entertainment. Two percent overall limit for miscellaneous deductions applies.
Reimbursement > Actual expenses	Excess reimbursement is included in gross income.	None	None
Nonaccountable Plans			
Reimbursement received	Full amount of reimbursement is included in gross income.	None	All employee business expenses are deductible as miscellaneous itemized deductions; 50% rule applies for meals and entertainment. Two percent overall limit for miscellaneous deductions applies.
No reimbursement	None	None	Same as for reimbursement received

▲ **Exhibit 8–3**

TREATMENT OF EMPLOYEE BUSINESS EXPENSES

▲ **EXAMPLE 18**   Assume the same facts as in example 15, except that Sarah either does not have to make an adequate accounting or does not have to return any excess reimbursement. That is, Santamaria's plan is a nonaccountable plan.

Discussion: In all of these examples, 15 to 17, the reporting is the same if the plan is nonaccountable. The reimbursement must be included in Sarah's gross income, and Sarah is allowed to deduct only actual costs as miscellaneous itemized deductions, subject to the 50% limitation on meals and entertainment. In each of these instances, Sarah is allowed a miscellaneous itemized deduction of $1,700 (the calculation follows). This is combined with her other miscellaneous itemized deductions and subjected to the 2% adjusted gross income limitation for miscellaneous itemized deductions.

Transportation costs	$ 600
Meals ($400 × 50%)	200
Lodging	800
Entertainment ($200 × 50%)	100
Total miscellaneous deduction	$1,700

Deductions for Self-Employed Taxpayers

The deductions for adjusted gross income that self-employed taxpayers are allowed to take for health insurance premiums and self-employment taxes are designed to provide some measure of equity in the treatment of employees and self-employed individuals. Recall that health insurance premiums paid by an employer for an employee are excluded from the employee's gross income. Because self-employed individuals are not employees, they cannot take advantage of this fringe benefit. In order to partially equalize the treatment of employees and self-employed individuals, the tax law allows self-employed individuals to deduct 30 percent of the cost of their health insurance premiums as a deduction for adjusted gross income.[11] The remaining premium cost is considered a personal medical expense that is deductible from adjusted gross income. If the self-employed taxpayer or spouse is eligible to be covered by employer-provided medical insurance, the deduction for adjusted gross income is not allowed.

▲ **EXAMPLE 19**   Rory is the sole proprietor of Rory's Western Wear. During the current year, Rory paid $1,800 for his own health insurance. How should Rory deduct the $1,800 health insurance cost?

Discussion: Because Rory is self-employed, he can deduct $540 ($1,800 × 30%) of the health insurance premiums as a deduction for adjusted gross income. The remaining $1,260 of the health insurance premium's cost is a personal medical expense that is combined with his other allowable medical expenses. Personal medical expenses (discussed later) are allowed as a personal itemized deduction.

   If Rory's wife Eleanor is covered by medical insurance provided by her employer, the entire $1,800 can be deducted only as an itemized medical expense.

The second deduction for adjusted gross income that self-employed taxpayers may take is for one-half of the self-employment tax paid. The **self-employment tax** is the method through which self-employed individuals contribute to the Social Security system. The self-employment tax rate for 1996 is 15.3 percent of self-employment income. This is equal to the rate paid by employees (7.65 percent), which is matched by employers. The employer's payment into the employee's Social Security account is not taxed to the employee. The deduction of one-half of the self-employment tax equalizes the treatment for employees and self-employed individuals. In determining self-employment income, the net earnings from self-employment are reduced by one-half of the self-employment tax paid.[12] The effect of this provision is that only 92.35 percent [100% − (50% × 15.3%)] of the net earnings from self-employment is subject to the self-employment tax.

▲ **EXAMPLE 20**   Ramona is the sole proprietor of Rangoon Foods. During 1996, Rangoon had a taxable income of $80,000. Assuming that Ramona had no other sources of self-employment income, what is Ramona's 1996 self-employment income subject to the self-employment tax?

Discussion: Only 92.35% of the net earnings from self-employment is subject to the self-employment tax. Thus, Ramona's self-employment income is $73,880 ($80,000 × 92.35%).

The amount of income subject to the self-employment tax is the lesser of the ceiling amount or 92.35 percent of self-employment earnings. The 15.3 percent self-employment tax rate consists of two components, Old Age, Survivors, and Disability Insurance (OASDI) and Medicare Health Insurance (MHI). For 1996, the OASDI component is levied at 12.4 percent on the first $62,700 of self-employment income, and the MHI component is levied at 2.9 percent of total self-employment income. In effect, the rate is 15.3 percent on the first $62,700 of self-employment income and 2.9 percent on income in excess of $62,700.

▲ **EXAMPLE 21**   In example 20, what are Ramona's 1996 self-employment tax and her deduction for self-employment taxes paid?

Discussion: Ramona's self-employment tax is $9,917.

Tax on $62,700 in Income	
$62,700 × 15.3%	$9,593
Tax on Income in Excess of $62,700	
$73,880 − $62,700 = $11,180 × 2.9%	324
Self-Employment Tax	$9,917

Ramona is allowed to deduct $4,959, half of the self-employment tax, as a deduction for adjusted gross income.

Retirement Plan Contribution Deductions

Employees who participate in qualified employer pension plans are allowed to defer recognition of income paid into and earnings on assets in such plans until they are withdrawn from the plan. Recall from Chapter 4 that employees' payments into a qualified employer-sponsored pension plan are excluded from the employee's gross income. Taxpayers who do not have access to an employer-sponsored pension plan have several options under which they can accumulate assets for retirement in a tax-deferred manner. These retirement plans are different from employer-provided plans in that the taxpayer makes contributions to the plan and takes deductions for adjusted gross income for the amounts contributed. As with employer-sponsored plans, earnings on amounts paid into these plans are deferred until they are withdrawn. The effect of this arrangement is to reduce adjusted gross income (and ultimately taxable income) by the amount contributed to the plan, providing the same tax relief as an employer-sponsored plan. Self-employed taxpayers are allowed to establish their own separate retirement savings plan (referred to as a *Keogh*, or *H.R. 10, Plan*). One type of plan in which all individuals may participate is an individual retirement account.

Individual Retirement Accounts.   All taxpayers are allowed to contribute as much as $2,000 per year of their earned income to an **individual retirement account (IRA).** Taxpayers who have no earned income are not eligible to establish IRA accounts. If a husband and wife both have earned sources of income, each may contribute the $2,000 maximum amount to separate IRA accounts. An IRA can also be established for a nonworking spouse. However, the total amount paid into the two IRAs, if one spouse does not work, cannot exceed $2,250 and no one account can receive more than $2,000.

▲ **EXAMPLE 22**   Irving and Gloria are married, and each has earned income. Irving makes $16,000 per year, and Gloria earns $28,000 per year. What is the maximum amount they can contribute to their individual retirement accounts?

Discussion: Because both Irving and Gloria have earned income, each may contribute the $2,000 maximum to his or her own account, a total of $4,000 between them.

▲ **EXAMPLE 23**   Assume that in example 22 only Gloria works and Irving stays home with the children. What is the maximum amount they can contribute to their individual retirement accounts?

Discussion: Irving is a nonworking spouse. Irving and Gloria can contribute a maximum total of $2,250 to their 2 accounts. They may divide the $2,250 between the 2 accounts in any manner they choose as long as no single account receives more than $2,000. They can divide the contributions equally between the 2 accounts, or 1 account could receive the maximum $2,000 while the other's account receives $250.

If neither spouse is covered by an employer-sponsored retirement plan, all allowable contributions made to their IRAs are deductible for adjusted gross income. The effect of the deduction is to reduce the taxpayer's earned income by the amount paid in to the IRA.

▲ **EXAMPLE 24**   Return to example 22. Neither Irving nor Gloria is covered by an employer-sponsored pension plan. If they each contribute the maximum allowable amount to their IRAs, what is their deduction for adjusted gross income?

Discussion: Because neither Irving nor Gloria is covered by an employer-sponsored plan, they may each contribute $2,000 to their plans and deduct $2,000 for adjusted gross income. This would give them a total deduction of $4,000 for adjusted gross income. Note that the effect of the deduction is to reduce their individual earned incomes by the $2,000 contribution. Irving is taxed on only $14,000 ($16,000 − $2,000) of his earned income, and Gloria is taxed on only $26,000 ($28,000 − $2,000) of her earned income. This gives them the same tax treatment as employees who contribute to employer-sponsored pension plans and receive an exclusion for the amounts they pay in to the plan.

Unmarried taxpayers who participate in an employer-sponsored plan must reduce the amount of their IRA deductions proportionately when their adjusted gross income reaches $25,000. The entire deduction must be reduced to zero when adjusted gross income reaches $35,000. If at least one spouse is covered by an employer-sponsored plan, the amount of the IRA deduction for a married couple must be reduced when adjusted gross income reaches $40,000 and is reduced to zero when adjusted gross income reaches $50,000.[13] Thus, in both cases the allowable deduction is reduced over a $10,000 range of adjusted gross income. When adjusted gross income exceeds the top end of the range, no deduction is allowed.

▲ EXAMPLE 25   Assume the same facts as in example 24, except that Gloria participates in an employer-sponsored retirement plan. Irving and Gloria continue to make the maximum contribution to their IRAs, and they have an adjusted gross income of $46,000. What is their allowable deduction for the $4,000 they contribute to their IRAs?

Discussion: Because 1 spouse participates in an employer-sponsored retirement plan, Irving and Gloria must reduce their $4,000 IRA deduction proportionately when their adjusted gross income exceeds $40,000. The entire deduction must be reduced to zero when adjusted gross income reaches $50,000. This gives a $10,000 range of adjusted gross income over which the $4,000 deduction is reduced. A general formula for calculating the percentage reduction for a married couple is

$$\frac{\text{Adjusted gross income } - \ \$40,000}{\$10,000}$$

Irving and Gloria's reduction:

$$\text{Percentage reduction in IRA deduction} = \frac{\$46,000 \ - \ \$40,000}{\$10,000}$$

$$= \frac{\$6,000}{\$10,000} = 60\%$$

Based on the reduction percentage, Irving and Gloria must reduce the amount of their IRA deduction to $1,600 [$4,000 − ($4,000 × 60%)].

Irving and Gloria may still contribute the $4,000 maximum to their IRA accounts. It is only the amount of the allowable deduction that must be reduced when 1 taxpayer is covered by a separate pension plan, not the allowable contribution amount. The tax benefit of making nondeductible contributions is that the earnings on the contributions are allowed to accumulate tax free until they are withdrawn. John and Gloria do not have to make the maximum contribution to get the $1,600 deduction. They may choose to contribute only the deductible amount, or they may contribute some amount less than the $4,000 maximum.

▲ EXAMPLE 26   Assume the same facts as in example 25, except that Irving and Gloria's adjusted gross income is $38,000. What is the amount of their IRA deduction?

Discussion: Although Gloria participates in an employer-sponsored plan, their adjusted gross income is below the level at which the IRA deduction is reduced. Therefore, they are allowed to deduct their entire $4,000 contribution.

▲ EXAMPLE 27   Assume the same facts as in example 25, except that Irving and Gloria's adjusted gross income is $56,000. What is the amount of their IRA deduction?

Discussion: Their adjusted gross income is beyond the IRA deduction phase-out level, and they are not allowed a deduction for their contribution.

Moving Expenses

Moving expenses are deductible if they meet two tests.[14] The *distance test* requires that the commuting distance from the old residence to the new job be 50 miles farther than the commuting distance was to the old job. This requirement effectively eliminates the deduction for moves within the same general area and for job changes in the same general area. The *time test* requires the taxpayer to be employed at the new location for 39 weeks in the 12-month period following the move. Self-employed individuals must work in the new location for 78 weeks during the succeeding 2-year period. The time requirements are waived for death, disability, or discharge or transfer that is not the fault of the employee.

Moving expenses are allowed as a deduction for adjusted gross income. However, only certain types of expenses associated with moving are deductible. The taxpayer is permitted to deduct only (1) the cost of moving household goods and personal effects to the new residence, and (2) the transportation and lodging costs of moving the taxpayer and family from the old residence to the new residence. No deduction is permitted for meals incurred in transporting the taxpayer and family from the old residence to the new residence. If the taxpayer drives from the old residence to the new residence, mileage is allowed at 10 cents per mile. There is no limit on the amount of moving expenses that are deductible so long as the expenses incurred are not lavish or unreasonable. For example, the cost of refitting drapes in the new residence and taking a vacation during the move are not part of the reasonable cost of a move and are disallowed.

▲ **EXAMPLE 28** Millie takes a job in New City during 1996. New City is 750 miles from Old City, where Millie had been working. She expects to meet the 39-week test. Millie incurs $2,900 in costs for moving her household goods and personal effects. In addition, she incurs $400 in lodging expenses, $100 in meal expenses, and pays $20 in tolls en route to New City. Before moving to New City, she flies to New City to find an apartment. The cost of the flight is $350, and she incurs lodging costs of $200 and meal expenses of $75. How much of these costs can Millie deduct as moving expenses?

Discussion: Millie's moving expense deduction is $3,395. She is allowed to deduct the cost of transporting her household goods and personal effects ($2,900). In addition, Millie is allowed to deduct a total of $495 [lodging of $400, tolls of $20, and $75 in mileage (750 miles @ 10 cents per mile)] traveling to New City. The meal expenses and the costs associated with finding an apartment are not deductible.

DEDUCTIONS FROM ADJUSTED GROSS INCOME

This class of deductions consists of expenditures that Congress has allowed for certain costs that individuals incur and that reduce the amount available to pay taxes. There is a minimum deduction allowable to all taxpayers called the **standard deduction**. As a matter of legislative grace and under the administrative convenience concept, taxpayers who incur minimum levels of the allowable itemized deductions may choose to use the minimum deduction instead of incurring the cost necessary to substantiate itemized deductions.

Standard Deduction

The amount of the standard deduction is based on the filing status of the taxpayer. The deduction is based on a statutorily determined amount for each category of filing status. Because costs are affected by inflation, the standard deduction amounts are adjusted upward each year for inflation.[15] Standard deduction amounts for 1995 and 1996 are provided in Table 8–1.

In addition to the regular standard deductions allowed all taxpayers, taxpayers who are either blind (as defined by the tax law)[16] or who have attained age 65 by the end of the tax year are allowed additional standard deductions. Single taxpayers are allowed an additional standard deduction of $1,000 in 1996 ($950 in 1995) for each condition. Married taxpayers and a surviving spouse are allowed an additional $800 in 1996 ($750 in 1995) for each condition.

▲ **EXAMPLE 29** Malcolm, a single taxpayer, is 62 and legally blind. What is Malcolm's 1996 standard deduction?

Discussion: Malcolm's standard deduction is equal to the sum of the $4,000 standard deduction for a single taxpayer and an additional standard deduction of $1,000 for his blindness, a total of $5,000.

Filing Status	1995	1996
Single taxpayers	$3,900	$4,000
Married taxpayers, filing jointly	6,550	6,700
Married taxpayers, filing separately	3,275	3,350
Head of household	5,750	5,900
Surviving spouse	6,550	6,700

▲ **Table 8–1**

STANDARD DEDUCTION
AMOUNTS—1995 & 1996

If Malcolm is 65 as of December 31, 1996, he is entitled to an additional $1,000 standard deduction for age, bringing his total standard deduction to $6,000. This is the maximum standard deduction allowed a single taxpayer.

▲ **EXAMPLE 30**   Carl and Wenona file a joint tax return for 1996. Carl is 67, and Wenona is 59. In addition, Wenona is legally blind. What is the amount of Carl and Wenona's 1996 standard deduction?

Discussion: Carl and Wenona's standard deduction is equal to the sum of the married, filing jointly, standard deduction, $6,700, and 2 additional standard deductions of $800 each (total $1,600) for Carl's age and Wenona's blindness, a total of $8,300.

Note that the additional standard deductions allowed for age and blindness are added to the general standard deduction amount for comparison with the taxpayer's itemized deductions. The additional standard deduction amounts are not added to the taxpayer's itemized deductions.

▲ **EXAMPLE 31**   Return to the facts of example 30. If Carl and Wenona's allowable itemized deductions total $8,000, what is their deduction from adjusted gross income for 1996?

Discussion: Carl and Wenona deduct the greater of their itemized deductions ($8,000) or their allowable standard deduction ($8,300). In this case, the $8,300 standard deduction is greater, and they will not itemize on their return.

▲ **EXAMPLE 32**   Assume that in example 31 Carl and Wenona's allowable itemized deductions total $11,000. What is their deduction from adjusted gross income in 1996?

Discussion: Carl and Wenona deduct the greater of their itemized deductions ($11,000) or their allowable standard deduction ($8,300). In this case, Carl and Wenona should choose to itemize their deductions to get the $11,000 deduction. NOTE: The $1,600 additional standard deduction Carl and Wenona receive for age and blindness is not added to the itemized deduction amount. In effect, taxpayers with such conditions who itemize their deductions do not receive any additional benefit because of their condition.

Itemized Deductions

Individuals are allowed to deduct certain personal expenditures as **deductions from adjusted gross income** in lieu of the standard deduction. That is, taxpayers itemize deductions only when the sum of their allowable deductions exceeds their standard deduction.

▲ **EXAMPLE 33**   Raymond is a single individual with total allowable itemized deductions in 1996 of $3,500. How much of a deduction from adjusted gross income is Raymond allowed on his 1996 return?

Discussion: Because the standard deduction for a single taxpayer in 1996 is $4,000, Raymond uses the standard deduction amount to calculate his 1996 taxable income.

▲ **EXAMPLE 34** Assume that Raymond's total allowable itemized deductions are $7,200 in 1996. How much can Raymond deduct on his 1996 return?

Discussion: Because Raymond's allowable itemized deductions exceed the $4,000 standard deduction, he deducts the $7,200 in itemized deductions in calculating his 1996 taxable income.

In allowing certain personal expenditures to be deducted, Congress has exercised its power under the legislative grace concept to restrict the amount of deductible expenditures. These restrictions limit deductions to amounts exceeding a stated percentage of the taxpayer's adjusted gross income. Only amounts in excess of the limit are deductible. Restricting these deductions provides an element of administrative convenience. That is, with these limitations, many taxpayers will not have sufficient amounts of deductions to itemize, choosing instead to use the standard deduction amount. The use of the standard deduction lowers compliance costs, both for the taxpayer, who does not have to keep records of small amounts of expenses, and the government, which does not have to audit the standard deduction. This chapter discusses in turn each general category of itemized deductions and any applicable limitations. Table 8–2 provides a summary of the categories of allowable itemized deductions and their limitations.

Medical Expenses. Individuals are allowed a deduction for their unreimbursed medical costs as well as those of their spouse and any dependents. An individual does not have to meet the gross income test or the joint return test to qualify for medical expense purposes.[17] A person who meets the support, relative, and residency tests is considered a dependent for purposes of the medical expense deduction. This treatment recognizes situations in which taxpayers are expending significant amounts on behalf of relatives who, because they earn too much money or are married, are not technically dependents. In addition, note that the medical expense area is the only context in which you are allowed a deduction for the payment of expenses of another taxpayer.

Medical expenses are defined as those expenditures incurred for "diagnosis, cure, mitigation, treatment, or prevention of disease," as well as those that are incurred because of problems "affecting any structure or function of the body."[18] This definition encompasses the majority of costs we usually think of as medical expenses—doctor bills, dentistry, optometry, surgery, medicine and drugs, hospital charges, and so on. Deductions for medicines and drugs are limited to prescription drugs and insulin. In addition to these typical costs, taxpayers can deduct the cost of health and accident insurance premiums and transportation costs of 10 cents per mile for travel to and from the place of medical care.[19] Exhibit 8–4 lists deductible and nondeductible medical costs.

Unreimbursed medical costs are deductible only to the extent that they exceed 7.5 percent of adjusted gross income. That is, medical costs below the 7.5-percent limit are effectively disallowed.[20] This limitation severely restricts the benefit of the medical expense deduction for taxpayers with high incomes and/or those covered by medical insurance. Although low-income taxpayers are more likely to have medical expenses that exceed the 7.5% limitation, most low-income taxpayers use the standard deduction and therefore receive no benefit for the medical expenses incurred.

▲ **Table 8–2**

SUMMARY OF ALLOWABLE ITEMIZED DEDUCTIONS

Type of Expense	Allowable Expenses	Limitations
Medical expenses	Unreimbursed medical expenses—doctors, dentists, optometrists, eyeglasses, hearing aids, medical insurance premiums, travel to medical care	Only prescription medicine and drugs and insulin allowed as medical expenses Total medical expenses limited to the excess of 7.5% of adjusted gross income
Taxes	State and local income taxes, property taxes	Property taxes must be ad valorem
Interest	Qualified home mortgage interest	Interest on up to $1,000,000 in acquisition debt on taxpayer's principal residence and 1 other residence Interest on up to $100,000 in home equity loan interest
	Investment interest	Investment interest deduction cannot exceed net investment income
Charitable contributions	Cash and property contributed to qualifying educational, religious, charitable, scientific, or literary organizations	Total deduction cannot exceed 50% of adjusted gross income Contributions of long-term capital gain property deducted at fair market value cannot exceed 30% of adjusted gross income
Casualty and theft losses	Losses on personal use property from casualty or theft	Amount of loss is the lesser of the decline in value of the property or its adjusted basis $100 statutory floor per occurrence 10% of adjusted gross income limitation for all casualties and thefts
Miscellaneous	Gambling losses, disabled work-related expenses, unrecovered annuity investment	Fully deductible
	Unreimbursed employee business expenses, investment expenses (other than interest), hobby deductions, costs related to tax returns	2% of adjusted gross income limitation

▲ **EXAMPLE 35**   Ari is a single individual with an adjusted gross income of $40,000. During the current year, he incurred several medical expenses. What is his allowable deduction for the following expenses?

Doctors	$2,500
Dentist	250
Optometrist	150
Prescription drugs	375
Aspirin, cold pills	45
Contact lenses	200
Crutch rental for broken leg	80
Health insurance premiums	1,300
Transportation—100 miles to and from doctors, dentists, etc.	
Reimbursements for medical care	$2,800

Discussion: All of these are allowable medical expenses, with the exception of the $45 for aspirin and cold pills, which are not prescription drugs. In addition, Ari is allowed a deduction of 10 cents per mile for the 100 miles of transportation costs. His total allowable medical expenses before reimbursement are $4,865 ($2,500 + $250 + $150 + $375 + $200 + $80 + $1,300 + $10). Unreimbursed medical expenses are $2,065 ($4,865 − $2,800). This is subject to the 7.5% of AGI limitation, which is $3,000 (7.5% × $40,000). Therefore, Ari is not entitled to a medical expense deduction because his unreimbursed expenses do not exceed the AGI limitation.

Taxes.   Deductions are allowed for amounts paid for state and local income taxes, real estate taxes, and other personal property taxes.[21] Because most individuals are cash basis taxpayers, the deduction allowed is for **taxes** paid during the year, not the ultimate total of the tax imposed. Thus, taxpayers who itemize deductions normally have an adjustment for state and local taxes paid in the year following the deduction. If the taxpayer obtains a state or local tax refund, the tax benefit rule requires that person to include the refund in the subsequent year's taxable income. Similarly, if the taxpayer pays additional taxes, these are added to the tax paid for the subsequent year to determine that year's deduction.

▲ **Exhibit 8–4**

EXAMPLES OF MEDICAL EXPENSES

Deductible Items	Nondeductible Items
The cost of all medical drugs, special foods, and drinks your doctor prescribes for treatment of an illness; pills or other birth control items your doctor prescribes; vitamins, iron, etc. your doctor prescribes; insulin.	Toothpaste Cosmetics Vitamins for general health Veterinarian's fees
Payments to or for a doctor, surgeon, dentist, osteopath, ophthalmologist, optometrist, psychiatrist, psychologist, hospital care, therapy, lab fees, diagnostic tests, X-ray examination or treatment, nursing care.	Illegal operations or drugs Cosmetic surgery Funeral or burial expenses
Special items or equipment such as false teeth, eyeglasses, hearing aids, crutches, prescribed elastic hose, artificial limbs, guide dogs for the blind or deaf, motorized wheelchair, hand controls on a car, special telephone for the deaf.	Maternity clothing Diaper service
Transportation to get medical care—to and from doctor, dentist, hospital, etc.	Life insurance premiums Loss-of-earnings insurance premiums
Health and accident insurance premiums, supplementary Medicare premiums.	Premiums of automobile insurance Basic Medicare premiums

▲ **EXAMPLE 36**   Alana's withholding for state income taxes totals $2,400 during 1996. Alana is single, and her itemized deductions—including state income taxes—total $10,000. In filing her state income tax return, Alana receives a refund of $200. What is the proper treatment of the refund?

Discussion: Because Alana's 1996 deduction is recovered through the $200 refund in 1997, the $200 is included in her 1997 gross income. NOTE: The tax benefit rule applies only to taxpayers who itemize deductions. A taxpayer who elects to use the standard deduction has not claimed a deduction for taxes paid. Therefore, a taxpayer who uses the standard deduction and receives a refund of state income taxes has no income to recognize.

▲ **EXAMPLE 37**   Assume the same facts as example 36, except that her total itemized deductions, including state income taxes, are $4,100 ($2,400 in state taxes + $1,700 in other itemized deductions). What is the proper tax treatment of the refund?

Discussion: Alana must include $100 of the refund as income. The actual amount of her state itemized deductions should have been $2,200 ($2,400 claimed minus the $200 refund). If Alana had deducted the actual amount of taxes ($2,200) in preparing her return, she would have had $3,900 in itemized deductions. Because the $3,900 is less than the standard deduction of $4,000, she would have prepared her return using the standard deduction. Under the tax benefit rule, the $100 benefit she derived by claiming $4,100 of itemized deductions, instead of the standard deduction of $4,000, must be included on her 1997 income tax return.

▲ **EXAMPLE 38**   Assume the same facts as in example 36, except that Alana owes an additional $300 in state income taxes when she files her 1996 state income tax return. How should Alana treat the $300 paid with the state return?

Discussion: Alana pays the $300 in additional state taxes in 1997. Because she is a cash basis taxpayer, the $300 in tax paid in 1997 should be deducted as state income taxes paid in 1997.

In order to be deductible, personal property taxes must be ad valorem, that is, based on the value of the property being taxed.

▲ **EXAMPLE 39**   State A charges a vehicle licensing fee that is based on the type of vehicle and its weight. State B's vehicle licensing fee is $25 plus 1% percent of the fair market value of the vehicle. Is either fee deductible as a tax?

Discussion: State A's fee is not based on the value of the vehicle and is not a deductible personal property tax. State B's fee is partially based on the value of the vehicle. Therefore, the fee in excess of the $25 fixed charge is deductible as a personal property tax.

An individual cannot use any of the following in calculating itemized tax deductions: federal taxes, including income and Social Security taxes; water use and sewer taxes; excise taxes on alcohol, tobacco, or firearms; gasoline taxes; utility taxes; assessments for local benefits such as sidewalks; and sales taxes.[22] Note that assessments for local benefits are not considered taxes and would be added to the basis of the property. It should be stressed that although these taxes are not deductible by individuals as itemized deductions, they may be deductible or capitalized as part of the cost when incurred in a trade or business (Chapter 6).

Interest Expense.   Itemized deductions for interest payments have been severely restricted in recent years. Personal interest (credit cards, auto loans, student loans) is specifically disallowed. The only interest deductible as an itemized deduction is qualified home mortgage interest and investment interest.[23] Each type of interest is subject to several restrictions.

HOME MORTGAGE INTEREST.   Only interest on debt that is secured by the taxpayer's principal residence and one other residence is deductible as **qualified home mortgage interest.**[24] The second residence either must qualify as a vacation home (see Chapter 6 for vacation home requirements) if it is rented out during the year or not be rented at all during the year in order to qualify as a second residence. If a second home is considered rental property (i.e., a rental loss is allowed), the portion of the interest expense attributable to the personal use of the home is considered personal interest and is not deductible. A *residence* includes a house, cooperative apartments, condominiums, and mobile homes and boats that have living accommodations (living quarters, cooking facilities, etc.).

Qualified home mortgage interest includes both acquisition debt and home equity debt. **Acquisition debt** is any debt incurred to acquire, construct, or substantially improve a qualified residence of the taxpayer. **Home equity debt** is any debt that is secured by a personal residence that is not acquisition debt. However, there is a cap on the level of indebtedness for each type of qualified home mortgage interest:

- Interest paid on acquisition debt of $1 million or less is deductible. Interest on debt in excess of $1 million is considered personal interest and is not deductible. Acquisition debt includes the cost of acquiring, constructing, or substantially improving a qualified residence.

- Interest paid on home equity debt of $100,000 or less is also deductible. However, total debt (acquisition plus home equity) cannot exceed the fair market value of the property. Home equity debt is any debt, other than acquisition debt, which is secured by the residence. The proceeds of home equity debt can be used for any purpose.

Points are prepaid interest amounts that must be paid in order to acquire financing. They are expressed as a percentage of the value of the loan and paid at loan acquisition. As such, they represent prepaid interest, which usually is capitalized and amortized over the term of the loan. A special provision in the tax law allows points paid to acquire an initial mortgage on a taxpayer's principal residence to be deducted in the year the points are paid.[25] However, points paid to refinance an existing mortgage must be capitalized and amortized as interest expense over the term of the loan. Loan origination fees that replace charges for services in obtaining the loan are not deductible as points. Prepayment penalties for the early payment of a mortgage are also deductible as qualified home mortgage interest.

▲ **EXAMPLE 40**   Anita purchases a new home in 1996, borrowing $80,000 from Local Bank to finance the purchase. Anita also pays $1,600 in points and $1,000 in loan origination fees. Interest paid on the $80,000 mortgage in 1996 totals $8,400. What is Anita's allowable 1996 interest deduction?

Discussion: Assuming that the $80,000 debt is secured by the property, Anita can deduct the $8,400 in mortgage interest and the $1,600 in points paid to obtain the mortgage—$10,000 in all. The loan origination fees are not deductible interest.

▲ **EXAMPLE 41**   Zane's home is worth $250,000. He purchased the home 20 years ago using a $100,000 mortgage. During the current year, Zane paid $5,400 in interest on the original mortgage, which has a balance of $45,000. Zane also borrowed $110,000 on a home equity loan and used the proceeds to pay off personal debts, buy a new sports car, and take a trip around the world. Zane paid $11,000 in interest (i.e., a 10% interest rate) on the home equity loan. How much is Zane's allowable interest deduction?

Discussion: The $5,400 paid on the original mortgage is qualified home mortgage interest. Although the total debt ($100,000 + $110,000) is less than the fair market value of the home, only $100,000 of the home equity is considered qualified debt. The deduction for the home equity loan would be $10,000 (10% × $100,000), for a total allowable interest deduction of $15,400. The excess home equity debt ($10,000) is considered personal debt, and the $1,000 in interest is nondeductible. NOTE: The $100,000 home equity loan is considered qualified debt, regardless of the use of the proceeds. In this case, even though Zane used the proceeds for purely personal purposes, the interest is deductible.

INVESTMENT INTEREST.   Interest paid on debt used to purchase portfolio investments is deductible. Thus, interest paid on an investment in a passive activity is not included in the investment interest deduction. Expenses related to passive activities are subject to the passive activity rules and are not included in the investment interest calculation. In addition, as stated in Chapter 5, interest paid to produce tax-exempt income is not deductible and therefore is not part of the investment interest deduction.

The deduction for **investment interest** is limited to the net investment income of the taxpayer for the year. Any interest not currently deductible because of this limitation may be carried forward indefinitely and applied to future years. **Net investment income** is defined as investment income less investment expenses (other than interest). *Investment income* consists of gross income from property held for investment purposes (i.e., not a passive activity), gains (losses) from the disposition of such properties, and portfolio income (as defined for passive loss rules). For tax years beginning after 1992, net long-term capital gains, which are taxed at the maximum 28% long-term capital gain rate, are not included in the investment income calculation. **Investment expenses** include all ordinary and necessary expenses directly connected to the production of the investment income.

▲ **EXAMPLE 42**   Kareem pays interest related to his investment activities totaling $40,000 in 1996. His investment income is $30,000, and investment expenses are $6,000. What is his 1996 investment interest deduction?

Discussion: The deduction is limited to $24,000 ($30,000 − $6,000), Kareem's net investment income. The $16,000 in disallowed interest is carried forward to 1997 for deduction against 1997 net investment income.

▲ **EXAMPLE 43**   Assume that in 1997, Kareem pays $36,000 in investment interest and has investment income of $44,000 and $5,000 in investment expenses. What is Kareem's 1997 investment interest deduction?

Discussion: Kareem's net investment income is $39,000 ($44,000 − $5,000). He is allowed to deduct the $36,000 in current-year interest and $3,000 of the previously disallowed interest. His carryover of disallowed investment interest to 1998 is $13,000 ($16,000 − $3,000).

Charitable Contributions.   Individuals are allowed to deduct contributions to organizations that are organized for religious, charitable, educational, scientific, or literary purposes.[26] Deductions are also allowed for contributions to organizations that work to prevent cruelty to animals or children and for contributions to government units. The top panel of Exhibit 8–5 contains examples of organizations that do and those that do not qualify as **charitable organizations.**

Most charitable contributions are made in cash and do not present valuation problems. However, when a taxpayer contributes property to a charitable organization, the type of property determines the amount of the contribution.[27] As indicated in the lower panel of Exhibit 8–5, property of a type that would produce ordinary income or short-term capital gain if it were sold is limited to the lesser of (1) the fair market value of the property on the date of the contribution, or (2) the adjusted basis of the property. This limitation makes it an unwise tax-planning strategy to donate ordinary income property that has a fair market value that is less than the adjusted basis (i.e., loss property).

> ▲ **EXAMPLE 44**   Tomas owns 2 properties that are ordinary income properties. Both properties have a fair market value of $10,000. Property A has an adjusted basis of $6,000, and property B has an adjusted basis of $25,000. Which property would be the better to contribute to his alma mater?
>
> *Discussion:*   If Tomas contributes property A, his deduction is only $6,000 (fair market value is greater than adjusted basis). A contribution of property B results in a deduction of $10,000 (fair market value is less than adjusted basis). However, if Tomas contributes property B, he loses the $15,000 ($10,000 − $25,000) in unrealized loss on the property. By contributing property A, his deduction is lower, but he avoids tax on the $4,000 ($10,000 − $6,000) in unrealized gain on the property.
>
> If Tomas wished to contribute property B, it would be better to sell the property, realize the ordinary loss of $15,000, and contribute the $10,000 in cash from the sale. The charitable contribution deduction would still be $10,000, and Tomas would have an ordinary loss deduction of $15,000 on the sale. Note that one big advantage of gifting property A is the avoidance of tax on the $4,000 in unrealized gain on property A.

Taxpayers can deduct the fair market value of contributions of property that would result in a long-term capital gain if the property were sold. However, the taxpayer may elect to reduce the amount of the contribution to the adjusted basis of the property in order to use a higher contribution ceiling, as discussed next.

> ▲ **EXAMPLE 45**   Assume that in example 44 both of Tomas's properties were long-term capital gain properties. Which is the better to contribute?
>
> *Discussion:*   Deductions for contributions of long-term capital gain property are allowed for the fair market value of the property. In this case, both properties would result in a deduction of $10,000. However, Tomas would be better off if he contributes property A and avoids the tax on the $4,000 in unrealized gain on the property.

There are three major limitations on the deductible amount of charitable contributions. The overall amount of the charitable contribution deduction cannot exceed 50 percent of the taxpayer's adjusted gross income. Contributions of capital gain property that are deducted at fair market value cannot exceed 30 percent of adjusted gross income. But a taxpayer who is willing to give up the deduction related to the property's appreciation (i.e., use the adjusted basis as the deductible amount) is not subject to the 30-percent limit. In addition, contributions to certain nonoperating private foundations are subject to rather complex limitations that

▲ **Exhibit 8–5**

SUMMARY OF
CHARITABLE
CONTRIBUTION RULES

Examples of Qualified Charities:	**Examples of Nonqualifying Organizations:**
Churches, mosques, synagogues	Chambers of Commerce and other business
Salvation Army, Red Cross, CARE, Goodwill,	leagues or organizations
United Way, Boy Scouts, Girl Scouts,	Civic leagues
Boys/Girls Club of America	Communist organizations
Fraternal orders (if gift used for charitable	International organizations
purpose)	Social clubs
Nonprofit schools and hospitals	Country clubs
Veterans' groups	
Certain cultural groups	
Federal, state, and local governments	

Examples of Allowable Contribution Items:	**Items That Are Not Deductible:**
Cash	Political contributions
Clothing	Raffle, bingo, or lottery tickets
Furniture	Tuition to a private school
Fixtures	The value of a person's time
Inventory	Value of blood donated to a blood bank or
Real property	Red Cross
Stocks, bonds	Gifts to individuals
Paintings, works of art	
Jewelry	
Automobiles	
Appliances	
Out-of-pocket costs for performing charitable	
work—special uniforms, mileage, etc.	

Type of Property:	Amount of Contribution:	Maximum Deduction (Limit):
Cash	Amount contributed	50% of adjusted gross income
Ordinary income or Short-term capital gain property	The lesser of 1. the fair market value at the time of the contribution or	50% of adjusted gross income
	2. the adjusted basis of the property	50% of adjusted gross income
Long-term capital gain property	Fair market value at the date of contribution	30% of adjusted gross income
	An election can be made to reduce the amount of the contribution to the adjusted basis of the property.	50% of adjusted gross income

are beyond the scope of this discussion. Any contributions in excess of the limitations are carried forward for deduction for five years.

▲ **EXAMPLE 46**   Antonia owns stock for which she paid $20,000 several years ago; she would like to donate the stock to the Girl Scouts. The stock is worth $25,000, and Antonia's adjusted gross income is $40,000. Assuming that she has made no other charitable contributions, what is her allowable deduction?

Discussion: Because the sale of the stock would produce a long-term capital gain if Antonia sold the stock, she is allowed to use the $25,000 fair market value as the amount of her contribution. However, deductions for contributions of property that are measured at fair market value are limited to 30% of adjusted gross income. In this case, Antonia's current deduction would be limited to $12,000 (30% × $40,000), with the $13,000 remainder carried forward for deduction in the subsequent 5 years.

Antonia has the option of measuring the amount of her contribution at her adjusted basis in the stock, $20,000. Property measured at the adjusted basis is subject to the general 50% of adjusted gross income limit for charitable contributions. By valuing her contribution at $20,000 (her basis), she could deduct the entire $20,000 in the current year. However, she would have no remaining deduction carryforward under this election.

Miscellaneous Itemized Deductions.   This category of deductions, **miscellaneous itemized deductions,** includes amounts expended for unreimbursed employee business expenses, investment expenses (other than investment interest), hobby-related deductions, and gambling losses to the extent of gambling winnings. In addition to the limitations imposed on specific types of deductions in this category (i.e., meals and entertainment), some expenditures are fully deductible, whereas others are subject to an annual limitation of 2 percent of adjusted gross income.[28]

FULLY DEDUCTIBLE EXPENDITURES.   Gambling losses (not to exceed the amount of gambling winnings), impairment-related work expenses of a disabled person, and the unrecovered investment in an annuity contract when the annuity ceases because of death (discussed in Chapter 3) are deductible without regard to the annual limitation imposed on other types of miscellaneous expenses. Thus, it is important to segregate these expenditures from other allowable miscellaneous deductions.

PARTIALLY DEDUCTIBLE EXPENDITURES.   Unreimbursed employee business expenses, investment expenses (other than investment interest), fees for tax advice and preparation, and hobby-related deductions are deductible only to the extent that the total expenditures in this category exceed 2 percent of the taxpayer's adjusted gross income. Examples of expenditures that qualify in this category are provided in Exhibit 8–6.

▲ **EXAMPLE 47**   Odakota has an adjusted gross income of $30,000 in the current year. Odakota incurred $800 in employment-related expenses that were not reimbursed by his employer and $200 for tax return preparation. What is Odakota's allowable miscellaneous itemized deduction?

Discussion: Of the $1,000 total allowable expenditures, only the amount in excess of $600 ($30,000 × 2%)—$400—is deductible.

The 2-percent limitation is an annual limitation that is imposed after any specific limitations imposed on each category of expenditure. For example, unreimbursed employee meals and entertainment are subject to the 50-percent limitation on meals and entertainment before the 2-percent annual limitation is applied. In addition, hobby expenses are limited to hobby income before application of the 2-percent annual limitation.[29]

▲ **EXAMPLE 48**   Lois paints in her spare time. During the current year, she sold some paintings at a local arts and crafts fair for $300. Her costs for painting supplies and transportation to and from the fair were $800. If Lois had an adjusted gross income of $25,000 (including the hobby income) and had no other miscellaneous itemized deductions, what is the effect of the hobby on her taxable income?

Discussion: Because her painting is considered a hobby, Lois must include the $300 in her gross income, and her allowable hobby deductions are limited to the $300 in income. The actual amount of the hobby expense deduction is subject to the 2% annual limitation. Because her allowable hobby deductions are less than $500 ($25,000 × 2%),

Fully Deductible Miscellaneous Expenditures:

Gambling losses (to extent of gambling winnings)
Impairment-related work expenses of a disabled person
Unrecovered investment in annuity contracts because of death

Partially Deductible Expenditures:	**Nondeductible Expenditures:**
Employee Business Expenses	Burial or funeral expenses
Certain employment agency fees	Fees and licenses, such as marriage
Certain employment-related education	licenses and dog tags
Dues to professional organizations	Fines and penalties
Subscriptions to professional journals	Home repairs
Small tools and supplies	Home insurance
Uniforms not adaptable to general use	Rent on a personal residence
Union dues and expenses	
Investment Expenses	
Legal and accounting fees	
Safe deposit box rental	
Investment counsel fees	
Clerical help and office rent in caring for	
investments	
Fees paid in connection with property held	
for the production of income	
Other Allowable Expenses	
Hobby-related deductions	
Fees for tax advice	
Fees for tax preparation	

none of her hobby costs is deductible. This results in her hobby increasing her taxable income by $300.

In regard to the limitation on investment interest discussed earlier, investment expenses are determined after applying the 2-percent annual limitation. However, any other miscellaneous itemized deductions are applied against the 2-percent limitation before investment expenses are reduced for purposes of the investment interest limitation.[30]

▲ **EXAMPLE 49**   Kareem, in example 42, pays interest related to his investment activities totaling $40,000 in 1996. His investment income is $30,000, and investment expenses are $6,000. Kareem has an adjusted gross income of $50,000 and no other allowable miscellaneous itemized deductions. What is his 1996 investment interest deduction?

Discussion: The investment interest deduction is limited to Kareem's net investment income. For purposes of this calculation, investment expenses are those allowable after applying the 2% annual miscellaneous itemized deduction limitation. Thus, Kareem's investment expense deduction is only $5,000 [$6,000 − ($50,000 × 2%)], and net investment income is $25,000 ($30,000 − $5,000). His allowable investment interest deduction is $25,000.

In comparing the results in this example to those in example 42, Kareem's investment interest deduction has increased by $1,000. This is because the 2% limitation reduces his deductible investment expenses to $5,000. Because Kareem receives no benefit for $1,000 of his investment expenses, they are not used in determining his net investment income.

▲ **EXAMPLE 50**   Assume that in example 49 Kareem also has $600 in allowable unreimbursed employee business expenses. What is his 1996 investment interest deduction?

Discussion: In determining the amount of investment expenses lost because of the 2% annual limitation, other deductions subject to the limitation must be taken against the limit first. In this case, the $600 in employee expenses is applied first against the $1,000 limit, leaving only $400 of the investment expenses subject to the limitation. This leaves Kareem with $5,600 ($6,000 − $400) in investment expenses and a net investment income of $24,400. Thus, only $24,400 of the investment interest is deductible. NOTE: The investment interest deduction of $24,400 is $600 less than the $25,000 in example 49 but $400 more than would be permitted (see example 42) if this provision did not exist.

ITEMIZED DEDUCTIONS AND EXEMPTIONS— REDUCTIONS BY HIGH-INCOME TAXPAYERS

The tax law requires that high-income taxpayers must reduce the amount of their allowable itemized deductions and personal and dependency exemption amounts. In general, taxpayers with adjusted gross incomes in excess of $117,950 in 1996 ($114,700 in 1995) must reduce their otherwise allowable itemized deductions by 3 percent of adjusted gross income in excess of $117,950 ($114,700 in 1995). In making this reduction to account for the **itemized deduction phase-out,** allowable deductions for medical expenses, investment interest, gambling losses, and casualty and theft losses are not subject to reduction. In addition, deductions subject to the 3-percent reduction rule may not be reduced by more than 80 percent of the otherwise allowable amount.[31]

▲ **EXAMPLE 51**   Charles and Aretha are a married couple filing a joint return in 1996. They have adjusted gross income of $250,000 and total itemized deductions of $22,000. Included in the $22,000 is $5,000 in allowable medical expenses and $7,000 in investment interest. How much of the $22,000 in itemized deductions may Charles and Aretha actually deduct on their return?

Discussion: The $12,000 in medical and investment interest expenses is not subject to the reduction rule. The remaining $10,000 is subject to reduction, but the reduction may not exceed $8,000 ($10,000 × 80%). The basic reduction is for 3% of AGI in excess of $117,950. This equals $3,962 [3% × ($250,000 − $117,950)]. Because the basic reduction is less than the $8,000 maximum reduction, total itemized deductions are reduced by $3,962. This leaves them with deductible itemized deductions of $18,038 ($22,000 − $3,962).

Note that if Charles and Aretha's AGI is $400,000, the 3% reduction rule would be $8,462 [3% × ($400,000 − $117,950)]. Because this is in excess of the $8,000 maximum reduction, they would reduce their total itemized deductions by the $8,000 maximum, resulting in a deduction of $14,000 ($22,000 − $8,000).

High-income taxpayers also must reduce their exemption deductions. The basic reduction is 2 percent of the allowable exemption amount for each $2,500 (or portion thereof) in adjusted gross income in excess of the threshold amount and is known as the **exemption deduction phase-out.** The threshold amount varies by filing status, as shown in Table 8–3.

Note that in Table 8–3 the third column shows the AGI level at which the phase-out ends. This means that taxpayers with AGIs in excess of these amounts are not be entitled to a deduction for personal and dependency exemptions.

▲ **EXAMPLE 52**   Martina is a single taxpayer with adjusted gross income of $140,000 in 1996. What is her allowable personal exemption amount?

Discussion: Because Martina's adjusted gross income is in excess of $117,950, she must reduce her $2,550 personal exemption by 2% for each $2,500 increment (or portion thereof) of adjusted gross income in excess of $117,950. Thus, the first step is to calculate the number of $2,500 increments:

1996		
Filing Status	**Threshold Amount**	**Phase-Out Ends**
Single	$117,950	$240,450
Head of household	$147,450	$269,950
Married, filing jointly	$176,950	$299,450
Married, filing separately	$ 88,475	$149,725
Surviving spouse	$176,950	$299,450
1995		
Filing Status	**Threshold Amount**	**Phase-Out Ends**
Single	$114,700	$237,200
Head of household	$143,350	$265,850
Married, filing jointly	$172,050	$294,550
Married, filing separately	$ 86,025	$147,275
Surviving spouse	$172,050	$294,550

▲ **Table 8–3**

THRESHOLD AGI FOR EXEMPTION PHASE-OUT: 1996, 1995

$$\$140,000 - \$117,950 = \$22,050 \text{ in excess of } \$117,950$$

$$\$22,050 \div \$2,500 = 8.82 \text{ increments} = 9 \text{ phase-out increments}$$

$$\text{Percentage of exemption lost} = 9 \times 2\% = 18\%$$

Because of the phase-out, Martina loses 18% of her exemption, leaving her 82% (100% − 18%) of her $2,550 exemption as her actual deduction, $2,091 ($2,550 × 82%).

▲ **EXAMPLE 53**   Bill and Catherine are a married couple, have 2 dependents, and file a joint return for 1996. Bill and Catherine's adjusted gross income is $320,000. What is their allowable exemption deduction?

Discussion: Bill and Catherine's adjusted gross income is greater than the top of the phase-out range for a married couple filing jointly ($299,450). Therefore, their exemption deductions are fully phased out, and they are not entitled to deductions for exemptions.

Two aspects to note in calculating the exemption phase-out are that the total exemption amount—not each individual exemption—is subject to the phase-out. Therefore, high-income taxpayers with larger numbers of exemptions lose more than taxpayers with the equivalent income but fewer exemptions. Second, each portion of a $2,500 increment results in a 2-percent reduction. Thus, in example 52, Martina lost a full 2 percent for the 0.82 increment. A rule of thumb to follow in doing this calculation is to always round up.

The tax law provides several restrictions on the use of exemptions and standard deductions by dependents. Any individual who can be claimed as a dependent of another is not allowed a personal exemption in the calculation of his or her own taxable income. Note that this requirement is not negotiable: If the dependency tests are met, no personal exemption deduction is allowed.

▲ **EXAMPLE 54**   Andreas, 20, is a full-time college student at City Tech. He earns $4,400 during 1996 that he uses to pay for living expenses. His father gives him an additional $9,600 to pay for college-related costs and additional living expenses. How much is Andreas's 1996 personal exemption?

EXEMPTION AND STANDARD DEDUCTION RESTRICTIONS ON DEPENDENTS

Discussion: Because Andreas meets all the tests for dependency, his father receives a dependency exemption for Andreas. Andreas is not allowed a personal exemption, because he qualifies as a dependent of his father.

The second restriction on a dependent is the amount of the allowable standard deduction. A dependent's standard deduction is the greater of

- $650 ($650 in 1995)

  or

- The dependent's earned income or the standard deduction amount for a single individual, whichever results in a smaller deduction

The intent of this provision is to deny the benefit of a full standard deduction to a dependent who has large amounts of unearned income. This takes away some of the incentive for high marginal tax rate taxpayers to shift significant amounts of unearned income to lower marginal tax rate dependents. However, dependents with earned sources of income are still allowed to use the standard deduction to reduce the tax on earned income.

▲ **EXAMPLE 55**   Return to the facts of example 54. What is Andreas's standard deduction amount for 1996?

Discussion: Because Andreas has earned income of $4,400, he is allowed a standard deduction of the full $4,000 single standard deduction. Assuming that Andreas has no deductions for AGI, his taxable income for 1996 is $400 ($4,400 − $4,000).

▲ **EXAMPLE 56**   Amy is a dependent of her parents; she earns $2,200 from a summer job and receives $1,200 in interest in 1996 from a savings account established by her grandfather. What is Amy's standard deduction?

Discussion: Because Amy is a dependent, her standard deduction is the greater of $650 or her earned income, $2,200. Her standard deduction is limited to the $2,200 in earned income. NOTE: Assuming that Amy has no deductions for AGI, her taxable income is $1,200. Thus, she has not been able to shield any of her unearned income through use of a personal exemption deduction or the standard deduction.

CALCULATING TAX LIABILITY

After determining the taxpayer's taxable income, the tax is computed using the appropriate rate schedule for the taxpayer's filing status. Individuals with taxable incomes of less than $100,000 generally use the tax tables provided by the IRS. A 1995 tax table and tax rate schedules for 1995 and 1996 can be found in Appendix A.

The next step in completing the tax liability calculation is to add any additional taxes due with the return and deduct any allowable tax credits to arrive at the net tax liability for the year (see Exhibit 8–1). Several other taxes are paid with an individual's income tax return. These taxes include the self-employment tax, the alternative minimum tax (see Chapter 14), recapture taxes, and the Social Security tax on unreported tip income. The net tax liability is then compared to amounts withheld from the taxpayer's salary and payments of estimated taxes to determine the amount of tax due (or the refund to be received) with the return.[32] If the amount of tax due is greater than $500 and more than 10 percent of the tax liability, the taxpayer may be penalized for the underpayment of estimated taxes.[33]

Tax on Unearned Income of a Minor Child

In 1986, Congress complicated the tax calculation for a minor child with significant amounts of unearned income (interest, dividends, royalties, etc.). The provision enacted is designed to eliminate the tax rate advantage that could have been gained under prior law by shifting unearned forms of income from the parents to a minor child. The basic thrust of the law is to tax the **net unearned income** of a child who has not attained the age of 14 **(minor child)** at the parent's marginal tax rate (the **kiddie tax**).[34] Although not specifically stated, this treatment is an extension of the assignment-of-income doctrine for investment income. That is, the substance of giving minor children investment property is to make an assignment of the parents' unearned income to the children in an attempt to lower taxes. For purposes of this calculation,

Net unearned income = Unearned income

Less: $650

Less: The greater of $650 or the costs of
producing the unearned income

Note that under this definition, any unearned income in excess of $1,300 ($650 + $650) is taxed at the parents' marginal tax rate. The remaining taxable income of the child is taxed at the child's marginal tax rate. This treatment has the effect of disallowing the assignment of unearned income in excess of $1,300 to a minor child.

▲ **EXAMPLE 57**   Dan and Madeline are a married couple with a taxable income of $55,000 in 1996. Their daughter, Dawn, 10, has interest income of $850 and dividend income of $950 in 1996. What is Dawn's 1996 tax liability?

Discussion: Because Dawn is younger than 14 and has unearned income in excess of $1,300, the tax on unearned income of a minor child applies.

Calculation of Dawn's Taxable Income	
Gross income ($850 + $950)	$1,800
Less: Standard deduction	(650)
Exemption	-0-
Taxable income	$1,150
Net Unearned Income Taxed at Parents' Rate	
$1,800 − $650 − $650 =	500
Remainder taxed at Dawn's rate	$ 650
Tax Calculation	
Tax on $500 at parents' marginal	
tax rate ($500 × 28%)	$ 140
Tax on $650 at Dawn's rate	
($650 × 15%)	98
Total tax due	$ 238

In most cases, parents whose children are subject to this special tax may calculate the tax and report it on their own return rather having the child file a separate return.

FILING REQUIREMENTS

Whether an individual is required to file a return depends on the taxpayer's gross income. General **filing requirements** for individuals are that they must file a return when their gross income exceeds the sum of (1) their standard deduction amount (including the additional amount for age but not for blindness), and (2) their allowable personal (not dependency) exemptions. There are three major exceptions to this general rule:

- Individuals with net earnings from self-employment in excess of $400 must file a return, regardless of their gross income level.

- Married taxpayers filing separate returns are required to file if their gross income exceeds $2,550, the personal exemption amount.

- Dependents with unearned income greater than $650 must file a return.[35]

> ▲ **EXAMPLE 58**   Matthew, who is a single taxpayer, is 66 and legally blind. In 1996, he receives $5,000 in Social Security and $7,800 in dividends. Is he required to file a tax return for 1996?
>
> *Discussion:*   Matthew must file a 1996 return, because his $7,800 gross income (the Social Security is not taxable in this case) is greater than the $7,550 filing requirement for a single taxpayer who is 65 or older. Note that the $1,000 additional standard deduction for blindness is not included in the filing requirement levels. As a result, Matthew must file a return, even though he will not have taxable income ($7,800 − $4,000 − $1,000 − $1,000 − $2,550 < 0).

Of course, taxpayers with gross income less than the required filing level will want to file when they are entitled to a refund of taxes. The filing levels for various taxpayers are given in Table 8–4.

SUMMARY

Calculating taxable income for an individual is complex because of several factors. First, unlike other income tax entities, individuals engage in both business and personal transactions. Congress has allowed individuals to take certain deductions for personal expenditures and has allowed for some element of convenience through use of the standard deduction. This causes a split of an individual's deductions into those for adjusted gross income and those from adjusted gross income. In addition, Congress has chosen to limit the availability and the amount of certain deductions to dependents and high-income taxpayers. To aid you in

▲ **Table 8–4**

1995 & 1996 FILING REQUIREMENTS

Filing Status	1995 Gross Income	1996 Gross Income
Single	$ 6,400	$ 6,550
Single—age 65 or older	7,350	7,550
Married, filing jointly	11,550	11,800
Married, filing jointly—one spouse 65 or older	12,300	12,600
Married, filing jointly—both 65 or older	13,050	13,400
Surviving spouse	9,050	9,250
Surviving spouse—age 65 or older	9,800	10,050
Married, filing separately	2,500	2,550
Head of household	8,250	8,450
Dependent with unearned income	650	650

your study, the appendix to this chapter contains a comprehensive example of the tax calculation for an individual taxpayer. You should review the example to get a feel for how an individual's tax return calculation is put together.

KEY TERMS

abandoned spouse (p. 333)
accountable plan (p. 335)
acquisition debt (p. 348)
adjusted gross income (p. 328)
charitable organization (p. 350)
citizen or residency test (p. 330)
deductions for adjusted gross
   income (p. 334)
deductions from adjusted gross
   income (p. 343)
dependency exemption (p. 328)
dependent (p. 329)
employer reimbursement plan
   (p. 335)
exemption deduction phase-out
   (p. 354)
filing requirements (p. 358)
filing status (p. 331)

gross income test (p. 329)
head of household (p. 333)
home equity debt (p. 348)
individual retirement account
   (IRA) (p. 340)
investment expense (p. 349)
investment interest (p. 349)
itemized deduction phase-out
   (p. 354)
joint return test (p. 331)
kiddie tax (p. 357)
married, filing jointly (p. 331)
married, filing separately (p. 332)
medical expenses (p. 344)
minor child (p. 357)
miscellaneous itemized
   deductions (p. 352)
moving expenses (p. 341)

multiple support agreement
   (p. 330)
net investment income (p. 349)
net unearned income (p. 357)
nonaccountable plan (p. 336)
personal exemption (p. 328)
points (p. 348)
qualified home mortgage interest
   (p. 348)
relationship, or member of
   household, test (p. 330)
self-employment tax (p. 338)
single (p. 332)
standard deduction (p. 342)
support test (p. 329)
surviving spouse (p. 332)
taxes (p. 346)

PRIMARY TAX LAW SOURCES

[1] Sec. 151—Allows a personal exemption deduction; requires the deduction to be adjusted annually for inflation; disallows a personal exemption deduction for a dependent.

[2] Sec. 152—Allows dependency exemption deductions; defines *dependent* and specifies the tests for dependency; requires the deduction to be adjusted annually for inflation.

[3] Reg. Sec. 1.151-3—Defines *child, student,* and *educational institution* for purposes of determining dependency exemptions.

[4] Reg. Sec. 1.152-3—Explains the rules for claiming dependency exemptions under multiple support agreements.

[5] Sec. 6013—Allows a married couple to file a joint return; specifies that marital status is determined on the last day of the tax year or at date of death of spouse.

[6] Sec. 2—Defines *surviving spouse* and *head of household*; allows an abandoned spouse to file as a head of household.

[7] Sec. 7703—Defines *abandoned spouse.*

[8] Sec. 62—Defines *adjusted gross income* for individual taxpayers and specifies the deductions allowed as deductions for adjusted gross income.

[9] Reg. Sec. 1.62-2—Provides the rules for reimbursements of employee business expenses.

[10] IRS Announcement 90-7—Provides an overview of the rules for reporting employee business expense reimbursements.

[11] Sec. 162(l)—Allows a self-employed individual to deduct for adjusted gross income 30% of the medical insurance premiums paid during the year.

[12] Sec. 1402—Defines *self-employment income* and provides for the tax to be paid on base amounts as specified in the Social Security Act for each tax year; allows the reduction of self-employment income by one-half of the Social Security tax paid.

[13] Sec. 219—Allows a deduction for contributions to an individual retirement account; prescribes the maximum amounts deductible and limitations on deductions

for active participants in other pension plans.

[14] Sec. 217—Allows a deduction for moving expenses and specifies the allowable expenses.

[15] Sec. 63—Defines *taxable income*; allows individual taxpayers to deduct the greater of their allowable itemized deductions or the standard deduction; specifies standard deduction amounts and requires their annual adjustment for inflation.

[16] Reg. Sec. 1.151-1—Defines *blindness* for purposes of additional standard deduction amount; provides examples of items that constitute support for purposes of the dependency exemption.

[17] Reg. Sec. 1.213-1—States that a medical dependent does not have to pass the gross income and joint return tests.

[18] Sec. 213—Allows the deduction of medical expenses as an itemized deduction for individual taxpayers; defines *medical expenses* and prescribes limitations on the amount of the deduction.

[19] Rev. Proc. 95-54—Provides the standard mileage rates for use of an automobile for medical and charitable purposes.

[20] Sec. 213—See footnote 18.

[21] Sec. 164—Specifies the allowable deductions for taxes.

[22] Reg. Sec. 1.164-2—Lists taxes that individuals cannot deduct as itemized deductions.

[23] Sec. 163—Specifies the allowable deductions for interest; disallows personal interest other than qualified home mortgage interest and investment interest.

[24] Reg. Sec. 1.163-10T—Provides the rules for determining the deduction for qualified residence interest.

[25] Sec. 461—Allows a current deduction for points paid to acquire a home mortgage.

[26] Sec. 170—Allows a deduction for contributions to qualifying charities.

[27] Reg. Sec. 1.170A-1—Provides general rules for determining amounts of charitable contributions; disallows a deduction for the contribution of time or services to a qualifying organization.

[28] Sec. 67—Defines *allowable miscellaneous itemized deductions*; provides for 2% of adjustment gross income limitation on miscellaneous itemized deductions; exempts certain miscellaneous itemized deductions from the 2% of adjusted gross income limit.

[29] Reg. Sec. 1.67-1T—Provides that any specific limitations on miscellaneous itemized deductions are to be applied before considering the 2% of adjusted gross income limitation.

[30] H.R. REP. NO. 841, 99th Cong., 2d Sess. (1986)—States that investment expenses are determined after applying the 2% of adjusted gross income limitation and that any other miscellaneous itemized deductions are applied against the 2% limit before any investment expenses are reduced.

[31] Sec. 68—Requires phase-out of itemized deductions by high-income taxpayers; specifies when deductions are phased out and requires the adjustment of the phase-out level annually for inflation.

[32] Sec. 31—Provides that amounts withheld as tax from salaries and wages are allowed as credits against that year's tax liability.

[33] Sec. 6654—Provides that all individuals must pay estimated taxes when their tax liability is expected to be greater than $500; imposes a penalty for not paying the proper amount of estimated tax.

[34] Sec. 1—Imposes a tax on the taxable income of different classes of individual taxpayers; specifies that the tax on the unearned income of a child younger than 14 (minor child) is taxed at the higher of the child's or the parents' marginal tax rate.

[35] Sec. 6012—Provides the general requirements for filing an income tax return.

DISCUSSION QUESTIONS

1. What is the difference between a personal exemption and a dependency exemption? Are all taxpayers allowed a personal exemption?

2. What are the five tests that must be met in order to claim a dependency exemption? Briefly explain each test.

3. Which parent is entitled to claim the dependency exemption for a child when the parents are divorced? Can the other parent ever claim the dependency exemption?

4. What is a multiple support agreement? When is a multiple support agreement necessary?

5. Why is a taxpayer's filing status important?

6. What is a surviving spouse? Explain the tax benefit available to a surviving spouse.

7. Under what circumstances can a married person file as a head of household?

8. What is (are) the main difference(s) between deductions for AGI and deductions from AGI?

9. Why are deductions for adjusted gross income "better" than deductions from adjusted gross income?

10. What is an accountable employee expense reimbursement plan? What is the significance of such a plan?

11. Why are self-employed taxpayers allowed to deduct a portion of their medical insurance premiums and self-employment tax for adjusted gross income?

12. Are all taxpayers allowed a deduction for an individual retirement account contribution? Explain.

13. What general requirements must be met in order to obtain a deduction for moving expenses?

14. What expenses associated with moving are allowed as a deduction?

15. What is the standard deduction? Explain its relationship to a taxpayer's itemized deductions.

16. One general requirement for deduction is that the expense be the taxpayer's, not that of another. Is this always true? Explain.

17. Explain the limitations placed on deductions for medical expenses.

18. What is an ad valorem tax? What is the significance of an ad valorem tax?

19. Which types of interest are deductible as itemized deductions? What (if any) limitations are imposed on the deduction?

20. In what year(s) are points paid to acquire a loan deductible? Explain.

21. Why is interest paid on a loan used to purchase municipal bonds not deductible?

22. What limits are placed on deductions for charitable contributions?

23. Explain how the deduction allowed for a charitable contribution of ordinary income property is different than the deduction for donation of long-term capital gain property.

24. What limitations are placed on miscellaneous itemized deductions?

25. The itemized deduction and exemption phase-outs are an example of what concept? Explain.

26. Which itemized deductions are not subject to the itemized deduction phase-out?

27. Explain the operation of the itemized deduction phase-out. What stops a taxpayer from losing all itemized deductions under the phase-out?

28. What is the standard deduction amount for a dependent? Under what conditions can a dependent claim the same standard deduction as a single individual who is not a dependent?

29. Why did Congress enact the "kiddie tax"?

30. What determines who must file a tax return?

PROBLEMS

31. Determine whether each of the following individuals can be claimed as a dependent in the current year. Assume that any tests not mentioned have been satisfied.
    a. Nico is 20 and a full-time college student who received a scholarship for $13,000 (tuition, books, and fees totaled $15,000). His father gave him an additional $10,000 to pay for room and board and other living expenses.
    b. Lawrence paid $8,000 of his mother's living expenses. His mother received $3,500 in Social Security benefits and $3,900 from a qualified employer retirement program, all of which was spent on her support.
    c. Megan's father had no sources of income. During the year, Megan paid all of her father's support. Her father is a citizen and resident of Australia.
    d. Tawana and Ralph are both college students. They are married and had income during the year totaling $6,400. Tawana and Ralph filed a joint return to receive a refund of the taxes withheld on the $6,400. Her parents gave them an additional $10,200 to help them through college.
    e. Assume the same facts as in part d, except that Tawana and Ralph had $8,000 in income.

32. Determine whether each of the following individuals can be claimed as a dependent in the current year. Assume that any tests not mentioned have been satisfied.
    a. Marvin's father, Bert, lives with him. Bert's only income is $8,000 in Social Security. Bert gives Marvin $2,800 per year to help him pay the household bills. Marvin pays all other costs of maintaining the household. During the current year, Marvin spent $12,000 in addition to the $2,800 his father gave him for food, rent, and other household costs.
    b. Darren and Darla were divorced during the current year. Darla has custody of their 3-year-old son. Darren pays Darla $300 per month in child support. Darla pays the other $200 per month it costs to support their son.
    c. Carlos is 25 and a college student. Carlos lives with his parents, who also give him $600 per month toward his college expenses. Carlos earns the other $4,500 he needs to cover his expenses with a part-time job at a convenience store.
    d. Andrew's mother, Julia, lives in a nursing home. Julia's $9,000 in Social Security is paid to the state, which pays the entire $14,000 cost of her nursing home. Andrew gives Julia $500 per month to pay other incidental costs not covered by the state.

33. Determine the filing status in each of the following situations:
    a. Angela was single for most of the year. She married Tim on December 30.
    b. Earl was divorced during the current year. Their son lives with Earl's former spouse. Earl lives alone.
    c. Rita is married to Bob, and they have 2 children, ages 2 and 4, at home. Bob and Rita had a fight in March; Bob left and never returned. Rita has no idea where Bob might be.
    d. Joe is single. Joe provides all the support for his parents, who live in a nursing home. Joe's parents' only source of income is Social Security.
    e. Sam's wife died in February of last year. Their children are all of legal age and none lives in the household. Sam has not remarried.
    f. Would your answer to part e change if Sam had a dependent son or daughter who still lived in the home?

34. What is the filing status of each of the following taxpayers?
    a. Tom was married to JoAnne until they separated on November 15. On December 27, a formal separation agreement was filed in court.
    b. Wanda is single. She provides a household for her 22-year-old son who works as a lifeguard at the local swimming pool. Her son earned $8,700 from his job this year.
    c. Randy is single. He gave his parents $10,000 to help them pay the cost of living in a retirement home in Florida. The cost of the retirement home is $15,000 per year. Randy's parents receive $6,000 per year in Social Security and $8,000 per year in taxable dividends.
    d. Andrea is married to Hal. They have 2 children who live at home. Hal became despondent over his job situation and left the country in April. Andrea has not heard from Hal since he left and doesn't know where he is.

35. During the current year, Carson paid $1,500 in child support and $2,000 in alimony to his ex-wife. What is Carson's allowable deduction, and how should it be deducted on his tax return?

36. Mona works for Leonardo Corporation as a sales representative. Leonardo gives her a travel allowance of $500 per month. During the current year, she spent the following amounts on valid travel expenses:

Transportation	$3,800
Meals	2,200
Lodging	2,400
Entertainment	1,600

How should Mona treat the $500 per month travel allowance and the travel costs she incurred if
   a. Leonardo's reimbursement plan is an accountable plan?
   b. Leonardo's reimbursement plan is a nonaccountable plan?

37. Alvin is an employee of York Co. During the year, Alvin incurred the following employment-related expenses:

Travel	$3,700
Meals	2,800
Lodging	3,500
Entertainment	2,000

   a. How should Alvin treat these expenses if York Co. has an accountable employee business expense reimbursement plan and Alvin is reimbursed
      1. $12,000?
      2. $9,000?
      3. $13,000?
   b. How would your answer to part a change if York's reimbursement plan was nonaccountable?
   c. How would your answer to part a change if Alvin is self-employed (i.e., he receives no reimbursements)?

38. The Ballaraat Corporation is cutting costs. The vice president of finance has asked the tax department to justify the company's continued use of an accountable employee expense reimbursement plan. You are the manager of the tax department. Prepare a letter to the vice president of finance explaining the tax consequences of not using an accountable employee expense reimbursement plan. Also discuss any nontax benefits of maintaining the plan.

39. Harold works for the Zanten Corporation. Ken is self-employed. Zanten pays all of Harold's medical insurance premiums, whereas Ken purchases medical insurance from his insurance agent. Explain how the payment for Ken's and Harold's medical insurance are treated for tax purposes. Does this treatment meet Adam Smith's equality criterion?

40. Evelyn is a self-employed engineer. During 1996, Evelyn's income from her engineering business was $50,000. Evelyn paid $3,900 for her medical insurance policy.
   a. How should the medical insurance policy payment be reflected on Evelyn's 1996 tax return?
   b. What is Evelyn's 1996 self-employment tax deduction?

41. Mae is single and earns a salary of $62,000. Mae also owns a house that she rents. During 1996, Mae receives $8,500 in rental income from the house. Her allowable expenses related to the rental property total $12,600. Assuming that Mae has no other sources of income and does not itemize her deductions, what is her 1996 taxable income?

42. Ferris and Jody are married and file a joint return. During the current year, Ferris had a salary of $32,000. Neither Ferris nor Jody is covered by an employer-sponsored pension plan. Determine the maximum IRA contribution and deduction amounts in each of the following cases:
    a. Jody earns $18,000, and their adjusted gross income is $47,000.
    b. Jody does not work, and their adjusted gross income is $33,000.
    c. Jody earns $12,000, and their adjusted gross income is $39,000.
    d. Assume the same facts as in part a, except that Ferris is covered by an employer-sponsored pension plan.
    e. Assume the same facts as in part c, except that Ferris is covered by an employer-sponsored pension plan.

43. Zorica and Pierre are married and file a joint return. Zorica earns $31,500 and Pierre $16,000. Their adjusted gross income is $49,000. Determine the maximum IRA contribution and deduction in each of the following cases:
    a. Neither Zorica nor Pierre is covered by an employee-sponsored pension plan.
    b. Only Zorica is covered by an employee-sponsored pension plan.
    c. Assume the same facts as in part b, except that Pierre works part time, earning $1,500, and their adjusted gross income is $36,500.

44. Kathy, who is single and 25, inherited $2,500 from her grandmother. A coworker has suggested that Kathy open an Individual Retirement Account with the $2,500. Her friend says that an IRA is a great way to save, because you don't have to pay tax on the income from the investment and you get a tax deduction for your contribution. Write a letter to Kathy explaining whether her friend's advice is correct. To the extent her friend's information is inaccurate, provide Kathy with the correct tax treatment, and explain how different facts may lead to different tax treatments.

45. Myron graduates from college this year and lands a job with the Collingwood Corporation in Dallas. After accepting the job with Collingwood, Myron travels to Dallas to find an apartment. Myron's grandmother gave him $2,000 as a graduation gift; he uses that money to pay a moving company to transport his household goods from Atlanta. He doesn't drive directly to Dallas but goes via Panama City to vacation with friends. In moving to Dallas via Panama City, he incurs the following expenses:

Transportation of household goods	$1,350
Lodging	675
Meals	330
Mileage (1,560 miles @ 9 cents per mile)	140
House-hunting trip:	
Transportation	325
Lodging	165
Meals	110

The expenses listed include $375 for lodging and $230 for meals in Panama City. The direct mileage between Atlanta and Dallas is 1,340 miles. When Myron arrives in Dallas, he is informed that the moving van has mechanical problems and will not arrive for two days. Instead of sleeping on the apartment floor, he stays in a local hotel. The hotel costs $55 per night, and he spends $60 for meals. What is Myron's allowable moving deduction?

46. Nina and Steve are married and live in Chariho. Steve accepts a new job in Hopkington, which is 80 miles from Chariho. Because Nina enjoys her job as a nurse at Chariho Hospital, they decide to move halfway between Chariho and Hopkington. Steve is aware that some moving costs are tax deductible and that certain requirements must be met to deduct moving expenses. Write a letter to Nina and Steve explaining the requirements that must be met and which expenses then become deductible. In your letter be sure to advise Steve and Nina whether their planned move qualifies for a deduction.

47. Determine the maximum deduction from AGI in the current year for each of the following taxpayers:
   a. Pedro and Juanita are married. They have total itemized deductions of $6,100.
   b. Avery is single and legally blind. His itemized deductions total $4,600.
   c. Janet is divorced. Her 25-year-old son lives with her while attending college. Her total itemized deductions are $4,700.
   d. Bruce is single. Bruce provides all the support for his parents who live in a nursing home. Bruce's parents' only source of income is Social Security. Bruce's itemized deductions total $8,000.

48. Alicia is 27 and has never been married. For 1996, her gross income totals $43,000, she has $1,400 in allowable for-AGI deductions and total itemized deductions of $6,100.
   a. What is Alicia's 1996 taxable income?
   b. What is Alicia's 1996 income tax?
   c. If Alicia has $6,550 withheld from her paycheck during 1996, is she entitled to a refund or does she owe additional taxes?

49. Arthur and Cora are married and have 2 dependent children. For 1996, they have a gross income of $81,000. Their allowable deductions for adjusted gross income total $2,100, and they have total allowable itemized deductions of $16,500.
   a. What is Arthur and Cora's 1996 taxable income?
   b. What is Arthur and Cora's 1996 income tax?
   c. If Arthur has $6,200 and Cora has $3,275 withheld from their paychecks during 1996, are they entitled to a refund, or do they owe additional taxes?

50. Jasper and June incurred the following medical expenses during the current year:

Medical insurance premiums	$4,550
Prescription drugs	650
Hearing aid	1,050
Root canal	1,600
Weight loss program	2,100

If Jasper and June were reimbursed for $2,200 of these costs, what is their allowable medical expense deduction if
   a. Their adjusted gross income is $42,000?
   b. Their adjusted gross income is $83,000?

51. Lian was injured in an automobile accident this year. She was hospitalized for 4 weeks and missed 3 months of work after getting out of the hospital. The costs related to her accident were

Hospitalization	$19,500
Prescription drugs	3,200
Doctor's fees	10,800
Wheelchair rental	650
Visits by home nursing service	2,300

Lian's employer-provided insurance policy paid $24,700 of the costs. She also received $5,200 in disability pay from her employer while she was absent from work. By the end of the year, Lian was able to pay only $4,300 of the costs that weren't covered by her medical insurance. What is Lian's allowed itemized deduction for medical expenses if her adjusted gross income was $35,000 before considering any of this information?

52. Jim resides in Minnesota and owns some business interests in Hawaii. During 1996, he pays the following taxes:

Minnesota state income tax withheld	$4,700
Hawaii estimated tax payments	1,800
Utility and telephone taxes	190
Additional Minnesota tax for 1994 because of an error	260
Interest and penalties on 1994 error	65
Sales tax paid on new automobile	620

Jim itemized his deductions on his 1995 tax return. He received a $340 refund of Minnesota taxes and paid an additional $440 in Hawaii taxes on his 1995 state income tax returns. What is Jim's allowable deduction for 1996 taxes paid?

53. Simon is single and a stock broker for a large investment bank. During 1996, he has withheld from his paycheck $2,000 for state taxes and $500 for city taxes. He also pays $150 when he files his 1995 state tax return in April 1996. In June 1997, Simon receives a state tax refund of $190. What is the proper tax treatment of the refund in 1997 if
    a. Simon uses the standard deduction?
    b. Simon has itemized deductions other than state and city income taxes of $3,900?
    c. Simon has itemized deductions other than state and city income taxes of $1,550?

54. Herbert buys a lot on May 1, 1996, for $24,000; he plans to build a new home on it. As part of the sales agreement, Herbert agrees to pay the entire $1,250 in property taxes on the property for the year. How much of the $1,250 can Herbert deduct? What is Herbert's basis in the lot?

55. Troy's 1994 tax return was audited. The auditor determined that Troy inadvertently understated his ending inventory in calculating his business income. The error created an additional tax liability of $5,000. The IRS charged interest on the additional tax liability of $600. Write a letter to Troy explaining whether the interest on the additional tax liability is deductible.

56. Robin purchased a new home costing $80,000 in the current year. She paid $8,000 down and borrowed the remaining $72,000 by securing a mortgage on the home. She also paid $1,750 in closing costs, which included $1,600 in points to obtain the mortgage. She paid $4,440 in interest on the mortgage during the year. What is Robin's allowable itemized deduction for interest paid?

57. Buford owed $90,000 on the mortgage on his residence. Because the interest rate on the mortgage was high relative to current interest rates, Buford refinanced the mortgage at a lower rate. He paid $1,350 in points to refinance the loan for 25 years. The refinancing took place on July 1. How much of the $1,350 in points is deductible in the current year?

58. Keith bought his home several years ago for $110,000. He paid $10,000 down on the purchase and borrowed the remaining $100,000. When the home was worth $140,000 and the balance on his mortgage was $70,000, Keith borrowed $50,000 using a home equity loan. Keith used the proceeds of the loan to pay off some gambling debts. During the year, Keith paid $6,800 in interest on the original home mortgage and $3,000 in interest on the home equity loan. What is Keith's allowable itemized deduction for interest paid?

59. Astrid originally borrowed $850,000 to acquire her home. When the balance on the original mortgage was $650,000, she purchased a ski chalet by borrowing $500,000, which was secured by a mortgage on the chalet. Astrid paid $62,000 in interest on her home mortgage and $34,000 in interest on the chalet's mortgage. What is Astrid's allowable itemized deduction for interest paid?

60. Mandy is interested in purchasing a new automobile for personal use. The dealer is offering a special 4.9% interest rate on new cars. Last fall, she opened a home equity line of credit with her bank. If she uses the line of credit to purchase the car, the interest rate will be 7.95%. Write a letter to Mandy explaining whether she should finance the purchase of her car through the dealer or use her home equity line of credit. Assume Mandy is in the 36% tax bracket.

61. Barbara had the following items of investment income during 1996:

Interest on savings account	$1,100
Cash stock dividends	1,800
Municipal bond interest	3,000
Net long-term capital gain from sale of stock	4,100

Barbara's only other source of income was her $56,000 salary. Barbara paid $11,000 in interest on a loan she used to purchase the stocks and bonds that produced the income listed. Assuming that she has no other deductions for adjusted gross income, what is Barbara's allowable deduction for investment interest paid?

62. Stoycho and Selen are married and have the following investment income for 1995 and 1996:

	1995	1996
Interest on U.S. Treasury notes	$1,500	$1,650
Cash dividends	1,850	2,030
Interest on savings	1,250	850
Interest on State of Montana bonds	2,700	2,700
Net long-term capital gain	2,000	3,575

Their adjusted gross income before considering the investment income is $72,000 in 1995 and $69,000 in 1996. Stoycho and Selen pay $8,500 in investment interest in 1995 and $6,100 in 1996.

Write a letter to Stoycho and Selen explaining how much investment interest they can deduct in 1995 and 1996.

63. Liang paid $16,000 in interest on debt that was used to purchase portfolio investments. He received $4,000 in dividends on stock, $2,500 in royalties, and $1,800 in interest on municipal bonds during the year. His investment-related expenses totaled $500. Liang's adjusted gross income was $80,000.
    a. Assuming that Liang had no other qualifying miscellaneous itemized deductions during the year and that none of the debt was used to acquire the municipal bonds, how much of the $16,000 in interest paid can he deduct?
    b. What would Liang's deduction be if he also had $1,200 in qualifying miscellaneous itemized deductions (employee business expenses)?
    c. Assume that in part b the qualifying expenses totaled $3,000.

64. Jana gave property worth $32,000 to her alma mater during the current year. She had purchased the property several years ago for $12,000.
    a. What is Jana's maximum deduction if the property is ordinary income property?
    b. What is Jana's maximum deduction if the property is capital gain property?
    c. How would your answer change if Jana's adjusted gross income was $48,000?

65. Lauren owns stock for which she paid $18,000 several years ago. She is considering donating the stock to the United Way. The fair market value of the stock is $38,000. Her adjusted gross income is $40,000. Lauren has $4,000-worth of other itemized deductions. Lauren expects that her adjusted gross income and itemized deductions will remain constant over the next 5 years. Assume a present value factor of 9%. Should she deduct the fair market value of the stock or elect to reduce the amount of her contribution to the adjusted basis of the property? Explain.

66. Determine the allowable charitable contribution in each of the following situations:
    a. Brett played in a charity golf tournament. The fee for the tournament was $1,000. The value of the greens fees, meals, and incidentals that Brett received was $100.
    b. Adrian purchased a statue at a church auction for $800. The fair market value of the statue was $50.
    c. James is a CPA. As a volunteer, he does the books for the local chapter of the United Way. James estimates that his normal fee for the work would be $450.

67. Miguel is a successful businessman who has been approached by St. Kilda University to make a donation to its capital campaign. Miguel agrees to contribute $50,000, but he is unsure which of the following assets he should contribute:

Asset	Basis	Fair Market Value
Ordinary income property	$28,000	$50,000
Long-term capital gain property	$67,000	$50,000
Long-term capital gain property	$21,000	$50,000

Write a letter to Miguel advising him which property he should contribute to St. Kilda's capital campaign.

68. Constance incurs $4,800 in valid employment-related expenses during the current year. Her employer reimburses her for only $3,600 of the expenses. She also incurs $1,400 in other allowable miscellaneous expenses. Constance's adjusted gross income is $37,000 without considering the effect of these expenses and the reimbursement. What is Constance's allowable deduction if
    a. Her employer's reimbursement plan is an accountable plan?
    b. Her employer's reimbursement plan is a nonaccountable plan?

69. Cody is a financial analyst for Woolwood, Inc. His adjusted gross income for the current year was $65,000. Cody incurred the following out-of-pocket expenses during the current year:

Dues to financial analysts' association	$ 320
Subscriptions to professional journals	375
Parking at work	1,200
Entertaining underwriters	450
Business suits	800
Tax return preparation fee	750
Legal fees paid for his divorce	1,650
Safe deposit box rental	80

What is Cody's allowable itemized deduction?

70. In his spare time, Don makes wooden boats as a hobby. In the current year, Don sells 1 boat to a friend for $400. Don estimates that it cost him $300 to make the boat and that he incurred another $200 in costs related to his boat hobby. How should Don treat the sale of the boat and the related expenses? Assume that Don's adjusted gross income is $30,000 and that he has no other qualifying miscellaneous itemized deductions.

71. Lee is a college professor with an adjusted gross income of $36,000. Lee had a lot of bad luck this year. First, a tornado blew off the roof of his house, causing $5,900 in damage. His insurance company would reimburse him only $1,600 for the roof damage. Later in the year, he was out at a local pub one night when his $625 car stereo was stolen. His insurance company would not pay anything for the stereo, because it was only worth $175 at the time and Lee's policy does not cover losses of less than $250. What is Lee's allowable casualty and theft loss for the year?

72. Michael owns a hair salon. During the current year, a tornado severely damaged the hair salon and destroyed his personal automobile, which was parked outside. It cost Michael $13,000 to make the necessary repairs to the hair salon. He had paid $27,000 for the automobile, which was worth $19,000 before the tornado. Michael's business insurance reimbursed him for $9,000 of the salon repair costs. His automobile insurance company paid only $15,000 for the automobile destruction. Michael's adjusted gross income was $30,000 before considering the effects of the tornado. Write a letter to Michael explaining his deductible casualty loss from the tornado.

73. Orley is a single individual with no dependents who had an adjusted gross income of $157,000 in 1996. Orley's itemized deductions totaled $23,000, which included $1,500 in deductible medical costs and $6,300 in investment interest.
    a. What is Orley's 1996 taxable income?
    b. Assume that Orley's adjusted gross income was $480,000. What is his 1996 taxable income?

74. Jeff and Marion are married with 3 dependents. Their adjusted gross income in 1996 is $165,000. Their itemized deductions total $47,200, including $7,400 in investment interest.
    a. What is their 1996 taxable income?
    b. Assume that their adjusted gross income is $243,600 and their itemized deductions remain the same. What is their 1996 taxable income?

75. Hal and Laura are married and have 3 dependent children. What is their total allowable exemption deduction in 1996 if
    a. Their adjusted gross income is $90,000?
    b. Their adjusted gross income is $249,000?
    c. Their adjusted gross income is $370,000?

76. Determine the taxable income of each of the following dependents in 1996:
    a. Louis is 11 and receives $850 in interest income.
    b. Jackson is 16. He earns $1,500 from his newspaper route and receives $300 in dividends on GCM stock.
    c. Loretta is 18. She earns $4,000 as a lifeguard during the summer. In addition, Loretta won a rescue contest and received a municipal bond worth $1,000. During the year, the bond paid $20 in interest.
    d. Eva is 8. Her income consists of municipal bond interest of $600, stock dividends of $1,400, and interest credited to her savings account of $350.
    e. Elaine is a college student. Her only income consists of $2,500 from her part-time job delivering pizzas. Her itemized deductions total $235.
    f. Greg is 2. Greg has certificates of deposit given to him by his grandparents that paid $1,900 in interest.

77. For each of the dependents in problem 76 calculate the income tax on their taxable income. In each case, assume that their parents' taxable income was $60,000.

78. Calculate the 1996 tax liability and the tax or refund due for each situation:
    a. Mark is single with no dependents and has a taxable income of $40,000. He has $8,125 withheld from his salary for the year.
    b. Harry and Linda are married and have taxable income of $40,000. Harry has $4,000 withheld from his salary. Linda makes estimated tax payments totaling $2,200.
    c. Aspra is single. His unmarried son lives with him throughout the year. Aspra pays all costs of maintaining the household. Aspra's taxable income is $40,000. Aspra's withholdings total $6,800, and he is entitled to a tax credit of $350.
    d. Randy and Raina are married. Because of martial discord, they are not living together at the end of the year, although they are not legally separated or divorced. Randy's taxable income is $22,000 and Raina's is $48,000. Randy makes estimated tax payments of $4,100, and Raina has $10,700 in tax withheld from her salary.

79. Calculate the 1996 tax liability and the tax or refund due for each situation:

  a. Seetharama is single with no dependents and has a taxable income of $48,700. He has $11,345 withheld from his salary for the year.

  b. Ward and Bari are married and have taxable income of $117,000. Ward makes estimated tax payments totaling $18,200. Bari has $9,200 withheld from her salary.

  c. Shaw is single. He provides 100% of the support for his mother, including the cost of maintaining her home. Shaw's taxable income is $85,000 and his withholdings total $22,800.

  d. Spencer and Gwen are married with 2 children, ages 6 and 8. In May, Spencer left town and Gwen does not know where he is. She has not initiated formal divorce proceedings. Gwen receives a salary statement from Spencer's former employer that lists income of $18,500. Gwen's taxable income, including Spencer's salary, is $34,000. Gwen has $5,100 in tax withheld from her salary. Spencer's employer withheld $3,600 from Spencer's salary.

80. Determine whether each of the following taxpayers must file a return in 1996:

  a. Jamie is a dependent who has wages of $2,700.

  b. Joel is a dependent who had interest income of $600.

  c. Martin is self-employed. His gross business receipts are $20,000, and business expenses are $23,000. His only other income is $1,950 in dividends from some stock he owns.

  d. Valerie is 68 and unmarried. Her income consists of $6,000 in Social Security benefits and $5,500 she receives from a qualified employer-provided pension plan.

  e. Raul and Yvonne are married and have 2 dependent children. Their only income is Raul's $13,000 salary.

INTEGRATIVE PROBLEMS

81. Robert and Susan (both are 39) are married and have 2 children. Their son Dylan is 8 and their daughter Harper is 3. Susan sells pharmaceuticals for the Bendigo Drug Co. Robert is a teacher at the local junior high school. In the summer, Robert earns extra money as a self-employed house painter. Their income from their jobs is as follows:

	Salary	Federal Tax Withheld	State Tax Withheld
Susan	$54,000	$6,320	$3,240
Robert	36,000	6,270	2,160

Bendigo has a cafeteria benefits plan that allows employees to select benefits equal to as much as 10% of their annual salary or receive the cash equivalent. Susan selected dental insurance, $100,000 in group term life insurance, disability insurance, and company-provided day care. The total cost to Bendigo of these benefits is $4,600. Susan takes the remaining benefits to which she is entitled in cash. Because Bendigo does not have an employee pension plan, Robert and Susan each contribute $2,000 to their individual retirement accounts.

The school district provides Robert with medical insurance and group term life insurance equal to 200% of his annual salary. Robert pays an additional $125 a month to cover Susan and the children under his medical plan. The school district also has a qualified contributory pension plan to which it contributes 8% of Robert's annual salary; he is required to contribute 4%. Robert is allowed to make additional contributions up to 4% of his salary, and he contributes the maximum.

In addition to the life insurance coverage provided by their employers, Robert and Susan purchase $100,000 in whole life insurance on each other, along with a disability insurance policy for Robert. See the checkbook analysis that follows for the costs of these policies.

Susan's job requires her to travel throughout her six-state region. Bendigo has an accountable reimbursement plan from which Susan receives $14,875 for the following expenses:

Transportation	$4,400
Lodging	5,950
Meals	3,850
Entertainment	2,900
Incidentals	400

In April, Susan and Robert go to the racetrack with Susan's client Annie and her husband. After wagering $150 without winning, Susan wins $2,500 on the last race. The racetrack withholds $750 for federal income taxes and $250 for state income taxes.

Robert hires college students to help him paint houses. This year, he is able to hire 8 students (two 4-person crews). Robert shuttles between sites, supervising the jobs, talking to prospective clients, and painting. Robert treats the college students as independent contractors. His business generates the following income and expenses:

Revenues	$85,000
Paint	22,000
Other material	4,500
Insurance	8,000
Payments to student help	31,500

During the year, Robert and Susan receive the following portfolio income:

Interest on savings account	$1,760
Interest on U.S. Treasury bills	400
Cash dividends on stock	1,240
Interest on City of Buffalo bonds	350
Interest on Puerto Rico government bonds	250

Robert and Susan own 3,000 shares of qualified small business stock that they purchased in 1991 for $30,000. Early in 1996, they sell all the shares for $12,500. Robert and Susan also sell 100 shares of Sobey Corporation stock for a short-term capital gain of $3,000 and 250 shares of the Bristol Corporation for a long-term capital loss of $7,500. They pay investment interest of $1,250 during the year.

Robert and Susan own a 4% interest in a limited partnership. The limited partnership reports the following information to them:

Ordinary loss	$1,600
Long-term capital gain	400
Charitable contribution	120
Cash distribution	2,800

During the year, the family spends 40 days at its summer home; they rent it to vacationers for 80 days. Information pertaining to the rental is as follows:

Rental income	$5,800
Interest on mortgage	4,350
Property taxes	1,150
Management fee	580
Repairs	325
Utilities	740
Insurance	290
Depreciation (unallocated)	6,000

One night, while returning home from a parent-teacher conference at school, Robert is involved in an automobile accident and is hospitalized for 7 days. Robert incurs $11,000 in medical expenses. His employer-provided policy reimburses him $8,800 of the costs. In addition, his disability policy pays him $2,400 for the time he misses from school.

The car is totally destroyed. The car was purchased in 1993 for $18,500, and Robert finds a similar car selling for $10,000. The insurance company reimburses him $7,200.

An analysis of Susan and Robert's checkbook reveals the following payments in 1996:

Automobile insurance	$ 870
Homeowners insurance	435
Life insurance	600
Disability insurance	130
Country club dues	1,400
Health club dues	330
Optometrist	270
Veterinarian	180
Prescription drugs	375
Over-the-counter medicine	245
Chamber of Commerce contribution	100
Contribution to candidate for Congress	200
United Way	350
St. Philip's Church	560
Randolph University	350
Auto registration on automobiles ($80 of which is a license fee)	640
Tax preparation fee	350

During 1996, Robert and Susan take out a $30,000 home equity loan that they use to pay off $10,000 in credit card debt. The remaining loan proceeds go to renovating the house. Interest paid on this loan totals $1,800 during 1996. Robert and Susan purchased their current home by paying $16,000 down and signing a $160,000 mortgage note, secured by the home. The home is worth $212,000, and the balance on the original mortgage is $134,000. They pay interest on their home mortgage of $12,400 during 1996. They also pay $155 in interest on their personal credit cards and $1,825 in property taxes on their home during 1996.

REQUIRED: Compute Robert and Susan's taxable income for 1996, the tax on this income, and the amount of any refund or additional tax due. You should provide a summary schedule of these calculations (in proper form) with a supplemental discussion of the treatment of each item given in the facts. If an item does not affect their taxable income calculation, you should discuss why it doesn't enter into the computation. See the appendix to this chapter for an example of the presentation required.

If you are using tax forms to solve this problem, you will need the following forms and schedules: Form 1040, Schedule A, Schedule B, Schedule C, Schedule D, Schedule E, Form 2106, Form 4684, and Form 8606. In addition, you should obtain a copy of the Form 1040 instructions to help you prepare the tax return.

82. In integrative problem 70 in Chapter 4, you were asked to calculate Carmin's gross income for 1996. This is the second phase, which provides the additional information necessary for you to calculate her taxable income, income tax liability, and additional tax (or refund due). NOTE: The gross income items from problem 70 still apply. However, some additional items might affect the amount of gross income that Carmin must report. That is, several items included in the gross income from integrative problem 70 are either not reported as gross income or need to be combined with the additional information in this problem to determine the correct treatment. Therefore, you should make the appropriate adjustments to gross income in integrative problem 70, and begin your tax calculation under the heading of Gross Income from Problem 70, As Adjusted.

From this point on, any items of gross income from the information in this problem should be listed to determine gross income for tax purposes. You do not need to list all the individual gross income items from integrative problem 70 in your solution. However, you should explain the adjustments made to the phase 1 gross income figure as part of your discussion of the solution.

Carmin has the following amounts withheld from her paycheck for the payment of state income taxes, federal taxes, and Social Security taxes:

State income taxes	$ 5,324
Federal income taxes	14,712
Social Security taxes	5,047

Because of her busy work schedule, Carmin is unable to provide her accountant with the tax documents necessary for filing her 1995 state and federal income tax return by the due date (April 15, 1996). In filing her extension on April 15, 1996, she makes a state tax payment of $325 and a federal tax payment of $850. Her return is eventually filed on June 25, 1996. In August 1996, she receives a federal refund of $112 and a state tax refund of $59.

Carmin pays $1,843 in real estate taxes on her principal residence. The real estate tax is used to pay for town schools and other municipal services. The town also has 5 separate fire districts, which levy a separate tax (i.e., fire tax) to fund each district's fire department. The fire tax is based on the assessed value of the taxpayer's home. Carmin pays $117 in fire tax during the year.

Carmin drives a 1995 Tarago 919 Wagon. Her car registration is $60 and covers the period 1/1/96 through 12/31/96. In addition, she pays $342 in property tax to the town, based on the book value of the car.

In addition to the medical costs presented in problem 70 in Chapter 4, Carmin incurs the following unreimbursed medical costs:

Dentist	$180
Doctor	220
Prescription drugs	425
Over-the-counter drugs	165
Optometrist	40
Emergency room charges	125
Chiropractor	290

On March 1, Carmin takes advantage of low interest rates and refinances her $75,000 home mortgage. The new home loan is for 15 years. Carmin and her ex-husband paid $90,000 for the house in 1984. The house is worth $135,000. She pays $547 in closing costs and $1,320 in points to obtain the loan. As part of the refinancing arrangement, she also obtains a $15,000 home equity loan. She uses the proceeds from the home equity loan to remodel the kitchen and bathroom and to reduce the balances on her credit cards. Her home mortgage interest for the year is $6,465, and her home equity interest is $1,342. She incurs interest on her Chargit credit card of $347 and $43 on her Myers Department store card. The interest on her car loan from Tarago Financing Corporation is $324.

Carmin receives the following information on her investment in Grubstake Mining and Development:

Ordinary income	$9,650
Short-term capital gain	1,200
Long-term capital loss	2,200
Charitable contribution	650

In May 1996, she contributes clothing to the Salvation Army. The original cost of the clothing was $830. She receives a statement from the Salvation Army valuing the donation at $265. In addition, she makes the following cash contributions:

Larkin College	$350
United Way	90
First Methodist Church	610
Amos House (homeless shelter)	125
Kappa Delta Delta Sorority	100
Local chamber of commerce	25

Carmin has a workshop of 600 square feet in her basement, where she makes pottery. She keeps her pottery wheel and kiln there and stores her raw materials and some finished pottery. She sells the majority of her work to craft and specialty shops throughout the state. Her sales to the large craft stores are net 30 days, whereas the small stores acquire her pottery on consignment. She has been operating in a businesslike way since 1986 and has always shown a profit. She has the following income and expenses from her business:

Sales	$15,465
Materials	3,246
Advertising	430
Booth rentals	525
Depreciation (kiln and wheel)	640

During the summer and fall, she travels throughout the state to weekend craft fairs, where she rents a booth to sell her pottery. Carmin uses her car and travels 1,845 miles to attend five shows during 1996. The total mileage on her car (e.g., business and personal mileage) during the year is 15,367 miles. Because each show lasts two days, she stays overnight at a nearby hotel. Her daughter Anika attends all the shows. Carmin and Anika's expenses are as follows:

Hotel*	$350
Meals—Carmin	280
Meals—Anika	180
Tolls	37
Parking	29

*The rate for double occupancy is the same as the single occupancy rate at all the hotels in which they stay.

The living area (not including the basement) of Carmin's house measures 2,400 square feet. When she started her business in 1986, the fair market value of the house was $100,000. Approximately 10% of the purchase price was attributable to the land. Carmin incurs the following expenses in operating her home:

Water	$110
Electric	445
Gas	780
Insurance	330

In April, Carmin's house is robbed. She apparently interrupted the burglar because all that's missing is an antique brooch she inherited from her grandmother and $250 in cash. Unfortunately, she didn't have a separate rider on her insurance policy covering the jewelry. Therefore, the insurance company reimburses her only $500 for the brooch. When her grandmother died in 1993, the fair market value of the pin was $5,500. Her insurance policy also limits to $100 the amount of cash that can be claimed in a theft.

Carmin's company has an accountable employee expense reimbursement plan from which Carmin receives $8,100 for the following expenses:

Airfare	$4,130
Hotel	2,245
Meals	1,300
Car rentals	640
Entertainment	475
Incidentals	210

During the year, she also pays $280 for business publications and $225 for a local accountant to prepare her 1995 tax return.

In 1994, Carmin loaned $12,000 to her ex-husband Ray so he could start a new business. Their loan agreement requires Ray to pay Carmin 8% interest on the unpaid balance of the loan on December 31 of each year and to begin repaying the loan in $4,000 annual installments on July 1, 1996. Carmin receives the interest on the loan during 1994 and 1995. In March 1996, Carmin receives a letter informing her that Ray has filed for bankruptcy. On February 22, 1997, the bankruptcy court awards all creditors 30% of their claims on Ray's assets.

REQUIRED: Calculate Carmin's taxable income on her 1996 tax return. Then do one (or both) of the following, according to your professor's instructions:

a. Include a brief explanation of how you determined each deduction and any item you did not treat as a deduction. Your solution to the problem should contain a list of each deduction and its amount, with the explanations attached.

b. Write a letter to Carmin explaining how you determined each deduction and any items you did not treat as a deduction. You should include a list of each deduction and its amount.

DISCUSSION CASES

83. Congress is working toward establishing a national health-care system. At the same time, the tax law permits unreimbursed medical expenses to be deducted only if they exceed 7.5% of the taxpayer's adjusted gross income. Why does Congress, apparently intent on providing an equitable national health-care plan, place a stringent limitation on the deduction of medical expenses? Who benefits the most from this limitation?

84. Chapter 8 discusses expenditures that are deductible either for adjusted gross income (e.g., alimony) or from adjusted gross income (e.g., medical expenses) and explains the advantage of having an expenditure classified as a deduction for adjusted gross income. Select an example of each type of deduction (i.e., for and from) and present an argument as to why that deduction is incorrectly classified. That is, why the expenditure that is a deduction for adjusted gross income should be reclassified as a deduction from adjusted gross income, and why the expenditure that is a deduction from adjusted gross income should be reclassified as a deduction for adjusted gross income.

TAX PLANNING CASE

85. Janek and Maliati are married and have 2 children. In addition to their principal residence, they own a vacation home in New Hampshire. The couple usually rents the house for 180 days during the year and uses it for personal purposes 15 days. Both Janek and Maliati are professors at Warren College. They anticipate that their adjusted gross income for the year, before considering the rental property, will be $135,000. Information concerning the rental property is as follows:

Rental income	$10,000
Management fee	1,450
Interest	6,000
Taxes	3,200
Utilities	1,400
Repairs	750
Depreciation (unallocated)	6,000

Next week, both Janek and Maliati need to tell the chairs of their respective departments whether they are going to teach during summer school. Each course pays $5,000, and each would teach 1 course. Their children want the family to spend an extra week (7 days) at their summer home. Janek and Maliati expect their itemized deductions to be

Medical expenses	$2,000
Real estate taxes (principal residence)	3,500
State income taxes	1,800
Interest (principal residence)	4,800
Home equity loan	1,600
Charitable contributions	2,200
Miscellaneous deductions	3,200

Janek is concerned that the family's decisions could have a dramatic effect on their tax liability. You are a graduate accounting student who is taking one of Janek's courses. He asks you to determine the tax consequences if

a. Both he and Maliati teach summer school, but the family does not spend an extra week in New Hampshire.

b. Both he and Maliati teach summer school, and the family spends an extra week in New Hampshire.

Specifically, Janek would like you to determine the increase or decrease in their tax liability for each scenario. He also would like you to explain the cause(s) of any changes in their tax liability for each scenario.

ETHICS DISCUSSION CASE

86. Tom, an executive for a large corporation, enjoys the challenge of preparing his tax return. Tom is aggressive in preparing his return and searches through all the available publications in an effort to reduce his tax liability. In all the years Tom has completed his return, he has never been audited. However, in preparing his 1995 tax return, Tom misinterpreted a complex change in the law and is being audited. Aware that he probably should have an expert represent him before the IRS, Tom has hired Josephine, a local CPA. During the audit process, Josephine finds expenses that Tom had failed to deduct. However, the IRS also disallowed some of Tom's other deductions. During a meeting, Josephine and the IRS agent agree on Tom's revised taxable income. When Josephine receives the auditor's change letter, she checks the agent's calculation and finds that the agent has miscalculated the new tax liability by $750 in Tom's favor. In fact, Tom will now receive a refund. When Tom receives his copy of the letter, he leaves a message on Josephine's voice mail congratulating her on her work. You are Josephine's assistant. Josephine asks you to write a letter to Tom explaining the course of action she must take.

Appendix to Chapter 8

Comprehensive Tax Return Illustration

Pierre and Charlotte are married and have 2 children, ages 14 and 17. Pierre, 47, is employed as a salesman for Old Line Boot Co. Charlotte, 49, runs a candle shop in a local mall. She is the sole owner of the candle shop; the business is not incorporated. Details regarding Pierre's employment with Old Line:

1996 commissions earned	$55,000
Federal income taxes withheld	5,500
State income taxes withheld	4,000

Employee Benefits Received

Health and accident insurance	$1,500
Group term life insurance ($100,000)	400
Subscriptions to trade journals	300
Contribution to qualified retirement plan	2,500

Old Line's qualified retirement program matches employee contributions to the plan of 5%, up to $50,000 in current-year compensation. Pierre contributes the maximum in 1996 (and Old Line matches the contribution). In addition to the benefits listed, Old Line has a flexible benefits program into which an employee may contribute as much as $4,000 per year to pay medical expenses, dependent insurance, and child-care costs not covered by Old Line's medical policy. Pierre elects to pay $3,000 into the plan. The first $3,000 in unreimbursed medical expenses is paid from the plan.

Old Line does not reimburse employees for business expenses. Instead, Old Line gives Pierre $150 per month for travel and other employment-related expenses. Pierre is not required to account for his expenses with Old Line. Pierre incurs the following employment-related expenditures:

Lodging	$800
Meals	300
Entertainment	600

In addition to these expenses, Pierre can document that he uses his personal automobile for business a total of 12,000 miles during 1996. However, he does not keep very good records of his actual expenses. He thinks he spends in the neighborhood of $1,500 for gas, oil, and repairs on the automobile for the year. Allocable depreciation on his automobile would be $1,000.

Charlotte has gross sales of $110,000 in her candle shop business for the year. She lists the following expenses:

Rent on business property	$12,000
Supplies purchased	800
Interest on debt to finance candle inventory	4,050
Utilities	2,500
Employee salaries	28,000
Candle purchases	60,000

Cost of special promotional candles	450
Employees' medical insurance premiums	1,400

Charlotte's inventory of candles on January 1 is $40,000. By December 31, it is $65,000. The promotional candles are imprinted with the shop's logo, and Charlotte has them passed out at a university football game.

Because she is not covered by Pierre's medical policy, Charlotte purchases her own policy at a cost of $1,600. In addition, Charlotte makes a $3,000 qualified contribution to her self-employed retirement plan during 1996.

In order to stay abreast of the latest developments in candle-making, Charlotte attends the annual candlemakers exhibition in Chicago. She spends 3 days attending the convention. At night, she visits friends and relatives living in the area. Her costs of the trip were

Airfare	$350
Lodging	600
Meals	180
Car rental, gasoline, etc.	160

In addition to these costs, she takes her biggest supplier out to dinner and a basketball game one night. At dinner, Charlotte tries to convince the supplier to offer her speedier delivery and better credit terms. The dinner costs Charlotte $200. Because of the popularity of the local basketball team, Charlotte has to purchase the 2 tickets from a scalper for $100 apiece (the face value of the tickets is $50 apiece).

Charlotte makes estimated tax payments to the federal government of $3,200 and $1,900 to the state. In addition, she pays her share of Social Security taxes on the salaries of her employees, $2,100, and state unemployment compensation taxes of $280.

Pierre and Charlotte pay $9,000 in mortgage interest, $850 in property taxes, and $1,300 in insurance on their home mortgage. Pierre and Charlotte regularly attend church and estimate that they put about $10 per week into the collection plate. In addition, they give clothing for which they had paid $800 to the Salvation Army. The Salvation Army estimates the value of the clothes at $160. Pierre and Charlotte also purchase $40-worth of Girl Scout cookies and a $100 raffle ticket for a new car given away by a local charity.

They had the following medical expenses during the year:

Dependent medical insurance premiums	$1,400
Doctor's fees	800
Dental costs	1,100
Eyeglasses for the boys	450
Surgery on son's broken leg	1,800
Hospital costs for surgery	3,800
Prescription drugs	385

Of these costs, Pierre's medical insurance pays $2,000, Charlotte's insurance covers $300, and they use the $3,000 put into Pierre's flexible benefits plan to pay other costs.

Pierre was divorced several years ago. He pays $6,000 in alimony to his former spouse and $3,000 in child support during 1996.

Pierre and Charlotte also receive $420 in interest on their personal savings account and $260 in dividends on some stock they own.

What are Pierre and Charlotte's taxable income, the tax on the taxable income, and their tax or refund due for the year?

Solution.   The first step in calculating the taxable income is to determine the taxpayers' gross income. Pierre's gross income from Old Line is

Commissions received		$55,000
Travel advance—$150 × 12		1,800
Reductions in taxable salary		
Retirement plan contributions	$2,500	
Salary reduction plan	3,000	(5,500)
Taxable employee benefits		
Group term life premiums—50 × $3.48		174
Total gross income from Old Line		$51,474

The medical insurance premiums and the trade journal subscriptions paid by Old Line are excludable employee fringe benefits. The premiums on the first $50,000 of group term life insurance are excludable, but premiums on Pierre's coverage in excess of $50,000 are taxable, per the IRS table (see Table 4–1, Chapter 4). NOTE: The $51,474 in gross income calculated here is reported to Pierre by Old Line on Pierre's annual statement of wages, Form W-2. Because Old Line does not have an accountable plan, Pierre must include the travel advance in his gross income. Pierre's employee business expenses are allowed as miscellaneous itemized deductions, because the plan is nonaccountable.

Calculating Charlotte's gross income is more complex, because she is in a trade or business. As such, she is allowed to deduct all ordinary and necessary business expenses for adjusted gross income on her individual income tax return. As a matter of form, the income (loss) from a trade or business is calculated separately, and the net figure reported as gross income. In addition, because Charlotte has inventories, she must report sales and cost of goods sold using the accrual basis. It is assumed in this example that Charlotte and Pierre elect to use the hybrid method, which accounts for all other income and expenses on the cash basis.

Charlotte's Business Income		
Sales		$110,000
Cost of goods sold:		
Beginning inventory	$ 40,000	
Purchases	60,000	
Goods available for sale	$100,000	
Less: Ending inventory	65,000	
Cost of goods sold		35,000
Gross profit		$ 75,000
Business expenses:		
Rent on business property	$12,000	
Supplies	800	
Business interest	4,050	
Utilities	2,500	
Employee salaries	28,000	
Social Security taxes on salaries	2,100	
State unemployment taxes	280	
Promotional candles	450	
Employees' medical insurance	1,400	
Travel	1,350	
Total deductible expenses		52,930
Net business income		$ 22,070

Charlotte is not allowed to deduct the insurance premiums she pays on her own medical insurance, because she is not an employee. The $3,000 contribution to her retirement plan is not a trade or business expense and may be deducted only as a separate deduction for adjusted gross income. The allowable travel deduction is figured as follows:

Airfare	$ 350
Lodging	600
Meals—$180 × 50%	90
Car rental	160
Entertainment—$300 × 50%	150
Total travel deduction	$1,350

All of Charlotte's days in Chicago constituted business days, and she is allowed to deduct all her costs. The entertainment cost is deductible, because the meal was directly related to her business (a valid business discussion was held), and the basketball game was associated with the business discussion at the meal. However, the deduction for tickets is limited to the face value of the tickets ($100 in this case).

Because Charlotte is self-employed, she will have to pay the 15.3% self-employment tax on her business income. The amount of her business income subject to tax is $20,382 ($22,070 × 92.35%). The tax amounts to $3,118 ($20,382 × 15.3%) and is added to the federal income tax and paid with the income tax return. Charlotte is allowed to deduct 50% of the tax, $1,559, as a deduction for adjusted gross income. Self-employed individuals are also allowed a for-adjusted gross income deduction of 30% of the cost of their medical insurance. However, this deduction is not allowed if the individual's spouse is covered by another plan or if the individual is eligible for coverage by the spouse's plan. In this case, Charlotte must treat her medical insurance as an itemized deduction.

In addition to the self-employment tax deduction and retirement plan contribution deduction, Pierre and Charlotte are allowed a deduction for adjusted gross income for the $6,000 in alimony paid. The child support payment is nondeductible. This leaves them with an adjusted gross income of $63,665: gross income of $74,224 ($51,474 + $22,070 + $420 + $260) and deductions for adjusted gross income of $10,559 ($6,000 + $1,559 + $3,000).

Pierre and Charlotte are allowed deductions from adjusted gross income for medical expenses, home mortgage interest, taxes, charitable contributions, and for Pierre's employee business expenses (miscellaneous itemized deductions). All the medical costs are allowable medical expenses, a total of $11,335. This is reduced by the $5,300 in reimbursements and 7.5% of adjusted gross income, for an actual deduction of $1,260.

Medical insurance premiums	
Dependents	$ 1,400
Charlotte	1,600
Doctors	800
Dental	1,100
Eyeglasses	450
Surgery	1,800
Hospital	3,800
Prescription drugs	385
Total allowable medical	$11,335
Less: Reimbursements	
Pierre's insurance	(2,000)
Salary reduction plan	(3,000)
Charlotte's insurance	(300)
Unreimbursed medical expenses	$ 6,035
Less: $63,665 × 7.5%	4,775
Deductible medical expenses	$ 1,260

The home mortgage interest of $9,000 is deductible, as is the $850 in property taxes paid on their home. The insurance on the home is a personal living expense and therefore not deductible. They are also entitled to a deduction of $5,900 ($4,000 + $1,900) for state income taxes paid. Their charitable contribution deduction is $680—$10 per week for 52 weeks of cash contributions to their church, a total of $520, and $160 for the clothing contribution (ordinary income property is valued at the lower of fair market value or adjusted basis). The Girl Scout cookies and the raffle ticket are not deductible charitable contributions.

Because Old Line's employee reimbursement plan is nonaccountable, Pierre must deduct his employee business expenses as miscellaneous itemized deductions. His total allowable deductions total $4,970, which is reduced by 2% of adjusted gross income for an allowable deduction of $3,697. In taking this deduction, Pierre is subject to the 50% limitation on meals and entertainment. In addition, because he has not kept adequate records of his automobile expenses, he must use the standard mileage method (31 cents per mile).

Lodging	$ 800
Meals—$300 × 50%	150
Entertainment—$600 × 50%	300
Automobile costs—12,000 × 0.31	3,720
Total	$4,970
Less: $63,665 × 2%	(1,273)
Deductible expenses	$3,697

Pierre and Charlotte's itemized deductions total $21,387, and they are entitled to 4 exemption deductions, a total of $10,200 ($2,550 × 4). This gives them a taxable income of $32,078 ($63,665 − $21,387 − $10,200). The tax on $32,078 for a married couple, filing jointly, in 1996 is $4,812 (32,078 × 15%). Charlotte's self-employment tax of $3,118 is added to the $4,812, for a total tax of $7,930. Pierre and Charlotte had $8,700 ($5,500 + $3,200) in tax withheld and paid, for a refund due of $770 ($7,930 − $8,700). Pierre and Charlotte's income tax calculation is shown here:

Pierre and Charlotte, 1996 Income Tax Calculation

Gross income			
Pierre's salary		$51,474	
Charlotte's business income		22,070	
Interest income		420	
Dividend income		260	$74,224
Deductions for adjusted gross income			
Alimony paid		$ 6,000	
Charlotte's self-employment tax		1,559	
Charlotte's retirement plan contribution		3,000	10,559
Adjusted gross income			$63,665
Deductions from adjusted gross income			
Medical expenses	$11,335		
Less: Reimbursements	(5,300)		
Unreimbursed medical	$6,035		
Less: $63,665 × 7.5%	(4,775)	$1,260	
Home mortgage interest		9,000	
Taxes			
Property taxes	$ 850		
State income taxes			
Pierre	4,000		
Charlotte	1,900	6,750	
Charitable contributions			
Cash payments	$ 520		
Clothing donated	160	680	
Miscellaneous itemized deductions			
Employee business expenses	$ 4,970		
Less: $63,665 × 2%	(1,273)	3,697	(21,387)
Personal and dependency exemptions ($2,550 × 4)			(10,200)
Taxable income			$32,078
Calculation of tax due/refund			
Tax on $32,078 − $32,078 × 15%			$ 4,812
Self-employment tax—$20,382 × 15.3%			3,118
Net tax			$ 7,930
Amounts withheld and paid in—$5,500 + $3,200			(8,700)
Refund of taxes withheld and paid in			$ 770

Other Tax Entities

▲ CHAPTER LEARNING OBJECTIVES

- Highlight the tax and nontax advantages of a corporation.
- Elaborate on the special rules for corporations, such as the dividends received deduction, passive activity losses, capital loss limitations, and charitable contributions limitations.
- Discuss the treatment of distributions to shareholders.
- Elaborate on the tax definitions of *trust* and *estate*.
- Explain the income taxation of fiduciaries.
- Highlight the tax and nontax advantages of a conduit entity.
- Explain the calculation of basis in a partnership and an S corporation.
- Discuss the legal characteristics of a partnership.
- Elaborate on the treatment of distributions made by the partnership.
- Discuss the requirements necessary to obtain S corporation status.
- Discuss income-splitting opportunities using multiple entities.

▲ CONCEPT REVIEW ▲

Accounting method A taxpayer must adopt an accounting method that clearly reflects income.

Annual accounting period All entities must report the results of their operations on an annual basis (the tax year). Each tax year stands on its own, apart from other tax years.

Basis This is the amount of unrecovered investment in an asset. As amounts are expended and/or recovered relative to an asset over time, the basis is adjusted in consideration of such changes. The **adjusted basis** of an asset is the original basis, plus or minus the changes in the amount of unrecovered investment.

Business purpose To be deductible, an expenditure or a loss must have a business or other economic purpose that exceeds any tax avoidance motive. The primary motive for the transaction must be to make a profit.

Capital recovery No income is realized until the taxpayer receives more than the amount invested to produce the income. The amount invested in an asset represents the maximum amount recoverable.

Conduit entity An entity for which the tax attributes flow through to its owners for tax purposes.

Entity All items of income, deductions, and so on are traced to the tax unit responsible for the item.

Legislative grace Any tax relief provided is the result of a specific act of Congress that must be strictly applied and interpreted. All income received is taxable unless a specific provision can be found in the tax law that excludes the income from taxation. Deductions must be approached with the philosophy that nothing is deductible unless a provision in the tax law allows the deduction.

Realization No income (or loss) is recognized until it has been realized. A realization involves a change in the form and/or the substance of a taxpayer's property rights that results from an arm's-length transaction.

Related party Family members and corporations that are owned by family members are considered related parties, as are certain other relationships between entities in which the power to control the substance of a transaction is evidenced through majority ownership.

Substance-over-form doctrine Transactions are to be taxed according to their true intention rather than some form that may have been contrived.

INTRODUCTION

Although individuals are the biggest group of taxpaying entities (discussed in Chapter 8) and generally the most commonly referred to in an entry-level tax course, many different legal, natural, economic, social, and cultural entities exist. Not all entities are taxpayers. Because of legislative grace, only three types of entities are taxable. Individuals, corporations, and fiduciaries (trusts and estates) are taxed on their income. All other entities are either exempt or are considered conduit entities. Whether an entity is taxable, tax exempt, or a conduit can depend on practical considerations or the theoretical foundations of the entities. For example, a university is an entity comprised of students, faculty, and staff personnel. It would be practically impossible for a taxing agency to assess or collect tax on all types of income earned only within the boundaries and population of the university (e.g., old tax exams traded for a history term paper). Also, that type of taxation would constitute a form of double taxation if the U.S. government also taxed the individual citizens of the university on their income.

One example of a tax conduit entity is the partnership. The partnership form of business theoretically was created primarily as an aggregation of owners, not as a separate entity. The income of the entity flows through to the individual owners in relation to their ownership shares.[1] This conduit entity pays no income tax.[2] The owners (partners) report the income on their personal tax returns. Other conduit entities are S corporations, limited liability entities, and sole proprietorships. (As discussed in Chapter 2, sole proprietorships are not pure conduits.)

This chapter presents a discussion of the role of taxable (corporations and fiduciaries) and conduit entities (partnerships and S corporations) within the U.S.

income tax system and describes the calculation of the tax bases for the various taxable entities. It also discusses components of the tax base and calculations that are unique to various entities. Finally, it presents planning opportunities and other uses of various entities.

CORPORATIONS

A **corporation** is an artificial entity created under the auspices of state law. As a separate legal entity, a corporation can enter into contracts in its name, own property, be sued, and must pay income tax based on its taxable income.

Attaining corporate status is fairly simple. Articles of incorporation are drafted and filed with the appropriate state agency (e.g., the Division of Corporations and Commercial Code of the state of Utah). Then the state grants a charter, and the corporation issues stock to shareholders. Once the corporation is formed and operating, it must hold stockholder meetings and record the minutes. Also, it must maintain stock transfer records and file annual reports with the appropriate state agency. It must follow a myriad of formal rules. All these requirements are costly, both in terms of time and actual money paid. For example, legal fees, charter and franchise fees, underwriter fees, and other organizational costs can be extensive.

Adhering to all the rules required by the state of incorporation provides the entity with a separate legal identity that has the nontax attributes of limited liability, unlimited life, and free transferability of ownership. These nontax factors generally are the impetus for operating a business in the corporate form.

When individuals are trying to choose the type of entity appropriate for their businesses, the single characteristic that is generally most important is limited liability. That is, an owner's liability extends only to the amount invested in the entity. Business creditors may not look beyond the assets of the entity to satisfy debts. Accordingly, owners with extensive assets in addition to their business investment generally choose the corporate entity form.

The limited liability attribute can be misleading for small business owners. That is, most shareholders of closely held corporations are required to personally guarantee loans to the corporation. Bankers and other creditors want assurance that the corporate debts are secured. Therefore, shareholders of closely held corporations often have only partial limited liability.

The need to raise relatively large sums of money also is a factor in choosing a corporate form. The characteristics of free transferability of ownership, continuity of life, limited liability, and centralized management are suitable for raising large amounts of money from many sources. For example, **free transferability of ownership** means that a corporate shareholder may sell or buy shares at any time without restriction. This characteristic led to the creation of major stock exchanges such as the American Stock Exchange and the New York Stock Exchange. **Continuity of life** and **centralized management** ensure that the business will continue to exist, regardless of which shareholders trade their stock and/or which managers come and go. **Limited liability** means that investors are not risking more of their personal assets than the amount they paid for the stock.

Corporate entities must pay tax on their taxable income.[3] Therefore, some entities that resemble corporations may try to avoid corporate status solely to avoid corporate taxation. Attempting to avoid corporate status for tax purposes raises a problem with the IRS.[4] The service may characterize an unincorporated entity as a corporation for tax purposes because of the actual corporate attributes of the entity. That is, the IRS may invoke the doctrine of substance over form, disregard the unincorporated nature of the entity, and assess corporate income tax.[5] Conversely, the IRS could ignore the form of an incorporated entity if it does not meet the actual attributes of a corporation.[6] Then the income becomes taxable directly to the shareholders as a conduit, because the entity is noncorporate.

▲ **EXAMPLE 1**   Allen and Brenda form Allbre Corporation under the laws of the state of Alaska. The corporation is used merely to hold most of Allen's and Brenda's personal assets, which they legally transferred to the corporation. The shareholders have no business purpose for the corporation. It was created to protect their personal assets from creditors of other risky, exploratory activities. Will Allbre Corporation hold up to IRS scrutiny as a corporation?

Discussion: For tax purposes, the entity will probably not be considered separate from the owners. Allbre has no business objective. For tax purposes, a corporation must have a reason to carry on a business and, accordingly, report the gains therefrom.[7]

In addition to having a business purpose, a corporation must, under tax law, have

- Associates (i.e., owners)
- Limited liability
- Continuity of life
- Centralized management
- Free transferability of interests.[8]

An unincorporated entity that has no more than two of four characteristics (associates and business purpose do not count in this assessment) will not be classified as a corporation for tax purposes.[9] (Associates and business purpose are considered common to both corporate and noncorporate business organizations).

▲ **EXAMPLE 2**   Colin and Dora are partners in the Coldo Partnership. Their partnership agreement provides that the partnership terminates upon the withdrawal of either partner, that a partner may not freely transfer his or her ownership interest in the partnership without the consent of the other partner, that both partners may participate in management activities, and that both partners are jointly and individually liable for the partnership debts. Could the IRS assert that the Coldo Partnership is a corporation for tax purposes?

Discussion: None of the determining corporate characteristics is present. Although the partnership has associates and a business purpose, these are not determinative. A majority (at least 3 of 4) of the other characteristics would cause a problem for Colin and Dora. In this case, Coldo does not have limited liability, continuity of life, centralized management, or free transferability of interest.

Income Tax Considerations

Although nontax factors generally outweigh tax considerations when choosing a business entity, tax issues do need to be addressed. For example, deciding whether a business should be a sole proprietorship or a corporation often begins with a comparison of the tax rates for these two entities.

Tax Rate Differentials.   Sole proprietorships operate as conduits that tax the individual owner on the income of the business. Therefore, tax rate tables for individuals are compared to corporate tax rates. Individuals are subject to four tax rate schedules.[10] Each schedule is for a different individual taxpaying entity and is based on filing status (i.e., married people who file a joint return or surviving spouses, heads of households, single people, and married people who file separate returns). The schedules for all taxable entities appear in Appendix A. Each individual schedule has a five-step progression for taxing taxable income.

The initial rate is 15 percent, followed by a second step rate of 28 percent; the third step rate is 31 percent, followed by a 36 percent rate; the top rate for all remaining taxable income is 39.6 percent. The amounts of taxable income at which the tax rates change from 15 percent to 28 percent and from 28 percent to 31 percent are different for each of the four individual tax rate schedules.

The **corporate tax rate** schedule for corporate taxpayers appears in Table 9–1. Because corporations do not marry, there is no need for different rate schedules based on filing status. Also, the corporate income tax rate schedule is not subject to inflation indexing as individual taxpayer rate schedules are. The corporate schedule includes four progressive rates:

- The rate is 15 percent for the first $50,000 of taxable income.
- The rate is 25 percent for the next $25,000 of taxable income.
- The rate is 34 percent for taxable income up to $10,000,000.
- The rate for all additional taxable income is 35 percent.

However, Congress felt that the benefits of the lower (15 percent and 25 percent) brackets should be available only to corporations with low amounts of income. Accordingly, a 5 percent surtax is levied on corporate taxpayers with income greater than $100,000 and less than $335,000. Therefore, a fifth marginal tax rate of 39 percent exists for income between $100,000 and $335,000. The effect of this surtax is to tax corporations with incomes greater than $335,000 and less than $10,000,000 at a flat rate of 34 percent. The Omnibus Budget Reconciliation Act of 1993 added a 35 percent rate for taxable income greater than $10,000,000. As with the 15 and 25 percent rates, the benefit of the 34 percent rate is phased out with a 3 percent surtax on taxable income in excess of $15,000,000. This adds a sixth marginal tax rate of 38 percent for income between $15,000,000 and $18,333,333. The effect is to tax corporations with incomes greater than $18,333,333 at a flat rate of 35 percent.

The top 1996 individual income tax rate of 39.6 percent allows business owners to use a corporation to shelter income taxes when taxable income exceeds $263,750. Also, as Figure 9–1 shows, a corporation is taxed at a lower rate than are married individuals filing jointly for taxable incomes between $40,100 and $75,000. Therefore, under the right circumstances, business owners can lower their income tax liabilities by incorporating. However, if the corporation distributes dividends to the individual owner-shareholder, the individual incurs additional income taxes. This situation is a classic case of double taxation, which may mitigate the tax advantage of incorporating. Double taxation occurs when dividends of a corporation (which are paid out of earnings that have previously been taxed) are taxed again to the shareholders receiving the dividends.

▲ **Table 9–1**

CORPORATE INCOME TAX RATE SCHEDULE

Taxable Income	Tax Rate
Not over $50,000	15%
Over $50,000 but not over $75,000	25%
Over $75,000 but not over $100,000	34%
Over $100,000 but not over $335,000	39%
Over $335,000 but not over $10,000,000	34%
Over $10,000,000 but not over $15,000,000	35%
Over $15,000,000 but not over $18,333,333	38%
Over $18,333,333	35%

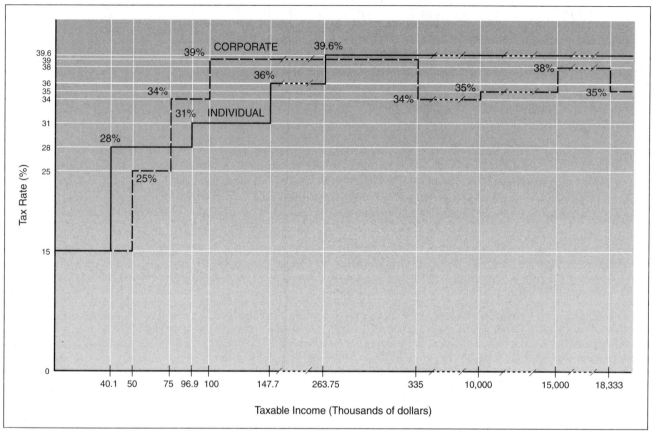

Tax Rate (%)

Taxable Income (Thousands of dollars)

▲ **Figure 9–1**

COMPARISON OF TAX
RATES (1996), CORPORATE
VERSUS INDIVIDUAL
(MARRIED)

▲ **EXAMPLE 3**   Ellen, a married individual, owns and operates a convenience store as a sole proprietorship. The net income from the convenience store consistently has been $50,000 a year. What would be the difference in tax dollars if the store is operated as a corporation rather than a sole proprietorship?

Discussion: Corporate taxes would be $7,500 ($50,000 × 15%). Because Ellen is married, her filing status is married, filing jointly, giving her a tax bill of $8,787 [$6,015 + ($9,900 × 28%)] in 1996, if she operates the store as a proprietorship. Accordingly, she saves $1,287 ($8,787 − $7,500) in taxes by incorporating. (This result assumes that after-tax corporate earnings are not distributed to the stockholder).

▲ **EXAMPLE 4**   Assume the same facts as in example 3, except that the corporate entity distributes a $20,000 cash dividend to Ellen. Now, what would be the difference in tax dollars if the store is operated as a corporation rather than a sole proprietorship?

Discussion: The corporate tax remains $7,500 (dividends are not deductions that reduce taxable income). However, Ellen has additional taxable income of $20,000 from the dividend she received. Her tax liability increases by $3,000 ($20,000 × 15%). Therefore, the total tax liability for Ellen and her corporation is $10,500 ($7,500 + $5,600). Because of the dividend, she owes $1,713 ($10,500 − $8,787) more in income tax than she would as a sole proprietor. NOTE: Instead of paying the $20,000 to Ellen as a dividend, her corporation could pay her the $20,000 as salary. Thus, the corporation's taxable income is reduced by $20,000, which saves corporate income taxes of $3,000 ($20,000 × 15%). This tax saving offsets the $3,000 in additional income taxes owed by Ellen upon receipt of the $20,000 salary.

▲ **EXAMPLE 5** Assume the same facts as in example 3, except the convenience store nets $200,000 annually. What would be the difference in tax dollars if the store is operated as a corporation rather than a sole proprietorship?

Discussion: Corporate taxes are $61,250 [($50,000 × 15%) + ($25,000 × 25%) + ($25,000 × 34%) + ($100,000 × 39%)]. The tax on $200,000 for a married couple filing jointly in 1996 is $56,495 [$37,667 + (36% × $52,300)], which is what Ellen would owe in tax from her business if she operated it as a proprietorship. Accordingly, she saves $4,755 ($61,250 − $56,495) by remaining with the sole proprietorship. This result assumes no dividends are distributed by the corporation to the shareholder. NOTE: The results of examples 3 and 5 are different because the store is making significantly different amounts of money—the marginal tax rate for corporations (34% plus the 5% surtax) is higher than the marginal tax rate for individuals (36%) at a $200,000 taxable income level. See Figure 9–1. Also, although the lowest marginal tax rate is the same for both entities (15%), the corporate tax rate schedule changes brackets at a higher amount of taxable income than does the tax rate schedule for individuals—$50,000 for corporations versus $40,100 for married individuals filing jointly.

Personal Service Corporations. This type of corporation is denied the benefit of the graduated corporate tax rates.

Personal service corporations are regular corporations in which

- The performance of personal services is the principal activity.
- The services are performed by owner-employees.
- The owner-employees together own more than 10 percent of the stock.[11]

Taxable income of a **personal service corporation (PSC)** is subject to a flat rate of 35 percent. The flat tax rate encourages owner-employees of PSCs to take corporate earnings out of the corporation as salary. Taxable incomes of married individuals up to $147,700 are taxed at rates lower than 35 percent.

▲ **EXAMPLE 6** A chiropractic clinic is formed as a corporation by four chiropractors who own all the stock in the corporation. During the current year, the clinic's gross profit before the chiropractors are paid is $500,000. They agree each will take a salary of $120,000. What are the tax effects to the corporation and the chiropractors?

Discussion: The clinic's taxable income becomes $20,000 ($500,000 − $480,000). The tax liability for the personal service corporation is $7,000 (35% × $20,000) because of the 35% flat tax rate. However, the chiropractors will not incur a marginal rate higher than 31% of their salaries. In fact, the marginal rate could be lower for individual chiropractors, depending on the number of exemptions, amount of itemized deductions, and amount of deductions for adjusted gross income that they can claim.

Owner-Employee Status. Another consideration in choosing the corporate form of doing business is the effect of a stockholder who also serves as a corporate employee. This consideration is especially important for the owner(s) of closely held corporations. These owners generally participate in the day-to-day activities of the business and have owner-employee status. Accordingly, they receive salaries and employee fringe benefits. From the corporate entity viewpoint, salaries and fringe benefits are deductible expenses that reduce taxable income.

The entity concept drives the ability of owners to be corporate employees for income tax purposes. Corporations are deemed separate entities, taxable on their own income. Accordingly, corporate owners (shareholders) can be employees of their corporation(s).

Attempts to reduce corporate taxable income through the use of the owner-employee status can have pitfalls. Chapter 5 describes some of them. The substance-over-form doctrine, dealing with the issues of lack of business purpose, unreasonableness of salary, and discriminatory fringe benefits, is the usual focus of IRS scrutiny. Closely held businesses are often objects of concern on these issues. Yet, benefits do accrue to owner-employees taking advantage of the corporate form of business.

FRINGE BENEFITS.   Recall from the discussion in Chapter 4 that employers receive significant tax advantages by paying certain expenses of their employees. Legislative grace excludes from taxation the following employee benefits:

- Employer-provided term life insurance up to $50,000 coverage
- Employer-sponsored accident and health-care plans
- Employer-provided educational assistance
- No additional cost services
- Qualified employee discounts
- Working-condition fringes
- De minimis fringes

The cost of these types of fringe benefits is deductible by a corporate employer. Thus, the benefits provide an owner-employee with a dual advantage. The value of the benefits is generally excludable from taxation for the owner-employee who receives them, and the corporation receives a tax deduction. These advantages are especially useful for the shareholder of a closely held corporation who is also an employee of the corporation.[12]

Caution must be exercised with fringe-benefit exclusions. The exclusion provisions are available only for employees. Owners (partners) of partnerships and sole proprietors are not considered employees. Therefore, they must include these types of benefits in their gross income, whereas their employees receive them tax free. Because of related party concerns about owner-employees and the legislative grace afforded fringe benefits, Congress has established a set of nondiscriminatory rules. That is, historically some employers have provided tax-free fringe benefits to only a few highly compensated employees or to corporate officers. Therefore, most types of fringe benefits must be offered at least equally to nonshareholder employees in order to retain the exclusion status for the recipients.

CHILDREN AS EMPLOYEES.   Another tax-planning strategy for reducing corporate taxable income is the valid employment of an owner-employee's children in the business. This strategy allows the corporation to deduct the wages or salaries as expenses, lowering taxable income, and it may permit the child to receive income tax free. That is, the child can earn as much as $4,000 in 1996 with no income tax liability because of the standard deduction amount for single individuals. Therefore, employing children in an incorporated business can allow a transfer of cash from parents to children free of income tax.

▲ EXAMPLE 7   Darianne is 12 and is paid $5 per hour by Momndad Corporation. Darianne's parents are the only stockholders of the corporation. How many hours could she work during 1996 and pay no income tax on her wages?

Discussion: Darianne could work 800 hours ($4,000 ÷ $5) during 1996 without paying income tax. Further, if Darianne contributes $2,000 to an IRA, she could earn as much as $6,000 by working 1,200 hours. This approach permits the corporation to take $2,000 more in business wage expense deduction.

Negative aspects of using children as employees include the incidence of payroll taxes and the possibility of the IRS's asserting that this related party transaction fails the test for reasonable amount of compensation.

UNREASONABLE COMPENSATION.   As discussed in Chapter 5, an expense must be reasonable in amount to be deductible. Related parties often face scrutiny of their transactions for reasonableness. Therefore, wages paid to children who are employees of their parents' corporation must be comparable to wages paid to any other employee for comparable services.

▲ EXAMPLE 8   Gregory Corporation has a single shareholder, Greg G. Gregory. The corporation hires Greg's 3 teenage children to answer telephone calls, take messages, prepare invoice forms, and do light cleanup. They are paid $4.25 per hour. Will the employment of the children pass IRS scrutiny?

Discussion: Because the children are actually working and the children's wages are not excessive (i.e. $4.25 per hour is the minimum wage), the IRS would find their compensation reasonable.

EMPLOYMENT TAXES.   Businesses are liable for the payment of Social Security (FICA) and federal and state unemployment compensation (FUTA and SUTA) taxes, referred to collectively as **employment taxes.** Therefore, additional business expenses are based on the 7.65-percent employer rate for FICA and the applicable rates for unemployment taxes, which may be as much as 6.2 percent. Accordingly, as much as 13.85 percent of the children's wages may be additional payroll-tax expense. If the business is organized by the parents as a sole proprietorship, they are not required to pay Social Security or other employment tax on their minor children's earnings.

DOUBLE TAXATION.   Obtaining cash distributions is generally the ultimate objective of corporate owners. In addition to salaries, cash is distributed to shareholders via dividends. Salaries are deductible expenses; dividend payments are not. Dividends are payments of already taxed earnings of corporations. When shareholders receive the dividends, the dividends are taxed again. This **double taxation** arises because the corporation is recognized as a separate taxpaying entity. It receives privileges afforded a legal person, and benefits accrue to its owners (e.g., limited liability, free transferability of interests, and continuity of life).

▲ EXAMPLE 9   Linh, a single individual, owns all the stock of Paige Corporation, which reports taxable income of $50,000 in 1996. The corporation distributes the $50,000 in earnings as a dividend. Assuming Linh's marginal tax rate is 28%, how much income tax do Paige Corporation and Linh pay?

Discussion: The total income tax liability resulting from the $50,000 income is $21,500 ($7,500 + $14,000). The corporate income tax is $7,500 ($50,000 x 15%). Linh includes the dividend in his individual 1996 taxable income and pays $14,000 ($50,000 x 28%) in income tax on the dividend amount. The corporate earnings are taxed twice—first at the corporate level and again at the individual stockholder level. Dividend payments are not deductible expenses.

Special Rules for Corporations

Calculating a corporation's taxable income is basically the same as calculating taxable income for individual taxpayers. However, several notable exceptions are unique to the corporate computation. The dividends-received deduction, passive loss limitation, capital loss limitation, charitable contributions, and organizational costs are special treatment items.

Dividends-Received Deduction. Double taxation occurs when corporate after-tax profits are distributed as dividends to shareholders. The corporation is not allowed a tax deduction for dividends paid, and the individual shareholders include the dividends in their gross income. Accordingly, if one corporation is a shareholder in another corporation, triple taxation results. To rectify this problem, legislative grace provides a deduction for dividends received by shareholders.

The **dividends-received deduction (DRD)** generally provides only partial relief of the triple taxation problem. However, the actual amount of the DRD depends on the percentage of ownership held by the recipient shareholder in the distributing corporation.[13] Generally, the DRD is 70 percent of the dividends received from U.S. taxable corporations. Table 9–2 presents the three different deduction rates and the related ownership percentages for dividend recipients.

The 70-percent and 80-percent DRDs are subject to certain limitations:

- The taxable income limitation creates a ceiling (maximum value) for the DRD. It is limited to 70 percent or 80 percent, respectively, of taxable income computed without the deductions for dividends received, any net operating loss (NOL) carryovers, and capital loss carrybacks to the current year.

- The taxable income limitation is disregarded if a loss (NOL) results after deducting the DRD using the general rules.

▲ **EXAMPLE 10** Hershal Corporation has the following income and expense items for the current tax year:

Dividend income received from less than 20%-owned domestic corporations	$100,000
Net income from operations	30,000

What is the amount of Hershal's DRD?

Discussion: Because Hershal owns less than 20% of the distributing corporations, the 70% deduction percentage applies. Under the general rule, the DRD is $70,000 (70% × $100,000 dividends). The taxable income limitation is $91,000 (70% × $130,000 taxable income before DRD). Because $70,000 is less than $91,000, Hershal Corporation may take the full 70% DRD.

▲ **EXAMPLE 11** Walker Corporation suffers a $20,000 net loss from operations for the current year and receives $180,000 in dividend income from corporations in which it owns 50% of the stock, resulting in a taxable income before the DRD of $160,000. What are the amounts of the DRD and the actual taxable income calculated for tax purposes?

Discussion: The DRD under the general rule is $144,000 (80% × $180,000). The taxable income limitation is $128,000 (80% × $160,000 in taxable income calculated without the DRD). Also, a loss does not result after deducting the DRD calculated under the general rule, so the taxable income limitation applies:

Net loss from operations	$ (20,000)
Dividend income	180,000
General rule DRD ($180,000 × 80%)	(144,000)
Taxable income calculated under the general rule	$ 16,000

Therefore, the DRD is limited to $128,000 (80% × $160,000), and the actual amount of taxable income for the current year is $32,000 ($160,000 − $128,000).

▲ **EXAMPLE 12** Cunningham Corporation incurs a net loss from operations of $70,000 for the current year. Cash dividends received from 30%-owned domestic corporations are $200,000, resulting in taxable income before the DRD of $130,000. What are the amounts of the DRD and the actual taxable income calculated for the current tax year?

% Ownership	Deduction Percentage
< 20%	70%
20%–80%	80%
80% or more	100%

Discussion: The DRD under the general rule is $160,000 ($200,000 × 80%). The taxable income limitation is $104,000 ($130,000 × 80%). The taxable income limitation does not apply in this case, because an NOL would result after the DRD, computed under the general rule, is subtracted from the operating loss and the dividend income:

Net loss from operations	$(70,000)
Dividend income	200,000
General rule DRD	(160,000)
NOL calculated under the general rule	$(30,000)

Therefore, the full $160,000 DRD is allowed.

As this example demonstrates, legislative grace permits income (dividends) to cause a net operating loss by applying the dividends-received deduction. Cunningham Corporation reports an NOL of $30,000 by deducting the full $160,000 DRD. If the taxable income limitation were in effect, Cunningham would report a taxable income of $26,000 ($130,000 − $104,000).

The dividends-received deduction provides small business owners who incorporate with an opportunity to partially shield from federal taxation the dividends they obtain from their invested capital.

▲ **EXAMPLE 13**   Conchita, a single taxpayer, operates Kapow Co., a garlic-packaging business, as a sole proprietorship. During the current year, the business income was $100,000. Conchita annually invests any excess cash in common stock of Tortilla's, Inc., a U.S. corporation. Tortilla paid Kapow $20,000 in dividends as of the end of the current year. What are the tax effects of the dividend income?

Discussion: Because the business operates as a sole proprietorship, the dividends are taxed at Conchita's marginal tax rate, 31%. Therefore, Conchita pays additional income tax of $6,200 ($20,000 × 31%), leaving her with after-tax dividend income of $13,800 ($20,000 − $6,200).

If Conchita incorporates her business, she can partially shield the dividend income from taxation because of the dividends-received deduction. Assuming Kapow Co., Inc., purchases the Tortilla's, Inc., stock, 70% of the dividends received by Kapow are deductible in determining corporate taxable income. Accordingly, only $6,000 [$20,000 − ($20,000 × 70%)] in dividend income is included in Kapow's taxable income. The $6,000 in added income results in increased taxes of $2,040 ($6,000 × 34%). Therefore, the after-tax dividend income is $17,960 ($20,000 − $2,040). A tax savings of $4,160 ($17,960 − $13,800) results when the corporate form of business is used.

Passive Activity Losses.   Generally, regular corporate taxpayers are not subject to the passive loss limitations discussed in Chapter 7.[14] Exceptions to this general rule concern personal service corporations (PSCs) and closely held regular corporations that are not PSCs.

PSCs are not permitted to use passive activity losses to reduce any of their income from personal services or income generated from their portfolio investments.

▲ **EXAMPLE 14**   A dental clinic is formed as a corporation by dentists who own all the stock in the corporation. The corporation acquires an interest in an oil exploration and drilling limited partnership. The partnership incurs operating losses that are passive. Can these losses be deducted in the current year?

Discussion: Because the dental clinic is a PSC (all owner-employees are providing the dental services), the passive activity losses (from the limited partnership) are suspended and cannot be used to offset the service income or any portfolio income of the corporation.

As demonstrated in example 14, architects, doctors, dentists, accountants, lawyers, and others whose primary income comes from providing services cannot avoid the passive activity loss limitations by incorporating. However, a closely held corporation that is not a personal service corporation can use the provision that permits use of passive activity losses to offset the corporation's active income—but not its portfolio income. Congress has effectively prevented shareholders from sheltering any portfolio income by transferring passive investments to their closely held corporations. However, closely held nonservice corporations are permitted to offset active income with passive activity losses.

▲ **EXAMPLE 15**   Kyle owns 55% of Boots, Inc. This entity is a rattlesnake-breeding ranch and boot factory formed as a corporation. During the current annual accounting period, Boots, Inc., has an operating income of $20,000, dividend income from investments in stock of other corporations of $3,000, interest income from savings and loan CDs of $2,000, and a loss from an investment in a limited partnership of $24,000. How much of the passive activity loss can be used to offset other income?

Discussion: Boots, Inc., is a closely held nonservice corporation, because Kyle owns more than 50% of the stock and the principal source of income is not from services. Accordingly, any corporate passive activity losses may be used to offset active income but may not be used to offset portfolio income. Therefore, the $24,000 passive activity loss may offset the $20,000 in operating (active) income. The $4,000 of loss remaining may not be used to offset the dividend or interest income. The $4,000 loss is carried over to the subsequent year to offset any passive or active income of that year.

An individual who owns a business operated as a sole proprietorship and also has passive activity losses cannot offset the operating (active) income with passive losses. Yet, if the individual incorporates the business and transfers the business assets and the passive activity investment assets to the corporation, the passive activity loss can shield the active income.

Capital Loss Limitations.   Corporations, in contrast to individuals, are not permitted to deduct net capital losses against other income (see Chapter 7 for this discussion). Corporations can use capital losses only to offset capital gains. When a corporation incurs a net capital loss for a tax year, it is allowed to carry the net capital loss back and use it to offset any net capital gains on which it paid tax in the previous three years. Any unused capital loss from the three-year carryback period may be carried forward to offset future capital gains for five years.[15] When carried back or forward, both short-term and long-term capital losses are treated as short-term capital losses.

▲ **EXAMPLE 16**   Gonzo, Inc., has the following income, gains, and losses for 1996 through 1999:

	1996	1997	1998	1999
Ordinary income	$50,000	$45,000	$40,000	$ 20,000
Net long-term capital gain (loss)	10,000	5,000	4,000	(30,000)
Total income	$60,000	$50,000	$44,000	$(10,000)

What is the effect of the net capital loss in 1999?

Discussion: Gonzo, Inc., cannot deduct any of the net capital loss to shield its 1999 ordinary income. Therefore, its taxable income is $20,000. The net capital loss is carried back to 1996 (3 years) and reduces the $10,000 in 1996 net capital gain to zero. Because Gonzo's 1996 marginal tax rate is a flat 25% for the taxable income from $50,000 to $60,000, Gonzo can file for a refund of $2,500 ($10,000 × 25%) for 1996. The new 1996 taxable income is $50,000. The $20,000 balance of the unused net capital loss is carried back to 1997 to offset that $5,000 net capital gain. Because Gonzo's total 1997 income decreases by $5,000 ($50,000 − $45,000) and the corporate rate is a flat 15% up to $50,000, Gonzo is due a refund of $750 ($5,000 × 15%) for 1997. Then, the unused net capital loss balance is carried to 1998, reducing the $4,000 net capital gain to zero and resulting in a tax refund of $600 ($4,000 × 15%) at a marginal rate of 15% for 1998. The 3-year carryback uses $19,000 ($10,000 + $5,000 + $4,000) of 1999's $30,000 net long-term capital loss. The remaining $11,000 ($30,000 − $19,000) of loss is carried forward as a short-term loss to reduce future capital gains over the next 5 years. The total refund Gonzo receives because of the carrybacks is $3,850 ($2,500 + $750 + $600).

	1996	1997	1998	1999	2000
Ordinary income	$ 50,000	$ 45,000	$ 40,000	$ 20,000	
Net long-term capital gain (loss)	10,000	5,000	4,000	(30,000)	
Capital loss carryback	(10,000)				
		(5,000)			
			(4,000)		(11,000)
Total income	$ 50,000	$ 45,000	$ 40,000	$ 20,000	
Tax refund	$ 2,500	$ 750	$ 600		

Charitable Contribution Limitations. Like individuals, corporations face certain limitations on the deductibility of **charitable contributions.** Generally, the rules governing charitable contributions made by corporations are the same as those pertaining to contributions made by individuals.[16] However, there are certain differences. For example, annual corporate charitable deductions are limited to 10 percent of taxable income (computed without regard to the charitable contribution deduction, NOL carrybacks, capital loss carrybacks, or the dividends-received deduction). Current-year contributions must be deducted against the limit before any carryover contributions may be deducted.

▲ **EXAMPLE 17**   King Corporation has the following items on its books for the current tax year:

Net income from operations	$125,000
Dividends received (70% rules)	10,000
Charitable contributions made in current year	15,000
Charitable contribution carryover from the previous year	3,000

What is the maximum amount of charitable contribution deduction allowed for the current year?

Discussion: The contribution deduction is limited to $13,500. For purposes of the 10% limitation only, King Corporation's taxable income is computed as follows:

Net income from operations	$125,000
Dividend income	10,000
Taxable income without the dividends-received deduction and the charitable contribution deduction	$135,000
Charitable contribution limit	× 10%
Maximum amount of charitable deduction	$ 13,500

Taxable income for the current year is $114,500.

Net income from operations		$125,000
Dividend income		10,000
		$135,000
Less:		
Charitable contributions	(13,500)	
Dividends-received deduction (70% × $10,000)	(7,000)	
Corporate taxable income		$114,500

NOTE: The current year's excess charitable contribution of $1,500 ($15,000 − $13,500) is carried over to the next tax year. It is subject to that year's limitation rules. The deductions of carryovers of excess charitable contributions are limited to 5 years subsequent to the year of the contribution. Any excess contribution not deducted after 5 years is lost forever.

Another difference between charitable contributions made by individuals and contributions by corporations affects accrual basis corporations. Generally, deductions are permitted only for actual contributions given during a tax year. However, accrual basis corporations may elect to deduct a pledge made during a given year so long as the actual contribution is made by the fifteenth day of the third month after the close of the year of the pledge.

A third difference between individual contributors and corporate contributors concerns donated inventory items. Generally, the value of **donated inventory** is the adjusted basis of the inventory. However, an exception is provided for a corporate taxpayer that donates inventory for either of two types of uses:

▪ Items given solely for the care of the ill, needy, or infants

▪ Items donated to a university or qualified research organization to be used for research, experimentation, or research training in the biological or physical sciences

The amount of deduction under this exception is the inventory's fair market value, less 50 percent of the income that would be recognized if the inventory were sold at its fair market value. However, there is a ceiling, or maximum amount of deduction, which is twice the basis of the donated inventory items.[17]

▲ **EXAMPLE 18**   Tech Corporation contributes some of its scientific software to the Department of Biophysics Research at Northwest University during the current year. As of the date of the contribution, the inventory had a fair market value of $50,000. Tech's basis in the software is $20,000. What is the amount of the charitable contribution deduction?

Discussion: The transaction qualifies under the exception for certain corporate inventory. Software given to a university for research or research training is qualified inventory. The amount of Tech's contribution is $35,000 [$50,000 − (50% × $30,000)].

▲ **EXAMPLE 19**   Assume the same facts as in example 18, except that the basis of the inventory is $10,000. What is the amount of the charitable contribution in this case?

Discussion: The amount of Tech's contribution (before any limitations) is $30,000 [$50,000 − (50% × $40,000)]. However, the actual amount of the contribution deduction is limited to $20,000 (2 x $10,000), the ceiling of twice the basis of the inventory.

Organizational Costs.   Because a corporation is a legal entity formed under state law, creating it requires various expenditures. Most expenses benefit future periods of the corporation's life. Specifically, **organizational costs** provide benefits over the life of the entity. Therefore, the corporation generally cannot deduct such expenditures until the corporation liquidates. Assets with an indefinite life may not be amortized for tax purposes. However, a corporation may elect to amortize qualified organizational expenses over a period of 60 months or more.[18] If the election to amortize these expenses is not made on the tax return for the first taxable year, the costs are not deductible until the corporation ceases business and liquidates. Organizational expenditures may include the following:

- Legal services incident to organization, such as drafting the corporate charter, bylaws, minutes of organizational meetings, terms of original stock certificates
- Necessary accounting services
- Expenses of temporary directors and of organizational meetings of directors or shareholders
- Fees paid to the state of incorporation[19]

Expenses that are not considered organizational expenditures include those incurred for the issue, or sales, of shares of corporate stock (e.g., commissions, printing costs). These costs are considered selling expenses and, accordingly, reduce stockholders' equity.

▲ **EXAMPLE 20**   NewCor, Inc., a calendar-year corporation, was formed during the current year and began business operations on October 1. NewCor, Inc., paid $4,200 to attorneys, accountants, and state regulatory agencies to organize the corporation. Can NewCor deduct any of the $4,200?

Discussion: If NewCor, Inc., files an election to amortize its organizational costs over 60 months, it may deduct $210 during the current year:

$$\$4,200 \div 60 \text{ months} = \$70 \text{ per month}$$
$$\$70 \times 3 \text{ months} = \$210$$

Calculation of Taxable Income

A corporation's taxable income calculation is similar to the computation of taxable income for an individual taxpayer. However, there are several important differences. Some differences involve the special items discussed earlier (the dividends-received deduction, the passive loss treatment, the capital loss limitation, the charitable contribution limitations, and organizational cost deductions). Other differences involve personal consumption-type expenses and exemptions that are allowed only to individuals. Corporations may not deduct personal use expenditures, nor is there a corporate standard deduction. Also, corporations are not permitted personal and dependency exemption deductions. Accordingly, there is no such thing as adjusted gross income for corporate taxpayers. The tax formula for corporations essentially involves a computation that is simpler than that for an individual. See Exhibit 9–1 for the formula for corporate taxpayers and Table 9–1 for corporate tax rates.

▲ **EXAMPLE 21**   Elway Corporation had the following items of income for its calendar year 1996:

Operating income	$250,000
Dividend income (5%-owned corporations)	20,000
Long-term capital gains	8,000
Long-term capital losses	(6,000)
Short-term capital gains	3,000
Capital loss carryover from 1995	(9,000)
Charitable cash contributions	50,000

What is the amount of the corporation's 1996 taxable income?

Discussion: The taxable income is $229,000. Netting the current year's capital gains and capital losses with the 1995 carryover results in a net short-term capital loss of $4,000 ($8,000 − $6,000 + $3,000 − $9,000). Because corporations can use capital losses only to reduce capital gains, Elway derives no benefit from the net capital loss in 1996. The net capital loss can be carried forward to offset future capital gains. The charitable contributions are subject to the taxable income limitation [$50,000 > (10% × $270,000 = $27,000)].

Operating income		$250,000
Dividend income		20,000
Gross income		$270,000
Less: Special deductions		
Dividends received		
(70% × $20,000)	$14,000	
Charitable contributions		
(10% × $270,000)	27,000	41,000
Taxable income		$229,000

NOTE: The $23,000 ($50,000 − $27,000) excess charitable contribution may be carried over to 1997.

Accounting Periods and Methods

A regular corporation generally has the same choices for its annual accounting period as individuals—calendar years or fiscal years. Compared to other entity forms (partnerships, S corporations), the selection of an annual accounting period is not restricted.[20] A new corporation may select its annual accounting period without prior approval of the IRS.

▲ **Exhibit 9–1**

CORPORATE INCOME TAX FORMULA

Gross income (all income less exclusions)		$ XXX
Less: Trade or business expenses		(XXX)
Less: Special deductions		
Dividends received	$XXX	
Passive losses	XXX	
Charitable contributions	XXX	
Organizational costs	XXX	(XXX)
Taxable income		$ XXX

▲ **EXAMPLE 22**   GnuCor, Inc., was incorporated during 1996. The corporate board of directors selected a fiscal year end of January 31. Is this action in compliance with the annual accounting period concept?

Discussion: Because GnuCor, Inc., is newly formed, no prior IRS approval is necessary. Therefore, the fiscal year will be recognized. Also, the corporation will have a different tax period than its individual shareholders. NOTE: If GnuCor, Inc., decides to change its fiscal year, IRS approval is necessary.

The selection of an accounting method is more restrictive for corporations than individuals. Regular corporations are generally denied the use of the cash method for tax purposes (unless the entity's average annual gross receipts are $5 million or less). Personal service corporations and S corporations may choose either the cash or accrual method.[21] Also, as discussed in Chapter 3, both individual and corporate taxpayers that have inventories must use the accrual method to account for sales and costs of goods sold inventories.

Distributions to Shareholders

Cash or other property distributed to a shareholder is generally taxable to the shareholder.[22] Also, the distributing corporation may not deduct the amount of dividends distributed for tax purposes (called **corporate distributions**). These rules originate from the tax definition of a **dividend**: a distribution by a corporation out of either its current or accumulated earnings and profits. **Earnings and profits (E&P)** generally represent undistributed, previously taxed corporate profits. Current earnings and profits are considered to be distributed first, followed by accumulated earnings and profits, if necessary.[23]

▲ **EXAMPLE 23**   Disco Corporation distributes a total of $100,000 to its shareholders during 1996. Accumulated earnings and profits are a deficit of $350,000 as of January 1, 1996. Current earnings and profits for 1996 are $300,000. How is the $100,000 distribution treated by the shareholder recipients?

Discussion: The amount of current earnings and profits is sufficient to classify the $100,000 as dividend income to the shareholders. A year-end deficit in accumulated earnings and profits of Disco Corporation will not change the outcome, because dividends are assumed to be paid out of the current year's E&P first.

If a corporate distribution exceeds both the current and accumulated earnings and profits, the capital recovery concept dictates that the distribution is tax free to shareholders. Therefore, the basis in the stock held by shareholders is reduced by the amount of the tax-free return of capital. If a shareholder receives a distribution in excess of the basis of the stock (excess capital recovery), the shareholder recognizes a capital gain.

▲ **EXAMPLE 24**   ABC Corporation distributes $200,000 in cash ($2 per share) when its current and cumulative earnings and profits are $50,000. What is the effect of the distribution on Jerry, who owns 500 shares of ABC stock for which she paid $10,000?

Discussion: The first 25% ($50,000 ÷ $200,000) of the distribution is a taxable dividend for Jerry of $250 [25% × ($2 × 500 shares)]. The remainder of Jerry's $1,000 distribution is deemed a recovery of capital to the extent of her basis in the shares of stock. Because Jerry's basis is $10,000, the remaining $750 of the dividend ($1,000 − $250) reduces the basis of her stock to $9,250 ($10,000 − $750). NOTE: If Jerry's basis had been less than $750, the distribution in excess of the basis causes recognition of a capital gain. The stock's basis then becomes zero.

The term *earnings and profits* is not technically defined in the tax law. Yet, it is designed to be a measure of a corporation's economic ability to pay dividends without impairing capital. Earnings and profits are conceptually analogous to the financial accounting term *retained earnings*, although several differences exist. Even without a technical definition, it is possible to determine earnings and profits by examining various transactions noted in tax law that affect them.[24] A detailed discussion of earnings and profits and their related transactions is beyond the scope of this text.

Multiple Corporations

The choice of the corporate form for doing business can offer many benefits. One benefit that has been effectively eliminated—because it was abused—is the use of multiple corporations to split income. That is, under prior law, tax planners made use of the entity concept that recognizes the corporate taxpayer as a single tax-paying unit. By carefully planning the income of each corporation (e.g., keeping each corporation's income at or below $50,000), all income of the taxpayer was taxed at the lowest marginal rate. Because lawmakers deemed that the use of multiple corporations lacked sound business purpose (tax saving was the dominant objective), corporate members of a controlled group (discussed later) must share the tax benefits of lower tax rates.

> ▲ **EXAMPLE 25**   Emanuel is the sole shareholder of a corporate business that earns $100,000 in taxable income annually. Therefore, the corporate tax liability is $22,250 [(15% × $50,000) + (25% × $25,000) + (34% × $25,000)]. Emanuel decided he could reduce his total corporate tax liability by splitting his business operations into two separate corporate entities reporting $50,000 in taxable income each. Therefore, the total tax liability of two corporations would be $15,000 ($50,000 × 15% × 2). This plan apparently saves $7,250. Will the plan pass IRS scrutiny?
>
> *Discussion:*   No. Emanuel's two corporations are members of a controlled group. Accordingly, each rate bracket must be shared by the two corporations. That is, the income of the two corporations is combined for purposes of computing the tax liability. The total tax liability becomes $22,250; the amount of tax is the same as if only 1 corporation had reported all the income.

Controlled Groups.   A **controlled group** is a group of two or more corporations that are owned directly or indirectly by the same shareholder(s).[25] The group of corporations may include a parent-subsidiary relationship, a brother-sister relationship, or a combination of these two types. If a parent or subsidiary group owns 80 percent or more of the stock of another corporation, the other corporation is included in the **parent-subsidiary relationship** (controlled group).

> ▲ **EXAMPLE 26**   Elvira Corporation owns 80% of Keith Corporation's stock and 45% of Mark Corporation's stock. Keith Corporation owns 35% of Mark Corporation's stock. Does a controlled group exist?
>
> *Discussion:*   Yes. Elvira, Keith, and Mark are members of the same parent-subsidiary controlled group. Elvira directly owns 80% of Keith Corporation's stock. Therefore, Elvira is the group's parent corporation. Also, Mark's stock is controlled by the 80% ownership group of Elvira (45%) and Keith corporations (35%). See Figure 9–2.

Another type of controlled group is a group of two or more corporations defined by two tests. Passing both tests, not just one, creates a **brother-sister re-**

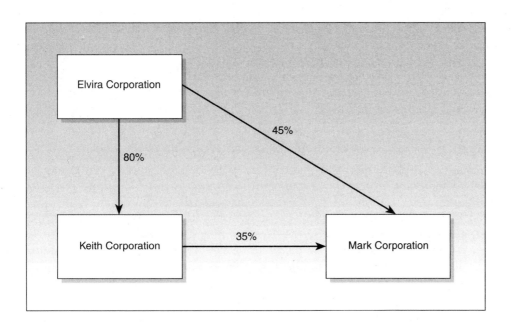

lationship. The first test (the 80-percent test) requires that five or fewer persons own 80 percent or more of the stock of each corporation in the group. The second test (the 50-percent test) requires that five or fewer persons own more than 50 percent of the stock of each corporation in the group (considering only the identical stock ownership that each person has with respect to each corporation). A shareholder's identical ownership is the percentage of stock held in common by the shareholder in each of the corporations. That percentage is equal to the smallest percentage of stock of any single corporation that the shareholder owns. For example, a person owning 20 percent of Rocket Corporation and 45 percent of Fueler Corporation has an identical ownership of 20 percent in the two corporations.

▲ **EXAMPLE 27**   DeWayne and Latifa own stock in Fritzy Corporation and Kragen Corporation:

	Stock Ownership Percentage		
Shareholder	Fritzy Corp.	Kragen Corp.	Identical Ownership
DeWayne	40%	55%	40%
Latifa	60%	45%	45%
Totals	100%	100%	85%

Are Fritzy and Kragen a brother-sister controlled group?

Discussion: Because 5 or fewer people (DeWayne and Latifa) own at least 80% of each corporation's stock (they together own 100% of each) and DeWayne and Latifa own more than 50% of each corporation's stock (they have an identical ownership of 85%), both the 80% test and the 50% test are satisfied. Accordingly, Fritzy and Kragen are a brother-sister controlled group.

FIDUCIARIES

A person who occupies a position of special confidence, especially a trustee, guardian, receiver, conservator, executor, or administrator, is considered a **fiduciary.** Such people have legal title to property, which they hold for the benefit of others, subject to strict duties under state law. Many, but not all, fiduciaries are required to file income tax returns on behalf of the entity (e.g., trust or estate) for which they are responsible.

Estates

An **estate** is created upon the death of an individual. Generally, the estate is merely a temporary, transitional entity. It holds the deceased person's property until the property is distributed to its beneficiaries. After all the property is transferred from the estate, its purpose has ended and it ceases to exist. During the estate's life, the property held by the executor may earn income. That income is taxed to the estate, and taxes are paid from estate assets. The taxable income of the estate is taxed using the fiduciary tax rates (see Table 9–3).

Trusts

A **trust** is a legal entity created when a person transfers ownership of property to a **trustee** to be held for the benefit of another person. Occasionally, a will directs the creation of a trust. This **testamentary trust** is funded by assets formerly held by the estate. The person who transfers the corpus, or trust assets, to the trustee is called the **grantor.** The directions given the trustee by the grantor are included in the trust instrument, or indenture. Often the trustee is a bank's trust department, another competent professional (e.g., an attorney or an accountant), or a trusted family member.

The trustee's primary purpose is to preserve the trust assets for the benefit of the beneficiaries. The trustee generally invests the corpus to earn the return desired by the grantor. If the grantor wants a beneficiary to receive an annual income distribution, the trustee must use her or his best judgment to bring the greatest return on investment without greatly risking the corpus. If the trustee is required to distribute all annual income to the trust beneficiaries, the trust is called a **simple trust.** All other trusts are called **complex trusts.** In addition, there is generally a **remainderman** who is the beneficiary and will receive the balance of the trust assets when the trust is terminated. The grantor may designate almost any mixture of trust income and/or corpus to be distributed to beneficiaries.

For a trust to be recognized as a taxable entity, no more than 5 percent of its assets may revert to the grantor or spouse (a **reversionary interest**) upon termi-

▲ Table 9–3

FIDUCIARY TAX RATES (ESTATES AND TRUSTS) (1996)

If Taxable Income Is		The Tax Is	Of the
Over—	But Not Over—		Amount Over—
$ -0-	$1,600	...........15 %	$ -0-
1,600	3,800	$ 240 + 28 %	1,600
3,800	5,800	856 + 31 %	3,800
5,800	7,900	1,476 + 36 %	5,800
7,900	....	2,232 + 39.6%	7,900

NOTE: Net long-term capital gain income is taxed at a maximum 28% rate.

nation (if the trust was created or had additional assets transferred to it after March 1, 1986). If a trust does not meet this requirement, trust income is taxed to the grantor.[26] This type of trust is known as a **grantor trust.**

▲ **EXAMPLE 28**   During 1995, Halah contributed common stock worth $200,000 to a simple trust managed by the trustee of the Second National Bank and Trust. Halah designated her teenage daughter Nadia as the beneficiary of the trust income. The trust instrument requires that the trust principal be returned to Halah upon Nadia's 24th birthday. In the current year, the Halah Trust earned $23,000 in dividend income. All $23,000 was distributed to Nadia. Who is responsible for reporting the $23,000 in dividend income?

Discussion: Because more than 5% of the trust assets revert to her at termination, Halah retains a reversionary interest in the trust assets. Therefore, Halah must include the $23,000 in her current gross income.

▲ **EXAMPLE 29**   Assume that Halah, in example 28, created the trust with her daughter Nadia as income beneficiary and the American Red Cross as the beneficiary of the trust principal upon Nadia's 24th birthday. During the current year, the Halah Trust earned $23,000 in dividend income, and all of it was distributed to Halah. Who is responsible for recognizing the $23,000 in income?

Discussion: Because Halah does not hold a reversionary interest in the trust assets (all assets go to the Red Cross at termination), the income beneficiary, Nadia, is taxed on the $23,000. The income retains the characteristics of dividends for Nadia.

Income Taxation of Fiduciaries

The general rules of individual income taxation govern fiduciary income taxation.[27] As with corporate taxation, a thorough understanding of taxation of individuals precedes the study of income taxation of fiduciaries—only a few tax rules are different for fiduciaries. The principal difference in the calculation of taxable income is the deduction for distributions to beneficiaries.

Most of the gross income received by a fiduciary consists of interest, dividends, royalties, and rents (i.e., forms of investment income). Therefore, the fiduciary's deductible expenses are those directly connected to the production of investment income, such as management or asset maintenance fees. The treatment of any tax-exempt income (e.g., municipal bond interest) is similar to its treatment for individuals. As with individuals, any allocable related expenses of tax-exempt income are not deductible by the fiduciary.

Unlike corporations, fiduciaries and beneficiaries are not subjected to double taxation on the income earned by an estate or trust. The fiduciary entity receives a deduction for income distributed to beneficiaries.[28] Then, beneficiaries report the amount of their receipts as income on their individual returns, much as owners of conduit entities do. Therefore, income is taxed just once. Either the fiduciary or the beneficiary pays the income tax. If not all of the current income is distributed, both fiduciary and beneficiary will pay some tax.

▲ **EXAMPLE 30**   During the current year, the Carson P. Taylor Trust earns interest income of $20,000. Patricia Taylor, the beneficiary, receives a $9,000 distribution from the trust. What are the tax effects of these events?

Discussion: Patricia reports $9,000 on her individual income tax return. The trust is taxed on its undistributed earnings, $11,000, less an allowable exemption of $100 (explained shortly).

Trusts that distribute income to beneficiaries follow the general distribution rules for conduit entities. That is, the income received by the beneficiary retains the same character it had when earned by the trust.

▲ **EXAMPLE 31**   The Barber Trust received $8,000 in dividends, $4,000 in corporate bond interest, $2,000 in capital gain income, and $6,000 in municipal bond tax-exempt interest. The trust distributes all its receipts to beneficiaries. What is the character of the receipts in the hands of the beneficiaries?

Discussion: Beneficiaries are deemed to have obtained the same $8,000 in dividends, $4,000 in interest, $2,000 in capital gains, and $6,000 in tax-exempt income as were earned by the trust. Therefore, the beneficiaries are not taxed on their share of the tax-exempt income. In addition, their share of the capital gain income will become part of their personal capital gain-and-loss netting.

Charitable Contributions.   Congress encourages fiduciaries to make donations to qualified charitable organizations by allowing unlimited charitable deductions, which is not true for individuals or corporations. Also, the annual accounting period concept is partially disregarded as a matter of legislative grace. A fiduciary may elect to deduct a contribution in one year but not actually make the payment until near the close of the following tax year.

One limitation on the generous deduction rules for charitable contributions involves tax-exempt income. If the fiduciary distributes to charitable organizations funds that are the result of tax-exempt income, that distribution does not qualify for a deduction against fiduciary taxable income.

▲ **EXAMPLE 32**   The Lawrence Trust receives $10,000 in tax-exempt interest and $30,000 in taxable dividends during the current tax year. Also, the trust gives $12,000 to the United Way. How much may the trust deduct as a charitable contribution for the current year?

Discussion: Twenty-five percent ($10,000 ÷ $40,000) of the year's income is tax exempt. Therefore, 25% of the charitable contribution is nondeductible. Only $9,000 (75% × $12,000) is deductible by the trust.

Accounting Periods.   Because the taxation of trust distributions could be deferred by choosing a fiscal year, Congress requires trusts to use a calendar year as their tax year.[29] Estates, however, are free to choose a tax year. Congress probably deemed death too high a price to pay for gaining favorable tax treatment for a beneficiary.

Exemption Amounts.   Fiduciaries, unlike individuals, are not allowed a standard deduction amount. This provision is consistent with the purpose of the standard deduction for individuals. Because fiduciaries (i.e., trusts or estates) do not have personal itemized deductions, there is no need for relief under the administrative convenience concept.

A fiduciary, like an individual taxpayer and unlike a corporation, may claim an exemption deduction.[30] The amount of the statutory exemption depends on the type of fiduciary (see Exhibit 9–2). Unlike the personal exemption amount for individuals, the exemption for fiduciaries is not indexed for inflation.

Income Tax Calculation

The fiduciary income tax formula is not much different from the corporate income tax formula. Fiduciaries deduct their expenses and specially allowed deductions (exemptions, beneficiary distributions, charitable contributions) from fiduciary income.

Estates	$600
Simple trusts	$300
Other trusts	$100

▲ **EXAMPLE 33**   During 1996, the Armstrong Trust receives $25,000 in dividend income from corporate stock and has a $15,000 long-term capital gain from the sale of stock. The trust expenses total $10,000. The trust agreement states that all net capital gains are characterized and accumulated as trust corpus. All ordinary income must be distributed annually. What are the amounts of the trust's taxable income and its income tax liability?

Discussion: The trust is a complex trust, because all income is not distributed to the beneficiaries. The $10,000 in trust expenses, the $25,000 in dividend income distributed to the beneficiaries, and the $100 trust exemption are deducted from the $40,000 in trust income, resulting in a taxable income of $4,900.

Armstrong Trust 1996	
Gross income ($25,000 + $15,000)	$40,000
Less: Expenses	(10,000)
Less: Income distributed to beneficiaries	(25,000)
Less: Exemption	(100)
Taxable income	$ 4,900

The income tax liability is determined by using the fiduciary rate schedule in Table 9–3:

$$[\$856 + 31\% (\$4,900 - \$3,800)] = \$1,197$$

▲ **EXAMPLE 34**   The Sadler Trust received $10,000 in dividend income, $5,000 in tax-exempt income, and $12,000 in long-term capital gains from the sale of corporate stock. Trust expenses not related to the tax-exempt income total $1,000. All trust income (after expenses) must be distributed annually. What is the trust's taxable income?

Discussion: Because all net trust income is distributed to the beneficiaries, the Sadler Trust is a simple trust. The amount distributed to beneficiaries is $26,000 ($10,000 + $12,000 + $5,000 − $1,000), resulting in a deduction of $21,000 ($26,000 − $5,000 in tax-exempt income) for the trust. The trust's taxable income is zero:

Sadler Trust	
Gross income ($10,000 + $12,000)	$22,000
Less: Expenses	(1,000)
Less: Income distributed to beneficiaries	(21,000)
Taxable income	$ -0-

Because all the income was distributed to beneficiaries, the trust has no taxable income and, accordingly, no tax liability. Therefore, the exemption amount is not needed. (Trusts cannot have net operating losses, because they are not a trade or business.) NOTE: The beneficiaries will include the dividend income, the tax-exempt income, and the long-term capital gains in their income per the categories from the trust.

Every entity is classified as either a taxable or a **conduit entity.** Tax conduits are characterized by the flow-through of their tax attributes directly to the owners of the entity.[31,32] The incidence of taxation of a conduit entity's income rests with the entity's owners.

CONDUIT ENTITIES

Trusts, as discussed in the previous section, are either taxable or conduit entities. The characterization depends on whether trust income is distributed to beneficiaries. The other types of tax conduits do not rely on distributions for characterization. Partnerships, S corporations, and sole proprietorships are required by tax law to allocate their income, gains, losses, deductions, and credits to owners, regardless of any distributions. This flow-through effect could force owners to recognize income without the benefit of the wherewithal to pay.

Accounting Periods

All entities must follow the annual accounting period concept. That is, the results of operations are reported annually, and each tax year stands apart from other tax years. Although conduits do not pay income tax, they are not immune from reporting their financial results to the government as other entities do.

Although conduits are required to report annually, partnerships and S corporations have restrictions on their selection of fiscal years.[33,34] Generally, most partnerships, S corporations, and conduit trusts must use a calendar year for tax purposes. The intent of this requirement is to reduce the ability to defer taxes when fiscal year conduit entities pass income through to owners.

> ▲ **EXAMPLE 35**   Henry and Laurel are equal partners in HL Partnership. Both partners are calendar-year taxpayers. The partnership chose a March 31 fiscal year end. For the year April 1, 1996, through March 31, 1997, HL Partnership reports $1,000,000 in net operating income. In what tax year will the individual partners report their respective shares of partnership income if the partnership tax year is valid?
>
> *Discussion:*   The initial result is that each partner reports $500,000 on her or his 1997 individual income tax return, due by April 15, 1998. This result defers reporting the income earned by HL for more than 13 months. However, this result is no longer valid. The partnership is required to have the same tax year as the partners' (calendar year). Therefore, HL must adopt a calendar year, and Henry and Laurel must report the $500,000 on their 1996 tax returns.

A partnership or S corporation may select a tax year other than the prescribed calendar year, with certain restrictions. These conduit entities may elect a fiscal year that results in a tax deferral of three months or less. For example, a partnership with calendar-year partners may select a September 30 (or October 31 or November 30) fiscal year end. However, the entity must make annual required payments on April 15 of the following year. The required payments are to offset the tax deferral advantage that calendar-year owners receive if their conduit entity uses a fiscal year.

The amount of the required payment is calculated as the previous year's taxable income multiplied by the maximum tax rate for individuals plus 1 percent and then by the deferral ratio. The deferral ratio equals the number of deferral months divided by 12 months.

> ▲ **EXAMPLE 36**   Big Orange Partnership elects a fiscal year end of September 30. For the tax year of October 1, 1996, through September 30, 1997, Big Orange's taxable income is $400,000. What is the amount of the required payment due for the privilege of selecting a 3-month deferral because of the fiscal year?
>
> *Discussion:*   The required payment is $37,000 [$400,000 × 37% (top individual rate + 1%) × 3/12 (the deferral ratio)]. The payment is due by April 15, 1998.

The required payment is effectively a deposit that approximates the value of the fiscal year deferral, resulting in no real tax advantage. Therefore, conduit entities must have good reasons other than tax deferral to elect fiscal years. Accordingly, businesses that have a natural business year other than the calendar year—and can establish that fact to the satisfaction of the IRS—do not have to make required payments (see Chapter 14).

Accounting Methods

A conduit entity can elect to use the cash, accrual, or hybrid method, following the basic rules for these methods. Also, special methods, such as those for installment sales or long-term construction contracts, must be used if the requirements for using the methods are met. Any of these elections or methods are determined at the entity level. Therefore, the conduit construct governs—owners report the items of income, deductions, gains, losses, and credits following the method(s) of determination for the entities. For example, a partnership electing the accrual method for income recognition forces its partners to report income of the partnership on the accrual method, even if the partners use the cash method.[35]

The characterization of income and deduction items occurs at the entity level. The items flowing through to owners cannot be reclassified by the owners. Also, because many items such as capital gains and losses, charitable contributions, rental income and expense, and certain other items are subject to special tax treatments, these items are reported separately. Therefore, any limitations (e.g., capital loss limitations) are applied at the owner level.

Basis in Partnerships and S Corporations

Basis in a partnership or S corporation may be the most critical attribute for owners. Basis establishes the amount of unrecovered investment in the conduit entity. Not only does basis establish the realized gain or loss on disposition of the investment through application of the capital recovery concept, it determines the taxability of distributions from the conduit entity to owners. Also, the amount of unrecovered basis determines whether an owner may recognize losses flowing from the conduit entity to the owner.

Basis is dynamic. Throughout the life of the investment, basis is adjusted to reflect the tax results of many entity transactions. Although S corporations and partnerships have a few different adjustments to their owners' bases, the primary adjustments are the same.

Basis is established when an investor purchases an ownership interest (e.g., shares of corporate stock or a partnership interest) in an entity. The cost of the investment is the initial basis amount.[36] (Exhibit 9–3 provides a general formula for determining the basis in an investment).

Instead of contributing cash to an entity, investors may contribute real or personal property. The tax results do not change for a contribution of property. The tax law permits a tax-free transaction when property is contributed in exchange for an ownership interest.[37] Therefore, the basis in the contributed property is substituted for the basis in the ownership interest.[38]

▲ **EXAMPLE 37**   Edith transfers $20,000 in cash and equipment that she uses in her sole proprietorship that has a fair market value of $12,000 (and an adjusted basis of $8,000) to the McDyss Partnership for a partnership interest worth $32,000. What is the amount of gain recognized by Edith, and what is the basis in her partnership interest?

Discussion: Edith does not recognize any gain on the transaction. Although she realizes a gain of $4,000 ($12,000 − $8,000) on the equipment, the tax law specifies that no gain or loss is recognized on the exchange of assets for a partnership interest. Only

Initial investment or contribution	$ XXX
Add: Additional forms of investment	
Share of entity income	XXX
Contribution of assets	XXX
Deduct: Returns of capital investment	
Share of entity losses	(XXX)
Withdrawals or dividends received	(XXX)
Adjusted basis in investment	$ XXX

the form of her ownership interest in the property has changed (sole proprietor versus partnership ownership)—she has a continuing ownership interest in the equipment through her partnership interest. In addition, Edith lacks the wherewithal to pay tax on the gain because the partnership interest is not liquid and cannot be used to pay taxes. Edith's basis in her partnership interest is $28,000 ($20,000 + $8,000). Because there is a continuity of ownership, Edith substitutes the basis of the property she transfers to the partnership for the basis of her partnership interest.

After the initial basis amount is determined, periodic increases and decreases occur. When a conduit entity reports net operating income or gains, those items flow through to owners who must recognize them on their personal tax returns. Because they are taxed to the owners, these items are added to the basis amount. They represent additional investments in the entity similar to an actual additional contribution to the entity of cash or other property.

▲ EXAMPLE 38   Lanier contributes land with a basis of $10,000 and a fair market value of $35,000 to the LMN Partnership for a 30% interest in the business. At the close of the year, LMN reports operating income of $50,000. No cash or property was distributed by LMN to Lanier during the year. What is Lanier's share of the income, and how does it affect the basis of her partnership interest?

Discussion: Lanier's share of the partnership income is $15,000 (30% × $50,000). Lanier reports the $15,000 on her personal income tax return. The basis of her partnership interest increases by the amount of the income recognized. Her initial basis, the $10,000 adjusted basis of the property contributed, plus income recognized, $15,000, equals an adjusted basis of $25,000 at the end of the year. NOTE: Lanier is required to include the partnership income in her gross income. Yet, Lanier received no cash or other property. The entity's assets increase because the operating earned income remains with the partnership. Lanier's share of the increase in partnership assets is analogous to an additional contribution of property to the partnership by the partner. Therefore, the basis in the ownership interest increases to reflect the partner's share of the additional assets of the partnership.

Not only will entity income and contributions to conduit entities affect an investor's basis amount but so will entity losses and withdrawals from conduit entities. Losses flow through to owners and are recognizable by them on their personal income tax returns. However, following the capital recovery concept, losses are recognized only to the extent a basis amount exists.

▲ EXAMPLE 39   Widdell has an initial basis of $5,000 in his 10% interest in the WW Partnership. WW Partnership reports a net operating loss of $60,000 for the current year. What amount can Widdell recognize for the current year?

Discussion: Widdell's share of the partnership loss is $6,000 (10% × $60,000). However, the amount of loss recognition is limited to the amount of basis. Therefore, Widdell is allowed to deduct only $5,000 of the loss. Widdell's total capital is recovered via the loss. NOTE: Widdell's remaining basis is zero, and the additional $1,000 loss is suspended until the basis amount again becomes positive—through future partnership income or additional capital contributions by Widdell.

Distribution of capital from conduit entities to owners is a true capital recovery. Withdrawals by partners and dividends to S corporation shareholders are nontaxable reductions of each owner's basis. However, if the withdrawal or dividend exceeds the amount of an owner's basis, the excess amount is a taxable capital gain.

▲ **EXAMPLE 40**   Edna and Lucille have been equal partners in the KAK Partnership for several years. At the close of the current year, Edna's basis in her ownership interest is $10,000, and Lucille's basis is $4,000. At that time, the partnership distributes cash in the amount of $5,000 to each partner. What are the tax and basis effects of these withdrawals?

Discussion: Edna receives her $5,000 tax free; it is merely a recovery of capital. Her basis is reduced to $5,000 ($10,000 − $5,000). Lucille receives $4,000 tax free as a recovery of capital. However, the excess $1,000 capital recovery is recognized as a capital gain. Lucille's basis amount is now zero.

	Edna	Lucille
Initial basis	$10,000	$4,000
Cash withdrawal	(5,000)	(5,000)
Remaining basis	$ 5,000	$ -0-
Taxable gain	$ -0-	$1,000

Basis computations are discussed further in the subsections about partnerships and S corporations. Each entity has basis adjustments that are unique.

Sole Proprietorships

The most common business form in the United States is the sole proprietorship. Individuals need do nothing formally to establish a sole proprietorship. This ease of formation results because the business is not separate from the individual owner from a tax perspective. Sometimes, the separation issue becomes blurred because of financial accounting rules that require proprietors to exclude reporting of nonbusiness items (e.g., personal expenses or nonbusiness income) from proprietorship financial reports. Schedule C of Form 1040 is the vehicle for reporting the items of proprietorship income, expenses, and credits. This reporting mechanism has the appearance of separating the proprietor from the proprietor's business. Yet, this reporting procedure reinforces the conduit nature of the sole proprietorship. The net operating income flows directly to the individual proprietor's Form 1040 as an item of gross income.

Because sole proprietorships are not separate taxable entities, owner-employee salaries and owner-employee fringe benefits are not deductible by sole proprietorships. Proprietors may take cash withdrawals from their businesses, but these payments are not going from one taxable entity to another. The only entity involved is the individual. Proprietorship cash draws are analogous to taking money from one pocket and putting it into another pocket in the same pair of pants. Partnerships also have these characteristics.

Sole proprietors cannot be employees of their businesses, because individuals cannot hire themselves. Therefore, salaries or fringe benefits such as group term life insurance are not available to proprietors. The business is not allowed a deduction for these items, and fringe-benefit recipients are not permitted exclusions for those benefits. Of course, wages and fringe-benefit payments on behalf of employees are deductible as proprietorship expenses.

As discussed in the first section of this chapter, a sole proprietor's child is not subject to Social Security taxes when validly employed in the parent's business. Sole proprietors can obtain multiple benefits by employing their children. Wages are deductible expenses of the business, and the parent-proprietor also saves 7.65 percent (employer's share of Social Security) of the child's wages. This procedure allows the parent-proprietor to put cash into the hands of children with positive results. Depending on the amount of the child's earned income, it is possible for the child to escape income taxation and Social Security taxation entirely (see examples 7 and 8).

Although a proprietor's child may escape payment of Social Security tax, the proprietor generally cannot. Self-employed individuals pay a tax on any self-employment income of $400 or more. As discussed in Chapter 8, self-employment income in 1996 is subject to a tax of 15.3% on the first $62,700 of self-employment income and 2.9% on the excess. A self-employed individual may deduct half of all self-employment taxes paid as a for-AGI deduction.

▲ **EXAMPLE 41**   Fletcher is a self-employed consultant with business net income of $50,000. How much self-employment tax is due?

Discussion: As discussed in Chapter 8, only 92.35% of self-employed income is subject to tax because of the deduction allowed for self-employment taxes paid. Fletcher's self-employment tax is $7,065 ($50,000 × 92.35% × 15.3%).

▲ **EXAMPLE 42**   How much of an income tax deduction is Fletcher, in example 41, allowed?

Discussion: Fletcher's income tax deduction is one-half of the total of self-employment taxes paid, $3,533 ($7,065 × 50%).

Partnerships

Although **partnerships** are considered conduits for the purpose of income taxation, they are treated as separate entities under local law. Therefore, partnerships can transact business and own property in their own names, separate from the partners. These common legal characteristics are similar to those for other business forms, such as corporations. Although partnerships are deemed aggregations of the partners' interests for income tax purposes, on occasion the characteristics become blurred. This section also introduces two new business forms, limited liability companies and limited liability partnerships, referred to collectively as *limited liability entities.*

Legal Characteristics.   Both corporations and partnerships are generally established with a business purpose and have two or more owners (associates). Therefore, the courts and Treasury regulations have settled on the absence of the four corporate characteristics to establish the existence of a partnership for tax purposes (see the discussion in the first section of this chapter). A general partnership is characterized as follows for tax purposes:

- A partner's liability is not limited.
- The life of the partnership depends on the life of the partner(s).
- All partners share in the partnership management.
- Partnership interests are not freely transferable.[39]

Certain types of partnerships can take on the corporate characteristic of limited liability in order to make capital acquisition easier. These limited partnerships have at least one partner whose liability is limited to the amount of his or her investment in the partnership. This attribute provides a measure of safety for the limited partners' personal assets. The limited partnership form of business has been a popular medium for investors in risky activities, such as mining or oil and gas exploration.

To obtain the limited liability attribute, limited partners give up any right to participate in the management of the business. Management is left to at least one general partner, whose liability is not limited and who is responsible for the on-going activities of the business.

Partners Are Not Employees.   The theoretical construct of the conduit entity provides that an employer/employee relationship cannot exist between a partnership and its partners. Remember that a partnership is generally considered a loose aggregation of owners (or owners' interests). Therefore, although **partners** receive compensatory payments for providing services to the business organization, they are not employees for purposes of payroll taxes and related withholding. Also, partners, like sole proprietors, are not allowed excludable employee benefits, such as group term life insurance, accident or health insurance, employer-provided meals and lodging, or death benefits. One exception to the lack of an employer/employee relationship concerns retirement plans. Under certain conditions, partners who also work for the partnership may participate in retirement plans of the organization. (The details of the restrictions placed on participating owners are beyond the scope of this text.)

Compensation to a partner may be classified in either of two ways. First, a partnership may offer a partner a guaranteed payment, determined without regard to the partnership's income. A **guaranteed payment** is a payment that must be made to a partner without regard to the profits of the partnership. This type of compensation is included as ordinary income to the partner and is a deductible compensation expense for the partnership.

▲ **EXAMPLE 43**   Bowlen Partnership pays Helena (a 20% owner) $5,000 monthly for managing the day-to-day affairs of the business. The partnership earned $200,000 during the current year without considering the $60,000 compensation paid to Helena. What are the tax effects for Helena and for the partnership of the $60,000 payment?

Discussion: Because the $60,000 was paid to Helena regardless of the partnership earnings (determined without regard to the amount of partnership earnings), it is a guaranteed payment. Therefore, Helena includes the $60,000 in her gross income and her self-employment income. The partnership may deduct the $60,000 as a compensation expense. Accordingly, the partnership's reported ordinary income is $140,000 ($200,000 − $60,000), and Helena's partnership share is $28,000 (20% × $140,000).

Helena's total ordinary income includes both the cash compensation classified as a guaranteed payment ($60,000) and her share of the partnership's ordinary income ($28,000). Therefore, Helena recognizes $88,000 in gross income and computes the applicable self-employment tax on these earnings—although she received payments of only $60,000.

If a partner receives compensatory payments based in any way on the partnership's gross or net income, the payments are classified as the partner's share of partnership profits. The partnership records the payments as nondeductible withdrawals, and the partner recognizes the income in the year of receipt.

▲ **EXAMPLE 44**   Preehya receives compensation set at 10% of the ABX Partnership's monthly net income, so long as there is income. Otherwise, no compensatory payment is made for that month. Are these payments considered guaranteed payments or Preehya's share of partnership profits?

Discussion: Because any compensation received is based on partnership income, these payments are treated as the partner's share of partnership profits and not as a guaranteed payment.

Basis of Partnership Interest.   Often, the primary motivation for an owner to invest in a partnership form of business is to obtain the flow-through tax effect of losses and/or other deductions. These losses are used to reduce the individual taxpayer's taxable income. Therefore, it is imperative that an owner have adequate basis. The basis amount establishes the maximum amount that a partner can deduct against other income in a given year. That is, the capital recovery concept dictates that losses may be used only to recover the amount of capital invested in the partnership and no more. A partner's basis may never go below zero.

▲ **EXAMPLE 45**   José contributes undeveloped land with a basis of $10,000 and fair market value of $50,000 to the JKL Partnership for a 20% interest. The partnership reports an annual operating loss of $40,000 for the current year. What is José's share of the partnership loss, and how does it affect his basis?

Discussion: José's share of partnership loss is $8,000 (20% × $40,000). José recognizes this amount on his personal tax return. After the loss, José's basis is $2,000 ($10,000 initial basis − $8,000 loss flow-through).

▲ **EXAMPLE 46**   Assume that the JKL Partnership, in example 45, reported a loss of $60,000. How would this result affect José?

Discussion: José's share of partnership loss is $12,000 (20% × $60,000). José's personal loss deduction is limited by the amount of his basis in his partnership interest. Therefore, José is limited to a loss deduction of $10,000 for the current year. His remaining basis amount is zero, and the additional $2,000 loss flow-through recognition is suspended until his basis increases enough to absorb it.

PARTNERSHIP DEBT.   Recall that basis begins with a person's contribution of assets or services in exchange for a capital interest. However, the use of the partnership form adds a unique complexity to basis calculations. Basis is increased by a partner's share of partnership liabilities, or **partnership debt.** Partnership debt assumed by a partner and the partner's share of partnership debt are deemed to be additional cash contributions by the partner to the partnership.[40] Likewise, basis is decreased by any partner's debt that is assumed by the partnership and by any decreases in the partner's share of partnership liabilities. Decreases in debt are deemed cash distributions to partners.[41] These allocations of debt have resulted in partnerships becoming the entity of choice for highly leveraged business ventures (e.g., real estate and natural resource exploration).

▲ **EXAMPLE 47**   Lou and Bud form the QED Partnership to develop and manage real estate. Each partner contributes $100,000 to the partnership. The partnership borrows a total of $1,000,000 from Texas Southwest Savings, Building, and Loan Association. What are the partners' bases amounts?

Discussion: Each partner adds the amount of his cash contribution ($100,000) to his share (50%) of the total partnership liability of $1,000,000. Each partner's basis is $600,000 [$100,000 + (50% × $1,000,000)].

▲ **EXAMPLE 48**   Tinker, Everett, and Cheryl form the Diamond Partnership by contributing the following:

Tinker: $100,000 cash for a 50% partnership interest.

Everett: $50,000 cash for a 25% partnership interest.

Cheryl: Real estate valued at $78,000 but encumbered by a mortgage of $28,000 that is assumed by the partnership. Cheryl's basis in the property is $32,000. She receives a 25% partnership interest.

What is the amount of each partner's basis in his or her partnership interest?

Discussion: Tinker and Everett add their respective shares of debt assumed by the partnership to their cash contributions to arrive at their bases in their partnership interests ($114,000 and $57,000, respectively). Cheryl adds her share of partnership debt (25%) to the basis of the property contributed to the partnership ($32,000) and subtracts the amount of debt relief ($28,000) that results from the partnership assuming the mortgage on the contributed real estate. Therefore, Cheryl's basis in her partnership interest is $11,000 ($32,000 + $7,000 − $28,000).

	Tinker	Everett	Cheryl
Basis of property or cash contributed	$100,000	$50,000	$32,000
Plus: Debt assumed by the partnership			
(50%)	14,000		
(25%)		7,000	7,000
Less: Debt relief			(28,000)
Basis of interest	$114,000	$57,000	$11,000

Partnership Distributions.

A partner's receipt of a cash or property distribution from a partnership is generally tax free and referred to as a **partnership distribution.**[42] This result is consistent with the capital recovery concept. That is, no gain is recognized until after the basis in the capital investment is recovered. Any excess of cash (or the basis of property) over the basis in a partner's interest is a recognizable gain for the recipient partner.[43]

▲ **EXAMPLE 49**   Sophia receives a partnership distribution of $10,000 cash from ECM Partnership. Sophia's basis in her partnership interest is $2,000 before the distribution. What is the effect of the distribution on Sophia?

Discussion: Sophia receives $2,000 as a tax-free recovery of capital. Sophia's basis reduces to zero. She recognizes $8,000 as a capital gain for the excess recovery of her investment in the partnership.

Initial basis	$2,000
Recovery of capital	(2,000)
Remaining basis	$ -0-
Excess distribution, capital gain recognized ($10,000 − $2,000)	$8,000

Partnership Terminations.

State laws vary on the situations that terminate a partnership. However, tax law provides two conditions that cause a partnership to terminate for tax purposes, regardless of state law provisions. Either of the following situations causes termination:

- If no partner continues to operate the business through the partnership, the partnership terminates.

- If at least 50 percent of the total interest in both partnership capital and profits is sold or exchanged within any 12-month period, a termination occurs.[44]

Terminations close the partnership tax year and force partners to include their shares of partnership income (or losses) for the short, closed year in their personal returns. This situation could cause partners to include more than 12 months of income on their personal returns for the termination year. Also, when a termination occurs, a liquidating distribution of partnership property is deemed to have been made. Partners are required to recognize gains or losses on these distributions, even if no property is actually distributed.

Limited Liability Companies (LLCs).   The limited liability company is a relatively new and unique form of business organization created under state laws. The **limited liability company (LLC)** combines the corporate characteristic of limited liability with the conduit tax treatment of partnerships. Whereas corporations are created by filing articles of incorporation, LLCs file articles of organization. The entity must have two or more members, have an objective to carry on a business, and establish a specific method for dividing the profits and losses from the business.

An unincorporated organization such as an LLC is not subject to corporate taxation, unless it has more corporate characteristics than noncorporate characteristics. As presented earlier in this chapter, the corporate characteristics on which the determination turns are

1. Limited liability of the owners
2. Free transferability of interests
3. Continuity of life
4. Centralization of management

That is, the test for conduit tax treatment hinges on whether the LLC has no more than one of the last three corporate characteristics in the list (items 2 through 4). If an LLC has at least two of the characteristics of items 2 through 4, it is taxed as a corporation, not as a conduit entity. So long as the entity possesses only one of the other three corporate characteristics, partnership tax treatment prevails.

The key planning feature of LLCs is limited liability. Owners have no personal liability for debts of the business. This feature provides a defense against astronomical lawsuits and exposure to unlimited personal liability.

Limited Liability Partnerships (LLPs).   Another new form of organization growing in popularity is the limited liability partnership. The **limited liability partnership (LLP)** is simply a general partnership with the added characteristic of limited liability for owners. States allowing this type of entity are responding to concerns about the traditional concepts of partner liability—general partners are unconditionally liable for partnership debts. Accordingly, an LLP permits the usual partnership conduit tax treatment but limits the liabilities of its owners (partners). Thus, an organization that seeks conduit tax treatment and limited personal liability for all owners has two options that provide virtually the same tax treatment—LLPs and LLCs. So nontax factors determine whether the entity should be an LLC or LLP.

Generally, it takes more effort (and cost) to operate as an LLC. Forming a board of directors, appointing operating officers, modifying membership agreements, registering with state regulatory agencies, paying franchise taxes or fees, and such are common requirements for LLCs but not for LLPs. The ease of converting to LLP status seems to favor that form. Also, some states' laws require the business organizations of such professionals as accountants and lawyers to use the partnership form. The LLP appears to be the logical choice for these service-related businesses.

During 1994, all the Big Six accounting firms converted from general partnerships to limited liability partnerships (LLPs). However, before taxpayers decide to establish an organization as an LLP or LLC, they should contact a professional tax adviser. Detailed examination of this topic is beyond the scope of this textbook.

S Corporations

Corporations, chartered under the laws of one of the 50 states, may obtain conduit entity tax status by making a valid election per Subchapter S of the Internal Revenue Code of 1986.[45] Therefore, the S corporation retains the legal characteristics of the corporate form (limited liability, free transferability of interests, continuity of life, and centralized management) while obtaining taxation characteristics similar to a partnership's.

Qualification Requirements.   S corporation status is attained when a qualified corporation elects this status. The election is effective for the current tax year if the election is filed at any time during the preceding year or on or before the fifteenth day of the third month of the current year. Therefore, a calendar-year corporate taxpayer desiring S corporation status for 1996 must file the election at any time from January 1, 1995, through March 15, 1996. The characteristics that qualify a corporation to make the election are that it

- Must be a domestic corporation
- Cannot be a member of an affiliated group of corporations (generally, an S corporation cannot own 80 percent or more of another corporation)
- May not have more than 35 shareholders (married individuals who are both shareholders are deemed to be one shareholder for S corporation status)
- Must have as its shareholders only individuals, estates, and certain trusts
- Cannot have a nonresident alien as a shareholder
- Has only one class of stock outstanding
- All shareholders consent to the election[46]

Every qualifying requirement must be met at the time of the election and at all times thereafter. The election terminates immediately when one or more of the qualifying characteristics is no longer met. As of the date of termination, the corporation becomes a taxable corporate entity.

▲ **EXAMPLE 50**   Pedry Corporation has been a qualified calendar-year S corporation since 1987. On April 1 of the current year, Hilda sells her 100 shares of Pedry stock to Holder Co., a limited partnership. Does this transaction affect the status of Pedry Corporation?

Discussion: Pedry's S corporation election terminates on April 1. Partnerships may not be shareholders in S corporations. Therefore, Pedry is an S corporation through March 31 and a taxable corporation from April 1 through December 31. NOTE: If the termination of the election is inadvertent, the S status may continue uninterrupted if the corporation corrects the disqualifying action. Therefore, if Hilda becomes aware of the results of her actions and can revoke the sale of the stock to the limited partnership, Pedry's S status will continue.

Revocation of the S Election. An S corporation may forfeit its election voluntarily. If holders of more than 50 percent of the total shares of stock consent to revoke the S status, the revocation is effective for the current year if made on or before the fifteenth day of the third month of the year.

▲ **EXAMPLE 51** RAD Corporation is a qualifying S corporation with 5 individual shareholders. Ralph owns 60% of the stock. Aileen, Alice, Doug, and Dorian each own 10% of the shares of stock. Ralph no longer desires S status. Therefore, on June 30 of the current year, he files an intent to terminate. Is the termination valid? If it is, when is it effective?

Discussion: The termination is valid, because Ralph owns more than 50% of the shares of RAD Corporation. The earliest effective date for the termination of S status is January 1 of the next tax year, because the termination was not made on or before the fifteenth day of March during the current year.

Once an election is terminated, the corporation may not make a new election for five years without special consent of the commissioner of the IRS.[47]

Change from C Corporation to S Corporation. In the early years of a business operation, losses are commonplace. Therefore, S corporations usually provide greater benefits to owners than corporations because of the conduit nature of S corporations. Even if a corporation with unused NOLs makes a valid election for S status, the NOL attribute does not carry over to the S corporation. In fact, the running of the carryforward period continues during S corporation status. If the S election is never revoked, unused NOLs from regular-corporation years expire after the 15-year carryforward period.[48] However, if S status is terminated and the corporation reverts to regular corporate status, any unused unexpired NOLs may be used to offset new corporation income. Therefore, to counteract these complications, a corporation that anticipates losses in future tax years should make the S election before the loss year.

Employee Status of Stockholders. Shareholder-employees of an electing S corporation are generally treated the same as other employees. Shareholder-employees must include salaries in their gross income. The S corporation may deduct the salary expense and the related payroll taxes. Likewise, employee fringe benefits paid by the S corporation for shareholder-employees who own no more than 2 percent of the corporate stock are deductible by the corporation. However, shareholder-employees exclude the value of the fringe benefits from their gross incomes only if the individual shareholder-employee owns 2 percent, or less, of the S corporation's stock.

Any S corporation shareholder who owns more than 2 percent of the stock is treated differently with regard to fringe benefits. The shareholder-employee is treated like a partner, and the cost of the fringe benefit is treated as a distribution of the corporation's earnings.[49] The S corporation may not deduct the cost of these fringe benefits as a business expense. Shareholder-employees owning more than 2 percent of the corporation's stock may deduct their fringe benefits on their individual tax returns if the benefits qualify as an itemized deduction.

▲ **EXAMPLE 52** Golic Corporation, an electing S corporation, has a company healthcare plan for all employees. Mike, an employee, owns 15% of the corporate stock, and Bob, also an employee, owns 1%. Mike's health benefits total $1,200 in the current year, and Bob's benefits total $1,800. How are the costs of these benefits treated by each shareholder-employee and by the S corporation?

Discussion: The $1,800 cost of Bob's benefits is a deductible business expense by the corporation and is excludable from gross income by Bob. Mike's $1,200 in benefits is not deductible by the corporation, because Mike owns more than 2% of the corporate stock. Mike recognizes the $1,200 as gross income. The $1,200 is deductible by Mike only to the extent that his medical expenses are allowable itemized deductions.

Distributions and Basis Adjustments.   Following the general rules for conduit entities, cash distributions from an S corporation to its shareholders are generally tax free and reduce the shareholders' basis in the corporate stock (see Exhibit 9–3). If distributions exceed a shareholder's basis, the excess amount is treated as a capital gain.[50] Recall that the capital recovery concept governs the treatment of distributions from conduit entities.

▲ **EXAMPLE 53**   Julio pays $20,000 for stock in an S corporation and receives shares equal to a 10% interest in the corporation in 1996. The S corporation reports taxable income of $150,000 in 1996. What are the tax effects of these events?

Discussion: Julio's initial basis in his ownership (stock) is the amount contributed, $20,000. Then, Julio's share of S corporation taxable income, $15,000 (10% × $150,000), is reported on his individual tax return. The recognition of the $15,000 allows Julio to increase the basis of his stock to $35,000 ($20,000 + $15,000). NOTE: Contrary to the wherewithal-to-pay concept, S corporation shareholders owe taxes on their shares of the corporate earnings but may receive no cash to pay the tax.

▲ **EXAMPLE 54**   Julio, in example 53, receives a cash distribution of $18,000 from the S corporation on December 31, 1996. What is the effect of this event?

Discussion: The $18,000 is a recovery of capital to the extent of Julio's basis. The basis amount is adjusted to reflect income flow-throughs (or gains, losses, deductions, etc.) before recovering capital amounts.[51] Therefore, the recoverable basis is $35,000. After the tax-free receipt of the $18,000, Julio's adjusted basis is $17,000 ($35,000 − $18,000).

▲ **EXAMPLE 55**   Assume Julio receives a distribution of $40,000 instead of the $18,000 in example 54. How does that change the tax effects of the distribution?

Discussion: Applying the capital recovery concept, the first $35,000 (Julio's basis) is tax free. The excess $5,000 ($40,000 − $35,000) is a capital gain. NOTE: The results of examples 53 to 55 do not change, even if the S corporation incurs debt. Recall from the discussion of partnerships that partnership debt causes the partners' bases to increase relative to their shares of the debt. This is not the case with S corporations and their shareholders. (See examples 47 and 48. Compare them to examples 53 to 55.)

See Exhibit 9–4 for a general comparison of the characteristics of conduit entities.

USES OF ENTITIES

A myriad of tax-planning opportunities exists when all the various taxable and conduit entities are considered. Recall the discussion of tax planning in Chapter 1. The primary objective of tax planning is to maximize wealth through timing of income and deductions and income splitting. However, do not lose sight of other objectives that may, or may not, have direct effects on this objective. For example, the corporate form of business offers the nontax benefit of limited liability. Often, this characteristic drives the choice of entity. However, individuals choosing the corporate form must be aware of the disadvantages (e.g., double taxation), as well as the advantages, that stem from tax rules for corporations.

Income Splitting

One basic tax-planning use of entities involves splitting income among two or more taxable entities. Income splitting can provide tax savings in a tax system like that of the United States in which progressive tax rates exist across taxable entities.

Characteristic	Limited Liability Companies	General Partnership	S Corporation	Sole Proprietors
Limited personal liability of owners	Yes	No; yes for LLPs	Yes	No
Double taxation	No	No	No	No
Permitted type and number of owners	No restriction on type; two or more members.	No restriction on type; two or more partners.	Individuals, estates, and certain trusts; from 1 to 35 shareholers.	N/A
Permitted classes of ownership interests	Multiple classes are permitted.	Multiple classes are permitted.	Limited to one class of stock.	N/A
Continuity of existence	Usually limited by articles and LLC bylaws or regulations.	Limited	Not limited	Limited
Transferability of interests	Usually limited by articles and LLC bylaws or regulations.	May be limited by partnership agreement and/or state law.	Limited by code restrictions on type and number of owners; may be limited by shareholder agreement.	Not limited
Necessary documentation	Articles of organization; state LLC laws.	State partnership laws.	Charter/articles of incorporation; bylaws; minutes of directors' & shareholders' meetings; stock records.	Minimal
State franchise tax imposed	Yes (generally)	No	Yes	No

▲ **Exhibit 9–4**

COMPARISON OF
CONDUIT ENTITY
CHARACTERISTICS

That is, net tax liabilities can be reduced by shifting income to the entity with the lowest marginal tax rate. For example, if one entity has a marginal rate of 34 percent and a second entity has a marginal rate of 15 percent, every dollar of income shifted from the first entity to the second saves 19 cents in taxes. (Many of the issues surrounding income splitting are discussed in this chapter in the subsection "Income Tax Considerations" under Corporations.)

▲ **EXAMPLE 56** Dino and Wilma operate their stone quarry and rock-polishing business as a sole proprietorship. The business generally earns $100,000 annually. The couple's 1996 joint tax liability on a taxable income of $88,200 ($100,000 − $6,700 standard deduction − $5,100 in personal exemptions) is $19,483 [$6,015 + 28% × ($88,200 − $40,100)]. Can the couple decrease their income tax liability by shifting business income to a corporate entity—by incorporating their business?

Discussion: They will see a decrease in tax liability if the shifted income is taxed at a marginal rate lower than that of individuals. Therefore, if no more than $50,000 in taxable income rests with the corporation, incorporation decreases the marginal tax rate from 28% to 15%. (See Figure 9–1 for the income levels at which rates change for corporations and individuals.)

If Dino and Wilma incorporate their business and pay themselves a total salary of $50,000, they shift $50,000 of their individual income to the corporation. Therefore, the corporate taxable income is $50,000 ($100,000 − $50,000 salary). The corporate tax liability is $7,500 ($50,000 $\times$ 15%), disregarding the effects of payroll taxes on the taxable income. Dino and Wilma's joint taxable income is $38,200 ($50,000 $-$ $6,700 standard deduction $-$ $5,100 in personal exemptions). Their joint individual income tax liability is $5,730 ($38,200 $\times$ 15%). The total tax liability is $13,230 ($7,500 + $5,730). A tax savings of $6,253 ($19,483 $-$ $13,230) results from incorporating the business.

▲ **EXAMPLE 57**   Cynthia is a sole proprietor, real estate property manager, and investor. She owns small rental houses and condominium units. Cynthia has her office in 1 room of her personal residence, and she properly deducts home-office and related business expenses (as discussed in Chapter 6). Her personal residence is 1 unit in the condominium complex. Is there a plan that uses an alternative entity form that may save tax dollars and increase Cynthia's net wealth?

Discussion: One alternative may be the use of the corporate form of business. That is, Cynthia incorporates her business and transfers ownership of all her real estate properties, and the accompanying mortgages, to the entity. Then, the corporation hires Cynthia to actively manage the properties. As a condition of employment, Cynthia is required to live in 1 of the properties (her former personal residence) so that she is available to tenants of the complex at all hours. Therefore, Cynthia may be able to exclude the value of her residence from her gross income (see Chapter 4). The corporation receives a deduction for insurance, utilities, and depreciation on the residence that otherwise would not be deductible for an individual. Accordingly, the total business income is reduced over what it would be under the former sole proprietorship.

A simple formula that allows individuals to select the best entity, or entities, to meet their personal objectives does not exist. Each taxpayer has a unique set of objectives, and these are intertwined with unique sets of personal and business attributes. All must be weighed and considered in developing a sound tax plan regarding the choice of entity.

S corporations and partnerships offer many similar advantages and disadvantages for investors. Primarily, the flow-through nature of their tax attributes makes these two forms of business quite popular. However, only S corporations provide limited liability to owners. Therefore, in addition to protecting the personal wealth of owners, the limited liability afforded by S corporation status makes capital acquisition easier. To obtain these S corporation benefits, owners are subject to many of the disadvantages of the corporate form in general. For example, state franchise fees, organizational costs, filing fees, and costs of record keeping can be substantial. Also, many states do not recognize the S election for state income tax purposes. (The S election is a federal tax alternative.) Therefore, a single corporation could be a conduit entity for federal income tax purposes and a taxable entity for state income tax authorities.

Partnerships and S corporations both present disadvantages for owner-employees. Although S corporations may hire and pay salaries to their shareholders who work for the organization, partnership owners cannot be employees. However, common fringe benefits paid for owners working for the business are generally not deductible by either business form.

The regular corporation provides limited liability for owners and offers the advantage of being a separate taxable entity, independent of its owners. Therefore, owners pay income tax on corporate earnings only if the corporation makes distributions to the owners (dividends). Also, owners may be employees of the corporation. Accordingly, the corporate entity may reduce corporate taxable income by deducting owner-employee salaries and fringe benefits. Of course, double taxation results when owners receive dividends.

There is no easy answer to the question of which entity to choose. Just try to weigh the objectives and the characteristics of the taxpayer with the attributes of the various entities.

SUMMARY

Not all entities are taxpayers. Only individuals, corporations, and fiduciaries are taxed on their income. Partnerships, S corporations, limited liability entities, and sole proprietorships are conduit entities and are not taxed. Conduit entity income flows through to the tax returns of the owners of the entities. The owners pay the income tax.

A corporation is a taxable legal entity separate from its owners. It has the nontax attributes of limited liability, unlimited life, centralized management, and transferability of ownership. However, if three or more of these characteristics are missing from an entity, the IRS may reclassify the entity as a conduit for tax purposes.

Generally, nontax factors outweigh tax considerations in regard to choosing a business entity. However, tax rate differentials between corporations and individuals often are critical in choosing which form to do business in. For businesses with net incomes of less than $100,000, the corporate form will probably reap tax savings in comparison with the sole proprietorship. Also, owner-employee status provides tax savings for a corporate entity that provides fringe benefits and hires children as employees.

Corporate entities receive a unique dividends-received deduction. Generally, 70 percent of the dividends received from U.S. corporations is deductible from corporate income to mitigate the effects of double, or triple, taxation. Also, the passive loss limitation rules do not affect corporate taxpayers. Exceptions exist for personal service corporations and closely held corporations. Corporations generally have no restrictions concerning their choices of annual accounting periods. However, the selection of an accounting method is fairly restrictive. Only small corporations (gross receipts of $5 million or less) are permitted to use the cash method.

Corporations face certain tax disadvantages, including capital loss limitations and charitable contribution limitations. Also, corporate distributions (dividends) are not deductible, and using multiple corporations to split income is not permitted.

Fiduciary taxation is special, because the fiduciary is responsible for reporting income and paying income taxes on behalf of such entities as trusts and estates. Fiduciary income taxation rules generally follow the rules for individual taxation. However, the law provides no standard deduction amount, allows unlimited charitable contributions, and provides an exemption amount.

Conduit entities (partnerships and S corporations) are characterized by the flow of their tax attributes through to the owners of the entity. The incidence of taxation of a conduit entity's income rests with the owners. However, this flow-through effect may cause owners to pay income taxes without having the benefit of the entity's wherewithal to pay.

Conduit entities must follow the annual accounting period concept and report their financial results as other entities do. Generally, conduits use a calendar year for tax purposes. However, a partnership or S corporation may select a tax year other than a calendar year if the entity makes certain annual payments or can establish a natural business year other than a calendar year to the satisfaction of the IRS.

Basis in a partnership or S corporation establishes the amount of unrecovered investment in the entity. Basis establishes realized gain or loss upon disposition of the investment through application of the capital recovery concept, and it determines the taxability of distributions from the conduit entity to owners. Also, the amount of unrecovered basis determines whether an owner may recognize losses flowing from the conduit entity to the owner.

Basis is dynamic. It is adjusted to reflect the tax results of many entity transactions. Generally, the bases of partnerships and S corporations are adjusted similarly. However, partnerships receive a unique benefit: Basis is increased by a partner's share of partnership debt. Therefore, a partnership can obtain a greater benefit from the flow-through of losses than can similarly situated S corporation shareholders.

Sole proprietorships, partnerships, limited liability companies, limited liability partnerships, and S corporations each offer certain advantages. Sole proprietorships are the easiest to create. Partnerships are almost as easy to form and offer the special basis adjustment rules for partnership debt. Limited liability companies and limited liability partnerships are generally treated as partnerships with the added characteristic of limited liability. S corporations are merely corporations that file the federal election to be treated as a conduit entity. However, the characteristics that qualify a corporation to make the election can be difficult to achieve and maintain. Yet, the corporate characteristics of limited liability, unlimited life, and free transferability of interest remain intact with the S corporation election.

Innumerable tax-planning opportunities exist when all the various entities are considered. For example, proper use of income splitting can provide substantial tax savings. However, a simple formula that allows individuals to select the best entity, or entities, for meeting their objectives does not exist. All of the taxpayer's objectives and characteristics need to be analyzed in conjunction with the attributes of the various entities.

KEY TERMS

brother-sister relationship (p. 400)
centralized management (p. 385)
charitable contribution (p. 395)
complex trust (p. 402)
conduit entity (p. 405)
continuity of life (p. 385)
controlled group (p. 400)
corporate distribution (p. 399)
corporate tax rate (p. 387)
corporation (p. 385)
dividend (p. 399)
dividends-received deduction
   (DRD) (p. 392)
donated inventory (p. 396)
double taxation (p. 391)

earnings and profits (p. 399)
employment taxes (p. 391)
estate (p. 402)
fiduciary (p. 402)
free transferability of ownership
   (p. 385)
grantor (p. 402)
grantor trust (p. 403)
guaranteed payment (p. 411)
limited liability (p. 385)
limited liability company (p. 414)
limited liability partnership
   (p. 414)
organizational costs (p. 397)

parent-subsidiary relationship
   (p. 400)
partners (p. 411)
partnership (p. 410)
partnership debt (p. 412)
partnership distribution (p. 413)
personal service corporation (PSC)
   (p. 389)
remainderman (p. 402)
reversionary interest (p. 402)
simple trust (p. 402)
testamentary trust (p. 402)
trust (p. 402)
trustee (p. 402)

[1] Sec. 704—Prescribes the allocation methods for partnership items and describes the limitations on recognizing losses.

[2] Sec. 701—States that a partnership is not subject to income tax and that each partner is liable for taxes only on his or her individual share.

[3] Sec. 11—Imposes income tax on corporate entities and provides the tax rates.

[4] Rev. Proc. 89-12, 1989-1 C.B. 798.— States that where the only general partner of a limited partnership is a corporation, partners must follow certain prescribed guidelines or the IRS may assert that the partnership is an association.

PRIMARY TAX LAW SOURCES

[5] Morrissey v. CIR, 296 U.S. 344 (1935)—Established in a landmark case that unincorporated businesses may be treated as associations taxed as corporations.

[6] Higgins v. Smith, 308 U.S. 473 (1940)—Held that if a corporation as defined by state law has as its only purpose the reduction of its owners' taxes, if it has no real business purpose, or if it has no economic function, the IRS may assert that it is a sham corporation.

[7] Moline Properties, Inc., 319 U.S. 436 (1943)—Held that, in general, so long as a business activity is carried on, a corporation will be considered a separate taxable entity.

[8] U.S. v. Kintner, 216 F.2d 418 (9th Cir. 1954)—Discussed the characteristics of a professional association that may cause it to be classified as a corporation. This case led to the promulgation of Reg. Sec. 301.7701-2.

[9] Reg. Sec. 301.7701-2—Lists the corporate characteristics that are determinative in defining whether an entity is considered an association for tax purposes.

[10] Sec. 1—Imposes income tax on all individuals and other noncorporate entities; provides the tax rate schedules for noncorporate taxpayers.

[11] Sec. 448(d)—Describes the criteria that establish a personal service corporation.

[12] Sec. 267—Describes the relationships that aid in defining closely held corporations.

[13] Sec. 243—Describes the procedures for calculating and determining the limitations on the dividends-received deduction.

[14] Sec. 469—Prescribes the treatment and definitions of *passive activity losses*.

[15] Sec. 1212—Provides the rules for the carryback and carryforward of capital losses by corporations.

[16] Sec. 170—Provides the rules for deducting charitable contributions.

[17] Sec. 170(e)(3)—Prescribes the treatment of inventory given to certain qualified charities by a corporation.

[18] Sec. 248—Permits the amortization and deduction of organizational expenses over a period of not less than 60 months at the election of the corporation.

[19] Reg. Sec. 1.248-1—Gives examples of items that are considered organizational expenditures and examples of items that are not considered organizational expenditures.

[20] Sec. 444—Restricts partnerships, S corporations, and personal service corporations to taxable years that are calendar years, natural business years, or specially electable fiscal years with a September, October, or November year end.

[21] Sec. 448—Describes the corporate exceptions for using the accrual method of accounting.

[22] Sec. 301—Provides the tax treatment of corporate dividend distributions.

[23] Sec. 316—Provides that distributions are made out of the earnings and profits of the current year first and that a distribution is a taxable dividend if paid out of the current or accumulated earnings and profits.

[24] Sec. 312—Describes the adjustments to taxable income for the determination of earnings and profits.

[25] Sec. 1563—Defines *controlled group*.

[26] Sec. 671—States that trust income and deductions are attributable to grantors.

[27] Sec. 641—States the general rules for the taxation of estates and trusts.

[28] Sec. 651—Permits a deduction for trusts distributing current income.

[29] Sec. 645—Requires that trusts use a calendar year as their tax year.

[30] Sec. 642—Provides the exemption amounts for fiduciaries.

[31] Sec. 701—Provides that partners, not partnerships, are subject to income tax.

[32] Sec. 1363—Explains that S corporations are not subject to income tax, and states that the S corporation computes its taxable income in a manner similar to that used by an individual taxpayer, except for the items that are subject to separate statement.

[33] Sec. 706—States that the taxable year adopted by a partnership must generally be the same as the taxable year used by partners who own more than 50 percent of the partnership.

[34] Sec. 1378—States that taxable years of S corporations may be only a permitted year. A permitted year is either a calendar year or a fiscal year approved by the IRS because it serves a business purpose.

[35] Sec. 703—States that elections related to the computation and reporting of partnership items are made at the partnership level and not by the individual partners.

[36] Sec. 705—Sets forth the rules for determining the basis of a partner's investment or interest in a partnership.

[37] Sec. 721—States that no gain or loss is recognized by the contributing partner or by the partnership upon the contribution of property to a partnership.

[38] Sec. 722—States that partners' bases in their interests in the partnership are the adjusted bases of the property contributed to attain the partnership interests.

[39] Sec. 761—Defines the terms *partnership*, *partner*, and *partnership agreement* for tax purposes.

[40] Sec. 752—Describes the effect of partnership debt on a partner's basis in that person's partnership interest.

[41] Reg. Sec. 1.752—Details how liabilities affect the basis of a partner's interest in a partnership.

[42] Sec. 733—Explains the effects of a distribution on the basis of a partner's interest.

[43] Sec. 731—Describes the situations in which partners recognize gain or loss on the distribution of partnership assets; provides that the partnership does not recognize any gain or loss upon the distribution of assets to a partner.

[44] Sec. 708(b)—Prescribes the conditions that cause termination of a partnership.

[45] Sec. 1362—Discusses the rules for election, disqualification, and revocation of S status.

[46] Sec. 1361—Provides the qualifying characteristics of corporations making the S election.

[47] Reg. Sec. 1.1372-5—Provides that the usual five-year wait for making the S corporation election after a revocation is unnecessary under certain circumstances.

[48] Sec. 172—Prescribes the procedures for net operating loss carrybacks and carryovers.

[49] Sec. 1372—Requires that the S corporation be treated as a partnership in regard to fringe benefits.

[50] Sec. 1368—Describes the tax effects of distributions by S corporations to their shareholders.

[51] Sec. 1367—Describes the rules for adjusting the basis of a shareholder's stock in the S corporation to account for income, losses, distributions, and expenses of the corporation.

Discussion Questions

1. How does the doctrine of substance over form affect the determination of corporate status?

2. Will an entity incorporated under state law be considered a corporation for tax purposes until it is dissolved and liquidated? Explain.

3. Herman, an unmarried individual with two dependent children, owns and operates a used car lot as a sole proprietorship. The net income from the business is consistently near $90,000 annually. Based solely on income taxes, consider whether the corporate form of business would produce savings.

4. Refer to question 3. What other factors should Herman consider when choosing between a sole proprietorship and a corporate form of doing business?

5. How do the highest marginal tax rates for individuals compare with the highest marginal tax rates for corporations?

6. Explain the advantages to taxpayers of hiring their children to work in their business enterprises.

7. Duane, the sole stockholder in the Flying R ranch, employs his 13-year-old son at a rate of $4.50. How many hours could Duane's son work during 1995 and pay no income tax on his wages?

8. An accounting firm is formed as a corporation by accountants who own all the stock in the corporation. The corporation acquires an interest in an exotic leather-importing limited partnership. The exotic leather partnership incurs operating losses. Can these losses be deducted currently?

9. Red Corporation owns 80% of Blue Corporation's stock and 45% of Yellow Corporation's stock. Blue Corporation owns 35% of Yellow Corporation's stock. Does a controlled group exist? Explain.

10. Explain the difference between a simple trust and a complex trust.

11. Trusts may be classified as either conduit entities or taxable entities. Explain how this result can occur.

12. A partnership is treated as an aggregation of the proprietary interests of the partners. Following this approach, what is the tax effect of
    a. Contributions of appreciated property to a partnership by its partners?
    b. Distributions of assets from a partnership to partners?
    c. Realization of income by a partnership?

13. Golden Partnership realizes operating income of $45,000 and a long-term capital gain of $6,000 during the current year. Susan Gold is a 1/3 partner. The partnership made no cash or property distributions this year. How do these events affect Susan's individual tax return for the current year?

14. How do liabilities affect the basis of a partner's interest in a partnership?

15. How can a partner deduct losses in excess of the cash or basis of property contributed to a partnership?

16. What situation may cause a partner to recognize a gain when she or he receives a distribution from the partnership?

17. Generally, each partner in a partnership is taxed as if she or he owns a portion of the underlying partnership assets and directly earns the income produced by the assets. If a partnership and its partners are cash basis taxpayers, which tax concept(s) is (are) being violated? Explain.

18. What are the major differences in the tax treatments of a partnership and a corporation?

19. Janice, Ellen, Dana, and Fred form a limited partnership with Janice as the only general partner. She will perform all management duties. Each partner owns a 1/4 interest in the limited partnership. The partnership agreement states that the 3 remaining partners must agree to any sale or transfer of the ownership interest of the fourth partner to an outsider. Which entity classification will the IRS most likely use for this business? Why?

20. Discuss the comparative advantages and disadvantages of general partnerships and limited partnerships.

21. Compare and contrast the characteristics of general partnerships, C corporations, S corporations, limited liability companies, and limited liability partnerships.

22. How are the following treated by each of the entities discussed in this chapter:
    a. Tax-exempt interest income?
    b. Cash dividend income?
    c. Net capital gains?

23. How do S corporation liabilities affect the basis of an S corporation shareholder's stock?

24. List the advantage(s) of the corporation form of organization.

25. Jillian is involved in oil exploration activities. Because of the riskiness of this business, Jillian wants to protect her personal assets such as her residence, stocks and bonds, rental property, and jewelry. She intends to create a corporation with a single purpose—to hold and protect these assets. Before obtaining a corporate charter and transferring her assets to the corporation, Jillian comes to you for advice. Write a letter to Jillian advising her on a plan for incorporation.

26. Billy Bob is the sole shareholder of Pony Ranch Corporation and is employed by the corporation to operate the business. The corporation provides excludable meals and lodging for Billy Bob at a cost of $12,000 annually. Billy Bob's marginal tax rate is 28%; the marginal tax rate of the corporation is 34%.
    a. What are the after-tax costs of the meal and lodging benefits for the corporation?
    b. What is the actual value of the benefits if they are not excludable for Billy Bob?

27. Under what conditions is the use of the corporate form of business beneficial based solely on the desire to lower marginal tax rates? Explain with examples.

28. During January 1996, Edgar purchases all the stock of Wooden Corporation for $80,000. Wooden's taxable income for 1996 is $100,000, and it pays $22,250 in income tax. None of Wooden's earnings were distributed as a dividend. Edgar sells all his stock on January 30, 1997, to Thurmal, Inc., for $157,750. Edgar tells you that he sold the stock now to avoid double taxation. Explain whether Edgar avoided double taxation.

29. Kelly, Gwen, and Tuoi incorporated their accounting business and own all the outstanding stock of the enterprise. During the current year, the corporation's taxable income is $200,000 after deducting salaries of $50,000 for each shareholder-employee.
    a. What is the corporate tax liability?
    b. What could the shareholders do to lower the corporate tax liability in the future?

30. The Boo-Ball Corporation receives dividend income from Flew-Ball, a domestic corporation, in the amount of $150,000. The Boo-Ball Corporation owns 70% of Flew-Ball Corporation. Boo-Ball's net income from operations is $25,000. What is the amount of Boo-Ball's dividends-received deduction?

31. The John Corporation suffers a $22,000 net loss from operations for the current year but receives $150,000 in dividend income from corporations in which it owns 50% of the stock. What are the amounts of the dividends-received deduction and the corporation's actual taxable income for the current year?

32. The Bat-Ball Corporation incurs a net loss from operations of $62,000 for the current year. The Bat-Ball Corporation received $175,000 in cash dividends from 30%-owned domestic corporations. What are the amounts of the dividends-received deduction and the actual taxable income for the current tax year?

33. 3Bears Corporation has $50,000 in taxable income before special deductions. Taxable income includes $60,000 in dividend income received from other corporations in which 3Bears owns less than a 20% interest. What is 3Bears's taxable income?

34. Adele owns 60% of Trouble, Inc. This entity is a perfume factory formed as a regular corporation. During the current annual accounting period, Trouble, Inc., had an operating income of $19,000, dividend income from investments in stock of other corporations of $2,800, interest income from First National of $2,200, and a loss from an investment in a limited partnership of $24,000. How much of the passive activity loss can be used to offset other income?

35. Elvira owns 100% of the stock of Midnite Corporation, a manufacturer of galobnotites. During the current year, Midnite has operating income of $50,000, dividend income of $16,000 from investments in other corporations, losses from investments in limited partnerships of $46,000, and pays $20,000 in dividends.
    a. What are the amounts of taxable income and tax liability reported by Midnite for the current year?
    b. Assume Midnite Corporation is operated as an S corporation. Explain why the amount of taxable income resulting from the items reported by both Midnite Corporation and Elvira are different from your answers in part a.

36. The Baker Corporation has the following entries on its books for the current tax year:

Net income from operations	$120,000
Dividends received (70% rules)	14,000
Charitable contributions made in current year	13,000
Charitable contribution carryover from the previous year	1,900

What is the maximum amount of charitable contribution deduction allowed for the current year? What is Baker's taxable income for the current year?

37. Fairplay Corporation has gross income of $150,000 and taxable income of $50,000. The company includes no special deductions in the calculation of its taxable income. While reviewing the tax return, Fairplay's accountant found $20,000 in charitable contributions improperly classified as advertising and promotion expense. He sent the return back to the tax department for correction. Write a letter to Fairplay's accountant explaining why the correction to taxable income must be made.

38. The New Tech Corporation contributes some of its scientific equipment inventory to the Computer Department of Great University during the current year. At the date of the contribution, the equipment has a fair market value of $38,000. New Tech's basis in the equipment is $12,000. What is the amount of the charitable contribution deduction? Would your answer change if New Tech's basis in the equipment was $16,000?

39. Mel's Super Groceries, Inc., donated $50,000-worth of canned food with a basis of $40,000 to St. Rebecca's Homeless Shelter, a qualified charitable organization. How much of a deduction may Mel's take for the charitable contribution of the canned food?

40. Big C Corporation, a calendar-year corporation, was formed during the current year and began business operations on September 1. Big C paid $8,000 to attorneys, accountants, and state regulatory agencies to organize the corporation. Big C also paid $6,000 in commissions on the sale of corporate stock. Write a letter to Big C Corporation's controller explaining how much of the $14,000 expenditure is deductible.

41. The Viking Corporation had the following items of income for its calendar year 1996:

Operating income	$350,000
Dividend income (12% owned corporations)	15,000
Long-term capital gains	9,000
Short-term capital gains	3,000
Capital loss carryover from 1995	8,000
Charitable cash contributions	12,000
Net operating loss carryover from 1995	35,000

a. What is the amount of the corporation's 1996 taxable income and tax liability?
b. Assume Viking is, and always has been, an S corporation wholly owned by Fran, a single taxpayer with no other income or deductions. Will either Viking Corporation or Fran realize any tax savings over the situation described in part a? Explain.

42. Charger, Inc., had the following items for 1996:

Net operating income	$ 40,000
Dividend income (50%-owned corporation)	100,000
Charitable cash contributions	20,000
Net operating loss carryover from 1995	10,000

a. What are the amounts of the corporation's 1996 taxable income and tax liability?
b. Assume Charger is, and always has been, an S corporation wholly owned by Suzanne, a married individual with no dependents and no other income or deductions. What are the tax liabilities of Charger and Suzanne?
c. Explain why the answers in parts a and b are different.

43. The Toy Corporation distributed $175,000 in cash ($1.75 per share) at a time when its accumulated earnings and profits were $40,000. What is the effect of the distribution on Bernice, who owns 500 shares of Toy stock for which she paid $8,000? Explain Bernice's tax results using income tax concepts.

44. Dance Corporation distributes $150,000 in cash to its shareholders during 1996. Accumulated earnings and profits are $25,000 as of January 1, 1996. Current earnings and profits for 1996 are $75,000. Jack, the sole shareholder of Dance Corporation, has a basis of $40,000 in the stock. What is the tax effect of this distribution for Jack?

45. Which of the following corporations are members of a brother-sister controlled group? Explain.

I.		Corporation	
		A	**B**
	Shareholder 1	90%	10%
	Shareholder 2	10%	90%

II.		Corporation	
		A	**B**
	Shareholder 1	70%	30%
	Shareholder 2	30%	70%

III.		Corporation	
		A	**B**
	Shareholder 1	79%	79%
	Shareholder 2	20%	1%
	Shareholder 3	1%	20%

IV.		Corporation	
		A	**B**
	Shareholder 1	90%	10%
	Shareholder 2	10%	-0-
	Shareholder 3	-0-	90%

46. Hiram owns 90% of Little Burro Corporation. Last year, Little Burro acquired 100% of the corporate stock of one of its suppliers, Small Bean, Inc. For the current year, Little Burro's taxable income is $100,000, and Small Bean's taxable income is $75,000. Discuss the income tax consequences for Hiram and the two corporations for the current year.

47. Dunston Corporation owns 100% of the stock of Bullinger, Inc., 50% of the stock of Carey Corporation, and 70% of the stock of Santo, Inc. Bullinger, Inc., owns 35% of the stock of Carey Corporation. All the corporations have only one class of stock outstanding. Which of these corporations comprise a parent-subsidiary controlled group?

48. Hobson transfers $400,000 in cash and property to a revocable grantor trust created in the current year. His daughter, Glenda, will receive the income from the trust for her life. Hobson's granddaughter, Wanda, is to receive the remainder at Glenda's death. The trust's income for the year consists of $48,000 in dividends and $9,000 in long-term capital gains. All the dividend income is distributed to Glenda. The capital gains are applied to trust principal and not distributed. Hobson's marginal tax rate is 31%. Glenda's marginal tax rate is 28%, and Wanda's marginal tax rate is 15%.
   a. What is the total amount of income tax liability attributable to the trust's income for the year?
   b. Explain and discuss alternative ways to structure the trust instrument.

49. Starita creates a trust and transfers property that will generate income for distribution to her minor child Terri, 12, until Terri reaches the age of 21. At that age, all trust property, including any accumulated income, is to be paid to Terri. During the current year, the trust distributes $10,000 for Terri's support and distributes and invests $6,000 in a bank CD in Terri's name. The balance of the trust income, $15,000, accumulates in the trust. Who is responsible for the tax on this year's trust income? Explain your reasoning, and discuss any other way to structure the trust instrument that may be beneficial to either Terri or Starita.

50. The Willow Trust receives $2,000 in municipal bond interest and $22,000 from U.S. government securities during the current year. The trust gives Planned Parenthood $1,000 annually. What is the amount of the charitable contribution deduction for the current year?

51. During the current year, Okner Trust receives $8,000 in dividend income from corporate stock, $2,000 in U.S. government security interest, and a $1,000 short-term capital gain. Trust administrative expenses total $500. The trust agreement states that all interest is distributed annually and all other forms of income and gains are accumulated as trust corpus. Determine the trust's taxable income and the trust's income tax liability.

52. Kyle Partnership begins operations in November 1995 and elects an October 31 fiscal year end. For the year ending October 31, 1996, the partnership has net income of $90,000. Write a letter to Kyle's partners explaining whether the elected fiscal year will pass IRS scrutiny. Include a discussion of the amount and reasoning for the deposit the partnership may need to make.

53. Fawn contributes undeveloped land with a basis of $15,000 and a fair market value of $90,000 to the Deer Partnership for a 25% interest in the partnership. What is Fawn's share of the partnership's operating income (loss), and how does the share affect Fawn's basis in each of the following situations?
    a. Deer Partnership reports an annual operating loss of $40,000 for the current year.
    b. Deer Partnership reports annual operating income of $25,000.
    c. Deer Partnership reports annual operating loss of $80,000.

54. Binh has a 50% interest in the Lamonica Partnership with a basis of $10,000 at the end of 1996 before accounting for his share of 1996's losses. The partnership suffered ordinary losses of $60,000 in 1996.
    a. How much of the partnership's 1996 losses may Binh deduct? What is Binh's adjusted basis at the end of 1996?
    b. Assume that in 1997 Binh makes additional capital contributions to Lamonica Partnership of $16,000, the partnership incurs $9,000 in additional debt, and the partnership realizes operating income of $2,000. How do the 1997 items affect Binh's adjusted basis?

55. Jacqui and Joanne plan to buy a bed-and-breakfast inn for $200,000. Jacqui will contribute $20,000 toward the purchase and will operate the enterprise. Joanne's primary role is that of investor. She will contribute $100,000. However, she will be an active participant because of her involvement in management decisions. They will borrow the balance of the purchase price from a local bank. Advise Jacqui and Joanne on a choice of business form. Consider that the enterprise is expected to realize operating losses of $50,000 annually for the first 3 years. During the fourth year, the inn should realize a meager profit.

56. John and Kathy form JK Partnership on January 1, 1996. John contributes $200,000 in cash for a 40% interest. Kathy contributes real estate valued at $450,000 and encumbered by a mortgage of $180,000, which is assumed by the partnership. Kathy's basis in the real estate is $100,000. She receives a 60% partnership interest. What is the amount of each partner's basis in his or her partnership interest?

57. Janice receives a partnership distribution of $31,000 in cash from AXE Partnership. Janice's basis in her partnership interest is $27,000 before the distribution. What is (are) the tax effect(s) of the distribution for Janice? What actions could Janice have taken before the distribution to change the results?

58. In January 1995, Waller pays $22,000 for 20% of the common stock of Baker, Inc., a qualified S corporation. Baker, Inc., reports a net loss from operations of $50,000 for 1995. For 1996, Baker, Inc., reports operating income of $20,000. On January 2, 1997, Baker, Inc., distributes $15,000 to Waller. What are the tax effects of these events for Waller?

59. Natrone pays $35,000 for stock in an S corporation and receives shares equal to a 20% interest in the corporation in the current year. At the same time, he pays $35,000 for a 20% interest in a general partnership. Both entities have outstanding mortgage debt of $60,000, and both report ordinary taxable income of $20,000. What is the maximum cash distribution each entity can make this year to Natrone without causing him to recognize income? Explain your answer(s) in terms of the underlying concepts and facts that support your calculations.

60. Lyra and Misha, a married couple, are the sole shareholders of Niki, Inc. Niki owns 80% of Gladly Corporation. During the current year, Gladly distributes a $20,000 cash dividend to Niki, Inc. Niki's taxable income before dividends is $75,000. Niki distributes all after-tax income to its shareholders. This distribution is the only source of income for Lyra and Misha.
    a. Determine the amount of after-tax income Lyra and Misha realize because of their corporate ownership.
    b. How will your answer in part a change if Niki, Inc., is an S corporation? Explain.

61. Monica and Mike, a married couple, recently incorporated their drapery business. To complete the entity transformation from sole proprietorship to corporation, they transferred ownership of sewing machines, cleaning equipment, assorted fabric, and $100,000 in municipal bonds to the corporation. The municipal bonds are collateral for bank loans to the corporation for business expansion. The business is expected to generate annual operating profits of $100,000. Tax-exempt interest will be $13,000 annually.
    a. Determine the amount of after-tax earnings and profits available to distribute as cash dividends.
    b. Will electing S corporation treatment save Monica and Mike and/or their corporation any money? Explain the result(s).

62. Last year, Linoa paid $25,000 for a 10% ownership interest in FasTrack Corporation. During the current year, FasTrack defaulted on a $100,000 loan to Third Security National Bank. Discuss the monetary implications for Linoa if the bank insists she repay the $100,000 loan under each of the following situations:
    a. FasTrack is a corporation.
    b. FasTrack is an S corporation.
    c. FasTrack is a partnership, and Linoa is a general partner.
    d. FasTrack is a partnership, and Linoa is a limited partner.

63. The laws of the country of Artichoke (a newly organized eastern European country) allow a legal entity called a *sharing association*. The characteristics of this legal entity are
    a. Its objective is to carry on a business for a profit.
    b. It has two or more owners.
    c. Transferability of its ownership interests is restricted.
    d. All owners share in management activities.
    e. Determination of the entity's life is independent of its owners.
    f. Owners have limited liability.
    Determine whether U.S. tax law will treat Artichoke's sharing association as a corporation or as a partnership.

64. Natalie operates her bookkeeping service as a corporation. She is the sole shareholder and is an employee functioning as the chief operating officer of the business. The corporation employs several other individuals and offers them good fringe benefits: group term life insurance, health insurance, disability insurance, and a 12% qualified pension plan. Natalie's good friend, Ricci, operates a custom software development company. The business is an S corporation, and Ricci is the sole shareholder. She is also an employee who serves as the manager. Upon Natalie's recommendation, Ricci copied the fringe-benefit package of Natalie's corporation. Assume both businesses are quite profitable.
    a. How do the employee benefits affect the tax bills of Natalie and her corporation?
    b. How do the employee benefits affect the tax bills of Ricci and her corporation?
    c. Write letters to both Natalie and Ricci explaining these tax ramifications.

65. Gena, the owner of Enterprise Business Systems, receives the benefits of $2,400-worth of premiums for health and accident insurance annually. The business's net operating income for the year is $50,000, before considering Gena's benefit. Determine the business's net income for the year and the tax effects for Gena for each of the following entities:

    a. A corporation   **c.** A sole proprietorship

    b. An S corporation   **d.** A partnership

DISCUSSION CASES

66. Four managers working for a certain Big Six accounting firm agree to join together and create their own tax-planning and management-consulting firm. Initially, Kelley, Barbara, Kuzuyo, and Leonard plan to operate their venture as a general partnership. All partners will share equally in decision making and business income and losses. The four individuals' ages range from 30 to 36. All have small children. Discuss the pros and cons of the various alternative business forms available to the individuals. Based upon known (and assumed) characteristics of the four owners, recommend the entity they should choose.

67. Astrid, a single individual, is a sales representative for several sporting goods manufacturers. She operates her enterprise as a sole proprietorship. Astrid has one employee, Melvin, who serves as office manager for the business. Gross revenues are $250,000 annually. Annual operating expenses are

Melvin's salary	$30,000
Payroll taxes & fees	3,000
Utilities	1,200
Rent	4,800
Selling expenses	8,000
Premiums paid for Melvin:	
$50,000 term life insurance policy	300
Health-care insurance policy	2,700

Astrid takes an annual draw of $3,000 to pay for insurance coverage equal to Melvin's. Astrid uses the remaining funds personally. Astrid is considering incorporating her business. Discuss the benefits that will accrue to Astrid by incorporating. Recommend any alternative courses of action.

TAX PLANNING CASES

68. John Johnson and his wife Joanne have 2 children, Joe, 16, and Jamie, 4. John is self-employed, and Joanne works as a swimming coach for Local University. John's business is manufacturing Jaugernauts. Through the years, Johnson's Jaugernauts has been fairly successful, providing a before-tax income of approximately $100,000 per year. The business has several employees, including a secretary-receptionist, 2 sales people, 4 production workers, and 2 truck drivers.

    Last year, Joanne entered a contest and won a sizable block of stock in a computer company. This stock is expected to produce approximately $10,000 per year in taxable dividends. Other than this stock, their investment assets consist mainly of savings accounts and certificates of deposits. However, in 1980 John invested in a tax shelter that provided him with tax write-offs until the Tax Reform Act of 1986 curtailed his loss deduction from the shelter (i.e., the losses are considered passive losses).

    John and Joanne have come to you for advice. They would like to rearrange their business and personal affairs to obtain a better tax situation. Discuss at least 3 actions (don't feel limited if you can think of more than 3) John and Joanne could take, and indicate the advantages and disadvantages of each action. Specific numerical calculations are not required, but if you think such an example would help explain your point, please feel free to use it.

69. For a number of years, Nina was a mechanical engineer for a chemical company. Nina always enjoyed working around her home in her spare time, doing necessary repairs and maintenance. However, she was always frustrated by the multitude of tools she had to carry around to do her various tasks. One evening, she drew up a design for a gizmo that could do the work of 12 different common home repair tools. At first, she made a few gizmos by hand and gave them to her friends as gag gifts. Their reaction to the gizmo was so enthusiastic that Nina took out a patent on it, got a loan from her friend at Local Bank, quit her job, and began a small-scale manufacturing operation.

In setting up her business, Nina took most of her advice from her brother-in-law, an assistant district attorney. Accordingly, she organized the business as a corporation and pays salaries to herself, her husband Stan, and their 3 children (the children are 2, 9, and 13). In addition, she put her investment portfolio inside the corporation.

After the first year of business, the corporate books show a loss of $25,000 after paying salaries of $30,000 to Nina, $20,000 to Stan (Stan continues to earn $18,000 from his full-time job), and $5,000 to each of the children.

a. What tax-related mistakes has Nina made regarding the business? Be specific. Indicate any negative effects that could arise from this arrangement.

b. Is there anything Nina can do to rectify the problems you identified? Explain, and indicate how each solution you propose cures or mitigates the problem.

70. Assume you are a CPA and a tax specialist. Your clients include Ale and Grains, Inc., an S corporation, and Gustav and Heidi Lager, a married couple who are shareholders and the operators of Ale and Grains. The S corporation has had 35 qualified shareholders for several years. Gustav and Heidi have come to you to let you know that they have just obtained a divorce. Both individuals will continue to operate Ale and Grains for the ownership group, and neither party plans to dispose of her or his ownership interest. They know that certain rules govern the number of shareholders allowed in an S corporation, but they tell you not to be concerned—because all that will change will be their mailing addresses. They refer to the doctrine of substance over form and how it fits this situation. Write a letter to Gustav, Heidi, and the other shareholders offering your advice. Refer to the AICPA Code of Professional Conduct and the Statements on Responsibilities in Tax Practice where necessary.

ETHICS DISCUSSION CASE

PROPERTY TRANSACTIONS

CHAPTER 10
ACQUISITIONS OF PROPERTY

CHAPTER 11
COST RECOVERY ON PROPERTY: DEPRECIATION,
DEPLETION, AND AMORTIZATION

CHAPTER 12
PROPERTY DISPOSITIONS

CHAPTER 13
NONRECOGNITION TRANSACTIONS

Acquisitions of Property

▲ CHAPTER LEARNING OBJECTIVES

■ Distinguish and define different types and classes of property.

■ Provide an overview of the property investment cycle from acquisition through disposition, and discuss the tax problems encountered throughout the cycle.

■ Explain the calculation of a property's adjusted basis.

■ Distinguish a realized from a recognized gain or loss on a disposition of property.

■ Explain how to determine the initial basis of purchased property.

■ Discuss the tax aspects of various ways to purchase the assets of a business.

■ Describe the rules for determining the initial basis of gift property, inherited property, personal use property converted to business use property, and property received from a spouse.

■ Explain the tax problems associated with determining the initial basis of securities.

10 Acquisitions of Property

...sses of Property — 436

. Property Investment Cycle — 437

Adjusted Basis — 438

Decrease in Basis — 440

Basis in Conduit Entities — 442

Property Dispositions — 444

.itial Basis — 445

rchase of Assets — 445

Determining the Amount Invested — 445

Basis of a Bargain Purchase — 447

Purchase of Multiple Assets — 447

Purchase of a Business — 448

Purchase of Corporate Stock — 450

Constructed Assets — 451

.cially Valued Property Acquisitions — 451

sis of Property Acquired by Gift — 452

General Rule for Gift Basis — 452

Split Basis Rule for Loss Property — 453

Holding Period — 454

sis of Property Acquired by Inheritance — 454

Primary Valuation Date — 455

Alternate Valuation Date — 455

Distribution Date — 456

Other Considerations — 456

perty Acquired From a Spouse — 457

rsonal use Property Converted to Business use — 458

General Rule for Basis — 459

Split Basis Rule — 459

sis in Securities — 460

Stock Dividends — 461

Transfers of Assets to a Controlled Corporation — 462

Wash Sale Stock Basis — 463

▲ CONCEPT REVIEW ▲

Accounting method   A taxpayer must adopt an accounting method that clearly reflects income.

All-inclusive income   All income received is taxable unless a specific provision can be found in the tax law that either excludes the income from taxation or defers its recognition to a future tax year.

Annual accounting period   All entities must report the results of their operations on an annual basis (the tax year). Each tax year stands on its own, apart from other tax years.

Arm's-length transaction   A transaction in which all parties to the transaction have bargained in good faith and for their individual benefit, not for the benefit of the transaction group.

Basis   This is the amount of unrecovered investment in an asset. As amounts are expended and/or recovered relative to an asset over time, the basis is adjusted in consideration of such changes. The **adjusted basis** of an asset is the original basis, plus or minus the changes in the amount of unrecovered investment.

Business purpose   To be deductible, an expenditure or a loss must have a business or other economic purpose that exceeds any tax avoidance motive. The primary motive for the transaction must be to make a profit.

Capital recovery   No income is realized until the taxpayer receives more than the amount invested to produce the income. The amount invested in an asset represents the maximum amount recoverable.

Conduit entity   An entity for which the tax attributes flow through to its owners for tax purposes.

Entity   All items of income, deduction, and so on are traced to the tax unit responsible for the item.

Legislative grace   Any tax relief provided is the result of a specific act of Congress that must be strictly applied and interpreted. All income received is taxable unless a specific provision can be found in the tax law that excludes the income from taxation. Deductions must be approached with the philosophy that nothing is deductible unless a provision in the tax law allows the deduction.

Realization   No income (or loss) is recognized until it has been realized. A realization involves a change in the form and/or the substance of a taxpayer's property rights that results from an arm's-length transaction.

Related party   Family members and corporations that are owned by family members are considered related parties, as are certain other relationships between entities in which the power to control the substance of a transaction is evidenced through majority ownership.

Substance-over-form doctrine   Transactions are to be taxed according to their true intention rather than some form that may have been contrived.

Chapter 5 discussed the general criteria for deducting expenses. Expenses incurred in a trade or business, for the production of income, and certain personal expenditures are deductible when they are paid or incurred. However, expenditures incurred in these activities that provide benefits that extend significantly beyond the end of the tax year cannot be deducted as a current expense. These expenditures, which provide long-lived benefits, are called *capital expenditures*. Thus, capital expenditures result in assets that provide economic or personal benefits that extend significantly beyond the end of the accounting period in which the expenditure is made. The term **property** is used in taxation to refer to long-lived assets that are owned by a taxpayer. Throughout the remaining chapters, the terms *property* and *asset* are used interchangeably to mean anything owned or possessed by a taxpayer.

The capital recovery concept provides the foundation for the tax accounting for property. According to this concept, the amount invested in an asset is recovered tax free before the taxpayer realizes any taxable income from the property investment. The two basic methods of recovering the capital invested in an asset are by deducting a portion of the cost of the asset against income during the life of the asset (e.g., through depreciation deductions) and by offsetting the invested

INTRODUCTION

amount against any amounts realized from the disposition of the asset at the end of its period of use. The amount of investment in an asset is the asset's basis. An asset's basis establishes the initial amount of capital investment that can be recovered tax free as a capital recovery, it is used to determine the amount of any annual deductions allowed for depreciation, and it represents the amount of unrecovered capital for determining gain or loss upon the disposition of the asset. Therefore, determining the correct basis of property is essential in order to properly account for the tax effects of investments in property.

The next four chapters discuss the tax aspects related to the acquisition, use, and disposition of property. This chapter begins with a discussion of the different classes of property and their characteristics. An overview of the property investment cycle is discussed next; it provides the framework for the study of chapters 10 through 13. The remainder of the chapter deals with problems involved in determining the initial basis of property when it is acquired.

CLASSES OF PROPERTY

For tax purposes, property is classified by both its use and its type. The use of property determines whether deductions are allowed for current-year expenditures (i.e., repairs, maintenance) relating to the property and for capital recovery deductions for depreciation, depletion, or amortization. In order to take any deductions relating to property, the property must have a business purpose: It must be used in a trade or business or held for the production of income. This is the general requirement for deductibility of expenses discussed in Chapter 5. Deductions for expenditures on property that is held for purely personal use are not generally allowed. Only those specifically allowed expenditures (discussed in Chapter 8) on **personal use property,** such as property taxes and home mortgage interest, are deductible. In addition, only casualty and theft losses on personal use property are deductible. Thus, proper classification of the use of an asset is essential to determining the effect of the property on taxable income.

▲ **EXAMPLE 1**   Ellen, a physician, purchased a television set for her patients to watch while they wait for their appointments. What is the proper classification of the television for Ellen?

Discussion: Because the television is used in relation to Ellen's business, it is classified as property used in a trade or business. Ellen may deduct any annual expenditures made relative to the television as an ordinary and necessary business expense. In addition, Ellen may deduct the appropriate amount of depreciation on the television during its tax life.

▲ **EXAMPLE 2**   When Ellen purchased the television in example 1, she purchased another television that she put in her family room at home. What is the proper classification of the second television set?

Discussion: The second television is used for personal purposes and therefore is a personal use asset. Ellen is not allowed any deductions for expenditures made relative to the second television, nor is she allowed to depreciate the television, because it is a personal use asset.

As these examples illustrate, the use of the property, not the type of property, is the key factor in determining deductibility. That is, any property can be used in any of the three basic categories. In addition, a single property may be used in more than one category. Such property is referred to as a **mixed-use property** (also called *mixed-use asset*). Proper accounting for mixed-use property requires a reasonable allocation of costs among the uses of the property.

> ▲ **EXAMPLE 3**   Don purchased a duplex at a cost of $80,000. Don resides in 1 unit and rents out the other unit. How should Don account for the duplex?
>
> *Discussion:*   The duplex is mixed-use property. The unit Don uses as his residence is a personal use asset and must be accounted for separately from the unit that is rented. Don will be allowed an itemized deduction only for the interest and property taxes from the personal use unit. However, on the rental unit he will be able to deduct all ordinary and necessary expenses of maintaining the unit. For example, if Don pays the utility bill of both units, only the portion that is reasonably allocable to the rental unit is deductible. In addition, Don may take the allowed depreciation deductions on the rental unit but is not allowed any depreciation deduction on the personal unit.

The type of property also affects the deductions allowed during the period the property is used. All property may be classified as tangible property or intangible property. **Tangible property** is any property that has a physical existence. That is, tangible property has form, shape, and substance. Land, buildings, machinery, equipment, automobiles, and furniture are all examples of tangible property. **Intangible property** lacks any physical characteristics and exists only because of economic rights the property possesses. Stocks, bonds, copyrights, trademarks, goodwill, and patents are examples of intangible property.

Tangible property is broken down further for tax purposes into real property and personal property. Real property consists of land and any structures permanently attached to land. A building and its structural components, such as the air-conditioning system, electrical wiring, and an elevator are considered real property. Real property is often referred to as **real estate,** and the terms are used interchangeably. Personal property is any tangible property that is not real property. Machinery, equipment, livestock, automobiles, computers, and paintings are all examples of personal property. Personal property is often referred to as **personalty,** and the terms are used interchangeably. Personal property is a *type* of property that is different from personal use property, which is a *use* of property. The type of property should not be confused with its use.

In contrast to the use of property, the type of property does not change from taxpayer to taxpayer. That is, land is always real property and a computer is always personal property, regardless of the use of the property. The type of property determines such things as the amount of allowable depreciation on the property. Personal property generally has a shorter useful life than real property, and the amount and timing of the depreciation deductions on the two properties are adjusted for the difference in useful lives. The allowable depreciation methods for different types of property are discussed in Chapter 11. Property type is also important in determining the tax effects of property dispositions. As will be discussed in Chapter 12, depreciable real property and depreciable personal property are subject to special rules that reclassify income from capital gain income to ordinary income at disposition. The type of property determines the amount of the gain that is reclassified. Table 10–1 provides a summary of the different types of property.

Generating income involves the acquisition and use of property to produce that income. That is, businesses acquire factories, equipment, supplies, and so on to produce products that are sold to generate income. Similarly, investors purchase

THE PROPERTY INVESTMENT CYCLE

▲ Table 10–1

SUMMARY OF
PROPERTY TYPES

Type of Property	Property Characteristics	Examples
Personal property (Personalty)	Property that has a physical existence and that is not real estate or permanently attached to real estate. Personal property has form, shape, and substance.	Machinery, equipment, automobiles, trucks, computers, furniture, fixtures, telephone systems, works of art, livestock, video equipment.
Real property (Real estate)	Land and any structures that are permanently attached to land. Real property has form, shape, and substance.	Land and land improvements such as landscaping, shrubbery, sidewalks, parking lots, and fences; buildings, grain silos, barns, sheds, greenhouses.
Intangible property	Property that lacks a physical existence; the rights to the property exist only on paper. Intangible property does not have form, shape, or physical substance.	Patents, copyrights, trademarks, goodwill, covenants not to compete, stocks, bonds, and other securities.
Personal use property	Any property that is used by the taxpayer for purely personal purposes. Personal use property can be personal property, real property, or intangible property.	Personal residence, clothing, furniture, home computer, lawnmower, personal automobile.

stocks and bonds to produce dividend and interest income as well as appreciation in the value of the security. Individuals acquire homes, furniture, clothing, and automobiles that they use in their personal activities. Acquisition of property begins a property investment cycle that has income tax effects throughout the period in which the taxpayer uses the property.

The property investment cycle and the tax accounting related to it are illustrated in Figure 10–1. In the top panel of Figure 10–1, the investment process begins with acquisition of the property. The most common method of acquiring property is by purchase. However, property may also be acquired through other means, such as by gift or inheritance. The initial basis of the property must be determined at acquisition. The **initial basis** of an asset is generally the cost of acquiring the asset and placing it into service. When assets are acquired by means other than purchase, special rules apply for determining the initial basis to assign to the asset for tax purposes. The cost of acquiring an asset by purchase and the special rules for other methods of acquisition are discussed later in this chapter.

Adjusted Basis

Under the capital recovery concept, a taxpayer is allowed to recover the amount of capital invested in an asset tax free. Thus, basis sets the limit on the maximum amount that can be recovered tax free. As an asset is used to generate income, it may be necessary to adjust the initial basis to account for additional capital investments in the asset or for recoveries of capital investment.[1] As Figure 10–1 illustrates, these adjustments result in an amount that is referred to as the *adjusted*

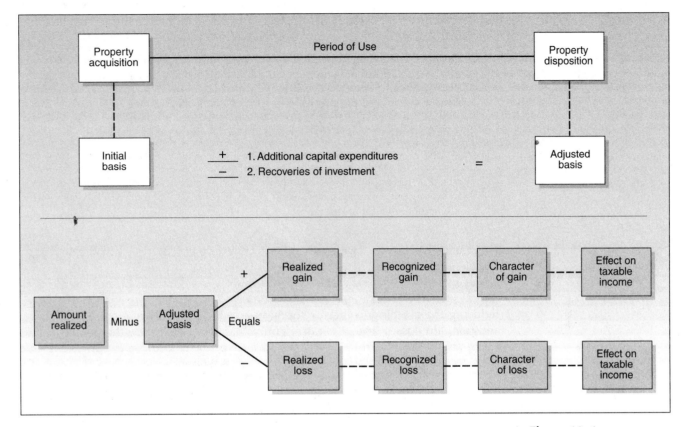

Property Investment Cycle

basis. **Adjusted basis** is equal to the initial basis, plus or minus the cumulative effects of the adjustments. Adjusted basis roughly corresponds to the book-value concept studied in financial accounting.

At any point in time, the remaining capital investment to be recovered is represented by an asset's adjusted basis. An asset's adjusted basis may never be less than zero (a negative number). For investments such as publicly traded corporate stocks, few, if any, adjustments to the initial basis are needed. But for other types of assets, such as depreciable assets used in a business, the adjusted basis calculation is made at least annually and on the date of an asset's disposition. Exhibit 10–1 presents a general format for computing an asset's adjusted basis.

Increases in Basis.   As Exhibit 10–1 indicates, there are two broad categories of increases in basis. An asset's basis is increased by expenditures that are an additional investment in the asset. Additional investments are expenditures made on behalf of the asset that cannot be deducted as a current period expense and must be capitalized as part of its basis.[2] Additional investments would include improvements to an asset that enlarge an asset (adding a room onto a building) or extends its useful life (putting a new roof on a building). In addition, any costs of defending the ownership of the property and special assessments for such local benefits as widening the street in front of a building are capitalized as part of the cost of the property.

Basis is also increased by items that constitute taxable income but are not withdrawn from the asset for personal or other use. The taxable income of a conduit entity that is allocated to the owner of the entity is added to the basis of the investment in the entity, because the owner is taxed on the income yet does not necessarily receive income.[3,4] This category of basis addition includes the bargain element that is recognized as income in a bargain purchase of property.

▲ **EXAMPLE 4**   Sterling is an employee of Shelf Road Development Co. The company recently subdivided some property and offered lots for sale at a price of $50,000 each. Shelf sold Sterling a lot for $20,000. The difference between the $50,000 fair market value and the $20,000 purchase price—$30,000—is taxable income to Sterling because the transaction is a bargain purchase. The purchase price is an attempt to compensate Sterling. How does Sterling's recognition of this income affect his basis in the property?

Discussion: The bargain purchase difference, $30,000, is added to Sterling's purchase price of $20,000 to reflect the income recognition that results from the bargain purchase. Therefore, Sterling will have to recognize the income from the bargain purchase, $30,000, only once. The property's basis becomes $50,000, which may reduce his capital gain when he sells the property.

Decreases in Basis.   Decreases in basis are grouped into three broad categories. The first group of decreases results from annual expense deductions that are allowed when the asset is used to earn income. The deduction of an expense is a capital recovery of an investment in an asset. The capital recovery results from reducing the taxable income for the year in which the deduction is claimed. In addition, any losses from a conduit entity that are allocated to the owner of the entity are subtracted from the basis of the investment, because the owner is entitled to the allowable loss deduction on the investment.

Basis is also reduced as a result of disposing of part of the asset. For example, a gift of half of a taxpayer's interest in an asset reduces the taxpayer's basis by half. If property is subject to a casualty, the asset's basis is reduced by the amount of loss deducted.

Special income items also reduce basis. For example, a payment received from a utility company for an easement for power lines does not constitute a realization, because the form or substance of the taxpayer's property rights does not change;

▲ **Exhibit 10–1**

COMPUTATION OF
ADJUSTED BASIS

Initial basis	$XXX
Increases in basis from	
■ Additional investments	
• Capital invested	
• Costs of protecting ownership	
• Special property tax assessments for local benefits	XXX
■ Reinvestment of income	
• Income taxed to owners of conduit entities	XXX
Decreases in basis from	
■ Annual tax deductions resulting in a reduction of tax liability	
• Depreciation, depletion, and amortization	
• Losses from conduit entities	(XXX)
■ Dispositions of all or part of interest in an asset	
• Casualty loss	
• Sale or gift of part of an asset	(XXX)
■ Capital recovery resulting from excluded income	
• Nontaxable dividends	
• Easements	(XXX)
Equals: Adjusted basis	$XXX*

*Adjusted basis cannot be less than zero.

such a payment is excluded from income. For tax purposes, the payment is treated as a capital recovery and a reduction in the basis of the land. Similarly, a shareholder who receives a nontaxable dividend from a corporation treats the payment as a recovery of the stock's basis. If the shareholder receives nontaxable dividends that ultimately reduce the stock's basis to zero, any additional nontaxable dividends mean the shareholder must recognize gain (from the "sale" of the asset).

▲ **EXAMPLE 5**   On July 1, 1996, Cynthia buys 500 shares of Watkins common stock at $35 per share ($17,500 total cost). On December 31, 1996, Watkins pays a $4 per share cash distribution. Watkins reports that $3 per share is taxable as a dividend and $1 per share is a nontaxable dividend. What is Cynthia's adjusted basis in the Watkins stock?

Discussion: Cynthia's adjusted basis in the Watkins stock after she receives the dividend is $34 per share. Cynthia must reduce her $17,500 initial basis by the $500 nontaxable dividend that is excluded from gross income ($1 × 500). Thus, Cynthia's adjusted basis on December 31, 1996, for the 500 shares is $17,000. The $3 per share taxable dividend is reported as gross income and does not affect the basis of the stock.

▲ **EXAMPLE 6**   James buys an office building in 1991. He pays $30,000 for the land and $170,000 for the building. Shortly after he acquires the property, the city imposes a $20,000 special property tax assessment to pave streets and install sidewalks. In addition, James pays $25,000 to remodel two rooms in the building to make them suitable for his use. When a dispute arises with a neighbor concerning property lines, James pays his attorney $2,000 to protect his interest in the land. Total depreciation deducted from 1991 through 1996 is $35,000. A fire in 1996 results in an $8,000 uninsured casualty loss to the building, which James deducts as a loss on his tax return. During 1996, James paid mortgage interest of $9,000, real estate taxes of $3,000, and maintenance service fees of $4,000 on the building. What is James's adjusted basis in the property on December 31, 1996?

Discussion: James's adjusted basis in the building is $152,000 and in the land is $52,000, computed as follows:

Expenditure	Building	Land	Current Expenses
Initial basis	$170,000	$30,000	
Remodel offices	25,000		
Special tax assessment for local benefits		20,000	
Attorney's fee to defend title		2,000	
Depreciation deducted	(35,000)		
Casualty loss from fire	(8,000)		
Mortgage interest			$(9,000)
Real estate taxes			(3,000)
Maintenance service fees			(4,000)
Adjusted basis	$152,000	$52,000	

The expenditures must be identified as adjustments to the basis of the land or the basis of the building or as current expenses. The $2,000 legal fee to defend title to the land increases the land's basis. The $20,000 in special tax assessments for local benefits is considered to attach to the basis of the land and also increases the land's basis. The $25,000 spent to remodel the building for his use is added to its basis. The $35,000 deduction for depreciation and the $8,000 casualty loss deduction are capital recoveries that reduce the basis of the building. The $9,000 mortgage interest, the $3,000 in real estate taxes, and the $4,000 in maintenance service fees are current expenses. They do not affect the basis of the building or the land.

The recovery of capital investment may occur at several different times. Assets that have definite useful lives may be recovered over the period of use through depreciation, depletion, or amortization deductions. To allocate the depreciation deduction to the correct accounting period, you must use tax accounting rules to correctly measure the basis subject to depreciation. If the basis of an asset is undervalued, depreciation deductions may be permanently lost. In addition, an asset's basis must be reduced by the larger of the depreciation allowable, based on tax accounting methods for computing depreciation, or by the amount of depreciation actually deducted on the taxpayer's returns.[5] Therefore, claiming smaller deductions than those to which the taxpayer is entitled can result in lost basis and unused deductions. On the other hand, a taxpayer who claims inflated depreciation deductions may be subject to penalties. Thus, proper determination of the basis in business assets is crucial to computing annual deductions for depreciation, depletion, and amortization. The example that follows highlights the importance of properly reporting depreciation deductions. Do not be concerned with depreciation methods until Chapter 11.

▲ **EXAMPLE 7**   Kalil Corporation uses a machine in its business that cost $10,000. Using tax depreciation methods, Kalil is entitled to total allowable depreciation on the machine of $9,000. However, because of clerical errors, Kalil actually deducted a total of $6,000 in allowed depreciation on its tax returns. Kalil sells the machine on July 1 for $5,000. What are the tax effects to Kalil of the clerical errors?

Discussion: Kalil Corporation must report a gain of $4,000 from the sale of the asset [$5,000 − ($10,000 − $9,000 allowable depreciation)]. The tax law requires Kalil to reduce its basis in the machine by the larger of the depreciation that it actually deducted or the amount it should have deducted based on tax deprecation methods. As a result, Kalil has lost the benefit of $3,000 in depreciation to which it was entitled under the capital recovery concept ($9,000 allowable − $6,000 allowed). Kalil Corporation might be able to salvage some of the lost basis by filing amended tax returns to correct the error.

Basis in Conduit Entities

Partnerships and S Corporations are conduit entities. As a result, the income and deductions of these entities are passed through and included in the gross income of the owners of the entity. Ownership of an interest in a **conduit entity** creates an interesting tax accounting problem. Effectively, owners must determine the adjusted basis of their investment using an equity accounting method. Using the equity accounting method, the investor increases and decreases the basis of the investment for items that change the amount that may be excluded from income under the capital recovery concept. These adjustments are fully explained in Chapter 9; Exhibit 10–2 presents the effect of these adjustments on adjusted basis.

The taxpayer's adjusted basis for the investment in the conduit entity can be zero, but it may not be a negative number, as explained in Chapter 9.

▲ **EXAMPLE 8**   Tina owns a 25% interest in Quality Conduit Entity. At the beginning of the current year, Tina's adjusted basis for her investment was $75,000. For the current year, Quality reports the following pass-through tax information:

Ordinary income	$100,000
Capital losses	10,000
Nondeductible expenses	5,000
Charitable contributions	1,600

Initial basis in stock (cost) or basis of	
investment at the beginning of the current year	$X,XXX
Increases in basis:	
• Additional capital invested during the year	
• Taxable and nontaxable income allocated to the	
owner for the current year	
• Liability adjustment	
—A partner's share of any increase in liabilities related to the partnership	XXX
Decreases in basis:	
• Cash received from the entity	
• Property received from the entity:	
—If a partnership, subtract the partnership's basis for the property	
—If an S corporation, subtract the fair market value of the property	
• Deductions, losses, and nondeductible expenses allocated to the owner	
for the current year	
• Liability adjustment	
—A partner's share of any decrease in liabilities related to the	
partnership	(XXX)
Equals: Adjusted basis in the conduit entity	$X,XXX

▲ **Exhibit 10–2**

CONDUIT ENTITY
BASIS COMPUTATION

During the year, Quality distributes $15,000 in cash to Tina. What is Tina's basis in Quality Conduit Entity at the end of the current year?

Discussion: At the end of the year, Tina's basis in Quality is $80,850. The adjusted basis is computed as follows:

Adjusted basis at beginning of year	$75,000
Add: Share of current income	25,000
Deduct: Share of deductions and losses	
Capital losses	(2,500)
Nondeductible expenses	(1,250)
Charitable contributions	(400)
Deduct: Cash received	(15,000)
Adjusted basis at end of year	$80,850

The capital loss and charitable contribution limitations are applied on Tina's personal tax return to determine the amounts that she may deduct. Tina must reduce her basis in the Quality stock, regardless of whether she can deduct the capital loss, the charitable contributions, or the nondeductible expenses on her personal tax return. These adjustments are illustrated in Chapter 9.

If all or a portion of the taxpayer's interest in the partnership or S corporation is sold, the adjusted basis reduces the sales price as a capital recovery to compute the gain or loss on the sale. Thus, the equity accounting method requires an investor in a partnership or S corporation to continuously record adjustments to the basis of the investment.

▲ **EXAMPLE 9**   Using the adjusted basis computed in example 8, what would Tina's gain or loss be if she sells her interest at the end of the current year for $100,000? $50,000?

Discussion: If Tina sells the investment in Quality for $100,000, she would report a $19,150 gain ($100,000 − $80,850) from the sale. If she sells the investment in Quality for $50,000, Tina would report a $30,850 loss. Tina's adjusted basis in the investment in Quality is subtracted from the sales price as a capital recovery.

Property Dispositions

The amount invested in an asset that has not been recovered through deductions related to its use for a business purpose is recovered at the date of its disposition. When an asset is sold, exchanged, abandoned, or otherwise disposed of, a realization of income occurs with respect to the **property disposition.** At this point, the tax effect of the realization must be determined. This process is illustrated in the lower panel of Figure 10–1. Capital is recovered upon disposition by offsetting the adjusted basis at the date of disposition with the amount realized from the disposition.[6] The **amount realized** from a disposition is the amount received from the disposition (generally the sales price of the property), less the expenses incurred to make the disposition. Thus, if the amount realized is greater than the adjusted basis, the taxpayer has a **realized gain** on the disposition. If the amount realized is less than the adjusted basis, the taxpayer has not fully recovered the capital investment and has a **realized loss** on the disposition. Calculating the amount realized and gains and losses realized on property dispositions is discussed in detail in Chapter 12.

As a general rule, taxpayers must recognize any gain realized on a property disposition under the all-inclusive income concept. *To recognize a gain* means to include it in the current year's taxable income calculation. However, gains from certain types of asset exchanges, involuntary conversions of property, and the sale of a principal residence may not be recognized in total in the year the disposition occurs. That is, provisions in the tax law allow gains from these transactions to be fully or partially deferred for recognition in a future tax year. Similarly, not all realized losses are recognized in the current year. Losses on certain types of transactions are disallowed (e.g., personal use losses) and therefore are never deductible, whereas other realized losses are deferred for future recognition (e.g., wash sale losses). Thus, after determining the amount of realized gain or loss from a disposition of property, you must determine the amount of gain or loss to be recognized in the current year. Chapter 13 discusses the tax treatments of commonly encountered transactions that are not recognized (nonrecognition transactions) in the year of realization.

The character of the recognized gain or loss determines its ultimate effect on taxable income for the current period. Thus far, all gains and losses have been characterized as being either ordinary (no special treatment) or capital. For individuals, capital gains are subject to a maximum tax rate of 28 percent, whereas net capital loss deductions are limited to $3,000 per year. In addition to ordinary gains and capital gains, sales of certain business assets produce what are referred to as *Section 1231 gains and losses.* Net Section 1231 gains receive long-term capital gain treatment, whereas net Section 1231 losses are deductible as ordinary losses. Because of the differences in treatment for the different types of gains, it is important to properly characterize each gain or loss. Chapter 12 discusses how to characterize the different types of gains and losses and their effect on taxable income for the year.

In order to properly characterize the gain or loss from a disposition of property, the holding period must be determined. The term *holding period* means the length of time an asset is owned. An asset's holding period normally begins on the day after it is acquired and ends on the day of its disposition.[7] In determining the holding period, include the day the asset is sold and exclude the day it was bought. The holding period of an asset acquired on January 1, 1996, begins on January 2, 1996. If the asset is still held on January 3, 1997, it is held for more than one year. Another way to remember this rule is that an asset that is held for one calendar year plus one day from its acquisition date is held for more than one year.

▲ **EXAMPLE 10**   Timothy purchases stock in Real Corporation on July 1, 1996. He sells the stock on July 3, 1997. What is Timothy's holding period?

Discussion: Timothy's holding period begins on July 2, 1996, and ends on July 3, 1997. Thus, Timothy held the stock for more than one year.

In certain types of acquisition transactions, the basis of another taxpayer or another asset is carried over to the basis of the asset acquired. The term **carryover basis** refers to all or part of an asset's basis that transfers from one owner to another or from one asset to another. Transactions resulting in a carryover basis are subject to special rules for determining the holding period. These rules require an adding on (tacking on) of the holding period of the previous asset or of a previous owner. Situations that involve a carryover basis are discussed later in this chapter and in Chapter 13.

INITIAL BASIS

Initial basis represents the taxpayer's total investment in an asset on its acquisition date. The initial basis of a purchased asset generally is the cost of acquiring and placing the asset into service. If an asset is acquired by means other than a purchase, its initial basis may be more difficult to determine. As stated earlier, the initial basis of a property has tax effects throughout the period in which the asset is used. In order to properly account for the investment in an asset throughout its tax life, you must determine the initial basis correctly. The remainder of this chapter discusses the tax rules and problems associated with different types of property acquisitions.

PURCHASE OF ASSETS

When an asset is purchased, it is necessary to determine the amount invested to establish an initial basis in a transaction. Once the total investment is determined, it must be assigned to the specific asset(s) purchased. If one asset is purchased, the assignment of the amount invested is straightforward. But in many transactions, such as the purchase of multiple assets or a business, the taxpayer must use a reasonable method to allocate a single purchase price to multiple assets. In addition, self-constructed assets require allocation of costs to the constructed asset.

Determining the Amount Invested

In an arm's-length transaction, the amount paid for an asset is assumed to be its fair market value. But for practical business reasons (e.g., a forced sale in liquidation of a business), a taxpayer might pay more or less than the true fair market value for an asset. When an asset is purchased with cash, the initial basis of the asset is easy to identify and is the same as the amount of cash paid. Measuring the basis of an asset can become complex when other forms of value are used to pay for the asset. The initial basis (amount invested) in an asset is equal to the purchase price of the asset plus any cost incurred to get the asset ready for its intended use.[8]

The purchase price of an asset is the sum of the

- Cash paid
- Fair market value of other property given to another entity in the exchange
- Fair market value of the taxpayer's services given to another entity in the exchange
- Increases in the taxpayer's liabilities related to the purchase (i.e., increases in debts owed by the taxpayer)

The purchase of an asset by using debt financing (e.g., assuming the seller's debt on the property or obtaining a bank loan to purchase the asset) results in an initial basis equal to the total amount paid for the asset.[9] Effectively, these buyers are treated as if they borrowed money and then used the cash to pay the seller for the asset. When the taxpayer pays off the debt, the asset's basis is not changed. The repayment of the debt merely reduces the lender's claims against the taxpayer. Depending on whether the asset is a business or personal use asset, interest paid on the loan may or may not yield an interest expense deduction, as previously discussed in chapters 5 and 8. The payment of interest expense on the loan does not affect the asset's basis.

▲ **EXAMPLE 11** Lorenzo purchased a new car by paying the dealer $2,000 cash down and signing an installment note to be paid monthly for $15,000 with interest at 13%. What is the initial basis of the car?

Discussion: Lorenzo's initial basis in the new car is $17,000. His basis includes the $2,000 cash plus the $15,000 note that increased his personal liability. The interest paid on the installment note does not affect the basis of the car. As he pays on the note each month, he reduces his indebtedness. The basis in the car is not affected by the repayment of the loan.

In addition to the purchase price of the property, any other costs incurred to get the property ready for its intended use are capitalized as part of the initial basis. Such costs would include commissions, sales tax paid on the purchase, legal fees, recording fees, accounting fees, transportation costs, installation and testing costs, licensing fees, title insurance, surveys, and any other cost that must be incurred to place the property in service.

▲ **EXAMPLE 12** Eve Corporation purchased an apartment building by paying $10,000 cash and borrowing $130,000 on a 12%, 30-year mortgage. Eve paid legal fees of $2,000 related to the purchase. Because the apartments were in a rundown condition, Eve spent $13,000 painting the apartments and $20,000 in other repair work before it could rent out the apartments. This is a list of items related to the purchase:

Cash down payment	$ 10,000
Mortgage	130,000
Legal fees	2,000
Painting	13,000
Repairs	20,000
Total	$175,000

What is Eve's initial basis in the apartment building?

Discussion: The purchase price of the building is $140,000 ($10,000 cash + $130,000 increase in liabilities). Eve Corporation will also add the $2,000 in legal fees to its basis as an acquisition cost. Painting and repair work are usually expensed as ongoing maintenance. However, in this case the painting and repair work had to be performed in order to get the apartments into condition to rent. Therefore, the costs are capitalized as a cost of getting the apartment building placed into service. The total initial basis in the apartment building is $175,000.

▲ **EXAMPLE 13** Holly purchased a new home for $85,000. To complete the sale and obtain a mortgage to finance the purchase, Holly paid the following:

Attorney fees for title opinion	$ 150
Points paid to acquire mortgage	2,000
Title insurance	250
Survey	125
Fee to record the deed	25
Total additional costs	$2,550

What is Holly's basis in the home?

Discussion: Holly's basis in her new home is $85,550. Her basis includes the $85,000 paid the seller plus $550 in costs paid to establish her ownership of the home. The $2,000 in points paid to acquire the mortgage is not related to the acquisition cost of the home. Points are prepaid interest charges on the mortgage that are deductible as interest in the year of acquisition (see Chapter 8).

If property taxes are owed on an asset when it is acquired and the buyer agrees to pay the taxes for the seller, the payment of the seller's taxes must be added to the asset's basis as part of the acquisition cost.[10] Thus, in the year real estate is acquired, property taxes must be allocated between the buyer and the seller. The taxes should be allocated according to the number of days each owned the property during the period covered by the tax assessment. The period covered by the assessment is called the *real property tax year.* For purposes of the allocation, the buyer's ownership period begins on the date of the sale.

▲ **EXAMPLE 14**   On March 1, 1996, Mark Corporation purchases a vacant city lot for $15,000 as an investment. The annual real estate tax on the lot is $120. The property tax year is a calendar year with the current year's tax payable on November 1, 1996. In the contract with the seller, Mark Corporation agrees to pay the $120 in real estate tax for the current year when the payment comes due on November 1. What is Mark's basis in the lot?

Discussion: Mark's basis in the lot is increased by the $19 [(59 ÷ 365) × $120] in real estate tax that it pays on behalf of the seller. The $101 in property tax related to the part of the year that the lot is owned by Mark Corporation is deductible as a property tax. Thus, Mark's basis in the lot is $15,019.

Basis of a Bargain Purchase

In Chapter 3, we applied the all-inclusive income concept to employee and shareholder **bargain purchases.** This concept requires recognition of income to the extent of the difference between the fair market value of an asset and its sales price. Because the bargain element (discount) is recognized as income, a basis is established in the asset. The asset's basis is equal to the amount paid plus the income recognized from the discount. Thus, the basis of an asset acquired in a bargain purchase is its fair market value on the date purchased. Likewise, a person who provides a service in exchange for an asset must recognize the fair market value of the asset received as income from services. The initial basis of the asset is its fair market value, and the fair market value of the asset is the amount of income recognized from the services. For these kinds of asset acquisitions, the asset's basis generally is the amount paid plus imputed income recognized for tax purposes. Again, the asset's basis usually is equal to its fair market value.

▲ **EXAMPLE 15**   Jack is an employee of Charles Construction Co. Charles is a home builder that is developing a new subdivision. Charles has built 5 new houses that are priced to sell for $150,000. To get a family in the subdivision and to thank Jack for his efforts as an employee, Charles sells a house to him for $100,000. What are the tax effects of the purchase for Jack?

Discussion: Jack has a $150,000 initial basis in his new home. Because of the bargain purchase rules, Jack has to recognize $50,000 in gross income. His basis in the new home is the sum of the $100,000 purchase price plus the $50,000 in income recognized from the bargain purchase.

Purchase of Multiple Assets

When more than one asset is bought for a single price (called a **multiple asset purchase**), the cost must be allocated to the individual assets in proportion to their fair market value on the date purchased.[11] This allocation of the purchase price is necessary because one or more of the assets may be subject to depreciation or the assets may be disposed of in different accounting periods. If the taxpayer does not make a reasonable allocation of the purchase price to the individual assets purchased, the IRS may decide to reallocate the cost.

An appraisal of the individual assets usually provides a reasonable basis for allocating the purchase price. As an alternative, the buyer and seller could agree, at arm's length, on an allocation of the purchase price. Another method that is commonly used to allocate the cost of real estate is based upon the property's tax-assessed value. As noted in Chapter 1, assessed values are usually less than actual fair market values. However, the assessed value does give a reasonable measure of the relative value of the assets (by ratio). Using this method, the purchase price is allocated to land and buildings according to the relative values placed on property by the tax assessor. The reasonable allocation of the purchase price of furniture and equipment is a more complex issue and generally should be based on appraisals, not assessed values. Allocating the cost of furniture and equipment should take into account the age and condition of each item.

▲ **EXAMPLE 16**   The Kay Partnership paid $150,000 for land and a building. At the date of purchase, the property tax valuations showed that the land was assessed at $10,000 and the building at $40,000. What is the basis of the land? the building?

Discussion: The basis in the land is $30,000, and the basis of the building is $120,000. The $150,000 purchase price should be allocated on a reasonable basis to the individual assets. Based on the property tax assessments, the purchase price should be allocated as follows:

Asset	Assessed Value	Percentage of Assessed Value		Purchase Price	Cost Basis
Land	$10,000	20%	×	$150,000	$ 30,000
Building	40,000	80%	×	150,000	120,000
Totals	$50,000	100%			$150,000

Purchase of a Business

A taxpayer who is interested in acquiring the assets of a business may purchase the assets directly from the owner. A purchase of assets results in the actual transfer of ownership of the assets to the purchaser. If the assets are owned by a corporation, the taxpayer may choose to buy the corporation's stock. The purchase of the corporation's stock results in ownership of the entity. Ownership of the entity results in indirect ownership of the corporation's assets. The tax effects of the two approaches for acquiring a business are explained in the discussion that follows.

Purchase of the Assets of a Business.   The purchase of the assets of a business results in a direct transfer of ownership of the assets. The main problem encountered in a direct purchase of assets is the allocation of the purchase price to the assets acquired. A taxpayer who purchases the assets of a business usually wants to allocate as much of the purchase price as possible to assets that will be subject to depreciation, amortization, or some other form of annual capital recovery and as little as possible to those assets that are not recoverable until they are sold. When the price paid exceeds the sum of the value of the individual assets, the excess price is considered **goodwill.** Before August 10, 1993, goodwill was considered to have an indefinite life. Thus, any cost allocated to goodwill purchased before August 10, 1993, was not subject to capital recovery until the owner disposed of the business. Therefore, taxpayers preferred to allocate their investment to assets that permitted a current recovery of their investment, such as depreciable equipment. In 1993, Congress enacted Section 197, which allows goodwill purchased after August 9, 1993, to be amortized over 15 years. (Chapter 11 discusses the effect of this new amortization rule for goodwill and other intangible assets.)

One approach to allocating the purchase price is for the buyer and seller to agree to a written allocation of the purchase price to individual assets. If the buyer and seller do not agree to an allocation, the purchase price must be allocated to all the acquired assets according to their relative fair market values. To identify the amount paid for goodwill, the purchase price is allocated to identifiable assets based on their relative market values. If the purchase price exceeds the total fair market value of the identifiable assets, the excess payment is considered goodwill.[12]

▲ **EXAMPLE 17** Sandra Corporation purchased the following business assets from Rafael:

Identifiable Asset	Rafael's Adjusted Basis	Fair Market Value
Accounts receivable	$ 100	$ 100
Furniture and fixtures	500	800
Equipment	300	600
Building	1,400	1,000
Land	100	300
Totals	$2,400	$2,800

Sandra Corporation paid $2,100 in cash and assumed $1,000 of Rafael's liabilities. Thus, Sandra's total cost for the assets is $3,100 ($2,100 cash + $1,000 increase in liabilities). What is Sandra's basis in the assets purchased?

Discussion: Sandra Corporation should allocate the purchase price according to the relative fair market values of the acquired assets. Because the $3,100 purchase price exceeds the total fair market value of $2,800, Sandra is considered to have paid $300 for goodwill. Each identifiable asset will have a tax basis equal to its fair market value on the date acquired by Sandra. Rafael's adjusted basis for the assets does not affect Sandra's allocation of the purchase price to the assets acquired.

▲ **EXAMPLE 18** Assume that in example 17 Sandra Corporation paid Rafael $2,100 for the assets and did not assume any of his liabilities. What is Sandra's basis in the assets purchased?

Discussion: Sandra should allocate the $2,100 purchase price to the identifiable assets acquired in proportion to their relative fair market values on the date acquired:

Identifiable Asset	FMV	Allocated % FMV	Basis
Accounts receivable	$ 100	3.6	$ 76
Furniture and fixtures	800	28.6	600
Equipment	600	21.4	449
Building	1,000	35.7	750
Land	300	10.7	225
Totals	$2,800	100.0	$2,100

100 ÷ 2800 = 3.6%

.036 × 2100 = 76

Because the amount paid for the identifiable assets is less than their total fair market value, none of the purchase price is allocated to goodwill. Rafael's adjusted basis for the assets is not relevant to Sandra's allocation of the purchase price to the assets acquired.

The relative market value allocation of the purchase price results in a reasonable assignment of a cost basis to each asset purchased. The use of a relative market value allocation is important for two reasons. First, the purchase price is objectively allocated among those assets subject to depreciation and amortization and those assets for which the cost is locked in until the asset is disposed of. For example, the basis of accounts receivable is recovered as the accounts are collected. The cost of buildings, furniture, and equipment is recovered through depreciation. The land is locked in and is not recoverable until its disposition. Second, the amounts subject to capital recovery are based on current costs paid by the buyer instead of the seller's adjusted basis.

Purchase of Corporate Stock.   The purchase of a corporation's stock to gain control over its business assets has a completely different result than the direct purchase of the assets. Because the corporation is a separate and distinct tax entity, the taxpayer owns shares of stock instead of the corporation's assets. Thus, the new owner controls the assets through the ownership of the entity, rather than through direct ownership of the individual business assets. As a separate entity, the corporation retains control over the assets, and it is entitled to the tax deductions and benefits resulting from the business use of the assets. The shareholder is entitled to receive a return on the amount invested in the stock in the form of dividends. Because of the entity concept, the corporation's tax basis in its assets does not change to reflect the amount the shareholder paid to purchase stock.

▲ **EXAMPLE 19**   Assume that in example 17 Sandra Corporation purchased 100% of Rafael Corporation's stock for $3,100 to gain control over its assets. The facts related to Rafael's assets are the same as in example 16. What is the tax effect of the stock purchase for Sandra?

Discussion: Sandra Corporation owns 100% of Rafael Corporation's stock with a tax basis of $3,100. Sandra and Rafael Corporation are separate tax entities. Sandra should expect to receive dividend income from the investment in the stock. When Sandra Corporation sells the stock in the future, it may reduce the sales price by the $3,100 basis to compute the gain or loss on the disposition.

▲ **EXAMPLE 20**   What are the tax effects of Sandra's purchase for Rafael Corporation?

Discussion: Rafael Corporation's basis in its assets is not affected by the purchase of its stock by a shareholder. Rafael Corporation will continue to use its assets in its business, and it will continue to compute depreciation and other capital recovery deductions according to the corporation's basis in the assets. The corporation is indifferent about who owns its stock and does not revalue its assets when ownership shares change hands.

The purchase of a corporation's stock instead of its assets has several pitfalls. The basis of the corporation's assets is not affected by the amount paid for its stock by a shareholder. Thus, there is a potential loss of depreciation deductions based on current values of the company's assets. The corporation keeps its tax history even though its controlling shareholders (owners) may change. As a result, the corporation must continue to use accounting methods adopted by previous owners. An additional serious problem with buying a corporation is that all the tax problems created by previous owners continue and could result in unexpected liabilities for the new owner.

Constructed Assets

Taxpayers who construct property for their own use must capitalize both the direct and indirect construction costs.[13] **Direct construction costs** are those costs actually incurred to physically construct the asset. Examples of direct costs include materials, labor, supplies, architectural fees, and payments to subcontractors. **Indirect construction costs** are other general costs of the business that indirectly support the construction project. Indirect costs include interest on funds to finance the construction, taxes, general administrative costs, depreciation on equipment, and pension costs for workers on the project. Because all the indirect costs are costs that are normally expensed in the period incurred, the effect of capitalizing them as part of the asset's cost is to delay the tax deduction for the costs. The value of the time the taxpayer devotes to the construction of the asset is not included in the property's basis.

▲ **EXAMPLE 21**   Fred is constructing a building for use in his business. The land cost $20,000, direct labor costs were $40,000, and the cost of construction materials totaled $35,000. Fred paid architects, subcontractors, and permit fees totaling $85,000. The interest on his construction loan was $10,000. In addition, Fred considers his allocation of $7,000 in indirect administrative costs to the construction activity to be reasonable. The value of Fred's time related to the building's construction was $4,000. Fred's income taxes for the year were $40,000. What is Fred's basis in the building?

Discussion: Fred's cost basis in the land is $20,000 and in the building is $177,000. His cost basis in the building includes direct labor, direct materials, other costs directly related to the construction of the building, and a reasonable allocation of indirect costs. The building's cost does not include the $4,000 value of Fred's time. The income taxes are not related to the construction and are not allocated to the building. Fred's cost basis in the building is composed of the following:

Direct labor	$ 40,000
Direct materials	35,000
Other direct costs	85,000
Construction interest	10,000
Allocated indirect costs	7,000
Cost basis in building	$177,000

Note that the effect of the requirement that indirect costs be allocated to the building is to reduce the current year's deductions by the $17,000 in interest and allocated indirect costs that are not allowed as current-year deductions. These costs will have to be recovered over the life of the building through depreciation deductions.

Although the general rule is that the initial basis of property is its cost as measured by the amount paid by the taxpayer to acquire and place the property in service, several situations require the use of a different basis. In the transfers considered next, the property's initial basis may be its fair market value, the adjusted basis in the hands of a prior owner, or a basis determined by referring to the basis in a related asset. The discussion that follows explains special valuation rules that apply when property has been acquired by means other than an arm's-length transaction.

SPECIALLY VALUED PROPERTY ACQUISITIONS

BASIS OF PROPERTY ACQUIRED BY GIFT

In Chapter 4, a **gift** was defined as a transfer of property proceeding from a "detached and disinterested generosity . . . out of affection, respect, admiration, charity, or like impulses."[14] Thus, by definition, a transfer of property from a donor to a donee is not a profit-motivated, arm's-length transaction. Neither the donor nor the donee recognizes any income or pays income tax on the transfer of gift property. However, the donor may be subject to a gift tax imposed on the transfer, based on the fair market value of the gift. Whether the donor must pay a gift tax depends on several factors, including the fair market value of the gift, total gifts made during the year, and exclusions and credits that the donor may use to reduce or eliminate the gift tax. Although computation of the gift tax is a topic that is beyond the scope of this discussion, considering the effect of the gift tax on the basis of an asset is necessary.

The receipt of property by gift and the payment of gift tax on the transfer ultimately have an income tax effect. The donee may have to determine the property's income tax basis on the date of gift in order to compute depreciation, depletion, or amortization deductions. In addition, the property's adjusted basis must be calculated upon disposition of the property to determine the income tax effect of the disposition. Depending on the property's adjusted basis in the hands of the donor, the fair market value of the asset on the date of gift, the amount of gift tax paid, and the amount received upon disposition of the property, the appropriate basis could be any one of three different amounts.

General Rule for Gift Basis

Because there is no realization upon the transfer of property from one taxpayer to another as a gift, the general rule for gift property is that the basis of the donor carries over to the donee. This result holds as long as the fair market value of the property on the date of gift is greater than the donor's adjusted basis for the property (i.e., the property has appreciated in value). Thus, the tax law allows the transfer of unrealized gains from one taxpayer to another through the use of gifts.

▲ **EXAMPLE 22**   Sanh owns stock worth $10,000 for which he paid $2,000 this year. Sanh is a 31% marginal tax rate payer. Sanh's son needs $10,000 to pay for college tuition next year. Sanh must sell the stock to come up with the cash necessary to pay his son's college expenses. Sanh's son is a 15% marginal tax rate payer. Should Sanh sell the stock or gift it to his son to sell?

Discussion: Sanh should gift the stock and have his son sell it. If Sanh sells the stock, the $8,000 gain will result in a tax of $2,480 ($8,000 × 31%). By gifting the stock to his son, the $8,000 gain is effectively transferred to the son through the carryover of basis. His son will pay a tax of only $1,200 ($8,000 × 15%) on the $8,000 gain. Thus, Sanh will save $1,280 ($2,480 − $1,200) by gifting the stock to his son to sell.

In addition to the carryover of basis, any gift tax paid by the donor on the net appreciation in the value of the property is treated as a capital expenditure and is added to the donee's basis. The donee's basis in gift property received is the donor's adjusted basis plus the gift tax paid on the asset's net appreciation (i.e., the increase in the asset's value while it was owned by the donor).[15] The pattern of the values in the transaction can be represented as follows:

Date Determined	Value Pattern	Basis
At the date of gift	Fair market value of gift *is greater than* donor's adjusted basis.	Donor's adjusted basis plus gift tax on net appreciation is used to compute gain, loss, and depreciation.

The calculation to determine the donee's basis on the date of the gift is

Donor's adjusted basis on date of gift $X,XXX

Plus: Gift tax paid by donor on net appreciation

$$\frac{\text{FMV of gift} \quad \text{Less} \quad \text{Donor's adjusted basis}}{\text{FMV of gift}} \times \text{Gift tax paid} = \text{XXX}$$

Equals: Donee's basis on date of gift $X,XXX

The sum of the donor's adjusted basis on the date of gift plus the gift tax related to the net appreciation in value may not be greater than the asset's fair market value on the date of gift. The application of this formula automatically imposes the fair market value limitation.

> ▲ **EXAMPLE 23**   Elena purchases 10 acres of land in 1976 for $40,000. On January 20, 1996, Elena gives the land to her son, Demetri. Elena pays $5,000 in gift tax on the transfer based on the land's $50,000 fair market value. What is Demetri's basis in the land received from Elena?
>
> *Discussion:*   Demetri has a basis of $41,000 in the land he receives from his mother. Demetri's basis is Elena's adjusted basis of $40,000 plus the $1,000 in gift tax paid on the appreciation in the value of the asset. The gift tax on the net appreciation while the land was owned by Elena is added to Demetri's basis [$1,000 = ($10,000 appreciation ÷ $50,000 fair market value of gift) × $5,000 gift tax paid)].

Split Basis Rule for Loss Property

Although the general rule for gifts allows the transfer of unrealized gains from one taxpayer to another, the result does not hold true for loss transfers. If the fair market value of the property at the date of the gift is less than the donor's basis, a split basis rule applies. A **split basis rule for gifts** means that the property has one basis for determining gains and a separate basis for determining losses upon disposition. Thus, the basis of a gift of a loss property depends on the sale price of the asset upon its disposition. The basis for determining gains is the donor's adjusted basis.[16] The basis for determining losses and for computing depreciation is the fair market value on the date of the gift.[17] The use of the split basis rule for gifts effectively eliminates the transfer of unrealized losses from one taxpayer to another by gift. The pattern of the gift values that invoke the special rules can be represented as follows:

Date Determined	Value Pattern	Basis
	Donor's adjusted basis	Donor's adjusted basis is used to compute gain.
On the date of gift	*is greater than*	
	fair market value of gift.	Fair market value is used to compute a loss and depreciation.

If the property is sold for an amount between the basis for gain and the basis for loss, the basis is assumed to be equal to the selling price.

Whenever the fair market value is less than the donor's basis at the date of the gift, any gift tax paid by the donor is not capitalized as part of the donee's basis in the gift property, because the property has not appreciated. Remember that only gift tax paid on net appreciation can be added to the donor's basis. As a result of not adding gift tax on a loss property, the donee's basis can never be more than the donor's adjusted basis.

▲ **EXAMPLE 24**   Assume that in example 23 Elena's adjusted basis is $40,000, the fair market value of the land on the date of gift is $28,000, and that Elena paid $3,000 in gift tax on the transfer based on the land's $28,000 fair market value. What is Demetri's basis in the land if Demetri sells the land for $46,000? for $24,000?

Discussion: Demetri's gain basis in the land is his mother's $40,000 adjusted basis. Because the fair market value of the property at the date of gift is less than Elena's adjusted basis, none of the gift tax can be added to basis. Demetri will report a $6,000 ($46,000 − $40,000) gain on the sale of the land.

   If Demetri sells the land for $24,000, his basis for computing a loss on the sale of the land is the $28,000 fair market value on the date of the gift. Demetri has a loss on the sale of $4,000 ($24,000 − $28,000).

Special Sales Price Basis.   At this point, the donee has a dilemma if the property is sold for less than its adjusted basis but for more than its fair market value on the date of gift. In this special situation, the donee should not report a gain or a loss. The property's basis is considered to be the same as the sales price.

▲ **EXAMPLE 25**   Refer to example 24. Assume that Demetri sells the land for $33,000.

Discussion: Demetri's gain basis is Elena's $40,000 adjusted basis. However, use of his gain basis produces a loss. His loss basis is the $28,000 fair market value on the date of gift. Here, use of the loss basis produces a gain. As a result, Demetri will not report gain or loss on the sale of the land. His basis ($33,000) will be the same as the sales price ($33,000).

Holding Period

The holding period for gifts follows the general rules for determining holding period. Whenever the donor's adjusted basis is used to compute a gain or loss on the donee's disposition of property received by gift, the donee's holding period includes the period of time the property was owned by both the donor and the donee.[18] As stated earlier, whenever a carryover basis is used, the holding period of the previous owner carries over to the new owner. However, if fair market value is used as the gift's basis, the donee's holding period begins on the date of gift. When fair market value is used, there is no carryover of basis and thus no carryover of holding period.

BASIS OF PROPERTY ACQUIRED BY INHERITANCE

When a person dies (decedent), a personal representative (executor) is appointed to determine the value of property owned by the person on the date of death, pay estate taxes, and distribute the remaining assets to the heirs of the estate. The property owned on the date of death is normally valued at its fair market value at the date of death,[19] or the executor may elect to use the fair market value on the alternate valuation date. The total value of the assets may be subject to a transfer tax called the *estate tax*. Whether an estate tax is paid depends on the size of the estate and the dollar amount of estate tax exemptions and credits that the estate can use to reduce the tax.

   Property passing from a decedent to an heir receives a fair market value basis. The property's new basis is stepped up or stepped down from the decedent's adjusted basis to its fair market value. Because of elections available to an executor, the executor can use one of three dates to establish the fair market value of assets owned on the date of death. These dates are the date of death, an alternate valuation date, and the distribution date. Because the assets owned at the date of the decedent's death are valued per the estate tax rules, the heirs have no control over the valuation of the assets.

Primary Valuation Date

The general rule for the initial basis of inherited property is its fair market value on the date of the deceased owner's death. The date of death is called the **primary valuation date.** Absent any special elections by the executor of the estate, the date of death is used to value the assets of the estate. The adjusted basis of the decedent does not carry over to an heir. Because fair market value establishes the heirs' basis, none of the estate tax paid may be used to increase the basis of inherited property. Under the holding period rules, **inherited property** is always treated as held for more than a year, even if the decedent bought it the day before dying and the heir sold it the day after the deceased's death.

▲ **EXAMPLE 26**   Sam dies on January 1, 1996. On the date of his death, he owned 100 shares of Dandy common stock. He purchased the stock 5 years ago for $500. The stock trades for $50 per share on January 1, 1996, $75 per share on April 15, 1996, and $45 per share on July 1, 1996. The Dandy stock is inherited by Betty, Sam's daughter. What is Betty's basis in the stock?

Discussion: Betty's initial basis for the stock is its $5,000 fair market value on the day of Sam's death (100 shares × $50). If Betty sells the stock on the day after she receives it from Sam's estate, she reports it as having been held for more than one year.

Alternate Valuation Date

The executor of the estate may elect not to use the primary valuation date to value the assets of the estate. The **alternate valuation date** is six months after the date of the decedent's death.

Alternate Valuation Date
6 Months after Death

1/1/96 ⟶ 7/1/96
Fair market   Fair market value
value at death   at alternate date

The alternate valuation date may be used only if *all three* of the following conditions are met:

■ The alternate value of the total estate is less than the value on the date of death.

■ The total estate tax based on the alternate value of the estate's assets is less than the tax due based on the date of death asset valuation.

■ The executor of the estate uses the alternative valuation date to compute the estate tax.[20]

▲ **EXAMPLE 27**   Refer to example 26. Assume that the executor elects to value Sam's estate on the alternate valuation date. The election reduces the amount of Sam's gross estate and the estate taxes. What is Betty's basis in the stock?

Discussion: Betty's basis for gain or loss on disposition of the stock is $4,500, its fair market value on July 1, 1996 (100 shares × $45). If Betty sells the stock on the day after she receives it from Sam's estate, she reports it as being held for more than one year.

Distribution Date

Although an executor may elect to use the alternate valuation date for the estate, specific assets may be distributed to beneficiaries before the end of the six-month period.

When the alternate valuation date has been elected and property is distributed before the six-month valuation date, its basis is its fair market value on the date it is distributed from the estate. The assets still held by the estate on the alternate valuation date are assigned a basis equal to their fair market value on the alternate date. Assets may not be valued at a date later than the alternate valuation date.

Alternate Valuation Date
6 Months after Death

1/1/96 ———————— Distribution Date ————————→ 7/1/96

Fair market value at death	Fair market value of an asset distributed before alternate valuation date	Fair market value at alternate date

▲ **EXAMPLE 28**   Refer to example 26. Assume that the executor elects the alternate valuation date. Also assume that the executor transfers the stock to Betty on April 15, 1996. The alternate valuation date election reduces the amount of Sam's gross estate and the estate taxes. What is Betty's basis in the stock?

Discussion: Betty's initial basis for gain or loss on disposition of the stock is its $7,500 fair market value on April 15, 1996 (100 shares × $75). The stock is valued in Sam's estate at $75 per share. If Betty sells the stock on the day after she receives it from Sam's estate, she reports it as being held for more than one year. Other assets still held by the estate at the end of the six-month period have a basis equal to their fair market value on the alternate valuation date.

▲ **EXAMPLE 29**   Refer to example 26. Assume that the executor elects the alternate valuation date. Also assume that the executor transfers the stock to Betty on October 15, 1996, when the shares are trading for $85. The alternate valuation date election reduces the amount of Sam's gross estate and the estate taxes. What is Betty's basis in the stock?

Discussion: Betty's basis for gain or loss on disposition of the stock is $4,500, its fair market value on July 1, 1996 (100 shares × $45). The latest that assets can be valued is the alternate valuation date. The value on the date of distribution applies only when the alternate date is elected and property is distributed before the alternate date.

Other Considerations

Any unrealized gain on property held by a decedent on the date of death escapes income taxation. On the other hand, unrealized losses at the date of death will never be allowed as an income tax deduction. If a taxpayer sells an appreciated asset and then dies before the sales proceeds are spent or given away, the gain is subject to income tax and the sales proceeds still held on the date of death are subject to the estate tax. If possible, a taxpayer should continue to own appreciated assets and let them pass through the estate to step up their basis to fair market value. When the estate or an heir sells the appreciated asset after the date of death, no income tax is paid on the appreciation in value during the time the decedent held the property. On the other hand, if a loss asset is sold before death, the loss can be deducted for income tax, whereas the fair market value of the asset (i.e., the sale proceeds) is subject to estate tax. Thus, the taxpayer can receive the benefit of a loss deduction for income tax purposes that would be lost if the property is held at death. The estate tax value would be about the same amount, because it is assessed on a stepped-down basis.

▲ **EXAMPLE 30**   Frank has a serious heart problem and is near death. He owns stock that has a cost basis of $10,000 and has a fair market value of $90,000. Should Frank sell the stock?

Discussion: If Frank sells the stock, he must report $80,000 in gain on the sale. Unless Frank can find a way to get the $90,000 in sale proceeds out of his estate, the full $90,000 may also be subject to estate tax. Thus, the appreciation on the stock is subject to both income and estate tax. By continuing to hold the stock, no income tax will be paid on the $80,000 unrealized appreciation in the value of the stock. Frank should not sell the stock.

▲ **EXAMPLE 31**   Based on the information in example 30, should Frank sell the stock if its fair market value is only $1,000?

Discussion: If the stock is worth only $1,000, Frank could sell the stock and recognize a $9,000 loss on the sale. If the sale proceeds are still held on the day he dies, only $1,000 would be included in his gross estate. Frank benefits by the amount of the income tax savings on the $9,000 tax loss if he sells the stock before he dies.

If a husband and wife own property as tenants by the entirety or as joint tenants with the right of survivorship, each is treated as owning half the property. When one dies, the survivor's basis in the property is the adjusted basis of the survivor's half-interest plus the fair market value of the other half-interest inherited from the deceased spouse.

▲ **EXAMPLE 32**   Ralph and Mae paid $50,000 for their home in 1970, which they own as tenants by the entirety. When Ralph died this year, estate tax appraisals placed the fair market value of the home at $140,000 on the date of death and $135,000 on the alternate valuation date. The executor of Ralph's estate elected the alternate valuation date. What is Mae's basis in the home?

Discussion: Mae's basis in the home is $92,500 ($25,000 + $67,500). Mae should add the cost basis of her half-interest ($25,000) to the fair market value on the valuation date used by the executor for the half-interest she inherited from Ralph ($67,500 = ¹/₂ × $135,000).

When people who are not married own a joint interest in property, the survivor's basis in the property is the amount the survivor actually paid toward the purchase of the asset plus the fair market value of the inherited interest.

▲ **EXAMPLE 33**   Assume in example 32 that Ralph and Mae are brother and sister. In addition, Mae paid $10,000 for a 20% joint tenant interest in the home, which cost $50,000 in 1970. The executor of Ralph's estate elected the alternate valuation date. What is Mae's basis in the home?

Discussion: Mae's basis in the home is $118,000 ($10,000 + $108,000). Mae should add the cost basis of her 20% interest ($10,000 = 20% × $50,000) to the fair market value on the valuation date used by the executor for the 80% interest she inherited from Ralph ($108,000 = 80% × $135,000).

PROPERTY ACQUIRED FROM A SPOUSE

When property is acquired from a spouse by gift or purchase, the basis of the property carries over from one person to the other. Because the transfer is to a related party, the realization concept is not applied, resulting in "giftlike" treatment. Neither spouse recognizes a gain or loss from the transaction, and the property has a carryover basis. Unlike a gift, the fair market value of the property at the time of the transfer is ignored. Thus, the spouse receiving the property assumes the adjusted basis of the spouse giving up the property for both gain and loss basis.

▲ **EXAMPLE 34**   Juan and Rosita are husband and wife. Juan owns a farm that has an adjusted basis to him of $150,000. Juan wants Rosita to own the farm as her separate asset. To accomplish the transfer of ownership, Rosita has agreed to purchase the farm from Juan for $300,000. What is Rosita's basis in the farm?

Discussion: If Rosita buys the farm from Juan for $300,000, her basis in the farm is $150,000. The purchase price is disregarded, because the transaction is treated as a gift (substance over form controls this situation). Also, Juan will not realize a taxable gain from the sale of the farm. Juan's adjusted basis carries over and becomes Rosita's basis. If Rosita and Juan decide that a sale is not appropriate and Juan makes a gift of the farm to Rosita, her basis remains at $150,000.

▲ **EXAMPLE 35**   What is Rosita's basis in the farm in example 34 if she buys it from Juan for $100,000?

Discussion: If Rosita buys the farm from Juan for $100,000, her basis in the farm is still $150,000. Regardless of the amount Rosita pays for the farm, the purchase price is disregarded. Juan will not realize a deductible loss from the sale of the farm. Juan's $150,000 adjusted basis becomes Rosita's basis.

The carryover basis rule also applies when property is received from a former spouse incident to a divorce.[21] Property received within one year after a marriage ends is considered incident to divorce. Later transfers are also subject to the carryover basis rule if they are related to the cessation of the marriage. Transfers made under the terms of a divorce or separation agreement within six years of the date the marriage ends are considered related to the cessation of the marriage.

▲ **EXAMPLE 36**   Kelly and Marsha divorce on June 1, 1994. Marsha owns the family home she inherited from her parents. Her basis in the home is $75,000, and its fair market value on June 1, 1994, is $100,000. Under the terms of their divorce agreement, Marsha retains possession of the family home until June 1, 1996. On that date, she is required to deed ownership of the home to Kelly. What is Kelly's basis in the home when it is transferred to him on June 1, 1996?

Discussion: When Kelly receives ownership of the home from Marsha on June 1, 1996, the transfer is considered related to the cessation of the marriage. As a result, the transfer receives giftlike treatment, and Marsha's $75,000 basis carries over to Kelly.

Because the original basis of the spouse carries over, the holding period of the original owner carries over to the subsequent owner. The holding period for the property includes the time owned by the acquiring spouse plus the time held by the spouse giving up the property.

PERSONAL USE PROPERTY CONVERTED TO BUSINESS USE

When property held for personal use is changed to property held for a business purpose, a split basis problem similar to the special valuation rule for gifts may develop. The split basis problem arises from the legislative grace concept's disallowance of personal deductions. Depending on the facts at the time the asset is changed to business use, the asset may have a basis equal to its adjusted basis, its fair market value, or its value on disposition. Because the asset may be subject to depreciation, depletion, or amortization while it is used in the business activity, the correct basis must be identified to compute the annual deduction.

General Rule for Basis

If the fair market value of personal use property is more than its adjusted basis on the date business use begins, the general basis rule applies. The asset's adjusted basis is used to compute depreciation and gain or loss on its disposition. As the asset is used in the business, its basis must be further reduced by depreciation allowed or allowable in computing taxable income.

> ▲ **EXAMPLE 37**   Mary purchases her home for $100,000 in 1992. The purchase price is properly allocated as $90,000 to the structure and $10,000 to the land. Because of tremendous growth in her business, she needs office space for her employees and herself. In 1996, she pays a contractor $15,000 to convert her home into suitable office space. At the date the home is changed to business property, the house is appraised at $130,000 and the land at $20,000. What is Mary's basis in the building for business purposes?
>
> *Discussion:*   Mary's basis in the office building is $105,000 ($90,000 + $15,000). Her business basis is her adjusted basis of $90,000 plus the $15,000 cost of improvements to prepare it for business use. The $10,000 basis of the land also carries over to the business.
>
> The $105,000 basis also is used to compute depreciation on the building. If Mary deducts depreciation totaling $8,000 and then sells the property, her adjusted basis is $107,000 ($105,000 building less $8,000 depreciation plus $10,000 basis of the land). Her gain or loss on the sale is computed by comparing the sales price to her $107,000 adjusted basis.

Split Basis Rule

If the fair market value of personal use property is less than its adjusted basis on the date it is changed to business use, it will have one basis for gain and a different basis for loss and depreciation.[22] An expense must be incurred for a business purpose to be deductible. The legislative grace concept prohibits the deduction of personal living expenses or losses related to a personal use asset. Because the property's loss of value occurred while it was held for personal use, the lost value cannot be deducted. The **split basis rules for business property** prevent the deduction of the disallowed personal loss through depreciation or as a loss from the sale of a business asset. The following basis rules apply when the personal use asset's fair market value is less than its adjusted basis on the date it changes to business property:

- The initial basis for gain is the property's adjusted basis on the conversion date.

- The initial basis for loss and depreciation is the property's fair market value on the conversion date.

- If the property is later sold for an amount that falls between the adjusted basis for gain and the adjusted basis for loss, the adjusted basis for the sale is the sales price.

The pattern of the values involved in this situation can be diagramed as follows:

Date Determined	Value Pattern	Basis
At the date business use begins	Adjusted basis *is greater than* fair market value	Adjusted basis is used to compute a gain. Fair market value is used to compute a loss and depreciation.

If the property is sold for an amount between the basis for gain and the basis for loss, the basis is assumed to be equal to the sales price.

▲ **EXAMPLE 38**   Latoya owns a personal use asset that cost her $50,000 five years ago. During the current year, when the asset's fair market value was $30,000, she started using the asset in her business. What is Latoya's basis in the asset for business purposes?

Discussion: The nondeductible loss in value related to personal use is $20,000 ($50,000 − $30,000 fair market value). Because the fair market value is less than adjusted basis, depreciation is calculated using the $30,000 fair market value. Using the lower value avoids deduction of the loss of value attributable to personal use. The basis for determining gain is the $50,000 adjusted basis before conversion to business use.

▲ **EXAMPLE 39**   Refer to example 38. Assume that after deducting $7,000 in depreciation on the asset, Latoya sells it for $60,000. What is Latoya's gain or loss on the sale?

Discussion: In order to determine the appropriate basis, Latoya must subtract the $7,000 in depreciation from both the gain basis and the loss basis to arrive at the adjusted basis for gain and for loss. Latoya's adjusted basis on the date of sale is calculated as follows:

	Gain Basis	Loss Basis
Initial basis at date converted	$50,000	$30,000
Less: Depreciation deducted while used in business (based on FMV)	(7,000)	(7,000)
Adjusted basis at date of sale	$43,000	$23,000

The $60,000 sales price means that the asset was sold at a gain. Therefore, the $43,000 adjusted basis for computing gain is used to determine that Latoya has a $17,000 gain on the sale.

▲ **EXAMPLE 40**   Assume the same facts as in example 39, except that Latoya sells the asset for $20,000. What is Latoya's gain or loss on the sale?

Discussion: The $20,000 sales price means that the asset is sold at a loss. Therefore, the $23,000 adjusted basis for determining loss is used to determine that Latoya has realized a loss of $3,000 on the sale.

▲ **EXAMPLE 41**   Assume the same facts as in example 39, except that Latoya sells the asset for $35,000. What is Latoya's gain or loss on the sale?

Discussion: When the $35,000 sales price is compared to the $43,000 gain basis, a loss results. Similarly, comparison with the $23,000 loss basis results in a gain. Therefore, the adjusted basis is equal to the selling price, and neither gain nor loss is realized on the sale.

Example 40 illustrates that any loss related to the period of personal use is not allowed as a deduction because of the split basis rule. The use of fair market value for computing depreciation also prevents taxpayers from recovering personal use losses through depreciation deductions. Also, note that the split basis rule is similar to the gift split basis rule in that it applies when property with an unrealized loss is converted from personal use to business use. Depreciation is calculated using the fair market value.

BASIS IN SECURITIES

Acquiring securities is usually straightforward. The initial basis is equal to the cost paid to acquire the security. The cost of a security includes the purchase price and any commissions paid on the purchase.[23] In certain circumstances, a taxpayer acquires securities subject to special rules or does so without paying a purchase price. These situations include the receipt of stock dividend shares, stock issued in a tax-free transfer to a controlled corporation, and shares acquired in a wash sale.

Stock Dividends

Most **stock dividends** are nontaxable dividends. When additional shares of a corporation's stock are received as a nontaxable dividend, part of the basis of the original stock must be allocated to the new stock received as a dividend.[24] Because the basis of the new shares is made by referring to the basis of the old shares, the holding period for the new shares of stock includes the holding period of the old shares. If the stock received as a dividend is the same class as the original stock, the allocation is made by using the following formula:

$$\text{Basis per share} = \text{Original cost} \div \text{Total shares held after dividend}$$

▲ **EXAMPLE 42**   Reginald owns 200 shares of Arko common stock for which he paid $22,000 on December 14, 1993. On July 8, 1996, Arko declares and distributes a 10% stock dividend. Reginald receives 20 additional shares of Arko common stock from the dividend. What is Reginald's basis in the 220 shares of stock he owns?

Discussion: Reginald must allocate part of the $22,000 original basis of the 200 shares to the basis of the 20 new shares. The total basis of the 220 shares remains at $22,000. However, the basis per share of the 220 shares is now $100. All 220 shares are deemed to have been held since December 15, 1993.

$$\text{Basis before dividend} = \$22,000 \div 200 = \$110 \text{ per share}$$
$$\text{Basis after dividend} \ \ = \$22,000 \div 220 = \$100 \text{ per share}$$

If the dividend shares are of a different class of stock than the original stock, the original basis is allocated according to the relative fair market values of the original stock and the stock received as a dividend.[25] Fair market values are determined on the date the new shares are distributed by the corporation. If, for example, preferred stock is distributed as a dividend to common stockholders, the allocation of the original basis is made by using the following formulas:

$$\frac{\text{Basis of}}{\text{preferred stock}} = \frac{\text{FMV of preferred stock}}{\left\{ \begin{array}{c} \text{FMV of preferred stock} \\ + \\ \text{FMV of common stock} \end{array} \right\}} \times \begin{array}{c} \text{Original} \\ \text{common stock} \\ \text{basis} \end{array}$$

$$\frac{\text{Basis of}}{\text{common stock}} = \frac{\text{FMV of common stock}}{\left\{ \begin{array}{c} \text{FMV of preferred stock} \\ + \\ \text{FMV of common stock} \end{array} \right\}} \times \begin{array}{c} \text{Original} \\ \text{common stock} \\ \text{basis} \end{array}$$

▲ **EXAMPLE 43**   Mac Corporation distributed to its common shareholders 1 share of preferred stock for each share of common stock they held on the record date. The common stock had a $50 per share market value, and the preferred stock had a $20 per share market value on the stock dividend distribution date. Asha, a Mac Corporation shareholder, owned 100 shares of common stock on the record date. She had purchased the common stock on March 9, 1990, for $3,000. Asha received 100 shares of preferred stock as a dividend. What is Asha's basis in the stock?

Discussion: Asha's $3,000 basis in the common stock must be allocated between the common and preferred stock in proportion to their relative market values on the date the stock dividend is distributed. Asha's basis in the preferred stock is $857, and her basis in the common stock is $2,143. The basis of each type of stock is determined as follows:

$$\text{Market value of preferred stock} = 100 \times \$20 = \$2,000$$
$$\text{Market value of common stock} = 100 \times \$50 = \underline{5,000}$$
$$\text{Total market value} \qquad\qquad\qquad\qquad \underline{\underline{\$7,000}}$$

Allocation of $3,000 original cost:

$$\text{Preferred} = (\$2,000 \div \$7,000) \times \$3,000 = \$857 \text{ or } \$8.57 \text{ per share}$$
$$\text{Common} = (\$5,000 \div \$7,000) \times \$3,000 = \$2,143 \text{ or } \$21.43 \text{ per share}$$

The holding period for both the common and preferred stock begins on March 10, 1990, the day after Asha originally purchased the common shares.

Taxable Stock Dividends.   Whenever the shareholder has the option of receiving cash or stock as a dividend, the dividend is taxable even if the shareholder elects to receive the stock. The amount of taxable income from the dividend is the fair market value of the shares on the date of distribution. In the case of a taxable stock dividend, the shareholder has a basis equal to the amount of income recognized.[26] The inclusion of the income recognized in the basis of the shares is necessary to ensure that the income is not taxed twice. Because the basis of the dividend is made by reference to the fair market value, the holding period of the shares begins on the date of distribution.

▲ **EXAMPLE 44**   Tanya purchases 500 shares of Upubco common stock on January 18, 1993, at a total cost of $4,600. On April 12, 1996, Upubco declares a 10% stock dividend with the option to receive $8 cash in lieu of taking the dividend shares. The dividend is distributed on June 15, 1996, when the fair market value of the stock is $8 per share. What are the tax effects for Tanya if she elects to take the cash option?

Discussion: Tanya recognizes the $400 [(500 × 10%) × $8] in cash received as income when she receives the cash. The basis of her original 500 shares is unaffected by the dividend.

▲ **EXAMPLE 45**   Assume that in example 44 Tanya elects to receive the stock instead of taking the cash option. What are the tax effects for Tanya?

Discussion: Because a cash option is available, Tanya must recognize the fair market value of the stock received on the date of distribution. Her taxable income is $400 [(500 × 10%) × $8]. Her basis in the 50 dividend shares is the $400 in income recognized. The holding period for the new shares begins on June 16, 1996. The basis of the original 500 shares is unaffected by the dividend.

Transfers of Assets to a Controlled Corporation

A special tax provision permits the transfer of assets and related liabilities to a corporation in exchange for the corporation's stock in a tax-free transaction. This provision is referred to as a *Section 351 transfer*. To qualify for this special treatment, the person(s) transferring property must own 80 percent or more of the corporation's stock immediately after the exchange of the property for stock.

The transfer is not taxable, because a realization is not deemed to occur with respect to the assets transferred. Whoever transfers the assets has a continuing proprietary interest in the assets that is represented by ownership of the corporation's stock. Thus, Section 351 permits a tax-free incorporation of a business by treating the transaction as a mere change in the form of the entity. As a result, the shareholder's basis in the stock received in the exchange generally is the same as the basis of the assets transferred to the corporation. The shareholder has a carryover basis in the stock. In some instances, a Section 351 transfer does require recognizing gain, which has the effect of increasing the shareholder's basis in the stock. Although this topic is best left for a corporate tax course, you should be aware of the availability of this tax-planning opportunity for incorporating a business tax free.

▲ **EXAMPLE 46**   Ted owned Ted's Store, a proprietorship. Ted's basis in the assets used in Ted's Store was $25,000. Also, Ted owed $1,000 in liabilities related to the business. Ted decided to incorporate Ted's Store in a tax-free transaction. The new corporation was named Video, Inc. Ted transferred all the proprietorship's assets and liabilities to the corporation in exchange for 100 shares of its stock. After the exchange, Ted owned 100% of Video, Inc.'s outstanding stock. What is the tax effect of the exchange?

Discussion: Ted's tax basis in the 100 shares of Video, Inc.'s stock is $24,000. The transfer of Ted's Store's assets and liabilities to the corporation is merely a change in the form of organization used to conduct the business. Ted's proprietary interest in the business assets used by Ted's Store is now represented by 100 shares of Video, Inc.'s stock instead of direct ownership of the individual assets. Ted's adjusted basis in Ted's Store's assets carries over to become the basis of the 100 shares of stock—$24,000 ($25,000 asset basis − $1,000 in liabilities assumed by Video, Inc.). Ted has a carryover basis in his Video, Inc., stock because the transaction is nontaxable.

Video, Inc.'s basis in the assets received from Ted is $25,000, and the corporation owes $1,000 in liabilities related to the assets. Because the transaction is nontaxable, Video, Inc., has a carryover basis in the assets it received from Ted in exchange for its stock. The assets are not marked up to fair market value, because the transfer is a change in the form of doing business, not a change in the ownership of the assets.

Wash Sale Stock Basis

A **wash sale** occurs when a security (stock, bond, option, etc.) is sold at a loss and is replaced within 30 days *before or after* the sale date with a substantially identical security.[27] Because the taxpayer's ownership interest has not changed as a result of the sale and repurchase of the stock, the transaction lacks economic substance. Thus, the form of a transaction has been used to create a paper tax loss. As a result, the substance-over-form doctrine applies to the artificial loss. The wash sale loss is not allowed as a current deduction. Deductions for wash sale losses were discussed in Chapter 7.

Because a wash sale loss cannot be used as a current deduction, the taxpayer still has an unrecovered investment in the stock sold. The capital recovery concept permits the unrecovered investment to be added to the basis of the new stock.

▲ **EXAMPLE 47**   Tracy purchases 100 shares of DHI stock for $20,000 in 1990. On December 31, 1996, Tracy sells all 100 shares for $15,000 so she can use the $5,000 capital loss to offset capital gains from other transactions. When the stock market reopens on January 4, 1997, Tracy repurchases 100 shares of DHI for $16,000. What are the tax effects for Tracy of the sale and repurchase of the DHI stock?

Discussion: Because the stock sold at a loss was replaced within 30 days of the sale date, the $5,000 wash sale loss cannot be deducted. The wash sale loss is added to Tracy's basis in the stock purchased on January 4, 1997. Tracy's basis in the DHI stock bought on January 4, 1997, is the sum of the $16,000 cost plus the $5,000 wash sale loss, a total basis of $21,000.

▲ **EXAMPLE 48**   On November 30, 1997, Tracy sells the 100 shares of DHI stock purchased on January 4, 1997, for $29,000. What is Tracy's gain on the sale?

Discussion: Tracy has a gain on the sale of $8,000 ($29,000 − $21,000). Note that the effect of adding the $5,000 in disallowed wash sale loss to the basis of the acquired shares is to decrease the gain on the subsequent sale by the $5,000 loss previously disallowed. That is, Tracy had a gain of $13,000 ($29,000 − $16,000) based on the actual purchase price of the shares. However, the wash sale loss basis adjustment brings the gain down to $8,000.

Example 48 illustrates that a loss from a wash sale is not disallowed forever. The loss is merely deferred until the taxpayer's interest in the replacement stock is disposed of in a taxable transaction. When the replacement stock is sold, the deferred loss is included in the amount subject to capital recovery. As a result, the deferred loss either decreases the gain or increases the loss that would otherwise have been recognized on the sale of the replacement stock.

Frequently, a taxpayer sells shares of stock and then repurchases either a larger or smaller number of replacement shares. If so, the wash sale rule applies on a first-in, first-out basis only to the extent the loss stock is replaced. As a result, a loss on shares of stock not replaced is deductible. Likewise, the basis of the shares of stock purchased in excess of the number of shares sold is not affected by the wash sale.

▲ **EXAMPLE 49**   Assume that in example 47 Tracy repurchases 150 shares of DHI for $24,000 on January 4, 1997. What is her basis in the replacement stock?

Discussion: The wash sale disallowance rule applies only to the shares sold at a loss that are replaced. Thus, the loss on the 100 shares sold is added to the basis of the first 100 shares repurchased during the 30 days before or after the wash sale date. The basis of the 50 shares that are not replacement stock under the wash sale rule is not affected. Tracy's basis is as follows:

Cost of 100 replacement shares	$16,000
Add: Deferred wash sale loss on 100 shares	5,000
Basis of 100 shares reacquired on 1/4/97	$21,000
Basis of extra 50 shares acquired 1/4/97	
($24,000 ÷ 150 = $160 × 50)	$ 8,000

▲ **EXAMPLE 50**   Assume that in example 47 Tracy repurchases only 50 shares of DHI for $8,000. What is her basis in the replacement stock?

Discussion: Because she repurchased only 50 of the 100 shares, the loss on the 50 shares replaced is disallowed and is added to the basis of the replacement shares. Tracy can deduct loss on the 50 shares she did not replace. Tracy's basis in the 50 replacement shares is the sum of the $8,000 replacement cost plus $2,500 [(50 ÷ 100) × $5,000] in deferred loss from the wash sale, $10,500.

SUMMARY

An asset owned by a taxpayer may be classified according to its business, investment, personal, or mixed use. Because deductions are permitted by legislative grace, a deduction for expenses and losses related to personal and mixed-use assets may be limited. Also, assets may be classified as real property, personal property, and intangible property. Personal property, as used in this classification scheme, refers to any tangible property that is not real estate; it does not refer to property held for personal use by the taxpayer.

Amounts allowed as a capital recovery for tax purposes reduce the amount of income that must be recognized under the all-inclusive income concept. If an asset is used for a business purpose, the full amount of the investment will usually be subject to capital recovery, either as the asset is used to earn income or upon its disposition. The tax law requires that a capital recovery be reported in the proper annual accounting period based on the taxpayer's accounting method.

An asset's initial basis on the date acquired must be adjusted over time for amounts that represent additional capital investments and recoveries. The adjusted investment amount is called the asset's *adjusted basis*. Adjusted basis represents the unrecovered capital investment in an asset.

The adjusted basis of an investment in a conduit entity is determined by using an equity accounting method. Thus, increases and decreases in the owner's investment in the conduit entity are reflected in the owner's accounting records and tax returns as the changes take place.

The initial basis of a purchased asset is its cost. Cost includes the purchase price of the asset plus any other costs incurred to acquire and place the asset into service. The purchase price is the sum of any amount paid for the asset in cash, the fair market value of property or services given to the seller, and the assumption of a liability by the buyer. If the purchase price includes more than one asset, it must be reasonably allocated to the individual assets acquired. If goodwill is among the purchased assets, a portion of the purchase price must be allocated to goodwill. The basis of a self-constructed asset includes all direct and indirect costs related to construction of the asset.

When property is received as a gift, the general rule provides that the donee receives a carryover of the donor's basis. If the fair market value of the gift is greater than the donor's basis, the gift tax paid by the donor on the net appreciation in the value of the asset is added to the donee's basis. When the fair market value of the gift is less than the donor's basis (the property has an unrealized loss) the split basis rule applies. The split basis rule provides that the donee's basis for gain is the donor's basis and the basis for loss is the fair market value of the gift. If the asset is sold for a price that falls between the special gain basis and loss basis, the basis is equal to the selling price and no gain or loss results from the disposition.

Inherited property generally has a basis equal to the asset's fair market value on the date of the original owners's death. As an alternative, the executor of the estate may elect to value the estate's assets six months later, on the alternate valuation date.

The transfer of property between spouses by gift or sale does not have an income tax effect. The basis of the property remains·the same in the hands of either spouse. The transfer between spouses is treated like a gift.

When property is converted from personal to business use, a split basis problem can result. The tax treatment is similar to the split basis rule for gifts. The basis for gain is the property's adjusted basis, and the basis for loss (and depreciation) is an adjusted fair market value. As with gifts, if the sales price falls between the gain basis and the loss basis, the basis is equal to the selling price.

The basis of a taxable stock dividend is the fair market value of the stock on the date it is distributed by the corporation. However, the basis of a nontaxable stock dividend is determined by allocating the taxpayer's investment in the original stock to the old shares and to the new shares received as a dividend.

Section 351 permits the tax-free incorporation of a business. The basis of the assets transferred to the corporation becomes the basis in the stock received from the corporation by the shareholders. A Section 351 transfer is merely a change in the form of the business entity, and no adjustments to the basis of the assets transferred to the corporation are made. A loss on a wash sale is added to the basis of the replacement securities.

Table 10–2 summarizes the basis rules discussed in this chapter. The table briefly states how the asset's basis is determined according to how an asset was acquired.

▲ **Table 10–2**

SUMMARY OF BASIS RULES

How Asset Was Acquired	Basis of Asset Acquired
Purchase of a single asset	Cost—Generally, the asset's fair market value on the date purchased plus any other costs incurred to obtain the asset and place it into service.
Purchase of several assets for a single price	Cost—The single purchase price is allocated to individual assets according to their relative fair market values on the date purchased.
Purchase of the assets of a business	Cost—The single purchase price is allocated to individual assets according to their relative fair market values on the date purchased. If the purchase price exceeds the total fair market value of the identifiable assets, the excess is allocated to goodwill.
Purchase of the stock of a corporation	Cost—Purchase price plus any other costs incurred to obtain the stock, such as commissions and legal fees.
Self-constructed assets	Cost—Total direct and indirect construction costs.
Gift:	
Fair market value on date of gift greater than donor's adjusted basis	Donor's adjusted basis plus gift tax on net appreciation.
Fair market value on date of gift less than donor's adjusted basis	Gain—Donor's adjusted basis (gift tax cannot be added to basis). Loss and depreciation—Fair market value on gift date. If asset is sold for an amount that is between the gain basis and the loss basis, the basis is deemed to be equal to the selling price.
Inheritance	Fair market value of the asset on the date of death or alternate valuation date.
Property acquired from a spouse by gift, purchase, or divorce settlement	Cost basis of spouse transferring property carries over to spouse receiving property.
Conversion of personal use property to business use	Gain—Adjusted basis. Loss and depreciation—Lesser of the adjusted basis or the fair market value when put into business use. If asset is sold for an amount that is between the gain basis and the loss basis, the basis is deemed to be equal to the selling price.
Conduit entity	Initial basis determined by how interest in entity was acquired; initial basis is adjusted for investments and recoveries of capital, using an equity accounting method.

(continued on next page)

How Asset Was Acquired	Basis of Asset Acquired
Stock dividend:	
Taxable	Fair market value of stock on distribution date.
Nontaxable	A part of old stock's basis is allocated to the new stock.
Nontaxable transfers to a controlled corporation	Basis of property transferred to corporation carries over to stock received from corporation.
Wash sale stock	Cost of replacement stock plus deferred loss on wash sale.

▲ **Table 10–2** *(continued)*

SUMMARY OF
BASIS RULES

KEY TERMS

adjusted basis (p. 439)
alternative valuation date (p. 455)
amount realized (p. 444)
bargain purchase (p. 447)
carryover basis (p. 445)
conduit entity (p. 442)
direct construction costs (p. 451)
gift (p. 452)
goodwill (p. 448)
indirect construction costs (p. 451)

inherited property (p. 455)
initial basis (p. 438)
intangible property (p. 437)
mixed-use property (p. 436)
multiple asset purchase (p. 447)
personalty (p. 437)
personal use property (p. 436)
primary valuation date (p. 455)
property (p. 435)

property disposition (p. 444)
real estate (p. 437)
realized gain (p. 444)
realized loss (p. 444)
split basis rule for gifts (p. 453)
split basis rules for business property (p. 459)
stock dividend (p. 461)
tangible property (p. 437)
wash sale (p. 463)

[1] Sec. 1016—Prescribes the adjustments that must be made to the basis of property.

[2] Reg. Sec. 1.1016-2—Gives examples of items that are added to basis as adjustments.

[3] Sec. 705—Prescribes the adjustments that must be made to a partner's basis.

[4] Sec. 1367—Prescribes the adjustments that must be made to an S corporation shareholder's basis.

[5] Reg. Sec. 1.1016-3—Requires adjustment of the basis of a depreciable asset even if depreciation was not claimed on the asset.

[6] Sec. 1001—Prescribes the computation of gain or loss on the disposition of property.

[7] Reg. Sec. 1.1223-1—Explains the rules for determining the holding period of assets in different circumstances.

[8] Sec. 1012—States that the general rule for the initial basis of a property is the property's cost.

[9] Crane v. Comm., 331 U.S. 1 (1947)—Held that mortgage debt must be included in the basis of property in order to properly reflect the economic cost of the property.

[10] Reg. Sec. 1.1001-1—Requires adjustment of the selling price (and therefore basis of the buyer) to account for property taxes paid as part of a sales agreement.

[11] Reg. Sec. 1.61-6(a)—Requires a reasonable apportionment of the cost of properties sold to the individual properties.

[12] Sec. 1060—Requires an allocation of the purchase price of the identifiable assets of a business, either by agreement with the seller or by the use of relative fair market values.

[13] Reg. Sec. 1.263A-1—Discusses the uniform capitalization rules as they apply to property constructed by taxpayers for their own use.

[14] Comm. v. Duberstein, 363 U.S. 278 at 283 (1960)—Held that a Cadillac received

PRIMARY TAX LAW SOURCES

by a taxpayer from a businessman to whom he occasionally gave names of potential customers was not a tax-free gift.

[15] Sec. 1015—States that the general rule for the basis of property received by gift is the donor's adjusted basis.

[16] Reg. Sec. 1.1015-1—Explains the split basis rule for gifts and gives examples of the application of the rule.

[17] Perkins v. Comm., 125 F.2d 150 (6th Cir. 1942)—Held that the basis amount for depreciation is the value of the property as of the gift transfer date when fair market value is less than the adjusted basis.

[18] Sec. 1223—Provides the rules for determining the holding period of property.

[19] Sec. 1014—States that the basis of property acquired from a decedent is its fair market value at the date of death, unless the executor elects to value the estate assets on the alternate valuation date.

[20] Sec. 2032—Provides the rules for an executor to elect to value the estate assets at the alternate valuation date.

[21] Sec. 1041—States that transfers between spouses (including transfers incident to a divorce) are treated as gifts for income-recognition and basis purposes.

[22] Reg. Sec. 1.167(g)-1—States that the basis for computing depreciation on personal use property that has been converted to business use is the lesser of the fair market value or the adjusted basis of the property at the date of the conversion.

[23] Reg. Sec. 1.263(a)—Gives examples of capital expenditures; specifically states that the commissions paid on the purchase of securities are capital expenditures.

[24] Sec. 307—Requires the allocation of the adjusted basis of securities to nontaxable dividend shares received.

[25] Reg. Sec. 1.307-1—Requires the allocation of adjusted basis using relative market values when stock of a different class is received in a nontaxable stock dividend.

[26] Sec. 301—States that the basis of stock received in a taxable stock dividend is its fair market value on the date of distribution.

[27] Sec. 1091—Defines a *wash sale* and prescribes the rules for treatment of disallowed losses on wash sales.

DISCUSSION QUESTIONS

1. What effect does a property's use have on the cost recovery allowable on the property?

2. What is the difference between a property's use and its type?

3. Explain the difference between tangible property and intangible property.

4. How is personal property different from personal use property?

5. Explain the role an asset's initial basis plays in determining the income to be recognized upon disposal of the the asset.

6. Explain the difference between a property's initial basis and its adjusted basis.

7. Larry is interested in acquiring a business owned by Jane. If Jane's business is organized as a corporation, what options are available to Larry in acquiring the business? Explain to Larry the difference in the options.

8. What tax problems does a taxpayer encounter when purchasing more than one asset for a single price? Explain.

9. What are the tax implications of a taxpayer's self-construction of assets for use in the taxpayer's trade or business?

10. List some costs, which are normally expensed, that must be capitalized when a taxpayer self-constructs an asset for use in a trade or business.

11. Why are gifts of property not income to the person receiving the gift?

12. A person who receives property as a gift makes no investment in order to receive the property. Why is a basis assignment to the gift property necessary, even though the donee has no investment in the property?

13. What is the general rule for determining the basis of gift property?

14. Janine is planning to make a gift of 50 shares of Acran, Inc., stock to her nephew to help with his college tuition. The stock originally cost Janine $5,000, and its current value is $4,000. Explain to Janine why the gift might not be the best way to achieve her goal.

15. What is the general rule for determining when the holding period of an asset begins?

16. What type(s) of asset acquisitions do not follow the general rule for determining when the holding period of the asset begins?

17. When is the primary valuation date for valuing inherited property? Does the executor of the estate have to do anything to use the primary valuation date?

18. When is the alternate valuation date for valuing inherited property? When elected, are all assets valued on the alternate date? Explain.

19. Are commissions paid to acquire securities a deductible expense? If not, are they ever deductible?

20. What are the tax effects if a sole proprietor converts the business to a corporation?

21. For each of the following assets, determine whether the asset is personal property, real property, intangible property, or personal use property:
    a. Festus purchased a revolver to use in his job as deputy sheriff.
    b. Anthony purchased a building to use as a hair salon. He also purchased 5 hair dryers and 5 specially made salon chairs.
    c. Jamie bought her father a new riding lawn mower for his birthday.
    d. Farmer Milton installed 3 miles of fencing around land on which he intends to graze cattle.
    e. Sidney bought all the assets of Hardcourt's Hardcourt Club for $460,000. The total fair market value of the identifiable assets of Hardcourt was $330,000.
    f. Egbert invented a new light bulb that will last for 20 years. He applied for and received a patent entitling him to exclusive use of the light bulb technology.

PROBLEMS

22. For each of the following assets, determine whether the asset is personal property, real property, intangible property, or personal use property:
    a. Woodrow spent $5,380 on trees and shrubs for use in his landscaping business.
    b. Woodrow spent $12,100 on a new tennis court for the backyard of his personal residence.
    c. Woodrow purchased the trade name Green Gopher Landscaping for $3,400 from the owner of a defunct business.
    d. Woodrow purchased an acre of land with the idea of eventually using it to grow shrubs for resale.
    e. Woodrow purchased an alarm system for the fences surrounding his landscaping business.
    f. Woodrow spent $2,600 on lights for the backyard of his residence.

23. Determine the adjusted basis of each of the following assets:
    a. Chin bought an apartment building at a cost of $180,000. The purchase price was properly allocated as $140,000 to the building and $40,000 to the land. Two years after purchasing the building, Chin installed a new roof at a cost of $5,000. Chin also paid a landscaping service $6,500 to plant some trees and shrubs and build a new walkway. Annual property taxes and maintenance costs on the building total $8,200. Chin has owned the building for 4 years and has deducted the allowable depreciation of $3,500 per year on the building.
    b. Stephanie purchased an automobile three years ago at a cost of $24,000. Stephanie uses the automobile 75% in her business and 25% personal. Stephanie purchased a 5-year repair warranty on the automobile for $3,000. To date, she has deducted the $5,400 in allowable depreciation on the business use portion of the automobile.

24. Determine the adjusted basis of each of the following assets:
    a. André purchases a parcel of land in 1993 at a cost of $17,000. In 1996, the adjoining property owner sues André, claiming that part of André's property belongs to him under the right of adverse possession. André incurs $4,000 in legal fees in successfully defending against the lawsuit. André pays annual property taxes of $300 on the land and has paid $3,700 in interest on the loan he took out to acquire the property.
    b. René purchases 1,000 shares of Cramdem Co. common stock for $8 per share on October 13, 1995. In 1996, Cramdem pays a taxable cash dividend of 30 cents per share. René sells 300 shares on August 22, 1997, for $3 per share. On December 2, 1997, Cramdem pays a nontaxable cash dividend of 10 cents per share.
    c. Rufus owns 12 acres of land he purchased as an investment for $5,000. He spent an additional $37,000 subdividing the land into residential parcels and having utility lines run to the property. After the subdividing and utility lines had been completed, he gifted two acres of the land to his sister as a wedding present.

25. Alberta owns 5 acres of land she purchased several years ago for $6,500. A new housing development is being built on the north side of her property. The owner of the development needs part of Alberta's land to run utility and sewer lines to the new development. The owner offers Alberta $13,000 for half of her land, but Alberta decides to wait to see if the land will appreciate further after the development is built. Alberta agrees to grant the developers an easement to run the utility and sewer lines through her property for $4,000. Write a letter to Alberta explaining the tax consequences of granting the easement.

26. Leineia owns 1,000 shares of Serous Corporation common stock. She paid $26 per share several years ago. On December 31, 1995, Serous Corporation distributes a $5 per share cash dividend. Serous reports that $3 per share is taxable and $2 is a nontaxable dividend. On February 3, 1996, Leineia receives an offer for the stock of $25 per share.
    a. What are the tax effects of the December 31 distribution?
    b. What are the potential tax effects of the sale?

27. Carl Corporation acquires a business use warehouse for $200,000 on January 2, 1989. From 1989 through 1995, Carl Corporation properly deducts $5,000 in depreciation expense annually. During 1995, Carl Corporation incurs a net operating loss. Therefore, Carl deducts no depreciation after 1995. Also, Carl has a $185,000 offer from Kelsa Co. to buy the warehouse. The sale will be completed on July 1, 1997, if Carl accepts the offer. Carla, the CEO of Carl Corporation, comes to your accounting firm for advice. You are asked to review the proposed sale. Write a memorandum explaining the tax results of the proposed transaction.

28. Hannibal owns a farm. He purchases a tractor in 1992 at a cost of $25,000. Because 1992 is a bad year, he does not deduct any depreciation on the tractor in 1992. He sells the tractor in 1996 for $13,000. He takes straight-line depreciation on the tractor of $12,500 for the years 1993 to 1996. The total allowable straight-line depreciation for the tractor for 1992 to 1996 is $15,000. What is Hannibal's gain (loss) on the sale of the tractor? Explain.

29. Jolene owns a dry-cleaning business. During the current year, a rainstorm leaked through her roof and shorted out a dry-cleaning machine. The cost of repairing the machine was $300, none of which was compensated by Jolene's insurance. The adjusted basis of the machine before the casualty was $14,000. What is Jolene's adjusted basis in the machine after the casualty?

30. During the current year, Horace's personal residence was damaged by a tornado. The residence had an adjusted basis of $70,000 before the tornado. The cost of repairing the damage was $15,000. Horace's insurance company reimbursed him $11,000 for the repairs. Horace itemizes his deductions and had an adjusted gross income of $37,000 for the year. What is Horace's adjusted basis in the residence after the tornado?

31. Amos and Thomas formed the Show Corporation during the current year. Amos owns 40% of Show's stock, Thomas owns 20%, and Arthur owns the remaining 40% of the stock. Amos paid $50,000 for his interest, and Thomas paid $25,000. Amos and Thomas are responsible for Show's daily operations and serve as co-chief executive officers. During the current year, Show Corporation had an operating income of $60,000 and paid out $10,000 in dividends. What are Amos's and Thomas's adjusted bases in the Show Corporation stock if

a. Show Corporation is organized as a corporation?

b. Show Corporation is organized as an S corporation?

32. Return to the facts of problem 31. Assume that Show Corporation is organized as an S corporation. In its second year of operations, Show had an operating loss of $40,000 and paid out $20,000 in dividends. On December 31, Amos gave a 10% interest in Show (i.e., 1/4 of his interest) to his son, Buddy. What is Amos's adjusted basis in the Show stock? What is Buddy's adjusted basis in the Show stock?

33. Paula purchases a 40% interest in Dancer Enterprises for $62,000 on January 2, 1996. Dancer is organized as a partnership and has an income of $30,000 in 1996. Dancer also distributes a total of $20,000 to the partners in 1996. What are the tax effects to Paula of her investment in Dancer? What is her adjusted basis in the partnership at the end of 1996?

34. Troy owns 600 of the 1,000 shares outstanding of Oiler Corporation. Troy's adjusted basis in the Oiler stock at the beginning of the current year is $89,000. Oiler Corporation is organized as an S Corporation and reports the following results for the current year:

Operating income before special items	$59,000
Charitable contributions	6,000
Nondeductible expenses	12,000
Cash dividends paid	25,000

a. What is Troy's adjusted basis in the Oiler Corporation stock at the end of the current year?

b. What is the amount of Troy's gain or loss if he sells the 600 shares to an unrelated person at the beginning of next year?

35. Thinh purchases an acre of undeveloped land on December 18, 1996, for $30,000. She makes a down payment of $10,000 and finances the balance with a 5-year, 8% mortgage. Her closing costs include attorney's fees of $200 and document filing fees of $60. During November 1997, Thinh receives an offer of $50,000 for the property. The offer includes a provision that the sale must be completed between December 10 and December 30. Thinh would like to sell, but she is concerned about the tax results of the transaction. Compare the tax and cash-flow results of selling on alternative dates in December.

36. Erin purchases 2 acres of land in 1996 by paying $4,000 in cash at closing and borrowing $40,000 to be repaid at $8,000 per year for the next 5 years with interest on the unpaid balance at 10%. In addition, Erin agrees to allow the seller to store some farm equipment on the land for 2 years (rental value of $1,000 per year). In return, the seller agrees to pay the $800 in points required to obtain the $40,000 loan. Erin also pays legal and abstracting fees of $700 on the purchase. What is Erin's initial basis in the land?

a. In 1997, Erin pays $250 in property tax on the land. In addition, the county paves the road that runs by the land and assesses each taxpayer $1,300 for the paving. What is Erin's adjusted basis in the land at the end of 1997?

b. In 1998, Erin sells 1 acre of the land to her brother for $18,000. What is Erin's gain (loss) on the sale of the land? What is her basis in the remaining acre of land?

37. Florian Corporation purchased a piece of land for investment purposes on April 1. Florian paid the seller $2,000 cash and agreed to pay the seller $3,000 per year for the next 5 years plus interest at 9% per year on the outstanding balance. As part of the purchase agreement, Florian agreed to pay all property taxes for the year, a total of $360. In addition, Florian paid legal fees of $500 connected with the purchase and gave the seller a car worth $4,000 (Florian's basis was $11,000). What is Florian Corporation's basis in the land?

38. Barbara wanted to go into the long-distance trucking business. She bought a used tractor and trailer for $82,000. However, the trailer wasn't suitable for Barbara's needs, so she sold it for $24,000 and purchased the trailer she needed for $30,000. What is Barbara's basis in the tractor? What is Barbara's basis in the trailer?

39. The Lester Partnership wanted to develop a shopping mall. The land it wanted for the mall was formerly a farm. The farmer wanted $260,000 for the land, $80,000 for the farm buildings, and $130,000 for the farmhouse. Although it wanted only the land, Lester agreed to the farmer's terms. Lester then paid Ace Wrecking Co. $20,000 to tear down the buildings. Lester was able to sell the scrap lumber from the buildings for $12,000. What is Lester's basis in the land?

40. On September 1, 1996, Mitzo Realty Partnership purchases a lot for future development for $60,000 from the Elm Trust. The trust's adjusted basis in the lot is $20,000. Real estate taxes attributable to the property are $1,000. The city in which the lot is located operates on a calendar year, and taxes are due on April 1 of the following year. The sales agreement provides that Mitzo will pay the property tax bill in 1997.
   a. What is Mitzo's initial basis in the lot?
   b. What is the amount of Elm Trust's gain on the sale?

41. Return to the facts of problem 40. Assume that the sales agreement provides that Elm Trust will pay its portion of the real estate taxes. The sales price remains at $60,000. On April 1, 1997, Mitzo Realty Partnership pays the $1,000 property tax bill.
   a. What is Mitzo's initial basis in the lot?
   b. What is the amount of Elm Trust's gain on the sale?

42. Fala is the sole shareholder of Campbell, Inc. During the current year, Campbell sold Fala land that had a fair market value of $44,000 for $20,000. Campbell had paid $30,000 for the land. What are the tax effects of the sale for Fala and Campbell? What is Fala's basis in the land?

43. Izzy is an employee of Kosmo's Kustom Kars, Inc. The company rebuilds classic automobiles for resale. Last year, Izzy bought a rebuilt 1956 Thunderbird for $20,000 from the company. A car like Izzy's Thunderbird generally sells for $30,000. On December 20 of the current year, Izzy receives an offer of $25,000 for the car. What are the tax results if Izzy completes the sale?

44. Evan purchased a condominium by paying $1,000 in cash and borrowing $77,000. He also paid $3,000 in legal fees, title search costs, and other closing fees in making the purchase. While having a drink to celebrate the closing of the purchase, the seller was distressed to learn that it was going to cost him $600 to have the furniture moved out of the condominium. The furniture was worth only $500, and the seller was going to give it to a local charity. Because Evan was going to rent out the condominium, he needed to furnish it to obtain the best rental price. Evan told the seller not to worry, he would take care of the furniture for him. The seller was so happy that he bought Evan another drink. Assume that the assessed property tax values of the land and the building were $4,000 and $18,000, respectively. Write a letter to Evan explaining the amount of basis to allocate to each asset.

45. Hester Corporation purchased a building by giving stock with a fair market value of $30,000 (original cost was $21,000) and borrowing $210,000. Hester paid closing costs of $10,000 on the purchase. For property tax purposes the land was assessed at $10,000 and the building at $40,000. Before buying property, Hester hired an independent appraiser and received appraisals of $21,000 on the land and $279,000 on the building. Compare initial bases of the properties using different allocation methods. What initial basis amounts should Hester use? Explain. Is there any other way to determine initial basis?

46. Earl purchased all the assets and assumed the liabilities of Buddy's Market Shop. Details concerning the adjusted basis and fair market value of Buddy's assets and liabilities are as follows:

Asset	Adjusted Basis	Fair Market Value
Inventory	$ 30,000	$ 40,000
Equipment	22,000	70,000
Land	10,000	15,000
Building	118,000	155,000
Liabilities	(60,000)	(60,000)

a. If Earl paid $250,000 for Buddy's net assets, what is Earl's basis in the assets purchased?

b. Assume that Buddy's Market Shop is a closely held corporation and that Earl paid $250,000 for all the stock. What is Earl's basis, and what is the basis of the assets of the corporation?

47. ABC Co. purchased all the assets of John's Saw Shop. Details on basis and fair market values of John's Saw Shop's assets are as follows:

Asset	Adjusted Basis	Fair Market Value
Inventory	$10,000	$20,000
Machinery & equipment	2,000	12,000
Land	8,000	22,000
Building	20,000	6,000

a. What is ABC's basis in the assets purchased if ABC paid $40,000 for them?

b. What is ABC's basis in the assets purchased if ABC paid $70,000 for them?

c. What is ABC's basis if John's Saw Shop is a corporation and ABC purchased all John's stock for $60,000?

48. Kieu Corporation constructs a new warehouse. It pays $90,000 for materials and $65,000 to the general contractor. Architectural fees total $18,000. The corporation pays $12,000 in interest on its loan to finance construction. The land costs $15,000, and the real estate taxes paid on the land during the construction period amount to $1,000. What is Kieu's initial basis in the warehouse?

49. Julia received 1,200 shares of Cookery Corporation stock from her grandfather as a wedding present. The shares were selling for $25 per share on the date of the gift. Grandfather had paid $12,000 for the shares 4 years earlier. Grandfather paid $4,000 in gift tax on the transfer of the shares to Julia.

a. What is Julia's basis in the Cookery Corporation shares?

b. Two months after her wedding, Julia wanted to take a trip to Europe. To get the money she needed for the trip, she sold 400 Cookery shares at $18 per share and paid a $400 commission on the sale. What is Julia's gain or loss on the sale of the 400 shares? What is her holding period for the shares?

50. Stockton paid $10,000 for 1,000 shares of Megacron, Inc., common stock on the day his niece Chama was born. Stockton's plan was to give the stock to Chama when she is ready to go to college. Eighteen years later, Chama is ready to leave for Eastern Private University. She needs the money for tuition. However, the market value of the stock is $6,000. Stockton's marginal tax rate is 31%. Chama's marginal tax rate is 15%.

a. Should Stockton sell the shares and give the proceeds to Chama? Explain.

b. What alternative course(s) of action does this situation offer?

51. For his 18th birthday, Kevin gave his son, Gabe, 5 Krugerrands. Kevin had paid $500 per Krugerrand 2 years earlier. On Gabe's birthday, Krugerrands were selling for $450. What is Gabe's basis in the Krugerrands? Explain.
    a. One month after his birthday, Gabe sold 2 of the Krugerrands for $525 each and used the money to buy a motorcycle. What is Gabe's gain or loss on the sale of the 2 Krugerrands? What is the holding period on the 2 Krugerrands he sold?
    b. Six months after Gabe's birthday, the Krugerrand market was nosediving. On the advice of his aunt, Gabe sold his 3 remaining Krugerrands for $375 each. What is Gabe's gain or loss on the sale of the 3 Krugerrands? What is the holding period on the 3 Krugerrands?
    c. Assume the same facts as in part b, except that Gabe sold the 3 Krugerrands for $475 each. What is Gabe's gain or loss on the sale of the 3 Krugerrands?

52. Florence's daughter, Eunice, needs $8,000 to start a new business. Florence has agreed to give Eunice the money she needs but will have to sell some securities she owns in order to raise that much cash. Florence has 1,400 shares of Tom Corporation common stock, which is selling for $6 per share. Florence's basis in the shares is $5 per share. Florence is in the 28% marginal tax rate bracket, and Eunice is in the 15% marginal tax rate bracket. Should Florence sell the shares and give the proceeds to her daughter? Explain.

53. Mikel's daughter, Liudmila, is planning to go to law school in the fall. Mikel has 1,000 shares of Konrad Corporation stock and has promised Liudmila that he will give her the stock to use for tuition, fees, books, and so on. Mikel purchased the stock for $25 per share plus commissions of $500 four years ago.
    a. Assume Mikel gives Liudmila the stock when its value is $19. Just before leaving for law school, she sells all the shares for $20 per share and pays $400 in commissions. What is Liudmila's gain or loss on the sale?
    b. Assume Mikel sells the shares for $20 per share and pays $400 in commissions. He gives the proceeds to Liudmila. Explain the differences in the tax consequences if he sells the shares and gives the proceeds to Liudmila or if he gives her the shares and she sells them.

54. Alex received an automobile from his mother as a graduation present. The auto had cost his mother $25,000 and had a fair market value of $9,000 on the date of the gift. No gift taxes were paid on the gift. Alex's first job will be as a traveling salesperson, and he will use the car in his business.
    a. What is Alex's basis for computing depreciation on the automobile? Explain.
    b. What is Alex's initial basis in the automobile? Explain.

55. Refer to problem 54. Alex used the automobile for 3 years and then sold it. During this period, he properly deducted a total of $3,600 in depreciation. What is Alex's gain (loss) on the automobile if he sold it for
    a. $4,000?
    b. $23,000?
    c. $9,000?

56. Yohanse's aunt Millie gave him a storage warehouse valued at $250,000 to use in his delivery business. The warehouse has been vacant since Millie received it through an inheritance from her grandfather several years ago. At that time, the warehouse had a value of $300,000 and a basis of $50,000.
    a. What is Yohanse's depreciable basis for the warehouse? Explain.
    b. What is Yohanse's initial basis in the warehouse? Explain.
    c. Determine the holding period for Yohanse's warehouse.

57. Refer to problem 56. Yohanse used the warehouse for 4 years and sold it. During this period, he properly deducted a total of $25,000 in depreciation. What is Yohanse's gain (loss) on the warehouse if he sold it for
    a. $285,000?
    b. $215,000?
    c. $245,000?

58. Tommi inherits Dierhopf Corporation common stock from her uncle Norvel. Norvel's adjusted basis in the stock is $200,000, and the fair market value is $380,000. Six months after Norvel's death, the stock's value is $420,000. Nine months after his death, the stock's value is $350,000.

    a. Can the executor elect the alternate valuation date? Explain.

    b. Assume the executor transfers the stock to Tommi 9 months after the date of death. What is Tommi's basis?

59. Jesse's grandfather died on April 13, 1996. Jesse inherited the following property:

Property	Basis	FMV—April 13	FMV—Oct. 13
Land	$ 5,000	$20,000	$13,000
Stock	14,000	10,000	12,000
Watch	50	500	500

    a. What is Jesse's basis in the inherited property?

    b. What is Jesse's basis in the property if the executor of the estate elects the alternate valuation date?

    c. Assume that the executor elected the alternate valuation date and distributed title to the land to Jesse on June 23, 1996, when the fair market value of the land was $17,000. What is Jesse's basis in her inherited property?

    d. Assume that the executor elected the alternate valuation date and distributed the property to Jesse on December 2, 1996, when the fair market values were $15,000 for the land, $11,500 for the stock, and $500 for the watch. What is Jesse's basis in her inherited property?

60. Taylor died on February 19, 1996. Among the assets in Taylor's estate were 500 shares of Dane Co. preferred stock. Taylor had paid $14 per share for the stock on August 13, 1989. Market values per share for Dane preferred stock on various dates were as follows:

February 19, 1996	$12
April 1, 1996	$18
August 19, 1996	$10
November 21, 1996	$16

    Taylor's will provided that his niece Sherry was to receive the Dane shares. What is Sherry's basis in the shares in each of the following circumstances?

    a. No elections are made by the executor, and the shares are given to Sherry on April 1, 1996.

    b. The executor validly elects the alternate valuation date, and Sherry receives the shares on November 21, 1996.

    c. The executor validly elects the alternate valuation date, and Sherry receives the shares on April 1, 1996.

61. Phong has terminal cancer. She and her husband own marketable securities that cost $5,000 twelve years ago. The market value is $20,000. She wonders whether she should sell her securities and distribute the proceeds to her son before she dies or just give the securities directly to him. Phong's marginal tax rate is 36%; her son's marginal tax rate is 15%. Write a letter to Phong explaining an optimal tax strategy for transferring assets to her son.

62. Return to the facts in problem 61. Assume that the securities have a fair market value of $1,000. What positive tax strategy exists in this situation? Explain.

63. Harry and Freddi, a married couple, purchased 100 shares of Opaque Mutual Fund in 1986 for $2,400 as joint tenants with the right of survivorship. Freddi died during the current year. Fair market value of the shares is $5,000 on the date of death. Six months later the value is $5,100. What is Harry's basis in the 100 shares?

64. Loretta and Louanne paid $40,000 for a truck to use in their remodeling business. They bought it as joint tenants (50:50 ownership) with the right of survivorship. Several months after the purchase, Loretta died tragically when scaffolding on which she was working broke. Louanne was appointed executor of Loretta's estate, and she decided to liquidate the business immediately. She received an offer of $36,000 for the truck.

   a. Assume Louanne accepted the offer. What is the tax treatment of the sale?

   b. What alternative courses of action can Louanne take to improve the tax results? (Assume the FMV of the truck is $38,000 as of the alternate valuation date.)

65. Jessica owns a house with a basis of $80,000 and a fair market value of $250,000. On June 2, 1996, she marries Rick. As part of their prenuptial agreement, Rick is to pay Jessica $75,000 for a one-half interest in the house. What are the tax effects of the sale of the half-interest to Rick?

66. Katherine and Patrick were divorced in the current year. As part of the divorce agreement, Patrick agreed to give Katherine his interest in their residence, which was worth $100,000. Patrick and Katherine had paid $80,000 for the house 5 years ago. What are the tax consequences to Patrick and Katherine of the agreement that made Katherine sole owner of the house? Explain.

67. Han owns a house that she lived in until this year. She paid $85,000 for the house on November 18, 1987, and it was appraised at $130,000 by an independent real estate appraiser in May of this year. She bought a new house on May 9 and converted her former residence into office space for her software consulting business. Property tax assessments value the structure at $100,000 and the land at $10,000. What is Han's basis in the office building?

68. Alexis purchased a duplex by paying $16,000 cash and assuming the seller's $70,000 mortgage. Alexis paid legal fees of $1,000 and spent $9,000 on painting and carpeting the 2 units before renting out 1 unit and moving into the other unit (i.e., 1 unit is her personal residence). Three years later, Alexis purchased a house and moved out of the duplex unit and rented it out. She had taken $4,800 in depreciation on the rental unit and had her unit repainted at a cost of $900 before renting it out. Because of a general decline in property values, the duplex was worth only $50,000 when she moved out of it. What is her adjusted basis in the duplex?

69. Phoebe opened a bait delivery service during the current year. In starting up the business, she decided to use her personal truck as a delivery vehicle. She had paid $15,000 for the truck, which was worth $9,000 when she turned it into a delivery truck. What is her initial basis in the truck? What is her basis for depreciation on the truck? Explain.

   a. After using the truck for 2 years, Phoebe sold the truck and used the $4,600 in proceeds as a down payment on a new delivery van. Phoebe had correctly deducted $2,700 in straight-line depreciation on the truck during the 2 years of business use. Write a letter to Phoebe explaining the amount of gain or loss resulting from the sale and why that is the result.

   b. Assume the same facts as in part a, except that Phoebe sold the truck for $7,200. What is her gain or loss on the sale?

70. On January 5, 1996, Henry purchases 500 shares of Wichmann, Inc., common stock at a cost of $24,700. On April 1, Henry purchases an additional 300 shares for $19,500. On November 13, 1996, Wichmann, Inc., declares and distributes a 30% stock dividend. On December 23, 1996, Wichmann distributes a cash dividend of 50 cents per share. On February 19, 1997, Henry sells 800 shares of the Wichmann, Inc., stock for $45 per share.

   a. How much income (loss) does Henry recognize in 1996 and 1997 on his Wichmann, Inc. stock?

   b. Explain how Henry can improve the tax results of the 1997 sale.

72. Monica owns 1,400 shares of Northeast Utilities common stoc... when its stock was selling for $10 per share, Northeast announced a 20% stock divi... dend. In lieu of receiving the dividend shares, stockholders had the option of receiving $2 per share in cash. Write a memo explaining the tax results of exercising the options.

73. Betty owns Betty's Car Repair Shop, a proprietorship. Betty's basis in the assets used in the business is $90,000. The fair market value of the assets is $140,000. Also, Betty owes $25,000 in liabilities related to the business. Betty has decided to incorporate the business using a tax-free transaction. She will name the new entity The Garage, Inc. Betty plans to transfer all assets and liabilities from the sole proprietorship to The Garage, Inc., in exchange for 1,000 shares of The Garage, Inc., common stock. After the exchange, Betty will own 100% of the outstanding stock of The Garage, Inc. What are the tax effects of the exchange for Betty and for The Garage, Inc.?

74. Abbie owns a fishing boat chartering business near San Diego. She owns 5 boats with appraised total value of $280,000. Abbie's adjusted basis in the boats is $50,000. She has outstanding debts relating to the business of $48,000. All the other equipment of the business is fully depreciated and has negligible fair market value. Abbie is concerned about her personal liability.
a. What actions may Abbie take to limit her personal exposure?
b. What is the tax treatment of her actions?

75. Eric owns 600 shares of Razor, Inc., stock for which he paid $3,500 in 1994. On December 14, 1996, Eric sells the 600 shares for $4 per share and pays a commission of $200 on the sale. On January 3, 1997, Eric purchases 500 shares of Razor, Inc., for $3 per share and pays a $100 commission on the purchase. What is Eric's recognized gain or loss on the sale of the 600 shares? What is his basis in the 500 shares purchased in 1997?

76. Steele bought 200 shares of Splendid, Inc., common stock 14 months ago for $9,000. He sells all the stock on December 20 of the current year for $15,000. On January 15 of the next year, he buys 250 shares of Splendid, Inc., stock for $17,500.
a. Explain what Steele is trying to accomplish with these transactions. Will it pass IRS scrutiny?
b. How will your explanation change if Steele sells the stock for $7,500 on December 20 and purchases 250 shares for $8,750 on January 15?

77. On November 14, 1996, Noel sells 2,000 shares of Marker, Inc., stock for $6,000. He had purchased the stock 2 years earlier for $10,000. Because the price of the stock continued to drop, Noel purchases additional shares of Marker stock on December 10, 1996. What are the tax effects of the sale of the stock and the basis in the new shares if Noel
a. Repurchases 2,000 shares for $5,000?
b. Repurchases 800 shares for $2,000?
c. Repurchases 4,000 shares for $9,000?

78. Lynn bought 100 shares of Filidelphia Corporation stock for $10,000 three years ago. On December 24, she sold 50 shares for $4,000. She plans to buy 100 more shares of Filidelphia stock for $7,000 on January 17. Explain the tax treatment of these transactions. Include a discussion of the underlying concepts that govern the results. What could Lynn do to change the results?

INTEGRATIVE PROBLEM

79. Art and Kris are married taxpayers with 3 dependent children. Art works as a gardener for Green, Inc. Kris, who is self-employed, sells custom golf clubs. During 1996, they have the following property transactions:

1. Art decides to open his own gardening company. He acquires the following assets to get the business started:

   a. Art purchases a small office building on March 28 for $5,000 cash and borrows $45,000 with interest at 9% for 30 years. For property tax purposes, the land is assessed at $2,000 and the building at $18,000.

   b. Art converts his personal truck into a business truck on April 1. Art paid $18,000 for the truck, which was worth $6,000 when it was converted to business use. Art paid $400 to have his business logo painted on the truck.

   c. Art purchases the following assets from Walt, a retired gardener, for $30,000 on April 5:

Asset	Walt's Basis	FMV
Gardening equipment	$ 3,000	$ 6,000
Gardening supplies	1,000	3,000
Shrubbery inventory	11,000	16,000
Totals	$15,000	$25,000

   d. Art's father gives him 2,000 shares of Galla Corporation stock to help him finance the cost of starting the new business. Art's father paid $5 per share for the stock in 1994, and it was worth $3 per share on the day Art received the stock. Art uses the stock as collateral for a loan he uses to pay Walt for the assets purchased in part c.

2. Kris wins a new automobile in a long-drive contest. The automobile has a list price of $28,000, but a local car dealer tells her that automobile would typically sell for $21,000. Kris intends to use the automobile in her business. Kris receives the automobile on March 3. Her records for the remainder of the year indicate that she drives the automobile 8,000 miles for business purposes and 4,000 miles for personal use. Kris purchases an extended warranty contract on the automobile from her local car dealer. The warranty costs $600 and provides additional coverage for 5 years from the date of purchase (March 5, 1996).

3. Kris's grandmother dies during 1996 and leaves Kris the family plate collection. The plates have been passed from generation to generation since the family first emigrated from Latvia. Kris doesn't know what the original cost of the plates was, but they were valued in her grandmother's estate at $38,000. The estate paid $8,200 in estate taxes on the plates.

4. Kris and Art's house is damaged by a tornado in 1996. They paid $44,000 for the house in 1987; $4,000 of the cost was properly allocated to the land. In 1990, they added a swimming pool at a cost of $15,000. Just before the casualty, they paid a landscaping company $3,600 to rework the landscaping in the yard. The value of the house before the casualty was $92,000. Repairs to the house cost $37,000, $23,000 of which was reimbursed by insurance. Art and Kris's 1996 adjusted gross income is $46,000.

5. Kris uses a room in their home exclusively and regularly as an office for her golf club business. The room is 10 feet by 12 feet. According to the original purchase documents, the total square footage of their house is 1,800 square feet. Kris began using the room as an office on May 24, 1993. At that time, she purchased a desk and a filing cabinet for $800. In 1994, she traded clubs that cost her $900 (fair market value was $1,600) for a photocopier. The 1996 casualty did not affect the home office.

6. On May 30, 1993, Kris purchased an automobile to use in her golf club business by paying $2,000 in cash and borrowing $13,000. During 1993, she drove the automobile 4,800 total miles and documented 3,600 business miles.

7. Art and Kris have a rental house. The house was acquired by Kris from her former husband in 1987 as part of their divorce settlement. They paid $80,000 for the house

tober 4, 1994, Corporate Golf Development distributed a 2-for-1 stock split.

b. Art and Kris received 1,000 shares of Zleine Corporation common stock as a wedding gift from Kris's uncle. Her uncle paid $4,000 for the stock in 1980. The fair market value of the stock on the date of the gift was $20,000. The uncle paid $500 in gift tax on the transfer.

9. Kris's father died on November 2, 1992. Kris inherited a parcel of land for which her father had paid $500 in 1971. On November 2, 1992, the land was appraised at $8,000. The executor of the estate elected to use the alternate valuation date. The value of the land on May 2, 1993, was $7,800. Kris received the land from the estate in August 1993 when it was worth $9,000.

Based on the information provided, determine the *initial basis* of each of Art and Kris's assets. If more than one basis is possible, list the alternatives and explain when each basis would apply.

DISCUSSION CASES

80. Monica is planning to start her own accounting, tax, and financial planning business. Her uncle Gus has given her file cabinets, a desk, computer equipment, and book cases that were in his den until he sold his house. Gus recently moved to a lakefront cottage and no longer needs the furniture and equipment. Gus's adjusted basis for all the items is $3,500, and the fair market value is $2,000. Monica will convert 20% of her personal residence into her office and will use it exclusively for her business. Monica's residence has a fair market value of $150,000 and an adjusted basis of $80,000 (10% is allocated to the land). What are the tax ramifications of the gifts and the conversion? What will be the depreciable basis of the property? Explain your answers in terms of the underlying concepts that govern the result.

81. Several years ago, Steve gave his nephew Rashan 600 shares of Dalmont Corporation common stock valued at $12,000 with a basis of $3,000. Steve's intent was to ensure that Rashan has money for college. Rashan is now a senior in high school, and the stock is worth $16,000. Rashan is considering selling the shares to put toward his first semester's tuition. His marginal tax rate is 15% and will remain at that rate throughout his college years because of part-time work. Steve is terminally ill and has no more than 16 months to live. He asks Rashan to give the shares of stock back to him and tells Rashan not to worry about it. Steve's will states that Rashan gets the 600 shares of Dalmont Corporation stock. Rashan is confused. He can cover his tuition, fees, and other college expenses for the first two years from savings and student loans. But he does not understand what Steve is trying to accomplish by asking for the stock. Explain all the tax ramifications to Rashan.

for his death. Although he intends to leave the bulk of his $200,000,000 estate to the Northern State Technical University School of Accounting, he does have a few nieces and nephews for whom he would like to provide (although not too lavishly). Listed here is a selection of assets he is thinking of giving to his nephews and nieces:

Asset	Fair Market Value	Basis	Suspended Loss
Keating S&L stock	$ 10,000	$ 200,000	
Impressionist painting	$5,000,000	-0-	
Land held as an investment	$2,000,000	$1,500,000	
Limited partnership interest	$ 100,000	$ 400,000	$1,300,000
Rental property	$4,000,000	$1,000,000	$2,500,000
General Motors stock	$2,000,000	$1,000,000	

1. Consider each of the following questions from Luther's point of view (what is best from the standpoint of his tax situation). Explain.
   a. Which of these properties would be best to give away to his favorite nephew? Why?
   b. Which of these properties would be the worst to give away? Why?
   c. Which property(ies) should Luther definitely retain? Why?
   d. Which property(ies) should Luther consider selling? Why?
2. Luther comes to your accounting firm for advice. Write a memorandum explaining your recommendations for optimizing Luther's tax situation in regard to the assets listed.

ETHICS
DISCUSSION CASE

83. Assume you are a CPA. A new client, Mark, a local chiropractor, has brought you the financial information for his business at the close of the past year. Previously, Mark prepared his own tax returns and had them reviewed by Blacke & Co. You find the information to be organized and fairly straightforward. Mark does bring one recent transaction to your attention. He sold an x-ray machine for $10,000 near the end of the past year. The machine had cost $25,000 three years earlier. Mark did not deduct depreciation expense in the year of acquisition. His business incurred an operating loss that year. Therefore, Mark "saved" some of his basis and did not report a loss as big as he could have. For the following year and for this year, Mark recorded depreciation of $5,000 annually. Mark tells you that he would like to "reclaim" the depreciation he did not deduct in the year of acquisition. He insists there will not be a problem, because he could have taken the depreciation 3 years ago. Also, by applying it to the adjusted basis for the sales transaction, he will not report a loss. So, the recognized loss will not be used to offset other income. Advise Mark on the propriety of this transaction. You may wish to consult the Statements on Responsibilities in Tax Practice. Write Mark a letter explaining his situation.

Cost Recovery on Property: Depreciation, Depletion, and Amortization

CHAPTER

11

▲ CHAPTER LEARNING OBJECTIVES

■ Discuss the recovery of the cost of long-lived assets and the general criteria for taking deductions for depreciation, depletion, or amortization on an investment in a long-lived asset.

■ Illustrate how the timing of the cost-recovery deduction affects the real after-tax return on an investment in property.

■ Identify the factors involved in and the general approach to calculating depreciation on assets acquired before 1981.

■ Discuss the general changes in the approach to calculating depreciation on assets acquired after 1980 under the Accelerated Cost Recovery System (ACRS).

■ Explain how to determine the amount of cost recovery on various classes of assets under the Modified Accelerated Cost Recovery System (MACRS).

■ Discuss the limitations on depreciation deductions for listed property in general and the specific limitation on depreciation of automobiles.

■ Explain the deduction for depletion and how to calculate depletion using the cost method and the statutory percentage method.

■ Discuss the amortization deduction for intangible assets.

Accounting method   A taxpayer must adopt an accounting method that clearly reflects income.

Administrative convenience   Those items for which the cost of compliance would exceed the revenue generated are not taxed.

Annual accounting period   All entities must report the results of their operations on an annual basis (the tax year). Each tax year stands on its own, apart from other tax years.

Basis   This is the amount of unrecovered investment in an asset. As amounts are expended and/or recovered relative to an asset over time, the basis is adjusted in consideration of such changes. The **adjusted basis** of an asset is the original basis, plus or minus the changes in the amount of unrecovered investment.

Business purpose   To be deductible, an expenditure or a loss must have a business or other economic purpose that exceeds any tax avoidance motive. The primary motive for the transaction must be to make a profit.

Capital recovery   No income is realized until the taxpayer receives more than the amount invested to produce the income. The amount invested in an asset represents the maximum amount recoverable.

Conduit entity   An entity for which the tax attributes flow through to its owners for tax purposes.

Entity   All items of income, deduction, and so on are traced to the tax unit responsible for the item.

Legislative grace   Any tax relief provided is the result of a specific act of Congress that must be strictly applied and interpreted. All income received is taxable unless a specific provision can be found in the tax law that excludes the income from taxation. Deductions must be approached with the philosophy that nothing is deductible unless a provision in the tax law allows the deduction.

Related party   Family members and corporations that are owned by family members are considered related parties, as are certain other relationships between entities in which the power to control the substance of a transaction is evidenced through majority ownership.

INTRODUCTION

Based on the legislative grace concept, business expenses are classified as related either to a trade or business or to a production-of-income activity. To be deductible, an expense must have a business purpose and be related to the current tax year. If an expenditure results in a long-lived asset that benefits several annual accounting periods, its cost is generally allocated on a reasonable basis to the tax years in which it is used to produce income. According to the capital recovery concept, a taxpayer does not realize taxable income until after the capital used to produce the income is recovered. An asset's basis is the maximum amount of investment in an asset that can be subtracted from income as a capital recovery. Tax **depreciation,** amortization, and depletion are tax accounting methods used to periodically recover the investment in assets. These accounting methods provide a reasonable allocation of bases to the annual accounting periods benefited by the use of the assets. The text first discusses the concept of capital recovery through depreciation. Then, it turns to tax accounting for depreciation, amortization, and depletion.

This chapter considers several different depreciation methods. Generally, a taxpayer can choose among three alternative depreciation methods. The method the taxpayer chooses determines the timing and the amount of the annual depreciation deduction. The timing and the amount of the depreciation expense affect the present value of the tax savings from the deduction (the time value of money effect). As a general rule, the earlier the taxpayer can claim a depreciation deduction, the greater its present value is.

▲ **EXAMPLE 1**   Angelo has $100,000 to invest in an asset. The cost of asset A will be deductible immediately. The cost of asset B cannot be deducted until it is sold. Both assets produce the same annual revenue and cost flows and will be held for 10 years. If Angelo is in a 31% marginal tax rate bracket during the 10-year period and the cost of capital is 10%, which asset will provide the greater real after-tax return?

Discussion: The deduction for both assets provides a $31,000 ($100,000 × 31%) tax savings. However, because asset A's tax savings occur in the first year, it results in real tax savings of $31,000. The present value of the future deduction for asset B is only $11,966 [$31,000 × 0.386 (the present value of $1 at 10% for 10 years)]. As a result of deferring the capital recovery on asset B for 10 years, its present value to Angelo is decreased by $19,034 ($31,000 − $11,966), compared to the immediate tax savings resulting from asset A.

More likely, a taxpayer will be faced with a situation in which the investment can be recovered as the asset is used to earn income.

▲ **EXAMPLE 2**   Tawana purchases an apartment building for $100,000 at the beginning of 1996 for use as rental property. Assume that Tawana is in the 31% marginal tax bracket, her cost of capital is 10%, and that she sells the building at the end of 10 years for $100,000, its original cost. To determine the effect of depreciation on the transaction, ignore the cost of the land, which is not included in the $100,000 cost basis of the building. Also, assume that the maximum marginal tax rate applicable to net long-term capital gains of 28% applies. What are the tax effects of the purchase, use, and disposition of the building?

Discussion: The $100,000 cost of the building is depreciated using the MACRS depreciation system (explained later in this chapter). The depreciation calculations and the annual tax savings at a 31% marginal tax rate discounted at 10% are as follows:

Year	MACRS Depreciation Rate	Annual Depreciation Deduction	31% Tax Rate Savings	10% PV Factor	PV of Tax Savings
1996	3.485	$ 3,485	$ 1,080	.909	$ 982
1997	3.636	3,636	1,127	.826	931
1998	3.636	3,636	1,127	.751	846
1999	3.636	3,636	1,127	.683	770
2000	3.636	3,636	1,127	.621	700
2001	3.636	3,636	1,127	.564	636
2002	3.636	3,636	1,127	.513	578
2003	3.636	3,636	1,127	.467	526
2004	3.636	3,636	1,127	.424	478
2005	3.637	3,637	1,127	.386	435
Totals		$36,210	$11,223		

Present value of tax savings on building $6,882

Sale of Building:

Sales price		$100,000
Less: Adjusted basis:		
Building—cost	$100,000	
Less: Depreciation	(36,210)	(63,790)
Gain on sale of property		$ 36,210
Tax on gain at capital gain rate (28% × $36,210)		$ 10,139
Present value factor		× .386
Present value of tax cost of gain on sale		(3,914)
Net tax savings from depreciation deduction		$2,968

paid out). When Tawana sells the building at the end of 10 years, she realizes and recognizes a $36,210 gain. The gain recognized stems from the depreciation deducted over the 10-year period in which the building was used. The gain on the sale of the building is taxed at the 28% capital gains rate for an individual. The present value of the tax to be paid on the gain from the sale of the building is $3,914 (a cash outflow). Thus, Tawana has been able to earn a $2,968 profit. The profit results from the timing differences in the present value (depreciation deductions versus gain on the sale) and from marginal tax rate differences (ordinary tax rates versus capital gains tax rate).

In example 2, note the following points:

- The earlier the depreciation deduction is taken, the greater will be the present value of the tax savings to the taxpayer.

- A taxpayer can receive an economic benefit by accelerating the recovery of basis and deferring income related to the property. In example 2, the property is sold for its original purchase price. Yet, the effect of depreciation is to provide the taxpayer with a positive present value.

- The taxpayer benefits when deductions can be claimed at regular tax rates and any gain from the sale of the property is taxed at a lower rate. The depreciation deductions in example 2 reduce ordinary income subject to tax at 31 percent. However, the gain on the sale of the building is subject to tax at the 28-percent long-term capital gains rate. Limitations on this effect are explained in Chapter 12.

CAPITAL RECOVERY FROM DEPRECIATION OR COST RECOVERY

The depreciation rules in effect when an asset is placed in service determine the depreciation method to be used during the life of the asset. An asset is placed in service when it is set up and ready for its intended use for a business purpose.[1] This general rule provides certainty and consistency when computing the depreciation deduction for a specific asset. However, frequent changes in the tax laws make the depreciation rules seem complex when computing depreciation for assets acquired over several years. As the time line in Figure 11–1 shows, depreciation methods have undergone three major changes since 1980. In addition, Congress has made several important but less dramatic changes in nearly every session. Taxpayers and tax advisers alike face significant difficulty in coping with the frequent changes in the depreciation rules.

Congress has established four different depreciation systems since the mid-1960s. Two systems, facts and circumstances and the Asset Depreciation Range (ADR), apply to assets placed in service before 1981. These systems were derived from financial accounting and required taxpayers to depreciate an asset's net cost over its estimated useful life in the business. Taxpayers had considerable freedom in selecting the actual computational method. Most taxpayers used one of the methods commonly taught in financial accounting—straight-line, sum-of-the-years' digits, or declining balance—all of which were appropriate for facts and circumstances depreciation systems. These methods require taxpayers to estimate an asset's useful life and its salvage value and to determine a method of allocating depreciation to the first and last year of the asset's life. The ADR system differed from facts and circumstances because it had specific classes for depreciable assets. For each class, the IRS specified the average life of assets in the class. Taxpayers did not have to determine their useful life. Also, ADR required the adoption of a convention for depreciating assets in their first year of use. That is, taxpayers did not have to be concerned with the actual date assets were placed in service. The

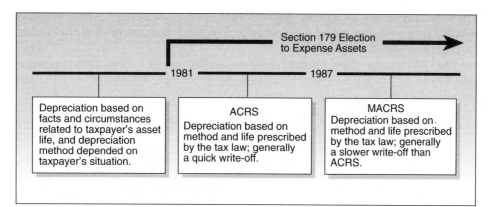

convention stated the percentage of depreciation allowed in the year assets were placed in service. Although the ADR system helped minimize taxpayer-IRS conflicts over useful life estimates, record-keeping complexities and other factors beyond the scope of this discussion doomed this system. Taxpayer-IRS disputes continued because of computational errors and the estimates taxpayers were using under the facts and circumstances system.

In 1981, Congress mandated the **Accelerated Cost Recovery System (ACRS)** in its effort to provide incentives for capital investment—and effectively eliminated the use of the facts and circumstances and ADR systems for assets placed in service after 1980. As part of the Economic Recovery Tax Act of 1981, this radically new approach to calculating depreciation was an attempt to influence the economy through tax legislation.[2] Unlike the facts and circumstances system and ADR, ACRS did not attempt to match an asset's depreciation to the annual accounting period that benefits from its use. Rather, the primary purpose of ACRS was to accelerate the capital recovery (i.e., present value of tax savings) taxpayers receive from depreciating property. In fact, ACRS and the current system, MACRS, both use the term *cost recovery* instead of *depreciation* to identify the deduction. Accordingly, in the discussion that follows, depreciation and cost recovery are used interchangeably to mean depreciation as it is generally understood.

Another factor that influenced the switch to ACRS from traditional depreciation methods was the concern over the complexity of the tax law. ACRS enhanced administrative convenience by standardizing the depreciation rules to help reduce the continuing conflict between the IRS and taxpayers over estimated useful life and salvage value. This was accomplished by having only five useful lives, by not subtracting an estimate of salvage value from an asset's depreciable basis, and by standardizing the conventions for depreciation in the year of an asset's acquisition and disposition.

The current depreciation system, the **Modified Accelerated Cost Recovery System (MACRS),** is used for assets placed in service after 1986. As its name indicates, MACRS is a modification of ACRS and operates in a similar manner. The primary difference between the two systems is that MACRS specifies longer recovery periods for depreciable assets, which results in slower depreciation than allowed by ACRS. Congress made these modifications because it was more concerned with raising revenue than stimulating the economy. The 1986 tax act reduced individual tax rates to 28 percent from a high of 50 percent and corporate tax rates to 34 percent from a high of 46 percent. In order to minimize the loss of revenue from tax rate reductions, Congress had to broaden the tax base. One way Congress did this was by specifying longer recovery periods for depreciable assets,

MACRS continues the use of a standardized depreciation calculation that reduces the complexity of the calculation.[3]

The Alternative Depreciation System (ADS) is an alternative to regular MACRS. Its primary use is for calculating the alternative minimum tax (discussed in Chapter 14). However, taxpayers may elect ADS for determining regular taxable income when there is no need for the greater MACRS deductions. A discussion of ADS follows the discussion of MACRS later in this chapter.

In addition to accelerating the recovery of an investment through ACRS and MACRS, Congress introduced the Section 179 election to expense certain depreciable assets placed in service after 1981. The Section 179 election replaces the deduction for additional first-year depreciation that was allowed before 1981. Initially, Section 179 allowed an expense deduction of as much as $5,000 in the year of acquisition on qualifying property. However, the 1986 act increased the limit to $10,000 for years after 1986. This limit has been increased to $17,500 for qualifying property placed in service after December 31, 1992.

SECTION 179 ELECTION TO EXPENSE ASSETS

Section 179 allows an annual current expense deduction for as much as $17,500 of the cost of qualifying depreciable property purchased for use in a trade or business. The deduction for expensed assets is treated as a depreciation deduction. This election allows many small businesses to expense assets as they are purchased instead of depreciating them over several years. The immediate deduction promotes administrative convenience by eliminating the need for extensive depreciation schedules for small purchases.

Qualified Taxpayers

Each year, individuals, corporations, S corporations, and partnerships may elect to deduct as an expense up to $17,500 in investment in qualified property to be used in an active trade or business.[4] A husband and wife are considered one entity for purposes of the election to expense. Although the phrase "active trade or business" is not defined in the tax law, it appears to have the same meaning as the phrase "trade or business" (Chapter 5). The elements of profit motivation, regularity, and continuity of the taxpayer's involvement in the activity and the absence of hobby, amusement, and similar motivations are important factors to consider when determining whether an activity qualifies for the Section 179 election. This interpretation is supported by the fact that the deduction is not allowed for assets purchased for use in an activity related to the production of income (an investment activity). However, the portion of a mixed-use asset that is used in a trade or business does qualify for immediate deduction under Section 179. Estates and trusts cannot use the Section 179 election to expense assets. The election is not available to these entities because they are formed to protect and conserve the entity's assets for the benefit of the beneficiaries and not to operate an active trade or business.

Qualified Property

The Section 179 expense deduction is allowed only on depreciable, tangible, personal property. Examples of eligible property include trucks, machinery, furniture, microcomputers, and store shelving. Real property, such as buildings and their structural components, does not qualify for the special election to expense. Also excluded from the deduction are land and improvements made directly to the land, such as a parking lot, sidewalks, or a swimming pool. In addition, qualifying property does not include intangible assets such as patents, copyrights, and goodwill.

▲ **EXAMPLE 3**   Kelly purchased a new computer and a new telephone system and installed a new roof and an air-conditioning system in her office building. Which of the expenditures qualify for the election to expense?

Discussion: The computer and the telephone system are depreciable, tangible, personal property and therefore qualify under Section 179. The roof and the air-conditioning system are integral parts of the office building. Therefore, the roof and the air-conditioning system are real property and do not qualify for immediate expensing.

Limitations on Deduction

The Section 179 election to expense deduction is subject to three limitations:

- A taxpayer's annual Section 179 deduction cannot exceed $17,500 for property placed in service after December 31, 1992. Before 1993, the limit was $10,000.

- If the taxpayer's investment in Section 179 property exceeds $200,000 for the tax year, the $17,500 annual deduction is reduced by one dollar for each dollar of investment over $200,000 for the tax year. If a taxpayer purchases more than $217,500 of qualifying property, the taxpayer may not take any election to expense deduction for any of the purchases.

- The Section 179 deduction allowed for a tax year cannot exceed the taxable income from the active conduct of all the taxpayer's trade or business activities.

Annual Deduction Limit.   The annual $17,500 deduction limit does not have to be prorated according to the length of time an asset is used during the year. Regardless of the date of acquisition, the taxpayer can deduct as an expense up to $17,500 of the total cost of qualifying assets purchased during the year. The $17,500 annual deduction limit applies to all tax entities entitled to use Section 179. Thus, the annual limit applies separately to a partnership and to its individual partners. The annual limit also applies separately to an S corporation and to its shareholders.[5] Because the partnership and S corporation are conduit entities, a portion of the entity's total deduction is allocated to each owner, who subtracts it as an expense on the personal tax return. However, the Section 179 deduction allocated to the taxpayer from the conduit entity plus the taxpayer's Section 179 deduction from all other sources cannot exceed the $17,500 annual limit. Any excess Section 179 election resulting from allocations from several entities must be carried forward to be used in subsequent years.

▲ **EXAMPLE 4**   Roberto is a 40% shareholder and full-time employee of an S corporation. During 1996, the S corporation invests $57,500 in equipment qualifying for the Section 179 deduction. Roberto also owns a sole proprietorship that constructs kitchen cabinets. The cabinet business qualifies as an active business for Roberto. During 1996, Roberto purchases $11,000-worth of equipment to use in his cabinet business. What is the maximum amount that Roberto can deduct as a Section 179 expense for 1996?

Discussion: Roberto's deductible Section 179 expenditures are limited to $17,500. The S corporation can elect to deduct $17,500 of its $57,500 in capital expenditures. The remaining $40,000 is subject to regular depreciation. The S corporation allocates $7,000 (40% × $17,500) of its Section 179 deduction to Roberto. Thus, Roberto's qualified Section 179 expenditures total $18,000 ($7,000 from the S corporation + $11,000 from only $17,500 as a Section 179 expense.

A taxpayer may choose to use all, part, or none of the $17,500 deduction. By electing to expense less than the limit for a tax year, the taxpayer can avoid a Section 179 deduction carryforward resulting from either the annual limitation or the trade or business income limitation.

▲ **EXAMPLE 5**   Based on the information in example 4, how should Roberto allocate his Section 179 deduction in 1996?

Discussion: Roberto should claim as a Section 179 deduction the $7,000 allocated to him from the S corporation plus $10,500 of the cost of the equipment purchased for use in the cabinet business. The remaining $500 cost of the equipment used in his cabinet business is depreciated, using regular depreciation methods.

If Roberto expenses the $11,000-worth of equipment he purchased for the cabinet business, he will lose $500 of the deduction allocated to him from the S corporation by exceeding the $17,500 annual limitation by $500 ($11,000 + $7,000 = $18,000) this year. The $500 carries forward to be used in subsequent years. Any amounts that flow to a taxpayer from a conduit entity should always be expensed under Section 179 before any amount is elected from another trade or business of the taxpayer.

After an asset's basis is reduced by the amount expensed under Section 179, the remaining basis is subject to regular depreciation under any valid method.

▲ **EXAMPLE 6**   Devra Corporation purchases a machine costing $39,000 for use in its business. Devra wants to expense $17,500 of the asset's cost under Section 179. If Devra makes the Section 179 election to expense $17,500 of the asset's cost, what is its depreciable basis in the machine?

Discussion: Devra's depreciable basis for regular depreciation is $21,500. The depreciable basis of the machine is its $39,000 cost, less the $17,500 it elects to expense under Section 179. The reduction of depreciable basis by amounts expensed under Section 179 is necessary to ensure that the total capital recovery on the machine does not exceed the $39,000 invested.

The Section 179 deduction can be allocated to reduce the basis of qualifying assets in any manner the taxpayer chooses. This allows the deduction to be allocated equally to all assets acquired during the year or to specific assets. This option is important. Two general rules apply to choosing assets to expense. First, do not use the Section 179 election to expense automobiles. As discussed later, automobiles are subject to annual depreciation deduction limits ($3,060 in 1996). For purposes of this annual limitation, the Section 179 expense is treated as a depreciation deduction. Because MACRS depreciation on most automobiles exceeds the first-year annual limitation amount, using the election to expense on an automobile does not result in additional tax savings. Second, based on time value of money concepts, taxpayers should take the depreciation deduction as early as possible. This is accomplished by expensing the assets with the longest life and using regular depreciation methods to depreciate assets with the shortest life.

▲ **EXAMPLE 7**   Gwendolyn purchases equipment costing $17,500 and a computer that also cost $17,500 for use in her business in 1996. Under MACRS, the equipment is 7-year property, and the computer is 5-year property. How should Gwendolyn allocate her $17,500 Section 179 expense deduction?

Discussion: If Gwendolyn wants to deduct the $17,500 maximum election to expense, she should elect to expense the $17,500 cost of the equipment. The $17,500 cost of the than if she elected to expense the computer.

Gwendolyn could elect to deduct less than the full $17,500 Section 179 limit. Because Section 179 is elective, Gwendolyn can decide how much to deduct and the specific assets to expense. This allows taxpayers who do not want or need the extra deductions in the current year to spread the deductions out through depreciation charges.

Annual Investment Limit. The $17,500 annual deduction limit is reduced dollar for dollar by the amount of the investment in qualifying property in excess of $200,000. As a result of this limitation, a taxpayer that purchases $217,500 or more of qualified property during the tax year cannot expense any amount under Section 179. Because of the $200,000 annual investment limitation, only relatively small businesses can use the election to expense.

▲ **EXAMPLE 8** During 1996, the Allen Partnership places $204,000 of Section 179 property in service for use in its business. What is Allen's maximum Section 179 deduction?

Discussion: Allen's election to expense is reduced to $13,500 by the $200,000 annual investment limit. Because the partnership invested $4,000 more than the $200,000 annual investment limitation ($204,000 − $200,000), it must reduce the annual deduction limit dollar for dollar by the excess ($17,500 - $4,000 = $13,500). NOTE: The $4,000 lost through the annual investment limit is not carried forward to future years. It is lost forever.

Handwritten margin notes:
Property 204,000
Limit Sec 179 200,000
4,000

Sec 179   17,500
− 4,000

Sec 179 deduction 13,500

Active Trade or Business Income Limit. The Section 179 deduction is limited to the total taxable income from the taxpayer's active conduct of any trade or business during the year. Total taxable income is the amount of taxable income computed before deducting the Section 179 expense. For purposes of the income limit, the taxpayer includes salaries and wages, income from a proprietorship, and any trade or business income allocated to the taxpayer from a partnership or S corporation in which the taxpayer actively participates (i.e., passive activities do not enter into the calculation). If the taxable income from the active conduct of a trade or business is less than the allowable Section 179 deduction, any expense election that is over the limit carries forward for use in subsequent years.

Handwritten margin note: $4,000 is lost forever

▲ **EXAMPLE 9** During 1996, Michael has a $5,000 net loss in his cabinet-making business. To supplement the family's income, Serena, Michael's wife, earns $7,000 working part time as a cashier at a local grocery store. In addition, they earn $1,000 in interest income on their savings account. Michael also purchases $8,000-worth of equipment for use in his business. For 1996, what is Serena and Michael's maximum Section 179 deduction?

Handwritten margin notes:
Salary 7000
Bus. Loss 5,000
Maximum Deduction 2000

Discussion: Their maximum deduction is $2,000, because Michael and Serena's taxable business income is only $2,000 ($7,000 salary - $5,000 business loss). The interest income cannot be counted, because it is from an investment. Thus, the business income limitation applies, and they can deduct only $2,000 for 1996. They can still elect to expense the full $8,000 Michael paid for the equipment. The $6,000 that they cannot deduct in 1996 carries forward, to be deducted as a Section 179 expense in subsequent years.

Handwritten margin note: $6,000 can be carried forward to future (8,000 − 2,000)

Any Section 179 deduction that is elected and not used because of the taxable income limit can be carried forward and used in a later year. The deductions are carried forward and used on a first-in, first-out basis against the $17,500 annual limit after current-year deductions. All or part of the deferred deduction can be used in a year in which the investment in qualifying property is less than the by the amount expensed under Section 179, even though the deduction cannot be used in the current year and is carried forward.[6] As stated earlier, a taxpayer does not have to use the full $17,500 expense deduction or expense the full cost of an asset. Instead of claiming the full deduction, the taxpayer can elect to expense an amount equal to the income limitation and avoid the carryover. This alternative is desirable if the taxpayer continuously invests in qualified property and would not expect to use the carryforward in the next tax year. The portion of an asset's basis not expensed remains subject to regular depreciation.

▲ EXAMPLE 10   Assume that in example 9 Michael purchases $16,000-worth of equipment in 1997. During 1997, Michael has $40,000 in taxable income from his business, and Serena earns a salary of $10,000. What is their maximum Section 179 deduction in 1997?

Discussion: Michael and Serena may elect to expense up to $17,500 as a Section 179 expense, because their taxable business income exceeds $17,500. Michael's current-year purchases of qualified property are less than $17,500, so the amount they can expense depends on the amount elected in 1996. If they elected to expense only the $2,000 income limit amount, they have no deduction to carry forward from 1996, and they can expense only the $16,000 in 1997 purchases. If they had elected to expense the full $8,000 purchase in 1996, they could also expense $1,500 ($17,500 limit − $16,000 current-year purchases) of the 1996 carryforward. This leaves $4,500 ($6,000 carryforward − $1,500 expensed) of the 1996 carryforward for use in 1998.

In this case, if they had anticipated continuing qualifying purchases in 1997, they should have elected to expense only the $2,000 limit in 1996. This would have allowed them to depreciate the remaining $6,000-worth of equipment rather than take it slowly over what may be a longer period.

Note the similarity to the loss limitations discussed in Chapter 7. The effect of the taxable active trade or business income limit is to prevent the Section 179 deduction from creating business losses that offset income from investment income sources.

MODIFIED ACCELERATED COST RECOVERY (MACRS)

MACRS took effect on January 1, 1987, after six years of ACRS rules. MACRS retains the basic straightforward ACRS approach to calculating the depreciation deduction. The computation is straightforward because the tax law specifies the recovery period, depreciation method, and the acquisition- and disposition-year conventions to be used. To simplify depreciation calculations, the IRS has developed tables incorporating these factors. Under MACRS, an asset's depreciable basis is multiplied by a percentage obtained from one of the IRS tables to determine the depreciation deduction. Therefore, the taxpayer's primary objective is to decide which table to use. To make that determination, a taxpayer must answer several questions:

■ Does the property qualify for MACRS treatment?

■ What is the asset's depreciable basis?

■ What is the depreciable asset's recovery period?

■ What is the appropriate first-year and last-year convention?

■ Is an accelerated or a slower cost-recovery method desirable?

These decisions lead a taxpayer to the appropriate IRS percentage tables. Then the depreciation deduction is calculated by multiplying the depreciable basis by the correct percentage from the table.

Property Subject to MACRS

MACRS applies to new and used tangible depreciable property. Tangible depreciable property includes buildings, land improvements, and equipment. Tangible property can be depreciated only if it is used in a trade or business or held for the production of income and has a determinable useful life.[7] Therefore, land, intangible assets, and personal use assets cannot be depreciated under MACRS. ✗

A taxpayer may not take a deduction for the periodic capital recovery of the basis of an asset held for personal use. A taxpayer can depreciate the business basis of a mixed-use asset but not the personal use part. An intangible asset used for both business and personal purposes, such as an extended (repair) warranty agreement on a car, can be amortized and deducted to the extent the asset is used for a business purpose. Table 11–1 illustrates examples of depreciable and non-depreciable assets that an individual might own.

> ▲ **EXAMPLE 11**   On January 1, 1996, Melody buys a new car that she plans to use 80% of the time in her business and 20% of the time for personal transportation. She also buys a 5-year extended repair warranty on her new car for $500. Can Melody deduct the cost of the extended warranty as an expense?
>
> *Discussion:*   The $500 paid for the extended warranty is not a current expense. The extended warranty is an intangible long-lived asset that provides benefits for 5 tax years. Because the asset provides business benefits, its cost is subject to amortization. The annual amortization is $100 ($500 ÷ 5 years). However, Melody is allowed a deduction of only $80 for the expense related to business use of the car (80% business use × $100). She cannot deduct the $20 expense related to personal use of the car.

A typical business asset that is not subject to depreciation is inventory. When inventory is sold, its cost basis is subtracted from sales as a deduction for the cost of goods sold.

> ▲ **EXAMPLE 12**   Mitch uses the following assets in his corner grocery store:
>
> No Inventory   Store building ✗
> Shelving ✗   No Land
> Black-topped parking lot ✗   Shopping carts ✗
>
> Which of the assets are subject to depreciation?

Depreciable Asset	Nondepreciable Asset
House held for rent to others	House used as taxpayer's personal residence
Auto used for a *business purpose* (e.g., if 60% of the miles an auto is driven relates to business use, 60% of the auto is a business asset subject to depreciation)	Auto used for commuting to and from work and for other personal uses
Furniture in business office	Furniture in taxpayer's personal residence
	Land (land is never depreciable)
Microcomputer used in a business	Microcomputer used by members of the family for personal recordkeeping and educational purposes

▲ **Table 11–1**

ASSETS OWNED BY INDIVIDUALS

[handwritten notes in margin: 500 ÷ 5 = 100 per year × 80% = $80 Allowed Deduction]

lot, and the shopping carts. These assets are used to conduct the grocery business, and they have a limited useful life in Mitch's business. The land cannot be depreciated, because it has an indefinite useful life. The sale of inventory results in a deduction for the cost of goods sold.

MACRS does not apply to any property that the taxpayer elects to depreciate using an accounting method that is based on units of production or any basis other than years of use. A taxpayer who uses the standard mileage rate method to compute an auto expense deduction has elected a special depreciation method. The auto is depreciated using a standard depreciation rate per mile (e.g., 12 cents per mile for 1996) and is not subject to MACRS. Therefore, a taxpayer can avoid the use of MACRS by electing to depreciate an asset using an alternative depreciation method not based on years of use. To be valid, the election must be made in the first year the asset is placed in service.

Basis Subject to Cost Recovery

Depreciable basis is the asset's original basis for depreciation, less any amount deducted under the Section 179 election to expense assets. Therefore, the basis rules discussed in Chapter 10 provide the starting point for computing the capital recovery deduction. An asset's basis for depreciation does not have to be reduced by its salvage value. The depreciable basis of an asset is the amount of basis that is subject to depreciation and is the amount used to determine the annual depreciation deduction.[8] The depreciable basis does not change during an asset's tax life unless additional capital expenditures are made for the asset. The total capital recovered as a depreciation deduction over an asset's useful life may never be more than its depreciable basis. Do not confuse the term *depreciable basis* with *adjusted basis*. **Adjusted basis** refers to the unrecovered capital of an asset at any point in time. An asset's adjusted basis decreases as cost-recovery deductions are taken. The capital recovery under MACRS does not necessarily relate to the true remaining useful life and salvage value of the asset. That is, an asset's depreciable basis can be fully recovered, even though the asset remains in service and salvage value exists.

▲ **EXAMPLE 13** In 1996, Estelle Corporation purchases office equipment costing $17,000 for use in its repair business. Because equipment is eligible to be expensed under Section 179, Estelle elects to expense $10,000 of the cost of the equipment. What is Estelle Corporation's depreciable basis in the equipment?

Discussion: Estelle's initial basis in the equipment is $17,000. The election to expense reduces the depreciable basis to $7,000 ($17,000 − $10,000). The corporation recovers its $17,000 investment in the equipment through $10,000 of expense in the year of purchase and $7,000 in depreciation charges over the tax life of the equipment.

If Estelle had elected to expense the entire $17,000 cost under Section 179, the corporation would fully recover its capital investment in 1996. The depreciable basis in the equipment then is zero, and the corporation is allowed no further capital recovery deductions on its initial $17,000 investment. However, the equipment remains in service and may provide several years of quality use.

MACRS Recovery Period

Each asset subject to MACRS must be placed in a MACRS class according to its **class life.** Table A11–1 (in the appendix to this chapter and partially reproduced here as Table 11–2) is an excerpt from IRS Revenue Procedure 87–56, which spec-

▲ **Table 11–2**

IRS TABLE OF MACRS CLASSES *(Partial Table)*

| Asset Class | Description of Assets Included | Class Life (in years) | Recovery Periods (in years) | |
			General Depreciation System	Alternative Depreciation System
Specific Depreciable Assets Used in All Business Activities, Except as Noted:				
00.11	Office Furniture, Fixtures, and Equipment: Includes furniture and fixtures that are not a structural component of a building. Includes such assets as desks, files, safes, and communications equipment. Does not include communications equipment that is included in other classes	10	7	10
00.22	Automobiles, Taxis	3	5	5
00.23	Buses	9	5	9
00.241	Light General Purpose Trucks: Includes trucks for use over the road (actual unloaded weight less than 13,000 pounds)	4	5	5
00.242	Heavy General Purpose Trucks: Includes heavy general purpose trucks, concrete ready mix-truckers, and ore trucks, for use over the road (actual unloaded weight 13,000 pounds or more)	6	5	6
00.25	Railroad Cars and Locomotives, except those owned by railroad transportation companies	15	7	15
00.26	Tractor Units For Use Over-The-Road	4	3	4
00.27	Trailers and Trailer-Mounted Containers	6	5	6
00.28	Vessels, Barges, Tugs, and Similar Water Transportation Equipment, except those used in marine construction	18	10	18
Certain Property for Which Recovery Periods Assigned:				
	A. Personal Property With No Class Life		7	12
	Section 1245 Real Property With No Class Life		7	40

ifies the class lives used to place assets in MACRS classes and determines recovery periods.[9] Revenue Procedure 87–56 gives the recovery periods for both MACRS (under the column labeled *General Depreciation System*) and ADS (under the column labeled *Alternative Depreciation System*) for broad classes of assets and industry groups. Specifying the recovery periods standardizes the depreciation calculation. Thus, MACRS eliminates several sources of potential conflict between the IRS and taxpayers concerning an asset's useful life and the calculation of the depreciation deduction.

MACRS provides 3-, 5-, 7-, 10-, 15-, and 20-year recovery periods for property other than real estate. Most personal property is in the 3-, 5-, or 7-year class. The 10-, 15-, and 20-year classes generally include land improvements and specialized types of buildings and other property. In addition, residential rental real estate is given a 27.5-year recovery period, whereas nonresidential real estate placed in service before May 13, 1993, is assigned a 31.5-year recovery period. The recovery period for nonresidential real estate placed in service after May 12, 1993, has been increased to 39 years. Table 11–3 lists the MACRS recovery classes and examples of

▲ Table 11–3

MACRS RECOVERY
CLASSES

Recovery Class	Examples of Property in Recovery Class
3 years	Tractor units for over-the road use Race horses older than 2 years and any other horse older than 12 years when placed in service Breeding hogs Special tools and handling devices used in manufacture of food and beverages, and rubber, glass, and fabricated metal products
5 years	Automobiles, taxis, buses, trucks, airplanes, helicopters, trailers, and trailer-mounted containers Computers and peripheral equipment Office machinery such as typewriters, copiers, calculators Assets used by general construction contractors and real estate developers Breeding and dairy cattle Logging machinery and sawmill equipment Qualified technological equipment Property used in research and experimentation Alternative energy property (e.g., geothermal, solar energy)
7 years	Office furniture, fixtures, and equipment Breeding or work horses 12 years or younger when placed in service Machinery used in various types of manufacturing Assets used to provide recreational services for a fee or admission charge, such as, bowling alleys, billiard and pool establishments, theaters, concert halls, and miniature golf courses Assets used to provide rides, attractions, and amusement in theme and amusement parks *Tangible* personal property with no class life
10 years	Water transportation equipment, such as vessels, barges, tugboats Single-purpose agricultural buildings Fruit- or nut-bearing trees and vines
15 years	Land improvements directly to or added to the land; includes sidewalks, roads, drainage facilities, fences, landscaping shrubbery Service station buildings and land improvements Car washes and related land improvements Billboards
20 years	Farm buildings Municipal sewers
27.5 years	Residential real estate Apartment buildings, houses, and mobile homes for which 80% or more of the gross rental income is from dwelling units
31.5 years	Nonresidential real estate placed in service before May 13, 1993 Office buildings, warehouses, factories, hotels, motels
39 years	Nonresidential real estate placed in service after May 12, 1993

property assigned to each class. If personal property is not listed in a specific asset class or identified with a specific industry in the revenue procedure, it is assigned a 7-year recovery period for MACRS and a 12-year recovery period for ADS.

▲ **EXAMPLE 14** Refer to the office equipment Estelle Corporation purchased in example 13. Using Table A11–1, what is the class life of the equipment and what are its recovery periods under MACRS and ADS?

Discussion: According to Table A11–1, this equipment has a class life of 10 years, a MACRS recovery period of 7 years, and an ADS recovery period of 10 years. Therefore, Estelle's $7,000 of depreciable basis must be recovered over either 7 years or 10 years. If Estelle chooses to maximize cost recovery with MACRS, the recovery period is 7 years (found under the *Recovery Period* column labeled *General Depreciation System*). If Estelle chooses to minimize cost recovery, Estelle elects ADS, and the recovery period is 10 years.

▲ **EXAMPLE 15**   In 1996, Drake purchases the following assets for use in his business:

Purchase Date	Asset	Cost
1/7	Truck (light)	$ 8,000
2/11	Machinery	5,000
4/5	Microcomputer	6,000
5/11	Land	50,000
6/1	Sidewalks	10,000
8/3	Warehouse	150,000
9/4	Office furniture	25,000

What are the MACRS and ADS recovery periods for each asset Drake places in service during 1996?

Discussion: Using Table A11–1, the recovery periods for MACRS (*General Depreciation System* column) and ADS (*Alternative Depreciation System* column) are as follows:

	Recovery Period	
Asset	MACRS	ADS
Truck	5	5
Machinery	7	10
Microcomputer	5	5
Land	not depreciable	
Sidewalks	15	20
Warehouse	39	40
Office furniture	7	10

MACRS Conventions

To avoid difficulties associated with computing depreciation for fractions of a year, Congress used the concept of administrative convenience and adopted three **depreciation conventions** for use under MACRS: a mid-year, mid-month, and mid-quarter convention.[10] All IRS percentage tables incorporate the appropriate convention for the first year. Generally, the mid-year convention applies to all ✳ classes of property except real estate.[11] The **mid-year convention** assumes that personal property is placed in service (and disposed of) in the middle of the year. Under this convention, a half-year of depreciation is allowed in both the first and last years of use. As a result, it takes four tax years to fully depreciate a three-year asset, six years to depreciate a five-year asset, and so forth for the other categories of property. Note that the IRS depreciation percentages listed in Table 11–4 incorporate the mid-year convention. In recovery year 1, the depreciation rate is significantly less than the rate for recovery year 2, even though an accelerated method of depreciation is in use. This happens because the year 1 rate is for only a half-year.

▲ **Table 11–4**

MACRS DEPRECIATION FOR PROPERTY OTHER THAN REAL ESTATE
Applicable convention: mid-year *(applicable methods: 200% or 150% declining balance, switching to straight-line)*

If the recovery year is	And the recovery period is					
	3 Years	5 Years	7 Years	10 Years	15 Years	20 Years
	The depreciation rate is					
1	33.33	20.00	14.29	10.00	5.00	3.750
2	44.45	32.00	24.49	18.00	9.50	7.219
3	14.81	19.20	17.49	14.40	8.55	6.677
4	7.41	11.52	12.49	11.52	7.70	6.177
5		11.52	8.93	9.22	6.93	5.713
6		5.76	8.92	7.37	6.23	5.285
7			8.93	6.55	5.90	4.888
8			4.46	6.55	5.90	4.522
9				6.56	5.91	4.462
10				6.55	5.90	4.461
11				3.28	5.91	4.462
12					5.90	4.461
13					5.91	4.462
14					5.90	4.461
15					5.91	4.462
16					2.95	4.461
17						4.462
18						4.461
19						4.462
20						4.461
21						2.231

The **mid-month convention** is used only for real estate. This convention allocates depreciation according to the number of months the real estate is in service. The mid-month convention assumes that real estate is placed in service (and disposed of) in the middle of the month. Therefore, the months of acquisition and disposition are counted only as half months. A taxpayer is never allowed a full year's depreciation in the year of acquisition or disposition under the mid-month convention.

The **mid-quarter convention** applies to personal property and assumes that all property is placed in service and disposed of in the middle of the quarter of the year of acquisition and disposition. Assets placed in service during the first quarter of the year are depreciated from the middle of the first quarter to the end of the year, or 10.5 months ÷ 12 of a full year's depreciation. The details of this convention are discussed later in this section.

Determining the appropriate convention to use to allocate first and last years' depreciation is one nuance of MACRS. However, note that each IRS table specifies the convention being used by that particular class life. The most important point underlying all the conventions is that the precise date of acquisition or disposition is not crucial in making the allocation, as was the case in computing depreciation under the facts and circumstances method.

▲ **EXAMPLE 16**   On March 10, 1997, Quynh purchases and places into service office furniture costing $20,000. Quynh does not elect to expense under Section 179. What is the correct convention for this property?

Discussion: The mid-year convention applies in this case because the office furniture is personal property. It is 7-year MACRS recovery property (see Table A11–1). The mid-year convention assumes the property is placed in service on July 1. The IRS depreciation percentage table that incorporates the mid-year convention for 7-year property is Table 11–4. The depreciation rate for year 1 is 14.29%. Multiplying this rate by the furniture's depreciable basis gives the first-year depreciation of $2,858 ($20,000 × 14.29%). Note that the 14.29% is based upon the 200% declining balance depreciation method and uses the mid-year convention. Thus, the MACRS depreciation can also be calculated without the percentage table: $2,857 = ($20,000 ÷ 7 years × 200% declining balance × 1/2 year). The $1 difference is the result of rounding. Using IRS percentage tables that incorporate the mid-year convention saves work and chance of errors.

The IRS tables provide the percentage for a full year of depreciation for each class of property. Therefore, the tables' percentages must be adjusted for the last year's depreciation if an asset is disposed of before the end of its recovery period.

▲ **EXAMPLE 17**   Assume that Quynh sells the office furniture in example 16 on December 14, 1999. How does the mid-year convention affect the allowable 1999 depreciation deduction on the office furniture?

Discussion: The 1999 depreciation deduction for the office furniture is $1,749. From Table 11–4, the depreciation percentage for 7-year property for the third year (1999) is 17.49%. A full year's depreciation would be $3,498 ($20,000 × 17.49%). However, under the mid-year convention only half the annual depreciation is allowed in the year of disposition—$1,749 ($3,498 × 1/2). The mid-year convention is built into the percentage tables only for property held for its total recovery period. Note that the adjusted basis of Quynh's office furniture is $10,495 [$20,000 − ($2,858 + $4,898 + $1,749)] at the sale date.

The mid-month convention applies only to real estate. It allocates depreciation according to the number of months the real estate is in service. However, the month of acquisition is counted as only a half month. Table 11–5 incorporates the mid-month convention for 39-year nonresidential real estate.

▲ **EXAMPLE 18**   Tomas Corporation's depreciable basis in a store building it purchased on May 31, 1993, is $100,000. What is the correct convention for this property, and how does it affect the first-year depreciation?

Discussion: Real estate always uses the mid-month convention. Accordingly, only one-half of the depreciation for May is allowed, regardless of the day in the month the building was actually placed in service. The building is considered to have been in service for 7.5 months (June through December plus one half-month for May) in 1993. Depreciation using the first-year depreciation rate of 1.605% is $1,605 ($100,000 × 1.605%). This rate is found in Table 11–5, reading across year 1 to column 5. Alternatively, the depreciation deduction can be calculated by using the straight-line method over 39 years and applying the mid-month convention. The deduction for 12 months in year 1 is $2,564 ($100,000 ÷ 39 years). Because Tomas placed the building in service in May, it is necessary to adjust the depreciation for the 7.5 months of service in 1993. Remember that the mid-month convention allows only one half-month of depreciation

If the recovery year is	And the month in the first recovery year the property is placed in service is											
	1	2	3	4	5	6	7	8	9	10	11	12
	The depreciation rate is											
1	2.461	2.247	2.033	1.819	1.605	1.391	1.177	0.963	0.749	0.535	0.321	0.107
2–39	2.564	2.564	2.564	2.564	2.564	2.564	2.564	2.564	2.564	2.564	2.564	2.564
40	0.107	0.321	0.535	0.749	0.963	1.177	1.391	1.605	1.819	2.033	2.247	2.461

▲ **Table 11–5**

MACRS DEPRECIATION FOR NONRESIDENTIAL REAL ESTATE PLACED IN SERVICE AFTER MAY 12, 1993 Applicable convention: mid-month *(applicable recovery period: 39 years)*

in the first month. So, $1,603 [$2,564 × (7.5 ÷ 12)] is the calculation for depreciation for 1993. (The $2 difference between this calculation and the amount in the table is the result of rounding).

If real estate is disposed of during the year, the percentages in the IRS tables must be adjusted to the month of disposition using the mid-month convention.

▲ **EXAMPLE 19**   Return to example 18. If Tomas sells the store building on March 1, 1999, how does the mid-month convention affect the 1999 depreciation deduction?

Discussion: The property is 39-year nonresidential rental property that was placed into service in the fifth month of Tomas's tax year. Therefore, the MACRS percentages from Table 11–5, column 5, are the depreciation schedule for the property. The asset is used in 1999, its seventh year. To determine the deduction for 1999, read across year 7 to column 5 to find 2.564%. The deduction for 12 months in year 7 is $2,564 ($100,000 × 2.564%). Because Tomas sold the asset in March, it has to adjust the annual table's deduction to claim 2.5 months' depreciation using the mid-month convention (January + February + 1/2 month for March). Tomas Corporation deducts $534 in depreciation [$2,564 × (2.5 months ÷ 12 months)] in 1999.

Mid-quarter Convention.   If more than 40 percent of the depreciable basis of personal property is placed in service during the last three months of the tax year, the taxpayer must use the mid-quarter convention. The mid-quarter convention applies only to personal property placed in service during the year. Real estate is never subject to the mid-quarter convention; it is always depreciated using the mid-month convention. This convention requires the calculation of depreciation from the middle of the quarter in which an asset is placed in service through the end of the year.

The first year's depreciation using the mid-quarter convention is computed by multiplying the depreciation on the asset for the full year by the applicable percentage for the quarter of acquisition:

Property Placed in Service during	Months Used	Percentage
1st quarter	10.5 ÷ 12	87.5
2nd quarter	7.5 ÷ 12	62.5
3rd quarter	4.5 ÷ 12	37.5
4th quarter	1.5 ÷ 12	12.5

Fortunately, MACRS percentage tables (see the appendix to this chapter, Tables A11–3 through A11–6) with appropriate depreciation percentages for the quarter of acquisition, are available for computing the depreciation deduction. Thus, the major problem is identifying those situations in which more than 40 percent of the personal property acquired during a year is placed in service in the last three months of the year.

▲ **EXAMPLE 20**   On February 2, 1996, the Rogers Partnership purchases a computer for $3,500. It buys office furniture for $6,000 on November 15, 1996. No other personal property is placed in service in 1996. Rogers does not elect to expense any of the property under Section 179. How much depreciation may the partnership deduct for 1996?

Discussion: Because more than 40% {63% = [$6,000 ÷ ($6,000 + $3,500)]} of the depreciable basis of personal property was placed in service during the last 3 months of the year, Rogers must use the mid-quarter convention. Rogers can use the mid-quarter convention MACRS percentage tables in the appendix to this chapter to calculate its depreciation. From Table A11–3, the depreciation on the computer placed in service in the first quarter is $1,225 ($3,500 × 35% for 5-year property). From Table

A11–6, the depreciation on the office furniture placed in service in the fourth quarter is $214 ($6,000 × 3.57% for 7-year property). The partnership's 1996 depreciation deduction is $1,439 ($1,225 + $214).

The use of the mid-quarter convention generally results in a smaller depreciation deduction than the mid-year convention because of the small portion of the first-year depreciation allowed on the fourth-quarter purchases. Therefore, taxpayers wishing to maximize deductions should plan their personal property purchases to avoid making more than 40 percent of such purchases during the last three months of the tax year. In certain situations, the Section 179 election can be used to avoid the mid-quarter convention by expensing assets purchased in the fourth quarter.[12]

▲ **EXAMPLE 21**   Ari purchases 5-year property costing $30,000 on April 4, 1996. He purchases other 5-year property costing $25,000 on November 3, 1996. He places no other personal property in service in 1996. What is Ari's maximum depreciation deduction for 1996?

Discussion: Ari's fourth-quarter purchases are 45% [$25,000 ÷ ($30,000 + $25,000)] of his total purchases during the year. Therefore, the mid-quarter convention applies. However, the 40% rule is based on the depreciable basis placed in service during the fourth quarter. Because the Section 179 election reduces the depreciable basis of assets expensed, Ari can reduce the depreciable basis placed in service during the fourth quarter by expensing $17,500 of the $25,000-worth of property purchased on November 3. This reduces the depreciable basis of the property to $7,500 and the percentage placed in service during the fourth quarter to 20% [$7,500 ÷ ($30,000 + $7,500)]. Ari is not subject to the mid-quarter convention and uses the general mid-year convention for personal property. The overall result is to give Ari a greater depreciation deduction on the property purchases:

	Mid-quarter		Mid-year	
April 4 property basis	$30,000		$ 30,000	
Depreciation %	× 25% (Table A11–4)		× 20% (Table 11–4)	
First-year depreciation	$ 7,500		$ 6,000	
November 3 property basis	$25,000		$ 25,000	
Less: Section 179 expense	-0-		(17,500)	
Depreciable basis	$25,000		$ 7,500	
Depreciation %	× 5% (Table A11–6)		× 20% (Table 11–4)	
First-year depreciation	$ 1,250		$ 1,500	
Total	$ 8,750	($7,500 + $1,250)	$ 25,000	($6,000 + $17,500
				+ $1,500)

Depreciation Method Alternatives

Under current tax law, taxpayers have three alternatives for calculating depreciation:

- Regular MACRS
- Straight-line over the MACRS recovery period
- Straight-line over the Alternative Depreciation System (ADS).

Figure 11–2 illustrates these choices for depreciating personal property. A taxpayer decides which to use by first choosing whether to maximize or minimize the depreciation deduction in the year of acquisition. The taxpayer would maximize by using the Section 179 election and regular MACRS for the remaining depreciable basis. Regular MACRS depreciates property in the 3-, 5-, 7-, and 10-

▲ **Figure 11–2**

TAXPAYERS' CHOICES FOR
DEPRECIATION: TO
MAXIMIZE OR MINIMIZE
(IN YEAR OF
ACQUISITION)

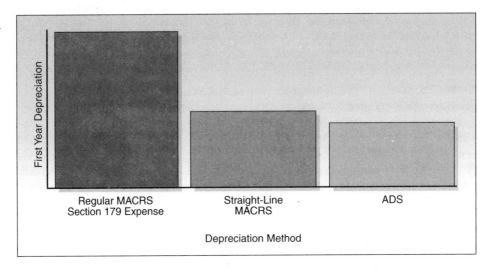

year classes using the 200-percent declining balance method with an optimal, automatic switch to straight-line in the IRS percentage tables. Assets in the 15- and 20-year classes are depreciated using the 150-percent declining balance method. The taxpayer who needs a slower depreciation rate can minimize the deduction by using straight-line (S-L) MACRS or ADS. Because of the longer recovery period, ADS produces the smallest depreciation deduction.

▲ **EXAMPLE 22**   On March 14, 1996, Lorange Mining Corporation purchases a bus costing $28,000 to transport its employees from its office building to the mines. What should Lorange do if it wants to recover its $28,000 cost as quickly as possible (i.e., maximize the cost recovery)?

Discussion: To maximize cost recovery, Lorange should elect to expense $17,500 of the cost under Section 179. This leaves a depreciable basis in the property of $10,500 ($28,000 - $17,500), which should be recovered using the regular MACRS 200% declining balance method over the 5-year recovery period for buses. This recovery period is found in Table A11–1 under the column labeled *General Depreciation System*. The regular MACRS method (using Table 11–4) provides the fastest depreciation write-off for the property's depreciable basis:

Initial basis	$ 28,000
Section 179 election	(17,500)
Depreciable basis	$ 10,500
MACRS % (Table 11–4)	× 20%
Year 1 depreciation	$ 2,100
Maximum cost recovery	$ 19,600 ($17,500 + $2,100)

▲ **EXAMPLE 23**   Assume that in example 22 Lorange wants to recover the $28,000 cost as slowly as possible (i.e., minimize the cost recovery). Which options should Lorange elect?

Discussion: The slowest cost recovery is obtained by not using Section 179 and by electing to use straight-line depreciation over the ADS life of the property. The ADS recovery period is always greater than or equal to the MACRS recovery period. Table A11–1 shows that the ADS recovery period is 9 years for buses. Remember that the MACRS recovery period is 5 years. Thus, the use of the ADS life generally stretches the depreciation deductions over a longer period, thereby diminishing the deduction amounts for each year in the recovery period:

Depreciable basis	$28,000
Full-year S-L deduction ($28,000 ÷ 9)	$ 3,111
Mid-year convention	× 1/2
First-year depreciation	$ 1,556

Lorange could also elect an intermediate recovery scheme by using the straight-line method over the MACRS life. This method depreciates the property more slowly than the regular MACRS 200% declining balance method but more rapidly than straight-line during the ADS life:

Depreciable basis	$28,000
MACRS S-L 5-year rate (Table A11–11)	× 10%
Depreciation deduction	$ 2,800

As the following comparison of depreciation methods for Lorange shows, using the ADS life instead of the regular MACRS method has the effect of stretching out the recovery period:

Year	Maximum Section 179 + MACRS	Intermediate MACRS S-L	Minimum ADS
1	$19,600	$2,800	$1,556
2	3,360	5,600	3,111
3	2,016	5,600	3,111
4	1,210	5,600	3,111
5	1,210	5,600	3,111
6	604	2,800	3,111
7			3,111
8			3,111
9			3,111
10			1,556

Under MACRS, real property is depreciated using the straight-line method. However, taxpayers may choose either MACRS straight-line or ADS. MACRS straight-line uses a 27.5-year recovery period for residential rental real estate and a 39-year recovery period for nonresidential real estate placed in service after May 12, 1993. For nonresidential real estate placed in service before May 13, 1993, the MACRS recovery period is 31.5 years. ADS generally uses a 40-year recovery period for real estate.

Using MACRS Percentage Tables

Once an asset's depreciable basis, recovery period, and appropriate convention are known, and the taxpayer has decided whether to use regular MACRS or to elect a straight-line depreciation method, percentage tables published by the IRS provide the depreciation rate. The asset's depreciable basis is multiplied by the depreciation rate to determine the annual deduction. All of the relevant IRS percentage tables are reproduced in the appendix to this chapter. The MACRS percentage table for property other than real estate appears in Table 11–4. The percentage tables are constructed to permit full capital recovery of an asset's basis over its recovery period. In addition, the percentage tables incorporate the proper first-year convention, and they make the switch from the declining balance to the straight-line method to optimize the deduction. In effect, the columns of the percentage tables are the depreciation schedule for each recovery period of an asset.

Using the tables standardizes the depreciation calculation and minimizes the possibility of error in the depreciation calculation—a taxpayer does not have to perform the mechanics of declining balance depreciation to benefit from the method.

▲ **EXAMPLE 24**   The Kwan Partnership purchases a machine in the 7-year MACRS recovery class on January 5, 1996, for $2,500. Assume that Kwan does not elect to expense any part of the asset's cost under Section 179. What amount may the partnership deduct as depreciation expense for each year of the asset's recovery period?

Discussion: Kwan may deduct a total of $2,500 over the machine's 7-year recovery period. Because the machine qualifies as 7-year property, it should use the 7-year column of Table 11–4. The deduction is determined each year by multiplying the $2,500 depreciable basis by the appropriate percentage for the year being calculated. This is the depreciation schedule for the asset:

Year	MACRS %		Depreciable Basis		Depreciation
1996	14.29	X	$2,500	=	$ 357
1997	24.49		2,500		612
1998	17.49		2,500		437
1999	12.49		2,500		312
2000	8.93		2,500		223
2001	8.92		2,500		223
2002	8.93		2,500		223
2003	4.46		2,500		113
Total depreciation					$2,500

Note that although the machine is 7-year class property, it takes 8 years to fully depreciate its cost. The mid-year convention used by MACRS assumes that assets are placed in service in the middle of the year and disposed of in the middle of the year. Thus, the first year and the eighth year are allowed only a half-year of depreciation.

Real estate depreciation begins with the selection of the correct IRS table for the type of real estate being depreciated (i.e., residential rental, or nonresidential). Table 11–6 provides percentages for residential rental real estate (27.5-year property). Table A11–8 provides percentages for nonresidential real estate placed in service before May 13, 1993 (31.5-year property), and Table 11–5 provides percentages for nonresidential real estate placed in service after May 12, 1993 (39-year property). The mid-month convention for depreciable real estate requires determining the month the property is placed in service and finding that month among the twelve columns in the appropriate percentage table. The column chosen becomes the depreciation schedule for the property. The rates in the table are percentages. If a column is added up, it will total 100%—representing complete cost recovery. Each row of the column is the depreciation year. For example, the year of acquisition is recovery year 1.

▲ **EXAMPLE 25**   On February 5, 1996, Pauline acquires an apartment building that costs $120,000. The basis allocated to the building is $100,000, and the basis of the land is $20,000. What is Pauline's depreciation deduction for the property for 1996?

Discussion: The land is not depreciable. The $100,000 building cost is depreciated using the schedule for 27.5-year residential real property. Pauline should use the IRS percentages in Table 11–6, reading across the row labeled *year 1* and down the column labeled *month 2* to find the first-year percentage, 3.182%. Pauline should deduct $3,182 ($100,000 × 3.182%) in depreciation on the building for 1996. The month-2 column of the table becomes the depreciation schedule for the building for the rest of its period of use.

▲ **Table 11–6**

MACRS DEPRECIATION
FOR RESIDENTIAL RENTAL
REAL ESTATE
Applicable convention:
mid-month *(applicable
recovery period: 27.5 years)*

If the recovery year is	And the month in the first recovery year the property is placed in service is											
	1	2	3	4	5	6	7	8	9	10	11	12
	The depreciation rate is											
1	3.485	3.182	2.879	2.576	2.273	1.970	1.667	1.364	1.061	0.758	0.455	0.152
2	3.636	3.636	3.636	3.636	3.636	3.636	3.636	3.636	3.636	3.636	3.636	3.636
3	3.636	3.636	3.636	3.636	3.636	3.636	3.636	3.636	3.636	3.636	3.636	3.636
4	3.636	3.636	3.636	3.636	3.636	3.636	3.636	3.636	3.636	3.636	3.636	3.636
5	3.636	3.636	3.636	3.636	3.636	3.636	3.636	3.636	3.636	3.636	3.636	3.636
6	3.636	3.636	3.636	3.636	3.636	3.636	3.636	3.636	3.636	3.636	3.636	3.636
7	3.636	3.636	3.636	3.636	3.636	3.636	3.636	3.636	3.636	3.636	3.636	3.636
8	3.636	3.636	3.636	3.636	3.636	3.636	3.636	3.636	3.636	3.636	3.636	3.636
9	3.636	3.636	3.636	3.636	3.636	3.636	3.636	3.636	3.636	3.636	3.636	3.636
10	3.637	3.637	3.637	3.637	3.637	3.637	3.636	3.636	3.636	3.636	3.636	3.636
11	3.636	3.636	3.636	3.636	3.636	3.636	3.637	3.637	3.637	3.637	3.637	3.637
12	3.637	3.637	3.637	3.637	3.637	3.637	3.636	3.636	3.636	3.636	3.636	3.636
13	3.636	3.636	3.636	3.636	3.636	3.636	3.637	3.637	3.637	3.637	3.637	3.637
14	3.637	3.637	3.637	3.637	3.637	3.637	3.636	3.636	3.636	3.636	3.636	3.636
15	3.636	3.636	3.636	3.636	3.636	3.636	3.637	3.637	3.637	3.637	3.637	3.637
16	3.637	3.637	3.637	3.637	3.637	3.637	3.636	3.636	3.636	3.636	3.636	3.636
17	3.636	3.636	3.636	3.636	3.636	3.636	3.637	3.637	3.637	3.637	3.637	3.637
18	3.637	3.637	3.637	3.637	3.637	3.637	3.636	3.636	3.636	3.636	3.636	3.636
19	3.636	3.636	3.636	3.636	3.636	3.636	3.637	3.637	3.637	3.637	3.637	3.637
20	3.637	3.637	3.637	3.637	3.637	3.637	3.636	3.636	3.636	3.636	3.636	3.636
21	3.636	3.636	3.636	3.636	3.636	3.636	3.637	3.637	3.637	3.637	3.637	3.637
22	3.637	3.637	3.637	3.637	3.637	3.637	3.636	3.636	3.636	3.636	3.636	3.636
23	3.636	3.636	3.636	3.636	3.636	3.636	3.637	3.637	3.637	3.637	3.637	3.637
24	3.637	3.637	3.637	3.637	3.637	3.637	3.636	3.636	3.636	3.636	3.636	3.636
25	3.636	3.636	3.636	3.636	3.636	3.636	3.637	3.637	3.637	3.637	3.637	3.637
26	3.637	3.637	3.637	3.637	3.637	3.637	3.636	3.636	3.636	3.636	3.636	3.636
27	3.636	3.636	3.636	3.636	3.636	3.636	3.637	3.637	3.637	3.637	3.637	3.637
28	1.970	2.273	2.576	2.879	3.182	3.485	3.636	3.636	3.636	3.636	3.636	3.636
29	0.000	0.000	0.000	0.000	0.000	0.000	0.152	0.455	0.758	1.061	1.364	1.667

[Handwritten margin notes:]

Race horse   50,000
D-L MACRS %,   × 16.67 %
  CAll-11   ―――――――
                               8,335
Depr Ded,   ―――――――

Mower $15,000
5 MACRS %.   × 7.14%
                             ―――――――
Depr Ded,   1,071
                             ―――――――

Total Depr Ded.   8,335
                  1,071
                 ――――――
                  9,406
                 ――――――

MACRS Straight-line Election

Taxpayers may depreciate personal property at a slower rate than the 200-percent
declining balance method of MACRS by making the MACRS straight-line election.
Taxpayers may desire the smaller straight-line deductions because of current low
income or loss. This election provides an intermediate recovery scheme by using
the straight-line method over the MACRS life. This method does not stretch out
the recovery period as long as the ADS straight-line method does. Table A11–11
provides the rate schedules under this election. Note that the MACRS mid-year
convention for both recovery year 1 and the final year of service is built into each
depreciation schedule. For example, an asset with a 5-year life is depreciated at a
rate of one-half of the regular straight-line rate, or 10% (1/2 × 20%), in the year
of acquisition. Also, note that depreciation is deducted over 6 years.

▲ **EXAMPLE 26**   On March 9, 1996, Antonia Stables Corporation places in service a 4-
year-old racehorse that cost $50,000 (3-year MACRS class) and a mower for its hay
field that cost $15,000 (7-year MACRS class). Antonia does not need the accelerated

depreciation deductions provided under MACRS and would like to spread out the deductions on the assets without using the recovery periods provided by the ADS election. What is Antonia's depreciation deduction for these two assets for 1996?

Discussion: Antonia's total depreciation deduction for 1996 is $9,406 ($8,335 + $1,071). The first-year depreciation for the horse is determined by using the straight-line method with the mid-year convention for the 3-year MACRS recovery period for racehorses older than two (Table A11–1). This results in a deduction of $8,335 {[$50,000 × 16.67% from Table A11–11 or ($50,000 ÷ 3) × 1/2]}. The first-year depreciation for the mower is determined by using the straight-line method with the mid-year convention for the 7-year MACRS recovery period for agricultural machinery (Table A11–1). This results in a deduction of $1,071 {[$15,000 × 7.14% from Table A11–11, or ($15,000 ÷ 7) × 1/2]}.

Note that this straight-line MACRS election lowers the first-year depreciation by $9,403 ($18,809 − $9,406) when compared to regular MACRS. Regular MACRS depreciation for the racehorse (3-year MACRS class) is $16,665 ($50,000 × 33.33% from Table 11–4), and regular MACRS for the mower (7-year MACRS class) is $2,144 ($15,000 × 14.29% from Table 11–4). Antonia's total first-year depreciation would be $18,809 ($16,665 + $2,144) if regular MACRS is used—without a Section 179 election.

Alternative Depreciation System (ADS)

The **Alternative Depreciation System (ADS)** generally spreads depreciation deductions over longer recovery periods than MACRS. Taxpayers may elect ADS for determination of regular taxable income. However, it is mandatory for calculation of the alternative minimum tax (discussed in Chapter 14).

A taxpayer may elect to use ADS for several reasons. First, the taxpayer may be experiencing a low income (or loss) period and does not need the greater MACRS deductions this year. By electing ADS, the taxpayer effectively defers the deduction to a future tax year when income is expected to be greater. A second reason for electing to use ADS is to avoid the alternative minimum tax. Taxpayers with large purchases of depreciable assets may become subject to the alternative minimum tax because of the greater MACRS depreciation deductions, which are not allowed in computing the alternative minimum tax. In some cases, by electing to take smaller depreciation deductions the taxpayer's final tax bill could actually drop.

The election to use ADS is made on a class-by-class, year-by-year basis for property other than real estate. For real estate, ADS is elected on a property-by-property basis in the year of acquisition.

If a taxpayer elects to use the Alternative Depreciation System, the depreciation is usually computed using the straight-line method over the specified, longer alternative recovery period. For computing the ADS deduction, an asset's life is determined by using the column for the Alternative Depreciation System in Table A11–1. For example, office fixtures have a regular MACRS (general depreciation system) recovery period of 7 years. Under ADS, the recovery period is 10 years. Residential rental real estate has a 27.5-year MACRS recovery period and a 40-year recovery period for ADS purposes. Nonresidential real estate has a 31.5-year or 39-year MACRS recovery period (depending on whether it was placed in service before or after May 13, 1993) and a 40-year recovery period for ADS purposes. However, automobiles have a 5-year recovery period under both MACRS and ADS. The deduction for the first and last years of an asset's recovery period must be calculated using the applicable mid-year, mid-quarter, or mid-month convention.

▲ **EXAMPLE 27**   Assume that in example 26 Antonia Stables Corporation wants to spread the deductions on the assets out for as long as possible. What is Antonia's depreciation deduction for these two assets for 1996?

Discussion: Antonia's smallest total depreciation deduction for 1996 is $2,833 ($2,083 + $750). The first-year depreciation for the racehorse is determined by using the straight-line method with the mid-year convention for the 12-year ADS recovery period for racehorses older than two (Table A11–1). This results in a deduction of $2,083 [($50,000 ÷ 12 years) × 1/2]. The first-year depreciation for the mower is determined by using the straight-line method with the mid-year convention for the 10-year ADS recovery period for agricultural machinery (Table A11–1). This results in a deduction of $750 [($15,000 ÷ 10 years) × 1/2]. Here is how the three depreciation methods for Antonia's new assets compare:

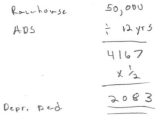

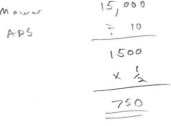

Regular MACRS	Straight-line MACRS	ADS
$18,809	$9,406	$2,833

Limitations on Listed Property

Because taxpayers have abused the opportunity to claim depreciation deductions for mixed-use property, Congress enacted listed property rules in 1984. The **listed property rules** require taxpayers to adequately substantiate the extent of an asset's business use.[13] If listed property is not predominately used in a trade or business, the business portion of the asset must be depreciated under the Alternative Depreciation System. Another important aspect of the listed property rules is that an annual dollar limitation is placed on the depreciation deduction for automobiles.[14]

Listed Property in General

Listed property includes the following categories:

■ Passenger autos—Any four-wheeled vehicle that is manufactured for use on public highways and that weighs 6,000 pounds or less; specifically excluded are ambulances, hearses, and vehicles used in the business of transporting people for hire (e.g., taxi cabs).

■ Other property used for transportation—Trucks, buses, airplanes, trains, boats, motorcycles, and any other vehicle used for transporting persons and goods; excluded are qualified nonpersonal use vehicles such as cement mixers, clearly marked police cars, combines, and several other vehicles. The exclusion is based on the nature (design) of the vehicle, which results in minimal personal use.

■ Property of a type that is generally used for purposes of entertainment, recreation, or amusement—Photographic, phonographic, communication, and video recording equipment, but these assets are excluded if they are used either exclusively at the taxpayer's regular business establishment or in connection with the taxpayer's principal trade or business. A regular business establishment includes a qualifying home office (see Chapter 6 for home office qualifications).

■ Any computer or peripheral equipment—Computers, printers, modems, and other property related to the computer; these assets are excluded if they are used exclusively at a regular business establishment. A regular business establishment includes a qualifying home office.

■ Any cellular telephone or similar communications equipment.

If more than 50 percent of an asset's total use for each year of its tax life is related to the taxpayer's trade or business, the asset is considered to be predominantly used in a trade or business and is treated the same as any other business asset. Using the asset in an investment activity (i.e., production-of-income use) is not counted as business use to satisfy the 50-percent test. When listed property is used 50 percent or less in the taxpayer's business, the asset is not considered predominantly used in a trade or business, and depreciation deductions are limited. The Section 179 expense election does not apply to the asset, and the annual depreciation deduction must be calculated using the Alternative Depreciation System (ADS).[15]

▲ **EXAMPLE 28**   On May 1, Sara places in service a computer that cost her $3,500. Sara uses the computer 60% of the time to manage her investments, 30% of the time in her consulting business, and 10% of the time for personal record keeping. Sara would like to maximize her depreciation deduction on the computer. What method must Sara use to compute her depreciation deduction?

Discussion: Sara must use ADS. Because Sara's trade or business use (30%) is not more than 50% of the computer's total use, she cannot use MACRS or make a Section 179 election. She must use the straight-line method to depreciate the business and investment portion (a total of 90%) over the 5-year ADS life. Her depreciation deduction is $315 [($3,500 × 90% = $3,150) ÷ 5 × 1/2].

▲ **EXAMPLE 29**   Assume that in example 28 Sara uses the computer 60% of the time in her consulting business, 30% of the time to manage her investments, and 10% of the time for personal record keeping. How should Sara compute her depreciation deduction?

Discussion: Sara's total depreciation deduction is $2,310 ($2,100 + $210). Sara may use MACRS. Because Sara's trade or business use (60%) is more than 50% of the computer's total use, she may use MACRS, and she can make a Section 179 election for the business portion of the asset. The computer is treated the same as other mixed-use business assets. The business and investment use of the asset (90%) is recovered as any other business asset would be.

	Business Use	Investment Use	Personal Use
Original basis	$2,100	$1,050	$350
Cost recovery:			
Election to expense	$2,100		
MACRS Depreciation			
(20% × $1,050)		$ 210	

Because Sara's business use is greater than 50%, she can elect to expense the business use of the computer, $2,100 (60% × $3,500). The investment use of the computer $1,050 (30% × $3,500) can be depreciated using the regular 5-year MACRS recovery period for computers $210 ($1,050 × 20% from Table 11–4). The personal use of the computer, $350 (10% × $3,500) is not subject to cost recovery.

Limitation on Passenger Autos.   Passenger autos are subject to a limitation on the annual amount of the deductible depreciation. The annual depreciation deduction for a passenger automobile cannot exceed a specified amount, which is pegged to the year a car is placed in service. Any depreciation that is disallowed because of the annual limitations may be deducted when the auto's recovery period ends. Table A11–10 lists the auto depreciation tables and the annual auto limits that are allowed for 100-percent business use of an auto placed in service in 1994, 1995, and 1996. If an auto is not used wholly for a business purpose, the amount of the annual **passenger automobile limitation** must be reduced by multiplying it by the business use percentage.[16] The depreciation subject to the first-year annual limitation includes any amount that is expensed using Section 179. As mentioned earlier, the annual limitation on the auto depreciation deduction makes it impractical to deduct any of the cost of an auto under Section 179.

▲ **EXAMPLE 30**   In 1996, Oscar purchases a new car for $20,000. Based on his mileage records, Oscar uses the car 80% of the time for a qualified business use. What is Oscar's depreciation deduction on the car for 1996?

Discussion: Automobiles are 5-year MACRS property. Oscar uses the automobile more than 50% of the time for business. Therefore, the allowable depreciation on a passenger automobile is the lesser of the regular MACRS depreciation or the passenger automobile limitation. Oscar's 1996 depreciation deduction for the car is limited to $2,448. Oscar would compute his depreciation deduction for 1996 as follows:

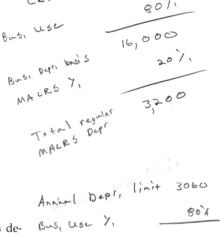

Regular MACRS Depreciation

Initial basis	$20,000
Business use percentage	× 80%
Business depreciable basis	$16,000
MACRS table percentage	× 20%
Total regular MACRS depreciation	$ 3,200

Passenger Automobile Limitation

Annual depreciation limit for an automobile placed in service in 1996 (from Table A11–10)	$ 3,060
Oscar's business use percentage	× 80%
Oscar's maximum depreciation on the auto	$ 2,448

Although the computed depreciation deduction using MACRS is $3,200, Oscar's deduction cannot exceed the annual limitation, adjusted for the percentage of business use, $2,448. Note that the effect of the auto depreciation limit is to make the Section 179 election a poor choice for an automobile, because the 179 election is considered depreciation for purposes of applying the auto limit.

Adequate Record Keeping.   Listed property is subject to special record-keeping requirements for documenting business use and amounts expended. To substantiate deductions, the taxpayer must be able to prove the

■ Amount of each expenditure related to the property, such as the cost of the property, repairs, insurance, and other expenses

■ Use of the asset, including documentation of the amount of business, investment, and other use of the asset

■ Date of the expenditure or use of the asset

■ Business purpose for the expenditure or the use of the asset

The best proof is written records that show the business use of the listed property. The records should contain receipts when possible and any other documentation necessary to prove the existence of these items. The most common method of substantiation is a diary or a log book in which the taxpayer records the necessary information as the expense is incurred.

DEPLETION

A taxpayer who owns an economic interest in a natural resource that wastes away through use is entitled to a capital recovery deduction for depletion. Minerals, oil and gas, other natural deposits, and timber are subject to depletion. **Depletion** is an accounting method used to recover the basis of an investment in a natural resource as it is used up to earn income. An investment in personal and real property (e.g., machinery, equipment, and buildings) related to recovering the natural resource remains subject to the depreciation rules and not depletion.

A taxpayer has an economic interest in a natural resource if two basic requirements are met. First, the investment in the natural resource must be still in place. *In place* means that the mineral deposit has not been removed from its original source (e.g., is still under ground). Second, capital recovery of the taxpayer's investment depends on the amount of income the taxpayer derives from the extraction of the natural resource.[17]

▲ **EXAMPLE 31**   DeWayne invested $90,000 in a coal mine. The $90,000 investment was allocated as follows: $25,000 as the basis in machinery and equipment, $50,000 as the basis in the coal deposit still in place below ground, and $15,000 as the basis of the residual value of the land. How should DeWayne recover his investment?

Discussion: DeWayne's $50,000 investment in the coal deposit in place is subject to depletion. The $25,000 investment in the machinery and equipment used to recover the coal is subject to depreciation. The basis of the land is not subject to depletion or depreciation. The basis of the land will be recovered at disposition.

Depletion Methods

Two methods are used to compute depletion of natural resources: the cost depletion method and the percentage (statutory) depletion method. Each year, the taxpayer is allowed to deduct the greater figure yielded by the two methods. Therefore, a taxpayer may use the cost method in one year and the percentage method in another year. Regardless of which depletion method is used, the deduction reduces the adjusted basis of the natural resource. A deduction for cost depletion is allowed until the depletable basis has been fully recovered.

In most cases, the taxpayer may continue to use percentage (statutory) depletion after the initial basis has been fully recovered. This use of percentage depletion violates the capital recovery concept by permitting total depletion deductions over the life of the natural resource to exceed the property's depletable basis. As a result, the taxpayer's depletion deduction can exceed the cost of the depletable asset. Although this is clearly a benefit for regular tax purposes, the depletion in excess of cost is not allowed for alternative minimum tax purposes.[18] As with the use of MACRS depreciation, taking depletion deductions in excess of cost could trigger the alternative minimum tax and make the use of percentage depletion undesirable.

▲ **EXAMPLE 32**   Assume that the coal mine in example 31 has operated for several years and that before deducting depletion for the current year DeWayne's adjusted basis for depletion of the coal deposit is $2,000. Further, assume that DeWayne's cost depletion for the current year is $2,000 and his percentage depletion is $2,500. What is DeWayne's current depletion deduction, and how does it affect his depletable basis?

Discussion: DeWayne is allowed to deduct the $2,500 in percentage depletion because it is greater than the $2,000 cost depletion. DeWayne's $2,000 adjusted basis in the coal deposit is reduced to zero by the percentage depletion deduction. At this point, DeWayne has claimed $500 more in capital recovery deductions than he had invested in the coal deposit ($2,500 deduction − $2,000 basis). Because DeWayne has fully recovered his basis, he cannot claim cost depletion in future years. However, he may continue to claim percentage depletion so long as he has gross income from the sale of the coal.

Cost Depletion

To compute **cost depletion,** you must know the basis subject to depletion, the recoverable quantity of the natural resource, and the quantity of the natural resource sold during the year. The basis of the natural resource subject to depletion is the basis that would be used to compute a gain on its sale.[19] For other assets, the basis construct has been used to describe the amount subject to capital recovery. For natural resources, *unrecovered basis* better describes the amount being recovered through depletion, because the estimate of the quantity of the resource to which the basis relates is subject to change each year. Cost depletion is calculated using a units-of-production method. The following computation is the general framework for calculating cost depletion using the units-of-production method:

$$\text{Cost Depletion} = \frac{\text{Basis of natural resource subject to capital recovery (unrecovered basis)}}{\text{Estimated number of mineral units to be recovered (e.g., tons of mineral, barrels of liquid)}} \times \begin{array}{c}\text{Number of units sold during tax year}\end{array}$$

The cost depletion computation allocates the unrecovered basis over the number of mineral units of the natural resource (useful life of the resource) to which the investment relates.

▲ **EXAMPLE 33** In example 31, DeWayne estimates that his $50,000 investment in the coal deposit will result in 350,000 recoverable tons of coal. During 1996, DeWayne mines and sells 40,000 tons of coal. What is DeWayne's cost depletion deduction for 1996?

Discussion: DeWayne's cost depletion deduction for 1996 is $5,714 [($50,000 basis ÷ 350,000 tons of coal) × 40,000 tons sold]. DeWayne's unrecovered basis of the coal deposit after deducting $5,714 for 1996's depletion is $44,286 ($50,000 - $5,714).

Because an estimate of the remaining recoverable units at the end of each year is used to make the computation, the cost depletion per unit will probably change for each tax year. Based on the annual accounting period concept, depletion deductions for prior years are not corrected because of a change in the estimate of recoverable units remaining. The adjustment related to a change in the estimate is allocated to current and future years by incorporating the new estimate in the formula.

▲ **EXAMPLE 34** Assume that during 1997 DeWayne in example 33 sells 105,000 tons of coal. Based on mining reports, DeWayne increases his estimate of recoverable coal by 5,000 tons. What is DeWayne's cost depletion deduction for 1997?

Discussion: DeWayne's cost depletion deduction for 1997 is $14,762. DeWayne's unrecovered basis in the coal deposit after deducting $14,762 for 1997's depletion is $29,524 ($44,286 − $14,762).

At the end of 1996, the estimated coal to be mined and sold is 310,000 tons (350,000 original estimate − 40,000 tons sold). The 5,000-ton revision in DeWayne's estimate increases the recoverable coal to 315,000 tons. The increase in the number of recoverable mineral units in 1997 affects 1997 and later years. DeWayne's 1997 cost depletion is $14,762 [($44,286 unrecovered basis ÷ 315,000 tons of coal) × 105,000 tons sold]. Based on the annual accounting period concept, the 1996 depletion deduction is not revised for the change in the estimate of recoverable mineral units in 1997.

Percentage Depletion

Percentage depletion (also called **statutory depletion**) is calculated by multiplying gross income from the sale of the natural resource by a statutory percentage.[20] The statutory percentage is the depletion rate specified by the tax law. For example, depletion (by percentage) is allowed for

Sulphur, uranium	22%
Gold, copper, silver, iron ore	15%
Asbestos, brucite, coal	10%
Gravel, peat, sand	5%

In addition, the tax law specifies a statutory depletion rate for many other natural resources, including oil and gas. The maximum allowable percentage depletion deduction for the tax year is limited to 50 percent of the taxable income from the natural resource before subtracting the depletion deduction.[21]

▲ **EXAMPLE 35**   In example 33, DeWayne sells the 40,000 tons of coal in 1996 for $1.20 per ton. After deducting operating expenses, DeWayne's taxable income from the property (before deducting percentage depletion) is $10,000. What is DeWayne's maximum depletion deduction for 1996?

Discussion: DeWayne's percentage depletion deduction is $4,800 (40,000 tons × $1.20 × 10% depletion rate for coal). Because 50% of the taxable income from the property, $5,000 ($10,000 × 50%), is greater than the computed percentage depletion, $4,800, the taxable income limit does not apply. However, because the cost depletion computed in example 33 is greater than the percentage depletion, DeWayne should deduct cost depletion for 1996. DeWayne's maximum 1996 depletion deduction is $5,714, using the cost depletion method. NOTE: Cost depletion is not subject to the 50% taxable income limit.

▲ **EXAMPLE 36**   In example 34, DeWayne sells the 105,000 tons of coal in 1997 for $1.50 per ton. After deducting operating expenses, DeWayne's taxable income from the property (before deducting percentage depletion) is $30,000. What is DeWayne's maximum depletion deduction for 1997?

Discussion: Based on the taxable income limitation, DeWayne's maximum allowable percentage depletion deduction is $15,000 ($30,000 × 50%). The tentative percentage depletion deduction is $15,750 (105,000 tons × $1.50 × 10% depletion). From example 34, cost depletion is $14,762, which is less than percentage depletion. However, the $15,000 taxable income limitation applies, because it is less than the $15,750 tentative percentage depletion deduction. Thus, the allowable percentage depletion is $15,000.

For 1997, DeWayne should deduct the $15,000 in percentage depletion, because it is greater than the $14,795 in cost depletion computed in example 34. As a result, DeWayne reduces his recoverable basis in the coal deposit by the percentage depletion deduction instead of the cost depletion deduction. DeWayne's recoverable basis in the coal deposit at the end of 1997 is $29,286 ($44,286 − $15,000 percentage depletion).

INTANGIBLE ASSETS

Patents, copyrights, agreements not to compete, franchises, and goodwill are all **intangible property.**[22] Capital recovery of the investment in an intangible asset is allowed as an expense deduction through amortization. The basis of an intangible is allocated on a straight-line basis over its useful life. To qualify for **amortization,** the intangible asset must be used for a business purpose and it must have a limited useful life that can be estimated with reasonable accuracy.

As a result of the limited life requirement, determining whether a specific intangible asset qualifies for amortization has required an analysis of the facts related to the taxpayer. Because goodwill does not have a useful life that can be estimated with reasonable accuracy, goodwill generally is not subject to amortization. However, in 1993 Congress enacted Section 197, which requires goodwill and other intangibles purchased after August 9, 1993, to be amortized over 15 years. In addition, a transitional relief rule allows taxpayers to elect to amortize

[Handwritten margin notes:
% Depletion
40,000 tons × $1.20 × 10% coal rate
= 4,800

Taxable income
10,000 × 50%
= 5,000

% Depletion
105,000 × $1.50 × 10%
= 15,750

Taxable income
30,000 × 50%
= 15,000

Must use 15,000 because the $15,750 is over the limit of $15,000]

over the 15-year period intangibles purchased after July 25, 1991. This section is a step toward simplifying tax law and offers an element of administrative convenience to the task of determining useful lives of intangibles. Also, through legislative grace, Congress now allows the amortization of goodwill that has been purchased.

Not all intangible assets are subject to the 15-year amortization period. Generally, intangibles subject to the 15-year amortization period are those that are acquired in connection with the purchase of assets constituting a trade or business. Exhibit 11–1 provides a list of qualifying intangible assets.

▲ **EXAMPLE 37**   Natasha is a partner in Future Designs. Natasha has decided to leave the partnership and move to a different state. In 1996, Future and Natasha enter an agreement not to compete. Future pays Natasha $50,000 for Natasha's agreement not to compete or interfere with Future's conduct of business within 250 miles of Future's home office for 5 years. The agreement is effective as of September 1, 1996. What is the tax effect of the transaction for Future and for Natasha?

Discussion: Future can amortize the $50,000 investment in the agreement not to compete by using straight-line amortization over 15 years. For 1996, Future can deduct $1,111 for 4 months' amortization of the investment in the agreement [($50,000 ÷ 15) × (4 ÷ 12)]. Based on the claim-of-right doctrine, Natasha must report the entire $50,000 payment she receives in 1996 as ordinary income related to services. Note that because the agreement not to compete is acquired in connection with the purchase of a trade or business, it must be amortized over the 15-year statutory period, not the 5-year term of the agreement.

▲ **EXAMPLE 38**   On January 1, 1996, Nisalke Co. sells all assets used in its business to Layden Co. The assets consist of real estate, a customer list, goodwill, a patent, and a covenant not to compete. The values allocated to each asset are as follows:

		Intangible Assets
Real estate	$10,000,000	
Customer list	800,000	800,000
Goodwill	500,000	500,000
Patent	1,000,000	1,000,000
Covenant	900,000	900,000
Total purchase price	$13,200,000	3,200,000
		÷ 15 yrs
		213,333 Total Amort for 1996

▲ **Exhibit 11–1**

INTANGIBLE ASSETS SUBJECT TO 15-YEAR AMORTIZATION

The real estate is subject to a recovery period of 39 years. The customer list has a 6-year useful life, the covenant not to compete lasts 3 years, and the patent has 10 years remaining on its useful life. What is Layden's intangible amortization amount for 1996?

Discussion: The four intangible assets must be amortized over 15 years. Total amortization for 1996 is $213,333 ($3,200,000 ÷ 15). Although the company receives the benefit of amortizing the $500,000 of goodwill now, the other intangibles are amortized for a period longer than their useful lives. If Section 197 had not been enacted, the total amortization for 1995 would have been $533,333 [$300,000 ($900,000 ÷ 3) from the covenant; $133,333 ($800,000 ÷ 6) from the customer list; $100,000 ($1,000,000 ÷ 10) from the patent; and zero from goodwill]. Layden reports $320,000 ($533,333 − $213,333) more in taxable income for the current tax year as a result of the 15-year amortization rule.

Certain intangible assets, such as sports franchises, are specifically excluded from the 15-year amortization period. Prior law continues to apply to the excluded assets, which are listed in Exhibit 11–2. For example, patents and copyrights not acquired in the purchase of a trade or business are amortized over periods of 17 years and 50 years plus the author's life, respectively. These amortization periods are useful lives that are set by statute.

170,000
÷ 17
$10,000
Deduction for Amorti

▲ **EXAMPLE 39** On January 4, 1996, Conroy Co. purchases from Technical Process Co., Inc., the patent to the process for extruding certain plastic forms. Conroy pays $170,000 for the newly developed patent process. The purchase does not represent an acquisition of Technical Process Co. What is the amount of patent amortization in 1996?

Discussion: Because the patent was not acquired as part of the purchase of a trade or business, the amortization period is 17 years (the legal life set by the government). Therefore, Conroy's 1996 deduction for amortization is $10,000 ($170,000 ÷ 17).

SUMMARY

The deduction for depreciation demonstrates the application of many concepts discussed in earlier chapters. It is well established that an annual deduction is allowed for the recovery of capital invested in a long-lived asset that is used up to earn income. The problem over the years has been how to determine the deduction for the capital recovery. The central concern of taxpayers is to recover their investment as quickly as possible to maximize the present value of depreciation deductions. However, Congress and the IRS have generally been concerned with protecting the collection of revenue. In addition, Congress has varied the amount of allowable depreciation as a method of stimulating capital investment.

▲ **Exhibit 11–2**

INTANGIBLE ASSETS
SPECIFICALLY EXCLUDED
FROM 15-YEAR
AMORTIZATION

- Interests in notional principal contracts and other similar financial instruments
- Stock, partnership interests
- Interests in land
- Certain computer software
- Interests in films, videotapes, books, and other like property, unless acquired in an acquisition of a trade or business
- Patents and copyrights, unless acquired in an acquisition of a trade or business
- Professional sports franchises
- Certain purchased mortgage service rights
- Interests under an existing lease of tangible property

Tangible real and personal property with a limited useful life used in a trade or business or in a production-of-income activity are subject to depreciation. An asset's depreciable basis is generally determined using the basis rules discussed in Chapter 10. Assets are depreciated according to the tax law in effect at the time the asset is placed in service. Before 1981, taxpayers usually used the facts and circumstances method to compute depreciation. The facts and circumstances method was a source of continuing controversy between taxpayers and the IRS, because the depreciation computation used a variety of estimates (e.g., estimated life and salvage value) and taxpayers had a wide variety of choices in regard to depreciation methods and acquisition- and disposition-year conventions.

ACRS was a revolutionary approach to depreciation that was introduced in 1981. Because ACRS more precisely prescribed how depreciation was to be calculated, it eliminated several areas of controversy that existed under the old system. Under ACRS, the tax law determined the recovery period, depreciation method, salvage value (none considered), and the first- and last-year conventions for real estate and personal property. Although buildings acquired from 1981 through 1986 are still being depreciated under ACRS, most personal property assets have been fully depreciated under the relatively short ACRS recovery periods.

As ACRS was being introduced, Congress added to the tax law the Section 179 election to expense assets. This election, which applies to personal property, primarily benefits small businesses. Initially, this election allowed taxpayers to expense as much as $5,000 in qualified investment in Section 179 property. The amount allowed as an expense was increased to $10,000 beginning in 1987 and to $17,500 beginning in 1993, subject to two limitations. The annual deduction under Section 179 is reduced dollar for dollar when the taxpayer places more than $200,000 in qualified property in service during the year. In addition, the annual election to expense is limited to the taxpayer's taxable active business income for the year. The Section 179 expense deduction is treated as regular depreciation. Therefore, any amount expensed under Section 179 reduces an asset's depreciable basis.

After 1986, MACRS is used to depreciate personal property and real estate. MACRS is a modification of ACRS that generally spreads the depreciation deduction over a longer time period. Table 11–7 presents an overview of MACRS. To depreciate property using MACRS, you need to know

- The property's depreciable basis
- The MACRS recovery period
- Whether regular MACRS or straight-line depreciation is to be used
- The applicable convention

Given this information, depreciation is calculated by multiplying the asset's depreciable basis by a prescribed percentage obtained from an IRS table. If an asset is disposed of before the end of its recovery period, the table's percentages have to be adjusted according to the applicable convention in order to claim depreciation for the fractional part of the last year in which the asset was used. Instead of using the declining balance method prescribed by MACRS, a taxpayer may elect to use the straight-line method with the same first- and last-year conventions as under regular MACRS. Listed property is subject to special record-keeping requirements and limitations. The depreciation deduction for automobiles is subject to an annual limit based on the year of acquisition and use.

A deduction for depletion is allowed when a taxpayer has an economic interest in a natural resource in place. The investment must be recovered from income received from its removal and sale. The depletion deduction is determined by

▲ **Table 11–7**

OVERVIEW OF THE
MODIFIED ACCELERATED
COST RECOVERY SYSTEM

MACRS Recovery Period Class	MACRS Method	MACRS Convention	Straight-Line Election	ADS
3-, 5-, 7-, 10-year	200% DB	Half-year Mid-quarter	SL over MACRS recovery period	SL over alternate MACRS recovery period
15-, 20-year	150% DB	Half-year Mid-quarter	SL over MACRS recovery period	SL over alternate MACRS recovery period
27.5-year residential rental real estate	SL	Mid-month	SL over MACRS recovery period	SL over alternate MACRS recovery period (40 years)
31.5-year Non-residential real estate	SL	Mid-month	SL over MACRS recovery period	SL over alternate MACRS recovery period (40 years)
39-year Nonresidential real estate	SL	Mid-month	SL over MACRS recovery period	SL over alternate MACRS recovery period (40 years)

using the cost or percentage depletion methods. A straight-line amortization deduction is allowed for intangible assets that have a useful life that can be estimated with reasonable accuracy. To lessen the difficulty of estimating useful lives, Congress enacted Section 197 in 1993. This provision allows certain purchased intangibles, including goodwill, to be amortized over 15 years.

KEY TERMS

Accelerated Cost Recovery System (ACRS) (p. 485)
adjusted basis (p. 492)
Alternative Depreciation System (ADS) (p. 504)
amortization (p. 510)
class life (p. 492)
cost depletion (p. 508)
depletion (p. 507)

depreciable basis (p. 492)
depreciation (p. 482)
depreciation convention (p. 495)
intangible property (p. 510)
listed property (p. 505)
listed property rules (p. 505)
mid-month convention (p. 496)
mid-quarter convention (p. 496)
mid-year convention (p. 495)

Modified Accelerated Cost Recovery System (MACRS) (p. 485)
passenger automobile limitation (p. 506)
percentage depletion (statutory depletion) (p. 509)
Section 179 (p. 486)

PRIMARY TAX LAW SOURCES

[1] Reg. Sec. 1.167(a)-2—Specifies the requirements that must be met in order to depreciate a property.

[2] S. REP. NO. 144, 97th Cong., 1st Sess., 47 (1981)—States congressional motives in enacting ACRS—that Congress felt that the old depreciation rules were unnecessarily complicated and did not provide

"the investment stimulus necessary that is essential for economic expansion."

[3] Sec. 168—Prescribes the calculations necessary for determining depreciation using cost recovery (ACRS and MACRS).

[4] Reg. Sec. 1.179-3—Provides definitions related to the Section 179 election to expense deduction.

[5] Reg. Sec. 1.179-2—Discusses dollar limitations on the Section 179 expense deduction and the application of the limitations to partnerships (and their partners) and S corporations (and their shareholders).

[6] Reg. Sec. 1.179-1—Requires the reduction of the unadjusted basis of an asset for any amounts expensed under Section 179.

[7] U.S. v. Ludley, 274 U.S. 295 (1927)—Stated the original depreciation theory: By using up a depreciable asset, a gradual sale is made of the asset.

[8] Prop. Reg. Sec. 1.168-2—Requires the use of the property's unadjusted basis in order to compute depreciation under the cost-recovery system.

[9] Rev. Proc. 87-56, 1987-2 C.B. 674—Provides the class lives of property that are necessary to compute depreciation deductions.

[10] Reg. Sec. 1.168(d)-1—Explains and gives examples of MACRS conventions.

[11] Sec. 168(d)(4)(A)—Describes the convention as half-year. For consistency, this text uses the term *mid-year*.

[12] Reg. Sec. 1.168(d)-1(b)(4)(i)—Specifies that depreciable basis for purposes of the 40-percent test reflect a reduction for any Sec. 179 expensing.

[13] Reg. Sec. 1.274–5T—Explains the substantiation requirements for various types of listed property.

[14] Sec. 280F—Defines *listed property* and provides limits on the deduction of depreciation when listed property is used 50 percent or less in a taxpayer's trade or business.

[15] Reg. Sec. 1.280F-3T—Explains the calculation of depreciation deductions on listed property when the trade or business use of the property is 50 percent or less.

[16] Reg. Sec. 1.280F-2T—Explains the limitations on depreciation deductions for passenger automobiles.

[17] Sec. 611—Specifies the requirements for a depletion deduction for natural resources.

[18] Sec. 57—States that the percentage depletion deduction in excess of the cost of the property is an addition to a taxpayer's alternative minimum taxable income.

[19] Sec. 612—Requires the use of basis for computing gain in the cost depletion calculation.

[20] Sec. 613—Specifies the calculation of percentage depletion and provides statutory rates for various types of depletable property.

[21] Reg. Sec. 1.613–2—Provides examples of the 50 percent of taxable income limit on percentage depletion deductions.

[22] Reg. Sec. 1.167(a)-3—Defines intangible assets for which a periodic expense deduction (through amortization) may be taken; specifically disallows any periodic deductions for goodwill.

DISCUSSION QUESTIONS

1. How does the allowable capital recovery period affect the potential return on the investment in an asset?

2. Which two tests must be met in order to claim a periodic recovery deduction on a capital expenditure?

3. What types of capital expenditures are not deductible over time (i.e., their cost is recovered upon disposition of the asset)?

4. What is the depreciable basis of an asset? What role does depreciable basis play in determining the annual cost recovery on a depreciable asset?

5. Compare facts and circumstances depreciation to MACRS cost recovery.

6. What was the purpose of changing from the facts and circumstances depreciation method to the ACRS method?

7. In general, which types of property may be expensed under Section 179, and what is the current maximum limit on the deduction?

8. What limitations are placed on the maximum amount to be expensed under Section 179?

9. Is the Section 179 election to expense an incentive to all businesses to invest in qualifying property?

10. In general, taxpayers want to depreciate property as rapidly as possible. Under what circumstances might a taxpayer not want to use accelerated depreciation? How can this be done under MACRS?

11. What is the purpose of the acquisition- and disposition-year convention?

12. What acquisition- and disposition-year conventions are used in MACRS and to what types of property does each of the conventions apply?

13. Why is the calculation of depreciation using MACRS generally considered easier and more efficient than the calculation using the facts and circumstances method?

14. What is the Alternate Depreciation System? How is it different from a straight-line election under MACRS?

15. Why might a taxpayer elect to depreciate assets using the Alternative Depreciation System (ADS)?

16. Why are restrictions placed on the cost recovery of listed property?

17. When a taxpayer purchases an automobile for use in trade or business, what limits are placed on the cost recovery on the automobile?

18. Which types of property are allowed a deduction for depletion?

19. How is cost depletion different from percentage depletion?

20. Which income tax concepts might taxpayers who take depletion deductions be violating?

21. How are the costs of intangible assets recovered?

PROBLEMS

22. Peter Corporation purchased the following assets during 1996. Identify which assets are not subject to cost recovery using depreciation, and state why that is so.
    a. Land
    b. Copyright
    c. Building
    d. Goodwill
    e. Inventory for sale in its store
    f. 500 shares of Excellent common stock
    g. A house to be rented out
    h. Equipment for use in its business
    i. An interest in an oil well
    j. A car that will be used 60% for business and 40% for personal use

23. State whether each of the following expenditures incurred during the current year should be treated as a repair expense or capitalized and depreciated using MACRS:
    a. Replacement of the carpeting in a rental apartment
    b. Replacement of the drill bit on a gas-powered post-hole digger
    c. Replacement of the water in the ponds of a catfish farm
    d. Replacement of spark plugs in a delivery truck
    e. Repainting the exterior of a personal use auto

24. For each of the following expenditures incurred during the current year, indicate whether it should be treated as a repair expense or capitalized and depreciated using MACRS:
    a. Replacement of the roof on an apartment building
    b. Replacement of the condenser in a central air conditioning unit
    c. Replacement of the tires on a delivery truck
    d. Addition of 10 tons of gravel to parking lot to restore surface
    e. Repainting of the interior and exterior of an apartment building

25. A taxpayer purchased $20,000-worth of property that qualified for the Section 179 deduction during the current year. The taxpayer would like to deduct the greatest depreciation expense possible (including the Section 179 deduction) on the property. For each of the following entities, indicate how the depreciation expense should be determined:
    a. An individual
    b. A corporation
    c. An S corporation
    d. A partnership
    e. A trust or an estate

26. Which of the following qualify for the Section 179 election to expense? Explain.
    a. Business office furniture
    b. Furniture for rental apartment
    c. Auto purchased for a car rental agency
    d. Screen porch added to a rental house
    e. Trademark purchased for a business
    f. Microwave oven for the employees' lounge in a manufacturing plant
    g. Computer with multimedia applications for use at home
    h. Two-year-old racehorse

27. Firefly, Inc., acquires business equipment in July 1996 for $211,000.
    a. What is Firefly's maximum Section 179 deduction for 1996? Explain.
    b. What happens to any portion of the annual limit not deducted in 1996? Explain.
    c. What is the depreciable basis of the equipment? Explain.

28. Chelko Partnership purchases machinery for $225,000 and places it in service in September 1996.
    a. What is the partnership's maximum Section 179 deduction for 1996? Explain.
    b. What happens to any portion of the annual limit not deducted in 1996? Explain.
    c. What is the depreciable basis of the machinery?
    d. Harvey owns a 10% interest in Chelko Partnership. Explain how Harvey benefits from the partnership's acquisition of the machinery.

29. In 1996, Theo purchases $16,000 of Section 179 property for use in his delivery business. During 1996, Theo has $13,000 in taxable income from his business.
    a. What is Theo's maximum Section 179 deduction in 1996? Explain.
    b. Theo's business taxable income for 1997 is $4,000. He purchased $1,000 of new Section 179 property in 1997. What is Theo's maximum Section 179 deduction in 1997?

30. During 1996, Belk Corporation purchases $19,000-worth of equipment for use in its business. Belk's current taxable income before considering the Section 179 deduction is $12,500.
    a. What is Belk's maximum Section 179 deduction in 1996? Explain.
    b. Belk's 1997 business taxable income—before a Section 179 deduction—is $2,000. What is Belk's maximum Section 179 deduction in 1997? Explain.

31. Terrell, Inc., purchases $215,000-worth of machinery in 1996. Its 1996 taxable income before considering the Section 179 deduction is $5,000.
    a. What is Terrell's maximum Section 179 deduction in 1996? Explain.
    b. What is the depreciable basis of the equipment?

32. Rufus operates Freedonia Co. as a sole proprietorship. In 1996, he purchases $205,000-worth of equipment. Rufus's taxable income from the business is $4,000.
    a. What is Rufus's maximum Section 179 deduction in 1996? Explain.
    b. What is the depreciable basis of the equipment? Explain.

33. Brad is a shareholder and full-time employee of an S corporation. During 1996, Brad earns a $30,000 salary from the S corporation and is allocated $32,000 as his share of its net operating loss. In addition, Brad owns a limited partnership interest from which he earns $12,000 during 1996. Kanika, Brad's wife, operates a small business as a proprietorship. During 1996, Kanika purchases $20,000-worth of equipment for use in her business, which had a taxable income of $13,000 before the Section 179 deduction.
    a. What is Brad and Kanika's maximum Section 179 deduction for 1996?
    b. Assume that Brad is allocated $5,000 in Section 179 expense from the S corporation for 1997 and Kanika purchases an additional $14,000-worth of equipment for use in her business. Also, assume that their taxable active business income is $75,000 for 1997. What is Brad and Kanika's maximum Section 179 deduction for 1997?

34. Jennifer owns a 1/4 interest in the Thomas Partnership. Jennifer also owns and operates an architectural consulting business. During the current year, the partnership purchases $36,000-worth of property qualifying under Section 179 and elects to expense $17,500. Jennifer purchases $20,000-worth of qualifying Section 179 property for use in her architectural consulting business. Write a letter to Jennifer explaining what she should do to maximize her cost recovery.

35. In each of the following situations, determine the depreciable basis of the asset:
    a. Rudy inherited his father's pickup truck. The truck was immediately placed in service in Rudy's delivery business. The fair market value of the truck at the date of Rudy's father's death was $8,000, and the value on the alternate valuation date was $7,500. The executor of the estate did not make any special elections. The truck originally cost Rudy's father $15,000.
    b. Maline purchased an office building to use as the main office of her mail order business. She paid the seller $25,000 in cash. In addition, she gave the seller her personal note for $100,000, plus 10 acres of real estate. At the date of the transaction, the real estate, which cost $10,000, was worth $25,000. Property tax records showed the land was assessed at $10,000 and the building was assessed at $40,000.
    c. Steve owned a computer that he bought for $5,000. The computer was used for personal family activities. When he started his business, Steve took the computer to his new office. The computer was worth $850 when he began using it in his business.
    d. Martha's aunt Mabel gave her a used table, which had been stored in Mabel's garage, to use in the conference room in Martha's office. Mabel had paid $1,200 for the table several years ago, and it was worth only $800 at the date of the gift. Mabel did not pay any gift tax on the transfer.

36. In each of the following situations, determine the depreciable basis of each asset:
    a. Helen purchases an automobile at a cost of $24,000. Helen uses the automobile 65% in her business and 35% personal. Helen purchases a 5-year warranty on the automobile for $3,000.
    b. Win buys an apartment building. She gives the seller $30,000 as a down payment and takes out a $220,000 loan with Evergreen Mortgage Co. for the balance. Property tax records show the land is assessed at $20,000 and the building is assessed at $180,000. Immediately after acquiring the apartment, Win installs a new roof at a cost of $5,000 and plants trees and shrubs around the building at a cost of $4,000.
    c. Dusty owns an automobile that he bought for $22,000 two years ago. The automobile was used predominantly for personal activities until Dusty begins to use it exclusively in his consulting business this year. When Dusty begins using the car for business, he has a complete tune-up performed for $350 and puts on new tires costing $400. The fair market value of the automobile on the conversion date is $14,000.
    d. Alison inherits an office building from her grandfather. The building is completely leased to commercial tenants for the next several years. The building cost her grandfather $200,000 forty years ago. The adjusted basis was zero when her grandfather died. The executor of the estate did not make any special elections and valued the property at its appraised fair market value of $1,000,000.

37. Determine the class life, MACRS recovery period, and ADS recovery period of each of the following assets:

a. Tugboat
b. Microcomputer
c. Taxi cab
d. Breeding hogs
e. Breeding cattle
f. Greenhouse
g. Office furniture
h. Land improvements

38. Determine the class life, MACRS recovery period, and ADS recovery period of each of the following assets acquired for a sports bar:

a. Pool table
b. Safe
c. Photocopying machines
d. Pickup truck
e. Electronic video games
f. Brewing tanks for the bar's microbrewery
g. Four-year-old racehorse named GofortheBrew purchased by the bar owners and raced locally
h. Point-of-sale computerized cash registers

39. For each asset in problem 38, determine the correct IRS percentage table, recovery period, and applicable convention.

40. Determine the correct IRS percentage table, recovery period, and applicable convention for each of the following assets:

a. Helicopter
b. Residential, 68-unit apartment building
c. The new Wings Field baseball stadium in Buffalo
d. Automobile
e. Commercial office building
f. Farm equipment storage building

41. Leon bought machinery (7-year MACRS property) on March 15, 1996, at a cost of $32,000. What is Leon's 1996 cost-recovery deduction if

a. He wants the maximum deduction allowable?
b. He wants the minimum deduction allowable?
c. How would your answer to part a change if Leon also purchased equipment in March and April costing $80,000 (7-year MACRS property) and a fleet of heavy-duty trucks (5-year MACRS property) costing $140,000?

42. Rograin Corporation purchased turning lathes costing $148,000 and a computer system costing $63,000 in June of the current year. The lathes are 7-year MACRS property, and the computer system is 5-year MACRS property.

a. What is Rograin's maximum Section 179 deduction?
b. Assuming that Rograin deducts the maximum Section 179 expense, what are the depreciable bases of the lathes and the computer system?
c. If Rograin wants to maximize its cost recovery this year, how much first-year depreciation may it deduct in addition to the Section 179 deduction?

43. In 1996, Rose purchases office furniture (7-year MACRS property) costing $30,000 for use in her consulting business. What is her maximum 1996 cost-recovery deduction on the furniture if her business income before any special elections is

a. $40,000?
b. $4,000?
c. Assume the same facts as in part b. In 1997, Rose purchases a computer workstation (5-year MACRS property) costing $6,000. What is Rose's maximum 1997 cost-recovery deduction if her business income before any special elections is $28,000 in that year?

44. Kringle Co. purchased 7-year MACRS property costing $9,000 in 1996. Kringle's 1996 business income before any cost-recovery deductions is $6,000. What is Kringle's maximum 1996 cost-recovery deduction on the property? Assume that Kringle plans to purchase more than $20,000-worth of personal property during the next 5 years.

45. Dikembe purchases 100 breeding hogs for $20,000 in April 1996.
   a. What is Dikembe's maximum 1996 cost-recovery deduction for the hogs?
   b. Dikembe's farming operation incurs a net loss this year and probably will next year before taking the cost recovery into consideration. What should Dikembe do in regard to his cost-recovery deductions?

46. Baker, Inc., purchases office furniture (7-year MACRS property) costing $35,000 and a computer system (5-year MACRS property) costing $35,000 in 1996. What is Baker's maximum cost-recovery deduction in 1996? (HINT: Maximize the Section 179 election effect.)

47. Chen Corporation purchased the following business assets during the current year:

Asset Purchased	Cost	Recovery Period
Office furniture	$12,000	7
Microcomputer	$ 8,000	5
Tugboat	$33,000	10

What is Chen's maximum current-year cost-recovery deduction on the assets purchased? (HINT: Maximize the Section 179 election effect.)

48. During 1996, Schottenheim Corporation buys 7 personal computers (PCs) and a small mainframe computer to use in its general sales offices. Schottenheim bought 4 PCs for $9,000 on March 29, 3 PCs for $8,000 on September 26, and the small mainframe for $28,000 on October 5. The corporation makes no other capital expenditures this year.
   a. What issues should the corporation consider when determining its 1996 cost-recovery deductions on the computers?
   b. The corporation has a contractual agreement to resell the small mainframe to the original vendor for $15,000 on March 1, 1999. How will the 1996 decisions affect the 1999 calculations if Schottenheim decides to sell that computer?

49. Harold purchases the following business assets on the dates indicated:

Asset	Date Purchased	Cost	Recovery Period
Photocopy equipment	2/14/96	$ 5,000	5
Dump truck	7/16/96	$25,000	5
Bus	11/24/96	$25,000	5

   a. What is Harold's 1996 cost-recovery deduction if he does not elect to expense any of the assets under Section 179?
   b. Determine the gain (loss) if Harold sells the bus for $15,000 on July 1, 1998.
   c. What could Harold do to maximize his 1996 deduction?

50. The Gladys Corporation buys equipment (7-year MACRS property) costing $54,000 on April 12, 1996. In 1999, new and improved models of the equipment make it obsolete, and Gladys sells the old equipment for $12,000 on December 27, 1999.
   a. What is Gladys Corporation's gain (loss) on the sale, assuming that Gladys takes the maximum cost-recovery deduction allowable on the equipment?
   b. What is Gladys Corporation's gain (loss) on the equipment, assuming that Gladys takes the minimum cost-recovery deduction allowable on the equipment?
   NOTE: The depreciation calculations from this problem will be needed for problem 63, Chapter 12.

51. Joan is interested in buying a special diagnostic machine for use in her medical practice. The machine will cost her $16,000, and it will have a $2,000 salvage value at the end of its 8-year life. Joan would like to know the actual cost of the machine after considering the effect of the present value of tax savings from depreciation. If Joan buys the machine, she will place it in service on April 1, 1996. Based on the following assumptions, what is Joan's after-tax cost? Assume that Joan is in the 28% marginal tax rate bracket and that the time value of money is worth 10%.

   a. Joan will depreciate the machine over 5 years using MACRS.

   b. Joan will depreciate the machine using the straight-line method over the 7-year ADS life.

   c. Joan will deduct the $16,000 investment as an expense in 1996.

52. During May 1996, just in time for the peak season, Happy Acres Amusement Park completes construction of a new roller coaster costing $200,000.

   a. Compare depreciation deductions using maximum, minimum, and intermediate cost-recovery methods over total applicable recovery periods.

   b. Under what conditions would the amusement park want to use a minimum method? an intermediate method?

53. Guadalupe purchases an office building to use in her business at a cost of $320,000. Guadalupe properly allocates $20,000 of the cost to the land and $300,000 to the building. Assuming that Guadalupe would like to deduct the maximum depreciation on the building, what is her first-year depreciation on the building if she purchased the building on

   a. June 30, 1992?

   b. June 30, 1994?

54. Refer to problem 53. Guadalupe sells the building on October 26, 1999. What is Guadalupe's 1999 depreciation deduction if she purchased the building on

   a. June 30, 1992?

   b. June 30, 1994?

55. Anton purchases a building on May 4, 1993, at a cost of $240,000. The land is properly allocated $30,000 of the cost. Anton sells the building on October 18, 1997, for $240,000. What is Anton's gain (loss) on the sale if he uses the regular MACRS system and the building is

   a. An apartment building?

   b. An office building?

   c. How would your answer(s) to parts a and b change if Anton makes a straight-line election on the building? Explain.

   d. How would your answers to parts a and b change if the building was purchased on May 4, 1995, and sold on October 18, 1999?

   NOTE: You will need the depreciation calculations from problem 55 in order to complete problem 68 in Chapter 12.

56. On July 19, 1991, Dorothy pays $145,000 for a building and immediately begins to operate her acting school from the site. She properly allocates $135,000 to the building and $10,000 to the land.

   a. What is the amount of Dorothy's 1991 depreciation deduction on the building?

   b. On April 11, 1996, Dorothy sells the property for $200,000. What is Dorothy's 1996 depreciation deduction? What is her adjusted basis in the property as of the sale date?

57. On October 1, 1996, Barbara pays $135,000 for a store building. She moves into the building and begins business on November 1. She properly allocates $125,000 of her cost to the building and $10,000 to the land. On November 21, 1996, she installs $25,000-worth of new display shelving. Barbara wants to claim the maximum allowable depreciation on the property she purchased. On January 2, 1999, Barbara sells the land and building for $145,000 and the display shelving for $15,000.

   a. What is Barbara's maximum depreciation deduction for 1996?

   b. What is Barbara's maximum depreciation deduction for 1999?

   c. What is Barbara's gain or loss on the sale of the land and building?

   d. What is Barbara's gain or loss on the sale of the shelving?

58. On February 23, 1996, Xuan pays $550,000 for a newly constructed apartment building. The tax assessor values the building at $400,000 and the land at $50,000. Before leasing apartments on May 1, Xuan acquires furniture and fixtures costing $100,000 for the apartment complex.

    a. Determine the depreciation for 1996 if Xuan wants to maximize the allowable depreciation deduction on her assets.

    b. Assume Xuan sells the property in 1999 for $750,000. What is the maximum depreciation for that year?

    c. What is the amount of gain or loss Xuan would recognize on the 1999 sale? Assume that 10% of the selling price is allocated to the furniture and fixtures.

59. Return to problem 58. Assume that Xuan tells you that she anticipates net operating losses from other activities in 1996. Write a letter to Xuan explaining the results of a depreciation minimization strategy.

60. Leroy purchases a computer and a desk for use in his home office. The computer costs $7,500, and the desk costs $1,000. During the first year, Leroy uses the computer and his desk 40% of the time in his consulting business and 20% of the time managing his investments. The remaining 40% of the use is for personal activities. What is Leroy's maximum cost-recovery deduction on the computer and the desk?

    Assume that Leroy uses the computer and the desk 70% of the time in his consulting business, 20% for managing his investments, and 10% for personal use purposes. What is his maximum first-year cost-recovery deduction?

61. Madina, a single individual, is a self-employed engineering consultant. In 1996, she bought a new automobile and personal computer. She paid $15,500 for the automobile on February 3. It is used 45% of the time for business. Madina paid $2,000 for the computer on October 22 and uses it 85% for business. Madina would like to know the amount of her maximum deduction for cost recovery in 1996. However, she is not sure she needs the maximum deduction amount, because her 1996 gross income from consulting is only $24,000. Write a letter to Madina in which you make a recommendation about her 1996 cost-recovery deductions.

62. On June 1, 1996, Kay buys a new car for $26,000. Kay drives her car 15,000 miles while on business, 3,000 miles for personal activities, and 2,000 miles in commuting to and from work. What is Kay's maximum depreciation deduction on the car for 1996?

63. On July 4, 1996, Lawrence invests $120,000 in a mineral property. He estimates that he will recover 800,000 units of the mineral from the deposit. During 1996, Lawrence recovers and sells 100,000 units of the mineral for $1.75 per unit.

    a. What are Lawrence's cost depletion deduction for 1996 and his adjusted basis for the mineral deposit after deducting depletion?

    b. If the percentage depletion rate for the mineral is 10%, what are his depletion deduction for 1996 and his adjusted basis for the mineral deposit after deducting depletion?

    c. If the statutory percentage depletion rate for the mineral is 10% and Lawrence's income from the mineral before the depletion deduction is $9,200, what are his depletion deduction for 1996 and his adjusted basis for the mineral deposit after deducting depletion?

64. Isidro purchases an interest in an oil-producing property for $50,000 on November 3, 1996. His geologist estimates 15,000 barrels of oil are recoverable. The entity sells 1,000 barrels for $20,000 during November and December 1996. Assume the percentage depletion rate for oil is 15%. Operating expenses related to the revenues are $3,000.

    a. Advise Isidro on the amount of depletion he should deduct in 1996.

    b. At the end of 1997, the geologist estimates the remaining number of recoverable barrels is 18,000. Isidro has an offer of $190,000 for his investment. In 1997, the entity sold only 3,000 barrels of oil. Gross revenues were $50,000 and operating expenses totaled $4,000. If Isidro sells the property, what is the amount of his realized gain?

    c. Write a memorandum explaining the details of Isidro's gain. Include a recommendation about whether he should accept or reject the offer.

65. On June 2, 1996, Lokar Corporation purchases a patent for $68,000 from the inventor of a new extrusion process. The patent has 12 years remaining on its legal life. Also, Lokar purchases substantially all the assets of the Barrios Corporation for $750,000 on September 8, 1996. The values of the assets as listed in the purchase agreement are as follows:

Inventory	$250,000
Manufacturing equipment	300,000
Patent on compression process	105,000
Goodwill	95,000

Assume negotiations have not been completed. The purchase agreement can be modified to reflect a reallocation of the purchase price to the individual assets. Advise Lokar on an optimum way to allocate the price.

a. Determine the maximum 1996 cost-recovery deductions for the assets purchased.

66. On April 18, 1996, Petros buys all the assets of Brigid's Muffler Shop. Included in the purchase price of $295,000 is a payment of $20,000 to Brigid not to open a competing shop in the state for a period of 5 years. Information on Brigid's assets at the date of sale is as follows:

Asset	Adjusted Basis	Fair Market Value
Inventory	$ 8,500	$ 15,000
Store equipment	3,500	25,000
Building	80,000	120,000
Patent	500	15,000
Land	5,000	10,000

The patent is on a special muffler that Brigid developed and patented 5 years ago. Petros would like to know the maximum amount of the deduction he will be allowed on the purchase of Brigid's assets for 1996.

67. In problem 79 of Chapter 10, you were asked to determine the initial basis of Art and Kris's business, investment, and personal use assets. In this problem, you are to determine the adjusted basis of the assets as of December 31, 1996. You should disclose all calculations made to arrive at the December 31, 1996, basis values. For depreciable assets and amortizable assets, present the basis in the following form:

INTEGRATIVE PROBLEMS

Asset: _____

Date acquired: _____

Initial basis: _____

Depreciation/Amortization life: _____

Depreciation/Amortization deducted to December 31, 1996: _____
   (per the schedule here)

Basis at December 31, 1996: _____

Depreciation/Amortization Schedule:

Year	Depreciable Basis	Depreciation Percentage	Depreciation

Additional Information

Kris's 1993 automobile: Although Kris keeps mileage records, her cost records are not good enough to use the actual cost method. Therefore, she deducts the standard mileage rate each year. For 1993 through 1996, Kris drives her old car 90,000 miles in all; 72,000 miles are business miles. (Assume that the depreciation portion of the standard mileage rate is 12 cents per mile for all years involved.)

Assume that Kris and Art have always deducted the maximum depreciation allowable. However, in 1996, because their income is less as a result of the opening of Art's new business, they do not wish to expense any eligible amounts.

68. Gloria has worked for several years in a friend's pottery shop. In 1992, she decides to open her own business. In August 1992, she leases a building and spends $3,000 installing shelving, counters, and display cabinets. Another pottery in a nearby town is going out of business, and Gloria buys the following assets for $12,000:

Asset	Fair Market Value
Inventory	$6,000
Pottery wheels	$2,400
Kiln	$1,200

In addition, Gloria purchases a computer system with point-of-sale terminals at a cost of $10,000.

Although business is slow at first, it begins to pick up during 1994. On March 14, 1995, she negotiates the purchase of the building she had been leasing for $80,000. The 1994 property tax statement had assessed the land at $2,000 and the building at $30,000.

During 1996, Gloria learns that her previous employer's wife has been transferred and he needs to sell his pottery. Because Gloria's business has been steadily improving, she decides to expand by buying out the business. On July 3, she purchases her former employer's business by investing $20,000 of her own cash and borrowing $120,000 from Local Bank. In the transaction, she receives the following assets:

Asset	Adjusted Basis	Fair Market Value
Land	$ 5,000	$10,000
Building	18,000	95,000
Inventory	11,000	15,000
Equipment	1,500	5,000

As part of her expansion, Gloria decides to begin providing delivery service for customers who place large orders. In August, she converts a van she had purchased for personal use in 1993 for $24,000 into a business van by paying $1,000 to have the shop's logo painted on the van. At the time of conversion, comparable vans are selling for $9,000.

a. Determine Gloria's maximum 1996 cost-recovery deduction on her business assets. Assume that she has always taken the maximum allowable cost-recovery deduction on her business assets but has never had enough business income to elect to expense assets under Section 179. In 1996, Gloria estimates that her net business income before any cost-recovery deductions will be at least $32,000, and she would like to take the maximum allowable deduction in 1996.

b. Write a letter to Gloria explaining the results of maximizing her 1996 allowable cost-recovery deductions.

69. Bonnie and Rick, a married couple, purchase a 2-bedroom condominium in Park City, Utah, on October 4 of the current year. The total purchase price is $118,000, including complete furnishings. Park County's tax assessor appraises the structure at $100,000 and the land and common area at $10,000. Furnishings (acquired 5 years ago by the previous owner) include:

create

1 sofa sleeper
1 end table
2 lamps
2 color TVs
1 set fireplace tools
1 dining table
7 chairs
12 dinner plates
1 refrigerator
1 microwave oven
1 coffee maker

8 place settings of silverware
12 water glasses
1 set of pots and pans
6 coffee mugs
1 queen-sized bed
1 king-sized bed
2 dressers
2 nightstands
2 table lamps
6 towels
4 sets of bed linens

Bonnie and Rick immediately place the property in service as a rental. They want to know their options in regard to deductions related to the rental property. Explain.

70. Fiona is a professional bass violinist with the St. Paul Symphony Orchestra. In February of the current year, she purchases at auction for $200,000 an eighteenth-century bass violin built by the renowned Asa Santavar. Fiona is thrilled by her acquisition. The violin is a treasured artwork and a quality investment. Also, it is an asset she will use almost daily in her profession. May Fiona deduct part of her expenditure this year? Explain.

DISCUSSION CASES

71. You are the resident tax expert for Wetzel's Pretzels, an international producer of junk food. The controller has come to you with the company's capital expenditures budget for next year. The budget shows that Wetzel's Pretzels plans to spend $1,000,000 next year on personal property. The largest single item in the budget is the purchase of new, high-tech pretzel twisters costing $450,000. The pretzel twisters are on order, but because of high demand for the technology, Wetzel's Pretzels will not receive the new twisters until November. The remaining $550,000 is for company automobiles, delivery trucks, personal computers, and office furniture. These items will be purchased throughout the year as needed.

The controller asks your advice on the tax aspects of these purchases. She is particularly interested in making sure that Wetzel's Pretzels is able to deduct the maximum amount regarding these purchases in the year of purchase.

How would you advise the controller? That is, are there any tax problems associated with these purchases? If so, suggest one or more ways in which Wetzel's can take advantage of the situation. Write a memorandum to the controller explaining your suggestions.

TAX PLANNING CASES

72. Maura is negotiating with Nagama Corporation, a seaweed food-supplement processor, to purchase all its assets. Maura and Nagama have generally agreed that the purchase price is $500,000. However, Maura is not sure how to classify the difference between the identifiable asset values and the total sales price in the sales agreement. The sale will close sometime between December 15 of the current year and January 10 of next year. An independent appraiser determined the values of the assets as follows:

	Adjusted Basis	FMV
Inventory of seaweed products	$10,000	$ 40,000
Machinery/equipment—5-year property	20,000	40,000
Machinery/equipment—7-year property	60,000	70,000
Patent on seaweed production process	-0-	150,000

Maura has served as director of marketing for Nagama for 16 years. Harry Nagama, the corporation's president, founder, and developer of the production process, tells Maura he will agree to a sales contract structured however she would like. Discuss Maura's options for classifying the difference between the identifiable assets and the purchase price.

a. What are the cost-recovery amounts related to the purchased assets in the year of acquisition?

b. Write a letter to Maura explaining her options.

ETHICS DISCUSSION CASE

73. Steem Advertising Corporation acquires 10 notebook-style personal computers in 1995 for its account executives to use. Steem pays $40,000 for the computers and bundled software. You are the newly hired CPA, and you expect to advise Steem on tax issues regarding tax years 1996 and 1997. Upon examining the firm's records for 1995, you find that each computer was expensed and deducted in 1995. Later, when examining one of the computers, you notice it has several games loaded in the hard drive. Also, you find several items of personal correspondence saved in a subdirectory of the word-processing software package.

a. What should you do? What are your obligations under the Statements on Responsibilities in Tax Practice?

b. Write a memorandum to your supervisor in the CPA firm explaining your observations and suggestions.

Appendix to Chapter 11

MACRS Class Lives and
MACRS Depreciation Schedules

Section 1. Purpose

REV. PROC. 87-56

The purpose of this revenue procedure is to set forth the class lives of property that are necessary to compute the depreciation allowances available under section 168 of the Internal Revenue Code, as amended by section 201(a) of the Tax Reform Act of 1986 (Act), 1986-3 (Vol. 1) C.B. 38. Rev. Proc. 87-57, page 17, this Bulletin, describes the applicable depreciation methods, applicable recovery periods, and applicable conventions that must be used in computing depreciation allowances under section 168.

Section 2. General Rules of Application

.01 In general. This revenue procedure specifies class lives and recovery periods for property subject to depreciation under the general depreciation system provided in section 168(a) of the Code or the alternative depreciation system provided in section 168(g).

.02 Definition of Class Life. Except with respect to certain assigned property described in section 3 of this revenue procedure, for purposes of both the general depreciation system and the alternative depreciation system, the term "class life" means the class life that would be applicable for any property as of January 1, 1986, under section 167(m) of the Code (determined without regard to paragraph 4 thereof and determined as if the taxpayer had made an election under section 167(m)). The class life that would be applicable for any property as of January 1, 1986, under section 167(m), is the asset guideline period (midpoint class life) for the asset guideline class in which such property is classified under Rev. Proc. 83-35, 1983-1 C.B. 745. However, for purposes of the alternative depreciation system, section 168(g)(3)(B) assigns a class life to certain property that is taken into account under section 168 rather than the class life that would be applicable as of January 1, 1986. The class life of property that is either determined as of January 1, 1986, under Rev. Proc. 83-35 or assigned under section 168(g)(3)(B) may be modified by the Secretary pursuant to authority granted under section 168(i)(1). See section 4 of this revenue procedure.

.03 Rev. Proc. 83-35. Rev. Proc. 83-35 sets out the asset guideline classes, asset guideline periods and ranges, and annual asset guideline repair allowance percentages for the Class Life Asset Depreciation Range System. The asset guideline periods (midpoint class lives) set out in Rev. Proc. 83-35 are also used in defining the classes of recovery property under the Accelerated Cost Recovery System (that is, section 168 of the Code as in effect prior to amendment by section 201 of the Act). Rev. Proc. 83-35 remains effective for property subject to depreciation under those systems. Rev. Proc. 83-35 does not apply to property subject to depreciation under section 168, other than as a basis for determining the class lives of such property under section 2.02 of this revenue procedure.

.04 Property with No Class Life.   Property that is neither described in an asset guideline class listed in section 5 of this revenue procedure nor assigned a class life under section 168(g)(3)(B) of the Code is treated as property having no class life for purposes of section 168 unless and until a class life is prescribed by the Secretary pursuant to the authority granted under section 168(i)(1). See section 4 of this revenue procedure. The general and alternative depreciation systems contain separate rules for classifying property that does not have a class life.

Section 5. Tables of Class Lives and Recovery Periods

.01   Except for property described in section 5.02, below, the class lives (if any) and recovery periods for property subject to depreciation under section 168 of the Code appear in the tables below. These tables are based on the definition of class life in section 2.02 of this revenue procedure and the assigned items described in section 3 of this revenue procedure.

.02   For purposes of depreciation under the general depreciation system, residential rental property has a recovery period of 27.5 years and nonresidential real property has a recovery period of 31.5 years. For purposes of the alternative depreciation system, residential rental and nonresidential real property each has a recovery period of 40 years.

.04   In addition to specifying class lives for each asset guideline class, the tables list certain property for which a recovery period is assigned, notwithstanding such property's class life (if any). See section 3 of this revenue procedure. The listed assigned property classes (denoted A-E) generally do not correspond to asset guideline classes for which class lives are specified in the tables. The class life (if any) of an item of assigned property described in classes A-E is determined by reference to the asset guideline class (if any) containing such item of property. If an item of assigned property described in classes A-E is not contained in any asset guideline class, such item of property has no class life.

Examples.   Qualified technological equipment as defined in section 168(i)(2) (class B) is assigned a recovery period of 5 years for both the general and alternative depreciation systems, notwithstanding such property's class life (if any). Property which is a computer or peripheral equipment, high technology telephone station equipment installed on the customer's premises or high technology medical equipment within the meaning of section 168(i)(2), may be described in asset guideline class 00.12 (class life 6 years), 48.13 (class life 10 years) or 57.0 (class life 9 years), respectively. Property used in connection with research and experimentation referred to in section 168(e)(3)(B) (class C) is assigned a recovery period of 5 years for the general depreciation system, notwithstanding its class life (if any). Such property's recovery period for the alternative depreciation system is based on its class life (if any). An item of property used in connection with research and experimentation has a class life if such property is contained in an asset guideline class.

.05 The following special rules are incorporated from Rev. Proc. 83-35, sections 2.02(iii) and (iv):

1 Asset guideline class 00.3, "Land Improvements," includes "other tangible property" that qualifies under section 1.48-1(d) of the Income Tax Regulations. However, a structure that is essentially an item of machinery or equipment or a structure that houses property used as an integral part of an activity specified in section 48(a)(1)(B)(i) of the Code, if the use of the structure is so closely related to the use of the property that the structure clearly can be expected to be replaced when the property it initially houses is replaced, is included in the asset guideline class appropriate to the equipment to which it is related.

▲ Table A11–1

IRS TABLE OF MACRS CLASSES *(Partial Table)*

Asset Class	Description of Assets Included	Class Life (in years)	Recovery Periods (in years)	
			General Depreciation System	Alternative Depreciation System
Specific Depreciable Assets Used in All Business Activities, Except as Noted:				
00.11	Office Furniture, Fixtures, and Equipment: Includes furniture and fixtures that are not a structural component of a building. Includes such assets as desks, files, safes, and communications equipment. Does not include communications equipment that is included in other classes	10	7	10
00.12	Information Systems: Includes computers and their peripheral equipment used in administering normal business transactions and the maintenance of business records, their retrieval and analysis. Information systems are defined as: 1) Computers: A computer is a programmable electronically activated device capable of accepting information, applying prescribed processes to the information, and supplying the results of these processes with or without human intervention. It usually consists of a central processing unit containing extensive storage, logic, arithmetic, and control capabilities. Excluded from this category are adding machines, electronic desk calculators, etc., and other equipment described in class 00.13. 2) Peripheral equipment consists of the auxiliary machines which are designed to be placed under control of the central processing unit. Nonlimiting examples are: Card readers, card punches, magnetic tape feeds, high speed printers, optical character readers, tape cassettes, mass storage units, paper tape equipment, keypunches, data entry devices, teleprinters, terminals, tape drives, disc drives, disc files, disc packs, visual image projector tubes, card sorters, plotters, and collators. Peripheral equipment may be used on-line or off-line. Does not include equipment that is an integral part of other capital equipment that is included in other classes of economic activity, i.e., computers used primarily for process or production control, switching, channeling, and automating distributive trades and services such as point of sale (POS) computer systems. Also, does not include equipment of a kind used primarily for amusement or entertainment of the user	6	5*	5*

*Property described in asset class 00.12 which is qualified technological equipment as defined in section 168(i)(2) is assigned a recovery period of 5 years notwithstanding its class life. See section 3 of the revenue procedure.

▲ **Table A11–1**
(continued)

IRS TABLE OF MACRS CLASSES *(Partial Table)*

Asset Class	Description of Assets Included	Class Life (in years)	Recovery Periods (in years) General Depreciation System	Alternative Depreciation System
Specific Depreciable Assets Used in All Business Activities, Except as Noted:				
00.13	Data Handling Equipment, except Computers: Includes only typewriters, calculators, adding and accounting machines, copiers, and duplicating equipment	6	5	6
00.21	Airplanes (airframes and engines), except those used in commercial or contract carrying of passengers or freight, and all helicopters (airframes and engines)	6	5	6
00.22	Automobiles, Taxis	3	5	5
00.23	Buses	9	5	9
00.241	Light General Purpose Trucks: Includes trucks for use over the road (actual unloaded weight less than 13,000 pounds)	4	5	5
00.242	Heavy General Purpose Trucks: Includes heavy general purpose trucks, concrete ready mix-trucks, and ore trucks, for use over the road (actual unloaded weight 13,000 pounds or more)	6	5	6
00.25	Railroad Cars and Locomotives, except those owned by railroad transportation companies	15	7	15
00.26	Tractor Units For Use Over-The-Road	4	3	4
00.27	Trailers and Trailer-Mounted Containers	6	5	6
00.28	Vessels, Barges, Tugs, and Similar Water Transportation Equipment, except those used in marine construction	18	10	18
00.3	Land Improvements: Includes improvements directly to or added to land, whether such improvements are section 1245 property or section 1250 property, provided such improvements are depreciable. Examples of such assets might include sidewalks, roads, canals, waterways, drainage facilities, sewers (not including municipal sewers in Class 51), wharves and docks, bridges, fences, landscaping, shubbery, or radio and television transmitting towers. Does not include land improvements that are explicitly included in any other class, and buildings and structural components as defined in section 1.48-1(e) of the regulations. Excludes public utility initial clearing and grading land improvements as specified in Rev. Rul. 72-403, 1972-2 C.B. 102	20	15	20

(continued on next page)

▲ **Table A11–1**
(continued)

IRS TABLE OF MACRS CLASSES *(Partial Table)*

Asset Class	Description of Assets Included	Class Life (in years)	Recovery Periods (in years) General Depreciation System	Recovery Periods (in years) Alternative Depreciation System
Specific Depreciable Assets Used in All Business Activities, Except as Noted:				
00.4	Industrial Steam and Electric Generation and/or Distribution Systems: Includes assets, whether such assets are section 1245 property or 1250 property, providing such assets are depreciable, used in the production and/or distribution of electricity with rated total capacity in excess of 500 Kilowatts and/or assets used in the production and/or distribution of steam with rated total capacity in excess of 12,500 pounds per hour for use by the taxpayer in its industrial manufacturing process or plant activity and not ordinarily available for sale to others. Does not include buildings and structural components as defined in section 1.48-1(e) of the regulations. Assets used to generate and/or distribute electricity or steam of the type described above but of lesser rated capacity are not included, but are included in the appropriate manufacturing equipment classes elsewhere specified. Also includes electric generating and steam distribution assets, which may utilize steam produced by a waste reduction and resource recovery plant, used by the taxpayer in its industrial manufacturing process or plant activity. Steam and chemical recovery boiler systems used for the recovery and regeneration of chemicals used in manufacturing, with rated capacity in excess of that described above, with specifically related distribution and return systems are not included but are included in appropriate manufacturing equipment classes elsewhere specified. An example of an excluded steam and chemical recovery boiler system is that used in the pulp and paper manufacturing industry	22	15	22
Depreciable Assets Used in the Following Activities:				
01.1	Agriculture: Includes machinery and equipment, grain bins, and fences but no other land improvements, that are used in the production of crops or plants, vines, and trees; livestock; the operation of farm dairies, nurseries, greenhouses, sod farms, mushroom cellars, cranberry bogs, apiaries, and fur farms; the performance of agriculture, animal husbandry, and horticultural services	10	7	10
01.11	Cotton Ginning Assets	12	7	12
01.21	Cattle, Breeding or Dairy	7	5	7
01.22	Horses, Breeding or Work	10	7	10

▲ Table A11–1
(continued)

IRS TABLE OF MACRS CLASSES *(Partial Table)*

Asset Class	Description of Assets Included	Class Life (in years)	Recovery Periods (in years) General Depreciation System	Recovery Periods (in years) Alternative Depreciation System
Depreciable Assets Used in the Following Activities:				
01.221	Any horse that is not a race horse and that is more than 12 years old at the time it is placed in service	10	3	10
01.222	Any race horse that is more than 2 years old at the time it is placed in service	*	3	12
01.23	Hogs, Breeding	3	3	3
01.24	Sheep and Goats, Breeding	5	5	5
01.3	Farm buildings except structures included in Class 01.4	25	20	25
01.4	Single purpose agricultural or horticultural structures (within the meaning of section 48(p) of the Code)	15	7	15
10.0	Mining: Includes assets used in the mining and quarrying of metallic and nonmetallic minerals (including sand, gravel, stone, and clay) and the milling, beneficiation and other primary preparation of such materials	10	7	10
13.1	Drilling of Oil and Gas Wells: Includes assets used in the drilling of onshore oil and gas wells and the provision of geophysical and other exploration services; and the provision of such oil and gas field services as chemical treatment, plugging and abandoning of wells and cementing or perforating well casings. Does not include assets used in the performance of any of these activities and services by integrated petroleum and natural gas producers for their own account	6	5	6
15.0	Construction: Includes assets used in construction by general building, special trade, heavy and marine construction contractors, operative and investment builders, real estate subdividers and developers, and others except railroads	6	5	6
20.1	Manufacture of Grain and Grain Mill Products: Includes assets used in the production of flours, cereals, livestock feeds, and other grain and grain mill products	17	10	17
57.0	Distributive Trades and Services: Includes assets used in wholesale and retail trade, and personal and professional services. Includes section 1245 assets used in marketing petroleum and petroleum products	9	5	+9

(continued on next page)

*Property described in asset class 00.12 which is qualified technological equipment as defined in section 168(i)(2) is assigned a recovery period of 5 years notwithstanding its class life. See section 3 of the revenue procedure.
+ Any high technology medical equipment as defined in section 168(i)(2)(C) which is described in asset guideline class 57.0 is assigned a 5-year recovery period for the alternative depreciation system.

▲ **Table A11–1**
(continued)

IRS TABLE OF MACRS CLASSES *(Partial Table)*

Asset Class	Description of Assets Included	Class Life (in years)	Recovery Periods (in years)	
			General Depreciation System	Alternative Depreciation System
Depreciable Assets Used in the Following Activities:				
57.1	Distributive Trades and Services-Billboard, Service Station Buildings and Petroleum Marketing Land Improvements: Includes section 1250 assets, including service station buildings and depreciable land improvements, whether section 1245 property or section 1250 property, used in the marketing of petroleum and petroleum products, but not including any of these facilities related to petroleum and natural gas trunk pipelines. Includes car wash buildings and related land improvements. Includes billboards, whether such assets are section 1245 property or section 1250 property. Excludes all other land improvements, buildings and structural components as defined in section 1.48-1(e) of the regulations	20	15	20
79.0	Recreation: Includes assets used in the provision of entertainment services on payment of a fee or admission charge, as in the operation of bowling alleys, billiard and pool establishments, theaters, concert halls, and miniature golf courses. Does not include amusement and theme parks and assets which consist primarily of specialized land improvements or structures, such as golf courses, sports stadia, race tracks, ski slopes, and buildings which house the assets used in entertainment services	10	7	10
80.0	Theme and Amusement Parks: Includes assets used in the provision of rides, attractions, and amusements in activities defined as theme and amusement parks, and includes appurtenances associated with a ride, attraction, amusement or theme setting within the park such as ticket booths, facades, shop interiors, and props, special purpose structures, and buildings other than warehouses, administration buildings, hotels, and motels. Includes all land improvements for or in support of park activities, (e.g., parking lots, sidewalks, waterways, bridges, fences, landscaping, etc.) and support functions (e.g., food and beverage retailing, souvenir vending and other nonlodging accommodations) if owned by the park and provided exclusively for the benefit of park patrons. Theme and amusement parks are defined as combinations of amusements, rides, and attractions which are permanently situated on park land and open to the			

▲ Table A11–1
(continued)

IRS TABLE OF MACRS CLASSES *(Partial Table)*

Asset Class	Description of Assets Included	Class Life (in years)	Recovery Periods (in years)	
			General Depreciation System	Alternative Depreciation System
Depreciable Assets Used in the Following Activities:				
80.0 *(cont.)*	public for the price of admission. This guideline class is a composite of all assets used in this industry except transportation equipment (general purpose trucks, cars, airplanes, etc., which are included in asset guideline classes with the prefix 00.2), assets used in the provision of administrative services (asset classes with the prefix 00.1), and warehouses, administration buildings, hotels and motels	12.5	7	12.5
Certain Property for Which Recovery Periods Assigned:				
	A. Personal Property With No Class Life		7	12
	Section 1245 Real Property With No Class Life		7	40
	B. Qualified Technological Equipment, as defined in section 168(i)(2).	+ +	5	5
	C. Property Used in Connection with Research and Experimentation referred to in section 168(e)(3)(B)	+ +	5	class life if no class life—12
	D. Alternative Energy Property described in sections 48(l)(3)(viii) or (iv), or section 48(l)(4) of the Code.	+ +	5	class life if no class life—12
	E. Biomass property described in section 48(l)(15) and is a qualifying small production facility within the meaning of section 3(17)(c) of the Federal Power Act, (16 U.S.C. 796(17)(C)), as in effect on September 1, 1986	+ +	5	class life if no class life—12

+ +The class life (if any) of property described in classes B, C, D, or E is determined by reference to the asset guideline classes in this revenue procedure. If an item of property described in paragraphs B, C, D, or E is not described in any asset guideline class, such item of property has no class life.

▲ Table A11–2

MACRS Depreciation for Property Other Than Real Estate Applicable convention: mid-year (*applicable methods: 200% or 150% declining balance, switching to straight-line*)

If the recovery year is	And the recovery period is					
	3 Years	5 Years	7 Years	10 Years	15 Years	20 Years
	The depreciation rate is					
1	33.33	20.00	14.29	10.00	5.00	3.750
2	44.45	32.00	24.49	18.00	9.50	7.219
3	14.81	19.20	17.49	14.40	8.55	6.677
4	7.41	11.52	12.49	11.52	7.70	6.177
5		11.52	8.93	9.22	6.93	5.713
6		5.76	8.92	7.37	6.23	5.285
7			8.93	6.55	5.90	4.888
8			4.46	6.55	5.90	4.522
9				6.56	5.91	4.462
10				6.55	5.90	4.461
11				3.28	5.91	4.462
12					5.90	4.461
13					5.91	4.462
14					5.90	4.461
15					5.91	4.462
16					2.95	4.461
17						4.462
18						4.461
19						4.462
20						4.461
21						2.231

▲ Table A11–3

MACRS Depreciation for Property Other Than Real Estate Applicable convention: mid-quarter; property placed in service in first quarter (*applicable methods: 200% or 150% declining balance, switching to straight-line*)

If the recovery year is	And the recovery period is					
	3 Years	5 Years	7 Years	10 Years	15 Years	20 Years
	The depreciation rate is					
1	58.33	35.00	25.00	17.50	8.75	6.563
2	27.78	26.00	21.43	16.50	9.13	7.000
3	12.35	15.60	15.31	13.20	8.21	6.482
4	1.54	11.01	10.93	10.56	7.39	5.996
5		11.01	8.75	8.45	6.65	5.546
6		1.38	8.74	6.76	5.99	5.130
7			8.75	6.55	5.90	4.746
8			1.09	6.55	5.91	4.459
9				6.56	5.90	4.459
10				6.55	5.91	4.459
11				0.82	5.90	4.459
12					5.91	4.460
13					5.90	4.459
14					5.91	4.460
15					5.90	4.459
16					0.74	4.460
17						4.459
18						4.460
19						4.459
20						4.460
21						0.557

If the recovery year is	And the recovery period is					
	3 Years	5 Years	7 Years	10 Years	15 Years	20 Years
			The depreciation rate is			
1	41.67	25.00	17.85	12.50	6.25	4.688
2	38.89	30.00	23.47	17.50	9.38	7.148
3	14.14	18.00	16.76	14.00	8.44	6.612
4	5.30	11.37	11.97	11.20	7.59	6.116
5		11.37	8.87	8.96	6.83	5.658
6		4.26	8.87	7.17	6.15	5.233
7			8.87	6.55	5.91	4.841
8			3.33	6.55	59.0	4.478
9				6.56	5.91	4.463
10				6.55	5.90	4.463
11				2.46	5.91	4.463
12					5.90	4.463
13					5.91	4.463
14					5.90	4.463
15					5.91	4.462
16					2.21	4.463
17						4.462
18						4.463
19						4.462
20						4.463
21						1.673

▲ **Table A11–4**

MACRS DEPRECIATION FOR PROPERTY OTHER THAN REAL ESTATE Applicable convention: mid-quarter; property placed in service in second quarter *(applicable methods: 200% or 150% declining balance, switching to straight-line)*

If the recovery year is	And the recovery period is					
	3 Years	5 Years	7 Years	10 Years	15 Years	20 Years
			The depreciation rate is			
1	25.00	15.00	10.71	7.50	3.75	2.813
2	50.00	34.00	25.51	18.50	9.63	7.289
3	16.67	20.40	18.22	14.80	8.66	6.742
4	8.33	12.24	13.02	11.84	7.80	6.237
5		11.30	9.30	9.47	7.02	5.769
6		7.06	8.85	7.58	6.31	5.336
7			8.86	6.55	5.90	4.936
8			5.53	6.55	5.90	4.566
9				6.56	5.91	4.460
10				6.55	5.90	4.460
11				4.10	5.91	4.460
12					5.90	4.460
13					5.91	4.461
14					5.90	4.460
15					5.91	4.461
16					3.69	4.460
17						4.461
18						4.460
19						4.461
20						4.460
21						2.788

▲ **Table A11–5**

MACRS DEPRECIATION FOR PROPERTY OTHER THAN REAL ESTATE Applicable convention: mid-quarter; property placed in service in third quarter *(applicable methods: 200% or 150% declining balance, switching to straight-line)*

▲ Table A11–6

MACRS DEPRECIATION FOR PROPERTY OTHER THAN REAL ESATE Applicable convention: mid-quarter; property placed in service in fourth quarter *(applicable methods: 200% or 150% declining balance, switching to straight-line)*

If the recovery year is	And the recovery period is					
	3 Years	5 Years	7 Years	10 Years	15 Years	20 Years
	The depreciation rate is					
1	8.33	5.00	3.57	2.50	1.25	0.938
2	61.11	38.00	27.55	19.50	9.88	7.430
3	20.37	22.80	19.68	15.60	8.89	6.872
4	10.19	13.68	14.06	12.48	8.00	6.357
5		10.94	10.04	9.98	7.20	5.880
6		9.58	8.73	7.99	6.48	5.439
7			8.73	6.55	5.90	5.031
8			7.64	6.55	5.90	4.654
9				6.56	5.90	4.458
10				6.55	5.91	4.458
11				5.74	5.90	4.458
12					5.91	4.458
13					5.90	4.458
14					5.91	4.458
15					5.90	4.458
16					5.17	4.458
17						4.458
18						4.459
19						4.458
20						4.459
21						3.901

Real Estate
27.5

▲ Table A11–7

MACRS Depreciation for Residential Rental Real Estate
Applicable convention: mid-month (*applicable recovery period: 27.5 years*)

If the recovery year is	And the month in the first recovery year the property is placed in service is											
	1	2	3	4	5	6	7	8	9	10	11	12
	The depreciation rate is											
1	3.485	3.182	2.879	2.576	2.273	1.970	1.667	1.364	1.061	0.758	0.455	0.152
2	3.636	3.636	3.636	3.636	3.636	3.636	3.636	3.636	3.636	3.636	3.636	3.636
3	3.636	3.636	3.636	3.636	3.636	3.636	3.636	3.636	3.636	3.636	3.636	3.636
4	3.636	3.636	3.636	3.636	3.636	3.636	3.636	3.636	3.636	3.636	3.636	3.636
5	3.636	3.636	3.636	3.636	3.636	3.636	3.636	3.636	3.636	3.636	3.636	3.636
6	3.636	3.636	3.636	3.636	3.636	3.636	3.636	3.636	3.636	3.636	3.636	3.636
7	3.636	3.636	3.636	3.636	3.636	3.636	3.636	3.636	3.636	3.636	3.636	3.636
8	3.636	3.636	3.636	3.636	3.636	3.636	3.636	3.636	3.636	3.636	3.636	3.636
9	3.636	3.636	3.636	3.636	3.636	3.636	3.636	3.636	3.636	3.636	3.636	3.636
10	3.637	3.637	3.637	3.637	3.637	3.637	3.636	3.636	3.636	3.636	3.636	3.636
11	3.636	3.636	3.636	3.636	3.636	3.636	3.637	3.637	3.637	3.637	3.637	3.637
12	3.637	3.637	3.637	3.637	3.637	3.637	3.636	3.636	3.636	3.636	3.636	3.636
13	3.636	3.636	3.636	3.636	3.636	3.636	3.637	3.637	3.637	3.637	3.637	3.637
14	3.637	3.637	3.637	3.637	3.637	3.637	3.636	3.636	3.636	3.636	3.636	3.636
15	3.636	3.636	3.636	3.636	3.636	3.636	3.637	3.637	3.637	3.637	3.637	3.637
16	3.637	3.637	3.637	3.637	3.637	3.637	3.636	3.636	3.636	3.636	3.636	3.636
17	3.636	3.636	3.636	3.636	3.636	3.636	3.637	3.637	3.637	3.637	3.637	3.637
18	3.637	3.637	3.637	3.637	3.637	3.637	3.636	3.636	3.636	3.636	3.636	3.636
19	3.636	3.636	3.636	3.636	3.636	3.636	3.637	3.637	3.637	3.637	3.637	3.637
20	3.637	3.637	3.637	3.637	3.637	3.637	3.636	3.636	3.636	3.636	3.636	3.636
21	3.636	3.636	3.636	3.636	3.636	3.636	3.637	3.637	3.637	3.637	3.637	3.637
22	3.637	3.637	3.637	3.637	3.637	3.637	3.636	3.636	3.636	3.636	3.636	3.636
23	3.636	3.636	3.636	3.636	3.636	3.636	3.637	3.637	3.637	3.637	3.637	3.637
24	3.637	3.637	3.637	3.637	3.637	3.637	3.636	3.636	3.636	3.636	3.636	3.636
25	3.636	3.636	3.636	3.636	3.636	3.636	3.637	3.637	3.637	3.637	3.637	3.637
26	3.637	3.637	3.637	3.637	3.637	3.637	3.636	3.636	3.636	3.636	3.636	3.636
27	3.636	3.636	3.636	3.636	3.636	3.636	3.637	3.637	3.637	3.637	3.637	3.637
28	1.970	2.273	2.576	2.879	3.182	3.485	3.636	3.636	3.636	3.636	3.636	3.636
29	0.000	0.000	0.000	0.000	0.000	0.000	0.152	0.455	0.758	1.061	1.364	1.667

▲ **Table A11–8**

MACRS DEPRECIATION
FOR NONRESIDENTIAL
REAL ESTATE PLACED IN
SERVICE BEFORE MAY 13,
1993
Applicable convention:
mid-month *(applicable
recovery period: 31.5 years)*

| If the recovery year is | And the month in the first recovery year the property is placed in service is | | | | | | | | | | | |
| | 1 | 2 | 3 | 4 | 5 | 6 | 7 | 8 | 9 | 10 | 11 | 12 |
	The depreciation rate is											
1	3.042	2.778	2.513	2.249	1.984	1.720	1.455	1.190	0.926	0.661	0.397	0.132
2	3.175	3.175	3.175	3.175	3.175	3.175	3.175	3.175	3.175	3.175	3.175	3.175
3	3.175	3.175	3.175	3.175	3.175	3.175	3.175	3.175	3.175	3.175	3.175	3.175
4	3.175	3.175	3.175	3.175	3.175	3.175	3.175	3.175	3.175	3.175	3.175	3.175
5	3.175	3.175	3.175	3.175	3.175	3.175	3.175	3.175	3.175	3.175	3.175	3.175
6	3.175	3.175	3.175	3.175	3.175	3.175	3.175	3.175	3.175	3.175	3.175	3.175
7	3.175	3.175	3.175	3.175	3.175	3.175	3.175	3.175	3.175	3.175	3.175	3.175
8	3.175	3.174	3.175	3.174	3.175	3.174	3.175	3.175	3.175	3.175	3.175	3.175
9	3.174	3.175	3.174	3.175	3.174	3.175	3.174	3.175	3.174	3.175	3.174	3.175
10	3.175	3.174	3.175	3.174	3.175	3.174	3.175	3.174	3.175	3.174	3.175	3.174
11	3.174	3.175	3.174	3.175	3.174	3.175	3.174	3.175	3.174	3.175	3.174	3.175
12	3.175	3.174	3.175	3.174	3.175	3.174	3.175	3.174	3.175	3.174	3.175	3.174
13	3.174	3.175	3.174	3.175	3.174	3.175	3.174	3.175	3.174	3.175	3.174	3.175
14	3.175	3.174	3.175	3.174	3.175	3.174	3.175	3.174	3.175	3.174	3.175	3.174
15	3.174	3.175	3.174	3.175	3.174	3.175	3.174	3.175	3.174	3.175	3.174	3.175
16	3.175	3.174	3.175	3.174	3.175	3.174	3.175	3.174	3.175	3.174	3.175	3.174
17	3.174	3.175	3.174	3.175	3.174	3.175	3.174	3.175	3.174	3.175	3.174	3.175
18	3.175	3.174	3.175	3.174	3.175	3.174	3.175	3.174	3.175	3.174	3.175	3.174
19	3.174	3.175	3.174	3.175	3.174	3.175	3.174	3.175	3.174	3.175	3.174	3.175
20	3.175	3.174	3.175	3.174	3.175	3.174	3.175	3.174	3.175	3.174	3.175	3.174
21	3.174	3.175	3.174	3.175	3.174	3.175	3.174	3.175	3.174	3.175	3.174	3.175
22	3.175	3.174	3.175	3.174	3.175	3.174	3.175	3.174	3.175	3.174	3.175	3.174
23	3.174	3.175	3.174	3.175	3.174	3.175	3.174	3.175	3.174	3.175	3.174	3.175
24	3.175	3.174	3.175	3.174	3.175	3.174	3.175	3.174	3.175	3.174	3.175	3.174
25	3.174	3.175	3.174	3.175	3.174	3.175	3.174	3.175	3.174	3.175	3.174	3.175
26	3.175	3.174	3.175	3.174	3.175	3.174	3.175	3.174	3.175	3.174	3.175	3.174
27	3.174	3.175	3.174	3.175	3.174	3.175	3.174	3.175	3.174	3.175	3.174	3.175
28	3.175	3.174	3.175	3.174	3.175	3.174	3.175	3.174	3.175	3.174	3.175	3.174
29	3.174	3.175	3.174	3.175	3.174	3.175	3.174	3.175	3.174	3.175	3.174	3.175
30	3.175	3.174	3.175	3.174	3.175	3.174	3.175	3.174	3.175	3.174	3.175	3.174
31	3.174	3.175	3.174	3.175	3.174	3.175	3.174	3.175	3.174	3.175	3.174	3.175
32	1.720	1.984	2.249	2.513	2.778	3.042	3.175	3.174	3.175	3.174	3.175	3.174
33	0.000	0.000	0.000	0.000	0.000	0.000	0.132	0.397	0.661	0.926	1.190	1.455

▲ **Table A11–9**

MACRS DEPRECIATION
FOR NONRESIDENTIAL
REAL ESTATE PLACED IN
SERVICE AFTER MAY 12,
1993
Applicable convention:
mid-month *(applicable
recovery period: 39 years)*

| If the recovery year is | And the month in the first recovery year the property is placed in service is | | | | | | | | | | | |
| | 1 | 2 | 3 | 4 | 5 | 6 | 7 | 8 | 9 | 10 | 11 | 12 |
	The depreciation rate is											
1	2.461	2.247	2.033	1.819	1.605	1.391	1.177	0.963	0.749	0.535	0.321	0.107
2–39	2.564	2.564	2.564	2.564	2.564	2.564	2.564	2.564	2.564	2.564	2.564	2.564
40	0.107	0.321	0.535	0.749	0.963	1.177	1.391	1.605	1.819	2.033	2.247	2.461

Recovery Year	Mid-Year Convention	Mid-Quarter Convention Car Placed in Service in				Maximum Depreciation Limit*	
		1st Quarter	2nd Quarter	3rd Quarter	4th Quarter	1994	1995 & 1996
1	20.00%	35.00%	25.00%	15.00%	5.00%	$2,960	$3,060
2	32.00%	26.00%	30.00%	34.00%	38.00%	$4,700	$4,900
3	19.20%	15.60%	18.00%	20.40%	22.80%	$2,850	$2,950
4	11.52%	11.01%	11.37%	12.24%	13.68%	$1,675	$1,775
5	11.52%	11.01%	11.37%	11.30%	10.94%	$1,675	$1,775
6	5.76%	1.38%	4.26%	7.06%	9.58%	$1,675	$1,775

*These amounts must be reduced if business use is less than 100%. The depreciation deduction for an automobile cannot exceed the amounts in the last column (adjusted for business use).

▲ **Table A11–10**

MACRS DEPRECIATION FOR A CAR PLACED IN SERVICE IN 1994, 1995, AND 1996, 200% DECLINING BALANCE METHOD

If the recovery year is	And the recovery period is					
	3 Years	5 Years	7 Years	10 Years	15 Years	20 Years
	The depreciation rate is					
1	16.67	10.00	7.14	5.00	3.33	2.50
2	33.33	20.00	14.29	10.00	6.67	5.00
3	33.33	20.00	14.29	10.00	6.67	5.00
4	16.67	20.00	14.29	10.00	6.67	5.00
5		20.00	14.29	10.00	6.67	5.00
6		10.00	14.29	10.00	6.67	5.00
7			14.29	10.00	6.67	5.00
8			7.14	10.00	6.67	5.00
9				10.00	6.67	5.00
10				10.00	6.67	5.00
11				5.00	6.67	5.00
12					6.67	5.00
13					6.67	5.00
14					6.67	5.00
15					6.67	5.00
16					3.33	5.00
17						5.00
18						5.00
19						5.00
20						5.00
21						2.50

▲ **Table A11–11**

OPTIONAL STRAIGHT-LINE MACRS DEPRECIATION FOR PROPERTY OTHER THAN REAL ESTATE Applicable Convention: Mid-Year

Property Dispositions

▲ CHAPTER LEARNING OBJECTIVES

■ Explain the calculation of realized gain or loss from the sale or other disposition of property.

■ Discuss what constitutes the amount realized from a disposition of property.

■ Differentiate a realized gain or loss from a property disposition and the amount of gain or loss that is recognized in the tax year of the disposition.

■ Describe capital assets and the year-end netting procedure used to determine the effect of capital asset transactions on taxable income.

■ Present year-end tax-planning strategies to take advantage of the capital asset netting procedure.

■ Describe Section 1231 assets and the year-end netting procedure used to determine the effect of Section 1231 transactions on taxable income.

■ Explain the reclassification of gain on the sale of depreciable assets as ordinary income under the depreciation recapture provisions.

■ Identify Section 1245 and Section 1250 assets and the depreciation recapture rule applicable to each type.

■ Provide a framework for analyzing the effect of a variety of different asset dispositions on taxable income for the year.

▲ CONCEPT REVIEW ▲

All-inclusive income   All income received is taxable unless a specific provision can be found in the tax law that either excludes the income from taxation or defers its recognition to a future tax year.

Annual accounting period   All entities must report the results of their operations on an annual basis (the tax year). Each tax year stands on its own, apart from other tax years.

Arm's-length transaction   A transaction in which all parties to the transaction have bargained in good faith and for their individual benefit, not for the benefit of the transaction group.

Basis   This is the amount of unrecovered investment in an asset. As amounts are expended and/or recovered relative to an asset over time, the basis is adjusted in consideration of such changes. The **adjusted basis** of an asset is the original basis, plus or minus the changes in the amount of unrecovered investment.

Business purpose   To be deductible, an expenditure or a loss must have a business or other economic purpose

that exceeds any tax avoidance motive. The primary motive for the transaction must be to make a profit.

Capital recovery   No income is realized until the taxpayer receives more than the amount invested to produce the income. The amount invested in an asset represents the maximum amount recoverable.

Legislative grace   Any tax relief provided is the result of a specific act of Congress that must be strictly applied and interpreted. All income received is taxable unless a specific provision can be found in the tax law that excludes the income from taxation. Deductions must be approached with the philosophy that nothing is deductible unless a provision in the tax law allows the deduction.

Realization   No income (or loss) is recognized until it has been realized. A realization involves a change in the form and/or the substance of a taxpayer's property rights that results from an arm's-length transaction.

Wherewithal to pay   Income is recognized in the period in which the taxpayer has the means to pay the tax on the income.

INTRODUCTION

A taxpayer realizes gain or loss on property when the form or substance of the property or its underlying property rights change as a result of an arm's-length transaction. Realization of gain or loss typically occurs upon disposition of property in a transaction with another entity. The most common way to dispose of an asset is by sale. However, property is also disposed of through exchanges, casualties and thefts, and abandonments or retirements.

Figure 12–1 presents an overview of the steps involved in analyzing a disposition of property. The first step is to calculate the amount realized from the disposition. Under the capital recovery concept, taxpayers do not recognize gain until they have recovered all capital invested in the property. The amount of unrecovered investment in the property is measured by the property's basis. As Chapter 10 explained, many properties are subject to adjustments to account for additional investment and deductions for cost recoveries throughout their lives. These adjustments give the property an adjusted basis at the date of disposition.

The second step is to calculate the gain or loss realized on the disposition. The gain or loss realized on a disposition is the difference between the amount realized from the disposition of the property and the adjusted basis of the property.

A gain on the disposition of a property represents an amount realized in excess of the unrecovered investment in the property. A gain is taxable under the all-inclusive income concept. On the other hand, a loss on a disposition represents a loss of capital invested in the property. As Figure 12–1 shows, some realized gains and losses are not recognized for tax purposes. Realized gains from certain types of transactions (like-kind exchanges, casualties and thefts, sales of personal residences) have been granted tax relief. Because these sale-and-replacement

▲ **Figure 12–1**

PROPERTY DISPOSITION
PROCEDURE

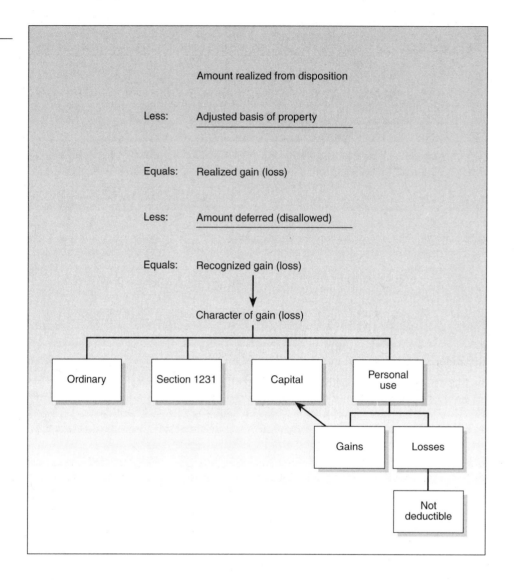

transactions require the reinvestment of the amount realized from the disposition, the taxpayer lacks the necessary wherewithal to pay. As a result, gains from these transactions are deferred for recognition in a future accounting period. Because these deferrals are a matter of legislative grace, few transactions qualify for this special relief. (The most common nontaxable transactions and their unique characteristics are discussed in Chapter 13.) Deductions for losses on dispositions are also subject to the legislative grace concept. Therefore, certain types of realized losses are deferred (e.g., like-kind exchanges, wash sales), whereas others are specifically disallowed (e.g., losses on sales of personal use property). Thus, the third step in the analysis of the disposition of property is to determine the amount of gain or loss that is to be recognized in the current tax year. A **recognized gain** or **a recognized loss** is one that is included in the calculation of the current year's taxable income.

▲ **EXAMPLE 1**   Ramona sold 600 shares of Barcelona stock to her father, Hermano, for $9,000. The stock had cost Ramona $15,000. One year later, Hermano sold the 600 shares for $12,000. What are Ramona's and Hermano's realized and recognized gains or losses on the sales of the Barcelona stock?

Discussion: Ramona has realized a loss of $6,000 ($9,000 − $15,000) on the sale of the stock. However, the loss is disallowed, because the sale is to a related party. Thus, Ramona has a nondeductible loss from the sale of the stock.

Her father realized a gain of $3,000 ($12,000 − $9,000) on his sale of the stock. However, under the related party rules, Hermano can use Ramona's disallowed loss to reduce his gain to zero (as discussed in Chapter 7, the disallowed loss cannot be used to create a loss on the second sale). Hermano has realized a gain on the sale of the stock, but it is not recognized because of the related party rules.

▲ **EXAMPLE 2**   Michael exchanged a computer used in his dental practice with an adjusted basis of $600 for a new computer. The new computer cost $3,000, but Michael was given a trade-in value of $1,000 for his old computer and had to pay only $2,000 out of pocket for the new computer. Has Michael realized a gain from the exchange of his computer? If so, is the gain recognized in the current period?

Discussion: The exchange of the computers is a disposition of the old computer. Michael has realized a gain of $400 ($1,000 trade-in value − $600 adjusted basis) on the exchange. The substance of the transaction is a sale of his old computer for $1,000 and the purchase of the new computer for $3,000.

In this case, Michael would not recognize any gain on the exchange in the current period. This is an exchange of business property for like-kind business property that can be deferred under the wherewithal-to-pay concept. Although Michael has realized a gain on the transaction, the net effect is that he pays out $2,000 in cash to effect the exchange. Michael has no assets remaining after the exchange with which to pay the tax on the realized gain. The definition of like-kind property and other rules regarding exchanges are discussed in Chapter 13.

After calculating the amount of gain or loss to be recognized, you must determine the character of the gain or loss. The tax law provides different treatments for gains and losses from different categories of property. As Figure 12–1 shows, all recognized gains and losses are categorized as one of the following:

1.   Ordinary gains and losses

2.   Capital gains and losses

3.   Section 1231 gains and losses

4.   Personal use gains and losses

Different procedures and rules apply to each category of gains and losses in determining the effect of the gains and losses on current taxable income. Exhibit 12–1 contains a representative list of assets in each of the four categories.

This chapter presents and discusses the basic treatments of dispositions of property. The first topic is how the amount of realized gain or loss is determined, followed by how to characterize recognized gains and losses as ordinary, capital, or Section 1231. The final, and perhaps the most complex, topic is reclassifying gains from the sale of depreciable property as ordinary income under the depreciation recapture rules. Detailed discussion of determining gains and losses deferred under the wherewithal-to-pay concept appears in Chapter 13.

REALIZED GAIN OR LOSS

Whenever a property disposition occurs, the taxpayer must calculate the realized gain or loss. Realized gain or loss is equal to the difference between the amount realized and the adjusted basis of the property.[1] The rules for determining a property's basis and the common adjustments to basis were discussed in Chapters

▲ **Exhibit 12–1**

CLASSIFICATION OF
ASSETS

Ordinary Income Assets	**Capital Assets**
Inventories, receivables	Stocks, bonds, options
Gains from depreciation	Rental property (if not considered a trade or
Losses on small business stock	business)
Depreciable property held ≤ 1 year	Investments in conduit entities
Sales of copyrights, artistic compositions,	Investments in passive activities
etc., by the person creating the property	Personal use property sold at a gain (but not
	at a loss)
Section 1231 Assets	**Personal Use Assets**
To qualify, the property must be used in a	Residence, automobile, clothing, furniture,
trade or business and held for more than	etc.
1 year	Any asset used for personal purposes (e.g.,
Land, buildings, equipment, machinery,	a computer used at home solely for
automobiles, computers, furniture, etc.	personal purposes)
Unharvested crops, timber, coal, domestic	
iron ore	
Livestock used for draft, breeding, dairy, or	
sporting purposes	

10 and 11. Thus, the primary focus of this section is on determining the amount realized from a disposition of property.

Amount Realized

The **amount realized** from a disposition must be calculated in order to determine whether the taxpayer has realized a gain or a loss. The amount realized is the gross sales price less all expenses incurred to complete the sale (selling expenses). The **gross sales price** is the price agreed upon by the seller and the buyer. In an arm's-length transaction, the gross sales price is equal to the fair market value of the property. Selling expenses include commissions, legal fees, title costs, advertising, and any other costs incurred to complete the disposition transaction. When the property sold has an objectively determined market value, this is a straightforward computation.

▲ **EXAMPLE 3**   Alvah sold 200 shares of Brett Co. stock for $25 per share. He paid $300 in commissions to his stockbroker for making the sale. Alvah had purchased the stock for $18 per share plus a $200 commission. What is Alvah's realized gain on the sale of the stock?

Discussion: The realized gain on the sale is $900, determined as follows:

Amount realized from sale ($5,000 − $300)	$4,700
Adjusted basis of shares sold ($3,600 + $200)	(3,800)
Realized gain on sale	$ 900

Note the effect of the commissions Alvah paid on the gain from the sale. Commissions paid to buy or sell property are never deducted as current expenses. When Alvah bought the stock, the $200 in commissions became part of the stock's basis (i.e., he had to pay the commissions in order to acquire the stock). When Alvah sold the stock, the commissions reduced the amount realized from the sale (i.e., they are a selling expense). On both sides of the transaction, the effect of the commissions is to reduce the amount of gain that Alvah realized from the stock investment.

The gross sales price of a property that does not have an objectively determined market value is any value received from the buyer less any value given back to the buyer. More formally, the gross selling price includes

Amounts received by the seller from the buyer

- Cash

- Fair market value of property received

- Fair market value of services received

- Amount of the seller's expenses paid by the buyer

- Amount of the seller's debt assumed by the buyer

LESS:
Amounts given by seller to the buyer

- Amount of the buyer's expenses paid by the seller

- Amount of the buyer's debt assumed by the seller

As you can see, the gross selling price is not always obvious. The terms of the sales agreement must be carefully analyzed in order to determine how much the buyer actually paid the seller for the property. In analyzing more complex situations, keep in mind that what you are determining is what the buyer actually paid the seller for the property.

▲ **EXAMPLE 4** Arnold had a tractor that Jack wanted to buy. Jack had $300 in cash. Arnold agreed to sell Jack the tractor for the $300 in cash if Jack would agree to mow Arnold's field for 1 year. Arnold usually pays a neighbor $1,000 per year to mow the field. What is the gross selling price of the tractor?

Discussion: The gross selling price is equal to the $300 in cash plus the $1,000 value of the mowing services Jack agreed to provide as part of the sale. Thus, Arnold sold the tractor to Jack for $1,300.

▲ **EXAMPLE 5** On April 1, Blake Corporation sold Zeke some land that it had bought for $8,000. Under the terms of the sale, Zeke was to pay Blake $13,000 in cash. In addition, Zeke also had to pay property taxes of $1,000 on the land for the entire year. Blake incurred commissions and legal fees of $1,600 related to the sale. What are the gross selling price, the amount realized, and Blake Corporation's gain (loss) on the sale of the land to Zeke?

Discussion: From Chapter 3, the payment of another's expenses in a business setting constitutes income to the person whose expenses are being paid. Therefore, the payment of Blake Corporation's share of the property taxes by Zeke is part of the sales price of the property. The gross selling price is equal to the $13,000 cash payment plus the $250 payment of Blake's property tax obligation ($1,000 × 3/12 for January, February, and March). Blake's amount realized is $11,650 ($13,250 − $1,600), resulting in a gain of $3,650 ($11,650 - $8,000) on the sale of the land.

Cash paid	$13,000
Blake's property taxes paid ($1,000 × 3/12)	250
Gross selling price	$13,250
Commissions and legal fees paid	(1,600)
Amount realized	$11,650
Adjusted basis of land sold	(8,000)
Gain realized	$ 3,650

Effect of Debt Assumptions

A buyer's assumption of the seller's debt increases the gross sales price.[2] Conversely, any debt of the buyer assumed by the seller in the transaction reduces the gross sales price. To understand why the assumption of debt by the buyer constitutes a realization of income for the seller, consider the following examples:

▲ **EXAMPLE 6**   The Lydia Partnership owns some land that has a fair market value of $70,000 on which it owes a debt of $40,000. The partnership sold the land to Kerry for $70,000 in cash (no debt assumption was part of the sales agreement). What is the gross selling price of the land? How much cash does the partnership have after the sale of the land?

Discussion: The gross selling price is the $70,000 in cash that Kerry paid to the Lydia Partnership. After receiving the $70,000, the partnership will have to pay off the $40,000 debt on the land, and it will have only $30,000 in cash remaining.

▲ **EXAMPLE 7**   Assume in example 6 that Kerry agreed to assume Lydia's debt on the land as part of the sales agreement. How much cash will Kerry pay to the partnership to purchase the land?

Discussion: Because the agreed-upon fair market value of the land is $70,000, Kerry will pay Lydia Partnership only $30,000 in cash if she assumes the $40,000 debt on the land. From Lydia's point of view, the transaction is equivalent to the transaction in example 6: In either case, the partnership receives $30,000 in cash from the sale after subtracting the debt on the property.

As these examples demonstrate, assuming another's debt is the same as paying cash to the debtor, who then uses it to pay off the debt. Therefore, any debt of the seller that is assumed by the buyer is always included in the amount realized by the seller.

In exchanges of property, parties often trade the debts they have on their properties. Trading debt along with the property often eliminates the need for the parties to obtain additional financing for the transaction.

▲ **EXAMPLE 8**   Doris and Cory each own land that they would like to trade. Details of the fair market values and the debts of each are as follows:

	Doris	Cory
Fair market value	$15,000	$25,000
Mortgage debt on land	(5,000)	(20,000)
Equity in land	$10,000	$ 5,000

Doris and Cory agree to exchange their land and assume each other's debt, with any difference paid in cash. Who will have to pay cash, and how much will that person have to pay?

Discussion: Cory will have to pay Doris $5,000. Although Cory's land is worth $10,000 more than Doris's land, Doris's land has a net of mortgage cash value of $10,000 ($15,000 − $5,000). Therefore, in a sale of her land with an assumption of her mortgage, she would expect to receive $10,000 in cash. On the other hand, Cory's net of mortgage cash value is only $5,000 ($25,000 − $20,000). Therefore, if Cory sold the land with the assumption of his mortgage, he would expect to receive $5,000. Because they are exchanging their land and their mortgages, they are really exchanging net mortgage value. Thus, Cory must pay Doris $5,000 to effect the exchange.

▲ **EXAMPLE 9**   What are the gross selling prices of Doris's and Cory's properties from the exchange in example 8?

Discussion: The gross selling prices realized by Doris and Cory will be the fair market values of their properties.

Doris realizes a gross selling price equal to $15,000:

Cash received from Cory	$ 5,000
Fair market value of land received	25,000
Mortgage assumed by Cory	5,000
Less: Assumption of Cory's mortgage	(20,000)
Gross selling price	$15,000

Cory realizes a gross selling price equal to $25,000:

Fair market value of land received	$15,000
Mortgage assumed by Doris	20,000
Less: Assumption of Doris's mortgage	(5,000)
Less: Cash paid to Doris	(5,000)
Gross selling price	$25,000

CHARACTER OF GAIN OR LOSS

After determining the amount of realized gain or loss to be recognized in the current period, you must classify the recognized gain or loss according to the character of the asset creating the gain or loss. Characterizing gains and losses from property dispositions follows the general classification scheme outlined for deductions and losses in chapters 5 through 7. In general, gains and losses on the sale of property used in a trade or business are considered ordinary gains and losses. However, gains on the sale of certain types of business assets, referred to as *Section 1231 property*, can be treated as capital gains under certain circumstances. This treatment is different from gains and losses from production-of-income activities, which are always considered capital gains and losses. Gains from the sale of personal use assets are capital gains, whereas losses on dispositions of personal use assets (other than casualty and theft losses) are specifically disallowed. Each asset type and the treatment of its gains and losses are discussed in turn.

CAPITAL GAINS AND LOSSES

Capital gains and losses result from the disposition of capital assets. Historically, net capital gains have received preferential treatment over other types of income, whereas deductions for capital losses have been limited. The various preferences and limitations applicable to capital gains have varied throughout the years, depending on the economic and political climate. In more recent times (i.e., before 1987), 60 percent of an individual's net long-term capital gains was allowed as a deduction for adjusted gross income. Thus, only 40 percent of a net long-term capital gain was subject to tax. During this period, the top marginal tax rate was 50 percent. This meant that the actual maximum marginal tax rate on a long-term capital gain was only 20 percent (40% × 50%). For a taxpayer in the 50-percent marginal tax rate bracket, classifying a gain as a capital gain produced significant tax savings.

The basic economic rationale for extending favorable treatment to long-term gains on capital assets is that such gains result from holding the property for a long time. During this holding period, inflation acts to reduce the purchasing power of the gains realized. The reduction of the gain subject to tax is often justified as necessary to offset the inflationary effects, which have less impact on assets held for a short time. Although this is true for assets held for lengthy periods, it is not necessarily true for the one-year holding period that qualifies a disposition for long-term capital gain treatment. A better justification for a differential rate of tax for long-term capital gains is that it provides incentives for investors to provide capital to companies on a more permanent basis, thereby expanding the amount of capital available to companies and lowering the cost of capital.

Whatever the rationale for extending preferential treatment to long-term capital gains, capital gains have been an important part of the tax law almost from its inception. Although much of the benefit of capital gains was removed in 1986 by the elimination of the 60-percent capital gains deduction, all the mechanisms for calculating net capital gains and losses for the year are still part of the tax law. More important, the limits on deductibility of net capital losses (discussed in Chapter 7) remained in effect after the 1986 repeal of the capital gains deduction.

 ## Capital Asset Definition

A **capital asset** is defined as any asset that is not

1. An inventory item
2. A receivable
3. Real or depreciable property used in a trade or business
4. A copyright, literary, musical, or artistic composition, letter or memorandum, or similar property held by the person creating the property or held by a person who received the property as a gift from its creator
5. Certain U.S. government publications[3]

A cursory examination of the list of properties that are not capital assets reveals that most trade or business assets are not capital assets. The first three categories excluded from capital asset status form the asset core of any business.

The fourth category consists of assets that are essentially inventories for their creators and are thus excluded from capital asset status. For example, an artist is in the trade or business of creating paintings. Artists who sell their paintings are like merchants who sell inventory. The exclusion of such property for anyone who receives it as a gift from its creator is intended to stop the conversion of ordinary income to capital gain income through gifts of the property. However, note that not all sales of paintings would constitute inventory sales. For example, a collector of art may purchase a painting for long-term appreciation. For the collector, the painting is a capital asset that creates a capital gain or loss upon disposition.

The last category of assets was added to the list of noncapital assets to stop former presidents of the United States from obtaining large charitable contribution deductions for giving their papers to nonprofit organizations after they left office. As such, it is not of concern to most taxpayers.

Long-Term versus Short-Term Classification

Preferential treatment for capital gains has always been limited to net long-term capital gains. Therefore, all capital gains and losses must be classified as either short or long term. In order to be a long-term gain or loss, the property must be held for more than one year. Gains and losses from property held exactly one year or less are short-term gains and losses.[4]

The holding period of an asset is generally the length of time the taxpayer actually owns the property. However, situations arise that do not fit this rule and that are inequitable if the law were strictly applied.

▲ **EXAMPLE 10**   Heidi received 100 shares of stock from her uncle Guiseppi as a graduation present. Guiseppi had paid $600 for the shares 5 years earlier. On the date of the gift, the shares were worth $2,000. One month after receiving the shares, Heidi sold them for $2,100, net of commissions. What is Heidi's gain on the sale of the stock? Is the gain short-term or long-term?

Discussion: Heidi's gain on the sale is $1,500 ($2,100 − $600). Because the fair market value of the shares on the date of the gift was greater than her uncle's basis, Heidi's basis is equal to her uncle's basis. Although Heidi has personally held the stock for only 1 month, the gain on the stock is the result of holding the shares for more than 5 years. Therefore, the gain on the sale of the stock is a long-term capital gain.

Example 10 illustrates a basic rule for determining the **holding period** of a property: Whenever a taxpayer's basis is determined, either in whole or in part, by reference to another asset's basis, the holding period of the other asset is included in the taxpayer's holding period. Under this rule, the prior holding period of any property with a carryover basis (see Chapter 10) is added to the current holding period. However, if the taxpayer's basis is made by reference to a market value at the date of acquisition, the holding period begins at the date of acquisition. The primary exception to the market value rule is for inherited property, which is always considered long term.[5]

▲ **EXAMPLE 11**   Rolf received a gift of stock from his mother, Sheila, as a graduation present. Sheila had paid $500 for the stock 5 years earlier. On the date of the gift, the stock was worth $400. Six months later, Rolf sold the stock for $350. What is Rolf's gain (loss) on the sale of the stock? Is the gain (loss) short term or long term?

Discussion: Because the fair market value of the stock at the date of the gift was less than Sheila's basis, the split basis rule for gifts applies. Rolf's basis for computing losses is equal to the fair market value of the stock on the date of the gift. Rolf has a loss of $50 ($350 − $400) on the sale. The loss is a short-term capital loss, because he held the stock for only 6 months. Rolf does not get his mother's holding period, because Rolf's basis is the fair market value at the date of acquisition.

▲ **EXAMPLE 12**   Assume the same facts as in example 11, except that Rolf sold the stock 6 months later for $600. What is Rolf's gain (loss) on the sale? Is the gain (loss) short term or long term?

Discussion: Under the split basis rule for gifts, Rolf's basis for determining gain is his mother's basis. Rolf has a gain of $100 ($600 − $500) on the sale of the stock. Because Rolf's basis is Sheila's basis, he receives his mother's holding period. Thus, Rolf has a $100 long-term capital gain on the sale.

Capital Gain-and-Loss Netting Procedure

Exhibit 12–2 presents the procedure for determining the net capital gain or loss for a tax year.[6] The first step in the process is to identify all gains and losses from the sale of capital assets during the year. The gains and losses are then separated into short-term and long-term gains and losses per the holding period of the property sold.

The second step is to combine all the capital gains and losses for the year into a single position. That is, the taxpayer has either gained in total from capital asset dispositions during the year or has lost in total during the year. This is accomplished by first netting together all short-term gains and losses to produce a single net short-term gain or loss amount for the year. The long-term gains and losses are also netted together to produce a net long-term gain or loss amount for the

▲ **Exhibit 12–2**

CAPITAL GAIN-AND-LOSS
NETTING PROCEDURE

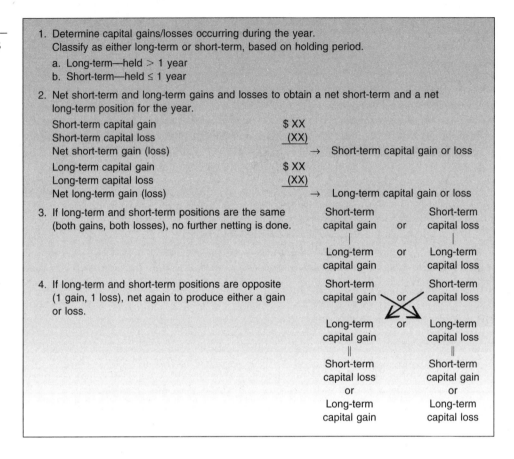

1. Determine capital gains/losses occurring during the year.
   Classify as either long-term or short-term, based on holding period.

   a. Long-term—held > 1 year
   b. Short-term—held ≤ 1 year

2. Net short-term and long-term gains and losses to obtain a net short-term and a net long-term position for the year.

Short-term capital gain	$ XX
Short-term capital loss	(XX)
Net short-term gain (loss)	→ Short-term capital gain or loss
Long-term capital gain	$ XX
Long-term capital loss	(XX)
Net long-term gain (loss)	→ Long-term capital gain or loss

3. If long-term and short-term positions are the same (both gains, both losses), no further netting is done.

4. If long-term and short-term positions are opposite (1 gain, 1 loss), net again to produce either a gain or loss.

year. If the result of these two nettings is the same—both are losses or both are gains—no further netting is required; a single position of gain or loss has been achieved. However, if the results of the first netting are opposite—one is a gain and one is a loss—a second netting is necessary to obtain a single position for the year, either a gain or a loss. In doing the capital gain-and-loss nettings, keep in mind that the ultimate goal of the netting is to reduce all capital gains and losses for the year to a single net position—the taxpayer has either gained or lost on the whole for the year and that is the position that ultimately affects the taxpayer's taxable income.

▲ **EXAMPLE 13**   Johanna had the following capital gains and losses for the current tax year:

Short-term capital gains	$ 5,000
Long-term capital gains	4,000
Short-term capital losses	(6,000)
Long-term capital losses	(12,000)

What is Johanna's net capital gain (loss) position for the year?

Discussion: Johanna has a net short-term capital loss of $1,000 and a net long-term capital loss of $8,000 for the year:

Short-term capital gains	$5,000	
Short-term capital losses	(6,000)	
Net short-term capital loss		$(1,000)

Long-term capital gains	$ 4,000	
Long-term capital losses	(12,000)	
Net long-term capital loss		$(8,000)

Because the short- and long-term positions are both losses, no further netting is necessary. Johanna's capital asset transactions for the year have produced a loss.

▲ **EXAMPLE 14**   Assume the same facts as in example 13, except that Johanna's long-term capital gains for the year totaled $20,000 instead of $4,000. What is Johanna's net capital gain (loss) position for the year?

Discussion: Johanna has a net long-term capital gain of $7,000 for the year:

Short-term capital gains	$5,000	
Short-term capital losses	(6,000)	
Net short-term capital loss		$(1,000)
Long-term capital gains	$20,000	
Long-term capital losses	(12,000)	
Net long-term capital gain		8,000
Net long-term capital gain		$ 7,000

Because the short-term position was a $1,000 loss and the long-term position was an $8,000 gain, the short-term and long-term positions are netted again to produce a single position for the year, which is a $7,000 long-term capital gain.

The tax law prescribes the treatment of the gain or loss after the position for the year has been determined. Table 12–1 summarizes these treatments for individuals and corporations.

▲ **Table 12–1**

TREATMENT OF CAPITAL GAINS AND LOSSES

Capital Gain/Loss Position	Individual Treatment	Corporate Treatment
Net short-term capital gain	Ordinary income.	Ordinary income.
Net short-term capital loss	Deductible loss for AGI; limited to $3,000 per year with indefinite carryforward of excess loss to future years' netting.	No current deduction; may carry back 3 years and forward 5 years to offset capital gains.
Net long-term capital gain	Taxed at a maximum rate of 28%.	Ordinary income.
Net long-term capital loss	Deductible loss for AGI; limited to $3,000 per year with indefinite carryforward of excess loss to future years' netting. Any short-term losses are applied against the $3,000 limit before long-term capital losses are deducted.	No current deduction; may carry back 3 years and forward 5 years to offset capital gains.

A review of Table 12–1 reveals that under current tax law only net long-term capital gains are accorded tax relief. Net long-term capital gains of individuals are subject to a maximum tax rate of 28 percent.[7] Under the current tax rate structure, only individuals in the 31-percent marginal tax brackets and higher receive any capital gains tax relief.

▲ **EXAMPLE 15**   Return to the facts of example 14. Johanna had a net long-term capital gain of $7,000 for the current year. Assuming that she is a single individual whose taxable income from all other sources was $100,000 during the current year, what amount of tax relief does Johanna receive on her $7,000 net long-term capital gain?

Discussion: Johanna's taxable income for the year is $107,000. From the tax rate schedules in Appendix A, Johanna is in the 31% marginal tax rate bracket. Therefore, the tax on her $7,000 net long-term capital gain is limited to a maximum rate of 28%. This yields a tax of $1,960 ($7,000 × 28%) on the capital gain versus a tax of $2,170 ($7,000 × 31%) at Johanna's marginal tax rate. Her tax savings from the net long-term capital gain is $210 [$7,000 × (31% − 28%)].

▲ **EXAMPLE 16**   Assume, in example 15, that Johanna's taxable income from other sources was only $30,000 during the current year. What amount of tax relief does Johanna receive on her $7,000 net long-term capital gain?

Discussion: Johanna's taxable income for the year is $37,000. From the tax rate schedules in Appendix A, Johanna is in the 28% marginal tax rate bracket. Because the maximum tax rate on long-term capital gains of 28% is equal to her marginal tax rate, Johanna receives no tax relief on her $7,000 net long-term capital gain.

Note also that short-term capital gains of individuals and all net capital gains of corporations are treated as ordinary income. They receive no special tax relief under current law. It would seem, then, that these capital gains and losses have no tax significance. Although this is true whenever an individual or a corporation has a net capital gain position for the year, the primary benefit of these gains is through the capital gain-and-loss netting procedure. That is, these gains can be used to offset and reduce capital losses occurring during the year. As shown in Table 12–1 (and covered in Chapter 7), capital loss deductions for both individuals and corporations are limited. Therefore, a tax benefit does result to the extent that a net short-term gain is used to offset a capital loss in the netting procedure.

The loss treatments in Table 12–1 are the same treatments studied in Chapter 7. The one refinement presented in this chapter is the ranking of the loss deductions for individuals. Individuals are allowed to deduct as much as $3,000 per year in net capital losses. When an individual has both a net short-term capital loss and a net long-term capital loss during the same year, the short-term losses are applied against the $3,000 limit first. Although this ranking has no effect under current law, it is an outgrowth of treatments of capital losses before 1987. Under prior law, each dollar of net long-term capital losses yielded only 50 cents of deductible loss. This means that a $2,000 net long-term capital loss yielded only a $1,000 deduction under prior law. Taking the fully deductible short-term losses first against the $3,000 limit was beneficial to the taxpayer under prior law. Under current law, both long-term and short-term capital losses are deductible dollar for dollar. However, the tax law still requires that short-term losses be deducted first.

▲ **EXAMPLE 17**   Return to the facts of example 13 in which Johanna had a net short-term capital loss of $1,000 and a net long-term capital loss of $8,000 during the current year. How much of the losses can Johanna deduct in the current year, and how much is carried forward to subsequent years?

Discussion: Johanna is allowed to deduct a maximum of $3,000 in capital losses per year with any excess loss carried forward to subsequent years. Johanna's total capital loss for the year is $9,000. Her $3,000 deduction is composed of the $1,000 short-term capital loss and $2,000 of the long-term capital loss. The remaining $6,000 of the net long-term capital loss is carried forward and used in the next year's netting as a $6,000 long-term capital loss carryforward.

Capital Gain Exclusion on Qualified Small Business Stock.

To stimulate investment in certain small businesses, the Omnibus Budget Reconciliation Act of 1993 added Section 1202 to the Code. The incentive provided by Section 1202 allows 50 percent of the gains (not reduced by any capital losses) from qualified small business stock that is held for more than five years to be excluded from taxation. The effect of the provision is to limit the marginal tax rate on such gains to a maximum of 14 percent (50% × 28% maximum capital gains rate). The maximum gain that can be excluded in a year is limited to the greater of 10 times the investor's basis in the stock or $10 million for each qualified small business. One-half of the exclusion amount is treated as a tax preference under the individual alternative minimum tax provisions (discussed in Chapter 14). This incentive provision is in addition to the loss deduction rules for certain qualifying small business stock discussed in Chapter 7. Thus, Congress has again used tax law to try to stimulate investment in small businesses.

▲ **EXAMPLE 18**   Isabel purchased 1,000 shares of qualified small business stock on November 19, 1996. On December 20, 2001, Isabel sells the 1,000 shares at a gain of $120,000. What is the effect of the sale of the stock on Isabel's tax liability, assuming that she had no other capital asset transactions in the year 2001 and is in the 36% marginal tax bracket?

Discussion: Because the stock is qualified small business stock that Isabel held for more than 5 years, she excludes 50% of the gain, $60,000, from her capital gain income. Because she has no other capital gains and losses during the year 2001, her net capital gain position is a net long-term capital gain of $60,000 ($120,000 gain − $60,000 exclusion). The gain is taxed at the 28% maximum capital gains tax rate, resulting in a tax liability of $16,800 ($60,000 × 28%). Note that tax on the gain is 14% of the total gain ($16,800 ÷ $120,000 = 14%).

▲ **EXAMPLE 19**   Assume the same facts as in example 18, except that Isabel has a net capital loss of $20,000 from her other capital asset transactions in the year 2001. What is the effect of the sale of the stock on Isabel's tax liability in the year 2001?

Discussion: The 50% exclusion is taken before the capital gain-and-loss netting. Therefore, Isabel is entitled to an exclusion of $60,000. The $60,000 long-term capital gain that remains after the exclusion is netted against the $20,000 capital loss, resulting in a net long-term capital gain of $40,000. Isabel's tax on the $40,000 net long-term capital gain is $11,200 ($40,000 × 28%).

Qualifying small business stock is stock originally issued after August 10, 1993, by a corporation that did not have gross assets in excess of $50 million after August 10, 1993, and before the stock issuance. The stock must be purchased at its original issue directly from the corporation or through its underwriter. That is, the stock cannot be acquired from another individual or entity. The small business issuing the stock must generally be an active corporation that uses substantially all its assets (at least 80 percent of the value) in the active conduct of a trade or business during the five-year holding period. Generally, only stock in manufacturing, retailing, and wholesaling businesses qualify for the exclusion. Banking, leasing, real estate, farming, mineral extraction, and hotels, motels, restaurants, or similar businesses are specifically denied treatment as qualified small business stock. In addition, the stock of certain service corporations does not qualify. Non-qualifying service corporations include those in the fields of health, law, engineering, accounting, architecture, performing arts, athletics, and financial and brokerage services.

Only noncorporate investors are eligible to claim the exclusion. Conduit entities, such as partnerships and S corporations, may hold qualified small business stock and may be able to pass the gain through to a partner or shareholder eligible for the exclusion.

▲ **EXAMPLE 20**   GARS Partnership was organized by 4 equal owners: 3 individuals (Garth, Adam, and Rachelle) and Solide Corporation. GARS Partnership purchased 10,000 shares of Mystuk Corporation stock directly from the corporation for $100,000 at its original issue on December 11, 1996. Mystuk is a pharmaceutical manufacturing enterprise, the gross assets of which have never exceeded $35 million. GARS held the stock until December 30, 2001, when it was sold for $220,000. What are the tax implications of the sale for GARS Partnership and the partners?

Discussion: Mystuk Corporation stock qualifies as small business stock. Its gross assets did not exceed $50 million after August 10, 1993, and before the stock was issued. Mystuk is an active manufacturer, and the original issue of the stock was after August 10, 1993. GARS realized a $120,000 gain ($220,000 − $100,000) on the stock sale. Because GARS is a conduit entity, the gain passes through to the partners. Each partner is allocated 25%, or $30,000, of the gain. Garth, Adam, and Rachelle can exclude $15,000 (50% × $30,000) of their individual shares of the gain. However, Solide Corporation must recognize all $30,000 of its share of the partnership's realized gain. Corporations are not allowed the benefits of the 50% exclusion.

Capital Gains and Losses—Planning Strategies

Before the end of any tax year, taxpayers should analyze their net capital gain or loss position for the year and determine whether there are any actions they might take to use the capital gain-and-loss netting procedures to their advantage. In this regard, the taxpayer may be in either a net capital gain position or a net capital loss position before the end of the year.

Net Capital Gain Position.   A taxpayer with a net capital gain position will have to pay tax on the net capital gains for the year. Therefore, the taxpayer should consider reducing the net capital gain by selling capital assets on which there is an unrealized loss. To obtain the maximum tax benefit, the taxpayer should take losses that cancel out the net capital gain to date. In addition, individuals can take $3,000 in losses over and above the net capital gain to take advantage of the net capital loss deduction provisions.

▲ **EXAMPLE 21**   Before the end of the current year, Ramsey has a net long-term capital gain of $20,000 on all capital asset transactions occurring throughout the year. What is Ramsey's optimal year-end tax-planning strategy for capital gains and losses?

Discussion: Any capital losses Ramsey realizes before the end of the year will reduce the $20,000 net long-term capital gain. Optimally, Ramsey will sell capital assets with unrealized losses to produce additional capital losses of $23,000. This will change his capital gain/loss position to a net loss of $3,000 ($20,000 − $23,000) for the year. He will then be able to deduct the entire $3,000 of net capital loss.

STRATEGY PITFALL: If Ramsey sells stock to create the $23,000 loss, he will not be able to repurchase any shares of the same company for 30 days. If he repurchases shares in the same company within 30 days, the wash sale rules disallow the loss on the shares replaced. Therefore, this strategy is contingent upon the taxpayer either not desiring to remain a shareholder in the loss shares or being willing to wait more than 30 days to replace the shares.

Net Capital Loss Position.   A taxpayer with a net capital loss position before the end of the year should act to avoid the limitations on capital loss deductions. For individuals, the optimal action is to take unrealized capital gains to reduce the net capital loss for the year to the $3,000 maximum deduction amount.

> ▲ **EXAMPLE 22**   Golda has a net capital loss of $15,000 before the end of the current tax year. What is Golda's optimal year-end tax-planning strategy for capital gains and capital losses?
>
> *Discussion:*   Because Golda can deduct only $3,000 of her $15,000 net capital loss, Golda should sell capital assets with unrealized gains to produce a capital gain of $12,000. The effect of the strategy is to fully use the net capital loss within the current period by offsetting the loss with a capital gain.
> Note that if Golda sells securities to produce the desired capital gain, nothing prevents her from repurchasing the shares, because there is no gain equivalent to the rules that disallow wash sale losses.

Example 22 illustrates the previously mentioned benefit of capital gains under current tax law—the ability to deduct capital gains against capital losses that would otherwise be nondeductible in the current period. Taxpayers in net capital loss situations may take capital gains that are essentially tax free in the current period and take advantage of the capital gain-and-loss netting procedure.

No

Short Sales.   Another tax-planning strategy available to taxpayers is a short sale against the box. This technique allows taxpayers to lock in gains on securities in the current period and defer recognition of the gain to the next period. The strategy provides a mechanism for deferring a gain to a period with lower marginal tax rates and takes advantage of the time value of money savings on the deferral of a gain.

A **short sale against the box** is a short sale of stock that the taxpayer already owns. Selling short is a technique for investing in a security that is expected to decline in value. Figure 12–2 illustrates the short-sale process.

In the first step of a true **short sale,** short sellers sell a security that they do not own and receive the net selling price from the buyer. Because short sellers do not actually own the securities, they borrow them from their brokers, who give the actual shares of stock to the buyers. At a later date, the short seller purchases the shares previously sold on the open market and gives them back to the broker to repay the shares borrowed at the initial short-sale date. This is called *closing the short sale.* The short seller's profit or loss is the difference between what the shares were sold for in the first step minus the price that the short seller paid to buy the shares back in the second step. Short sellers are betting that the shares sold short will decline in value and they will be able to buy them back for less than they were initially sold.

The potential deferral mechanism of the short sale is that the gain or loss on the short sale cannot be determined until the buy-back price is known at the closing of the short sale (i.e., step 2 is completed). Thus, shares sold short in December and repurchased in January do not produce a recognized gain or loss until January.[8]

> ▲ **EXAMPLE 23**   Galen sold short 100 shares of Harvest Co. common stock on December 22 for $25 per share. He paid a commission on the short sale of $2 per share. By

▲ **Figure 12–2**

SHORT SALES

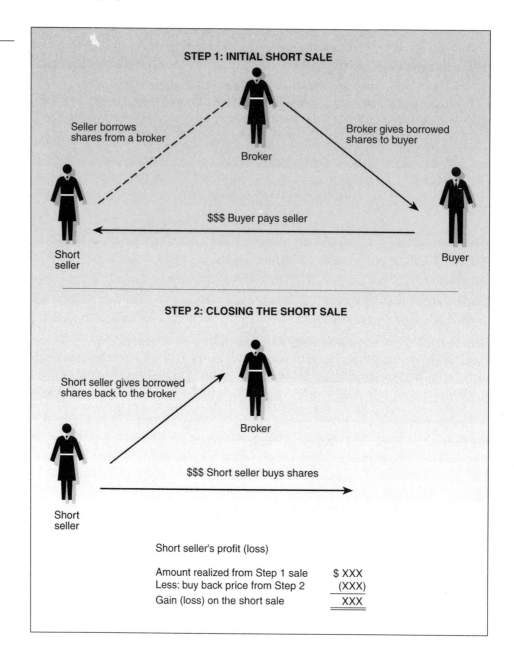

STEP 1: INITIAL SHORT SALE

Broker

Seller borrows
shares from a broker

Broker gives borrowed
shares to buyer

$$$ Buyer pays seller

Short
seller

Buyer

STEP 2: CLOSING THE SHORT SALE

Short seller gives borrowed
shares back to the broker

Broker

$$$ Short seller buys shares

Short
seller

Short seller's profit (loss)

Amount realized from Step 1 sale	$ XXX
Less: buy back price from Step 2	(XXX)
Gain (loss) on the short sale	XXX

January 5 of the next year, Harvest Co. stock had declined in value to $13 per share. Galen purchased the 100 shares sold short for $13 per share and paid $1 per share in commissions on the purchase. Galen gave the 100 shares to his broker to close the December 22 short sale. What is Galen's gain (loss) on the short-sale, and when is it recognized for tax purposes?

Discussion: Galen realized $2,300 [100 × ($25 − $2)] from the short sale, and he has a basis in the shares purchased to close the short sale of $1,400 [100 × ($13 + $1)]. Galen has realized a gain of $900 ($2,300 − $1,400) on the short sale that will not be recognized for tax purposes until January when the short sale is closed.

▲ **EXAMPLE 24**   Assume the same facts as in example 23, except that the value of the Harvest Co. stock increased and Galen had to repurchase the shares for $35 per share and he paid a $3 per-share commission on the purchase. What is Galen's gain (loss) on the short sale, and when is it recognized for tax purposes?

Discussion: In this case, Galen's basis in the repurchased shares is $3,800 [100 × ($35 + $3)]. Galen has realized a loss of $1,500 ($2,300 − $3,800) on the short sale that is recognized for tax purposes in January.

In a short sale against the box, a short sale is made of shares that the taxpayer already owns. That is, the taxpayer executes step 1 of the short-sale process. Shares are sold, and borrowed shares are given to the buyer. The short sale is then closed by giving the shares already owned (rather than buying them on the market) to the broker in the next tax year. This allows the taxpayer to lock in a gain on the shares owned in the current tax year while deferring recognition of the gain until the next tax year.

▲ **EXAMPLE 25**   Priscilla owns 500 shares of Rocker common stock that she acquired early this year at a cost of $20 per share. The stock has increased in value this year and is worth $45 per share in December. Priscilla is afraid that the stock will soon decline in value and would like to take her profit. The problem is that she is already in the 31% marginal tax rate bracket this year and would like to take the gain next year when she anticipates being in a lower tax bracket. What options are available to Priscilla? What are the consequences of these options?

Discussion: Priscilla has 3 options. She can sell the stock in the current year and pay tax on the gain at her 31% marginal tax rate (because Priscilla has held the stock less than 1 year, it will be taxed as ordinary income). Her second option is to wait and sell the stock next year and pay tax in the next year. The risk of this option is that the stock will decline in value before she sells and she will lose some of her profit.

The third option is to sell the 500 shares short at the current market value and complete the short sale next year by giving the 500 shares she owns to the broker. Ignoring transaction costs, this option would allow her to realize the $22,500 (500 × $45) of current market value and defer recognition of her $12,500 [$22,500 − (500 × $20)] gain on the short sale until the next year, when the short sale is completed.

Note the difference in the basic short sale and the short sale against the box: In a true short sale, the profit (loss) on the shares sold short is not known until the short sale is closed by purchasing the shares. In a short sale against the box, the profit is known when the initial short sale is made, because the short seller knows the basis of the shares that will be used to complete the short sale. This technique allows taxpayers to lock in gains on stocks near the end of the year and defer recognition of the gains until the next tax year.

Worthless Securities.   When a security becomes worthless, a technical disposition does not take place. However, the tax law recognizes the loss of investment suffered by the taxpayer in such situations; taxpayers with **worthless securities** are deemed to have realized the loss on the last day of the tax year in which the security is determined to be worthless. The realized loss is equal to the basis of the worthless security. The last day of the tax year is the date of realization in determining the holding period of the security for classification of the loss as short or long term.[9]

▲ **EXAMPLE 26**   Zev owns 500 shares of Newstart Co. that he purchased on November 4, 1995, for $20,000. In April 1996, Newstart declares bankruptcy, and Zev is unable to sell his shares. The bankruptcy court liquidates the company, and the shareholders receive no cash for their stock. How should Zev treat the loss on his Newstart stock?

Discussion: The Newstart stock is deemed to be worthless on December 31, 1996, which is when Zev realizes the loss of his $20,000 basis. The loss is a long-term capital loss, because Zev has held the stock for more than one year (November 4, 1995, to December 31, 1996). NOTE: If the stock in Newstart was qualified small business stock, Zev could deduct the loss as an ordinary loss (see Chapter 7).

Basis of Securities Sold.   When taxpayers sell only some of the securities they hold, the shares being sold must be identified if the securities were purchased at different times and at different prices. Because securities are generic, it is often difficult to precisely identify specific shares as from a specific purchase. The tax law provides that, in the absence of a specific identification of the shares sold, the shares are sold in a first-in, first-out order (FIFO).[10]

▲ **EXAMPLE 27**   DeWitt sold 400 shares of Rubble, Inc., common stock for $8,000 and paid a $500 commission on the sale. DeWitt had purchased his Rubble shares as follows:

Purchase Date	Number of Shares	Total Cost
February 1995	200	$3,000
November 1995	300	$3,000

What is DeWitt's gain or loss on the sale of the 400 shares?

Discussion: DeWitt's amount realized on the sale of the 400 shares is $7,500 ($8,000 − $500). Because he purchased the 500 shares at two different times and at different prices, he must either specifically identify the shares sold or determine the basis of the 400 shares in first-in, first-out order. Assuming that DeWitt cannot specifically identify the 400 shares, his basis would be $5,000:

Basis of 200 shares from February purchase	$3,000
Basis of 200 shares from November purchase	
$3,000 ÷ 300 = $10 per share × 200 shares	2,000
Basis of 400 shares	$5,000

DeWitt would realize a gain of $2,500 ($7,500 − $5,000) on the sale of the shares.

The first-in, first-out rule for the sale of securities can be overridden by directing in writing that certain lots of securities are to be sold. Thus, a taxpayer who has purchased shares at different times and at different prices can determine the amount of gain or loss to be recognized on a particular sale of shares.

▲ **EXAMPLE 28**   Cathi owns 600 shares of Wetzel's Pretzels common stock. Cathi purchased the 600 shares as follows:

Purchase Date	Number of Shares	Total Cost
October 1992	200	$ 6,000
May 1993	200	$ 9,000
December 1994	200	$14,000

Before December 28, 1996, Cathi has a net capital gain of $7,000. On December 28, 1996, Wetzel's Pretzel's stock is trading for $60 per share. If Cathi wants to sell some Wetzel's Pretzel stock to decrease her 1996 taxable income, what should she do?

Discussion: The optimal strategy in a net capital gain situation is to take capital losses to reduce capital gain income. In this case, Cathi should direct her broker, in writing, to sell the 200 shares purchased in December 1994. Ignoring sales commissions, the sale would result in a $2,000 [(200 × $60) − $14,000] capital loss, reducing her net capital gain to $5,000.

If Cathi does not specify in writing the precise shares to be sold, the October 1992 shares would be sold under the FIFO rule, resulting in a $6,000 ($12,000 − $6,000) capital gain. However, by specifying that the loss shares be sold, Cathi can control whether she has a gain or a loss on the sale.

The discussion of capital assets noted that most business assets do not receive capital gain (loss) treatment. Therefore, dispositions of assets used in a trade or business would generally produce ordinary gains and losses. However, Congress has provided capital gain relief for certain long-lived business assets. The rationale for this treatment is that long-lived assets sold at a gain have characteristics common to capital assets and deserve the same treatment in order to negate inflationary gains and to promote capital investment in long-lived business assets. The assets accorded this special relief are referred to as *Section 1231 property.* The basic intention of Section 1231 is to provide long-term capital gain status to net **Section 1231 gains** for a tax year while preserving the ordinary loss deduction for years in which a business has net **Section 1231 losses.** Therefore, this provision provides the best of both worlds—preferential capital gain treatment for net gains and ordinary loss deductions for net losses.

Definition of Section 1231 Property

Assets eligible for the preferential treatment under Section 1231 include

1. Property used in a trade or business that is held for more than one year and that is depreciable property or real property
2. Timber, coal, and domestic iron ore
3. Cattle and horses held for draft, breeding, dairy and sporting purposes that are held for 24 months or more
4. Other livestock held for draft, breeding, dairy, and sporting purposes that are held for 12 months or more
5. Unharvested crops

The assets qualifying for Section 1231 treatment must be held for more than one year, consistent with the holding period requirement for long-term capital gains. Assets that are held for less than a year are never given Section 1231 treatment and always produce ordinary income. The first category affects most businesses, because the category includes all fixed assets of a business. Note that **Section 1231 property** is property that is used primarily to operate the business. Property such as inventory that is sold to produce the income of the business generally is not Section 1231 property. However, the last three categories are inventory-type items for which Congress has applied the legislative grace concept in order to grant the special treatment provided by Section 1231.

Section 1231 Netting Procedure

As with capital gains and losses, the tax treatments accorded Section 1231 property apply to the net gain or loss on all Section 1231 transactions occurring during a tax year. The netting procedure involves two separate nettings of transactions occurring during the current tax year and a separate netting of any net Section 1231 gains in the current year against net 1231 loss deductions taken during the previous five years. Figure 12–3 outlines the netting procedure.[11]

The first step in the **Section 1231 netting procedure** is to net together all casualty (theft) gains and losses on Section 1231 property to produce a single net casualty gain or loss for the year. If the result of the first netting is a loss, all casualty gains and losses for the year are considered ordinary losses. This results in a net ordinary casualty loss deduction for the year. If the result of the first netting is a gain, the net casualty gain is carried into the second netting. The purpose of this separate netting of casualty and theft losses is to provide the maximum benefit possible for casualty and theft losses—ordinary loss deductions for net casualty losses and capital gain treatment of net casualty gains.

In the second netting, all other Section 1231 gains and losses occurring during the year are netted together with any net casualty gain from the first netting. As in the first netting, if the result of the second netting is a loss, all gains and losses for the year are considered ordinary. This results in a net ordinary loss deduction for Section 1231 transactions for the year.

▲ **Figure 12–3**

Section 1231 Netting

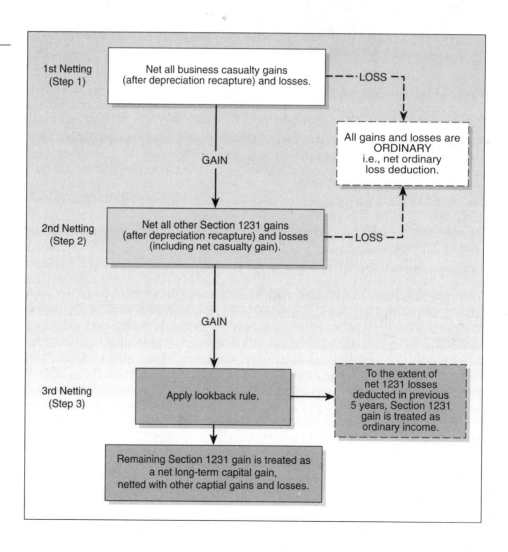

▲ **EXAMPLE 29** After summarizing the results of all its transactions for the year, *Step 1*
Bemigi Corporation had the following gains and losses from Section 1231 property:

Casualty gains	$23,000
Casualty losses	(5,000)
Section 1231 gains	35,000
Section 1231 losses	(60,000)

[handwritten:]
Casualty gains #23,000
Casualty loses (5,000)
Net casualty gain 18,000

What is the effect of the Section 1231 transactions on Bemigi's taxable income for the current year?

Discussion: In order to determine the tax effect, Bemigi must go through the Section 1231 netting procedure:

Step 1: Net all casualty gains and losses

Casualty gains	$23,000
Casualty losses	(5,000)
Net casualty gain	$18,000

[handwritten:]
Net casualty gain 18,000
Sect. 1231 gain 35,000
Sect 1231 loss (60,000)
Net Sect 1231 loss (7,000)

Because this netting results in a gain, the net gain is carried to the second netting.

Step 2: Net all other 1231 gains and losses with the net casualty gain

Net casualty gain	$ 18,000
Section 1231 gains	35,000
Section 1231 losses	(60,000)
Net Section 1231 loss	$ (7,000)

Because the Section 1231 netting produced a loss, all Section 1231 gains and losses for the year are considered ordinary losses. The result is that the Section 1231 transactions reduce Bemigi's taxable income by $7,000. This is a favorable result, because there are no restrictions on the deductibility of an ordinary loss.

When the result of the second netting is a gain, another netting must take place. This netting is required by the **lookback recapture rule,** which effectively nets the current-year net Section 1231 gain against any Section 1231 ordinary loss deductions taken in the previous five years. Any current-year net Section 1231 gain in excess of Section 1231 ordinary losses deducted in the previous five years is treated as a long-term capital gain. After applying the lookback rule's netting, the Section 1231 gain is added to other long-term capital gains and combined with other capital gains and losses in the capital gain-and-loss netting.

▲ **EXAMPLE 30** Assume that Bemigi Corporation had the following Section 1231 gains and losses in the next year (according to the results in example 29). What is the tax treatment of the Section 1231 gains and losses if Bemigi's only Section 1231 transactions during the previous 5 years were those that produced the $7,000 Section 1231 loss in example 29?

Casualty loss	$(8,000)
Section 1231 gains	33,000
Section 1231 losses	(6,000)

[handwritten:]
Sec 1231 gain 33,000
Sec 1231 losses (6,000)
Net Sec 1231 gain 27,000

Discussion: The Section 1231 netting procedure results in the following:

[handwritten:]
Net Sec 1231 gain 27,000
Sec 1231 loss from last year (7,000)
20,000

Step 1: The casualty loss is an ordinary loss. It is not carried to the second netting.

Step 2: Net together the other Section 1231 gains and losses.

Section 1231 gains	$33,000
Section 1231 losses	(6,000)
Net Section 1231 gain	$27,000

Step 3: Because the second netting produced a net Section 1231 gain for the year, ordinary loss deductions taken under Section 1231 during the previous 5 years must be recaptured as ordinary income before any long-term capital gain treatment is allowed.

Net Section 1231 gain	$27,000
Section 1231 loss deduction from last year	(7,000)
Long-term capital gain	$20,000

The results of the Section 1231 netting are summarized as follows:

Ordinary casualty loss deduction	$(8,000)
Ordinary income under lookback rule	7,000
Long-term capital gain	20,000

The ordinary income from the lookback recapture rule and the ordinary loss from the casualty are combined (added or subtracted) in the calculation of Bemigi's taxable income. The $20,000 long-term capital gain is combined with any other capital gains and losses in the capital gain-and-loss netting procedure to determine its effect on taxable income.

Once ordinary Section 1231 loss deductions have been recaptured as ordinary income, they do not have to be recaptured again. The intent of the lookback rule is to net together ordinary loss deductions against net Section 1231 gains to equalize the characterization of gains and losses over the five-year lookback period. Once an ordinary loss deduction of one year has been offset by Section 1231 gain of a later year, there is no need for further recapture.

▲ **EXAMPLE 31**   Assume that in the year after that described in example 30, Bemigi Corporation had the following Section 1231 gains and losses:

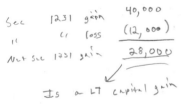

Section 1231 gains	$40,000
Section 1231 losses	(12,000)

What is the effect of the Section 1231 gains and losses on Bemigi's taxable income?

Discussion: Bemigi has a net Section 1231 gain of $28,000 ($40,000 − $12,000) for the year. Because Bemigi recaptured all of its Section 1231 ordinary loss deductions last year, the entire $28,000 gain is a long-term capital gain. The $28,000 long-term capital gain is combined with other capital gains and capital losses in the capital gain-and-loss netting procedure.

Given that the current treatment of long-term capital gains is not of great benefit to many taxpayers (see Table 12–1), why is the Section 1231 capital gain relief important? As with any net capital gain, one benefit under current law is the reduction of otherwise currently nondeductible capital losses. Without the Section 1231 provisions, many taxpayers would pay tax on their gains from selling business assets while realizing little or no current relief from net capital losses.

▲ **EXAMPLE 32**   Assume that in example 30, which produced a net long-term capital gain of $20,000 from the Section 1231 netting, Bemigi also had the following capital gains and losses for the year. What is the treatment of the capital gains and losses?

Short-term capital gains	$13,000
Long-term capital losses	(30,000)

Discussion: The capital gain-and-loss netting procedure produces a net short-term capital gain of $3,000:

Short-term capital gain		$13,000
Long-term capital gain from Section 1231	$20,000	
Long-term capital loss	(30,000)	
Net long-term capital loss		(10,000)
Net short-term capital gain		$ 3,000

Note that without the long-term capital gain from the Section 1231 netting, Bemigi would have had a long-term capital loss of $17,000 ($13,000 − $30,000) for the year. As a corporation, Bemigi would not be allowed to deduct any of the capital loss in the current year. The capital loss would be carried back 3 years and used to offset net capital gains. If Bemigi had no capital gains in the carryback period, it could carry the capital loss forward for 5 years. However, because the Section 1231 netting produced a capital gain, Bemigi has effectively deducted the $17,000 loss in the current year.

Dispositions of Rental Activities

Guidelines for determining whether a rental activity is a trade or business were discussed in Chapter 5. We noted that because rental expenses are deductions for adjusted gross income, classification of a rental activity as a trade or business or a production-of-income activity does not affect the current deductibility of the rental expenses. However, the importance of the classification is in the treatment of the gain or loss from the disposition of the rental property. If the rental property is held for the production of income, any gain or loss on its disposition is a capital gain or loss. On the other hand, if the rental activity constitutes a trade or business, any gain or loss on the property is a Section 1231 gain or loss. Because the capital gain and Section 1231 netting procedures both treat net gains as capital gains, the main difference in treatments is for rental property sold at a loss.

▲ **EXAMPLE 33**   Teresa owns a rental property that has an adjusted basis of $120,000. During the current year, she sold the property for $100,000. Assuming that she had no other property transactions during the year, how much of the loss is deductible if the rental activity is considered a trade or business for Teresa? a production-of-income activity for Teresa?

Discussion: Teresa has realized a loss of $20,000 on the sale of the rental property. If the rental activity is a trade or business, the loss is a Section 1231 loss that is deductible in full as an ordinary loss. (With no other transactions during the year, the result of the 1231 netting procedure would be a $20,000 loss.)

If the rental activity is a production-of-income activity, the loss is a capital loss. Because she has no other property transactions during the current year, Teresa has a net capital loss of $20,000. Her current capital loss deduction is limited to $3,000.

In extending capital gain relief on assets held for more than one year through the capital gain and Section 1231 provisions, Congress was concerned that only gains derived from appreciation in the value of the property were granted tax relief. In many instances, the entire gain on the disposition of a property is derived from appreciation.

DEPRECIATION RECAPTURE

▲ **EXAMPLE 34**   Raquel purchases 300 shares of Houston Co. stock on September 4, 1992, at a cost of $4,500. On April 5, 1996, Raquel sells the 300 shares of stock for $8,500. Is Raquel's $4,000 gain on the sale derived from appreciation in the value of the stock?

Discussion: Raquel's $4,000 gain is totally derived from appreciation in the price of the Houston Co. stock. Because Raquel is not allowed to recover any of her $4,500 investment in the stock until the stock is sold, any gain on the sale of the stock is attributable solely to price appreciation.

We can conclude from example 34 that when the investment in the asset is recovered only at disposition, any gain on the sale is derived from price appreciation. However, through depreciation deductions, taxable entities recover capital investments in many assets while the asset is used to produce income. As an asset is depreciated, the basis in the asset is reduced. When the asset is disposed of, the gain or loss is measured as the difference between the amount realized and the adjusted basis of the asset. As a result, some—and perhaps all—of the gain on the sale of a depreciable asset derives from depreciation previously deducted on the asset.

▲ **EXAMPLE 35**   In 1994, Latifa Corporation purchases a computer to be used solely in its trade or business at a cost of $15,000. Latifa elects to use straight-line depreciation on the computer. In 1996, when the adjusted basis of the computer is $9,000, the corporation sells the computer for $10,000. How much of Latifa's $1,000 gain on the sale derives from the depreciation it took on the computer?

Discussion: The entire $1,000 gain is attributable to depreciation. That is, the computer has not appreciated in value from its original acquisition cost. It has actually lost $5,000 in value since Latifa purchased it. Only because Latifa took $6,000 in depreciation on the computer (reducing its basis) did the corporation have a gain.

Example 35 illustrates the basic rationale for disallowing long-term capital gain treatment for gains from depreciation deductions. Although the computer has lost $5,000 in value, the $6,000 in depreciation taken on the computer has resulted in a gain of $1,000 on the sale of the computer. This gain is created by the depreciation that was deducted as an ordinary expense for the business, reducing the tax on ordinary income. Allowing long-term capital gain treatment on the sale of the computer would allow an ordinary deduction to create a capital gain on the disposition. As previously discussed, one purpose of the preferential treatment for capital gains and Section 1231 property is that the gains have been artificially increased by inflation. However, with depreciable assets, a portion of the gain is created through ordinary deductions. The purpose of the depreciation recapture rules is to reclassify gains from depreciation as ordinary income.

Recapture can be seen as giving back the ordinary deduction that created the gain. Only the gain remaining in excess of the recaptured amount is accorded capital gain or Section 1231 treatment. Thus, **depreciation recapture** is the reclassification as ordinary income of all or part of a gain on the disposition of a capital asset or a Section 1231 asset. The recaptured amount does not receive preferential treatment in the calculation of taxable income.

There are two primary recapture provisions, referred to as *Section 1245 recapture* and *Section 1250 recapture*. All depreciable assets must be classified as either a Section 1245 property or a Section 1250 property and the appropriate recapture rule applied when the asset is disposed of at a gain. In studying these provisions, keep in mind that the intent of the two provisions is to reclassify gains from depreciation as ordinary income. Depreciation deductions do not create losses. Therefore, the depreciation recapture provisions do not apply to depreciable assets sold at a loss.

Section 1245 Recapture Rule

Section 1245 property is subject to a full recapture of all depreciation taken as ordinary income.[12] The practical effect of this provision is to deny capital gain or Section 1231 treatment on any Section 1245 property that is disposed of at less than its original cost.

▲ **EXAMPLE 36**   Reactor Tractor Co. purchases machinery in 1994 at a cost of $40,000. In 1996, when the adjusted basis of the machinery is $15,000, Reactor sells the machinery for $26,000. The machinery is Section 1245 property. What is the character of the $11,000 gain on the sale of the machinery?

Discussion: Machinery used in a trade or business is a Section 1231 property. However, Reactor is required to recapture as ordinary income any gain on the sale that derives from depreciation before any of the gain is considered Section 1231 gain. In this case, the $11,000 gain is totally derived from the $25,000 ($40,000 − $15,000) in depreciation taken on the machinery. Therefore, all gain on the sale is ordinary income. None of the gain is eligible for treatment under the Section 1231 netting procedure.

▲ **EXAMPLE 37**   Assume the same facts as in example 36, except that the machinery is sold for $47,000, resulting in a gain on the sale of $32,000. What is the character of the $32,000 gain on the sale of the machinery?

Discussion: Of the total gain on the sale, $25,000 derives from the reduction in basis for depreciation and is recaptured as ordinary income. The remaining $7,000 of gain derives from price appreciation in the machinery and is characterized as gain from the sale of a Section 1231 asset.

Amount realized	$47,000
Adjusted basis ($40,000 − $25,000)	(15,000)
Gain on sale	$32,000
Gain from depreciation—ordinary income	(25,000)
Gain from price appreciation—Section 1231 gain	$ 7,000

These two examples illustrate a basic result of the **Section 1245 recapture rule:** No capital gain or Section 1231 treatment results from the sale of a Section 1245 property unless it is sold for more than its original cost. Note that the $7,000 in Section 1231 gain in example 37 is the appreciation in price from the $40,000 original cost to the $47,000 selling price. This result always holds for a Section 1245 property.

Section 1250 Recapture Rule

The recapture rule for gains on the sale of Section 1250 assets is more generous than under Section 1245. Under the **Section 1250 recapture rule,** only gains that are attributable to excess depreciation are recaptured as ordinary income. *Excess depreciation* is defined as the total depreciation taken to date, less the allowable straight-line depreciation on the asset.[13] Note that if a Section 1250 asset has been depreciated using the straight-line method, no recapture of depreciation occurs, because no excess depreciation has been deducted on the asset.

▲ **EXAMPLE 38**   Ragwood Co. purchased a factory building in 1980 at a cost of $800,000. The factory building is sold in 1996 for $700,000. The maximum allowable

[Handwritten margin notes:]

Amt. realized on sale $ 700,000
Adj. Basis (800,000 - 600,000)   (200,000)
Gain on Sale   500,000

Depr. Recapture
(600,000 - 400,000)   (200,000)

Section 1231 gain   300,000

Amt. realized on sale   700,000
Adj Basis (800,000 - 400,000)   (400,000)
Gain on Sale   300,000
    Sec 1231 gain

depreciation on the building as of the date of sale was $600,000. Straight-line depreciation for the same period would have been $400,000. The building is a Section 1250 property. What is the character of the gain on the sale of the building if Ragwood took the maximum allowable depreciation deduction on the building?

Discussion: The gain on the sale of the building is $500,000. The factory building is a Section 1231 property. However, before any of the gain is Section 1231 gain, the excess depreciation of $200,000 must be recaptured as ordinary income. This leaves $300,000 of Section 1231 gain:

Amount realized on sale	$ 700,000
Adjusted basis ($800,000 − $600,000)	(200,000)
Gain on sale	$ 500,000
Depreciation recapture—ordinary income	
($600,000 − $400,000)	(200,000)
Section 1231 gain	$ 300,000

▲ **EXAMPLE 39**   Assume that in example 38 Ragwood had deducted straight-line depreciation during the time it held the factory building. What is the character of the gain on the sale of the building?

Discussion: Using straight-line depreciation, the gain on the sale of the building would have been $300,000 [$700,000 − ($800,000 − $400,000)]. Because Ragwood used the straight-line method to depreciate the building, there is no excess depreciation to recapture. Thus, the entire $300,000 gain is Section 1231 gain.

A comparison of these examples reveals the basic result of the Section 1250 recapture rule: The Section 1231 gain (or capital gain) is always equal to the gain that would have occurred had straight-line depreciation been used. The gain remaining after depreciation recapture on a Section 1250 property is equal to the sum of the straight-line depreciation plus any price appreciation in the property. Note that this recapture result is more generous than that under Section 1245, which allows only true price appreciation to result in Section 1231 or capital gain.

▲ **EXAMPLE 40**   A depreciable asset used in a trade or business that was purchased for $80,000 was sold for $95,000. Actual depreciation deducted on the asset totaled $35,000. Allowable straight-line depreciation for the same period would have been $20,000. What is the character of the gain if the asset is a Section 1245 property? a Section 1250 property?

Discussion: The gain on the sale of the asset is $50,000 [$95,000 − ($80,000 − $35,000)]. The character of the gain under Section 1245 and Section 1250 is calculated as follows:

	Section 1245	Section 1250
Gain on Sale	$ 50,000	$ 50,000
Depreciation recapture—ordinary income		
Section 1245—all depreciation	(35,000)	
Section 1250—excess depreciation		
($35,000 − $20,000)		(15,000)
Section 1231 gain	$ 15,000	$ 35,000

Under Section 1245, the Section 1231 gain is equal to the price appreciation in the asset ($95,000 − $80,000). Under Section 1250, the Section 1231 gain is equal to the sum of the $15,000 price appreciation and the $20,000 straight-line depreciation deduction that is not recaptured under Section 1250.

The depreciation recapture rules apply to all depreciable assets.[14] There are no exceptions in the tax law that override the depreciation recapture rules. Whenever a gain is recognized on a depreciable asset, the applicable recapture rule must be applied to determine the character of the gain. In applying the recapture rules, any amounts expensed under Section 179 are considered depreciation. As a final reminder, the depreciation recapture rules apply only to gains caused by depreciation; losses are not subject to recapture.

Installment Sales of Depreciable Assets.   In an installment sale, gain is recognized proportionately in the years in which the taxable entity receives the sales proceeds (see Chapter 3). A special provision overrides the general installment sales recognition rules when a depreciable asset is sold in an installment sale. This provision requires all income characterized as ordinary income because of depreciation recapture to be recognized in the year of the sale.[15] Only the capital gain or Section 1231 gain on an installment sale is recognized using the installment sales method.

▲ **EXAMPLE 41**   Joe sold an apartment building he had purchased in 1985 as an investment. Joe had paid $190,000 for the building and had taken depreciation of $90,000 on the building up to the date of sale. Straight-line depreciation on the building would have been $50,000. The terms of the sale required the buyer to pay Joe $20,000 at closing and $50,000 per year for the next 4 years, with interest on the unpaid balance at 8%. The apartment building is Section 1250 property. How much gain must Joe recognize on the sale of the building in the year of sale, and what is the character of the gain to be recognized?

Discussion: The sale of the apartment building is an installment sale. Joe must use the installment sales method to recognize income from the sale, unless he elects to recognize the entire gain of $120,000 in the year of sale. Joe's realized gain and the character of the gain are calculated as follows:

Amount realized [$20,000 + ($50,000 × 4)]	$220,000
Adjusted basis ($190,000 − $90,000)	(100,000)
Realized gain on sale	$120,000
Section 1250 recapture—ordinary income	
Excess depreciation ($90,000 − $50,000)	(40,000)
Long-term capital gain	$ 80,000

Because the apartment building is depreciable property, the $40,000 in ordinary income from the recapture of depreciation must be recognized in the year of sale. Only the $80,000 long-term capital gain is recognized using the installment sales method. Joe would recognize $7,273 in long-term capital gain in the year of sale using the installment sales method:

$$\text{Gain recognized} = \frac{\text{Capital gain}}{\text{Contract price}} \times \text{Cash received}$$

$$\text{Gain recognized} = \frac{\$80,000}{\$220,000} \times \$20,000 = \$7,273$$

As each $50,000 installment payment is received, Joe will recognize $18,182 in long-term capital gain:

$$\text{Gain recognized} = \frac{\$80,000}{\$220,000} \times \$50,000 = \$18,182$$

Over the 5-year period of the installment sale, Joe's recognized gain and its character are as follows:

Character of Gain	Year 1	Year 2	Year 3	Year 4	Year 5	Total Gain
Ordinary	$40,000					$ 40,000
Capital	$ 7,273	$18,182	$18,182	$18,182	$18,181	$ 80,000
Total gain recognized						$120,000

Section 1245 and Section 1250 Properties

In order to apply the proper recapture rule, you must determine the type of depreciable property. Depreciable assets fall into two basic categories: tangible personal property and real property (see Chapter 11). Historically, the distinction between **Section 1245 property** and **Section 1250 property** was between these two basic classes of property. All depreciable tangible personal property was Section 1245 property, and all depreciable real property was Section 1250 property. Note that assets that are not depreciable because (1) they have indefinite lives (e.g., land) or (2) they are capital assets or Section 1231 assets that are not depreciable, are not subject to depreciation recapture. In 1981, the ACRS depreciation system drastically increased the allowable depreciation deductions on real property by allowing accelerated depreciation over a 15-year life. In allowing this rapid acceleration of depreciation on real property, Congress took back some of the benefit by reclassifying most real property as Section 1245 property using the accelerated ACRS method.

Table 12–2 compares the asset classifications for assets purchased before 1981 and those purchased after 1981. The key difference in classification of assets ac-

▲ **Table 12–2**

SECTION 1245 AND 1250 PROPERTIES

	Section 1245	Section 1250

Assets acquired before 1981	Depreciable personal property:
	  Autos, trucks, equipment
	  Machinery, computers
	  Greenhouses, grain silos
	  Patents, copyrights
	  Leaseholds
	  Livestock
		Depreciable real property:
		  Office buildings
		  Apartment buildings
		  Warehouses
		  Factory buildings
		  Low-income housing

Assets acquired 1981–1986	Depreciable personal property Depreciable real property that does not qualify as Section 1250 property	Residential rental property Low-income housing Any real property that has been depreciated using the straight-line method Real property used predominantly outside the U.S.

Assets acquired after 1986	Depreciable personal property:
	  Autos, trucks, equipment
	  Machinery, computers
	  Greenhouses, grain silos
	  Patents, copyrights
	  Leaseholds
	  Livestock
		Depreciable real property:
		  Office buildings
		  Apartment buildings
		  Warehouses
		  Factory buildings
		  Low-income housing

quired from 1981 through 1986 is for real property. Note that only four types of real property purchased from 1981 through 1986 qualify for the more generous Section 1250 treatment:

- Residential rental property
- Low-income housing
- Any real property that is depreciated using the straight-line method
- Real property used predominantly outside the United States

The third general category causes most of the confusion. For example, a factory building purchased in 1977 (before 1981) is always a Section 1250 property, regardless of the depreciation method used. The same factory building purchased in 1983 would be a Section 1245 property if the regular ACRS (accelerated) method was used. However, if the owner of the factory building had elected to use the straight-line method, the building would be a Section 1250 property. On the other hand, an apartment building is always considered Section 1250 property, regardless of when it is purchased or which depreciation method is used.

You should note, in the last row of Table 12–2, that any real property purchased after 1986 is Section 1250 property. This result occurs because all real property purchased after 1986 is subject to the MACRS depreciation system. Under MACRS, all real property is depreciated using the straight-line method. Thus, all real property purchased after 1986 is once again Section 1250 property, and the original distinction between Section 1245 and Section 1250 properties is restored. The practical effect of this reclassification and the use of straight-line depreciation for real property under MACRS is that there is no excess depreciation to recapture on real property purchased after 1986.

SUMMARY

Whenever property is disposed of, the realized gain or loss from the disposition must be calculated. Dispositions of property occur as a result of sales, exchanges, casualties and thefts, and abandonments and retirements. The realized gain or loss is equal to the amount realized, less the adjusted basis of the property. The amount realized from a disposition is the gross selling price, less the costs incurred in making the disposition. The gross selling price is equal to the net value received by the taxpayer for the property.

All realized gains and losses are not recognized in the period in which they are realized. Gains from certain types of transactions (discussed in Chapter 13) are deferred for future recognition. Losses from other types of transactions (wash sales, related party sales) are also deferred. Losses on the sale of personal use assets are never deductible. Thus, after the realized gain or loss on a disposition has been calculated, the amount that must be recognized in the current period must be determined.

Recognized gains and losses are then categorized according to the use of the property creating the gain or loss. All property can be categorized as ordinary income property, capital gain property, Section 1231 property, or personal use property. Once categorized, gains and losses are treated according to the rules for the particular category of property.

Ordinary gains and losses receive no special treatment in the calculation of taxable income. Losses on the sale of personal use property are not deductible, whereas gains on personal use property are subject to tax as capital gains. Thus, the primary distinction as to the effect on income involves ordinary income property, capital gain property, and Section 1231 property.

Before any gain on the sale of a depreciable asset is characterized as a capital gain or a Section 1231 gain, the appropriate depreciation recapture rule must be applied. Thus, gains on disposition of depreciable capital assets and Section 1231 property will produce ordinary income to the extent permitted under the depreciation recapture rules. This requires that the appropriate depreciation recapture be calculated before proceeding with the capital asset and Section 1231 netting. In addition, because the ultimate result of the Section 1231 netting is to tax net Section 1231 gains as long-term capital gains, the Section 1231 netting must be performed before the capital gain-and-loss netting. The year-end process for property dispositions is charted in Exhibit 12–3.

Section 1231 netting is done after applying the applicable depreciation recapture rules. If the netting results in a loss, all Section 1231 gains and losses for the year are considered ordinary gains and losses. If the Section 1231 netting results in a gain, the resulting gain is treated as a long-term capital gain that is combined with other capital gains and losses in the capital gain-and-loss netting procedure.

The goal of the capital gain-and-loss netting procedure is to reduce all gains and losses for the year to a net position that is either a gain or a loss. This is accomplished by determining a net short-term gain or loss for the year and a net long-term gain or loss for the year. If the short-term and long-term positions are the same, no further netting is required. If the two positions are opposite, a second netting of the short-term and long-term positions is required to reduce the transactions to one net position for the year, either a gain or a loss.

The preferential treatment for net capital gains is that net long-term capital gains of individuals are limited to a maximum tax rate of 28 percent. Net capital loss deductions are limited. For individuals, only $3,000 in net capital losses is deductible, with any remaining loss carried forward indefinitely. Corporations can

▲ **Exhibit 12–3**

SUMMARY OF THE
PROPERTY DISPOSITION
PROCESS

1. Determine the amount of realized and recognized gain or loss from each property disposition occurring during the year.
2. Classify all recognized gains and losses as
   a. Ordinary income property
   b. Capital gain property
   c. Section 1231 property
   d. Personal use property
3. All depreciable property sold at a gain is classified as either Section 1245 or Section 1250 property, and the appropriate depreciation recapture rule is applied. Any gain remaining is either a capital gain or a section 1231 gain, according to the classification made in step 2. *Depreciable property sold at a loss is not subject to recapture.*
4. Perform the Section 1231 netting procedure. If the netting results in a loss, the loss is ordinary. If the netting process results in a gain, the net Section 1231 gain is a long-term capital gain.
5. Perform the capital gain-and-loss netting procedure. Include in the netting any long-term capital gain from the Section 1231 netting.
6. Apply the treatment rules for capital gains and losses to the results of the capital gain-and-loss netting.
   a. Net long-term capital gains of individuals are subject to a maximum tax rate on the gain of 28%.
   b. Deductions for net long-term capital losses are limited:
      1. Individuals can deduct only $3,000 in net capital losses per year.
      2. Corporations can deduct net capital losses only against capital gains. This is done by allowing a three-year carryback and five-year carryforward for deduction of a current-year net capital loss.

deduct capital losses only against capital gains. Thus, a current-year capital loss can be deducted only against capital gains from the previous three years (carryback period) and in the succeeding five years (carryforward period).

Because of the different treatments accorded various types of gains and losses, the proper characterization of gains and losses on dispositions is crucial to the proper calculation of taxable income.

KEY TERMS

amount realized (p. 546)
capital asset (p. 550)
depreciation recapture
 (p. 566)
gross sales price (p. 546)
holding period (p. 551)
lookback recapture rule
 (p. 563)

recognized gain (p. 544)
recognized loss (p. 544)
Section 1231 gain (p. 561)
Section 1231 loss (p. 561)
Section 1231 netting procedure
 (p. 562)
Section 1231 property (p. 561)
Section 1245 property (p. 570)

Section 1245 recapture rule
 (p. 567)
Section 1250 property (p. 570)
Section 1250 recapture rule
 (p. 567)
short sale (p. 557)
short sale against the box (p. 557)
worthless security (p. 559)

PRIMARY TAX LAW SOURCES

[1] Sec. 1001—Defines gain or loss on the sale or other disposition of property.

[2] Reg. Sec. 1.001-2—Discusses the effect of discharges of liabilities on the amount realized from the sale or other disposition of property.

[3] Sec. 1221—Defines *capital assets.*

[4] Sec. 1222—Defines *holding periods for short-term and long-term capital gains and losses.*

[5] Sec. 1223—Provides rules for determining the holding period of property in different circumstances.

[6] Reg. Sec. 1.1222-1—Defines the *capital gain-and-loss netting procedure.*

[7] Sec. 1—Limits the tax on net long-term capital gains of individuals to a maximum of 28 percent.

[8] Sec. 1233—Defines a *short sale* and provides the tax rules for short sales.

[9] Sec. 165—Treats losses from worthless securities as occurring on the last day of the tax year in which the security becomes worthless.

[10] Reg. Sec. 1.1012-1—Provides rules for identifying securities sold, including what constitutes specific identification of a security sold.

[11] Reg. Sec. 1.1231-1—Explains the Section 1231 netting procedure and gives examples of its application.

[12] Reg. Sec. 1.1245-1—Explains the general operation of Section 1245 and gives examples of the application of Section 1245 in various situations.

[13] Reg. Sec. 1.1250-2—Defines *excess depreciation* and gives examples of the calculation of excess depreciation for purposes of recapture under Section 1250.

[14] Reg. Sec. 1.1245-6—States that all other nonrecognition provisions of the tax law are overridden by Section 1245. A similar provision is found in Section 1.1250-1 of the Treasury regulations relating to Section 1250 recapture.

[15] Sec. 453—Requires amounts recaptured under Section 1245 or Section 1250 to be recognized in the year of disposition when property is sold on an installment basis.

DISCUSSION QUESTIONS

1. Whenever a disposition of property occurs, a gain or loss on the disposition has been realized. However, not all gains and losses realized in the current period are recognized for tax purposes. What is the difference between a realized gain (loss) and a recognized gain (loss)?

2. In determining the amount of a realized gain or loss to be recognized in the current year, certain types of gains and losses are deferred, whereas others are disallowed. What is the difference between deferring a gain or loss realized in the current period and disallowing the recognition of a current period loss? Give at least one example of each that has been studied to date in this course.

3. What effect does the assumption of a seller's debt have on the amount realized from the disposition of the property?

4. Are brokerage commissions paid on the sale of stock a current period expense? Explain.

5. In a transaction in which the seller of property agrees to take other property from the buyer as part of the sales price, why is the buyer's adjusted basis unimportant in determining the amount realized by the seller?

6. Why is a distinction made between long-term capital gain (loss) property and short-term capital gain (loss) property?

7. What is (are) the current tax advantage(s) of selling an asset at a long-term capital gain?

8. What is the purpose of the capital gain-and-loss netting procedure?

9. Evaluate the following statement:

   Corporations can never deduct net capital losses.

10. Under what conditions may a taxpayer exclude a portion of a realized capital gain?

11. What basic tax-planning strategy should a taxpayer with a large net capital gain for the year pursue before the end of the year?

12. What is a short sale against the box? When should it be used?

13. When is a security deemed worthless for tax purposes?

14. How should taxpayers determine the basis of securities sold when their portfolios contain several purchases of the same stock at different prices? Explain.

15. When does a taxpayer realize a loss on a worthless security? What is the amount of realized loss? What rules govern the recognition of a loss on a worthless security? Explain.

16. What is a Section 1231 property?

17. What is the tax advantage of selling a Section 1231 property at a gain?

18. One primary problem in properly accounting for property dispositions is differentiating capital assets and Section 1231 property. Why is it important to correctly identify as either a capital asset or a Section 1231 property an asset that has been disposed of? Explain.

19. Explain the lookback rule as it applies to the Section 1231 netting procedure.

20. Why is it important to determine whether a rental property constitutes a trade or business or an investment activity for the taxpayer owning the property?

21. The chapter noted that all depreciable property is subject to the depreciation recapture rules. What is the intent of the depreciation recapture rules?

22. How are the recapture provisions for Section 1245 and Section 1250 property different?

23. Is an installment sale of a depreciable property treated the same as an installment sale of property that is not subject to depreciation?

24. Are buildings always Section 1250 property? If not, explain the circumstances under which a building would not be Section 1250 property.

25. Some tax theorists have noted that in the majority of cases a sale of a depreciable asset will not be accorded capital gain treatment. What would prompt tax theorists to make this statement?

26. Determine the amount realized in each of the following property dispositions:
    a. Herbert sold some land he owned to Elroy in exchange for $21,000 in cash and 2 breeding hogs worth $1,900 each (adjusted basis of $500 each). In closing the sale, Herbert incurred legal feels of $500, title search costs of $200, and document filing fees of $50.
    b. Saada Corporation sold a building it owned to Paris. Paris will finance the purchase by obtaining a $150,000 loan and will pay an additional $25,000 in cash. As part of the sales agreement, Saada agreed to pay the $3,000 in points that Paris had to pay to obtain the loan. The corporation incurred commission costs of $9,000 and $5,000 in various legal fees in making the sale.
    c. Andrew and Sandra agreed to exchange land that each owned. Andrew's land was worth $40,000, and Sandra's land was worth $43,000. Therefore, in the exchange of the land, Andrew had to pay Sandra $3,000.
    d. Artworld, Inc., sold its building to Paula for $20,000 in cash. As part of the sales agreement, Paula agreed to assume Artworld's $95,000 mortgage on the property.

27. Determine the amount realized in each of the following property dispositions:
    a. Umberto wanted to buy Kevin's truck. Because Umberto had no cash and could not obtain a loan to finance the purchase, Kevin agreed to let Umberto pay him $320 a month for 6 months. In addition, Umberto agreed to put a new roof on Kevin's house as part of the truck purchase. Umberto estimated that his cost of reroofing the house would be $750, although he would have charged Kevin $2,500 if Kevin were a paying customer.
    b. During the current year, a tornado totally destroyed a warehouse that Ajax, Inc., used in its manufacturing operation. The warehouse had a fair market value of $195,000. Ajax's insurance company paid $170,000 on the destruction of the warehouse. The president of Ajax was upset that the insurance company did not pay full fair market value, because Ajax had paid annual insurance premiums of $10,000 for the last 10 years on the warehouse.
    c. Paloma Pitchfork Co. sold an apartment complex it owned to Greedy Investors, Inc. The terms of the sale called for Greedy to pay $40,000 cash, assume Paloma's $520,000 mortgage debt on the property, and give Paloma 10,000 shares of Horticulture, Inc., common stock. Greedy had paid $16 per share for the Horticulture stock, which is currently trading for $5 per share.
    d. Melinda and Nancy agreed to exchange apartment buildings and the related mortgage debt on each building. Melinda's apartment building was worth $250,000 and was encumbered by a mortgage of $100,000. Nancy's building was worth $300,000 and had a $200,000 mortgage. In addition to exchanging the properties and the underlying debt, Nancy paid Melinda $50,000 cash to complete the exchange.

28. Tuyen is negotiating the sale of her lakefront property near Wabasha. Nils is offering
    - Cash of $10,000
    - A parcel of land near Red Wing valued at $5,000 with an adjusted basis of $3,000
    - A ski boat valued at $9,000 with an adjusted basis of $15,000
    - Installation of new heating and air conditioning in Tuyen's Rochester residence (Nils's labor and equipment costs are valued at $4,500)
    - Payment of $2,000 in real estate taxes due on the property
    - Assumption of the $130,000 balance of the mortgage on the property
    - Payment of the $900 in attorney fees and $50 in filing fees to complete the transaction

    In addition, Tuyen is offering to transfer her pontoon boat and outboard motor to Nils. The boat and motor have a fair market value of $8,500 and an adjusted basis of $10,000. Also, she would assume the $3,000 mortgage balance on the Red Wing real estate.

    Tuyen's brother tells her she should not accept an offer of less than $150,000 for the Wabasha property. Write a letter to Tuyen explaining how much she would realize if she accepts Nils's offer as presented.

29. Determine the amount of gain or loss realized and the amount of gain or loss to be recognized in each of the following dispositions:

   a. On October 1, the Rufus Partnership sold land to Gerald for which it had paid $30,000. Gerald agreed to pay Rufus $17,000 and to assume Rufus's $11,000 mortgage on the land. In addition, Gerald agreed to pay the $1,600 in property taxes on the land for the entire year.

   b. Carrie sold to her brother Dolph for $5,000 stock that had cost her $8,000. Several years later, Dolph sold the stock for $11,000.

   c. Jill wanted to refurnish her new home. As part of her refurnishing plan, she sold all her old living room furniture for $2,000; it had cost her $3,900. She used the $2,000 as a down payment on new furniture costing $5,600.

   d. Upon obtaining a job in New City, Gary sold his house for $120,000. Gary paid selling expenses of $7,600 on the sale. Gary had paid $50,000 for the house and had added a den at a cost of $22,000 and a new swimming pool costing $16,000 during the time he held the house.

30. Determine the amount of gain or loss realized and the amount of gain or loss to be recognized in each of the following dispositions:

   a. Jorge owned 800 shares of Archer Co. stock. Jorge had purchased 300 of the shares at a cost of $9,000 and 500 of the shares at a cost of $10,000. During the current year, Jorge instructed his broker to sell 400 of the shares when the market value of the shares hit $29. Jorge paid a $300 commission on the sale.

   b. Alana owned 300 shares of Courtney common stock that had cost her $6,000. On February 1, she sold the 300 shares for $4,800 and paid a $300 commission on the sale. On February 19, Alana purchased 500 shares of Courtney common stock for $5,300 plus a $400 commission on the purchase.

   c. Janet went down to the local flea market one Saturday morning and purchased a painting for $20. Although she didn't really want the painting, she felt that the frame alone was worth $20. When she returned home, she took the old painting out of the frame and found another painting hidden in the back. She took the new painting to a local art dealer who told her the painting was almost certainly a Pistachio and worth at least $20,000. Janet decided that she would wait a couple of years, get another expert's opinion, and see if she could sell the painting for more than $20,000.

   d. Enrique owned some land that he was holding as an investment. A local developer wanted to build a new housing project on the north side of his land. The local utility company wanted to run utility lines along the east side of Enrique's land. Enrique had paid $8,000 for the land but did not want to sell the land yet, because he thought the new housing project would greatly enhance its value. Enrique agreed to accept $2,000 from the utility company for an easement to run its lines along the edge of his property. Enrique estimates that the lines will use up about 1/50 of his land.

31. During 1996, James sold some land he had purchased in 1992 as an investment. In 1992, he had paid $4,000 in cash and borrowed $22,000 to purchase the land. He had paid legal fees of $440 and commissions of $560 on the purchase. He sold the land on October 1, 1996, to DeWayne, who gave James 200 shares of Aardvark common stock with a fair market value of $9,600 (DeWayne had paid $3,700 for the stock) and assumed James's debt on the land, which was $20,800 at the time of sale. James paid legal fees of $400 and $1,800 of commissions on the sale. DeWayne paid legal fees of $575 and commissions of $980 related to the purchase. In addition, DeWayne agreed to pay the property taxes of $800 on the land for the entire year.

   Assume you are a staff accountant in a CPA firm. Write a memorandum to your supervisor explaining James's gain or loss on the land sale, James's basis in the common stock received, DeWayne's gain or loss on the transaction, and DeWayne's basis in the land.

32. Ronald and Linh each own land that they would like to trade. The land values and the debts of each are as follows:

	Ronald	Linh
Fair market value	$20,000	$35,000
Mortgage debt on land	15,000	32,000

Ronald and Linh agree to exchange their land and assume each other's debt, with any difference paid in cash.

a. Who will have to pay cash, and how much will that person have to pay?

b. What are the gross selling prices of Ronald's and Linh's properties from the exchange?

33. Elvira owns an office building, and Jared Partnership owns an apartment building. Each property is encumbered by a mortgage. Elvira and the Jared Partnership agree to exchange their properties and their mortgages, with any difference to be paid in cash. The fair market values, mortgages, and adjusted bases for the properties are as follows:

	Elvira's Building	Jared Partnership Building
Fair market value	$220,000	$250,000
Mortgage debt	80,000	150,000
Adjusted basis	100,000	175,000

a. Write a letter to Elvira explaining who will have to pay cash to complete the exchange, the amount of her gross selling price, and the amount of gain or loss she will realize on the exchange.

b. Write a letter to the Jared Partnership explaining who will have to pay cash to complete the exchange, the amount of the gross selling price of its property, and the amount of gain or loss it will realize on the exchange.

34. Guerda owned 1,000 shares of Ditchdirt common stock. During the current year, she sold 350 shares of the stock for $12 per share and paid a commission of $250 on the sale. Guerda had purchased the 1,000 shares as follows:

Purchase Date	# of Shares	Purchase Price	Commissions Paid
1/14/94	100	$ 850	$ 50
6/13/94	150	$1,100	$100
10/30/94	400	$3,600	$400
2/22/95	250	$3,200	$300
11/29/95	100	$1,150	$150

What is Guerda's gain or loss on the sale of the stock?

35. Return to the facts of problem 34. Assume that Guerda later sold an additional 400 shares of the Ditchdirt stock for $18 per share, paying a commission of $500 on the sale. What is Guerda's gain or loss on the sale of the stock?

36. Return to the facts of problem 34. Assume that Guerda sold the remaining 250 shares of Ditchdirt stock for $12 per share and paid a commission of $200 on the sale. What is Guerda's gain or loss on the sale?

37. Return to the facts of problem 34. What tax-planning strategy can be used to achieve more favorable tax results? Use this strategy to determine Guerda's gain or loss on the sale.

38. Classify each of the following assets as ordinary income property, capital asset property, Section 1231 property, or personal use property. If more than one classification is possible, explain the circumstances that would determine the proper classification of the property.

a. Sarah is a sculptor. During the current year, she gave one of her statues to her niece as a gift.

b. Petros sells facsimiles of Greek artifacts in a store he owns. Because of a cash-flow problem during the current year, he sold some accounts receivable to a discounter for 75% of face value.

c. Lana is a college professor. She owns an apartment building and rents apartments out to students.

d. Ryan uses his automobile 75% of the time in his job as a real estate salesperson. The remaining use of the automobile is for personal purposes.

e. Fred owns a used car business. During the current year, he purchased a piece of land across the street from his used car business. Fred intends to expand his business and feels that he will ultimately need the space for the extra inventory he wants to purchase over the next few years.

f. Althea got a tip from a friend that a new golf course was going to be developed south of town. Because she thought the surrounding land was sure to appreciate in value after the golf course was built, Althea purchased several plots of land near where her friend told her the golf course was to be built.

39. Classify each of the following assets as ordinary income property, capital asset property, Section 1231 property, or personal use property. If more than one classification is possible, explain the circumstances that would determine the proper classification of the property.

a. Letters written by then-Vice President Harry Truman to Helena Desponsa on the day Franklin Delano Roosevelt died. Desponsa still holds the letters.

b. Ritva is a home-building contractor. She built her own principal residence.

c. Domingos, a real estate broker, owns undeveloped land as an investment.

d. Chas Automotive Plaza, Inc., owns cars held for resale to customers.

e. Arcie, Inc., bought a utility van from Chas Automotive Plaza to use in its concrete installation business.

f. Anne Marie Arcie, the president of Arcie, Inc., bought a car to use for commuting to the corporate offices from her home.

40. Spencer purchases 100 shares of Reality Virtual Corporation common stock for $1,200 on July 30, 1996. He sells 75 shares of this stock for $525 on December 27, 1996. On January 12, 1997, Spencer purchases 300 shares of Reality Virtual stock; the price is $2 per share.

a. What are the tax effects of these transactions?

b. What is the adjusted basis of Spencer's stock on April 15, 1997, when the FMV of the stock is $9 per share?

41. Mort begins investing in stocks in 1996. Listed here are Mort's stock transactions for 1996 and 1997. Determine Mort's gain or loss on his stock transactions for 1996 and 1997. In addition, for each sale of stock, determine whether the gain or loss is short term or long term.

Stock	Transaction Date	Transaction	Price Per Share	Commissions Paid
Pepper Farm	5/24/96	Purchased 50 shares	$ 8	$ 50
Acala Steel	10/5/96	Purchased 200 shares	$14	$200
Horton, Inc.	12/10/96	Purchased 300 shares	$ 3	$100
Acala Steel	12/28/96	Sold 50 shares	$18	$ 70
Horton, Inc.	2/4/97	Purchased 200 shares	$ 2	$ 30
Pepper Farm	2/15/97	Sold 25 shares	$12	$ 25
Horton, Inc.	3/1/97	Sold 100 shares	$ 2	$ 20
Pepper Farm	8/13/97	Sold 25 shares	$13	$ 35
Angor Mills	11/11/97	Purchased 800 shares	$ 6	$400
Angor Mills	12/4/97	Sold 300 shares	$ 9	$250
Horton, Inc.	12/19/97	Sold 400 shares	$ 7	$250

42. Rudy had the following capital gains and losses for the current year. What is the effect of the capital asset transactions on Rudy's taxable income? Explain, and show any calculations.

Short-term capital loss	$13,500
Long-term capital gain	$ 9,600
Long-term capital loss	$ 2,300

43. The Judith Corporation had the following gains and losses from sales of capital assets during the current year. What is the effect of the capital asset transactions on Judith's taxable income? Explain, and show any calculations.

Short-term capital gain	$1,400
Short-term capital loss	$2,900
Long-term capital loss	$6,200

44. Return to the facts of problem 43. Assume that Judith is an individual taxpayer. What is the effect of the capital asset transactions on Judith's taxable income? Compare this result with the result in problem 43.

45. Tate had the following gains and losses from sales of capital assets during the current year. What is the effect of the capital asset transactions on Tate's taxable income? Explain, and show any calculations.

Short-term capital gain	$ 1,700
Long-term capital gain	$14,200
Long-term capital loss	$ 3,400

46. Troy had the following gains and losses from sales of capital assets during the current year. What is the effect of the capital asset transactions on Troy's taxable income? Explain, and show any calculations.

Short-term capital gain	$8,600
Short-term capital loss	$ 300
Long-term capital gain	$4,700
Long-term capital loss	$6,600

47. For each of the following capital asset dispositions, determine whether the taxpayer has realized a gain or loss on the disposition and whether that gain or loss is short term or long term:

   a. Ari received some stock from his grandfather Stephan for Christmas. Stephan had paid $4,300 for the stock 3 years earlier. The stock had a fair market value of $7,000 on December 24. Ari sold the stock on December 28 for $7,100 and paid a commission of $500 on the sale.

   b. Joan owns 600 shares of Archibald common stock that she had purchased in 1994 for $7,920. On July 1, 1996, Archibald declares and distributes a 10% stock dividend. Joan sells the 660 shares of Archibald stock on November 14, 1996, for $13,400 and pays a $700 commission on the sale.

   c. On April 1, 1996, LeRoy sells to his son for $3,000 shares of stock for which he had paid $8,000 two years earlier. His son sells the shares for $11,000 on June 14, 1996.

   d. Lee owns 800 shares of Bolstead, Inc., stock that she had purchased for $20,000 on October 11, 1995. On July 5, 1996, Lee sells 400 shares of Bolstead stock for $7,000. On July 27, 1996, Lee purchases an additional 600 shares of Bolstead stock for $6,000. On December 3, 1996, Lee sells the remaining 1,000 shares of Bolstead stock for $12,000.

48. For each of the following capital asset dispositions, determine whether the taxpayer has realized a gain or loss and whether that gain or loss is short term or long term:

   a. Larry's aunt June dies on May 4, 1996. As part of her will, Larry receives some land that June had purchased in 1978 for $2,000. On May 4, 1996, the land is worth $40,000. Larry receives title to the land on October 15, 1996, and sells it on November 27, 1996, for $40,000. Larry pays $3,000 in commissions and other selling expenses in making the sale.

   b. Sterling receives 4,000 shares of Suburb Corporation stock as a birthday present from his mother-in-law on May 6, 1996. His mother-in-law had paid $18,000 for the stock 8 years earlier. On May 6, 1996, the stock has a fair market value of $4,000. On June 18, 1996, Sterling sells 1,000 shares of the stock for $800.

   c. Assume the same facts as in part b. Suburb Corporation becomes the target of a takeover attempt in July, and its stock soars. Sterling sells the remaining 3,000 shares for $19,000 on August 6, 1996.

   d. Bert owns 1,000 shares of Crooner Capital Corporation common stock for which he paid $8,000 in 1990. On March 13, 1996, Crooner declares a dividend of 1 share of preferred stock for each 10 shares of common stock owned. On the date the preferred shares are distributed, Crooner common shares are selling for $7 per share, and its preferred shares are selling for $10 per share. On November 14, 1996, Bert sells the 100 preferred shares for $1,100.

49. For each of the following capital asset dispositions, determine whether the taxpayer has realized a gain or a loss and whether that gain or loss is short term or long term:

    a. Marino inherited antique pottery from the estate of his grandmother on March 10, 1996. He immediately sold the pottery for $15,000 to a collector who had made the offer to the executor of the estate several weeks before. The estate valuation of the pottery is $13,000. Marino's grandmother paid $20,000 for the pottery during an October 1995 visit to a flea market. She was convinced the pottery was a valuable investment—that she was getting a "steal" and the pottery would substantially appreciate over time.

    b. Jackie received 100 shares of stock as a birthday gift from her Uncle Horace. Horace acquired the shares twenty-two years ago for $4 per share. The stock's value on Jackie's birthday was $36 per share. Jackie sold half her shares for $1,500 five months after her birthday and paid a broker $50 to complete the sale.

    c. Melody was snorkeling while on her 1996 spring break in Cancun. She found a small bag lodged between some rocks about 25 yards off shore; it contained several jewels. Melody reported the find to the local authorities. However, no one had ever reported a loss of jewels, and Melody was allowed to keep them. Upon returning home, she took the jewels to an appraiser, who set their value at $18,000. Because she needed money to pay for her college tuition, dormitory room and board, and books, Melody sold the jewels to a local jewelry store for $16,000.

    d. Xuan owns 700 shares of Fredrick common stock that he purchased in 1994 for $2,100. On October 1, 1995, Fredrick declared and distributed a 20% stock dividend. Xuan purchased another 100 shares of Fredrick common stock for $20 per share on December 1, 1995. Xuan sold all his shares for $15,100 on February 12, 1996.

50. In 1996, Harry sells the automobile he has used in his job as a salesman for $3,000. The automobile cost $14,000 four years earlier. Harry used the automobile 80% of the time in his job and 20% of the time for personal purposes. At the date of sale, Harry had taken $8,000 in depreciation on the automobile. Write a letter to Harry explaining his amount of realized gain or loss from the sale and how much he must recognize for tax purposes.

51. Yorgi purchases qualified small business stock in Gnu Co., Inc., on January 17, 1996, for $100,000. Yorgi sells the shares of stock for $500,000 on December 30, 2002. The stock retains its qualified small business status through the date of the sale.

    a. Determine the amount of realized and recognized gain on the sale.

    b. What is Yorgi's effective tax rate on this transaction? (Assume Yorgi's marginal tax rate is 31% in the year 2002).

52. During August 1996, Madeline invests $500,000 in Qual Co., Inc., buying 100,000 shares of stock. Her stockbroker told her this would be an excellent investment because these securities are qualified small business stock. He predicts the stock will triple in value over the next three years. At the end of 1996, Madeline's shares are valued at $594,000. Madeline is encouraged. She decides to cash out of this investment in December 1997 if the stock continues to appreciate. Madeline comes to you for advice. Write a letter advising her what she should do.

53. Neila holds an extensive portfolio of securities. She sells 500 shares of Bolero Corporation stock for $10,000 and pays $500 in sales commissions on September 23 of the current year. Neila acquired the stock for $4,500 plus $450 in commissions in 1992. Write a memorandum to Neila recommending an optimal year-end tax-planning strategy for her capital gains and losses.

54. Jeremy owns 2,000 shares of Quilliam Quantum common stock that he acquired several years ago for $25 per share. For the current year, Jeremy's net capital gain position is a long-term capital gain. Jeremy also has a nonbusiness bad debt outstanding that he believes will result in a $33,000 loss next year when bankruptcy proceedings for the debtor are concluded. In late December of the current year, Quilliam common stock is selling for $40 per share. Jeremy does not want to take the gain on the stock this year in anticipation of the large loss on the nonbusiness bad debt next year. However, he is concerned that the Quilliam stock may decline in value before the end of the current year. What options are available to Jeremy? Explain, and show any calculations related to the options.

55. On December 12, 1996, Ben sells short 400 shares of Westie Corporation stock at $10 per share. He buys 500 shares of Westie stock on January 8, 1997, at $13 per share. On January 15, 1997, Ben closes the short sale by delivering 400 of the shares purchased on January 8.
   a. What is Ben's gain or loss on the short sale, and when is it recognized?
   b. Assume that the facts remain the same, except that Ben's January 8 purchase is at $9 per share. Explain how your answers in part a will change.

56. Chikako owns 300 shares of Leem, Inc., common stock, which she purchased on January 15, 1996, for $50 per share. On December 3, 1996, the stock has a market value of $76 per share. However, Chikako has heard rumors that Leem's 1996 earnings are much lower than expected, which means its stock price is likely to fall. Chikako wants to take her profit, but she would rather postpone recognition of the gain until 1997 when her marginal tax rate is expected to be down to 28%. Her stock broker tells her to sell the 300 shares short at $76. He will charge her $400 to complete the sale. Explain how Chikako will complete the short sale and the tax results of the transaction(s).

57. Opal's neighbor, Jilian, persuades her to invest in Schaake Corporation, a new venture, on March 4, 1996. Opal pays $20,000 for 2,000 shares of common stock. On February 6, 1997, Schaake Corporation declares bankruptcy and closes its doors forever. The venture failed. Opal never receives a return on her investment or a reimbursement of her original investment. What are the tax consequences to Opal?

58. Fred's Foam Foundations (FFF) is a sole proprietorship that Fred started in 1991. Before 1996, FFF had not disposed of any property it owned. During 1996, FFF has the following gains and losses:

Casualty loss on foam truck	$3,200
Section 1231 gains	$6,300
Section 1231 losses	$1,200

What is the effect of these transactions on Fred's 1996 taxable income? Explain, and show the calculations.

59. Refer to the facts in problem 58. In 1997, FFF has the following gains and losses:

Casualty gain on building	$ 7,300
Section 1231 gains	$ 2,000
Section 1231 losses	$14,100

What is the effect of these transactions on Fred's 1997 taxable income? Explain, and show the required calculations.

60. In 1996, Sondra Corporation recognizes $32,000 in Section 1231 gains and $18,000 in Section 1231 losses. In 1992, Sondra reported $15,000 in Section 1231 losses and no Section 1231 gains. No other Section 1231 gains or losses were recognized by Sondra during the 1991–1995 period. What is the tax treatment for Sondra's 1996 Section 1231 gains and losses?

61. Rhinelander Corporation has the following net Section 1231 gains and losses for 1992 through 1996:

1992	$ 13,000
1993	$(7,000)
1994	$(18,000)
1995	$ 16,000
1996	$ 3,000

  a. What is the proper characterization of the net Section 1231 gains and losses for 1992–1996 for Rhinelander Corporation?

  b. Assume that in 1997 Rhinelander has a net Section 1231 gain of $14,000. What is the proper characterization of the $14,000 gain?

62. Tawana purchases some rental property in 1996 at a cost of $200,000. In 1997, Tawana is experiencing cash-flow problems and wants to sell the rental property. The adjusted basis of the rental property is $185,000.

  a. What are the tax consequences to Tawana if she can sell the rental property for $220,000? If there is any uncertainty in the tax consequences, explain why there is an uncertainty and what the resolution of the uncertainty will have on the ultimate tax consequences of the sale.

  b. What are the tax consequences for Tawana if she can sell the rental property for $150,000? If there is any uncertainty in the tax consequences, explain why there is an uncertainty and what the resolution of the uncertainty will have on the ultimate tax consequences of the sale.

63. The Gladys Corporation buys equipment (7-year MACRS property) costing $54,000 on April 12, 1996. In 1999, new and improved models of the equipment make it obsolete, and Gladys sells the old equipment for $12,000 on December 27, 1999.

  a. What is the character of Gladys Corporation's gain (loss) on the sale, assuming that Gladys took the maximum cost-recovery deductions allowable on the equipment?

  b. What is the character of Gladys Corporation's gain (loss) on the equipment, assuming that Gladys took the minimum cost-recovery deduction allowable on the equipment?

  NOTE: The depreciation calculations for this problem were done for problem 50, Chapter 11.

64. Alex purchases a building in 1985 at a cost of $450,000. ACRS depreciation on the building totals $290,000, whereas straight-line depreciation would be $245,000 for the same period. Alex sells the building in 1996 for $500,000.

  a. What is Alex's gain on sale if he deducts the ACRS depreciation on the building?

  b. If the building is an apartment building that Alex rents to individuals, what is the character of the gain? Assume that Alex holds the building as an investment.

  c. How would your answer to part b change if the building were sold for $105,000?

65. Alex purchases a building in 1985 at a cost of $450,000. ACRS depreciation on the building totals $290,000, whereas straight-line depreciation would be $245,000 for the same period. Alex sells the building in 1996 for $500,000.

  a. What is Alex's gain on sale if he deducts the straight-line depreciation on the building?

  b. If the building is an apartment building that Alex rents to individuals, what is the character of the gain? Assume that Alex holds the building as an investment.

  c. How would your answer to part b change if the building were sold for $105,000?

66. Alex purchases an apartment building in 1985 at a cost of $450,000. ACRS depreciation on the building totals $290,000, whereas straight-line depreciation would be $245,000 for the same period. Alex sells the building in 1996 for $500,000. The sales agreement calls for the buyer to pay Alex $100,000 in 1996 and $50,000 per year for the next 8 years, with interest on the unpaid balance at 9%. If Alex used the ACRS method to depreciate the building, how much gain would he have to recognize in 1996 and what would be the character of the gain?

67. Manuel is negotiating the sale of two of his rental properties. He has an offer of $500,000 for each condo—a $50,000 down payment on each property with balances paid in equal installments over 15 years plus 8% on the unpaid balance. Manuel bought one condo in 1985 for $400,000 and has deducted depreciation of $185,000 using ACRS (accelerated depreciation). Straight-line depreciation would have been $125,000 if he had elected to use it. Manuel paid $300,000 for the condo he bought in 1988, and he has deducted depreciation of $81,800 using the MACRS rates for residential real estate. Compare the realized gains or losses and the recognized gains or losses of the two properties, assuming Manuel sells both. Explain the differences.

68. Anton purchases a building on May 4, 1993, at a cost of $240,000. The land is properly allocated $30,000 of the cost. Anton sells the building on October 18, 1997, for $240,000. What is Anton's gain (loss) on the sale if he uses the regular MACRS system and the building is

a. An apartment building?

b. An office building?

NOTE: The depreciation calculations for this problem were done for problem 55, Chapter 11.

INTEGRATIVE PROBLEM

69. In problem 79 in Chapter 10 and problem 67 in Chapter 11, the initial basis and the basis of Art and Kris's assets were determined as of December 31, 1996. During 1997, Art and Kris have the following transactions related to the assets:

a. Kris has stopped using for business purposes the automobile she acquired in 1993 after winning the automobile in 1996. She tries to sell the old car but has little luck until November 1996, when she agrees to sell it for $4,000. However, the buyer does not have the cash, and the actual sale does not occur until February 1997.

b. In June, one of Art's employees drops a torch while working in the shop and starts a fire. The cost of repairing the damage caused by the fire is $25,000. Art's insurance policy reimburses him $19,000 for the fire damage.

c. The real estate market begins to deteriorate in 1997. Art and Kris decide to sell their rental house before it loses any more value. They sell the house for $95,000 on June 4, 1997. They pay $250 to advertise the property for sale. In addition, they pay $5,000 in brokerage commissions and $475 in legal fees on the sale. Because their renters had a one-year rental agreement, Art and Kris have to pay the renters $700 to vacate the lease.

d. The land that Art inherited is next to a new housing development. The developer needs to run the utility lines through Art's property and attempts to buy the land from Art. Art does not want to sell the land because he and Kris intend to build their dream home on the property one day. The developer agrees to pay Art $1,000 for an easement to run the utility lines along one side of Art's property.

e. While assessing the damage caused by the fire, the contractor Art hired to repair the damage finds an antique cash register that had been sealed behind one wall. Art sells the cash register to a local dealer for $2,200.

f. To help pay for the uninsured portion of the fire damage, Art sells his gardening equipment for $7,000. He uses $5,000 of the proceeds to purchase some older gardening equipment.

g. Art raises the additional cash he needs to complete the building repairs by selling 1,000 shares of Galla Corporation stock for $1.50 per share (he pays brokerage commissions of $100). He also sells 300 shares of Corporate Golf Development stock for $14 per share (brokerage commissions are $250).

h. Kris decides to upgrade her home office by adding a new deluxe computer workstation. Because the workstation has a built-in desk and filing cabinet, she no longer needs her old desk and filing cabinet. She gives the old desk and filing cabinet to the housekeeper. The housekeeper agrees to clean the house for 10 weeks in exchange for the desk and filing cabinet. The housekeeper normally charges $30 per week.

i. In December, Art and Kris's stockbroker advises them that bad news about the Zleine Corporation is likely to be forthcoming and probably will cause the stock's value to decline. Because of their current income situation, the broker advises Art and Kris to sell the stock short to protect their gain. On December 17, they sell the 1,000 shares of Zleine stock short for $23 per share. Brokerage commissions on the short sale are $1,400. They close the short sale on January 27, 1998, by delivering the 1,000 shares to the broker.

j. In addition to these transactions, Art tells you that a company in which he and Kris had invested went bankrupt in 1995. They had purchased the stock from Art's brother for $37,500 in 1990. The company was dissolved in 1995, and the shareholders received nothing from the bankruptcy proceeding. Art and Kris had no other capital asset transactions in 1995 and 1996.

REQUIRED: For each of these transactions, determine the realized and recognized gain or loss and the character of the gain or loss. Do the appropriate year-end netting procedures, and determine the effect of the transactions on Art and Kris's 1997 adjusted gross income. Assume that Art and Kris's adjusted gross income before considering these transactions was $47,000.

70. Duke Plumbing and Wallpaper Co. has been in business since 1979. During the current year, it had the following property transactions:

    a. A warehouse purchased in 1987 for $200,000 was sold for $190,000. Depreciation taken on the building to date of sale totaled $133,000.

    b. Wallpaper that had a cost of $75,000 became obsolete when a new type of wallpaper was developed. Duke was unable to sell the wallpaper and ended up throwing it in the trash.

    c. Two of Duke's service trucks collided in the parking lot, destroying both trucks. The older truck had cost $18,000 and had an adjusted basis of $4,000. The fair market value of the older truck was $9,000, which was reimbursed by Duke's insurance company. The newer truck had been purchased 3 months earlier for $22,000. The newer truck had a fair market value of $17,000, which was reimbursed by Duke's insurance company.

    d. Plumbing equipment purchased in January for $6,000 was sold in November for $3,500. The equipment was advertised as being the easiest equipment of its kind to use in installing new plumbing fixtures. However, it was so complicated to operate that none of Duke's employees could figure out how to use it, and Duke decided it was easier to do it the old-fashioned way.

    e. Duke's computer system became obsolete and was sold for $1,300. Duke had paid $12,000 for the system 4 years earlier and had taken $9,000 in depreciation on the system as of the date of sale.

    f. Because the 2 service trucks that were destroyed (in part c) had to be replaced, Duke decided to sell its other service truck and buy 3 new trucks. The third service truck had cost $19,000 two years earlier and had an adjusted basis of $13,000. Duke received $15,000 from the sale of the truck.

    g. An antique plumbing plunger for which Duke had paid $5,000 and was fully depreciated was sold for $8,600.

    h. Duke decided not to replace the warehouse it sold in part a. The office building it had erected in 1989 at a cost of $140,000 to service the warehouse was no longer of any use and was sold for $158,000. The office building had an adjusted basis of $122,000.

    REQUIRED: For each of these transactions, determine the gain or loss that must be recognized on the transaction and the character of the gain or loss. Determine the effect of all the transactions on Duke's taxable income for the year.

71. Barney is a farmer who had the following transactions during 1996:

    a. A barn that had cost $34,000 in 1990 with an adjusted basis of $19,000 was destroyed by a tornado. Barney's insurance paid him $23,000 for the casualty.

COMPREHENSIVE PROBLEMS

b. Barney's prize bull, for which he had paid $17,000 and which had an adjusted basis of $9,000, was in the barn when the tornado hit. Although the bull was not killed, he was injured severely enough that he could no longer breed. The bull was worth only $300 after the casualty (at stud he was valued at more than $20,000), but he had been such a favorite of Barney's that Barney kept him and put him out to pasture. Barney's insurance company refused to pay anything for the bull's injuries.

c. Breeding cattle that had cost $17,500 in 1994 with an adjusted basis of $6,720 were sold for $21,000.

d. A tractor that had cost $18,000 and had an adjusted basis of $8,500 was sold for $4,200.

e. Stock in Old Mill Co. that Barney had purchased on November 13, 1995, for $32,000 became worthless when Old Mill went out of business on April 1, 1996.

f. A horse Barney had purchased in February for $8,000 as a gift for his daughter came up lame and had to be sold for $1,000.

g. Barney sold 80 acres of farmland for $39,000. Barney had received the land as a gift from his uncle when he first went into farming. Barney's uncle had paid $2,000 for the land, which was worth $5,000 at the time of the gift.

What is the effect of these transactions on Barney's taxable income for 1996? In solving this problem, first determine the amount and character of gain (loss) on each of the transactions. Then, perform the appropriate netting procedures. Your answer should be a summary of the gains (losses) as they would appear on Barney's tax return. Write a letter to Barney explaining the tax results of his transactions.

DISCUSSION CASES

72. As a gift for her granddaughter Ella's 13th birthday, Melanie purchases 500 shares of Soft'n Sales Corporation stock on July 10, 1996. Melanie buys the stock directly from the underwriter for a total of $20,000. Soft'n Sales has just gone public, and Melanie believes the stock will be a good investment for Ella's college education. Melanie tells Ella that she will receive control of the stock on her 18th birthday so long as Ella maintains an A average in high school.

Soft'n Sales is a software development enterprise in San Diego. It just introduced a new database program that is currently number one in sales. In about 10 months it will introduce a new spreadsheet program that integrates with the database program. Other new products are in developmental stages. At the date of the public offering, Soft'n Sales's gross assets total $10 million. These assets include mostly intangibles, equipment, and raw materials for product development. The company owns no real estate and holds no investment securities. All capital is reinvested within the enterprise.

The year 2001 arrives. Explain Melanie's options for transferring the stock to Ella to use for college expenses. What are the tax implications of each option?

73. Christoffe sold 1,000 shares of HoTech Corporation preferred stock for $37 per share on August 3 of the current year. Sales commissions totaled $300. The stock's price has been falling since HoTech's management was sued for patent infringement four months ago. The price is expected to keep falling until the law suit is settled. Christoffe received the stock as a Christmas gift from his wife last year. She paid $48 per share plus a $400 commission. The year-end is approaching, and he wants to optimize his tax position. Christoffe's current portfolio contains the following corporate stock:

Stock	Number of Shares	Date Acquired	Adjusted Basis per Share	FMV
MURF Corp.	1,000	1/12/90	$11	$28
Tellics, Inc.	2,000	10/2/91	$15	$29
HIGG Corp.	200	12/9/93	$41	$90

Make recommendations to Christoffe.

TAX PLANNING CASES

74. At the beginning of 1996 Heather owned the following stocks:

Stock	Date Purchased	# of Shares	Per Share Price	Commissions
Clutch common	11/30/95	250	$40	$ 500
Pauley preferred	4/13/95	100	$10	$ 100
Leines common	10/14/92	1,000	$35	$2,000

In addition to these stocks, Heather had received 400 shares of Poor Boy preferred stock from her grandfather as a gift on December 25, 1995. The shares were selling for $25 per share on December 24, 1995. No gift tax was paid on the transfer of the stock. Her grandfather had purchased the shares for $5 per share in 1972.

During 1996, Heather had the following stock transactions:

Stock	Transaction	Date	Sales Price	Commissions Paid
Poor Boy	Sold 100 shares	3/12	$ 2,200	$200
Leines	Sold 400 shares	6/8	$ 5,300	$300
Clutch	Sold 200 shares	10/18	$ 4,700	$270
Ragtop common	Purchased 2,000	12/18	$20,000	$600
Leines	Purchased 200	12/25	$ 3,550	$450

  a. What is Heather's net capital gain (loss) for 1996?

  b. On December 28, 1996, Heather's stocks have the following fair market values:

Pauley	$13 per share
Clutch	$28 per share
Leines	$23 per share
Poor Boy	$37 per share
Ragtop	$ 4 per share

Assuming that the commission paid on any sale is equal to 5% of the selling price, what action(s) would you recommend to Heather to minimize her 1996 tax? Discuss the potential tax effects of selling each of the stocks Heather owns at the end of the year.

  c. Assume that in addition to the stock sales, Heather sold some land she had inherited from her father. Her father had paid $5,000 for the land in 1982. Her father died on April 14, 1991, when the land was worth $12,000. Heather sold the land on May 21, 1996, for $50,000. Legal fees and commissions of $5,500 were paid on the sale. What is Heather's net capital gain (loss) for 1996?

  d. Given the fair market values, what action would you recommend Heather take to minimize her 1996 tax? Explain.

75. Rosie has owned a successful luncheonette for several years. Tired of the long hours and eager to try another way of life, Rosie has decided to buy a fishing boat and start a charter service near Key West. The only obstacle is the sale of the following assets of the luncheonette to fund her fishing boat endeavor:

Asset	Date Acquired	Adjusted Basis	Original Cost
Building	1/12/83	$ 5,000 ($6,600 if SL depreciation used)	$50,000
Land	1/12/83	$10,000	$10,000
Equipment	2/9/92	$ 7,800	$25,000
Supplies	Current year	$ 5,000	$ 5,000

Hank, Rosie's part-time cook, has offered her $175,000 for the luncheonette, which Rosie believes is a fair price. However, she is concerned about the tax consequences of the sale. For example, she wonders how to allocate the sales price among the assets to receive the most advantageous tax results. Write a letter to Rosie about the best way to make the allocations and explaining the tax effects of your recommendations.

76. Twenty years ago, Consuela Guererro invented and patented a high-speed burrito-stuffing machine. Through the years, Consuela has jealously guarded her invention, allowing its use in only El Consuela's, a chain of restaurants in which she owns 60% of the stock (her basis in the stock is $200,000). On the advice of her accountant, the patent is owned and manufacturing of the burrito stuffer is done exclusively by Consuela's wholly owned corporation, Stuff, Inc. (Consuela's basis in the Stuff, Inc., stock is $250,000.)

Consuela has been approached by the Frijoles Co. about acquiring her burrito-stuffing operation. Specifically, Frijoles would like to acquire Stuff, Inc.'s patent and burrito-stuffer manufacturing operation. Consuela is tired after spending so many years fighting off the competition, and she has agreed to sell to Frijoles. Consuela feels that the patent and manufacturing equipment are worth at least $2,000,000, although they are carried on Stuff, Inc.'s books at their adjusted basis of $100,000. Consuela wants your advice on how best to structure her exit from the burrito-stuffing business. She intends to retain her ownership interest in El Consuela's.

   a. From Consuela's point of view, should she sell the burrito-stuffer assets owned by Stuff, Inc., directly to Frijoles, or should she sell her stock in Stuff, Inc.? (Consider not only the tax aspects of the alternatives but also how each alternative could influence the proposed $2,000,000 purchase price.)

   b. Write a letter to Consuela explaining her alternatives for disposing of her ownership in the burrito-stuffing business.

   c. Consider part a from Frijoles' point of view.

   d. Write a letter to Frijoles Co. explaining its alternatives for acquiring the burrito-stuffing business.

ETHICS DISCUSSION CASE

77. You are a CPA who works for a local accounting firm. While having lunch at Willie's Diner last Thursday, you overheard Beth Murray describe how Bart (her spouse) was able to get a $2,000 business loss, free car maintenance for 2 years, and $4,000 cash to spend on their vacation in exchange for an old truck. You didn't think too much about the conversation until you returned to your office. While you were at lunch, Bart Murray dropped off the tax information for his business, Bart's Mobile Glass Service, for the past year. Your curiosity gets the best of you. You open the packet of information and immediately look for the truck sale information. The only documentation you find is a hand-written memo stating, "1990 Dodge truck sold for $4,000 and loss on sale = $2,000." The memo is initialed by Bart Murray. Attached to the memo is a photocopy of a check from Haroldene Harvey's Auto Castle, Inc., for $4,000. Haroldene Harvey is also your client. You know that Haroldene and Bart are neighbors and good friends. Your review of Bart Murray's asset and depreciation schedules confirms that the truck had an adjusted basis of $6,000 as of the sale date. What are your obligations under the Statements on Responsibilities in Tax Practice (Appendix D)? Write a memorandum to the managing partner explaining what should be done about the situation involving Bart Murray.

Nonrecognition Transactions

▲ CHAPTER LEARNING OBJECTIVES

- ■ Introduce three commonly encountered classes of property transactions for which the nonrecognition (deferral) of gains is allowed.

- ■ Discuss the rationale for nonrecognition (deferral) of gain on the three classes of property transactions.

- ■ Explain the common characteristics of the three classes of nonrecognition transactions and how the characteristics affect the nonrecognition of gain calculations and adjustments.

- ■ Describe the basic nonrecognition rules for like-kind exchanges of property and the calculation of the basis of property received in a like-kind exchange.

- ■ Identify properties that qualify as like-kind for the deferral of gains and losses on exchanges.

- ■ Explain the effects of "boot" paid and received in like-kind exchanges.

- ■ Describe involuntary conversions of property and how gains (but not losses) may be deferred when a qualified replacement property is purchased.

- ■ Discuss what constitutes a qualified replacement property for property that is involuntarily converted.

- ■ Describe the provisions for deferring gain (but not loss) on the sale and timely replacement of a taxpayer's principal residence.

- ■ Explain when a taxpayer may elect to exclude up to $125,000 of gain on the sale of a principal residence.

▲ CONCEPT REVIEW ▲

All-inclusive income All income received is taxable unless a specific provision can be found in the tax law that either excludes the income from taxation or defers its recognition to a future tax year.

Annual accounting period All entities must report the results of their operations on an annual basis (the tax year). Each tax year stands on its own, apart from other tax years.

Basis This is the amount of unrecovered investment in an asset. As amounts are expended and/or recovered relative to an asset over time, the basis is adjusted in consideration of such changes. The **adjusted basis** of an asset is the original basis, plus or minus the changes in the amount of unrecovered investment.

Legislative grace Any tax relief provided is the result of a specific act of Congress that must be strictly applied and interpreted. All income received is taxable unless a specific provision can be found in the tax law that excludes the income from taxation. Deductions must be ap-

proached with the philosophy that nothing is deductible unless a provision in the tax law allows the deduction.

Realization No income (or loss) is recognized until it has been realized. A realization involves a change in the form and/or the substance of a taxpayer's property rights that results from an arm's-length transaction.

Related party Family members and corporations that are owned by family members are considered related parties, as are certain other relationships between entities in which the power to control the substance of a transaction is evidenced through majority ownership.

Substance over form Transactions are to be taxed according to their true intention rather than some form that may have been contrived.

Wherewithal to pay Income is recognized in the period in which the taxpayer has the means to pay the tax on the income.

INTRODUCTION

Chapter 12 noted that a gain or a loss realized on a disposition of property may not be recognized in the year the transaction takes place. Earlier discussions of nonrecognition focused on realized losses that are permanently disallowed (e.g., personal use losses) and those that are deferred (e.g., wash sales) for recognition. In addition, gains on certain types of dispositions are not recognized in the period in which they are realized.

Under the all-inclusive income concept, any gain realized on a disposition of property is taxable (i.e., recognized in the period of realization). However, Congress has granted tax relief to certain types of transactions. These transactions are referred to as **nonrecognition transactions.** It should be noted that, with one exception, these transactions are not nontaxable in the sense that tax will never be paid on the realized gain. Rather, recognition of these gains is deferred until a future period. One exception to the deferral-of-gain treatment is a special provision that allows taxpayers who have attained age 55 to exclude up to $125,000 in gain on the sale of their principal residence.

The purpose of this chapter is to discuss commonly encountered nonrecognition transactions. Three common classes of nonrecognition transactions are

- Exchanges of like-kind property
- Involuntary conversions of property
- Sale of a principal residence

Although each type of nonrecognition transaction is distinct, the underlying rationale for deferral of gains from each class is the same. In addition, these transactions share characteristics and mechanisms for deferring gains and losses upon their disposition.

There are two interrelated reasons that the three classes of transactions have been granted tax relief. First, in each transaction, the initial realization is considered part of a continuing investment process. That is, although one asset has been disposed of, another asset with similar characteristics has taken its place. Under the substance-over-form doctrine, the new property acquired in the transaction is viewed as a continuation of the original investment. This view represents a refinement of the realization concept, which postpones recognition of appreciation in value until the taxpayer disposes of a property. In effect, the nonrecognition provisions mandate deferral of the tax consequences if a disposition and its timely replacement provide the taxpayer with a continuing interest in a similar property.

RATIONALE FOR NONRECOGNITION

▲ **EXAMPLE 1**   Archibald, Inc.'s warehouse was destroyed by a fire. The warehouse had an adjusted basis of $100,000 and a fair market value before the fire of $325,000. Archibald received $300,000 from its insurance company for the loss of the warehouse. Archibald used the $300,000 to purchase another warehouse costing $400,000. What is Archibald's realized gain (loss) on the casualty?

Insurance   300,000
Adj. Basis   (100,000)
Realized gain on casualty   200,000
Recognized gain   0
Deferred Gain   200,000 ✓

Discussion: Archibald has realized a gain of $200,000 ($300,000 − $100,000) on the casualty. The loss on business property fully destroyed is the adjusted basis of the property, $100,000. However, the receipt of the $300,000 in insurance proceeds results in a gain of $200,000 on the casualty.

Amount realized from insurance	$300,000
Adjusted basis of warehouse	(100,000)
Realized gain on the casualty	$200,000
Recognized gain	-0-
Deferred gain	$200,000

A casualty loss on business property is an involuntary conversion. Because the warehouse is critical to Archibald's business, it was replaced. Thus, the new warehouse is a continuation of the investment in the original warehouse, and Archibald may defer the gain on the involuntary conversion. In effect, the tax law views the destruction of the warehouse and its replacement as not constituting a realization of the appreciation in the value of the warehouse.

The second rationale for not recognizing these transactions is that the taxpayer lacks the wherewithal to pay the tax on the realized gain, because the amount realized on the transaction is reinvested in the replacement asset. A primary requirement for total deferral of gain in all three classes of transactions is that any amounts realized from the disposition must be fully reinvested in a replacement asset.

▲ **EXAMPLE 2**   In example 1, does Archibald have the wherewithal to pay tax on the $200,000 realized gain on the warehouse?

Discussion: In acquiring the replacement warehouse, Archibald reinvested the entire $300,000 it received from its insurance company. It does not have any cash remaining to pay the tax on the $200,000 gain. Archibald does not have the wherewithal to pay tax on the gain, because all the insurance proceeds were used to replace the warehouse.

COMMONALITIES OF NONRECOGNITION TRANSACTIONS

The continuity of investment criteria and lack of wherewithal to pay for the three classes of nontaxable transactions provide five distinctive commonalities in the tax treatment of these transactions. Figure 13–1 illustrates these factors. First, the wherewithal-to-pay concept provides the rationale for deferring gain. Thus, all three nonrecognition transactions provide for the deferral of realized gains. Deferring gains is mandatory for like-kind exchanges and the sale of a principal residence. However, deferring gains from involuntary conversions is usually

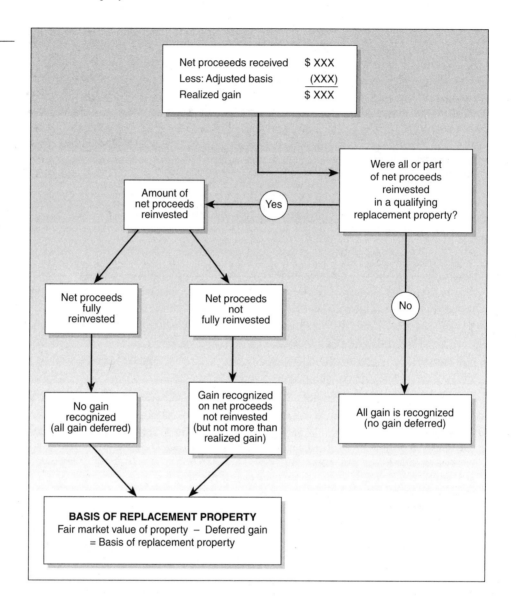

elective. On the loss side, deferring realized losses on like-kind exchanges is mandatory. Losses on involuntary conversions are never deferred and are recognized in the period of realization. A loss on the sale of a principal residence is a personal use loss that is never deductible and therefore not deferrable.

Second, classification of a nonrecognition transaction as a continuation of an investment requires a replacement asset. Each type of nonrecognition transaction requires the purchase of a qualified replacement asset within a specified time period. The time allowed for the qualified replacement varies with each type of nonrecognition transaction. As you can see in Figure 13–1, the transaction is taxable and treated as any other disposition of property if a qualified replacement property is not purchased within the allowable time period.

The third factor common to these transactions also is a result of the wherewithal-to-pay concept. Although the transactions qualify for nonrecognition, gains on all the transactions must be recognized when the taxpayer has the wherewithal to pay the tax on some portion of the realized gain. As depicted in Figure

13–1, no gain is recognized so long as the entire proceeds received in the nonre-cognition transaction are reinvested in a qualified replacement asset. However, if all the proceeds are not reinvested, the taxpayer has the wherewithal to pay tax in the amount of those proceeds not reinvested. In general, the amount of gain to be recognized is the portion of the amount realized that the taxpayer has not reinvested in a replacement asset.

▲ **EXAMPLE 3**   Assume that in example 1 Archibald purchased a qualifying replace-ment warehouse at a cost of $275,000. What amount of gain must Archibald recognize on the casualty?

Discussion: Archibald realized a gain of $200,000 on the destruction of the ware-house. Although the replacement of the warehouse qualifies for nonrecognition, Ar-chibald must recognize gain on the warehouse for any proceeds from the casualty that were not reinvested in acquiring the replacement warehouse. Therefore, Archibald must recognize $25,000 ($300,000 in insurance proceeds − $275,000 to replace the ware-house) of the gain on the warehouse casualty.

When recognizing gains on nontaxable transactions, keep in mind that the amount of gain recognized can never exceed the amount of the gain realized on the transaction. This is an application of the capital recovery concept, which limits the amount of income to the amount realized in excess of the capital invested in the asset.

▲ **EXAMPLE 4**   Gecko Co. suffered a fire that destroyed its office building. The build-ing was worth $200,000 before the fire and had an adjusted basis of $170,000. Gecko received $200,000 in insurance proceeds and bought a qualifying replacement building for $150,000. What are Gecko's realized and recognized gains on the casualty?

Discussion: Gecko has a realized gain of $30,000 ($200,000 − $170,000) on the casu-alty. After purchasing the replacement building, Gecko has $50,000 of the insurance proceeds available to pay tax. However, the maximum gain that can be recognized is the amount of the realized gain. Therefore, Gecko's recognized gain is $30,000 (no gain is deferred).

The fourth common attribute is the mechanism used to defer gains and losses from the transaction. Recall that a *deferral* means that a realized gain (or loss) is not recognized in the current period but will be recognized in some future period. The mechanism for effecting the deferral is through an adjustment of the replacement asset's basis.[1] A general formula for adjusting the basis of the replacement asset is

Basis of replacement asset = Fair market value of replacement

Less:	Gain deferred
or	
Plus:	Loss deferred (exchanges only)
Equals:	Basis of replacement asset

The rationale for adjusting the basis of the replacement asset lies in the capital recovery concept. In a gain deferral situation, the realized gain on the transaction is an excess capital recovery that is not being taxed in the period of realization. Moreover, without the basis adjustment, the deferred gain would never be rec-ognized. As a continuation of investment, the amount of capital recovery allowed on the replacement asset must be reduced by the amount of any gain deferred. In subsequent periods, the amount of capital recovery taken on the replacement asset through depreciation and at disposition of the replacement asset will be reduced by the amount of the gain deferred. While the replacement asset is being used, taxable income will increase by the amount of the gain deferred in calculating the replacement asset's basis.

▲ **EXAMPLE 5**   Jordan owns land with a fair market value of $10,000. Jordan had purchased the land as an investment in 1991 for $6,000. In 1996, he trades the land in a qualifying like-kind exchange for another parcel of land that is worth $10,000. What are Jordan's realized and recognized gains on the like-kind exchange and the basis in the new parcel of land?

Discussion: Jordan has realized a gain of $4,000 on the exchange of the land. However, all of it is deferred, because Jordan has no wherewithal to pay the tax on the $4,000 gain. The basis of the new parcel of land is $6,000:

Amount realized (fair market value of land received)	$10,000
Adjusted basis of land exchanged	(6,000)
Realized gain on exchange	$ 4,000
Recognized gain on exchange	-0-
Deferred gain on exchange	$ 4,000

Basis of new parcel = $10,000 − $4,000 = $6,000

By reducing the basis in the second parcel, Jordan will not be able to recover the deferred gain tax free when he disposes of the second parcel in a taxable transaction. When Jordan disposes of the second parcel in a taxable transaction, his realized gain will be a combination of the $4,000 in gain deferred on the exchange and any subsequent gain (loss) in value of the second parcel.

▲ **EXAMPLE 6**   In 1997, Jordan sells the second parcel of land for $13,000. What are his realized and recognized gains on the sale?

Discussion: Jordan has realized a gain of $7,000 ($13,000 − $6,000) on the sale of the land. The sale of the land is a taxable transaction, and he must recognize the entire $7,000 gain.

The $7,000 recognized gain is composed of 2 separate gains on the individual parcels. The first parcel yielded a $4,000 gain, which was not recognized on the exchange for the second parcel. The second parcel was worth $10,000 when Jordan received it in the exchange. It appreciated in value by $3,000 while Jordan held it. Thus, Jordan's $7,000 gain is the result of a $4,000 gain on his initial land investment and a $3,000 gain on the subsequent investment acquired in the like-kind exchange. Over the 2-year period, the same amount of gain is recognized for the exchange deferral as would have been recognized if no deferral had been allowed on the exchange:

	Gain Recognized		
	1996	**1997**	**Total**
No gain deferral allowed	$4,000	$3,000	$7,000
With exchange deferral	-0-	$7,000	$7,000

Note in examples 5 and 6 that Jordan's basis in the new parcel of land is equal to his basis in the parcel of land exchanged (carryover basis). This reflects the fact that Jordan made no additional investment to obtain the second parcel of land. The amount of his investment has not changed in continuing his investment in land, resulting in a carryover of his initial $6,000 investment to the investment in the second parcel. However, the general basis adjustment takes into account any additional investment made to acquire the replacement asset.

▲ **EXAMPLE 7**   Assume that in example 5 Jordan exchanges his land for another parcel of land that is worth $12,000. Because his land is worth only $10,000, Jordan has to pay $2,000 to make the exchange. What are Jordan's realized and recognized gains on the exchange and his basis in the new parcel of land?

Discussion: Jordan realizes a gain of $4,000 on the exchange of the land. However, all gain from the like-kind exchange is deferred, because Jordan has no wherewithal to pay the tax on the $4,000 gain. The basis of the new parcel of land is $8,000:

Amount realized ($12,000 − $2,000)	$10,000
Adjusted basis	(6,000)
Realized gain on exchange	$ 4,000
Recognized gain on exchange	-0-
Deferred gain on exchange	$ 4,000

Basis of new parcel = $12,000 − $4,000 = $8,000

The $8,000 basis in the second parcel of land is the $6,000 invested in the first parcel (which remains unrealized) and the additional $2,000 Jordan paid to acquire the second parcel.

▲ **EXAMPLE 8**   Assume that in example 5 Jordan exchanges his land for another parcel of land that is worth $7,000. Because his land is worth $10,000, Jordan receives $3,000 in the exchange. What are Jordan's realized and recognized gains on the exchange and his basis in the new parcel of land?

Discussion: Jordan has realized a $4,000 gain on the exchange. However, Jordan has $3,000 in cash after the exchange that is available to pay tax. Therefore, he must recognize $3,000 of the $4,000 gain, leaving only $1,000 of the gain to be deferred. His basis in the new land is $6,000:

Amount realized ($7,000 + $3,000)	$10,000
Adjusted basis	(6,000)
Realized gain on exchange	$ 4,000
Recognized gain on exchange (cash received)	3,000
Deferred gain on exchange	$ 1,000

Basis of new parcel = $7,000 − $1,000 = $6,000

The final commonality is the carryover of the tax attributes of the first asset to the replacement asset to reflect the replacement asset's status as a continuation of the investment in the first asset. These attributes include the holding period of the first asset and any unrecognized depreciation recapture on the first asset.[2,3] These carryovers are essential to give full effect to the second asset as the continuation of the investment in the first asset.

▲ **EXAMPLE 9**   Kolby Co. purchases machinery in 1993 at a cost of $30,000. In 1996, Kolby exchanges the machinery for other machinery with a fair market value of $20,000. MACRS depreciation on the machinery was $18,500. The exchange qualifies as a like-kind exchange. What are Kolby's realized gain, recognized gain, and basis in the new machinery?

Discussion: Kolby has a realized gain of $8,500 on the exchange. Because Kolby has no wherewithal to pay after the exchange, the entire gain is deferred. The basis of the new machinery is $11,500:

Amount realized (FMV of new machinery)	$20,000
Adjusted basis ($30,000 − $18,500)	(11,500)
Realized gain on exchange	$ 8,500
Recognized gain on exchange	-0-
Deferred gain on exchange	$ 8,500

Basis of new machinery = $20,000 − $8,500 = $11,500

▲ **EXAMPLE 10** Assume that Kolby immediately sells the machinery received in the exchange in example 9 for $20,000. What are the amount of recognized gain on the sale and the character of the gain on the sale?

Discussion: Kolby's realized and recognized gain on the sale is $8,500 ($20,000 − $11,500). Machinery used in a trade or business is Section 1231 property. However, because the machinery is depreciable property, it is subject to the depreciation recapture rules under Section 1245 (see Chapter 12).

Although Kolby has taken no depreciation on the machinery sold, the tax attributes of the initial machinery attach to the machinery sold. As a continuation of the original investment in the machinery, the machinery sold is considered to have been held since 1993 when the initial purchase took place. In addition, characterization of any gain on a taxable disposition of the machinery must view the $18,500 in depreciation taken on the initial machinery as having been taken on the machinery sold. Thus, the entire $8,500 in gain is recaptured as ordinary income under Section 1245.

Carrying over the depreciation recapture for nonrecognition transactions gives the gain from disposition of the replacement the attributes of the original asset. This effectively eliminates the use of nonrecognition transactions to avoid the depreciation recapture rules.

LIKE-KIND EXCHANGES

A realized gain or loss is never recognized on an exchange of business or investment property for other like-kind property for business or investment use. Realized gain or loss on a transaction that qualifies as an exchange of like-kind property for other like-kind property must always be deferred.[4] However, gains on like-kind exchanges must be recognized when the taxpayer has the wherewithal to pay the tax after the exchange is completed. The wherewithal to pay is evidenced by the receipt of other nonqualifying property with the like-kind property (in tax jargon, other nonqualifying property is called **boot,** so named because, along with the like-kind property, one party has received nonqualified property "to boot"). Thus, gains are recognized to the extent that boot is received in the exchange. However, realized losses on like-kind exchanges are never recognized, even when boot is received in the deal.

Exchange Requirement

To qualify for nonrecognition, a direct exchange of like-kind property must occur. Thus, a sale of property and a purchase of like-kind property from another would not be considered an exchange, unless the two transactions were interdependent. If the sale and purchase transactions are interdependent, the transactions are treated as an exchange under the substance-over-form doctrine.

▲ **EXAMPLE 11** Sarah sold her business car to Karen for $3,000. The auto had an adjusted basis of $4,500 at the date of sale. Sarah used the $3,000 as a down payment on a new business car she purchased from Alpha Auto Sales for $19,000. What are the tax effects for Sarah of the sale and purchase of the autos?

Discussion: Because the 2 transactions are not interdependent, an exchange of like-kind property has not occurred. Sarah realizes and recognizes a loss on the sale of her business car of $1,500 ($3,000 − $4,500). Her basis in the new car for business is the $19,000 purchase price.

Classifying the transaction in example 11 as a sale has important tax implications. As a sale, Sarah can deduct the loss she realizes on the transaction.

However, if the transaction had been characterized as an exchange, Sarah would not be allowed to recognize the loss. Nonrecognition of gains and losses on exchanges of like-kind property is mandatory. Thus, a taxpayer wishing to recognize a loss on the disposition of an asset that is to be replaced must be careful not to make the sale and purchase transactions interdependent. Sale and repurchase from a dealer in property usually collapse under IRS scrutiny and are treated as an exchange of property.

▲ **EXAMPLE 12**   Assume that in example 11 Sarah sold her old auto to Alpha Auto Sales for $3,000. She deposited the check in the bank and wrote a separate check to Alpha Auto Sales for $19,000 to purchase the new auto. What are the tax effects for Sarah of the sale and purchase of the autos?

Discussion: Because the sale and purchase transactions were made with the same dealer in property, the IRS would collapse the 2 transactions and treat them as a direct exchange of property. That is, although the form of the transaction is a sale and a purchase, the substance of the transaction is an exchange of autos between Sarah and Alpha Auto Sales.

Because the transaction is an exchange of like-kind business property for like-kind business property, Sarah is not allowed to recognize the $1,500 loss on the exchange. The loss is added to the basis of the new auto. Thus, instead of recognizing a $1,500 loss and having an auto with a basis of $19,000 (example 11), Sarah has no recognized loss and her basis in the auto is $20,500 ($19,000 + $1,500).

The direct exchange of property requirement does not mean that the exchange must be simultaneous. Taxpayers are allowed to structure transactions through third parties that qualify as exchanges if they meet certain time requirements for identifying properties and closing the transaction.

▲ **EXAMPLE 13**   Percy Corporation would like to obtain land owned by Olivia. Olivia does not want to sell the land, because she would have to recognize a large gain, but she is willing to trade for land owned by Bake. Under a binding contract, Olivia delivers title to her land to Percy, and Percy agrees to purchase the land from Bake and deliver title to the land to Olivia. Percy purchases the land from Bake and delivers title to Olivia. Does the transaction qualify as an exchange?

Discussion: The transaction between Percy Corporation and Olivia qualifies as a direct exchange of property if the transaction meets the time requirements for completing the transaction.

The transaction between Percy Corporation and Bake is not an exchange. It is a sale of property by Bake to Percy and is not part of the exchange transaction.

The exchange illustrated in example 13 is referred to as a **deferred (third-party) exchange.** The deferred exchange rules allow a transaction to be structured as an exchange when the two parties do not have property that they want to exchange directly.[5] The rules for structuring such exchanges require that the property to be exchanged be identified within 45 days of the date of the first property transfer. In addition, the exchange must be completed within 180 days of the first property transfer. In example 13, the land owned by Bake would have to be identified as being part of the exchange within 45 days of the transfer of land from Olivia to Percy Corporation. In addition, Percy would have 180 days to purchase the land from Bake and transfer title to the land to Olivia to qualify the transaction as an exchange. Application of the deferred exchange rules can be quite complex in practice and is generally beyond the scope of this text. However, you should know that exchanges can still be made when one party does not own the property the other party desires to receive in the exchange.

Like-Kind Property Requirements

The **like-kind exchange rules** require that the property being transferred in an exchange be used either in a trade or business or held as an investment. This excludes personal use property (residences, personal automobiles, etc.) from the nonrecognition rules for like-kind exchanges. In addition, stock-in-trade (inventories); other property held primarily for sale; stocks, bonds, notes, other securities; partnership interests; and intangible assets are specifically excluded from the exchange nonrecognition rules. Exchanges of these assets generally result in recognized gains and losses.

The property received in the exchange must be like-kind property and be held for business or investment use. This is interpreted as meaning that the property is of like kind in the taxpayer's hands, not the prior owner's. Thus, a taxpayer can make a like-kind exchange with a dealer in property, even though the dealer does not hold the property for business or investment use. In addition, the requirement that both the property exchanged and the property received be held for business or investment use is interpreted as meaning that business use property can be exchanged for property to be held as an investment and vice versa, so long as the two properties are of like kind.

> ▲ **EXAMPLE 14**   Ace Trucking Co. owned a parcel of land it had acquired several years earlier as an investment. Ace needed more land for parking its trucking fleet, so it exchanged the investment land for a parcel of land adjacent to its truck barn. Is the exchange of land eligible for treatment as a like-kind exchange?
>
> *Discussion:* Exchanging land held for investment purposes for land to be used in a trade or business is a like-kind exchange. Investment property can be exchanged for business use property so long as both properties are of like kind. In this case, the two parcels of land are of like kind.

Central to the exchange nonrecognition provisions is that the properties exchanged are like kind. The Treasury regulations on like-kind exchanges give the following interpretation of what constitutes **like-kind property:**

> The words "like kind" have reference to the nature or character of the property and not to its grade or quality. One kind or class of property may not be exchanged for property of a different kind or class. The fact that any real estate involved is improved or unimproved is not material, for that fact relates only to the grade or quality of the property and not to its kind or class.[6]

According to the IRS interpretation, *like-kind property* means that the properties exchanged must be of the same class of property. Only two classes of property are eligible for exchange treatment—tangible personal property and real property. The exchange requirement allows any real property to be exchanged for any other real property in a like-kind exchange. For example, unimproved land exchanged for an office building is a like-kind exchange, because both properties are real property.

Until July 1, 1992, any personal property could be exchanged for any other personal property and receive like-kind exchange treatment. To qualify as like-kind property, personal property exchanges after July 1, 1992, must be of like class.[7] *Like class* is defined as being within the same general asset class as defined for cost-recovery purposes (see Table A11–1 in the appendix to Chapter 11). The **general asset classes** are as follows:

00.11   Office furniture, fixtures, and equipment
00.12   Information systems (computers and peripheral equipment)
00.13   Data-handling equipment, except computers

00.21   Airplanes (airframes and engines), except those used in commercial or contract-carrying of passengers or freight, and all helicopters

00.22   Automobiles, taxis

00.23   Buses

00.241 Light general purpose trucks

00.242 Heavy general purpose trucks

00.25   Railroad cars and locomotives, except those owned by railroad transportation companies

00.26   Tractor units for use over the road

00.27   Trailers and trailer-mounted containers

00.28   Vessels, barges, tugs, and similar water-transportation equipment, except those used in marine construction

00.4   Industrial steam and electrical generation and/or distribution systems

▲ **EXAMPLE 15**   Peter Peppers, Inc., exchanged an automobile for a delivery van. Are the two properties of like kind?

Discussion: Exchanging an automobile used in a trade or business for a delivery van to be used in a trade or business is not a like-kind exchange, because the properties are not of like class. Automobiles are in class 00.22, whereas a delivery van would be in class 00.241 (light general purpose trucks).

▲ **EXAMPLE 16**   Sherry exchanged a computer she used in her trade or business for a laser printer. Are the two properties of like kind?

Discussion: The properties are like-kind properties. Both fall into asset class 00.12, computers and peripheral equipment.

▲ **EXAMPLE 17**   Clemons exchanged a parcel of land he held as an investment for an office building to be used in his business. Are the two properties of like kind?

Discussion: An exchange of real property for other real property is a like-kind exchange. It does not matter that the land is unimproved property and the building is improved property. Clemons's exchange is a like-kind exchange.

If both properties being exchanged do not fall within one of the general asset classes, the properties are like kind if they fall within the same product class. **Product class** is defined as the four-digit product class of the *Standard Industrial Classification Manual* **(SIC Codes).**[8] Two sample classes are shown in Exhibit 13–1. Additional selected SIC product classes appear in the appendix to this chapter. An asset cannot have both an asset class and a product class for purposes of determining like-kind exchange treatment. Therefore, if one asset being exchanged is in a general asset class and the other asset is not, the two properties are not like kind (even if both are in the same product class).

▲ **EXAMPLE 18**   Andrea exchanged an automobile used in her trade or business for a motor home to be used in her trade or business. Are the two properties of like kind?

Discussion: Automobiles are in general asset class 00.22. Mobile homes are not included in any general asset class but are in Product Class 3711 (Exhibit 13–1). Because the automobile is in a general asset class and the mobile home is not, the properties are not like kind. Note that this result holds even though automobiles are included in Product Class 3711.

▲ **EXAMPLE 19**   Franny's Firewood, Inc., exchanged a log splitter for a mechanical rake. Are the two properties of like kind?

Discussion: Neither the log splitter nor the rake falls within a general asset class. Both assets are in Product Class 3531. Therefore, the log splitter and the rake are like-kind properties.

▲ **Exhibit 13–1**

SAMPLE SIC PRODUCT CLASS CODES

3711 Motor Vehicles and Passenger Car Bodies

Ambulances
Amphibian motor vehicles, except tanks
Assembling complete automobiles
Automobiles
Bodies, passenger automobile
Brooms, powered
Car bodies
Cars, armored
Cars, electric: for highway use

Chassis, motor vehicle
Fire department vehicles
Flushers, street
Hearses
Mobile lounges
Motor buses, except trackless trolley
Motor homes, self-contained
Motor trucks, except off-highway
Motor vehicles, including amphibian

Patrol wagons
Personnel carriers, for highway use
Road oilers
Snowplows
Station wagons
Street sprinklers and sweepers
Taxicabs
Tractors, truck: for highway use
Universal carriers, military

3531 Construction Machinery and Equipment

Aerial work platforms
Aggregate spreaders
Asphalt plants
Automobile wrecker hoists
Backfillers, self-propelled
Backhoes
Ballast distributors
Batching plants, bituminous
Batching plants, for aggregate concrete
Blades for graders, scrapers, dozers,
    and snowplows
Breakers, paving
Buckets, excavating: clamshell, concrete,
    dragline, drag scraper, shovel
Bulldozers, construction
Cabs, construction machinery
Capstans, ship
Carriers, crane
Chip spreaders, self-propelled
Chippers, commercial: brush, limb,
    and log
Concrete buggies, powered
Concrete plants
Concrete grouting equipment
Concrete gunning equipment
Construction machinery, except mining
Cranes, construction
Cranes, except industrial plant
Crushers, mineral: portable
Derricks, except oil and gas field
Distributors (construction machinery)
Ditchers, ladder
Dozers, tractor mounted: material moving
Draglines, powered
Drags, road (construction and road
    maintenance equipment)

Dredging machinery
Excavators: e.g., cable, clamshell, crane,
    derrick, dragline, power shovel
Extractors, piling
Finishers and spreaders, construction
Finishers, concrete and bituminous
Grader attachments, elevating
Graders, road (construction machinery)
Grapples: rock, wood, etc.
Grinders, stone: portable
Hammer mills (rock and ore crushing
    machines), portable
Hammers, pile driving
Line markers, self-propelled
Locomotive cranes
Log splitters
Logging equipment
Mixers: e.g., concrete, ore, sand, slag,
    plaster, mortar, bituminous
Mortar mixers
Mud jacks
Pavers
Pile-driving equipment
Planers, bituminous
Plaster mixers
Plows, construction: excavating and
    grading
Post hole diggers, powered
Power cranes, draglines, and shovels
Pulverizers, stone: portable
Railway track equipment: e.g., rail-layers,
    ballast distributors
Rakes, land clearing: mechanical
Road construction and maintenance
    machinery

Rock crushing machinery, portable
Rollers, road
Rollers, sheepsfoot and vibratory
Sand mixers
Scarifiers, road
Scrapers, construction
Screeds and screeding machines
Screeners, portable
Ship cranes and derricks
Shovel loaders
Shovels, power
Silos, cement (batch plant)
Slag mixers
Snowplow attachments
Soil compactors: vibratory
Spreaders and finishers, construction
Subgraders, construction equipment
Subsoiler attachments, tractor-mounted
Surfacers, concrete grinding
Tampers, powered
Tamping equipment, rail
Teeth, bucket and scarifier
Tractors, construction
Tractors, crawler
Tractors, track-laying
Trenching machines
Trucks, off-highway
Vibrators for concrete construction
Wellpoint systems
Winches, all types
Work platforms, elevated

SOURCE: U.S. Office of Management and Budget, *Standard Industrial Classification Manual*, Washington, D.C.: Executive Office of the President, 1987.

▲ **EXAMPLE 20**   Assume that in example 19 Franny's had exchanged the log splitter for a snowplow. Are the two properties of like kind?

Discussion: Neither the log splitter nor the snowplow falls within a general asset class. The log splitter is in Product Class 3531, and the snowplow is in Product Class 3711. Because the two assets are not in the same product class, they are not like-kind properties.

The following is a list of exchanges that never qualify for like-kind exchange treatment:

- Exchanges involving personal use property
- Exchanges of stocks, bonds, and inventories
- Exchanges of intangible property
- Exchanges of tangible personal property for real property
- Exchanges of livestock of a different sex
- Exchanges of partnership interests

Effect of Boot

When properties of different values are exchanged, the party with the lower-valued property must equalize the transaction by transferring cash, securities, or other property not of like kind (boot). Boot does not taint the like-kind nature of the exchange. However, any gain or loss realized on the transfer of the nonqualifying property must be recognized.

▲ **EXAMPLE 21**   Geraldine traded in her old cash register, which was worth $10,000, for a new cash register with a fair market value of $25,000. In obtaining the new cash register, Geraldine gave the dealer $5,000 in cash and stock with a fair market value of $10,000. Geraldine had adjusted bases of $7,000 in the old cash register and $4,000 in the stock. What are the tax consequences of the exchange?

Discussion: The exchange of the cash registers is a like-kind exchange for Geraldine. Her realized gain on the exchange is $3,000, none of which is recognized. Her basis in the new cash register is $22,000:

Amount realized (trade-in value)	$10,000
Adjusted basis	(7,000)
Realized gain	$ 3,000
Recognized gain (no boot received)	-0-
Deferred gain	$ 3,000

Basis in new cash register = $25,000 − $3,000 = $22,000

Although the exchange of the cash registers is tax free, stock is not like-kind property, and its disposition as part of the exchange transaction is a taxable transaction. Geraldine has a gain, realized and recognized, of $6,000 ($10,000 − $4,000) on the transfer of the stock.

Receipt of Boot.   The receiver of boot in a like-kind exchange has the where-withal to pay tax on the exchange to the extent of the boot received. Therefore, a gain on a like-kind exchange is recognized to the extent of any boot received (but never more than the realized gain on the exchange). Losses on like-kind exchanges are never recognized, even when boot is received. The most common form of boot payment is cash. However, anything of value can be used to equalize the exchange. Therefore, receipts of other assets, services, and assumptions of debt constitute boot.[9]

▲ **EXAMPLE 22**   Endorra Corporation owns a building with a fair market value of $70,000 and an adjusted basis of $40,000. The corporation exchanges the building for land with a fair market value of $45,000 and receives $25,000 in cash. Both properties are investment properties for Endorra. What are Endorra Corporation's realized gain, recognized gain, and basis in the land?

Discussion: The exchange of a building for land is a like-kind exchange. Endorra Corporation realizes a gain of $30,000 on the building. Because it is in receipt of $25,000 in cash boot, the corporation must recognize $25,000 of the gain. Endorra's basis in the land is $40,000:

Amount realized ($45,000 + $25,000)	$70,000
Adjusted basis	(40,000)
Realized gain	$30,000
Recognized gain (cash boot received)	(25,000)
Deferred gain	$ 5,000

$$\text{Basis in land} = \$45,000 - \$5,000 = \$40,000$$

▲ **EXAMPLE 23**   Assume that Endorra had a $10,000 mortgage on the building. As part of the exchange, the owner of the land agrees to assume the $10,000 mortgage and pay the corporation $15,000 in cash. What are Endorra's realized gain, recognized gain, and basis in the land?

Discussion: Endorra realizes a gain of $30,000 on the building. The corporation is in receipt of $25,000 in boot from the $10,000 mortgage assumption and the $15,000 in cash. Therefore, it must recognize a gain of $25,000. Endorra Corporation's basis in the land is $40,000:

Amount realized ($45,000 + $10,000 + $15,000)	$70,000
Adjusted basis	(40,000)
Realized gain	$30,000
Recognized gain (liability assumed + cash received)	(25,000)
Deferred gain	$ 5,000

$$\text{Basis in land} = \$45,000 - \$5,000 = \$40,000$$

Example 23 illustrates that the assumption of a liability is considered boot received and therefore subject to current taxation. This occurs because a buyer who assumes a mortgage in essence gives cash to the seller, which the seller uses to pay off the existing mortgage. In example 23, the owner of the land could have paid Endorra $25,000 in cash to effect the exchange. Endorra would then have used $10,000 of the cash to pay off its mortgage, leaving the corporation with $15,000 in cash. This treatment of debt assumptions makes the taxation of exchanges neutral with respect to debt. That is, the same result is obtained regardless of whether the property being exchanged includes the assumption of debt on the property. However, if a mortgage is assumed and boot is paid in the transaction, the boot paid is offset by the boot received in the mortgage assumption.[10]

▲ **EXAMPLE 24**   Assume that in example 22 Endorra's mortgage on the building is $30,000. In order to make the exchange for the land, the corporation has to pay $5,000. What are Endorra's realized gain, recognized gain, and basis in the land?

Discussion: Endorra realizes a gain of $30,000 on the building. The corporation is in receipt of mortgage boot of $30,000, but it is allowed to offset the mortgage boot with the $5,000 cash boot it paid to make the exchange. Thus, Endorra recognizes a gain of $25,000 on the exchange. The corporation's basis in the land is $40,000:

Amount realized ($45,000 + $30,000 − $5,000)	$70,000
Adjusted basis	(40,000)
Realized gain	$30,000
Recognized gain (liability assumed − cash boot paid)	(25,000)
Deferred gain	$ 5,000

$$\text{Basis in land} = \$45,000 - \$5,000 = \$40,000$$

Note that the amount by which the cash boot offsets the mortgage is equal to the amount by which Endorra could have reduced its mortgage ($25,000) and then traded the mortgaged building for the land in an even exchange.

The tax law does not allow the receiver of money or other boot property to use liabilities assumed in the exchange to offset the boot received.

▲ **EXAMPLE 25**   Raul owned land with a fair market value of $30,000 and an adjusted basis of $8,000. Raul traded the land for another parcel of land with a fair market value of $35,000 and encumbered by a $10,000 mortgage. In the exchange, Raul assumed the $10,000 mortgage and received $5,000 in cash. What are Raul's realized gain, recognized gain, and his basis in the land acquired in the exchange?

Discussion: Raul has realized a gain of $22,000 on the exchange of the land. Raul must recognize a gain equal to the $5,000 in cash boot. He cannot offset the $5,000 cash boot with the $10,000 he paid in mortgage boot. His basis in the new land is $18,000:

Amount realized ($35,000 + $5,000 − $10,000)	$30,000
Adjusted basis	(8,000)
Realized gain	$22,000
Recognized gain (cash boot received)	(5,000)
Deferred gain	$17,000

$$\text{Basis in land} = \$35,000 - \$17,000 = \$18,000$$

The $18,000 basis in the land consists of the $8,000 basis in the original parcel of land, plus the extra $10,000 in debt Raul took on in the exchange.

When both properties being exchanged are encumbered by mortgages and the mortgages on the properties are exchanged, the mortgages are netted out. Only the party that has the larger mortgage is considered to have received mortgage boot. The party with the smaller mortgage is a net payer of mortgage boot and does not recognize gain from the net mortgage boot paid.

▲ **EXAMPLE 26**   Tara owns an office building, and the Barney Partnership owns an apartment building. Each property is encumbered by a mortgage. They agree to exchange their properties and their mortgages, with any difference to be paid in cash. The fair market values (FMV), mortgages, and adjusted bases for each property are listed here. Who must pay the cash to make the exchange, and how much must that taxpayer pay? What are the tax effects of the exchange for Tara and the Barney Partnership?

	Tara's Office Building	Barney's Apartment Building
FMV	$220,000	$250,000
Mortgage	$ 80,000	$150,000
Adjusted basis	$100,000	$175,000

Discussion: The partnership must pay Tara $40,000 to make the exchange. Tara's property has a net of mortgage value of $140,000 ($220,000 − $80,000), and Barney's net of mortgage value is $100,000 ($250,000 − $150,000). Therefore, the partnership must pay the $40,000 difference in the net value being exchanged.

Tara realizes a gain of $120,000 on her office building. She will have to recognize the $40,000 in cash boot she receives, but she is not allowed to offset the $40,000 with the $70,000 ($80,000 − $150,000) of net mortgage boot she pays on the exchange. Her basis in the apartment building is $170,000:

Amount realized ($250,000 + $40,000 + $80,000 − $150,000)	$220,000
Adjusted basis	(100,000)
Realized gain	$120,000
Recognized gain (cash boot received)	(40,000)
Deferred gain	$ 80,000

Basis in apartments = $250,000 − $80,000 = $170,000

Tara's basis in the apartment building is her $100,000 basis in the office building plus the additional $70,000 ($150,000 − $80,000) of debt she takes on in the exchange.

  Barney realizes a gain of $75,000 on its apartment building. The partnership is in receipt of net mortgage boot of $70,000 ($150,000 − $80,000). However, it is allowed to use the $40,000 cash boot paid to Tara to offset the mortgage boot paid to Tara. Therefore, the partnership will recognize a gain of only $30,000. Barney's basis in the office building is $175,000:

Amount realized ($220,000 + $150,000 − $80,000 − $40,000)		$250,000
Adjusted basis		(175,000)
Realized gain		$ 75,000
Recognized gain - net mortgage boot:		
Barney's mortgage assumed by Tara	$150,000	
Tara's mortgage assumed by Barney	(80,000)	
Net mortgage boot received	$ 70,000	
Less: Cash boot paid	(40,000)	
Net boot received		(30,000)
Deferred gain		$ 45,000

Basis in office building = $220,000 − $45,000 = $175,000

The recognition of gains on like-kind exchanges to the extent of any boot received is based on the wherewithal-to-pay concept. However, this concept is not applicable to losses—losses do not require that resources be available for payment of tax on the transaction. Therefore, losses on like-kind exchanges are never recognized, even when boot is received in the exchange.

▲ **EXAMPLE 27** Genevieve exchanged an apartment building held as an investment for a parcel of land. The apartment building had a fair market value of $43,000 and an adjusted basis of $65,000. Because the land was worth only $30,000, Genevieve received $13,000 in cash in the exchange. What are Genevieve's realized and recognized gain (loss) on the exchange and her basis in the land?

Discussion: Genevieve has a realized loss of $22,000 on the exchange. Losses on like-kind exchanges are never recognized. Her basis in the land is $52,000:

Amount realized ($30,000 + $13,000)	$ 43,000
Adjusted basis	(65,000)
Realized loss	$(22,000)
Recognized loss	-0-
Deferred loss	$(22,000)

Basis in land = $30,000 + $22,000 = $52,000

Note that in this case, Genevieve's basis in the land is not equal to the basis she had in the building, because she has recovered $13,000 of her investment with no tax consequences. Thus, her unrecovered investment is $52,000 ($65,000 − $13,000).

Related Party Exchanges

Tax law subjects transactions involving related parties to careful scrutiny. Many transactions between related parties are either disallowed or subject to special limitations. Like-kind exchange treatment is allowed for qualifying exchanges between related parties. However, for related party exchanges occurring after July 10, 1989, each party to the exchange must hold the property received in the exchange for two years to continue its qualification as a like-kind exchange. If either party disposes of the property received in the exchange sooner than two years, both parties must immediately recognize the tax effects of the initial exchange. Note that the recognition takes places in the year of the disposition. The year in which the original exchange occurred is not amended under the annual accounting period concept.

▲ **EXAMPLE 28**   Fred owns land with a fair market value of $85,000 and an adjusted basis of $5,000. Dan wants to buy the land from Fred. Nance Corporation, which is wholly owned by Fred, owns an apartment building with a fair market value of $85,000 and an adjusted basis of $70,000. In December 1996, Fred exchanges his land for Nance Corporation's apartment building. What are the tax consequences to Fred and Nance Corporation?

Discussion: An exchange of land for an apartment building is a like-kind exchange. The fact that Fred and Nance are related parties will not affect the nonrecognition of the exchange transaction in 1996. Fred has a realized gain of $80,000 ($85,000 − $5,000), none of which is recognized in 1996. Fred's basis in the apartments is $5,000. Nance has a realized gain of $15,000 ($85,000 − $70,000), none of which is recognized in 1996. Nance's basis in the land is $70,000. So long as both Fred and Nance hold the properties for two full years from the date of the exchange, no gains will be recognized from the exchange.

	Fred	Nance Corporation
Amount realized	$85,000	$85,000
Adjusted basis	(5,000)	(70,000)
Realized gain	$80,000	$15,000
Recognized gain	-0-	-0-
Deferred gain	$80,000	$15,000
Basis in property received	$5,000 ($85,000 − $80,000)	$70,000 ($85,000 − $15,000)

▲ **EXAMPLE 29**   In January 1997, Nance Corporation sells the land acquired from Fred to Dan for $85,000. What are the tax consequences to Fred and Nance Corporation of the sale to Dan?

Discussion: Because Nance sold the land acquired from Fred without holding it for two full years, the original exchange no longer qualifies as a like-kind exchange. Fred must recognize his $80,000 in realized gain on the land in 1997. This gives him a basis in the apartment buildings of $85,000. Nance must recognize the $15,000 gain realized on the apartment building in 1997, leaving Nance with a basis of $85,000 in the land. The sale of the land to Dan results in no realization of gain ($85,000 − $85,000).

	Fred	Nance Corporation
Amount realized	$85,000	$85,000
Adjusted basis	(5,000)	(70,000)
Realized gain	$80,000	$15,000
Recognized gain	(80,000)	(15,000)
Deferred gain	$ -0-	$ -0-
Basis in property received (FMV)	$85,000	$85,000

Carryover of Tax Attributes

When property is exchanged in a qualifying like-kind exchange, the tax attributes of the asset carry over and are attributed to the new asset acquired in the exchange. As a continuation of investment, the holding period of the new asset includes the period during which the initial asset was held. More important, if the asset being exchanged is a depreciable asset, the recapture potential of the first asset carries to the second asset. The recapture potential of an asset is the maximum amount of recapture on the asset at the time of the exchange. For a Section 1245 asset, the recapture potential is equal to the depreciation taken on the asset as of the date it is exchanged. The recapture potential of a Section 1250 asset is the excess depreciation taken on the asset as of the date of the exchange.

▲ **EXAMPLE 30**   Kelly purchased a machine used in her business that had a fair market value of $16,000 by trading in an old machine and giving $9,000. Kelly had paid $14,000 for the old machine, which had an adjusted basis of $3,000 at the date of the trade. What are the tax effects for Kelly of the exchange?

Discussion: Kelly has realized a gain of $4,000 on the old machine. Kelly will not have to recognize any of the gain, because she did not receive any boot in the exchange. Her basis in the new machine is $12,000:

Amount realized ($16,000 − $9,000)	$7,000
Adjusted basis ($14,000 − $11,000)	(3,000)
Realized gain	$4,000
Recognized gain	-0-
Deferred gain	$4,000

Basis in new machine = $16,000 − $4,000 = $12,000

In addition, the $11,000 in depreciation taken on the old machine is attributed to the new machine as the carryover of the recapture potential. That is, the first $11,000 of any gain on a taxable disposition of the second machine will be ordinary income from the recapture of the depreciation deductions taken on the old machine. In addition, any depreciation deductions on the new machine will also be subject to recapture.

▲ **EXAMPLE 31**   Three years after acquiring the new machine in example 30, Kelly sold the machine for $14,000. Depreciation taken on the machine was $6,200. What is the character of the gain on the sale of the machine?

Discussion: Kelly must recognize a gain of $8,200 [$14,000 − ($12,000 − $6,200)] on the sale of the machine. Machinery used in a trade or business is a Section 1245 asset. Kelly must recognize any gain on the sale of the asset as ordinary income to the extent of the depreciation taken on the machine. Although Kelly has deducted only $6,200 in depreciation on the machine sold, the $11,000 in depreciation taken on the previous machine is attributed to the new machine. Therefore, Kelly is considered to have deducted $17,200 in depreciation on the machine she sold for purposes of applying the depreciation recapture rules, and her $8,200 gain on the sale is ordinary income.

Amount realized	$14,000
Adjusted basis ($12,000 − $6,200)	(5,800)
Realized gain	$ 8,200
Recognized gain [ordinary income to the extent of the total depreciation deduction of $17,200 ($11,000 + $6,200)]	(8,200)
Deferred gain	$ -0-

An **involuntary conversion** occurs whenever a gain or loss is realized from a transaction that occurs against the taxpayer's will. That is, an involuntary conversion is a disposition of property that is beyond the control of the taxpayer. Involuntary conversions result when property is destroyed or damaged in a casualty or theft, when a government unit condemns property under its power of eminent domain, or when a foreign government seizes or nationalizes property. Property that is sold under a threat or imminence of a condemnation or seizure is considered an involuntary conversion. In addition, the selling of livestock because of disease or drought is treated as an involuntary conversion.

INVOLUNTARY CONVERSIONS

Treatment of Involuntary Conversion Gains and Losses

The key to understanding the tax treatment of involuntary conversions is that the disposition of the property was not within the taxpayer's control. Although the taxpayer may have been fully insured and realized a gain on the conversion, replacement of the income-producing capacity of an asset involuntarily converted may take months or years. This puts the business at a distinct disadvantage. Because of the detrimental nature of involuntary conversions, the tax law provides the maximum relief possible.

To provide tax relief, losses on involuntary conversions of business or investment property are always recognized in full. Personal casualty and theft losses are deductible, subject to the event and adjusted gross income limitations discussed in Chapter 7. However, a condemnation loss on a personal use asset is not deductible.

When an involuntary conversion results in a gain, taxpayers may elect to defer the gain if they purchase qualified replacement property. This provision allows taxpayers who suffer an involuntary conversion the maximum allowable relief. Under the wherewithal-to-pay concept, any involuntary conversion proceeds that are not reinvested in a qualified replacement property must be recognized.[11] However, the amount of gain recognized can never exceed the gain realized on the involuntary conversion.

▲ **EXAMPLE 32**   Bolder Co.'s truck storage shed was destroyed by an avalanche. The shed had cost $160,000 and had an adjusted basis of $70,000 when it was destroyed. The shed was worth $200,000, and Bolder received $180,000 from its insurance company for the casualty. What is the minimum amount of gain Bolder must recognize in each of the following cases? What is the basis of the replacement shed in each case?

Case A
Bolder purchased a qualified replacement shed for $230,000.

Discussion: Bolder has realized a gain of $110,000 on the casualty. Because Bolder used all the insurance proceeds to replace the shed, Bolder has no wherewithal to pay tax on the gain. None of the gain must be recognized. Bolder's basis in the new shed is $120,000:

Amount realized (insurance proceeds)		$180,000
Adjusted basis		(70,000)
Realized gain		$110,000
Recognized gain:		
Insurance proceeds received	$180,000	
Amount reinvested in new shed	230,000	
Insurance proceeds remaining after replacement		-0-
Deferred gain		$110,000

Basis of new shed = $230,000 − $110,000 = $120,000

Note that the basis of the new shed ($120,000) is equal to the $70,000 basis of the old shed plus the additional $50,000 ($230,000 − $180,000) of out-of-pocket cost of purchasing the replacement shed.

Case B
Bolder purchased a qualified replacement shed costing $150,000.

Discussion: After replacing the shed, Bolder has $30,000 of the insurance proceeds remaining. Bolder must recognize $30,000 of the $110,000 gain on the shed. Bolder's basis in the new shed is $70,000:

Realized gain		$110,000
Recognized gain:		
Insurance proceeds received	$180,000	
Amount reinvested in new shed	(150,000)	
Insurance proceeds remaining		
after replacement		(30,000)
Deferred gain		$ 80,000

Basis of new shed = $150,000 − $80,000 = $70,000

In an involuntary conversion, the taxpayer typically receives insurance proceeds or a cash payment for the property from the government condemning or seizing the property. In the rare case of a direct conversion to another piece of property (no cash payment received), no gain on the conversion is recognized. Direct conversions are analogous to like-kind exchanges. Therefore, tax law treats direct conversions as such. The basis of the property converted is carried over to the basis of the property received.[12] If the direct conversion results in a loss, the loss on the conversion is recognized.

▲ **EXAMPLE 33**   Kari's warehouse is condemned by the city development authority so the land can be used as a site for new low-income housing. Kari's adjusted basis in the warehouse is $130,000. In consideration for her old warehouse the development authority transfers to Kari title to a warehouse with a fair market value of $400,000 in a new industrial park. What are Kari's tax consequences of the involuntary conversion?

Discussion: Kari's realized gain on the involuntary conversion is $270,000 ($400,000 - $130,000). Because this is a direct conversion, Kari must defer the gain. The basis in her replacement warehouse is $130,000 ($400,00 - $270,000).

Amount realized	$400,000
Adjusted basis	(130,000)
Realized gain	$270,000
Recognized gain	-0-
Deferred gain	$270,000

Basis in the replacement property = $400,000 - $270,000 = $130,000

The deferral of gain realized on an involuntary conversion is not mandatory. A taxpayer may choose to recognize the entire gain on an involuntary conversion. A gain deferral provides a time value of money savings on the income tax deferred and is usually the preferred alternative. However, situations do arise in which a gain on an involuntary conversion can be recognized without paying additional tax. For example, a taxpayer with a large net capital loss that could not otherwise be deducted in the current year may elect to recognize gain if the property involuntarily converted produces either a capital gain or a Section 1231 gain (which is treated as a long-term capital gain). In such cases, the recognized gain is offset by the capital loss, with no additional tax required of the taxpayer. Because the gain is fully recognized, the basis of the replacement property is not reduced, resulting in larger deductions on the property in future tax years.

▲ **EXAMPLE 34** A rental property Cecilia held as an investment is destroyed by a flood in 1996. Cecilia had purchased the property in 1990, and it had an adjusted basis of $95,000 when it was destroyed. Cecilia receives $115,000 in insurance proceeds, which she uses to buy a qualifying rental property costing $140,000. Cecilia has a net capital loss of $33,000 from her other capital asset transactions during 1996. What are the tax consequences if Cecilia recognizes the $20,000 gain on the involuntary conversion in 1996?

Discussion: The $20,000 realized gain ($115,000 − $95,000) is a capital gain. Because the property was depreciated using the MACRS system, there is no excess depreciation to recapture if the gain is recognized. The entire gain would be a long-term capital gain that would be netted against the $33,000 net capital loss. Cecilia would then have a net capital loss of $13,000. If Cecilia elects to recognize the gain, she pays no additional tax in 1996. In addition, her basis in the replacement property would be $140,000, versus a basis of $120,000 if she elects to defer the gain. The election to recognize the gain does not increase her 1996 tax liability and she may deduct the additional $20,000 of basis in the new property through depreciation over the life of the new property.

Amount realized	$115,000
Adjusted basis	(95,000)
Realized gain	$ 20,000
Recognized long-term capital gain	(20,000)
Deferred gain	$ -0-
Basis in the new purchased property	$140,000
Net capital losses	$ (33,000)
Long-term capital gain	20,000
Net capital loss	$ (13,000)

As example 34 illustrates, cases in which an election to recognize a gain on an involuntary conversion can prove beneficial. However, don't forget that the depreciation recapture rules may reclassify most, if not all, of the gain as ordinary income. Under such circumstances, recognition of the gain may not provide the desired offset of the net capital loss. The important point is that by making the deferral of a gain on an involuntary conversion elective rather than mandatory (as in like-kind exchanges), the taxpayer is given maximum flexibility in obtaining the optimal tax result for the particular situation. Combined with the recognition of losses on involuntary conversions, the tax law provides taxpayers who suffer an involuntary conversion the maximum tax relief possible.

Qualified Replacement Property

Taxpayers may defer gains on involuntary conversions only if they purchase qualified replacement property within two years of the close of the tax year in which the involuntary conversion occurred; this time limit is referred to as the involuntary conversion replacement period. Qualified replacement property must be "property similar or related in service or use."[13] This requirement is referred to as the *functional use test*. The functional use test requires that the replacement property perform the same function or have the same use to the taxpayer as the property involuntarily converted. The functional use test is applicable to all business and investment property—other than a condemnation of real property—that is subject to an involuntary conversion. The replacement requirement for condemned business or investment real property is that the taxpayer must purchase like-kind property.[14] As discussed earlier, *like kind* means that the taxpayer can purchase any other type of real property. Thus, the replacement requirements for condemnations of real property are more generous than for other types of conversions.

▲ **EXAMPLE 35**   One of Sno-Cone, Inc.'s ice-making factories was destroyed by a fire. Sno-Cone used the insurance proceeds from the fire to purchase another ice-making factory. Is the new ice-making factory a qualified replacement property?

Discussion: Sno-Cone must replace the factory with property that has the same functional use. Because the new ice-making facility performs the same function as the factory involuntarily converted, it is a qualified replacement property.

▲ **EXAMPLE 36**   Assume that Sno-Cone did not need to purchase another ice-making facility to maintain its production capacity and used the insurance proceeds to purchase a lollipop factory. Is the lollipop factory a qualified replacement property?

Discussion: The lollipop factory does not perform the same function in Sno-Cone, Inc.'s business as the ice-making factory. It is not a qualified replacement property.

▲ **EXAMPLE 37**   Assume the same facts as in example 36, except that the ice-making factory was condemned and bought by the local government. Is the purchase of the lollipop factory a qualified replacement property?

Discussion: Sno-Cone must replace the condemned business real property with like-kind property. Because a lollipop factory is real property, it is like-kind property that is a qualified replacement property for condemned real property.

In general, qualified replacement property must be purchased within two years after the close of the tax year in which the involuntary conversion occurred. If a property is sold under a threat of condemnation, the replacement period begins at the date of the threat of condemnation. In addition, the replacement period for condemned business or investment real property is extended to three years.

SALE OF A PRINCIPAL RESIDENCE

A realized loss on the sale or exchange of a taxpayer's personal residence is not deductible because of the restrictions on loss deductions for personal use assets. On the other hand, a realized gain from the sale or exchange of a personal residence is taxable under the all-inclusive income concept. However, taxpayers who purchase a qualified replacement residence must defer the gain they realize. As with all nonrecognition transactions, any proceeds from the sale of a principal residence that are not reinvested in acquiring the replacement residence must be recognized and are subject to tax under the wherewithal-to-pay concept.

Principal Residence

To be eligible for gain deferral, both the old and the new residences must be used as the principal residence of the taxpayer. A **principal residence** is where the taxpayer lives most of the time. A taxpayer can have only one principal residence at a time. A principal residence can be a house, mobile home, cooperative apartment, condominium, or a houseboat, provided it is where the taxpayer lives. Ordinarily, it is not difficult to determine whether the old and new properties constitute the taxpayer's residences. However, the distinction is crucial, because the deferral provisions do not apply to the sale of a vacation home, even if the proceeds are used to purchase a home that is occupied year-round. Similarly, gain on the sale of a principal residence cannot be deferred if the proceeds are invested in a vacation home.

▲ **EXAMPLE 38**   Althea owned a ski cabin that she held as a rental property. Althea lived in an apartment that she rented from an unrelated party. Althea sold the ski cabin at a gain and used the proceeds to purchase a house, which she moved into and used as her residence. Can the gain on the sale of the rental property be deferred?

Discussion: Althea is taxed on the gain realized from the sale of the ski cabin. Both the residence sold and the residence purchased must be Althea's principal residence. She had held the ski property for investment; it was not where Althea lived during the year.

If the old residence ceases to be the taxpayer's principal residence before the sale takes place, the nonrecognition provisions do not apply. Abandonment or conversion of the old residence to a rental property before sale would disqualify the property from the nonrecognition provisions. However, temporarily renting out a residence while it is being advertised for sale will not normally change the status of a principal residence. In determining whether a residence is a principal residence, the tax law looks at "all the facts and circumstances" about the residence, including "the good faith of the taxpayer." [15]

▲ **EXAMPLE 39**   The Smith family owned and lived in a house in St. Louis for many years. In February 1996, Francine Smith is transferred by her company to Mississippi. The Smiths move to Mississippi the next month. Because they are unable to sell their house before they move, they rent the house out on a month-to-month rental contract to help pay the cost of maintaining both the St. Louis property and a new home in Mississippi until the St. Louis house can be sold. Is the St. Louis house a principal residence?

Discussion: All the facts and circumstances indicate that renting the St. Louis house was not an attempt to convert the house to a rental property. Rather, the month-to-month rental of the property to defray the costs of holding two residences would indicate a continuing desire to sell the property, not an intent to convert it to rental property.

Replacement Period

To qualify for nonrecognition, the old residence must be replaced by a new residence within a period that begins two years before the sale of the old residence and ends two years after the sale of the old residence; this period is referred to as the *principal residence replacement period.* Allowing the two-year replacement period before and after the sale of the old residence recognizes the realities of the marketplace: Many people must move before they are able to sell their old residence.

▲ **EXAMPLE 40**   Assume that in example 39 the Smith family purchases a new residence in Mississippi in June 1996. The St. Louis house is sold in November 1996. Does the Mississippi residence meet the two-year replacement period requirement?

Discussion: The Mississippi residence was purchased within two years of the sale of the St. Louis residence. The replacement period requirements are satisfied.

Once the replacement is made in June 1996, the Smiths have until June 1998 to sell the St. Louis home. If the St. Louis home is not sold by then, they cannot defer any gain on the sale of the St. Louis residence.

In addition to acquiring the property during the two-year period, the taxpayer must occupy and use the new residence as a principal residence during that period. The occupancy and use requirements have been strictly interpreted by the courts to mean actual physical occupancy and actual use of the property as a principal residence.

▲ **EXAMPLE 41**   In 1969, President Richard Nixon purchased the "San Clemente White House" as a replacement for his New York City residence. He used the San Clemente property on weekends and holidays with the intent of living there full time after his presidential term ended. Does the San Clemente property qualify as a replacement principal residence for the New York City residence sold in 1969?

Discussion: Congress's Joint Committee on Internal Revenue Taxation determined that the use of a house on weekends with an intent to occupy after leaving the White House did not meet the actual occupancy and use test. It was determined that there were no statutory exceptions that would allow a taxpayer not to physically occupy and use the property as a principal residence during the two-year replacement period. Although Nixon occupied San Clemente as his principal residence sooner than he had initially anticipated, he did not do so within two years of the sale of his New York City residence, and his gain deferral was denied.[16]

To discourage use of the nonrecognition provisions as a deferral technique in a rising real estate market, the tax law does not allow deferral on subsequent sales for a two-year period. Therefore, a taxpayer who buys more than one principal residence during the two-year period following the sale of an old residence must use the last residence purchased as the replacement residence for calculating the deferral of gain on the sale of the old residence. Gains on other sales during the two-year period are recognized.

▲ **EXAMPLE 42**   Joe Bob sells his principal residence on March 14, 1996. He purchases a qualified replacement residence on July 4, 1996. On January 6, 1997, he sells the second residence and uses the proceeds to purchase another principal residence on April 28, 1997. Can Joe Bob defer the gain from the sale of both residences?

Discussion: Because Joe Bob sold the first replacement residence sooner than two years from the sale of his first principal residence, he cannot defer the gain on its sale. He defers the gain on the March 14, 1996, sale, using the residence purchased on April 28, 1997, to calculate the gain deferral.

The two-year resale rule would work a hardship on an employee who is transferred and therefore has no control over the timing of the sales and purchases. The provision is waived for any sale that is caused by a change in the location of employment. To qualify as a change in location, the move must meet the distance and time tests for deducting moving expenses.

▲ **EXAMPLE 43**   Assume that in example 42 Joe Bob sells his residence on January 6, 1997, because he is being transferred to another state by his employer. Can Joe Bob defer the gain from the sale of both residences?

Discussion: Because a change in the location of his employment necessitates the sale of the first replacement residence, Joe Bob can defer the gain on the sale of both residences.

Deferral of Gain

As with all nonrecognition provisions, a gain on the sale of a principal residence is not recognized if the taxpayer does not have the wherewithal to pay the tax on the gain after purchasing the replacement property. So long as the proceeds received from the sale of the residence are fully reinvested in the new residence, no gain on sale is recognized. However, realized gains are recognized to the extent that proceeds from the sale are not reinvested.

The amount that must be reinvested in the new residence is the adjusted sales price of the old residence. The **adjusted sales price** is equal to the amount realized on the sale, less fixing-up expenses. Fixing-up expenses are noncapital expenditures that prepare the residence for sale, are incurred within 90 days before the sale, and paid within 30 days after the sale. The reduction of the amount realized from the sale by the fixing-up expenses reflects the fact that such costs are nondeductible, because they are related to a personal use asset, yet the amount expended on such costs is not available for reinvestment by the taxpayer. Exhibit

13–2 presents the framework for calculating the amount of deferred gain on the sale of a principal residence.

▲ **EXAMPLE 44**   Walter sold his principal residence for $113,000. Walter paid selling expenses of $9,000 and incurred $4,000 in fixing-up expenses to prepare the residence for sale. Walter's adjusted basis in the residence was $84,000. What are Walter's recognized gain and his basis in the new residence in each of the qualified replacement cases that follow?

	Case A	Case B	Case C
Replacement residence cost	$126,000	$95,000	$75,000

Discussion: In each case, Walter has realized a gain of $20,000. Walter's adjusted sales price, which he must reinvest, is $100,000:

Amount realized ($113,000 − $9,000)	$104,000
Adjusted basis	(84,000)
Realized gain on sale	$ 20,000

Adjusted sales price = $104,000 − $4,000 = $100,000

	Case A	Case B	Case C
Realized gain on sale	$ 20,000	$ 20,000	$ 20,000
Recognized Gain			
Adjusted sales price	$100,000	$100,000	$100,000
Cost of new residence	126,000	95,000	75,000
Excess—Recognized gain	-0-	$ 5,000	$ 20,000
Deferred Gain	$ 20,000	$ 15,000	$ -0-
Basis of New Residence			
Cost of new residence	$126,000	$ 95,000	$ 75,000
Less: Deferred gain	(20,000)	(15,000)	-0-
Basis	$106,000	$ 80,000	$ 75,000

In case A, the entire adjusted sales price has been reinvested in acquiring the new $126,000 residence, and none of the $20,000 gain is recognized. In case B, $5,000 of the adjusted sales price was not reinvested and is taxed under the wherewithal-to-pay concept. In case C, $25,000 of the adjusted sales price was not reinvested. However,

Amount realized on sale (selling price less selling expenses)	$XXX
Less: Adjusted basis	(XXX)
Realized gain on sale	$XXX
Calculation of Deferred Gain	
Amount realized $XXX	
Less: Fixing-up expenses (XXX)	
Adjusted sales price $XXX	
Cost of new residence (XXX)	
Recognized gain—Excess (if any) of adjusted sales price over cost of new residence	(XXX)
Deferred gain	$XXX
Calculation of Basis of New Residence	
Cost of new residence	$XXX
Less: Deferred gain	(XXX)
Basis of replacement residence	$XXX

▲ **Exhibit 13–2**

SALE OF PRINCIPAL RESIDENCE GAIN DEFERRAL CALCULATION

the amount of recognized gain cannot exceed the gain realized on the sale. The full $20,000 in realized gain is recognized in case C.

The provisions for deferring gain on the sale of a principal residence also require deferral of gain when a new principal residence is acquired by exchange. In addition, a gain resulting from the condemnation of a principal residence may be deferred by using either the rules for involuntary conversions or the sale of principal residence provisions. Under no circumstances may a loss from the sale, exchange, or condemnation of a principal residence be deferred. These are personal use losses that are not deductible and therefore not deferrable. The only loss on a principal residence that is deductible is a casualty loss, which is deductible under the personal casualty loss rules.

▲ **EXAMPLE 45**   Courtney sold her principal residence for $63,000, paying selling expenses of $2,000. Fixing-up expenses were $500. Courtney's adjusted basis in the residence was $76,000. Courtney purchased another principal residence for $82,000. What are the tax effects of the sale and purchase of the principal residences for Courtney?

Discussion: Courtney has realized a loss of $15,000 [($63,000 − $2,000) − $76,000] on the sale of her residence. A loss on the sale of a principal residence is a personal use loss, which is not deductible. The basis in the new residence is her $82,000 cost. The $15,000 loss is not deferred into the basis of the new residence.

Amount realized ($63,000 − $2,000)	$61,000
Adjusted basis	(76,000)
Realized loss	$15,000
Recognized loss	-0-
Deferred loss	$ -0-

Basis in the new residence is Courtney's cost = $82,000

SALE OF A PRINCIPAL RESIDENCE— TAXPAYERS OLDER THAN 55

For many taxpayers, the principal residence represents the largest single investment asset they own. Older taxpayers who have owned the same residence for many years often have very large gains when they sell the property. Much of this gain comes from inflation in property values and corresponding deflation in the purchasing power of the dollar during the long period the property was held. To afford older citizens some tax relief when they realize these big gains and either do not replace the property or purchase a much smaller property, Congress has provided a one-time exclusion of up to $125,000 in gain on the sale of a principal residence.[17] An *exclusion from income* means that the income will never be subject to tax. Thus, an election to exclude gain does not require that a replacement residence be purchased.

Gain Exclusion Requirements

To be eligible to elect the exclusion of gain, the taxpayer must meet the following requirements:

■ The taxpayer or the taxpayer's spouse must have attained age 55 before the closing date of the sale.

■ The taxpayer or the taxpayer's spouse may not have previously made an election to exclude gain on the sale of a principal residence.

■ The residence must have been owned and used as the principal residence of the taxpayer or the taxpayer's spouse during three of the previous five years. For purposes of the three-year residence test, up to two years of living in a nursing facility while taxpayers are incapable of caring for themselves can be counted in the three-year period.

One-Time Exclusion of Gain

The election to exclude gain is available only once during the lifetime of a taxpayer. The $125,000 exclusion is the maximum amount that can be excluded when making the one-time election to exclude. You are not allowed to exclude a series of gains up to a total gain of $125,000. Taxpayers who are eligible for exclusion and who buy a replacement residence should try to defer the gain under the sale of principal residence rules to avoid wasting their one-time election. However, taxpayers who purchase a much smaller residence, and therefore can defer little or none of the gain, probably should use the gain exclusion to take advantage of the time value of money savings on the excluded gain.

▲ **EXAMPLE 46**   Horatio and Maude are both older than 55. They sold their principal residence for $175,000 and moved in with their son and his family. Selling expenses were $9,000. Their adjusted basis in the residence was $28,000. What is their recognized gain on the sale of the residence?

Discussion: Horatio and Maude realized a gain of $138,000 on the sale. Because at least 1 of them is older than 55, they may elect to exclude up to $125,000 of the gain. The election to exclude leaves them with a recognized gain of $13,000:

Amount realized on sale ($175,000 − $9,000)	$166,000
Adjusted basis	(28,000)
Realized gain	$138,000
Less: Maximum $125,000 gain exclusion	(125,000)
Recognized gain	$ 13,000

▲ **EXAMPLE 47**   Assume the same facts as in example 46, except that Horatio and Maude purchased a new principal residence costing $180,000. Should they use their election to exclude gain on the sale?

Discussion: Because Horatio and Maude purchased a new principal residence, they must use the deferral rules for sale of a principal residence if they do not elect to take their $125,000 gain exclusion. In this case, they have reinvested the entire adjusted sales price in the new residence and can defer the entire gain. Thus, they should not elect to use their one-time gain exclusion:

Realized gain		$138,000
Recognized gain		
Adjusted sales price	$166,000	
Cost of new residence	180,000	
Recognized gain (no excess)		-0-
Deferred gain		$138,000

Basis in new residence = $180,000 − $138,000 = $42,000

The limit of one election to exclude for the taxpayer or the taxpayer's spouse precludes using the election when one spouse has used the election before marrying the current spouse.[18]

▲ **EXAMPLE 48**   Lee and Kathleen married in 1990. In 1996, they sell their principal residence at a gain of $80,000 and do not buy another principal residence. Lee is 53, and Kathleen is 59. In 1987, while Kathleen was married to Gary (who was 56 at the time), Gary and Kathleen elected to exclude the gain on the sale of their principal residence. Can Lee and Kathleen exclude the $80,000 gain on the sale of their principal residence?

Discussion: Because Kathleen previously used the one-time election to exclude gain (while she was married to Gary), Lee and Kathleen are not eligible to exclude the $80,000 gain. This result holds, even though Lee has never used the election. If one spouse "spends" the election to exclude gain in a previous marriage (or while single), the election is no longer available in a subsequent marriage.

Interaction of Deferral and Exclusion Provisions

If an eligible taxpayer has a gain in excess of $125,000 and makes a qualified replacement, the election to exclude and the deferral of gain on sale of a principal residence may both be used to minimize current gain recognition. Using both provisions is necessary only when the gain on sale cannot be fully deferred through use of the deferral provisions. This is often the case when an eligible taxpayer buys less expensive housing when purchasing a new residence. When both provisions are being used, the $125,000 excludable gain cannot be taxed and therefore does not have to be invested in a replacement residence. Thus, the adjusted sales price for calculating the gain deferral is reduced by the $125,000 in excluded gain.

▲ **EXAMPLE 49**   Hal and Renee are both older than 55. During the current year, they sold their house for $265,000. Selling expenses were $18,000, and they incurred $4,000 in fixing-up expenses. The adjusted basis of the house was $67,000. They purchased a $90,000 condominium to use as their residence. What are the amount of gain they must recognize on the sale and the basis in the condominium?

Discussion: Hal and Renee have realized a gain of $180,000 on the sale of the house. They may elect to exclude $125,000 of the gain. Because they bought a new residence, they must use the sale of principal residence deferral rules on the remaining $55,000 of gain. This results in a recognized gain of $28,000 and a basis in the condominium of $63,000:

Amount realized ($265,000 − $18,000)	$247,000
Adjusted basis	(67,000)
Realized gain	$180,000
Excluded gain	(125,000)
Gain remaining for deferral	$ 55,000

Gain Deferral

Adjusted Sales Price		
Amount realized from sale	$247,000	
Less: Fixing-up expenses	(4,000)	
Less: Excluded gain	(125,000)	
Adjusted sales price	$118,000	
Cost of condominium	(90,000)	
Recognized gain		(28,000)
Deferred gain		$ 27,000

Basis in condominium = $90,000 − $27,000 = $63,000

The key factor in applying the exclusion and deferral provisions to the same transaction is that the $125,000 is never subject to tax. Thus, it does not have to be reinvested, and the adjusted sales price is reduced to determine the amount of gain recognized on the purchase of the new residence. This subtraction occurs because adjusted sales price represents the wherewithal to pay.

SUMMARY

The all-inclusive income concept requires that all gains are subject to tax when they are realized in an arm's-length transaction. However, Congress has provided current period tax relief for gains from like-kind exchanges, involuntary conversions, and the sale of a principal residence. Although each nonrecognition transaction has unique characteristics, the three classes of transactions have five distinctive commonalities. First, the rationale for nonrecognition of these transactions comes from the wherewithal-to-pay concept. Because this concept is a basis for not recognizing gains, all the transactions allow for the deferral of gains. The deferral is mandatory for like-kind exchanges and the sale of a principal residence. Gains on involuntary conversions are deferred at the election of the taxpayer. Losses on like-kind exchanges must be deferred. Involuntary conversion losses are

▲ **Table 13–1**

CHARACTERISTICS OF NONRECOGNITION TRANSACTIONS

Characteristic	Like-Kind Exchanges	Involuntary Conversions	Sale of Principal Residence	
			Deferral	Exclusion
Property eligible for nonrecognition	Business or investment property other than inventories, securities, intangible assets, and partnership interests.	Property used in a trade or business or held for investment.	Principal residence of the taxpayer.	Principal residence of the taxpayer.
Replacement property requirement	Like-kind business or investment property. Like-kind property is property of the same general class.	Property must have the same functional use to the taxpayer as the property converted. Condemned real property must be replaced with like-kind property.	Principal residence of the taxpayer.	No property purchase required.
Replacement period	Property to be received in the exchange must be identified within 45 days and transaction completed within 180 days of first transfer of property.	Two years from the end of the tax year of the conversion. Taxpayer has 3 years to replace condemned real property.	Replacement period begins 2 years before sale and ends 2 years after sale.	No property purchase required.
Realized gains	Deferral of gains is mandatory. Gains are recognized to the extent of boot received in the exchange.	Deferral of gains is elective. If deferral is elected, any proceeds not reinvested must be recognized.	Deferral of gains is mandatory. Any part of the adjusted sales price that is not reinvested must be recognized.	Taxpayers who are at least 55 may elect to exclude up to $125,000 in gain.
Realized losses	Deferral of losses is mandatory.	Losses are recognized.	Losses are not deductible or deferred.	Losses are not deductible or deferred.
Basis of replacement property	Gains: reduce by deferred gain. Losses: increase by deferred loss.	Reduce basis by deferred gain.	Reduce basis by deferred gain.	None. Property purchase not required.

deducted in the period of realization. Realized losses on a principal residence cannot be deducted or deferred.

Each nonrecognition transaction is viewed as the continuation of an ongoing investment in the asset disposed of in the transaction. Therefore, each nonrecognition transaction requires the acquisition of a qualified replacement property within a prescribed period in order for gain to be deferred.

Gains are fully deferred when the entire proceeds of the realization are reinvested in a replacement property. However, any amount realized on a nonrecognition disposition that is not reinvested in a qualifying replacement property is subject to tax under the wherewithal-to-pay concept. The amount of gain to be recognized cannot exceed the gain realized on the transaction.

The deferral of gains (and losses on like-kind exchanges) is effected through an adjustment of the basis of the replacement property. The basis of the replacement property is reduced for any gain deferred on the nonrecognition transaction. Losses on like-kind exchanges are deferred by increasing the basis of the replacement property.

As a continuation of the original investment in the property on which gain has been realized, the tax attributes of the original property attach to the replacement property. Under this attribution, the holding period of the replacement property includes the holding period of the original property. In addition, any depreciation recapture potential on the original property is attributed to the replacement. The recapture potential of a property is the maximum amount of depreciation recapture on the property as of the date of disposition.

A special provision allows taxpayers who are at least 55 years old as of the date of sale of a principal residence to exclude a maximum of $125,000 in gain. The exclusion is a once-in-a-lifetime election and cannot be used if the taxpayer or the taxpayer's spouse has previously elected to exclude gain on the sale of a principal residence. If an election to exclude is made and the taxpayer also acquires a qualified replacement residence, the taxpayer must use the sale of principal residence deferral rules to defer any gain on sale in excess of the $125,000 exclusion.

Table 13–1 compares and summarizes the characteristics and requirements for nonrecognition in each of the nonrecognition transactions.

KEY TERMS

adjusted sales price (p. 612)
boot (p. 596)
deferred (third-party) exchange
   (p. 597)
general asset class (p. 598)

involuntary conversion (p. 607)
like-kind exchange rules (p. 598)
like-kind property (p. 598)
nonrecognition transaction
   (p. 590)

principal residence (p. 610)
product class (p. 599)
SIC Codes (p. 599)

PRIMARY TAX LAW SOURCES

[1] Reg. Sec. 1.1031(c)-1—Requires adjustment of the basis of property acquired in a nontaxable exchange. Similar provisions are found in Reg. Sec. 1.1033(b)-1 for involuntarily converted property and Reg. Sec. 1.1034-1 for replacement of a principal residence.

[2] Sec. 1223—The general rule for holding period requires a carryover of holding period when a carryover basis is used.

[3] Reg. Sec. 1.1250-3—Requires the carryover of excess depreciation on any Section 1250 property acquired in a tax-free trans-

action. Reg. Sec. 1.1245-4 contains a similar provision applicable to Section 1245 property.

[4] Sec. 1031—Provides rules for like-kind exchanges of property.

[5] Reg. Sec. 1.1031(k)-1—Provides the rules for deferred exchanges and gives examples of qualifying exchanges.

[6] Reg. Sec. 1.1031(a)-1—Gives the general definition of *like-kind property* for purposes of Section 1031.

[7] Reg. Sec. 1.1031(a)-2—Expands on the definition of *like-kind property* as it applies to personal property.

[8] U.S. Office of Management and Budget, *Standard Industrial Classification Manual* (Washington, D.C.: Executive Office of the President, 1987).

[9] Reg. Sec. 1.1031(b)-1—Discusses the treatment of boot in like-kind exchanges.

[10] Reg. Sec. 1.1031(d)-2—Provides rules for treatment of mortgage assumptions in like-kind exchanges.

[11] Sec. 1033—Provides rules for deferring gains on involuntary conversions.

[12] Reg. Sec. 1.1033(a)-2—Provides the rules for direct conversions of property.

[13] Sec. 1033—See footnote 11.

[14] Reg. Sec. 1.1033(g)-1—Allows condemned real property used in a trade or business or for the production of income to be replaced with like-kind property.

[15] Reg. Sec. 1034-1—Discusses what constitutes a taxpayer's principal residence for purposes of Section 1034.

[16] JOINT COMM. ON INTERNAL REVENUE TAXATION, EXAMINATION OF PRESIDENT NIXON'S TAX RETURNS FOR 1969 THROUGH 1972, H.R. REP. NO. 966, 93d Cong., 2d Sess. 117–118 (1974).

[17] Sec. 121—Allows taxpayers who have attained age 55 to exclude up to $125,000 in gain on the sale of a principal residence.

[18] Reg. Sec. 1.121-2—Discusses limitations on the exclusion of gain from the sale of a principal residence.

DISCUSSION QUESTIONS

1. How does the wherewithal-to-pay concept affect the recognition of gains on asset dispositions? What else is necessary for nonrecognition of a gain upon disposition of an asset?

2. How is the tax treatment of a deferred gain similar to and different from the treatment of an excluded gain?

3. When a gain on a property disposition is deferred, the basis of the replacement property is reduced by the amount of gain deferred. Which concept supports this treatment? Explain.

4. When a gain on a depreciable property is deferred through a nonrecognition transaction, the tax attributes of the first property carry over to the second property. Why is this important, particularly with respect to like-kind exchanges of property?

5. What is boot? How does boot affect the recognition of gains (losses) on like-kind exchanges?

6. What constitutes an exchange of assets?

7. Does an exchange have to occur simultaneously to qualify for nonrecognition? Explain.

8. Define *like-kind property* as it applies to like-kind exchanges, and give examples of like-kind properties and properties that are not of like kind.

9. Why does the assumption of a mortgage when exchanging related assets constitute boot?

10. Discuss the restrictions placed on like-kind exchanges between related parties. Include the reasoning behind the restriction in your discussion.

11. What is the recapture potential of an asset?

12. The rules for gain/loss recognition on involuntary conversions are more liberal than those for exchanges. What features of an involuntary conversion contribute to the difference in treatments for the two types of transactions?

13. How long does a taxpayer who suffers an involuntary conversion of an asset have to replace the asset to qualify for nonrecognition? Explain.

14. What is a principal residence of a taxpayer?

15. Losses on exchanges must be deferred. A loss on an involuntary conversion is never deferred. In contrast, a loss on the sale of a principal residence is never recognized. Explain why losses on the sale of a principal residence are treated differently than losses on exchanges and involuntary conversions.

16. How long does a taxpayer have to replace a principal residence? Why is the replacement period different from that for an involuntary conversion replacement?

17. In general, taxpayers cannot defer gain on more than one sale of principal residence every two years. Explain the rationale for this restriction and the circumstances under which the two-year period provision is waived.

18. How much must be reinvested in a replacement residence to completely defer any gain on the sale of a principal residence?

19. What are the requirements for excluding gain on the sale of a principal residence?

PROBLEMS

20. Honre Corporation's warehouse and Filip Co.'s office building were located side by side until a fire raced through both structures, completely destroying them. The warehouse had an adjusted basis of $250,000 and a fair market value (FMV) before the fire of $450,000. Honre Corporation's fire insurance policy covered the FMV and paid $450,000. Honre decided not to replace the warehouse because it already had adequate storage space. Filip Co.'s office building had an adjusted basis of $400,000 and a FMV before the fire of $750,000. Filip's fire insurance covered a maximum structural loss of only $600,000 and paid that amount. Filip used the $600,000 to build a new office building on its old site.

    Honre Corporation has a taxable transaction. Filip Co. does not. Compare these tax results using only the attributes and commonalities of nonrecognition transactions. (Do not use the specific rules of involuntary conversions.)

21. Which of the following transfers meet the exchange requirement for deferral under like-kind exchange provisions?
    a. Bonita sells her rental condominium in Park City and uses the proceeds as a down payment to buy a rental condominium in Breckenridge.
    b. Enrique Corporation sells its old pasta machine to Angelo Distributing Co. and after shopping around for a few days purchases a new Angelo Model 5 Pasta Machine from Angelo Distributing Co.
    c. Habit Partnership trades 3 of its delivery vans to Cal's Cars and Trucks for 2 new delivery vans.
    d. Louise owns an apartment building in Milwaukee, which Rebecca offers to purchase. Louise is willing to part with the property but does not want to recognize the substantial gain on the sale. Louise is willing to exchange the apartment for a lakefront resort lodge in Minnesota. Rebecca finds such a property and buys it from Ole. Then Rebecca exchanges the resort for Louise's apartment building.
    e. Phong sells his drill press to Cower Co. and purchases a new drill press from Tomzack Manufacturing Corporation with the proceeds from the sale.

22. Bonnie wants to trade her Snow Bird, Utah, condominium, which she has held for investment, for investment property in Steamboat Springs or Crested Butte, Colorado. On April 20, 1996, Bonnie transfers title to the Snow Bird property to Thanh/Hao Partnership, which transfers $200,000 cash to a real estate broker to hold in escrow until Bonnie finds a replacement property. The broker is commissioned to find suitable property for Bonnie. Discuss what must occur for Bonnie to achieve deferral status under the like-kind exchange provisions.

23. Which of the following exchanges of property are like-kind exchanges?
    a. Waldo traded in his business auto for a computer to use in his business.
    b. Germaine exchanged an interest in a condominium she used as a principal residence for a tract of undeveloped land.
    c. Jorge traded his racehorse for a mare to use for breeding.
    d. Arnold traded stock in Palmtree Co. for stock in Webster Co.
    e. Lorraine traded 5 Reggie Jackson baseball cards for 1 Robin Ventura baseball card.

24. Which of the following exchanges of property are like-kind exchanges?
    a. Horace traded his personal residence for another personal residence.
    b. Lian traded an apartment building she rented out for a warehouse to use in her business.
    c. Arthur owns a hardware store. He traded some roofing materials for a cash register.
    d. Wenona traded in an automobile she used 75% of the time for business purposes. She expects to use the new automobile for business purposes about 75% of the time.
    e. Ace Construction Co. traded a used dump truck for a crane.

25. Which of the following exchanges of property are like-kind exchanges?
    a. A hotel in Ft. Lauderdale, Florida, for an apartment complex in Bangor, Maine.
    b. A corporate jet for a warehouse in Detroit.
    c. Typewriters for a computer workstation.
    d. An orange grove in Anaheim, California, for a cherry orchard in Bountiful, Utah.
    e. A resort hotel on Mission Bay near San Diego for a resort hotel in Tijuana, Baja, Mexico.
    f. Children's clothing inventory for store fixtures and shelving.

26. Murray Corporation exchanged land with a fair market value of $23,000 and an adjusted basis of $16,000 for an automobile. Does Murray have a recognized gain on the exchange? Explain.

27. Return to problem 26. Assume that Murray Corporation exchanged the land for another parcel of land worth $30,000. How much boot must be paid to make the exchange, and who must pay the boot? Does Murray have a recognized gain on the exchange?

28. Jalapeno Co. traded in its old delivery van for a new delivery van. The old van had cost $25,000 and had an adjusted basis of $9,000. Jalapeno was given a $7,000 trade-in allowance on the new van and paid the remaining $22,000 of the $29,000 purchase price in cash.
    a. What is Jalapeno's realized gain (loss) on the exchange?
    b. How much of the realized gain (loss) is recognized on the exchange?
    c. How much of the realized gain (loss) is deferred?
    d. What is the basis of the new delivery van?

29. Pauline's Pastry Shop decided to remodel its offices this year. As part of the remodeling, Pauline's traded furniture with a cost of $9,400 that had been expensed in the year of purchase (Section 179 expense election) for new furniture costing $19,500. Pauline's received a $6,000 credit for the old furniture and borrowed the remaining $13,500 from Easy Finance Co.
    a. What is Pauline's realized gain (loss) on the old furniture?
    b. How much of the realized gain (loss) is recognized on the exchange?
    c. How much of the realized gain (loss) is deferred?
    d. What is the basis of the new furniture?

30. Beaver Corporation owns a parcel of land with a fair market value (FMV) of $95,000 and a basis of $40,000. Beaver exchanges the land for a building with a FMV of $65,000. The corporation also receives $30,000 in cash. Both properties are investment properties for Beaver.
    a. What is Beaver's amount realized on the exchange?
    b. What is Beaver's realized gain (loss) on the exchange?
    c. How much of the realized gain (loss) must Beaver recognize?
    d. What is the character of the recognized gain (loss)?
    e. What is Beaver's basis in the building it acquired?

31. Tinh exchanges business equipment with an adjusted basis of $65,000 (initial basis was $95,000) for business equipment worth $60,000 and $15,000 in cash.
    a. What is Tinh's realized gain (loss) on the old equipment?
    b. How much of the realized gain (loss) is recognized on the exchange?
    c. What is the character of the recognized gain?
    d. What is the basis of Tinh's new business equipment?

32. Armando owns a pizza parlor. Because his business was declining, he traded his old pizza oven in on a smaller oven that was worth $24,000. The old oven had cost $32,000 and had an adjusted basis of $17,000. Because Armando's oven was worth $26,000, he agreed to take the $2,000 difference in olive oil and pepperoni.
    a. What is Armando's realized gain (loss) on the old oven?
    b. How much of the realized gain (loss) is recognized on the exchange?
    c. What is the character of the recognized gain (loss)?
    d. How much of the realized gain (loss) is deferred?
    e. What is the basis of the new oven?

33. Reginald exchanged an apartment building he held as an investment for an office building to use in his tuxedo rental business. The apartment building was worth $130,000 and had a $20,000 mortgage. The office building was worth $110,000. The owner of the office building agreed to assume Reginald's $20,000 mortgage to equalize the exchange. The apartments had cost $200,000 and had an adjusted basis of $160,000.
    a. What is Reginald's realized gain (loss) on the apartment building?
    b. How much of the realized gain (loss) is recognized on the exchange?
    c. What is the character of the recognized gain (loss)?
    d. How much of the realized gain (loss) is deferred?
    e. What is the basis of the office building acquired in the exchange?

34. Fremont Corporation and Hawkins Corporation exchanged equipment. The particulars regarding each company's equipment are as follows:

	Fremont	Hawkins
Fair market value	$39,000	$48,000
Adjusted basis	18,000	54,000
Cash paid	9,000	

What are Fremont's and Hawkins's realized and recognized gains (losses) on the exchange and the bases in the equipment they acquire in the exchange?

35. Shirley has an old tractor that has an adjusted basis of $3,000 and a fair market value of $1,000. Shirley wants to trade the tractor in on a new tractor that costs $28,000. Write a memorandum to Shirley advising her about how to structure the transaction to optimize her tax situation.

36. Elrod traded an apartment building he owned for a piece of undeveloped land. The land had a fair market value of $50,000. The owner of the land assumed Elrod's $38,000 mortgage on the apartment building in the exchange. Elrod had purchased the apartment building in 1989 for $86,000, and it had an adjusted basis of $62,000 when it was traded. What are Elrod's realized and recognized gains (losses) on the exchange and his basis in the land he received in the exchange?

37. Olga traded in a computer she had used in her trade or business for a new computer. The old computer had cost Olga $7,000 and had an adjusted basis of $1,400. The computer dealer gave Olga a $3,000 trade-in allowance on the old computer, and Olga paid the remaining $6,500 price of the new computer in cash. What are Olga's realized and recognized gains on the trade-in of her old computer? What is the basis of the new computer?

38. Return to the facts of problem 37. Two years after acquiring the new computer, Olga sold it for $8,200. The adjusted basis of the computer was $6,400. What is the character of the recognized gain on the sale of the computer?

39. Evelyn's Excavating Service traded an excavator for a new backhoe. The excavator had a fair market value of $37,000 and an adjusted basis of $24,000. The backhoe was worth $34,000. The owner of the backhoe agreed to assume Evelyn's $8,000 loan on the excavator, and Evelyn's paid $5,000 in cash in the exchange. What are Evelyn's realized and recognized gains (losses) on the exchange and Evelyn's basis in the backhoe?

The owner of the backhoe, Susan, had an adjusted basis in the backhoe of $18,000. How much of the realized gain must Susan recognize on the exchange? What is the basis in the excavator?

40. Oscar and Harriet agreed to exchange apartment buildings and the mortgages on the buildings, with any difference to be paid in cash. Particulars of their respective buildings are as follows:

	Oscar	Harriet
Fair market value	$98,000	$86,000
Mortgage	63,000	47,000
Adjusted basis	47,000	72,000

a. How much cash must be paid, and who must pay the cash to equalize the exchange?
b. What are Oscar's realized and recognized gains on the exchange and his basis in the apartment building acquired in the exchange?
c. What are Harriet's realized and recognized gains on the exchange and her basis in the apartment building acquired in the exchange?

41. On July 8, 1996, Cynthia and her daughter Constance agree to exchange land they held for investment. Both tracts of land are worth $18,000. Cynthia had acquired her land 4 years earlier at a cost of $9,000. Constance had paid $16,000 for her land investment the previous year. What are the tax effects for Cynthia and Constance of the exchange?

On February 15, 1998, Constance sells the land acquired in the exchange for $21,000. What are the tax effects of the sale? Explain.

42. Walker Corporation acquires a business automobile with a fair market value of $20,000 by trading an old automobile and giving $14,000. Walker had paid $12,000 for the old automobile, which had an adjusted basis of $1,000 at the date of the trade. Two years after acquiring the new automobile, Walker sells it for $15,000. Depreciation taken on the automobile is $7,000. How much gain or loss should Walker recognize on the sale and how should it be characterized?

43. Which of the following are qualified replacement properties for properties involuntarily converted? Explain.
a. The proceeds from a warehouse destroyed by a fire were used to purchase a manufacturing plant. The warehouse and the manufacturing plant are both used in the taxpayer's manufacturing business.
b. Assume the same facts as in part a, except that the warehouse was held as an investment and rented out to businesses. The manufacturing plant will also be rented out to a manufacturing business.
c. An office building used in a trade or business was condemned. The proceeds from the condemnation were used to buy an apartment complex that will be used as an investment activity.
d. The insurance proceeds from the destruction of a construction crane were used to buy a fleet of fork lifts. The crane and the fork lifts are used in the taxpayer's construction business.
e. An antique vase was stolen from the lobby of a business. The insurance proceeds were used to buy a painting, which was hung in the same lobby.

44. Which of the following are qualified replacement properties for properties involuntarily converted? Explain.

 a. The city of Marble River announces plans to condemn Heima's rental apartment complex on July 2, 1996. On August 7, 1996, Heima purchases a warehouse to use as a rental. The city pays Heima $890,000 on November 1, 1996, as the condemnation proceedings come to a close.

 b. The city of Marble River also announces plans to condemn Heima's principal residence on July 2, 1996. He receives a check for $150,000 on the November 1, 1996, condemnation closing date. On March 29, 1998, Heima purchases a new residence.

 c. Lila uses the insurance proceeds from the destruction of her commercial fishing boat by Hurricane Fredd to buy new fishing equipment and nets for her other fishing boat.

 d. Milo uses the insurance proceeds from a fire that totally destroyed his warehouse near the pier to buy 100% of the common stock of Storage Space Corporation, a company that owns and operates 3 warehouse facilities.

45. A fire in the factory of Franny's Famous Frankfurters destroyed several stuffing machines. The machines had an adjusted basis of $146,000 and a fair market value of $180,000. Franny's insurance company reimbursed Franny's $144,000 for the destruction of the machines. Franny's used the insurance proceeds to buy some secondhand stuffers costing $120,000. What are Franny's realized and recognized gains (losses) on the fire and the basis in the replacement stuffers?

46. Grant Industries' warehouse is condemned by the city on August 18, 1996. Because of widespread publicity leading up to the condemnation, Grant anticipates the condemnation and purchases a replacement warehouse on April 15, 1996, for $670,000. The city pays Grant $430,000 for the condemned property, which had an adjusted basis to Grant of $220,000.

 a. What is Grant's realized gain (loss) on the condemnation?

 b. What is the minimum amount of gain Grant must recognize on the condemnation?

 c. If Grant elects to recognize the minimum amount of gain on the condemnation, what is the basis in the new warehouse?

47. Refer to the facts of problem 46. Write a letter to Grant Industries explaining why it might want to recognize the entire gain on the condemnation.

48. One of Reddy's Fancy Dog Food factories was destroyed by a tornado. The factory had an adjusted basis of $450,000. Reddy's received $600,000 from its insurance company to cover the loss. What is the minimum amount of gain that must be recognized in each of the following situations and the basis of any property purchased with the insurance proceeds?

 a. Reddy's decided that the lost production could be made up by its other factories and used the proceeds to pay a cash dividend to its shareholders.

 b. Reddy's purchased another factory for $650,000.

 c. Reddy's purchased another factory for $500,000.

 d. Reddy's purchased another factory for $400,000.

49. A fire totally destroys a manufacturing plant owned by Ansel Corporation in 1996. The plant, located in Louisiana, had been used for more than 30 years and was fully depreciated at the date of the fire. Ansel's insurance pays $500,000 for the destruction. In analyzing qualified replacement properties, Ansel is able to buy a qualified replacement manufacturing plant for $460,000 in Oklahoma. What is the minimum amount of gain Ansel must recognize on the insurance proceeds? What is the basis of the Oklahoma manufacturing plant? Explain.

50. MacKenzie owns a boat rental business. During the current year, a tidal wave swept through the harbor where MacKenzie kept her boats anchored. Four boats were totally destroyed by the tidal wave, but the rest of the rental fleet escaped serious damage. MacKenzie replaced the 4 boats within 6 months of the tidal wave. Details on each boat destroyed and the cost of its replacement are as follows:

Boat	Insurance Proceeds	Adjusted Basis	Replacement Cost
Sailboat	$ 46,000	$21,000	$ 42,000
Yacht	$124,000	$88,000	$140,000
Speedboat	$ 67,000	$78,000	$ 80,000
Fishing boat	$123,000	$96,000	$ 92,000

   a. What is the realized gain (loss) on each of the boats?
   b. What is the minimum amount of gain or loss that must be recognized on each of the boats?
   c. Assuming that MacKenzie elects to recognize the minimum amount of gain or loss on each boat, what is the basis of each replacement boat?

51. Alley's automobile dealership, which had an adjusted basis of $400,000, is destroyed by a hurricane in 1996. Alley's receives $600,000 from its insurance company to cover the loss. Alley's has begun to rebuild the dealership at an estimated cost of $750,000. Assume that the rebuilding costs at least $750,000.
   a. What is the minimum gain Alley's must recognize on the hurricane damage?
   b. Alley's is organized as a corporation. Because of the slump in the automobile industry, Alley's has net operating losses totaling $400,000 that it is carrying forward from the previous 5 years. Alley's expects to have another operating loss in 1996. Write a letter to Alley's explaining how to account for the involuntary conversion results and why you advise taking those measures.

52. Aretha sold her house for $180,000. Aretha paid commissions of $8,000 and incurred $3,000 in valid fixing-up expenses readying the house for sale. Aretha had purchased the house for $65,000 and made capital improvements costing $15,000 on the house before the sale date. How much gain must Aretha recognize in each of the following cases?
   a. Aretha moved to Brazil and did not buy another residence, preferring to move from town to town and live with the locals in each town.
   b. Aretha bought a new residence costing $212,000. What is Aretha's basis in the new residence?
   c. Aretha bought a new residence costing $135,000. What is Aretha's basis in the new residence?
   d. Aretha bought a condominium for $72,000 that she used as her residence. What is Aretha's basis in the condominium?

53. In each of the following principal residence sale and replacements, determine the amount of realized gain (loss), the recognized gain (loss), and the basis of the replacement property:

Case	Selling Price	Selling Expenses	Fixing-up Expenses	Adjusted Basis	New Residence Cost
A	$ 40,000	$ 2,200	$ 300	$ 43,000	$ 50,000
B	170,000	15,000	1,300	62,000	190,000
C	95,000	6,000	1,000	45,000	76,000
D	220,000	19,000	3,000	185,000	138,000
E	80,000	4,000	500	27,000	-0-

54. In each of the following cases, determine the amount of realized gain (loss), the recognized gain (loss), and the basis of any property acquired:

   a. Cheryl sold her house for $73,000. She paid $4,000 in commissions on the sale and had $1,000 of valid fixing-up expenses. Cheryl had paid $83,000 for the house 4 years earlier. She bought another house costing $78,000.

   b. Alexandra was transferred to San Diego by her employer. She sold the house she had lived in for 1 year for $62,000 and paid selling expenses of $3,000. The house had cost Alexandra $55,000. Alexandra used the proceeds of the sale to purchase a sailboat for $57,000. The sailboat was fully equipped, and Alexandra lived in the sailboat after moving to San Diego.

   c. Oswald sold his principal residence for $320,000 and paid selling expenses of $20,000 on the sale. Oswald had purchased the house for $80,000. Oswald used the proceeds from the sale to purchase a cooperative apartment to live in and a cabin at the lake that he used on weekends. The apartment cost $200,000, and the cabin cost $180,000.

   d. Ushi is transferred by her employer to North Carolina in March 1996. Ushi is unable to sell her home in Texas (which had a basis of $113,000) before moving to North Carolina. She rents out the Texas house on a 6-month rental contract, figuring that she can sell it within that period. In July 1996, she purchases a new residence in North Carolina at a cost of $137,000. The Texas property has not sold at the end of the 6-month lease, and she continues to rent it out on a month-to-month basis. The Texas house finally sells in November 1997 for $132,000. Ushi pays $10,000 in expenses relating to the sale.

55. After trying to sell his house for several years, Randy traded the house for a condominium owned by Dorr Real Estate. As part of the exchange, Randy agreed to give Dorr Real Estate 400 shares of Peat Pollyperk common stock that had a fair market value of $10,000 (Randy had paid $3,000 for the stock 4 years earlier). Randy's basis in the house was $72,000. Condominiums in the same complex as Randy's had been selling for $90,000. What are the tax effects of the trade for Randy? Explain. What are the tax effects of the trade for Dorr Real Estate? Explain.

56. The city of Stillcreek decided to expand the runway at the local airport. To get the land for the expansion, it condemned the property it needed and paid the owners the current appraised value. Buster's house was condemned, and he was paid $80,000 for his property. Buster had purchased the property for $70,000 and had made $30,000 in improvements to the property. Buster used the proceeds to purchase a new residence for $85,000.

   a. What is Buster's realized gain (loss) on the condemnation of his residence?

   b. How much of the realized gain (loss) must Buster recognize?

   c. What is the basis of the new residence?

57. Manuel and Rita sold their home for $196,000, incurring selling expenses of $13,000. They had purchased the residence for $16,000 and had made capital improvements totaling $20,000 during the 20 years they lived in the house. They moved to Texas and purchased a mobile home for $62,000.

   a. Assuming that both Manuel and Rita are younger than 55 at the date of the sale, what are the tax consequences of the sale?

   b. How would your answer to part a change if Manuel is 62 and Rita is 49?

58. Mai, 58, is a single taxpayer and an attorney with Khang, Armstong, and Associates. During the current year, she sells her residence in the suburbs for $300,000. Just before the sale, Mai spent $5,000 for painting, new wallpaper, and cleaning. Realtors' commissions, attorney fees, and filing fees to complete the sale total $12,000. She bought the house twelve years ago for $60,000.

   Mai buys a new downtown condominium for $152,000 a few weeks after she sells her suburban residence.

   a. What is the amount of Mai's recognized gain (loss) on the sale if she does not make the special election to exclude a portion of the gain?

   b. What is the amount of Mai's recognized gain (loss) on the sale if she makes the special election to exclude a portion of the gain?

59. Joe was divorced from Estelle several years ago. As part of the divorce agreement, Joe received the house that he and Estelle had purchased for $30,000 in the early years of their marriage. Joe retired this year and wants to sell his house and buy a cabin in Colorado to live out his golden years. A real estate appraiser told Joe that his house would probably sell for $260,000, net of commissions and other closing costs. Joe has his eye on a cabin in his favorite area of Colorado that is listed for sale at $114,000. Joe would like some advice on the tax consequences of the sale of his house and the purchase of the cabin. Write a letter to Joe with your advice.

60. Five years ago, Ace owned 2 fine racehorses—OntheInside and AtthePost. These horses were born and raised on Ace's horse farm. Thus, his $2,000 tax basis for each horse was quite low compared with their market value. Because of his compulsive gambling, Ace was forced to trade the horses for more conservative business property.

COMPREHENSIVE
PROBLEM

In the trade, Ace received $150,000-worth of heavy equipment for use in his new earth-moving business. Shortly after the trade, Ace decided the business was too dirty for him. Thus, Ace traded the heavy equipment on which he had deducted $10,000 in depreciation for 4 single-family homes to be held for rental purposes.

The homes, with a combined value of $350,000, were taken subject to a $200,000 mortgage. After paying off the mortgage and deducting $15,000 in depreciation on the homes, Ace traded them for a 25-unit apartment building worth $750,000.

When the building burned down the day after the trade, the insurance company paid Ace $740,000. Ace used $5,000 of the proceeds to buy back OntheInside and AtthePost, because he loved the old hay burners. He used the remaining $735,000 to buy a farm to go back into the horse-breeding business.

a. How much gain did Ace realize and how much must he recognize when he traded the horses for the equipment? What is his basis in the equipment?

b. How much gain did Ace realize and how much must he recognize when he traded the equipment for the 4 single-family homes? What is his basis in the houses?

c. How much gain did Ace realize and how much must he recognize when he traded the 4 single-family homes for the apartment building? What is his basis in the apartment building?

d. How much gain did Ace realize and how much must he recognize when the apartment building was involuntary converted and was replaced with the farm land and racehorses?

e. What are the bases in the farm land and horses?

61. Glenda, 34 and single, has lived for 5 years in a house with an adjusted basis of $85,000. In May 1996, she decides to move so that her daughter can attend school in a different school district. She lists her house with a Realtor for $140,000. In July 1996, Glenda purchases a new residence for $200,000 and moves in.

Six months later, she lowers the asking price for the old house to $120,000. Six months after that, Glenda drops the price to $105,000. Finally, after living in the new house for 20 months and becoming frustrated that her old house has not sold, Glenda considers moving back to her former residence. Her Realtor tells her the new house will sell fairly easily. Advise Glenda on the tax consequences of her choices.

62. In October 1996, fire completely destroys the principal residence of Olaf, who is 66, single, and lives in Bemidji, Minnesota. Olaf owned the home for 16 years; his adjusted basis is $58,000. Olaf receives insurance proceeds of $200,000.

Olaf plans to move to Scottsdale, Arizona, no later than 1999 to be near his daughter. That is the year she is scheduled to finish her five-year tour of duty with the U.S. Foreign Service and is planning to return to her home in Scottsdale. Olaf also owns a condominium at Hilton Head, South Carolina. He paid $120,000 for the apartment in February 1995. Olaf has never used the one-time election to exclude gain on the sale of a personal residence. Write a letter to Olaf advising him on his options and their tax consequences.

63. In 1992, Joe and Jill sold their principal residence for $250,000. Their adjusted basis in the property was $136,000. Because both were older than 55 at the date of the sale, they elected to exclude $125,000 from their realized gain. To complete the sale, Joe and Jill had to take back a second mortgage for $20,000. The buyers borrowed $205,000 from a local bank and put down $25,000 in cash.

In 1996, Joe and Jill are notified that the buyers have defaulted on the second mortgage and filed for bankruptcy. A large manufacturing plant near the house has closed, and the housing market is overstocked; the value of the house has dropped significantly—below the amount remaining on the bank's mortgage. Joe and Jill want to deduct the loss on the second mortgage. The IRS Hot Line adviser tells them the loss is not recognizable, because they have no basis in the mortgage debt. Joe and Jill never reported as income the payments they received on the second mortgage. Advise Joe and Jill on the deductibility of the defaulted mortgage.

TAX PLANNING CASES

64. Outdoor Amusements Center is a sole proprietorship owned by Adrian. The center's facilities include a go-cart track, miniature golf course, and 10 trampolines. In July, a tornado destroyed all the trampolines. Miraculously, the go-cart and miniature golf facilities sustained no significant damage in the tornado.

Adrian had bought the trampolines two years earlier for $35,000. The trampolines were insured, and Adrian received a check for $35,000 from her insurance company in early August. By early September, all the trampolines had been replaced at a cost of $40,000.

a. Does Adrian have to recognize any gain because of the tornado damage to the trampolines? Explain. NOTE: The trampolines are 7-year MACRS property. Adrian has always deducted the maximum depreciation possible on the trampolines.

b. Adrian owns some stock in GoGoKarts, Inc. She paid $20,000 for the stock several years earlier. Because of the sluggishness of the economy and a recent rise in oil prices, the stock is worth only $5,000. Her broker has recommended that she sell the stock and realize the tax savings from the loss. However, Adrian is hesitant to sell, because she believes that GoGoKarts will eventually rebound. She would like to know the tax advantages she would realize in the current year from such a sale and how the trampoline casualty could affect those advantages. Assuming that she has no other gains from property transactions during the year, should she sell the stock? Write a memorandum to Adrian explaining your suggestion.

65. Thelma owns and operates a fishing boat charter service on Santa Catalina Island. While vacationing in the northeastern part of the United States, Thelma met Doug and his sister Lara, owners of DL Enterprises. DL owns two fishing boat charter services. One is in Portsmouth, New Hampshire, and one is in Newport, Oregon. Doug would like to relocate one of the businesses to a warmer climate. So, Thelma, Doug, and Lara decide to trade businesses. Thelma will relocate to Newport, and Doug will move to Santa Catalina. Lara will remain in Portsmouth and operate that business. Doug insists that Thelma sign a covenant not to compete for 5 years. The following are the assets involved in the exchange:

	FMV	
	Thelma	Doug/Lara
Boats	$500,000	$550,000
Equipment	60,000	20,000
Covenant not to compete	40,000	

Also, Doug and Lara pay Thelma $30,000 in cash. Thelma's adjusted bases are $325,000 for the boats and $70,000 for the equipment. Write a letter to Thelma advising her on the income tax consequences of the proposed exchange. Include any alternatives that may produce better tax results.

66. You are a staff accountant in the tax department of Coopers & Marwick, CPAs. While discussing some tax-planning matters with one of your office's biggest (in total billings) and best clients, McDonald Krump, you learn that he sold his personal residence in 1994. He replaced the residence (estate) shortly thereafter. During your conversations, Krump mentioned he "took a bath" on the sale of the former residence but will eventually recoup his loss through use of tax deferral provisions. Because you are an expert on real estate matters, your curiosity is getting the best of you in regard to Krump's sale and subsequent purchase. Therefore, after hours you snoop through copies of Krump's 1994 tax returns and working papers. You find the following in regard to the sale of his residence:

Amount realized	$2,200,000
Adjused basis	2,600,000
Loss realized	$ (400,000)
Cost of replacement	$3,300,000
Plus deferred loss	400,000
Basis of replacement residence	$3,700,000

The working papers were approved and initialed by Jacob Deerborn, the senior tax partner in your office. Deerborn also signed the form as the "paid preparer" representing your firm. Coincidently, Deerborn, Krump, and your father belong to the same country club and play at least one round of golf together weekly. What are your obligations under the Statements on Responsibilities in Tax Practice? Discuss your obligations.

Appendix to Chapter 13

Selected SIC Product Classes

3711 Motor Vehicles and Passenger Car Bodies

Ambulances
Amphibian motor vehicles, except tanks
Assembling complete automobiles
Automobiles
Bodies, passenger automobile
Brooms, powered
Car bodies
Cars, armored
Cars, electric: for highway use
Chassis, motor vehicle
Fire department vehicles
Flushers, street
Hearses
Mobile lounges
Motor buses, except trackless trolley
Motor homes, self-contained
Motor trucks, except off-highway
Motor vehicles, including amphibian
Patrol wagons
Personnel carriers, for highway use
Road oilers
Snowplows
Station wagons
Street sprinklers and sweepers
Taxicabs
Tractors, truck: for highway use
Universal carriers, military

3531 Construction Machinery and Equipment

Aerial work platforms
Aggregate spreaders
Asphalt plants
Automobile wrecker hoists
Backfillers, self-propelled
Backhoes
Ballast distributors
Batching plants, bituminous
Batching plants, for aggregate concrete
Blades for graders, scrapers, dozers, and snowplows
Breakers, paving
Buckets, excavating: clamshell, concrete, dragline, drag scraper, shovel
Bulldozers, construction
Cabs, construction machinery
Capstans, ship
Carriers, crane
Chip spreaders, self-propelled
Chippers, commercial: brush, limb, and log
Concrete buggies, powered
Concrete grouting equipment
Concrete gunning equipment
Concrete plants
Construction machinery, except mining
Cranes, construction
Cranes, except industrial plant
Crushers, mineral: portable
Derricks, except oil and gas field
Distributors (construction machinery)
Ditchers, ladder
Dozers, tractor mounted: material moving
Draglines, powered
Drags, road (construction and road maintenance equipment)
Dredging machinery
Excavators: e.g., cable, clamshell, crane, derrick, dragline, power shovel
Extractors, piling
Finishers and spreaders, construction
Finishers, concrete and bituminous
Grader attachments, elevating
Graders, road (construction
machinery)
Grapples: rock, wood, etc.
Grinders, stone: portable
Hammer mills (rock and ore crushing machines), portable
Hammers, pile driving
Line markers, self-propelled
Locomotive cranes
Log splitters
Logging equipment
Mixers: e.g., concrete, ore, sand, slag, plaster, mortar, bituminous
Mortar mixers
Mud jacks
Pavers
Pile-driving equipment
Planers, bituminous
Plaster mixers
Plows, construction: excavating and grading
Post hole diggers, powered
Power cranes, draglines, and shovels
Pulverizers, stone: portable
Railway track equipment: e.g.,

rail layers, ballast distributors
Rakes, land clearing: mechanical
Road construction and maintenance machinery
Rock crushing machinery, portable
Rollers, road
Rollers, sheepsfoot and vibratory
Sand mixers
Scarifiers, road
Scrapers, construction
Screeds and screeding machines
Screeners, portable
Ship cranes and derricks

Shovel loaders
Shovels, power
Silos, cement (batch plant)
Slag mixers
Snowplow attachments
Soil compactors: vibratory
Spreaders and finishers, construction
Subgraders, construction equipment
Subsoiler attachments, tractor-mounted
Surfacers, concrete grinding

Tampers, powered
Tamping equipment, rail
Teeth, bucket and scarifier
Tractors, construction
Tractors, crawler
Tractors, tracklaying
Trenching machines
Trucks, off-highway
Vibrators for concrete construction
Wellpoint systems
Winches, all types
Work platforms, elevated

2451 Mobile Homes

Buildings, mobile: commercial use
Mobile buildings for commercial use (e.g., offices, banks)

Mobile classrooms
Mobile dwellings
Mobile homes, except recreational

3589 Service Industry Machinery, Not Elsewhere Classified

Cafeteria food warming equipment
Carpet sweepers, except household electric vacuum sweepers
Carwashing machinery, including coin-operated
Cookers, steam: restaurant type
Cooking equipment, commercial
Corn popping machines, commercial
Dirt sweeping units, industrial
Dishwashing machines, commercial
Floor sanding, washing, and

polishing machines: commercial type
Food warming equipment, commercial
Fryers, commercial
Garbage disposers, commercial
Janitors' carts
Mop wringers
Ovens, cafeteria food warming: portable
Ovens, microwave (cooking equipment): commercial
Pressure cookers, steam: commercial
Sanding machines, floor

Scrubbing machines
Servicing machines, coin-operated: except drycleaning and laundry
Sewage treatment equipment
Sewer processing equipment
Sewer cleaning equipment, power
Sludge processing equipment
Vacuum cleaners and sweepers, electric industrial and commercial
Water purification equipment
Water type conditioners
Water filters and softeners
Water treatment equipment

3546 Power-Driven Handtools

Buffing machines, hand: electric
Cartridge-activated hand power tools
Caulking hammers
Chain saws, portable
Chipping hammers, electric
Drills, hand: electric
Flexible shaft metalworking machines, portable

Grinders, pneumatic and electric: portable (metalworking machinery)
Grinders, snagging
Guns, pneumatic: chip removal
Hammers: portable electric and pneumatic: e.g., chipping, riveting, caulking
Handtools, power-driven:

woodworking or metalworking
Masonry and concrete drilling tools, power: portable
Powder-actuated hand tools
Riveting hammers
Sanders, hand: electric
Saws, portable hand held: power-driven—woodworking or metalworking.

3537 Industrial Trucks, Tractors, Trailers, and Stackers

Adapters for multiweapon rack loading on aircraft
Aircraft engine cradles
Aircraft loading hoists
Boat cradles
Bomb lifts
Bomb trucks
Cabs for industrial trucks and tractors
Cars, industrial: except automotive cars and trucks and mining cars
Containers, air cargo: metal
Cranes, mobile industrial truck
Die and strip handlers
Docks, loading: portable,
Dollie (hand or power trucks), industrial: except mining
Drum cradles

Engine stands and racks, metal
Forklift trucks
Hoists, aircraft loading
Hoppers, end dump
Hospital dollies
Industrial truck cranes
Industrial trucks and tractors
Laundry containers on wheels
Lift trucks, industrial: fork, platform, straddle, etc.
Mobile straddle carriers
Pallet assemblies for landing mats
Pallet loaders and unloaders
Palletizers and depalletizers
Pallets, metal
Platforms, cargo: metal
Ramps, aircraft—loading
Ramps, loading: portable, adjustable, and hydraulic

Skid boxes, metal
Skids, metal
Stackers, power (industrial truck stackers)
Stacking carts
Stacking machines, automatic
Stands, ground servicing aircraft
Straddle carriers, mobile
Tables, lift: hydraulic
Tractors, industrial: for use in plants, depots, docks, and terminals
Truck trailers for use in plants, depots, docks, and terminals
Trucks, industrial (except mining): for freight, baggage, etc.
Tunnell kiln cars

3523 Farm Machinery and Equipment

Agricultural implements and machinery
Ammonia applicators and attachments (agricultural machinery)
Bale throwers
Balers, farm: e.g., hay, straw, cotton
Barn cleaners
Barn stanchions and standards
Blowers and cutters, ensilage
Blowers, forage
Brooders
Cabs, agricultural machinery
Calf savers (farm equipment)
Cattle feeding, handling, and watering equipment
Cattle oilers (farm equipment)
Chicken brooders
Cleaning machines for fruits, grains, and vegetables: farm
Combines (harvester-threshers)
Conveyors, farm (agricultural machinery)
Corn pickers and shellers, farm
Corrals, portable
Cotton picker and stripper harvesting machinery

Cream separators, farm
Crop driers, farm
Crushers, feed (agricultural machinery)
Cultivators, agricultural field and row crop
Cutters, ensilage
Dairy equipment, farm
Drags (agricultural equipment)
Driers: grain, hay, and seed (agricultural implements)
Dusters, mechanical: agricultural
Elevators, farm
Farm machinery and equipment
Feed grinders, crushers, and mixers (agricultural machinery)
Feeders, chicken
Fertilizing machinery, farm
Field type rotary tillers (agricultural machinery)
Fruit, vegetables, berry, and grape harvesting machines
Gates, holding (farm equipment)
Grading, cleaning, and sorting machines: fruit, grain, and vegetable
Grain drills, including legume

planters (agricultural machinery)
Grain stackers
Greens mowing equipment
Grounds mowing equipment
Hair clippers for animal use, hand and electric
Hammer and roughage mills (agricultural machinery)
Harrows: disc, spring, and tine
Harvesting machines
Haying machines: mowers, rakes, loaders, stackers, balers, presses
Hog feeding, handling, and watering equipment
Hulling machinery, agricultural
Incubators, except laboratory and infant
Irrigation equipment, self-propelled
Land rollers and levelers (agricultural machinery)
Listers
Loaders, farm type (general utility)
Milking machines
Mowers and mower-conditioners, hay

Peanut combines, diggers, packers, and threshers (agricultural equipment)
Planting machines, agricultural
Plows, agricultural: disc, moldboard, chisel, etc.
Potato diggers, harvesters, and planters
Poultry brooders, feeders, and waterers
Poultry vision control devices
Presses and balers, farm: hay, cotton,
Rakes, hay
Rotary hoes
Roughage mills

Seeders (agricultural machinery)
Separators, grain and berry: farm
Shears, sheep: power
Shellers, nut
Shredders (agricultural machinery)
Silo fillers (agricultural machinery)
Soil pulverizers and packers (agricultural machinery)
Sorting machines for agricultural products
Sprayers, hand: agricultural
Spraying machines (agricultural machinery)

Spreaders, fertilizer
Tractors, wheel: farm type
Trailers and wagons, farm
Transplanters
Turf equipment, commercial
Vine pullers
Volume guns (irrigation equipment)
Water troughs
Weeding machines, farm
Windmills for pumping water (agricultural machinery)
Tobacco curers
Windrowers (agricultural machinery)

3553 Woodworking Machinery

Bandsaws, woodworking
Box making machines for wooden boxes
Cabinet makers' machinery
Furniture makers' machinery (woodworking)
Jointers (woodworking machines)
Lathes, wood turning: including accessories
Mortisers (woodworking machines)
Pattern makers' machinery (woodworking)

Planers, woodworking
Planing mill machinery
Presses, woodworking: particleboard, hardboard, medium density fiberboard (MDF), and plywood
Sanding machines, except portable floor sanders (woodworking machinery)
Sawmill machines
Saws, power: bench and table (woodworking machinery), except portable

Scarifing machines (woodworking machinery)
Shapers, woodworking machinery
Surfacers (woodworking machines)
Tenoners (woodworking machines)
Veneer mill machines
Venetian blind machines (woodworking machinery)
Woodworking machines

TAX CONSIDERATIONS

CHAPTER 14
OTHER FACTORS AFFECTING TAX LIABILITY

CHAPTER 15
TAX RESEARCH

Other Factors Affecting Tax Liability

▲ CHAPTER LEARNING OBJECTIVES

■ Discuss taxpayer's selection of an accounting period and the restrictions on accounting periods imposed on partnerships and S corporations.

■ Explain the restrictions placed on the use of the cash method of accounting.

■ Expand on the tax treatment of long-term contracts to include the lookback method computation that must be done at the completion of the contract and the exemption from the percentage-of-completed-contract method of accounting for long-term contracts.

■ Explain basic tax accounting for inventories, including using the lower of cost-or-market method of valuation and the election to use the last in, first out inventory flow assumption.

■ Discuss the use of tax credits to achieve various policy goals.

■ Provide an overview of the tax credits available to businesses and the income tax rules applicable to several of the most commonly encountered business tax credits.

■ Discuss the use of tax credits for individuals and explain the provisions of the individual tax credits.

■ Present an overview of the alternative minimum tax system and its purpose in the income tax system.

■ Discuss the general computation of the alternative minimum tax and provide an overview of the income tax items that affect the calculation of the tax.

▲ CONCEPT REVIEW ▲

Ability to pay   A tax should be based on the amount that the taxpayer can afford to pay, relative to other taxpayers.

Accounting method   A taxpayer must adopt an accounting method that clearly reflects income.

Administrative convenience   Those items for which the cost of compliance would exceed the revenue generated are not taxed.

Annual accounting period   All entities must report the results of their operations on an annual basis (the tax year). Each tax year stands on its own, apart from other tax years.

Conduit entity   An entity for which the tax attributes flow through to its owners for tax purposes.

Entity   All items of income, deductions, and so on are traced to the tax unit responsible for the item.

Legislative grace   Any tax relief provided is the result of a specific act of Congress that must be strictly applied and interpreted. All income received is taxable unless a specific provision can be found in the tax law that excludes the income from taxation. Deductions must be approached with the philosophy that nothing is deductible unless a provision in the tax law allows the deduction.

INTRODUCTION

In addition to the income and deduction items discussed throughout the text, other factors affect the determination of a taxpayer's tax liability. The selection of a tax entity's annual accounting period and its accounting method can have a significant effect on the amount and timing of the entity's taxable income. Special methods of accounting for the treatment of individual items, such as long-term contracts and inventories, have similar income effects. Tax credits, which are given for engaging in certain specified types of transactions and activities, may significantly reduce a taxpayer's liability. Finally, all taxpayers must pay a defined minimum amount of tax on their income. This minimum amount is called the *alternative minimum tax.*

This chapter discusses each of these additional factors that could affect the tax liability. The purpose of the chapter is not to provide an in-depth discussion of all the other relevant factors in calculating the tax liability. Rather, it is designed to acquaint the reader with various aspects that have the greatest potential for affecting the tax liability.

ACCOUNTING PERIODS

The annual accounting period concept requires all tax entities to report the results of their operations on an annual basis. The period for which an entity reports is referred to as the **taxable year.** A taxable year may be either a calendar year (ending on December 31) or a fiscal year.[1] A **fiscal year** is defined as

1. A period of 12 months ending on the last day of any month other than December.
    or

2. A 52- to 53-week taxable year. The 52- to 53-week fiscal year ends on the same day of the same week each year. The year must end either the last time a particular day occurs during the month (e.g., the last Wednesday in October) or the day that occurs closest to the end of a particular month (e.g., the Friday closest to March 31, even if that Friday happens to be April 2).

The primary rationale for allowing taxpayers to select fiscal taxable years is to make the closing of the books and preparation of the tax return of the taxpayer easier and more cost efficient. That is, many businesses have both peak and slow periods. By allowing them the flexibility to close their books and prepare their returns after the end of peak seasons, businesses are able to comply with the tax law in a more timely and efficient manner. In addition, the fiscal year provision gives the government an element of administrative convenience. By spreading the filing of returns out over other periods, the government is able to process and audit returns with fewer personnel than would be required if all tax entities filed their returns on the basis of a calendar year.

▲ **EXAMPLE 1**   Rondo Corporation manufactures toys. Its peak sales season revolves around Christmas sales. Rondo's production facilities operate at full capacity from April through June to satisfy Christmas sales demand. The production facilities are shut down in July and August each year for maintenance. From September through March, the production facilities operate at 30% to 60% of capacity, depending on demand.

Discussion: By selecting a fiscal year ending July 31 or August 31, Rondo can more efficiently close its books and prepare its tax returns. During this time, there is no production to account for and the record-keeping staff has more time to make the entries necessary to close the books and compile the information necessary to prepare its tax return.

▲ **EXAMPLE 2**   Roland, a CPA, is busy preparing tax returns from December through April. From May through the middle of November, Roland and his staff have several not-for-profit audits that keep them busy. From November 15 through December 15, business is slack. Can Roland elect a fiscal year ending November 15 to report his income?

Discussion: A fiscal year must end either on the last day of any month other than December or on the same day of the same week each year. Thus, Roland could not elect a fiscal year ending November 15. Roland does have several options for meeting his needs. First, he could elect a fiscal year ending on November 30. This would allow him some slack time to close his books and prepare his tax return. A second option would be to elect a 52- to 53-week year. Under this option, he could elect to close his books on the last Friday of November. This would be past his busy season and allow him a few more days to close his books and prepare his return than the November 30 fiscal year.

A taxable entity establishes a taxable year by keeping its books on the basis of that year and filing its first tax return based on that taxable year.[2] This requires the entity to formally close its books on that date and file a timely tax return for the selected tax year. If the entity does not close its books on that date or if it does not keep formal books, it must use a calendar year. In addition, if the entity closes its books on a date that does not qualify as a fiscal year (e.g., November 15), it must use a calendar year for tax purposes. Because of the record-keeping requirement, most individuals (who do not keep formal books) use calendar years.

▲ **EXAMPLE 3**   Maldonado Corporation begins operations during 1996. It would like to use a fiscal year ending on July 31 to report its income. What must Maldonado do to establish a July 31 fiscal year?

Discussion: To establish a July 31 fiscal year, Maldonado must keep its books on the basis of a July 31 fiscal year and file its first tax return on that basis. This requires Maldonado to close its books on July 31, 1996, and file its first tax return on the 1996 results up to July 31.

Under the entity concept, each tax entity is responsible for reporting its own results to the government. This concept is extended to the selection of the taxable year by not allowing the books of one entity to establish the taxable year of another entity.

▲ **EXAMPLE 4**   Fred and Dalena are equal partners in Golf Millionaires, Inc. The partnership keeps its books on the basis of a fiscal year ending March 31 and reports its results to the government on that basis. Fred and Dalena receive the bulk of their income from Golf Millionaires and therefore do not keep separate books. Can Fred and Dalena elect to use a March 31 fiscal year?

Discussion: Fred and Dalena may not use the books of their partnership to establish their individual tax years. Under the entity concept, each tax entity is considered separate and apart from other entities. Because Fred and Dalena do not keep individual books, they must use a calendar year to report their income. NOTE: As discussed later, Golf Millionaires may not be eligible to use a March 31 fiscal year.

Taxpayers are generally free to choose which accounting period they will use as their taxable year. However, the tax law limits the choices of several types of entities.

Limitations on Choice of Taxable Year

Without any restrictions on the selection of a taxable year, owners of conduit entities could obtain a tax deferral benefit by having the entity select a taxable year different from that of the owners'.

▲ **EXAMPLE 5**   Return to the facts of example 4. If Golf Millionaires is allowed to use a March 31 fiscal year while its 2 owners use a calendar year, Fred and Dalena will effectively be allowed a 9-month deferral on the reporting of their income from Golf Millionaires. This happens because income from a conduit entity is deemed to be earned on the last day of the entity's tax year. Because Fred and Dalena would receive their income from Golf Millionaires on March 31, they would not report it on their individual returns until December 31, resulting in a 9-month deferral of income.

Because of this potential deferral, in 1986 Congress enacted a set of rules that limits the choice of taxable years for partnerships and S corporations. In addition, trusts are required to use a calendar year.

Partnership Limitations.   The selection of a partnership tax year is done on a hierarchical basis that attempts to match the tax years of the partnership to the partners'.[3] First, the partnership must use the same tax year as that used by those partners having a majority interest (more than 50 percent), called the **majority-interest tax year,** in partnership profits and capital.

▲ **EXAMPLE 6**   Carla, Ted, and Don are partners in the CTD Partnership. Carla owns 60% of CTD. Ted and Don each own 20% of CTD. Carla, Ted, and Don all use calendar years. What taxable year must CTD use?

Discussion: Because more than 50% of the partnership interests use a calendar year, CTD must also use a calendar year. Note that the effect of this rule is to have the partnership's year-end match the year-ends of the majority of the partners'.

▲ **EXAMPLE 7**   Assume that in example 6 Carla established a January 31 fiscal year. What taxable year must CTD use?

Discussion: Because Carla owns more than 50% of CTD, CTD must use the same fiscal year as Carla, January 31. As in example 6, the effect of this rule is to match 60% of the partnership's profits to Carla's taxable year, with only 40% subject to deferral.

If the majority-interest partners do not have the same tax year, the partnership must use the tax year of its principal partners, referred to as the **principal partner tax year.** A principal partner is a partner with at least a 5-percent interest.[4]

▲ **EXAMPLE 8**   Conrad Limited Partnership is owned by 20 limited partners each of which has a 4% interest in the partnership profits and capital. Hal is the general partner and owns 10% of the partnership. The remaining 10% is owned by Morgan Corporation. Both Hal and Morgan have fiscal years that end on July 31. The tax years of the 20 limited partners are diverse; there is no majority-interest tax year. What tax year must Conrad Limited use?

Discussion: Because there is no majority-interest tax year, the partnership must use the tax year of the principal partners. In this case, none of the limited partners qualifies as principal partner, because each owns less than a 5% interest in the partnership. Hal and Morgan Corporation are the only principal partners. Because the 2 principal partners have the same tax year, the partnership must use that tax year—a fiscal year ending July 31.

When the principal partners do not have the same tax year, the partnership must use the tax year that results in the least aggregate deferral of income of the partners.[5] Because the purpose of the partnership limitations is to effect the least amount of deferral, under this rule a partnership will always use the tax year of at least one of the partners (i.e., at least one partner gets no deferral). The deferral of each partner for each tax year possible is determined by the number of months that fall between the end of the partnership's tax year and the end of the partner's tax year. The aggregate deferral is determined by adding the products of the number of months of deferral for each partner multiplied by each partner's ownership interest. The tax year that produces the shortest deferral is the **least aggregate deferral tax year.**

▲ **EXAMPLE 9**   Tiger and Tetra are equal partners in Tetra Tigers Tinkers (TTT). Tiger uses the calendar year. Tetra has a fiscal year ending November 30. What tax year must TTT use?

Discussion: Because TTT can meet neither the majority-interest rule nor the principal partner rule, it must determine its taxable year by using the least aggregate deferral method. The 2 options are the fiscal years of the 2 partners, December 31 and November 30. The aggregate deferral is counted as the number of months from the end of the partnership year multiplied by the ownership percentage for each partner. These are then added to obtain the total deferral:

Using December 31 Year-End	
Tiger (0 months × 50%)	-0-
Tetra (11 months × 50%)	5.5
Total deferral	5.5

Using November 30 Year-End	
Tiger (1 month × 50%)	0.5
Tetra (0 months × 50%)	-0-
Total deferral	0.5

The use of a November 30 year-end by TTT will result in the least aggregate deferral of income to the partners.

A partnership can use a taxable year other than that prescribed by the hierarchical rules if it can establish to the IRS's satisfaction that a valid business purpose exists for having a different tax year.[6] To establish a **business purpose tax year,** the partnership must obtain permission from the IRS to use the particular tax year. To obtain IRS approval, the partnership must establish that the year selected does not create for either the partnership or its partners significant deferral of income or shifting of deductions. The type of business purpose tax year granted most frequently is the natural business year. The natural business year test (discussed in the next section) also applies to S corporations.

S Corporation Limitations.   In general, an S corporation must use a calendar year.[7] However, it can choose an alternate year under the ownership tax year or the natural business year exceptions. An **ownership tax year** is the tax year of more than 50 percent of the owners of the corporation.[8] Thus, the ownership tax year is similar in concept to the majority-interest tax year of a partnership.

> ▲ **EXAMPLE 10**   Ragweed Corporation is an S corporation that is equally owned by Arthur, Bake, and Charlene. Arthur uses a calendar year. Bake and Charlene use a fiscal year ending March 31. What is the ownership tax year?
>
> *Discussion:*   Bake and Charlene have the same tax year and own more than 50% of the corporation. Therefore, the ownership tax year is Bake and Charlene's tax year— the fiscal year ending March 31. Ragweed can use either a calendar year or a fiscal year ending March 31.

A **natural business year** is defined as "the annual accounting period encompassing all related income and expenses."[9] In order to establish a natural business year, an S corporation (or a partnership) must have peak and off-peak business periods. The natural business year is the end of the peak business period. The natural business year recognizes that the income and expenses of some businesses are reflected more accurately when the books are closed at the end of the peak season. In addition, businesses with peak and off-peak periods can more easily and efficiently close their books and prepare their tax returns at the end of their busiest seasons.

> ▲ **EXAMPLE 11**   Atkins Department Store is an S corporation. The bulk of Atkins's business occurs during the Christmas season and through January, dealing with returns and exchanges of merchandise. During the rest of the year, business is relatively slow. What is Atkins's natural business year?
>
> *Discussion:*   Based on the facts presented, Atkins's peak season ends by the end of January. Therefore, Atkins's natural business year would be a fiscal year ending January 31. This tax year would allow Atkins to close its books and prepare its returns at the beginning of its off-peak season. Note also that by closing the books on January 31, returns and exchanges from the busiest sales period will be reflected in the income for that tax year, providing a more accurate reflection of annual income.

A mechanical test is used to determine a natural business year.[10] Under this test, an annual accounting period qualifies as a natural business year if the gross receipts from sales or services for the final two months of the current year and each of the two preceding years equal or exceed 25 percent of the gross receipts for the entire 12-month period.

> ▲ **EXAMPLE 12**   Rocco's Rebels is a manufacturer of toys. Rocco's heaviest sales period occurs during August and September when retailers are stocking their shelves for Christmas. Gross sales for August and September and the 12-month periods ending on September 30 of the current year and each of the 2 preceding years are as follows:

	Aug. & Sept.	12-Month Period
Current year	$35,000	$125,000
Preceding year 1	$31,250	$120,000
Preceding year 2	$25,000	$100,000

Does September 30 qualify as a natural business year under the gross receipts test?

Discussion: In order to qualify under the gross receipts test, the gross receipts for the last 2 months of the fiscal year (August and September) must equal or exceed 25% of the current year's and the 2 preceding years'. Here is the calculation of the gross receipts percentage for the 3 applicable periods:

Current year $35,000 ÷ $125,000 = 28%

Preceding year 1 $31,250 ÷ $120,000 = 26%

Preceding year 2 $25,000 ÷ $100,000 = 25%

Because the gross receipts for August and September for the current and 2 preceding years equal or exceed 25% in each of those years, September 30 qualifies as a natural business year.

ACCOUNTING METHODS

Taxpayers are required to maintain the accounting records necessary to enable them to file their annual tax returns. In order to properly characterize income and deduction items, taxpayers must select an accounting method. An **accounting method** is defined as the method or system by which taxpayers determine the amount of their income, gains, losses, deductions, and credits, as well as the proper time to recognize these items. As such, the tax law recognizes two distinct types of accounting methods: (1) **overall accounting methods,** which refer to the general accounting method adopted by taxpayers in keeping their books, and (2) **individual accounting treatments,** which are the individual treatments of specific items when the tax law provides the taxpayer with options for the treatment of an item. The three acceptable overall methods are the cash method, the accrual method, and the hybrid method. Depreciation methods, accounting for inventories, installment sales accounting, and accounting for long-term contracts are all examples of individual accounting treatments.

In selecting an overall method of accounting, taxpayers are required to use for taxable income computation the method of accounting that they regularly use for their books. The method must be used consistently from period to period and must clearly reflect the income of the taxpayer. The commissioner of the Internal Revenue Service has the authority to reject the use of any method that does not clearly reflect the income of the taxpayer.[11] Once adopted, an accounting method must be used consistently from one tax period to the next. Taxpayers wishing to change their methods of accounting must generally obtain prior approval from the IRS. When such consent is granted, the taxpayer must make transitional adjustments to income for the change as prescribed in the tax law.[12] The purpose of the transitional adjustments is to prevent the taxpayer from getting a tax advantage (e.g., getting a double deduction or never having to recognize an item of income because of differences in the two methods) by changing accounting method. In general, the required adjustments spread the effect of making the change in method out over several tax years.

We have already discussed the general operation of the overall accounting methods and applications of the methods to income and deductions. This text also has covered operation of the MACRS depreciation system and its options, as well as the general calculations required in accounting for installment sales and long-term contracts. The sections that follow present and discuss restrictions on the use of the cash method by certain taxpayers and additional information on how to account for long-term contracts. This chapter also introduces and discusses the general rules applicable to accounting for inventories.

Restrictions on Use of the Cash Method

As with accounting periods, taxpayers generally have a significant degree of latitude in selecting their accounting method. However, certain provisions restrict the choice for certain types of taxpayers. For example, the basic requirement that a taxpayer keep books on the basis of the method selected limits most individuals to using the cash method; most people do not keep the records necessary to compute taxable income on the accrual basis. Another basic restriction imposed on taxpayers who have inventories of goods is that they must use the accrual basis to account for sales and cost of goods sold. This requires taxpayers with inventories to select either the accrual or hybrid method to compute their taxable income. In addition, three types of entities must use the accrual method:

- Corporations
- Partnerships that have at least one partner that is a regular corporation
- Any tax shelter activity[13]

For purposes of these restrictions, any method that accounts for some but not all items on the cash basis (i.e., the hybrid method) is considered a cash method. Therefore, these three types of entities cannot use the hybrid method of accounting. The restriction on corporations is designed to prevent a corporation from manipulating its cash receipt-and-disbursement policies to obtain a tax advantage. The partnership restriction is a logical extension of the corporate restriction to prevent using a partnership to defer taxes through the cash method. Similarly, tax shelter activities (as defined in the tax law) are not allowed to use the cash method to increase losses by manipulating income and expense items.[14]

The restrictions on corporations and partnerships are somewhat mitigated by two exceptions. First, corporations and partnerships in which a corporation is a partner may still elect to use the cash method (if they are otherwise eligible to do so) if its average annual gross receipts for the previous three years are $5 million or less. This provision makes the exception somewhat useless for corporations. That is, corporations eligible to use the cash method cannot have inventories. In order to have sales in excess of $5 million, it is likely that the corporation would be engaged in the sale of inventories and be required to use the accrual method under the general rule for inventories. Because it is rare (perhaps impossible) for a large number of corporations that do not have inventories to have sales in excess of $5 million, the exception that provides the choice of methods is negated.

▲ **EXAMPLE 13**   For 3 years, Jackamani Corporation has had average annual sales of $3,600,000. What accounting methods may Jackamani select if Jackamani is in the financial consulting business and does not have inventories?

Discussion: Because Jackamani's average annual gross receipts for the previous 3 years are less than $5,000,000, Jackamani is exempted from the restriction on accounting methods that applies to corporations. In addition, because Jackamani does not have inventories, it is not required to use the accrual method. Therefore, Jackamani can use either the cash method or the accrual method.

▲ **EXAMPLE 14**　Assume the same facts as in example 13, except that Jackamani is a manufacturer of tack for racehorses.

Discussion:　Although Jackamani meets the $5,000,000 average annual sales exception, it must use the accrual method because it has inventories. NOTE: Jackamani may also elect to use the hybrid method and use the accrual method only to account for sales and cost of goods sold.

▲ **EXAMPLE 15**　Assume the same facts as in example 13, except that Jackamani has average annual gross sales of $7,000,000. In addition, Jackamani is an S corporation. What accounting methods may Jackamani select?

Discussion:　Because Jackamani is an S corporation, the corporation exception does not apply. In addition, Jackamani does not have inventories and therefore may elect to use either the cash method or the accrual method.

A second exception allows a corporation or a partnership with a corporate partner that is engaged in farming to use the cash method, regardless of the amount of its gross receipts. However, if the corporation is also engaged in a separate nonfarming business, it must account for that portion of its business by using the accrual method, unless one of the other exceptions applies. A farming business includes the raising and/or harvesting of crops and livestock, the operation of a nursery or sod farm, and the raising and harvesting of trees bearing fruit, nuts, or other crops, or ornamental trees. A farming business does not include the processing of commodities or products beyond the activities normally incident to the growing, raising, or harvesting of the products.[15]

▲ **EXAMPLE 16**　Kumquat Korporation (KK) owns a large grove of kumquat trees. When the kumquats are ready for harvest, the corporation picks, washes, inspects, and packages the kumquats for distribution. Can KK use the cash method of accounting?

Discussion:　Picking, washing, inspecting, and packaging the kumquats all are activities incidental to the raising of the fruit. Therefore, KK may use the cash method to account for its activities.

▲ **EXAMPLE 17**　Assume the same facts as in example 16, except that KK also uses some kumquats to make preserves, which it sells to fruit wholesalers. Can KK use the cash method of accounting?

Discussion:　The preserve-making operation is not incident to the raising of the fruit. Because it involves inventories, KK must use the accrual method to account for the preserve-making operation. However, KK can still elect to account for its farming operation using the cash method.

Long-Term Construction Contracts

Taxpayers are generally required to account for long-term construction contracts using the percentage-of-completed-contract method.[16] A long-term construction contract is any contract for the manufacture, building, installation, or construction of property that is not completed within the tax year in which the contract is entered into. Under the **percentage-of-completed-contract method,** income from long-term contracts is recognized during each period according to the degree of completion of the project during that period. The degree of completion must be based on estimated costs rather than the degree of the project's physical completion. The formula for determining each year's gross income recognition is

$$\frac{\text{Contract}}{\text{price}} \times \frac{\text{Actual costs incurred during the year}}{\text{Total estimated contract costs}} = \frac{\text{Gross}}{\text{income}}$$

The purpose of requiring the percentage of completed contract method is to ensure that the accounting by taxpayers entering into long-term contracts clearly reflects income. Before 1986, taxpayers had the option of recognizing income under the completed contract method. Under this method, all income and related costs were deferred until the tax year in which the project was completed. As Exhibit 14–1 illustrates, using this method could result in significant time value of money savings. In Exhibit 14–1, note that although Ace Construction Co. recognizes the same amount of income and pays the same amount of tax on the contract over the two-year period, deferring the payment of $113,750 in taxes from 1996 to 1997 under the completed contract method results in a time value of money savings of $10,351 when discounted at 10%. Although this does not appear to be large in relation to the size of this particular contract, when projects are spread out over periods of three to five years, the savings can be significant.

The Lookback Method. Because the percentage-of-completed-contract method uses the taxpayer's estimated total contract costs to determine each period's income recognition, the taxpayer could underpay the tax due each period by inflating the estimated contract costs. To remove the incentive to overestimate

---

▲ **Exhibit 14–1**

COMPARISON OF PERCENTAGE-OF-COMPLETED-CONTRACT AND COMPLETED CONTRACT METHODS

Basic Facts: Early in 1996, Ace Construction Co. enters into a contract to build a bridge for Logan County. The contract price is $2,500,000. Ace estimates its total costs of constructing the bridge to be $2,000,000. In 1996, Ace incurs $1,300,000 in costs. The bridge is completed in 1997 with Ace incurring additional costs of $700,000. Ace is in the 35% marginal tax rate bracket.

Recognition of Gross Profit from Contract

		Percentage-of-Completed-Contract Method	Completed Contract Method
1996	$2,500,000 $\times \dfrac{\$1,300,000}{\$2,000,000}$ − $1,300,000	$325,000	$ -0-
1997	$2,500,000 $\times \dfrac{\$\ 700,000}{\$2,000,000}$ − $700,000	$175,000	
	$2,500,000 − ($1,300,000 + $700,000)		$500,000
Total income recognized		$500,000	$500,000

Income Taxes Paid

		Percentage-of-Completed-Contract Method	Completed Contract Method
1996	$325,000 × 35%	$113,750	$ -0-
1997	$175,000 × 35%	61,250	
	$500,000 × 35%		175,000
Total taxes paid		$175,000	$175,000

Time Value of Money Savings at 10%

$113,750 − ($113,750 × 0.909) = $10,351

costs, upon completion of the contract the taxpayer must use the **lookback method** to determine whether each year's taxes have been under- or overpaid according to the actual total costs of the contract. If the taxpayer has underpaid (i.e., costs were overestimated), the taxpayer must pay interest on the income deferred by the underpayment. Conversely, if an overpayment has been made, the taxpayer receives interest on the overpayment.

The purpose of the lookback method is to compensate for any deferral or acceleration of income that results from using estimated costs rather than actual costs in applying the percentage-of-completed-contract method. This is accomplished by charging the taxpayer interest on any underpayment or paying the taxpayer interest on any overpayment of tax because of differences in actual and estimated costs. Thus, any time value of money savings that a taxpayer could obtain by underestimating costs during the life of the contract is offset by the interest charge on the resulting underpayment.

Calculating the interest due (receivable) under the lookback method has three basic steps:

1. At the completion of a contract, recalculate the tax due for each year of the contract using the actual contract costs.

2. Compute the difference between the actual amount paid for each period and the amounts calculated in step 1.

3. Calculate the interest charge for each amount calculated in step 2 from the end of the period being calculated to the end of the period of completion, using the applicable federal interest rate. The amount of interest payable (due) is equal to the sum of the individual period interest charges.[17]

▲ **EXAMPLE 18**   Assume the same facts as in Exhibit 14–1, except that the costs incurred in 1997 to complete the contract were only $500,000. The actual total cost of the project was only $1,800,000 (not the $2,000,000 originally estimated). In 1996, Ace would compute the income to be recognized using the estimated $2,000,000 cost, recognize gross profit of $325,000 on the contract, and pay a tax of $113,750 on the income reported. How much interest must Ace pay in 1997 under the lookback method if the interest rate is 6%?

Discussion: Under the lookback method, Ace must recompute the 1996 tax using the $1,800,000 in actual costs. This results in a gross profit of $505,556 and a tax based on actual costs of $176,945:

Step 1—Recalculate 1996 Gross Profit

$$\$2,500,000 \times \frac{\$1,300,000}{\$1,800,000} - \$1,300,000 = \$505,556$$

Step 2—Tax on Recomputed Gross Profit

$$\$505,556 \times 35\% = \$176,945$$

The third step requires Ace to pay interest at 6% on the $63,195 ($176,945 − $113,750) underpayment of tax that resulted from the use of the $2,000,000 estimate in 1996. This results in an interest payment of $3,792 ($63,195 × 6%).

If a taxpayer underestimates the total contract costs, the gross profit recognized in the years before completion will be overstated, and an overpayment of tax will occur. In this case, the taxpayer is entitled to a refund of interest on the overpaid tax. It should also be noted that the lookback method is a hypothetical calculation of the tax that would have been paid during the period of the contract, not an actual recalculation in the sense that the taxpayer must file an amended return for each year. Under the annual accounting period concept, each tax year is deemed to stand on its own, apart from other tax years. Thus, the interest paid (due) under the lookback method is reported in the period in which the contract is completed.

The lookback method is generally applicable to all contracts that must be accounted for with the percentage-of-completed-contract method. However, two exceptions to the use of the lookback method apply to small contracts. The lookback method does not apply to

1. Home construction contracts
    or
2. Any contract completed within two years of the commencement of the contract, if the gross contract price does not exceed
    a. $1 million
        or
    b. 1 percent of the average annual gross receipts for the three tax years preceding the tax year of completion

The intention of these exceptions is to exclude those contracts from the lookback method for which only a small amount of interest would be payable (due). In addition, exempting small contracts from the lookback rule adds an element of administrative convenience for both taxpayers and the government in the calculation of the amounts payable (due) under the method.

Taxpayers Exempt from Percentage-of-Completed-Contract Method. Three categories of contracts are exempted from using the percentage-of-completed-contract method. Contracts that can be accounted for using the completed contract method must meet one of the following tests:

■ Home construction contract—Eighty percent or more of the estimated cost of the contract must be attributable either to a dwelling unit or to improvements to real property related to a dwelling unit and located on the same site as a dwelling unit.

■ Two-year test—Any contract that, at the time of commencement of the contract, is estimated to be completed within two years.

■ Gross receipts test—Any contract entered into by a taxpayer whose average annual gross receipts for the preceding three tax years are less than $10 million.

As with the exceptions to the lookback rule, the intent of these exceptions is to allow taxpayers who would not obtain a significant deferral from using the percentage-of-completed-contract method to use the administratively simple completed contract method.

Accounting for Inventories

When inventories are an income-producing factor, the entity must use the accrual method to account for cost of goods sold.[18] Inventories include goods held for resale, as well as inventories of raw materials and supplies that will become part of the merchandise produced by a manufacturer. The inventory method selected by a taxpayer must conform to the best accounting practices in the taxpayer's trade or business, and it must clearly reflect income. The best accounting practices in a trade or business are synonymous with generally accepted accounting practices. In most cases, tax accounting and financial accounting for inventories are similar. However, the commissioner of the IRS has the authority to determine whether an inventory method clearly reflects income, and conflicts often arise.

> ▲ **EXAMPLE 19**   Thor Corporation is a manufacturer of power tools. During the current year, it wrote down the cost of obsolete parts. The parts were kept on hand, and the selling price of the parts was not reduced. The practice is generally acceptable in Thor's trade or business. Can Thor write down the parts for tax purposes?
>
> *Discussion:* The tax law allows obsolete or slow-moving inventory to be written down only if the selling price of the inventory is reduced. Although Thor's write-down conformed to generally accepted accounting principles, the commissioner of the IRS determined that the write-down did not clearly reflect income, because Thor did not reduce the selling price of the obsolete parts. The Supreme Court ruled in favor of the commissioner, and Thor was not allowed to write down the obsolete parts for tax purposes.[19]

Example 19 illustrates that generally accepted accounting principles may be used in accounting for inventory only when the tax law does not specify the treatment or when the tax law allows alternative treatments.

Exhibit 14–2 provides the formula for calculating costs of goods sold. As you can see, the taxpayer must determine inventories at the beginning and end of the year and must record purchases of goods during the year. A manufacturer must also keep inventories of raw materials, supplies, and work in process to determine the cost of goods manufactured during the tax year. Taxpayers have several options in determining the cost of inventory items. Inventories may be valued either at cost or at the lower of cost-or-market value. In order to determine the cost of items on hand at the end of the period, an inventory flow assumption must be adopted. Taxpayers are generally required to use the first-in, first-out (FIFO) assumption, although they could elect to use either the average cost method or last-in, first-out (LIFO) inventory valuation.

Determining Inventory Cost.   The cost of inventories and purchases must be determined. In the case of purchased inventory, cost is equal to the invoice price of the merchandise, less trade discounts, plus freight, and other transportation costs. Manufacturers must use the **full absorption costing method** to determine inventory cost. Under this method, all direct costs (direct materials and direct labor), as well as overhead costs, must be included in the cost of goods manufactured.

As of 1986, manufacturers and certain retailers and wholesalers are required to determine the cost of their inventories using the uniform capitalization rules.[20] Retailers and wholesalers with average annual gross revenue of less than $10

▲ **Exhibit 14–2**

COST-OF-GOODS-SOLD CALCULATION

Acne Retailers sells widgets that it purchases from various manufacturers. At the beginning of 1996, Acne has $22,000-worth of widgets on hand. During the year, Acne purchases widgets costing $94,000. At the end of 1996, Acne has $17,000-worth of widgets in its inventory. What is Acne's 1996 cost of goods sold?	
Beginning inventory	$ 22,000
Add: Purchases of inventory	94,000
Goods available for sale	$116,000
Less: Ending inventory	(17,000)
Equals: Cost of goods sold	$ 99,000

million are exempt from these rules. In addition, farmers and ranchers who elect to use the cash method are not required to maintain inventories and thus are exempt.

The **uniform capitalization (unicap) rules** require a "reasonable allocation" of all direct and indirect costs to the cost of inventory. Indirect costs include all costs other than selling and general and administrative costs that are not related to production (e.g., general accounting salaries). Thus, many costs that are normally expensed for financial accounting purposes, such as storage costs, purchasing agents' salaries, and general and administrative costs that benefit production, must be allocated to the cost of inventory. Exhibit 14–3 provides a list of costs that must be capitalized under the unicap rules.

The imposition of the unicap rules has created an administrative nightmare for businesses. Because these rules do not conform to generally accepted accounting principles, firms are forced to keep two sets of inventory records to comply with the rules. In addition, the unicap rules further complicate the calculation of deferred taxes for financial accounting purposes. These are significant costs, which raises the question of whether the additional tax revenue generated under the unicap rules significantly exceeds the cost of implementing the rules.

LOWER OF COST-OR-MARKET VALUATION.   Taxpayers may elect to use the lower of cost-or-market valuation to determine inventory values.[21] *Cost* refers to the amount determined under the cost method using the unicap rules. *Market for purchased merchandise* means the bid price for the particular inventory item in the volume in which it is normally purchased by the taxpayer. For manufactured goods, market is the total reproduction cost at current bid prices.

The **lower of cost-or-market method** requires a comparison of cost and market for each inventory item. Comparison of the total cost and total market value of nonsimiliar inventory items is not permitted.

▲ **EXAMPLE 20**   Ward Manufacturing produces 4 different products. The cost and market value at the end of Ward's tax year for each of the products is provided. What is Ward's inventory value if it elects to use the lower of cost-or-market method?

Product	Cost	Market
A	$14,000	$15,000
B	8,000	3,000
C	23,000	21,000
D	12,000	5,000

Cost	Treatment
Direct materials	Capitalize
Direct labor	Capitalize
Indirect materials (consumed in production operation)	Capitalize
Indirect labor (worked in production process, but not directly on product)	Capitalize
Storage, handling, and insurance on materials or merchandise	Capitalize
Fringe benefits for direct and indirect labor	Capitalize
Pension costs for direct and indirect labor	Capitalize
Depreciation on production facilities	Capitalize
Property taxes, insurance, maintenance, etc. on production facilities	Capitalize
Interest paid related to production facilities	Capitalize
Mixed service costs (personnel costs, data processing, purchasing)	Allocated

▲ **Exhibit 14–3**

TREATMENT OF COSTS UNDER UNIFORM CAPITALIZATION RULES

Discussion: Ward must take the lower of cost or market for each of the 4 individual inventory items. The lower value for each inventory item is added to obtain the total inventory value. This results in a total inventory value of $43,000. Ward cannot compare the total cost of the 4 products with the total market value to compute the lower of cost or market.

Product	Cost	Market	Lower of Cost-or-Market Value
A	$14,000	$15,000	$14,000
B	8,000	3,000	3,000
C	23,000	21,000	21,000
D	12,000	5,000	5,000
Total	$57,000	$44,000	$43,000

Inventory Flow Assumptions. Merchandise that can be readily identified with specific invoices or production records is valued by reference to the invoice or production records. This type of valuation is referred to as the *specific identification method* and is used by dealers in large or unique items (e.g., automobile and heavy equipment dealers, antique store owners). However, such specific identification procedures are not economically feasible for businesses that have many units of a particular product that are not easily identifiable with specific invoices or production records. In such cases, an inventory flow assumption must be made. An inventory flow assumption prescribes the order in which goods in inventory are assumed to be sold. The FIFO method is generally required for tax purposes. However, taxpayers may elect to use either the average cost method or the LIFO method. The application of these flow assumptions follows those used in financial accounting.

▲ **EXAMPLE 21** Maynard Corporation's inventory records for the current year for its designer hairbrushes disclose the following:

Date	Units Purchased	Cost per Unit	Total Cost
Beginning Inventory	200	$3	$ 600
February 13	400	$5	2,000
July 24	600	$6	3,600
November 18	300	$7	2,100
Totals	1,500		$8,300

A physical count of the hairbrushes at the end of the year shows that Maynard has 250 on hand. What is Maynard's ending inventory value using the average cost, FIFO, and LIFO methods?

Discussion: Maynard's ending inventory value under each assumption is calculated as follows:

Average Cost Method:
Average cost per unit = Total cost ÷ Total units available
= $8,300   ÷ 1,500 = $ 5.53 per unit
Multiplied by ending inventory units   × 250
Equals ending inventory value $1,383

FIFO Method

Under the FIFO method, the first units in inventory are assumed to be sold first. The 250 units on hand at the end of the year are the last 250 units purchased. The 300 units purchased on November 18 cost $7 per unit. Under a FIFO flow assumption, the ending inventory value would be $1,750 (250 × $7).

LIFO Method

The LIFO method assumes that the last units purchased are the first units sold. The 250 units on hand at the end of the year are the first 250 units purchased. The ending inventory under LIFO is composed of the 200 units of beginning inventory and 50 of the units purchased on February 13. This gives an inventory value of $850:

Beginning inventory (200 × $3)	$600
February 13 purchase (50 × $5)	250
LIFO inventory cost	$850

Taxpayers have considerable leeway in selecting which inventory flow assumption to use for tax purposes. However, in order to use the average cost method, the taxpayer must be able to show that it is applicable to all goods in its inventory, not to just one particular line of inventory. This requires the taxpayer to use average cost on all inventory items, not just a select few. Because the LIFO flow assumption usually results in a larger cost of goods sold (with less taxable income) than the other methods, it is subject to several limitations.

Electing LIFO.   A taxpayer wishing to switch to LIFO must file an application with the IRS for the tax year in which the change is to be made. The LIFO application must specify the precise inventories of the taxpayer to which the method is to be applied.[22] Approval is automatic. However, once elected, a taxpayer cannot switch to another inventory method without the written consent of the commissioner of the IRS.

LIFO is deemed to be a cost-based method of inventory valuation. Taxpayers cannot use the lower of cost-or-market valuation method in tandem with a LIFO assumption. If a taxpayer who has been using the lower of cost-or-market method makes a LIFO election, any previous write-downs to the beginning inventory (the previous year's ending inventory) for the year of change must be added to income to restore the inventory to a cost basis.

▲ **EXAMPLE 22**   Roger Corporation elects to use the LIFO inventory method beginning in 1996. Roger's ending inventory for 1995 is valued at $23,000 using the lower of cost-or-market method. The cost of the 1995 ending inventory is $26,000. What is the effect of the change to LIFO on Roger's 1996 taxable income?

Discussion: Because LIFO is a cost-based method, Roger must restore the $3,000 ($26,000 − $23,000) lower of cost-or-market write-down to the 1996 beginning inventory. If this higher inventory figure had been used to compute 1995 cost of goods, cost of goods sold would have been $3,000 less, and taxable income would have increased by the $3,000 write-down. Therefore, in converting the 1996 beginning inventory to a cost basis, Roger must add the $3,000 1995 write-down to its 1996 income.

A final requirement for the use of LIFO for tax purposes is that the taxpayer must also use it for financial reporting purposes. This is known as the *financial conformity rule.*[23] This rule prevents taxpayers from using the LIFO advantage for tax purposes while reporting higher income for financial reporting by using another inventory flow assumption.

INCOME TAX CREDITS

A tax credit is a direct reduction in the tax liability of the taxpayer receiving the credit. As such, tax credits are not part of the tax base used to compute the tax liability. Because they are not part of the base and reduce the tax liability dollar for dollar, tax credits are neutral with respect to the marginal tax rate of the taxpayer. That is, in contrast to tax deductions, a $100 tax credit is worth a $100 reduction in taxes to taxpayers in the 15- and 31-percent marginal tax rate brackets.

Most tax credits are nonrefundable—if the amount of the credit exceeds the tax liability, the taxpayer is not entitled to a refund of the excess. Although most business tax credits are nonrefundable, they generally provide that any amount of credit not used in the current year may be carried forward and used in future years; these are known as **nonrefundable tax credits.** Tax credits available only to individuals are not allowed this carryforward, although the earned income credit is refundable. A **refundable tax credit** means that the taxpayer is entitled to a refund of the excess credit. This is a form of negative income tax—the taxpayer not only pays no tax but receives a payment from the government that is based on the income of the taxpayer.

The neutrality of tax credits with respect to marginal tax rates allows Congress to target specific activities with the certainty that taxpayers engaging in the activity will receive the expected tax relief. Tax credits are used to

- Encourage investment in specific types of assets or engage in specific activities
- Provide equitable treatment among taxpayers
- Provide tax relief for low-income, elderly, and disabled taxpayers

As you can see, certain credits are used to encourage investment by businesses, whereas others are geared specifically to tax relief for individuals. The discussion that follows delineates those tax credits available to businesses and those targeted specifically for individuals.

Business Tax Credits

There are numerous tax credits for engaging in certain types of business activities. Congress enacted each credit for a specific purpose. Table 14–1 provides a list of business tax credits and a summary of their individual purposes. The list is quite extensive; this chaper discusses some of the more important ones.

Investment Tax Credit.   Congress has used the **investment tax credit (ITC)** since 1962 to stimulate the economy by allowing a credit for a percentage of the cost of qualifying property (generally, only personal property has been allowed the ITC). Congress has turned the ITC on and off many times since the first credit was enacted. In 1986, Congress repealed the ITC, and it is not in force today. However, history suggests that Congress will not hesitate to reinstate the credit if it feels it is necessary to get the economy moving. Because the ITC is a nonrefundable credit, some businesses may have unused ITCs that they continue to carry over and use.

Foreign Tax Credit.   Taxpayers may claim a tax credit for foreign taxes paid on foreign source income.[24] Alternatively, the taxpayer may elect to deduct the foreign taxes paid in computing taxable income.[25] In most cases, the value of the credit exceeds the value of the deduction, and taxpayers find it advantageous to use the tax credit. The purpose of the **foreign tax credit** is to alleviate the effects of double taxation on businesses that pay taxes to another country on the income

Business Tax Credit	Purpose of Credit
Investment tax credit (currently repealed)	To encourage new investment in equipment, which is a stimulant to the economy and increases employment
Foreign tax credit	To provide relief from double taxation of foreign source income
Research & experimental credit	To encourage research in new technology, which will strengthen the country's technological base
Targeted jobs credit	To encourage employers to hire unemployed workers from disadvantaged groups
Rehabilitation tax credit	To encourage the rehabilitation of older buildings and structures to preserve them for future generations
Business energy credits	To encourage energy conservation and promote the use of alternative fuels
Low-income housing credit	To encourage construction of low-income housing
Disabled access credit	To encourage small businesses to provide access for disabled people
Alcohol fuels credit	To encourage the use of fuels with an alcohol base
Oil recovery credit	To encourage domestic production of oil through use of tertiary recovery methods
Reforestation credit	To provide relief to commercial timber products businesses for replanting and seeding trees

▲ **Table 14–1**

BUSINESS TAX CREDITS & THEIR PURPOSE

earned in that country. The maximum tax credit allowed is the tax that is assessed by the United States on the foreign source income.[26] That is, taxpayers may use the foreign tax credit only to offset taxes that would have been paid to the United States on the foreign source income:

$$\text{Limit} = \frac{\text{Foreign source taxable income}}{\text{Worldwide taxable income}} \times \begin{array}{l}\text{U.S. income tax}\\\text{before tax credits}\end{array}$$

Note that the formula sets a maximum allowable credit. If the actual foreign taxes paid are less than the limit, the actual foreign tax is the amount of the allowable credit. When the foreign taxes paid exceed the limit, the unused portion can be carried back two years and forward for five years, subject to each year's individual foreign tax credit limit.

▲ **EXAMPLE 23** Geraldo Corporation engages in operations in several foreign countries as well as in the United States. During the current year, Geraldo's worldwide taxable income was $800,000. Geraldo's foreign source income was $200,000, on which it paid total foreign taxes of $30,000. What is Geraldo's allowable foreign tax credit?

Discussion: The foreign tax credit on Geraldo's foreign source income is limited to the lesser of the actual taxes paid or the limit calculated by the formula. Geraldo's U.S. tax on $800,000 in taxable income is $272,000 ($800,000 × 34%). This produces a limit of $68,000:

$$\text{Limit} = \frac{\$200,000}{\$800,000} \times \$272,000 = \$68,000$$

Because the actual taxes paid are less than the limit, Geraldo's foreign tax credit is the $30,000 in actual foreign taxes paid.

▲ **EXAMPLE 24**   Assume the same facts as in example 23, except that Geraldo paid $85,000 in foreign taxes. What is Geraldo's foreign tax credit?

Discussion: Geraldo's foreign tax credit is limited to the $68,000 calculated in example 23. The $17,000 ($85,000 − $68,000) excess may be carried back 2 years and used to offset tax paid, subject to each year's foreign tax credit limit. If the entire credit is not used in the carryback period, any unused portion may be carried forward for 5 years and used, subject to each year's individual limit on foreign taxes paid.

Research and Experimental Credit.   The purpose of the **research and experimental (R&E) tax credit** is to encourage research and development of new technologies and processes. Two separate credits are allowed. The first credit is for incremental research expenditures. The incremental credit is equal to 20 percent of the qualified research expenditures in the current year in excess of the base amount.[27]

Qualified expenditures must be technical in nature, intended to be useful in the development of a new or improved business component of the taxpayer, or be elements of a process of experimentation for a functional purpose. Obviously, this characterization of qualified expenditures leads to numerous interpretations that are beyond the scope of this text.[28] The basic point is that the credit is meant to encourage expenditures on new technology and for experimentation leading to new technology, not for fine-tuning existing processes or custom orders of a particular product.

The base amount for computing the credit is equal to the product of (1) the fixed base percentage, which is the ratio of the taxpayer's total qualified research expenses for the base period of 1984 to 1988 to its total gross receipts for the same period (limited to a maximum of 16 percent), and (2) the taxpayer's average annual gross receipts for the four previous years. The minimum base amount may not be less than 50 percent of the current year's expenditures.[29]

▲ **EXAMPLE 25**   Creator Corporation spent $400,000 on qualified research activities during the current year. Its fixed base percentage is 13%, and average annual gross receipts for the previous 4 years were $1,300,000. What is Creator's base amount for computing the incremental research credit?

Discussion: The base amount is the fixed base percentage multiplied by the average annual gross receipts for the 4 previous years. Creator's base amount for the current year is $169,000 ($1,300,000 × 13%) per this calculation. However, the minimum base amount is 50% of current-year expenditures, $200,000 ($400,000 × 50%). Therefore, for purposes of computing the incremental research credit, Creator's base amount is $200,000, the minimum amount allowable.

▲ **EXAMPLE 26**   Refer to example 25. What is Creator's current-year incremental research expenditure credit?

Discussion: The incremental research expenditure credit is equal to 20% of the excess of the current year's expenditures, minus the base amount. Creator's credit is $40,000 [20% × ($400,000 − $200,000)].

The deduction for research and experimental expenditures must be reduced by the amount of the credit.

▲ **EXAMPLE 27**   Refer to examples 25 and 26. What is Creator Corporation's allowable deduction for research and experimentation expenditures?

Discussion: The $400,000 in qualified expenditures must be reduced by the $40,000 tax credit. Therefore, Creator can deduct only $360,000 of the qualified expenditures in calculating its taxable income.

The second component of the R&E credit is the basic research credit. This credit is equal to 20 percent of qualified expenditures for research that is intended to advance scientific knowledge without a specific commercial objective. In order to qualify, two conditions must be met: The payments must be made in cash under a written agreement, and the research must be performed or controlled by a university, college, or other nonprofit scientific research organization. Amounts expended for the basic research credit cannot be used in the calculation of the incremental research credit.

Rehabilitation Tax Credit.   Although the investment tax credit provided incentive for investing in personal property (e.g., machinery and equipment), the credit was not available for the purchase of real property. Congress felt that some incentive was needed for rejuvenating inner cities and historic structures; it created two types of **rehabilitation tax credits:** a 10-percent older buildings credit and a 20-percent historic structures credit.[30] The older buildings credit applies to structures placed in service before 1936. To qualify for the historic structures credit, a building must be certified as historic by the Department of the Treasury and must be located in a registered historic district or listed on the National Register of Historic Places. Both tax credits can be taken on a building that qualifies for both credits. To avoid a double tax benefit, the basis of the building or structure must be reduced by the amount of credit taken.

In order to qualify for the 10-percent older buildings credit, the rehabilitation expenditures must be incurred to improve or rehabilitate property that is used in the taxpayer's trade or business or that is held for investment purposes. The credit for historic structures is not as restrictive—residential real estate can qualify for the historic structures credit but not for the older buildings credit. The structure must also be "substantially rehabilitated." A *substantial rehabilitation* means that the rehabilitation expenditures exceed the greater of the property's adjusted basis or $5,000. In addition, at least 75 percent of the external walls (including at least 50-percent use as external walls) and at least 75 percent of the internal structural framework must remain in place.

▲ **EXAMPLE 28**   Eskimo Joe's purchased a building in downtown Stillwater at a cost of $20,000. The building was originally placed in service in 1928. Joe's spent $50,000 to rehabilitate the building for use as a restaurant. The external walls remained in place, and only minor modifications were made to the existing internal structural framework. Do the expenditures qualify for the rehabilitation expenditure credit?

Discussion: The expenditures qualify for the 10% rehabilitation credit because the building is used in Eskimo Joe's trade or business, the property was originally placed in service before 1936, the $50,000 of rehabilitation expenditures exceed Eskimo Joe's $20,000 basis [the greater of Eskimo Joe's adjusted basis ($20,000) in the property or $5,000)], and the 75% tests for external walls and internal structural framework are met. Eskimo Joe's tax credit is $5,000 ($50,000 × 10%). Joe's adjusted basis in the building is $65,000 ($20,000 + $50,000 − $5,000).

▲ **EXAMPLE 29**   Assume the same facts as in example 28, except that the building has been certified by the Department of Treasury as a historic structure and is listed on the National Register of Historic Places. What would be the total amount of rehabilitation credits Eskimo Joe's could take on the building?

Discussion: Because the rehabilitation expenditures qualify for both the 10-percent older buildings credit and the 20-percent historic structures credit, Eskimo Joe's tax credit is $15,000 (30% × $50,000). Joe's adjusted basis in the building would be $55,000 ($20,000 + $50,000 − $15,000).

In order to retain the full benefit of the tax credit, the property must be held five full years. If a rehabilitated structure is sold before the end of the five-year period, the credit is recaptured (added to the tax liability) in proportion to the number of years (or portions thereof) the actual holding period fell short of the five-year required holding period.

▲ **EXAMPLE 30**   Assume that the building in example 28 is rehabilitated on June 4, 1996. Eskimo Joe's takes the proper credit on its 1996 tax return. On February 4, 1999, Eskimo Joe's sells the building. How much of the $5,000 rehabilitation tax credit must be recaptured in 1999?

Discussion: Eskimo Joe's has not held the building 5 full years. Eskimo Joe's must recapture the credit attributable to the portion of the 5-year holding period requirement it did not meet. In this case, the building was held for 2 years and 8 months. Therefore, Eskimo Joe's held the property for only 2 full years, leaving 3 years (2 full years plus a portion of a third) subject to recapture. Eskimo Joe's must recapture $3,000 ($5,000 × 3/5) of the credit by adding it to its 1999 tax liability.

Individual Tax Credits

In contrast to business tax credits, which are designed mainly to provide an incentive for businesses to invest in certain activities, the tax credits available for individuals are generally intended to provide tax relief to certain classes of taxpayers. Congress has favored the use of credits (rather than deductions) in these situations, because the amount of the relief is equal for taxpayers in different marginal tax brackets. In addition, because the credits are targeted for low-income taxpayers, many of whom do not itemize deductions, the use of a credit assures that these taxpayers get the intended relief. One of the credits, the earned income credit, is refundable. This allows the taxpayer to receive a refund of tax in excess of any amounts paid during the year. In effect, this feature allows the government to provide a cash subsidy to taxpayers (an effect not possible with deductions).

Table 14–2 lists the tax credits available only to individual taxpayers and the purpose of each credit. Note the brevity of the list, compared with that for busi-

▲ **Table 14–2**

INDIVIDUAL TAX CREDITS & THEIR PURPOSE

Individual Tax Credit	Purpose of Credit
Earned income credit	To provide tax relief to low-income taxpayers
Child and dependent care credit	To provide tax relief to taxpayers who incur child and dependent care expenses so that they can be employed
Tax credit for the elderly and the disabled	To provide extra tax relief to low-income taxpayers who either are elderly or retired because of a permanent and total disability
Residential mortgage interest credit (currently expired)	To increase home ownership in areas that are experiencing prolonged economic depression

nesses. One characteristic of the individual credits is that they begin to phase out (i.e., are reduced) when some measure of the taxpayer's income (e.g., earned income or adjusted gross income) reaches a predetermined level. The use of a phase-out rule gives a larger credit to lower-income taxpayers and either reduces or eliminates the credit for those with higher incomes. The earned income credit and the credit for child and dependent care illustrate the operation of individual tax credits.

Earned Income Credit.   The **earned income credit (EIC)** provides tax relief to low-income taxpayers. Unlike the other individual tax credits, the EIC is refundable. That is, even if the taxpayer has no tax liability, the taxpayer can receive a refund equal to the amount of the credit. Because the amount of credit is dependent on the taxpayer's earned income and phases out after the taxpayer's income reaches a predetermined level, married taxpayers are required to file a joint return in order to take the EIC. This prevents taxpayers from filing separate returns and obtaining a credit based only on each spouse's income. By filing a separate return, the couple would be able to receive a higher credit or in some cases qualify for the credit when their combined income would exceed the maximum allowable earned income (EI).

Another factor in determining the amount of the taxpayer's earned income credit is the number of qualifying children living in the taxpayer's home. A qualifying child must be younger than 19 (24, if a full-time student); the child, stepchild, foster child, or a descendant of the taxpayer; and reside for more than half the year with the taxpayer. To be eligible for the earned income credit, a taxpayer must meet all of the following requirements:

1. The taxpayer's principal place of abode for more than one-half of the year must be in the United States.

2. The taxpayer or the taxpayer's spouse must be older than 25 but not older than 65.

3. The taxpayer or taxpayer's spouse cannot be a dependent of another taxpayer.[31]

The general formula for calculating the earned income credit is the lesser of the following:

1. Maximum credit allowed = Earned income (EI) up to maximum allowable for the category × Credit percentage for the category.
    or

2. Maximum credit allowed − [(Greater of AGI or EI − EI/AGI phase-out income level) × Phase-out percentage for the category].

Applying the phase-out rate to the greater of the taxpayer's earned income or adjusted gross income yields two results. First, the EIC does not begin to phase out until adjusted gross income (or earned income, if greater) reaches $11,610 ($5,280 for taxpayers with no children). Second, the EIC is phased out completely when adjusted gross income (or earned income, if greater) reaches $28,495 ($9,500 for taxpayers with no children and $25,078 for taxpayers with one child) in 1996.

The 1996 credit percentages appear in the third column of Table 14–3. Multiplying the maximum earned income level in column 2 by the credit percentage

▲ Table 14–3

1996 EARNED INCOME
CREDIT

Category	Maximum Earned Income	Credit Percentage	EI/AGI Phase-out Income Level	Phase-Out Percentage	Maximum EI/AGI Income	Maximum Credit Allowed
No children	$4,220	7.65%	$ 5,280	7.65%	$ 9,500	$ 323
One child	$6,330	34.00%	$11,610	15.98%	$25,078	$2,152
More than 2 children	$8,890	40.00%	$11,610	21.06%	$28,495	$3,556

in column 3 yields the maximum credit allowed, set forth in the last column. For a taxpayer with no children, the maximum credit is $323 ($4,220 × 7.65%); for a taxpayer with one child the maximum credit is $2,152 ($6,330 × 34%); for a taxpayer with two or more children, the maximum credit is $3,556 ($8,890 × 40%). The earned income levels in Table 14–3 are indexed for inflation and increase each year. Note that if the taxpayer's income equals the maximum earned income in column 2 ($4,220 for a taxpayer with no children), the taxpayer owes no tax for the year and is due a refund of the full amount of the credit, $323.

▲ **EXAMPLE 31**   Bo and April are married and have 1 dependent child who lives in their home during the entire tax year. Bo and April have earned income of $14,000 in 1996. They have no other sources of income or deductions. What are Bo and April's income tax liability and their basic EIC for 1996?

Discussion: Bo and April's taxable income is zero, and they have no tax liability:

Gross income = Earned income = Adjusted gross income	$14,000
Less:	
Standard deduction	(6,700)
Less:	
Personal and dependency exemptions ($2,550 × 3)	(7,650)
Taxable income	$ -0-

Bo and April's Basic EIC is $1,770.

The lesser of
1. $6,330 × 34% = $2,152
   or
2. $2,152 − [($14,000 − $11,610) × 15.98% = $1,770

Although Bo and April owe no tax, they are entitled to a refund of the $1,770 EIC and any amounts withheld from their income during the year.

Because the credit is refundable, taxpayers who expect to receive the credit can fill out a form and get an advance from their employer based on an estimate of the amount of their credit. Any EIC advanced is reported as a reduction of the EIC on the taxpayer's return. The advanced EIC is limited to 60 percent of the maximum credit available for taxpayers with one child.

Child and Dependent Care Credit.   Taxpayers who pay someone to care for their child and/or other dependent so the taxpayers can work are eligible for a credit based on the amount of their expenses and their earned income level; it is known as the **child and dependent care credit.** This credit is designed to encourage taxpayers who work and have children to provide them with adequate care while they are at work. It also provides tax relief to lower-income working families who have children at home. The child and dependent care credit is a nonrefundable credit.

To qualify for the credit, two conditions must be met:

1. The taxpayer must incur employment-related expenses.
2. The expenses must be for the care of qualified individuals.

An employment-related expense is one that must be paid to enable the taxpayer to work and must be paid for either household services or for the care of a qualified individual. Generally, the expenses must be incurred within the taxpayer's home, although out-of-the-home expenses for dependents younger than 13 and for a disabled dependent or spouse (if the disabled person spends at least eight hours per day in the home) also qualify. The exception for the disabled encourages individuals to keep disabled dependents or a spouse in the home rather than institutionalize them.[32]

A qualifying individual includes any dependent younger than 13 or a dependent or a spouse of the taxpayer who is physically or mentally incapacitated.

▲ **EXAMPLE 32**   Aria is a CPA, and her husband is an auto mechanic. They employ a housekeeper who cleans the house and cooks and takes care of their 6-year-old son. Are Aria and her husband entitled to a credit for child and dependent care?

Discussion: The expenditures for the housekeeper are eligible for the credit. They allow Aria and her husband to be employed, are spent for household services, and their 6-year-old son is a qualifying individual (he is younger than 13).

▲ **EXAMPLE 33**   Assume the same facts as in example 32. Because her husband's shop is open 7 days a week, he doesn't have time to take care of their yard. They hired a lawn service to fertilize and mow the lawn. Does the cost of the lawn service qualify for the child and dependent care credit?

Discussion: The child and lawn care services do allow Aria and her husband to be employed. However, the lawn care services are not paid for either household services or for the care of a qualifying dependent. Therefore, they are not eligible costs for the credit. However, the housekeeper costs are still eligible for the credit.

▲ **EXAMPLE 34**   Julie's husband Paul was injured in an accident at work several years ago and is confined to a wheelchair. Because he is unable to take care of himself, Julie leaves Paul at a day-care center while she works. Is Julie eligible for the child and dependent care credit?

Discussion: Because her husband is disabled, Julie may leave him outside the home. She is eligible for the credit so long as Paul spends at least 8 hours per day at home.

The amount of the credit is generally 30 percent of the qualified expenditures incurred, limited to $2,400 ($4,800 with two or more qualifying individuals). The 30-percent rate is reduced by 1 percent for each $2,000 (or portion thereof) of the taxpayer's adjusted gross income in excess of $10,000. The maximum reduction is limited to 10 percent, leaving a minimum allowable credit of 20 percent. The 20-percent minimum credit limit is reached when the taxpayer's adjusted gross income exceeds $28,000.[33]

▲ **EXAMPLE 35**   Jorge is a single parent with 2 dependent children living with him. During 1996, Jorge has an adjusted gross income of $23,000 and pays $3,000 in qualified child-care expenses. Assuming that both children are younger than 13, what is Jorge's child and dependent care credit?

Discussion: Because his AGI is in excess of $10,000, Jorge must reduce the 30% general credit rate by 1% for each $2,000 (or portion thereof) of AGI in excess of $10,000. Jorge's credit is $690:

Amount of qualified child care expenses			$3,000
Basic credit rate		30%	
Reduction for excess AGI:			
Jorge's AGI	$23,000		
Less:	(10,000)		
Excess AGI	$13,000		
Divided by number of $2,000	÷ 2,000		
increments (rounded up)	7		
Reduction % per increment	× ___1%	7%	× 23%
Child care credit			$ 690

The expenditures qualifying for the credit cannot exceed the earned income of the taxpayer. For married taxpayers, the lower earned income of the two is used for the purpose of the limit. The purpose of the limit on expenditures is consistent with the purpose of the credit—to allow the taxpayer to be gainfully employed. If the expense of child care is in excess of the income earned by working, the employment does not provide a net gain to the household income.

▲ **EXAMPLE 36** Doug and Dorothy are married and have 2 dependent children younger than 13. Dorothy is an airline pilot who earns $150,000 per year. Doug is interested in art and is employed part time at an art gallery. Doug earned $3,000 at the art gallery. Qualified child-care expenses were $8,000. What is Doug and Dorothy's child and dependent care credit?

Discussion: Qualifying child-care expenditures are limited to the earned income of the lesser-paid spouse. In this case, Doug's earned income ($3,000) is less than the amount expended for child care ($8,000). Only the $3,000 is eligible for the credit. Because their AGI is in excess of $28,000, they are allowed the minimum 20% credit. This results in a child and dependent care credit of $600 ($3,000 × 20%).

THE ALTERNATIVE MINIMUM TAX

In exercising its power of legislative grace, Congress in many instances has chosen to use the tax system to encourage taxpayers to engage in various transactions it deems socially or economically desirable. This text has discussed many provisions that provide tax relief on transactions that depart from the treatment prescribed by the general concepts of taxation. As the number of such relief provisions proliferated through the years, Congress became increasingly aware that many taxpayers were carefully planning their affairs to take maximum advantage of these provisions. The result of this planning documented in various reports by the Treasury Department and academic studies showed that a large number of corporations and individuals with quite large economic incomes were paying little or no taxes.

Because Congress was hesitant to single out any one incentive by repealing its relief provisions, the politicians decided to impose an additional tax on those taxpayers who take too much advantage of a specified set of tax incentives. The set of tax incentives that became subject to this new tax is called *tax preference items.* Tax preference items are provisions in the tax law that treat certain items of income or deduction preferentially as compared with other items. In addition, in order to be considered a tax preference item, Congress must specify the item as such (i.e., all items that depart from the general concepts of taxation are not tax preference items).

In 1969, Congress enacted the first tax on preference items. This initial tax was called the *add-on minimum tax,* because the tax on preference items was paid in addition to the regular income tax liability. So as not to totally discourage taxpayers from engaging in tax preference activities, the first tax was 10 percent of tax preference items in excess of $30,000 (i.e., the first $30,000 of tax preference items was exempt from the tax). With minor adjustments, this system remained in effect until 1978. However, studies indicated that the tax was not very successful in its goal of assuring that all taxpayers paid their fair share of taxes. A new system of taxing preference items was initiated in 1978 called the **alternative minimum tax (AMT).** As its name implies, this tax is an alternative calculation of the tax liability that results in the minimum amount of tax that the taxpayer must pay. In effect, the AMT is a separate, parallel tax system. Within this system, many preference items allowed in the calculation of the regular tax liability are either not allowed or the amount of tax relief provided is greatly diminished.

There are two aspects of the AMT system that need to be pointed out before we discuss the mechanics of the system. First, using a parallel system of tax rules requires all but the smallest taxpaying units to keep a separate set of accounting records to compute the tax. Second, changes in the system in 1986, 1989, and 1993 have greatly increased the number of taxpayers who are subject to the tax. For example, the top **alternative minimum tax rate** paid by individual taxpayers has been increased to 28 percent, compared with a top marginal regular tax rate of 39.6 percent. The narrow spread between the two rates has subjected individual taxpayers with fairly minimal amounts of preference items to the tax. Thus, it has become an increasingly important aspect of individual taxation in recent years. The system is extremely complex. The discussion that follows provides an overview of the system and the effects it can have on taxpayers.

Basic AMT Computation

As a separate tax system, the AMT is calculated by applying a tax rate to a tax base.[34] The tax base is called **alternative minimum taxable income (AMTI).** Exhibit 14–4 provides the general calculation of the AMT. The starting point for the calculation of AMTI is regular taxable income, the taxable income as computed under the general tax system that has been discussed throughout the text. As shown in Exhibit 14–4, AMTI is determined by making two separate categories of

		▲ Exhibit 14–4
Regular taxable income	$XXX	Basic AMT Calculation
Add (Subtract): Adjustments	XXX	
Add: Preferences	XXX	
Add (Subtract): Net operating loss adjustment	(XXX)	
Equals: Tentative alternative minimum taxable income	$XXX	
Subtract: Applicable exemption amount	(XXX)	
Equals: Alternative minimum taxable income	$XXX	
Times: Tax rate (20% for corporations, 26% and 28% for individuals)	× XX%	
Equals: Tentative minimum tax before foreign tax credit	$XXX	
Subtract: AMT foreign tax credit	(XXX)	
Equals: Tentative minimum tax	$XXX	
Subtract: Regular tax liability	(XXX)	
Equals: Alternative minimum tax (if positive)	$XXX	

modifications to the regular taxable income. The first modification is for adjustments and the second is for preferences. *Adjustments* are generally made to items that are treated differently in the current period but that will reverse themselves in future periods. As such, adjustments may be either positive or negative (generally positive in the first period and negative in future periods as the difference in treatment reverses itself). The net operating loss adjustment has been singled out in the computation, because it must be made after considering all other adjustments and preferences. *Preferences* are items that are never allowed for AMT purposes. Because they are never allowed, they do not reverse over time and thus are always positive adjustments in calculating AMTI.

As with the first add-on minimum tax, the AMT recognizes that there should be some allowable level of preference items through the use of exemption amounts. However, these exemption amounts are phased out at varying levels of tentative AMTI, resulting in reduced (possibly no) exemption amounts for taxpayers with large amounts of tax preference items. Subtraction of the applicable exemption amount yields the tax base, AMTI. The tentative tax is calculated by applying a flat rate to AMTI. Corporate taxpayers pay an AMT rate of 20%. All other taxpayers, individuals and fiduciaries, are subject to an AMT rate of 26 percent on the first $175,000 of AMTI and 28 percent on AMTI in excess of $175,000. Multiplication of the AMTI by the AMT rate yields the tentative minimum tax amount before foreign tax credits. Foreign tax credits are the only tax credits allowed against the AMT liability. Subtraction of the allowable foreign tax credit provides what is referred to as the *tentative minimum tax liability*. It is tentative because it must be compared with the regular tax liability to determine whether the AMT is applicable. Because the AMT is the minimum amount of tax that the taxpayer must pay, if the regular tax liability is greater than the tentative minimum tax, the AMT is not applicable and the taxpayer pays the regular tax liability. On the other hand, if the tentative minimum tax is greater than the regular tax, the taxpayer is subject to the AMT. Although the full amount of the tentative AMT is paid, the tax law views the taxpayer as paying the tax in two separate components—the regular tax liability and the additional tax imposed because of the AMT. Thus, as a definition, the AMT is equal to the tentative minimum tax in excess of the regular tax liability.

▲ **EXAMPLE 37**   Nigel Corporation's regular tax liability during the current year is $650,000. Nigel's tentative alternative minimum tax is $800,000. How much AMT must Nigel pay, and what is Nigel's total tax liability?

Discussion: Because Nigel's tentative minimum tax is greater than its regular tax liability, it is subject to the AMT and must pay the $800,000 tax calculated using the AMT rules. Nigel is deemed to pay $650,000 in regular tax liability and an AMT of $150,000 ($800,000 − $650,000).

▲ **EXAMPLE 38**   Assume the same facts as in example 37, except that Nigel's regular tax liability is $900,000. How much AMT must Nigel pay, and what is Nigel's total tax liability?

Discussion: Because Nigel's regular tax liability exceeds the tentative minimum tax, Nigel must pay the $900,000 regular tax liability. No AMT is due (AMT cannot be negative). Note that the purpose of the AMT is to ensure that taxpayers pay a certain minimum amount of tax. When the regular tax liability exceeds this minimum amount, the regular tax liability is the amount that must be paid.

The remainder of the chapter discusses the individual components of the AMT calculation. Because of the great technical complexity of many of the adjustments and preferences, this book makes no attempt to present every detail of every item that affects the AMT. The purpose of the discussion is to provide a basic understanding of the approach the AMT uses to tax those taxpayers whose use of tax incentives is excessive (as defined by the AMT).

AMT Adjustments.   The purpose of the AMT adjustments is to account for the effect of items that must be determined using either alternative calculations or alternative accounting methods for AMT purposes. Many of these adjustments are extremely technical. Further complicating the AMT calculation is that not all adjustments apply to all types of taxpayers. Table 14–4 provides a brief description of the AMT adjustments by type of taxpayer affected.[35]

Adjustment Item	Brief General Description
Applicable to All Taxpayers	
Depreciation on property placed in service after 12/31/86	AMT depreciation calculated using ADS system (longer life and straight-line method).
Mining exploration & development costs	Must be amortized over 10 years for AMT purposes.
Long-term contracts	Taxpayers using completed contract method must use percentage-of-completed-contract method for AMT purposes.
Amortization of pollution control facilities	Must be amortized over a longer period for AMT.
Gains deferred on installment sales	Gains may not be deferred on installment sales for AMT purposes.
Gain/loss on properties subject to AMT rules that affect basis	Any AMT adjustments that affect the basis of property must be reflected in the gain/loss on the property when it is disposed of.
Net operating loss deduction	NOL is recalculated using AMT rules for income and deductions. NOL deduction is limited to 90% of AMTI (after all other adjustments and preferences).
Applicable to Individuals and Fiduciaries	
Limitation on deductions from AGI	Most deductions from AGI disallowed or reduced; no personal exemption or standard deduction.
Exercise of incentive stock options	Excess of fair market value over option price at date of exercise is included in AMTI.
Research and development expenditures	Amounts expensed in excess of 10-year amortization are added back.
Certain tax shelter farming activities	Losses not deductible against current period passive losses; can only deduct against future period income from farming activities.
Applicable to Corporate Taxpayers	
Adjusted current earnings	Three-fourths of the excess of adjusted current earnings (a measure based on financial accounting income) over AMTI before the ACE adjustment.

▲ **Table 14–4**

AMT ADJUSTMENT ITEMS

In general, the use of the AMT calculation or method results in either acceleration of income items or deferral of deduction items. The net effect of either is a higher taxable income in the initial period(s) of difference. However, most **alternative minimum tax adjustment** items are not disallowed for AMT purposes; they are merely spread out (in the case of deductions) or accelerated (in the case of income items), with the difference in the two calculations being temporary, not permanent. That is, the initial differences reverse themselves over time and therefore have the opposite effect on AMTI. Thus, adjustments can be either positive or negative in the calculation of AMTI. This effect is best illustrated by the depreciation adjustment, which applies to property placed in service after December 31, 1986 (i.e., property subject to the MACRS depreciation system). The AMT requires depreciation to be computed using the alternative depreciation system (discussed in Chapter 11). The ADS system uses the straight-line method and longer depreciation lives than MACRS. The use of ADS in calculating depreciation causes AMT depreciation to be lower initially. However, in later years, the ADS depreciation will exceed the MACRS depreciation, and the effect of the adjustment will reverse itself in the AMTI calculation.

▲ **EXAMPLE 39**   Ortno Corporation purchases depreciable property costing $45,000 in 1996. The property is 3-year MACRS property and has an ADS life of 5 years. What is Ortno's AMT adjustment for each of the applicable years? Assume that Ortno uses straight-line depreciation on the property for regular tax purposes.

Discussion: Ortno must add the excess of MACRS depreciation over the allowable ADS depreciation for AMT purposes. When depreciation under ADS exceeds MACRS, the difference is subtracted in computing AMTI. The adjustments for the 5-year ADS life are as follows:

Year	MACRS Depreciation	ADS Depreciation	AMT Adjustment
1996	$ 7,500	$ 4,500	$ 3,000
1997	15,000	9,000	6,000
1998	15,000	9,000	6,000
1999	7,500	9,000	(1,500)
2000	-0-	9,000	(9,000)
2001	-0-	4,500	(4,500)
Total	$45,000	$45,000	$ -0-

Note that over the 5-year ADS life, the difference between the MACRS and ADS depreciation deduction reverses itself. This is reflected in the AMT adjustment by reducing AMTI when the ADS depreciation exceeds MACRS depreciation. Thus, over the 5-year ADS life, the effect of the depreciation difference is zero.

The use of different calculation methods for AMT purposes requires the taxpayer to keep a separate set of accounting records to verify the AMT calculations. This is especially important when the calculation difference affects the basis of an asset. That is, because the methods compute adjustments to basis differently under the AMT, the asset has a different basis for AMT purposes than for regular tax purposes. When the asset is sold or otherwise disposed of, the gain or loss for regular tax purposes is different than for the AMT. This requires another adjustment to AMTI in order to reflect the difference.

▲ **EXAMPLE 40**   Refer to the property purchased by Ortno Corporation in example 39. Assume that Ortno sells the property in the year 2000 for $15,000. What is the effect of the sale on Ortno's AMTI (i.e., what adjustment must be made)?

Discussion: Because the allowable depreciation is different under the 2 systems, the basis of the property at the date of sale is also different. For regular tax purposes, the property is fully depreciated (zero basis), resulting in a gain of $15,000 on the sale. The AMT basis of the property is $9,000 [$45,000 − $36,000 (4.5 years of depreciation)], which results in an AMT gain of $6,000. The $9,000 ($15,000 − $6,000) difference in the gains is subtracted in the AMTI calculation as an adjustment. The $9,000 adjustment is the amount of gain that is included in regular taxable income that should not be included in AMTI because of the reduced depreciation deductions for AMT purposes.

The primary adjustments that are required of individual taxpayers are for deductions from adjusted gross income that are either modified or not allowed for AMT purposes. The only itemized deductions allowed from AGI for AMT purposes are

1. Medical expenses in excess of 10% of AGI (i.e., not 7.5%)

2. Charitable contributions

3. Casualty and theft losses

4. Qualified housing interest

5. Investment interest

6. Miscellaneous itemized deductions not subject to the 2 percent of AGI reduction (gambling losses and premature cessation of annuities)

Therefore, individuals must add back excess medical expenses, taxes, interest other than qualified housing and investment interest, miscellaneous itemized deductions subject to the 2-percent limitation, and personal and dependency exemption amounts deducted in arriving at taxable income. In addition, the standard deduction is not allowed and is added back by taxpayers who do not itemize. However, the 3 percent of AGI phase-out rule for itemized deductions is not applicable for AMT purposes. Therefore, the amount of any itemized deduction reduction from the phase-out rule is subtracted in the AMTI calculation.

Qualified housing interest for AMT purposes is more restrictive than the itemized deduction allowed for qualified residence interest. Interest on a qualified residence is allowed for AMT purposes only if the loan was used to acquire, construct, or substantially improve the residence. Thus, under the AMT, home equity loan interest is deductible only if the proceeds of the loan were used to improve the residence.

▲ **EXAMPLE 41**   George and Cassandra purchased a home in 1988 at a cost of $100,000. They initially borrowed $85,000 to purchase the home. In 1996, when the home was worth $125,000, they took out a home equity loan for $40,000 that they used to purchase a personal automobile. How much of the loan interest related to their residence is deductible for regular tax and for AMT purposes?

Discussion: Interest on both loans is deductible for regular tax purposes. The home equity loan only has to be secured by the principle residence and be less than $100,000 to qualify for deduction. However, the interest paid on the home equity loan is not deductible for AMT purposes, because it was not used to improve the residence. Therefore, the home equity loan interest will be added as an adjustment in the calculation of AMTI.

Two factors cause the calculation of investment interest to be redone for AMT purposes. First, any interest earned on tax-exempt securities is excluded for regular tax purposes. However, certain private activity bond interest is subject to the AMT through its inclusion as a preference item (see the discussion of preferences).

Therefore, investment income must be increased by any such interest earned by the taxpayer for AMT purposes. Second, recall from Chapter 8 that in the definition of net investment income, investment expenses are those expenses that remain after applying the 2-percent miscellaneous itemized deduction limit. In determining investment expenses for regular tax purposes, any other miscellaneous itemized deductions are taken against the 2-percent limit first. For AMT purposes, none of the other miscellaneous deductions is allowed, necessitating a recalculation of investment expenses.

▲ **EXAMPLE 42**   Vanessa has total taxable investment income of $14,000 in the current year. Vanessa also received $2,000 in private activity bond interest that is exempt from regular tax. Vanessa's investment expenses were $3,000, and she paid interest related to the investments of $15,000. Vanessa's AGI is $40,000, and she had other miscellaneous itemized deductions totaling $1,600. What is Vanessa's allowable investment interest deduction for regular tax and AMT purposes?

Discussion: Vanessa's investment interest deduction is limited to her net investment income (investment income − investment expenses). For regular tax purposes, her investment interest deduction is $11,000:

Investment income		$14,000
Less: Investment expenses		
Miscellaneous itemized deduction limit—		
2% × $40,000 =	$ 800	
Other miscellaneous itemized deductions	1,600	
Amount of limit applied to investment expenses	$ -0-	
Deductible investment expenses		(3,000)
Net investment income		$11,000

For AMT purposes, the $2,000 in private activity bond interest is taxable. Therefore, Vanessa's AMT investment income is increased to $16,000. The other miscellaneous itemized deductions are not allowed for AMT, and the $800 limit is applied to Vanessa's investment expenses, lowering them to $2,200. This results in an investment interest deduction for AMT purposes of $13,800:

Investment income ($14,000 + $2,000)		$16,000
Less: Investment expenses		
Miscellaneous itemized deduction limit	$ 800	
Investment expenses	3,000	
Deductible investment expenses		(2,200)
Net investment income		$13,800

The additional $2,800 ($13,800 − $11,000) of investment interest allowed as an AMT deduction is shown as a subtraction adjustment in the calculation of AMTI.

The final adjustment is the **AMT net operating loss deduction.** For AMT purposes, the NOL deduction must be recomputed using the AMT rules for income and deductions.

▲ **EXAMPLE 43**   Worth Corporation suffers a net operating loss of $90,000 in 1996. In calculating the loss, Worth has total net positive adjustments and credits of $20,000. What is Worth's AMT net operating loss?

Discussion: For AMT purposes, the NOL must be calculated using the adjustment and preference items. Therefore, the NOL is reduced by the $20,000 in positive adjustments and preferences to $70,000. Worth can carry the NOL back to 1993 and obtain a refund of taxes. The $90,000 loss is used against 1993's regular taxable income, and the $70,000 is used in 1993's AMT calculation in determining the amount of the refund.

A further limitation on the AMT net operating loss deduction is that it cannot exceed 90 percent of alternative minimum taxable income, computed after all other adjustments and preferences.

▲ **EXAMPLE 44**   Assume the same facts as in example 43. In 1993, Worth had a taxable income of $40,000, and its AMTI before the NOL carryback was $60,000. How much of the 1996 NOL can Worth deduct against its 1993 income for regular tax and AMT purposes?

Discussion: The $90,000 regular NOL can be fully used against the 1993 regular taxable income, reducing it to zero. The AMT net operating loss is limited to $54,000 (90% × $60,000 AMTI) in the calculation of AMTI.

Note that the different NOL rules for the 2 systems create a disparity in the amount of NOL carryforward. For regular tax purposes, Worth has an NOL carryforward to 1994 of $50,000 ($90,000 − $40,000), whereas the AMT carryforward is only $16,000 ($70,000 − $54,000). As with most of the other adjustments, this creates a separate and parallel set of carryforwards.

AMT Preferences.   Preferences are different from adjustments in two distinct ways. First, **alternative minimum tax preferences** apply to all taxpayers. There are no specific preferences for corporate and noncorporate taxpayers, as is the case with adjustments. Second, preferences are always added in the computation of AMTI. Although the preference items reflect differences in how the two systems treat such items (as is the case with adjustments), preference items either do not reverse or Congress has determined that the taxpayer should not have the benefit of any reversal. Because preference reversals are not allowed, there is no correlative adjustment to the basis of the property for AMT purposes, as is the case with adjustments. The list of preference items is much shorter than the number of adjustment items. Table 14–5 lists the preference items and provides a brief description of the AMT treatment of the item.[36]

The preference item that can have the greatest effect on individual taxpayers is the private activity bond interest tax preference. Interest paid on debt by state and local governments is excluded from gross income to enable municipalities to

Preference Item	Brief General Description
Percentage depletion in excess of basis	Percentage depletion deductions in excess of the basis of the property are disallowed.
Intangible drilling costs on oil & gas properties	Limited to 65% of the net income from each property.
Tax-exempt interest from private activity bonds	Interest is taxable for AMT purposes.
Excess depreciation on property placed in service before 1/1/1987	Depreciation in excess of straight-line is not allowed for AMT purposes.
Reserves for bad debts of financial institutions	Financial institutions must use the specific write-off method for bad debts.

▲ **Table 14–5**

AMT PREFERENCE ITEMS

raise capital at lower rates than comparable taxable debt instruments. Many municipalities have used this exclusion to float bond issues for private activities, such as the construction of industrial facilities. To attract new jobs to the community, these facilities are then leased to private businesses. The indirect effect of such arrangements is to give the private business financing at a lower rate than it could obtain by financing its own facilities. Congress reacted to this perceived inequity by disallowing the exclusion of interest on private activity bonds for AMT purposes. A **private activity bond** is one in which the proceeds are used by anyone other than a government unit. Examples of private activity bonds include industrial development bonds, mortgage subsidy bonds, and student loan bonds. Fortunately, the issuers of the bonds have the obligation to disclose to purchasers whether the bond is a private activity bond or a wholly exempt bond. However, taxpayers who purchase private activity bonds have the responsibility for properly reporting the interest earned on their returns.

AMT Exemptions.   After making all the required adjustments and adding the preference items to taxable income, the result is the tentative alternative minimum taxable income. In determining the AMTI tax base, an exemption amount is allowed as a reduction of the tentative AMTI. The exemption amount is designed to eliminate taxpayers with relatively moderate amounts of taxable income who do not have significant amounts of adjustments and/or preferences from the AMT. The exemption amount starts at a tentative amount based on the type of taxpayer and is then reduced by 25 percent of every dollar by which the tentative AMTI exceeds a specified level for each type of taxpayer. Table 14–6 provides the exemption amounts and their phase-out ranges by type of taxpayer. Note that the effect of the phase-out is to deny exemption amounts to taxpayers whose AMTI exceeds the amounts in the last column of the table.

The practical effect of the exemption is that average individual taxpayers may ignore the AMT with little risk of it applying to them. However, corporations and individuals with more substantial incomes need to be aware of what could happen when they engage in transactions that result in AMT adjustments and preferences. Because of the complexity of the AMT calculation, the aid of a tax specialist is virtually a necessity for high-income individuals.

AMT Tax Credits.   In general, the only tax credit allowed against the tentative AMT is the foreign tax credit.[37] As a result, all other tax credits (e.g., child-care credit) are lost when the AMT applies. Although the foreign tax credit is allowed

▲ Table 14–6

AMT EXEMPTION
AMOUNTS AND
PHASE-OUTS

Type of Entity	Filing Status	Initial Exemption	Phase-Out begins at AMTI of	No exemption if AMTI exceeds
Corporation	N.A.	$40,000	$150,000	$310,000
Fiduciary	N.A.	$22,500	$ 75,000	$165,000
Individual	Single and head of household	$33,750	$112,500	$247,500
Individual	Married couple filing jointly	$45,000	$150,000	$330,000
Individual	Married couple filing separately	$22,500	$ 75,000	$165,000

for AMT purposes, it is limited to 90 percent of the tentative AMT. The purpose of this limit is to prevent a taxpayer with substantial foreign source income from using the credit to completely avoid paying U.S. tax.

THE AMT CREDIT AGAINST THE REGULAR TAX.   Most adjustments made in calculating AMTI are merely timing differences. The AMT calculation for these items accelerates income for AMT purposes so that it is reported earlier than it would be for regular tax purposes. This creates a form of double jeopardy when a taxpayer is subject to the AMT in earlier years and the regular tax in later years when the timing difference reverses. That is, the accelerated income is taxed first under the AMT and again later, when the timing difference reverses for regular tax purposes.

▲ **EXAMPLE 45**   Perry Corporation uses the completed contract method to account for its home construction contracts. During the current year, Perry entered into a contract to build a home and expected $200,000 in profit. The home is 40% complete at the end of the current year and is completed in the subsequent year. Assuming that Perry has no other taxable income in each of the 2 years, what is Perry's tax liability in each year?

Discussion: Under the completed contract method, no income is recognized until the year in which the contract is completed. Therefore, Perry will have no regular taxable income in the first year and will report $200,000 in taxable income in the second year. For AMT purposes, the completed contract method is not allowed. Perry must make an adjustment in calculating AMTI to account for the profit it would have recognized using the percentage-of-completed-contract method. This will result in Perry's paying an AMT of $8,000 in the first year.

Regular taxable income	$ -0-
Add: Adjustment for completed contract method	
Amount recognized under percentage	
of completion method ($200,000 × 40%)	80,000
Less: AMT exemption	(40,000)
Equals: AMTI	$40,000
Times: Corporate AMT rate	× 20%
Equals: Tentative minimum tax	$ 8,000
Less: Regular tax liability	-0-
Equals: AMT	$ 8,000

In the second year, the entire $200,000 will be reported for regular tax purposes. The regular tax on $200,000 for a corporation is $61,250. In calculating the AMT, Perry has a negative adjustment of $80,000 [$200,000 reported for regular tax − $120,000 ($200,000 × 60%) reported using the percentage-of-completed-contract method]. The net result is that no AMT is due in the second year, and Perry pays the $61,250 in regular tax:

Regular taxable income	$200,000
Less: Adjustment for completed contract method	(80,000)
Less: AMT exemption	(40,000)
Equals: AMTI	$ 80,000
Times: Corporate AMT rate	× 20%
Equals: Tentative minimum tax	$ 16,000
Less: Regular tax liability	(61,250)
Equals: AMT	$ -0-

The result of the reversal of income recognition on the contract is to tax the $80,000 recognized for AMT purposes in the first year under the AMT and to tax the same $80,000 again in the second year when the regular tax applies.

To avoid double taxation of reversal items, Congress enacted a minimum tax credit that can only be used to reduce the regular tax liability in later years when the regular tax exceeds the alternative minimum tax. The **AMT minimum tax credit** is calculated each year in which the AMT applies. The amount of the credit is the difference between the actual AMT for the year and a recomputed AMT. The recomputed AMT is the AMT that would have been paid if the reversal adjustments did not enter into the AMTI calculation. That is, the AMT is recalculated using only preference items and those adjustments that do not reverse. The credit is carried forward and used to reduce the regular tax liability in those years in which the regular tax is greater than the AMT. The credit may be used only to reduce the regular tax to the tentative AMT amount.[38]

▲ **EXAMPLE 46**   Assume the same facts as in example 45. What is Perry's minimum tax credit in the first year and its tax liability in the second year?

Discussion: The minimum tax credit is the difference between the AMT as computed, $8,000, and the AMT recomputed without the timing differences. In this case, without the $80,000 adjustment in the first year, Perry's AMT would have been zero and no AMT would have been paid. Thus, the minimum tax credit to carry forward to year 2 is $8,000 ($8,000 − $0). In the second year, the regular tax and the AMT would have been calculated as in example 45, resulting in a regular tax liability of $61,250. Perry is allowed to reduce the $61,250 by the $8,000 minimum tax credit from the first year, resulting in a net tax due of $53,250.

Tax Planning and the AMT.   Given the narrowness of the gap between the 28-percent top AMT individual rate and the 39.6-percent maximum tax rate that applies to high-income individuals, it is easy to trigger the AMT. Thus, it is important for tax-planning purposes to consider AMT implications along with the regular tax. Although the overall goal of tax planning remains the maximization of wealth via the minimization of taxes, it should be recognized that too small a reduction in the regular tax may trigger the AMT. When an individual expects the AMT to apply, a strategy opposite to that for regular tax purposes is often appropriate. A rule of thumb to follow for regular tax-planning purposes is to defer income and accelerate deductions. Because the AMT tax rate for individuals is lower than that for the regular tax, a taxpayer subject to the AMT would generally be better off to accelerate income into the AMT year and defer deductions to a regular tax year.

▲ **EXAMPLE 47**   Eve is a financial consultant with several large clients. Her contract with her large clients allows her to bill them for services monthly or quarterly, at her option. In reviewing her current-year tax situation, Eve has determined that she will be subject to the alternative minimum tax at the 26 percent rate. Because of several reversing adjustments, Eve does not think that she will be subject to the AMT next year, but she will be in the 31% marginal tax rate bracket. If Eve submits monthly bills for November to her large clients, she estimates that she will receive $40,000 before the end of the year. What is Eve's tax savings on the $40,000 of income if she submits the monthly bills?

Discussion: Because Eve is subject to the AMT, she will pay $10,400 ($40,000 × 26%) in tax. Delaying the billing to next year will result in a tax of $12,400 ($40,000 × 31%). Billing this year saves $2,000 ($12,400 − $10,400) in taxes. However, because she will have to pay the tax a year earlier, Eve should also consider the time value of money effect. Assuming a 10% time value of money, the present value of paying the tax next year is $11,272 ($12,400 × 0.909 PV factor). Eve's real tax savings by billing in the current year is $872 ($11,272 − $10,400).

Although the planning result in example 47 is a straightforward application of the basic strategy, the complexity of the AMT calculation makes it difficult to apply the basic strategy in most situations. For example, should a taxpayer eligible to use the completed contract method of accounting for long-term contracts elect to use the percentage-of-completed-contract method to avoid paying the AMT? General answers to such questions do not usually hold up. The only reliable way for taxpayers to make such decisions is through the use of long-term planning projections that show the effect of all alternative courses of action possible. In order to make such long-term projections, taxpayers need to be aware of the adjustments and preferences that can trigger the AMT and consider them when evaluating investment opportunities.

KEY TERMS

accounting method (p. 642)
alternative minimum tax (AMT) (p. 661)
alternative minimum taxable income (AMTI) (p. 661)
alternative minimum tax adjustment (p. 664)
alternative minimum tax preference (p. 667)
alternative minimum tax rate (p. 661)
AMT minimum tax credit (p. 670)
AMT net operating loss deduction (p. 666)
business purpose tax year (p. 641)
child and dependent care credit (p. 658)

earned income credit (EIC) (p. 657)
fiscal year (p. 637)
foreign tax credit (p. 652)
full absorption costing method (p. 648)
individual accounting treatments (p. 642)
investment tax credit (ITC) (p. 652)
least aggregate deferral tax year (p. 640)
lower of cost-or-market method (p. 649)
lookback method (p. 646)
majority-interest tax year (p. 639)

natural business year (p. 641)
nonrefundable tax credit (p. 652)
overall accounting methods (p. 642)
ownership tax year (p. 641)
percentage-of-completed-contract method (p. 644)
principal partner tax year (p. 640)
private activity bond (p. 668)
refundable tax credit (p. 652)
rehabilitation tax credit (p. 655)
research and experimental (R&E) credit (p. 654)
taxable year (p. 637)
uniform capitalization (unicap) rules (p. 649)

PRIMARY TAX LAW SOURCES

[1] Sec. 441—Allows taxpayers to use either a calendar year or a fiscal year to compute taxable income. Defines *fiscal year*.

[2] Reg. Sec. 1.441-1T—Explains how to establish a tax year.

[3] Sec. 706—Provides the rules for selecting a partnership tax year.

[4] Reg. Sec. 1.706-1—Defines a *principal partner* for purposes of selecting a partnership tax year and illustrates the principal partner tax year.

[5] Reg. Sec. 1.706-1T—Explains the computation of the least aggregate deferral tax year for a partnership.

[6] Rev. Rul. 87-57—Explains the factors necessary for a partnership to establish a business purpose tax year.

[7] Sec. 1378—Defines the tax years that can be used by an S corporation.

[8] Rev. Proc. 87-32—Explains the ownership tax year test and how to adopt an ownership tax year.

[9] Reg. Sec. 1.706-1—Defines *natural business year.*

[10] Rev. Proc. 87-32—Provides examples of the test for a natural business year.

[11] Sec. 446—Defines the general rules for methods of accounting and provides the

authority for the IRS to change a taxpayer's method of accounting.

[12] Sec. 481—Prescribes the adjustments necessary when a taxpayer makes a change in an accounting method.

[13] Sec. 448—Requires corporations, partnerships with a corporate partner, and tax shelter activities to use the accrual method.

[14] Reg. Sec. 1.448-1T—Defines *tax shelter activity*.

[15] Reg. Sec. 1.448-1T—Defines *farming business* and gives examples of the exception that allows a farming business to use the cash method.

[16] Sec. 460—Requires the use of the percentage-of-completed-contract method for long-term construction contracts.

[17] Reg. Sec. 1.460-6—Illustrates the application of the lookback method.

[18] Sec. 471—Requires the use of the accrual method to calculate cost of goods sold when inventories are an income-producing factor.

[19] Thor Power Tool Co. v. Comm., 439 U.S. 522 (1979)—Held that the clear reflection of income is a more important factor than industry practice in determining the appropriateness of an accounting method.

[20] Reg. Sec. 1.263A-1T—Prescribes the application of the unicap rules as they apply to inventories.

[21] Reg. Sec. 1.471-4—Discusses the rules and definitions applicable to the use of lower of cost-or-market valuation.

[22] Reg. Sec. 1.472-3—Prescribes the procedures necessary to make a LIFO election.

[23] Reg. Sec. 1.472-2—Discusses the financial conformity rule and gives examples of its application.

[24] Sec. 27—Allows the foreign tax credit.

[25] Sec. 911—Provides for the exclusion of as much as $70,000 in foreign earned income in lieu of the foreign tax credit.

[26] Sec. 901—Specifies the calculation of and the limitations on the foreign tax credit.

[27] Sec. 41—Allows a tax credit for increasing research activities.

[28] Reg. Sec. 1.41-2—Defines *qualified research expenses*.

[29] Omnibus Budget Reconciliation Act of 1989. Pub. L. No. 101-239, 103 Stat. 2106.

[30] Sec. 47—Allows a tax credit for qualified rehabilitation expenditures.

[31] Sec. 32—Allows the earned income credit and prescribes the limitations on the amount of the credit.

[32] Reg. Sec. 1.44A-1—Discusses the general requirements and defines the terms applicable to the child and dependent care credit.

[33] Sec. 21—Allows a tax credit for child and dependent care expenses and prescribes the limits on the amount of the credit.

[34] Sec. 55—Requires the calculation of the alternative minimum tax and defines its calculation.

[35] Sec. 56—Prescribes the adjustment items that must be taken into account in calculating the alternative minimum tax.

[36] Sec. 57—Prescribes the preference items that must be added in calculating the alternative minimum taxable income.

[37] Sec. 59—Allows a credit for foreign tax paid (subject to limitations) against the tentative alternative minimum tax.

[38] Sec. 53—Allows the AMT credit against the regular tax and defines the calculation of the credit.

DISCUSSION QUESTIONS

1. What is the difference between a calendar year and a fiscal year?

2. Under what circumstances might a taxpayer find the use of a fiscal year advantageous?

3. How does a taxpayer select a taxable year?

4. Why do most individuals use calendar years rather than fiscal years?

5. Why are restrictions placed on the selection of a tax year by partnerships and S corporations?

6. What is the difference between an overall method of accounting and an individual accounting treatment?

7. What are the general requirements a taxpayer must meet in selecting an accounting method?

8. Which types of tax entities generally cannot elect to use the cash method of accounting?

9. Explain the two exceptions under which an entity that is generally not allowed to use the cash method of accounting still may elect to use the cash method.

10. What is the general accounting requirement for taxpayers who have long-term construction contracts?

11. What is the purpose of the lookback method of accounting for long-term construction contracts?

12. Do all taxpayers with long-term construction contracts have to use the percentage-of-completed-contract method of accounting? Explain.

13. What is the "cost" of inventory?

14. Briefly explain the uniform capitalization rules as they apply to inventories.

15. Do the uniform capitalization rules promote or hinder administrative convenience? Explain.

16. What restrictions are placed on taxpayers who elect to value their inventories at the lower of cost-or-market value?

17. What must a taxpayer do to make an election to use LIFO?

18. Why are tax credits rather than a deduction used to provide tax relief?

19. What is the difference between a refundable tax credit and a nonrefundable tax credit?

20. Why are tax credits often used? Give examples of tax credits that meet the purposes indicated.

21. What is the purpose of the foreign tax credit?

22. Are all foreign taxes paid automatically eligible for the foreign tax credit? (What limitations, if any, are imposed?)

23. What is the purpose of the research and experimental tax credit?

24. What types of expenditures qualify for the rehabilitation expenditure tax credit?

25. What restrictions are placed on the rehabilitation expenditures tax credit?

26. How are business tax credits different from individual tax credits?

27. What are the general criteria for eligibility for the earned income credit?

28. What are the general criteria for eligibility for the child and dependent care credit?

29. What are *qualifying dependents* for purposes of the child and dependent care credit?

30. Does the child care credit help promote a progressive tax rate structure? Explain.

31. What is the purpose of the alternative minimum tax?

32. Why is the alternative minimum tax a more important planning consideration now than it was before 1986?

33. What is the tax base for the alternative minimum tax? Explain the general computation of the base.

34. What is the basic difference between an AMT adjustment and a preference?

35. Why is MACRS depreciation on real property included as an AMT adjustment? Explain.

36. Why can AMT adjustments be negative?

37. What is the AMT exemption amount? Is it available for all taxpayers?

38. What tax credits are allowed for AMT purposes? Are there any limits on the amount of credit that can be used for AMT purposes?

39. What is the purpose of the AMT credit against the regular tax?

PROBLEMS

40. What tax year must be used by each of the following taxpayers? Explain.
    a. Rodney works for Big Co. His only other source of income is from interest and dividends. Although Rodney usually itemizes his deductions, he does not keep any formal books or records, relying instead on wage statements and other documents in preparing his return.
    b. John and Gloria own Spoke and Pedal Cyclery as equal partners. John and Gloria both use calendar years to report their income.
    c. Fax, Inc., is an S corporation wholly owned by Helena. Helena uses a calendar year to report her income.
    d. Assume the same facts as in part c, except that Fax, Inc., is a corporation.
    e. Bloodworth Trust holds assets for the benefit of Albert's children. The children use fiscal years ending June 30 to report their income.

41. What tax year must each of the following taxpayers use? Explain.
    a. Brayanth works for Gippsland Corporation. Brayanth's income for the year includes salary, interest, dividend income, and a long-term capital gain. Although he itemizes his deductions, he keeps no formal books or records, relying instead on his wage statement, canceled checks, and other formal documents furnished to him for preparing his return.
    b. Assume the same facts as in part a, except that Brayanth is self-employed as a plumber and keeps meticulous books and records.
    c. Cindy and Derek are partners in a pet shop. Cindy owns 55% and Derek owns 45%. Cindy reports her income using a July 31 fiscal year, whereas Derek uses a calendar year.
    d. Syme, Inc., is an S corporation wholly owned by Jeremiah. Jeremiah uses a calendar year to report his income.
    e. Assume the same facts as in part d, except that Syme, Inc., is a corporation.
    f. The Hackett Trust holds assets for the benefit of the Schnappauf children. The children use a fiscal year that ends October 31 to report their income.

42. Determine the tax year that must be used by each of the following partnerships. Explain.
    a. MNO Partnership is owned equally by Jane, Larry, and Ruby. Jane and Larry use a fiscal year ending on October 31, and Ruby uses a calendar year.
    b. Terry is the general partner of the LBO Partnership. Terry owns 25% of the partnership. The remaining 75% is owned by limited partners, none of whom owns more than a 3% interest.
    c. Kurt and Connie own the Alfa Partnership. Kurt owns 60% of Alfa and has a fiscal year ending June 30. Connie owns the remaining 40% of Alfa and reports her income using a calendar year.

43. Determine the tax year that must be used by each of the following partnerships. Explain.
    a. The Tullamarine Group is a partnership; Theresa owns 60%, Ulma owns 20%, and Lois owns 20%. Theresa uses a calendar tax year, and Ulma and Lois use a fiscal year that ends November 30.
    b. Sven is the general partner of Yoroke Partners. Sven owns 15% of the partnership. The remaining 85% is owned by 17 limited partners, each of whom owns a 5% interest. Sven uses a fiscal year that ends October 30, whereas 12 limited partners use a fiscal year that ends September 30. The other 5 limited partners use a calendar year.
    c. Vivian and Monica are equal partners in the Racecourse Inn. Vivian uses a fiscal year that ends September 30, and Monica uses a fiscal year that ends November 30.

44. Determine the tax year(s) that can be used by each of the following S corporations. Explain.
    a. Red, Ed, and Ling are equal owners of RET Corporation. Red and Ed use a calendar year. Ling uses a fiscal year ending July 31.
    b. Assume the same facts as in part a, except that Red and Ed each own a 15% interest in RET and Ling owns the remaining 70%.
    c. Assume the same facts as in part a. RET's business is seasonal, with March and April the heaviest revenue months. Revenues for the current and 2 previous years were as follows:

	March & April	12-Month Period
Current year	$40,000	$140,000
1st preceding year	$35,000	$130,000
2nd preceding year	$30,000	$120,000

    d. Assume the same facts as in part c, except that revenues for the second preceding year totaled $150,000.

45. Determine the tax year(s) that must be used by each of the following S corporations. Explain.
    a. Will, Dan, and Tom are equal owners of Rheen Corporation and each has a different fiscal year. Will has a fiscal year that ends April 30, Dan's ends May 31, and Tom's ends November 30.
    b. Assume the same facts as in part a, except that Tom and Dan each own a 20% interest in Rheen and Will owns the remaining 60%.
    c. Assume the same facts as in part b. Rheen's business is seasonal; the heaviest revenue months are July and August. Revenues for three years are as follows:

	July & August	12-Month Period
Current year	$90,000	$300,000
1st preceding year	$80,000	$260,000
2nd preceding year	$60,000	$230,000

46. Which accounting method must each of the following taxpayers use? Explain.
    a. Rodney works for Big Co. His only other source of income is from interest and dividends. Although Rodney usually itemizes his deductions, he does not keep any formal books or records, relying instead on wage statements and other documents in preparing his return.
    b. Fax, Inc., is an S corporation wholly owned by Helena. Helena uses a calendar year to report her income.
    c. Assume the same facts as in part b, expect that Fax, Inc., is a corporation. Fax, Inc.'s annual revenues have never exceeded $250,000 in any year.
    d. Assume the same facts as in part c, except that Fax, Inc.'s annual revenues usually are between $8,000,000 and $9,000,000.
    e. Spoke and Pedal Cyclery is organized as a partnership. Spoke and Pedal is owned by John and Gloria as equal partners.

47. Which accounting method must each of the following taxpayers use? Explain.
   a. Earlene is the sole proprietor of The Sports Store. The Sports Store sells athletic equipment and clothing. Earlene keeps adequate records of the store's operation but does not keep formal records of her other individual income and expense items.
   b. Archer Partnership is owned equally by Adolph and the Blake Corporation. Adolph reports his income on the cash basis, whereas Blake uses the accrual method of accounting.
   c. Wheaton Corporation is owned by Carol and her family. The corporation raises grain that it harvests and sells to wholesalers.
   d. Assume the same facts as in part c, except that some grain is sold at the bakery that Wheaton owns. The bakery processes the grain into various products that it sells to wholesalers.

48. Kim and Brendan, who are long-time friends, have decided to buy a golf equipment store and go into business together. They will be equal partners. Kim reports his income by calendar year, and Brendan uses a fiscal year that ends September 30. One of the attractions of owning the golf equipment store is that the business is seasonal and will allow them to take long vacations. The peak revenue months are June and July. The owner provides them with the following information:

	July & August	12-Month Period
Current year	$200,000	$500,000
1st preceding year	$280,000	$700,000
2nd preceding year	$325,000	$850,000

   a. If Kim and Brendan form a corporation, what options, if any, do they have in choosing their tax year and method of accounting?
   b. If Kim and Brendan form a partnership, what options, if any, do they have in choosing their tax year and method of accounting?
   c. If Kim and Brendan form an S corporation, what options, if any, do they have in choosing their tax year and method of accounting?

49. WCM is a construction company that is solely owned by Bill. WCM is primarily engaged in the construction of single-family dwellings and small business offices. During the current year, WCM entered into 2 contracts. One contract is for building a house. The second contract is for construction of a small shopping mall. Information regarding the 2 contracts is as follows:

		Current Year	Second Year	Third Year
Home Contract				
Contract price	$250,000			
Total estimated costs	$225,000			
Costs incurred		$125,000	$100,000	
Shopping Mall				
Contract price	$750,000			
Total estimated costs	$600,000			
Costs incurred		$180,000	$240,000	$200,000

   a. Determine the gross profit to be recognized for each year of each contract, assuming that WCM uses
      ■ The completed contract method of accounting
      ■ The percentage-of-completed-contract method
   b. Under what conditions can WCM use the completed contract method?

50. Bridge & Ball Works builds highways, bridges, and other major construction projects. Because of its size it is required to use the percentage-of-completed-contract method to account for its construction contracts. The current interest rate is 7%. Determine the amount of gross profit to be recognized in each year and any other additions or subtractions to income from the following contract:

Contract price	$2,400,000
Total estimated costs	(2,000,000)
Estimated gross profit	$ 400,000

Actual Costs Incurred

Year 1	$ 700,000
Year 2	800,000
Year 3	300,000
Total actual costs	$1,800,000

51. BGL is a construction firm specializing in building hotels and office complexes. BGL is required to use the percentage-of-completion-method to account for its construction contracts. The current interest rate is 9%. Determine the amount of gross profit that GBL must recognize in each year and any other additions or subtractions to income from the following contract:

Contract price	$3,500,000
Total estimated costs	2,800,000
Estimated gross profit	$ 700,000

Actual Costs Incurred

Year 1	$ 800,000
Year 2	1,200,000
Year 3	1,000,000
Total actual costs	$3,000,000

52. Artho Corporation sells 3 different products. Information on the ending inventory of each product is as follows:

	Total Cost	Total Market Value
Item #1	$ 4,500	$ 3,800
Item #2	$12,000	$16,600
Item #3	$40,000	$32,400

What are all the ending inventory values possible for Artho? Explain Artho's options in this regard.

53. The Aeroflight Co. sells 4 different golf balls. Information on the ending inventory of each golf ball is as follows:

Type of Golf Ball	Total Cost	Total Market Value
HT 90	$3,700	$ 2,100
LT 90	$6,350	$ 5,150
HT 100	$8,200	$10,400
LT 100	$9,700	$ 8,500

What are all the ending inventory values possible for Aeroflight? Explain Aeroflight's options in this regard.

54. Provided here is information regarding the purchase and sale (in chronological order) of an inventory item during the current year:

	Number of Units	Cost per Unit
Beginning inventory	300	$15
Purchase	400	$18
Sale	650	
Purchase	1,000	$20
Sale	750	
Purchase	300	$18
Sale	200	

Determine the ending inventory value for each of the following inventory flow assumptions:

a. FIFO   **b.** LIFO   **c.** Average cost

55. The Mulgrave Co. owns a chain of retail computer stores. The company provides you with the following information regarding the purchase and sale (in chronological order) of one model, the LCD 466, during the current year:

	Number of Units	Cost per Unit
Beginning inventory	150	$2,000
Purchased	300	$2,300
Sold	200	
Purchased	550	$2,400
Sold	400	
Purchased	200	$2,200
Sold	350	

Determine the ending inventory value for each of the following inventory flow assumptions:

a. FIFO   **b.** LIFO   **c.** Average cost

56. Groff Corporation has been valuing its inventory using the lower of cost-or-market method for many years. During the current year, Groff elects to switch to the LIFO inventory valuation method. At the beginning of the year, product A had a cost of $24,000 and a market value of $18,000. Write a memo to Malcolm, the controller of Groff, explaining what adjustments must be made to the beginning inventory if the company switches to the LIFO method of inventory.

57. Flagler Corporation paid $62,500 in foreign taxes on $250,000 of foreign source income during the current year. Flagler's total taxable income was $800,000. What is Flagler's foreign tax credit?

    Assume that Flagler paid $112,500 on its foreign source income. What is Flagler's foreign tax credit?

58. Clinton Corporation spent $800,000 on qualified research activities during the current year. Clinton's fixed base percentage is 10%, and its annual average gross receipts for the 4 preceding years were $2,000,000. What is Clinton's allowable incremental research and experimentation tax credit?

    Assume that Clinton's annual average gross receipts for the preceding 4 years were $10,000,000. What is Clinton's allowable incremental research tax credit?

59. Lavinia owns an advertising agency. In February 1996, Lavinia purchases for $32,000 a building that was originally placed in service in 1918. Lavinia spends $65,000 rehabilitating the building for use as her advertising agency office. The rehabilitation is completed in November 1996.

   a. What criteria must Lavinia meet to qualify for the older buildings rehabilitation tax credit?

   b. Assuming that Lavinia meets all qualifying criteria, what are the amounts for Lavinia's older buildings credit and the basis of the building?

   c. What criteria must Lavinia meet to qualify for the historic structures credit?

   d. Assume the criteria in part c were met and that the building qualifies for both credits. What is the total of the rehabilitation credits for 1996? What is the basis of the building?

60. Return to the facts of problem 59, and assume that Lavinia sells the building in April 1999.

   a. How much of the older buildings tax credit must Lavinia recapture?

   b. Assuming the building qualified for both credits, how much of the historic structures credit must Lavinia recapture?

61. Determine the total allowable 1996 earned income credit in each of the following situations:

   a. Judy is single and earned $5,500 in salary for the year. In addition, she received $2,300 in unemployment compensation during the year.

   b. Monica is a single parent with 1 dependent child. Monica earned $12,500 from her job as a taxicab driver. She also received $4,700 in child support from her ex-husband.

   c. Paul and Yvonne are married and have 3 dependent children. Their earned income is $21,300, and they received $1,900 in interest income from their savings account.

   d. Hattie is married to Herbert, and they have 2 dependent children. During February, Herbert left and hasn't been seen or heard from since. Hattie earned $16,400 from her job. During January and February, Herbert earned $4,800, but Hattie has no idea how much he earned for the entire year.

62. Determine the total allowable 1996 earned income credit in each of the following situations:

   a. Rina is single and earns $6,300 in salary for the year. In addition, she receives $1,450 in unemployment compensation during the year.

   b. Lachlan is single with 1 dependent child. During the year he earns 8,000 as a waiter and receives alimony of $10,000 and child support of $5,000.

   c. Zorica is a single parent with 2 dependent children. Zorica earns $19,000 from her job as a mechanic. She also receives $3,000 in child support from her ex-husband.

   d. Elliot and Pam are married and have 3 dependent children. Elliot earns $12,000 and Pam $9,000 from their jobs. They receive $2,000 in interest on New York State bonds and $1,000 in dividend income.

63. Determine the amount of the child and dependent care credit to which each of the following taxpayers is entitled:

    a. Michael and Gladys are married and have a 7-year-old child. Their adjusted gross income is $44,000, and they paid $1,900 in qualified child-care expenses during the year. Michael earned $12,000 and Gladys earned $30,000 from their jobs.

    b. Jill is a single parent with an 11-year-old daughter. Jill's adjusted gross income was $24,500, and she paid $2,100 in qualified child-care expenses.

    c. Cory is a single parent who earned $9,000 and received other nontaxable government assistance totaling $5,700 during the year. She paid $1,600 in qualified child-care expenses during the year.

    d. Roosevelt and Myrtle are married and have 2 children. Roosevelt earns $94,000, and Myrtle has a part-time job from which she earned $4,400 during the year. They paid $4,700 in qualified child-care expenses during the year.

    e. Randy is single and earns $80,000 per year. He maintains a home for his father, who has been confined to a wheelchair since he had a stroke several years ago. Randy's father receives $6,000 in Social Security but has no other income. Because his father requires constant attention, Randy hires a helper to take care of his father while he is at work. Randy paid the helper $13,000 during the current year.

64. Determine the amount of the child and dependent care credit to which each of the following taxpayers is entitled:

    a. Caryle and Philip are married and have a 4-year-old daughter. Their adjusted gross income is $38,000, and they pay $2,100 in qualified child-care expenses during the year. Caryle earns $18,000, and Philip earns $20,000 in salary.

    b. Natalie is a single parent with an 8-year-old son. Natalie's adjusted gross income is $24,500, and she pays $1,900 in qualified child-care expenses.

    c. Leanne and Ross are married and have 3 children, ages 6, 4, and 1. Their adjusted gross income is $78,000, and they pay $6,500 in qualified child-care expenses during the year. Leanne earns $48,000, and Philip earns $30,000 in salary.

    d. Malcolm and Mirella are married and have 2 children. Mirella earns $55,000, and Malcolm has a part-time job from which he earns $4,000 during the year. They pay $4,800 in qualified child-care expenses during the year.

    e. Andrew is a single parent with a 14-year-old son. Because he does not arrive home from work until 7 P.M., Andrew has hired someone to take care of his son after school and cook him supper. Andrew's adjusted gross income is $59,000, and he pays $2,700 in child-care expenses.

    f. Assume the same facts as in part e, except that Andrew's son is 12 years old.

65. Determine the total amount of tax due and the amount of the alternative minimum tax in each of the following situations:

    a. Wilbur Corporation's regular tax liability is $180,000, and its tentative minimum tax is $150,000.

    b. Gene's regular tax liability is $27,000, and her tentative minimum tax is $42,000.

66. Stan purchases machinery costing $54,000 for use in his business in 1996. The machinery is 7-year MACRS property and has an ADS life of 12 years. Prepare a depreciation schedule using the regular MACRS method and the ADS depreciation. Indicate how much of an adjustment Stan must make in computing his alternative minimum tax each year.

67. Assume that in problem 66, Stan sells the machinery in the year 2002 for $28,500. Determine the effect of the sale on Stan's regular taxable income and his alternative minimum taxable income for the year 2002.

68. Alice and Frank had the following items on their current-year tax return:

Adjusted gross income			$54,000
Less: Deductions from adjusted gross income			
Medical expenses	$4,500		
Less: 7.5% × $54,000	(4,050)	$ 450	
Home mortgage interest		5,300	
Home equity loan interest		1,200	
State income taxes		2,725	
Property taxes		950	
Charitable contributions (cash)		575	
Miscellaneous itemized deductions	$1,480		
Less: 2% × $54,000	(1,080)	400	(11,600)
Less: Exemptions (2 × $2,550)			(5,100)

Determine the amount of the adjustments that Alice and Frank will have to make in computing their alternative minimum tax.

69. Joan and Matthew are married with 2 children and reported the following items on their current-year tax return:

Adjusted gross income			$135,000
Less: Deductions from adjusted gross income			
Medical expenses	$12,000		
Less: 7.5% × $135,000	(10,125)	$ 1,875	
Home mortgage interest		13,500	
Home equity loan (for college education)		9,000	
State income taxes		11,000	
Property taxes		6,500	
Charitable contributions		7,000	
Miscellaneous itemized deductions	$ 3,000		
Less: 2% × $135,000	(2,700)	300	(49,175)
Less: Exemptions (4 × $2,550)			(10,200)

Determine Joan and Matthew's regular tax liability and, if applicable, the amount of their alternative minimum tax. Write a memo to Joan and Matthew explaining the adjustments they will have to make in computing their alternative minimum tax.

70. Pauline is considering investing in bonds. Her broker has given her several options to consider. The first option is to invest in city bonds with an interest rate of 6%. The second option involves the purchase of private activity bonds (subject to the AMT) that yield 7.5% interest. A third option is the purchase of High-Flier Utility bonds yielding 9% interest. Assuming that Pauline's marginal tax rate is 28%, write a letter to her explaining which option she should choose. In your letter, be sure to consider all circumstances that could affect the after-tax return on the bond.

71. Determine the AMT exemption amount for each of the following taxpayers:
    a. Nominal Corporation has an alternative minimum taxable income of $140,000.
    b. Janine is a single individual with an alternative minimum taxable income of $155,000.
    c. Jagged Corporation has an alternative minimum taxable income of $220,000.
    d. Peter and Wendy have an alternative minimum taxable income of $110,000.
    e. Popup Corporation has an alternative minimum taxable income of $540,000.

DISCUSSION CASES

72. Harry and Matilda are married and have the following tax return data for 1996:

Income		
Salaries		$100,000
Cash dividends		4,000
Tax-exempt bond interest		8,000
Total income		$112,000
Exclusions		
Tax-exempt bond interest		(8,000)
Gross income		$104,000
Deductions for adjusted gross income		
Loss on rental property	$14,000	
NOL carryforward	50,000	(64,000)
Adjusted gross income		$ 40,000
Deductions from adjusted gross income (after limitations)		
Medical expenses	$ 3,000	
Taxes	14,500	
Home mortgage interest	15,200	
Home equity loan interest	9,000	
Charitable contributions	6,200	
Misc. itemized deductions	3,500	(51,400)
Personal and dependency exemptions		(10,200)
Taxable income		$(21,600)

Do Harry and Matilda owe any income tax for 1996? Explain why they might owe tax in 1996, and discuss the items on their tax return that could cause them to pay income tax in 1996. Be sure to adequately explain each item. Calculations are not required.

73. Alex and Jeff have differing views on the current tax system. Alex believes that any tax system that has two tax structures, a regular tax and an alternative minimum tax, is inefficient and inequitable. In fact, the system violates all canons of taxation espoused by Adam Smith. Jeff, however, feels that Congress should use the tax code as a vehicle for encouraging taxpayers to engage in various social and economic transactions. Therefore, he argues that the alternative minimum tax is necessary to ensure that each taxpayer pays some amount of tax. With whom do you agree? Why?

TAX PLANNING CASE

74. Reg and Rhonda are married and have 2 children, ages 5 and 3. Rhonda has not worked since the birth of their first child. Now that the children are older, she would like to return to work and has a job offer that would pay her $22,000 per year. In order for her to take the job, the children will have to be put into a day-care center. The day-care center will cost $400 per month. Given the high cost of the day-care center, Reg and Rhonda are wondering whether it is worth it for Rhonda to take the job. They project their current-year taxable income (without considering Rhonda's job) as $40,000. Write a letter to Rhonda explaining how much additional cash (after taxes) she will earn if she accepts the job. You should include in your letter the nontax factors Rhonda should consider before taking the job.

75. Nina is the auditor for Geiger Construction, a local builder. Geiger recently completed the renovation of a historic building in downtown Kingston. The building, which consists of 5 separate shops, is owned by the Restoring Historic Kingston Partnership (RHKP). Nina is also the tax accountant for Merlin, one of the limited partners in RHKP. In preparing Merlin's 1996 tax return, the partner information return from RHKP (which Nina did not prepare) indicates that Merlin is entitled to both an older buildings credit and a historic structures credit. Nina properly deducts both credits. Later that year, Nina is conducting the audit of Geiger Construction, and she compliments the owner on the wonderful job the company did in restoring the building while meeting the requirements necessary for the building to qualify for the historic rehabilitation credits. Marshall, the owner of Geiger Construction, informs Nina that because of an unforeseen structural problem, the company was not able to meet the historic rehabilitation requirements. The company could preserve only 50%, not the required 75%, of the external walls. What is Nina's obligation (refer to Statements on Responsibilities in Tax Practice), if any, with respect to Merlin's filed tax return? Does she have any obligation to Merlin's other partners? to the preparer of the partnership return?

**ETHICS
DISCUSSION CASE**

Tax Research

▲ CHAPTER LEARNING OBJECTIVES

■ Explain the difference between primary and secondary tax authorities.

■ Identify the different types of legislative, administrative, and judicial primary authorities.

■ Describe the hierarchy or different levels of importance attributable to each of the primary authorities.

■ Prepare citations to each of the primary authorities.

■ Identify and describe the purpose of the different types of secondary authorities.

■ Understand the difference between tax planning and tax compliance.

■ Describe the basic steps involved in tax research.

■ Apply the tax research process to a comprehensive problem.

■ Describe the basic methods used by the IRS to select tax returns that will be examined.

■ Explain the different types of examinations and ways in which the IRS attempts to settle disputes with taxpayers administratively.

Tax research is the process by which the tax consequences of a completed or proposed transaction are determined. The tax treatment of any transaction must be based on some supporting authority. Indeed, all the rules in this text originated in some supporting authoritative pronouncement. Tax research is simply the means by which these authoritative pronouncements are located, evaluated, and applied to a specific set of facts.

All tax authorities fall into one of two classes: primary and secondary. **Primary authorities** relate to the three principal functions of government: legislative, executive/administrative, and judicial. The legislative authorities include the Constitution, tax treaties, the law as enacted by Congress (i.e., Internal Revenue Code), and the meaning of the law as described by the various congressional committee reports that accompany enactment of the law.

The tax law as enacted by Congress contains general language, so interpretations are necessary. The administrative authorities are the official interpretations of the law prepared by the Department of the Treasury and the Internal Revenue Service. These sources consist of regulations, revenue rulings, revenue procedures, and some other miscellaneous pronouncements. Whenever the IRS and a taxpayer disagree about the interpretation and application of a specific Code provision, the courts may be called upon to decide the matter. Decisions by the various trial and appellate courts are the judicial authorities. All legislative, administrative, and judicial primary authorities are commonly referred to as the *tax law*. Figure 15–1 summarizes these primary sources of authority.

Secondary authorities serve primarily as tools for locating the relevant primary authorities. They also provide information that leads to better understanding, interpretation, and application of the primary authorities. Secondary authorities include all other statements, pronouncements, explanations, or interpretations of the law that are not primary; they consist chiefly of tax services, citators, computer software systems that research tax databases, and tax journals and newsletters.

This chapter first examines more closely the different types of primary and secondary authorities and the hierarchy, or different levels of importance, attributable to each type. This is followed by a step-by-step discussion of how these authorities are used to determine the tax consequences related to a specific set of facts. The chapter concludes with an overview of the audit-and-appeals process as prescribed by the Internal Revenue Service.

Legislative Sources

The legislative primary authorities consist of the U.S. Constitution, new tax laws enacted by Congress and incorporated in the Internal Revenue Code, reports issued by congressional committees as new laws are enacted, and treaties with other countries, which are negotiated by the president with the advice and consent of the Senate. Collectively, these authorities are sometimes referred to as *statutory authorities*. They are generally accorded a higher level of authority than other administrative or judicial primary authorities.

The U.S. Constitution.   The authority for the imposition of the federal income tax is found in Article I, Section 7, of the U.S. Constitution. It grants Congress the authority to impose taxes to pay debts and provide for the common defense and general welfare of the United States. It also requires that all tax legislation originate in the House of Representatives. Early attempts at an income tax were

▲ **Figure 15–1**

PRIMARY SOURCES OF
TAX LAW AUTHORITY

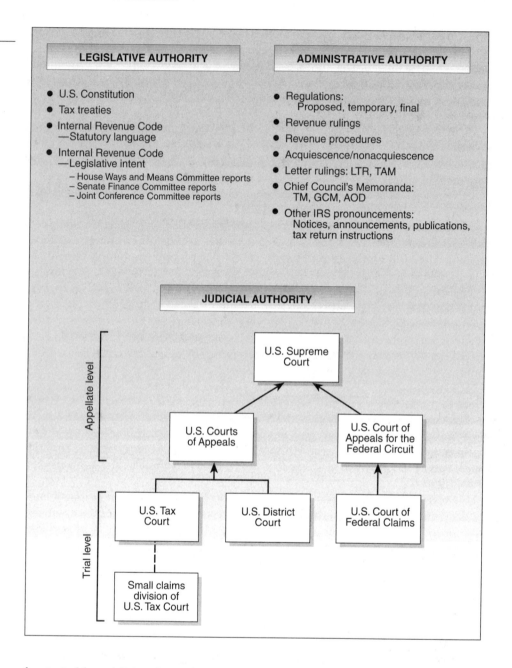

LEGISLATIVE AUTHORITY

- U.S. Constitution
- Tax treaties
- Internal Revenue Code
  —Statutory language
- Internal Revenue Code
  —Legislative intent
    – House Ways and Means Committee reports
    – Senate Finance Committee reports
    – Joint Conference Committee reports

ADMINISTRATIVE AUTHORITY

- Regulations:
    Proposed, temporary, final
- Revenue rulings
- Revenue procedures
- Acquiescence/nonacquiescence
- Letter rulings: LTR, TAM
- Chief Council's Memoranda:
    TM, GCM, AOD
- Other IRS pronouncements:
    Notices, announcements, publications,
    tax return instructions

JUDICIAL AUTHORITY

U.S. Supreme
Court

U.S. Courts
of Appeals

U.S. Court of
Appeals for the
Federal Circuit

U.S. Tax
Court

U.S. District
Court

U.S. Court of
Federal Claims

Small claims
division of
U.S. Tax Court

Appellate level

Trial level

frustrated by additional requirements in Article I that direct taxes be apportioned among the states in proportion to the Census. As a result, most early attempts to raise revenue for the federal government were in the form of an excise tax. A tax based on income became an integral source of federal revenue with ratification of the Sixteenth Amendment to the Constitution in 1913. The Sixteenth Amendment permits a tax on income, from whatever source derived, without apportionment among the states and without regard to the Census.

Although the constitutional authority for an income tax is clear, tax protesters frequently have challenged it on the ground that it violates other constitutional rights. For example, protesters have claimed that their right to due process is violated, that they have religious or conscientious objections to defense expenditures, and that the filing of tax returns violates their protection from self-incrimination. Tax protesters' activities include filing incomplete tax returns, modifying return forms in such a way that they cannot be processed by the IRS, or claiming deductions for items clearly not allowed. The various methods are intended to hinder the administration of the tax law or frustrate the collection of the tax due. Tax protesters have not been successful in the courts and are subject to substantial penalties for their protest activities and for failure to file a proper return and pay the tax due.

Internal Revenue Code of 1986.   The most important source of current federal income tax law is the Internal Revenue Code of 1986, as amended (the Code, or I.R.C.). What is commonly referred to as the *Internal Revenue Code*, or simply *the Code*, is actually Title 26 of the *United States Code*. The *U.S. Code* is a consolidated and coordinated compilation of all laws enacted by Congress. All laws dealing with the same subject are brought together under one title. Other titles of the *U.S. Code* include Title 10, dealing with armed forces, and Title 28, dealing with the judiciary and judicial procedure.

Whenever Congress enacts a new tax law, the amendments are integrated into the I.R.C. The Code has been amended almost annually since it was comprehensively overhauled in 1986. The Code was comprehensively reorganized and amended in 1954, and from that time until 1986 it was referred to as the *Internal Revenue Code of 1954.*

STRUCTURE.   The Code has many different subdivisions, each with a different designation. For example, there are subtitles, chapters, subchapters, parts, and subparts. The contents of the Code can be broadly defined by examining the names of its nine subtitles, which appear in Exhibit 15–1.

Each subtitle is further subdivided into chapters. Exhibit 15–2 shows that Subtitle A, which deals with income taxes, has chapters numbered 1 through 6 and that one chapter has been repealed. Each chapter may again be subdivided into numerous subchapters. Exhibit 15–3 lists some of the more common subchapters of Chapter 1, which deals with normal taxes and surtaxes. Each subchapter may also be subdivided into parts and subparts.

The basic reference to a particular part of the Code is typically by section number. Reference to larger divisions, such as subtitles and chapters, is generally omitted. The section numbers run consecutively from 1 to 9602, although many numbers in the sequence are missing to allow for further expansion of the tax law. Each section of the Code may be further subdivided into subsections, paragraphs, subparagraphs, and clauses. Exhibit 15–4 provides a comprehensive

▲ **Exhibit 15–1**

SUBTITLES OF THE
INTERNAL REVENUE CODE

Subtitle	Name	Beginning Code Section Number
A	Income Taxes	Sec. 1
B	Estate and Gift Taxes	Sec. 2001
C	Employment Taxes	Sec. 3101
D	Miscellaneous Excise Taxes	Sec. 4001
E	Alcohol, Tobacco, and Certain Other Excise Taxes	Sec. 5001
F	Procedure and Administration	Sec. 6001
G	The Joint Committee on Taxation	Sec. 8001
H	Financing of Presidential Election Campaigns	Sec. 9001
I	Trust Fund Code	Sec. 9501

Chapter	Name	Beginning Code Section Number
1	Normal Taxes and Surtaxes	Sec. 1
2	Tax on Self-Employment Income	Sec. 1401
3	Withholding of Tax on Nonresident Aliens and Foreign Corporations	Sec. 1441
4	[Repealed]	
5	Tax on Transfers To Avoid Income Tax	Sec. 1491
6	Consolidated Returns	Sec. 1501

example of the arrangement for Section 170(b)(1)(A) dealing with percentage limitations on charitable contributions.

Some words of caution about reading the Code are warranted. You must always read the entire section, not just the smallest subdivision that may contain the apparent answer to a tax question. Frequently, other divisions of the section contain special rules or definitions that could be applicable.

For example, Section 170(a) generally allows a deduction for any charitable contribution to a qualified organization, including an educational institution. However, Section 170(l) limits the deduction to 80 percent of the amount otherwise allowable if the contribution entitles the donor to purchase tickets for seating at an athletic event in an athletic stadium of the educational institution (so-called donor seating).

Similarly, you must review other sections within the subpart, part, or other larger division that contains the particular section for similar limitations or cross-references to other parts of the Code that may be relevant. Section 168, for example, provides the general rules for computing the accelerated cost-recovery deduction for depreciable property, including automobiles. It is located in Part VI, entitled "Itemized Deductions for Individuals and Corporations," of Subchapter A. Section 280F, however, which is located in Part IX, entitled "Items Not Deductible," limits the depreciation deduction in cases in which expensive cars are purchased or they are not used at least 50 percent of the time in a trade or business.

Occasionally, the Code will specify that certain conditions must be met before the ultimate treatment can be determined. Under these circumstances, it is im-

▲ Exhibit 15–3

PARTIAL LIST OF
SUBCHAPTERS OF
CHAPTER 1 OF SUBTITLE A

Subchapter	Name	Beginning Code Section Number
A	Determination of Tax Liability	Sec. 1
B	Computation of Taxable Income	Sec. 61
C	Corporate Distributions and Adjustments	Sec. 301
D	Deferred Compensation	Sec. 401
E	Accounting Periods and Methods of Accounting	Sec. 441
I	Natural Resources	Sec. 611
J	Estates, Trusts, Beneficiaries, and Decedents	Sec. 641
K	Partners and Partnerships	Sec. 701
N	Tax Based on Income from Sources within or without the United States	Sec. 861
O	Gain or Loss on Disposition of Property	Sec. 1001
P	Capital Gain or Loss	Sec. 1201
S	Tax Treatment of S Corporations and Their Shareholders	Sec. 1361

▲ **Exhibit 15–4**

SUBDIVISIONS OF
SECTION 170

Title 26:	Internal Revenue Code
Subtitle A:	Income Tax
Chapter 1:	Normal Taxes and Surtaxes
Subchapter B:	Computation of Taxable Income
Part VI:	Itemized Deductions for Individuals and Corporations
Section:	Sec. 170 CHARITABLE, ETC., CONTRIBUTIONS AND GIFTS
Subsection:	(a) ALLOWANCE OF DEDUCTION
Paragraph:	(1) GENERAL RULE—There shall be allowed as a deduction any charitable contribution. . . . only if verified under regulations prescribed by the Secretary.
	. . . .
Subsection:	(b) PERCENTAGE LIMITATIONS
Paragraph:	(1) INDIVIDUALS—In the case of an individual, the deduction provided in subsection (a) shall be limited as provided in the succeeding subparagraphs.
Subparagraph:	(A) GENERAL RULE—Any charitable contribution to a [church] . . . shall be allowed to the extent that the aggregate of such contributions does not exceed 50 percent of the taxpayer's contribution base for the taxable year.
	. . . .

portant to understand, for example, whether conditions 1, 2, *and* 3 must be satisfied or whether condition 1, 2, *or* 3 will satisfy. Obviously, the ultimate treatment can be drastically different, depending on which of the interpretations is applicable.

THE LEGISLATIVE PROCESS.   Figure 15–2 presents a diagram of the process by which amendments to the Code are enacted. Typically, amendments to the Code are initiated by the president or a member of Congress as a *bill*. In accordance with the constitutional requirements, the bill is introduced in the House of Representatives, where it is referred to the Ways and Means Committee, which has jurisdiction over all tax matters. After hearings and deliberations, a bill approved by the committee is sent back to the full House. Under what is referred to as the *closed rule*, the House can only approve or disapprove the bill as written by the Ways and Means Committee. Bills approved by the House are sent to the Senate.

The bill follows a similar path in the Senate. It is first referred to the Finance Committee, which has jurisdiction over all tax matters in the Senate. The Senate Finance Committee may accept the bill as approved by the House, make some amendments to it, or make so many amendments that the resulting bill is really a substitute. After the committee approves the bill, it is referred to the full Senate. In contrast with the House's closed rule procedure, any senator may propose changes to the bill when it is being considered by the full Senate. Usually, the versions passed by the House and Senate are not the same, and any differences are resolved by a joint conference committee. Members of the joint conference committee are the most senior, or ranking, members of the House Ways and Means Committee and the Senate Finance Committee.

After the conference committee negotiates a resolution of the differences in the House and Senate versions of a bill, it is sent back to both the House and the Senate, where it can only be approved or disapproved. If the bill is passed by both the House and Senate, it is sent to the president. The president may approve

▲ **Figure 15–2**
THE LEGISLATIVE PROCESS FOR A TAX LAW

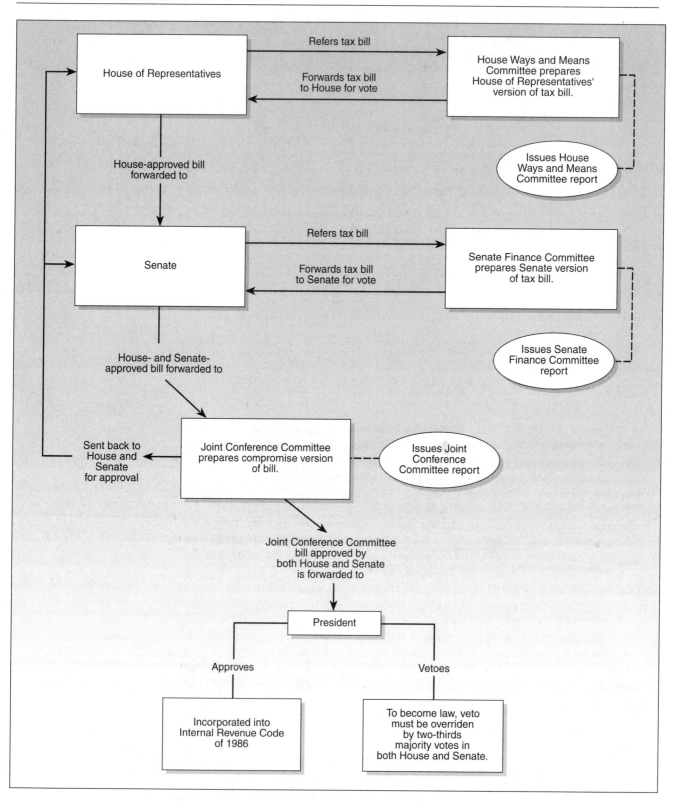

the bill by signing it, or the president may veto it. A veto can be overridden by a two-thirds majority of both the House and Senate.

Several documents that accompany a bill through the legislative process provide insight into Congress's intent in enacting the new legislation. As each committee approves a bill, it writes a report that describes why the change in the law was considered necessary, explains each change, and often provides examples of how a particular rule is to be applied. Accordingly, the House Ways and Means Committee report, Senate Finance Committee report, and Joint Conference Committee report provide information that helps the IRS, taxpayers, and the courts understand and interpret the bill as it was approved at each stage of the process.

After a bill is enacted, the Joint Committee on Taxation prepares a general explanation of the bill as approved by the president. This report is commonly referred to as the *blue book* because of the color of its binding. The Joint Committee on Taxation should not be confused with the Joint Conference Committee. The Joint Conference Committee is an integral part of the legislative process that develops a new bill.[1] The Joint Committee on Taxation's primary responsibility is to oversee the operation and administration of the tax system as a whole. It is not directly involved in the legislative process of enacting a new bill.

Tax Treaties.   Although the Code is the primary source of tax law in the United States, Congress also enters into tax treaties with various countries. Tax treaties are separate laws that define how citizens of the two countries are to be taxed on income derived from working or investing in the other country. As such, they are important for individuals and corporations that do business in foreign countries. At times, the provisions of a tax treaty may override provisions of the Code.[2] Because of their variety and complexity, details of specific tax treaties are beyond the scope of this text.

Administrative Sources

The agency within the administrative branch of government with overall responsibility for the administration of the Internal Revenue Code is the Treasury Department.[3] This responsibility is fulfilled by the Internal Revenue Service, a branch of the Treasury Department that is directly responsible for interpreting, administering, and enforcing the tax laws. The official in charge of the IRS is called the *commissioner* and is given general legal assistance by the Office of the Chief Counsel.[4]

The Treasury Department provides overall interpretive guidance by issuing Treasury regulations. In fulfilling its function, the IRS issues revenue rulings, revenue procedures, and a variety of other pronouncements.[5] It is important to keep in mind that regulations, rulings, and other pronouncements have different levels of authority, or weight. This is analogous to saying that a Supreme Court decision is more important than a decision of some lower court. These varying levels of authority play an important role in the tax research process described later in the chapter.

Treasury Regulations.   A Treasury regulation is the Treasury Department's official explanation of a related provision in the Internal Revenue Code. Regulations are the only administrative interpretations that require an intensive review and public comment process before they can be issued in final form. Regulations may be classified as interpretative or legislative. An **interpretative regulation** is issued under the general authority of the Treasury Department to provide official interpretations of I.R.C. provisions. A **legislative regulation** is issued when Congress specifically delegates the authority to the Treasury Department to write the specific rules for a designated Code section. For example, Section 469(l) specifically requires the Treasury Department to prescribe such regulations as may be necessary or appropriate to carry out all the provisions of Section 469. Because of this specific delegation of authority to Treasury by Congress, legislative regulations have a higher level of authority than interpretative regulations.

A regulation may be issued in a proposed, temporary, or final form. **Proposed regulations** are issued to let the public know what the IRS believes is the proper interpretation of a related Code provision and to provide an opportunity for the public to comment before they are issued in final form. Proposed regulations are not binding on taxpayers or the IRS until they are issued as **final regulations.** **Temporary regulations** are issued to provide taxpayers with guidance until a final regulation is issued. Section 7805(e), added in 1988, requires all temporary regulations to also be issued as proposed regulations and specifies that the regulation will expire if it is not amended or issued as a final regulation within three years. A regulation issued in its final form represents the Treasury Department's official interpretation and may be different from the position taken in a proposed or temporary regulation.

Revenue Rulings and Procedures.

Although regulations provide valuable interpretative information, they include only statements of general principles and cannot address every situation that could arise under a given Code section. **Revenue rulings** are interpretations by the IRS of the Code and regulations as they apply to specific factual situations. They represent official policy of the IRS and are binding on the IRS until they are revoked, amended, or otherwise changed. They do not, however, carry the same force and effect as a regulation and will be held invalid by a court if they are found to conflict with the intent of the regulation or I.R.C. provision to which they relate.

Revenue procedures are issued to explain internal IRS administrative practices and procedures. For example, a revenue procedure may explain the means by which employers may submit withholding information on computer tapes instead of paper documents. Familiarity with these pronouncements facilitates the processing of the taxpayer's returns and assures compliance with other administrative matters when dealing with the IRS.

The IRS issues hundreds of revenue rulings and procedures every year. Because of the great volume, they are not subject to as extensive a review process as regulations. Because of the lower level of review, revenue rulings and revenue procedures are given less weight than regulations as an authoritative source of the tax law.

Acquiescence and Nonacquiescence.

Whenever the IRS loses in a U.S. Tax Court proceeding, it will notify taxpayers as to whether it agrees or disagrees with the decision by issuing an **acquiescence** or **nonacquiescence.** These will not be issued if the IRS loses in any other court or for memorandum decisions of the U.S. Tax Court. (Other forums for resolving disputes between the IRS and taxpayers and the distinction between regular and memorandum decisions by the tax court are more fully discussed later in the chapter.)

It is important to understand that issuance of an acquiescence or nonacquiescence by the IRS is equivalent to a revenue ruling. Recall that a revenue ruling is the IRS's interpretation and application of the law to a specific factual situation.

When the tax court interprets and applies the law to a specific factual situation, the IRS can in essence make a ruling by signifying that it agrees (or disagrees) with the decision. Like a revenue ruling, an acquiescence or nonacquiescence is binding on the IRS in other, similar, factual situations unless it is later withdrawn.

Other Pronouncements.   The IRS issues various other interpretive pronouncements to aid taxpayers in complying with the tax law. A **private letter ruling (LTR)** is issued by the National Office of the IRS in response to specific questions raised by taxpayers and typically deals with prospective transactions. By issuing revenue procedures, the IRS restricts the areas in which it will issue private letter rulings. An LTR applies only to the taxpayer requesting the ruling and does not bind the IRS to take the same position when dealing with a different taxpayer. If the IRS believes that the transaction represented in an LTR may be of importance to taxpayers in general, it may issue a revenue ruling.

A **technical advice memorandum (TAM)** may be thought of as an LTR for a completed transaction.[6] A TAM originates as a request for assistance by a local office of the IRS and typically arises as part of an ongoing audit. Like the LTR, the TAM is issued by the National Office of the IRS and is not binding on the IRS. LTRs and TAMs are generically referred to as **letter rulings,** and although they are not officially published by the government, they are unofficially made available to the public by many private publishers such as Commerce Clearing House and Research Institute of America. Although they are accorded a lower level of authority, letter rulings are a useful source in determining the current position of the IRS on an issue.

Chief counsel's memoranda are issued by the Office of Chief Counsel of the IRS and include technical memoranda, general counsel's memoranda, and actions on decisions. These documents originate in the process of preparing other authoritative pronouncements and are frequently relied on by IRS personnel in disputes with taxpayers. **Technical memoranda (TM)** are used to explain Treasury regulations. Over the last few years, the use of TM has decreased and been replaced with what is referred to as the *preamble* to Treasury regulations. **General counsel's memoranda (GCM)** explain the authority and reasoning used to prepare revenue rulings, private letter rulings, and technical advice memoranda. **Actions on decisions (AOD)** explain whether the Chief Counsel's Office believes that an adverse court decision should be appealed. If the unfavorable decision is rendered by the tax court, the AOD may suggest that an acquiescence or nonacquiescence be issued. Like letter rulings, these documents are not binding on the service and are not officially published by the government. Nevertheless, they are helpful in understanding the position of the IRS and are made unofficially available by private publishers.

The IRS does publish a variety of other items that are designed to help taxpayers comply with the tax law. These include notices, announcements, IRS publications, and tax return instructions. Caution is warranted, however, because these items are sometimes incomplete and misleading. And, although they are published by the IRS, the taxpayer may not rely on them as an authoritative source for a position taken on a tax return.

Judicial Sources

If a taxpayer and the IRS disagree on the interpretation and application of the Code, the matter may have to be resolved in court. Court decisions are official interpretations and applications of the Code by the judicial branch of government and therefore represent the third source of primary authority. All litigation must start in a trial court. It is the trial court's responsibility to determine the facts and then interpret and apply the law. Whenever the taxpayer or the IRS loses at the trial level, either party may appeal the decision to a higher court. No appellate court, including the Supreme Court, holds another trial (lawyers' arguments must be based on the record of the original trial). These courts' primary responsibility is to determine whether the law was correctly applied to the facts. Only rarely will an appellate court disturb the findings of fact by the trial court. Losses at the first appellate level may be further appealed to the Supreme Court, decisions of which are final and binding on all lower courts.

Trial Courts.   Taxpayers may choose one of three different courts in which to initiate litigation: U.S. District Court, U.S. Court of Federal Claims, and U.S. Tax Court. These courts of original jurisdiction are referred to as the **trial courts.** Taxpayers willing to pay the tax in dispute and then sue for a refund have the option of taking their case to a U.S. District Court or the U.S. Court of Federal Claims. Each **U.S. District Court** hears cases on legal issues involving the entire *United States Code*, of which the Internal Revenue Code is but one small part. Therefore, district court judges must be generalists in matters of federal law and are not specialists in federal tax law. District courts are located throughout the country— each is assigned to serve a specific geographic area. In order to have a jury trial, taxpayers must file in district court. The **U.S. Court of Federal Claims** hears cases concerning any monetary claim against the federal government. Because income tax refunds are only one type of claim that can be filed against the federal government, claims court judges are not specialists in federal tax law. Unlike the district courts, the claims court does not allow jury trials.

As an alternative, taxpayers may choose not to pay the additional tax and then file a petition in **U.S. Tax Court** for relief. There are two distinct advantages in choosing the tax court. First, as indicated, the case can be taken to the tax court without first paying the tax. This is why the tax court is often referred to as the "poor person's court." Second, the tax court offers an opportunity for the issues to be decided by a court that specializes in tax matters.

The tax court has traditionally issued two types of decisions: regular and memorandum. **Tax Court regular decisions** are those that are presumed to have value as precedents or involve issues that have not previously been considered. All other decisions are **Tax Court memorandum decisions.** Regular decisions are generally regarded as stronger authorities than memorandum decisions. Although the distinction has become somewhat blurred over the years, recall that the IRS will issue an acquiescence or nonacquiescence only for regular decisions.

In cases in which the amount of tax in dispute is less than $10,000, a taxpayer may elect to use the small claims division of the tax court. The purpose of the small claims division is to allow taxpayers to obtain a ruling on their case with a minimal amount of formality, delay, and expense. Caution is warranted, however, because small claims cases cannot be appealed, the decisions are not published, and the decisions cannot be used as precedents in other courts.

Both the tax court and the claims court are referred to as *national courts* because they hear cases from taxpayers living anywhere in the United States. A district court can hear cases only from taxpayers who live within the specific geographical area over which the court presides.[7] Taxpayers must consider these jurisdictional differences, whether to pay first, whether the technical expertise of the tax court is desirable, the advantages of a jury, and prior decisions on similar issues when selecting a trial court.

Appellate Courts.   Decisions of the district courts and tax court are appealed to one of 12 regional **U.S. Courts of Appeals** (previously the U.S. Circuit Courts of Appeals and occasionally still referred to as such). Each circuit court has a specific geographical area over which it has sole jurisdiction. Decisions of the U.S. Claims Court must be appealed to the **U.S. Court of Appeals for the Federal Circuit** in Washington, D.C. Decisions by all appellate courts have precedence over trial court decisions. For example, if a circuit court has previously ruled on an issue, all the district courts within that circuit must follow that decision in any future cases.

The tax court will also follow the holdings of a circuit court but only for taxpayers residing within the specific geographical jurisdiction of the appellate court. Outside that circuit, the tax court may hold differently on exactly the same facts and issues. This so-called *Golsen* rule has been justified by the tax court on the ground that it is a trial court with national jurisdiction. The claims court is bound to follow only decisions of the U.S. Court of Appeals for the Federal Circuit.

Although trial courts are bound only by the decisions of their own circuit court, they frequently look to other circuit court decisions as well as decisions of other trial courts in forming their own opinions. Similarly, each circuit court does not need to follow prior decisions of other circuit courts but does look to these decisions for guidance.

Supreme Court.   All decisions of appellate courts may be further appealed to the **U.S. Supreme Court.** Unlike the circuit courts, which must rule on every case that is appealed from the trial courts, the Supreme Court does not have to accept every case that is appealed from the circuit courts. The Supreme Court decides which cases it wants to review by granting a writ of certiorari. Granting the writ of certiorari simply means that at least four of the nine justices on the Court feel the case is important enough for them to review it. Conversely, denying a writ of certiorari means only that the Court does not think the case is important enough for it to review at that time. It does not reverse or in any other way directly affect the decision of the lower court. Review will, however, strengthen the authority or importance of the case in the hierarchy of primary authorities. The Court limits its review of tax cases to those of major importance or to those in which the decisions of the circuit courts conflict.

If the Supreme Court agrees to review a decision, its interpretation and application of the law are the final authority, and all lower courts, taxpayers, and the IRS must follow its decision. If Congress is unhappy with the Court's interpretation and application of the law, its only recourse is to follow the legislative process described earlier and amend the Code.

Citations to Primary Authorities

Whenever a reference is made to any primary authority, it is important to include a citation indicating where the full text of the document may be found. This is an especially crucial part of the tax research process described later in this chapter. Although it is beyond the scope of this text to discuss citation formats in any great depth, a brief review is necessary. Exhibit 15–5 illustrates citations to most of the primary authorities previously discussed and provides the basis for the discussion that follows.

Committee Reports.   All reports issued by the House Ways and Means Committee, the Senate Finance Committee, and the Joint Conference Committee are

▲ Exhibit 15–5

CITATIONS TO PRIMARY
AUTHORITIES

Primary Authority	Citation
Committee report	HOUSE COMMITTEE ON WAYS AND MEANS, H.REP.NO. 432, 98th Cong., 2d Sess. (March 5, 1984).
Internal Revenue Code	Sec. 469(e)(1)(A).
Treasury regulation—final	Reg. Sec. 1.269-1(a)(3).
Treasury regulation—proposed	Prop. Reg. Sec. 1.704-3(c).
Treasury regulation—temporary	Temp. Reg. Sec. 1.441-1T(a)(2).
Revenue ruling—permanent	Rev. Rul. 54-56, 1954-2 C.B. 108.
Revenue ruling—temporary	Rev. Rul. 84-101, I.R.B. No. 28, 5.
Revenue procedure—permanent	Rev. Proc. 88-12, 1988-1 C.B. 17.
Revenue procedure—temporary	Rev. Proc. 93-15, I.R.B. 3, 12.
Private letter ruling	LTR 8450056 (PLR).
U.S. Tax Court—regular decision	J.B. Linderman, 60 T.C. 609 (1973).
U.S. Tax Court—memorandum decision	Thomas E. Lesslie, 36 TCM 495 (1977), T.C. Memo ¶77, 111.
Acquiescence	Phillip G. Larson, 66 T.C. 159 (1976), *acq.* 1979–1 C.B. 1.
U.S. District Court	Arnold v. U.S., 289 F. Supp. 206, 68-2 USTC ¶9590, 22 A.F.T.R.2d 5661 (D.Ct. N.Y., 1968).
U.S. Court of Federal Claims	Zuchman v. U.S., 524 F.2d 729, 75-2 USTC ¶9778, 36 A.F.T.R.2d 75-6193 (Cl.Ct., 1975).
U.S. Courts of Appeals	Comm. v. Percy W. Phillips, 275 F.2d 33, 60-1 USTC ¶9294, 5 A.F.T.R.2d 855 (4th Cir. 1960).
U.S. Supreme Court	Commissioner v. Duberstein, 80 S. Ct. 1190, 60-2 USTC ¶9515, 5 A.F.T.R.2d 1626 (1960).

cited in the same general manner. The example in Exhibit 15–5 is for a House Ways and Means Committee report and tells the reader that it is the 432nd report issued by the House of Representatives during the second session of the 98th Congress and was issued on March 5, 1984. The name of the committee frequently is omitted from the citation. This generally occurs when reference to the committee that issued the report is made in a related text discussion.

Code and Regulations.　References to the Code have been introduced previously. Spelling out *Internal Revenue Code* or inserting *I.R.C.* is usually omitted in practice, because it is understood that the reference is to the Internal Revenue Code of 1986, as amended. The last group of numbers in any Code citation should reflect the smallest subdivision of a section that relates to the tax issue under consideration.

Treasury regulations follow a similar citation pattern, but they are preceded by a number that specifies the general area of tax to which the regulation relates. Most regulations start with *1*, signifying that they deal with income taxes. Other common numbers are *20*, relating to estate taxes; *25*, involving gift taxes; and *301* or *601*, dealing with administrative rules. The first numbers after the period state the related Code section. The Code section number is followed by a hyphen and the number of the regulation. Several different regulations may be issued under the same Code section. The last group of numbers gives the smallest subdivision of the regulation that is appropriate. Proposed and temporary regulations follow the same format, except that they are preceded by *Prop.* or *Temp.* In addition— and only for temporary regulations—a *T* follows the regulation number. Again, spelling out *Treasury* or inserting *Treas.* is usually omitted in practice; common practice is to abbreviate *Section* as *Sec.*, instead of using the symbol for *section*, §.

Other IRS Pronouncements.   All other pronouncements of the IRS are initially published weekly by the U.S. Government Printing Office in the ***Internal Revenue Bulletin* (I.R.B.).** Semiannually, the last six months of the I.R.B. are reorganized and published in a permanent document called the ***Cumulative Bulletin* (C.B.).** Citations to most IRS documents should be to the C.B. Whenever the latest C.B. does not include the referenced document, a temporary citation is made to the I.R.B.

As Exhibit 15–5 illustrates, revenue rulings and procedures are cited similarly. The numbers following *Rev. Rul.* provide the reader with the following information: the ruling was the 56th ruling issued in 1954 and can be found on page 108 of the second volume of the 1954 *Cumulative Bulletin*. The temporary citation yields this information: The ruling is the 101st ruling issued in 1984 and can be found on page 5 of the 28th weekly issue of the *Internal Revenue Bulletin*. Revenue procedures read the same way.

Letter rulings, including private letter rulings and technical advice memoranda, are given an official seven-digit number. The first two digits provide the year the ruling was issued, the next two indicate the week, and the final three digits are the number assigned to that ruling for that week. The citation in Exhibit 15–5 tells the reader that the ruling was issued in 1984, during the 50th week and was the 56th ruling issued that week. Sometimes, the citation includes a designation after the number that tells the reader which type of letter ruling is being cited [i.e., either a private letter ruling (PLR) or a technical advice memorandum (TAM)].

Court Decisions.   All judicial citations follow the same format: case name, volume number of the reporter in which the case is published, name of the reporter, and the page of the reporter on which the case begins. Sometimes, the year of the decision or the name of the court is added in parentheses at the end. A **reporter** is a series of books published by the federal government or by a private publishing company that provides the full text of court decisions. The two biggest private publishers of reporters are the Research Institute of America (RIA, formerly Prentice-Hall) and Commerce Clearing House (CCH). Complete citations typically include one citation to a government reporter and at least one additional citation to a CCH or RIA reporter. Different reporters are cited for each court that renders a decision.

TAX COURT.   Regular decisions of U.S. Tax Court are published by the Government Printing Office (GPO) in a reporter called ***Reports of the United States Tax Court* (T.C.).** CCH and RIA also publish regular tax court decisions in separate special decision reporters. Both are called *Tax Court Reporter*. However, common tax practice is to cite only T.C., the official GPO reporter. The citation for the *Linderman* case in Exhibit 15–5 provides the information that the case can be found on page 609 of volume 60 of *Reports of the United States Tax Court* and that it was decided in 1973.

Memorandum decisions of U.S. Tax Court are not published in any government reporter. They are, however, published by both RIA (*T.C. Memorandum Decisions*) and CCH (*Tax Court Memorandum Decisions*). Common practice is to cite RIA's reporter as *T.C. Memo* and CCH's as *TCM*. As Exhibit 15–5 illustrates, citations for both services follow exactly the same format. For example, the *Lesslie* case can be found on page 495 of volume 36 of *Tax Court Memorandum Decisions* (TCM) and in the 1977 volume of T.C. Memo, at paragraph 77,111. A complete citation would include citations to both reporters.

Whenever the IRS issues an acquiescence (*acq.*) or nonacquiescence (*nonacq.*) to an unfavorable regular decision of U.S. Tax Court, it should be included in the citation, as it is for the *Larson* case in Exhibit 15–5. This informs the reader that the acquiescence can be found on page 1 of volume 1 of the 1979 *Cumulative Bulletin*.

ALL OTHER COURTS EXCEPT THE U.S. SUPREME COURT.   The U.S. government does not officially publish the decisions of the district courts, claims court, or the appellate courts in any reporter. West Publishing Co., however, is treated as the official publisher, and any citation to decisions from these courts should include a citation to one of its reporters. This includes the **Federal Supplement (F. Supp.)** for all district court cases and the **Federal Reporter, 2d series (F.2d)** for claims court and appellate court cases.

These decisions are also reported by RIA in *American Federal Tax Reports* (A.F.T.R. and A.F.T.R.2d) and by Commerce Clearing House in *U.S. Tax Cases* (USTC). The CCH and RIA reporters include only tax cases, whereas the West reporters include all cases decided by the respective courts. A complete citation should cite all three reporters. For example, the citation for the *Arnold* case in Exhibit 15–5 provides the following information: The case can be found on page 206 of volume 289 of the *Federal Supplement;* it is a case decided by the U.S. District Court for New York in 1968; it can also be found at paragraph 9590 of volume 68-2 of *U.S. Tax Cases* and on page 5661 of volume 22 of *American Federal Tax Reports*, second series. Decisions of the appellate courts and the claims court are cited the same way.

SUPREME COURT.   Decisions of the United States Supreme Court are officially printed by the government in the **United States Reports (U.S.)** reporter. Because of their importance, these decision are also published by West Publishing in **Supreme Court Reports (S. Ct.)** and are included in the A.F.T.R. and *U.S. Tax Cases* series. A complete citation should include reference to either the S. Ct. or U.S. reporters and both the A.F.T.R. and USTC reporters. The *Duberstein* case in Exhibit 15–5 is an example of a citation that provides references to all three sources.

SECONDARY SOURCES OF FEDERAL INCOME TAX LAW

Answers to federal tax questions must be based on the primary authorities. However, as we have discussed, the number of these authorities is vast, they are constantly changing, and they are not indexed or coordinated in any logical fashion. The most important role of secondary authorities is to provide help in locating the legislative, administrative, or judicial primary authorities that provide the answers about the tax consequences related to a specific factual situation. Tax services, including computerized versions, and citators are two types of secondary authorities that are used for this purpose. Secondary authorities, including textbooks, journals, and editorial comments in tax services, may also be used to help understand and interpret the law. These are unofficial interpretations only and have no legal authority.

Tax Services

Tax services, one type of secondary authority, principally are tools for locating the primary authorities related to various factual circumstances. They generally consist of a multivolume set of loose-leaf binders that are constantly updated. Tax services fall into two major categories, based on the amount of editorial discussion provided by the publisher. The first category consists of those services with limited editorial discussion and numerous brief interpretations and citations to the primary authorities (other than the Code and regulations, which are provided in full text). These abridged interpretations, or annotations, are indexed according to the Code section to which they relate. They consist chiefly of brief interpretations of revenue rulings and procedures, court cases, letter rulings, and other miscellaneous pronouncements. The researcher must know the Code section that relates to the tax question or may use a topical index to find the appropriate section. Services in this category include *Standard Federal Tax Reporter (CCH)* and *United States Tax Reporter (RIA)*. It is important to remember that the researcher using these services should not rely on the synopses given in the annotations, because they represent only the editors' interpretation of the related authority. The researcher should always read the full text of the appropriate primary authority before reaching any conclusions.

The second category of tax services contains extensive editorial discussion and interpretation of the law, with citations to the primary authorities provided in the footnotes. These services also provide full text of the Code and regulations but are arranged by topical headings determined by the editor. An index is useful for locating the relevant part of the service that discusses the related Code, regulations, and other primary authorities. Services in this category include the Research Institute of America's *Federal Tax Coordinator 2d*, the Bureau of National Affairs's *Tax Management Portfolios*, and *Mertens Law of Federal Income Taxation*, published by Callaghan and Co. The researcher should always read the entire text of the authority cited in the footnotes to be sure that the analysis and interpretation provided in the editorial discussion are proper.

Both categories of tax services should always be checked for current developments, which usually appear in a separate volume. In addition, the publishers of most services provide paperback versions of the Code and regulations, which are convenient and may provide answers to some basic questions. Abridged paperback versions of most tax services, called *tax guides*, are also available from the publishers. Because their coverage is limited, these should be used only for orientation purposes and not for research.

Citators

Citators are used primarily to determine the history of a judicial decision and how that decision has been criticized, approved, or otherwise commented upon in other court decisions. This type of information also is available for revenue rulings, revenue procedures, and certain other administrative pronouncements. Citators are a valuable tool in the "validation" step of tax research, described later in this chapter. Citators refer to the case being evaluated as the **cited case,** and any cases discussing that case are called the **citing cases.** Cited cases are listed alphabetically, followed by the citing cases and rulings.

The history of a cited case refers to all other decisions by higher or lower courts in the same case. For example, if the cited case has been appealed to a higher court, the citator provides the name of the appellate court and whether it affirmed, reversed, or modified the decision of the cited case. Similarly, if the cited case is an appellate court decision, the citator provides the name of the trial court and states whether the cited case affirmed, reversed, or otherwise modified the decision of the lower court. For revenue rulings, citators provide historical citations to related rulings that revoke, modify, or supersede the cited ruling and to any earlier rulings affected by the cited ruling. Citators further provide *citing references*, which provide other rulings or court cases that have discussed the cited ruling.

The citator also gives information about how the decision of the cited case has been interpreted by other courts. These courts can, in their decisions, agree or disagree with the cited case, differentiate the facts or law in their case from the cited case, or may simply refer to the cited case without comment. Some citators use abbreviations to indicate which of these reasons are specified by the citing court. These notations are most useful when the citing cases are numerous.

The citators most frequently used are Research Institute of America's *Federal Tax Citator,* which comes as a multivolume set separate from its tax service, and Commerce Clearing House's two-volume set, which is included in its tax service. As a final step, the researcher using these citators must always check their supplements or current development sections.

Tax Periodicals

Numerous publications, law school journals, and newsletters dealing with tax matters also serve as secondary authorities and sources of tax information. These are especially valuable for planning and notification of new developments. Examples of these sources include *Journal of Taxation, TAXES—The Tax Magazine, Tax Adviser, Estate Planning, University of Virginia Law Review, Tax Notes,* and *Daily Tax Report.* Some tax services, or a separate service such as *Federal Tax Articles* (published by Commerce Clearing House), provide topical indexes to articles in these and other publications.

Computer-Assisted Tax Research

One additional and important secondary source of tax information is referred to as **computer-assisted tax research (CATR).** The researcher can use a computer to gain access to a large tax database containing the full text of virtually all primary and secondary authorities. The researcher uses key words that appear in the document to find a specific authority. The system can also search the database for particular words that must be absent from the document, before or after a specified date, or within so many words of a specified term. Numerous other search terms and strategies are available.

The major CATR systems are LEXIS and WESTLAW and have several useful features. To be complete, tax libraries must keep on hand printed versions of tax services, reporters, cumulative bulletins, newsletters, and the like. Most libraries will not have all the authorities, because they are expensive, require a considerable amount of storage space, and involve staff time to keep them current. In contrast, a CATR system is complete, and all the researcher needs is a terminal with a modem, keyboard, screen, and printer. Cost is a bit more controversial. Some argue that CATR technology is still too expensive to be cost effective. After all, the client ultimately bears the cost of these systems. Others, however, contend that when convenience, completeness, and timeliness are factored in, a CATR system is less expensive than maintaining a traditional tax library.

A recent expansion of the CATR concept is the use of CD-ROM technology, which puts tax databases on compact disks. Instead of using the telephone to access an external database, the researcher has at hand virtually every primary and secondary authority, stored on only a few compact disks. The CDs and a CD reader are acquired for a one-time, up-front cost. The CD-ROM systems eliminate the cost of telephone and search time on an external database, learning time for new staffers to become proficient, and other costs typically associated with on-line CATR systems. In other words, the variable cost of the traditional CATR system is converted to the more fixed cost of the CATR CD-ROM system. The biggest disadvantage of these systems is the difficulty of keeping the material current. Some systems give their purchasers access to an on-line system for up-to-the-minute research, replace the CDs periodically with those that contain more current material, and/or send users monthly floppy disks that contain current information.

TAX RESEARCH

Tax research is simply the process by which the answers to tax questions are determined. From an initial set of facts, the researcher identifies the tax issues to be resolved. The researcher must locate the governing Code section and any administrative or judicial interpretations and evaluate and apply them to the facts. The researcher must draw conclusions and communicate the results and recommendations to the interested parties.

Tax Compliance versus Tax Planning

Tax research usually becomes important for either a transaction that has already been completed or for one that is being contemplated. Finding the answer to a completed transaction is commonly referred to as *compliance work* and typically arises during the preparation of a tax return. Determining the tax consequence of transactions that have not yet been completed is called *tax planning*. In planning situations, tax research is undertaken in order to find the "best" way to accomplish a desired result. Frequently, the best method depends on both tax and nontax considerations.

▲ **EXAMPLE 1**   Edna, a client, tells you she would like to give her son some apartment buildings that she owns. She wants to know the best way to transfer this property to him.

Discussion: The alternatives might include a sale, a gift, or transferring the property to a trust, with Edna's son as beneficiary. Each method has different tax consequences. You also know that Edna does not really trust her son and is quite worried that he will simply take all the profits and let the building deteriorate. This nontax factor may lead you to conclude that the "best" method would be to set up a trust, even if the tax consequences are not the most favorable.

Whether tax research is for compliance or planning, it is important to use a systematic procedure for your research. The basic steps involved in this process are

1.   Establish the facts and determine the issues.
2.   Locate the relevant authorities.
3.   Assess the importance of the authorities.
4.   Reach conclusions, make recommendations, and communicate the results.

Step 1: Establish the Facts and Determine the Issues

All tax research begins with determining the facts. The facts help define the initial tax issues and the apparently applicable Code provisions and any administrative or judicial interpretations. Reviewing these authorities most likely leads to the need for more information. Such additional information may yield citations of other applicable authorities, which again may require the researcher to track down further factual information. Following the trail of facts and authorities is an inherent part of the tax research process.

▲ **EXAMPLE 2**   Let us return to your client, Edna. Assume she sold the property to her son and that the sale resulted in a loss. Is the loss deductible?

Discussion: The applicable statutory provision is Sec. 267 of the Code. Sec. 267(a)(1) disallows losses between persons specified in Sec. 267(b), which includes members of family, as defined in Sec. 267(c)(4). Sec. 267(c)(4) specifies that members of a family include the taxpayer's brothers and sisters, spouse, ancestors, and lineal descendants. Your initial conclusion is that the loss will be disallowed as a deduction. But further discussion with the taxpayer yields the information that the son is really a stepson who was never legally adopted. This additional fact changes your conclusion. Under the authority of Reg. Sec. 1.267(c)-1(a)(4), only legally adopted lineal descendants are members of the family. Edna may take the loss as a deduction.

Facts relevant to a tax situation include the taxpayer's method of accounting, the marital status of the taxpayer, whether the parties to a transaction are related, the domicile and citizenship of the taxpayer, and whether the taxpayer is a partner or S corporation shareholder. When the taxpayer is a corporation, relevant tax facts include whether it is an S or C corporation, whether it is tax exempt, and whether it is a financial institution, insurance company, or personal holding company. In some cases, the facts are well established, and the only issue is how the tax law is interpreted and how that interpretation applies to the facts. These are generally referred to as *questions of law*, in contrast to questions of fact.

Step 2: Locate the Relevant Authorities

Secondary authorities are most useful for locating the applicable primary authorities. Usually, this means research begins with the index to one of the tax services. The index provides a reference to the part of the service that contains the full text of the relevant Code section and regulations, as well as annotations of court decisions and administrative pronouncements. Remember that any editorial commentary included in the tax services is secondary authority only. All conclusions and recommendations must be based on primary authorities. Further, conclusions should never be based on the annotations provided by the editorial staff of the publishers of the tax services. You must examine and evaluate the full text of the court case, revenue ruling, or other primary authority, as indicated in step 3.

Step 3: Assess the Importance of the Authorities

Once you have located the apparently applicable authorities, you must evaluate them to determine whether they actually are applicable to the facts and issues and to assess their importance. Determining whether the authority is relevant to the tax issues under consideration is accomplished by reading the full text of the document. Determining the importance, or relative weight, of the authorities is more difficult. In many cases, the Code and regulations do not provide a conclusive answer to the issues involved in a specific set of facts. You may have to rely on other administrative or judicial authorities, and these are frequently in conflict. To determine the inherent strength or weakness of these authorities, you need a general understanding of the hierarchy of the authorities and how to use a citator.

Code and Regulations. Sometimes, simply reading the applicable Code section yields the answer to a tax question. More often, however, the statutory language is ambiguous or does not directly address the issues identified. Under these circumstances, the secondary authorities—especially the citators and annotations in the tax services—are useful for finding other primary authorities that may be helpful in evaluating and applying the statute. In relatively rare circumstances, you will find no other regulations, IRS pronouncements, or court decisions that conclusively deal with the issue. When this occurs, you must examine the legislative history of the provision, as provided by the committee reports, for congressional intent. One other point bears repeating. Compliance work frequently requires determining the answer to a transaction that occurred some years earlier. Accordingly, it is important to be sure that the version of the Code or Treasury regulation you are using applies to the period in which the transaction occurred.

The Code is generally considered the highest authority, because it is the law as enacted by Congress. If the issue deals with international tax matters, treaties as enacted by Congress may supersede provisions in the Code. The courts can invalidate a section of the Code or a treaty only if it violates the U.S. Constitution.

Treasury regulations, representing the official interpretation of the law by the Treasury Department, are often referred to as having *the force and effect of the law.* The courts can invalidate them only by determining that they are inconsistent with the statute to which they relate. In assessing the importance of Treasury regulations, it is important to remember that there are different types of regulations. Temporary regulations are accorded the same weight as final regulations. Proposed regulations carry no authority, because they are only indications of what the Treasury Department may decide. They are not binding on either the taxpayer or the IRS. Recall that there also are interpretive and legislative regulations. Legislative regulations, by their very nature, are accorded more authority than interpretive regulations.

Pronouncements.   Revenue rulings, issued by the IRS, represent agency policy and are binding on the IRS and its personnel until they are revoked, modified, superseded, or withdrawn. Although they are accorded considerable importance, they do not have the force and effect of a Treasury regulation, primarily because they are subjected to only a limited review before they are issued. The courts frequently find that a ruling is inconsistent with the Code section or regulation it is interpreting. It is important to use a citator to determine not only the current status of the ruling but also *how* the ruling has been evaluated by the courts. Because an acquiescence or nonacquiescence by the IRS to an adverse tax court decision is tantamount to a revenue ruling, acquiescenses and nonacquiescenses are accorded the same weight as revenue rulings. This procedure should be followed in assessing the importance of any other IRS pronouncement.

Court Decisions.   Numerous factors affect the strength of a court decision. One factor is whether the decision was issued by a trial or appellate court. A decision by the U.S. Court of Appeals for the Third Circuit would be more authoritative than a trial court decision. An opinion by the Supreme Court would be the highest authority.

Another important factor is whether the decision was issued by the tax court or some other trial court. Recall that the tax court is generally considered to have more technical expertise than other trial courts.

▲ EXAMPLE 3   On a very technical question, your research turns up an applicable tax court decision that provides favorable support for the position your client wants to take. You also find a district court decision on substantially identical facts but with opposite results.

Discussion: If the two cases are identical in all other respects, the tax court decision is the higher authority. Similarly, a regular decision of the U.S. Tax Court generally carries more weight than a memorandum decision.

Other factors to be considered in determining the level of authority of a court decision include whether the decision is unanimous or split and the jurisdictional issues regarding the taxpayer's residence, discussed earlier. All the factors can be determined by actually reading the case.

The most important factor determining the relative importance or weight accorded a court decision is how other courts have viewed the decision. Using a citator is crucial for determining how the opinion stacks up with other decisions on the same issue. A strong decision would be one with a long history of favorable evaluation by other courts.

Step 4: Reach Conclusions, Make Recommendations, and Communicate the Results

The final research step is both objective and subjective. You must reach objective conclusions about each primary authority and how it applies to the facts and issues under consideration. In reporting to the client, you must include all your conclusions, whether they result in a favorable outcome for the taxpayer or not. These objective conclusions state what you believe is the current state of the law.

From these conclusions, you must subjectively determine which of the often-conflicting interpretations is the correct one to recommend. Your recommendation should include a research memorandum that encompasses a statement of the relevant facts, the tax issues considered, the conclusions and recommendations reached for each issue, and the authorities, reasoning, and analysis used to arrive at each conclusion and recommendation. Always provide citations to supporting primary authorities.

The research memorandum provides the basis for a separate letter to the taxpayer, which, although containing basically the same information, is less detailed. The importance of the research memorandum and letter cannot be over emphasized. All your research will be wasted if you do not communicate the results effectively.

COMPREHENSIVE RESEARCH EXAMPLE

Step 1: Establish the Facts and Determine the Issues

Sam, a surgeon, and his wife Sara own and rent out a vacation home. During the year, they use the home 20 days and rent it for 40 days. Rental income for the year was $4,000. Total expenses are as follows:

Interest and taxes	$4,200
Utilities and maintenance	1,500
Depreciation	6,000

Sam has asked for assistance in determining the tax treatment of these expenditures.

Step 2: Locate the Relevant Authorities

Using the index to any of the tax services leads to Sec. 280A, "Disallowance Of Certain Expenses in Connection with Business Use of Home, Rental of Vacation Homes, Etc." A review of the editorial discussion and annotations indicates that Prop. Reg. Sec. 1.280A-3 and *Bolton v. Commissioner*, 694 F.2d 556, 51 A.F.T.R.2d 83-305, 83-20 USTC ¶9699 (9th Cir. 1982), affirming 77 T.C. 104 (1981), may also be applicable.

Step 3: Assess the Importance of the Authorities

Completion of this step requires review of each authority identified to determine its applicability. Always examine the relevant Code section first. If questions remain unanswered, you must look to the administrative and judicial interpretations to see if they provide definitive answers or at least some direction.

The Code.   Exhibit 15–6 provides the relevant portions of Sec. 280A. The general rule of Sec. 280A(a) limits a taxpayer's business deductions for expenses incurred for a dwelling unit if that unit was used as a personal residence during the taxable year. Under Sec. 280A(d)(1), the general rule of Sec. 280A(a) applies if the taxpayer's personal use of the dwelling unit exceeds the greater of 14 days or 10 percent of the number of days the unit is rented. Because Sam and Sara's personal use of

▲ **Exhibit 15–6**

CODE SECTION 280A

Sec. 280A Disallowance of **Certain Expenses** in Connection with Business Use of Home, Rental of Vacation Homes, etc.

(a) **General rule.** Except as otherwise provided in this section, in the case of a taxpayer who is an individual or an S corporation, no deduction otherwise allowable under this chapter shall be allowed with respect to the use of a dwelling unit which is used by the taxpayer during the taxable years as a residence.

(b) **Exception for interest, taxes, casualty losses, etc.** Subsection (a) shall not apply to any deduction allowable to the taxpayer without regard to its connection with his trade or business (or with his income-producing activity).

(c) **Exceptions for certain business or rental use; limitation on deductions for such use.**

. . . .

  (3) **Rental use.** Subsection (a) shall not apply to any item which is attributable to the rental of the dwelling unit or portion thereof (determined after the application of subsection (e)).

. . . .

  (5) **Limitation on deductions.** In the case of a use described in paragraph (1), (2), or (4), and in the case of a use described in paragraph (3) where the dwelling unit is used by the taxpayer during the taxable year as a residence, the deductions allowed under this chapter for the taxable year by reason of being attributed to such use shall not exceed the excess of—

  (A) the gross income derived from such use for the taxable year, over
  (B) the sum of—
      (i) the deductions allocable to such use which are allowable under this chapter for the taxable year whether or not such unit (or portion thereof) was so used, and
      (ii) the deductions allocable to the trade or business (or rental activity) in which such use occurs (but which are not allocable to such use) for such taxable year. . . .

(e) **Expenses attributable to rental.**

  (1) **In general.** In any case where a taxpayer who is an individual or an S corporation uses a dwelling unit for personal purposes on any day during the taxable year (whether or not he is treated under this section as using such unit as a residence), the amount deductible under this chapter with respect to expenses attributable to the rental of the unit (or portion thereof) for the taxable year shall not exceed an amount which bears the same relationship to such expenses as the number of days during each year that the unit (or portion thereof) is rented at a fair rental bears to the total number of days during such year that the unit (or portion thereof) is used.

  (2) **Exception for deductions otherwise allowable.** This subsection shall not apply with respect to deduction which would be allowable under this chapter for the taxable year whether or not such unit (or portion thereof) was rented.

the vacation home exceeds both 14 days and 10 percent of the rental days, the general limitation applies.

Sec. 280A(b) provides that nonbusiness expenditures otherwise deductible (e.g., taxes, interest, and casualty losses) are not subject to the general limitation in Sec. 280A(a). Sec. 280A(c)(3) provides another exception to the general limitation by allowing a deduction for "any item attributable to rental of the unit" (e.g., utilities, maintenance, and depreciation). The latter so-called maintenance expenditures, however, must first be allocated to the rental use under the rules of Sec. 280A(e)(1) and then are limited under the rules of Sec. 280A(c)(5).

Sec. 280A(e)(1) requires that the maintenance expenditures attributable to the rental use be allocated using the following formula:

$$\frac{\text{Number of days in the tax year the unit is rented}}{\text{Total number of days in the tax year the unit is used}}$$

All maintenance expenditures are multiplied by this ratio to arrive at a tentative deduction figure. Applying the formula to the facts for Sam and Sara results in the following calculation:

$$\frac{40 \text{ (days rented)}}{60 \text{ (days used)}} = 66.67\% \times \$7{,}500 = \$5{,}000$$

In other words, of the total maintenance expenditures of $7,500, the maximum amount allocable to the rental activity that may be deducted is $5,000.

Sec. 280A(c)(5) may further limit deductions for maintenance expenditures. It provides that all expenses (interest, taxes, casualty losses, and maintenance expenditures) allocable to the rental activity cannot exceed the gross rental income. Further, it requires that deductions allowed (e.g., interest, taxes, and casualty losses), whether the unit was used as a rental or not, be allocated to the rental activity and to the amount otherwise allowable as itemized deductions. Any maintenance expenditures are then allowable to the extent that gross rental income exceeds the interest, taxes, and casualty losses allocable to the rental use. Although Sec. 280A(e) does provide the rules for allocating the maintenance expenditures, it provides no guidance for allocating the interest, taxes, and casualty losses. As the editorial commentary in the tax service noted, this has been an area of dispute, with the proposed regulations suggesting one method and the court in *Bolton* suggesting another allocation method.

Regulations.   Prop. Reg. Sec. 1.280A-3(c)(1) requires that interest and taxes be allocated in the same fashion as maintenance expenditures under Sec. 280A(e)(1). For Sam and Sara, a tentative conclusion is that the allocation used should be 40:60 (as suggested in the proposed regulation), which would yield the following calculations:

	Total	Rental Use	Itemized Deduction	Not Deductible
Gross rental income	$4,000	$4,000	—	—
Interest & taxes	(4,200)	(2,800)	$1,400	
Excess		$1,200		
Maintenance	(7,500)	(1,200)		$6,300
Total		$ -0-	$1,400	$6,300

Court Decision.   In *Bolton*, the U.S. Court of Appeals for the Ninth Circuit affirmed a decision of the U.S. Tax Court, which held that the interpretation provided in the proposed regulation was inconsistent with the statute, its history, and the legislative purpose behind Sec. 280A. The courts held that interest and taxes, unlike maintenance expenditures, are expenses that continue or accrue on a daily basis throughout the year. Accordingly, they should be allocated according to a ratio of days rented to total days in the year.

For Sam and Sara, a tentative conclusion using an allocation of 40:60 for the maintenance expenditures and 40:365 for interest and taxes, as suggested in *Bolton*, would be as follows:

	Total	Rental Use	Itemized Deduction	Not Deductible
Gross rental income	$4,000	$4,000	—	—
Interest & taxes	(4,200)	(460)	$3,740	
Excess		$3,540		
Maintenance	(7,500)	(3,540)		$3,960
Total		$ -0-	$3,740	$3,960

It should be noted that the proposed regulations were initially issued on August 7, 1980, and amended on July 21, 1983. The ninth circuit's decision in *Bolton* was rendered on December 2, 1982, which was before the last revision to the proposed regulations. The citator provides the information that the IRS has not issued an acquiescence or nonacquiescence to the unfavorable tax court decision, that the ninth circuit's decision has been cited in numerous tax court regular and memorandum decisions, and that its decision has been followed by the tenth circuit in *Edith McKinney v. Comm.*, 732 F.2d 416, 52 A.F.T.R.2d 83-6281, 83-2 USTC ¶9655 (10th Cir. 1983).

Step 4: Reach Conclusions, Make Recommendations, and Communicate the Results

The conclusion reached by the court in *Bolton* is much more favorable for Sara and Sam than the position taken by the proposed regulations. The tax court's allocation formula results in a smaller allocation of interest and taxes to the rental unit, an increase in itemized deductions, and a decrease in taxable income for the current year.

A recommendation to Sara and Sam to follow the allocation formula in *Bolton* should be accompanied by some words of caution. The proposed regulations, which were struck down, have not been amended to reflect the tax court and ninth circuit decisions. The failure to amend the proposed regulations could be a signal that the IRS will continue to litigate similar cases in hopes of receiving a favorable decision in another circuit. You should prepare a research memorandum and letter to Sara and Sam that reflects these findings and conclusions.

THE AUDIT AND APPEAL PROCESS WITHIN THE IRS

The federal income tax system is based on self-assessment, which requires taxpayers to report and pay their taxes correctly. IRS examinations, or audits, can vary from a letter that requests supporting information by mail to a full-scale, continuous examination of large corporations in which teams of IRS agents work at each taxpayer's office. Taxpayers who do not agree to changes suggested by the IRS during an audit can appeal the matter to a higher administrative level within the IRS. Generally, taxpayers cannot be charged with any additional taxes, interest, or penalties without first being formally notified. Whenever settlement cannot be reached with the IRS, the taxpayer can initiate litigation in one of the trial courts described previously.

Tax Return Selection Processes

The IRS cannot possibly examine every return that is filed. It does examine as many returns as possible, given its staffing and facility levels. Currently, this amounts to about only 2 percent of all returns filed. The IRS uses five general methods to verify that taxpayers are properly self-assessing their taxes. One of the most important is a computerized return selection program called the **Discriminant Function System (DIF).** Through mathematical analysis of historical data, this program selects those returns with the highest probability of containing errors. Selected returns are typically examined only for specific items such as charitable contributions or employee business expenses. A related program is the **Taxpayer Compliance Measurement Program (TCMP).** Returns are randomly selected from different income levels, and every item on the return is comprehensively audited. The results are used to set the parameters for the **DIF** computer selection program. The IRS has suspended the TCMP audits for 1996 because of reductions to its budget.

Virtually all returns are checked for mathematical, tax calculation, and clerical errors during the initial processing of the returns. If an error is discovered under this **document perfection program,** the IRS recalculates the amount of tax due and sends an explanation to the taxpayer. Another program of increasing importance is called the **information-matching program.** Information returns from banks, employers, and others on forms such as the W-2 for wages and withholding and the 1099 for miscellaneous income are matched to the taxpayer's return. For any omitted or incorrect items, the IRS recomputes the tax and sends an explanation to the taxpayer. Finally, a number of **special audit programs** are designed by the IRS and combine computer and manual selection based on various standards that are changed periodically. Some of the standards used include the size of the refund, the amount of adjusted gross income reported, the amount or type of deduction claimed, and so on.

Types of Examinations

There are three basic types of IRS examinations. **Correspondence examinations** are those that can be routinely handled by mail. Most originate at the IRS service centers and involve routine requests for supporting documents such as canceled checks or some other written instruments. A written reply to the questions raised, along with copies of supporting documents, usually completes the examination.

Office examinations are conducted at the local district office of the IRS and usually involve middle-income, nonbusiness returns and small sole proprietorships. The taxpayer is notified by letter of the date and time of the exam, as well as the items for which proof is requested. Most taxpayers appear for themselves, although some may be represented by their return preparers or other tax advisers. The audit is relatively informal, and the IRS agent has considerable discretion in resolving factual questions such as substantiation of travel expenses. For questions of law, however, the agent must follow IRS policy as expressed in Treasury regulations, revenue rulings and procedures, and the like, even if the taxpayer has court decisions that indicate otherwise.

Field examinations are conducted at the taxpayer's place of business and can involve any item on the income tax return as well as any items on the payroll and excise tax returns. These examinations are handled by more experienced IRS agents, and almost all taxpayers are represented by their tax advisers. As with office examinations, IRS agents must follow their own rulings on matters of law and are accorded a great deal of latitude in settling matters of fact.

Settlement Procedures

After the examination, the agent prepares a report, known as the **revenue agent's report (RAR)**, describing how each issue was settled and the amount of any additional tax or refund due the taxpayer. The agent also prepares a **waiver of restrictions on assessment (Form 870)**, which states that the taxpayer waives any restrictions against assessment and collection of the tax by the IRS. Both items are mailed to the taxpayer in a letter commonly called the **30-day letter**, along with an IRS publication describing the taxpayer's appeal rights.

A signed Form 870 means that the taxpayer agrees to the proposed changes, but it is not binding on either the taxpayer or the IRS. The taxpayer merely agrees to pay the additional tax due while reserving the right to file for a refund in a subsequent court action. Generally, the IRS rejects a settlement reached by its agents only if there is fraud or a misrepresentation of a material fact.

Administrative Appeals

A taxpayer who does not agree with the agent's report may request a meeting with agents from the **IRS Appeals Division** within 30 days of the date of the letter. If the additional tax due exceeds $2,500, the taxpayer must include a written response to the agent's findings; the taxpayer's response is called a **protest letter.** When the amount is less than $2,500 or is the result of a correspondence or office examination, no written protest is required.

The administrative appeal process allows taxpayers one additional opportunity to reach a settlement before resorting to the courts. The appeals division has the authority to consider the **hazards of litigation.** For example, when the facts or the law are uncertain, or both, the appeals division may settle issues it does not want to litigate, even if the IRS position has some merit. After what may be lengthy negotiations, taxpayers who finally reach an agreement with the IRS, or who simply don't want to pursue the matter, sign the Form 870 (or Form 870-AD, if the IRS has conceded some issues) and pay the full amount of the deficiency plus any penalties and interest.

Taxpayers unable to reach an agreement in the appeals division, or who have bypassed the appeals division by failing to respond to the 30-day letter, are sent a **statutory notice of deficiency.** This letter is the official notification by the IRS that it intends to assess or charge the taxpayer for some additional taxes and is commonly referred to as a **90-day letter.**

Taxpayers who are not interested in going to court can simply wait 90 days to have the deficiency formally assessed and then pay any additional amounts due. Taxpayers who want to litigate in district court or the claims court first must pay the amounts due and file for a refund in the court of their choice. Taxpayers who do not want to pay first must file a petition with the U.S. Tax Court within 90 days of the date of the letter. The decision to take an unresolved issue to court involves a number of additional factors and typically is made only with the advice of legal counsel specializing in tax litigation.

SUMMARY

Tax research is the process by which the primary tax law authorities are located, evaluated, and applied to a specific factual situation. The different types of primary authorities are related to the three principal functions of government: legislative, administrative, and judicial. Legislative authorities include the Constitution, treaties, the Internal Revenue Code of 1986, and the committee reports issued by Congress as new tax laws are enacted. Administrative authorities consist of Treasury regulations, revenue rulings, revenue procedures, and other miscellaneous pronouncements issued by the Internal Revenue Service. Judicial authorities include decisions by the various trial and appellate courts in tax-related matters.

Secondary authorities are all other publications that are helpful in locating, evaluating, and applying the primary authorities to the specific factual situation under consideration. They consist primarily of tax services, citators, and computer software systems that research tax databases, tax journals, and tax newsletters.

A systematic procedure must be followed in order to locate, evaluate, and apply the primary authorities to a specific factual situation. The steps involved in this process are to establish the facts and identify the issues, locate the relevant authorities, evaluate and apply the authorities to the facts, reach conclusions and make recommendations, and communicate the results to interested parties.

This chapter also reviewed the audit and appeal process within the Internal Revenue Service. Among the procedures used by the IRS to select returns for examination are the Taxpayer Compliance Measurement Program, the document perfection program, the information-matching program, and a number of special audit programs. Selected returns are subject to correspondence, office, or field examinations. An appeal process is available within the IRS if the taxpayer disagrees with the results of the examination. Taxpayers unable to reach an agreement with the IRS through the appeals process may proceed to court for ultimate resolution of the tax issues.

KEY TERMS

30-day letter (p. 709)
90-day letter (p. 709)
acquiescence (p. 692)
action on decision (AOD) (p. 693)
chief counsel's memorandum
  (p. 693)
citator (p. 699)
cited case (p. 699)
citing case (p. 699)
computer-assisted tax research
  (CATR) (p. 700)
correspondence examination
  (p. 708)
Cumulative Bulletin (C.B.) (p. 697)
Discriminant Function System
  (DIF) (p. 708)

document perfection program
  (p. 708)
Federal Reporter, 2d series (F.2d)
  (p. 698)
Federal Supplement, (F. Supp.)
  (p. 698)
Federal Tax Citator (p. 700)
field examination (p. 709)
final regulation (p. 692)
general counsel's memorandum
  (GCM) (p. 693)
hazards of litigation (p. 709)
information-matching program
  (p. 708)
Internal Revenue Bulletin (I.R.B.)
  (p. 697)

interpretive regulation (p. 691)
IRS Appeals Division (p. 709)
legislative regulation (p. 692)
letter ruling (p. 693)
nonacquiescence (p. 692)
office examination (p. 708)
primary authorities (p. 685)
private letter ruling (LTR)
  (p. 693)
proposed regulation (p. 692)
protest letter (p. 709)
reporter (p. 697)
*Reports of the United States Tax
  Court* (T.C.) (p. 697)
revenue agent's report (RAR)
  (p. 709)

revenue procedure (p. 692)
revenue ruling (p. 692)
secondary authorities (p. 685)
special audit program (p. 708)
statutory notice of deficiency
(p. 709)
Supreme Court Reports (S. Ct.)
(p. 698)
Tax Court memorandum decision
(p. 694)
Tax Court regular decision (p. 694)

tax service (p. 698)
*Taxpayer Compliance Measurement
Program* (TCMP) (p. 708)
technical advice memorandum
(TAM) (p. 693)
technical memorandum (TM)
(p. 693)
temporary regulation (p. 692)
trial court (p. 694)
United States Reports (U.S.)
(p. 698)

U.S. Court of Federal Claims
(p. 694)
U.S. Courts of Appeals (p. 695)
U.S. Court of Appeals for the
Federal Circuit (p. 695)
U.S. District Court (p. 694)
U.S. Supreme Court (p. 695)
U.S. Tax Court (p. 694)
waiver of restrictions on
assessment (Form 870) (p. 709)

PRIMARY TAX LAW SOURCES

[1] See Secs. 8001–8023 for information on the organization, membership, powers, and other matters relating to the Joint Committee on Taxation.

[2] Sec. 894—Requires application of the Internal Revenue Code to give due regard to any treaty obligations of the United States.

[3] Sec. 7801—Specifies the powers and the duties of the secretary of the Treasury.

[4] Sec. 7802—Establishes the position of commissioner of the Internal Revenue Service, whose duties are to be prescribed by the secretary of the Treasury.

[5] Sec. 7805—Authorizes the secretary of the Treasury to issue the rules and regulations necessary for the enforcement of the income tax law.

[6] The abbreviations given here are those commonly used in citing various tax materials. However, some of these abbreviations are different from those specified by *The Bluebook, A Uniform System of Citation* (the lawyer's bible) and do not appear in the list of abbreviations used by the *Cumulative Bulletin*, to which the *Bluebook* defers on tax matters. Thus, tax researchers occasionally may encounter cites to Tech. Adv. Mem. instead of TAM, to Tech. Mem. instead of TM, and to PLR instead of LTR.

[7] See Secs. 7401–7434 for organization, jurisdiction, and other procedural matters relating to the Tax Court. Similar matters for district court cases involving tax-related issues are covered in Sections 7401–7434.

DISCUSSION QUESTIONS

1. Differentiate primary tax law authorities and secondary tax law authorities.

2. Briefly describe the three categories of primary authorities and the different types of authorities within each category.

3. Name the different types of secondary authorities.

4. On what grounds have tax protesters challenged the income tax?

5. The Internal Revenue Code is just one part of the *U.S. Code*. Explain.

6. Name the different subdivisions of the Internal Revenue Code.

7. What would be the general nature of Sec. 612? Sec. 6601?

8. How many chapters are there within Subtitle A?

9. What are some of the things to look out for when reading the Code?

10. Give examples of how the Code is sometimes used to achieve economic and social objectives.

11. Briefly describe the process by which a new tax law is passed.

12. What are the three reports that are issued as part of the legislative process?

13. How are the Joint Conference Committee and the Joint Committee on Taxation different?

14. What is a Treasury regulation? Are they binding on the courts?

15. Differentiate an interpretive regulation and a legislative regulation.

16. Differentiate a proposed regulation and a temporary regulation.

17. What are revenue rulings? revenue procedures?

18. How are a revenue ruling and a Treasury regulation different? a revenue ruling and a private letter ruling?

19. What does it mean when the IRS issues an acquiescence or nonacquiescence?

20. What is the difference between a revenue ruling and a case in which the IRS has issued an acquiescence?

21. Name the other types of pronouncements issued by the IRS, and briefly describe their content.

22. What are the three trial courts? Which is most important?

23. What is meant by the *Golsen* rule?

24. Do district courts have to follow the decisions of all circuit courts?

25. What does it mean when the Supreme Court issues a writ of certiorari?

26. Assume that the Supreme Court interprets a certain Code section in a manner that members of Congress believe is contrary to what they meant when they originally enacted that part of the Code. What (if anything) can Congress do?

27. Interpret the following citations:
    a. SENATE FINANCE COMMITTEE, S. REP. NO. 2, 97th Cong., 2d Sess. (April 15, 1982).
    b. LTR 8101067.
    c. Rev. Proc. 78-172, 1978-2 C.B. 22.
    d. Lacy v. Comm., 344 F.2d 123, 89-1 USTC ¶1221, 43 A.F.T.R. 89-2233 (9th Cir. 1989).

28. Provide the correct citations for the following:
    a. The fifteenth revenue procedure issued in 1993 and found on page 12 of the third *Internal Revenue Bulletin* issued in 1993.
    b. Subsection (a) of the first temporary income tax regulation interpreting Section 63.
    c. An acquiescence issued by the IRS on page 1 of volume 1 of the 1992 *Cumulative Bulletin* related to *Chasteen v. Comm.*, which was reported on page 132 of volume 77 of *Reports of the United States Tax Court* in 1991.

29. Why is it that some court decisions will have two or three different citations?

30. Describe the two major categories of tax services.

31. When can a researcher rely on an editorial opinion expressed in the tax services?

32. Differentiate a cited case and a citing case.

33. What is meant by the history of a cited case?

34. Assume that you have found an excellent article in *Tax Notes* that provides a favorable interpretation of Sec. 469. Can you rely on that article as authority for your position? In general, what role do tax periodicals and newsletters play in tax research?

35. What are some of the advantages and disadvantages of CATR?

36. Briefly describe the steps involved in tax research.

37. Briefly describe the different types of programs used by the IRS to select a return for audit.

38. What are the three different types of IRS examinations?

39. What is included in the 30-day letter, and what options does the taxpayer have after receiving one?

40. What does the 90-day letter represent, and what are the choices the taxpayer has after receiving one?

Income Problems

41. Gary is an internal auditor for Bodine Information Systems (BIF). In 1993, BIF opened a large production plant in Las Vegas, Nevada. Subsequently, Gary has had to spend several months each year at the Las Vegas facility. Gary has always fancied himself a proficient blackjack player. During his trips to Las Vegas, he stays at a hotel on the Strip and spends a considerable amount of his off-duty time gambling.

   In February 1994, Gary applies for (and receives) a $20,000 line of credit at the hotel to be used for gambling. The line of credit allows him to receive gambling chips in exchange for signing markers. The markers are negotiable drafts payable to the hotel and drawn on Gary's personal bank account. The hotel's practice is to hold the markers for 60 days, at which time Gary pays them with a personal check.

   By the beginning of 1995, Gary is gambling heavily at the hotel. He requests and receives an increase in his credit limit to $100,000. Gary continues to lose heavily, and through some accounting oversights by the hotel, his debt has risen to $325,000 by October 1995. The checks that Gary writes to cover the markers are returned for insufficient funds, and the hotel immediately cuts off his credit. The hotel subsequently files suit in state court, seeking repayment of the $325,000 owed on the markers.

   In early 1996, Gary negotiates a settlement with the hotel whereby he will settle the debt for 4 monthly payments of $25,000 ($100,000). Gary pays the $100,000 per the terms of the agreement. He seeks your advice as to the tax consequences of the settlement with the hotel. That is, does he have to include in his gross income the amount of the debt he didn't have to repay?

42. Adrian is a salesperson who represents several different wholesale companies. On January 2, 1996, she receives by mail a commission check from Ace Distributors in the amount of $10,000 and dated December 30, 1995. Adrian is concerned about the year in which the $10,000 is taxable. Although the check is dated 1995, she contends that it would have been unreasonable for her to drive the 50 miles to the Ace offices on a Saturday (December 30, 1995, is a Saturday) to collect the check. Further, Adrian maintains that even if she had made the trip on Saturday to collect the check, by the time she returned home, her bank would have closed and she could not have received credit for the check until Monday. Adrian would like you to determine whether she should include the $10,000 on her 1995 or 1996 tax return.

43. Hawaii law requires the state to deposit a portion of its annual pineapple income in the Hawaiian Long-lasting Fund. All income from the fund is deposited in the state's general fund. The fund's general manager is permitted to use the funds to buy only certain income-producing assets, such as government and corporate obligations, preferred and common stock of U.S. corporations, and equity interests in partnerships and other entities that invest in real estate. Each year, a portion of the fund's income is transferred to a dividend fund that distributes the dividends to native Hawaiians.

   At issue is whether such payments constitute income to native Hawaiians and, if so, what type of income is being received—is any income generated from the distributions either investment income or passive activity income?

44. After Maria and Tatsuo are divorced, their 2 minor children continue to live with Maria. Pursuant to their divorce decree, Tatsuo pays Maria $1,000 per month in child support and $1,800 per month in alimony. The divorce decree specifies that, in the event of a court-ordered increase in child support, the alimony payment amount will decrease by the amount of the child support increase. That is, Tatsuo's total monthly payment cannot exceed $2,800. Read the following authorities and determine how much gross income Maria has from the payments received from Tatsuo:

   Sec. 71.
   Temp. Reg. Sec. 1.71–1T.
   Madeline Davis Heller, 68 TCM 838 (1994).

45. Lorissa owes Waterbury State Bank $200,000. During the current year, she is unable to make the required payments on the loan and negotiates the following terms to extinguish the debt. Lorissa transfers to Waterbury ownership of investment property with a value of $90,000 and a basis of $55,000, common stock with a value of $50,000 and a basis of $70,000. Lorissa also pays Waterbury $5,000 cash and Waterbury forgives the remaining amount of debt. Before the agreement, Lorissa's assets are $290,000 and her liabilities are $440,000.

Read and analyze the following authorities and determine how much gross income Lorissa has from the extinguishment of the debt:

Sec. 108.
Reg. Sec. 1.61–12.
Reg. Sec. 1.1001–2.
Julian S. Danenberg, 73 T.C. 370 (1979).
James J. Gehl, 102 T.C. 74 (1994).

46. Henry invests $50,000 in an entity called Forward Investments on January 20, 1995. Under the terms of the investment agreement, the $50,000 is considered a loan that Forward will use to invest in derivative contracts. Henry is to receive 2% of the amount Forward earns each month from his investment plus 10 percent simple interest on funds left invested for a full year. Henry can withdraw part or all of his investment at any time on 10 days' notice to Forward.

During 1995, Henry receives quarterly statements of earnings on his investment in Forward. As of December 31, 1995, the statements indicate that Henry has earned $9,600. In January 1996, Henry hears a rumor that Forward Investments was not a legitimate investment broker. On January 26, 1996, Henry withdraws his investment, receiving $60,050 (the $50,000 original investment plus $10,050 in earnings). In late February, Henry learns that Forward Investments is a pyramid scheme through which early investors were paid earnings out of capital contributions made by later investors. The U.S. Securities and Exchange Commission files suit against Forward in March 1996.

Henry wants to know the taxability of the amounts he received from Forward. He thinks that he never really earned any income from his investment because he was paid out of later investors' capital contributions. Write Henry a letter explaining the income tax effects of the payments he received from Forward Investments.

Deduction Problems

47. Mason is the owner of Brickman, Inc., which specializes in laying brick patios, terraces, and walkways. In 1996, Mason bids on a contract with State University to build several large terraces as well as the walkways adjoining the terraces. Although he is the low bidder, Mason is approached by Don, purchasing agent for State University, who lets Mason know that in order to secure the contract, Mason must make a cash payment to a firm that is building a swimming pool for Don. Mason makes the required payment and secures the contract. Later, Don demands, and Mason makes, a payment to a rancher for the purchase of a horse for Don's children. The payments made by Mason are not illegal under state law. Mason seeks your advice as to the deductibility of these payments.

Read and analyze the following authorities, and determine whether Mason can deduct the payments he made to Don:

Sec. 162.
Raymond Bertolini Trucking v. Comm., 736 F.2d 1120 (6th Cir. 1984).
Car-Ron Asphalt Paving Co. Inc. v. Comm., 758 F.2d 1132 (6th Cir. 1985).

48. Jefferson is a grade school teacher whose annual income from teaching is $20,000. Jefferson has always enjoyed bowling, and in 1996 his local pro urges him to turn professional. He subsequently begins working for his pro as an unpaid assistant and enters an apprenticeship program with the Professional Bowlers' Association of America (PBA). As an apprentice, he accumulates credits toward becoming a member of the PBA by taking approved classes, working as an assistant pro, and playing in pro tournaments. Jefferson expects to be approved as a full member of the PBA next year.

Although Jefferson continues to teach full time, he goes to the bowling alley each day after school and practices after fulfilling his duties as an unpaid assistant. During the summer months, he spends 12 to 15 hours each day at the bowling alley. In addition, he participates in as many PBA tournaments as he can work into his schedule.

Jefferson has come to you for advice on the deductibility of the expenses he has incurred in his bowling career. Since deciding to turn pro, he has won money in tournaments every year. However, his expenses have exceeded his earnings by $5,000 to $10,000 per year.

49. Seaweed Salvagers is a corporation engaged in the production of various foodstuffs from seaweed. Seaweed's primary salvaging plant is located in California. Because the salvaging technology hasn't changed through the years, Seaweed's primary salvaging equipment was purchased in the early 1970s. At that time, the primary insulation material used in the machines was asbestos. In 1986, the Occupational Safety and Health Administration lowered the standard for concentrations of allowable airborne asbestos fibers in the workplace. In addition, California requires employers to monitor airborne concentration levels to ensure that they do not exceed permissible exposure levels.

To comply with these requirements and to provide its workers with a safe workplace, Seaweed institutes an asbestos abatement program. After careful study, Seaweed determines that the major asbestos problem occurs during ordinary repairs and maintenance of the equipment. Initially, Seaweed institutes a program of continuous monitoring and encapsulation during repair and maintenance periods. However, Seaweed finds that this is inadequate because (a) it did not ensure that all parts of the plant are in compliance, (b) repairs and maintenance costs are increasing dramatically, and (c) the extra down time during maintenance and repairs causes production to drop to a level that is financially unprofitable.

During the current year, Seaweed begins removing the asbestos insulation from the machinery and replacing it with an alternative, environmentally friendly insulation material. The new insulation material is about 15% less efficient than the asbestos material and results in no energy or other cost savings. The cost of replacing the insulation in 1 machine is about $13,000. The annual repair and maintenance cost of 1 machine averages $45,000. Each machine has an estimated fair market value of $600,000.

Seaweed believes that it should be able to expense the cost of removing the asbestos insulation and replacing it with the alternative insulation. Read and analyze the following authorities, and determine whether Seaweed can deduct the asbestos removal costs:

Sec. 263.
Reg. Sec. 1.162-4.
Reg. Sec. 1.263(a)-1.
Indopco Inc. v. Comm., 112 S. Ct. 1038 (1992).
LTR 9240004.
Rev. Rul. 94-38.

50. Hanna and Helmut, a married couple, have the following items of income during 1996:

Salaries (earned equally)	$28,000
Taxable interest	13,000
Tax-exempt interest	3,000
Social Security benefits	8,000

Hanna is covered by her employer's retirement plan; Helmut is not covered by any type of pension plan. Hanna and Helmut would like to make the maximum deductible contribution to their individual retirement account (IRA).

Hanna and Helmut seek your advice in determining their maximum IRA contribution deduction in 1996 as well as their 1996 adjusted gross income. Read and analyze the following authorities to determine Hanna and Helmut's maximum IRA contribution deduction and their adjusted gross income for 1996. Write a letter to Hanna and Helmut explaining their maximum 1996 IRA contribution and what their adjusted gross income will be for 1996.

> Sec. 219.
>
> Sec. 86.
>
> Announcement 88-38.

51. Don and Rosetta purchase a new residence on February 19, 1993, for $100,000. Because they are unable to obtain conventional financing, they negotiate the following terms with the seller. They put down $5,000, and the seller agrees to finance the remaining $95,000 with an interest-only note for 3 years. The note carries an interest rate of 10% (simple interest, payable annually on February 19) and requires payment of the principal amount on or before February 19, 1996. On January 15, 1996, Don and Rosetta obtain a 30-year mortgage from First International Savings and Loan and pay the $95,000 balance due on the original note. As part of the refinancing, Don and Rosetta pay points (from their own funds) totaling $2,850. The payment of points is customary where Don and Rosetta live, and the amount is in line with what other lenders are charging. Don and Rosetta would like to know the proper tax treatment of the refinancing points they paid.

Don and Rosetta seek your advice in determining the deduction for the points they paid to acquire the mortgage from First International Savings and Loan. Write Don and Rosetta a letter explaining their 1996 deduction for the points.

52. Larry is a professional gambler, specializing in dog racing. He spends 50 to 60 hours per week studying racing forms and placing bets at the track. During the current year, Larry has winnings of $240,000 on $380,000 of bets placed. Larry has no other business income. His wife Jane is employed as a university professor and earns $55,000 annually. They also have $15,000 in income from various investments. Because Larry devotes all of his time to his dog-racing activities, he feels that he should be able to deduct the loss he incurred in his "business" against their other income.

Read and analyze the following authorities to determine the deduction Larry is allowed for his dog-racing losses:

> Sec. 162.
>
> Sec. 165.
>
> Commissioner v. Groetzinger, 480 U.S. 23 (1987).
>
> Pete C. Valenti, 68 TCM 730 (1994).

Loss Problems

53. Sterling is a college professor with an extensive stock portfolio. Last year, Sterling met Wheeler, a stockbroker with the firm of Ransom, LaForge, and Adkins. In order to get Sterling's business, Wheeler offered to use his investment expertise on Sterling's behalf, for which he would receive 1/4 of any profits and would also assume 1/4 of any losses if Sterling would give Wheeler $300,000 to invest. Sterling accepted Wheeler's offer. During 1995, Wheeler makes a net profit of $120,000 on trades with Sterling's money. On January 31, 1996, Sterling pays Wheeler $30,000 per their agreement. In addition, Sterling pays normal brokerage commissions on the purchases and sales that Wheeler executes in making the $120,000 net profit on the $300,000 investment. The commissions are properly included in the calculation of the net profit. Sterling would like to know the proper tax treatment of the $30,000 payment he made to Wheeler.

54. Kimberly is a developer of apartment complexes. In 1994, Kimberly forms Deckside Apartments, a partnership, and initiates development of the Deckside Apartment complex. The Staten Investment Fund agrees to provide financing for the development at an annual interest rate of 10%, secured by a mortgage on the property. However, state law limits the annual interest rate for noncorporate borrowers to 8%. To avoid this state usury law, Kimberly incorporates Hump Day, Inc., under state law. Kimberly is the only shareholder of Hump Day, Inc. The next day, Deckside Apartments and Hump Day, Inc., enter into a written agreement under which the corporation holds title to the apartments solely for the purpose of obtaining financing. Hump Day cannot convey, assign, or encumber the property without the permission of Deckside, has no obligation to maintain the property, assumes no liability regarding the financing, and is held harmless from any liability it might sustain as the agent for Deckside.

    Staten Investment Fund agrees to provide the financing to Hump Day, Inc., as the corporate nominee of Deckside, provided that Kimberly personally guarantees the note. Upon completion of the apartments, Kimberly, through Hump Day, Inc., obtains the permanent financing from Staten and pays off the short-term construction loans that she had obtained for the construction of the apartments. An apartment manager is hired to oversee the operation of the apartments. All rents collected are deposited to and expenses paid from an account opened by the partnership.

    During 1996, the apartments generate substantial operating losses. Kimberly seeks your advice as to the proper treatment of these losses.

55. Fingeland's Forest Choppers is a corporation engaged in the production of timber and lumber. In 1994, Fingeland's reforests a clear-cut area by planting nursery-grown seedlings. In 1995, a severe drought kills 80% of the seedlings, forcing Fingeland's to replant the entire area in 1996. The loss is not covered by insurance. Fingeland's had capitalized the cost of preparing the site for reforestation and the seedling planting costs in a deferred reforestation account in 1994.

    Fingeland's would like to know whether it can deduct as a casualty loss the costs it incurred to replant the clear-cut area in 1996.

    Read and analyze the following authorities, and determine whether Fingeland's can deduct the costs as a casualty loss, and if so, in what year the loss is deductible.

    Sec. 165.
    Sec. 611.
    Reg. Sec. 1.611-3.
    Rev. Rul. 81-2.
    Rev. Rul. 87-59.
    Rev. Rul. 90-61.

    Write a memorandum to your supervisor explaining your conclusions on Fingeland's deduction of the costs of replanting the clear-cut area in 1996.

56. Mae and Vernon are equal owners of Denson, Inc., an S corporation. Denson owns 5,000 shares of stock in Cowboy Country. Denson paid $300,000 for the Cowboy Country stock, which is qualified small business stock. During the current year, Denson sells 4,000 shares of Cowboy Country for $100,000. Denson's accountant is preparing the current-year tax return and is unsure of the reporting of the stock sale to Mae and Vernon.

Read and analyze the following authorities and determine how the sale of the stock should be reported to Mae and Vernon:

> Sec. 1244.
> Sec. 1363.
> Reg. Sec. 1.1244(a)-1.
> Virgil D. Rath, 101 T.C. 196 (1994).

Property Problems

57. Dagwood has come to you with a pressing problem. In November 1988, he purchased an office building that he had rented out to various businesses. On May 2, 1996, a fire swept through the building, totally destroying it. To make matters worse, his lifelong accountant was trapped in the building and perished in the fire (along with all of Dagwood's income tax records). The following is all of the information Dagwood has available about the building.

Dagwood is sure that he purchased the building in November 1988, because he has a property tax statement indicating that the land was revalued at $30,000 and the building at $300,000 for property tax purposes at that time. The date is further supported by a canceled check dated November 28, 1988, for $550,000, payable to the company from which he had purchased the property. Although he doesn't have the tax records to support any deductions on the property, he's confident that his former accountant took the maximum deductions allowable on the property as it had always produced a loss for income tax purposes.

He recently received a check for $400,000 from his insurance company for the destruction of the building. In the interim, Dagwood has been obtaining estimates of the cost of putting another office building on the property. However, his analysis of the construction costs, combined with the potential rental income generated by the building, indicates that putting another office building on the property would not be profitable in either the short or the long term. He has received an offer to sell the land for $84,000. If he does sell the land, he is considering purchasing an upscale apartment building in another part of town.

Before he proceeds with the sale of the land and the purchase of the apartment building, he needs to know the tax effects of the fire and the sale of the land. Dagwood is afraid that he may have a big tax bill to pay and won't be able to afford the apartment building after he settles up with the IRS.

Read and analyze the following authorities and determine how much gain or loss, if any, Dagwood will have to recognize from the fire if he purchases the apartment building:

> Sec. 1033.
> Rev. Rul. 64-237.
> Rev. Rul. 59-361.
> Henry G. Masser, 30 T.C. 741 (1958).

58. On November 3, 1994, Jim and Pam sell their principal residence for $150,000, incurring selling expenses of $10,000. They had purchased the residence in 1988 at a cost of $90,000 and had made no significant improvements to it before the sale. In filing their 1994 return, they properly defer recognition of the gain on the sale, as they anticipate purchasing a new principal residence of equal or greater value within 2 years.

In 1995, before they purchase a new home, Jim and Pam divorce. In February 1996, Jim purchases a personal residence for $80,000. Pam does not purchase a new residence before November 3, 1996.

Read and analyze the following authorities, and determine how much gain, if any, Jim must report on the sale of the residence:

Sec. 1034.
Reg. Sec. 1.1034-1.
Rev. Rul. 74-250.
Rev. Rul. 80-5.

59. Martha, 65, sells her residence on March 15, 1996, for $165,000 net of commissions and other selling costs. She purchased the residence on February 20, 1993, for $105,000. Before the purchase, Martha sold her previous home on January 5, 1993, for $95,000. Martha had paid $80,000 for the residence and had made $10,000 in capital improvements before the sale. Martha moves to a retirement community and therefore does not plan to purchase another residence.

Martha asks you to prepare her 1996 tax return. In going over her previous year returns, you find that the accountant who prepared her 1993 tax return had elected to exclude the $5,000 gain on the 1993 sale rather than defer the gain. When you ask Martha about this, she is confused. She tells you that she knows that if you sell one house for $95,000 and purchase another house for $105,000, none of the gain is taxable. Because no gain was shown on the 1993 return, she signed it without reviewing the details.

Determine the amount of gain Martha will have to report on the 1996 sale. Write her a letter explaining why she does or does not have to report the gain and any actions she must take to ensure this result.

60. Marjorie is a software systems engineer for Hustead Corporation. In November 1993, she inherited two parcels of land in Brower Township from her grandfather. Her grandfather's estate valued the two parcels, which are adjacent to each other and total 25 acres, at $11,000. Marjorie thought the parcels were worth more than $11,000, so she asked the estate's appraiser why the parcels weren't valued higher. The appraiser told her that the zoning on the land allows only one residence per every two acres, which severely diminishes the resale value.

In 1994, Marjorie applied to Brower Township for a change of zoning. The Brower Township Board of Supervisors denied her application in November 1994. Marjorie filed a constitutional challenge to Brower Township's zoning ordinance in 1995. The board of supervisors denied her constitutional challenge. Marjorie filed an appeal of the denial in Brower County District Court on September 25, 1995. On October 5, 1995, the Brower Township Board of Supervisors began consideration of a new zoning ordinance. Under the ordinance, Marjorie's land would be rezoned to a designation that would allow three residences per acre. At this point, Marjorie withdrew her court appeal, pending the outcome of the new zoning ordinance. On January 10, 1996, the new zoning ordinance was adopted. Marjorie estimated that the value of the land increased to at least $21,000 as a result of the rezoning.

Marjorie incurred $14,000 in attorney's fees and other costs in challenging the zoning ordinance. She paid $3,500 of the expenditures in 1995 and $10,500 in 1996. She would like to know the proper income tax treatment of these expenses. Can Marjorie deduct the costs of challenging the zoning ordinance? Write a memorandum explaining the deductibility of the costs of challenging the zoning ordinance.

Accounting Methods/Procedure Problems

61. The Kona Rural Electric Co-op (KREC) is an accrual basis public utility. All new customers are required to pay a deposit equal to 3 times the customer's estimated monthly bill or $100, whichever is greater. The purpose of the deposit is to ensure that timely payment is made on accounts. The funds so received are not segregated from other KREC funds and are used in the ordinary course of business. Interest at the rate of 5% is paid annually on the deposits. Customers may elect to receive a check for the interest or may accept the payment as a credit on their monthly bill.

KREC's policy is to refund the deposit when a customer discontinues service or when the customer has made timely monthly payments for 8 consecutive months or for 9 of 12 consecutive months. When deposits are refunded, interest is paid on the deposit through the date of the refund. KREC's experience with the deposit requirement is that 80% of all deposits are returned within 1 year of receipt. Approximately 5% of all deposits are ultimately used to satisfy delinquent customer accounts.

KREC would like to know whether the deposits should be included in income when they are received or deferred until they are used to satisfy customer accounts.

62. Tomiko owns the copyright to several classic Motown songs. In 1994, he became aware that Tinseltown Records was selling several of his songs without his permission. He sues Tinseltown seeking $1,000,000 in damages. In 1996, the court awards Tomiko $500,000 in compensatory damages, $50,000 in prejudgment interest, postjudgment interest to the date of payment, and court costs. Tinseltown is aware that Tomiko is likely to appeal the judgment and offers to settle for $600,000 with no payment of postjudgment interest or court costs. On the advice of his attorney, Tomiko rejects the settlement offer.

On December 29, 1996, Tomiko receives a check for $600,000 from Tinseltown. An accompanying letter notes that the payment is in full settlement of the order of the court. Tomiko believes that if he cashes the check, he will forfeit his right to appeal the judgment, the postjudgment interest, and court costs. Accordingly, he immediately returns the check to Tinseltown via overnight mail, stating in a letter that his appeal rights are not exhausted and he is returning the check until such time as the issue is settled. Tinseltown remails the check on December 31, 1996. Included with the check is a letter advising Tomiko that Tinseltown intends to deduct the $600,000 in 1996 and that the funds are available for his unrestricted use. On January 15, 1997, Tomiko files an appeal seeking an increase in the damage award. The next day, he deposits Tinseltown's check into his business account. On June 5, 1997, the appeals court rejects Tomiko's appeal for higher damages. Tomiko is a cash basis taxpayer. In what year should he include the $600,000 in income?

Read the following authorities, and determine the proper year for Tomiko to include the $600,000 in income:

Sec. 451.
Reg. Sec. 1.451-2.
Walter I. Bones, 4 T.C. 415 (1944).
Fromson v. Comm., 74 A.F.T.R.2d, 5642 (1994), 94-2 USTC ¶50, 425.

63. Ernie's Farm and Garden Implement Store sells, repairs, and services farm and garden equipment. In 1995, the state attorney general began to investigate customers' complaints that Ernie's was adding a delivery and handling fee to each product—fees that are illegal under state law. In 1996, Ernie's entered into a consent judgment under which it was to make restitution of every delivery and handling fee charged to customers after April 1, 1991. The judgment also required Ernie's to give the attorney general's office a list of every customer entitled to restitution and to issue a coupon in the name of each customer.

The coupons offered each customer the option of a $50 discount on the purchase of any part or service or $90 toward the purchase of any new or used equipment. If not satisfied with the coupon offer, the customer could redeem the coupon for $40 in cash. Ernie's mailed out 1,860 coupons in April and May 1996. As of December 31, 1996, 835 coupons had been redeemed. They were redeemed as follows: 405 for cash refunds, 390 for $50 discounts for parts and services, and 40 for $90 discounts on equipment purchases.

The controller of Ernie's is not certain that the company can deduct the amounts it gave customers for refunds or discounts in 1996 and has asked your firm for advice. Your supervisor has assigned you to determine Ernie's 1996 deduction. Write a memorandum to your supervisor explaining Ernie's 1996 deduction for the coupons.

64. Lydia and Andre are divorcing this year. Because they are hotly contesting the terms of the settlement, they will not file a joint return for the current year. Lydia receives a Form 1099-INT from Andre's accountant and a letter stating that Lydia should include 50% of the $6,200 interest on their savings account in her taxable income. Andre's Social Security number is listed on the account (Lydia's is not) and the Form 1099-INT was issued in his name, although they own the account as joint tenants with the right of survivorship. Under applicable state law, both spouses have an equal right to jointly held property. Lydia doesn't think that she should be taxed on this income because the account is in Andre's name and he was issued the Form 1099-INT. Lydia has come to you for advice. Write a letter to Lydia explaining who is taxed on the $6,200 in interest.

TAX RATE SCHEDULES
AND TAX TABLES

- 1996 Individual Tax Rate Schedules
- 1995 Individual Tax Rate Schedules
- 1996 Corporate Tax Rate Schedule
- 1996 Estate and Trust Tax Rate Schedule
- 1995 Estate and Trust Tax Rate Schedule
- 1995 Individual Tax Table

▲ 1996 INDIVIDUAL TAX RATE SCHEDULES

▲ Table A–1

SINGLE TAXPAYERS

If Taxable Income Is Over	But Not Over	The Tax Is	of the Amount Over
$ 0	24,000	.................15%	$ 0
24,000	58,150	$ 3,600.00 + 28%	24,000
58,150	121,300	13,162.00 + 31%	58,150
121,300	263,750	32,738.50 + 36%	121,300
263,750	....	84,020.50 + 39.6%	263,750

▲ Table A–2

MARRIED TAXPAYERS FILING JOINTLY AND SURVIVING SPOUSE

If Taxable Income Is Over	But Not Over	The Tax Is	of the Amount Over
$ 0	40,100	.................15%	$ 0
40,100	96,900	$ 6,015.00 + 28%	40,100
96,900	147,700	21,919.00 + 31%	96,900
147,700	263,750	37,667.00 + 36%	147,700
263,750	....	79,445.00 + 39.6%	263,750

▲ Table A–3

HEAD OF HOUSEHOLD

If Taxable Income Is Over	But Not Over	The Tax Is	of the Amount Over
$ 0	32,150	.................15%	$ 0
32,150	83,050	$ 4,822.50 + 28%	32,150
83,050	134,500	19,074.50 + 31%	83,050
134,500	263,750	35,024.00 + 36%	134,500
263,750	....	81,554.00 + 39.6%	263,750

▲ Table A–4

MARRIED TAXPAYERS FILING SEPARATELY

If Taxable Income Is Over	But Not Over	The Tax Is	of the Amount Over
$ 0	20,050	.................15%	$ 0
20,050	48,450	$ 3,007.50 + 28%	20,050
48,450	73,850	10,959.50 + 31%	48,450
73,850	131,875	18,833.50 + 36%	73,850
131,875	....	39,722.50 + 39.6%	131,875

▲ 1995 INDIVIDUAL TAX RATE SCHEDULES

If Taxable Income Is Over	But Not Over	The Tax Is	of the Amount Over
$ 0	23,350	................15%	$ 0
23,350	56,550	$ 3,502.50 + 28%	23,350
56,550	117,950	12,798.50 + 31%	56,550
117,950	256,500	31,832.50 + 36%	117,950
256,500	....	81,710.50 + 39.6%	256,500

▲ Table A–5

SINGLE TAXPAYERS

If Taxable Income Is Over	But Not Over	The Tax Is	of the Amount Over
$ 0	39,000	................15%	$ 0
39,000	94,250	$ 5,850.00 + 28%	39,000
94,250	143,600	21,320.00 + 31%	94,250
143,600	256,500	36,618.50 + 36%	143,600
256,500	....	77,262.50 + 39.6%	256,500

▲ Table A–6

MARRIED TAXPAYERS FILING JOINTLY AND SURVIVING SPOUSE

If Taxable Income Is Over	But Not Over	The Tax Is	of the Amount Over
$ 0	31,250	................15%	$ 0
31,250	80,750	$ 4,687.50 + 28%	31,250
80,750	130,800	18,547.50 + 31%	80,750
130,800	256,500	34,063.00 + 36%	130,800
256,500	....	79,315.00 + 39.6%	256,500

▲ Table A–7

HEAD OF HOUSEHOLD

If Taxable Income Is Over	But Not Over	The Tax Is	of the Amount Over
$ 0	19,500	................15%	$ 0
19,500	47,125	$ 2,925.00 + 28%	19,500
47,125	71,800	10,660.00 + 31%	47,125
71,800	128,250	18,309.25 + 36%	71,800
128,250	....	38,631.25 + 39.6%	128,250

▲ Table A–8

MARRIED TAXPAYERS FILING SEPARATELY

▲ 1996 CORPORATE TAX RATE SCHEDULE

▲ Table A–9

If Taxable Income Is Over	But Not Over	The Tax Is	of the Amount Over
$ 0	50,000	................15%	$ 0
50,000	75,000	$ 7,500 + 25%	50,000
75,000	100,000	13,750 + 34%	75,000
100,000	335,000	22,250 + 39%	100,000
335,000	10,000,000	113,900 + 34%	335,000
10,000,000	15,000,000	3,400,000 + 35%	10,000,000
15,000,000	18,333,333	5,150,000 + 38%	15,000,000
18,333,333	....	6,416,667 + 35%	18,333,333

▲ 1996 ESTATE AND TRUST TAX RATE SCHEDULE

▲ Table A–10

If Taxable Income Is Over	But Not Over	The Tax Is	of the Amount Over
$ 0	1,600	................15%	$ 0
1,600	3,800	$ 240.00 + 28%	1,600
3,800	5,800	856.00 + 31%	3,800
5,800	7,900	1,476.00 + 36%	5,800
7,900	....	2,232.00 + 39.6%	7,900

▲ 1995 ESTATE AND TRUST TAX RATE SCHEDULE

▲ Table A–11

If Taxable Income Is Over	But Not Over	The Tax Is	of the Amount Over
$ 0	1,550	................15%	$ 0
1,550	3,700	$ 232.50 + 28%	1,550
3,700	5,600	834.50 + 31%	3,700
5,600	7,650	1,423.50 + 36%	5,600
7,650	....	2,161.50 + 39.6%	7,650

▲ 1995 INDIVIDUAL TAX TABLES

1995 Tax Table

Use if your taxable income is less than $100,000. If $100,000 or more, use the Tax Rate Schedules.

Example. Mr. and Mrs. Brown are filing a joint return. Their taxable income on line 37 of Form 1040 is $25,300. First, they find the $25,300–25,350 income line. Next, they find the column for married filing jointly and read down the column. The amount shown where the income line and filing status column meet is $3,799. This is the tax amount they must enter on line 38 of their Form 1040.

Sample Table

At least	But less than	Single	Married filing jointly *	Married filing separately	Head of a household
			Your tax is—		
25,200	25,250	4,028	3,784	4,528	3,784
25,250	25,300	4,042	3,791	4,542	3,791
25,300	25,350	4,056	(3,799)	4,556	3,799
25,350	25,400	4,070	3,806	4,570	3,806

If line 37 (taxable income) is— At least	But less than	Single	Married filing jointly *	Married filing separately	Head of a house-hold	If line 37 (taxable income) is— At least	But less than	Single	Married filing jointly *	Married filing separately	Head of a house-hold	If line 37 (taxable income) is— At least	But less than	Single	Married filing jointly *	Married filing separately	Head of a house-hold
			Your tax is—						**Your tax is—**						**Your tax is—**		
0	5	0	0	0	0	1,300	1,325	197	197	197	197	2,700	2,725	407	407	407	407
5	15	2	2	2	2	1,325	1,350	201	201	201	201	2,725	2,750	411	411	411	411
15	25	3	3	3	3	1,350	1,375	204	204	204	204	2,750	2,775	414	414	414	414
25	50	6	6	6	6	1,375	1,400	208	208	208	208	2,775	2,800	418	418	418	418
50	75	9	9	9	9	1,400	1,425	212	212	212	212	2,800	2,825	422	422	422	422
75	100	13	13	13	13	1,425	1,450	216	216	216	216	2,825	2,850	426	426	426	426
100	125	17	17	17	17	1,450	1,475	219	219	219	219	2,850	2,875	429	429	429	429
125	150	21	21	21	21	1,475	1,500	223	223	223	223	2,875	2,900	433	433	433	433
150	175	24	24	24	24	1,500	1,525	227	227	227	227	2,900	2,925	437	437	437	437
175	200	28	28	28	28	1,525	1,550	231	231	231	231	2,925	2,950	441	441	441	441
200	225	32	32	32	32	1,550	1,575	234	234	234	234	2,950	2,975	444	444	444	444
225	250	36	36	36	36	1,575	1,600	238	238	238	238	2,975	3,000	448	448	448	448
250	275	39	39	39	39	1,600	1,625	242	242	242	242						
275	300	43	43	43	43	1,625	1,650	246	246	246	246	**3,000**					
300	325	47	47	47	47	1,650	1,675	249	249	249	249						
325	350	51	51	51	51	1,675	1,700	253	253	253	253	3,000	3,050	454	454	454	454
350	375	54	54	54	54	1,700	1,725	257	257	257	257	3,050	3,100	461	461	461	461
375	400	58	58	58	58	1,725	1,750	261	261	261	261	3,100	3,150	469	469	469	469
400	425	62	62	62	62	1,750	1,775	264	264	264	264	3,150	3,200	476	476	476	476
425	450	66	66	66	66	1,775	1,800	268	268	268	268	3,200	3,250	484	484	484	484
450	475	69	69	69	69	1,800	1,825	272	272	272	272	3,250	3,300	491	491	491	491
475	500	73	73	73	73	1,825	1,850	276	276	276	276	3,300	3,350	499	499	499	499
500	525	77	77	77	77	1,850	1,875	279	279	279	279	3,350	3,400	506	506	506	506
525	550	81	81	81	81	1,875	1,900	283	283	283	283	3,400	3,450	514	514	514	514
550	575	84	84	84	84	1,900	1,925	287	287	287	287	3,450	3,500	521	521	521	521
575	600	88	88	88	88	1,925	1,950	291	291	291	291	3,500	3,550	529	529	529	529
600	625	92	92	92	92	1,950	1,975	294	294	294	294	3,550	3,600	536	536	536	536
625	650	96	96	96	96	1,975	2,000	298	298	298	298	3,600	3,650	544	544	544	544
650	675	99	99	99	99							3,650	3,700	551	551	551	551
675	700	103	103	103	103	**2,000**						3,700	3,750	559	559	559	559
700	725	107	107	107	107							3,750	3,800	566	566	566	566
725	750	111	111	111	111	2,000	2,025	302	302	302	302	3,800	3,850	574	574	574	574
750	775	114	114	114	114	2,025	2,050	306	306	306	306	3,850	3,900	581	581	581	581
775	800	118	118	118	118	2,050	2,075	309	309	309	309	3,900	3,950	589	589	589	589
800	825	122	122	122	122	2,075	2,100	313	313	313	313	3,950	4,000	596	596	596	596
825	850	126	126	126	126	2,100	2,125	317	317	317	317						
850	875	129	129	129	129	2,125	2,150	321	321	321	321	**4,000**					
875	900	133	133	133	133	2,150	2,175	324	324	324	324						
900	925	137	137	137	137	2,175	2,200	328	328	328	328	4,000	4,050	604	604	604	604
925	950	141	141	141	141	2,200	2,225	332	332	332	332	4,050	4,100	611	611	611	611
950	975	144	144	144	144	2,225	2,250	336	336	336	336	4,100	4,150	619	619	619	619
975	1,000	148	148	148	148	2,250	2,275	339	339	339	339	4,150	4,200	626	626	626	626
1,000						2,275	2,300	343	343	343	343	4,200	4,250	634	634	634	634
						2,300	2,325	347	347	347	347	4,250	4,300	641	641	641	641
1,000	1,025	152	152	152	152	2,325	2,350	351	351	351	351	4,300	4,350	649	649	649	649
1,025	1,050	156	156	156	156	2,350	2,375	354	354	354	354	4,350	4,400	656	656	656	656
1,050	1,075	159	159	159	159	2,375	2,400	358	358	358	358	4,400	4,450	664	664	664	664
1,075	1,100	163	163	163	163	2,400	2,425	362	362	362	362	4,450	4,500	671	671	671	671
1,100	1,125	167	167	167	167	2,425	2,450	366	366	366	366	4,500	4,550	679	679	679	679
1,125	1,150	171	171	171	171	2,450	2,475	369	369	369	369	4,550	4,600	686	686	686	686
1,150	1,175	174	174	174	174	2,475	2,500	373	373	373	373	4,600	4,650	694	694	694	694
1,175	1,200	178	178	178	178	2,500	2,525	377	377	377	377	4,650	4,700	701	701	701	701
1,200	1,225	182	182	182	182	2,525	2,550	381	381	381	381	4,700	4,750	709	709	709	709
1,225	1,250	186	186	186	186	2,550	2,575	384	384	384	384	4,750	4,800	716	716	716	716
1,250	1,275	189	189	189	189	2,575	2,600	388	388	388	388	4,800	4,850	724	724	724	724
1,275	1,300	193	193	193	193	2,600	2,625	392	392	392	392	4,850	4,900	731	731	731	731
						2,625	2,650	396	396	396	396	4,900	4,950	739	739	739	739
						2,650	2,675	399	399	399	399	4,950	5,000	746	746	746	746
						2,675	2,700	403	403	403	403						

Continued on next page

* This column must also be used by a qualifying widow(er).

1995 Tax Table—*Continued*

If line 37 (taxable income) is—		And you are—				If line 37 (taxable income) is—		And you are—				If line 37 (taxable income) is—		And you are—			
At least	But less than	Single	Married filing jointly *	Married filing sepa-rately	Head of a house-hold	At least	But less than	Single	Married filing jointly *	Married filing sepa-rately	Head of a house-hold	At least	But less than	Single	Married filing jointly *	Married filing sepa-rately	Head of a house-hold
		Your tax is—						Your tax is—						Your tax is—			
5,000						**8,000**						**11,000**					
5,000	5,050	754	754	754	754	8,000	8,050	1,204	1,204	1,204	1,204	11,000	11,050	1,654	1,654	1,654	1,654
5,050	5,100	761	761	761	761	8,050	8,100	1,211	1,211	1,211	1,211	11,050	11,100	1,661	1,661	1,661	1,661
5,100	5,150	769	769	769	769	8,100	8,150	1,219	1,219	1,219	1,219	11,100	11,150	1,669	1,669	1,669	1,669
5,150	5,200	776	776	776	776	8,150	8,200	1,226	1,226	1,226	1,226	11,150	11,200	1,676	1,676	1,676	1,676
5,200	5,250	784	784	784	784	8,200	8,250	1,234	1,234	1,234	1,234	11,200	11,250	1,684	1,684	1,684	1,684
5,250	5,300	791	791	791	791	8,250	8,300	1,241	1,241	1,241	1,241	11,250	11,300	1,691	1,691	1,691	1,691
5,300	5,350	799	799	799	799	8,300	8,350	1,249	1,249	1,249	1,249	11,300	11,350	1,699	1,699	1,699	1,699
5,350	5,400	806	806	806	806	8,350	8,400	1,256	1,256	1,256	1,256	11,350	11,400	1,706	1,706	1,706	1,706
5,400	5,450	814	814	814	814	8,400	8,450	1,264	1,264	1,264	1,264	11,400	11,450	1,714	1,714	1,714	1,714
5,450	5,500	821	821	821	821	8,450	8,500	1,271	1,271	1,271	1,271	11,450	11,500	1,721	1,721	1,721	1,721
5,500	5,550	829	829	829	829	8,500	8,550	1,279	1,279	1,279	1,279	11,500	11,550	1,729	1,729	1,729	1,729
5,550	5,600	836	836	836	836	8,550	8,600	1,286	1,286	1,286	1,286	11,550	11,600	1,736	1,736	1,736	1,736
5,600	5,650	844	844	844	844	8,600	8,650	1,294	1,294	1,294	1,294	11,600	11,650	1,744	1,744	1,744	1,744
5,650	5,700	851	851	851	851	8,650	8,700	1,301	1,301	1,301	1,301	11,650	11,700	1,751	1,751	1,751	1,751
5,700	5,750	859	859	859	859	8,700	8,750	1,309	1,309	1,309	1,309	11,700	11,750	1,759	1,759	1,759	1,759
5,750	5,800	866	866	866	866	8,750	8,800	1,316	1,316	1,316	1,316	11,750	11,800	1,766	1,766	1,766	1,766
5,800	5,850	874	874	874	874	8,800	8,850	1,324	1,324	1,324	1,324	11,800	11,850	1,774	1,774	1,774	1,774
5,850	5,900	881	881	881	881	8,850	8,900	1,331	1,331	1,331	1,331	11,850	11,900	1,781	1,781	1,781	1,781
5,900	5,950	889	889	889	889	8,900	8,950	1,339	1,339	1,339	1,339	11,900	11,950	1,789	1,789	1,789	1,789
5,950	6,000	896	896	896	896	8,950	9,000	1,346	1,346	1,346	1,346	11,950	12,000	1,796	1,796	1,796	1,796
6,000						**9,000**						**12,000**					
6,000	6,050	904	904	904	904	9,000	9,050	1,354	1,354	1,354	1,354	12,000	12,050	1,804	1,804	1,804	1,804
6,050	6,100	911	911	911	911	9,050	9,100	1,361	1,361	1,361	1,361	12,050	12,100	1,811	1,811	1,811	1,811
6,100	6,150	919	919	919	919	9,100	9,150	1,369	1,369	1,369	1,369	12,100	12,150	1,819	1,819	1,819	1,819
6,150	6,200	926	926	926	926	9,150	9,200	1,376	1,376	1,376	1,376	12,150	12,200	1,826	1,826	1,826	1,826
6,200	6,250	934	934	934	934	9,200	9,250	1,384	1,384	1,384	1,384	12,200	12,250	1,834	1,834	1,834	1,834
6,250	6,300	941	941	941	941	9,250	9,300	1,391	1,391	1,391	1,391	12,250	12,300	1,841	1,841	1,841	1,841
6,300	6,350	949	949	949	949	9,300	9,350	1,399	1,399	1,399	1,399	12,300	12,350	1,849	1,849	1,849	1,849
6,350	6,400	956	956	956	956	9,350	9,400	1,406	1,406	1,406	1,406	12,350	12,400	1,856	1,856	1,856	1,856
6,400	6,450	964	964	964	964	9,400	9,450	1,414	1,414	1,414	1,414	12,400	12,450	1,864	1,864	1,864	1,864
6,450	6,500	971	971	971	971	9,450	9,500	1,421	1,421	1,421	1,421	12,450	12,500	1,871	1,871	1,871	1,871
6,500	6,550	979	979	979	979	9,500	9,550	1,429	1,429	1,429	1,429	12,500	12,550	1,879	1,879	1,879	1,879
6,550	6,600	986	986	986	986	9,550	9,600	1,436	1,436	1,436	1,436	12,550	12,600	1,886	1,886	1,886	1,886
6,600	6,650	994	994	994	994	9,600	9,650	1,444	1,444	1,444	1,444	12,600	12,650	1,894	1,894	1,894	1,894
6,650	6,700	1,001	1,001	1,001	1,001	9,650	9,700	1,451	1,451	1,451	1,451	12,650	12,700	1,901	1,901	1,901	1,901
6,700	6,750	1,009	1,009	1,009	1,009	9,700	9,750	1,459	1,459	1,459	1,459	12,700	12,750	1,909	1,909	1,909	1,909
6,750	6,800	1,016	1,016	1,016	1,016	9,750	9,800	1,466	1,466	1,466	1,466	12,750	12,800	1,916	1,916	1,916	1,916
6,800	6,850	1,024	1,024	1,024	1,024	9,800	9,850	1,474	1,474	1,474	1,474	12,800	12,850	1,924	1,924	1,924	1,924
6,850	6,900	1,031	1,031	1,031	1,031	9,850	9,900	1,481	1,481	1,481	1,481	12,850	12,900	1,931	1,931	1,931	1,931
6,900	6,950	1,039	1,039	1,039	1,039	9,900	9,950	1,489	1,489	1,489	1,489	12,900	12,950	1,939	1,939	1,939	1,939
6,950	7,000	1,046	1,046	1,046	1,046	9,950	10,000	1,496	1,496	1,496	1,496	12,950	13,000	1,946	1,946	1,946	1,946
7,000						**10,000**						**13,000**					
7,000	7,050	1,054	1,054	1,054	1,054	10,000	10,050	1,504	1,504	1,504	1,504	13,000	13,050	1,954	1,954	1,954	1,954
7,050	7,100	1,061	1,061	1,061	1,061	10,050	10,100	1,511	1,511	1,511	1,511	13,050	13,100	1,961	1,961	1,961	1,961
7,100	7,150	1,069	1,069	1,069	1,069	10,100	10,150	1,519	1,519	1,519	1,519	13,100	13,150	1,969	1,969	1,969	1,969
7,150	7,200	1,076	1,076	1,076	1,076	10,150	10,200	1,526	1,526	1,526	1,526	13,150	13,200	1,976	1,976	1,976	1,976
7,200	7,250	1,084	1,084	1,084	1,084	10,200	10,250	1,534	1,534	1,534	1,534	13,200	13,250	1,984	1,984	1,984	1,984
7,250	7,300	1,091	1,091	1,091	1,091	10,250	10,300	1,541	1,541	1,541	1,541	13,250	13,300	1,991	1,991	1,991	1,991
7,300	7,350	1,099	1,099	1,099	1,099	10,300	10,350	1,549	1,549	1,549	1,549	13,300	13,350	1,999	1,999	1,999	1,999
7,350	7,400	1,106	1,106	1,106	1,106	10,350	10,400	1,556	1,556	1,556	1,556	13,350	13,400	2,006	2,006	2,006	2,006
7,400	7,450	1,114	1,114	1,114	1,114	10,400	10,450	1,564	1,564	1,564	1,564	13,400	13,450	2,014	2,014	2,014	2,014
7,450	7,500	1,121	1,121	1,121	1,121	10,450	10,500	1,571	1,571	1,571	1,571	13,450	13,500	2,021	2,021	2,021	2,021
7,500	7,550	1,129	1,129	1,129	1,129	10,500	10,550	1,579	1,579	1,579	1,579	13,500	13,550	2,029	2,029	2,029	2,029
7,550	7,600	1,136	1,136	1,136	1,136	10,550	10,600	1,586	1,586	1,586	1,586	13,550	13,600	2,036	2,036	2,036	2,036
7,600	7,650	1,144	1,144	1,144	1,144	10,600	10,650	1,594	1,594	1,594	1,594	13,600	13,650	2,044	2,044	2,044	2,044
7,650	7,700	1,151	1,151	1,151	1,151	10,650	10,700	1,601	1,601	1,601	1,601	13,650	13,700	2,051	2,051	2,051	2,051
7,700	7,750	1,159	1,159	1,159	1,159	10,700	10,750	1,609	1,609	1,609	1,609	13,700	13,750	2,059	2,059	2,059	2,059
7,750	7,800	1,166	1,166	1,166	1,166	10,750	10,800	1,616	1,616	1,616	1,616	13,750	13,800	2,066	2,066	2,066	2,066
7,800	7,850	1,174	1,174	1,174	1,174	10,800	10,850	1,624	1,624	1,624	1,624	13,800	13,850	2,074	2,074	2,074	2,074
7,850	7,900	1,181	1,181	1,181	1,181	10,850	10,900	1,631	1,631	1,631	1,631	13,850	13,900	2,081	2,081	2,081	2,081
7,900	7,950	1,189	1,189	1,189	1,189	10,900	10,950	1,639	1,639	1,639	1,639	13,900	13,950	2,089	2,089	2,089	2,089
7,950	8,000	1,196	1,196	1,196	1,196	10,950	11,000	1,646	1,646	1,646	1,646	13,950	14,000	2,096	2,096	2,096	2,096

* This column must also be used by a qualifying widow(er).

Continued on next page

1995 Tax Table—*Continued*

Left panel (14,000–17,000)

If line 37 (taxable income) is— At least	But less than	And you are— Single	Married filing jointly*	Married filing separately	Head of a household
14,000					
14,000	14,050	2,104	2,104	2,104	2,104
14,050	14,100	2,111	2,111	2,111	2,111
14,100	14,150	2,119	2,119	2,119	2,119
14,150	14,200	2,126	2,126	2,126	2,126
14,200	14,250	2,134	2,134	2,134	2,134
14,250	14,300	2,141	2,141	2,141	2,141
14,300	14,350	2,149	2,149	2,149	2,149
14,350	14,400	2,156	2,156	2,156	2,156
14,400	14,450	2,164	2,164	2,164	2,164
14,450	14,500	2,171	2,171	2,171	2,171
14,500	14,550	2,179	2,179	2,179	2,179
14,550	14,600	2,186	2,186	2,186	2,186
14,600	14,650	2,194	2,194	2,194	2,194
14,650	14,700	2,201	2,201	2,201	2,201
14,700	14,750	2,209	2,209	2,209	2,209
14,750	14,800	2,216	2,216	2,216	2,216
14,800	14,850	2,224	2,224	2,224	2,224
14,850	14,900	2,231	2,231	2,231	2,231
14,900	14,950	2,239	2,239	2,239	2,239
14,950	15,000	2,246	2,246	2,246	2,246
15,000					
15,000	15,050	2,254	2,254	2,254	2,254
15,050	15,100	2,261	2,261	2,261	2,261
15,100	15,150	2,269	2,269	2,269	2,269
15,150	15,200	2,276	2,276	2,276	2,276
15,200	15,250	2,284	2,284	2,284	2,284
15,250	15,300	2,291	2,291	2,291	2,291
15,300	15,350	2,299	2,299	2,299	2,299
15,350	15,400	2,306	2,306	2,306	2,306
15,400	15,450	2,314	2,314	2,314	2,314
15,450	15,500	2,321	2,321	2,321	2,321
15,500	15,550	2,329	2,329	2,329	2,329
15,550	15,600	2,336	2,336	2,336	2,336
15,600	15,650	2,344	2,344	2,344	2,344
15,650	15,700	2,351	2,351	2,351	2,351
15,700	15,750	2,359	2,359	2,359	2,359
15,750	15,800	2,366	2,366	2,366	2,366
15,800	15,850	2,374	2,374	2,374	2,374
15,850	15,900	2,381	2,381	2,381	2,381
15,900	15,950	2,389	2,389	2,389	2,389
15,950	16,000	2,396	2,396	2,396	2,396
16,000					
16,000	16,050	2,404	2,404	2,404	2,404
16,050	16,100	2,411	2,411	2,411	2,411
16,100	16,150	2,419	2,419	2,419	2,419
16,150	16,200	2,426	2,426	2,426	2,426
16,200	16,250	2,434	2,434	2,434	2,434
16,250	16,300	2,441	2,441	2,441	2,441
16,300	16,350	2,449	2,449	2,449	2,449
16,350	16,400	2,456	2,456	2,456	2,456
16,400	16,450	2,464	2,464	2,464	2,464
16,450	16,500	2,471	2,471	2,471	2,471
16,500	16,550	2,479	2,479	2,479	2,479
16,550	16,600	2,486	2,486	2,486	2,486
16,600	16,650	2,494	2,494	2,494	2,494
16,650	16,700	2,501	2,501	2,501	2,501
16,700	16,750	2,509	2,509	2,509	2,509
16,750	16,800	2,516	2,516	2,516	2,516
16,800	16,850	2,524	2,524	2,524	2,524
16,850	16,900	2,531	2,531	2,531	2,531
16,900	16,950	2,539	2,539	2,539	2,539
16,950	17,000	2,546	2,546	2,546	2,546

Middle panel (17,000–20,000)

If line 37 (taxable income) is— At least	But less than	And you are— Single	Married filing jointly*	Married filing separately	Head of a household
17,000					
17,000	17,050	2,554	2,554	2,554	2,554
17,050	17,100	2,561	2,561	2,561	2,561
17,100	17,150	2,569	2,569	2,569	2,569
17,150	17,200	2,576	2,576	2,576	2,576
17,200	17,250	2,584	2,584	2,584	2,584
17,250	17,300	2,591	2,591	2,591	2,591
17,300	17,350	2,599	2,599	2,599	2,599
17,350	17,400	2,606	2,606	2,606	2,606
17,400	17,450	2,614	2,614	2,614	2,614
17,450	17,500	2,621	2,621	2,621	2,621
17,500	17,550	2,629	2,629	2,629	2,629
17,550	17,600	2,636	2,636	2,636	2,636
17,600	17,650	2,644	2,644	2,644	2,644
17,650	17,700	2,651	2,651	2,651	2,651
17,700	17,750	2,659	2,659	2,659	2,659
17,750	17,800	2,666	2,666	2,666	2,666
17,800	17,850	2,674	2,674	2,674	2,674
17,850	17,900	2,681	2,681	2,681	2,681
17,900	17,950	2,689	2,689	2,689	2,689
17,950	18,000	2,696	2,696	2,696	2,696
18,000					
18,000	18,050	2,704	2,704	2,704	2,704
18,050	18,100	2,711	2,711	2,711	2,711
18,100	18,150	2,719	2,719	2,719	2,719
18,150	18,200	2,726	2,726	2,726	2,726
18,200	18,250	2,734	2,734	2,734	2,734
18,250	18,300	2,741	2,741	2,741	2,741
18,300	18,350	2,749	2,749	2,749	2,749
18,350	18,400	2,756	2,756	2,756	2,756
18,400	18,450	2,764	2,764	2,764	2,764
18,450	18,500	2,771	2,771	2,771	2,771
18,500	18,550	2,779	2,779	2,779	2,779
18,550	18,600	2,786	2,786	2,786	2,786
18,600	18,650	2,794	2,794	2,794	2,794
18,650	18,700	2,801	2,801	2,801	2,801
18,700	18,750	2,809	2,809	2,809	2,809
18,750	18,800	2,816	2,816	2,816	2,816
18,800	18,850	2,824	2,824	2,824	2,824
18,850	18,900	2,831	2,831	2,831	2,831
18,900	18,950	2,839	2,839	2,839	2,839
18,950	19,000	2,846	2,846	2,846	2,846
19,000					
19,000	19,050	2,854	2,854	2,854	2,854
19,050	19,100	2,861	2,861	2,861	2,861
19,100	19,150	2,869	2,869	2,869	2,869
19,150	19,200	2,876	2,876	2,876	2,876
19,200	19,250	2,884	2,884	2,884	2,884
19,250	19,300	2,891	2,891	2,891	2,891
19,300	19,350	2,899	2,899	2,899	2,899
19,350	19,400	2,906	2,906	2,906	2,906
19,400	19,450	2,914	2,914	2,914	2,914
19,450	19,500	2,921	2,921	2,921	2,921
19,500	19,550	2,929	2,929	2,932	2,929
19,550	19,600	2,936	2,936	2,946	2,936
19,600	19,650	2,944	2,944	2,960	2,944
19,650	19,700	2,951	2,951	2,974	2,951
19,700	19,750	2,959	2,959	2,988	2,959
19,750	19,800	2,966	2,966	3,002	2,966
19,800	19,850	2,974	2,974	3,016	2,974
19,850	19,900	2,981	2,981	3,030	2,981
19,900	19,950	2,989	2,989	3,044	2,989
19,950	20,000	2,996	2,996	3,058	2,996

Right panel (20,000–23,000)

If line 37 (taxable income) is— At least	But less than	And you are— Single	Married filing jointly*	Married filing separately	Head of a household
20,000					
20,000	20,050	3,004	3,004	3,072	3,004
20,050	20,100	3,011	3,011	3,086	3,011
20,100	20,150	3,019	3,019	3,100	3,019
20,150	20,200	3,026	3,026	3,114	3,026
20,200	20,250	3,034	3,034	3,128	3,034
20,250	20,300	3,041	3,041	3,142	3,041
20,300	20,350	3,049	3,049	3,156	3,049
20,350	20,400	3,056	3,056	3,170	3,056
20,400	20,450	3,064	3,064	3,184	3,064
20,450	20,500	3,071	3,071	3,198	3,071
20,500	20,550	3,079	3,079	3,212	3,079
20,550	20,600	3,086	3,086	3,226	3,086
20,600	20,650	3,094	3,094	3,240	3,094
20,650	20,700	3,101	3,101	3,254	3,101
20,700	20,750	3,109	3,109	3,268	3,109
20,750	20,800	3,116	3,116	3,282	3,116
20,800	20,850	3,124	3,124	3,296	3,124
20,850	20,900	3,131	3,131	3,310	3,131
20,900	20,950	3,139	3,139	3,324	3,139
20,950	21,000	3,146	3,146	3,338	3,146
21,000					
21,000	21,050	3,154	3,154	3,352	3,154
21,050	21,100	3,161	3,161	3,366	3,161
21,100	21,150	3,169	3,169	3,380	3,169
21,150	21,200	3,176	3,176	3,394	3,176
21,200	21,250	3,184	3,184	3,408	3,184
21,250	21,300	3,191	3,191	3,422	3,191
21,300	21,350	3,199	3,199	3,436	3,199
21,350	21,400	3,206	3,206	3,450	3,206
21,400	21,450	3,214	3,214	3,464	3,214
21,450	21,500	3,221	3,221	3,478	3,221
21,500	21,550	3,229	3,229	3,492	3,229
21,550	21,600	3,236	3,236	3,506	3,236
21,600	21,650	3,244	3,244	3,520	3,244
21,650	21,700	3,251	3,251	3,534	3,251
21,700	21,750	3,259	3,259	3,548	3,259
21,750	21,800	3,266	3,266	3,562	3,266
21,800	21,850	3,274	3,274	3,576	3,274
21,850	21,900	3,281	3,281	3,590	3,281
21,900	21,950	3,289	3,289	3,604	3,289
21,950	22,000	3,296	3,296	3,618	3,296
22,000					
22,000	22,050	3,304	3,304	3,632	3,304
22,050	22,100	3,311	3,311	3,646	3,311
22,100	22,150	3,319	3,319	3,660	3,319
22,150	22,200	3,326	3,326	3,674	3,326
22,200	22,250	3,334	3,334	3,688	3,334
22,250	22,300	3,341	3,341	3,702	3,341
22,300	22,350	3,349	3,349	3,716	3,349
22,350	22,400	3,356	3,356	3,730	3,356
22,400	22,450	3,364	3,364	3,744	3,364
22,450	22,500	3,371	3,371	3,758	3,371
22,500	22,550	3,379	3,379	3,772	3,379
22,550	22,600	3,386	3,386	3,786	3,386
22,600	22,650	3,394	3,394	3,800	3,394
22,650	22,700	3,401	3,401	3,814	3,401
22,700	22,750	3,409	3,409	3,828	3,409
22,750	22,800	3,416	3,416	3,842	3,416
22,800	22,850	3,424	3,424	3,856	3,424
22,850	22,900	3,431	3,431	3,870	3,431
22,900	22,950	3,439	3,439	3,884	3,439
22,950	23,000	3,446	3,446	3,898	3,446

* This column must also be used by a qualifying widow(er).

Continued on next page

1995 Tax Table—*Continued*

23,000 / 24,000 / 25,000

At least	But less than	Single	Married filing jointly*	Married filing separately	Head of a household
23,000					
23,000	23,050	3,454	3,454	3,912	3,454
23,050	23,100	3,461	3,461	3,926	3,461
23,100	23,150	3,469	3,469	3,940	3,469
23,150	23,200	3,476	3,476	3,954	3,476
23,200	23,250	3,484	3,484	3,968	3,484
23,250	23,300	3,491	3,491	3,982	3,491
23,300	23,350	3,499	3,499	3,996	3,499
23,350	23,400	3,510	3,506	4,010	3,506
23,400	23,450	3,524	3,514	4,024	3,514
23,450	23,500	3,538	3,521	4,038	3,521
23,500	23,550	3,552	3,529	4,052	3,529
23,550	23,600	3,566	3,536	4,066	3,536
23,600	23,650	3,580	3,544	4,080	3,544
23,650	23,700	3,594	3,551	4,094	3,551
23,700	23,750	3,608	3,559	4,108	3,559
23,750	23,800	3,622	3,566	4,122	3,566
23,800	23,850	3,636	3,574	4,136	3,574
23,850	23,900	3,650	3,581	4,150	3,581
23,900	23,950	3,664	3,589	4,164	3,589
23,950	24,000	3,678	3,596	4,178	3,596
24,000					
24,000	24,050	3,692	3,604	4,192	3,604
24,050	24,100	3,706	3,611	4,206	3,611
24,100	24,150	3,720	3,619	4,220	3,619
24,150	24,200	3,734	3,626	4,234	3,626
24,200	24,250	3,748	3,634	4,248	3,634
24,250	24,300	3,762	3,641	4,262	3,641
24,300	24,350	3,776	3,649	4,276	3,649
24,350	24,400	3,790	3,656	4,290	3,656
24,400	24,450	3,804	3,664	4,304	3,664
24,450	24,500	3,818	3,671	4,318	3,671
24,500	24,550	3,832	3,679	4,332	3,679
24,550	24,600	3,846	3,686	4,346	3,686
24,600	24,650	3,860	3,694	4,360	3,694
24,650	24,700	3,874	3,701	4,374	3,701
24,700	24,750	3,888	3,709	4,388	3,709
24,750	24,800	3,902	3,716	4,402	3,716
24,800	24,850	3,916	3,724	4,416	3,724
24,850	24,900	3,930	3,731	4,430	3,731
24,900	24,950	3,944	3,739	4,444	3,739
24,950	25,000	3,958	3,746	4,458	3,746
25,000					
25,000	25,050	3,972	3,754	4,472	3,754
25,050	25,100	3,986	3,761	4,486	3,761
25,100	25,150	4,000	3,769	4,500	3,769
25,150	25,200	4,014	3,776	4,514	3,776
25,200	25,250	4,028	3,784	4,528	3,784
25,250	25,300	4,042	3,791	4,542	3,791
25,300	25,350	4,056	3,799	4,556	3,799
25,350	25,400	4,070	3,806	4,570	3,806
25,400	25,450	4,084	3,814	4,584	3,814
25,450	25,500	4,098	3,821	4,598	3,821
25,500	25,550	4,112	3,829	4,612	3,829
25,550	25,600	4,126	3,836	4,626	3,836
25,600	25,650	4,140	3,844	4,640	3,844
25,650	25,700	4,154	3,851	4,654	3,851
25,700	25,750	4,168	3,859	4,668	3,859
25,750	25,800	4,182	3,866	4,682	3,866
25,800	25,850	4,196	3,874	4,696	3,874
25,850	25,900	4,210	3,881	4,710	3,881
25,900	25,950	4,224	3,889	4,724	3,889
25,950	26,000	4,238	3,896	4,738	3,896

26,000 / 27,000 / 28,000

At least	But less than	Single	Married filing jointly*	Married filing separately	Head of a household
26,000					
26,000	26,050	4,252	3,904	4,752	3,904
26,050	26,100	4,266	3,911	4,766	3,911
26,100	26,150	4,280	3,919	4,780	3,919
26,150	26,200	4,294	3,926	4,794	3,926
26,200	26,250	4,308	3,934	4,808	3,934
26,250	26,300	4,322	3,941	4,822	3,941
26,300	26,350	4,336	3,949	4,836	3,949
26,350	26,400	4,350	3,956	4,850	3,956
26,400	26,450	4,364	3,964	4,864	3,964
26,450	26,500	4,378	3,971	4,878	3,971
26,500	26,550	4,392	3,979	4,892	3,979
26,550	26,600	4,406	3,986	4,906	3,986
26,600	26,650	4,420	3,994	4,920	3,994
26,650	26,700	4,434	4,001	4,934	4,001
26,700	26,750	4,448	4,009	4,948	4,009
26,750	26,800	4,462	4,016	4,962	4,016
26,800	26,850	4,476	4,024	4,976	4,024
26,850	26,900	4,490	4,031	4,990	4,031
26,900	26,950	4,504	4,039	5,004	4,039
26,950	27,000	4,518	4,046	5,018	4,046
27,000					
27,000	27,050	4,532	4,054	5,032	4,054
27,050	27,100	4,546	4,061	5,046	4,061
27,100	27,150	4,560	4,069	5,060	4,069
27,150	27,200	4,574	4,076	5,074	4,076
27,200	27,250	4,588	4,084	5,088	4,084
27,250	27,300	4,602	4,091	5,102	4,091
27,300	27,350	4,616	4,099	5,116	4,099
27,350	27,400	4,630	4,106	5,130	4,106
27,400	27,450	4,644	4,114	5,144	4,114
27,450	27,500	4,658	4,121	5,158	4,121
27,500	27,550	4,672	4,129	5,172	4,129
27,550	27,600	4,686	4,136	5,186	4,136
27,600	27,650	4,700	4,144	5,200	4,144
27,650	27,700	4,714	4,151	5,214	4,151
27,700	27,750	4,728	4,159	5,228	4,159
27,750	27,800	4,742	4,166	5,242	4,166
27,800	27,850	4,756	4,174	5,256	4,174
27,850	27,900	4,770	4,181	5,270	4,181
27,900	27,950	4,784	4,189	5,284	4,189
27,950	28,000	4,798	4,196	5,298	4,196
28,000					
28,000	28,050	4,812	4,204	5,312	4,204
28,050	28,100	4,826	4,211	5,326	4,211
28,100	28,150	4,840	4,219	5,340	4,219
28,150	28,200	4,854	4,226	5,354	4,226
28,200	28,250	4,868	4,234	5,368	4,234
28,250	28,300	4,882	4,241	5,382	4,241
28,300	28,350	4,896	4,249	5,396	4,249
28,350	28,400	4,910	4,256	5,410	4,256
28,400	28,450	4,924	4,264	5,424	4,264
28,450	28,500	4,938	4,271	5,438	4,271
28,500	28,550	4,952	4,279	5,452	4,279
28,550	28,600	4,966	4,286	5,466	4,286
28,600	28,650	4,980	4,294	5,480	4,294
28,650	28,700	4,994	4,301	5,494	4,301
28,700	28,750	5,008	4,309	5,508	4,309
28,750	28,800	5,022	4,316	5,522	4,316
28,800	28,850	5,036	4,324	5,536	4,324
28,850	28,900	5,050	4,331	5,550	4,331
28,900	28,950	5,064	4,339	5,564	4,339
28,950	29,000	5,078	4,346	5,578	4,346

29,000 / 30,000 / 31,000

At least	But less than	Single	Married filing jointly*	Married filing separately	Head of a household
29,000					
29,000	29,050	5,092	4,354	5,592	4,354
29,050	29,100	5,106	4,361	5,606	4,361
29,100	29,150	5,120	4,369	5,620	4,369
29,150	29,200	5,134	4,376	5,634	4,376
29,200	29,250	5,148	4,384	5,648	4,384
29,250	29,300	5,162	4,391	5,662	4,391
29,300	29,350	5,176	4,399	5,676	4,399
29,350	29,400	5,190	4,406	5,690	4,406
29,400	29,450	5,204	4,414	5,704	4,414
29,450	29,500	5,218	4,421	5,718	4,421
29,500	29,550	5,232	4,429	5,732	4,429
29,550	29,600	5,246	4,436	5,746	4,436
29,600	29,650	5,260	4,444	5,760	4,444
29,650	29,700	5,274	4,451	5,774	4,451
29,700	29,750	5,288	4,459	5,788	4,459
29,750	29,800	5,302	4,466	5,802	4,466
29,800	29,850	5,316	4,474	5,816	4,474
29,850	29,900	5,330	4,481	5,830	4,481
29,900	29,950	5,344	4,489	5,844	4,489
29,950	30,000	5,358	4,496	5,858	4,496
30,000					
30,000	30,050	5,372	4,504	5,872	4,504
30,050	30,100	5,386	4,511	5,886	4,511
30,100	30,150	5,400	4,519	5,900	4,519
30,150	30,200	5,414	4,526	5,914	4,526
30,200	30,250	5,428	4,534	5,928	4,534
30,250	30,300	5,442	4,541	5,942	4,541
30,300	30,350	5,456	4,549	5,956	4,549
30,350	30,400	5,470	4,556	5,970	4,556
30,400	30,450	5,484	4,564	5,984	4,564
30,450	30,500	5,498	4,571	5,998	4,571
30,500	30,550	5,512	4,579	6,012	4,579
30,550	30,600	5,526	4,586	6,026	4,586
30,600	30,650	5,540	4,594	6,040	4,594
30,650	30,700	5,554	4,601	6,054	4,601
30,700	30,750	5,568	4,609	6,068	4,609
30,750	30,800	5,582	4,616	6,082	4,616
30,800	30,850	5,596	4,624	6,096	4,624
30,850	30,900	5,610	4,631	6,110	4,631
30,900	30,950	5,624	4,639	6,124	4,639
30,950	31,000	5,638	4,646	6,138	4,646
31,000					
31,000	31,050	5,652	4,654	6,152	4,654
31,050	31,100	5,666	4,661	6,166	4,661
31,100	31,150	5,680	4,669	6,180	4,669
31,150	31,200	5,694	4,676	6,194	4,676
31,200	31,250	5,708	4,684	6,208	4,684
31,250	31,300	5,722	4,691	6,222	4,695
31,300	31,350	5,736	4,699	6,236	4,709
31,350	31,400	5,750	4,706	6,250	4,723
31,400	31,450	5,764	4,714	6,264	4,737
31,450	31,500	5,778	4,721	6,278	4,751
31,500	31,550	5,792	4,729	6,292	4,765
31,550	31,600	5,806	4,736	6,306	4,779
31,600	31,650	5,820	4,744	6,320	4,793
31,650	31,700	5,834	4,751	6,334	4,807
31,700	31,750	5,848	4,759	6,348	4,821
31,750	31,800	5,862	4,766	6,362	4,835
31,800	31,850	5,876	4,774	6,376	4,849
31,850	31,900	5,890	4,781	6,390	4,863
31,900	31,950	5,904	4,789	6,404	4,877
31,950	32,000	5,918	4,796	6,418	4,891

* This column must also be used by a qualifying widow(er).

Continued on next page

1995 Tax Table—*Continued*

If line 37 (taxable income) is—		And you are—			
At least	But less than	Single	Married filing jointly *	Married filing separately	Head of a household
		Your tax is—			

32,000

At least	But less than	Single	Married filing jointly *	Married filing separately	Head of a household
32,000	32,050	5,932	4,804	6,432	4,905
32,050	32,100	5,946	4,811	6,446	4,919
32,100	32,150	5,960	4,819	6,460	4,933
32,150	32,200	5,974	4,826	6,474	4,947
32,200	32,250	5,988	4,834	6,488	4,961
32,250	32,300	6,002	4,841	6,502	4,975
32,300	32,350	6,016	4,849	6,516	4,989
32,350	32,400	6,030	4,856	6,530	5,003
32,400	32,450	6,044	4,864	6,544	5,017
32,450	32,500	6,058	4,871	6,558	5,031
32,500	32,550	6,072	4,879	6,572	5,045
32,550	32,600	6,086	4,886	6,586	5,059
32,600	32,650	6,100	4,894	6,600	5,073
32,650	32,700	6,114	4,901	6,614	5,087
32,700	32,750	6,128	4,909	6,628	5,101
32,750	32,800	6,142	4,916	6,642	5,115
32,800	32,850	6,156	4,924	6,656	5,129
32,850	32,900	6,170	4,931	6,670	5,143
32,900	32,950	6,184	4,939	6,684	5,157
32,950	33,000	6,198	4,946	6,698	5,171

33,000

At least	But less than	Single	Married filing jointly *	Married filing separately	Head of a household
33,000	33,050	6,212	4,954	6,712	5,185
33,050	33,100	6,226	4,961	6,726	5,199
33,100	33,150	6,240	4,969	6,740	5,213
33,150	33,200	6,254	4,976	6,754	5,227
33,200	33,250	6,268	4,984	6,768	5,241
33,250	33,300	6,282	4,991	6,782	5,255
33,300	33,350	6,296	4,999	6,796	5,269
33,350	33,400	6,310	5,006	6,810	5,283
33,400	33,450	6,324	5,014	6,824	5,297
33,450	33,500	6,338	5,021	6,838	5,311
33,500	33,550	6,352	5,029	6,852	5,325
33,550	33,600	6,366	5,036	6,866	5,339
33,600	33,650	6,380	5,044	6,880	5,353
33,650	33,700	6,394	5,051	6,894	5,367
33,700	33,750	6,408	5,059	6,908	5,381
33,750	33,800	6,422	5,066	6,922	5,395
33,800	33,850	6,436	5,074	6,936	5,409
33,850	33,900	6,450	5,081	6,950	5,423
33,900	33,950	6,464	5,089	6,964	5,437
33,950	34,000	6,478	5,096	6,978	5,451

34,000

At least	But less than	Single	Married filing jointly *	Married filing separately	Head of a household
34,000	34,050	6,492	5,104	6,992	5,465
34,050	34,100	6,506	5,111	7,006	5,479
34,100	34,150	6,520	5,119	7,020	5,493
34,150	34,200	6,534	5,126	7,034	5,507
34,200	34,250	6,548	5,134	7,048	5,521
34,250	34,300	6,562	5,141	7,062	5,535
34,300	34,350	6,576	5,149	7,076	5,549
34,350	34,400	6,590	5,156	7,090	5,563
34,400	34,450	6,604	5,164	7,104	5,577
34,450	34,500	6,618	5,171	7,118	5,591
34,500	34,550	6,632	5,179	7,132	5,605
34,550	34,600	6,646	5,186	7,146	5,619
34,600	34,650	6,660	5,194	7,160	5,633
34,650	34,700	6,674	5,201	7,174	5,647
34,700	34,750	6,688	5,209	7,188	5,661
34,750	34,800	6,702	5,216	7,202	5,675
34,800	34,850	6,716	5,224	7,216	5,689
34,850	34,900	6,730	5,231	7,230	5,703
34,900	34,950	6,744	5,239	7,244	5,717
34,950	35,000	6,758	5,246	7,258	5,731

35,000

At least	But less than	Single	Married filing jointly *	Married filing separately	Head of a household
35,000	35,050	6,772	5,254	7,272	5,745
35,050	35,100	6,786	5,261	7,286	5,759
35,100	35,150	6,800	5,269	7,300	5,773
35,150	35,200	6,814	5,276	7,314	5,787
35,200	35,250	6,828	5,284	7,328	5,801
35,250	35,300	6,842	5,291	7,342	5,815
35,300	35,350	6,856	5,299	7,356	5,829
35,350	35,400	6,870	5,306	7,370	5,843
35,400	35,450	6,884	5,314	7,384	5,857
35,450	35,500	6,898	5,321	7,398	5,871
35,500	35,550	6,912	5,329	7,412	5,885
35,550	35,600	6,926	5,336	7,426	5,899
35,600	35,650	6,940	5,344	7,440	5,913
35,650	35,700	6,954	5,351	7,454	5,927
35,700	35,750	6,968	5,359	7,468	5,941
35,750	35,800	6,982	5,366	7,482	5,955
35,800	35,850	6,996	5,374	7,496	5,969
35,850	35,900	7,010	5,381	7,510	5,983
35,900	35,950	7,024	5,389	7,524	5,997
35,950	36,000	7,038	5,396	7,538	6,011

36,000

At least	But less than	Single	Married filing jointly *	Married filing separately	Head of a household
36,000	36,050	7,052	5,404	7,552	6,025
36,050	36,100	7,066	5,411	7,566	6,039
36,100	36,150	7,080	5,419	7,580	6,053
36,150	36,200	7,094	5,426	7,594	6,067
36,200	36,250	7,108	5,434	7,608	6,081
36,250	36,300	7,122	5,441	7,622	6,095
36,300	36,350	7,136	5,449	7,636	6,109
36,350	36,400	7,150	5,456	7,650	6,123
36,400	36,450	7,164	5,464	7,664	6,137
36,450	36,500	7,178	5,471	7,678	6,151
36,500	36,550	7,192	5,479	7,692	6,165
36,550	36,600	7,206	5,486	7,706	6,179
36,600	36,650	7,220	5,494	7,720	6,193
36,650	36,700	7,234	5,501	7,734	6,207
36,700	36,750	7,248	5,509	7,748	6,221
36,750	36,800	7,262	5,516	7,762	6,235
36,800	36,850	7,276	5,524	7,776	6,249
36,850	36,900	7,290	5,531	7,790	6,263
36,900	36,950	7,304	5,539	7,804	6,277
36,950	37,000	7,318	5,546	7,818	6,291

37,000

At least	But less than	Single	Married filing jointly *	Married filing separately	Head of a household
37,000	37,050	7,332	5,554	7,832	6,305
37,050	37,100	7,346	5,561	7,846	6,319
37,100	37,150	7,360	5,569	7,860	6,333
37,150	37,200	7,374	5,576	7,874	6,347
37,200	37,250	7,388	5,584	7,888	6,361
37,250	37,300	7,402	5,591	7,902	6,375
37,300	37,350	7,416	5,599	7,916	6,389
37,350	37,400	7,430	5,606	7,930	6,403
37,400	37,450	7,444	5,614	7,944	6,417
37,450	37,500	7,458	5,621	7,958	6,431
37,500	37,550	7,472	5,629	7,972	6,445
37,550	37,600	7,486	5,636	7,986	6,459
37,600	37,650	7,500	5,644	8,000	6,473
37,650	37,700	7,514	5,651	8,014	6,487
37,700	37,750	7,528	5,659	8,028	6,501
37,750	37,800	7,542	5,666	8,042	6,515
37,800	37,850	7,556	5,674	8,056	6,529
37,850	37,900	7,570	5,681	8,070	6,543
37,900	37,950	7,584	5,689	8,084	6,557
37,950	38,000	7,598	5,696	8,098	6,571

38,000

At least	But less than	Single	Married filing jointly *	Married filing separately	Head of a household
38,000	38,050	7,612	5,704	8,112	6,585
38,050	38,100	7,626	5,711	8,126	6,599
38,100	38,150	7,640	5,719	8,140	6,613
38,150	38,200	7,654	5,726	8,154	6,627
38,200	38,250	7,668	5,734	8,168	6,641
38,250	38,300	7,682	5,741	8,182	6,655
38,300	38,350	7,696	5,749	8,196	6,669
38,350	38,400	7,710	5,756	8,210	6,683
38,400	38,450	7,724	5,764	8,224	6,697
38,450	38,500	7,738	5,771	8,238	6,711
38,500	38,550	7,752	5,779	8,252	6,725
38,550	38,600	7,766	5,786	8,266	6,739
38,600	38,650	7,780	5,794	8,280	6,753
38,650	38,700	7,794	5,801	8,294	6,767
38,700	38,750	7,808	5,809	8,308	6,781
38,750	38,800	7,822	5,816	8,322	6,795
38,800	38,850	7,836	5,824	8,336	6,809
38,850	38,900	7,850	5,831	8,350	6,823
38,900	38,950	7,864	5,839	8,364	6,837
38,950	39,000	7,878	5,846	8,378	6,851

39,000

At least	But less than	Single	Married filing jointly *	Married filing separately	Head of a household
39,000	39,050	7,892	5,857	8,392	6,865
39,050	39,100	7,906	5,871	8,406	6,879
39,100	39,150	7,920	5,885	8,420	6,893
39,150	39,200	7,934	5,899	8,434	6,907
39,200	39,250	7,948	5,913	8,448	6,921
39,250	39,300	7,962	5,927	8,462	6,935
39,300	39,350	7,976	5,941	8,476	6,949
39,350	39,400	7,990	5,955	8,490	6,963
39,400	39,450	8,004	5,969	8,504	6,977
39,450	39,500	8,018	5,983	8,518	6,991
39,500	39,550	8,032	5,997	8,532	7,005
39,550	39,600	8,046	6,011	8,546	7,019
39,600	39,650	8,060	6,025	8,560	7,033
39,650	39,700	8,074	6,039	8,574	7,047
39,700	39,750	8,088	6,053	8,588	7,061
39,750	39,800	8,102	6,067	8,602	7,075
39,800	39,850	8,116	6,081	8,616	7,089
39,850	39,900	8,130	6,095	8,630	7,103
39,900	39,950	8,144	6,109	8,644	7,117
39,950	40,000	8,158	6,123	8,658	7,131

40,000

At least	But less than	Single	Married filing jointly *	Married filing separately	Head of a household
40,000	40,050	8,172	6,137	8,672	7,145
40,050	40,100	8,186	6,151	8,686	7,159
40,100	40,150	8,200	6,165	8,700	7,173
40,150	40,200	8,214	6,179	8,714	7,187
40,200	40,250	8,228	6,193	8,728	7,201
40,250	40,300	8,242	6,207	8,742	7,215
40,300	40,350	8,256	6,221	8,756	7,229
40,350	40,400	8,270	6,235	8,770	7,243
40,400	40,450	8,284	6,249	8,784	7,257
40,450	40,500	8,298	6,263	8,798	7,271
40,500	40,550	8,312	6,277	8,812	7,285
40,550	40,600	8,326	6,291	8,826	7,299
40,600	40,650	8,340	6,305	8,840	7,313
40,650	40,700	8,354	6,319	8,854	7,327
40,700	40,750	8,368	6,333	8,868	7,341
40,750	40,800	8,382	6,347	8,882	7,355
40,800	40,850	8,396	6,361	8,896	7,369
40,850	40,900	8,410	6,375	8,910	7,383
40,900	40,950	8,424	6,389	8,924	7,397
40,950	41,000	8,438	6,403	8,938	7,411

* This column must also be used by a qualifying widow(er).

Continued on next page

1995 Tax Table—*Continued*

Left column group

If line 37 (taxable income) is—		And you are—			
At least	But less than	Single	Married filing jointly *	Married filing separately	Head of a house-hold
		Your tax is—			
41,000					
41,000	41,050	8,452	6,417	8,952	7,425
41,050	41,100	8,466	6,431	8,966	7,439
41,100	41,150	8,480	6,445	8,980	7,453
41,150	41,200	8,494	6,459	8,994	7,467
41,200	41,250	8,508	6,473	9,008	7,481
41,250	41,300	8,522	6,487	9,022	7,495
41,300	41,350	8,536	6,501	9,036	7,509
41,350	41,400	8,550	6,515	9,050	7,523
41,400	41,450	8,564	6,529	9,064	7,537
41,450	41,500	8,578	6,543	9,078	7,551
41,500	41,550	8,592	6,557	9,092	7,565
41,550	41,600	8,606	6,571	9,106	7,579
41,600	41,650	8,620	6,585	9,120	7,593
41,650	41,700	8,634	6,599	9,134	7,607
41,700	41,750	8,648	6,613	9,148	7,621
41,750	41,800	8,662	6,627	9,162	7,635
41,800	41,850	8,676	6,641	9,176	7,649
41,850	41,900	8,690	6,655	9,190	7,663
41,900	41,950	8,704	6,669	9,204	7,677
41,950	42,000	8,718	6,683	9,218	7,691
42,000					
42,000	42,050	8,732	6,697	9,232	7,705
42,050	42,100	8,746	6,711	9,246	7,719
42,100	42,150	8,760	6,725	9,260	7,733
42,150	42,200	8,774	6,739	9,274	7,747
42,200	42,250	8,788	6,753	9,288	7,761
42,250	42,300	8,802	6,767	9,302	7,775
42,300	42,350	8,816	6,781	9,316	7,789
42,350	42,400	8,830	6,795	9,330	7,803
42,400	42,450	8,844	6,809	9,344	7,817
42,450	42,500	8,858	6,823	9,358	7,831
42,500	42,550	8,872	6,837	9,372	7,845
42,550	42,600	8,886	6,851	9,386	7,859
42,600	42,650	8,900	6,865	9,400	7,873
42,650	42,700	8,914	6,879	9,414	7,887
42,700	42,750	8,928	6,893	9,428	7,901
42,750	42,800	8,942	6,907	9,442	7,915
42,800	42,850	8,956	6,921	9,456	7,929
42,850	42,900	8,970	6,935	9,470	7,943
42,900	42,950	8,984	6,949	9,484	7,957
42,950	43,000	8,998	6,963	9,498	7,971
43,000					
43,000	43,050	9,012	6,977	9,512	7,985
43,050	43,100	9,026	6,991	9,526	7,999
43,100	43,150	9,040	7,005	9,540	8,013
43,150	43,200	9,054	7,019	9,554	8,027
43,200	43,250	9,068	7,033	9,568	8,041
43,250	43,300	9,082	7,047	9,582	8,055
43,300	43,350	9,096	7,061	9,596	8,069
43,350	43,400	9,110	7,075	9,610	8,083
43,400	43,450	9,124	7,089	9,624	8,097
43,450	43,500	9,138	7,103	9,638	8,111
43,500	43,550	9,152	7,117	9,652	8,125
43,550	43,600	9,166	7,131	9,666	8,139
43,600	43,650	9,180	7,145	9,680	8,153
43,650	43,700	9,194	7,159	9,694	8,167
43,700	43,750	9,208	7,173	9,708	8,181
43,750	43,800	9,222	7,187	9,722	8,195
43,800	43,850	9,236	7,201	9,736	8,209
43,850	43,900	9,250	7,215	9,750	8,223
43,900	43,950	9,264	7,229	9,764	8,237
43,950	44,000	9,278	7,243	9,778	8,251

Middle column group

If line 37 (taxable income) is—		And you are—			
At least	But less than	Single	Married filing jointly *	Married filing separately	Head of a house-hold
		Your tax is—			
44,000					
44,000	44,050	9,292	7,257	9,792	8,265
44,050	44,100	9,306	7,271	9,806	8,279
44,100	44,150	9,320	7,285	9,820	8,293
44,150	44,200	9,334	7,299	9,834	8,307
44,200	44,250	9,348	7,313	9,848	8,321
44,250	44,300	9,362	7,327	9,862	8,335
44,300	44,350	9,376	7,341	9,876	8,349
44,350	44,400	9,390	7,355	9,890	8,363
44,400	44,450	9,404	7,369	9,904	8,377
44,450	44,500	9,418	7,383	9,918	8,391
44,500	44,550	9,432	7,397	9,932	8,405
44,550	44,600	9,446	7,411	9,946	8,419
44,600	44,650	9,460	7,425	9,960	8,433
44,650	44,700	9,474	7,439	9,974	8,447
44,700	44,750	9,488	7,453	9,988	8,461
44,750	44,800	9,502	7,467	10,002	8,475
44,800	44,850	9,516	7,481	10,016	8,489
44,850	44,900	9,530	7,495	10,030	8,503
44,900	44,950	9,544	7,509	10,044	8,517
44,950	45,000	9,558	7,523	10,058	8,531
45,000					
45,000	45,050	9,572	7,537	10,072	8,545
45,050	45,100	9,586	7,551	10,086	8,559
45,100	45,150	9,600	7,565	10,100	8,573
45,150	45,200	9,614	7,579	10,114	8,587
45,200	45,250	9,628	7,593	10,128	8,601
45,250	45,300	9,642	7,607	10,142	8,615
45,300	45,350	9,656	7,621	10,156	8,629
45,350	45,400	9,670	7,635	10,170	8,643
45,400	45,450	9,684	7,649	10,184	8,657
45,450	45,500	9,698	7,663	10,198	8,671
45,500	45,550	9,712	7,677	10,212	8,685
45,550	45,600	9,726	7,691	10,226	8,699
45,600	45,650	9,740	7,705	10,240	8,713
45,650	45,700	9,754	7,719	10,254	8,727
45,700	45,750	9,768	7,733	10,268	8,741
45,750	45,800	9,782	7,747	10,282	8,755
45,800	45,850	9,796	7,761	10,296	8,769
45,850	45,900	9,810	7,775	10,310	8,783
45,900	45,950	9,824	7,789	10,324	8,797
45,950	46,000	9,838	7,803	10,338	8,811
46,000					
46,000	46,050	9,852	7,817	10,352	8,825
46,050	46,100	9,866	7,831	10,366	8,839
46,100	46,150	9,880	7,845	10,380	8,853
46,150	46,200	9,894	7,859	10,394	8,867
46,200	46,250	9,908	7,873	10,408	8,881
46,250	46,300	9,922	7,887	10,422	8,895
46,300	46,350	9,936	7,901	10,436	8,909
46,350	46,400	9,950	7,915	10,450	8,923
46,400	46,450	9,964	7,929	10,464	8,937
46,450	46,500	9,978	7,943	10,478	8,951
46,500	46,550	9,992	7,957	10,492	8,965
46,550	46,600	10,006	7,971	10,506	8,979
46,600	46,650	10,020	7,985	10,520	8,993
46,650	46,700	10,034	7,999	10,534	9,007
46,700	46,750	10,048	8,013	10,548	9,021
46,750	46,800	10,062	8,027	10,562	9,035
46,800	46,850	10,076	8,041	10,576	9,049
46,850	46,900	10,090	8,055	10,590	9,063
46,900	46,950	10,104	8,069	10,604	9,077
46,950	47,000	10,118	8,083	10,618	9,091

Right column group

If line 37 (taxable income) is—		And you are—			
At least	But less than	Single	Married filing jointly *	Married filing separately	Head of a house-hold
		Your tax is—			
47,000					
47,000	47,050	10,132	8,097	10,632	9,105
47,050	47,100	10,146	8,111	10,646	9,119
47,100	47,150	10,160	8,125	10,660	9,133
47,150	47,200	10,174	8,139	10,676	9,147
47,200	47,250	10,188	8,153	10,691	9,161
47,250	47,300	10,202	8,167	10,707	9,175
47,300	47,350	10,216	8,181	10,722	9,189
47,350	47,400	10,230	8,195	10,738	9,203
47,400	47,450	10,244	8,209	10,753	9,217
47,450	47,500	10,258	8,223	10,769	9,231
47,500	47,550	10,272	8,237	10,784	9,245
47,550	47,600	10,286	8,251	10,800	9,259
47,600	47,650	10,300	8,265	10,815	9,273
47,650	47,700	10,314	8,279	10,831	9,287
47,700	47,750	10,328	8,293	10,846	9,301
47,750	47,800	10,342	8,307	10,862	9,315
47,800	47,850	10,356	8,321	10,877	9,329
47,850	47,900	10,370	8,335	10,893	9,343
47,900	47,950	10,384	8,349	10,908	9,357
47,950	48,000	10,398	8,363	10,924	9,371
48,000					
48,000	48,050	10,412	8,377	10,939	9,385
48,050	48,100	10,426	8,391	10,955	9,399
48,100	48,150	10,440	8,405	10,970	9,413
48,150	48,200	10,454	8,419	10,986	9,427
48,200	48,250	10,468	8,433	11,001	9,441
48,250	48,300	10,482	8,447	11,017	9,455
48,300	48,350	10,496	8,461	11,032	9,469
48,350	48,400	10,510	8,475	11,048	9,483
48,400	48,450	10,524	8,489	11,063	9,497
48,450	48,500	10,538	8,503	11,079	9,511
48,500	48,550	10,552	8,517	11,094	9,525
48,550	48,600	10,566	8,531	11,110	9,539
48,600	48,650	10,580	8,545	11,125	9,553
48,650	48,700	10,594	8,559	11,141	9,567
48,700	48,750	10,608	8,573	11,156	9,581
48,750	48,800	10,622	8,587	11,172	9,595
48,800	48,850	10,636	8,601	11,187	9,609
48,850	48,900	10,650	8,615	11,203	9,623
48,900	48,950	10,664	8,629	11,218	9,637
48,950	49,000	10,678	8,643	11,234	9,651
49,000					
49,000	49,050	10,692	8,657	11,249	9,665
49,050	49,100	10,706	8,671	11,265	9,679
49,100	49,150	10,720	8,685	11,280	9,693
49,150	49,200	10,734	8,699	11,296	9,707
49,200	49,250	10,748	8,713	11,311	9,721
49,250	49,300	10,762	8,727	11,327	9,735
49,300	49,350	10,776	8,741	11,342	9,749
49,350	49,400	10,790	8,755	11,358	9,763
49,400	49,450	10,804	8,769	11,373	9,777
49,450	49,500	10,818	8,783	11,389	9,791
49,500	49,550	10,832	8,797	11,404	9,805
49,550	49,600	10,846	8,811	11,420	9,819
49,600	49,650	10,860	8,825	11,435	9,833
49,650	49,700	10,874	8,839	11,451	9,847
49,700	49,750	10,888	8,853	11,466	9,861
49,750	49,800	10,902	8,867	11,482	9,875
49,800	49,850	10,916	8,881	11,497	9,889
49,850	49,900	10,930	8,895	11,513	9,903
49,900	49,950	10,944	8,909	11,528	9,917
49,950	50,000	10,958	8,923	11,544	9,931

* This column must also be used by a qualifying widow(er).

Continued on next page

1995 Tax Table—Continued

If line 37 (taxable income) is—		And you are—			
At least	But less than	Single	Married filing jointly *	Married filing separately	Head of a household
		Your tax is—			

50,000

At least	But less than	Single	Married filing jointly	Married filing separately	Head of a household
50,000	50,050	10,972	8,937	11,559	9,945
50,050	50,100	10,986	8,951	11,575	9,959
50,100	50,150	11,000	8,965	11,590	9,973
50,150	50,200	11,014	8,979	11,606	9,987
50,200	50,250	11,028	8,993	11,621	10,001
50,250	50,300	11,042	9,007	11,637	10,015
50,300	50,350	11,056	9,021	11,652	10,029
50,350	50,400	11,070	9,035	11,668	10,043
50,400	50,450	11,084	9,049	11,683	10,057
50,450	50,500	11,098	9,063	11,699	10,071
50,500	50,550	11,112	9,077	11,714	10,085
50,550	50,600	11,126	9,091	11,730	10,099
50,600	50,650	11,140	9,105	11,745	10,113
50,650	50,700	11,154	9,119	11,761	10,127
50,700	50,750	11,168	9,133	11,776	10,141
50,750	50,800	11,182	9,147	11,792	10,155
50,800	50,850	11,196	9,161	11,807	10,169
50,850	50,900	11,210	9,175	11,823	10,183
50,900	50,950	11,224	9,189	11,838	10,197
50,950	51,000	11,238	9,203	11,854	10,211

51,000

At least	But less than	Single	Married filing jointly	Married filing separately	Head of a household
51,000	51,050	11,252	9,217	11,869	10,225
51,050	51,100	11,266	9,231	11,885	10,239
51,100	51,150	11,280	9,245	11,900	10,253
51,150	51,200	11,294	9,259	11,916	10,267
51,200	51,250	11,308	9,273	11,931	10,281
51,250	51,300	11,322	9,287	11,947	10,295
51,300	51,350	11,336	9,301	11,962	10,309
51,350	51,400	11,350	9,315	11,978	10,323
51,400	51,450	11,364	9,329	11,993	10,337
51,450	51,500	11,378	9,343	12,009	10,351
51,500	51,550	11,392	9,357	12,024	10,365
51,550	51,600	11,406	9,371	12,040	10,379
51,600	51,650	11,420	9,385	12,055	10,393
51,650	51,700	11,434	9,399	12,071	10,407
51,700	51,750	11,448	9,413	12,086	10,421
51,750	51,800	11,462	9,427	12,102	10,435
51,800	51,850	11,476	9,441	12,117	10,449
51,850	51,900	11,490	9,455	12,133	10,463
51,900	51,950	11,504	9,469	12,148	10,477
51,950	52,000	11,518	9,483	12,164	10,491

52,000

At least	But less than	Single	Married filing jointly	Married filing separately	Head of a household
52,000	52,050	11,532	9,497	12,179	10,505
52,050	52,100	11,546	9,511	12,195	10,519
52,100	52,150	11,560	9,525	12,210	10,533
52,150	52,200	11,574	9,539	12,226	10,547
52,200	52,250	11,588	9,553	12,241	10,561
52,250	52,300	11,602	9,567	12,257	10,575
52,300	52,350	11,616	9,581	12,272	10,589
52,350	52,400	11,630	9,595	12,288	10,603
52,400	52,450	11,644	9,609	12,303	10,617
52,450	52,500	11,658	9,623	12,319	10,631
52,500	52,550	11,672	9,637	12,334	10,645
52,550	52,600	11,686	9,651	12,350	10,659
52,600	52,650	11,700	9,665	12,365	10,673
52,650	52,700	11,714	9,679	12,381	10,687
52,700	52,750	11,728	9,693	12,396	10,701
52,750	52,800	11,742	9,707	12,412	10,715
52,800	52,850	11,756	9,721	12,427	10,729
52,850	52,900	11,770	9,735	12,443	10,743
52,900	52,950	11,784	9,749	12,458	10,757
52,950	53,000	11,798	9,763	12,474	10,771

53,000

At least	But less than	Single	Married filing jointly	Married filing separately	Head of a household
53,000	53,050	11,812	9,777	12,489	10,785
53,050	53,100	11,826	9,791	12,505	10,799
53,100	53,150	11,840	9,805	12,520	10,813
53,150	53,200	11,854	9,819	12,536	10,827
53,200	53,250	11,868	9,833	12,551	10,841
53,250	53,300	11,882	9,847	12,567	10,855
53,300	53,350	11,896	9,861	12,582	10,869
53,350	53,400	11,910	9,875	12,598	10,883
53,400	53,450	11,924	9,889	12,613	10,897
53,450	53,500	11,938	9,903	12,629	10,911
53,500	53,550	11,952	9,917	12,644	10,925
53,550	53,600	11,966	9,931	12,660	10,939
53,600	53,650	11,980	9,945	12,675	10,953
53,650	53,700	11,994	9,959	12,691	10,967
53,700	53,750	12,008	9,973	12,706	10,981
53,750	53,800	12,022	9,987	12,722	10,995
53,800	53,850	12,036	10,001	12,737	11,009
53,850	53,900	12,050	10,015	12,753	11,023
53,900	53,950	12,064	10,029	12,768	11,037
53,950	54,000	12,078	10,043	12,784	11,051

54,000

At least	But less than	Single	Married filing jointly	Married filing separately	Head of a household
54,000	54,050	12,092	10,057	12,799	11,065
54,050	54,100	12,106	10,071	12,815	11,079
54,100	54,150	12,120	10,085	12,830	11,093
54,150	54,200	12,134	10,099	12,846	11,107
54,200	54,250	12,148	10,113	12,861	11,121
54,250	54,300	12,162	10,127	12,877	11,135
54,300	54,350	12,176	10,141	12,892	11,149
54,350	54,400	12,190	10,155	12,908	11,163
54,400	54,450	12,204	10,169	12,923	11,177
54,450	54,500	12,218	10,183	12,939	11,191
54,500	54,550	12,232	10,197	12,954	11,205
54,550	54,600	12,246	10,211	12,970	11,219
54,600	54,650	12,260	10,225	12,985	11,233
54,650	54,700	12,274	10,239	13,001	11,247
54,700	54,750	12,288	10,253	13,016	11,261
54,750	54,800	12,302	10,267	13,032	11,275
54,800	54,850	12,316	10,281	13,047	11,289
54,850	54,900	12,330	10,295	13,063	11,303
54,900	54,950	12,344	10,309	13,078	11,317
54,950	55,000	12,358	10,323	13,094	11,331

55,000

At least	But less than	Single	Married filing jointly	Married filing separately	Head of a household
55,000	55,050	12,372	10,337	13,109	11,345
55,050	55,100	12,386	10,351	13,125	11,359
55,100	55,150	12,400	10,365	13,140	11,373
55,150	55,200	12,414	10,379	13,156	11,387
55,200	55,250	12,428	10,393	13,171	11,401
55,250	55,300	12,442	10,407	13,187	11,415
55,300	55,350	12,456	10,421	13,202	11,429
55,350	55,400	12,470	10,435	13,218	11,443
55,400	55,450	12,484	10,449	13,233	11,457
55,450	55,500	12,498	10,463	13,249	11,471
55,500	55,550	12,512	10,477	13,264	11,485
55,550	55,600	12,526	10,491	13,280	11,499
55,600	55,650	12,540	10,505	13,295	11,513
55,650	55,700	12,554	10,519	13,311	11,527
55,700	55,750	12,568	10,533	13,326	11,541
55,750	55,800	12,582	10,547	13,342	11,555
55,800	55,850	12,596	10,561	13,357	11,569
55,850	55,900	12,610	10,575	13,373	11,583
55,900	55,950	12,624	10,589	13,388	11,597
55,950	56,000	12,638	10,603	13,404	11,611

56,000

At least	But less than	Single	Married filing jointly	Married filing separately	Head of a household
56,000	56,050	12,652	10,617	13,419	11,625
56,050	56,100	12,666	10,631	13,435	11,639
56,100	56,150	12,680	10,645	13,450	11,653
56,150	56,200	12,694	10,659	13,466	11,667
56,200	56,250	12,708	10,673	13,481	11,681
56,250	56,300	12,722	10,687	13,497	11,695
56,300	56,350	12,736	10,701	13,512	11,709
56,350	56,400	12,750	10,715	13,528	11,723
56,400	56,450	12,764	10,729	13,543	11,737
56,450	56,500	12,778	10,743	13,559	11,751
56,500	56,550	12,792	10,757	13,574	11,765
56,550	56,600	12,806	10,771	13,590	11,779
56,600	56,650	12,822	10,785	13,605	11,793
56,650	56,700	12,837	10,799	13,621	11,807
56,700	56,750	12,853	10,813	13,636	11,821
56,750	56,800	12,868	10,827	13,652	11,835
56,800	56,850	12,884	10,841	13,667	11,849
56,850	56,900	12,899	10,855	13,683	11,863
56,900	56,950	12,915	10,869	13,698	11,877
56,950	57,000	12,930	10,883	13,714	11,891

57,000

At least	But less than	Single	Married filing jointly	Married filing separately	Head of a household
57,000	57,050	12,946	10,897	13,729	11,905
57,050	57,100	12,961	10,911	13,745	11,919
57,100	57,150	12,977	10,925	13,760	11,933
57,150	57,200	12,992	10,939	13,776	11,947
57,200	57,250	13,008	10,953	13,791	11,961
57,250	57,300	13,023	10,967	13,807	11,975
57,300	57,350	13,039	10,981	13,822	11,989
57,350	57,400	13,054	10,995	13,838	12,003
57,400	57,450	13,070	11,009	13,853	12,017
57,450	57,500	13,085	11,023	13,869	12,031
57,500	57,550	13,101	11,037	13,884	12,045
57,550	57,600	13,116	11,051	13,900	12,059
57,600	57,650	13,132	11,065	13,915	12,073
57,650	57,700	13,147	11,079	13,931	12,087
57,700	57,750	13,163	11,093	13,946	12,101
57,750	57,800	13,178	11,107	13,962	12,115
57,800	57,850	13,194	11,121	13,977	12,129
57,850	57,900	13,209	11,135	13,993	12,143
57,900	57,950	13,225	11,149	14,008	12,157
57,950	58,000	13,240	11,163	14,024	12,171

58,000

At least	But less than	Single	Married filing jointly	Married filing separately	Head of a household
58,000	58,050	13,256	11,177	14,039	12,185
58,050	58,100	13,271	11,191	14,055	12,199
58,100	58,150	13,287	11,205	14,070	12,213
58,150	58,200	13,302	11,219	14,086	12,227
58,200	58,250	13,318	11,233	14,101	12,241
58,250	58,300	13,333	11,247	14,117	12,255
58,300	58,350	13,349	11,261	14,132	12,269
58,350	58,400	13,364	11,275	14,148	12,283
58,400	58,450	13,380	11,289	14,163	12,297
58,450	58,500	13,395	11,303	14,179	12,311
58,500	58,550	13,411	11,317	14,194	12,325
58,550	58,600	13,426	11,331	14,210	12,339
58,600	58,650	13,442	11,345	14,225	12,353
58,650	58,700	13,457	11,359	14,241	12,367
58,700	58,750	13,473	11,373	14,256	12,381
58,750	58,800	13,488	11,387	14,272	12,395
58,800	58,850	13,504	11,401	14,287	12,409
58,850	58,900	13,519	11,415	14,303	12,423
58,900	58,950	13,535	11,429	14,318	12,437
58,950	59,000	13,550	11,443	14,334	12,451

* This column must also be used by a qualifying widow(er).

Continued on next page

1995 Tax Table—*Continued*

If line 37 (taxable income) is— At least	But less than	Single	Married filing jointly *	Married filing separately	Head of a household
59,000					
59,000	59,050	13,566	11,457	14,349	12,465
59,050	59,100	13,581	11,471	14,365	12,479
59,100	59,150	13,597	11,485	14,380	12,493
59,150	59,200	13,612	11,499	14,396	12,507
59,200	59,250	13,628	11,513	14,411	12,521
59,250	59,300	13,643	11,527	14,427	12,535
59,300	59,350	13,659	11,541	14,442	12,549
59,350	59,400	13,674	11,555	14,458	12,563
59,400	59,450	13,690	11,569	14,473	12,577
59,450	59,500	13,705	11,583	14,489	12,591
59,500	59,550	13,721	11,597	14,504	12,605
59,550	59,600	13,736	11,611	14,520	12,619
59,600	59,650	13,752	11,625	14,535	12,633
59,650	59,700	13,767	11,639	14,551	12,647
59,700	59,750	13,783	11,653	14,566	12,661
59,750	59,800	13,798	11,667	14,582	12,675
59,800	59,850	13,814	11,681	14,597	12,689
59,850	59,900	13,829	11,695	14,613	12,703
59,900	59,950	13,845	11,709	14,628	12,717
59,950	60,000	13,860	11,723	14,644	12,731
60,000					
60,000	60,050	13,876	11,737	14,659	12,745
60,050	60,100	13,891	11,751	14,675	12,759
60,100	60,150	13,907	11,765	14,690	12,773
60,150	60,200	13,922	11,779	14,706	12,787
60,200	60,250	13,938	11,793	14,721	12,801
60,250	60,300	13,953	11,807	14,737	12,815
60,300	60,350	13,969	11,821	14,752	12,829
60,350	60,400	13,984	11,835	14,768	12,843
60,400	60,450	14,000	11,849	14,783	12,857
60,450	60,500	14,015	11,863	14,799	12,871
60,500	60,550	14,031	11,877	14,814	12,885
60,550	60,600	14,046	11,891	14,830	12,899
60,600	60,650	14,062	11,905	14,845	12,913
60,650	60,700	14,077	11,919	14,861	12,927
60,700	60,750	14,093	11,933	14,876	12,941
60,750	60,800	14,108	11,947	14,892	12,955
60,800	60,850	14,124	11,961	14,907	12,969
60,850	60,900	14,139	11,975	14,923	12,983
60,900	60,950	14,155	11,989	14,938	12,997
60,950	61,000	14,170	12,003	14,954	13,011
61,000					
61,000	61,050	14,186	12,017	14,969	13,025
61,050	61,100	14,201	12,031	14,985	13,039
61,100	61,150	14,217	12,045	15,000	13,053
61,150	61,200	14,232	12,059	15,016	13,067
61,200	61,250	14,248	12,073	15,031	13,081
61,250	61,300	14,263	12,087	15,047	13,095
61,300	61,350	14,279	12,101	15,062	13,109
61,350	61,400	14,294	12,115	15,078	13,123
61,400	61,450	14,310	12,129	15,093	13,137
61,450	61,500	14,325	12,143	15,109	13,151
61,500	61,550	14,341	12,157	15,124	13,165
61,550	61,600	14,356	12,171	15,140	13,179
61,600	61,650	14,372	12,185	15,155	13,193
61,650	61,700	14,387	12,199	15,171	13,207
61,700	61,750	14,403	12,213	15,186	13,221
61,750	61,800	14,418	12,227	15,202	13,235
61,800	61,850	14,434	12,241	15,217	13,249
61,850	61,900	14,449	12,255	15,233	13,263
61,900	61,950	14,465	12,269	15,248	13,277
61,950	62,000	14,480	12,283	15,264	13,291

If line 37 (taxable income) is— At least	But less than	Single	Married filing jointly *	Married filing separately	Head of a household
62,000					
62,000	62,050	14,496	12,297	15,279	13,305
62,050	62,100	14,511	12,311	15,295	13,319
62,100	62,150	14,527	12,325	15,310	13,333
62,150	62,200	14,542	12,339	15,326	13,347
62,200	62,250	14,558	12,353	15,341	13,361
62,250	62,300	14,573	12,367	15,357	13,375
62,300	62,350	14,589	12,381	15,372	13,389
62,350	62,400	14,604	12,395	15,388	13,403
62,400	62,450	14,620	12,409	15,403	13,417
62,450	62,500	14,635	12,423	15,419	13,431
62,500	62,550	14,651	12,437	15,434	13,445
62,550	62,600	14,666	12,451	15,450	13,459
62,600	62,650	14,682	12,465	15,465	13,473
62,650	62,700	14,697	12,479	15,481	13,487
62,700	62,750	14,713	12,493	15,496	13,501
62,750	62,800	14,728	12,507	15,512	13,515
62,800	62,850	14,744	12,521	15,527	13,529
62,850	62,900	14,759	12,535	15,543	13,543
62,900	62,950	14,775	12,549	15,558	13,557
62,950	63,000	14,790	12,563	15,574	13,571
63,000					
63,000	63,050	14,806	12,577	15,589	13,585
63,050	63,100	14,821	12,591	15,605	13,599
63,100	63,150	14,837	12,605	15,620	13,613
63,150	63,200	14,852	12,619	15,636	13,627
63,200	63,250	14,868	12,633	15,651	13,641
63,250	63,300	14,883	12,647	15,667	13,655
63,300	63,350	14,899	12,661	15,682	13,669
63,350	63,400	14,914	12,675	15,698	13,683
63,400	63,450	14,930	12,689	15,713	13,697
63,450	63,500	14,945	12,703	15,729	13,711
63,500	63,550	14,961	12,717	15,744	13,725
63,550	63,600	14,976	12,731	15,760	13,739
63,600	63,650	14,992	12,745	15,775	13,753
63,650	63,700	15,007	12,759	15,791	13,767
63,700	63,750	15,023	12,773	15,806	13,781
63,750	63,800	15,038	12,787	15,822	13,795
63,800	63,850	15,054	12,801	15,837	13,809
63,850	63,900	15,069	12,815	15,853	13,823
63,900	63,950	15,085	12,829	15,868	13,837
63,950	64,000	15,100	12,843	15,884	13,851
64,000					
64,000	64,050	15,116	12,857	15,899	13,865
64,050	64,100	15,131	12,871	15,915	13,879
64,100	64,150	15,147	12,885	15,930	13,893
64,150	64,200	15,162	12,899	15,946	13,907
64,200	64,250	15,178	12,913	15,961	13,921
64,250	64,300	15,193	12,927	15,977	13,935
64,300	64,350	15,209	12,941	15,992	13,949
64,350	64,400	15,224	12,955	16,008	13,963
64,400	64,450	15,240	12,969	16,023	13,977
64,450	64,500	15,255	12,983	16,039	13,991
64,500	64,550	15,271	12,997	16,054	14,005
64,550	64,600	15,286	13,011	16,070	14,019
64,600	64,650	15,302	13,025	16,085	14,033
64,650	64,700	15,317	13,039	16,101	14,047
64,700	64,750	15,333	13,053	16,116	14,061
64,750	64,800	15,348	13,067	16,132	14,075
64,800	64,850	15,364	13,081	16,147	14,089
64,850	64,900	15,379	13,095	16,163	14,103
64,900	64,950	15,395	13,109	16,178	14,117
64,950	65,000	15,410	13,123	16,194	14,131

If line 37 (taxable income) is— At least	But less than	Single	Married filing jointly *	Married filing separately	Head of a household
65,000					
65,000	65,050	15,426	13,137	16,209	14,145
65,050	65,100	15,441	13,151	16,225	14,159
65,100	65,150	15,457	13,165	16,240	14,173
65,150	65,200	15,472	13,179	16,256	14,187
65,200	65,250	15,488	13,193	16,271	14,201
65,250	65,300	15,503	13,207	16,287	14,215
65,300	65,350	15,519	13,221	16,302	14,229
65,350	65,400	15,534	13,235	16,318	14,243
65,400	65,450	15,550	13,249	16,333	14,257
65,450	65,500	15,565	13,263	16,349	14,271
65,500	65,550	15,581	13,277	16,364	14,285
65,550	65,600	15,596	13,291	16,380	14,299
65,600	65,650	15,612	13,305	16,395	14,313
65,650	65,700	15,627	13,319	16,411	14,327
65,700	65,750	15,643	13,333	16,426	14,341
65,750	65,800	15,658	13,347	16,442	14,355
65,800	65,850	15,674	13,361	16,457	14,369
65,850	65,900	15,689	13,375	16,473	14,383
65,900	65,950	15,705	13,389	16,488	14,397
65,950	66,000	15,720	13,403	16,504	14,411
66,000					
66,000	66,050	15,736	13,417	16,519	14,425
66,050	66,100	15,751	13,431	16,535	14,439
66,100	66,150	15,767	13,445	16,550	14,453
66,150	66,200	15,782	13,459	16,566	14,467
66,200	66,250	15,798	13,473	16,581	14,481
66,250	66,300	15,813	13,487	16,597	14,495
66,300	66,350	15,829	13,501	16,612	14,509
66,350	66,400	15,844	13,515	16,628	14,523
66,400	66,450	15,860	13,529	16,643	14,537
66,450	66,500	15,875	13,543	16,659	14,551
66,500	66,550	15,891	13,557	16,674	14,565
66,550	66,600	15,906	13,571	16,690	14,579
66,600	66,650	15,922	13,585	16,705	14,593
66,650	66,700	15,937	13,599	16,721	14,607
66,700	66,750	15,953	13,613	16,736	14,621
66,750	66,800	15,968	13,627	16,752	14,635
66,800	66,850	15,984	13,641	16,767	14,649
66,850	66,900	15,999	13,655	16,783	14,663
66,900	66,950	16,015	13,669	16,798	14,677
66,950	67,000	16,030	13,683	16,814	14,691
67,000					
67,000	67,050	16,046	13,697	16,829	14,705
67,050	67,100	16,061	13,711	16,845	14,719
67,100	67,150	16,077	13,725	16,860	14,733
67,150	67,200	16,092	13,739	16,876	14,747
67,200	67,250	16,108	13,753	16,891	14,761
67,250	67,300	16,123	13,767	16,907	14,775
67,300	67,350	16,139	13,781	16,922	14,789
67,350	67,400	16,154	13,795	16,938	14,803
67,400	67,450	16,170	13,809	16,953	14,817
67,450	67,500	16,185	13,823	16,969	14,831
67,500	67,550	16,201	13,837	16,984	14,845
67,550	67,600	16,216	13,851	17,000	14,859
67,600	67,650	16,232	13,865	17,015	14,873
67,650	67,700	16,247	13,879	17,031	14,887
67,700	67,750	16,263	13,893	17,046	14,901
67,750	67,800	16,278	13,907	17,062	14,915
67,800	67,850	16,294	13,921	17,077	14,929
67,850	67,900	16,309	13,935	17,093	14,943
67,900	67,950	16,325	13,949	17,108	14,957
67,950	68,000	16,340	13,963	17,124	14,971

* This column must also be used by a qualifying widow(er).

Continued on next page

1995 Tax Table—*Continued*

If line 37 (taxable income) is—		And you are—			
At least	But less than	Single	Married filing jointly *	Married filing separately	Head of a household
		Your tax is—			
68,000					
68,000	68,050	16,356	13,977	17,139	14,985
68,050	68,100	16,371	13,991	17,155	14,999
68,100	68,150	16,387	14,005	17,170	15,013
68,150	68,200	16,402	14,019	17,186	15,027
68,200	68,250	16,418	14,033	17,201	15,041
68,250	68,300	16,433	14,047	17,217	15,055
68,300	68,350	16,449	14,061	17,232	15,069
68,350	68,400	16,464	14,075	17,248	15,083
68,400	68,450	16,480	14,089	17,263	15,097
68,450	68,500	16,495	14,103	17,279	15,111
68,500	68,550	16,511	14,117	17,294	15,125
68,550	68,600	16,526	14,131	17,310	15,139
68,600	68,650	16,542	14,145	17,325	15,153
68,650	68,700	16,557	14,159	17,341	15,167
68,700	68,750	16,573	14,173	17,356	15,181
68,750	68,800	16,588	14,187	17,372	15,195
68,800	68,850	16,604	14,201	17,387	15,209
68,850	68,900	16,619	14,215	17,403	15,223
68,900	68,950	16,635	14,229	17,418	15,237
68,950	69,000	16,650	14,243	17,434	15,251
69,000					
69,000	69,050	16,666	14,257	17,449	15,265
69,050	69,100	16,681	14,271	17,465	15,279
69,100	69,150	16,697	14,285	17,480	15,293
69,150	69,200	16,712	14,299	17,496	15,307
69,200	69,250	16,728	14,313	17,511	15,321
69,250	69,300	16,743	14,327	17,527	15,335
69,300	69,350	16,759	14,341	17,542	15,349
69,350	69,400	16,774	14,355	17,558	15,363
69,400	69,450	16,790	14,369	17,573	15,377
69,450	69,500	16,805	14,383	17,589	15,391
69,500	69,550	16,821	14,397	17,604	15,405
69,550	69,600	16,836	14,411	17,620	15,419
69,600	69,650	16,852	14,425	17,635	15,433
69,650	69,700	16,867	14,439	17,651	15,447
69,700	69,750	16,883	14,453	17,666	15,461
69,750	69,800	16,898	14,467	17,682	15,475
69,800	69,850	16,914	14,481	17,697	15,489
69,850	69,900	16,929	14,495	17,713	15,503
69,900	69,950	16,945	14,509	17,728	15,517
69,950	70,000	16,960	14,523	17,744	15,531
70,000					
70,000	70,050	16,976	14,537	17,759	15,545
70,050	70,100	16,991	14,551	17,775	15,559
70,100	70,150	17,007	14,565	17,790	15,573
70,150	70,200	17,022	14,579	17,806	15,587
70,200	70,250	17,038	14,593	17,821	15,601
70,250	70,300	17,053	14,607	17,837	15,615
70,300	70,350	17,069	14,621	17,852	15,629
70,350	70,400	17,084	14,635	17,868	15,643
70,400	70,450	17,100	14,649	17,883	15,657
70,450	70,500	17,115	14,663	17,899	15,671
70,500	70,550	17,131	14,677	17,914	15,685
70,550	70,600	17,146	14,691	17,930	15,699
70,600	70,650	17,162	14,705	17,945	15,713
70,650	70,700	17,177	14,719	17,961	15,727
70,700	70,750	17,193	14,733	17,976	15,741
70,750	70,800	17,208	14,747	17,992	15,755
70,800	70,850	17,224	14,761	18,007	15,769
70,850	70,900	17,239	14,775	18,023	15,783
70,900	70,950	17,255	14,789	18,038	15,797
70,950	71,000	17,270	14,803	18,054	15,811

If line 37 (taxable income) is—		And you are—			
At least	But less than	Single	Married filing jointly *	Married filing separately	Head of a household
		Your tax is—			
71,000					
71,000	71,050	17,286	14,817	18,069	15,825
71,050	71,100	17,301	14,831	18,085	15,839
71,100	71,150	17,317	14,845	18,100	15,853
71,150	71,200	17,332	14,859	18,116	15,867
71,200	71,250	17,348	14,873	18,131	15,881
71,250	71,300	17,363	14,887	18,147	15,895
71,300	71,350	17,379	14,901	18,162	15,909
71,350	71,400	17,394	14,915	18,178	15,923
71,400	71,450	17,410	14,929	18,193	15,937
71,450	71,500	17,425	14,943	18,209	15,951
71,500	71,550	17,441	14,957	18,224	15,965
71,550	71,600	17,456	14,971	18,240	15,979
71,600	71,650	17,472	14,985	18,255	15,993
71,650	71,700	17,487	14,999	18,271	16,007
71,700	71,750	17,503	15,013	18,286	16,021
71,750	71,800	17,518	15,027	18,302	16,035
71,800	71,850	17,534	15,041	18,318	16,049
71,850	71,900	17,549	15,055	18,336	16,063
71,900	71,950	17,565	15,069	18,354	16,077
71,950	72,000	17,580	15,083	18,372	16,091
72,000					
72,000	72,050	17,596	15,097	18,390	16,105
72,050	72,100	17,611	15,111	18,408	16,119
72,100	72,150	17,627	15,125	18,426	16,133
72,150	72,200	17,642	15,139	18,444	16,147
72,200	72,250	17,658	15,153	18,462	16,161
72,250	72,300	17,673	15,167	18,480	16,175
72,300	72,350	17,689	15,181	18,498	16,189
72,350	72,400	17,704	15,195	18,516	16,203
72,400	72,450	17,720	15,209	18,534	16,217
72,450	72,500	17,735	15,223	18,552	16,231
72,500	72,550	17,751	15,237	18,570	16,245
72,550	72,600	17,766	15,251	18,588	16,259
72,600	72,650	17,782	15,265	18,606	16,273
72,650	72,700	17,797	15,279	18,624	16,287
72,700	72,750	17,813	15,293	18,642	16,301
72,750	72,800	17,828	15,307	18,660	16,315
72,800	72,850	17,844	15,321	18,678	16,329
72,850	72,900	17,859	15,335	18,696	16,343
72,900	72,950	17,875	15,349	18,714	16,357
72,950	73,000	17,890	15,363	18,732	16,371
73,000					
73,000	73,050	17,906	15,377	18,750	16,385
73,050	73,100	17,921	15,391	18,768	16,399
73,100	73,150	17,937	15,405	18,786	16,413
73,150	73,200	17,952	15,419	18,804	16,427
73,200	73,250	17,968	15,433	18,822	16,441
73,250	73,300	17,983	15,447	18,840	16,455
73,300	73,350	17,999	15,461	18,858	16,469
73,350	73,400	18,014	15,475	18,876	16,483
73,400	73,450	18,030	15,489	18,894	16,497
73,450	73,500	18,045	15,503	18,912	16,511
73,500	73,550	18,061	15,517	18,930	16,525
73,550	73,600	18,076	15,531	18,948	16,539
73,600	73,650	18,092	15,545	18,966	16,553
73,650	73,700	18,107	15,559	18,984	16,567
73,700	73,750	18,123	15,573	19,002	16,581
73,750	73,800	18,138	15,587	19,020	16,595
73,800	73,850	18,154	15,601	19,038	16,609
73,850	73,900	18,169	15,615	19,056	16,623
73,900	73,950	18,185	15,629	19,074	16,637
73,950	74,000	18,200	15,643	19,092	16,651

If line 37 (taxable income) is—		And you are—			
At least	But less than	Single	Married filing jointly *	Married filing separately	Head of a household
		Your tax is—			
74,000					
74,000	74,050	18,216	15,657	19,110	16,665
74,050	74,100	18,231	15,671	19,128	16,679
74,100	74,150	18,247	15,685	19,146	16,693
74,150	74,200	18,262	15,699	19,164	16,707
74,200	74,250	18,278	15,713	19,182	16,721
74,250	74,300	18,293	15,727	19,200	16,735
74,300	74,350	18,309	15,741	19,218	16,749
74,350	74,400	18,324	15,755	19,236	16,763
74,400	74,450	18,340	15,769	19,254	16,777
74,450	74,500	18,355	15,783	19,272	16,791
74,500	74,550	18,371	15,797	19,290	16,805
74,550	74,600	18,386	15,811	19,308	16,819
74,600	74,650	18,402	15,825	19,326	16,833
74,650	74,700	18,417	15,839	19,344	16,847
74,700	74,750	18,433	15,853	19,362	16,861
74,750	74,800	18,448	15,867	19,380	16,875
74,800	74,850	18,464	15,881	19,398	16,889
74,850	74,900	18,479	15,895	19,416	16,903
74,900	74,950	18,495	15,909	19,434	16,917
74,950	75,000	18,510	15,923	19,452	16,931
75,000					
75,000	75,050	18,526	15,937	19,470	16,945
75,050	75,100	18,541	15,951	19,488	16,959
75,100	75,150	18,557	15,965	19,506	16,973
75,150	75,200	18,572	15,979	19,524	16,987
75,200	75,250	18,588	15,993	19,542	17,001
75,250	75,300	18,603	16,007	19,560	17,015
75,300	75,350	18,619	16,021	19,578	17,029
75,350	75,400	18,634	16,035	19,596	17,043
75,400	75,450	18,650	16,049	19,614	17,057
75,450	75,500	18,665	16,063	19,632	17,071
75,500	75,550	18,681	16,077	19,650	17,085
75,550	75,600	18,696	16,091	19,668	17,099
75,600	75,650	18,712	16,105	19,686	17,113
75,650	75,700	18,727	16,119	19,704	17,127
75,700	75,750	18,743	16,133	19,722	17,141
75,750	75,800	18,758	16,147	19,740	17,155
75,800	75,850	18,774	16,161	19,758	17,169
75,850	75,900	18,789	16,175	19,776	17,183
75,900	75,950	18,805	16,189	19,794	17,197
75,950	76,000	18,820	16,203	19,812	17,211
76,000					
76,000	76,050	18,836	16,217	19,830	17,225
76,050	76,100	18,851	16,231	19,848	17,239
76,100	76,150	18,867	16,245	19,866	17,253
76,150	76,200	18,882	16,259	19,884	17,267
76,200	76,250	18,898	16,273	19,902	17,281
76,250	76,300	18,913	16,287	19,920	17,295
76,300	76,350	18,929	16,301	19,938	17,309
76,350	76,400	18,944	16,315	19,956	17,323
76,400	76,450	18,960	16,329	19,974	17,337
76,450	76,500	18,975	16,343	19,992	17,351
76,500	76,550	18,991	16,357	20,010	17,365
76,550	76,600	19,006	16,371	20,028	17,379
76,600	76,650	19,022	16,385	20,046	17,393
76,650	76,700	19,037	16,399	20,064	17,407
76,700	76,750	19,053	16,413	20,082	17,421
76,750	76,800	19,068	16,427	20,100	17,435
76,800	76,850	19,084	16,441	20,118	17,449
76,850	76,900	19,099	16,455	20,136	17,463
76,900	76,950	19,115	16,469	20,154	17,477
76,950	77,000	19,130	16,483	20,172	17,491

* This column must also be used by a qualifying widow(er).

Continued on next page

1995 Tax Table—*Continued*

If line 37 (taxable income) is— At least	But less than	Single	Married filing jointly *	Married filing separately	Head of a household
77,000					
77,000	77,050	19,146	16,497	20,190	17,505
77,050	77,100	19,161	16,511	20,208	17,519
77,100	77,150	19,177	16,525	20,226	17,533
77,150	77,200	19,192	16,539	20,244	17,547
77,200	77,250	19,208	16,553	20,262	17,561
77,250	77,300	19,223	16,567	20,280	17,575
77,300	77,350	19,239	16,581	20,298	17,589
77,350	77,400	19,254	16,595	20,316	17,603
77,400	77,450	19,270	16,609	20,334	17,617
77,450	77,500	19,285	16,623	20,352	17,631
77,500	77,550	19,301	16,637	20,370	17,645
77,550	77,600	19,316	16,651	20,388	17,659
77,600	77,650	19,332	16,665	20,406	17,673
77,650	77,700	19,347	16,679	20,424	17,687
77,700	77,750	19,363	16,693	20,442	17,701
77,750	77,800	19,378	16,707	20,460	17,715
77,800	77,850	19,394	16,721	20,478	17,729
77,850	77,900	19,409	16,735	20,496	17,743
77,900	77,950	19,425	16,749	20,514	17,757
77,950	78,000	19,440	16,763	20,532	17,771
78,000					
78,000	78,050	19,456	16,777	20,550	17,785
78,050	78,100	19,471	16,791	20,568	17,799
78,100	78,150	19,487	16,805	20,586	17,813
78,150	78,200	19,502	16,819	20,604	17,827
78,200	78,250	19,518	16,833	20,622	17,841
78,250	78,300	19,533	16,847	20,640	17,855
78,300	78,350	19,549	16,861	20,658	17,869
78,350	78,400	19,564	16,875	20,676	17,883
78,400	78,450	19,580	16,889	20,694	17,897
78,450	78,500	19,595	16,903	20,712	17,911
78,500	78,550	19,611	16,917	20,730	17,925
78,550	78,600	19,626	16,931	20,748	17,939
78,600	78,650	19,642	16,945	20,766	17,953
78,650	78,700	19,657	16,959	20,784	17,967
78,700	78,750	19,673	16,973	20,802	17,981
78,750	78,800	19,688	16,987	20,820	17,995
78,800	78,850	19,704	17,001	20,838	18,009
78,850	78,900	19,719	17,015	20,856	18,023
78,900	78,950	19,735	17,029	20,874	18,037
78,950	79,000	19,750	17,043	20,892	18,051
79,000					
79,000	79,050	19,766	17,057	20,910	18,065
79,050	79,100	19,781	17,071	20,928	18,079
79,100	79,150	19,797	17,085	20,946	18,093
79,150	79,200	19,812	17,099	20,964	18,107
79,200	79,250	19,828	17,113	20,982	18,121
79,250	79,300	19,843	17,127	21,000	18,135
79,300	79,350	19,859	17,141	21,018	18,149
79,350	79,400	19,874	17,155	21,036	18,163
79,400	79,450	19,890	17,169	21,054	18,177
79,450	79,500	19,905	17,183	21,072	18,191
79,500	79,550	19,921	17,197	21,090	18,205
79,550	79,600	19,936	17,211	21,108	18,219
79,600	79,650	19,952	17,225	21,126	18,233
79,650	79,700	19,967	17,239	21,144	18,247
79,700	79,750	19,983	17,253	21,162	18,261
79,750	79,800	19,998	17,267	21,180	18,275
79,800	79,850	20,014	17,281	21,198	18,289
79,850	79,900	20,029	17,295	21,216	18,303
79,900	79,950	20,045	17,309	21,234	18,317
79,950	80,000	20,060	17,323	21,252	18,331

If line 37 (taxable income) is— At least	But less than	Single	Married filing jointly *	Married filing separately	Head of a household
80,000					
80,000	80,050	20,076	17,337	21,270	18,345
80,050	80,100	20,091	17,351	21,288	18,359
80,100	80,150	20,107	17,365	21,306	18,373
80,150	80,200	20,122	17,379	21,324	18,387
80,200	80,250	20,138	17,393	21,342	18,401
80,250	80,300	20,153	17,407	21,360	18,415
80,300	80,350	20,169	17,421	21,378	18,429
80,350	80,400	20,184	17,435	21,396	18,443
80,400	80,450	20,200	17,449	21,414	18,457
80,450	80,500	20,215	17,463	21,432	18,471
80,500	80,550	20,231	17,477	21,450	18,485
80,550	80,600	20,246	17,491	21,468	18,499
80,600	80,650	20,262	17,505	21,486	18,513
80,650	80,700	20,277	17,519	21,504	18,527
80,700	80,750	20,293	17,533	21,522	18,541
80,750	80,800	20,308	17,547	21,540	18,555
80,800	80,850	20,324	17,561	21,558	18,571
80,850	80,900	20,339	17,575	21,576	18,586
80,900	80,950	20,355	17,589	21,594	18,602
80,950	81,000	20,370	17,603	21,612	18,617
81,000					
81,000	81,050	20,386	17,617	21,630	18,633
81,050	81,100	20,401	17,631	21,648	18,648
81,100	81,150	20,417	17,645	21,666	18,664
81,150	81,200	20,432	17,659	21,684	18,679
81,200	81,250	20,448	17,673	21,702	18,695
81,250	81,300	20,463	17,687	21,720	18,710
81,300	81,350	20,479	17,701	21,738	18,726
81,350	81,400	20,494	17,715	21,756	18,741
81,400	81,450	20,510	17,729	21,774	18,757
81,450	81,500	20,525	17,743	21,792	18,772
81,500	81,550	20,541	17,757	21,810	18,788
81,550	81,600	20,556	17,771	21,828	18,803
81,600	81,650	20,572	17,785	21,846	18,819
81,650	81,700	20,587	17,799	21,864	18,834
81,700	81,750	20,603	17,813	21,882	18,850
81,750	81,800	20,618	17,827	21,900	18,865
81,800	81,850	20,634	17,841	21,918	18,881
81,850	81,900	20,649	17,855	21,936	18,896
81,900	81,950	20,665	17,869	21,954	18,912
81,950	82,000	20,680	17,883	21,972	18,927
82,000					
82,000	82,050	20,696	17,897	21,990	18,943
82,050	82,100	20,711	17,911	22,008	18,958
82,100	82,150	20,727	17,925	22,026	18,974
82,150	82,200	20,742	17,939	22,044	18,989
82,200	82,250	20,758	17,953	22,062	19,005
82,250	82,300	20,773	17,967	22,080	19,020
82,300	82,350	20,789	17,981	22,098	19,036
82,350	82,400	20,804	17,995	22,116	19,051
82,400	82,450	20,820	18,009	22,134	19,067
82,450	82,500	20,835	18,023	22,152	19,082
82,500	82,550	20,851	18,037	22,170	19,098
82,550	82,600	20,866	18,051	22,188	19,113
82,600	82,650	20,882	18,065	22,206	19,129
82,650	82,700	20,897	18,079	22,224	19,144
82,700	82,750	20,913	18,093	22,242	19,160
82,750	82,800	20,928	18,107	22,260	19,175
82,800	82,850	20,944	18,121	22,278	19,191
82,850	82,900	20,959	18,135	22,296	19,206
82,900	82,950	20,975	18,149	22,314	19,222
82,950	83,000	20,990	18,163	22,332	19,237

If line 37 (taxable income) is— At least	But less than	Single	Married filing jointly *	Married filing separately	Head of a household
83,000					
83,000	83,050	21,006	18,177	22,350	19,253
83,050	83,100	21,021	18,191	22,368	19,268
83,100	83,150	21,037	18,205	22,386	19,284
83,150	83,200	21,052	18,219	22,404	19,299
83,200	83,250	21,068	18,233	22,422	19,315
83,250	83,300	21,083	18,247	22,440	19,330
83,300	83,350	21,099	18,261	22,458	19,346
83,350	83,400	21,114	18,275	22,476	19,361
83,400	83,450	21,130	18,289	22,494	19,377
83,450	83,500	21,145	18,303	22,512	19,392
83,500	83,550	21,161	18,317	22,530	19,408
83,550	83,600	21,176	18,331	22,548	19,423
83,600	83,650	21,192	18,345	22,566	19,439
83,650	83,700	21,207	18,359	22,584	19,454
83,700	83,750	21,223	18,373	22,602	19,470
83,750	83,800	21,238	18,387	22,620	19,485
83,800	83,850	21,254	18,401	22,638	19,501
83,850	83,900	21,269	18,415	22,656	19,516
83,900	83,950	21,285	18,429	22,674	19,532
83,950	84,000	21,300	18,443	22,692	19,547
84,000					
84,000	84,050	21,316	18,457	22,710	19,563
84,050	84,100	21,331	18,471	22,728	19,578
84,100	84,150	21,347	18,485	22,746	19,594
84,150	84,200	21,362	18,499	22,764	19,609
84,200	84,250	21,378	18,513	22,782	19,625
84,250	84,300	21,393	18,527	22,800	19,640
84,300	84,350	21,409	18,541	22,818	19,656
84,350	84,400	21,424	18,555	22,836	19,671
84,400	84,450	21,440	18,569	22,854	19,687
84,450	84,500	21,455	18,583	22,872	19,702
84,500	84,550	21,471	18,597	22,890	19,718
84,550	84,600	21,486	18,611	22,908	19,733
84,600	84,650	21,502	18,625	22,926	19,749
84,650	84,700	21,517	18,639	22,944	19,764
84,700	84,750	21,533	18,653	22,962	19,780
84,750	84,800	21,548	18,667	22,980	19,795
84,800	84,850	21,564	18,681	22,998	19,811
84,850	84,900	21,579	18,695	23,016	19,826
84,900	84,950	21,595	18,709	23,034	19,842
84,950	85,000	21,610	18,723	23,052	19,857
85,000					
85,000	85,050	21,626	18,737	23,070	19,873
85,050	85,100	21,641	18,751	23,088	19,888
85,100	85,150	21,657	18,765	23,106	19,904
85,150	85,200	21,672	18,779	23,124	19,919
85,200	85,250	21,688	18,793	23,142	19,935
85,250	85,300	21,703	18,807	23,160	19,950
85,300	85,350	21,719	18,821	23,178	19,966
85,350	85,400	21,734	18,835	23,196	19,981
85,400	85,450	21,750	18,849	23,214	19,997
85,450	85,500	21,765	18,863	23,232	20,012
85,500	85,550	21,781	18,877	23,250	20,028
85,550	85,600	21,796	18,891	23,268	20,043
85,600	85,650	21,812	18,905	23,286	20,059
85,650	85,700	21,827	18,919	23,304	20,074
85,700	85,750	21,843	18,933	23,322	20,090
85,750	85,800	21,858	18,947	23,340	20,105
85,800	85,850	21,874	18,961	23,358	20,121
85,850	85,900	21,889	18,975	23,376	20,136
85,900	85,950	21,905	18,989	23,394	20,152
85,950	86,000	21,920	19,003	23,412	20,167

* This column must also be used by a qualifying widow(er).

Continued on next page

1995 Tax Table—Continued

If line 37 (taxable income) is— / And you are—

Your tax is— (* This column must also be used by a qualifying widow(er).)

86,000 / 89,000 / 92,000

At least	But less than	Single	Married filing jointly *	Married filing separately	Head of a household
86,000	86,050	21,936	19,017	23,430	20,183
86,050	86,100	21,951	19,031	23,448	20,198
86,100	86,150	21,967	19,045	23,466	20,214
86,150	86,200	21,982	19,059	23,484	20,229
86,200	86,250	21,998	19,073	23,502	20,245
86,250	86,300	22,013	19,087	23,520	20,260
86,300	86,350	22,029	19,101	23,538	20,276
86,350	86,400	22,044	19,115	23,556	20,291
86,400	86,450	22,060	19,129	23,574	20,307
86,450	86,500	22,075	19,143	23,592	20,322
86,500	86,550	22,091	19,157	23,610	20,338
86,550	86,600	22,106	19,171	23,628	20,353
86,600	86,650	22,122	19,185	23,646	20,369
86,650	86,700	22,137	19,199	23,664	20,384
86,700	86,750	22,153	19,213	23,682	20,400
86,750	86,800	22,168	19,227	23,700	20,415
86,800	86,850	22,184	19,241	23,718	20,431
86,850	86,900	22,199	19,255	23,736	20,446
86,900	86,950	22,215	19,269	23,754	20,462
86,950	87,000	22,230	19,283	23,772	20,477
89,000	89,050	22,866	19,857	24,510	21,113
89,050	89,100	22,881	19,871	24,528	21,128
89,100	89,150	22,897	19,885	24,546	21,144
89,150	89,200	22,912	19,899	24,564	21,159
89,200	89,250	22,928	19,913	24,582	21,175
89,250	89,300	22,943	19,927	24,600	21,190
89,300	89,350	22,959	19,941	24,618	21,206
89,350	89,400	22,974	19,955	24,636	21,221
89,400	89,450	22,990	19,969	24,654	21,237
89,450	89,500	23,005	19,983	24,672	21,252
89,500	89,550	23,021	19,997	24,690	21,268
89,550	89,600	23,036	20,011	24,708	21,283
89,600	89,650	23,052	20,025	24,726	21,299
89,650	89,700	23,067	20,039	24,744	21,314
89,700	89,750	23,083	20,053	24,762	21,330
89,750	89,800	23,098	20,067	24,780	21,345
89,800	89,850	23,114	20,081	24,798	21,361
89,850	89,900	23,129	20,095	24,816	21,376
89,900	89,950	23,145	20,109	24,834	21,392
89,950	90,000	23,160	20,123	24,852	21,407
92,000	92,050	23,796	20,697	25,590	22,043
92,050	92,100	23,811	20,711	25,608	22,058
92,100	92,150	23,827	20,725	25,626	22,074
92,150	92,200	23,842	20,739	25,644	22,089
92,200	92,250	23,858	20,753	25,662	22,105
92,250	92,300	23,873	20,767	25,680	22,120
92,300	92,350	23,889	20,781	25,698	22,136
92,350	92,400	23,904	20,795	25,716	22,151
92,400	92,450	23,920	20,809	25,734	22,167
92,450	92,500	23,935	20,823	25,752	22,182
92,500	92,550	23,951	20,837	25,770	22,198
92,550	92,600	23,966	20,851	25,788	22,213
92,600	92,650	23,982	20,865	25,806	22,229
92,650	92,700	23,997	20,879	25,824	22,244
92,700	92,750	24,013	20,893	25,842	22,260
92,750	92,800	24,028	20,907	25,860	22,275
92,800	92,850	24,044	20,921	25,878	22,291
92,850	92,900	24,059	20,935	25,896	22,306
92,900	92,950	24,075	20,949	25,914	22,322
92,950	93,000	24,090	20,963	25,932	22,337

87,000 / 90,000 / 93,000

At least	But less than	Single	Married filing jointly *	Married filing separately	Head of a household
87,000	87,050	22,246	19,297	23,790	20,493
87,050	87,100	22,261	19,311	23,808	20,508
87,100	87,150	22,277	19,325	23,826	20,524
87,150	87,200	22,292	19,339	23,844	20,539
87,200	87,250	22,308	19,353	23,862	20,555
87,250	87,300	22,323	19,367	23,880	20,570
87,300	87,350	22,339	19,381	23,898	20,586
87,350	87,400	22,354	19,395	23,916	20,601
87,400	87,450	22,370	19,409	23,934	20,617
87,450	87,500	22,385	19,423	23,952	20,632
87,500	87,550	22,401	19,437	23,970	20,648
87,550	87,600	22,416	19,451	23,988	20,663
87,600	87,650	22,432	19,465	24,006	20,679
87,650	87,700	22,447	19,479	24,024	20,694
87,700	87,750	22,463	19,493	24,042	20,710
87,750	87,800	22,478	19,507	24,060	20,725
87,800	87,850	22,494	19,521	24,078	20,741
87,850	87,900	22,509	19,535	24,096	20,756
87,900	87,950	22,525	19,549	24,114	20,772
87,950	88,000	22,540	19,563	24,132	20,787
90,000	90,050	23,176	20,137	24,870	21,423
90,050	90,100	23,191	20,151	24,888	21,438
90,100	90,150	23,207	20,165	24,906	21,454
90,150	90,200	23,222	20,179	24,924	21,469
90,200	90,250	23,238	20,193	24,942	21,485
90,250	90,300	23,253	20,207	24,960	21,500
90,300	90,350	23,269	20,221	24,978	21,516
90,350	90,400	23,284	20,235	24,996	21,531
90,400	90,450	23,300	20,249	25,014	21,547
90,450	90,500	23,315	20,263	25,032	21,562
90,500	90,550	23,331	20,277	25,050	21,578
90,550	90,600	23,346	20,291	25,068	21,593
90,600	90,650	23,362	20,305	25,086	21,609
90,650	90,700	23,377	20,319	25,104	21,624
90,700	90,750	23,393	20,333	25,122	21,640
90,750	90,800	23,408	20,347	25,140	21,655
90,800	90,850	23,424	20,361	25,158	21,671
90,850	90,900	23,439	20,375	25,176	21,686
90,900	90,950	23,455	20,389	25,194	21,702
90,950	91,000	23,470	20,403	25,212	21,717
93,000	93,050	24,106	20,977	25,950	22,353
93,050	93,100	24,121	20,991	25,968	22,368
93,100	93,150	24,137	21,005	25,986	22,384
93,150	93,200	24,152	21,019	26,004	22,399
93,200	93,250	24,168	21,033	26,022	22,415
93,250	93,300	24,183	21,047	26,040	22,430
93,300	93,350	24,199	21,061	26,058	22,446
93,350	93,400	24,214	21,075	26,076	22,461
93,400	93,450	24,230	21,089	26,094	22,477
93,450	93,500	24,245	21,103	26,112	22,492
93,500	93,550	24,261	21,117	26,130	22,508
93,550	93,600	24,276	21,131	26,148	22,523
93,600	93,650	24,292	21,145	26,166	22,539
93,650	93,700	24,307	21,159	26,184	22,554
93,700	93,750	24,323	21,173	26,202	22,570
93,750	93,800	24,338	21,187	26,220	22,585
93,800	93,850	24,354	21,201	26,238	22,601
93,850	93,900	24,369	21,215	26,256	22,616
93,900	93,950	24,385	21,229	26,274	22,632
93,950	94,000	24,400	21,243	26,292	22,647

88,000 / 91,000 / 94,000

At least	But less than	Single	Married filing jointly *	Married filing separately	Head of a household
88,000	88,050	22,556	19,577	24,150	20,803
88,050	88,100	22,571	19,591	24,168	20,818
88,100	88,150	22,587	19,605	24,186	20,834
88,150	88,200	22,602	19,619	24,204	20,849
88,200	88,250	22,618	19,633	24,222	20,865
88,250	88,300	22,633	19,647	24,240	20,880
88,300	88,350	22,649	19,661	24,258	20,896
88,350	88,400	22,664	19,675	24,276	20,911
88,400	88,450	22,680	19,689	24,294	20,927
88,450	88,500	22,695	19,703	24,312	20,942
88,500	88,550	22,711	19,717	24,330	20,958
88,550	88,600	22,726	19,731	24,348	20,973
88,600	88,650	22,742	19,745	24,366	20,989
88,650	88,700	22,757	19,759	24,384	21,004
88,700	88,750	22,773	19,773	24,402	21,020
88,750	88,800	22,788	19,787	24,420	21,035
88,800	88,850	22,804	19,801	24,438	21,051
88,850	88,900	22,819	19,815	24,456	21,066
88,900	88,950	22,835	19,829	24,474	21,082
88,950	89,000	22,850	19,843	24,492	21,097
91,000	91,050	23,486	20,417	25,230	21,733
91,050	91,100	23,501	20,431	25,248	21,748
91,100	91,150	23,517	20,445	25,266	21,764
91,150	91,200	23,532	20,459	25,284	21,779
91,200	91,250	23,548	20,473	25,302	21,795
91,250	91,300	23,563	20,487	25,320	21,810
91,300	91,350	23,579	20,501	25,338	21,826
91,350	91,400	23,594	20,515	25,356	21,841
91,400	91,450	23,610	20,529	25,374	21,857
91,450	91,500	23,625	20,543	25,392	21,872
91,500	91,550	23,641	20,557	25,410	21,888
91,550	91,600	23,656	20,571	25,428	21,903
91,600	91,650	23,672	20,585	25,446	21,919
91,650	91,700	23,687	20,599	25,464	21,934
91,700	91,750	23,703	20,613	25,482	21,950
91,750	91,800	23,718	20,627	25,500	21,965
91,800	91,850	23,734	20,641	25,518	21,981
91,850	91,900	23,749	20,655	25,536	21,996
91,900	91,950	23,765	20,669	25,554	22,012
91,950	92,000	23,780	20,683	25,572	22,027
94,000	94,050	24,416	21,257	26,310	22,663
94,050	94,100	24,431	21,271	26,328	22,678
94,100	94,150	24,447	21,285	26,346	22,694
94,150	94,200	24,462	21,299	26,364	22,709
94,200	94,250	24,478	21,313	26,382	22,725
94,250	94,300	24,493	21,328	26,400	22,740
94,300	94,350	24,509	21,343	26,418	22,756
94,350	94,400	24,524	21,359	26,436	22,771
94,400	94,450	24,540	21,374	26,454	22,787
94,450	94,500	24,555	21,390	26,472	22,802
94,500	94,550	24,571	21,405	26,490	22,818
94,550	94,600	24,586	21,421	26,508	22,833
94,600	94,650	24,602	21,436	26,526	22,849
94,650	94,700	24,617	21,452	26,544	22,864
94,700	94,750	24,633	21,467	26,562	22,880
94,750	94,800	24,648	21,483	26,580	22,895
94,800	94,850	24,664	21,498	26,598	22,911
94,850	94,900	24,679	21,514	26,616	22,926
94,900	94,950	24,695	21,529	26,634	22,942
94,950	95,000	24,710	21,545	26,652	22,957

* This column must also be used by a qualifying widow(er).

Continued on next page

1995 Tax Table—*Continued*

If line 37 (taxable income) is—		And you are—				If line 37 (taxable income) is—		And you are—			
At least	But less than	Single	Married filing jointly *	Married filing separately	Head of a household	At least	But less than	Single	Married filing jointly *	Married filing separately	Head of a household
		Your tax is—						Your tax is—			

95,000

						98,000					
95,000	95,050	24,726	21,560	26,670	22,973	98,000	98,050	25,656	22,490	27,750	23,903
95,050	95,100	24,741	21,576	26,688	22,988	98,050	98,100	25,671	22,506	27,768	23,918
95,100	95,150	24,757	21,591	26,706	23,004	98,100	98,150	25,687	22,521	27,786	23,934
95,150	95,200	24,772	21,607	26,724	23,019	98,150	98,200	25,702	22,537	27,804	23,949
95,200	95,250	24,788	21,622	26,742	23,035	98,200	98,250	25,718	22,552	27,822	23,965
95,250	95,300	24,803	21,638	26,760	23,050	98,250	98,300	25,733	22,568	27,840	23,980
95,300	95,350	24,819	21,653	26,778	23,066	98,300	98,350	25,749	22,583	27,858	23,996
95,350	95,400	24,834	21,669	26,796	23,081	98,350	98,400	25,764	22,599	27,876	24,011
95,400	95,450	24,850	21,684	26,814	23,097	98,400	98,450	25,780	22,614	27,894	24,027
95,450	95,500	24,865	21,700	26,832	23,112	98,450	98,500	25,795	22,630	27,912	24,042
95,500	95,550	24,881	21,715	26,850	23,128	98,500	98,550	25,811	22,645	27,930	24,058
95,550	95,600	24,896	21,731	26,868	23,143	98,550	98,600	25,826	22,661	27,948	24,073
95,600	95,650	24,912	21,746	26,886	23,159	98,600	98,650	25,842	22,676	27,966	24,089
95,650	95,700	24,927	21,762	26,904	23,174	98,650	98,700	25,857	22,692	27,984	24,104
95,700	95,750	24,943	21,777	26,922	23,190	98,700	98,750	25,873	22,707	28,002	24,120
95,750	95,800	24,958	21,793	26,940	23,205	98,750	98,800	25,888	22,723	28,020	24,135
95,800	95,850	24,974	21,808	26,958	23,221	98,800	98,850	25,904	22,738	28,038	24,151
95,850	95,900	24,989	21,824	26,976	23,236	98,850	98,900	25,919	22,754	28,056	24,166
95,900	95,950	25,005	21,839	26,994	23,252	98,900	98,950	25,935	22,769	28,074	24,182
95,950	96,000	25,020	21,855	27,012	23,267	98,950	99,000	25,950	22,785	28,092	24,197

96,000

						99,000					
96,000	96,050	25,036	21,870	27,030	23,283	99,000	99,050	25,966	22,800	28,110	24,213
96,050	96,100	25,051	21,886	27,048	23,298	99,050	99,100	25,981	22,816	28,128	24,228
96,100	96,150	25,067	21,901	27,066	23,314	99,100	99,150	25,997	22,831	28,146	24,244
96,150	96,200	25,082	21,917	27,084	23,329	99,150	99,200	26,012	22,847	28,164	24,259
96,200	96,250	25,098	21,932	27,102	23,345	99,200	99,250	26,028	22,862	28,182	24,275
96,250	96,300	25,113	21,948	27,120	23,360	99,250	99,300	26,043	22,878	28,200	24,290
96,300	96,350	25,129	21,963	27,138	23,376	99,300	99,350	26,059	22,893	28,218	24,306
96,350	96,400	25,144	21,979	27,156	23,391	99,350	99,400	26,074	22,909	28,236	24,321
96,400	96,450	25,160	21,994	27,174	23,407	99,400	99,450	26,090	22,924	28,254	24,337
96,450	96,500	25,175	22,010	27,192	23,422	99,450	99,500	26,105	22,940	28,272	24,352
96,500	96,550	25,191	22,025	27,210	23,438	99,500	99,550	26,121	22,955	28,290	24,368
96,550	96,600	25,206	22,041	27,228	23,453	99,550	99,600	26,136	22,971	28,308	24,383
96,600	96,650	25,222	22,056	27,246	23,469	99,600	99,650	26,152	22,986	28,326	24,399
96,650	96,700	25,237	22,072	27,264	23,484	99,650	99,700	26,167	23,002	28,344	24,414
96,700	96,750	25,253	22,087	27,282	23,500	99,700	99,750	26,183	23,017	28,362	24,430
96,750	96,800	25,268	22,103	27,300	23,515	99,750	99,800	26,198	23,033	28,380	24,445
96,800	96,850	25,284	22,118	27,318	23,531	99,800	99,850	26,214	23,048	28,398	24,461
96,850	96,900	25,299	22,134	27,336	23,546	99,850	99,900	26,229	23,064	28,416	24,476
96,900	96,950	25,315	22,149	27,354	23,562	99,900	99,950	26,245	23,079	28,434	24,492
96,950	97,000	25,330	22,165	27,372	23,577	99,950	100,000	26,260	23,095	28,452	24,507

97,000

97,000	97,050	25,346	22,180	27,390	23,593
97,050	97,100	25,361	22,196	27,408	23,608
97,100	97,150	25,377	22,211	27,426	23,624
97,150	97,200	25,392	22,227	27,444	23,639
97,200	97,250	25,408	22,242	27,462	23,655
97,250	97,300	25,423	22,258	27,480	23,670
97,300	97,350	25,439	22,273	27,498	23,686
97,350	97,400	25,454	22,289	27,516	23,701
97,400	97,450	25,470	22,304	27,534	23,717
97,450	97,500	25,485	22,320	27,552	23,732
97,500	97,550	25,501	22,335	27,570	23,748
97,550	97,600	25,516	22,351	27,588	23,763
97,600	97,650	25,532	22,366	27,606	23,779
97,650	97,700	25,547	22,382	27,624	23,794
97,700	97,750	25,563	22,397	27,642	23,810
97,750	97,800	25,578	22,413	27,660	23,825
97,800	97,850	25,594	22,428	27,678	23,841
97,850	97,900	25,609	22,444	27,696	23,856
97,900	97,950	25,625	22,459	27,714	23,872
97,950	98,000	25,640	22,475	27,732	23,887

$100,000 or over — use the Tax Rate Schedules on page 53

* This column must also be used by a qualifying widow(er).

TAX RETURN PROBLEM

INTRODUCTION

This tax return problem represents an accumulation of material for preparing the tax return of the Schmidt family. The information is presented in three phases, which correspond to the three major components of computing tax—gross income, deductions and losses, and property transactions. If your instructor assigns these problems at the end of each major segment (i.e., Chapter 4, Chapter 8, and Chapter 13), you should complete the appropriate portions of the forms using the instructions at the end of each part of the problem. The instructions vary according to whether you are preparing the tax return manually or with a tax software package.

Completing the tax return problem will help you understand the reporting procedures for the information in each major segment of the text. In addition, the tax return project will aid you in reviewing the major topics discussed in the book and serve as an overview for the course.

THE SCHMIDT FAMILY

Karl and Jan Schmidt are married and live in Avondale, Kentucky. Karl is 38 and Jan is 36. The Schmidts have two children, Elise, 6, and Jon, 4. Jan also has a daughter, Samantha, 12, from a previous marriage. Jan has custody of Samantha and is entitled to the dependency exemption in even-numbered tax years (e.g., 1992, 1994). Karl owns an automobile repair shop that specializes in fixing imported cars. During 1995, Karl decided to expand his operations by increasing the repair area of his garage by 2,000 square feet. However, because of a quirk in the zoning regulations, Karl had to build a separate structure next to his original facility. Jan is an associate professor of marketing at Cardinal University and a partner in a consulting business with two other professors from the university. In February 1996, the Schmidts provided you with the following basic information for preparing their 1995 federal income tax return:

1. The Schmidts use the cash method of accounting and file their return on a calendar-year basis.

2. Unless otherwise stated, assume that the Schmidts want to minimize the current year's tax liability. That is, they would like to defer income when possible and take the largest deductions possible, a practice they have followed in the past.

3. Karl's Social Security number is 407-74-1339.

4. Jan's Social Security number is 401-96-7645.

5. Samantha's Social Security number is 405-74-4998.

6. Elise's Social Security number is 404-72-1824.

7. Jon's Social Security number is 404-73-1919.

8. They have no foreign bank accounts or foreign trusts.

9. The Schmidts live at 456 Castlerock Drive, Avondale, Kentucky 40278.

10. The Schmidts do not wish to contribute to the presidential election campaign.

PHASE I—CHAPTERS 1 to 4

The first phase of the tax return problem is designed to introduce you to some of the tax forms and supporting documentation (Forms W-2, 1099-INT, etc.) needed to complete a basic tax return. The first four chapters focus on the income aspects of individual taxation. Accordingly, this phase of the tax return focuses on the basic concepts of income.

1. Jan's W-2 is provided (Exhibit B–1). The W-2 reflects her salary of $62,000 and a summer research grant of $8,500. Cardinal University requires her to con-

tribute 5% of her salary to a pension plan, and the university contributes an amount equal to 10% of her salary. Jan elected to defer the tax on all contributions to the plan.

2. During the year, the Schmidts received four 1099-INTs for interest income (see exhibits B–2 to B–5) and five 1099-DIVs (see exhibits B–6 to B–10) for dividends.

3. Jan is a one-third partner in The Clayton Group, a management consulting partnership. During the year, Jan received a cash distribution of $5,000 from the partnership. As of February, the partnership had not furnished her with any other information regarding the operations of the partnership.

4. The Schmidts filed their 1994 federal income tax return on April 14, 1995. Because of a computer error at the IRS Service Center in Cincinnati, Ohio, where they filed their return, the Schmidts did not receive their refund of $1,242 until October 16, 1995. Because of the delay in processing their return, the $1,242 refund included $24 in interest.

5. On May 19, 1995, they received their 1994 Kentucky state income tax refund. In January 1996, the state mailed the Schmidts a Form 1099-G (see Exhibit B–11). The Schmidts' total itemized deductions during 1994 were $26,479.

6. During 1995, the Avondale Parents and Teachers Organization (PTO) held a raffle to raise money for the public schools. Karl won the grand prize, a trip for four to Disney World. The trip included airfare, four nights' lodging, and $500 in cash. The airfare and lodging are valued at $2,200. However, Karl has noticed similar packages advertised in the newspaper for $1,499. The PTO failed to issue Karl a Form 1099-MISC.

7. A paper Jan presented at the Midwestern Telemarketing Association meeting was selected as the outstanding paper. In recognition of her achievement, she received a plaque along with a check for $350 (see Exhibit B–12).

8. The Schmidts received a Form W-2G in January 1996 (see Exhibit B–13) relating to their winnings at the Flemington Racetrack in October 1995.

9. On September 10, 1995, Jan received a check for $27,926 from the Essendon Insurance Corporation. Jan was one of four beneficiaries of a life insurance policy on the life of her uncle, Herman Power. Mr. Power died on July 18, 1992. The delay in receiving her share of the insurance proceeds was caused by her cousin David's contesting the will (David is Herman's son). The $27,796 payment included $2,796 in interest (see Exhibit B–14). Her uncle paid $43,546 in premiums on the policy.

10. Jan's divorce agreement requires that her former husband pay her alimony of $3,000 per year until Jan turns 62. The yearly payment is to be reduced to $1,500 when Samantha is no longer a full-time student.

11. To complete phase I, you will need Form 1040, Schedule B, and Schedule D.

INSTRUCTIONS: If you are using tax software to prepare the tax return and/or are not completing phases II and/or III of the problem, ignore the instructions that follow.

If you are preparing the return manually, you cannot complete some of the forms (e.g., Form 1040) used in phase I until you receive additional information, provided in phase II or phase III. Therefore, as a general rule, you should only post the information to the appropriate form and not compute totals for that form. The following specific instructions will assist you in preparing Part I of the return.

a. The only form that can be totaled is Schedule B.

b. Only post the appropriate information to Schedule D. Do not total any column. More information is provided in phases II and III of the tax return problem.

c. Do not calculate total income or adjusted gross income on page 1 of Form 1040.

d. Post the appropriate information on page 2 of Form 1040, but do not total this page, compute the federal tax liability, or determine the refund or balance due.

PHASE II— CHAPTERS 5 to 8

This is the second phase of the tax return problem that you began at the end of Chapter 4. This phase of the tax return incorporates material from chapters 5, 6, 7, and 8 by providing you with information concerning the Schmidts' deductions for 1995. The Schmidts provided you with the following information for preparing their 1995 tax return:

1. Karl operates his imported car repair business as sole proprietorship and keeps his records on the cash basis. He employs four people; three work full time (two mechanics and an administrative assistant) and a college student works part time. Karl provided the following notations from his business records:

Accounts receivable 1/1/95	$ 6,500
Accounts receivable 12/31/95	3,350
1995 Billings	548,000
Cost of new repair shop building	56,000
Parts and supplies	326,800
Purchase of computer equipment	5,910
Gross salaries	105,000
Social Security taxes	8,033
Employee withholding:	
Social Security taxes	8,033
Federal taxes	27,500
State taxes	6,750
Other payroll taxes	650
Workers compensation insurance	4,700
Advertising	7,500
Insurance	8,350
Utilities	3,250
Interest	14,340
Property taxes	6,980
Office supplies	1,425
Postage	220
Accounting fees	840
Legal fees	450
Cost of new tow truck	42,000

Karl made federal estimated tax payments of $4,500 per quarter on April 15, 1995, June 15, 1995, September 15, 1995, and January 15, 1996. Karl also made estimated tax payments of $750 per quarter to the state of Kentucky on April 15, 1995, June 15, 1995, September 15, 1995, and December 31, 1995.

2. On January 3, 1995, Jan purchased a new car for her consulting business. The partnership agreement requires that she pay for the cost of her local trans-

portation. The car, a Toronado, cost $19,000. Jan paid $6,000 in cash and financed the balance through TCE Motor Credit. She used the car 40% of the time in her consulting business and drove the car a total of 14,000 miles during 1995, with 5,600 miles documented as use in her consulting business. The total expenses for the 14,000 miles are as follows: car maintenance expenses, $140; insurance, $650; and gas, $870. The correct depreciation expense for 1995 is $760.

3. In 1989, the Schmidts paid $15,000 for a limited partnership interest in a real estate venture. The limited partnership has never shown a profit, and the Schmidts accumulated $6,250 in suspended losses from the limited partnership before 1995. On March 20, 1996, they received a Schedule K-1 from the limited partnership (see Exhibit B–15).

4. Jan sold an acre of land on November 12, 1995, for $46,000. She bought the land from her brother for $24,000 on February 22, 1989. Her brother purchased the land in 1985 for $30,000.

5. Karl and Jan each contributed $2,000 to their respective individual retirement accounts (IRAs) for 1995. Jan participates in the university's pension plan. Karl's retirement vehicle is his IRA account. Karl has a basis in his IRA of $12,000 and Jan has a basis of $6,500.

6. On August 13, 1995, a tornado went through the Schmidts' neighborhood and tore the roof off their garage. The tornado also damaged a riding lawn mower, a tabletop saw, and an antique car Karl was restoring in the garage. The cost of fixing the roof was $5,250, and they received $4,000 from their insurance company to repair it. The information concerning the property damage is as follows:

Property	Original Cost	FMV Before	FMV After	Insurance Payment
Antique car	$5,000	$20,000	$12,700	$4,000
Tabletop saw	1,250	950	-0-	650
Riding mower	1,480	1,050	450	300

7. In 1995, the Schmidts incurred the following unreimbursed medical expenses:

Medical premiums	$3,000
Doctors	1,200
Dentist	800
Orthodontist	3,000
Chiropractor	400
Optometrist	350
Veterinarian fees (pet cat)	220
Prescription drugs	430
Over-the-counter drugs (aspirin, cough syrup)	240

In January 1995, Jan and Karl joined a health club. They paid a $500 initiation fee and total monthly dues of $50.

8. In 1995, the Schmidts paid $2,340 in property taxes on their Avondale house. In November 1995, the town of Avondale built new sidewalks in the Schmidts' neighborhood. They received a $2,400 assessment (payable over three years) for the new sidewalks. They paid $800 of the assessment in 1995. They also paid licensing fees of $210 on Karl's car and $350 on Jan's car. The licensing

fees are based on the value of the automobile and include a fixed $30 registration fee.

9. During 1996, the Schmidts received two 1098 forms for interest on bank loans; they also have investment interest, interest on Jan's car loan, and interest on their personal credit cards:

Commonwealth Bank, account #675689 (see Exhibit B–16)
Commonwealth Bank, home equity account #675689H (see Exhibit B–17)
TCE Motor Credit, Toronado (see Exhibit B–18)
Pinehurst Investment Group, investment interest (see Exhibit B–19)

Budnick's Department Store	$165
Cenco Oil	30
Rialto Bank & Trust credit card	435

Karl and Jan purchased their house on May 27, 1988, for $90,000. The original mortgage on the house was $80,000. The loan balance at the end of 1995 was $70,000. In 1992, they took out a $35,000 home equity loan. They used the proceeds of the loan to pay off medical expenses and credit card debts and to purchase a new automobile. The house is worth $122,000 today.

10. Karl and Jan made charitable contributions of cash in 1995 to the Louisville United Way ($500), Avondale Methodist Church ($1,300), the American Cancer Society ($250), and Huntingdale College ($400). They also contributed $350 to the Cal Hudson for Governor Committee. On August 31, 1995, they donated the following items to the Salvation Army:

	FMV	Original Cost	Date Acquired
3 sport coats	$175	$650	Various
4 dresses	200	630	Various
2 bicycles	80	220	Various
Kitchen table	$120	450	3/7/86

All the charitable organizations gave Karl and Jan statements acknowledging their contributions.

On December 20, the Schmidts donated 200 shares of Sanco stock to Huntingdale College. The fair market value of the shares on the date of the gift was $10,000. They acquired the shares on April 19, 1987, for $3,550. The basis of the stock includes all brokerage commissions.

11. The Schmidts have the following expenses:

Type	Amount
1994 tax preparation fee (paid in 1995)	$850
Safety deposit box	60
Investment journals	350
Publications (related to Jan's university job)	450

12. Other information:
a. The name of Karl's business is Schmidt's Imported Car Repair and Service and his employer I.D. number is 05–6724958. The address of the business is 750 Ridgewood Drive, Avondale, Kentucky 40222.
b. The Salvation Army's address is 421 Yukon Avenue, Avondale, Kentucky 40222.

c. Huntingdale College's address is 500 Hilltop Boulevard, Martindale, West Virginia 39878.

d. To complete phase II, you will need the following forms: Schedule A, Schedule C (2 copies), and Schedule E, and Forms 4684, 4952, 8283, 8582, and 8606 (2 copies).

e. NOTE: If you are not completing phase III, assume that Karl's depreciation deduction is $22,952 and that Jan's income from The Clayton Group was $16,400. You will also need separate Schedule SE's for Karl and Jan.

INSTRUCTIONS: If you are using tax software to prepare the tax return, and/or are not completing phase III of the problem, ignore the instructions that follow.

As in phase I, some forms in phase II cannot be completed without additional information, provided in phase III. The following instructions will aid you in doing this phase of the return:

a. The only forms that can be completed at the end of phase II are Forms 8283 and 8606.

b. Do not calculate total income or adjusted gross income on page 1 of Form 1040.

c. Post the appropriate information on page 2 of Form 1040, but do not total this page, compute the federal tax liability, or determine the refund or balance due.

d. Do not calculate a total for any of the Schmidts' itemized deductions (e.g., interest, taxes) on Schedule A.

e. Do not total Karl's expenses on Schedule C.

f. Complete Form 4684 only to the point that adjusted gross income is requested.

g. Complete only Part I of Form 4952.

h. Complete only Part 1, lines 2a through 2d, of Form 8582.

This is the third and final phase of the Schmidt tax return. This phase incorporates the material in chapters 9 to 13 and the child-care credit information presented in Chapter 14. This phase requires you to analyze the various types of property transactions discussed in chapters 9 through 13.

PHASE III— CHAPTERS 9 to 13

1. The Schmidts have a summer house on Lake Hamilton. During the year, they used the house for 28 days and rented it for 56 days. They purchased the house on May 16, 1989, for $85,000. The land represents 12% of the purchase price. During 1995, they purchased the following assets for the house: a washing machine ($400) on March 17, 1995, a dryer ($300) on May 16, 1995, and a microwave oven ($240) on July 16, 1995. For the year, the Schmidts provided the following income and expenses for the Lake Hamilton rental property:

Rent	$4,200
Interest	(see Exhibit B–20)
Repairs	450
Management fee	480
Property taxes	1,100
Insurance	300
Utilities	700

2. On April 5, 1987, Karl and Jan acquired a rental property for $80,000. They paid $10,000 down and financed the balance with Lonsdale Savings & Loan. The land represents 10% of the purchase price. The property is in a neighboring town, and Karl actively participates in managing the property. The

property has been rented continuously since May 1987, and—with the exception of the first year—has never shown a loss. Over the last few years they purchased the following assets for the house: a refrigerator ($800) on June 12, 1992, an oven ($740) on June 20, 1994, and a kitchen sink ($580) on June 5, 1995.

Income	$7,200
Repairs	520
Property tax	950
Interest	(see Exhibit B–21)
Insurance	480

3. On March 25, 1996, Jan received a Schedule K-1 from her consulting partnership (see Exhibit B–22).

4. During 1995, the Schmidts sold marketable securities. Jan's brother-in-law is a broker with Pinehurst Investment Group and manages their portfolio. The selling price is net of broker commissions (see Exhibit B–23).

Asset	Date Acquired	Date Sold	Selling Price	Basis
200 shares Faxon Industries	10/23/92	8/18/95	$ 7,700	$ *
50 shares Vaughn, Inc.	3/17/91	10/27/95	1,000	**
120 shares Armadale, Inc.	4/30/90	12/20/95	4,840	3,340
80 shares Vas Corp.	1/7/95	10/27/95	4,960	5,600
240 shares Brighton Bros., Inc.	1/8/91	5/31/95	6,240	14,380

*Jan inherited 200 shares of Faxon Industries from her grandmother. The fair market value at the date of death was $2,200. Her grandmother's basis in the stock was $3,500.
**Karl's uncle gave him 50 shares of Vaughn, Inc. At the date of the gift, the fair market value of the stock was $600. His uncle's basis in the stock was $1,200.

5. Karl provided you with the following schedule of business assets that have a remaining depreciable basis:

Asset	Placed in Service	Cost
Original building	6/17/87	$120,000
1995 addition	4/17/95	56,000
Tow truck	6/23/95	42,000
Alignment equipment	8/15/94	12,000
Hydraulic lift	6/20/93	3,000
Computer system	4/14/95	5,910

During the year Karl placed in service $1,800-worth of small tools. The land value for the original building is worth 10% of the total cost.

6. On September 12, 1995, Karl donated his old computer system with an adjusted basis of $-0- to the Avondale Elementary School. The fair market value of the computer system was $700.

7. On May 19, 1995, Karl sold a tow truck not listed in his schedule of business assets for $13,000. He purchased the truck for $35,000 on February 23, 1991. Karl did not elect to expense any of the cost of the truck in 1991.

8. The Schmidts paid $4,300 in qualified child-care expenses for their two children.

9. Other information:
   a. The address of their summer home on Lake Hamilton is 167 Walter Road, Murray, Kentucky 41597.
   b. The duplex is located at 400 Richard Street, Avondale, Kentucky 40223.
   c. The child care is provided by the Growing Family Center, located at 456 Harbor Avenue, Avondale, Kentucky 40224. The center's employer I.D. number is 05–6998991.

INSTRUCTIONS: To complete phase III, you need the following additional forms: Schedule SE (2 copies), Form 2441, Form 4562 (3 copies), and Form 4797. You now have all the information necessary to complete the forms and schedules that you did not finish in phases I and II.

▲ **Exhibit B–1**

a Control number 31968		OMB No. 1545-0008	This information is being furnished to the Internal Revenue Service. If you are required to file a tax return, a negligence penalty or other sanction may be imposed on you if this income is taxable and you fail to report it.	

b Employer's identification number 05-9472281	1 Wages, tips, other compensation *$67,497.68*	2 Federal income tax withheld *$14,174*
c Employer's name, address, and ZIP code *Cardinal University* *44 Crum Lane* *Louisville, KY 40292*	3 Social security wages *$61,200*	4 Social security tax withheld *$3,794.40*
	5 Medicare wages and tips *$67,497.68*	6 Medicare tax withheld *$978.72*
	7 Social security tips	8 Allocated tips
d Employee's social security number 401-96-7645	9 Advance EIC payment	10 Dependent care benefits
e Employee's name, address, and ZIP code *Jan Schmidt* *456 Castlerock Drive* *Avondale, Kentucky 40278*	11 Nonqualified plans	12 Benefits included in box 1
	13 See Instrs. for box 13 *C – $97.68* *E – $3,100*	14 Other

15 Statutory employee ☐	Deceased ☐	Pension plan ☐	Legal rep. ☐	Hshld. emp. ☐	Subtotal ☐	Deferred compensation ☐

16 State *KY*	Employer's state I.D. No. *KY-9472281*	17 State wages, tips, etc. *$67,497.68*	18 State income tax *$3,038*	19 Locality name *Louisville*	20 Local wages, tips, etc. *$67,497*	21 Local income tax *$1,484*

Department of the Treasury—Internal Revenue Service

Form **W-2** Wage and Tax Statement **1995**

Copy C For EMPLOYEE'S RECORDS (See Notice on back.)

Notice to Employee

Refund.—Even if you do not have to file a tax return, you should file to get a refund if box 2 shows Federal income tax withheld, or if you can take the earned income credit.

Earned Income Credit (EIC).—You must file a tax return if any amount is shown in box 9.

You may be able to take the EIC for 1995 if **(1)** you do not have a qualifying child and you earned less than $9,230, **(2)** you have one qualifying child and you earned less than $24,396, or **(3)** you have more than one qualifying child and you earned less than $26,673. **Any EIC that is more than your tax liability is refunded to you, but only if you file a tax return.** If you have at least one qualifying child, you may get as much as $1,257 of the EIC in advance by completing Form W-5. Your 1995 income tax return instructions and Pub. 596 explain the EIC in detail. You can get these items by calling 1-800-TAX-FORM (829-3676).

Corrections.—If your name, social security number (SSN), or address is incorrect, correct Copies B, C, and 2 and ask your employer to correct your employment record. Be sure to ask the employer to file **Form W-2c,** Statement of Corrected Income and Tax Amounts, with the Social Security Administration (SSA) to correct any name, address, amount, or SSN error reported to the SSA on Copy A of Form W-2. If your name and SSN are correct but are not the same as shown on your social security card, you should ask for a new card at any Social Security office or call 1-800-SSA-1213.

Credit for Excess Taxes.—If more than one employer paid you wages during 1995 and more than the maximum social security employee tax, railroad retirement (RRTA) tax, or combined social security and RRTA tax was withheld, you may claim the excess as a credit against your Federal income tax. See your income tax return instructions.

Box 1.—Enter this amount on the wages line of your tax return.

Box 2.—Enter this amount on the Federal income tax withheld line of your tax return.

Box 8.—This amount is **not** included in boxes 1, 5, or 7. For information on how to report tips on your tax return, see your tax return instructions.

Box 9.—Enter this amount on the advance earned income credit payment line of your tax return.

Box 10.—This amount is the total dependent care benefits your employer paid to you (or incurred on your behalf). Any amount over $5,000 is included in box 1. This amount may be taxable unless you complete Schedule 2 of Form 1040A or Form 2441.

Box 11.—This amount is a distribution made to you from a nonqualified deferred compensation or section 457 plan and is included in box 1. Or, it may be a contribution by your employer to a nonqualified deferred compensation plan that is included in box 3 and/or 5.

Box 12.—You may be able to deduct expenses that are related to fringe benefits; see the instructions for your tax return.

Box 13.—The following list explains the codes shown in box 13. You may need this information to complete your tax return.

A—Uncollected social security tax on tips (see "Total tax" in Form 1040 instructions)

B—Uncollected Medicare tax on tips (see "Total tax" in Form 1040 instructions)

C—Cost of group-term life insurance coverage over $50,000

D—Elective deferrals to a section 401(k) cash or deferred arrangement

E—Elective deferrals to a section 403(b) salary reduction agreement

F—Elective deferrals to a section 408(k)(6) salary reduction SEP

G—Elective and nonelective deferrals to a section 457(b) deferred compensation plan

H—Elective deferrals to a section 501(c)(18)(D) tax-exempt organization plan (see Form 1040 instructions for how to deduct)

J—Sick pay not includible as income

K—Tax on excess golden parachute payments

L—Nontaxable part of employee business expense reimbursements

M—Uncollected social security tax on cost of group-term life insurance coverage over $50,000 (former employees only) (see Form 1040 instructions)

N—Uncollected Medicare tax on cost of group-term life insurance coverage over $50,000 (former employees only) (see Form 1040 instructions)

P—Excludable moving expense reimbursements

Q—Military employee basic quarters and subsistence

Box 15.—If the "Pension plan" box is marked, special limits may apply to the amount of IRA contributions you may deduct. If the "Deferred compensation" box is marked, the elective deferrals in box 13 (for all employers, and for all such plans to which you belong) are generally limited to $9,240. Elective deferrals for section 403(b) contracts are limited to $9,500 ($12,500 in limited circumstances, see Pub. 571). The limit for section 457(b) plans is $7,500. Amounts over that must be included in income. See instructions for Form 1040.

▲ **Exhibit B–2**

Instructions for Recipient

Box 1.—Shows interest paid to you during the calendar year by the payer. This does not include interest shown in box 3.

If you receive a Form 1099-INT for interest paid on a tax-exempt obligation, please see the instructions for your income tax return.

Box 2.—Shows interest or principal forfeited because of early withdrawal of time savings. You may deduct this on your Federal income tax return only on the specific line of Form 1040 under "Adjustments to Income."

Box 3.—Shows interest on U.S. Savings Bonds, Treasury bills, Treasury bonds, and Treasury notes. This may or may not be all taxable. See **Pub. 550,** Investment Income and Expenses. This interest is exempt from state and local income taxes. **This interest is not included in box 1.**

Box 4.—Shows backup withholding. For example, persons not furnishing their taxpayer identification number to the payer become subject to backup withholding at a 31% rate. See **Form W-9,** Request for Taxpayer Identification Number

and Certification, for information on backup withholding. **Include this amount on your income tax return as tax withheld.**

Box 5.—Shows foreign tax paid. You may choose to claim this tax as a deduction or a credit on your Federal income tax return. See **Pub. 514,** Foreign Tax Credit for Individuals.

Nominees.—If your Federal identification number is shown on this form and the form includes amounts belonging to another person, you are considered a nominee recipient. You must file Form 1099-INT for each of the other owners showing the amounts allocable to each. You must also furnish a Form 1099-INT to each of the other owners. File Form(s) 1099-INT with **Form 1096,** Annual Summary and Transmittal of U.S. Information Returns, with the Internal Revenue Service Center for your area. On each Form 1099-INT, list yourself as the "payer" and the other owner as the "recipient." On Form 1096, list yourself as the "filer." A husband or wife is not required to file a nominee return to show amounts owned by the other.

☐ CORRECTED (if checked)

PAYER'S name, street address, city, state, and ZIP code		Payer's RTN (optional)	OMB No. 1545-0112	
Rialto Bank & Trust *751 Beddoe Avenue* *Prospect, KY 40317*			**19**95 Form **1099-INT**	**Interest Income**
PAYER'S Federal identification number *06-7411139*	RECIPIENT'S identification number *401-96-7645*	**1** Interest income not included in box 3 $ *167*		**Copy B** **For Recipient**
RECIPIENT'S name *Jan Schmidt*		**2** Early withdrawal penalty $	**3** Interest on U.S. Savings Bonds and Treas. obligations $	This is important tax information and is being furnished to the Internal Revenue Service. If you are
Street address (including apt. no.) *456 Castlerock Drive* City, state, and ZIP code		**4** Federal income tax withheld $		required to file a return, a negligence penalty or other sanction may be
Avondale, KY 40278 Account number (optional)		**5** Foreign tax paid $	**6** Foreign country or U.S. possession	imposed on you if this income is taxable and the IRS determines that it has not been reported.

Form **1099-INT**   (Keep for your records.)   Department of the Treasury - Internal Revenue Service

▲ Exhibit B–3

	☐ CORRECTED (if checked)	

PAYER'S name, street address, city, state, and ZIP code	Payer's RTN (optional)	OMB No. 1545-0112	
Commonwealth Bank *139 Celia Street* *Burwood, KY 43121*		**19**95 Form **1099-INT**	**Interest Income**

PAYER'S Federal identification number	RECIPIENT'S identification number	**1** Interest income not included in box 3		**Copy B**
06-9881470	*407-74-1339*	$ *341*		**For Recipient**
RECIPIENT'S name *Karl & Jan Schmidt*	**2** Early withdrawal penalty $ *43*	**3** Interest on U.S. Savings Bonds and Treas. obligations $	This is important tax information and is being furnished to the Internal Revenue Service. If you are required to file a return, a negligence penalty or other sanction may be imposed on you if this income is taxable and the IRS determines that it has not been reported.
Street address (including apt. no.) *456 Castlerock Drive*	**4** Federal income tax withheld $		
City, state, and ZIP code *Avondale, KY 40278*	**5** Foreign tax paid	**6** Foreign country or U.S. possession	
Account number (optional)			
	$		

Form **1099-INT**   (Keep for your records.)   Department of the Treasury - Internal Revenue Service

▲ Exhibit B–4

	☐ CORRECTED (if checked)	

PAYER'S name, street address, city, state, and ZIP code	Payer's RTN (optional)	OMB No. 1545-0112	
Lonsdale Savings & Loan *227 Little Collins Street* *Gembrook, KY 40251*		**19**95 Form **1099-INT**	**Interest Income**

PAYER'S Federal identification number	RECIPIENT'S identification number	**1** Interest income not included in box 3		**Copy B**
05-2798133	*407-74-1339*	$ *478*		**For Recipient**
RECIPIENT'S name *Karl Schmidt*	**2** Early withdrawal penalty $	**3** Interest on U.S. Savings Bonds and Treas. obligations $	This is important tax information and is being furnished to the Internal Revenue Service. If you are required to file a return, a negligence penalty or other sanction may be imposed on you if this income is taxable and the IRS determines that it has not been reported.
Street address (including apt. no.) *456 Castlerock Drive*	**4** Federal income tax withheld $ *97*		
City, state, and ZIP code *Avondale, KY 40278*	**5** Foreign tax paid	**6** Foreign country or U.S. possession	
Account number (optional)			
	$		

Form **1099-INT**   (Keep for your records.)   Department of the Treasury - Internal Revenue Service

▲ **Exhibit B–5**

☐ CORRECTED (if checked)

PAYER'S name, street address, city, state, and ZIP code *U.S. Treasury* *202 New Jersey Avenue* *Washington, D.C. 34862*	Payer's RTN (optional)	OMB No. 1545-0112 **19**~~**95**~~ Form **1099-INT**	**Interest Income**

PAYER'S Federal identification number *05-3222471*	RECIPIENT'S identification number *407-74-1339*	**1** Interest income not included in box 3 $		**Copy B** **For Recipient**

| RECIPIENT'S name

Karl & Jan Schmidt | | **2** Early withdrawal penalty

$ | **3** Interest on U.S. Savings Bonds and Treas. obligations

$ *289* | This is important tax information and is being furnished to the Internal Revenue Service. If you are required to file a return, a negligence penalty or other sanction may be imposed on you if this income is taxable and the IRS determines that it has not been reported. |

Street address (including apt. no.)

456 Castlerock Drive

4 Federal income tax withheld

$

City, state, and ZIP code

Avondale, KY 40278

5 Foreign tax paid

6 Foreign country or U.S. possession

Account number (optional)

$

Form **1099-INT**   (Keep for your records.)   Department of the Treasury - Internal Revenue Service

▲ Exhibit B–6

Instructions for Recipient

Box 1a.—Gross dividends include any amounts shown in boxes 1b, 1c, 1d, and 1e. If an amount appears in box 1c or 1d or both, you must file **Form 1040.** If you file **Form 1040A,** report the amount in box 1a. If you file **Schedule 1 (Form 1040A)** or **Schedule B (Form 1040)** to report dividends, report the amount in box 1a. If you file Form 1040 without Schedule B, report the sum of boxes 1b and 1e on the "Dividend income" line and box 1c on **Schedule D (Form 1040)** or the "Capital gain or (loss)" line (write "CGD" on the dotted line).

The amount shown may be a distribution from an employee stock ownership plan (ESOP). Although you should report the ESOP distribution as a dividend on your income tax return, treat it as a plan distribution, not as investment income, for any other purpose.

Box 1b.—Ordinary dividends are fully taxable and are included in box 1a.

Box 1c.—Capital gain distributions are included in box 1a.

Box 1d.—This part of the distribution is nontaxable because it is a return of your cost (or other basis). You must reduce your cost (or other basis) by this amount for figuring gain or loss when you sell your stock. But if you get back all your cost (or other basis), you must report future nontaxable distributions as capital gains, even though this form shows them as nontaxable. This amount is included in box 1a. For more information, see **Pub. 550,** Investment Income and Expenses.

Box 1e.—Any amount shown is your share of the expenses of a nonpublicly offered regulated investment company, generally a nonpublicly offered mutual fund, which is included as a dividend in box 1a. The full amount shown in box 1a must be reported as income on your tax return. You can deduct the expenses shown in box 1e on the "Other expenses" line on **Schedule A (Form 1040)** subject to the 2% limit. Generally, the actual amount you should have received or had credited to you is the amount in box 1a less the amount in box 1e.

Box 2.—Shows backup withholding. For example, persons not furnishing their taxpayer identification number to the payer become subject to backup withholding at a 31% rate on certain payments. See **Form W-9,** Request for Taxpayer Identification Number and Certification, for information on backup withholding. **Include this amount on your income tax return as tax withheld.**

Box 3.—You may elect to claim the amount shown as a deduction or a credit. See **Pub. 514,** Foreign Tax Credit for Individuals.

Nominees.—If your Federal identification number is shown on this form and the form includes amounts belonging to another person, you are considered a nominee recipient. You must file Form 1099-DIV for each of the other owners showing the income allocable to each, and you must furnish a Form 1099-DIV to each. File Form(s) 1099-DIV with **Form 1096,** Annual Summary and Transmittal of U.S. Information Returns, at the Internal Revenue Service Center for your area. On each Form 1099-DIV, list yourself as the "payer" and the other owner as the "recipient." On Form 1096, list yourself as the "filer." A husband or wife is not required to file a nominee return to show amounts owned by the other.

☐ CORRECTED (if checked)

PAYER'S name, street address, city, state, and ZIP code	1a Gross dividends and other distributions on stock (Total of 1b, 1c, 1d, and 1e) $ 684	OMB No. 1545-0110 **1995**	**Dividends and Distributions**
Hawthorn Mutual Fund *44 Jolimont Avenue* *Hawthorn, CT 06497*	1b Ordinary dividends $ 466	Form **1099-DIV**	

PAYER'S Federal identification number *05-1712328*	RECIPIENT'S identification number *407-74-1339*	1c Capital gain distributions $ 218	2 Federal income tax withheld $	**Copy B** **For Recipient**
RECIPIENT'S name *Karl & Jan Schmidt*		1d Nontaxable distributions $	3 Foreign tax paid $	This is important tax information and is being furnished to the Internal Revenue Service. If you are required to file a return, a negligence penalty or other sanction may be imposed on you if this income is taxable and the IRS determines that it has not been reported.
Street address (including apt. no.) *456 Castlerock Drive*		1e Investment expenses $	4 Foreign country or U.S. possession	
City, state, and ZIP code *Avondale, KY 40278*		**Liquidation Distributions**		
Account number (optional)		5 Cash $	6 Noncash (Fair market value) $	

Form **1099-DIV**　　　　　　(Keep for your records.)　　　　Department of the Treasury - Internal Revenue Service

▲ **Exhibit B–7**

☐ CORRECTED (if checked)

PAYER'S name, street address, city, state, and ZIP code		**1a** Gross dividends and other distributions on stock (Total of 1b, 1c, 1d, and 1e) $ 185	OMB No. 1545-0110	
Faxon Industries *432 Spalding Circle* *Boise, Idaho 87641*		**1b** Ordinary dividends $ 185	19**95** Form **1099-DIV**	**Dividends and Distributions**
PAYER'S Federal identification number 05-1624087	RECIPIENT'S identification number 401-96-7645	**1c** Capital gain distributions $	**2** Federal income tax withheld $	**Copy B** **For Recipient**
RECIPIENT'S name *Jan Schmidt*		**1d** Nontaxable distributions $	**3** Foreign tax paid $	This is important tax information and is being furnished to the Internal Revenue Service. If you are required to file a return, a negligence penalty or other sanction may be imposed on you if this income is taxable and the IRS determines that it has not been reported.
Street address (including apt. no.) *456 Castlerock Drive*		**1e** Investment expenses $	**4** Foreign country or U.S. possession	
City, state, and ZIP code *Avondale, KY 40278*		**Liquidation Distributions**		
Account number (optional)		**5** Cash $	**6** Noncash (Fair market value) $	

Form **1099-DIV**   (Keep for your records.)   Department of the Treasury - Internal Revenue Service

▲ **Exhibit B–8**

☐ CORRECTED (if checked)

PAYER'S name, street address, city, state, and ZIP code		**1a** Gross dividends and other distributions on stock (Total of 1b, 1c, 1d, and 1e) $ 322	OMB No. 1545-0110	
Armadale Inc. *1747 Toorak Court* *Madison, Wisconsin 57794*		**1b** Ordinary dividends $ 322	19**95** Form **1099-DIV**	**Dividends and Distributions**
PAYER'S Federal identification number 05-4255871	RECIPIENT'S identification number 407-74-1339	**1c** Capital gain distributions $	**2** Federal income tax withheld $ 64	**Copy B** **For Recipient**
RECIPIENT'S name *Karl & Jan Schmidt*		**1d** Nontaxable distributions $	**3** Foreign tax paid $	This is important tax information and is being furnished to the Internal Revenue Service. If you are required to file a return, a negligence penalty or other sanction may be imposed on you if this income is taxable and the IRS determines that it has not been reported.
Street address (including apt. no.) *456 Castlerock Drive*		**1e** Investment expenses $	**4** Foreign country or U.S. possession	
City, state, and ZIP code *Avondale, KY 40278*		**Liquidation Distributions**		
Account number (optional)		**5** Cash $	**6** Noncash (Fair market value) $	

Form **1099-DIV**   (Keep for your records.)   Department of the Treasury - Internal Revenue Service

▲ **Exhibit B–9**

CORRECTED (if checked)

PAYER'S name, street address, city, state, and ZIP code	1a Gross dividends and other distributions on stock (Total of 1b, 1c, 1d, and 1e) $ 98	OMB No. 1545-0110	**Dividends and Distributions**
Brighton Bros. Inc. 179 Dandenong Road St. Kilda, Kansas 62749	1b Ordinary dividends $ 98	**1995** Form **1099-DIV**	

PAYER'S Federal identification number 05-0041927	RECIPIENT'S identification number 407-74-1339	1c Capital gain distributions $	2 Federal income tax withheld $	**Copy B** For Recipient
RECIPIENT'S name Karl Schmidt		1d Nontaxable distributions $	3 Foreign tax paid $	This is important tax information and is being furnished to the Internal Revenue Service. If you are required to file a return, a negligence penalty or other sanction may be imposed on you if this income is taxable and the IRS determines that it has not been reported.
Street address (including apt. no.) 456 Castlerock Drive		1e Investment expenses $	4 Foreign country or U.S. possession	
City, state, and ZIP code Avondale, KY 40278		**Liquidation Distributions**		
Account number (optional)		5 Cash $	6 Noncash (Fair market value) $	

Form **1099-DIV**   (Keep for your records.)   Department of the Treasury - Internal Revenue Service

▲ **Exhibit B–10**

CORRECTED (if checked)

PAYER'S name, street address, city, state, and ZIP code	1a Gross dividends and other distributions on stock (Total of 1b, 1c, 1d, and 1e) $ 520	OMB No. 1545-0110	**Dividends and Distributions**
The Frankston Corporation 750 Mornington Hwy Louisville, Ky 40311	1b Ordinary dividends $ 520	**1995** Form **1099-DIV**	

PAYER'S Federal identification number 05-0179844	RECIPIENT'S identification number 401-96-7645	1c Capital gain distributions $	2 Federal income tax withheld $	**Copy B** For Recipient
RECIPIENT'S name Jan Schmidt		1d Nontaxable distributions $	3 Foreign tax paid $	This is important tax information and is being furnished to the Internal Revenue Service. If you are required to file a return, a negligence penalty or other sanction may be imposed on you if this income is taxable and the IRS determines that it has not been reported.
Street address (including apt. no.) 456 Castlerock Drive		1e Investment expenses $	4 Foreign country or U.S. possession	
City, state, and ZIP code Avondale, KY 40278		**Liquidation Distributions**		
Account number (optional)		5 Cash $	6 Noncash (Fair market value) $	

Form **1099-DIV**   (Keep for your records.)   Department of the Treasury - Internal Revenue Service

▲ **Exhibit B–11**

Instructions for Recipient

Box 1.—Shows the total unemployment compensation paid to you this year. This amount is taxable income to you. For details, see the instructions for your Federal income tax return. If you expect to receive these benefits next year, see Form 1040-ES for estimated tax payments.

Box 2.—Shows refunds, credits, or offsets of state or local income tax you received. If there is an entry in this box, it may be taxable to you if you deducted the tax paid as an itemized deduction on your Federal income tax return. Even if you did not receive the amount shown, for example, because it was credited to your estimated tax, it is still taxable if it was deducted. Any interest received on this must be included as interest income on your return. See the instructions for Form 1040 or 1040A.

Box 3.—Identifies the tax year for which the refund, credit, or offset shown in box 2 was made. If there is no entry in this box, the refund is for 1994 taxes.

Box 4.—Shows backup withholding. For example, persons not furnishing their taxpayer identification number to the payer become subject to backup withholding at a 31% rate on certain payments. See **Form W-9,** Request for Taxpayer Identification Number and Certification, for information on backup withholding. **Include this on your income tax return as tax withheld.**

Box 6.—Shows the amount of taxable grants you received from the Federal, state, or local government.

Box 7.—Shows the amount of Department of Agriculture payments that are taxable to you. If the payer shown is anyone other than the Department of Agriculture, it means the payer has received a payment, as a nominee, that is taxable to you. This may represent the entire agricultural subsidy payment received on your behalf by the nominee, or it may be your pro rata share of the original payment. See **Pub. 225,** Farmer's Tax Guide, and the instructions for **Schedule F (Form 1040),** Profit or Loss From Farming, for information about where to report this income.

Box 8.—If this box is checked, the refund, credit, or offset in box 2 is attributable to an income tax that applies exclusively to income from a trade or business and is not a tax of general application. The amount, if taxable, should not be reported on page 1 of Form 1040, but should be reported on Schedule C, C-EZ, or F (Form 1040), as appropriate.

☐ CORRECTED (if checked)

PAYER'S name, street address, city, state, and ZIP code		**1** Unemployment compensation $	OMB No. 1545-0120	**Certain Government Payments**
State of Kentucky *Boone Highway* *Frankfort, KY 41744*		**2** State or local income tax refunds, credits, or offsets $ *734*	**19****95** Form **1099-G**	
PAYER'S Federal identification number *05-0000042*	RECIPIENT'S identification number *407-74-1339*	**3** Box 2 amount is for tax year *1994*	**4** Federal income tax withheld $	**Copy B**
RECIPIENT'S name *Karl & Jan Schmidt*		**5**	**6** Taxable grants $	**For Recipient** This is important tax information and is being furnished to the Internal Revenue Service. If you are required to file a return, a negligence penalty or other sanction may be imposed on you if this income is taxable and the IRS determines that it has not been reported.
Street address (including apt. no.) *456 Castlerock Drive*		**7** Agriculture payments $	**8** The amount in box 2 applies to income from a trade or business ▶ ☐	
City, state, and ZIP code *Avondale, KY 40278*				
Account number (optional)				

Form **1099-G**   (Keep for your records.)   Department of the Treasury - Internal Revenue Service

▲ **Exhibit B–12**

☐ CORRECTED (if checked)

PAYER'S name, street address, city, state, and ZIP code	**1** Rents $	OMB No. 1545-0115	**Miscellaneous Income**
Midwestern Telemarketing Association *1457 Nell Street* *Grand Rapids, Iowa 74599*	**2** Royalties $	19**95**	
	3 Other income $ *350*	Form **1099-MISC**	

PAYER'S Federal identification number *05-9473215*	RECIPIENT'S identification number *401-96-7645*	**4** Federal income tax withheld $	**5** Fishing boat proceeds $	**Copy B**
RECIPIENT'S name *Jan Schmidt*		**6** Medical and health care payments $	**7** Nonemployee compensation $	**For Recipient**
Street address (including apt. no.) *456 Castlerock Drive*		**8** Substitute payments in lieu of dividends or interest $	**9** Payer made direct sales of $5,000 or more of consumer products to a buyer (recipient) for resale ▶ ☐	This is important tax information and is being furnished to the Internal Revenue Service. If you are required to file a return, a negligence penalty or other sanction may be imposed on you if this income is taxable and the IRS determines that it has not been reported.
City, state, and ZIP code *Avondale, KY 40278*		**10** Crop insurance proceeds $	**11** State income tax withheld $	
Account number (optional)		**12** State/Payer's state number		

Form **1099-MISC**   (Keep for your records.)   Department of the Treasury - Internal Revenue Service

Instructions for Recipient

Amounts shown on this form may be subject to self-employment tax computed on **Schedule SE (Form 1040)**. See **Pub. 533**, Self-Employment Tax, for information on self-employment income. If no income or social security and Medicare taxes were withheld by the payer, you may have to make estimated tax payments if you are still receiving these payments. See **Form 1040-ES**, Estimated Tax for Individuals.

If you are an individual, report the taxable amounts shown on this form on your tax return, as explained below. (Others, such as fiduciaries or partnerships, report the amounts on the corresponding lines of your tax return.)

Boxes 1 and 2.—Report rents from real estate on Schedule E (Form 1040). If you provided significant services to the tenant, sold real estate as a business, or rented personal property as a business, report on Schedule C or C-EZ (Form 1040). For royalties on timber, coal, and iron ore, see **Pub. 544**, Sales and Other Dispositions of Assets.

Box 3.—Report on the "Other income" line on Form 1040 and identify the payment. If it is trade or business income, report this amount on Schedule C, C-EZ, or F (Form 1040). The amount shown may be payments you received as the beneficiary of a deceased employee, prizes, awards, taxable damages, or other taxable income.

Box 4.—Shows backup withholding. For example, persons not furnishing their taxpayer identification number to the payer become subject to backup withholding at a 31% rate on certain payments. See **Form W-9**, Request for Taxpayer Identification Number and Certification, for information on backup withholding. **Include this on your income tax return as tax withheld.**

Box 5.—An amount in this box means the fishing boat operator considers you self-employed. Report this amount on Schedule C or C-EZ (Form 1040). See **Pub. 595**, Tax Guide for Commercial Fishermen.

Box 6.—Report on Schedule C or C-EZ (Form 1040).

Box 7.—Generally, payments for services reported in this box are income from self-employment. Since you received this form, rather than Form W-2, the payer may have considered you self-employed and did not withhold social security or Medicare taxes. Report self-employment income on Schedule C, C-EZ, or F (Form 1040), and **compute the self-employment tax on Schedule SE (Form 1040)**. However, if you are not self-employed, report this amount on Form 1040 on the "Wages, salaries, tips, etc." line. Call the IRS for information about how to report any social security and Medicare taxes.

If "EPP" is shown, this is excess golden parachute payments subject to a 20% excise tax. See your Form 1040 instructions for the "Total Tax" line. The unlabeled amount is your total compensation.

Box 8.—Report as "Other income" on your tax return. This amount is substitute payments in lieu of dividends or tax-exempt interest received by your broker on your behalf after transfer of your securities for use in a short sale.

Box 9.—An entry in the checkbox means sales to you of consumer products on a buy-sell, deposit-commission, or any other basis for resale have amounted to $5,000 or more. The person filing this return does not have to show a dollar amount in this box. Any income from your sale of these products should generally be reported on Schedule C or C-EZ (Form 1040).

Box 10.—Report on the "Crop insurance proceeds. . ." line on Schedule F (Form 1040).

▲ Exhibit B–13

Instructions to Winner

Box 1.—The payer must furnish a Form W-2G to you if you receive:

1. $600 or more in gambling winnings and the payout is at least 300 times the amount of the wager (except winnings from bingo, slot machines, and keno);

2. $1,200 or more in gambling winnings from bingo or slot machines;

3. $1,500 or more in proceeds (the amount of winnings less the amount of the wager) from keno; or

4. Any gambling winnings subject to Federal income tax withholding.

Generally, report all gambling winnings on the "Other income" line of Form 1040. You can deduct gambling losses as an itemized deduction, but you cannot deduct more than your winnings. Keep an accurate diary or similar record of your winnings and losses, and be able to prove those amounts by receipts, tickets, statements, or similar items.

Box 2.—Any Federal income tax withheld on these winnings is shown in this box. Federal income tax must be withheld at the rate of 28% on certain winnings less the wager. Whether Federal income tax must be withheld depends on the type and amount of the winnings, including winnings from identical wagers, and the odds.

If you did not provide your social security number to the payer, the amount in this box may be backup withholding at a 31% rate.

Include the amount shown in box 2 on your tax return as Federal income tax withheld.

Signature.—You must sign Form W-2G if you are the only person entitled to the winnings and the winnings are subject to regular gambling withholding.

Other Winners.—Prepare **Form 5754,** Statement by Person(s) Receiving Gambling Winnings, if another person is entitled to any part of these winnings.

☐ CORRECTED

PAYER'S name, address, ZIP code, and Federal identification number *Flemington Racetrack* *Secretariat Drive* *Lexington, KY 42771*	**1** Gross winnings *$1,369*	**2** Federal income tax withheld *$ 383*	OMB No. 1545-0238
	3 Type of wager *Trifecta*	**4** Date won *10 : 23 : 95*	**Form W-2G**
	5 Transaction	**6** Race	**Certain Gambling Winnings**
	7 Winnings from identical wagers	**8** Cashier	
WINNER'S name, address (including apt. no.), and ZIP code *Jan Schmidt* *456 Castlerock Drive* *Avondale, KY 40278*	**9** Winner's taxpayer identification no. *401-96-7645*	**10** Window	For Paperwork Reduction Act Notice and instructions for completing this form, see **Instructions for Forms 1099, 1098, 5498, and W-2G.**
	11 First I.D.	**12** Second I.D.	
	13 State/Payer's state identification no.	**14** State income tax withheld .	

Under penalties of perjury, I declare that, to the best of my knowledge and belief, the name, address, and taxpayer identification number that I have furnished correctly identify me as the recipient of this payment and any payments from identical wagers, and that no other person is entitled to any part of these payments. **Signature ▶** **Date ▶**	**Copy D** **For Payer**

Form **W-2G**   Department of the Treasury - Internal Revenue Service

▲ Exhibit B–14

Essendon Insurance Corporation
150 Monkhurst Highway
Hazleton, Connecticut 06457

Re: Policy # HB3456992

September 5, 1995

Dear Ms. Schmidt:

Enclosed please find a check for $27,796. As you are aware, an injunction issued by the probate court prevented the distribution of the assets of Mr. Herman Powers's estate until the matter could be resolved by the court. As a result, we were unable to distribute your share of the life insurance proceeds until the dispute was settled.

Effective August 24, 1995, we received permission from the probate court to distribute your share of the proceeds from Mr. Powers's life insurance policy. The enclosed check consists of your one-fourth share of the $100,000 life insurance policy ($25,000) along with your pro rata share of the accrued interest. The interest income of $2,796 is calculated beginning 30 days after the death of Mr. Powers (August 17, 1993) through September 4, 1995. A portion of the payment you receive may be taxable, so we suggest you contact your tax adviser to determine the taxable portion, if any, of the payment.

If you have any questions concerning the payment, please feel free to contact me at (203) 591-4359.

Sincerely,

Fred Hashway
Senior Claims Manager

▲ **Exhibit B–15**

SCHEDULE K-1 (Form 1065)	**Partner's Share of Income, Credits, Deductions, etc.**	OMB No. 1545-0099

Department of the Treasury
Internal Revenue Service

► See separate instructions.

19 95

For calendar year 1995 or tax year beginning _____ , 1995, and ending _____ , 19 ____

Partner's identifying number ► *407-74-1339*	**Partnership's identifying number** ► *05 1478956*

Partner's name, address, and ZIP code	Partnership's name, address, and ZIP code
Karl & Jan Schmidt	*Wyatt Properties*
456 Castlerock Drive	*1150 Southern Highway*
Avondale, KY 40278	*Dallas, Texas 76198*

A This partner is a ☐ general partner ☒ limited partner
☐ limited liability company member

B What type of entity is this partner? ► *Individual*

C Is this partner a ☒ domestic or a ☐ foreign partner?

D Enter partner's percentage of:

	(i) Before change or termination	(ii) End of year
Profit sharing	_____ %	_____ %
Loss sharing	_____ %	*1* %
Ownership of capital	_____ %	*1* %

E IRS Center where partnership filed return: *Austin, TX*

F Partner's share of liabilities (see instructions):

Nonrecourse . . . . $ _____

Qualified nonrecourse financing . $ *3,000*

Other . . . . $ _____

G Tax shelter registration number . ► _____

H Check here if this partnership is a publicly traded partnership as defined in section 469(k)(2) . . . . ☐

I Check applicable boxes: **(1)** ☒ Final K-1 **(2)** ☐ Amended K-1

J Analysis of partner's capital account:

(a) Capital account at beginning of year	(b) Capital contributed during year	(c) Partner's share of lines 3, 4, and 7, Form 1065, Schedule M-2	(d) Withdrawals and distributions	(e) Capital account at end of year (combine columns (a) through (d))
8,750	*0*	*624*	(*150*)	*9,097*

	(a) Distributive share item		(b) Amount	(c) 1040 filers enter the amount in column (b) on:
Income (Loss)	**1** Ordinary income (loss) from trade or business activities . . .	1		See pages 5 and 6 of Partner's Instructions for Schedule K-1 (Form 1065).
	2 Net income (loss) from rental real estate activities	2	*624*	
	3 Net income (loss) from other rental activities	3		
	4 Portfolio income (loss):			
	a Interest	4a		Sch. B, Part I, line 1
	b Dividends	4b		Sch. B, Part II, line 5
	c Royalties	4c		Sch. E, Part I, line 4
	d Net short-term capital gain (loss)	4d		Sch. D, line 5, col. (f) or (g)
	e Net long-term capital gain (loss).	4e		Sch. D, line 13, col. (f) or (g)
	f Other portfolio income (loss) *(attach schedule)*	4f		Enter on applicable line of your return.
	5 Guaranteed payments to partner	5		See page 6 of Partner's Instructions for Schedule K-1 (Form 1065).
	6 Net gain (loss) under section 1231 (other than due to casualty or theft)	6		
	7 Other income (loss) *(attach schedule)*	7		Enter on applicable line of your return.
Deductions	**8** Charitable contributions (see instructions) *(attach schedule)* . .	8	*127*	Sch. A, line 15 or 16
	9 Section 179 expense deduction	9		See page 7 of Partner's Instructions for Schedule K-1 (Form 1065).
	10 Deductions related to portfolio income *(attach schedule)* . . .	10		
	11 Other deductions *(attach schedule)*	11		
Investment Interest	**12a** Interest expense on investment debts	12a		Form 4952, line 1
	b (1) Investment income included on lines 4a, 4b, 4c, and 4f above	b(1)		See page 7 of Partner's Instructions for Schedule K-1 (Form 1065).
	(2) Investment expenses included on line 10 above	b(2)		
Credits	**13a** Low-income housing credit:			
	(1) From section 42(j)(5) partnerships for property placed in service before 1990	a(1)		Form 8586, line 5
	(2) Other than on line 13a(1) for property placed in service before 1990	a(2)		
	(3) From section 42(j)(5) partnerships for property placed in service after 1989	a(3)		
	(4) Other than on line 13a(3) for property placed in service after 1989	a(4)		
	b Qualified rehabilitation expenditures related to rental real estate activities	13b		See page 8 of Partner's Instructions for Schedule K-1 (Form 1065).
	c Credits (other than credits shown on lines 13a and 13b) related to rental real estate activities.	13c		
	d Credits related to other rental activities	13d		
	14 Other credits	14		

For Paperwork Reduction Act Notice, see Instructions for Form 1065.   Cat. No. 11394R   **Schedule K-1 (Form 1065) 1995**

▲ Exhibit B–15
(continued)

Schedule K-1 (Form 1065) 1995 Page **2**

(a) Distributive share item	(b) Amount	(c) 1040 filers enter the amount in column (b) on:
Self-employment		
15a Net earnings (loss) from self-employment	15a	Sch. SE, Section A or B
b Gross farming or fishing income	15b	See page 8 of Partner's Instructions for Schedule K-1 (Form 1065).
c Gross nonfarm income	15c	
Adjustments and Tax Preference Items		
16a Depreciation adjustment on property placed in service after 1986	16a	
b Adjusted gain or loss	16b	See pages 8 and 9 of Partner's Instructions for Schedule K-1 (Form 1065) and Instructions for Form 6251.
c Depletion (other than oil and gas)	16c	
d (1) Gross income from oil, gas, and geothermal properties	d(1)	
(2) Deductions allocable to oil, gas, and geothermal properties	d(2)	
e Other adjustments and tax preference items *(attach schedule)*	16e	
Foreign Taxes		
17a Type of income ▶		Form 1116, check boxes
b Name of foreign country or U.S. possession ▶		
c Total gross income from sources outside the United States *(attach schedule)*	17c	Form 1116, Part I
d Total applicable deductions and losses *(attach schedule)*	17d	
e Total foreign taxes (check one): ▶ ☐ Paid ☐ Accrued	17e	Form 1116, Part II
f Reduction in taxes available for credit *(attach schedule)*	17f	Form 1116, Part III
g Other foreign tax information *(attach schedule)*	17g	See Instructions for Form 1116.
Other		
18 Section 59(e)(2) expenditures: **a** Type ▶		See page 9 of Partner's Instructions for Schedule K-1 (Form 1065).
b Amount	18b	
19 Tax-exempt interest income	19	Form 1040, line 8b
20 Other tax-exempt income	20	
21 Nondeductible expenses	21	See page 9 of Partner's Instructions for Schedule K-1 (Form 1065).
22 Distributions of money (cash and marketable securities)	22	
23 Distributions of property other than money	23	
24 Recapture of low-income housing credit:		
a From section 42(j)(5) partnerships	24a	Form 8611, line 8
b Other than on line 24a	24b	

Supplemental Information

25 Supplemental information required to be reported separately to each partner *(attach additional schedules if more space is needed)*:

▲ **Exhibit B–16**

Instructions for Payer/Borrower

A person (including a financial institution, a governmental unit, and a cooperative housing corporation) who is engaged in a trade or business and, in the course of such trade or business, received from you at least $600 of mortgage interest (including certain points) on any one mortgage in the calendar year must furnish this statement to you.

If you received this statement as the payer of record on a mortgage on which there are other borrowers entitled to a deduction for the interest and points shown on this form, please furnish each of the other borrowers with information about the proper distribution of these amounts. Each borrower is entitled to deduct only the amount he or she paid and points paid by the seller that represent his or her share of the amount allowable as a deduction for mortgage interest and points.

If your mortgage payments were subsidized by a government agency, you may not be able to deduct the amount of the subsidy.

Box 1.—Shows the mortgage interest received by the interest recipient during the year. This amount includes interest on any obligation secured by real property, including a home equity, line of credit, or credit card loan. This amount does not include points, government subsidy payments, or seller payments on a "buy-down" mortgage. Such amounts are deductible by you only in certain circumstances. **Caution:** *If you prepaid interest in 1995 that accrued in full by January 15, 1996, this prepaid interest may be included in box 1. However, even though the prepaid amount may* be included in box 1, you cannot deduct the prepaid amount in 1995. For more information, see **Pub. 936,** Home Mortgage Interest Deduction. If you are a mortgage credit certificate holder who can claim the mortgage interest credit, see **Form 8396,** Mortgage Interest Credit. If the interest was paid on a mortgage, home equity, line of credit, or credit card loan secured by your personal residence, you may be subject to a deduction limitation as explained in the instructions for **Schedule A (Form 1040).**

Box 2.—Not all points are reportable to you. This form shows points you or the seller paid this year for the purchase of your principal residence that are required to be reported to you. Generally, these points are fully deductible in the year paid, but you must subtract seller-paid points from the basis of your residence. Other points not reported in this box may be deductible. See Pub. 936. Also see your Form 1040 instructions.

Box 3.—**Do not deduct this amount.** It is a refund (or credit) from the interest recipient/lender for overpayment(s) of interest you made in a prior year or years. Generally, list the total amount shown in box 3 on the "Other income" line on your 1995 Form 1040. However, do not report the refund as income if you did not itemize deductions in the year(s) you paid the interest. No adjustment to your prior year(s) tax return(s) is necessary. For more information, see Pub. 936 and **Pub. 525,** Taxable and Nontaxable Income.

Box 4.—This box is for use by the interest recipient to furnish other information to you, such as real estate taxes or insurance paid from escrow.

☐ VOID ☐ CORRECTED		
RECIPIENT'S/LENDER'S name, street address, city, state, and ZIP code *Commonwealth Bank* *139 Celia Street* *Burwood, KY 43121*	OMB No. 1545-0901 **1995** Form **1098**	**Mortgage Interest Statement**

RECIPIENT'S Federal identification no. 06-9881470	PAYER'S social security number *407-74-1339*	1 Mortgage interest received from payer(s)/borrower(s) $ *7,360*	**Copy C For Recipient**
PAYER'S/BORROWER'S name *Karl & Jan Schmidt*		2 Points paid on purchase of principal residence $	For Paperwork Reduction Act Notice and instructions for completing this form, see **Instructions for Forms 1099, 1098, 5498, and W-2G.**
Street address (including apt. no.) *456 Castlerock Drive*		3 Refund of overpaid interest $	
City, state, and ZIP code *Avondale, KY 40278*		4	
Account number (optional) *#675689*			

Form **1098**   Department of the Treasury - Internal Revenue Service

Recipients/Lenders, Please Note—

Specific information needed to complete this form and forms in the 1099 series is given in the **1995 Instructions for Forms 1099, 1098, 5498, and W-2G.** A chart in those instructions gives a quick guide to which form must be filed to report a particular payment. You can order those instructions and additional forms by calling 1-800-TAX-FORM (1-800-829-3676).

Furnish Copy B of this form to the recipient by January 31, 1996.

File Copy A of this form with the IRS by February 28, 1996.

▲ Exhibit B–17

Instructions for Payer/Borrower

A person (including a financial institution, a governmental unit, and a cooperative housing corporation) who is engaged in a trade or business and, in the course of such trade or business, received from you at least $600 of mortgage interest (including certain points) on any one mortgage in the calendar year must furnish this statement to you.

If you received this statement as the payer of record on a mortgage on which there are other borrowers entitled to a deduction for the interest and points shown on this form, please furnish each of the other borrowers with information about the proper distribution of these amounts. Each borrower is entitled to deduct only the amount he or she paid and points paid by the seller that represent his or her share of the amount allowable as a deduction for mortgage interest and points.

If your mortgage payments were subsidized by a government agency, you may not be able to deduct the amount of the subsidy.

Box 1.—Shows the mortgage interest received by the interest recipient during the year. This amount includes interest on any obligation secured by real property, including a home equity, line of credit, or credit card loan. This amount does not include points, government subsidy payments, or seller payments on a "buy-down" mortgage. Such amounts are deductible by you only in certain circumstances. **Caution:** *If you prepaid interest in 1995 that accrued in full by January 15, 1996, this prepaid interest may be included in box 1. However, even though the prepaid amount may* be included in box 1, you cannot deduct the prepaid amount in 1995. For more information, see **Pub. 936,** Home Mortgage Interest Deduction. If you are a mortgage credit certificate holder who can claim the mortgage interest credit, see **Form 8396,** Mortgage Interest Credit. If the interest was paid on a mortgage, home equity, line of credit, or credit card loan secured by your personal residence, you may be subject to a deduction limitation as explained in the instructions for **Schedule A (Form 1040).**

Box 2.—Not all points are reportable to you. This form shows points you or the seller paid this year for the purchase of your principal residence that are required to be reported to you. Generally, these points are fully deductible in the year paid, but you must subtract seller-paid points from the basis of your residence. Other points not reported in this box may be deductible. See Pub. 936. Also see your Form 1040 instructions.

Box 3.—Do not deduct this amount. It is a refund (or credit) from the interest recipient/lender for overpayment(s) of interest you made in a prior year or years. Generally, list the total amount shown in box 3 on the "Other income" line on your 1995 Form 1040. However, do not report the refund as income if you did not itemize deductions in the year(s) you paid the interest. No adjustment to your prior year(s) tax return(s) is necessary. For more information, see Pub. 936 and **Pub. 525,** Taxable and Nontaxable Income.

Box 4.—This box is for use by the interest recipient to furnish other information to you, such as real estate taxes or insurance paid from escrow.

☐ VOID ☐ CORRECTED

RECIPIENT'S/LENDER'S name, street address, city, state, and ZIP code			
Commonwealth Bank *139 Celia Street* *Burwood, KY 43121*		OMB No. 1545-0901 **19**95 Form **1098**	**Mortgage Interest Statement**
RECIPIENT'S Federal identification no. 06-9881470	PAYER'S social security number *407-74-1339*	1 Mortgage interest received from payer(s)/borrower(s) $ *2,690*	**Copy C For Recipient**
PAYER'S/BORROWER'S name *Karl & Jan Schmidt*		2 Points paid on purchase of principal residence $	For Paperwork Reduction Act Notice and instructions for completing this form, see **Instructions for Forms 1099, 1098, 5498, and W-2G.**
Street address (including apt. no.) *456 Castlerock Drive*		3 Refund of overpaid interest $	
City, state, and ZIP code *Avondale, KY 40278*		4	
Account number (optional) *#675689 H*			

Form **1098**

Department of the Treasury - Internal Revenue Service

Recipients/Lenders, Please Note—

Specific information needed to complete this form and forms in the 1099 series is given in the **1995 Instructions for Forms 1099, 1098, 5498, and W-2G.** A chart in those instructions gives a quick guide to which form must be filed to report a particular payment. You can order those instructions and additional forms by calling 1-800-TAX-FORM (1-800-829-3676).

Furnish Copy B of this form to the recipient by January 31, 1996.

File Copy A of this form with the IRS by February 28, 1996.

▲ Exhibit B–18

TCE Motor Credit
1432 Motown Credit
Flint, MI 48502

January 30, 1996

Dear Ms. Schmidt:

Per your request, a summary of transactions for account #345-1289 is provided below:

Principle balance as of January 3, 1995	$13,000
1995 Payments	$ 2,990
Payments applied to principal balance	$ 1,540
1995 interest paid	$ 1,450
Principal balance as of December 31, 1995	$11,460

If you have any questions concerning your account, please feel free to contact me at (313) 276-4550.

Sincerely,

Agnes Hightower
Account Representative

▲ Exhibit B–19

Pinehurst Investment Group
275 Norman Way
Pinehurst, NC 22798

January 25, 1996

Dear Ms. Schmidt:

The following is important tax information and is provided to you so that you can prepare your 1995 tax return. None of this information has been provided to the IRS.

1995 investment interest	$1,450
Management expenses	$ 740

If you have any questions concerning this information, please feel free to contact me at (919) 691-8867.

Sincerely,

Roberta Edwards
Senior Investment Adviser

▲ Exhibit B–20

Instructions for Payer/Borrower

A person (including a financial institution, a governmental unit, and a cooperative housing corporation) who is engaged in a trade or business and, in the course of such trade or business, received from you at least $600 of mortgage interest (including certain points) on any one mortgage in the calendar year must furnish this statement to you.

If you received this statement as the payer of record on a mortgage on which there are other borrowers entitled to a deduction for the interest and points shown on this form, please furnish each of the other borrowers with information about the proper distribution of these amounts. Each borrower is entitled to deduct only the amount he or she paid and points paid by the seller that represent his or her share of the amount allowable as a deduction for mortgage interest and points.

If your mortgage payments were subsidized by a government agency, you may not be able to deduct the amount of the subsidy.

Box 1.—Shows the mortgage interest received by the interest recipient during the year. This amount includes interest on any obligation secured by real property, including a home equity, line of credit, or credit card loan. This amount does not include points, government subsidy payments, or seller payments on a "buy-down" mortgage. Such amounts are deductible by you only in certain circumstances. **Caution:** *If you prepaid interest in 1995 that accrued in full by January 15, 1996, this prepaid interest may be included in box 1. However, even though the prepaid amount may*

be included in box 1, you cannot deduct the prepaid amount in 1995. For more information, see **Pub. 936,** Home Mortgage Interest Deduction. If you are a mortgage credit certificate holder who can claim the mortgage interest credit, see **Form 8396,** Mortgage Interest Credit. If the interest was paid on a mortgage, home equity, line of credit, or credit card loan secured by your personal residence, you may be subject to a deduction limitation as explained in the instructions for **Schedule A (Form 1040).**

Box 2.—Not all points are reportable to you. This form shows points you or the seller paid this year for the purchase of your principal residence that are required to be reported to you. Generally, these points are fully deductible in the year paid, but you must subtract seller-paid points from the basis of your residence. Other points not reported in this box may be deductible. See Pub. 936. Also see your Form 1040 instructions.

Box 3.—Do not deduct this amount. It is a refund (or credit) from the interest recipient/lender for overpayment(s) of interest you made in a prior year or years. Generally, list the total amount shown in box 3 on the "Other income" line on your 1995 Form 1040. However, do not report the refund as income if you did not itemize deductions in the year(s) you paid the interest. No adjustment to your prior year(s) tax return(s) is necessary. For more information, see Pub. 936 and **Pub. 525,** Taxable and Nontaxable Income.

Box 4.—This box is for use by the interest recipient to furnish other information to you, such as real estate taxes or insurance paid from escrow.

☐ VOID ☐ CORRECTED		

RECIPIENT'S/LENDER'S name, street address, city, state, and ZIP code		OMB No. 1545-0901	**Mortgage Interest Statement**
Murray Savings Bank *325 Main Street* *Murray, KY 41597*		**19 95** Form **1098**	

RECIPIENT'S Federal identification no. 06-4752681	PAYER'S social security number *407-74-1339*	1 Mortgage interest received from payer(s)/borrower(s) $ *6,400*	**Copy C** **For Recipient**
PAYER'S/BORROWER'S name *Karl & Jan Schmidt*		2 Points paid on purchase of principal residence $	For Paperwork Reduction Act Notice and instructions for completing this form, see
Street address (including apt. no.) *456 Castlerock Drive*		3 Refund of overpaid interest $	**Instructions for Forms 1099,**
City, state, and ZIP code *Avondale, KY 40278*		4	**1098, 5498,**
Account number (optional)			**and W-2G.**

Form **1098**   Department of the Treasury - Internal Revenue Service

Recipients/Lenders, Please Note—

Specific information needed to complete this form and forms in the 1099 series is given in the **1995 Instructions for Forms 1099, 1098, 5498, and W-2G.** A chart in those instructions gives a quick guide to which form must be filed to report a particular payment. You can order those instructions and additional forms by calling 1-800-TAX-FORM (1-800-829-3676).

Furnish Copy B of this form to the recipient by January 31, 1996.

File Copy A of this form with the IRS by February 28, 1996.

▲ **Exhibit B–21**

Instructions for Payer/Borrower

A person (including a financial institution, a governmental unit, and a cooperative housing corporation) who is engaged in a trade or business and, in the course of such trade or business, received from you at least $600 of mortgage interest (including certain points) on any one mortgage in the calendar year must furnish this statement to you.

If you received this statement as the payer of record on a mortgage on which there are other borrowers entitled to a deduction for the interest and points shown on this form, please furnish each of the other borrowers with information about the proper distribution of these amounts. Each borrower is entitled to deduct only the amount he or she paid and points paid by the seller that represent his or her share of the amount allowable as a deduction for mortgage interest and points.

If your mortgage payments were subsidized by a government agency, you may not be able to deduct the amount of the subsidy.

Box 1.—Shows the mortgage interest received by the interest recipient during the year. This amount includes interest on any obligation secured by real property, including a home equity, line of credit, or credit card loan. This amount does not include points, government subsidy payments, or seller payments on a "buy-down" mortgage. Such amounts are deductible by you only in certain circumstances. **Caution:** *If you prepaid interest in 1995 that accrued in full by January 15, 1996, this prepaid interest may be included in box 1. However, even though the prepaid amount may*

be included in box 1, you cannot deduct the prepaid amount in 1995. For more information, see **Pub. 936,** Home Mortgage Interest Deduction. If you are a mortgage credit certificate holder who can claim the mortgage interest credit, see **Form 8396,** Mortgage Interest Credit. If the interest was paid on a mortgage, home equity, line of credit, or credit card loan secured by your personal residence, you may be subject to a deduction limitation as explained in the instructions for **Schedule A (Form 1040).**

Box 2.—Not all points are reportable to you. This form shows points you or the seller paid this year for the purchase of your principal residence that are required to be reported to you. Generally, these points are fully deductible in the year paid, but you must subtract seller-paid points from the basis of your residence. Other points not reported in this box may be deductible. See Pub. 936. Also see your Form 1040 instructions.

Box 3.—Do not deduct this amount. It is a refund (or credit) from the interest recipient/lender for overpayment(s) of interest you made in a prior year or years. Generally, list the total amount shown in box 3 on the "Other income" line on your 1995 Form 1040. However, do not report the refund as income if you did not itemize deductions in the year(s) you paid the interest. No adjustment to your prior year(s) tax return(s) is necessary. For more information, see Pub. 936 and **Pub. 525,** Taxable and Nontaxable Income.

Box 4.—This box is for use by the interest recipient to furnish other information to you, such as real estate taxes or insurance paid from escrow.

☐ VOID ☐ CORRECTED

RECIPIENT'S/LENDER'S name, street address, city, state, and ZIP code		OMB No. 1545-0901	**Mortgage Interest Statement**
Lonsdale Savings & Loan *227 Little Collins Street* *Gembrook, KY 40251*		19**95** Form **1098**	
RECIPIENT'S Federal identification no. 05-2798133	PAYER'S social security number 407-74-1339	1 Mortgage interest received from payer(s)/borrower(s) $ *5,740*	**Copy C** **For Recipient**
PAYER'S/BORROWER'S name *Karl & Jan Schmidt*		2 Points paid on purchase of principal residence $	For Paperwork Reduction Act Notice and instructions for completing this form, see **Instructions for Forms 1099, 1098, 5498, and W-2G.**
Street address (including apt. no.) *456 Castlerock Drive*		3 Refund of overpaid interest $	
City, state, and ZIP code *Avondale, KY 40278*		4	
Account number (optional)			

Form **1098**

Department of the Treasury - Internal Revenue Service

Recipients/Lenders, Please Note—

Specific information needed to complete this form and forms in the 1099 series is given in the **1995 Instructions for Forms 1099, 1098, 5498, and W-2G.** A chart in those instructions gives a quick guide to which form must be filed to report a particular payment. You can order those instructions and additional forms by calling 1-800-TAX-FORM (1-800-829-3676).

Furnish Copy B of this form to the recipient by January 31, 1996.

File Copy A of this form with the IRS by February 28, 1996.

▲ Exhibit B–22

SCHEDULE K-1 (Form 1065)	Partner's Share of Income, Credits, Deductions, etc.	OMB No. 1545-0099

Department of the Treasury
Internal Revenue Service

► See separate instructions.

1995

For calendar year 1995 or tax year beginning   , 1995, and ending   , 19

Partner's identifying number ► *401-96-7645*   Partnership's identifying number ► *05 : 9724684*

Partner's name, address, and ZIP code	Partnership's name, address, and ZIP code
Jan Schmidt	*The Clayton Group*
456 Castlerock Drive	*415 Princes Highway*
Avondale, KY 40278	*Louisville, KY 40016*

A This partner is a ☒ general partner ☐ limited partner
☐ limited liability company member

B What type of entity is this partner? ► *Individual*

C Is this partner a ☐ domestic or a ☐ foreign partner?

D Enter partner's percentage of:
    (i) Before change or termination   (ii) End of year
Profit sharing . . . . % *33* %
Loss sharing . . . . % *33* %
Ownership of capital . . . . . % *33* %

E IRS Center where partnership filed return:

F Partner's share of liabilities (see instructions):
Nonrecourse . . . . $ _____
Qualified nonrecourse financing . $ *20,000*
Other . . . . $

G Tax shelter registration number . ► _____

H Check here if this partnership is a publicly traded partnership as defined in section 469(k)(2) . . . . ☐

I Check applicable boxes: **(1)** ☒ Final K-1 **(2)** ☐ Amended K-1

J Analysis of partner's capital account:

(a) Capital account at beginning of year	(b) Capital contributed during year	(c) Partner's share of lines 3, 4, and 7, Form 1065; Schedule M-2	(d) Withdrawals and distributions	(e) Capital account at end of year (combine columns (a) through (d))
27,500	*0*	*16,400*	(*5,000*)	*38,550*

	(a) Distributive share item		(b) Amount	(c) 1040 filers enter the amount in column (b) on:
Income (Loss)	**1** Ordinary income (loss) from trade or business activities . . .	**1**	*16,400*	See pages 5 and 6 of Partner's Instructions for Schedule K-1 (Form 1065).
	2 Net income (loss) from rental real estate activities	**2**		
	3 Net income (loss) from other rental activities	**3**		
	4 Portfolio income (loss):			
	a Interest	**4a**		Sch. B, Part I, line 1
	b Dividends	**4b**		Sch. B, Part II, line 5
	c Royalties	**4c**		Sch. E, Part I, line 4
	d Net short-term capital gain (loss)	**4d**		Sch. D, line 5, col. (f) or (g)
	e Net long-term capital gain (loss).	**4e**		Sch. D, line 13, col. (f) or (g)
	f Other portfolio income (loss) *(attach schedule)*	**4f**		Enter on applicable line of your return.
	5 Guaranteed payments to partner	**5**		See page 6 of Partner's Instructions for Schedule K-1 (Form 1065).
	6 Net gain (loss) under section 1231 (other than due to casualty or theft)	**6**		
	7 Other income (loss) *(attach schedule)*	**7**		Enter on applicable line of your return.
Deductions	**8** Charitable contributions (see instructions) *(attach schedule)* . .	**8**		Sch. A, line 15 or 16
	9 Section 179 expense deduction	**9**	*350*	See page 7 of Partner's Instructions for Schedule K-1 (Form 1065).
	10 Deductions related to portfolio income *(attach schedule)* . . .	**10**		
	11 Other deductions *(attach schedule)*	**11**		
Investment Interest	**12a** Interest expense on investment debts	**12a**		Form 4952, line 1
	b (1) Investment income included on lines 4a, 4b, 4c, and 4f above	**b(1)**		See page 7 of Partner's Instructions for Schedule K-1 (Form 1065).
	(2) Investment expenses included on line 10 above	**b(2)**		
Credits	**13a** Low-income housing credit:			
	(1) From section 42(j)(5) partnerships for property placed in service before 1990	**a(1)**		
	(2) Other than on line 13a(1) for property placed in service before 1990	**a(2)**		
	(3) From section 42(j)(5) partnerships for property placed in service after 1989	**a(3)**		Form 8586, line 5
	(4) Other than on line 13a(3) for property placed in service after 1989	**a(4)**		
	b Qualified rehabilitation expenditures related to rental real estate activities	**13b**		
	c Credits (other than credits shown on lines 13a and 13b) related to rental real estate activities.	**13c**		See page 8 of Partner's Instructions for Schedule K-1 (Form 1065).
	d Credits related to other rental activities	**13d**		
	14 Other credits	**14**		

For Paperwork Reduction Act Notice, see Instructions for Form 1065.   Cat. No. 11394R   Schedule K-1 (Form 1065) 1995

▲ Exhibit B–22

(continued)

	(a) Distributive share item		(b) Amount	(c) 1040 filers enter the amount in column (b) on:
Self-employment	**15a** Net earnings (loss) from self-employment	**15a**	*16,400*	Sch. SE, Section A or B
	b Gross farming or fishing income.	**15b**		} See page 8 of Partner's Instructions for Schedule K-1 (Form 1065).
	c Gross nonfarm income.	**15c**		
Adjustments and Tax Preference Items	**16a** Depreciation adjustment on property placed in service after 1986	**16a**		} See pages 8 and 9 of Partner's Instructions for Schedule K-1 (Form 1065) and Instructions for Form 6251.
	b Adjusted gain or loss	**16b**		
	c Depletion (other than oil and gas)	**16c**		
	d (1) Gross income from oil, gas, and geothermal properties . .	**d(1)**		
	(2) Deductions allocable to oil, gas, and geothermal properties	**d(2)**		
	e Other adjustments and tax preference items *(attach schedule)*	**16e**		
Foreign Taxes	**17a** Type of income ▶			Form 1116, check boxes
	b Name of foreign country or U.S. possession ▶			}
	c Total gross income from sources outside the United States *(attach schedule)*	**17c**		} Form 1116, Part I
	d Total applicable deductions and losses *(attach schedule)* . . .	**17d**		
	e Total foreign taxes (check one): ▶ ☐ Paid ☐ Accrued . . .	**17e**		Form 1116, Part II
	f Reduction in taxes available for credit *(attach schedule)* . . .	**17f**		Form 1116, Part III
	g Other foreign tax information *(attach schedule)*	**17g**		See Instructions for Form 1116.
Other	**18** Section 59(e)(2) expenditures: **a** Type ▶			} See page 9 of Partner's Instructions for Schedule K-1 (Form 1065).
	b Amount	**18b**		
	19 Tax-exempt interest income	**19**		Form 1040, line 8b
	20 Other tax-exempt income.	**20**		} See page 9 of Partner's Instructions for Schedule K-1 (Form 1065).
	21 Nondeductible expenses	**21**		
	22 Distributions of money (cash and marketable securities) . . .	**22**		
	23 Distributions of property other than money	**23**		
	24 Recapture of low-income housing credit:			
	a From section 42(j)(5) partnerships	**24a**		} Form 8611, line 8
	b Other than on line 24a.	**24b**		

25 Supplemental information required to be reported separately to each partner *(attach additional schedules if more space is needed):*

Supplemental Information

....

....

....

....

....

....

....

....

....

....

....

....

....

....

....

....

....

....

....

....

▲ **Exhibit B–23**

Instructions for Recipient

Brokers and barter exchanges must report proceeds from transactions to the Internal Revenue Service. This form is used to report these proceeds.

Box 1a.—Shows the trade date of the transaction. For aggregate reporting, no entry will be present.

Box 1b.—For broker transactions, may show the CUSIP (Committee on Uniform Security Identification Procedures) number of the item reported.

Box 2.—Shows the proceeds from transactions involving stocks, bonds, other debt obligations, commodities, or forward contracts. Losses on forward contracts are shown in parentheses. This box does not include proceeds from regulated futures contracts. The broker must indicate whether gross proceeds or gross proceeds less commissions and option premiums were reported to the IRS. Report this amount on **Schedule D (Form 1040),** Capital Gains and Losses.

Box 3.—Shows the fair market value of any trade credits or scrip credited to your account for exchanges of property or services as well as cash received through a barter exchange. Report bartering income in the proper part of Form 1040. See **Pub. 525,** Taxable and Nontaxable Income, for information on how to report this income.

Box 4.—Shows backup withholding. For example, persons not furnishing their taxpayer identification number to the payer become subject to backup withholding at a 31% rate on certain payments. See **Form W-9,** Request for Taxpayer Identification Number and Certification, for information on backup withholding. **Include this amount on your income tax return as tax withheld.**

Box 5.—Shows a brief description of the item or service for which the proceeds or bartering income is being reported. For regulated futures contracts and forward contracts, "RFC" or other appropriate description, and any amount subject to backup withholding, may be shown.

Box 6.—Shows the profit or (loss) realized on regulated futures or foreign currency contracts closed during 1995.

Box 7.—Shows any year-end adjustment to the profit or (loss) shown in box 6 due to open contracts on December 31, 1994.

Box 8.—Shows the unrealized profit or (loss) on open contracts held in your account on December 31, 1995. These are considered sold as of that date. This will become an adjustment reported in box 7 in 1996.

Box 9.—Boxes 6, 7, and 8 are used to figure the aggregate profit or (loss) on regulated futures or foreign currency contracts for the year. Include this figure on your 1995 **Form 6781,** Gains and Losses From Section 1256 Contracts and Straddles.

☐ CORRECTED (if checked)

PAYER'S name, street address, city, state, and ZIP code		**1a** Date of sale	OMB No. 1545-0715	**Proceeds From Broker and Barter Exchange Transactions**
Pinehurst Investment Group *275 Norman Way* *Pinehurst, NC 22798*		**1b** CUSIP No.	**1995** Form **1099-B**	
		2 Stocks, bonds, etc. $ *24,740*	Reported to IRS ⎰ ☐ Gross proceeds ⎱ ☒ Gross proceeds less commissions and option premiums	
PAYER'S Federal identification number *06-7975218*	RECIPIENT'S identification number *407-74-1339*	**3** Bartering $	**4 Federal income tax withheld** $	**Copy B** **For Recipient**
RECIPIENT'S name *Karl & Jan Schmidt*		**5** Description		This is important tax information and is being furnished to the Internal Revenue Service. If you are required to file a return, a negligence penalty or other sanction may be imposed on you if this income is taxable and the IRS determines that it has not been reported.
Street address (including apt. no.) *456 Castlerock Drive* City, state, and ZIP code *Avondale, KY 40278*		**Regulated Futures Contracts**		
		6 Profit or (loss) realized in 1995 $	**7** Unrealized profit or (loss) on open contracts–12/31/94 $	
Account number (optional)		**8** Unrealized profit or (loss) on open contracts–12/31/95 $	**9** Aggregate profit or (loss) $	

Form **1099-B**   (Keep for your records.)   Department of the Treasury - Internal Revenue Service

TAX FORMS

Form 1040EZ	Income Tax Return for Single and Joint Filers With No Dependents	C–3
Form 1040A	U.S. Individual Income Tax Return (Short Form)	C–4
Schedule 1	Interest and Dividend Income	C–6
Schedule 2	Child and Dependent Care Expenses	C–7
Schedule 3	Credit for the Elderly or the Disabled	C–9
Form 1040	U.S. Individual Income Tax Return	C–11
Schedule A	Itemized Deductions	C–13
Schedule B	Interest and Dividend Income	C–14
Schedule C	Profit or Loss From Business	C–15
Schedule C-EZ	Net Profit From Business	C–17
Schedule D	Capital Gains and Losses	C–18
Schedule E	Supplemental Income and Loss	C–20
Schedule EIC	Earned Income Credit	C–22
Table EIC	Earned Income Credit (EIC) Table	C–23
Schedule F	Profit or Loss From Farming	C–25
Schedule H	Household Employment Taxes	C–27
Schedule R	Credit for the Elderly or the Disabled	C–29
Schedule SE	Self-Employment Tax	C–31
Form 1040X	Amended U.S. Individual Income Tax Return	C–33
Form 1065	U.S. Partnership Return of Income	C–35
Schedule K–1	Partner's Share of Income, Credits, Deductions, etc.	C–39

Form 1116	Foreign Tax Credit	C–41
Form 1120	U.S. Corporation Income Tax Return	C–43
Form 1120S	U.S. Income Tax Return for an S Corporation	C–47
Schedule K–1	Shareholder's Share of Income, Credits, Deductions, etc.	C–51
Form 2106	Employee Business Expenses	C–53
Form 2106-EZ	Unreimbursed Employee Business Expenses	C–55
Form 2119	Sale of Your Home	C–56
Form 2120	Multiple Support Declaration	C–57
Form 2210	Underpayment of Estimated Tax by Individuals, Estates, and Trusts	C–58
Form 2441	Child and Dependent Care Expenses	C–61
Form 2555	Foreign Earned Income	C–63
Form 2848	Power of Attorney and Declaration of Representative	C–66
Form 3800	General Business Credit	C–68
Form 3903	Moving Expenses	C–70
Form 4562	Depreciation and Amortization	C–71
Form 4684	Casualties and Thefts	C–73
Form 4797	Sales of Business Property	C–75
Form 4868	Application for Automatic Extension of Time To File U.S. Individual Income Tax Return	C–77
Form 4952	Investment Interest Expense Deduction	C–78
Form 5329	Additional Taxes Attributable to Qualified Retirement Plans (Including IRAs), Annuities, and Modified Endowment Contracts	C–79
Form 6251	Alternative Minimum Tax—Individuals	C–81
Form 6252	Installment Sale Income	C–82
Form 7004	Application for Automatic Extension of Time To File Corporation Income Tax Return	C–83
Form 8283	Noncash Charitable Contributions	C–84
Form 8332	Release of Claim to Exemption for Child of Divorced or Separated Parents	C–86
Form 8453	U.S. Individual Income Tax Declaration for Electronic Filing	C–87
Form 8582	Passive Activity Loss Limitations	C–88
Form 8606	Nondeductible IRAs	C–89
Form 8615	Tax for Children Under Age 14 Who Have Investment Income of More Than $1,300	C–90
Form 8814	Parents' Election To Report Child's Interest and Dividends	C–91
Form 8829	Expenses for Business Use of Your Home	C–92

Department of the Treasury—Internal Revenue Service

Form 1040EZ

Income Tax Return for Single and Joint Filers With No Dependents **1995**

OMB No. 1545-0675

Use the IRS label here

Your first name and initial   Last name

If a joint return, spouse's first name and initial   Last name

Home address (number and street). If you have a P.O. box, see page 11.   Apt. no.

City, town or post office, state, and ZIP code. If you have a foreign address, see page 11.

Your social security number

Spouse's social security number

See instructions on back and in Form 1040EZ booklet.

Presidential Election Campaign (See page 11.)

Note: *Checking "Yes" will not change your tax or reduce your refund.*

Do you want $3 to go to this fund?   ▶

If a joint return, does your spouse want $3 to go to this fund?   ▶

Yes   No

Dollars   Cents

Income

Attach Copy B of Form(s) W-2 here. Enclose, but do not attach, any payment with your return.

1 Total wages, salaries, and tips. This should be shown in box 1 of your W-2 form(s). Attach your W-2 form(s).   1

2 Taxable interest income of $400 or less. If the total is over $400, you cannot use Form 1040EZ.   2

3 Unemployment compensation (see page 14).   3

4 Add lines 1, 2, and 3. This is your **adjusted gross income.** If less than $9,230, see page 15 to find out if you can claim the earned income credit on line 8.   4

Note: *You* **must** *check Yes or No.*

5 Can your parents (or someone else) claim you on their return?

☐ **Yes.** Do worksheet on back; enter amount from line G here.

☐ **No.** If **single,** enter 6,400.00. If **married,** enter 11,550.00. For an explanation of these amounts, see back of form.   5

6 Subtract line 5 from line 4. If line 5 is larger than line 4, enter 0. This is your **taxable income.**   ▶ 6

Payments and tax

7 Enter your Federal income tax withheld from box 2 of your W-2 form(s).   7

8 **Earned income credit** (see page 15). Enter type and amount of nontaxable earned income below.

Type _____ $ _____   8

9 Add lines 7 and 8 (don't include nontaxable earned income). These are your **total payments.**   9

10 **Tax.** Use the amount on **line 6** to find your tax in the tax table on pages 29–33 of the booklet. Then, enter the tax from the table on this line.   10

Refund or amount you owe

11 If line 9 is larger than line 10, subtract line 10 from line 9. This is your **refund.**   11

12 If line 10 is larger than line 9, subtract line 9 from line 10. This is the **amount you owe.** See page 22 for details on how to pay and what to write on your payment.   12

I have read this return. Under penalties of perjury, I declare that to the best of my knowledge and belief, the return is true, correct, and accurately lists all amounts and sources of income I received during the tax year.

Sign your return

Keep a copy of this form for your records.

Your signature

Spouse's signature if joint return

Date   Your occupation

Date   Spouse's occupation

For IRS Use Only — Please do not write in boxes below.

1   2   3   4   5

6   7   8   9   10

Form

1040A (99)

Department of the Treasury—Internal Revenue Service

U.S. Individual Income Tax Return   **1995**   IRS Use Only—Do not write or staple in this space.

OMB No. 1545-0085

Label

(See page 19.)

Use the IRS label. Otherwise, please print or type.

L A B E L   H E R E

Your first name and initial | Last name

If a joint return, spouse's first name and initial | Last name

Home address (number and street). If you have a P.O. box, see page 19. | Apt. no.

City, town or post office, state, and ZIP code. If you have a foreign address, see page 19.

Your social security number

Spouse's social security number

For Privacy Act and Paperwork Reduction Act Notice, see page 11.

Presidential Election Campaign Fund (See page 19.)

Do you want $3 to go to this fund? . . . .

If a joint return, does your spouse want $3 to go to this fund?

Yes | No

Note: Checking "Yes" will not change your tax or reduce your refund.

Check the box for your filing status

(See page 20.)

Check only one box.

1 ☐ Single

2 ☐ Married filing joint return (even if only one had income)

3 ☐ Married filing separate return. Enter spouse's social security number above and full name here. ▶ _____

4 ☐ Head of household (with qualifying person). (See page 21.) If the qualifying person is a child but not your dependent, enter this child's name here. ▶ _____

5 ☐ Qualifying widow(er) with dependent child (year spouse died ▶ 19____). (See page 22.)

Figure your exemptions

(See page 22.)

If more than seven dependents, see page 25.

6a ☐ **Yourself.** If your parent (or someone else) can claim you as a dependent on his or her tax return, **do not** check box 6a. But be sure to check the box on line 18b on page 2.

b ☐ **Spouse**

c **Dependents:**

(1) First name Last name	(2) Dependent's social security number. If born in 1995, see page 25.	(3) Dependent's relationship to you	(4) No. of months lived in your home in 1995

No. of boxes checked on 6a and 6b ____

No. of your children on 6c who:

• lived with you ____

• didn't live with you due to divorce or separation (see page 26)

Dependents on 6c not entered above

d If your child didn't live with you but is claimed as your dependent under a pre-1985 agreement, check here . . . . ▶ ☐

e Total number of exemptions claimed.

Add numbers entered on lines above ☐

Figure your adjusted gross income

Attach Copy B of your Forms W-2 and 1099-R here.

If you didn't get a W-2, see page 27.

Enclose, but do not attach, any payment.

7 Wages, salaries, tips, etc. This should be shown in box 1 of your W-2 form(s). Attach Form(s) W-2.   **7**

8a **Taxable** interest income (see page 28). If over $400, attach Schedule 1.   **8a**

b **Tax-exempt** interest. DO NOT include on line 8a.   **8b**

9 Dividends. If over $400, attach Schedule 1.   **9**

10a Total IRA distributions.   **10a** | 10b Taxable amount (see page 29).   **10b**

11a Total pensions and annuities.   **11a** | 11b Taxable amount (see page 29).   **11b**

12 Unemployment compensation (see page 32).   **12**

13a Social security benefits.   **13a** | 13b Taxable amount (see page 33).   **13b**

14 Add lines 7 through 13b (far right column). This is your **total income.** ▶   **14**

15a Your IRA deduction (see page 35).   **15a**

b Spouse's IRA deduction (see page 35).   **15b**

c Add lines 15a and 15b. These are your **total adjustments.**   **15c**

16 Subtract line 15c from line 14. This is your **adjusted gross income.** If less than $26,673 and a child lived with you (less than $9,230 if a child didn't live with you), see "Earned income credit" on page 47. ▶   **16**

51A5AAA

Cat. No. 11327A

1995 Form 1040A page 1

1995 Form 1040A page 2

Figure your standard deduction, exemption amount, and taxable income	**17**	Enter the amount from line 16.	17	

18a Check if: ☐ **You** were 65 or older   ☐ Blind   ☐ **Spouse** was 65 or older   ☐ Blind } **Enter number of boxes checked ▶** 18a

b If your parent (or someone else) can claim you as a dependent, check here. .   .   .   . ▶ 18b ☐

c If you are married filing separately and your spouse itemizes deductions, see page 40 and check here. .   .   .   .   .   . ▶ 18c ☐

19 Enter the **standard deduction** shown below for your filing status. **But if you checked any box on line 18a or b,** go to page 40 to find your standard deduction. **If you checked box 18c,** enter -0-.

• Single—$3,900   • Married filing jointly or Qualifying widow(er)—$6,550

• Head of household—$5,750   • Married filing separately—$3,275   19

20 Subtract line 19 from line 17. If line 19 is more than line 17, enter -0-.   20

21 Multiply $2,500 by the total number of exemptions claimed on line 6e.   21

22 Subtract line 21 from line 20. If line 21 is more than line 20, enter -0-. This is your **taxable income.** ▶ 22

Figure your tax, credits, and payments

If you want the IRS to figure your tax, see the instructions for line 22 on page 41.

23 Find the tax on the amount on line 22. Check if from: ☐ Tax Table (pages 65–70) or   ☐ Form 8615 (see page 42).   23

24a Credit for child and dependent care expenses. Attach Schedule 2.   24a

b Credit for the elderly or the disabled. Attach Schedule 3.   24b

c Add lines 24a and 24b. These are your **total credits.**   24c

25 Subtract line 24c from line 23. If line 24c is more than line 23, enter -0-.   25

26 Advance earned income credit payments from Form W-2.   26

27 Household employment taxes. Attach Schedule H.   27

28 Add lines 25, 26, and 27. This is your **total tax.** ▶ 28

29a Total Federal income tax withheld. If any is from Form(s) 1099, check here. ▶ ☐   29a

b 1995 estimated tax payments and amount applied from 1994 return.   29b

c **Earned income credit.** Attach Schedule EIC if you have a qualifying child.   29c
Nontaxable earned income: amount ▶ _____ and type ▶

d Add lines 29a, 29b, and 29c (don't include nontaxable earned income). These are your **total payments.** ▶ 29d

Figure your refund or amount you owe

30 If line 29d is more than line 28, subtract line 28 from line 29d. This is the amount you **overpaid.**   30

31 Amount of line 30 you want **refunded to you.**   31

32 Amount of line 30 you want **applied to your 1996 estimated tax.**   32

33 If line 28 is more than line 29d, subtract line 29d from line 28. This is the **amount you owe.** For details on how to pay, including what to write on your payment, see page 55.   33

34 Estimated tax penalty (see page 55). Also, include on line 33.   34

Sign your return

Keep a copy of this return for your records.

Under penalties of perjury, I declare that I have examined this return and accompanying schedules and statements, and to the best of my knowledge and belief, they are true, correct, and accurately list all amounts and sources of income I received during the tax year. Declaration of preparer (other than the taxpayer) is based on all information of which the preparer has any knowledge.

▶ Your signature	Date	Your occupation
▶ Spouse's signature. If joint return, BOTH must sign.	Date	Spouse's occupation

Paid preparer's use only

Preparer's signature ▶	Date	Check if self-employed ☐	Preparer's SSN
Firm's name (or yours if self-employed) and address ▶		EIN	
		ZIP code	

N1A5AAA

✿ *Printed on recycled paper*

1995 Form 1040A page 2

Schedule 1
(Form 1040A)

Department of the Treasury—Internal Revenue Service

Interest and Dividend Income
for Form 1040A Filers   (99)   **1995**

OMB No. 1545-0085

Name(s) shown on Form 1040A | Your social security number

Part I

Interest income

(See pages 28 and 71.)

Note: *If you received a Form 1099–INT, Form 1099–OID, or substitute statement from a brokerage firm, enter the firm's name and the total interest shown on that form.*

1	List name of payer. If any interest is from a seller-financed mortgage and the buyer used the property as a personal residence, see page 71 and list this interest first. Also, show that buyer's social security number and address.		**Amount**	
		1		

2	Add the amounts on line 1.	2	
3	Excludable interest on series EE U.S. savings bonds issued after 1989 from Form 8815, line 14. You **must** attach Form 8815 to Form 1040A.	3	
4	Subtract line 3 from line 2. Enter the result here and on Form 1040A, line 8a.	4	

Part II

Dividend income

(See pages 28 and 72.)

Note: *If you received a Form 1099–DIV or substitute statement from a brokerage firm, enter the firm's name and the total dividends shown on that form.*

5	List name of payer	**Amount**	
		5	

5/15AAA

| 6 | Add the amounts on line 5. Enter the total here and on Form 1040A, line 9. | 6 | |

For Paperwork Reduction Act Notice, see Form 1040A instructions.   Cat. No. 12075R   **1995 Schedule 1 (Form 1040A) page 1**

 Printed on recycled paper

Schedule 2
(Form 1040A)

Department of the Treasury—Internal Revenue Service
Child and Dependent Care
Expenses for Form 1040A Filers   (99)   **1995**

OMB No. 1545-0085

Name(s) shown on Form 1040A	Your social security number

You need to understand the following terms to complete this schedule: **Qualifying person(s), Dependent care benefits, Qualified expenses,** and **Earned income.** See **Important terms** on page 73.

Part I

Persons or organizations who provided the care

You MUST complete this part.

1

(a) Care provider's name	(b) Address (number, street, apt. no., city, state, and ZIP code)	(c) Identifying number (SSN or EIN)	(d) Amount paid (see page 75)

(If you need more space, use the bottom of page 2.)

2 Add the amounts in column (d) of line 1.   **2**

3 Enter the number of **qualifying persons** cared for in 1995 . . . . ▶ ☐

Did you receive **dependent care benefits?**	**NO** ——————▶ Complete only Part II below.
	YES ——————▶ Complete Part III on the back now.

Part II

Credit for child and dependent care expenses

4 Enter the amount of **qualified expenses** you incurred and paid in 1995. DO NOT enter more than $2,400 for one qualifying person or $4,800 for two or more persons. If you completed Part III, enter the amount from line 25.   **4**

5 Enter YOUR **earned income.**   **5**

6 If married filing a joint return, enter YOUR SPOUSE'S earned income (if student or disabled, see page 76); **all others,** enter the amount from line 5.   **6**

7 Enter the **smallest** of line 4, 5, or 6.   **7**

8 Enter the amount from Form 1040A, line 17.   **8**

9 Enter on line 9 the decimal amount shown below that applies to the amount on line 8.

If line 8 is—		Decimal amount is	If line 8 is—		Decimal amount is
Over	But not over		Over	But not over	
$0	10,000	.30	$20,000	22,000	.24
10,000	12,000	.29	22,000	24,000	.23
12,000	14,000	.28	24,000	26,000	.22
14,000	16,000	.27	26,000	28,000	.21
16,000	18,000	.26	28,000	No limit	.20
18,000	20,000	.25			

9   × .

10 Multiply **line 7** by the decimal amount on line 9. Enter the result. Then, see page 76 for the amount of credit to enter on Form 1040A, line 24a.   **10**   =

Caution: *If you paid a person who worked in your home, you may have to pay employment taxes. See the instructions for Form 1040A, line 27, on page 43.*

5/25AAA

For Paperwork Reduction Act Notice, see Form 1040A instructions.   Cat. No. 10749I   **1995 Schedule 2 (Form 1040A) page 1**

1995 Schedule 2 (Form 1040A) page 2

Part III

Dependent care benefits

Complete this part **only** if you received these benefits.

11	Enter the total amount of **dependent care benefits** you received for 1995. This amount should be shown in box 10 of your W-2 form(s). DO NOT include amounts that were reported to you as wages in box 1 of Form(s) W-2.	11	
12	Enter the amount forfeited, if any. See page 77.	12	
13	Subtract line 12 from line 11.	13	

14	Enter the total amount of **qualified expenses** incurred in 1995 for the care of the qualifying person(s).	14	
15	Enter the **smaller** of line 13 or 14.	15	
16	Enter YOUR **earned income.**	16	
17	If married filing a joint return, enter YOUR SPOUSE'S earned income (if student or disabled, see the line 6 instructions); if married filing a separate return, see the instructions for the amount to enter; **all others,** enter the amount from line 16.	17	
18	Enter the **smallest** of line 15, 16, or 17.	18	

19	**Excluded benefits.** Enter here the **smaller** of the following: ● The amount from line 18, or ● $5,000 ($2,500 if married filing a separate return **and** you were required to enter your spouse's earned income on line 17).	19	
20	**Taxable benefits.** Subtract line 19 from line 13. Also, include this amount on Form 1040A, line 7. In the space to the left of line 7, write "DCB."	20	

To claim the child and dependent care credit, complete lines 21–25 below, and lines 4–10 on the front of this schedule.

21	Enter the amount of qualified expenses you incurred and paid in 1995. DO NOT include on this line any excluded benefits shown on line 19.	21	
22	Enter $2,400 ($4,800 if two or more qualifying persons).	22	
23	Enter the amount from line 19.	23	
24	Subtract line 23 from line 22. If zero or less, **STOP.** You cannot take the credit. **Exception.** If you paid 1994 expenses in 1995, see the line 10 instructions.	24	
25	Enter the **smaller** of line 21 or 24 here **and** on line 4 on the front of this schedule.	25	

N/25AAA

1995 Schedule 2 (Form 1040A) page 2

Schedule 3

(Form 1040A)

Department of the Treasury—Internal Revenue Service

Credit for the Elderly or the Disabled for Form 1040A Filers

(99) **1995**

OMB No. 1545-0085

Name(s) shown on Form 1040A

Your social security number

You may be able to take this credit and reduce your tax if by the end of 1995:

- You were age 65 or older, **OR**
- You were under age 65, you retired on **permanent and total** disability, and you received taxable disability income.

But you must also meet other tests. See the separate instructions for Schedule 3.

Note: *In most cases, the IRS can figure the credit for you. See page 42 of the Form 1040A instructions.*

Part I Check the box for your filing status and age	**If your filing status is:**	**And by the end of 1995:**	**Check only one box:**
	Single, Head of household, or Qualifying widow(er) with dependent child	**1** You were 65 or older.	1 ☐
		2 You were under 65 and you retired on permanent and total disability	2 ☐
	Married filing a joint return	**3** Both spouses were 65 or older	3 ☐
		4 Both spouses were under 65, but only one spouse retired on permanent and total disability	4 ☐
		5 Both spouses were under 65, and both retired on permanent and total disability	5 ☐
		6 One spouse was 65 or older, and the other spouse was under 65 and retired on permanent and total disability .	6 ☐
		7 One spouse was 65 or older, and the other spouse was under 65 and **NOT** retired on permanent and total disability	7 ☐
	Married filing a separate return	**8** You were 65 or older and you lived apart from your spouse for all of 1995	8 ☐
		9 You were under 65, you retired on permanent and total disability, and you lived apart from your spouse for all of 1995	9 ☐

Did you check box 1, 3, 7, or 8? — Yes ➔ Skip Part II and complete Part III on the back.

— No ➔ Complete Parts II and III.

Part II

Statement of permanent and total disability

5/35AAA

Complete this part **only** if you checked box 2, 4, 5, 6, or 9 above.

IF: **1** You filed a physician's statement for this disability for 1983 or an earlier year, or you filed a statement for tax years after 1983 and your physician signed line B on the statement, **AND**

2 Due to your continued disabled condition, you were unable to engage in any substantial gainful activity in 1995, check here ▶ ☐. You do not have to file another statement for 1995. If you **did not** check this box, have your physician complete the statement below.

Physician's statement (See instructions at bottom of page 2.)

I certify that _____

Name of disabled person

was permanently and totally disabled on January 1, 1976, or January 1, 1977, **OR** was permanently and totally disabled on the date he or she retired. If retired after 1976, enter the date retired ▶ _____

Physician: Sign your name on **either** line A or B below.

A The disability has lasted or can be expected to last continuously for at least a year . . . .

Physician's signature	Date

B There is no reasonable probability that the disabled condition will ever improve . . . .

Physician's signature	Date

Physician's name	Physician's address

For Paperwork Reduction Act Notice, see Form 1040A instructions.

Cat. No. 12064K

1995 Schedule 3 (Form 1040A) page 1

1995 Schedule 3 (Form 1040A) page 2

Part III
Figure your credit

10 **If you checked (in Part I):**   **Enter:**
   Box 1, 2, 4, or 7 . . . . $5,000
   Box 3, 5, or 6 . . . . $7,500
   Box 8 or 9 . . . . $3,750   **10**

| Did you check box 2, 4, 5, 6, or 9 in Part I? | ── Yes ──▶ | You **must** complete line 11. |
| | ── No ──▶ | Enter the amount from line 10 on line 12 and go to line 13. |

11 • If you checked box 6 in Part I, add $5,000 to the taxable disability income of the spouse who was under age 65. Enter the total.

   • If you checked box 2, 4, or 9 in Part I, enter your taxable disability income.

   • If you checked box 5 in Part I, add your taxable disability income to your spouse's taxable disability income. Enter the total.

   TIP: For more details on what to include on line 11, see the instructions.   **11**

12 If you completed line 11, enter the **smaller** of line 10 or line 11; **all others,** enter the amount from line 10.   **12**

13 Enter the following pensions, annuities, or disability income that you (and your spouse if filing a joint return) received in 1995.

   a Nontaxable part of social security benefits, and
   Nontaxable part of railroad retirement benefits treated as social security. See instructions.   **13a**

   b Nontaxable veterans' pensions and any other pension, annuity, or disability benefit that is excluded from income under any other provision of law. See instructions.   **13b**

   c Add lines 13a and 13b. (Even though these income items are not taxable, they **must** be included here to figure your credit.) If you did not receive any of the types of nontaxable income listed on line 13a or 13b, enter -0- on line 13c.   **13c**

14 Enter the amount from Form 1040A, line 17.   **14**

15 **If you checked (in Part I):**   **Enter:**
   Box 1 or 2 . . . . $7,500
   Box 3, 4, 5, 6, or 7 . . . . $10,000
   Box 8 or 9 . . . . $5,000   **15**

16 Subtract line 15 from line 14. If zero or less, enter -0-.   **16**

17 Enter one-half of line 16.   **17**

18 Add lines 13c and 17.   **18**

19 Subtract line 18 from line 12. If zero or less, **stop; you cannot** take the credit. Otherwise, go to line 20.   **19**

20 Multiply line 19 by 15% (.15). Enter the result here and on Form 1040A, line 24b.   **20**

N/35AAA

Instructions for physician's statement

Taxpayer.—If you retired after 1976, enter the date you retired in the space provided in Part II.

Physician.—A person is permanently and totally disabled if **both** of the following apply:

   1. He or she cannot engage in any substantial gainful activity because of a physical or mental condition, and

   2. A physician determines that the disability has lasted or can be expected to last continuously for at least a year or can lead to death.

 Printed on recycled paper

Form **1040**

Department of the Treasury—Internal Revenue Service
U.S. Individual Income Tax Return 19**95** (99) IRS Use Only—Do not write or staple in this space.

For the year Jan. 1–Dec. 31, 1995, or other tax year beginning , 1995, ending , 19 | OMB No. 1545-0074

Label
(See instructions on page 11.)

Use the IRS label. Otherwise, please print or type.

L A B E L   H E R E

Your first name and initial | Last name | Your social security number

If a joint return, spouse's first name and initial | Last name | Spouse's social security number

Home address (number and street). If you have a P.O. box, see page 11. | Apt. no.

City, town or post office, state, and ZIP code. If you have a foreign address, see page 11.

For Privacy Act and Paperwork Reduction Act Notice, see page 7.

Presidential Election Campaign
(See page 11.)

Yes | No | Note: Checking "Yes" will not change your tax or reduce your refund.

Do you want $3 to go to this fund? . . . .

If a joint return, does your spouse want $3 to go to this fund? . . . .

Filing Status
(See page 11.)

Check only one box.

1 ☐ Single

2 ☐ Married filing joint return (even if only one had income)

3 ☐ Married filing separate return. Enter spouse's social security no. above and full name here. ▶ _____

4 ☐ Head of household (with qualifying person). (See page 12.) If the qualifying person is a child but not your dependent, enter this child's name here. ▶ _____

5 ☐ Qualifying widow(er) with dependent child (year spouse died ▶ 19). (See page 12.)

Exemptions
(See page 12.)

If more than six dependents, see page 13.

6a ☐ **Yourself.** If your parent (or someone else) can claim you as a dependent on his or her tax return, **do not** check box 6a. But be sure to check the box on line 33b on page 2 .

b ☐ **Spouse** . . . .

c **Dependents:**

(1) First name Last name	(2) Dependent's social security number. If born in 1995, see page 13.	(3) Dependent's relationship to you	(4) No. of months lived in your home in 1995

No. of boxes checked on 6a and 6b _____

No. of your children on 6c who:
• lived with you _____
• didn't live with you due to divorce or separation (see page 14) _____

Dependents on 6c not entered above _____

d If your child didn't live with you but is claimed as your dependent under a pre-1985 agreement, check here ▶ ☐

e Total number of exemptions claimed . . . .

Add numbers entered on lines above ▶ _____

Income

Attach Copy B of your Forms W-2, W-2G, and 1099-R here.

If you did not get a W-2, see page 14.

Enclose, but do not attach, your payment and payment voucher. See page 33.

7 Wages, salaries, tips, etc. Attach Form(s) W-2 . . . . | 7

8a **Taxable** interest income (see page 15). Attach Schedule B if over $400 . . . . . | 8a

b **Tax-exempt** interest (see page 15). DON'T include on line 8a | 8b

9 Dividend income. Attach Schedule B if over $400 . . . . . . | 9

10 Taxable refunds, credits, or offsets of state and local income taxes (see page 15) . . | 10

11 Alimony received . . . . | 11

12 Business income or (loss). Attach Schedule C or C-EZ . . . . . . | 12

13 Capital gain or (loss). If required, attach Schedule D (see page 16) . . . . . | 13

14 Other gains or (losses). Attach Form 4797 . . . . | 14

15a Total IRA distributions . | 15a | b Taxable amount (see page 16) | 15b

16a Total pensions and annuities | 16a | b Taxable amount (see page 16) | 16b

17 Rental real estate, royalties, partnerships, S corporations, trusts, etc. Attach Schedule E | 17

18 Farm income or (loss). Attach Schedule F . . . . | 18

19 Unemployment compensation (see page 17) . . . . | 19

20a Social security benefits | 20a | b Taxable amount (see page 18) | 20b

21 Other income. List type and amount—see page 18 .... | 21

22 Add the amounts in the far right column for lines 7 through 21. This is your **total income** ▶ | 22

Adjustments to Income

23a Your IRA deduction (see page 19) . . . . . . | 23a

b Spouse's IRA deduction (see page 19) . . . . . | 23b

24 Moving expenses. Attach Form 3903 or 3903-F . . . | 24

25 One-half of self-employment tax . . . . | 25

26 Self-employed health insurance deduction (see page 21) | 26

27 Keogh & self-employed SEP plans. If SEP, check ▶ ☐ | 27

28 Penalty on early withdrawal of savings . . . . . | 28

29 Alimony paid. Recipient's SSN ▶ | 29

30 Add lines 23a through 29. These are your **total adjustments** . . . . ▶ | 30

Adjusted Gross Income

31 Subtract line 30 from line 22. This is your **adjusted gross income**. If less than $26,673 and a child lived with you (less than $9,230 if a child didn't live with you), see "Earned Income Credit" on page 27 ▶ | 31

Cat. No. 11320B   Form **1040** (1995)

Form 1040 (1995)

Tax Compu-tation

(See page 23.)

32	Amount from line 31 (adjusted gross income)		32	

33a Check if: ☐ **You** were 65 or older, ☐ Blind; ☐ **Spouse** was 65 or older, ☐ Blind.
Add the number of boxes checked above and enter the total here . . . ▶ 33a

b If your parent (or someone else) can claim you as a dependent, check here . ▶ 33b ☐

c If you are married filing separately and your spouse itemizes deductions or you are a dual-status alien, see page 23 and check here . . . . . . ▶ 33c ☐

34 Enter the larger of your: { **Itemized deductions** from Schedule A, line 28, **OR**
Standard deduction shown below for your filing status. **But if you checked any box on line 33a or b,** go to page 23 to find your standard deduction. If you checked **box 33c,** your standard deduction is zero.
• Single—$3,900 • Married filing jointly or Qualifying widow(er)—$6,550
• Head of household—$5,750 • Married filing separately—$3,275 }

34		

35 Subtract line 34 from line 32 . . . . | 35 |

36 If line 32 is $86,025 or less, multiply $2,500 by the total number of exemptions claimed on line 6e. If line 32 is over $86,025, see the worksheet on page 23 for the amount to enter . | 36 |

If you want the IRS to figure your tax, see page 35.

37 **Taxable income.** Subtract line 36 from line 35. If line 36 is more than line 35, enter -0- | 37 |

38 Tax. Check if from **a** ☐ Tax Table, **b** ☐ Tax Rate Schedules, **c** ☐ Capital Gain Tax Worksheet, or **d** ☐ Form 8615 (see page 24). Amount from Form(s) 8814 ▶ **e** _____ | 38 |

39 Additional taxes. Check if from **a** ☐ Form 4970 **b** ☐ Form 4972 . . . . | 39 |

40 Add lines 38 and 39 . . . . ▶ | 40 |

Credits

(See page 24.)

41 Credit for child and dependent care expenses. Attach Form 2441 | 41 |

42 Credit for the elderly or the disabled. Attach Schedule R . . | 42 |

43 Foreign tax credit. Attach Form 1116 . . . . . . | 43 |

44 Other credits (see page 25). Check if from **a** ☐ Form 3800 **b** ☐ Form 8396 **c** ☐ Form 8801 **d** ☐ Form (specify) ____ | 44 |

45 Add lines 41 through 44 . . . . | 45 |

46 Subtract line 45 from line 40. If line 45 is more than line 40, enter -0- . . . . ▶ | 46 |

Other Taxes

(See page 25.)

47 Self-employment tax. Attach Schedule SE . . . . | 47 |

48 Alternative minimum tax. Attach Form 6251 . . . . | 48 |

49 Recapture taxes. Check if from **a** ☐ Form 4255 **b** ☐ Form 8611 **c** ☐ Form 8828 . | 49 |

50 Social security and Medicare tax on tip income not reported to employer. Attach Form 4137 . | 50 |

51 Tax on qualified retirement plans, including IRAs. If required, attach Form 5329 . . . | 51 |

52 Advance earned income credit payments from Form W-2 . . . . | 52 |

53 Household employment taxes. Attach Schedule H . . . . | 53 |

54 Add lines 46 through 53. This is your **total tax** . . . . ▶ | 54 |

Payments

Attach Forms W-2, W-2G, and 1099-R on the front.

55 Federal income tax withheld. If any is from Form(s) 1099, check ▶ ☐ | 55 |

56 1995 estimated tax payments and amount applied from 1994 return . | 56 |

57 **Earned income credit.** Attach Schedule EIC if you have a qualifying child. Nontaxable earned income: amount ▶ _____
and type ▶ ------------------------- | 57 |

58 Amount paid with Form 4868 (extension request) . . . . | 58 |

59 Excess social security and RRTA tax withheld (see page 32) | 59 |

60 Other payments. Check if from **a** ☐ Form 2439 **b** ☐ Form 4136 | 60 |

61 Add lines 55 through 60. These are your **total payments** . . . . ▶ | 61 |

Refund or Amount You Owe

62 If line 61 is more than line 54, subtract line 54 from line 61. This is the amount you **OVERPAID**. . | 62 |

63 Amount of line 62 you want **REFUNDED TO YOU**. . . . . ▶ | 63 |

64 Amount of line 62 you want **APPLIED TO YOUR 1996 ESTIMATED TAX** ▶ | 64 |

65 If line 54 is more than line 61, subtract line 61 from line 54. This is the **AMOUNT YOU OWE.** For details on how to pay and use **Form 1040-V,** Payment Voucher, see page 33 . . ▶ | 65 |

66 Estimated tax penalty (see page 33). Also include on line 65 | 66 |

Sign Here

Keep a copy of this return for your records.

Under penalties of perjury, I declare that I have examined this return and accompanying schedules and statements, and to the best of my knowledge and belief, they are true, correct, and complete. Declaration of preparer (other than taxpayer) is based on all information of which preparer has any knowledge.

Your signature	Date	Your occupation
Spouse's signature. If a joint return, BOTH must sign.	Date	Spouse's occupation

Paid Preparer's Use Only

Preparer's signature ▶	Date	Check if self-employed ☐	Preparer's social security no.
Firm's name (or yours if self-employed) and address ▶		EIN	
		ZIP code	

✪ Printed on recycled paper

SCHEDULES A&B
(Form 1040)

Department of the Treasury
Internal Revenue Service   (99)

Schedule A—Itemized Deductions

(Schedule B is on back)

▶ **Attach to Form 1040.** ▶ **See Instructions for Schedules A and B (Form 1040).**

OMB No. 1545-0074

1995

Attachment
Sequence No. **07**

Name(s) shown on Form 1040

Your social security number

Medical and Dental Expenses		Caution: *Do not include expenses reimbursed or paid by others.*			
	1	Medical and dental expenses (see page A-1)	**1**		
	2	Enter amount from Form 1040, line 32 . ⌐2⌐			
	3	Multiply line 2 above by 7.5% (.075)	**3**		
	4	Subtract line 3 from line 1. If line 3 is more than line 1, enter -0-		**4**	
Taxes You Paid (See page A-1.)	5	State and local income taxes	**5**		
	6	Real estate taxes (see page A-2)	**6**		
	7	Personal property taxes	**7**		
	8	Other taxes. List type and amount ▶ _____ _____	**8**		
	9	Add lines 5 through 8		**9**	
Interest You Paid (See page A-2.)	10	Home mortgage interest and points reported to you on Form 1098	**10**		
	11	Home mortgage interest not reported to you on Form 1098. If paid to the person from whom you bought the home, see page A-3 and show that person's name, identifying no., and address ▶ _____ _____ _____	**11**		
Note: Personal interest is not deductible.	12	Points not reported to you on Form 1098. See page A-3 for special rules	**12**		
	13	Investment interest. If required, attach Form 4952. (See page A-3.)	**13**		
	14	Add lines 10 through 13		**14**	
Gifts to Charity If you made a gift and got a benefit for it, see page A-3.	15	Gifts by cash or check. If you made any gift of $250 or more, see page A-3	**15**		
	16	Other than by cash or check. If any gift of $250 or more, see page A-3. If over $500, you **MUST** attach Form 8283	**16**		
	17	Carryover from prior year	**17**		
	18	Add lines 15 through 17		**18**	
Casualty and Theft Losses	19	Casualty or theft loss(es). Attach Form 4684. (See page A-4.)		**19**	
Job Expenses and Most Other Miscellaneous Deductions (See page A-5 for expenses to deduct here.)	20	Unreimbursed employee expenses—job travel, union dues, job education, etc. If required, you **MUST** attach Form 2106 or 2106-EZ. (See page A-5.) ▶ _____ _____	**20**		
	21	Tax preparation fees	**21**		
	22	Other expenses—investment, safe deposit box, etc. List type and amount ▶ _____	**22**		
	23	Add lines 20 through 22	**23**		
	24	Enter amount from Form 1040, line 32 ⌐24⌐			
	25	Multiply line 24 above by 2% (.02)	**25**		
	26	Subtract line 25 from line 23. If line 25 is more than line 23, enter -0-		**26**	
Other Miscellaneous Deductions	27	Other—from list on page A-5. List type and amount ▶ _____ _____		**27**	
Total Itemized Deductions	28	Is Form 1040, line 32, over $114,700 (over $57,350 if married filing separately)? **NO.** Your deduction is not limited. Add the amounts in the far right column for lines 4 through 27. Also, enter on Form 1040, line 34, the **larger** of this amount or your standard deduction. **YES.** Your deduction may be limited. See page A-5 for the amount to enter.	▶	**28**	

For Paperwork Reduction Act Notice, see Form 1040 instructions.

Cat. No. 11330X

Schedule A (Form 1040) 1995

OMB No. 1545-0074   Page **2**

Name(s) shown on Form 1040. Do not enter name and social security number if shown on other side.

Your social security number

Schedule B—Interest and Dividend Income

Attachment
Sequence No. **08**

Part I
Interest Income

(See pages 15 and B-1.)

Note: If you received a Form 1099-INT, Form 1099-OID, or substitute statement from a brokerage firm, list the firm's name as the payer and enter the total interest shown on that form.

Note: *If you had over $400 in taxable interest income, you must also complete Part III.*

1 List name of payer. If any interest is from a seller-financed mortgage and the buyer used the property as a personal residence, see page B-1 and list this interest first. Also, show that buyer's social security number and address ▶

	Amount
1	

2 Add the amounts on line 1 . . . . | **2** |

3 Excludable interest on series EE U.S. savings bonds issued after 1989 from Form 8815, line 14. You MUST attach Form 8815 to Form 1040 . . . . | **3** |

4 Subtract line 3 from line 2. Enter the result here and on Form 1040, line 8a ▶ | **4** |

Part II
Dividend Income

(See pages 15 and B-1.)

Note: If you received a Form 1099-DIV or substitute statement from a brokerage firm, list the firm's name as the payer and enter the total dividends shown on that form.

Note: *If you had over $400 in gross dividends and/or other distributions on stock, you must also complete Part III.*

5 List name of payer. Include gross dividends and/or other distributions on stock here. Any capital gain distributions and nontaxable distributions will be deducted on lines 7 and 8 ▶

	Amount
5	

6 Add the amounts on line 5 . . . . | **6** |

7 Capital gain distributions. Enter here and on Schedule D* . | **7** | |

8 Nontaxable distributions. (See the inst. for Form 1040, line 9.) | **8** | |

9 Add lines 7 and 8 . . . . | **9** |

10 Subtract line 9 from line 6. Enter the result here and on Form 1040, line 9 . ▶ | **10** |

If you do not need Schedule D to report any other gains or losses, see the instructions for Form 1040, line 13, on page 16.

Part III
Foreign Accounts and Trusts

(See page B-2.)

If you had over $400 of interest or dividends **or** had a foreign account or were a grantor of, or a transferor to, a foreign trust, you must complete this part.

	Yes	No

11a At any time during 1995, did you have an interest in or a signature or other authority over a financial account in a foreign country, such as a bank account, securities account, or other financial account? See page B-2 for exceptions and filing requirements for Form TD F 90-22.1 . . . . .

b If "Yes," enter the name of the foreign country ▶

12 Were you the grantor of, or transferor to, a foreign trust that existed during 1995, whether or not you have any beneficial interest in it? If "Yes," you may have to file Form 3520, 3520-A, or 926 .

For Paperwork Reduction Act Notice, see Form 1040 instructions.   ✱ *Printed on recycled paper*   **Schedule B (Form 1040) 1995**

| SCHEDULE C
(Form 1040)

Department of the Treasury
Internal Revenue Service   (99) | **Profit or Loss From Business**
(Sole Proprietorship)
▶ Partnerships, joint ventures, etc., must file Form 1065.
▶ Attach to Form 1040 or Form 1041.   ▶ See Instructions for Schedule C (Form 1040). | OMB No. 1545-0074
1995
Attachment
Sequence No. **09** |

Name of proprietor | Social security number (SSN)

A Principal business or profession, including product or service (see page C-1)

B Enter principal business code
(see page C-6) ▶ | | | |

C Business name. If no separate business name, leave blank.

D Employer ID number (EIN), if any

E Business address (including suite or room no.) ▶ --
City, town or post office, state, and ZIP code

F Accounting method: **(1)** ☐ Cash   **(2)** ☐ Accrual   **(3)** ☐ Other (specify) ▶ ------------------

G Method(s) used to
value closing inventory: **(1)** ☐ Cost   **(2)** ☐ Lower of cost
or market   **(3)** ☐ Other (attach
explanation)   **(4)** ☐ Does not apply (if
checked, skip line H) | Yes | No

H Was there any change in determining quantities, costs, or valuations between opening and closing inventory? If "Yes," attach
explanation . . . .

I Did you "materially participate" in the operation of this business during 1995? If "No," see page C-2 for limit on losses. . .

J If you started or acquired this business during 1995, check here . . . . ▶ ☐

Part I   **Income**

1	Gross receipts or sales. **Caution:** If this income was reported to you on Form W-2 and the "Statutory employee" box on that form was checked, see page C-2 and check here . . . . . . ▶ ☐	**1**	
2	Returns and allowances	**2**	
3	Subtract line 2 from line 1	**3**	
4	Cost of goods sold (from line 40 on page 2)	**4**	
5	**Gross profit.** Subtract line 4 from line 3	**5**	
6	Other income, including Federal and state gasoline or fuel tax credit or refund (see page C-2) . . .	**6**	
7	**Gross income.** Add lines 5 and 6 . . . . ▶	**7**	

Part II   **Expenses.** Enter expenses for business use of your home **only** on line 30.

8	Advertising	**8**			19	Pension and profit-sharing plans	**19**	
9	Bad debts from sales or services (see page C-3) . .	**9**			20	Rent or lease (see page C-4):		
					a Vehicles, machinery, and equipment .	**20a**	
10	Car and truck expenses (see page C-3)	**10**			**b** Other business property . .	**20b**	
11	Commissions and fees. . .	**11**			21	Repairs and maintenance . .	**21**	
12	Depletion.	**12**			22	Supplies (not included in Part III) .	**22**	
13	Depreciation and section 179 expense deduction (not included in Part III) (see page C-3) . .	**13**			23	Taxes and licenses	**23**	
					24	Travel, meals, and entertainment:		
					a Travel	**24a**	
14	Employee benefit programs (other than on line 19) . . .	**14**			**b** Meals and entertainment		
15	Insurance (other than health) .	**15**			**c** Enter 50% of line 24b subject to limitations (see page C-4) .		
16	Interest:							
a	Mortgage (paid to banks, etc.) .	**16a**			**d** Subtract line 24c from line 24b .	**24d**	
b	Other	**16b**			25	Utilities	**25**	
17	Legal and professional services	**17**			26	Wages (less employment credits) .	**26**	
					27	Other expenses (from line 46 on page 2)		
18	Office expense	**18**					**27**	

28	**Total expenses** before expenses for business use of home. Add lines 8 through 27 in columns . . ▶	**28**	
29	Tentative profit (loss). Subtract line 28 from line 7	**29**	
30	Expenses for business use of your home. Attach **Form 8829**	**30**	
31	**Net profit or (loss).** Subtract line 30 from line 29. • If a profit, enter on **Form 1040, line 12,** and ALSO on **Schedule SE, line 2** (statutory employees, see page C-5). Estates and trusts, enter on Form 1041, line 3. • If a loss, you MUST go on to line 32.	**31**	

32 If you have a loss, check the box that describes your investment in this activity (see page C-5).
• If you checked 32a, enter the loss on **Form 1040, line 12,** and ALSO on **Schedule SE, line 2**
(statutory employees, see page C-5). Estates and trusts, enter on Form 1041, line 3.
• If you checked 32b, you MUST attach **Form 6198.**

32a ☐ All investment is at risk.
32b ☐ Some investment is not at risk.

For Paperwork Reduction Act Notice, see Form 1040 instructions.   Cat. No. 11334P   Schedule C (Form 1040) 1995

Part III   **Cost of Goods Sold** (see page C-5)

33	Inventory at beginning of year. If different from last year's closing inventory, attach explanation . .	33
34	Purchases less cost of items withdrawn for personal use	34
35	Cost of labor. Do not include salary paid to yourself	35
36	Materials and supplies	36
37	Other costs	37
38	Add lines 33 through 37	38
39	Inventory at end of year	39
40	**Cost of goods sold.** Subtract line 39 from line 38. Enter the result here and on page 1, line 4 . .	40

Part IV   **Information on Your Vehicle.** Complete this part **ONLY** if you are claiming car or truck expenses on line 10 and are not required to file Form 4562 for this business. See the instructions for line 13 on page C-3 to find out if you must file.

41   When did you place your vehicle in service for business purposes? (month, day, year) ▶ ..../........./........ .

42   Of the total number of miles you drove your vehicle during 1995, enter the number of miles you used your vehicle for:

  a Business .... **b** Commuting .... **c** Other ....

43   Do you (or your spouse) have another vehicle available for personal use? . . . . ☐ **Yes**   ☐ **No**

44   Was your vehicle available for use during off-duty hours? . . . . ☐ **Yes**   ☐ **No**

45a   Do you have evidence to support your deduction? . . . . ☐ **Yes**   ☐ **No**
  b   If "Yes," is the evidence written? . . . . ☐ **Yes**   ☐ **No**

Part V   **Other Expenses.** List below business expenses not included on lines 8–26 or line 30.

46	**Total other expenses.** Enter here and on page 1, line 27	46

♻ *Printed on recycled paper*

SCHEDULE C-EZ (Form 1040) Department of the Treasury Internal Revenue Service	**Net Profit From Business** (Sole Proprietorship) ▶ **Partnerships, joint ventures, etc., must file Form 1065.** ▶ **Attach to Form 1040 or Form 1041. ▶ See instructions on back.**	OMB No. 1545-0074 19**95** Attachment Sequence No. **09A**
Name of proprietor		Social security number (SSN)

Part I   General Information

You May Use This Schedule Only If You:

• Had gross receipts from your business of $25,000 or less.
• Had business expenses of $2,000 or less.
• Use the cash method of accounting.
• Did not have an inventory at any time during the year.
• Did not have a net loss from your business.
• Had only one business as a sole proprietor.

And You:

• Had no employees during the year.
• Are not required to file **Form 4562,** Depreciation and Amortization, for this business. See the instructions for Schedule C, line 13, on page C-3 to find out if you must file.
• Do not deduct expenses for business use of your home.
• Do not have prior year unallowed passive activity losses from this business.

A Principal business or profession, including product or service

B Enter principal business code (see page C-6) ▶

C Business name. If no separate business name, leave blank.

D Employer ID number (EIN), if any

E Business address (including suite or room no.). Address not required if same as on Form 1040, page 1.

City, town or post office, state, and ZIP code

Part II   Figure Your Net Profit

1 **Gross receipts.** If more than $25,000, you **must** use Schedule C.
Caution: *If this income was reported to you on Form W-2 and the "Statutory employee" box on that form was checked, see **Statutory Employees** in the instructions for Schedule C, line 1, on page C-2 and check here* . . . . ▶ ☐ | **1** |

2 **Total expenses.** If more than $2,000, you **must** use Schedule C. See instructions . . . . . | **2** |

3 **Net profit.** Subtract line 2 from line 1. If less than zero, you **must** use Schedule C. Enter on **Form 1040, line 12,** and ALSO on **Schedule SE, line 2.** (Statutory employees **do not** report this amount on Schedule SE, line 2. Estates and trusts, enter on Form 1041, line 3.) . . . . . | **3** |

Part III   Information on Your Vehicle. Complete this part **ONLY** if you are claiming car or truck expenses on line 2.

4 When did you place your vehicle in service for business purposes? (month, day, year) ▶ ..... / ..... / ....

5 Of the total number of miles you drove your vehicle during 1995, enter the number of miles you used your vehicle for:

a Business .... **b** Commuting .... **c** Other ....

6 Do you (or your spouse) have another vehicle available for personal use? . . . . ☐ **Yes** ☐ **No**

7 Was your vehicle available for use during off-duty hours? . . . . ☐ **Yes** ☐ **No**

8a Do you have evidence to support your deduction? . . . . ☐ **Yes** ☐ **No**

b If "Yes," is the evidence written? . . . . ☐ **Yes** ☐ **No**

For Paperwork Reduction Act Notice, see Form 1040 instructions.   Cat. No. 14374D   **Schedule C-EZ (Form 1040) 1995**

SCHEDULE D
(Form 1040)

Department of the Treasury
Internal Revenue Service (99)

Capital Gains and Losses

▶ **Attach to Form 1040.**   ▶ **See Instructions for Schedule D (Form 1040).**

▶ **Use lines 20 and 22 for more space to list transactions for lines 1 and 9.**

OMB No. 1545-0074

1995

Attachment
Sequence No. **12**

Name(s) shown on Form 1040

Your social security number

Part I Short-Term Capital Gains and Losses—Assets Held One Year or Less

	(a) Description of property (Example: 100 sh. XYZ Co.)	(b) Date acquired (Mo., day, yr.)	(c) Date sold (Mo., day, yr.)	(d) Sales price (see page D-3)	(e) Cost or other basis (see page D-3)	(f) LOSS If (e) is more than (d), subtract (d) from (e)	(g) GAIN If (d) is more than (e), subtract (e) from (d)
1							
2	Enter your short-term totals, if any, from line 21 . . . . **2**						
3	**Total short-term sales price amounts.** Add column (d) of lines 1 and 2 . . . **3**						
4	Short-term gain from Forms 2119 and 6252, and short-term gain or loss from Forms 4684, 6781, and 8824 . . . . **4**						
5	Net short-term gain or loss from partnerships, S corporations, estates, and trusts from Schedule(s) K-1 . . . . **5**						
6	Short-term capital loss carryover. Enter the amount, if any, from line 9 of your 1994 Capital Loss Carryover Worksheet **6**						
7	Add lines 1 through 6 in columns (f) and (g) **7**					( )	
8	**Net short-term capital gain or (loss).** Combine columns (f) and (g) of line 7 . . . . . ▶ **8**						

Part II Long-Term Capital Gains and Losses—Assets Held More Than One Year

9							
10	Enter your long-term totals, if any, from line 23 . . . . **10**						
11	**Total long-term sales price amounts.** Add column (d) of lines 9 and 10 . . . **11**						
12	Gain from Form 4797; long-term gain from Forms 2119, 2439, and 6252; and long-term gain or loss from Forms 4684, 6781, and 8824 . . . . . **12**						
13	Net long-term gain or loss from partnerships, S corporations, estates, and trusts from Schedule(s) K-1 . . . . **13**						
14	Capital gain distributions **14**						
15	Long-term capital loss carryover. Enter the amount, if any, from line 14 of your 1994 Capital Loss Carryover Worksheet **15**						
16	Add lines 9 through 15 in columns (f) and (g) **16**					( )	
17	**Net long-term capital gain or (loss).** Combine columns (f) and (g) of line 16 . . . . . ▶ **17**						

Part III Summary of Parts I and II

18	Combine lines 8 and 17. If a loss, go to line 19. If a gain, enter the gain on Form 1040, line 13. **Note:** *If both lines 17 and 18 are gains, see the* **Capital Gain Tax Worksheet** *on page 24* . .	**18**
19	If line 18 is a loss, enter here and as a (loss) on Form 1040, line 13, the **smaller** of these losses:	
a	The loss on line 18; **or**	
b	($3,000) or, if married filing separately, ($1,500)	**19** ( )
	Note: *See the* **Capital Loss Carryover Worksheet** *on page D-3 if the loss on line 18 exceeds the loss on line 19 or if Form 1040, line 35, is a loss.*	

For Paperwork Reduction Act Notice, see Form 1040 instructions.   Cat. No. 11338H   Schedule D (Form 1040) 1995

Schedule D (Form 1040) 1995   Attachment Sequence No. **12**   Page **2**

Name(s) shown on Form 1040. Do not enter name and social security number if shown on other side. | **Your social security number**

Part IV **Short-Term Capital Gains and Losses—Assets Held One Year or Less** *(Continuation of Part I)*

(a) Description of property (Example: 100 sh. XYZ Co.)	(b) Date acquired (Mo., day, yr.)	(c) Date sold (Mo., day, yr.)	(d) Sales price (see page D-3)	(e) Cost or other basis (see page D-3)	(f) LOSS If (e) is more than (d), subtract (d) from (e)	(g) GAIN If (d) is more than (e), subtract (e) from (d)
20						

21 Short-term totals. Add columns (d), (f), and (g) of line 20. Enter here and on line 2 .   **21**

Part V **Long-Term Capital Gains and Losses—Assets Held More Than One Year** *(Continuation of Part II)*

22						

23 Long-term totals. Add columns (d), (f), and (g) of line 22. Enter here and on line 10 .   **23**

✪ *Printed on recycled paper*

SCHEDULE E
(Form 1040)

Department of the Treasury
Internal Revenue Service (99)

Supplemental Income and Loss

(From rental real estate, royalties, partnerships,
S corporations, estates, trusts, REMICs, etc.)

▶ **Attach to Form 1040 or Form 1041.**   ▶ **See Instructions for Schedule E (Form 1040).**

OMB No. 1545-0074

1995

Attachment
Sequence No. **13**

Name(s) shown on return | Your social security number

Part I | **Income or Loss From Rental Real Estate and Royalties** Note: *Report income and expenses from your business of renting personal property on Schedule C or C-EZ (see page E-1). Report farm rental income or loss from Form 4835 on page 2, line 39.*

1 Show the kind and location of each **rental real estate property:**

A ....

B ....

C ....

2 For each rental real estate property listed on line 1, did you or your family use it for personal purposes for more than the greater of 14 days or 10% of the total days rented at fair rental value during the tax year? (See page E-1.)

	Yes	No
A		
B		
C		

Income:

		Properties			Totals
		A	**B**	**C**	(Add columns A, B, and C.)
3 Rents received	**3**				**3**
4 Royalties received	**4**				**4**

Expenses:

5 Advertising	**5**				
6 Auto and travel (see page E-2) .	**6**				
7 Cleaning and maintenance . . .	**7**				
8 Commissions	**8**				
9 Insurance	**9**				
10 Legal and other professional fees	**10**				
11 Management fees	**11**				
12 Mortgage interest paid to banks, etc. (see page E-2)	**12**				**12**
13 Other interest	**13**				
14 Repairs	**14**				
15 Supplies	**15**				
16 Taxes	**16**				
17 Utilities	**17**				
18 Other (list) ▶....................	**18**				
19 Add lines 5 through 18	**19**				**19**
20 Depreciation expense or depletion (see page E-2)	**20**				**20**
21 Total expenses. Add lines 19 and 20	**21**				
22 Income or (loss) from rental real estate or royalty properties. Subtract line 21 from line 3 (rents) or line 4 (royalties). If the result is a (loss), see page E-2 to find out if you must file **Form 6198**. . .	**22**				
23 Deductible rental real estate loss. **Caution:** *Your rental real estate loss on line 22 may be limited. See page E-3 to find out if you must file **Form 8582**. Real estate professionals must complete line 42 on page 2*	**23**	( )	( )	( )	

24 **Income.** Add positive amounts shown on line 22. **Do not** include any losses	**24**		
25 **Losses.** Add royalty losses from line 22 and rental real estate losses from line 23. Enter the total losses here .	**25**	(	)
26 Total rental real estate and royalty income or (loss). Combine lines 24 and 25. Enter the result here. If Parts II, III, IV, and line 39 on page 2 do not apply to you, also enter this amount on Form 1040, line 17. Otherwise, include this amount in the total on line 40 on page 2	**26**		

For Paperwork Reduction Act Notice, see Form 1040 instructions.   Cat. No. 11344L   **Schedule E (Form 1040) 1995**

Schedule E (Form 1040) 1995   Attachment Sequence No. **13**   Page **2**

Name(s) shown on return. Do not enter name and social security number if shown on other side.	Your social security number

Note: *If you report amounts from farming or fishing on Schedule E, you must enter your gross income from those activities on line 41 below. Real estate professionals must complete line 42 below.*

Part II   **Income or Loss From Partnerships and S Corporations**   **Note:** *If you report a loss from an at-risk activity, you MUST check either column (e) or (f) of line 27 to describe your investment in the activity. See page E-4. If you check column (f), you must attach Form 6198.*

27	(a) Name	(b) Enter **P** for partnership; **S** for S corporation	(c) Check if foreign partnership	(d) Employer identification number	Investment At Risk?	
					(e) All is at risk	(f) Some is not at risk
A						
B						
C						
D						
E						

	Passive Income and Loss		Nonpassive Income and Loss		
	(g) Passive loss allowed (attach **Form 8582** if required)	**(h)** Passive income from **Schedule K–1**	**(i)** Nonpassive loss from **Schedule K–1**	**(j)** Section 179 expense deduction from **Form 4562**	**(k)** Nonpassive income from **Schedule K–1**
A					
B					
C					
D					
E					
28a Totals					
b Totals					

29 Add columns (h) and (k) of line 28a **29**

30 Add columns (g), (i), and (j) of line 28b . . . . **30** ( )

31 Total partnership and S corporation income or (loss). Combine lines 29 and 30. Enter the result here and include in the total on line 40 below **31**

Part III   **Income or Loss From Estates and Trusts**

32	(a) Name	(b) Employer identification number
A		
B		

	Passive Income and Loss		Nonpassive Income and Loss	
	(c) Passive deduction or loss allowed (attach **Form 8582** if required)	**(d)** Passive income from **Schedule K–1**	**(e)** Deduction or loss from **Schedule K–1**	**(f)** Other income from **Schedule K–1**
A				
B				
33a Totals				
b Totals				

34 Add columns (d) and (f) of line 33a **34**

35 Add columns (c) and (e) of line 33b . . . . **35** ( )

36 Total estate and trust income or (loss). Combine lines 34 and 35. Enter the result here and include in the total on line 40 below **36**

Part IV   **Income or Loss From Real Estate Mortgage Investment Conduits (REMICs)—Residual Holder**

37	(a) Name	(b) Employer identification number	(c) Excess inclusion from **Schedules Q,** line 2c (see page E-4)	(d) Taxable income (net loss) from **Schedules Q,** line 1b	(e) Income from **Schedules Q,** line 3b

38 Combine columns (d) and (e) only. Enter the result here and include in the total on line 40 below   **38**

Part V   **Summary**

39 Net farm rental income or (loss) from **Form 4835.** Also, complete line 41 below **39**

40 TOTAL income or (loss). Combine lines 26, 31, 36, 38, and 39. Enter the result here and on Form 1040, line 17 ▶   **40**

41 **Reconciliation of Farming and Fishing Income.** Enter your **gross** farming and fishing income reported on Form 4835, line 7; Schedule K-1 (Form 1065), line 15b; Schedule K-1 (Form 1120S), line 23; and Schedule K-1 (Form 1041), line 13 (see page E-4) **41**

42 **Reconciliation for Real Estate Professionals.** If you were a real estate professional (see page E-3), enter the net income or (loss) you reported anywhere on Form 1040 from all rental real estate activities in which you materially participated under the passive activity loss rules . . **42**

✺ *Printed on recycled paper*

| SCHEDULE EIC (Form 1040A or 1040)
Department of the Treasury
Internal Revenue Service (99) | **Earned Income Credit**
(Qualifying Child Information)
▶ Attach to Form 1040A or 1040.
▶ See instructions on back. | OMB No. 1545-0074
19**95**
Attachment Sequence No. **43** |

| Name(s) shown on return | Your social security number |

Before You Begin . . .

- Answer the questions on page 47 of the Form 1040A instructions or page 27 of the Form 1040 instructions to see if you can take this credit.
- If you can take the credit, fill in the worksheet on page 48 (1040A) or page 28 (1040) to figure your credit. **But if you want the IRS to figure it for you, see page 42 (1040A) or page 35 (1040).**

Then, you **must** complete and attach Schedule EIC only if you have a qualifying child (see boxes on back).

Information About Your Qualifying Child or Children

If you have more than two qualifying children, you only have to list two to get the maximum credit.

Caution: If you don't attach Schedule EIC and fill in all the lines that apply, it will take us longer to process your return and issue your refund.	**(a) Child 1**	**(b) Child 2**
	First name Last name	First name Last name
1 Child's name		
2 Child's year of birth	19___	19___
3 If the child was born **before 1977** AND—		
a was **under age 24** at the end of 1995 **and** a student, check the "Yes" box, **OR**	☐ Yes	☐ Yes
b was permanently and totally disabled (see back), check the "Yes" box	☐ Yes	☐ Yes
4 Enter the child's social security number. If born in 1995, see instructions on back		
5 Child's relationship to you (for example, son, grandchild, etc.) .		
6 Number of months child lived with you in the United States in 1995	months	months

TIP: Do you want the earned income credit added to your take-home pay in 1996? To see if you qualify, get **Form W-5** from your employer or by calling the IRS at 1-800-TAX-FORM (1-800-829-3676).

5/E5AAA

For Paperwork Reduction Act Notice, see Form 1040A or 1040 instructions.   Cat. No. 13339M   **Schedule EIC (Form 1040A or 1040) 1995**

1995 Earned Income Credit (EIC) Table

Caution: This is **not** a tax table.

To find your credit: First, read down the "At least — But less than" columns and find the line that includes the amount you entered on line 6 or line 8 of the **Earned Income Credit Worksheet** on page 28. Next, read across to the column that includes the number of qualifying children you have. Then, enter the credit from that column on line 7 or line 9 of that worksheet, whichever applies.

If the amount on line 6 or line 8 of the worksheet on page 28 is—		And you have—			If the amount on line 6 or line 8 of the worksheet on page 28 is—		And you have—			If the amount on line 6 or line 8 of the worksheet on page 28 is—		And you have—			If the amount on line 6 or line 8 of the worksheet on page 28 is—		And you have—		
At least	But less than	No children	One child	Two children	At least	But less than	No children	One child	Two children	At least	But less than	No children	One child	Two children	At least	But less than	No children	One child	Two children
		Your credit is—					Your credit is—					Your credit is—					Your credit is—		
$1	$50	$2	$9	$9	3,000	3,050	231	1,029	1,089	6,000	6,050	245	2,049	2,169	9,000	9,050	16	2,094	3,110
50	100	6	26	27	3,050	3,100	235	1,046	1,107	6,050	6,100	241	2,066	2,187	9,050	9,100	12	2,094	3,110
100	150	10	43	45	3,100	3,150	239	1,063	1,125	6,100	6,150	238	2,083	2,205	9,100	9,150	8	2,094	3,110
150	200	13	60	63	3,150	3,200	243	1,080	1,143	6,150	6,200	234	2,094	2,223	9,150	9,200	4	2,094	3,110
200	250	17	77	81	3,200	3,250	247	1,097	1,161	6,200	6,250	230	2,094	2,241	9,200	9,250	*	2,094	3,110
250	300	21	94	99	3,250	3,300	251	1,114	1,179	6,250	6,300	226	2,094	2,259	9,250	11,300	0	2,094	3,110
300	350	25	111	117	3,300	3,350	254	1,131	1,197	6,300	6,350	222	2,094	2,277	11,300	11,350	0	2,089	3,103
350	400	29	128	135	3,350	3,400	258	1,148	1,215	6,350	6,400	218	2,094	2,295	11,350	11,400	0	2,081	3,093
400	450	33	145	153	3,400	3,450	262	1,165	1,233	6,400	6,450	215	2,094	2,313	11,400	11,450	0	2,073	3,083
450	500	36	162	171	3,450	3,500	266	1,182	1,251	6,450	6,500	211	2,094	2,331	11,450	11,500	0	2,065	3,073
500	550	40	179	189	3,500	3,550	270	1,199	1,269	6,500	6,550	207	2,094	2,349	11,500	11,550	0	2,057	3,063
550	600	44	196	207	3,550	3,600	273	1,216	1,287	6,550	6,600	203	2,094	2,367	11,550	11,600	0	2,049	3,053
600	650	48	213	225	3,600	3,650	277	1,233	1,305	6,600	6,650	199	2,094	2,385	11,600	11,650	0	2,041	3,043
650	700	52	230	243	3,650	3,700	281	1,250	1,323	6,650	6,700	195	2,094	2,403	11,650	11,700	0	2,033	3,033
700	750	55	247	261	3,700	3,750	285	1,267	1,341	6,700	6,750	192	2,094	2,421	11,700	11,750	0	2,025	3,022
750	800	59	264	279	3,750	3,800	289	1,284	1,359	6,750	6,800	188	2,094	2,439	11,750	11,800	0	2,017	3,012
800	850	63	281	297	3,800	3,850	293	1,301	1,377	6,800	6,850	184	2,094	2,457	11,800	11,850	0	2,009	3,002
850	900	67	298	315	3,850	3,900	296	1,318	1,395	6,850	6,900	180	2,094	2,475	11,850	11,900	0	2,001	2,992
900	950	71	315	333	3,900	3,950	300	1,335	1,413	6,900	6,950	176	2,094	2,493	11,900	11,950	0	1,993	2,982
950	1,000	75	332	351	3,950	4,000	304	1,352	1,431	6,950	7,000	173	2,094	2,511	11,950	12,000	0	1,985	2,972
1,000	1,050	78	349	369	4,000	4,050	308	1,369	1,449	7,000	7,050	169	2,094	2,529	12,000	12,050	0	1,977	2,962
1,050	1,100	82	366	387	4,050	4,100	312	1,386	1,467	7,050	7,100	165	2,094	2,547	12,050	12,100	0	1,969	2,952
1,100	1,150	86	383	405	4,100	4,150	314	1,403	1,485	7,100	7,150	161	2,094	2,565	12,100	12,150	0	1,961	2,942
1,150	1,200	90	400	423	4,150	4,200	314	1,420	1,503	7,150	7,200	157	2,094	2,583	12,150	12,200	0	1,953	2,931
1,200	1,250	94	417	441	4,200	4,250	314	1,437	1,521	7,200	7,250	153	2,094	2,601	12,200	12,250	0	1,945	2,921
1,250	1,300	98	434	459	4,250	4,300	314	1,454	1,539	7,250	7,300	150	2,094	2,619	12,250	12,300	0	1,937	2,911
1,300	1,350	101	451	477	4,300	4,350	314	1,471	1,557	7,300	7,350	146	2,094	2,637	12,300	12,350	0	1,929	2,901
1,350	1,400	105	468	495	4,350	4,400	314	1,488	1,575	7,350	7,400	142	2,094	2,655	12,350	12,400	0	1,921	2,891
1,400	1,450	109	485	513	4,400	4,450	314	1,505	1,593	7,400	7,450	138	2,094	2,673	12,400	12,450	0	1,913	2,881
1,450	1,500	113	502	531	4,450	4,500	314	1,522	1,611	7,450	7,500	134	2,094	2,691	12,450	12,500	0	1,905	2,871
1,500	1,550	117	519	549	4,500	4,550	314	1,539	1,629	7,500	7,550	130	2,094	2,709	12,500	12,550	0	1,897	2,861
1,550	1,600	120	536	567	4,550	4,600	314	1,556	1,647	7,550	7,600	127	2,094	2,727	12,550	12,600	0	1,889	2,851
1,600	1,650	124	553	585	4,600	4,650	314	1,573	1,665	7,600	7,650	123	2,094	2,745	12,600	12,650	0	1,881	2,840
1,650	1,700	128	570	603	4,650	4,700	314	1,590	1,683	7,650	7,700	119	2,094	2,763	12,650	12,700	0	1,873	2,830
1,700	1,750	132	587	621	4,700	4,750	314	1,607	1,701	7,700	7,750	115	2,094	2,781	12,700	12,750	0	1,865	2,820
1,750	1,800	136	604	639	4,750	4,800	314	1,624	1,719	7,750	7,800	111	2,094	2,799	12,750	12,800	0	1,857	2,810
1,800	1,850	140	621	657	4,800	4,850	314	1,641	1,737	7,800	7,850	107	2,094	2,817	12,800	12,850	0	1,849	2,800
1,850	1,900	143	638	675	4,850	4,900	314	1,658	1,755	7,850	7,900	104	2,094	2,835	12,850	12,900	0	1,841	2,790
1,900	1,950	147	655	693	4,900	4,950	314	1,675	1,773	7,900	7,950	100	2,094	2,853	12,900	12,950	0	1,833	2,780
1,950	2,000	151	672	711	4,950	5,000	314	1,692	1,791	7,950	8,000	96	2,094	2,871	12,950	13,000	0	1,825	2,770
2,000	2,050	155	689	729	5,000	5,050	314	1,709	1,809	8,000	8,050	92	2,094	2,889	13,000	13,050	0	1,817	2,760
2,050	2,100	159	706	747	5,050	5,100	314	1,726	1,827	8,050	8,100	88	2,094	2,907	13,050	13,100	0	1,809	2,749
2,100	2,150	163	723	765	5,100	5,150	314	1,743	1,845	8,100	8,150	85	2,094	2,925	13,100	13,150	0	1,801	2,739
2,150	2,200	166	740	783	5,150	5,200	310	1,760	1,863	8,150	8,200	81	2,094	2,943	13,150	13,200	0	1,793	2,729
2,200	2,250	170	757	801	5,200	5,250	306	1,777	1,881	8,200	8,250	77	2,094	2,961	13,200	13,250	0	1,785	2,719
2,250	2,300	174	774	819	5,250	5,300	303	1,794	1,899	8,250	8,300	73	2,094	2,979	13,250	13,300	0	1,777	2,709
2,300	2,350	178	791	837	5,300	5,350	299	1,811	1,917	8,300	8,350	69	2,094	2,997	13,300	13,350	0	1,769	2,699
2,350	2,400	182	808	855	5,350	5,400	295	1,828	1,935	8,350	8,400	65	2,094	3,015	13,350	13,400	0	1,761	2,689
2,400	2,450	186	825	873	5,400	5,450	291	1,845	1,953	8,400	8,450	62	2,094	3,033	13,400	13,450	0	1,753	2,679
2,450	2,500	189	842	891	5,450	5,500	287	1,862	1,971	8,450	8,500	58	2,094	3,051	13,450	13,500	0	1,745	2,669
2,500	2,550	193	859	909	5,500	5,550	283	1,879	1,989	8,500	8,550	54	2,094	3,069	13,500	13,550	0	1,737	2,658
2,550	2,600	197	876	927	5,550	5,600	280	1,896	2,007	8,550	8,600	50	2,094	3,110	13,550	13,600	0	1,729	2,648
2,600	2,650	201	893	945	5,600	5,650	276	1,913	2,025	8,600	8,650	46	2,094	3,110					
2,650	2,700	205	910	963	5,650	5,700	272	1,930	2,043	8,650	8,700	42	2,094	3,110					
2,700	2,750	208	927	981	5,700	5,750	268	1,947	2,061	8,700	8,750	39	2,094	3,110					
2,750	2,800	212	944	999	5,750	5,800	264	1,964	2,079	8,750	8,800	35	2,094	3,110					
2,800	2,850	216	961	1,017	5,800	5,850	260	1,981	2,097	8,800	8,850	31	2,094	3,110					
2,850	2,900	220	978	1,035	5,850	5,900	257	1,998	2,115	8,850	8,900	27	2,094	3,110					
2,900	2,950	224	995	1,053	5,900	5,950	253	2,015	2,133	8,900	8,950	23	2,094	3,110					
2,950	3,000	228	1,012	1,071	5,950	6,000	249	2,032	2,151	8,950	9,000	20	2,094	3,110					

* If the amount on line 6 or line 8 of the worksheet is at least $9,200 **but** less than $9,230, your credit is $1. Otherwise, you **cannot** take the credit.

1995 Earned Income Credit (EIC) Table *Continued*

At least	But less than	No children	One child	Two children
13,600	13,650	0	1,721	2,638
13,650	13,700	0	1,713	2,628
13,700	13,750	0	1,705	2,618
13,750	13,800	0	1,697	2,608
13,800	13,850	0	1,689	2,598
13,850	13,900	0	1,681	2,588
13,900	13,950	0	1,673	2,578
13,950	14,000	0	1,665	2,567
14,000	14,050	0	1,657	2,557
14,050	14,100	0	1,649	2,547
14,100	14,150	0	1,641	2,537
14,150	14,200	0	1,633	2,527
14,200	14,250	0	1,625	2,517
14,250	14,300	0	1,617	2,507
14,300	14,350	0	1,609	2,497
14,350	14,400	0	1,601	2,487
14,400	14,450	0	1,593	2,477
14,450	14,500	0	1,585	2,466
14,500	14,550	0	1,577	2,456
14,550	14,600	0	1,569	2,446
14,600	14,650	0	1,561	2,436
14,650	14,700	0	1,553	2,426
14,700	14,750	0	1,545	2,416
14,750	14,800	0	1,537	2,406
14,800	14,850	0	1,530	2,396
14,850	14,900	0	1,522	2,386
14,900	14,950	0	1,514	2,375
14,950	15,000	0	1,506	2,365
15,000	15,050	0	1,498	2,355
15,050	15,100	0	1,490	2,345
15,100	15,150	0	1,482	2,335
15,150	15,200	0	1,474	2,325
15,200	15,250	0	1,466	2,315
15,250	15,300	0	1,458	2,305
15,300	15,350	0	1,450	2,295
15,350	15,400	0	1,442	2,284
15,400	15,450	0	1,434	2,274
15,450	15,500	0	1,426	2,264
15,500	15,550	0	1,418	2,254
15,550	15,600	0	1,410	2,244
15,600	15,650	0	1,402	2,234
15,650	15,700	0	1,394	2,224
15,700	15,750	0	1,386	2,214
15,750	15,800	0	1,378	2,204
15,800	15,850	0	1,370	2,193
15,850	15,900	0	1,362	2,183
15,900	15,950	0	1,354	2,173
15,950	16,000	0	1,346	2,163
16,000	16,050	0	1,338	2,153
16,050	16,100	0	1,330	2,143
16,100	16,150	0	1,322	2,133
16,150	16,200	0	1,314	2,123
16,200	16,250	0	1,306	2,113
16,250	16,300	0	1,298	2,102
16,300	16,350	0	1,290	2,092
16,350	16,400	0	1,282	2,082
16,400	16,450	0	1,274	2,072
16,450	16,500	0	1,266	2,062
16,500	16,550	0	1,258	2,052
16,550	16,600	0	1,250	2,042
16,600	16,650	0	1,242	2,032
16,650	16,700	0	1,234	2,022
16,700	16,750	0	1,226	2,011
16,750	16,800	0	1,218	2,001
16,800	16,850	0	1,210	1,991
16,850	16,900	0	1,202	1,981
16,900	16,950	0	1,194	1,971
16,950	17,000	0	1,186	1,961

At least	But less than	No children	One child	Two children
17,000	17,050	0	1,178	1,951
17,050	17,100	0	1,170	1,941
17,100	17,150	0	1,162	1,931
17,150	17,200	0	1,154	1,920
17,200	17,250	0	1,146	1,910
17,250	17,300	0	1,138	1,900
17,300	17,350	0	1,130	1,890
17,350	17,400	0	1,122	1,880
17,400	17,450	0	1,114	1,870
17,450	17,500	0	1,106	1,860
17,500	17,550	0	1,098	1,850
17,550	17,600	0	1,090	1,840
17,600	17,650	0	1,082	1,829
17,650	17,700	0	1,074	1,819
17,700	17,750	0	1,066	1,809
17,750	17,800	0	1,058	1,799
17,800	17,850	0	1,050	1,789
17,850	17,900	0	1,042	1,779
17,900	17,950	0	1,034	1,769
17,950	18,000	0	1,026	1,759
18,000	18,050	0	1,018	1,749
18,050	18,100	0	1,010	1,738
18,100	18,150	0	1,002	1,728
18,150	18,200	0	994	1,718
18,200	18,250	0	986	1,708
18,250	18,300	0	978	1,698
18,300	18,350	0	970	1,688
18,350	18,400	0	962	1,678
18,400	18,450	0	954	1,668
18,450	18,500	0	946	1,658
18,500	18,550	0	938	1,647
18,550	18,600	0	930	1,637
18,600	18,650	0	922	1,627
18,650	18,700	0	914	1,617
18,700	18,750	0	906	1,607
18,750	18,800	0	898	1,597
18,800	18,850	0	890	1,587
18,850	18,900	0	882	1,577
18,900	18,950	0	874	1,567
18,950	19,000	0	866	1,556
19,000	19,050	0	858	1,546
19,050	19,100	0	850	1,536
19,100	19,150	0	842	1,526
19,150	19,200	0	834	1,516
19,200	19,250	0	826	1,506
19,250	19,300	0	818	1,496
19,300	19,350	0	810	1,486
19,350	19,400	0	802	1,476
19,400	19,450	0	794	1,466
19,450	19,500	0	786	1,455
19,500	19,550	0	778	1,445
19,550	19,600	0	770	1,435
19,600	19,650	0	762	1,425
19,650	19,700	0	754	1,415
19,700	19,750	0	746	1,405
19,750	19,800	0	738	1,395
19,800	19,850	0	731	1,385
19,850	19,900	0	723	1,375
19,900	19,950	0	715	1,364
19,950	20,000	0	707	1,354
20,000	20,050	0	699	1,344
20,050	20,100	0	691	1,334
20,100	20,150	0	683	1,324
20,150	20,200	0	675	1,314
20,200	20,250	0	667	1,304
20,250	20,300	0	659	1,294
20,300	20,350	0	651	1,284
20,350	20,400	0	643	1,273

At least	But less than	No children	One child	Two children
20,400	20,450	0	635	1,263
20,450	20,500	0	627	1,253
20,500	20,550	0	619	1,243
20,550	20,600	0	611	1,233
20,600	20,650	0	603	1,223
20,650	20,700	0	595	1,213
20,700	20,750	0	587	1,203
20,750	20,800	0	579	1,193
20,800	20,850	0	571	1,182
20,850	20,900	0	563	1,172
20,900	20,950	0	555	1,162
20,950	21,000	0	547	1,152
21,000	21,050	0	539	1,142
21,050	21,100	0	531	1,132
21,100	21,150	0	523	1,122
21,150	21,200	0	515	1,112
21,200	21,250	0	507	1,102
21,250	21,300	0	499	1,091
21,300	21,350	0	491	1,081
21,350	21,400	0	483	1,071
21,400	21,450	0	475	1,061
21,450	21,500	0	467	1,051
21,500	21,550	0	459	1,041
21,550	21,600	0	451	1,031
21,600	21,650	0	443	1,021
21,650	21,700	0	435	1,011
21,700	21,750	0	427	1,000
21,750	21,800	0	419	990
21,800	21,850	0	411	980
21,850	21,900	0	403	970
21,900	21,950	0	395	960
21,950	22,000	0	387	950
22,000	22,050	0	379	940
22,050	22,100	0	371	930
22,100	22,150	0	363	920
22,150	22,200	0	355	909
22,200	22,250	0	347	899
22,250	22,300	0	339	889
22,300	22,350	0	331	879
22,350	22,400	0	323	869
22,400	22,450	0	315	859
22,450	22,500	0	307	849
22,500	22,550	0	299	839
22,550	22,600	0	291	829
22,600	22,650	0	283	818
22,650	22,700	0	275	808
22,700	22,750	0	267	798
22,750	22,800	0	259	788
22,800	22,850	0	251	778
22,850	22,900	0	243	768
22,900	22,950	0	235	758
22,950	23,000	0	227	748
23,000	23,050	0	219	738
23,050	23,100	0	211	727
23,100	23,150	0	203	717
23,150	23,200	0	195	707
23,200	23,250	0	187	697
23,250	23,300	0	179	687
23,300	23,350	0	171	677
23,350	23,400	0	163	667
23,400	23,450	0	155	657
23,450	23,500	0	147	647
23,500	23,550	0	139	636
23,550	23,600	0	131	626
23,600	23,650	0	123	616
23,650	23,700	0	115	606
23,700	23,750	0	107	596
23,750	23,800	0	99	586

At least	But less than	No children	One child	Two children
23,800	23,850	0	91	576
23,850	23,900	0	83	566
23,900	23,950	0	75	556
23,950	24,000	0	67	545
24,000	24,050	0	59	535
24,050	24,100	0	51	525
24,100	24,150	0	43	515
24,150	24,200	0	35	505
24,200	24,250	0	27	495
24,250	24,300	0	19	485
24,300	24,350	0	11	475
24,350	24,400	0	*	465
24,400	24,450	0	0	455
24,450	24,500	0	0	444
24,500	24,550	0	0	434
24,550	24,600	0	0	424
24,600	24,650	0	0	414
24,650	24,700	0	0	404
24,700	24,750	0	0	394
24,750	24,800	0	0	384
24,800	24,850	0	0	374
24,850	24,900	0	0	364
24,900	24,950	0	0	353
24,950	25,000	0	0	343
25,000	25,050	0	0	333
25,050	25,100	0	0	323
25,100	25,150	0	0	313
25,150	25,200	0	0	303
25,200	25,250	0	0	293
25,250	25,300	0	0	283
25,300	25,350	0	0	273
25,350	25,400	0	0	262
25,400	25,450	0	0	252
25,450	25,500	0	0	242
25,500	25,550	0	0	232
25,550	25,600	0	0	222
25,600	25,650	0	0	212
25,650	25,700	0	0	202
25,700	25,750	0	0	192
25,750	25,800	0	0	182
25,800	25,850	0	0	171
25,850	25,900	0	0	161
25,900	25,950	0	0	151
25,950	26,000	0	0	141
26,000	26,050	0	0	131
26,050	26,100	0	0	121
26,100	26,150	0	0	111
26,150	26,200	0	0	101
26,200	26,250	0	0	91
26,250	26,300	0	0	80
26,300	26,350	0	0	70
26,350	26,400	0	0	60
26,400	26,450	0	0	50
26,450	26,500	0	0	40
26,500	26,550	0	0	30
26,550	26,600	0	0	20
26,600	26,650	0	0	10
26,650	26,673	0	0	2
26,673 or more		0	0	0

* If the amount on line 6 or line 8 of the worksheet is at least $24,350 **but** less than $24,396, your credit is $4. Otherwise, you **cannot** take the credit.

SCHEDULE F
(Form 1040)

Department of the Treasury
Internal Revenue Service   (99)

Profit or Loss From Farming

▶ Attach to Form 1040, Form 1041, or Form 1065.

▶ See Instructions for Schedule F (Form 1040).

OMB No. 1545-0074

1995

Attachment
Sequence No. **14**

Name of proprietor	Social security number (SSN)

A Principal product. Describe in one or two words your principal crop or activity for the current tax year.

B Enter principal agricultural activity code (from page 2) ▶

D Employer ID number (EIN), if any

C Accounting method: **(1)** ☐ Cash   **(2)** ☐ Accrual

E Did you "materially participate" in the operation of this business during 1995? If "No," see page F-2 for limit on passive losses.   ☐ Yes   ☐ No

Part I Farm Income—Cash Method. Complete Parts I and II (Accrual method taxpayers complete Parts II and III, and line 11 of Part I.)
Do not include sales of livestock held for draft, breeding, sport, or dairy purposes; report these sales on Form 4797.

1	Sales of livestock and other items you bought for resale	**1**	
2	Cost or other basis of livestock and other items reported on line 1	**2**	
3	Subtract line 2 from line 1		**3**
4	Sales of livestock, produce, grains, and other products you raised		**4**
5a	Total cooperative distributions (Form(s) 1099-PATR) **5a**	**5b** Taxable amount	**5b**
6a	Agricultural program payments (see page F-2) **6a**	**6b** Taxable amount	**6b**
7	Commodity Credit Corporation (CCC) loans (see page F-2):		
a	CCC loans reported under election		**7a**
b	CCC loans forfeited or repaid with certificates **7b**	**7c** Taxable amount	**7c**
8	Crop insurance proceeds and certain disaster payments (see page F-2):		
a	Amount received in 1995 **8a**	**8b** Taxable amount	**8b**
c	If election to defer to 1996 is attached, check here ▶ ☐	**8d** Amount deferred from 1994	**8d**
9	Custom hire (machine work) income		**9**
10	Other income, including Federal and state gasoline or fuel tax credit or refund (see page F-3)		**10**
11	**Gross income.** Add amounts in the right column for lines 3 through 10. If accrual method taxpayer, enter the amount from page 2, line 51. ▶		**11**

Part II Farm Expenses—Cash and Accrual Method. Do not include personal or living expenses such as taxes, insurance, repairs, etc., on your home.

12	Car and truck expenses (see page F-3—also attach **Form 4562**)	**12**		**25**	Pension and profit-sharing plans	**25**	
13	Chemicals	**13**		**26**	Rent or lease (see page F-4):		
14	Conservation expenses. Attach **Form 8645.**	**14**		**a**	Vehicles, machinery, and equipment	**26a**	
15	Custom hire (machine work)	**15**		**b**	Other (land, animals, etc.)	**26b**	
16	Depreciation and section 179 expense deduction not claimed elsewhere (see page F-4)	**16**		**27**	Repairs and maintenance	**27**	
				28	Seeds and plants purchased	**28**	
				29	Storage and warehousing	**29**	
17	Employee benefit programs other than on line 25	**17**		**30**	Supplies purchased	**30**	
18	Feed purchased	**18**		**31**	Taxes	**31**	
19	Fertilizers and lime	**19**		**32**	Utilities	**32**	
20	Freight and trucking	**20**		**33**	Veterinary, breeding, and medicine	**33**	
21	Gasoline, fuel, and oil	**21**		**34**	Other expenses (specify):		
22	Insurance (other than health)	**22**		**a**		**34a**	
23	Interest:			**b**		**34b**	
a	Mortgage (paid to banks, etc.)	**23a**		**c**		**34c**	
b	Other	**23b**		**d**		**34d**	
24	Labor hired (less employment credits)	**24**		**e**		**34e**	
				f		**34f**	

35	**Total expenses.** Add lines 12 through 34f ▶	**35**	
36	**Net farm profit or (loss).** Subtract line 35 from line 11. If a profit, enter on **Form 1040, line 18,** and ALSO on **Schedule SE, line 1.** If a loss, you MUST go on to line 37 (estates, trusts, and partnerships, see page F-5)	**36**	
37	If you have a loss, you MUST check the box that describes your investment in this activity (see page F-5). If you checked 37a, enter the loss on **Form 1040, line 18,** and ALSO on **Schedule SE, line 1.** If you checked 37b, you MUST attach **Form 6198.**	**37a** ☐ All investment is at risk. **37b** ☐ Some investment is not at risk.	

For Paperwork Reduction Act Notice, see Form 1040 instructions.   Cat. No. 11346H   **Schedule F (Form 1040) 1995**

Part III   **Farm Income—Accrual Method** (see page F-5)

Do not include sales of livestock held for draft, breeding, sport, or dairy purposes; report these sales on Form 4797 and do not include this livestock on line 46 below.

38	Sales of livestock, produce, grains, and other products during the year	**38**
39a	Total cooperative distributions (Form(s) 1099-PATR) [39a _____]	39b Taxable amount	**39b**
40a	Agricultural program payments . . . . . [40a _____]	40b Taxable amount	**40b**
41	Commodity Credit Corporation (CCC) loans:	
a	CCC loans reported under election	**41a**
b	CCC loans forfeited or repaid with certificates [41b _____]	41c Taxable amount	**41c**
42	Crop insurance proceeds	**42**
43	Custom hire (machine work) income	**43**
44	Other income, including Federal and state gasoline or fuel tax credit or refund	**44**
45	Add amounts in the right column for lines 38 through 44	**45**
46	Inventory of livestock, produce, grains, and other products at beginning of the year.	**46**
47	Cost of livestock, produce, grains, and other products purchased during the year.	**47**
48	Add lines 46 and 47	**48**
49	Inventory of livestock, produce, grains, and other products at end of year	**49**
50	Cost of livestock, produce, grains, and other products sold. Subtract line 49 from line 48*	**50**
51	**Gross income.** Subtract line 50 from line 45. Enter the result here and on page 1, line 11 . . . . . ▶	**51**

*If you use the unit-livestock-price method or the farm-price method of valuing inventory and the amount on line 49 is larger than the amount on line 48, subtract line 48 from line 49. Enter the result on line 50. Add lines 45 and 50. Enter the total on line 51.

Part IV   **Principal Agricultural Activity Codes**

Caution: *File **Schedule C** (Form 1040), Profit or Loss From Business, or **Schedule C-EZ** (Form 1040), Net Profit From Business, instead of Schedule F if:*

• *Your principal source of income is from providing agricultural services such as soil preparation, veterinary, farm labor, horticultural, or management for a fee or on a contract basis, or*

• *You are engaged in the business of breeding, raising, and caring for dogs, cats, or other pet animals.*

Select one of the following codes and write the 3-digit number on page 1, line B:

120 **Field crop,** including grains and nongrains such as cotton, peanuts, feed corn, wheat, tobacco, Irish potatoes, etc.

160 **Vegetables and melons,** garden-type vegetables and melons, such as sweet corn, tomatoes, squash, etc.

170 **Fruit and tree nuts,** including grapes, berries, olives, etc.

180 **Ornamental floriculture and nursery products**

185 **Food crops grown under cover,** including hydroponic crops

211 **Beefcattle feedlots**

212 **Beefcattle,** except feedlots

215 **Hogs, sheep, and goats**

240 **Dairy**

250 **Poultry and eggs,** including chickens, ducks, pigeons, quail, etc.

260 **General livestock,** not specializing in any one livestock category

270 **Animal specialty,** including bees, fur-bearing animals, horses, snakes, etc.

280 **Animal aquaculture,** including fish, shellfish, mollusks, frogs, etc., produced within confined space

290 **Forest products,** including forest nurseries and seed gathering, extraction of pine gum, and gathering of forest products

300 **Agricultural production,** not specified

Printed on recycled paper

SCHEDULE H
(Form 1040)

Department of the Treasury
Internal Revenue Service

Household Employment Taxes

(For Social Security, Medicare, Withheld Income, and Federal Unemployment (FUTA) Taxes)

▶ **Attach to Form 1040, 1040A, 1040NR, 1040NR-EZ, 1040-SS, 1040-T, or 1041.**

▶ **See separate instructions.**

OMB No. 1545-0074

1995

Attachment
Sequence No. **44**

Name of employer (as shown on return)

Social security number

Employer identification number

A Did you pay **any one** household employee cash wages of $1,000 or more in 1995? (If any household employee was your spouse, your child under age 21, your parent, or anyone under age 18, see the line A instructions on page 3 before you answer this question.)

☐ **Yes.** Skip questions B and C and go to Part I.
☐ **No.** Go to question B.

B Did you withhold Federal income tax during 1995 for any household employee?

☐ **Yes.** Skip question C and go to Part I.
☐ **No.** Go to question C.

C Did you pay **total** cash wages of $1,000 or more in **any** calendar **quarter** of 1994 or 1995 to household employees? (**Do not** count cash wages paid in 1994 or 1995 to your spouse, your child under age 21, or your parent.)

☐ **No.** **Stop.** Do not file this schedule.
☐ **Yes.** Skip Part I and go to Part II on the back.

Part I   **Social Security, Medicare, and Income Taxes**

1	Total cash wages subject to social security taxes (see page 4) . .	**1**	
2	Social security taxes. Multiply line 1 by 12.4% (.124)	**2**	
3	Total cash wages subject to Medicare taxes (see page 4)	**3**	
4	Medicare taxes. Multiply line 3 by 2.9% (.029)	**4**	
5	Federal income tax withheld, if any	**5**	
6	Add lines 2, 4, and 5	**6**	
7	Advance earned income credit (EIC) payments, if any	**7**	
8	**Total social security, Medicare, and income taxes.** Subtract line 7 from line 6	**8**	

9 Did you pay **total** cash wages of $1,000 or more in **any** calendar **quarter** of 1994 or 1995 to household employees? (**Do not** count cash wages paid in 1994 or 1995 to your spouse, your child under age 21, or your parent.)

☐ **No.** **Stop.** Take the amount from line 8 above and enter it on Form 1040, line 53, or Form 1040A, line 27. If you are not required to file Form 1040 or 1040A, see the line 9 instructions on page 4.

☐ **Yes.** Go to Part II on the back.

For Paperwork Reduction Act Notice, see Form 1040 instructions.   Cat. No. 12187K   **Schedule H (Form 1040) 1995**

Schedule H (Form 1040) 1995   Page **2**

Part II	**Federal Unemployment (FUTA) Tax**		

		Yes	No
10	Did you pay unemployment contributions to only one state?		
11	Did you pay all state unemployment contributions for 1995 by April 15, 1996? Fiscal year filers, see page 4 . .		
12	Were all wages that are taxable for FUTA tax also taxable for your state's unemployment tax?		

Next: If you answered **"Yes"** to **all** of the questions above, complete Section A.

If you answered **"No"** to **any** of the questions above, skip Section A and complete Section B.

Section A

13	Name of the state where you paid unemployment contributions ▶	
14	State reporting number as shown on state unemployment tax return ▶	
15	Contributions paid to your state unemployment fund (see page 5) .	**15**
16	Total cash wages subject to FUTA tax (see page 5)	**16**
17	**FUTA tax.** Multiply line 16 by .008. Enter the result here, skip Section B, and go to Part III . .	**17**

Section B

18 Complete all columns below that apply (if you need more space, see page 5):

(a) Name of state	(b) State reporting number as shown on state unemployment tax return	(c) Taxable wages (as defined in state act)	(d) State experience rate period		(e) State experience rate	(f) Multiply col. (c) by .054	(g) Multiply col. (c) by col. (e)	(h) Subtract col. (g) from col. (f). If zero or less, enter -0-.	(i) Contributions paid to state unemployment fund
			From	To					

19	Totals		**19**		
20	Add columns (h) and (i) of line 19	**20**			
21	Total cash wages subject to FUTA tax (see the line 16 instructions on page 5)	**21**			
22	Multiply line 21 by 6.2% (.062)	**22**			
23	Multiply line 21 by 5.4% (.054)	**23**			
24	Enter the **smaller** of line 20 or line 23	**24**			
25	**FUTA tax.** Subtract line 24 from line 22. Enter the result here and go to Part III	**25**			

Part III	**Total Household Employment Taxes**		

26	Enter the amount from line 8	**26**	
27	Add line 17 (or line 25) and line 26	**27**	
28	Are you required to file Form 1040 or 1040A?		

☐ **Yes. Stop.** Take the amount from line 27 above and enter it on Form 1040, line 53, or Form 1040A, line 27. **Do not** complete Part IV below.

☐ **No.** You may have to complete Part IV. See page 5 for details.

Part IV	**Address and Signature**—Complete this part **only** if required. See the line 28 instructions on page 5.

Address (number and street) or P.O. box if mail is not delivered to street address	Apt., room, or suite no.

City, town or post office, state, and ZIP code

Under penalties of perjury, I declare that I have examined this schedule, including accompanying statements, and to the best of my knowledge and belief, it is true, correct, and complete. No part of any payment made to a state unemployment fund claimed as a credit was, or is to be, deducted from the payments to employees.

▶ _____   ▶ _____

Employer's signature   Date

✪ *Printed on recycled paper*

Schedule R
(Form 1040)

Department of the Treasury
Internal Revenue Service (99)

Credit for the Elderly or the Disabled

► **Attach to Form 1040.**   ► **See separate instructions for Schedule R.**

OMB No. 1545-0074

1995

Attachment
Sequence No. **16**

Name(s) shown on Form 1040

Your social security number

You may be able to take this credit and reduce your tax if by the end of 1995:

● You were age 65 or older, **OR** ● You were under age 65, you retired on **permanent and total** disability, and you received taxable disability income.

But you must also meet other tests. See the separate instructions for Schedule R.

Note: *In most cases, the IRS can figure the credit for you. See page 35 of the Form 1040 instructions.*

Part I   **Check the Box for Your Filing Status and Age**

If your filing status is:	And by the end of 1995:	Check only one box:
Single, Head of household, or Qualifying widow(er) with dependent child	**1** You were 65 or older **1**	☐
	2 You were under 65 and you retired on permanent and total disability . . . **2**	☐
	3 Both spouses were 65 or older **3**	☐
	4 Both spouses were under 65, but only one spouse retired on permanent and total disability **4**	☐
Married filing a joint return	**5** Both spouses were under 65, and both retired on permanent and total disability **5**	☐
	6 One spouse was 65 or older, and the other spouse was under 65 and retired on permanent and total disability **6**	☐
	7 One spouse was 65 or older, and the other spouse was under 65 and **NOT** retired on permanent and total disability **7**	☐
Married filing a separate return	**8** You were 65 or older and you lived apart from your spouse for all of 1995 . . **8**	☐
	9 You were under 65, you retired on permanent and total disability, and you lived apart from your spouse for all of 1995. . . . . **9**	☐

Did you check box 1, 3, 7, or 8?	── Yes ──► Skip Part II and complete Part III on back.
	── No ──► Complete Parts II and III.

Part II   **Statement of Permanent and Total Disability** (Complete **only** if you checked box 2, 4, 5, 6, or 9 above.)

IF: 1 You filed a physician's statement for this disability for 1983 or an earlier year, or you filed a statement for tax years after 1983 and your physician signed line B on the statement, **AND**

    2 Due to your continued disabled condition, you were unable to engage in any substantial gainful activity in 1995, check this box . . . . ► ☐

● If you checked this box, you do not have to file another statement for 1995.
● If you **did not** check this box, have your physician complete the statement below.

Physician's Statement (See instructions at bottom of page 2.)

I certify that _____
Name of disabled person

was permanently and totally disabled on January 1, 1976, or January 1, 1977, **OR** was permanently and totally disabled on the date he or she retired. If retired after 1976, enter the date retired. ► _____

Physician: Sign your name on **either** line A or B below.

A The disability has lasted or can be expected to last continuously for at least a year . . . .

B There is no reasonable probability that the disabled condition will ever improve . . . . .

Physician's signature	Date
Physician's signature	Date

Physician's name	Physician's address

For Paperwork Reduction Act Notice, see Form 1040 instructions.   Cat. No. 11359K   **Schedule R (Form 1040) 1995**

Part III   **Figure Your Credit**

10   If you checked (in Part I):   **Enter:**

Box 1, 2, 4, or 7 . . . . $5,000 ⎫

Box 3, 5, or 6 . . . . $7,500 ⎬ **10**

Box 8 or 9 . . . . $3,750 ⎭

┌─────────────────┐
│ **Did you check** │ ──── **Yes** ───► You **must** complete line 11.
│ **box 2, 4, 5, 6,** │
│ **or 9 in Part I?** │ ──── **No** ───► Enter the amount from line 10 on
└─────────────────┘   line 12 and go to line 13.

11   If you checked:

  • Box 6 in Part I, add $5,000 to the taxable disability income of the   ⎫
    spouse who was under age 65. Enter the total.   │

  • Box 2, 4, or 9 in Part I, enter your taxable disability income.   ⎬ **11**

  • Box 5 in Part I, add your taxable disability income to your spouse's   │
    taxable disability income. Enter the total.   ⎭

  TIP: For more details on what to include on line 11, see the instructions.

12   If you completed line 11, enter the **smaller** of line 10 or line 11; **all others,** enter the amount
        from line 10 . . . .   **12**

13   Enter the following pensions, annuities, or disability income that you
        (and your spouse if filing a joint return) received in 1995.

  a   Nontaxable part of social security benefits, and   ⎫
        Nontaxable part of railroad retirement benefits treated as   ⎬ . . .   **13a**
        social security. See instructions.   ⎭

  b   Nontaxable veterans' pensions, and   ⎫
        Any other pension, annuity, or disability benefit that is   ⎬ . . .   **13b**
        excluded from income under any other provision of law.   │
        See instructions.   ⎭

  c   Add lines 13a and 13b. (Even though these income items are not
        taxable, they **must** be included here to figure your credit.) If you did
        not receive any of the types of nontaxable income listed on line 13a
        or 13b, enter -0- on line 13c **13c**

14   Enter the amount from Form 1040, line 32   **14**

15   If you checked (in Part I):   **Enter:**

Box 1 or 2 . . . . $7,500 ⎫

Box 3, 4, 5, 6, or 7 . . . . $10,000 ⎬   **15**

Box 8 or 9 . . . . $5,000 ⎭

16   Subtract line 15 from line 14. If zero or less,
        enter -0- **16**

17   Enter one-half of line 16 . . . .   **17**

18   Add lines 13c and 17 . . . .   **18**

19   Subtract line 18 from line 12. If zero or less, **stop;** you **cannot** take the credit. Otherwise, go to
        line 20 . . . .   **19**

20   Multiply line 19 by 15% (.15). Enter the result here and on Form 1040, line 42. **Caution:** *If you
        file Schedule C, C-EZ, D, E, or F (Form 1040), your credit may be limited. See the instructions
        for line 20 for the amount of credit you can claim* **20**

Instructions for Physician's Statement

Taxpayer

If you retired after 1976, enter the date
you retired in the space provided in
Part II.

Physician

A person is permanently and totally
disabled if **both** of the following apply:

  1. He or she cannot engage in any
substantial gainful activity because of a
physical or mental condition, and

  2. A physician determines that the
disability has lasted or can be expected
to last continuously for at least a year or
can lead to death.

  Printed on recycled paper

SCHEDULE SE **(Form 1040)** Department of the Treasury Internal Revenue Service (99)	**Self-Employment Tax** ► See Instructions for Schedule SE (Form 1040). ► Attach to Form 1040.	OMB No. 1545-0074 **1995** Attachment Sequence No. **17**

Name of person with **self-employment** income (as shown on Form 1040)	Social security number of person with **self-employment** income ►

Who Must File Schedule SE

You must file Schedule SE if:

- You had net earnings from self-employment from **other than** church employee income (line 4 of Short Schedule SE or line 4c of Long Schedule SE) of $400 or more, **OR**

- You had church employee income of $108.28 or more. Income from services you performed as a minister or a member of a religious order **is not** church employee income. See page SE-1.

Note: *Even if you have a loss or a small amount of income from self-employment, it may be to your benefit to file Schedule SE and use either "optional method" in Part II of Long Schedule SE. See page SE-3.*

Exception. If your only self-employment income was from earnings as a minister, member of a religious order, or Christian Science practitioner **and** you filed Form 4361 and received IRS approval not to be taxed on those earnings, **do not** file Schedule SE. Instead, write "Exempt–Form 4361" on Form 1040, line 47.

May I Use Short Schedule SE or MUST I Use Long Schedule SE?

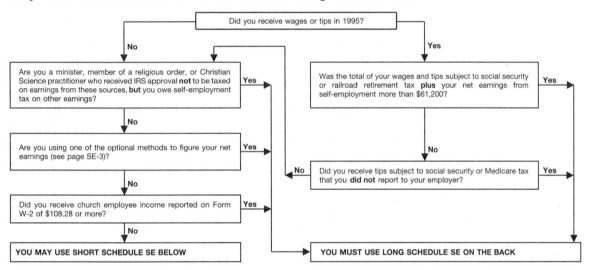

Section A—Short Schedule SE. Caution: *Read above to see if you can use Short Schedule SE.*

1	Net farm profit or (loss) from Schedule F, line 36, and farm partnerships, Schedule K-1 (Form 1065), line 15a	**1**
2	Net profit or (loss) from Schedule C, line 31; Schedule C-EZ, line 3; and Schedule K-1 (Form 1065), line 15a (other than farming). Ministers and members of religious orders see page SE-1 for amounts to report on this line. See page SE-2 for other income to report	**2**
3	Combine lines 1 and 2	**3**
4	**Net earnings from self-employment.** Multiply line 3 by 92.35% (.9235). If less than $400, **do not** file this schedule; you do not owe self-employment tax . . . . ►	**4**
5	**Self-employment tax.** If the amount on line 4 is: • $61,200 or less, multiply line 4 by 15.3% (.153). Enter the result here and on **Form 1040, line 47.** • More than $61,200, multiply line 4 by 2.9% (.029). Then, add $7,588.80 to the result. Enter the total here and on **Form 1040, line 47.**	**5**
6	**Deduction for one-half of self-employment tax.** Multiply line 5 by 50% (.5). Enter the result here and on **Form 1040, line 25** . . . . | **6** |	

For Paperwork Reduction Act Notice, see Form 1040 instructions.   Cat. No. 11358Z   **Schedule SE (Form 1040) 1995**

Name of person with **self-employment** income (as shown on Form 1040)	Social security number of person with **self-employment** income ▶		

Section B—Long Schedule SE

Part I Self-Employment Tax

Note: *If your only income subject to self-employment tax is* **church employee income,** *skip lines 1 through 4b. Enter -0- on line 4c and go to line 5a. Income from services you performed as a minister or a member of a religious order is not church employee income. See page SE-1.*

A If you are a minister, member of a religious order, or Christian Science practitioner **and** you filed Form 4361, but you had $400 or more of **other** net earnings from self-employment, check here and continue with Part I . . . . ▶ ☐

1	Net farm profit or (loss) from Schedule F, line 36, and farm partnerships, Schedule K-1 (Form 1065), line 15a. **Note:** *Skip this line if you use the farm optional method. See page SE-3.* . .	**1**		
2	Net profit or (loss) from Schedule C, line 31; Schedule C-EZ, line 3; and Schedule K-1 (Form 1065), line 15a (other than farming). Ministers and members of religious orders see page SE-1 for amounts to report on this line. See page SE-2 for other income to report. **Note:** *Skip this line if you use the nonfarm optional method. See page SE-3.*	**2**		
3	Combine lines 1 and 2	**3**		
4a	If line 3 is more than zero, multiply line 3 by 92.35% (.9235). Otherwise, enter amount from line 3	**4a**		
b	If you elected one or both of the optional methods, enter the total of lines 15 and 17 here . .	**4b**		
c	Combine lines 4a and 4b. If less than $400, **do not** file this schedule; you do not owe self-employment tax. **Exception.** If less than $400 and you had **church employee income,** enter -0- and continue ▶	**4c**		
5a	Enter your **church employee income** from Form W-2. **Caution:** *See page SE-1 for definition of church employee income* **5a**			
b	Multiply line 5a by 92.35% (.9235). If less than $100, enter -0-	**5b**		
6	**Net earnings from self-employment.** Add lines 4c and 5b	**6**		
7	Maximum amount of combined wages and self-employment earnings subject to social security tax or the 6.2% portion of the 7.65% railroad retirement (tier 1) tax for 1995	**7**	61,200	00
8a	Total social security wages and tips (total of boxes 3 and 7 on Form(s) W-2) and railroad retirement (tier 1) compensation **8a**			
b	Unreported tips subject to social security tax (from Form 4137, line 9) **8b**			
c	Add lines 8a and 8b	**8c**		
9	Subtract line 8c from line 7. If zero or less, enter -0- here and on line 10 and go to line 11 . ▶	**9**		
10	Multiply the **smaller** of line 6 or line 9 by 12.4% (.124)	**10**		
11	Multiply line 6 by 2.9% (.029).	**11**		
12	**Self-employment tax.** Add lines 10 and 11. Enter here and on **Form 1040, line 47**	**12**		
13	**Deduction for one-half of self-employment tax.** Multiply line 12 by 50% (.5). Enter the result here and on **Form 1040, line 25** **13**			

Part II Optional Methods To Figure Net Earnings (See page SE-3.)

Farm Optional Method. You may use this method **only** if:
- Your gross farm income[1] was not more than $2,400, **or**
- Your gross farm income[1] was more than $2,400 and your net farm profits[2] were less than $1,733.

14	Maximum income for optional methods	**14**	1,600	00
15	Enter the **smaller** of: two-thirds (⅔) of gross farm income[1] (not less than zero) **or** $1,600. Also, include this amount on line 4b above	**15**		

Nonfarm Optional Method. You may use this method **only** if:
- Your net nonfarm profits[3] were less than $1,733 and also less than 72.189% of your gross nonfarm income,[4] **and**
- You had net earnings from self-employment of at least $400 in 2 of the prior 3 years.

Caution: *You may use this method no more than five times.*

16	Subtract line 15 from line 14	**16**		
17	Enter the **smaller** of: two-thirds (⅔) of gross nonfarm income[4] (not less than zero) **or** the amount on line 16. Also, include this amount on line 4b above	**17**		

[1]From Schedule F, line 11, and Schedule K-1 (Form 1065), line 15b. [3]From Schedule C, line 31; Schedule C-EZ, line 3; and Schedule K-1 (Form 1065), line 15a.
[2]From Schedule F, line 36, and Schedule K-1 (Form 1065), line 15a. [4]From Schedule C, line 7; Schedule C-EZ, line 1; and Schedule K-1 (Form 1065), line 15c.

✱ *Printed on recycled paper*

Form 1040X
(Rev. October 1995)

Department of the Treasury—Internal Revenue Service

Amended U.S. Individual Income Tax Return

▶ See separate instructions.

OMB No. 1545-0091

This return is for calendar year ▶ 19　, OR fiscal year ended ▶　, 19　.

Please print or type

Your first name and initial	Last name	Your social security number
If a joint return, spouse's first name and initial	Last name	Spouse's social security number
Home address (number and street). If you have a P.O. box, see instructions.	Apt. no.	Telephone number (optional) ( )
City, town or post office, state, and ZIP code. If you have a foreign address, see instructions.		For Paperwork Reduction Act Notice, see page 1 of separate instructions.

A If the name or address shown above is different from that shown on the original return, check here . . . . ▶ ☐

B Has original return been changed or audited by the IRS or have you been notified that it will be? . . . ☐ Yes ☐ No
If notified that it will be, identify the IRS office ▶

C If you are amending your return to include any item (loss, credit, deduction, other tax benefit, or income) relating to a tax shelter required to be registered, attach **Form 8271,** Investor Reporting of Tax Shelter Registration Number, and check here . . . . ▶ ☐

D Filing status claimed. **Note:** *You cannot change from joint to separate returns after the due date has passed.*

On original return ▶ ☐ Single ☐ Married filing joint return ☐ Married filing separate return ☐ Head of household ☐ Qualifying widow(er)
On this return ▶ ☐ Single ☐ Married filing joint return ☐ Married filing separate return ☐ Head of household ☐ Qualifying widow(er)

Income and Deductions (see instructions) USE PART II ON PAGE 2 TO EXPLAIN ANY CHANGES		**A.** As originally reported or as previously adjusted (see instructions)	**B.** Net change— Increase or (Decrease)—explain on page 2	**C.** Correct amount
1 Adjusted gross income (see instructions)	1			
2 Itemized deductions or standard deduction	2			
3 Subtract line 2 from line 1	3			
4 Exemptions. If changing, fill in Parts I and II on page 2 . .	4			
5 Taxable income. Subtract line 4 from line 3	5			
Tax Liability **6** Tax (see instructions). Method used in col. C _____	6			
7 Credits (see instructions)	7			
8 Subtract line 7 from line 6. Enter the result but not less than zero .	8			
9 Other taxes (see instructions)	9			
10 Total tax. Add lines 8 and 9	10			
Payments **11** Federal income tax withheld and excess social security, Medicare, and RRTA taxes withheld. If changing, see instructions	11			
12 Estimated tax payments	12			
13 Earned income credit	13			
14 Credits for Federal tax paid on fuels, regulated investment company, etc.	14			
15 Amount paid with Form 4868, Form 2688, or Form 2350 (applications for extension of time to file) .	15			
16 Amount of tax paid with original return plus additional tax paid after it was filed	16			
17 Total payments. Add lines 11 through 16 in column C	17			

Refund or Amount You Owe

18 Overpayment, if any, as shown on original return or as previously adjusted by the IRS . . .	18	
19 Subtract line 18 from line 17 (see instructions)	19	
20 **AMOUNT YOU OWE.** If line 10, column C, is more than line 19, enter the difference and see instructions .	20	
21 If line 10, column C, is less than line 19, enter the difference	21	
22 Amount of line 21 you want **REFUNDED TO YOU**	22	
23 Amount of line 21 you want **APPLIED TO YOUR 19**　**ESTIMATED TAX** ▏ 23 ▏		

Sign Here
Keep a copy of this return for your records.

Under penalties of perjury, I declare that I have filed an original return and that I have examined this amended return, including accompanying schedules and statements, and to the best of my knowledge and belief, this amended return is true, correct, and complete. Declaration of preparer (other than taxpayer) is based on all information of which the preparer has any knowledge.

▶ _____ _____ ▶ _____ _____
　Your signature　　　　　　 Date　　　　　Spouse's signature. If a joint return, BOTH must sign.　　Date

Paid Preparer's Use Only

Preparer's signature ▶	Date	Check if self-employed ☐	Preparer's social security no.
Firm's name (or yours if self-employed) and address ▶		EIN	
		ZIP code	

Cat. No. 11360L

Form **1040X** (Rev. 10-95)

Form 1040X (Rev. 10-95)   Page **2**

Part I Exemptions. See Form 1040, Form 1040A, or Form 1040-T instructions.	**A.** Number originally reported	**B.** Net change	**C.** Correct number
If you are **not changing your exemptions,** do not complete this part. If claiming **more exemptions,** complete lines 24–30 and, if applicable, line 31. If claiming **fewer exemptions,** complete lines 24–29.			

24	Yourself and spouse	**24**		
	Caution: *If your parents (or someone else) can claim you as a dependent (even if they chose not to), you cannot claim an exemption for yourself.*			
25	Your dependent children who lived with you	**25**		
26	Your dependent children who did not live with you due to divorce or separation	**26**		
27	Other dependents	**27**		
28	Total number of exemptions. Add lines 24 through 27	**28**		

29 Multiply the number of exemptions claimed on line 28 by the amount listed below for the tax year you are amending. Enter the result here and on line 4.

Tax Year	Exemption Amount	But see the instructions if the amount on line 1 is over:
1995	$2,500	$86,025
1994	2,450	83,850
1993	2,350	81,350
1992	2,300	78,950

29

30 Dependents (children and other) not claimed on original return:
Note: *If amending your 1995 return,* **do not** *complete column (b) below.*

(a) First Name Last Name	(b) Check if under age 1	(c) If age 1 or older (or born before 11/1/95 if a 1995 return), enter dependent's social security number	(d) Dependent's relationship to you	(e) No. of months lived in your home

No. of your children on line 30 who lived with you ▶ ☐

No. of your children on line 30 who **didn't** live with you due to divorce or separation (see instructions) ▶ ☐

No. of dependents on line 30 not entered above ▶ ☐

31 If your child listed on line 30 didn't live with you but is claimed as your dependent under a pre-1985 agreement, check here ▶ ☐

Part II Explanation of Changes to Income, Deductions, and Credits

Enter the line number from page 1 for each item you are changing and give the reason for each change. Attach all supporting forms and schedules for items changed. If you don't, your Form 1040X may be returned. Be sure to include your name and social security number on any attachments.

If the change relates to a net operating loss carryback or a general business credit carryback, attach the schedule or form that shows the year in which the loss or credit occurred. See instructions. Also, check here . . . . ▶ ☐

_____

_____

_____

_____

_____

_____

_____

Part III Presidential Election Campaign Fund. Checking below will not increase your tax or reduce your refund.

If you did not previously want to have $3 go to the fund but now want to, check here . . . . ▶ ☐
If a joint return and your spouse did not previously want to have $3 go to the fund but now wants to, check here . . ▶ ☐

✿ *Printed on recycled paper*

Form **1065**	**U.S. Partnership Return of Income**	OMB No. 1545-0099
Department of the Treasury Internal Revenue Service	For calendar year 1995, or tax year beginning .... , 1995, and ending .... , 19 .... . ▶ See separate instructions.	**1995**

A Principal business activity	Use the IRS label. Other-wise, please print or type.	Name of partnership	**D** Employer identification number
B Principal product or service		Number, street, and room or suite no. (If a P.O. box, see page 10 of the instructions.)	**E** Date business started
C Business code number		City or town, state, and ZIP code	**F** Total assets (see page 10 of the instructions) $

G Check applicable boxes: **(1)** ☐ Initial return **(2)** ☐ Final return **(3)** ☐ Change in address **(4)** ☐ Amended return

H Check accounting method: **(1)** ☐ Cash **(2)** ☐ Accrual **(3)** ☐ Other (specify) ▶ ....

I Number of Schedules K-1. Attach one for each person who was a partner at any time during the tax year ▶ ....

Caution: *Include **only** trade or business income and expenses on lines 1a through 22 below. See the instructions for more information.*

Income

1a Gross receipts or sales	**1a**			
b Less returns and allowances.	**1b**		**1c**	
2 Cost of goods sold (Schedule A, line 8)			**2**	
3 Gross profit. Subtract line 2 from line 1c			**3**	
4 Ordinary income (loss) from other partnerships, estates, and trusts *(attach schedule)* . . .			**4**	
5 Net farm profit (loss) *(attach Schedule F (Form 1040))*			**5**	
6 Net gain (loss) from Form 4797, Part II, line 20.			**6**	
7 Other income (loss) *(attach schedule)*			**7**	
8 **Total income (loss).** Combine lines 3 through 7			**8**	

Deductions (see page 11 of the instructions for limitations)

9 Salaries and wages (other than to partners) (less employment credits)			**9**	
10 Guaranteed payments to partners			**10**	
11 Repairs and maintenance			**11**	
12 Bad debts			**12**	
13 Rent			**13**	
14 Taxes and licenses			**14**	
15 Interest			**15**	
16a Depreciation (if required, attach Form 4562)	**16a**			
b Less depreciation reported on Schedule A and elsewhere on return	**16b**		**16c**	
17 Depletion **(Do not deduct oil and gas depletion.)**			**17**	
18 Retirement plans, etc.			**18**	
19 Employee benefit programs			**19**	
20 Other deductions *(attach schedule)*			**20**	
21 **Total deductions.** Add the amounts shown in the far right column for lines 9 through 20 .			**21**	
22 **Ordinary income (loss)** from trade or business activities. Subtract line 21 from line 8 . .			**22**	

Please Sign Here	Under penalties of perjury, I declare that I have examined this return, including accompanying schedules and statements, and to the best of my knowledge and belief, it is true, correct, and complete. Declaration of preparer (other than general partner or limited liability company member) is based on all information of which preparer has any knowledge.
	▶ Signature of general partner or limited liability company member .... ▶ Date ....

Paid Preparer's Use Only	Preparer's signature ▶		Date	Check if self-employed ▶ ☐	Preparer's social security no.
	Firm's name (or yours if self-employed) and address ▶			EIN ▶	
				ZIP code ▶	

For Paperwork Reduction Act Notice, see page 1 of separate instructions.   Cat. No. 11390Z   Form **1065** (1995)

Schedule A   **Cost of Goods Sold** (see page 13 of the instructions)

1	Inventory at beginning of year	**1**	
2	Purchases less cost of items withdrawn for personal use	**2**	
3	Cost of labor	**3**	
4	Additional section 263A costs *(attach schedule)*	**4**	
5	Other costs *(attach schedule)*	**5**	
6	**Total.** Add lines 1 through 5	**6**	
7	Inventory at end of year	**7**	
8	**Cost of goods sold.** Subtract line 7 from line 6. Enter here and on page 1, line 2	**8**	

9a Check all methods used for valuing closing inventory:

    (i) ☐ Cost as described in Regulations section 1.471-3

    (ii) ☐ Lower of cost or market as described in Regulations section 1.471-4

    (iii) ☐ Other (specify method used and attach explanation) ▶ --

  b Check this box if there was a writedown of "subnormal" goods as described in Regulations section 1.471-2(c) . . . . ▶ ☐

  c Check this box if the LIFO inventory method was adopted this tax year for any goods *(if checked, attach Form 970)* . . ▶ ☐

  d Do the rules of section 263A (for property produced or acquired for resale) apply to the partnership? . . ☐ **Yes** ☐ **No**

  e Was there any change in determining quantities, cost, or valuations between opening and closing inventory? ☐ **Yes** ☐ **No**
     If "Yes," attach explanation.

Schedule B   **Other Information**

		Yes	No
1	What type of entity is filing this return?		
	Check the applicable box ▶ ☐ General partnership ☐ Limited partnership ☐ Limited liability company		
2	Are any partners in this partnership also partnerships?		
3	Is this partnership a partner in another partnership?		
4	Is this partnership subject to the consolidated audit procedures of sections 6221 through 6233? If "Yes," see **Designation of Tax Matters Partner** below		
5	Does this partnership meet **ALL THREE** of the following requirements?		
a	The partnership's total receipts for the tax year were less than $250,000;		
b	The partnership's total assets at the end of the tax year were less than $600,000; **AND**		
c	Schedules K-1 are filed with the return and furnished to the partners on or before the due date (including extensions) for the partnership return.		
	If "Yes," the partnership is not required to complete Schedules L, M-1, and M-2; Item F on page 1 of Form 1065; or Item J on Schedule K-1		
6	Does this partnership have any foreign partners?		
7	Is this partnership a publicly traded partnership as defined in section 469(k)(2)?		
8	Has this partnership filed, or is it required to file, **Form 8264,** Application for Registration of a Tax Shelter? . .		
9	At any time during calendar year 1995, did the partnership have an interest in or a signature or other authority over a financial account in a foreign country (such as a bank account, securities account, or other financial account)? (See page 14 of the instructions for exceptions and filing requirements for Form TD F 90-22.1.) If "Yes," enter the name of the foreign country. ▶ ---------------------------		
10	Was the partnership the grantor of, or transferor to, a foreign trust that existed during the current tax year, whether or not the partnership or any partner has any beneficial interest in it? If "Yes," you may have to file Forms 3520, 3520-A, or 926		
11	Was there a distribution of property or a transfer (e.g., by sale or death) of a partnership interest during the tax year? If "Yes," you may elect to adjust the basis of the partnership's assets under section 754 by attaching the statement described under **Elections Made By the Partnership** on page 5 of the instructions		

Designation of Tax Matters Partner (see page 14 of the instructions)

Enter below the general partner designated as the tax matters partner (TMP) for the tax year of this return:

Name of designated TMP ▶		Identifying number of TMP ▶	
Address of designated TMP ▶			

Schedule K	Partners' Shares of Income, Credits, Deductions, etc.	
	(a) Distributive share items	**(b) Total amount**

Income (Loss)

1	Ordinary income (loss) from trade or business activities (page 1, line 22)	**1**
2	Net income (loss) from rental real estate activities *(attach Form 8825)* . .	**2**
3a	Gross income from other rental activities . . . . [3a]	
b	Expenses from other rental activities *(attach schedule)* . . . . [3b]	
c	Net income (loss) from other rental activities. Subtract line 3b from line 3a	**3c**
4	Portfolio income (loss): **a** Interest income	**4a**
b	Dividend income	**4b**
c	Royalty income	**4c**
d	Net short-term capital gain (loss) *(attach Schedule D (Form 1065))*	**4d**
e	Net long-term capital gain (loss) *(attach Schedule D (Form 1065))*	**4e**
f	Other portfolio income (loss) *(attach schedule)*	**4f**
5	Guaranteed payments to partners	**5**
6	Net gain (loss) under section 1231 (other than due to casualty or theft) *(attach Form 4797)*	**6**
7	Other income (loss) *(attach schedule)*	**7**

Deductions

8	Charitable contributions *(attach schedule)*	**8**
9	Section 179 expense deduction *(attach Form 4562)*	**9**
10	Deductions related to portfolio income (itemize)	**10**
11	Other deductions *(attach schedule)*	**11**

Investment Interest

12a	Interest expense on investment debts	**12a**
b (1)	Investment income included on lines 4a, 4b, 4c, and 4f above	**12b(1)**
(2)	Investment expenses included on line 10 above.	**12b(2)**

Credits

13a	Low-income housing credit:	
(1)	From partnerships to which section 42(j)(5) applies for property placed in service before 1990 .	**13a(1)**
(2)	Other than on line 13a(1) for property placed in service before 1990	**13a(2)**
(3)	From partnerships to which section 42(j)(5) applies for property placed in service after 1989	**13a(3)**
(4)	Other than on line 13a(3) for property placed in service after 1989	**13a(4)**
b	Qualified rehabilitation expenditures related to rental real estate activities *(attach Form 3468)*	**13b**
c	Credits (other than credits shown on lines 13a and 13b) related to rental real estate activities	**13c**
d	Credits related to other rental activities	**13d**
14	Other credits	**14**

Self-Employment

15a	Net earnings (loss) from self-employment	**15a**
b	Gross farming or fishing income	**15b**
c	Gross nonfarm income	**15c**

Adjustments and Tax Preference Items

16a	Depreciation adjustment on property placed in service after 1986	**16a**
b	Adjusted gain or loss	**16b**
c	Depletion (other than oil and gas)	**16c**
d (1)	Gross income from oil, gas, and geothermal properties	**16d(1)**
(2)	Deductions allocable to oil, gas, and geothermal properties	**16d(2)**
e	Other adjustments and tax preference items *(attach schedule)*	**16e**

Foreign Taxes

17a	Type of income ▶ . . . . **b** Foreign country or U.S. possession ▶	
c	Total gross income from sources outside the United States *(attach schedule)*	**17c**
d	Total applicable deductions and losses *(attach schedule)*	**17d**
e	Total foreign taxes (check one): ▶ ☐ Paid ☐ Accrued	**17e**
f	Reduction in taxes available for credit *(attach schedule)*	**17f**
g	Other foreign tax information *(attach schedule)*	**17g**

Other

18	Section 59(e)(2) expenditures: **a** Type ▶ . . . . **b** Amount ▶	**18b**
19	Tax-exempt interest income	**19**
20	Other tax-exempt income	**20**
21	Nondeductible expenses	**21**
22	Distributions of money (cash and marketable securities)	**22**
23	Distributions of property other than money	**23**
24	Other items and amounts required to be reported separately to partners *(attach schedule)*	

Analysis

25a	Income (loss). Combine lines 1 through 7 in column (b). From the result, subtract the sum of lines 8 through 12a, 17e, and 18b	**25a**

b Analysis by type of partner:	**(a) Corporate**	**(b) Individual**		**(c) Partnership**	**(d) Exempt organization**	**(e) Nominee/Other**
		i. Active	ii. Passive			
(1) General partners						
(2) Limited partners						

Form 1065 (1995)   Page **4**

Note: *If Question 5 of Schedule B is answered "Yes," the partnership is not required to complete Schedules L, M-1, and M-2.*

Schedule L   Balance Sheets

Assets	Beginning of tax year		End of tax year	
	(a)	(b)	(c)	(d)
1 Cash .				
2a Trade notes and accounts receivable .				
b Less allowance for bad debts .				
3 Inventories .				
4 U.S. government obligations .				
5 Tax-exempt securities .				
6 Other current assets *(attach schedule)*				
7 Mortgage and real estate loans .				
8 Other investments *(attach schedule)* .				
9a Buildings and other depreciable assets .				
b Less accumulated depreciation .				
10a Depletable assets .				
b Less accumulated depletion .				
11 Land (net of any amortization) .				
12a Intangible assets (amortizable only).				
b Less accumulated amortization .				
13 Other assets *(attach schedule)* .				
14 **Total** assets .				
Liabilities and Capital				
15 Accounts payable .				
16 Mortgages, notes, bonds payable in less than 1 year.				
17 Other current liabilities *(attach schedule)* .				
18 All nonrecourse loans .				
19 Mortgages, notes, bonds payable in 1 year or more .				
20 Other liabilities *(attach schedule)* .				
21 Partners' capital accounts .				
22 **Total** liabilities and capital .				

Schedule M-1   Reconciliation of Income (Loss) per Books With Income (Loss) per Return
(see page 23 of the instructions)

1	Net income (loss) per books .		6	Income recorded on books this year not included on Schedule K, lines 1 through 7 (itemize):
2	Income included on Schedule K, lines 1 through 4, 6, and 7, not recorded on books this year (itemize):		a	Tax-exempt interest $ ....
3	Guaranteed payments (other than health insurance) .		7	Deductions included on Schedule K, lines 1 through 12a, 17e, and 18b, not charged against book income this year (itemize):
4	Expenses recorded on books this year not included on Schedule K, lines 1 through 12a, 17e, and 18b (itemize):		a	Depreciation $ ....
a	Depreciation $			
b	Travel and entertainment $		8	Add lines 6 and 7 .
			9	Income (loss) (Schedule K, line 25a). Subtract line 8 from line 5 .
5	Add lines 1 through 4 .			

Schedule M-2   Analysis of Partners' Capital Accounts

1	Balance at beginning of year .		6	Distributions: **a** Cash .
2	Capital contributed during year .			**b** Property .
3	Net income (loss) per books .		7	Other decreases (itemize): ....
4	Other increases (itemize):			
			8	Add lines 6 and 7 .
5	Add lines 1 through 4 .		9	Balance at end of year. Subtract line 8 from line 5

♻ *Printed on recycled paper*

SCHEDULE K-1
(Form 1065)
Department of the Treasury
Internal Revenue Service

Partner's Share of Income, Credits, Deductions, etc.
▶ See separate instructions.

For calendar year 1995 or tax year beginning   , 1995, and ending   , 19

OMB No. 1545-0099

1995

Partner's identifying number ▶

Partnership's identifying number ▶

Partner's name, address, and ZIP code

Partnership's name, address, and ZIP code

A This partner is a ☐ general partner ☐ limited partner
☐ limited liability company member

B What type of entity is this partner? ▶ ....

C Is this partner a ☐ domestic or a ☐ foreign partner?

D Enter partner's percentage of:

	(i) Before change or termination	**(ii)** End of year
Profit sharing	.... %	.... %
Loss sharing	.... %	.... %
Ownership of capital	.... %	.... %

E IRS Center where partnership filed return:

F Partner's share of liabilities (see instructions):

Nonrecourse . . . . $ ....

Qualified nonrecourse financing . $ ....

Other . . . . $ ....

G Tax shelter registration number . ▶ ....

H Check here if this partnership is a publicly traded partnership as defined in section 469(k)(2) . . . . ☐

I Check applicable boxes: **(1)** ☐ Final K-1 **(2)** ☐ Amended K-1

J Analysis of partner's capital account:

(a) Capital account at beginning of year	**(b)** Capital contributed during year	**(c)** Partner's share of lines 3, 4, and 7, Form 1065, Schedule M-2	**(d)** Withdrawals and distributions	**(e)** Capital account at end of year (combine columns (a) through (d))
			( )	

	(a) Distributive share item		**(b)** Amount	**(c)** 1040 filers enter the amount in column (b) on:
Income (Loss)	**1** Ordinary income (loss) from trade or business activities . . .	**1**		See pages 5 and 6 of Partner's Instructions for Schedule K-1 (Form 1065).
	2 Net income (loss) from rental real estate activities	**2**		
	3 Net income (loss) from other rental activities	**3**		
	4 Portfolio income (loss):			
	a Interest	**4a**		Sch. B, Part I, line 1
	b Dividends	**4b**		Sch. B, Part II, line 5
	c Royalties	**4c**		Sch. E, Part I, line 4
	d Net short-term capital gain (loss)	**4d**		Sch. D, line 5, col. (f) or (g)
	e Net long-term capital gain (loss)	**4e**		Sch. D, line 13, col. (f) or (g)
	f Other portfolio income (loss) *(attach schedule)*	**4f**		Enter on applicable line of your return.
	5 Guaranteed payments to partner	**5**		See page 6 of Partner's Instructions for Schedule K-1 (Form 1065).
	6 Net gain (loss) under section 1231 (other than due to casualty or theft)	**6**		
	7 Other income (loss) *(attach schedule)*	**7**		Enter on applicable line of your return.
Deductions	**8** Charitable contributions (see instructions) *(attach schedule)* . .	**8**		Sch. A, line 15 or 16
	9 Section 179 expense deduction	**9**		See page 7 of Partner's Instructions for Schedule K-1 (Form 1065).
	10 Deductions related to portfolio income *(attach schedule)* . . .	**10**		
	11 Other deductions *(attach schedule)*	**11**		
Investment Interest	**12a** Interest expense on investment debts	**12a**		Form 4952, line 1
	b (1) Investment income included on lines 4a, 4b, 4c, and 4f above	**b(1)**		See page 7 of Partner's Instructions for Schedule K-1 (Form 1065).
	(2) Investment expenses included on line 10 above	**b(2)**		
Credits	**13a** Low-income housing credit:			
	(1) From section 42(j)(5) partnerships for property placed in service before 1990	**a(1)**		Form 8586, line 5
	(2) Other than on line 13a(1) for property placed in service before 1990	**a(2)**		
	(3) From section 42(j)(5) partnerships for property placed in service after 1989	**a(3)**		
	(4) Other than on line 13a(3) for property placed in service after 1989	**a(4)**		
	b Qualified rehabilitation expenditures related to rental real estate activities	**13b**		
	c Credits (other than credits shown on lines 13a and 13b) related to rental real estate activities	**13c**		See page 8 of Partner's Instructions for Schedule K-1 (Form 1065).
	d Credits related to other rental activities	**13d**		
	14 Other credits	**14**		

For Paperwork Reduction Act Notice, see Instructions for Form 1065.

Cat. No. 11394R

Schedule K-1 (Form 1065) 1995

Schedule K-1 (Form 1065) 1995   Page **2**

(a) Distributive share item		(b) Amount	(c) 1040 filers enter the amount in column (b) on:
Self-employment **15a** Net earnings (loss) from self-employment	15a		Sch. SE, Section A or B
b Gross farming or fishing income.	15b		See page 8 of Partner's Instructions for Schedule K-1 (Form 1065).
c Gross nonfarm income.	15c		
Adjustments and Tax Preference Items **16a** Depreciation adjustment on property placed in service after 1986	16a		See pages 8 and 9 of Partner's Instructions for Schedule K-1 (Form 1065) and Instructions for Form 6251.
b Adjusted gain or loss	16b		
c Depletion (other than oil and gas)	16c		
d (1) Gross income from oil, gas, and geothermal properties . .	d(1)		
(2) Deductions allocable to oil, gas, and geothermal properties .	d(2)		
e Other adjustments and tax preference items *(attach schedule)*	16e		
Foreign Taxes **17a** Type of income ▶ -----------------------------------			Form 1116, check boxes
b Name of foreign country or U.S. possession ▶ ---------------			
c Total gross income from sources outside the United States *(attach schedule)*	17c		Form 1116, Part I
d Total applicable deductions and losses *(attach schedule)*. .	17d		
e Total foreign taxes (check one): ▶ ☐ Paid ☐ Accrued . .	17e		Form 1116, Part II
f Reduction in taxes available for credit *(attach schedule)* . .	17f		Form 1116, Part III
g Other foreign tax information *(attach schedule)*	17g		See Instructions for Form 1116.
Other **18** Section 59(e)(2) expenditures: **a** Type ▶ ---------------------			See page 9 of Partner's Instructions for Schedule K-1 (Form 1065).
b Amount	18b		
19 Tax-exempt interest income	19		Form 1040, line 8b
20 Other tax-exempt income.	20		See page 9 of Partner's Instructions for Schedule K-1 (Form 1065).
21 Nondeductible expenses	21		
22 Distributions of money (cash and marketable securities) . . .	22		
23 Distributions of property other than money	23		
24 Recapture of low-income housing credit:			
a From section 42(j)(5) partnerships	24a		Form 8611, line 8
b Other than on line 24a.	24b		

25 Supplemental information required to be reported separately to each partner *(attach additional schedules if more space is needed)*:

Supplemental Information

Printed on recycled paper

Form **1116** Department of the Treasury Internal Revenue Service	**Foreign Tax Credit** (Individual, Estate, Trust, or Nonresident Alien Individual) ▶ Attach to Form 1040, 1040NR, 1041, or 990-T. ▶ See separate instructions.	OMB No. 1545-0121 19**95** Attachment Sequence No. **19**

Name	Identifying number as shown on page 1 of your tax return

*Report all amounts in U.S. dollars except where specified in Part II. Use a separate Form 1116 for each category of income listed below. Check only **one** box. Before you check a box, read **Categories of Income** on page 3 of the instructions. Complete this form for credit for taxes on:*

a ☐ Passive income

b ☐ High withholding tax interest

c ☐ Financial services income

d ☐ Shipping income

e ☐ Dividends from a DISC or former DISC

f ☐ Certain distributions from a foreign sales corporation (FSC) or former FSC

g ☐ Lump-sum distributions (see page 3 of the instructions before completing form)

h ☐ General limitation income—all other income from sources outside the United States (including income from sources within U.S. possessions)

i Resident of (name of country) ▶

Note: *If you paid taxes to one foreign country or U.S. possession, use column A in Part I and line A in Part II. If you paid taxes to **more than one** foreign country or U.S. possession, use a separate column and line for each country or possession. However, see the exception under **How To Complete Form 1116** on page 1 of the Instructions.*

Part I **Taxable Income or Loss From Sources Outside the United States for Separate Category Checked Above**

		Foreign Country or U.S. Possession			Total
		A	**B**	**C**	(Add cols. A, B, and C.)
j	Enter the name of the foreign country or U.S. possession . . . . ▶				
1	Gross income from sources within country shown above and of the type checked above. See page 5 of the instructions:				**1**
	Applicable deductions and losses. (See pages 5 and 6 of the instructions.):				
2	Expenses directly allocable to the income on line 1 (attach statement)				
3	Pro rata share of other deductions not directly allocable:				
a	Certain itemized deductions or standard deduction. See instructions				
b	Other deductions (attach statement)				
c	Add lines 3a and 3b				
d	Gross foreign source income. See instructions .				
e	Gross income from all sources. See instructions				
f	Divide line 3d by line 3e				
g	Multiply line 3c by line 3f				
4	Pro rata share of interest expense. See instructions:				
a	Home mortgage interest from line 5 of the worksheet on page 6 of the instructions . . .				
b	Other interest expense				
5	Losses from foreign sources				
6	Add lines 2, 3g, 4a, 4b, and 5				**6**
7	Subtract line 6 from line 1. Enter the result here and on line 14. . . . . ▶				**7**

Part II **Foreign Taxes Paid or Accrued** (See page 6 of the instructions.)

Country	Credit is claimed for taxes (you must check one) **(k)** ☐ Paid **(l)** ☐ Accrued	Foreign taxes paid or accrued								
		In foreign currency				In U.S. dollars				
		Taxes withheld at source on:			**(q)** Other foreign taxes paid or accrued	Taxes withheld at source on:			**(u)** Other foreign taxes paid or accrued	**(v)** Total foreign taxes paid or accrued (add cols. (r) through (u))
	(m) Date paid or accrued	**(n)** Dividends	**(o)** Rents and royalties	**(p)** Interest		**(r)** Dividends	**(s)** Rents and royalties	**(t)** Interest		
A										
B										
C										

8 Add lines A through C, column (v). Enter the total here and on line 9 . . . . ▶ **8**

For Paperwork Reduction Act Notice, see page 1 of separate instructions. Cat. No. 11440U Form **1116** (1995)

Form 1116 (1995)   Page **2**

Part III   **Figuring the Credit**

9   Enter amount from line 8. This is the total foreign taxes paid or accrued
    for the category of income checked above Part I .   .   .   . | 9 |

10 Carryback or carryover (attach detailed computation) .   .   .   .   . | 10 |

11 Add lines 9 and 10 .   .   .   . | 11 |

12 Reduction in foreign taxes. See page 7 of the instructions .   .   .   . | 12 |

13 Subtract line 12 from line 11. This is the total amount of foreign taxes available for credit .   .   .   . | 13 |

14 Enter amount from line 7. This is your taxable income or (loss) from
    sources outside the United States (before adjustments) for the
    category of income checked above Part I. See page 7 of the
    instructions .   .   .   . | 14 |

15 Adjustments to line 14. See page 7 of the instructions .   .   .   .   . | 15 |

16 Combine the amounts on lines 14 and 15. This is your net foreign
    source taxable income. (If the result is zero or less, you have no foreign
    tax credit for the category of income you checked above Part I. Skip
    lines 17 through 21.) .   .   .   . | 16 |

17 **Individuals:** Enter amount from Form 1040, line 35. If you are a
    nonresident alien, enter amount from Form 1040NR, line 34.
    Estates and trusts: Enter your taxable income without the deduction
    for your exemption .   .   .   . | 17 |

    Caution: *If you figured your tax using the maximum tax rate on capital gains, see page 8 of the instructions.*

18 Divide line 16 by line 17. If line 16 is more than line 17, enter the figure "1" .   .   .   . | 18 |

19 **Individuals:** Enter amount from Form 1040, line 40, **less** any amounts on Form 1040, lines 41, 42,
    and any mortgage interest credit (from Form 8396) on line 44. If you are a nonresident alien, enter
    amount from Form 1040NR, line 39, less any amount on Form 1040NR, line 40 and any mortgage
    interest credit (from Form 8396) on line 42.
    Estates and trusts: Enter amount from Form 1041, Schedule G, line 1c, or Form 990-T, lines 36 and 37 . | 19 |

20 Multiply line 19 by line 18 (maximum amount of credit) .   .   .   .   .   . | 20 |

21 Enter the amount from line 13 or line 20, whichever is smaller. (If this is the only Form 1116 you are
    completing, skip lines 22 through 29 and enter this amount on line 30. Otherwise, complete the
    appropriate lines in Part IV.) .   .   .   .   ▶ | 21 |

Part IV   **Summary of Credits From Separate Parts III** (See page 8 of the instructions.)

22 Credit for taxes on passive income .   .   .   . | 22 |

23 Credit for taxes on high withholding tax interest .   .   .   . | 23 |

24 Credit for taxes on financial services income .   .   .   . | 24 |

25 Credit for taxes on shipping income .   .   .   . | 25 |

26 Credit for taxes on dividends from a DISC or former DISC .   .   .   . | 26 |

27 Credit for taxes on certain distributions from a FSC or former FSC .   . | 27 |

28 Credit for taxes on lump-sum distributions .   .   .   . | 28 |

29 Credit for taxes on general limitation income (all other income from
    sources outside the United States) .   .   .   . | 29 |

30 Add lines 22 through 29.   .   .   .   . | 30 |

31 Reduction of credit for international boycott operations. See instructions for line 12 on page 7 .   . | 31 |

32 Subtract line 31 from line 30. This is your foreign tax credit. Enter here and on Form 1040, line 43;
    Form 1040NR, line 41; Form 1041, Schedule G, line 2a; or Form 990-T, line 39a .   .   .   .   .   ▶ | 32 |

✿ *Printed on recycled paper*

Form **1120**	**U.S. Corporation Income Tax Return**	OMB No. 1545-0123
Department of the Treasury Internal Revenue Service	For calendar year 1995 or tax year beginning .... , 1995, ending .... , 19 ... ▶ Instructions are separate. See page 1 for Paperwork Reduction Act Notice.	**1995**

A Check if a:
1 Consolidated return (attach Form 851) ☐
2 Personal holding co. (attach Sch. PH) ☐
3 Personal service corp. (as defined in Temporary Regs. sec. 1.441-4T— see instructions) ☐

Use IRS label. Otherwise, print or type.

Name

Number, street, and room or suite no. (If a P.O. box, see page 6 of instructions.)

City or town, state, and ZIP code

B Employer identification number

C Date incorporated

D Total assets (see page 6 of instructions)
$

E Check applicable boxes: (1) ☐ Initial return (2) ☐ Final return (3) ☐ Change of address

Income

1a	Gross receipts or sales [........] **b** Less returns and allowances [........] **c** Bal ▶	1c
2	Cost of goods sold (Schedule A, line 8)	2
3	Gross profit. Subtract line 2 from line 1c	3
4	Dividends (Schedule C, line 19)	4
5	Interest	5
6	Gross rents	6
7	Gross royalties	7
8	Capital gain net income (attach Schedule D (Form 1120))	8
9	Net gain or (loss) from Form 4797, Part II, line 20 (attach Form 4797)	9
10	Other income (see page 7 of instructions—attach schedule) . . .	10
11	**Total income.** Add lines 3 through 10 . . . . ▶	11

Deductions (See instructions for limitations on deductions.)

12	Compensation of officers (Schedule E, line 4)	12
13	Salaries and wages (less employment credits)	13
14	Repairs and maintenance	14
15	Bad debts	15
16	Rents	16
17	Taxes and licenses	17
18	Interest	18
19	Charitable contributions (see page 9 of instructions for 10% limitation)	19
20	Depreciation (attach Form 4562)	20	
21	Less depreciation claimed on Schedule A and elsewhere on return . .	21a	21b
22	Depletion	22
23	Advertising	23
24	Pension, profit-sharing, etc., plans	24
25	Employee benefit programs	25
26	Other deductions (attach schedule)	26
27	**Total deductions.** Add lines 12 through 26 . . . . ▶	27
28	Taxable income before net operating loss deduction and special deductions. Subtract line 27 from line 11	28
29	**Less:** **a** Net operating loss deduction (see page 11 of instructions) . .	29a	
	b Special deductions (Schedule C, line 20)	29b	29c

Tax and Payments

30	**Taxable income.** Subtract line 29c from line 28	30
31	**Total tax** (Schedule J, line 10)	31
32	**Payments: a** 1994 overpayment credited to 1995	32a	
b	1995 estimated tax payments . .	32b	
c	Less 1995 refund applied for on Form 4466	32c ( ) **d** Bal ▶	32d
e	Tax deposited with Form 7004		32e
f	Credit from regulated investment companies (attach Form 2439) . . .	32f
g	Credit for Federal tax on fuels (attach Form 4136). See instructions . .	32g	32h
33	Estimated tax penalty (see page 12 of instructions). Check if Form 2220 is attached . . . ▶ ☐	33
34	**Tax due.** If line 32h is smaller than the total of lines 31 and 33, enter amount owed	34
35	**Overpayment.** If line 32h is larger than the total of lines 31 and 33, enter amount overpaid	35
36	Enter amount of line 35 you want: **Credited to 1996 estimated tax** ▶ [........] **Refunded** ▶	36

Sign Here

Under penalties of perjury, I declare that I have examined this return, including accompanying schedules and statements, and to the best of my knowledge and belief, it is true, correct, and complete. Declaration of preparer (other than taxpayer) is based on all information of which preparer has any knowledge.

▶ Signature of officer _____ Date _____ ▶ Title _____

Paid Preparer's Use Only

Preparer's signature ▶	Date	Check if self-employed ☐	Preparer's social security number
Firm's name (or yours if self-employed) and address ▶		EIN ▶	
		ZIP code ▶	

Cat. No. 11450Q

Schedule A — Cost of Goods Sold (See page 12 of instructions.)

1	Inventory at beginning of year	1	
2	Purchases	2	
3	Cost of labor	3	
4	Additional section 263A costs (attach schedule)	4	
5	Other costs (attach schedule)	5	
6	**Total.** Add lines 1 through 5	6	
7	Inventory at end of year	7	
8	**Cost of goods sold.** Subtract line 7 from line 6. Enter here and on page 1, line 2	8	

9a Check all methods used for valuing closing inventory:
(i) ☐ Cost as described in Regulations section 1.471-3
(ii) ☐ Lower of cost or market as described in Regulations section 1.471-4
(iii) ☐ Other (Specify method used and attach explanation.) ▶ ----------------------------------

b Check if there was a writedown of subnormal goods as described in Regulations section 1.471-2(c) . . . . ▶ ☐
c Check if the LIFO inventory method was adopted this tax year for any goods (if checked, attach Form 970) . . . . ▶ ☐
d If the LIFO inventory method was used for this tax year, enter percentage (or amounts) of closing inventory computed under LIFO   9d
e Do the rules of section 263A (for property produced or acquired for resale) apply to the corporation? . . . . . ☐ Yes ☐ No
f Was there any change in determining quantities, cost, or valuations between opening and closing inventory? If "Yes," attach explanation . . . . ☐ Yes ☐ No

Schedule C — Dividends and Special Deductions (See page 13 of instructions.)

		(a) Dividends received	(b) %	(c) Special deductions (a) × (b)
1	Dividends from less-than-20%-owned domestic corporations that are subject to the 70% deduction (other than debt-financed stock)		70	
2	Dividends from 20%-or-more-owned domestic corporations that are subject to the 80% deduction (other than debt-financed stock)		80	
3	Dividends on debt-financed stock of domestic and foreign corporations (section 246A)		see instructions	
4	Dividends on certain preferred stock of less-than-20%-owned public utilities		42	
5	Dividends on certain preferred stock of 20%-or-more-owned public utilities		48	
6	Dividends from less-than-20%-owned foreign corporations and certain FSCs that are subject to the 70% deduction		70	
7	Dividends from 20%-or-more-owned foreign corporations and certain FSCs that are subject to the 80% deduction		80	
8	Dividends from wholly owned foreign subsidiaries subject to the 100% deduction (section 245(b))		100	
9	**Total.** Add lines 1 through 8. See page 13 of instructions for limitation			
10	Dividends from domestic corporations received by a small business investment company operating under the Small Business Investment Act of 1958		100	
11	Dividends from certain FSCs that are subject to the 100% deduction (section 245(c)(1))		100	
12	Dividends from affiliated group members subject to the 100% deduction (section 243(a)(3))		100	
13	Other dividends from foreign corporations not included on lines 3, 6, 7, 8, or 11			
14	Income from controlled foreign corporations under subpart F (attach Form(s) 5471)			
15	Foreign dividend gross-up (section 78)			
16	IC-DISC and former DISC dividends not included on lines 1, 2, or 3 (section 246(d))			
17	Other dividends			
18	Deduction for dividends paid on certain preferred stock of public utilities			
19	**Total dividends.** Add lines 1 through 17. Enter here and on line 4, page 1 ▶			
20	**Total special deductions.** Add lines 9, 10, 11, 12, and 18. Enter here and on line 29b, page 1 ▶			

Schedule E — Compensation of Officers (See instructions for line 12, page 1.)

Complete Schedule E only if total receipts (line 1a plus lines 4 through 10 on page 1, Form 1120) are $500,000 or more.

(a) Name of officer	(b) Social security number	(c) Percent of time devoted to business	Percent of corporation stock owned		(f) Amount of compensation
			(d) Common	(e) Preferred	
1		%	%	%	
		%	%	%	
		%	%	%	
		%	%	%	
		%	%	%	

2 Total compensation of officers
3 Compensation of officers claimed on Schedule A and elsewhere on return
4 Subtract line 3 from line 2. Enter the result here and on line 12, page 1

Schedule J — Tax Computation (See page 14 of instructions.)

1 Check if the corporation is a member of a controlled group (see sections 1561 and 1563) . . . . ▶ ☐

Important: Members of a controlled group, see instructions on page 14.

2a If the box on line 1 is checked, enter the corporation's share of the $50,000, $25,000, and $9,925,000 taxable income brackets (in that order):

(1) $ _____   (2) $ _____   (3) $ _____

b Enter the corporation's share of:

(1) Additional 5% tax (not more than $11,750) $ _____

(2) Additional 3% tax (not more than $100,000) $ _____

3 Income tax. Check this box if the corporation is a qualified personal service corporation as defined in section 448(d)(2) (see instructions on page 15). . . . . ▶ ☐ | **3** |

4a Foreign tax credit (attach Form 1118) . . . . | **4a** |

b Possessions tax credit (attach Form 5735) . . . . | **4b** |

c Check: ☐ Nonconventional source fuel credit ☐ QEV credit (attach Form 8834) | **4c** |

d General business credit. Enter here and check which forms are attached:

☐ 3800 ☐ 3468 ☐ 5884 ☐ 6478 ☐ 6765 ☐ 8586 ☐ 8830

☐ 8826 ☐ 8835 ☐ 8844 ☐ 8845 ☐ 8846 ☐ 8847 . . . . | **4d** |

e Credit for prior year minimum tax (attach Form 8827) . . . . | **4e** |

5 **Total credits.** Add lines 4a through 4e . . . . | **5** |

6 Subtract line 5 from line 3 . . . . | **6** |

7 Personal holding company tax (attach Schedule PH (Form 1120)) . . . . . | **7** |

8 Recapture taxes. Check if from: ☐ Form 4255 ☐ Form 8611 . . . . | **8** |

9a Alternative minimum tax (attach Form 4626) . . . . | **9a** |

b Environmental tax (attach Form 4626) . . . . | **9b** |

10 **Total tax.** Add lines 6 through 9b. Enter here and on line 31, page 1 . . . . . | **10** |

Schedule K — Other Information (See page 17 of instructions.)

	Yes	No

1 Check method of accounting: **a** ☐ Cash

b ☐ Accrual **c** ☐ Other (specify) ▶ _____

2 See page 19 of the instructions and state the principal:

a Business activity code no. ▶ _____

b Business activity ▶ _____

c Product or service ▶ _____

3 Did the corporation at the end of the tax year own, directly or indirectly, 50% or more of the voting stock of a domestic corporation? (For rules of attribution, see section 267(c).) . . . .

If "Yes," attach a schedule showing: (a) name and identifying number, (b) percentage owned, and (c) taxable income or (loss) before NOL and special deductions of such corporation for the tax year ending with or within your tax year.

4 Is the corporation a subsidiary in an affiliated group or a parent-subsidiary controlled group? . . . . . .

If "Yes," enter employer identification number and name of the parent corporation ▶ _____

_____

5 Did any individual, partnership, corporation, estate or trust at the end of the tax year own, directly or indirectly, 50% or more of the corporation's voting stock? (For rules of attribution, see section 267(c).) . . . .

If "Yes," attach a schedule showing name and identifying number. (Do not include any information already entered in **4** above.) Enter percentage owned ▶ _____

6 During this tax year, did the corporation pay dividends (other than stock dividends and distributions in exchange for stock) in excess of the corporation's current and accumulated earnings and profits? (See secs. 301 and 316.) . . . .

If "Yes," file Form 5452. If this is a consolidated return, answer here for the parent corporation and on **Form 851,** Affiliations Schedule, for each subsidiary.

7 Was the corporation a U.S. shareholder of any controlled foreign corporation? (See sections 951 and 957.) . . .

If "Yes," attach Form 5471 for each such corporation. Enter number of Forms 5471 attached ▶ _____

8 At any time during the 1995 calendar year, did the corporation have an interest in or a signature or other authority over a financial account in a foreign country (such as a bank account, securities account, or other financial account)? .

If "Yes," the corporation may have to file Form TD F 90-22.1.

If "Yes," enter name of foreign country ▶ _____

9 Was the corporation the grantor of, or transferor to, a foreign trust that existed during the current tax year, whether or not the corporation has any beneficial interest in it? If "Yes," the corporation may have to file Forms 926, 3520, or 3520-A .

10 Did one foreign person at any time during the tax year own, directly or indirectly, at least 25% of: **(a)** the total voting power of all classes of stock of the corporation entitled to vote, or **(b)** the total value of all classes of stock of the corporation? If "Yes,"

a Enter percentage owned ▶ _____

b Enter owner's country ▶ _____

c The corporation may have to file Form 5472. Enter number of Forms 5472 attached ▶ _____

11 Check this box if the corporation issued publicly offered debt instruments with original issue discount . ▶ ☐

If so, the corporation may have to file Form 8281.

12 Enter the amount of tax-exempt interest received or accrued during the tax year ▶ $ _____

13 If there were 35 or fewer shareholders at the end of the tax year, enter the number ▶ _____

14 If the corporation has an NOL for the tax year and is electing to forego the carryback period, check here ▶ ☐

15 Enter the available NOL carryover from prior tax years (Do not reduce it by any deduction on line 29a.) ▶ $ _____

Form 1120 (1995)   Page **4**

Schedule L	Balance Sheets	Beginning of tax year		End of tax year	
	Assets	**(a)**	**(b)**	**(c)**	**(d)**
1	Cash				
2a	Trade notes and accounts receivable . . .				
b	Less allowance for bad debts	( )		( )	
3	Inventories				
4	U.S. government obligations				
5	Tax-exempt securities (see instructions) . .				
6	Other current assets (attach schedule) . .				
7	Loans to stockholders				
8	Mortgage and real estate loans				
9	Other investments (attach schedule) . . .				
10a	Buildings and other depreciable assets . .				
b	Less accumulated depreciation	( )		( )	
11a	Depletable assets				
b	Less accumulated depletion	( )		( )	
12	Land (net of any amortization)				
13a	Intangible assets (amortizable only) . . .				
b	Less accumulated amortization	( )		( )	
14	Other assets (attach schedule)				
15	Total assets				
	Liabilities and Stockholders' Equity				
16	Accounts payable				
17	Mortgages, notes, bonds payable in less than 1 year				
18	Other current liabilities (attach schedule) . .				
19	Loans from stockholders				
20	Mortgages, notes, bonds payable in 1 year or more				
21	Other liabilities (attach schedule)				
22	Capital stock: **a** Preferred stock . . .				
	b Common stock . . .				
23	Paid-in or capital surplus				
24	Retained earnings—Appropriated (attach schedule)				
25	Retained earnings—Unappropriated . . .				
26	Less cost of treasury stock		( )		( )
27	Total liabilities and stockholders' equity				

Note: *You are not required to complete Schedules M-1 and M-2 below if the total assets on line 15, column (d) of Schedule L are less than $25,000.*

Schedule M-1	Reconciliation of Income (Loss) per Books With Income per Return (See page 18 of instructions.)

1	Net income (loss) per books		7	Income recorded on books this year not included on this return (itemize):	
2	Federal income tax				
3	Excess of capital losses over capital gains .			Tax-exempt interest $	
4	Income subject to tax not recorded on books this year (itemize):			....	
	....		8	Deductions on this return not charged against book income this year (itemize):	
5	Expenses recorded on books this year not deducted on this return (itemize):			**a** Depreciation . . . . $..............	
a	Depreciation . . . . $..............			**b** Contributions carryover $	
b	Contributions carryover $			....	
c	Travel and entertainment $			....	
	....		9	Add lines 7 and 8	
6	Add lines 1 through 5		10	Income (line 28, page 1)—line 6 less line 9	

Schedule M-2	Analysis of Unappropriated Retained Earnings per Books (Line 25, Schedule L)

1	Balance at beginning of year		5	Distributions: **a** Cash	
2	Net income (loss) per books			**b** Stock	
3	Other increases (itemize):			**c** Property	
	....		6	Other decreases (itemize):	
	....			....	
	....		7	Add lines 5 and 6	
4	Add lines 1, 2, and 3		8	Balance at end of year (line 4 less line 7)	

✳ *Printed on recycled paper*

Form **1120S**	**U.S. Income Tax Return for an S Corporation**	OMB No. 1545-0130
Department of the Treasury Internal Revenue Service	▶ **Do not file this form unless the corporation has timely filed Form 2553 to elect to be an S corporation.** ▶ See separate instructions.	**1995**

For calendar year 1995, or tax year beginning _____ , 1995, and ending _____ , 19 ____

A Date of election as an S corporation	**Use IRS label. Other- wise, please print or type.**	Name	**C** Employer identification number
B Business code no. (see Specific Instructions)		Number, street, and room or suite no. (If a P.O. box, see page 9 of the instructions.)	**D** Date incorporated
		City or town, state, and ZIP code	**E** Total assets (see Specific Instructions) $

F Check applicable boxes: (1) ☐ Initial return   (2) ☐ Final return   (3) ☐ Change in address   (4) ☐ Amended return

G Check this box if this S corporation is subject to the consolidated audit procedures of sections 6241 through 6245 (see instructions before checking this box) . ▶ ☐

H Enter number of shareholders in the corporation at end of the tax year . . . . ▶

Caution: *Include **only** trade or business income and expenses on lines 1a through 21. See the instructions for more information.*

Income

1a	Gross receipts or sales |_____| **b** Less returns and allowances |_____| **c** Bal ▶	**1c**	
2	Cost of goods sold (Schedule A, line 8)	**2**	
3	Gross profit. Subtract line 2 from line 1c	**3**	
4	Net gain (loss) from Form 4797, Part II, line 20 *(attach Form 4797)* . . .	**4**	
5	Other income (loss) *(attach schedule)*	**5**	
6	**Total income (loss).** Combine lines 3 through 5 . . . . ▶	**6**	

Deductions (see page 10 of the instructions for limitations)

7	Compensation of officers	**7**	
8	Salaries and wages (less employment credits)	**8**	
9	Repairs and maintenance.	**9**	
10	Bad debts	**10**	
11	Rents	**11**	
12	Taxes and licenses	**12**	
13	Interest	**13**	
14a	Depreciation *(if required, attach Form 4562)* . . . **14a**		
b	Depreciation claimed on Schedule A and elsewhere on return . **14b**		
c	Subtract line 14b from line 14a	**14c**	
15	Depletion **(Do not deduct oil and gas depletion.)** . . .	**15**	
16	Advertising	**16**	
17	Pension, profit-sharing, etc., plans	**17**	
18	Employee benefit programs	**18**	
19	Other deductions *(attach schedule)*	**19**	
20	**Total deductions.** Add the amounts shown in the far right column for lines 7 through 19 ▶	**20**	
21	Ordinary income (loss) from trade or business activities. Subtract line 20 from line 6	**21**	

Tax and Payments

22	**Tax: a** Excess net passive income tax *(attach schedule)*. . . . **22a**		
b	Tax from Schedule D (Form 1120S) **22b**		
c	Add lines 22a and 22b (see page 13 of the instructions for additional taxes)	**22c**	
23	**Payments: a** 1995 estimated tax payments and amount applied from 1994 return **23a**		
b	Tax deposited with Form 7004 . . . . **23b**		
c	Credit for Federal tax paid on fuels *(attach Form 4136)* . . . **23c**		
d	Add lines 23a through 23c	**23d**	
24	Estimated tax penalty. Check if Form 2220 is attached . . . . ▶☐	**24**	
25	**Tax due.** If the total of lines 22c and 24 is larger than line 23d, enter amount owed. See page 3 of the instructions for depositary method of payment . . . . ▶	**25**	
26	**Overpayment.** If line 23d is larger than the total of lines 22c and 24, enter amount overpaid ▶	**26**	
27	Enter amount of line 26 you want: **Credited to 1996 estimated tax ▶** |_____| **Refunded ▶**	**27**	

Please Sign Here

Under penalties of perjury, I declare that I have examined this return, including accompanying schedules and statements, and to the best of my knowledge and belief, it is true, correct, and complete. Declaration of preparer (other than taxpayer) is based on all information of which preparer has any knowledge.

▶ _____   _____   ▶ _____
    Signature of officer   Date   Title

Paid Preparer's Use Only

Preparer's signature ▶		Date	Check if self- employed ▶ ☐	Preparer's social security number
Firm's name (or yours if self-employed) and address ▶			EIN ▶	
			ZIP code ▶	

For Paperwork Reduction Act Notice, see page 1 of separate instructions.   Cat. No. 11510H   Form **1120S** (1995)

Schedule A	Cost of Goods Sold (see page 14 of the instructions)

1	Inventory at beginning of year	1		
2	Purchases	2		
3	Cost of labor	3		
4	Additional section 263A costs (attach schedule)	4		
5	Other costs (attach schedule)	5		
6	**Total.** Add lines 1 through 5	6		
7	Inventory at end of year	7		
8	**Cost of goods sold.** Subtract line 7 from line 6. Enter here and on page 1, line 2	8		

9a Check all methods used for valuing closing inventory:

   (i) ☐ Cost as described in Regulations section 1.471-3

   (ii) ☐ Lower of cost or market as described in Regulations section 1.471-4

   (iii) ☐ Other (specify method used and attach explanation) ▶ --

  b Check if there was a writedown of "subnormal" goods as described in Regulations section 1.471-2(c) . . . . ▶ ☐

  c Check if the LIFO inventory method was adopted this tax year for any goods (if checked, attach Form 970) . . . . . . ▶ ☐

  d If the LIFO inventory method was used for this tax year, enter percentage (or amounts) of closing
     inventory computed under LIFO 9d

  e Do the rules of section 263A (for property produced or acquired for resale) apply to the corporation? . . . . ☐ Yes ☐ No

  f Was there any change in determining quantities, cost, or valuations between opening and closing inventory? . . ☐ Yes ☐ No
     If "Yes," attach explanation.

Schedule B	Other Information

		Yes	No
1	Check method of accounting: **(a)** ☐ Cash **(b)** ☐ Accrual **(c)** ☐ Other (specify) ▶ ----------------------------		
2	Refer to the list on page 24 of the instructions and state the corporation's principal:		
	(a) Business activity ▶ ---------------------------- **(b)** Product or service ▶ ----------------------------		
3	Did the corporation at the end of the tax year own, directly or indirectly, 50% or more of the voting stock of a domestic corporation? (For rules of attribution, see section 267(c).) If "Yes," attach a schedule showing: **(a)** name, address, and employer identification number and **(b)** percentage owned.		
4	Was the corporation a member of a controlled group subject to the provisions of section 1561?		
5	At any time during calendar year 1995, did the corporation have an interest in or a signature or other authority over a financial account in a foreign country (such as a bank account, securities account, or other financial account)? (See page 14 of the instructions for exceptions and filing requirements for Form TD F 90-22.1.)		
	If "Yes," enter the name of the foreign country ▶ ----------------------------		
6	Was the corporation the grantor of, or transferor to, a foreign trust that existed during the current tax year, whether or not the corporation had any beneficial interest in it? If "Yes," the corporation may have to file Forms 3520, 3520-A, or 926		
7	Check this box if the corporation has filed or is required to file **Form 8264,** Application for Registration of a Tax Shelter . . . . ▶ ☐		
8	Check this box if the corporation issued publicly offered debt instruments with original issue discount . . ▶ ☐		
	If so, the corporation may have to file **Form 8281,** Information Return for Publicly Offered Original Issue Discount Instruments.		
9	If the corporation: **(a)** filed its election to be an S corporation after 1986, **(b)** was a C corporation before it elected to be an S corporation **or** the corporation acquired an asset with a basis determined by reference to its basis (or the basis of any other property) in the hands of a C corporation, and **(c)** has net unrealized built-in gain (defined in section 1374(d)(1)) in excess of the net recognized built-in gain from prior years, enter the net unrealized built-in gain reduced by net recognized built-in gain from prior years (see page 14 of the instructions) . . . . . ▶ $ ----------------		
10	Check this box if the corporation had subchapter C earnings and profits at the close of the tax year (see page 15 of the instructions) . . . . ▶ ☐		

Designation of Tax Matters Person (see page 15 of the instructions)

Enter below the shareholder designated as the tax matters person (TMP) for the tax year of this return:

Name of designated TMP ▶	Identifying number of TMP ▶

Address of designated TMP ▶

Form 1120S (1995)   Page **3**

Schedule K	Shareholders Shares of Income, Credits, Deductions, etc.		
	(a) Pro rata share items		**(b)** Total amount

Income (Loss)	**1** Ordinary income (loss) from trade or business activities (page 1, line 21)	**1**	
	2 Net income (loss) from rental real estate activities *(attach Form 8825)*	**2**	
	3a Gross income from other rental activities **3a**		
	b Expenses from other rental activities *(attach schedule)*. . **3b**		
	c Net income (loss) from other rental activities. Subtract line 3b from line 3a	**3c**	
	4 Portfolio income (loss):		
	a Interest income	**4a**	
	b Dividend income	**4b**	
	c Royalty income	**4c**	
	d Net short-term capital gain (loss) *(attach Schedule D (Form 1120S))*	**4d**	
	e Net long-term capital gain (loss) *(attach Schedule D (Form 1120S))*	**4e**	
	f Other portfolio income (loss) *(attach schedule)*	**4f**	
	5 Net gain (loss) under section 1231 (other than due to casualty or theft) *(attach Form 4797)*	**5**	
	6 Other income (loss) *(attach schedule)*	**6**	
Deductions	**7** Charitable contributions *(attach schedule)*	**7**	
	8 Section 179 expense deduction *(attach Form 4562)*.	**8**	
	9 Deductions related to portfolio income (loss) (itemize)	**9**	
	10 Other deductions *(attach schedule)*	**10**	
Investment Interest	**11a** Interest expense on investment debts	**11a**	
	b (1) Investment income included on lines 4a, 4b, 4c, and 4f above	**11b(1)**	
	(2) Investment expenses included on line 9 above	**11b(2)**	
Credits	**12a** Credit for alcohol used as a fuel *(attach Form 6478)*	**12a**	
	b Low-income housing credit:		
	(1) From partnerships to which section 42(j)(5) applies for property placed in service before 1990	**12b(1)**	
	(2) Other than on line 12b(1) for property placed in service before 1990.	**12b(2)**	
	(3) From partnerships to which section 42(j)(5) applies for property placed in service after 1989	**12b(3)**	
	(4) Other than on line 12b(3) for property placed in service after 1989	**12b(4)**	
	c Qualified rehabilitation expenditures related to rental real estate activities *(attach Form 3468)*	**12c**	
	d Credits (other than credits shown on lines 12b and 12c) related to rental real estate activities	**12d**	
	e Credits related to other rental activities.	**12e**	
	13 Other credits	**13**	
Adjustments and Tax Preference Items	**14a** Depreciation adjustment on property placed in service after 1986	**14a**	
	b Adjusted gain or loss	**14b**	
	c Depletion (other than oil and gas)	**14c**	
	d (1) Gross income from oil, gas, or geothermal properties	**14d(1)**	
	(2) Deductions allocable to oil, gas, or geothermal properties	**14d(2)**	
	e Other adjustments and tax preference items *(attach schedule)*	**14e**	
Foreign Taxes	**15a** Type of income ▶		
	b Name of foreign country or U.S. possession ▶		
	c Total gross income from sources outside the United States *(attach schedule)*	**15c**	
	d Total applicable deductions and losses *(attach schedule)*	**15d**	
	e Total foreign taxes (check one): ▶ ☐ Paid ☐ Accrued	**15e**	
	f Reduction in taxes available for credit *(attach schedule)*	**15f**	
	g Other foreign tax information *(attach schedule)*	**15g**	
Other	**16** Section 59(e)(2) expenditures: **a** Type ▶		
	b Amount	**16b**	
	17 Tax-exempt interest income	**17**	
	18 Other tax-exempt income	**18**	
	19 Nondeductible expenses	**19**	
	20 Total property distributions (including cash) other than dividends reported on line 22 below	**20**	
	21 Other items and amounts required to be reported separately to shareholders *(attach schedule)*		
	22 Total dividend distributions paid from accumulated earnings and profits	**22**	
	23 **Income (loss).** (Required only if Schedule M-1 must be completed.) Combine lines 1 through 6 in column (b). From the result, subtract the sum of lines 7 through 11a, 15e, and 16b	**23**	

Form 1120S (1995)   Page **4**

Schedule L	**Balance Sheets**	Beginning of tax year		End of tax year	
	Assets	(a)	(b)	(c)	(d)
1	Cash				
2a	Trade notes and accounts receivable . .				
b	Less allowance for bad debts				
3	Inventories				
4	U.S. Government obligations				
5	Tax-exempt securities				
6	Other current assets (attach schedule) . .				
7	Loans to shareholders				
8	Mortgage and real estate loans				
9	Other investments (attach schedule) . .				
10a	Buildings and other depreciable assets .				
b	Less accumulated depreciation				
11a	Depletable assets				
b	Less accumulated depletion				
12	Land (net of any amortization)				
13a	Intangible assets (amortizable only) . . .				
b	Less accumulated amortization				
14	Other assets (attach schedule)				
15	Total assets				
	Liabilities and Shareholders Equity				
16	Accounts payable				
17	Mortgages, notes, bonds payable in less than 1 year				
18	Other current liabilities (attach schedule) .				
19	Loans from shareholders				
20	Mortgages, notes, bonds payable in 1 year or more				
21	Other liabilities (attach schedule) . . .				
22	Capital stock				
23	Paid-in or capital surplus				
24	Retained earnings				
25	Less cost of treasury stock	(	)	(	)
26	Total liabilities and shareholders equity . .				

Schedule M-1	**Reconciliation of Income (Loss) per Books With Income (Loss) per Return** (You are not required to complete this schedule if the total assets on line 15, column (d), of Schedule L are less than $25,000.)

1	Net income (loss) per books		5	Income recorded on books this year not included on Schedule K, lines 1 through 6 (itemize):	
2	Income included on Schedule K, lines 1 through 6, not recorded on books this year (itemize):			a Tax-exempt interest $	
	....			....	
3	Expenses recorded on books this year not included on Schedule K, lines 1 through 11a, 15e, and 16b (itemize):		6	Deductions included on Schedule K, lines 1 through 11a, 15e, and 16b, not charged against book income this year (itemize):	
a	Depreciation $			a Depreciation $	
b	Travel and entertainment $			....	
	....		7	Add lines 5 and 6	
4	Add lines 1 through 3		8	Income (loss) (Schedule K, line 23). Line 4 less line 7	

Schedule M-2	**Analysis of Accumulated Adjustments Account, Other Adjustments Account, and Shareholders Undistributed Taxable Income Previously Taxed** (see page 22 of the instructions)

		(a) Accumulated adjustments account	**(b)** Other adjustments account	**(c)** Shareholders undistributed taxable income previously taxed
1	Balance at beginning of tax year . . .			
2	Ordinary income from page 1, line 21 . .			
3	Other additions			
4	Loss from page 1, line 21	( )		
5	Other reductions	( )	( )	
6	Combine lines 1 through 5			
7	Distributions other than dividend distributions .			
8	Balance at end of tax year. Subtract line 7 from line 6			

| SCHEDULE K-1
(Form 1120S)

Department of the Treasury
Internal Revenue Service | **Shareholder's Share of Income, Credits, Deductions, etc.**
▶ See separate instructions.
For calendar year 1995 or tax year
beginning , 1995, and ending , 19 | OMB No. 1545-0130

1995 |

Shareholder's identifying number ▶	Corporation's identifying number ▶
Shareholder's name, address, and ZIP code	Corporation's name, address, and ZIP code

A Shareholder's percentage of stock ownership for tax year (see Instructions for Schedule K-1) . . . . ▶ .... %
B Internal Revenue Service Center where corporation filed its return ▶ ....
C Tax shelter registration number (see Instructions for Schedule K-1) . . . . ▶ ....
D Check applicable boxes: **(1)** ☐ Final K-1   **(2)** ☐ Amended K-1

		(a) Pro rata share items		(b) Amount	(c) Form 1040 filers enter the amount in column (b) on:
Income (Loss)	**1**	Ordinary income (loss) from trade or business activities . . .	1		See pages 4 and 5 of the Shareholder's Instructions for Schedule K-1 (Form 1120S).
	2	Net income (loss) from rental real estate activities	2		
	3	Net income (loss) from other rental activities	3		
	4	Portfolio income (loss):			
	a	Interest	4a		Sch. B, Part I, line 1
	b	Dividends	4b		Sch. B, Part II, line 5
	c	Royalties	4c		Sch. E, Part I, line 4
	d	Net short-term capital gain (loss).	4d		Sch. D, line 5, col. (f) or (g)
	e	Net long-term capital gain (loss)	4e		Sch. D, line 13, col. (f) or (g)
	f	Other portfolio income (loss) (attach schedule)	4f		(Enter on applicable line of your return.)
	5	Net gain (loss) under section 1231 (other than due to casualty or theft)	5		See Shareholder's Instructions for Schedule K-1 (Form 1120S).
	6	Other income (loss) (attach schedule)	6		(Enter on applicable line of your return.)
Deductions	**7**	Charitable contributions (attach schedule)	7		Sch. A, line 15 or 16
	8	Section 179 expense deduction	8		See page 6 of the Shareholder's Instructions for Schedule K-1 (Form 1120S).
	9	Deductions related to portfolio income (loss) (attach schedule) .	9		
	10	Other deductions (attach schedule)	10		
Investment Interest	**11a**	Interest expense on investment debts	11a		Form 4952, line 1
	b	**(1)** Investment income included on lines 4a, 4b, 4c, and 4f above	b(1)		See Shareholder's Instructions for Schedule K-1 (Form 1120S).
		(2) Investment expenses included on line 9 above	b(2)		
Credits	**12a**	Credit for alcohol used as fuel	12a		Form 6478, line 10
	b	Low-income housing credit:			
		(1) From section 42(j)(5) partnerships for property placed in service before 1990.	b(1)		
		(2) Other than on line 12b(1) for property placed in service before 1990	b(2)		Form 8586, line 5
		(3) From section 42(j)(5) partnerships for property placed in service after 1989	b(3)		
		(4) Other than on line 12b(3) for property placed in service after 1989	b(4)		
	c	Qualified rehabilitation expenditures related to rental real estate activities	12c		See page 7 of the Shareholder's Instructions for Schedule K-1 (Form 1120S).
	d	Credits (other than credits shown on lines 12b and 12c) related to rental real estate activities	12d		
	e	Credits related to other rental activities.	12e		
	13	Other credits	13		
Adjustments and Tax Preference Items	**14a**	Depreciation adjustment on property placed in service after 1986	14a		See page 7 of the Shareholder's Instructions for Schedule K-1 (Form 1120S) and Instructions for Form 6251
	b	Adjusted gain or loss	14b		
	c	Depletion (other than oil and gas)	14c		
	d	**(1)** Gross income from oil, gas, or geothermal properties . . .	d(1)		
		(2) Deductions allocable to oil, gas, or geothermal properties .	d(2)		
	e	Other adjustments and tax preference items (attach schedule) .	14e		

For Paperwork Reduction Act Notice, see page 1 of Instructions for Form 1120S.   Cat. No. 11520D   **Schedule K-1 (Form 1120S) 1995**

Schedule K-1 (Form 1120S) (1995)   Page **2**

(a) Pro rata share items		(b) Amount	(c) Form 1040 filers enter the amount in column (b) on:
Foreign Taxes	**15a** Type of income ▶		Form 1116, Check boxes
	b Name of foreign country or U.S. possession ▶		
	c Total gross income from sources outside the United States *(attach schedule)*	**15c**	Form 1116, Part I
	d Total applicable deductions and losses *(attach schedule)*	**15d**	
	e Total foreign taxes (check one): ▶ ☐ Paid ☐ Accrued	**15e**	Form 1116, Part II
	f Reduction in taxes available for credit *(attach schedule)*	**15f**	Form 1116, Part III
	g Other foreign tax information *(attach schedule)*	**15g**	See Instructions for Form 1116
Other	**16** Section 59(e)(2) expenditures: **a** Type ▶		See Shareholder's Instructions for Schedule K-1 (Form 1120S).
	b Amount	**16b**	
	17 Tax-exempt interest income	**17**	Form 1040, line 8b
	18 Other tax-exempt income	**18**	
	19 Nondeductible expenses	**19**	See page 7 of the Shareholder's Instructions for Schedule K-1 (Form 1120S).
	20 Property distributions (including cash) other than dividend distributions reported to you on Form 1099-DIV	**20**	
	21 Amount of loan repayments for Loans From Shareholders	**21**	
	22 Recapture of low-income housing credit:		
	a From section 42(j)(5) partnerships	**22a**	Form 8611, line 8
	b Other than on line 22a	**22b**	

23 Supplemental information required to be reported separately to each shareholder *(attach additional schedules if more space is needed)*:

Supplemental Information

Form **2106**

Department of the Treasury
Internal Revenue Service (99)

Employee Business Expenses

▶ See separate instructions.

▶ Attach to Form 1040 or Form 1040-T.

OMB No. 1545-0139

1995

Attachment
Sequence No. **54**

Your name	Social security number	Occupation in which expenses were incurred

Part I   Employee Business Expenses and Reimbursements

STEP 1   Enter Your Expenses

			Column A Other Than Meals and Entertainment		Column B Meals and Entertainment
1	Vehicle expense from line 22 or line 29	1			
2	Parking fees, tolls, and transportation, including train, bus, etc., that **did not** involve overnight travel	2			
3	Travel expense while away from home overnight, including lodging, airplane, car rental, etc. **Do not** include meals and entertainment	3			
4	Business expenses not included on lines 1 through 3. **Do not** include meals and entertainment	4			
5	Meals and entertainment expenses (see instructions)	5			
6	**Total expenses.** In Column A, add lines 1 through 4 and enter the result. In Column B, enter the amount from line 5	6			

Note: *If you were not reimbursed for any expenses in Step 1, skip line 7 and enter the amount from line 6 on line 8.*

STEP 2   Enter Amounts Your Employer Gave You for Expenses Listed in STEP 1

7	Enter amounts your employer gave you that were **not** reported to you in box 1 of Form W-2. Include any amount reported under code "L" in box 13 of your Form W-2 (see instructions) . . .	7		

STEP 3   Figure Expenses To Deduct on Schedule A (Form 1040) or Form 1040-T, Section B

8	Subtract line 7 from line 6	8		
	Note: *If **both columns** of line 8 are zero, **stop here.** If Column A is less than zero, report the amount as income on Form 1040, line 7, or Form 1040-T, line 1.*			
9	In Column A, enter the amount from line 8 (if zero or less, enter -0-). In Column B, multiply the amount on line 8 by 50% (.50) .	9		
10	Add the amounts on line 9 of both columns and enter the total here. **Also, enter the total on Schedule A (Form 1040), line 20, or Form 1040-T, Section B, line n.** (Qualified performing artists and individuals with disabilities, see the instructions for special rules on where to enter the total.) . . . . ▶	10		

For Paperwork Reduction Act Notice, see instructions.   Cat. No. 11700N   Form **2106** (1995)

Form 2106 (1995)   Page **2**

Part II	**Vehicle Expenses** (See instructions to find out which sections to complete.)			

Section A.—General Information | | **(a)** Vehicle 1 | **(b)** Vehicle 2

11	Enter the date vehicle was placed in service	**11**	/ /	/ /
12	Total miles vehicle was driven during 1995	**12**	miles	miles
13	Business miles included on line 12	**13**	miles	miles
14	Percent of business use. Divide line 13 by line 12	**14**	%	%
15	Average daily round trip commuting distance	**15**	miles	miles
16	Commuting miles included on line 12	**16**	miles	miles
17	Other personal miles. Add lines 13 and 16 and subtract the total from line 12	**17**	miles	miles

18	Do you (or your spouse) have another vehicle available for personal purposes?	☐ Yes	☐ No

19 If your employer provided you with a vehicle, is personal use during off-duty hours permitted? ☐ Yes   ☐ No   ☐ Not applicable

20	Do you have evidence to support your deduction?	☐ Yes	☐ No
21	If "Yes," is the evidence written?	☐ Yes	☐ No

Section B.—Standard Mileage Rate (Use this section only if you own the vehicle.)

22	Multiply line 13 by 30¢ (.30). Enter the result here and on line 1. (Rural mail carriers, see instructions.)	**22**		

Section C.—Actual Expenses | | **(a)** Vehicle 1 | | **(b)** Vehicle 2 | |

23	Gasoline, oil, repairs, vehicle insurance, etc.	**23**				
24a	Vehicle rentals	**24a**				
b	Inclusion amount (see instructions)	**24b**				
c	Subtract line 24b from line 24a	**24c**				
25	Value of employer-provided vehicle (applies only if 100% of annual lease value was included on Form W-2—see instructions)	**25**				
26	Add lines 23, 24c, and 25 . .	**26**				
27	Multiply line 26 by the percentage on line 14 . . .	**27**				
28	Depreciation. Enter amount from line 38 below	**28**				
29	Add lines 27 and 28. Enter total here and on line 1.	**29**				

Section D.—Depreciation of Vehicles (Use this section only if you own the vehicle.)

			(a) Vehicle 1		**(b)** Vehicle 2	
30	Enter cost or other basis (see instructions)	**30**				
31	Enter amount of section 179 deduction (see instructions) .	**31**				
32	Multiply line 30 by line 14 (see instructions if you elected the section 179 deduction) . . .	**32**				
33	Enter depreciation method and percentage (see instructions) .	**33**				
34	Multiply line 32 by the percentage on line 33 (see instructions) . .	**34**				
35	Add lines 31 and 34	**35**				
36	Enter the limitation amount from the table in the line 36 instructions	**36**				
37	Multiply line 36 by the percentage on line 14 . . .	**37**				
38	Enter the **smaller** of line 35 or line 37. Also, enter this amount on line 28 above	**38**				

✹ *Printed on recycled paper*

Form **2106-EZ** Department of the Treasury Internal Revenue Service (99)	**Unreimbursed Employee Business Expenses** ▶ See instructions on back. ▶ Attach to Form 1040 or Form 1040-T.	OMB No. 1545-1441 **1995** Attachment Sequence No. **54A**	

Your name	Social security number	Occupation in which expenses were incurred

Part I General Information

You May Use This Form ONLY if All of the Following Apply:

- You are an employee deducting expenses attributable to your job.
- You **do not** get reimbursed by your employer for any expenses (amounts your employer included in box 1 of your Form W-2 are not considered reimbursements).
- If you are claiming vehicle expense,
  a You own your vehicle, and
  b You are using the standard mileage rate for 1995 **and** also used it for the year you first placed the vehicle in service.

Part II Figure Your Expenses

1	Vehicle expense using the standard mileage rate. Complete Part III and multiply line 8a by 30¢ (.30)	1	
2	Parking fees, tolls, and transportation, including train, bus, etc., that **did not** involve overnight travel	2	
3	Travel expense while away from home overnight, including lodging, airplane, car rental, etc. **Do not** include meals and entertainment	3	
4	Business expenses not included on lines 1 through 3. **Do not** include meals and entertainment .	4	
5	Meals and entertainment expenses: $ _____ x 50% (.50)	5	
6	**Total expenses.** Add lines 1 through 5. Enter here and **on line 20 of Schedule A (Form 1040), or Form 1040-T, Section B, line n.** (Qualified performing artists and individuals with disabilities, see the instructions for special rules on where to enter this amount.)	6	

Part III Information on Your Vehicle. Complete this part **ONLY** if you are claiming vehicle expense on line 1.

7 When did you place your vehicle in service for business purposes? (month, day, year) ▶ .... / .... / ....

8 Of the total number of miles you drove your vehicle during 1995, enter the number of miles you used your vehicle for:

a Business .... **b** Commuting .... **c** Other ....

9 Do you (or your spouse) have another vehicle available for personal use? . . . . ☐ Yes ☐ No

10 Was your vehicle available for use during off-duty hours? . . . . ☐ Yes ☐ No

11a Do you have evidence to support your deduction? . . . . ☐ Yes ☐ No

b If "Yes," is the evidence written? . . . . ☐ Yes ☐ No

For Paperwork Reduction Act Notice, see back of form.   Cat. No. 20604Q   Form **2106-EZ** (1995)

Form 2119 — Sale of Your Home

Form **2119**

Department of the Treasury
Internal Revenue Service

Sale of Your Home

▶ Attach to Form 1040 for year of sale.
▶ See separate instructions. ▶ Please print or type.

OMB No. 1545-0072

1995

Attachment Sequence No. **20**

Your first name and initial. If a joint return, also give spouse's name and initial.   Last name   Your social security number

Fill in Your Address Only If You Are Filing This Form by Itself and Not With Your Tax Return

Present address (no., street, and apt. no., rural route, or P.O. box no. if mail is not delivered to street address)   Spouse's social security number

City, town or post office, state, and ZIP code

Part I — Gain on Sale

1. Date your former main home was sold (month, day, year) . . . . ▶ **1** __ / __ / __
2. Have you bought or built a new main home? . . . . □ Yes □ No
3. If any part of either main home was ever rented out or used for business, check here ▶ □ and see page 3.
4. Selling price of home. Do not include personal property items you sold with your home . . **4**
5. Expense of sale (see page 3) **5**
6. Subtract line 5 from line 4 . . . . **6**
7. Adjusted basis of home sold (see page 3) **7**
8. **Gain on sale.** Subtract line 7 from line 6 . . . . **8**

Is line 8 more than zero?

Yes ▶ If line 2 is "Yes," you **must** go to Part II or Part III, whichever applies. If line 2 is "No," go to line 9.

No ▶ **Stop;** see **Loss on the Sale of Your Home** on page 1.

9. If you haven't replaced your home, do you plan to do so within the **replacement period** (see page 1)? . □ Yes □ No
   - If line 9 is "Yes," stop here, attach this form to your return, and see **Additional Filing Requirements** on page 1.
   - If line 9 is "No," you **must** go to Part II or Part III, whichever applies.

Part II — One-Time Exclusion of Gain for People Age 55 or Older—

By completing this part, you are electing to take the one-time exclusion (see page 2). If you are not electing to take the exclusion, go to Part III now.

10. Who was age 55 or older on the date of sale? . . . . □ You □ Your spouse □ Both of you
11. Did the person who was 55 or older own and use the property as his or her main home for a total of at least 3 years of the 5-year period before the sale? See page 2 for exceptions. If "No," go to Part III now . . . □ Yes □ No
12. At the time of sale, who owned the home? . . . . □ You □ Your spouse □ Both of you
13. Social security number of spouse at the time of sale if you had a different spouse from the one above. If you were not married at the time of sale, enter "None" . . . . ▶ **13**
14. **Exclusion.** Enter the **smaller** of line 8 or $125,000 ($62,500 if married filing separate return). Then, go to line 15 . . . . **14**

Part III — Adjusted Sales Price, Taxable Gain, and Adjusted Basis of New Home

15. If line 14 is blank, enter the amount from line 8. Otherwise, subtract line 14 from line 8 . . **15**
   - If line 15 is zero, stop and attach this form to your return.
   - If line 15 is more than zero and line 2 is "Yes," go to line 16 now.
   - If you are reporting this sale on the installment method, stop and see page 4.
   - All others, stop and **enter the amount from line 15 on Schedule D, col. (g), line 4 or line 12.**
16. Fixing-up expenses (see page 4 for time limits) **16**
17. If line 14 is blank, enter amount from line 16. Otherwise, add lines 14 and 16 . . . . . . **17**
18. **Adjusted sales price.** Subtract line 17 from line 6 . . . . **18**
19a. Date you moved into new home ▶ __ / __ / __   b Cost of new home (see page 4) **19b**
20. Subtract line 19b from line 18. If zero or less, enter -0- **20**
21. **Taxable gain.** Enter the **smaller** of line 15 or line 20 . . . . . . **21**
   - If line 21 is zero, go to line 22 and attach this form to your return.
   - If you are reporting this sale on the installment method, see the line 15 instructions and go to line 22.
   - All others, **enter the amount from line 21 on Schedule D, col. (g), line 4 or line 12,** and go to line 22.
22. Postponed gain. Subtract line 21 from line 15 . . . . **22**
23. **Adjusted basis of new home.** Subtract line 22 from line 19b **23**

Sign Here Only If You Are Filing This Form by Itself and Not With Your Tax Return

Under penalties of perjury, I declare that I have examined this form, including attachments, and to the best of my knowledge and belief, it is true, correct, and complete.

Your signature   Date   Spouse's signature   Date

▶ _____ ▶ _____
If a joint return, both must sign.

For Paperwork Reduction Act Notice, see separate instructions.   Cat. No. 11710J   Form **2119** (1995)

Printed on recycled paper

Form **2120**
(Rev. January 1994)

Department of the Treasury
Internal Revenue Service

Multiple Support Declaration

▶ **Attach to Form 1040 or Form 1040A of Person
Claiming the Dependent.**

OMB No. 1545-0071
Expires 1-31-97

Attachment
Sequence No. **50**

Name of person claiming the dependent

Social security number

During the calendar year 19 ...., I paid over 10% of the support of

Name of person

I could have claimed this person as a dependent except that I did not pay over 50% of his or her support. I understand that this person named above is being claimed as a dependent on the income tax return of

Name

Address

I agree not to claim this person as a dependent on my Federal income tax return for any tax year that began in this calendar year.

Your signature

Your social security number

Date

Address (number, street, apt. no.)

City, state, and ZIP code

Instructions

Paperwork Reduction Act Notice

We ask for the information on this form to carry out the Internal Revenue laws of the United States. You are required to give us the information. We need it to ensure that you are complying with these laws and to allow us to figure and collect the right amount of tax.

The time needed to complete and file this form will vary depending on individual circumstances. The estimated average time is: **Recordkeeping**, 7 minutes; **Learning about the law or the form**, 2 minutes; **Preparing the form**, 7 minutes; and **Copying, assembling, and sending the form to the IRS**, 10 minutes.

If you have comments concerning the accuracy of these time estimates or suggestions for making this form more simple, we would be happy to hear from you. You can write to both the IRS and the Office of Management and Budget at the addresses listed in the instructions of the tax return with which this form is filed.

Purpose of Form

When two or more individuals together pay over 50% of another person's support, Form 2120 or a similar statement is used to allow one of them to claim the person as a dependent for tax purposes.

The similar statement must contain the same information that is required by this form.

Who Can Claim the Dependent

To claim someone as a dependent, you must pay over 50% of that person's living expenses (support).

If no one meets this support test, but two or more of you together provide over 50% of a person's support, then one of you can claim that person as a dependent.

To claim the dependent, you must meet **all three** of the following requirements:

1. You paid over 10% of the support, and

2. All others who paid over 10% agree not to claim the person as a dependent, and

3. The other four dependency tests are met. See **Dependents** in the Form 1040 or Form 1040A instructions.

All contributors who provided over 10% support must choose which one of them will claim the dependent. If you will be claiming the dependent, see **How To File** below.

If you are a 10% contributor but **will not** be claiming the dependent, complete and sign a Form 2120 or similar statement. Give it to the person claiming the dependent.

How To File

If you are claiming the dependent, you must attach to your tax return a Form 2120 or similar statement that is completed and signed by each of the 10% contributors who are not claiming the dependent for the tax year. Be sure your name and social security number are at the top of each Form 2120 or similar statement.

Additional Information

See **Pub. 501**, Exemptions, Standard Deduction, and Filing Information, for more information.

Cat. No. 11712F

Form **2120** (Rev. 1-94)

Form **2210**	**Underpayment of**	OMB No. 1545-0140

Estimated Tax by Individuals, Estates, and Trusts

Department of the Treasury
Internal Revenue Service

► See separate instructions.

► Attach to Form 1040, 1040A, 1040-T, 1040NR, 1040NR-EZ, or 1041.

1995

Attachment
Sequence No. **06A**

Name(s) shown on tax return	Identifying number

Note: *In most cases, you **do not** need to file Form 2210. The IRS will figure any penalty you owe and send you a bill. File Form 2210 **only** if one or more boxes in Part I apply to you. If you do not need to file Form 2210, you still may use it to figure your penalty. Enter the amount from line 20 or line 36 on the penalty line of your return, but do not attach Form 2210.*

Part I   **Reasons For Filing**—If 1a, b, or c below applies to you, you may be able to lower or eliminate your penalty. But you MUST check the boxes that apply and file Form 2210 with your tax return. If 1d below applies to you, check that box and file Form 2210 with your tax return.

1   Check whichever boxes apply (if none apply, see the **Note** above):

a ☐ You request a **waiver.** In certain circumstances, the IRS will waive all or part of the penalty. See **Waiver of Penalty** on page 1 of the instructions.

b ☐ You use the **annualized income installment method.** If your income varied during the year, this method may reduce the amount of one or more required installments. See page 4 of the instructions.

c ☐ You had Federal income tax withheld from wages and you treat it as paid for estimated tax purposes when it was **actually** withheld instead of in equal amounts on the payment due dates. See the instructions for line 22.

d ☐ Your required annual payment (line 13 below) is based on your 1994 tax and you filed or are filing a joint return for either 1994 or 1995 but not for both years.

Part II   **Required Annual Payment**

2	Enter your 1995 tax after credits (see instructions)	**2**	
3	Other taxes (see instructions)	**3**	
4	Add lines 2 and 3	**4**	
5	Earned income credit	**5**	
6	Credit for Federal tax paid on fuels	**6**	
7	Add lines 5 and 6	**7**	
8	Current year tax. Subtract line 7 from line 4	**8**	
9	Multiply line 8 by 90% (.90)	**9**	
10	Withholding taxes. **Do not** include any estimated tax payments on this line (see instructions) .	**10**	
11	Subtract line 10 from line 8. If less than $500, stop here; **do not** complete or file this form. You do not owe the penalty	**11**	
12	Enter the tax shown on your 1994 tax return (110% of that amount if the adjusted gross income shown on that return is more than $150,000, or if married filing separately for 1995, more than $75,000). **Caution:** *See instructions*	**12**	
13	**Required annual payment.** Enter the **smaller** of line 9 or line 12	**13**	

Note: *If line 10 is equal to or more than line 13, stop here; you do not owe the penalty. Do not file Form 2210 unless you checked box 1d above.*

Part III   **Short Method (Caution:** *Read the instructions to see if you can use the short method. If you checked box **1b** or **c** in Part I, skip this part and go to Part IV.*)

14	Enter the amount, if any, from line 10 above	**14**	
15	Enter the total amount, if any, of estimated tax payments you made	**15**	
16	Add lines 14 and 15	**16**	
17	**Total underpayment for year.** Subtract line 16 from line 13. If zero or less, stop here; you do not owe the penalty. Do not file Form 2210 unless you checked box 1d above	**17**	
18	Multiply line 17 by .06066	**18**	
19	● If the amount on line 17 was paid **on or after** 4/15/96, enter -0-.		
	● If the amount on line 17 was paid **before** 4/15/96, make the following computation to find the amount to enter on line 19. Amount on line 17 ✕ Number of days paid before 4/15/96 ✕ .00025	**19**	
20	**PENALTY.** Subtract line 19 from line 18. Enter the result here and on Form 1040, line 66; Form 1040A, line 34; Form 1040-T, line 42; Form 1040NR, line 66; Form 1040NR-EZ, line 26; or Form 1041, line 26 . . . . ►	**20**	

For Paperwork Reduction Act Notice, see page 1 of separate instructions.   Cat. No. 11744P   Form **2210** (1995)

Part IV **Regular Method** (See the instructions if you are filing Form 1040NR or 1040NR-EZ.)

		Payment Due Dates			
		(a) 4/15/95	**(b)** 6/15/95	**(c)** 9/15/95	**(d)** 1/15/96

Section A—Figure Your Underpayment

21	**Required installments.** If box 1b applies, enter the amounts from Schedule AI, line 26. Otherwise, enter ¼ of line 13, Form 2210, in each column	**21**				
22	Estimated tax paid and tax withheld (see instructions). For column (a) only, also enter the amount from line 22 on line 26. If line 22 is equal to or more than line 21 for all payment periods, stop here; you do not owe the penalty. Do not file Form 2210 unless you checked a box in Part I	**22**				
	Complete lines 23 through 29 of one column before going to the next column.					
23	Enter amount, if any, from line 29 of previous column	**23**				
24	Add lines 22 and 23	**24**				
25	Add amounts on lines 27 and 28 of the previous column	**25**				
26	Subtract line 25 from line 24. If zero or less, enter -0-. For column (a) only, enter the amount from line 22 .	**26**				
27	If the amount on line 26 is zero, subtract line 24 from line 25. Otherwise, enter -0-	**27**				
28	**Underpayment.** If line 21 is equal to or more than line 26, subtract line 26 from line 21. Then go to line 23 of next column. Otherwise, go to line 29 . ▶	**28**				
29	Overpayment. If line 26 is more than line 21, subtract line 21 from line 26. Then go to line 23 of next column	**29**				

Section B—Figure the Penalty (Complete lines 30 through 35 of one column before going to the next column.)

			(a)	(b)	(c)	(d)
Rate Period 1	**April 16, 1995—June 30, 1995**		4/15/95	6/15/95		
	30 Number of days FROM the date shown above line 30 TO the date the amount on line 28 was paid **or** 6/30/95, whichever is earlier	**30**	Days:	Days:		
	31 Underpayment on line 28 (see instructions) × (Number of days on line 30)/365 × .10 ▶	**31**	$	$		
Rate Period 2	**July 1, 1995—December 31, 1995**		6/30/95	6/30/95	9/15/95	
	32 Number of days FROM the date shown above line 32 TO the date the amount on line 28 was paid **or** 12/31/95, whichever is earlier	**32**	Days:	Days:	Days:	
	33 Underpayment on line 28 (see instructions) × (Number of days on line 32)/365 × .09 ▶	**33**	$	$	$	
Rate Period 3	**January 1, 1996—April 15, 1996**		12/31/95	12/31/95	12/31/95	1/15/96
	34 Number of days FROM the date shown above line 34 TO the date the amount on line 28 was paid **or** 4/15/96, whichever is earlier	**34**	Days:	Days:	Days:	Days:
	35 Underpayment on line 28 (see instructions) × (Number of days on line 34)/366 × .09 ▶	**35**	$	$	$	$

36	**PENALTY.** Add all amounts on lines 31, 33, and 35 in all columns. Enter the total here and on Form 1040, line 66; Form 1040A, line 34; Form 1040-T, line 42; Form 1040NR, line 66; Form 1040NR-EZ, line 26; or Form 1041, line 26 . . . . ▶	**36**	$

Form 2210 (1995)   Page **3**

Schedule AI—Annualized Income Installment Method (see instructions)

Estates and trusts, **do not** use the period ending dates shown to the right. Instead, use the following: 2/28/95, 4/30/95, 7/31/95, and 11/30/95.

		(a) 1/1/95–3/31/95	(b) 1/1/95–5/31/95	(c) 1/1/95–8/31/95	(d) 1/1/95–12/31/95

Part I   Annualized Income Installments   Caution: *Complete lines 20–26 of one column before going to the next column.*

			(a)	(b)	(c)	(d)
1	Enter your adjusted gross income for each period (see instructions). (Estates and trusts, enter your taxable income without your exemption for each period.)	1				
2	Annualization amounts. (Estates and trusts, see instructions.)	2	4	2.4	1.5	1
3	Annualized income. Multiply line 1 by line 2	3				
4	Enter your itemized deductions for the period shown in each column. If you do not itemize, enter -0- and skip to line 7. (Estates and trusts, enter -0-, skip to line 9, and enter the amount from line 3 on line 9.)	4				
5	Annualization amounts	5	4	2.4	1.5	1
6	Multiply line 4 by line 5 (see instructions if line 3 is more than $57,350)	6				
7	In each column, enter the full amount of your standard deduction from Form 1040, line 34; Form 1040A, line 19; or Form 1040-T, line 20 (Form 1040NR or 1040NR-EZ filers, enter -0-. **Exception:** Indian students and business apprentices, enter standard deduction from Form 1040NR, line 33 or Form 1040NR-EZ, line 10.)	7				
8	Enter the **larger** of line 6 or line 7	8				
9	Subtract line 8 from line 3	9				
10	In each column, multiply $2,500 by the total number of exemptions claimed (see instructions if line 3 is more than $86,025). (Estates and trusts and Form 1040NR or 1040NR-EZ filers, enter the exemption amount shown on your tax return.)	10				
11	Subtract line 10 from line 9	11				
12	Figure your tax on the amount on line 11 (see instructions)	12				
13	Form 1040 filers only, enter your self-employment tax from line 35 below	13				
14	Enter other taxes for each payment period (see instructions)	14				
15	Total tax. Add lines 12, 13, and 14	15				
16	For each period, enter the same type of credits as allowed on Form 2210, lines 2, 5, and 6 (see instructions)	16				
17	Subtract line 16 from line 15. If zero or less, enter -0-	17				
18	Applicable percentage	18	22.5%	45%	67.5%	90%
19	Multiply line 17 by line 18	19				
20	Add the amounts in all preceding columns of line 26	20				
21	Subtract line 20 from line 19. If zero or less, enter -0-	21				
22	Enter ¼ of line 13 on page 1 of Form 2210 in each column	22				
23	Enter amount from line 25 of the preceding column of this schedule	23				
24	Add lines 22 and 23 and enter the total	24				
25	Subtract line 21 from line 24. If zero or less, enter -0-	25				
26	Enter the **smaller** of line 21 or line 24 here and on Form 2210, line 21 ▶	26				

Part II   Annualized Self-Employment Tax

			(a)	(b)	(c)	(d)
27a	Net earnings from self-employment for the period (see instructions)	27a				
b	Annualization amounts	27b	4	2.4	1.5	1
c	Multiply line 27a by line 27b	27c				
28	Social security tax limit	28	$61,200	$61,200	$61,200	$61,200
29	Enter actual wages subject to social security tax or the 6.2% portion of the 7.65% railroad retirement (tier 1) tax	29				
30	Annualization amounts	30	4	2.4	1.5	1
31	Multiply line 29 by line 30	31				
32	Subtract line 31 from line 28. If zero or less, enter -0-	32				
33	Multiply the smaller of line 27c or line 32 by .124	33				
34	Multiply line 27c by .029	34				
35	Add lines 33 and 34. Enter the result here and on line 13 above ▶	35				

✱ *Printed on recycled paper*

Form **2441**

Department of the Treasury
Internal Revenue Service (99)

Child and Dependent Care Expenses

▶ Attach to Form 1040.

▶ See separate instructions.

OMB No. 1545-0068

1995

Attachment
Sequence No. **21**

Name(s) shown on Form 1040

Your social security number

You need to understand the following terms to complete this form:
Qualifying Person(s), Dependent Care Benefits, Qualified Expenses, and **Earned Income.** See **Important Terms** on page 1 of the Form 2441 instructions.

Part I **Persons or Organizations Who Provided the Care**—You **must** complete this part.
(If you need more space, use the bottom of page 2.)

1	(a) Care provider's name	(b) Address (number, street, apt. no., city, state, and ZIP code)	(c) Identifying number (SSN or EIN)	(d) Amount paid (see instructions)

2 Add the amounts in column (d) of line 1 . . . . **2**

3 Enter the number of **qualifying persons** cared for in 1995 . . . . ▶

| Did you receive **dependent care benefits?** | —— NO ——▶ Complete only Part II below. |
| | —— YES ——▶ Complete Part III on the back now. |

Part II **Credit for Child and Dependent Care Expenses**

4 Enter the amount of **qualified expenses** you incurred and paid in 1995. DO NOT enter more than $2,400 for one qualifying person or $4,800 for two or more persons. If you completed Part III, enter the amount from line 25 . . . . **4**

5 Enter YOUR **earned income** **5**

6 If married filing a joint return, enter YOUR SPOUSE'S earned income (if student or disabled, see the instructions); **all others,** enter the amount from line 5 . . . . **6**

7 Enter the **smallest** of line 4, 5, or 6 . . . . **7**

8 Enter the amount from Form 1040, line 32 . . . . **8**

9 Enter on line 9 the decimal amount shown below that applies to the amount on line 8

If line 8 is—		Decimal amount is	If line 8 is—		Decimal amount is
Over	But not over		Over	But not over	
$0—10,000		.30	$20,000—22,000		.24
10,000—12,000		.29	22,000—24,000		.23
12,000—14,000		.28	24,000—26,000		.22
14,000—16,000		.27	26,000—28,000		.21
16,000—18,000		.26	28,000—No limit		.20
18,000—20,000		.25			

9 ✕ .

10 Multiply **line 7** by the decimal amount on line 9. Enter the result. Then, see the instructions for the amount of credit to enter on Form 1040, line 41 . . . . **10**

Caution: *If you paid a person who worked in your home, you may have to pay employment taxes. See the instructions for Form 1040, line 53, on page 26.*

For Paperwork Reduction Act Notice, see separate instructions.

Cat. No. 11862M

Form **2441** (1995)

Part III Dependent Care Benefits—Complete this part **only** if you received these benefits.

11 Enter the total amount of **dependent care benefits** you received for 1995. This amount should be shown in box 10 of your W-2 form(s). DO NOT include amounts that were reported to you as wages in box 1 of Form(s) W-2 11

12 Enter the amount forfeited, if any. See the instructions 12

13 Subtract line 12 from line 11 13

14 Enter the total amount of **qualified expenses** incurred in 1995 for the care of the qualifying person(s) 14

15 Enter the **smaller** of line 13 or 14 15

16 Enter YOUR **earned income** 16

17 If married filing a joint return, enter YOUR SPOUSE'S earned income (if student or disabled, see the line 6 instructions); if married filing a separate return, see the instructions for the amount to enter; **all others,** enter the amount from line 16 . . 17

18 Enter the **smallest** of line 15, 16, or 17 18

19 **Excluded benefits.** Enter here the **smaller** of the following:

   • The amount from line 18, or
   • $5,000 ($2,500 if married filing a separate return **and** you were required to enter your spouse's earned income on line 17).   19

20 **Taxable benefits.** Subtract line 19 from line 13. Also, include this amount on Form 1040, line 7. On the dotted line next to line 7, write "DCB" 20

To claim the child and dependent care credit, complete
lines 21–25 below, and lines 4–10 on the front of this form.

21 Enter the amount of qualified expenses you incurred and paid in 1995. DO NOT include on this line any excluded benefits shown on line 19 21

22 Enter $2,400 ($4,800 if two or more qualifying persons) . . . 22

23 Enter the amount from line 19 23

24 Subtract line 23 from line 22. If zero or less, **STOP.** You cannot take the credit. **Exception.** If you paid 1994 expenses in 1995, see the line 10 instructions 24

25 Enter the **smaller** of line 21 or 24 here **and** on line 4 on the front of this form 25

 Printed on recycled paper

Form **2555**	**Foreign Earned Income**	OMB No. 1545-0067

Form **2555**

Department of the Treasury
Internal Revenue Service

Foreign Earned Income

▶ See separate instructions.   ▶ Attach to Form 1040.

OMB No. 1545-0067

1995

Attachment
Sequence No. **34**

For Use by U.S. Citizens and Resident Aliens Only

Name shown on Form 1040

Your social security number

Part I   General Information

1 Your foreign address (including country)

2 Your occupation

3 Employer's name ▶

4a Employer's U.S. address ▶

b Employer's foreign address ▶

5 Employer is (check any that apply): ▶   **a** ☐ A foreign entity   **b** ☐ A U.S. company   **c** ☐ Self
d ☐ A foreign affiliate of a U.S. company   **e** ☐ Other (specify) ▶

6a If, after 1981, you filed Form 2555 to claim either of the exclusions or Form 2555-EZ to claim the foreign earned income exclusion, enter the last year you filed the form. ▶

b If you did not file Form 2555 or 2555-EZ after 1981 to claim either of the exclusions, check here ▶ ☐ and go to line 7 now.

c Have you ever revoked either of the exclusions?   ☐ Yes ☐ No

d If you answered "Yes," enter the type of exclusion and the tax year for which the revocation was effective. ▶

7 Of what country are you a citizen/national? ▶

8a Did you maintain a separate foreign residence for your family because of adverse living conditions at your tax home? See **Second foreign household** on page 3 of the instructions   ☐ Yes ☐ No

b If "Yes," enter city and country of the separate foreign residence. Also, enter the number of days during your tax year that you maintained a second household at that address. ▶

9 List your tax home(s) during your tax year and date(s) established. ▶

Next, complete either Part II or Part III. If an item does not apply, write "NA." If you do not give the information asked for, any exclusion or deduction you claim may be disallowed.

Part II   Taxpayers Qualifying Under Bona Fide Residence Test (See page 2 of the instructions.)

10 Date bona fide residence began ▶ _____ , and ended ▶

11 Kind of living quarters in foreign country ▶ **a** ☐ Purchased house   **b** ☐ Rented house or apartment   **c** ☐ Rented room
d ☐ Quarters furnished by employer

12a Did any of your family live with you abroad during any part of the tax year?   ☐ Yes ☐ No

b If "Yes," who and for what period? ▶

13a Have you submitted a statement to the authorities of the foreign country where you claim bona fide residence that you are not a resident of that country? (See instructions.)   ☐ Yes ☐ No

b Are you required to pay income tax to the country where you claim bona fide residence? (See instructions.)   ☐ Yes ☐ No

If you answered "Yes" to 13a and "No" to 13b, you do not qualify as a bona fide resident. Do not complete the rest of this part.

14 If you were present in the United States or its possessions during the tax year, complete columns (a)-(d) below. **Do not** include the income from column (d) in Part IV, but report it on Form 1040.

(a) Date arrived in U.S.	(b) Date left U.S.	(c) Number of days in U.S. on business	(d) Income earned in U.S. on business (attach computation)	(a) Date arrived in U.S.	(b) Date left U.S.	(c) Number of days in U.S. on business	(d) Income earned in U.S. on business (attach computation)

15a List any contractual terms or other conditions relating to the length of your employment abroad. ▶

b Enter the type of visa under which you entered the foreign country. ▶

c Did your visa limit the length of your stay or employment in a foreign country? If "Yes," attach explanation   ☐ Yes ☐ No

d Did you maintain a home in the United States while living abroad?   ☐ Yes ☐ No

e If "Yes," enter address of your home, whether it was rented, the names of the occupants, and their relationship to you. ▶

For Paperwork Reduction Act Notice, see page 1 of separate instructions.   Cat. No. 11900P   Form **2555** (1995)

Form 2555 (1995) .   Page **2**

Part III   Taxpayers Qualifying Under Physical Presence Test (See page 2 of the instructions.)

16   The physical presence test is based on the 12-month period from ▶.............................. through ▶ ....

17   Enter your principal country of employment during your tax year. ▶...

18   If you traveled abroad during the 12-month period entered on line 16, complete columns (a)–(f) below. Exclude travel between foreign countries that did not involve travel on or over international waters, or in or over the United States, for 24 hours or more. If you have no travel to report during the period, enter "Physically present in a foreign country or countries for the entire 12-month period." **Do not** include the income from column (f) below in Part IV, but report it on Form 1040.

(a) Name of country (including U.S.)	(b) Date arrived	(c) Date left	(d) Full days present in country	(e) Number of days in U.S. on business	(f) Income earned in U.S. on business (attach computation)

Part IV   All Taxpayers

Note: *Enter on lines 19 through 23 all income, including noncash income, you earned and actually or constructively received during your 1995 tax year for services you performed in a foreign country. If any of the foreign earned income received this tax year was earned in a prior tax year, or will be earned in a later tax year (such as a bonus), see the instructions. Do not include income from line 14, column (d), or line 18, column (f). Report amounts in U.S. dollars, using the exchange rates in effect when you actually or constructively received the income.*

If you are a cash basis taxpayer, report on Form 1040 all income you received in 1995, no matter when you performed the service.

1995 Foreign Earned Income		Amount (in U.S. dollars)
19 Total wages, salaries, bonuses, commissions, etc..	19	
20 Allowable share of income for personal services performed (see instructions):		
a In a business (including farming) or profession	20a	
b In a partnership. List partnership's name and address and type of income. ▶	20b	
21 Noncash income (market value of property or facilities furnished by employer—attach statement showing how it was determined):		
a Home (lodging)	21a	
b Meals	21b	
c Car . . .	21c	
d Other property or facilities. List type and amount. ▶	21d	
22 Allowances, reimbursements, or expenses paid on your behalf for services you performed:		
a Cost of living and overseas differential	22a	
b Family	22b	
c Education	22c	
d Home leave	22d	
e Quarters.	22e	
f For any other purpose. List type and amount. ▶	22f	
g Add lines 22a through 22f	22g	
23 Other foreign earned income. List type and amount. ▶	23	
24 Add lines 19 through 21d, line 22g, and line 23	24	
25 Total amount of meals and lodging included on line 24 that is excludable (see instructions) . .	25	
26 Subtract line 25 from line 24. Enter the result here and on line 27 on page 3. This is your **foreign earned income** . . . . ▶	26	

Form 2555 (1995)

Part V   All Taxpayers

27	Enter the amount from line 26	27	

Are you claiming the housing exclusion or housing deduction?
Yes. Complete Part VI.
No. Go to Part VII.

Part VI   For Taxpayers Claiming the Housing Exclusion AND/OR Deduction

28	Qualified housing expenses for the tax year (see instructions)	28	
29	Number of days in your qualifying period that fall within your 1995 tax year (see instructions) . . . . [29]		
30	Multiply $24.82 by the number of days on line 29. If 365 entered on line 29, enter $9,060.00 here .	30	
31	Subtract line 30 from line 28. If zero or less, do not complete the rest of this part or any of Part IX	31	
32	Enter employer-provided amounts (see instructions) . . . . . . [32]		
33	Divide line 32 by line 27. Enter the result as a decimal (to two places), but do not enter more than "1.00".	33	✕ .
34	**Housing exclusion.** Multiply line 31 by line 33. Enter the result but do not enter more than the amount on line 32. Also, complete Part VIII . . . . ▶	34	

Note: *The housing deduction is figured in Part IX. If you choose to claim the foreign earned income exclusion, complete Parts VII and VIII before Part IX.*

Part VII   For Taxpayers Claiming the Foreign Earned Income Exclusion

35	Maximum foreign earned income exclusion	35	$70,000	00
36	• If you completed Part VI, enter the number from line 29. • All others, enter the number of days in your qualifying period that fall within your 1995 tax year (see the instructions for line 29). [36]		
37	• If line 36 and the number of days in your 1995 tax year (usually 365) are the same, enter "1.00." • Otherwise, divide line 36 by the number of days in your 1995 tax year and enter the result as a decimal (to two places).	37	✕ .
38	Multiply line 35 by line 37	38	
39	Subtract line 34 from line 27	39	
40	**Foreign earned income exclusion.** Enter the **smaller** of line 38 or line 39. Also, complete Part VIII ▶	40	

Part VIII   For Taxpayers Claiming the Housing Exclusion, Foreign Earned Income Exclusion, or Both

41	Add lines 34 and 40	41	
42	Deductions allowed in figuring your adjusted gross income (Form 1040, line 31) that are allocable to the excluded income. See instructions and attach computation	42	
43	Subtract line 42 from line 41. Enter the result here and in parentheses on Form 1040, line 21. Next to the amount write "Form 2555." On Form 1040, subtract this amount from your income to arrive at total income on Form 1040, line 22 . . . . ▶	43	

Part IX   For Taxpayers Claiming the Housing Deduction—Complete this part only if (a) line 31 is more than line 34 and (b) line 27 is more than line 41.

44	Subtract line 34 from line 31	44	
45	Subtract line 41 from line 27	45	
46	Enter the **smaller** of line 44 or line 45	46	

Note: *If line 45 is **more than** line 46 and you couldn't deduct all of your 1994 housing deduction because of the 1994 limit, use the worksheet on page 4 of the instructions to figure the amount to enter on line 47. Otherwise, go to line 48.*

47	Housing deduction carryover from 1994 (from worksheet on page 4 of the instructions) . . .	47	
48	**Housing deduction.** Add lines 46 and 47. Enter the total here and on Form 1040 to the left of line 30. Next to the amount on Form 1040, write "Form 2555." Add it to the total adjustments reported on that line . . . . ▶	48	

✪ *Printed on recycled paper*

Form **2848**
(Rev. December 1995)

Department of the Treasury
Internal Revenue Service

Power of Attorney
and Declaration of Representative

▶ **For Paperwork Reduction and Privacy Act Notice, see the instructions.**

OMB No. 1545-0150

For IRS Use Only

Received by:

Name _____

Telephone ( )_____

Function _____

Date   /   /

Part I   **Power of Attorney** (Please type or print.)

1   **Taxpayer Information** (Taxpayer(s) must sign and date this form on page 2, line 9.)

Taxpayer name(s) and address	Social security number(s)	Employer identification number
	Daytime telephone number ( )	Plan number (if applicable)

hereby appoint(s) the following representative(s) as attorney(s)-in-fact:

2   **Representative(s)** (Representative(s) must sign and date this form on page 2, Part II.)

Name and address

CAF No. ....
Telephone No. (   ) ....
Fax No. (   ) ....
Check if new: Address ☐   Telephone No. ☐

Name and address

CAF No. ....
Telephone No. (   ) ....
Fax No. (   ) ....
Check if new: Address ☐   Telephone No. ☐

Name and address

CAF No. ....
Telephone No. (   ) ....
Fax No. (   ) ....
Check if new: Address ☐   Telephone No. ☐

to represent the taxpayer(s) before the Internal Revenue Service for the following tax matters:

3   **Tax Matters**

Type of Tax (Income, Employment, Excise, etc.)	Tax Form Number (1040, 941, 720, etc.)	Year(s) or Period(s)

4   **Specific Use Not Recorded on Centralized Authorization File (CAF).**—If the power of attorney is for a specific use not recorded on CAF, check this box. (See **Line 4—Specific uses not recorded on CAF** on page 3.). . . . . ▶ ☐

5   **Acts Authorized.**—The representatives are authorized to receive and inspect confidential tax information and to perform any and all acts that I (we) can perform with respect to the tax matters described on line 3, for example, the authority to sign any agreements, consents, or other documents. The authority does not include the power to receive refund checks (see line 6 below), the power to substitute another representative unless specifically added below, or the power to sign certain returns (see **Line 5—Acts authorized** on page 4).

List any specific additions or deletions to the acts otherwise authorized in this power of attorney: ....
....
....

Note: *In general, an unenrolled preparer of tax returns cannot sign any document for a taxpayer. See Revenue Procedure 81-38, printed as Pub. 470, for more information.*

Note: *The tax matters partner/person of a partnership or S corporation is not permitted to authorize representatives to perform certain acts. See the instructions for more information.*

6   **Receipt of Refund Checks.**—If you want to authorize a representative named on line 2 to receive, **BUT NOT TO ENDORSE OR CASH**, refund checks, initial here _____ and list the name of that representative below.

Name of representative to receive refund check(s) ▶

Cat. No. 11980J

Form **2848** (Rev. 12-95)

Form 2848 (Rev. 12-95)   Page **2**

7 **Notices and Communications.**—Original notices and other written communications will be sent to you and a copy to the first representative listed on line 2 unless you check one or more of the boxes below.

   a If you want the first representative listed on line 2 to receive the original, and yourself a copy, of such notices or communications, check this box . . . . ▶ ☐

   b If you also want the second representative listed to receive a copy of such notices and communications, check this box . . . . ▶ ☐

   c If you do not want any notices or communications sent to your representative, check this box . . . . ▶ ☐

8 **Retention/Revocation of Prior Power(s) of Attorney.**—The filing of this power of attorney automatically revokes all earlier power(s) of attorney on file with the Internal Revenue Service for the same tax matters and years or periods covered by this document. If you do not want to revoke a prior power of attorney, check here . . . . ▶ ☐
YOU MUST ATTACH A COPY OF ANY POWER OF ATTORNEY YOU WANT TO REMAIN IN EFFECT.

9 **Signature of Taxpayer(s).**—If a tax matter concerns a joint return, **both** husband and wife must sign if joint representation is requested, otherwise, see the instructions. If signed by a corporate officer, partner, guardian, tax matters partner/person, executor, receiver, administrator, or trustee on behalf of the taxpayer, I certify that I have the authority to execute this form on behalf of the taxpayer.

▶ **IF NOT SIGNED AND DATED, THIS POWER OF ATTORNEY WILL BE RETURNED.**

Signature	Date	Title (if applicable)
Print Name		
Signature	Date	Title (if applicable)
Print Name		

Part II **Declaration of Representative**

Under penalties of perjury, I declare that:

- I am not currently under suspension or disbarment from practice before the Internal Revenue Service;
- I am aware of regulations contained in Treasury Department Circular No. 230 (31 CFR, Part 10), as amended, concerning the practice of attorneys, certified public accountants, enrolled agents, enrolled actuaries, and others;
- I am authorized to represent the taxpayer(s) identified in Part I for the tax matter(s) specified there; and
- I am one of the following:

   a Attorney—a member in good standing of the bar of the highest court of the jurisdiction shown below.

   b Certified Public Accountant—duly qualified to practice as a certified public accountant in the jurisdiction shown below.

   c Enrolled Agent—enrolled as an agent under the requirements of Treasury Department Circular No. 230.

   d Officer—a bona fide officer of the taxpayer's organization.

   e Full-Time Employee—a full-time employee of the taxpayer.

   f Family Member—a member of the taxpayer's immediate family (i.e., spouse, parent, child, brother, or sister).

   g Enrolled Actuary—enrolled as an actuary by the Joint Board for the Enrollment of Actuaries under 29 U.S.C. 1242 (the authority to practice before the Service is limited by section 10.3(d)(1) of Treasury Department Circular No. 230).

   h Unenrolled Return Preparer—an unenrolled return preparer under section 10.7(a)(7) of Treasury Department Circular No. 230.

▶ **IF THIS DECLARATION OF REPRESENTATIVE IS NOT SIGNED AND DATED, THE POWER OF ATTORNEY WILL BE RETURNED.**

Designation—Insert above letter **(a–h)**	Jurisdiction (state) or Enrollment Card No.	Signature	Date

Form **3800**

Department of the Treasury
Internal Revenue Service

General Business Credit

▶ **Attach to your tax return.**

▶ **See separate instructions.**

OMB No. 1545–0895

1995

Attachment
Sequence No. **22**

Name(s) shown on return

Identifying number

Part I — Tentative Credit

1a	Current year investment credit (Form 3468, Part I)	**1a**	
b	Current year jobs credit (Form 5884, Part I)	**1b**	
c	Current year credit for alcohol used as fuel (Form 6478)	**1c**	
d	Current year credit for increasing research activities (Form 6765, Part I)	**1d**	
e	Current year low-income housing credit (Form 8586, Part I)	**1e**	
f	Current year enhanced oil recovery credit (Form 8830, Part I)	**1f**	
g	Current year disabled access credit (Form 8826, Part I)	**1g**	
h	Current year renewable electricity production credit (Form 8835, Part I)	**1h**	
i	Current year Indian employment credit (Form 8845, Part I)	**1i**	
j	Current year credit for employer social security and Medicare taxes paid on certain employee tips (Form 8846, Part I)	**1j**	
k	Current year credit for contributions to selected community development corporations (Form 8847, Part I)	**1k**	
l	Current year trans-Alaska pipeline liability fund credit (see instructions)	**1l**	
m	**Current year general business credit.** Add lines 1a through 1l	**1m**	
2	Passive activity credits included on line 1m (see instructions)	**2**	
3	Subtract line 2 from line 1m	**3**	
4	Passive activity credits allowed for 1995 (see instructions)	**4**	
5	Carryforward of general business, WIN, or ESOP credit to 1995 (see instructions for the schedule to attach)	**5**	
6	Carryback of general business credit to 1995 (see instructions)	**6**	
7	**Tentative general business credit.** Add lines 3 through 6	**7**	

Part II — General Business Credit Limitation Based on Amount of Tax

8a	Individuals. Enter amount from Form 1040, line 40			
b	Corporations. Enter amount from Form 1120, Schedule J, line 3 (or Form 1120-A, Part I, line 1)	}	**8**	
c	Other filers. Enter regular tax before credits from your return.			
9a	Credit for child and dependent care expenses (Form 2441, line 10)	**9a**		
b	Credit for the elderly or the disabled (Schedule R (Form 1040), line 20)	**9b**		
c	Mortgage interest credit (Form 8396, line 11)	**9c**		
d	Foreign tax credit (Form 1116, line 32, or Form 1118, Sch. B, line 12) .	**9d**		
e	Possessions tax credit (Form 5735)	**9e**		
f	Orphan drug credit (Form 6765)	**9f**		
g	Credit for fuel from a nonconventional source	**9g**		
h	Qualified electric vehicle credit (Form 8834, line 19)	**9h**		
i	Add lines 9a through 9h		**9i**	
10	Net regular tax. Subtract line 9i from line 8		**10**	
11	Tentative minimum tax (see instructions):			
a	Individuals. Enter amount from Form 6251, line 26			
b	Corporations. Enter amount from Form 4626, line 13 . . . . . . }		**11**	
c	Estates and trusts. Enter amount from Form 1041, Schedule I, line 37			
12	Net income tax:			
a	Individuals. Add line 10 above and line 28 of Form 6251			
b	Corporations. Add line 10 above and line 15 of Form 4626 . . . . } .		**12**	
c	Estates and trusts. Add line 10 above and line 41 of Form 1041, Schedule I			
13	If line 10 is more than $25,000, enter 25% (.25) of the excess (see instructions)		**13**	
14	Subtract line 11 or line 13, whichever is greater, from line 12. If zero or less, enter -0- . . .		**14**	
15	**General business credit allowed for current year.** Enter the **smaller** of line 7 or line 14. Enter here and on Form 1040, line 44; Form 1120, Schedule J, line 4d; Form 1120-A, Part I, line 2a; or the appropriate line of your tax return. (Individuals, estates, and trusts, see instructions if the credit for increasing research activities is claimed. C corporations, see instructions for Schedule A if any regular investment credit carryforward is claimed. See the instructions if the corporation has undergone a post-1986 "ownership change.")		**15**	

For Paperwork Reduction Act Notice, see page 2 of this form.   Cat. No. 12392F   Form **3800** (1995)

Schedule A— Additional General Business Credit Allowed By Section 38(c)(2) (Before Repeal by the Revenue Reconciliation Act of 1990)—Only Applicable to C Corporations

16	Enter the portion of the credit shown on line 5, page 1, that is attributable to the regular investment credit under section 46 (before amendment by the Revenue Reconciliation Act of 1990) . . .	**16**		
17	Tentative minimum tax (from line 11, page 1)	**17**			
18	Multiply line 17 by 25% (.25)	**18**		
19	Enter the amount from line 14, page 1	**19**			
20	Enter the portion of the credit shown on line 7, page 1, that is NOT attributable to the regular investment credit under section 46 (before amendment by the Revenue Reconciliation Act of 1990)	**20**			
21	Subtract line 20 from line 19 (if zero or less, enter -0-)	**21**		
22	Subtract line 21 from line 16 (if zero or less, enter -0-)	**22**		
23	For purposes of this line only, refigure the amount on line 11, Form 4626, by using zero on line 6, Form 4626, and enter the result here .	**23**			
24	Multiply line 23 by 10% (.10)	**24**		
25	Net income tax (from line 12, page 1)	**25**		
26	General business credit (from line 15, page 1)	**26**		
27	Subtract line 26 from line 25	**27**		
28	Subtract line 24 from line 27	**28**		
29	Enter the smallest of line 18, line 22, or line 28	**29**		
30	Subtract line 29 from line 17	**30**		
31	Enter the greater of line 30 or line 13, page 1	**31**		
32	Subtract line 31 from line 25	**32**		
33	Enter the smaller of line 32 or line 10, page 1. Enter this amount also on line 15, page 1, instead of the amount previously figured on that line. Write "Sec. 38(c)(2)" in the margin next to your entry on line 15, page 1	**33**		
34	If line 32 is greater than line 33, enter the excess here and see the instructions on how to claim the additional credit	**34**		

Paperwork Reduction Act Notice

We ask for the information on this form to carry out the Internal Revenue laws of the United States. You are required to give us the information. We need it to ensure that you are complying with these laws and to allow us to figure and collect the right amount of tax.

The time needed to complete and file this form will vary depending on individual circumstances. The estimated average time is:

Recordkeeping . . . .11 hr., 43 min.

Learning about the law or the form . . . . 1 hr.

Preparing and sending the form to the IRS . . 1 hr., 14 min.

If you have comments concerning the accuracy of these time estimates or suggestions for making this form simpler, we would be happy to hear from you. You can write to the IRS at the address listed in the instructions for the tax return with which this form is filed.

Form **3903**	**Moving Expenses**	OMB No. 1545-0062

Department of the Treasury
Internal Revenue Service

▶ **Attach to Form 1040.**

▶ **See instructions on back.**

1995

Attachment
Sequence No. **62**

Name(s) shown on Form 1040

Your social security number

Caution: *If you are a member of the armed forces, see the instructions before completing this form.*

1   Enter the number of miles from your **old home** to your **new workplace** . . | **1** | miles

2   Enter the number of miles from your **old home** to your **old workplace** . . . | **2** | miles

3   Subtract line 2 from line 1. Enter the result but not less than zero . . . . | **3** | miles

Is line 3 at least 50 miles?

Yes ▶   Go to line 4. Also, see **Time Test** in the instructions.

No ▶   You **cannot** deduct your moving expenses. Do not complete the rest of this form.

4   Transportation and storage of household goods and personal effects . . . . | **4** |

5   Travel and lodging expenses of moving from your old home to your new home. **Do not** include meals . . . . | **5** |

6   Add lines 4 and 5 . . . . | **6** |

7   Enter the total amount your employer paid for your move (including the value of services furnished in kind) that is **not** included in the wages box (box 1) of your W-2 form. This amount should be identified with code **P** in box 13 of your W-2 form. . . . . | **7** |

Is line 6 more than line 7?

Yes ▶   Go to line 8.

No ▶   You **cannot** deduct your moving expenses. If line 6 is less than line 7, subtract line 6 from line 7 and include the result in income on Form 1040, line 7.

8   Subtract line 7 from line 6. Enter the result here and on Form 1040, line 24. This is your **moving expense deduction** . . . . | **8** |

For Paperwork Reduction Act Notice, see back of form.   Cat. No. 12490K   Form **3903** (1995)

Form 4562

Department of the Treasury
Internal Revenue Service (99)

Depreciation and Amortization
(Including Information on Listed Property)

▶ See separate instructions.   ▶ Attach this form to your return.

OMB No. 1545-0172

1995

Attachment
Sequence No. **67**

Name(s) shown on return	Business or activity to which this form relates	Identifying number

Part I — Election To Expense Certain Tangible Property (Section 179) (Note: *If you have any "Listed Property," complete Part V before you complete Part I.*)

1	Maximum dollar limitation. If an enterprise zone business, see page 1 of the instructions . .	**1**	$17,500
2	Total cost of section 179 property placed in service during the tax year. See page 2 of the instructions	**2**	
3	Threshold cost of section 179 property before reduction in limitation	**3**	$200,000
4	Reduction in limitation. Subtract line 3 from line 2. If zero or less, enter -0-	**4**	
5	Dollar limitation for tax year. Subtract line 4 from line 1. If zero or less, enter -0-. If married filing separately, see page 2 of the instructions	**5**	

(a) Description of property	(b) Cost	(c) Elected cost
6		

7	Listed property. Enter amount from line 27.	**7**	
8	Total elected cost of section 179 property. Add amounts in column (c), lines 6 and 7 . . .	**8**	
9	Tentative deduction. Enter the smaller of line 5 or line 8	**9**	
10	Carryover of disallowed deduction from 1994. See page 2 of the instructions	**10**	
11	Taxable income limitation. Enter the smaller of taxable income (not less than zero) or line 5 (see instructions)	**11**	
12	Section 179 expense deduction. Add lines 9 and 10, but do not enter more than line 11 . .	**12**	
13	Carryover of disallowed deduction to 1996. Add lines 9 and 10, less line 12 ▶	**13**	

Note: *Do not use Part II or Part III below for listed property (automobiles, certain other vehicles, cellular telephones, certain computers, or property used for entertainment, recreation, or amusement). Instead, use Part V for listed property.*

Part II — MACRS Depreciation For Assets Placed in Service ONLY During Your 1995 Tax Year (Do Not Include Listed Property.)

Section A—General Asset Account Election

14   If you are making the election under section 168(i)(4) to group any assets placed in service during the tax year into one or more general asset accounts, check this box. See page 2 of the instructions . . . . ▶ ☐

(a) Classification of property	(b) Month and year placed in service	(c) Basis for depreciation (business/investment use only—see instructions)	(d) Recovery period	(e) Convention	(f) Method	(g) Depreciation deduction
Section B—General Depreciation System (GDS) (See page 2 of the instructions.)						
15a 3-year property						
b 5-year property						
c 7-year property						
d 10-year property						
e 15-year property						
f 20-year property						
g Residential rental property			27.5 yrs.	MM	S/L	
			27.5 yrs.	MM	S/L	
h Nonresidential real property			39 yrs.	MM	S/L	
				MM	S/L	
Section C—Alternative Depreciation System (ADS) (See page 4 of the instructions.)						
16a Class life					S/L	
b 12-year			12 yrs.		S/L	
c 40-year			40 yrs.	MM	S/L	

Part III — Other Depreciation (Do Not Include Listed Property.) (See page 4 of the instructions.)

17	GDS and ADS deductions for assets placed in service in tax years beginning before 1995	**17**	
18	Property subject to section 168(f)(1) election	**18**	
19	ACRS and other depreciation	**19**	

Part IV — Summary (See page 4 of the instructions.)

20	Listed property. Enter amount from line 26.	**20**	
21	**Total.** Add deductions on line 12, lines 15 and 16 in column (g), and lines 17 through 20. Enter here and on the appropriate lines of your return. Partnerships and S corporations—see instructions . .	**21**	
22	For assets shown above and placed in service during the current year, enter the portion of the basis attributable to section 263A costs	**22**	

For Paperwork Reduction Act Notice, see page 1 of the separate instructions.   Cat. No. 12906N   Form **4562** (1995)

Form 4562 (1995)   Page **2**

Part V	Listed Property—Automobiles, Certain Other Vehicles, Cellular Telephones, Certain Computers, and Property Used for Entertainment, Recreation, or Amusement

Note: *For any vehicle for which you are using the standard mileage rate or deducting lease expense, complete **only** 23a, 23b, columns (c) through (i) of Section A, all of Section B, and Section C if applicable.*

Section A—Depreciation and Other Information (Caution: *See page 5 of the instructions for limitations for automobiles.***)**

23a Do you have evidence to support the business/investment use claimed? ☐ **Yes** ☐ **No**   **23b** If "Yes," is the evidence written? ☐ **Yes** ☐ **No**

(a) Type of property (list vehicles first)	(b) Date placed in service	(c) Business/ investment use percentage	(d) Cost or other basis	(e) Basis for depreciation (business/investment use only)	(f) Recovery period	(g) Method/ Convention	(h) Depreciation deduction	(i) Elected section 179 cost
24 Property used more than 50% in a qualified business use (See page 5 of the instructions.):								
		%						
		%						
		%						
25 Property used 50% or less in a qualified business use (See page 5 of the instructions.):								
		%				S/L –		
		%				S/L –		
		%				S/L –		

26 Add amounts in column (h). Enter the total here and on line 20, page 1 . . . . . | **26** |

27 Add amounts in column (i). Enter the total here and on line 7, page 1 . . . . | **27** |

Section B—Information on Use of Vehicles

Complete this section for vehicles used by a sole proprietor, partner, or other "more than 5% owner," or related person.
If you provided vehicles to your employees, first answer the questions in Section C to see if you meet an exception to completing this section for those vehicles.

		(a) Vehicle 1		(b) Vehicle 2		(c) Vehicle 3		(d) Vehicle 4		(e) Vehicle 5		(f) Vehicle 6	
28	Total business/investment miles driven during the year (DO NOT include commuting miles)												
29	Total commuting miles driven during the year												
30	Total other personal (noncommuting) miles driven												
31	Total miles driven during the year. Add lines 28 through 30.												
		Yes	No	Yes	No	Yes	No	Yes	No	Yes	No	Yes	No
32	Was the vehicle available for personal use during off-duty hours?												
33	Was the vehicle used primarily by a more than 5% owner or related person?												
34	Is another vehicle available for personal use?												

Section C—Questions for Employers Who Provide Vehicles for Use by Their Employees

*Answer these questions to determine if you meet an exception to completing Section B for vehicles used by employees who **are not** more than 5% owners or related persons.*

		Yes	No
35	Do you maintain a written policy statement that prohibits all personal use of vehicles, including commuting, by your employees?		
36	Do you maintain a written policy statement that prohibits personal use of vehicles, except commuting, by your employees? See page 6 of the instructions for vehicles used by corporate officers, directors, or 1% or more owners		
37	Do you treat all use of vehicles by employees as personal use?		
38	Do you provide more than five vehicles to your employees, obtain information from your employees about the use of the vehicles, and retain the information received?		
39	Do you meet the requirements concerning qualified automobile demonstration use? See page 6 of the instructions . .		

Note: *If your answer to 35, 36, 37, 38, or 39 is "Yes," you need not complete Section B for the covered vehicles.*

Part VI	Amortization

(a) Description of costs	(b) Date amortization begins	(c) Amortizable amount	(d) Code section	(e) Amortization period or percentage	(f) Amortization for this year
40 Amortization of costs that begins during your 1995 tax year:					

41 Amortization of costs that began before 1995 . . . . | **41** |

42 **Total.** Enter here and on "Other Deductions" or "Other Expenses" line of your return . . . | **42** |

✿ *Printed on recycled paper*

Form **4684**

Department of the Treasury
Internal Revenue Service

Casualties and Thefts

▶ See separate instructions.
▶ Attach to your tax return.
▶ **Use a separate Form 4684 for each different casualty or theft.**

OMB No. 1545-0177

1995

Attachment
Sequence No. **26**

Name(s) shown on tax return

Identifying number

SECTION A—Personal Use Property (Use this section to report casualties and thefts of property **not** used in a trade or business or for income-producing purposes.)

1   Description of properties (show type, location, and date acquired for each):

Property **A** ....

Property **B** ....

Property **C** ....

Property **D** ....

Properties (Use a separate column for each property lost or damaged from one casualty or theft.)

		A	B	C	D
2	Cost or other basis of each property	**2**				
3	Insurance or other reimbursement (whether or not you filed a claim). See instructions	**3**				
	Note: *If line 2 is **more than** line 3, skip line 4.*					
4	Gain from casualty or theft. If line 3 is **more than** line 2, enter the difference here and skip lines 5 through 9 for that column. See instructions if line 3 includes insurance or other reimbursement you did not claim, or you received payment for your loss in a later tax year	**4**				
5	Fair market value **before** casualty or theft . . .	**5**				
6	Fair market value **after** casualty or theft	**6**				
7	Subtract line 6 from line 5	**7**				
8	Enter the **smaller** of line 2 or line 7	**8**				
9	Subtract line 3 from line 8. If zero or less, enter -0-	**9**				

10	Casualty or theft loss. Add the amounts on line 9. Enter the total	**10**	
11	Enter the amount from line 10 or $100, whichever is **smaller**	**11**	
12	Subtract line 11 from line 10	**12**	
	Caution: *Use only one Form 4684 for lines 13 through 18.*		
13	Add the amounts on line 12 of all Forms 4684	**13**	
14	Combine the amounts from line 4 of all Forms 4684	**14**	
15	● If line 14 is **more than** line 13, enter the difference here and on Schedule D. Do not complete the rest of this section (see instructions). ● If line 14 is **less than** line 13, enter -0- here and continue with the form. ● If line 14 is **equal to** line 13, enter -0- here. Do not complete the rest of this section.	**15**	
16	If line 14 is **less than** line 13, enter the difference	**16**	
17	Enter 10% of your adjusted gross income (Form 1040, line 32). Estates and trusts, see instructions	**17**	
18	Subtract line 17 from line 16. If zero or less, enter -0-. Also enter result on Schedule A (Form 1040), line 19. Estates and trusts, enter on the "Other deductions" line of your tax return	**18**	

For Paperwork Reduction Act Notice, see page 1 of separate instructions.   Cat. No. 12997O   Form **4684** (1995)

Form 4684 (1995)   Attachment Sequence No. **26**   Page **2**

Name(s) shown on tax return. Do not enter name and identifying number if shown on other side. | Identifying number

SECTION B—Business and Income-Producing Property (Use this section to report casualties and thefts of property used in a trade or business or for income-producing purposes.)

Part I — Casualty or Theft Gain or Loss (Use a separate Part I for each casualty or theft.)

19 Description of properties (show type, location, and date acquired for each):

Property **A** ....
Property **B** ....
Property **C** ....
Property **D** ....

Properties (Use a separate column for each property lost or damaged from one casualty or theft.)

	A	B	C	D
20 Cost or adjusted basis of each property				
21 Insurance or other reimbursement (whether or not you filed a claim). See the instructions for line 3. **Note:** If line 20 is **more than** line 21, skip line 22.				
22 Gain from casualty or theft. If line 21 is **more than** line 20, enter the difference here and on line 29 or line 34, column (c), except as provided in the instructions for line 33. Also, skip lines 23 through 27 for that column. See the instructions for line 4 if line 21 includes insurance or other reimbursement you did not claim, or you received payment for your loss in a later tax year				
23 Fair market value **before** casualty or theft				
24 Fair market value **after** casualty or theft				
25 Subtract line 24 from line 23				
26 Enter the **smaller** of line 20 or line 25				

Note: If the property was totally destroyed by casualty or lost from theft, enter on line 26 the amount from line 20.

27 Subtract line 21 from line 26. If zero or less, enter -0-				

28 Casualty or theft loss. Add the amounts on line 27. Enter the total here and on line 29 **or** line 34 (see instructions). | 28 |

Part II — Summary of Gains and Losses (from separate Parts I)

(a) Identify casualty or theft	(b) Losses from casualties or thefts		(c) Gains from casualties or thefts includible in income
	(i) Trade, business, rental or royalty property	(ii) Income-producing property	

Casualty or Theft of Property Held One Year or Less

29	( )	( )	
	( )	( )	
30 Totals. Add the amounts on line 29	( )	( )	

31 Combine line 30, columns (b)(i) and (c). Enter the net gain or (loss) here and on Form 4797, line 15. If Form 4797 is not otherwise required, see instructions | 31 |

32 Enter the amount from line 30, column (b)(ii) here and on Schedule A (Form 1040), line 22. Partnerships, S corporations, estates and trusts, see instructions | 32 |

Casualty or Theft of Property Held More Than One Year

33 Casualty or theft gains from Form 4797, line 34 | 33 |

| 34 | ( ) | ( ) | |
| | ( ) | ( ) | |

35 Total losses. Add amounts on line 34, columns (b)(i) and (b)(ii) | 35 ( ) | ( ) |
36 Total gains. Add lines 33 and 34, column (c) | 36 |
37 Add amounts on line 35, columns (b)(i) and (b)(ii) | 37 |
38 If the loss on line 37 is **more than** the gain on line 36:
a Combine line 35, column (b)(i) and line 36, and enter the net gain or (loss) here. Partnerships and S corporations see the note below. All others enter this amount on Form 4797, line 15. If Form 4797 is not otherwise required, see instructions | 38a |
b Enter the amount from line 35, column (b)(ii) here. Partnerships and S corporations see the note below. Individuals enter this amount on Schedule A (Form 1040), line 22. Estates and trusts, enter on the "Other deductions" line of your tax return | 38b |
39 If the loss on line 37 is **equal to** or **less than** the gain on line 36, combine these lines and enter here. Partnerships, see the note below. All others, enter this amount on Form 4797, line 3 | 39 |

Note: Partnerships, enter the amount from line 38a, 38b, or line 39 on Form 1065, Schedule K, line 7. S corporations, enter the amount from line 38a or 38b on Form 1120S, Schedule K, line 6.

Form **4797**	**Sales of Business Property**	OMB No. 1545-0184

(Also Involuntary Conversions and Recapture Amounts Under Sections 179 and 280F(b)(2))

Department of the Treasury
Internal Revenue Service   (99)

► **Attach to your tax return.**   ► **See separate instructions.**

1995

Attachment
Sequence No. **27**

Name(s) shown on return

Identifying number

1 Enter here the gross proceeds from the sale or exchange of real estate reported to you for 1995 on Form(s) 1099-S (or a substitute statement) that you will be including on line 2, 11, or 22 . . . . **1**

Part I **Sales or Exchanges of Property Used in a Trade or Business and Involuntary Conversions From Other Than Casualty or Theft—Property Held More Than 1 Year**

(a) Description of property	(b) Date acquired (mo., day, yr.)	(c) Date sold (mo., day, yr.)	(d) Gross sales price	(e) Depreciation allowed or allowable since acquisition	(f) Cost or other basis, plus improvements and expense of sale	(g) LOSS ((f) minus the sum of (d) and (e))	(h) GAIN ((d) plus (e) minus (f))
2							

3 Gain, if any, from Form 4684, line 39 . . . . **3**

4 Section 1231 gain from installment sales from Form 6252, line 26 or 37 . . . . **4**

5 Section 1231 gain or (loss) from like-kind exchanges from Form 8824 . . . . **5**

6 Gain, if any, from line 34, from other than casualty or theft **6**

7 Add lines 2 through 6 in columns (g) and (h) . . . . **7** ( )

8 Combine columns (g) and (h) of line 7. Enter gain or (loss) here, and on the appropriate line as follows: **8**

Partnerships—Enter the gain or (loss) on Form 1065, Schedule K, line 6. Skip lines 9, 10, 12, and 13 below.

S corporations—Report the gain or (loss) following the instructions for Form 1120S, Schedule K, lines 5 and 6. Skip lines 9, 10, 12, and 13 below, unless line 8 is a gain and the S corporation is subject to the capital gains tax.

All others—If line 8 is zero or a loss, enter the amount on line 12 below and skip lines 9 and 10. If line 8 is a gain and you did not have any prior year section 1231 losses, or they were recaptured in an earlier year, enter the gain as a long-term capital gain on Schedule D and skip lines 9, 10, and 13 below.

9 Nonrecaptured net section 1231 losses from prior years (see instructions) **9**

10 Subtract line 9 from line 8. If zero or less, enter -0-. Also enter on the appropriate line as follows (see instructions): **10**

S corporations—Enter this amount on Schedule D (Form 1120S), line 13, and skip lines 12 and 13 below.

All others—If line 10 is zero, enter the amount from line 8 on line 13 below. If line 10 is more than zero, enter the amount from line 9 on line 13 below, and enter the amount from line 10 as a long-term capital gain on Schedule D.

Part II **Ordinary Gains and Losses**

11 Ordinary gains and losses not included on lines 12 through 18 (include property held 1 year or less):

12 Loss, if any, from line 8 . . . . **12**

13 Gain, if any, from line 8, or amount from line 9 if applicable **13**

14 Gain, if any, from line 33 . . . . **14**

15 Net gain or (loss) from Form 4684, lines 31 and 38a **15**

16 Ordinary gain from installment sales from Form 6252, line 25 or 36 . . . . **16**

17 Ordinary gain or (loss) from like-kind exchanges from Form 8824 . . . . **17**

18 Recapture of section 179 expense deduction for partners and S corporation shareholders from property dispositions by partnerships and S corporations (see instructions) **18**

19 Add lines 11 through 18 in columns (g) and (h) . . . . **19** ( )

20 Combine columns (g) and (h) of line 19. Enter gain or (loss) here, and on the appropriate line as follows: . . . **20**

a For all except individual returns: Enter the gain or (loss) from line 20 on the return being filed.

b For individual returns:

(1) If the loss on line 12 includes a loss from Form 4684, line 35, column (b)(ii), enter that part of the loss here and on line 22 of Schedule A (Form 1040). Identify as from "Form 4797, line 20b(1)." See instructions . . . . **20b(1)**

(2) Redetermine the gain or (loss) on line 20, excluding the loss, if any, on line 20b(1). Enter here and on Form 1040, line 14 . **20b(2)**

For Paperwork Reduction Act Notice, see page 1 of separate instructions.   Cat. No. 13086I   Form **4797** (1995)

Part III   Gain From Disposition of Property Under Sections 1245, 1250, 1252, 1254, and 1255

21	(a) Description of section 1245, 1250, 1252, 1254, or 1255 property:	(b) Date acquired (mo., day, yr.)	(c) Date sold (mo., day, yr.)
A			
B			
C			
D			

Relate lines 21A through 21D to these columns ▶		Property A	Property B	Property C	Property D
22	Gross sales price (**Note:** *See line 1 before completing.*)	22				
23	Cost or other basis plus expense of sale	23				
24	Depreciation (or depletion) allowed or allowable	24				
25	Adjusted basis. Subtract line 24 from line 23	25				
26	Total gain. Subtract line 25 from line 22	26				
27	**If section 1245 property:**					
a	Depreciation allowed or allowable from line 24	27a				
b	Enter the **smaller** of line 26 or 27a	27b				
28	**If section 1250 property:** If straight line depreciation was used, enter -0- on line 28g, except for a corporation subject to section 291.					
a	Additional depreciation after 1975 (see instructions)	28a				
b	Applicable percentage multiplied by the **smaller** of line 26 or line 28a (see instructions)	28b				
c	Subtract line 28a from line 26. If residential rental property or line 26 is not more than line 28a, skip lines 28d and 28e	28c				
d	Additional depreciation after 1969 and before 1976	28d				
e	Enter the **smaller** of line 28c or 28d	28e				
f	Section 291 amount (corporations only)	28f				
g	Add lines 28b, 28e, and 28f	28g				
29	**If section 1252 property:** Skip this section if you did not dispose of farmland or if this form is being completed for a partnership.					
a	Soil, water, and land clearing expenses	29a				
b	Line 29a multiplied by applicable percentage (see instructions)	29b				
c	Enter the **smaller** of line 26 or 29b	29c				
30	**If section 1254 property:**					
a	Intangible drilling and development costs, expenditures for development of mines and other natural deposits, and mining exploration costs (see instructions)	30a				
b	Enter the **smaller** of line 26 or 30a	30b				
31	**If section 1255 property:**					
a	Applicable percentage of payments excluded from income under section 126 (see instructions)	31a				
b	Enter the **smaller** of line 26 or 31a (see instructions)	31b				

Summary of Part III Gains. Complete property columns A through D, through line 31b before going to line 32.

32	Total gains for all properties. Add property columns A through D, line 26	32
33	Add property columns A through D, lines 27b, 28g, 29c, 30b, and 31b. Enter here and on line 14	33
34	Subtract line 33 from line 32. Enter the portion from casualty or theft on Form 4684, line 33. Enter the portion from other than casualty or theft on Form 4797, line 6	34

Part IV   Recapture Amounts Under Sections 179 and 280F(b)(2) When Business Use Drops to 50% or Less
See instructions.

			(a) Section 179	(b) Section 280F(b)(2)
35	Section 179 expense deduction or depreciation allowable in prior years	35		
36	Recomputed depreciation. See instructions	36		
37	Recapture amount. Subtract line 36 from line 35. See the instructions for where to report	37		

✪ *Printed on recycled paper*

1995 Form 4868  Department of the Treasury
Internal Revenue Service

General Instructions

Note: *Form 1040-T references are to a new form sent to certain individuals on a test basis.*

A Change To Note

We have combined Form 4868-V (payment voucher) and Form 4868 into one, smaller, detachable Form 4868. The form is at the bottom of this page.

Purpose of Form

Use Form 4868 to apply for 4 more months to file **Form 1040EZ, Form 1040A, Form 1040, or Form 1040-T.**

To get the extra time you **MUST:**

● Properly estimate your 1995 tax liability using the information available to you,

● Enter your tax liability on line 6a of Form 4868,

● Sign your Form 4868, **AND**

● File Form 4868 by the regular due date of your return.

If you cannot pay the entire balance due, see the instructions for line 6c.

You do not have to explain why you are asking for the extension. We will contact you only if your request is denied.

Do not file Form 4868 if you want the IRS to figure your tax or you are under a court order to file your return by the regular due date.

If you need an additional extension, see **Additional Time** on page 3.

Note: *An extension of time to file your 1995 calendar year income tax return also extends the time to file a gift or generation-skipping transfer (GST) tax return **(Form 709 or 709-A)** for 1995.*

Out of the Country

If you already had 2 extra months to file because you were a U.S. citizen or resident and were out of the country, use this form to obtain an additional 2 months to file. Write "Taxpayer Abroad" across the top of Form 4868. "Out of the country" means either **(a)** you live outside the United States and Puerto Rico **and** your main place of work is outside the United States and Puerto Rico, **or (b)** you are in military or naval service outside the United States and Puerto Rico.

When To File Form 4868

File Form 4868 by April 15, 1996. If you are filing a fiscal year return, file Form 4868 by the regular due date of your return.

If you had 2 extra months to file your return because you were out of the country, file Form 4868 by June 17, 1996, for a 1995 calendar year return.

For Paperwork Reduction Act Notice, see page 3.

Cat. No. 13141W

Form **4868** (1995)

▼ DETACH HERE ▼

Form **4868**
Department of the Treasury
Internal Revenue Service

Application for Automatic Extension of Time To File U.S. Individual Income Tax Return

OMB No. 1545-0188

19**95**

1 Your name(s) (see instructions)		**2a Amount due—**
Address (see instructions)	3 Your social security number	Add lines 6c, d, and e ▶ $
City, town or post office, state, and ZIP code	4 Spouse's social security no.	**b Amount you are paying** ▶ $

5 I request an automatic 4-month extension of time to August 15, 1996, to file my individual tax return for the calendar year 1995 or to _____ , 19 ____ , for the fiscal tax year ending _____ , 19 ____ .

6 Individual Income Tax—See instructions.

Gift or GST Tax Return(s)—See instructions.

Check here **ONLY** if filing a gift or GST tax return . . . . } Yourself ▶ ☐ Spouse ▶ ☐

a Total tax liability for 1995 . . . . . $ _____

b Total payments for 1995 . . . . . $ _____

c Balance due. Subtract 6b from 6a . . $ _____

d Amount of gift or GST tax **you** are paying $ _____

e Your spouse's gift/GST tax payment $ _____

Under penalties of perjury, I declare that I have examined this form, including accompanying schedules and statements, and to the best of my knowledge and belief, it is true, correct, and complete; and, if prepared by someone other than the taxpayer, that I am authorized to prepare this form.

▶ _____ _____
Your signature   Date

▶ _____ _____
Spouse's signature, if filing jointly   Date

▶ _____ _____
Preparer's signature (other than taxpayer)   Date

Form **4952**

Department of the Treasury
Internal Revenue Service   (99)

Investment Interest Expense Deduction

► **Attach to your tax return.**

OMB No. 1545-0191

1995

Attachment
Sequence No. **12A**

Name(s) shown on return

Identifying number

Part I   Total Investment Interest Expense

1	Investment interest expense paid or accrued in 1995. See instructions.	**1**	
2	Disallowed investment interest expense from 1994 Form 4952, line 7	**2**	
3	**Total investment interest expense.** Add lines 1 and 2	**3**	

Part II   Net Investment Income

4a	Gross income from property held for investment (excluding any net gain from the disposition of property held for investment)	**4a**	
b	Net gain from the disposition of property held for investment . . .	**4b**	
c	Net capital gain from the disposition of property held for investment	**4c**	
d	Subtract line 4c from line 4b. If zero or less, enter -0-	**4d**	
e	Enter all or part of the amount on line 4c that you elect to include in investment income. Do not enter more than the amount on line 4b. See instructions . . . . ►	**4e**	
f	Investment income. Add lines 4a, 4d, and 4e. See instructions	**4f**	
5	Investment expenses. See instructions	**5**	
6	**Net investment income.** Subtract line 5 from line 4f. If zero or less, enter -0-	**6**	

Part III   Investment Interest Expense Deduction

7	Disallowed investment interest expense to be carried forward to 1996. Subtract line 6 from line 3. If zero or less, enter -0-	**7**	
8	**Investment interest expense deduction.** Enter the smaller of line 3 or 6. See instructions . .	**8**	

Paperwork Reduction Act Notice

We ask for the information on this form to carry out the Internal Revenue laws of the United States. You are required to give us the information. We need it to ensure that you are complying with these laws and to allow us to figure and collect the right amount of tax.

The time needed to complete and file this form will vary depending on individual circumstances. The estimated average time is:

Recordkeeping	13 min.
Learning about the law or the form	15 min.
Preparing the form	21 min.
Copying, assembling, and sending the form to the IRS . .	10 min.

If you have comments concerning the accuracy of these time estimates or suggestions for making this form simpler, we would be happy to hear from you. See the instructions for the tax return with which this form is filed.

General Instructions

Section references are to the Internal Revenue Code unless otherwise noted. Form 1040-T references are to a new form sent to certain individuals on a test basis.

A Change To Note

If you had a carryover of disallowed interest expense from 1983, 1984, 1985, or 1986, that carryover may need to be refigured based on Rev. Rul. 95-16, 1995-1 C.B. 9. Under Rev. Rul. 95-16, the carryover of disallowed investment interest expense from any tax year is not limited by the taxable income for that year. The amount you enter on line 2 of the 1995 Form 4952 could be affected by this change.

Purpose of Form

Interest expense paid by an individual, estate, or trust on a loan allocable to property held for investment may not be fully deductible in the current year. Use Form 4952 to figure the amount of investment interest expense deductible for the current year and the amount, if any, to carry forward to future years.

For more details, get **Pub. 550,** Investment Income and Expenses.

Who Must File

If you are an individual, estate, or a trust, and you claim a deduction for investment interest expense, you must complete and attach Form 4952 to your tax return, unless **all** the following apply.

● Your only investment income was from interest or dividends.

● You have no other deductible expenses connected with the production of interest or dividends.

● Your investment interest expense is not more than your investment income.

● You have no disallowed investment interest expense from 1994.

Allocation of Interest Expense Under Temporary Regulations Section 1.163-8T

If you paid or accrued interest on a loan and used the loan proceeds for more than one purpose, you may have to allocate the interest paid. This is necessary because different rules apply to investment interest, personal interest, trade or business interest, home mortgage interest, and passive activity interest. See Pub. 550.

Form **5329**	**Additional Taxes Attributable to Qualified Retirement Plans (Including IRAs), Annuities, and Modified Endowment Contracts**	OMB No. 1545-0203
Department of the Treasury Internal Revenue Service	(Under Sections 72, 4973, 4974, and 4980A of the Internal Revenue Code) ▶ Attach to Form 1040. See separate instructions.	**19**95 Attachment Sequence No. **29**

Name of individual subject to additional tax. (If married filing jointly, see page 2 of the instructions.)	Your social security number

Fill in Your Address Only If You Are Filing This Form by Itself and Not With Your Tax Return ▷

Home address (number and street), or P.O. box if mail is not delivered to your home	Apt. no.
City, town or post office, state, and ZIP code	If this is an amended return, check here ▶ ☐

If you are subject to the 10% tax on early distributions **only,** see **Who Must File** in the instructions before continuing. You may be able to report this tax directly on Form 1040 without filing Form 5329.

Part I   **Tax on Early Distributions**

Complete this part if a taxable distribution was made from your qualified retirement plan (including an IRA), annuity contract, or modified endowment contract before you reached age 59½ (or was incorrectly indicated as such on your Form 1099-R—see instructions). **Note:** *You must include the amount of the distribution on line 15b or 16b of Form 1040 or on the appropriate line of Form 4972.*

1	Early distributions included in gross income (see page 2 of the instructions)	**1**	
2	Distributions excepted from additional tax (see page 2 of the instructions). Enter appropriate exception number from instructions ▶ _____	**2**	
3	Amount subject to additional tax. Subtract line 2 from line 1	**3**	
4	**Tax due.** Multiply line 3 by 10% (.10). Enter here and on Form 1040, line 51	**4**	

Part II   **Tax on Excess Contributions to Individual Retirement Arrangements**

Complete this part if, either in this year or in earlier years, you contributed more to your IRA than is or was allowable and you have an excess contribution subject to tax.

5	Excess contributions for 1995 (see page 3 of the instructions). Do not include this amount on Form 1040, line 23a or 23b			**5**	
6	Earlier year excess contributions not previously eliminated (see page 3 of the instructions)	**6**			
7	Contribution credit. If your actual contribution for 1995 is less than your maximum allowable contribution, see page 3 of the instructions; otherwise, enter -0-	**7**			
8	1995 distributions from your IRA account that are includible in taxable income	**8**			
9	1994 tax year excess contributions (if any) withdrawn after the due date (including extensions) of your 1994 income tax return, and 1993 and earlier tax year excess contributions withdrawn in 1995 . . .	**9**			
10	Add lines 7, 8, and 9	**10**			
11	Adjusted earlier year excess contributions. Subtract line 10 from line 6. Enter the result, but not less than zero			**11**	
12	Total excess contributions. Add lines 5 and 11			**12**	
13	**Tax due.** Enter the **smaller** of 6% (.06) of line 12 or 6% (.06) of the value of your IRA on the last day of 1995. Also enter this amount on Form 1040, line 51			**13**	

For Paperwork Reduction Act Notice, see page 1 of separate instructions.   Cat. No. 13329Q   Form **5329** (1995)

Form 5329 (1995)   Page **2**

Part III	Tax on Excess Accumulation in Qualified Retirement Plans (Including IRAs)			

14	Minimum required distribution (see page 3 of the instructions)	14		
15	Amount actually distributed to you	15		
16	Subtract line 15 from line 14. If line 15 is more than line 14, enter -0-	16		
17	**Tax due.** Multiply line 16 by 50% (.50). Enter here and on Form 1040, line 51	17		

Part IV	Tax on Excess Distributions From Qualified Retirement Plans (Including IRAs)		Column A Regular Distributions	Column B Lump-Sum Distributions
Complete Column A for regular distributions. Complete Column B for lump-sum distributions.				
18	Total amount of regular retirement or lump-sum distributions	18		
19	Amount excluded from additional tax. Enter appropriate exception number from page 4 of the instructions ▶ _____	19		
20	Subtract line 19 from line 18	20		
21	Enter the **larger** of the threshold amount or the 1995 recovery of the grandfather amount (from Worksheet 1 or 2). See page 4 of the instructions	21		
22	Excess distributions. Subtract line 21 from line 20. If less than zero, enter -0-	22		
23	Tentative tax. Multiply line 22 by 15% (.15)	23		
24	Early distributions tax offset (see page 4 of the instructions)	24		
25	Subtract line 24 from line 23	25		
26	**Tax due.** Combine columns (a) and (b) of line 25. Enter here and on Form 1040, line 51 . . .	26		

Acceleration Elections (see the instructions for Part IV)

1 If you elected the discretionary method in 1987 or 1988 and wish to make an acceleration election beginning in 1995 under Temporary Regulations section 54.4981A-1T, Q&A b-12, check here ▶ ☐ .
2 If you previously made an acceleration election and wish to revoke that election, check here ▶ ☐ .

Signature. *Complete **ONLY** if you are filing this form by itself and not with your tax return.*

Please Sign Here	Under penalties of perjury, I declare that I have examined this form, including accompanying schedules and statements, and to the best of my knowledge and belief, it is true, correct, and complete. Declaration of preparer (other than taxpayer) is based on all information of which preparer has any knowledge.	
	▶ Your signature	▶ Date

Paid Preparer's Use Only	Preparer's signature ▶	Date	Check if self-employed ▶ ☐	Preparer's social security no.
	Firm's name (or yours, if self-employed) and address ▶		EIN ▶	
			ZIP code ▶	

✪ *Printed on recycled paper*

Tax Forms

Form **6251**

Department of the Treasury
Internal Revenue Service

Alternative Minimum Tax—Individuals

▶ See separate instructions.

▶ Attach to Form 1040, Form 1040NR, or Form 1040-T.

OMB No. 1545-0227

19**95**

Attachment
Sequence No. **32**

Name(s) shown on Form 1040

Your social security number

Part I	**Adjustments and Preferences**	

1 If you itemized deductions on Schedule A (Form 1040) (or you entered the amount from Form 1040-T, Section B, line t, on Form 1040-T, line 20), go to line 2. Otherwise, enter your standard deduction from Form 1040, line 34 (or Form 1040-T, line 20), and go to line 6 . . . . **1**

2 Medical and dental. Enter the smaller of Schedule A (Form 1040), line 4 **or** 2½% of Form 1040, line 32 (Form 1040-T filers, enter the smaller of Section B, line c **or** 2½% of Form 1040-T, line 16) . . . **2**

3 Taxes. Enter the amount from Schedule A (Form 1040), line 9 (or the total of lines d through g of Form 1040-T, Section B) . **3**

4 Certain interest on a home mortgage not used to buy, build, or improve your home **4**

5 Miscellaneous itemized deductions. Enter the amount from Schedule A (Form 1040), line 26 (or Form 1040-T, Section B, line r) **5**

6 Refund of taxes. Enter any tax refund from Form 1040, line 10 or line 21 (or Form 1040-T, line 4 or line 9) . **6** ( )

7 Investment interest. Enter difference between regular tax and AMT deduction **7**

8 Post-1986 depreciation. Enter difference between regular tax and AMT depreciation **8**

9 Adjusted gain or loss. Enter difference between AMT and regular tax gain or loss **9**

10 Incentive stock options. Enter excess of AMT income over regular tax income **10**

11 Passive activities. Enter difference between AMT and regular tax income or loss **11**

12 Beneficiaries of estates and trusts. Enter the amount from Schedule K-1 (Form 1041), line 8 . . . . **12**

13 Tax-exempt interest from private activity bonds issued after 8/7/86 . . . . **13**

14 Other. Enter the amount, if any, for each item and enter the total on line 14.

a Charitable contributions .   h Loss limitations . . . .
b Circulation expenditures .   i Mining costs . . . .
c Depletion .   j Patron's adjustment . .
d Depreciation (pre-1987) .   k Pollution control facilities .
e Installment sales .   l Research and experimental
f Intangible drilling costs .   m Tax shelter farm activities .
g Long-term contracts .   n Related adjustments . . **14**

15 **Total Adjustments and Preferences.** Combine lines 1 through 14 . . . . . . ▶ **15**

Part II	**Alternative Minimum Taxable Income**	

16 Enter the amount from **Form 1040, line 35 (or Form 1040-T, line 21).** If less than zero, enter as a (loss) . ▶ **16**

17 Net operating loss deduction, if any, from Form 1040, line 21. Enter as a positive amount **17**

18 If Form 1040, line 32 (or Form 1040-T, line 16), is over $114,700 (over $57,350 if married filing separately), and you itemized deductions, enter the amount, if any, from line 9 of the worksheet for Schedule A (Form 1040), line 28 (or line 9 of the worksheet for Section B, line t, of Form 1040-T). . . . . . . **18** ( )

19 Combine lines 15 through 18 . . . . ▶ **19**

20 Alternative tax net operating loss deduction. See page 5 of the instructions **20**

21 **Alternative Minimum Taxable Income.** Subtract line 20 from line 19. (If married filing separately and line 21 is more than $165,000, see page 5 of the instructions.) . . . . ▶ **21**

Part III	**Exemption Amount and Alternative Minimum Tax**	

22 **Exemption Amount.** (If this form is for a child under age 14, see page 6 of the instructions.)

If your filing status is:	And line 21 is not over:	Enter on line 22:	
Single or head of household	$112,500	$33,750	
Married filing jointly or qualifying widow(er) . .	150,000	45,000	**22**
Married filing separately	75,000	22,500	

If line 21 is **over** the amount shown above for your filing status, see page 6 of the instructions.

23 Subtract line 22 from line 21. If zero or less, enter -0- here and on lines 26 and 28 . . . . . ▶ **23**

24 If line 23 is $175,000 or less ($87,500 or less if married filing separately), multiply line 23 by 26% (.26). Otherwise, multiply line 23 by 28% (.28) and subtract $3,500 ($1,750 if married filing separately) from the result . . . **24**

25 Alternative minimum tax foreign tax credit. See page 6 of the instructions **25**

26 Tentative minimum tax. Subtract line 25 from line 24 . . . . ▶ **26**

27 Enter your tax from Form 1040, line 38 (plus any amount from Form 4970 included on Form 1040, line 39), minus any foreign tax credit from Form 1040, line 43 (Form 1040-T filers, enter the amount from Form 1040-T, line 26) **27**

28 **Alternative Minimum Tax.** (If this form is for a child under age 14, see page 7 of the instructions.) Subtract line 27 from line 26. If zero or less, enter -0-. Enter here and on Form 1040, line 48 (or Form 1040-T, line 31) ▶ **28**

For Paperwork Reduction Act Notice, see separate instructions.   *Printed on recycled paper*   Cat. No. 13600G   Form **6251** (1995)

Form **6252**	**Installment Sale Income**	OMB No. 1545-0228

Form **6252**

Department of the Treasury
Internal Revenue Service

Installment Sale Income

▶ See separate instructions.   ▶ Attach to your tax return.
▶ Use a separate form for each sale or other disposition of
property on the installment method.

OMB No. 1545-0228

1995

Attachment
Sequence No. **79**

Name(s) shown on return

Identifying number

1 Description of property ▶ ....

2a Date acquired (month, day, year) ▶ ⌊ / / ⌋ **b** Date sold (month, day, year) ▶ ⌊ / / ⌋

3 Was the property sold to a related party after May 14, 1980? See instructions . . . . ☐ Yes ☐ No

4 If the answer to question 3 is "Yes," was the property a marketable security? If "Yes," complete Part III. If
"No," complete Part III for the year of sale and for 2 years after the year of sale. . . . . ☐ Yes ☐ No

Part I **Gross Profit and Contract Price.** Complete this part for the year of sale only.

5	Selling price including mortgages and other debts. Do not include interest whether stated or unstated	**5**	
6	Mortgages and other debts the buyer assumed or took the property subject to, but not new mortgages the buyer got from a bank or other source .	**6**	
7	Subtract line 6 from line 5	**7**	
8	Cost or other basis of property sold	**8**	
9	Depreciation allowed or allowable	**9**	
10	Adjusted basis. Subtract line 9 from line 8	**10**	
11	Commissions and other expenses of sale.	**11**	
12	Income recapture from Form 4797, Part III. See instructions . .	**12**	
13	Add lines 10, 11, and 12	**13**	
14	Subtract line 13 from line 5. If zero or less, **stop here.** Do not complete the rest of this form .	**14**	
15	If the property described on line 1 above was your main home, enter the total of lines 14 and 22 from Form 2119. Otherwise, enter -0-	**15**	
16	**Gross profit.** Subtract line 15 from line 14	**16**	
17	Subtract line 13 from line 6. If zero or less, enter -0-	**17**	
18	**Contract price.** Add line 7 and line 17	**18**	

Part II **Installment Sale Income.** Complete this part for the year of sale and any year you receive a payment or have certain debts you must treat as a payment on installment obligations.

19	Gross profit percentage. Divide line 16 by line 18. For years after the year of sale, see instructions	**19**	
20	**For year of sale only**—Enter amount from line 17 above; otherwise, enter -0-	**20**	
21	Payments received during year. See instructions. Do not include interest whether stated or unstated	**21**	
22	Add lines 20 and 21	**22**	
23	Payments received in prior years. See instructions. Do not include interest whether stated or unstated **23**		
24	**Installment sale income.** Multiply line 22 by line 19	**24**	
25	Part of line 24 that is ordinary income under recapture rules. See instructions	**25**	
26	Subtract line 25 from line 24. Enter here and on Schedule D or Form 4797. See instructions .	**26**	

Part III **Related Party Installment Sale Income.** Do not complete if you received the final payment this tax year.

27 Name, address, and taxpayer identifying number of related party ....

....

28 Did the related party, during this tax year, resell or dispose of the property ("second disposition")? . . . ☐ Yes ☐ No

29 **If the answer to question 28 is "Yes," complete lines 30 through 37 below unless one of the following conditions is met. Check only the box that applies.**

a ☐ The second disposition was more than 2 years after the first disposition (other than dispositions
of marketable securities). If this box is checked, enter the date of disposition (month, day, year) ▶ ⌊ / / ⌋

b ☐ The first disposition was a sale or exchange of stock to the issuing corporation.

c ☐ The second disposition was an involuntary conversion where the threat of conversion occurred after the first disposition.

d ☐ The second disposition occurred after the death of the original seller or buyer.

e ☐ It can be established to the satisfaction of the Internal Revenue Service that tax avoidance was not a principal purpose
for either of the dispositions. If this box is checked, attach an explanation. See instructions.

30	Selling price of property sold by related party	**30**	
31	Enter contract price from line 18 for year of first sale	**31**	
32	Enter the **smaller** of line 30 or line 31	**32**	
33	Total payments received by the end of your 1995 tax year. See instructions	**33**	
34	Subtract line 33 from line 32. If zero or less, enter -0-	**34**	
35	Multiply line 34 by the gross profit percentage on line 19 for year of first sale	**35**	
36	Part of line 35 that is ordinary income under recapture rules. See instructions	**36**	
37	Subtract line 36 from line 35. Enter here and on Schedule D or Form 4797. See instructions .	**37**	

For Paperwork Reduction Act Notice, see separate instructions.   Cat. No. 13601R   Form **6252** (1995)

✿ Printed on recycled paper

Form **7004**
(Rev. June 1995)

Department of the Treasury
Internal Revenue Service

Application for Automatic Extension of Time To File Corporation Income Tax Return

OMB No. 1545-0233

Name of corporation	Employer identification number

Number, street, and room or suite no. (If a P.O. box or outside the United States, see instructions.)

City or town, state, and ZIP code

Check type of return to be filed:

☐ Form 1120	☐ Form 1120-FSC	☐ Form 1120-ND	☐ Form 1120-REIT	☐ Form 1120-SF
☐ Form 1120-A	☐ Form 1120-H	☐ Form 1120-PC	☐ Form 1120-RIC	☐ Form 990-C
☐ Form 1120-F	☐ Form 1120-L	☐ Form 1120-POL	☐ Form 1120S	☐ Form 990-T

Form 1120-F filers: Check here if you do not have an office or place of business in the United States . . . . ▶ ☐

1a I request an automatic 6-month (or, for certain corporations, 3-month) extension of time

until ...., 19....... , to file the income tax return of the corporation named above for ▶ ☐ calendar

year 19 ......or ▶ ☐ tax year beginning ...., 19......., and ending ...., 19........

b If this tax year is for less than 12 months, check reason:

☐ Initial return   ☐ Final return   ☐ Change in accounting period   ☐ Consolidated return to be filed

2 If this application also covers subsidiaries to be included in a consolidated return, complete the following:

Name and address of each member of the affiliated group	Employer identification number	Tax period

3	Tentative tax (see instructions)			**3**	
4	**Credits:**				
a	Overpayment credited from prior year.	**4a**			
b	Estimated tax payments for the tax year	**4b**			
c	Less refund for the tax year applied for on Form 4466	**4c** ( ) **Bal ▶**	**4d**		
e	Credit from regulated investment companies		**4e**		
f	Credit for Federal tax on fuels		**4f**		
5	Total. Add lines 4d through 4f			**5**	
6	**Balance due.** Subtract line 5 from line 3. **Deposit this amount electronically or with a Federal Tax Deposit (FTD) Coupon** (see instructions)			**6**	

Signature.—Under penalties of perjury, I declare that I have been authorized by the above-named corporation to make this application, and to the best of my knowledge and belief, the statements made are true, correct, and complete.

(Signature of officer or agent)	(Title)	(Date)

For Paperwork Reduction Act Notice, see instructions.   Cat. No. 13804A   Form **7004** (Rev. 6-95)

Form **8283**	**Noncash Charitable Contributions**	OMB No. 1545-0908
(Rev. October 1995)	▶ **Attach to your tax return if you claimed a total deduction of over $500 for all contributed property.**	
Department of the Treasury Internal Revenue Service	▶ **See separate instructions.**	Attachment Sequence No. **55**

Name(s) shown on your income tax return	Identifying number

Note: *Figure the amount of your contribution deduction before completing this form. See your tax return instructions.*

Section A—List in this section **only** items (or groups of similar items) for which you claimed a deduction of $5,000 or less. Also, list certain publicly traded securities even if the deduction is over $5,000 (see instructions).

Part I   **Information on Donated Property**—If you need more space, attach a statement.

1	**(a)** Name and address of the donee organization	**(b)** Description of donated property
A		
B		
C		
D		
E		

Note: *If the amount you claimed as a deduction for an item is $500 or less, you do not have to complete columns (d), (e), and (f).*

	(c) Date of the contribution	**(d)** Date acquired by donor (mo., yr.)	**(e)** How acquired by donor	**(f)** Donor's cost or adjusted basis	**(g)** Fair market value	**(h)** Method used to determine the fair market value
A						
B						
C						
D						
E						

Part II   **Other Information**—Complete line 2 if you gave less than an entire interest in property listed in Part I. Complete line 3 if restrictions were attached to a contribution listed in Part I.

2   If, during the year, you contributed less than the entire interest in the property, complete lines a – e.

a   Enter the letter from Part I that identifies the property ▶ _____ . If Part II applies to more than one property, attach a separate statement.

b   Total amount claimed as a deduction for the property listed in Part I: **(1)** For this tax year ▶ _____
(2) For any prior tax years ▶ _____ .

c   Name and address of each organization to which any such contribution was made in a prior year (complete only if different than the donee organization above):

Name of charitable organization (donee)

Address (number, street, and room or suite no.)

City or town, state, and ZIP code

d   For tangible property, enter the place where the property is located or kept ▶ _____

e   Name of any person, other than the donee organization, having actual possession of the property ▶ _____

3   If conditions were attached to any contribution listed in Part I, answer questions a – c and attach the required statement (see instructions).

		Yes	No
a	Is there a restriction, either temporary or permanent, on the donee's right to use or dispose of the donated property?		
b	Did you give to anyone (other than the donee organization or another organization participating with the donee organization in cooperative fundraising) the right to the income from the donated property or to the possession of the property, including the right to vote donated securities, to acquire the property by purchase or otherwise, or to designate the person having such income, possession, or right to acquire?		
c	Is there a restriction limiting the donated property for a particular use?		

For Paperwork Reduction Act Notice, see separate instructions.   Cat. No. 62299J   Form **8283** (Rev. 10-95)

Form 8283 (Rev. 10-95)   Page **2**

Name(s) shown on your income tax return	Identifying number

Section B—Appraisal Summary—List in this section only items (or groups of similar items) for which you claimed a deduction of more than $5,000 per item or group. **Exception.** Report contributions of certain publicly traded securities only in Section A.

If you donated art, you may have to attach the complete appraisal. See the **Note** in Part I below.

Part I   **Information on Donated Property**—To be completed by the taxpayer and/or appraiser.

4   Check type of property:

☐ Art* (contribution of $20,000 or more)   ☐ Real Estate   ☐ Gems/Jewelry   ☐ Stamp Collections
☐ Art* (contribution of less than $20,000)   ☐ Coin Collections   ☐ Books   ☐ Other

*Art includes paintings, sculptures, watercolors, prints, drawings, ceramics, antique furniture, decorative arts, textiles, carpets, silver, rare manuscripts, historical memorabilia, and other similar objects.

Note: *If your total art contribution deduction was $20,000 or more, you must attach a complete copy of the signed appraisal. See instructions.*

5	**(a)** Description of donated property (if you need more space, attach a separate statement)	**(b)** If tangible property was donated, give a brief summary of the overall physical condition at the time of the gift	**(c)** Appraised fair market value
A			
B			
C			
D			

	(d) Date acquired by donor (mo., yr.)	**(e)** How acquired by donor	**(f)** Donor's cost or adjusted basis	**(g)** For bargain sales, enter amount received	**(h)** Amount claimed as a deduction	**(i)** Average trading price of securities
					See instructions	
A						
B						
C						
D						

Part II   **Taxpayer (Donor) Statement**—List each item included in Part I above that is separately identified in the appraisal as having a value of $500 or less. See instructions.

I declare that the following item(s) included in Part I above has to the best of my knowledge and belief an appraised value of not more than $500 (per item). Enter identifying letter from Part I and describe the specific item. See instructions. ▶ _____

Signature of taxpayer (donor) ▶ _____   Date ▶ _____

Part III   **Declaration of Appraiser**

I declare that I am not the donor, the donee, a party to the transaction in which the donor acquired the property, employed by, or related to any of the foregoing persons, or married to any person who is related to any of the foregoing persons. And, if regularly used by the donor, donee, or party to the transaction, I performed the majority of my appraisals during my tax year for other persons.

Also, I declare that I hold myself out to the public as an appraiser or perform appraisals on a regular basis; and that because of my qualifications as described in the appraisal, I am qualified to make appraisals of the type of property being valued. I certify that the appraisal fees were not based on a percentage of the appraised property value. Furthermore, I understand that a false or fraudulent overstatement of the property value as described in the qualified appraisal or this appraisal summary may subject me to the penalty under section 6701(a) (aiding and abetting the understatement of tax liability). I affirm that I have not been barred from presenting evidence or testimony by the Director of Practice.

Sign Here | Signature ▶ _____   Title ▶ _____   Date of appraisal ▶ _____

Business address (including room or suite no.)	Identifying number

City or town, state, and ZIP code

Part IV   **Donee Acknowledgment**—To be completed by the charitable organization.

This charitable organization acknowledges that it is a qualified organization under section 170(c) and that it received the donated property as described in Section B, Part I, above on ▶ _____
                                                                                          (Date)

Furthermore, this organization affirms that in the event it sells, exchanges, or otherwise disposes of the property described in Section B, Part I (or any portion thereof) within 2 years after the date of receipt, it will file **Form 8282**, Donee Information Return, with the IRS and give the donor a copy of that form. This acknowledgment does not represent agreement with the claimed fair market value.

Name of charitable organization (donee)	Employer identification number	
Address (number, street, and room or suite no.)	City or town, state, and ZIP code	
Authorized signature	Title	Date

✪ *Printed on recycled paper*

Form **8332**
(Rev. March 1993)

Department of the Treasury
Internal Revenue Service

Release of Claim to Exemption
for Child of Divorced or Separated Parents

ATTACH to noncustodial parent's return each year exemption claimed.

OMB No. 1545-0915
Expires 3-31-96

Attachment
Sequence No. **51**

Name(s) of parent claiming exemption

Social security number

Part I   **Release of Claim to Exemption for Current Year**

I agree not to claim an exemption for_____
                                            Name(s) of child (or children)

for the tax year 19_____ .

_____   _____   _____
Signature of parent releasing claim to exemption   Social security number   Date

If you choose not to claim an exemption for this child (or children) for future tax years, complete Part II.

Part II   **Release of Claim to Exemption for Future Years** *(If completed, see Noncustodial Parent below.)*

I agree not to claim an exemption for_____
                                            Name(s) of child (or children)

for the tax year(s)_____ .
                       (Specify. See instructions.)

_____   _____   _____
Signature of parent releasing claim to exemption   Social security number   Date

General Instructions

Paperwork Reduction Act Notice.—We ask for the information on this form to carry out the Internal Revenue laws of the United States. You are required to give us the information. We need it to ensure that you are complying with these laws and to allow us to figure and collect the right amount of tax.

The time needed to complete and file this form will vary depending on individual circumstances. The estimated average time is: **Recordkeeping,** 7 min.; **Learning about the law or the form,** 5 min.; **Preparing the form,** 7 min.; and **Copying, assembling, and sending the form to the IRS,** 14 min.

If you have comments concerning the accuracy of these time estimates or suggestions for making this form more simple, we would be happy to hear from you. You can write to both the IRS and the Office of Management and Budget at the addresses listed in the instructions for the return with which this form is filed.

Purpose of Form.—If you are a **custodial parent,** you may use this form to release your claim to your child's exemption. To do so, complete this form and give it to the **noncustodial parent** who will claim the child's exemption. Then, the noncustodial parent must attach this form or a similar statement to his or her tax return each year the exemption is claimed.

You are the **custodial parent** if you had custody of the child for most of the year. You are the **noncustodial parent** if you had custody for a shorter period of time or did not have custody at all.

Instead of using this form, you (the custodial parent) may use a similar

statement as long as it contains the same information required by this form.

Children of Divorced or Separated Parents.—Special rules apply to determine if the support test is met for children of parents who are divorced or legally separated under a decree of divorce or separate maintenance or separated under a written separation agreement. The rules also apply to children of parents who did not live together at any time during the last 6 months of the year, even if they do not have a separation agreement.

The general rule is that the custodial parent is treated as having provided over half of the child's support if:

1. The child received over half of his or her total support for the year from both of the parents, **AND**

2. The child was in the custody of one or both of his or her parents for more than half of the year.

Note: *Public assistance payments, such as Aid to Families with Dependent Children, are not support provided by the parents.*

If both **1** and **2** above apply, and the other four dependency tests in the instructions for Form 1040 or Form 1040A are also met, the custodial parent can claim the child's exemption.

Exception. The general rule does not apply if **any** of the following applies:

● The custodial parent agrees not to claim the child's exemption by signing this form or similar statement. The noncustodial parent **must** attach this form or similar statement to his or her tax return for the tax year. See **Custodial Parent** later.

● The child is treated as having received over half of his or her total support from a

person under a multiple support agreement **(Form 2120,** Multiple Support Declaration).

● A pre-1985 divorce decree or written separation agreement states that the noncustodial parent can claim the child as a dependent. But the noncustodial parent must provide at least $600 for the child's support during the year. The noncustodial parent must also check the box on line 6d of Form 1040 or Form 1040A. This rule does not apply if the decree or agreement was changed after 1984 to say that the noncustodial parent cannot claim the child as a dependent.

Additional Information.—For more details, get **Pub. 504,** Divorced or Separated Individuals.

Specific Instructions

Custodial Parent.—You may agree to release your claim to the child's exemption for the current tax year or for future years, or both.

● Complete **Part I** if you agree to release your claim to the child's exemption for the current tax year.

● Complete **Part II** if you agree to release your claim to the child's exemption for any or all future years. If you do, write the specific future year(s) or "all future years" in the space provided in Part II.

Noncustodial Parent.—Attach Form 8332 or a similar statement to your tax return for the tax year in which you claim the child's exemption. You may claim the exemption **only** if the other four dependency tests in the Form 1040 or Form 1040A instructions are met.

Note: *If the custodial parent completed Part II, you **must** attach a copy of this form to your tax return for each future year in which you claim the exemption.*

Declaration Control Number (DCN)

00 – ⬚⬚⬚⬚⬚⬚ – ⬚⬚⬚⬚⬚ – 6

IRS Use Only—Do not write or staple in this space.

Form **8453**

Department of the Treasury
Internal Revenue Service

U.S. Individual Income Tax Declaration for Electronic Filing

For the year January 1–December 31, 1995
▶ See instructions on back.

OMB No. 1545-0936

1995

Use the IRS label. Otherwise, please print or type.

L A B E L H E R E

Your first name and initial	Last name	Your social security number
If a joint return, spouse's first name and initial	Last name	Spouse's social security number
Home address (number and street). If a P.O. box, see instructions.	Apt. no.	Telephone number (optional) ( )
City, town or post office, state, and ZIP code		For Paperwork Reduction Act Notice, see instructions.

Part I   Tax Return Information (Whole dollars only)

1 Total income (Form 1040, line 22; Form 1040A, line 14; Form 1040EZ, line 4) **1**
2 Total tax (Form 1040, line 54; Form 1040A, line 28; Form 1040EZ, line 10) **2**
3 Federal income tax withheld (Form 1040, line 55; Form 1040A, line 29a; Form 1040EZ, line 7). If any is from Form(s) 1099, check here ▶ ☐ . . . **3**
4 Refund (Form 1040, line 63; Form 1040A, line 31; Form 1040EZ, line 11) **4**
5 Amount you owe (Form 1040, line 65; Form 1040A, line 33; Form 1040EZ, line 12) **5**

Part II   Direct Deposit of Refund (Optional–See instructions.)

Attach Copy B of Forms W-2, W-2G, and 1099-R here.

6 Name of financial institution and, if applicable, branch name ▶ --

7 Routing transit number (RTN)   The first two numbers of the RTN must be 01 through 12 or 21 through 32.

8 Depositor account number (DAN)

9 Type of account: ☐ Checking   ☐ Savings
10 Ownership of account: ☐ Self   ☐ Spouse   ☐ Self and Spouse

Part III   Declaration of Taxpayer (Sign only after Part I is completed.)

11 ☐   I consent that my refund be directly deposited as designated in Part II, and declare that the information shown on lines 6 through 10 is correct. If I have filed a joint return, this is an irrevocable appointment of the other spouse as an agent to receive the refund.

☐   I do not want direct deposit of my refund or am not receiving a refund.

If I have filed a balance due return, I understand that if the IRS does not receive full and timely payment of my tax liability, I will remain liable for the tax liability and all applicable interest and penalties. If I have filed a joint Federal and state tax return and there is an error on my state return, I understand my Federal return will be rejected.

Under penalties of perjury, I declare that the information I have given my ERO and the amounts in Part I above agree with the amounts on the corresponding lines of the electronic portion of my 1995 Federal income tax return. To the best of my knowledge and belief, my return is true, correct, and complete. I consent to my ERO sending my return, this declaration, and accompanying schedules and statements to the IRS. I also consent to the IRS sending my ERO and/or transmitter an acknowledgment of receipt of transmission and an indication of whether or not my return is accepted, and, if rejected, the reason(s) for the rejection.

Sign Here ▶

| Your signature | Date | ▶ Spouse's signature. If a joint return, BOTH must sign. | Date |

Part IV   Declaration of Electronic Return Originator (ERO) and Paid Preparer (See instructions.)

I declare that I have reviewed the above taxpayer's return and that the entries on Form 8453 are complete and correct to the best of my knowledge. If I am only a collector, I am not responsible for reviewing the return and only declare that this form accurately reflects the data on the return. If Part II is completed, I declare that I have verified the taxpayer's proof of account and it agrees with the name shown on this form. The taxpayer will have signed this form before I submit the return. I will give the taxpayer a copy of all forms and information to be filed with the IRS, and have followed all other requirements in **Pub. 1345,** Handbook for Electronic Filers of Individual Income Tax Returns (Tax Year 1995). If I am also the Paid Preparer, under penalties of perjury I declare that I have examined the above taxpayer's return and accompanying schedules and statements, and to the best of my knowledge and belief, they are true, correct, and complete. This declaration is based on all information of which I have any knowledge.

ERO's Use Only

ERO's signature ▶	Date	Check if also paid preparer ☐	Check if self-employed ☐	Your social security number
Firm's name (or yours if self-employed) and address ▶			EIN	
			ZIP code	

Under penalties of perjury, I declare that I have examined the above taxpayer's return and accompanying schedules and statements, and to the best of my knowledge and belief, they are true, correct, and complete. This declaration is based on all information of which I have any knowledge.

Paid Preparer's Use Only

Preparer's signature ▶	Date	Check if self-employed ☐	Preparer's social security no.
Firm's name (or yours if self-employed) and address ▶		EIN	
		ZIP code	

Cat. No. 62766T   Form **8453** (1995)

Form **8582**	Passive Activity Loss Limitations	OMB No. 1545-1008
Department of the Treasury Internal Revenue Service	▶ See separate instructions. ▶ Attach to Form 1040 or Form 1041.	19**95** Attachment Sequence No. **88**
Name(s) shown on return		Identifying number

Part I   **1995 Passive Activity Loss**

Caution: *See the instructions for Worksheets 1 and 2 on page 8 before completing Part I.*

Rental Real Estate Activities With Active Participation (For the definition of active participation see **Active Participation in a Rental Real Estate Activity** on page 4 of the instructions.)

1a Activities with net income (from Worksheet 1, column (a)) . . .	**1a**		
b Activities with net loss (from Worksheet 1, column (b))	**1b** ( )		
c Prior year unallowed losses (from Worksheet 1, column (c)) . .	**1c** ( )		
d Combine lines 1a, 1b, and 1c		**1d**	

All Other Passive Activities

2a Activities with net income (from Worksheet 2, column (a)) . . .	**2a**		
b Activities with net loss (from Worksheet 2, column (b))	**2b** ( )		
c Prior year unallowed losses (from Worksheet 2, column (c)) . .	**2c** ( )		
d Combine lines 2a, 2b, and 2c		**2d**	

3 Combine lines 1d and 2d. If the result is net income or zero, see the instructions for line 3 on page 8. If this line and line 1d are losses, go to line 4. Otherwise, enter -0- on line 9 and go to line 10 .   **3**

Part II   **Special Allowance for Rental Real Estate With Active Participation**

Note: *Enter all numbers in Part II as positive amounts. See page 8 of the instructions for examples.*

4 Enter the **smaller** of the loss on line 1d or the loss on line 3	**4**	
5 Enter $150,000. If married filing separately, see page 8 of the instructions	**5**	
6 Enter modified adjusted gross income, but not less than zero (see page 8 of the instructions)	**6**	
Note: *If line 6 is equal to or greater than line 5, skip lines 7 and 8, enter -0- on line 9, and then go to line 10. Otherwise, go to line 7.*		
7 Subtract line 6 from line 5	**7**	
8 Multiply line 7 by 50% (.5). **Do not** enter more than $25,000. If married filing separately, see page 9 of the instructions	**8**	
9 Enter the **smaller** of line 4 or line 8	**9**	

Part III   **Total Losses Allowed**

10 Add the income, if any, on lines 1a and 2a and enter the total	**10**	
11 **Total losses allowed from all passive activities for 1995.** Add lines 9 and 10. See pages 10 and 11 of the instructions to find out how to report the losses on your tax return	**11**	

For Paperwork Reduction Act Notice, see separate instructions.   Cat. No. 63704F   Form **8582** (1995)

Form **8606**

Department of the Treasury
Internal Revenue Service

Nondeductible IRAs
(Contributions, Distributions, and Basis)

▶ **Please see What Records Must I Keep? on page 2.**
▶ **Attach to Form 1040, Form 1040A, or Form 1040NR.**

OMB No. 1545-1007

1995

Attachment
Sequence No. **47**

Name. If married, file a separate Form 8606 for each spouse. See instructions.

Your social security number

**Fill in Your Address Only
If You Are Filing This
Form by Itself and Not
With Your Tax Return**

Home address (number and street, or P.O. box if mail is not delivered to your home)

Apt. no.

City, town or post office, state, and ZIP code

Contributions, Nontaxable Distributions, and Basis

1	Enter your IRA contributions for 1994 that you choose to be nondeductible. Include those made during 1/1/95–4/17/95 that were for 1994. See instructions	1	
2	Enter your total IRA basis for 1993 and earlier years. See instructions	2	
3	Add lines 1 and 2	3	

Did you receive any IRA distributions (withdrawals) in 1994?

No ──▶ Enter the amount from line 3 on line 12. Then, **stop** and read **When and Where To File** on page 2.

Yes ──▶ Go to line 4.

4	Enter only those contributions included on line 1 that were made during 1/1/95–4/17/95. This amount will be the same as line 1 if all of your nondeductible contributions for 1994 were made in 1995 by 4/17/95. See instructions	4	
5	Subtract line 4 from line 3	5	
6	Enter the total value of **ALL** your IRAs as of 12/31/94 plus any outstanding rollovers. See instructions	6	
7	Enter the total IRA distributions received during 1994. Do not include amounts rolled over before 1/1/95. See instructions	7	
8	Add lines 6 and 7	8	
9	Divide line 5 by line 8 and enter the result as a decimal (to at least two places). Do not enter more than "1.00"	9	× .
10	Multiply line 7 by line 9. This is the amount of your **nontaxable distributions for 1994**	10	
11	Subtract line 10 from line 5. This is the **basis in your IRA(s) as of 12/31/94**	11	
12	Add lines 4 and 11. This is your **total IRA basis for 1994 and earlier years**	12	

Taxable Distributions for 1994

13	Subtract line 10 from line 7. Enter the result here and on Form 1040, line 15b; Form 1040A, line 10b; or Form 1040NR, line 16b, whichever applies	13	

**Sign Here Only If You
Are Filing This Form
by Itself and Not With
Your Tax Return**

Under penalties of perjury, I declare that I have examined this form, including accompanying attachments, and to the best of my knowledge and belief, it is true, correct, and complete.

▶ Your signature

▶ Date

Paperwork Reduction Act Notice

We ask for the information on this form to carry out the Internal Revenue laws of the United States. You are required to give us the information. We need it to ensure that you are complying with these laws and to allow us to figure and collect the right amount of tax.

The time needed to complete and file this form will vary depending on individual circumstances. The estimated average time is: **Recordkeeping, 26 min.; Learning about the law or the form, 7 min.; Preparing the form, 21 min.;** and **Copying, assembling, and sending the form to the IRS, 20 min.**

If you have comments concerning the accuracy of these time estimates or suggestions for making this form more

simple, we would be happy to hear from you. You can write to both the IRS and the Office of Management and Budget at the addresses listed in the Instructions for Form 1040, Form 1040A, or Form 1040NR.

General Instructions

Section references are to the Internal Revenue Code.

Purpose of Form

Use Form 8606 to report your IRA contributions that you choose to be nondeductible. For example, if you cannot deduct all of your contributions because of the income limits for IRAs, you may want to make nondeductible contributions.

Also use Form 8606 to figure the basis in your IRA(s) and the taxable part of any distributions you received in 1994 if you have ever made nondeductible contributions.

Your **basis** is the total of all your nondeductible IRA contributions minus the total of all nontaxable IRA distributions received. It is to your advantage to keep track of your basis because it is used to figure the nontaxable part of future distributions.

Note: *To figure your deductible IRA contributions, use the Instructions for Form 1040 or Form 1040A, whichever applies.*

Who Must File

You must file Form 8606 for 1994 if:

● You made nondeductible contributions to your IRA for 1994, **or**

● You received IRA distributions in 1994 **and** you have ever made nondeductible contributions to any of your IRAs.

Cat.No. 63966F

Form **8606** (1994)

Form **8615**

Department of the Treasury
Internal Revenue Service

Tax for Children Under Age 14
Who Have Investment Income of More Than $1,300

▶ Attach ONLY to the child's Form 1040, Form 1040A, Form 1040NR, or Form 1040-T.

OMB No. 1545-0998

1995

Attachment
Sequence No. **33**

Child's name shown on return

Child's social security number

A Parent's name (first, initial, and last). **Caution:** *See instructions on back before completing.*

B Parent's social security number

C Parent's filing status (check one):

☐ Single   ☐ Married filing jointly   ☐ Married filing separately   ☐ Head of household   ☐ Qualifying widow(er)

Step 1   Figure child's net investment income

1	Enter child's investment income, such as taxable interest and dividend income. See instructions. If this amount is $1,300 or less, **stop;** do not file this form	**1**		
2	If the child DID NOT itemize deductions on Schedule A (Form 1040 or Form 1040NR) or Section B (Form 1040-T), enter $1,300. If the child ITEMIZED deductions, see instructions	**2**		
3	Subtract line 2 from line 1. If the result is zero or less, **stop;** do not complete the rest of this form but ATTACH it to the child's return	**3**		
4	Enter child's **taxable** income from Form 1040, line 37; Form 1040A, line 22; Form 1040NR, line 36; or Form 1040-T, line 25	**4**		
5	Enter the **smaller** of line 3 or line 4. . . . . ▶	**5**		

Step 2   Figure tentative tax based on the tax rate of the parent listed on line A

6	Enter parent's **taxable** income from Form 1040, line 37; Form 1040A, line 22; Form 1040EZ, line 6; Form 1040NR, line 36; Form 1040NR-EZ, line 13; or Form 1040-T, line 25. If the parent transferred property to a trust, see instructions	**6**		
7	Enter the total net investment income, if any, from Forms 8615, line 5, of ALL OTHER children of the parent identified above. **Do not** include the amount from line 5 above	**7**		
8	Add lines 5, 6, and 7	**8**		
9	Tax on line 8 based on the **parent's** filing status. See instructions. If from Capital Gain Tax Worksheet, enter amount from line 4 of that worksheet here ▶ _____	**9**		
10	Enter parent's tax from Form 1040, line 38; Form 1040A, line 23; Form 1040EZ, line 10; Form 1040NR, line 37; Form 1040NR-EZ, line 14; or Form 1040-T, line 26. If from **Capital Gain Tax Worksheet,** enter amount from line 4 of that worksheet here ▶ _____	**10**		
11	Subtract line 10 from line 9. If line 7 is blank, enter on line 13 the amount from line 11; skip lines 12a and 12b	**11**		
12a	Add lines 5 and 7 . . . . **12a**			
b	Divide line 5 by line 12a. Enter the result as a decimal (rounded to two places)	**12b**	✕ .	
13	Multiply line 11 by line 12b . . . . ▶	**13**		

Step 3   Figure child's tax—If lines 4 and 5 above are the same, enter -0- on line 15 and go to line 16.

14	Subtract line 5 from line 4 . . . . **14**			
15	Tax on line 14 based on the **child's** filing status. See instructions. If from Capital Gain Tax Worksheet, enter amount from line 4 of that worksheet here ▶ _____	**15**		
16	Add lines 13 and 15	**16**		
17	Tax on line 4 based on the **child's** filing status. See instructions. If from Capital Gain Tax Worksheet, check here . . . . ▶ ☐	**17**		
18	Enter the **larger** of line 16 or line 17 here and on Form 1040, line 38; Form 1040A, line 23; Form 1040NR, line 37; or Form 1040-T, line 26. Be sure to check the box (or, on Form 1040-T, fill in the space) for "Form 8615" even if line 17 is more than line 16 . . . . ▶	**18**		

General Instructions

Caution: *At the time this form was printed, Congress was considering legislation that would change the tax treatment of capital gains. For information on the changes, get* **Pub. 553,** *Highlights of 1995 Tax Changes.*

Purpose of Form.—For children under age 14, investment income over $1,300 is taxed at the parent's rate if the parent's rate is higher than the child's rate. If the child's investment income is more than $1,300, use this form to figure the child's tax.

Investment Income.—As used on this form, "investment income" includes all taxable income other than earned income as defined on page 2. It includes taxable interest, dividends, capital gains, rents, royalties, etc. It also includes pension and annuity income and income (other than earned income) received as the beneficiary of a trust.

Who Must File.—Generally, Form 8615 must be filed for any child who was under age 14 on January 1, 1996, had more than $1,300 of investment income, and is required to file a tax return. If neither

parent was alive on December 31, 1995, do not use Form 8615. Instead, figure the child's tax in the normal manner.

Note: *The parent may be able to elect to report the child's interest and dividends on his or her return. If the parent makes this election, the child will not have to file a return or Form 8615. For more details, see the child's tax return instruction booklet or get* **Form 8814,** *Parents' Election To Report Child's Interest and Dividends.*

Additional Information.—For more details, get **Pub. 929,** Tax Rules for Children and Dependents.

For Paperwork Reduction Act Notice, see back of form.   Cat. No. 64113U   Form **8615** (1995)

Form **8814**

Department of the Treasury
Internal Revenue Service

**Parents' Election To Report
Child's Interest and Dividends**
▶ See instructions below and on back.
▶ Attach to parents' Form 1040 or Form 1040NR.

OMB No. 1545-1128

1995

Attachment
Sequence No. **40**

Name(s) shown on your return

Your social security number

A Child's name (first, initial, and last)

B Child's social security number

C If more than one Form 8814 is attached, check here . . . . ▶

Step 1	**Figure amount of child's interest and dividend income to report on your return**

1a Enter your child's **taxable** interest income. If this amount is different from the amounts shown on the child's Forms 1099-INT and 1099-OID, see the instructions . . . . | **1a** |

b Enter your child's **tax-exempt** interest income. **DO NOT** include this amount on line 1a . . . . | **1b** |

2a Enter your child's gross dividends, including any Alaska Permanent Fund dividends. If none, enter -0- on line 2c and go to line 3. If your child received any capital gain distributions or dividends as a nominee, see the instructions . . . . | **2a** |

b Enter your child's nontaxable distributions that are included on line 2a. These should be shown in box 1d of Form 1099-DIV . . . . | **2b** |

c Subtract line 2b from line 2a . . . . | **2c** |

3 Add lines 1a and 2c. If the total is $1,000 or less, skip lines 4 and 5 and go to line 6. If the total is $5,000 or more, **do not** file this form. Your child **must** file his or her own return to report the income . . . . | **3** |

4 Base amount . . . . | **4** | 1,000 | 00 |

5 Subtract line 4 from line 3. If you checked the box on line C above or if line 2a includes any capital gain distributions, see the instructions. Also, include this amount in the total on Form 1040, line 21, or Form 1040NR, line 21. In the space next to line 21, enter "Form 8814" and show the amount. Go to line 6 below . . . . ▶ | **5** |

Step 2	**Figure your tax on the first $1,000 of child's interest and dividend income**

6 Amount not taxed . . . . | **6** | 500 | 00 |

7 Subtract line 6 from line 3. If the result is zero or less, enter -0- . . . . | **7** |

8 **Tax.** Is the amount on line 7 less than $500?
 NO. Enter $75 here and see the **Note** below.
 YES. Multiply line 7 by 15% (.15). Enter the result here and see the **Note** below. | **8** |

Note: *If you checked the box on line C above, see the instructions. Otherwise, include the amount from line 8 in the tax you enter on Form 1040, line 38, or Form 1040NR, line 37. Also, enter the amount from line 8 in the space provided next to line 38 on Form 1040, or next to line 37 on Form 1040NR.*

General Instructions

Purpose of Form.—Use this form if you elect to report your child's income on your return. If you do, your child will not have to file a return. You can make this election if your child meets **all** of the following conditions:

● Was under age 14 on January 1, 1996.

● Is required to file a 1995 return.

● Had income only from interest and dividends, including Alaska Permanent Fund dividends.

● Had gross income for 1995 that was less than $5,000.

● Had no estimated tax payments for 1995.

● Did not have any overpayment of tax shown on his or her 1994 return applied to the 1995 return.

● Had no Federal income tax withheld from his or her income.

 You must also qualify as explained on page 2 of these instructions.

 Step 1 of the form is used to figure the amount of your child's income to report on your return. **Step 2** is used to figure an additional tax that must be added to your tax.

How To Make the Election.—To make the election, complete and attach Form 8814 to your tax return and file your return by the due date (including extensions). A separate Form 8814 must be filed for **each** child whose income you choose to report.

Caution: *The Federal income tax on your child's income may be less if you file a tax return for the child instead of making this election. This is because you cannot take certain deductions that your child would be entitled to on his or her own return. For details, see **Deductions You May Not Take** on page 2.*

For Paperwork Reduction Act Notice, see back of form. Cat. No. 10750J Form **8814** (1995)

Form **8829**

Expenses for Business Use of Your Home

▶ File only with Schedule C (Form 1040). Use a separate Form 8829 for each home you used for business during the year.

▶ See separate instructions.

Department of the Treasury
Internal Revenue Service   (99)

OMB No. 1545-1266

1995

Attachment
Sequence No. **66**

Name(s) of proprietor(s)

Your social security number

Part I   Part of Your Home Used for Business

1	Area used regularly and exclusively for business, regularly for day care, or for inventory storage. See instructions	1	
2	Total area of home	2	
3	Divide line 1 by line 2. Enter the result as a percentage	3	%

• **For day-care facilities not used exclusively for business, also complete lines 4–6.**

• **All others, skip lines 4–6 and enter the amount from line 3 on line 7.**

4	Multiply days used for day care during year by hours used per day .	4		hr.
5	Total hours available for use during the year (365 days × 24 hours). See instructions	5	8,760	hr.
6	Divide line 4 by line 5. Enter the result as a decimal amount . . .	6	.	

7	Business percentage. For day-care facilities not used exclusively for business, multiply line 6 by line 3 (enter the result as a percentage). All others, enter the amount from line 3 . . . . . ▶	7	%

Part II   Figure Your Allowable Deduction

8	Enter the amount from Schedule C, line 29, **plus** any net gain or (loss) derived from the business use of your home and shown on Schedule D or Form 4797. If more than one place of business, see instructions	8	

See instructions for columns (a) and (b) before completing lines 9–20.

		(a) Direct expenses	(b) Indirect expenses		
9	Casualty losses. See instructions	9			
10	Deductible mortgage interest. See instructions .	10			
11	Real estate taxes. See instructions	11			
12	Add lines 9, 10, and 11.	12			
13	Multiply line 12, column (b) by line 7	13			
14	Add line 12, column (a) and line 13.			14	
15	Subtract line 14 from line 8. If zero or less, enter -0- .			15	
16	Excess mortgage interest. See instructions . .	16			
17	Insurance	17			
18	Repairs and maintenance	18			
19	Utilities	19			
20	Other expenses. See instructions	20			
21	Add lines 16 through 20	21			
22	Multiply line 21, column (b) by line 7	22			
23	Carryover of operating expenses from 1994 Form 8829, line 41 . .	23			
24	Add line 21 in column (a), line 22, and line 23			24	
25	Allowable operating expenses. Enter the **smaller** of line 15 or line 24			25	
26	Limit on excess casualty losses and depreciation. Subtract line 25 from line 15			26	
27	Excess casualty losses. See instructions	27			
28	Depreciation of your home from Part III below	28			
29	Carryover of excess casualty losses and depreciation from 1994 Form 8829, line 42	29			
30	Add lines 27 through 29			30	
31	Allowable excess casualty losses and depreciation. Enter the **smaller** of line 26 or line 30 . .			31	
32	Add lines 14, 25, and 31			32	
33	Casualty loss portion, if any, from lines 14 and 31. Carry amount to **Form 4684**, Section B .			33	
34	Allowable expenses for business use of your home. Subtract line 33 from line 32. Enter here and on Schedule C, line 30. If your home was used for more than one business, see instructions ▶			34	

Part III   Depreciation of Your Home

35	Enter the **smaller** of your home's adjusted basis or its fair market value. See instructions . .	35	
36	Value of land included on line 35	36	
37	Basis of building. Subtract line 36 from line 35	37	
38	Business basis of building. Multiply line 37 by line 7	38	
39	Depreciation percentage. See instructions	39	%
40	Depreciation allowable. Multiply line 38 by line 39. Enter here and on line 28 above. See instructions	40	

Part IV   Carryover of Unallowed Expenses to 1996

41	Operating expenses. Subtract line 25 from line 24. If less than zero, enter -0-	41	
42	Excess casualty losses and depreciation. Subtract line 31 from line 30. If less than zero, enter -0- .	42	

For Paperwork Reduction Act Notice, see page 1 of separate instructions.   ✲   *Printed on recycled paper*   Cat. No. 13232M   Form **8829** (1995)

STATEMENTS ON RESPONSIBILITIES IN TAX PRACTICE

1991 Revision
Statements 1–8 and Interpretation 1–1

Issued by the Tax Executive Committee
of the American Institute of Certified Public Accountants

CONTENTS

Foreword   D-4

Introduction   D-5
The Program   D-5
The Significance of the Statements   D-5
The Objectives   D-5
The Program in Perspective   D-5
The Scope and Purpose of the Statements   D-6
Authority of the Tax Executive Committee   D-6
The Procedures   D-6

Statement No. 1: Tax Return Positions   D-7
Introduction   D-7
Statement   D-7
Explanation   D-7

Interpretation No. 1–1: Realistic Possibility Standard   D-9
Background   D-9
General Interpretation   D-9
Specific Illustrations   D-10

Statement No. 2: Answers to Questions on Returns   D-14
Introduction   D-14
Statement   D-14
Explanation   D-14

Statement No. 3: Certain Procedural Aspects of Preparing Returns   D-15
Introduction   D-15
Statement   D-15
Explanation   D-15

Statement No. 4: Use of Estimates   D-17
Introduction   D-17
Statement   D-17
Explanation   D-17

Statement No. 5: Departure from a Position Previously Concluded in an Administrative Proceeding or Court Decision   D-19
   Introduction   D-19
   Statement   D-19
   Explanation   D-19

Statement No. 6: Knowledge of Error: Return Preparation   D-21
   Introduction   D-21
   Statement   D-21
   Explanation   D-21

Statement No. 7: Knowledge of Error: Administrative Proceedings   D-23
   Introduction   D-23
   Statement   D-23
   Explanation   D-23

Statement No. 8: Form and Content of Advice to Clients   D-25
   Introduction   D-25
   Statement   D-25
   Explanation   D-25

Statements on Responsibilities in Tax Practice are published for the guidance of members of the Institute and do not constitute enforceable standards. The statements have been approved by at least two-thirds of the members of the Responsibilities in Tax Practice Committee and the Tax Executive Committee.

Statements containing recommended standards of responsibilities that are more restrictive than those established by the Internal Revenue Code, the Treasury Department, or the Institute's Code of Professional Conduct depend for their authority on the general acceptability of the opinions expressed. These statements are not intended to be retroactive.

FOREWORD

This booklet contains the current version of the Statements on Responsibilities in Tax Practice (SRTPs) plus Interpretation 1-1, "Realistic Possibility Standard." The original Statements on Responsibilities in Tax Practice were issued between 1964 and 1977 to provide a body of advisory opinions on good standards of tax practice, delineating the CPA's responsibilities to the client, the public, the government, and the profession. Statement Nos. 1 through 9 and the Introduction were codified in 1976 as *Statements on Responsibilities in Tax Practice.* Statement No. 10 was issued in 1977.

The original statements concerning the CPA's responsibility to sign the return (Statement Nos. 1 and 2, "Signature of Preparers" and "Signature of Reviewer: Assumption of Preparer's Responsibility") were withdrawn in 1982 after Treasury Department regulations were issued adopting substantially the same standards for all tax return preparers. Statement Nos. 6 and 7, concerning the responsibility of a CPA who becomes aware of an error, were revised in 1991. The first interpretation of the Statements on Responsibilities in Tax Practice, Interpretation 1-1, was approved in December 1990. The previously issued statements have been renumbered as indicated in the Appendix, and the current statements should be cited as "SRTP No. 1," "SRTP No. 2," etc.

This publication is intended to be part of an ongoing process that will require changes to and interpretations of current statements and additions of new statements in recognition of the accelerating rate of change in tax laws and the increasing importance of tax practice to CPAs.

Statements on Responsibilities in Tax Practice are developed by the Responsibilities in Tax Practice Committee and approved by the Tax Executive Committee. This revision was approved by the 1990–91 Responsibilities in Tax Practice Committee and the 1990–91 Tax Executive Committee, but acknowledgment is also due to the many members whose efforts over the years went into the development of these statements.

Donald H. Skadden
Vice President—Taxation

INTRODUCTION

The Program

.01   The program contemplates publication and dissemination of a numbered series of Statements on Responsibilities in Tax Practice by the Institute's Tax Executive Committee.

The Significance of the Statements

.02   The statements constitute a body of advisory opinion on what are appropriate standards of tax practice, outlining the extent of a CPA's responsibility to clients, the public, the government, and the profession. Each statement covers a particular aspect of tax practice. The statements, which are educational and advisory, take into account applicable legal requirements of tax practice as well as the Tax Division's opinions as to appropriate standards of responsibilities in tax practice.

The Objectives

.03   The principal objectives of the program are—

a.   To recommend appropriate standards of responsibilities in tax practice and to promote their uniform application by CPAs.

b.   To encourage the development of increased understanding of the responsibilities of CPAs by the Treasury Department and Internal Revenue Service and to urge their officials to promote the application of commensurate standards of responsibilities by their personnel.

c.   To foster increased public understanding of, compliance with, and confidence in our tax system through awareness of the recommended standards of responsibilities of CPAs in tax practice.

The Program in Perspective

.04   There are numerous guides to help determine practice responsibilities. The CPA is required to follow the statutes, regulations, and rules governing practice before the Internal Revenue Service (for example, Treasury Department Circular 230). The Institute's Code of Professional Conduct requires the observance of high ethical standards. These statements are published to clarify the CPA's dual responsibilities to the tax system and clients.

.05   Although the CPA has no separate enforceable statement of standards of conduct relating solely to tax practice, the Institute's Code of Professional Conduct requires attitudes and habits of truthfulness and integrity in all of a CPA's practice, including tax practice. Rule 102 of the Code of Professional Conduct states:

> In the performance of any professional service, a member shall maintain objectivity and integrity, shall be free of conflicts of interest, and shall not knowingly misrepresent facts or subordinate his or her judgment to others.

.06   The statements are not intended to establish a code of conduct in tax practice that is separate and apart from the general ethical precepts of the Institute's Code of Professional Conduct. That Code imposes upon individual members obligations to maintain high standards of technical competence and integrity in dealing with clients and the public in all phases of the professional activities of members, including tax practice.

.07   In this environment, the Tax Executive Committee concludes that while the Code of Professional Conduct is a major factor in molding the CPA's professional behavior, it is in the public interest and in the self-interest of the CPA to develop separate statements of recommended standards of responsibilities of CPAs in tax practice for the guidance of taxpayers and CPAs alike.

The Scope and Purpose of the Statements

.08   The statements generally are confined to discussions of the considerations relating to *federal income tax* practice, including the preparation of tax returns, tax planning, and representation before the Internal Revenue Service. The Tax Executive Committee will consider development of statements of responsibilities in other areas of tax practice in the future as part of its ongoing program to review, revise, and add statements as necessary or appropriate.

.09   The primary purpose of the program is educational. The statements do not have the force of authority, in contrast, for example, to the regulations contained in Treasury Department Circular 230, the Internal Revenue Code or its regulations, or the AICPA Code of Professional Conduct. Statements containing recommended standards of responsibilities that are more restrictive than those established by the Internal Revenue Code, the Treasury Department, or the AICPA Code of Professional Conduct are advisory opinions and CPAs should use them as guides.

Authority of the Tax Executive Committee

.10   By resolution of the Institute's Council, the Tax Executive Committee is authorized to express opinions on matters of broad policy related to taxation including the issuance of Statements on Responsibilities in Tax Practice.

The Procedures

.11   The statements present the opinion of at least two-thirds of the members of the Responsibilities in Tax Practice Committee and two-thirds of the Tax Executive Committee.

.12   Drafts of a proposed statement are given appropriate exposure before the Tax Executive Committee issues a statement.

.13   Details of the procedural aspects of issuing the statements can be found in the AICPA *Tax Division Administrative Manual.*

Statement on Responsibilities in Tax Practice No. 1
Issued August 1988

Tax Return Positions

Introduction

.01   This statement sets forth the standards a CPA should follow in recommending tax return positions and in preparing or signing tax returns including claims for refunds. For this purpose, a "tax return position" is (1) a position reflected on the tax return as to which the client has been specifically advised by the CPA or (2) a position as to which the CPA has knowledge of all material facts and, on the basis of those facts, has concluded that the position is appropriate.

Statement

.02   With respect to tax return positions, a CPA should comply with the following standards:

a.   A CPA should not recommend to a client that a position be taken with respect to the tax treatment of any item on a return unless the CPA has a good faith belief that the position has a realistic possibility of being sustained administratively or judicially on its merits if challenged.

b.   A CPA should not prepare or sign a return as an income tax return preparer if the CPA knows that the return takes a position that the CPA could not recommend under the standard expressed in paragraph .02a.

c.   Notwithstanding paragraphs .02a and .02b, a CPA may recommend a position that the CPA concludes is not frivolous so long as the position is adequately disclosed on the return or claim for refund.

d.   In recommending certain tax return positions and in signing a return on which a tax return position is taken, a CPA should, where relevant, advise the client as to the potential penalty consequences of the recommended tax return position and the opportunity, if any, to avoid such penalties through disclosure.

.03   The CPA should not recommend a tax return position that—

a.   Exploits the Internal Revenue Service audit selection process; or

b.   Serves as a mere "arguing" position advanced solely to obtain leverage in the bargaining process of settlement negotiation with the Internal Revenue Service.

.04   A CPA has both the right and responsibility to be an advocate for the client with respect to any positions satisfying the aforementioned standards.

Explanation

.05   Our self-assessment tax system can only function effectively if taxpayers report their income on a tax return that is true, correct, and complete. A tax return is primarily a taxpayer's representation of facts, and the taxpayer has the final responsibility for positions taken on the return.

.06   CPAs have a duty to the tax system as well as to their clients. However, it is well-established that the taxpayer has no obligation to pay more taxes than are legally owed, and the CPA has a duty to the client to assist in achieving the result. The aforementioned standards will guide the CPA in meeting responsibilities to the tax system and to clients.

.07   The standards suggested herein require that a CPA in good faith believe that the position is warranted in existing law or can be supported by a good faith argument for an extension, modification, or reversal of existing law. For example, the CPA may reach such a conclusion on the basis of well-reasoned articles, treatises, IRS General Counsel Memoranda, a General Explanation of a Revenue Act prepared by the staff of the Joint Committee on Taxation and Internal Revenue Service written determinations (for example, private letter rulings), whether or not such sources are treated as "authority" under section 6661. A position would meet these standards even though, for example, it is later abandoned due to practical or procedural aspects of an IRS administrative hearing or in the litigation process.

.08   Where the CPA has a good faith belief that more than one position meets the standards suggested herein, the CPA's advice concerning alternative acceptable positions may include a discussion of the likelihood that each such position might or might not cause the client's tax return to be examined and whether the position would be challenged in an examination.

.09   In some cases, a CPA may conclude that a position is not warranted under the standard set forth in the preceding paragraph, .02a. A client may, however, still wish to take such a tax return position. Under such circumstances, the client should have the opportunity to make such an assertion, and the CPA should be able to prepare and sign the return provided the position is adequately disclosed on the return or claim for refund and the position is not frivolous. A "frivolous" position is one which is knowingly advanced in bad faith and is patently improper.

.10   The CPA's determination of whether information is adequately disclosed by the client is based on the facts and circumstances of the particular case. No detailed rules have been formulated, for purposes of this statement, to prescribe the manner in which information should be disclosed.

.11   Where particular facts and circumstances lead the CPA to believe that a taxpayer penalty might be asserted, the CPA should so advise the client and should discuss with the client issues related to disclosure on the tax return. Although disclosure is not required if the position meets the standard in paragraph .02a, the CPA may nevertheless recommend that a client disclose a position. Disclosure should be considered when the CPA believes it would mitigate the likelihood of claims of taxpayer penalties under the Internal Revenue Code or would avoid the possible application of the six-year statutory period for assessment under section 6501(e). Although the CPA should advise the client with respect to disclosure, it is the client's responsibility to decide whether and how to disclose.

Statement on Responsibilities in Tax Practice Interpretation No. 1-1
Issued December 1990

REALISTIC POSSIBILITY STANDARD

Background

.01   The AICPA Tax Division issues Statements on Responsibilities in Tax Practice (SRTPs). The primary purpose of these advisory statements on appropriate standards of tax practice is educational. This interpretation does not have the force of authority, in contrast, for example, to the regulations contained in Treasury Department Circular 230 or the preparer penalty provisions of the Internal Revenue Code.

.02   SRTP No. 1, "Tax Return Positions," contains the standards a CPA should follow in recommending tax return positions and in preparing or signing tax returns and claims for refunds. In general, a CPA should have "a good-faith belief that the [tax return] position [being recommended] has a realistic possibility of being sustained administratively or judicially on its merits if challenged" (see SRTP No. 1, paragraph .02*a*). This is referred to here as the "realistic possibility standard." If a CPA concludes that a tax return position does not meet the realistic possibility standard, the CPA may still recommend the position to the client or, if the position is not frivolous and is adequately disclosed on the tax return or claim for refund, the CPA may prepare and sign a return containing the position.

.03   A "frivolous" position is one which is knowingly advanced in bad faith and is patently improper (see SRTP No. 1, paragraph .09). The CPA's determination of whether information is adequately disclosed on the client's tax return or claim for refund is based on the facts and circumstances of the particular case (see SRTP No. 1, paragraph .10).

.04   If the CPA believes there is a possibility that a tax return position might result in penalties being asserted against the client, the CPA should so advise the client and should discuss with the client the opportunity, if any, of avoiding such penalties through disclosure (see SRTP No. 1, paragraph .11).

General Interpretation

.05   To meet the realistic possibility standard, a CPA should have a good-faith belief that the position is warranted by existing law or can be supported by a good-faith argument for an extension, modification, or reversal of existing law through the administrative or judicial process. The CPA should have an honest belief that the position meets the realistic possibility standard. Such a belief must be based on sound interpretations of the tax law. A CPA should not take into account the likelihood of audit or detection when determining whether this standard has been met (see SRTP No. 1, paragraph .03*a*).

.06   The realistic possibility standard cannot be expressed in terms of percentage odds. The realistic possibility standard is less stringent than the "substantial authority" and the "more likely than not" standards that apply under the Internal Revenue Code to substantial understatements of liability by taxpayers. It is more strict than the "reasonable basis" standard under regulations issued prior to the Revenue Reconciliation Act of 1989.

.07   In determining whether a tax return position meets the realistic possibility standard, a CPA may rely on authorities in addition to those evaluated when determining whether substantial authority exists. Accordingly, CPAs may rely on well-reasoned treatises, articles in recognized professional tax publications, and other reference tools and sources of tax analyses commonly used by tax advisors and preparers of returns.

.08   In determining whether a realistic possibility exists, the CPA should do all of the following:[1]

a.   Establish relevant background facts.

b.   Distill the appropriate questions from these facts.

c.   Search for authoritative answers to those questions.

d.   Resolve the questions by weighing the authorities uncovered by that search.

e.   Arrive at a conclusion supported by the authorities.

.09   The CPA should consider the weight of each authority in order to conclude whether a position meets the realistic possibility standard. In determining the weight of an authority, the CPA should consider its persuasiveness, relevance, and source. Thus, the type of authority is a significant factor. Other important factors include whether the facts stated by the authority are distinguishable from those of the client and whether the authority contains an analysis of the issue or merely states a conclusion.

.10   The realistic possibility standard may be met despite the absence of certain types of authority. For example, a CPA may conclude that the realistic possibility standard has been met when the position is supported only by a well-reasoned construction of the applicable statutory provision.

.11   In determining whether the realistic possibility standard has been met, the extent of research required is left to the judgment of the CPA with respect to all the facts and circumstances known to the CPA. The CPA may conclude that more than one position meets the realistic possibility standard.

Specific Illustrations

.12   The following illustrations deal with general fact patterns. Accordingly, the application of the guidance discussed above to variances in such general facts or to particular facts or circumstances may lead to different conclusions. In each illustration there is no authority other than that indicated.

> *Illustration 1.*   The CPA's client has engaged in a transaction that is adversely affected by a new statutory provision. Prior law supports a position favorable to the client. The client believes, and the CPA concurs, that the new statute is inequitable as applied to the client's situation. The statute is clearly drafted and unambiguous. The committee reports discussing the new statute contain general comments that do not specifically address the client's situation.

The CPA should recommend the return position supported by the new statute. A position contrary to a clear, unambiguous statute would ordinarily be considered a frivolous position.

---

1. See Ray M. Sommerfeld, et al., *Tax Research Techniques,* 3rd rev. ed. (New York: AICPA, 1989), for a discussion of this process.

Illustration 2. The facts are the same as in illustration 1 except that the committee reports discussing the new statute specifically address the client's situation and take a position favorable to the client.

In a case where the statute is clearly and unambiguously against the taxpayer's position but a contrary position exists based on committee reports specifically addressing the client's situation, a return position based on either the statutory language or the legislative history satisfies the realistic possibility standard.

Illustration 3. The facts are the same as in illustration 1 except that the committee reports can be interpreted to provide some evidence or authority in support of the taxpayer's position; however, the legislative history does not specifically address the situation.

In a case where the statute is clear and unambiguous, a contrary position based on an interpretation of committee reports that do not explicitly address the client's situation does not meet the realistic possibility standard. However, since the committee reports provide some support or evidence for the taxpayer's position, such a return position is not frivolous. The CPA may recommend the position to the client if it is adequately disclosed on the tax return.

Illustration 4. A client is faced with an issue involving the interpretation of a new statute. Following its passage, the statute was widely recognized to contain a drafting error, and a technical correction proposal has been introduced. The IRS issues an announcement indicating how it will administer the provision. The IRS pronouncement interprets the statute in accordance with the proposed technical correction.

Return positions based on either the existing statutory language or the IRS pronouncement satisfy the realistic possibility standard.

Illustration 5. The facts are the same as in illustration 4 except that no IRS pronouncement has been issued.

In the absence of an IRS pronouncement interpreting the statute in accordance with the technical correction, only a return position based on the existing statutory language will meet the realistic possibility standard. A return position based on the proposed technical correction may be recommended if it is adequately disclosed, since it is not frivolous.

Illustration 6. A client is seeking advice from a CPA regarding a recently amended Internal Revenue Code section. The CPA has reviewed the Code section, committee reports that specifically address the issue, and a recently published IRS Notice. The CPA has concluded in good faith that, based on the Code section and the committee reports, the IRS's position as stated in the Notice does not reflect congressional intent.

The CPA may recommend the position supported by the Internal Revenue Code section and the committee reports since it meets the realistic possibility standard.

Illustration 7. The facts are the same as in illustration 6 except that the IRS pronouncement is a temporary regulation.

In determining whether the position meets the realistic possibility standard, the CPA should determine the weight to be given the regulation by analyzing factors such as whether the regulation is legislative, interpretative, or inconsistent with the statute. If the CPA concludes that the position does not meet the realistic possibility standard, the position may nevertheless be recommended if it is adequately disclosed, since it is not frivolous.

Illustration 8.   A tax form published by the IRS is incorrect, but completion of the form as published provides a benefit to the client. The CPA knows that the IRS has published an announcement acknowledging the error.

In these circumstances, a return position in accordance with the published form is a frivolous position.

Illustration 9.   The client wants to take a position that the CPA has concluded is frivolous. The client maintains that even if the return is examined by the IRS, the issue will not be raised.

The CPA should not consider the likelihood of audit or detection when determining whether the realistic possibility standard has been met. The CPA should not prepare or sign a return that contains a frivolous position even if it is disclosed.

Illustration 10.   Congress passes a statute requiring the capitalization of certain expenditures. The client believes, and the CPA concurs, that in order to comply fully, the client will need to acquire new computer hardware and software and implement a number of new accounting procedures. The client and the CPA agree that the costs of full compliance will be significantly greater than the resulting increase in tax due under the new provision. Because of these cost considerations, the client makes no effort to comply. The client wants the CPA to prepare and sign a return on which the new requirement is simply ignored.

The return position desired by the client is frivolous, and the CPA should neither prepare nor sign the return.

Illustration 11.   The facts are the same as in illustration 10 except that the client has made a good-faith effort to comply with the law by calculating an estimate of expenditures to be capitalized under the new provision.

In this situation, the realistic possibility standard has been met. When using estimates in the preparation of a return, the CPA should refer to SRTP No. 4, ''Use of Estimates.''

Illustration 12.   On a given issue, the CPA has located and weighed two authorities. The IRS has published its clearly enunciated position in a Revenue Ruling. A court opinion is favorable to the client. The CPA has considered the source of both authorities and has concluded that both are persuasive and relevant.

The realistic possibility standard is met by either position.

Illustration 13.   A tax statute is silent on the treatment of an item under the statute. However, the committee reports explaining the statute direct the IRS to issue regulations that will require a specified treatment of the item. No regulations have been issued at the time the CPA must recommend a position on the tax treatment of the item.

The CPA may recommend the position supported by the committee reports, since it meets the realistic possibility standard.

Illustration 14.   The client wants to take a position that the CPA concludes meets the realistic possibility standard based on an assumption regarding an underlying nontax legal issue. The CPA recommends that the client seek advice from its legal counsel, and the client's attorney gives an opinion on the nontax legal issue.

A legal opinion on a nontax legal issue may, in general, be relied upon by a CPA. The CPA must, however, use professional judgment when relying on a legal opinion. If, on its face, the opinion of the client's attorney appears to be unreasonable, unsubstantiated, or unwarranted, the CPA should consult his or her attorney before relying on the opinion.

> *Illustration 15.* The client has obtained from its attorney an opinion on the tax treatment of an item and requests that the CPA rely on the opinion.

The authorities on which a CPA may rely include well-reasoned sources of tax analysis. If the CPA is satisfied as to the source, relevance, and persuasiveness of the legal opinion, the CPA may rely on that opinion when determining whether the realistic possibility standard has been met.

Statement on Responsibilities in Tax Practice No. 2
Issued August 1988

ANSWERS TO QUESTIONS ON RETURNS

Introduction

.01   This statement considers whether a CPA may sign the preparer's declaration on a tax return where one or more questions on the return have not been answered. The term "questions" includes requests for information on the return, in the instructions, or in the regulations, whether or not stated in the form of a question.

Statement

.02   A CPA should make a reasonable effort to obtain from the client, and provide, appropriate answers to all questions on a tax return before signing as preparer.

Explanation

.03   It is recognized that the questions on tax returns are not of uniform importance, and often they are not applicable to the particular taxpayer. Nevertheless, aside from administrative convenience to the Internal Revenue Service, there are at least two considerations which dictate that a CPA should be satisfied that a reasonable effort has been made to provide appropriate answers to the questions on the return which are applicable to the taxpayer:

a. A question may be of importance in determining taxable income or loss, or the tax liability shown on the return, in which circumstance the omission tends to detract from the quality of the return.

b. The CPA must sign the preparer's declaration stating that the return is true, correct, and complete.

.04   While an effort should be made to provide an answer to each question on the return that is applicable to the taxpayer, reasonable grounds may exist for omitting an answer. For example, reasonable grounds may include the following:

a. The information is not readily available and the answer is not significant in terms of taxable income or loss, or the tax liability shown on the return.

b. Genuine uncertainty exists regarding the meaning of the question in relation to the particular return.

c. The answer to the question is voluminous; in such cases, assurance should be given on the return that the data will be supplied upon examination.

.05   The fact that an answer to a question might prove disadvantageous to the client does not justify omitting an answer.

.06   Where reasonable grounds exist for omission of an answer to an applicable question, a CPA is not required to provide on the return an explanation of the reason for the omission. In this connection, the CPA should consider whether the omission of an answer to a question may cause the return to be deemed incomplete.

Statement on Responsibilities in Tax Practice No. 3
Issued August 1988

CERTAIN PROCEDURAL ASPECTS OF PREPARING RETURNS

Introduction

.01 This statement considers the responsibility of the CPA to examine or verify certain supporting data or to consider information related to another client when preparing a client's tax return.

Statement

.02 In preparing or signing a return, the CPA may in good faith rely without verification upon information furnished by the client or by third parties. However, the CPA should not ignore the implications of information furnished and should make reasonable inquiries if the information furnished appears to be incorrect, incomplete, or inconsistent either on its face or on the basis of other facts known to the CPA. In this connection, the CPA should refer to the client's returns for prior years whenever feasible.

.03 Where the Internal Revenue Code or income tax regulations impose a condition to deductibility or other tax treatment of an item (such as taxpayer maintenance of books and records or substantiating documentation to support the reported deduction or tax treatment), the CPA should make appropriate inquiries to determine to his or her satisfaction whether such condition has been met.

.04 The individual CPA who is required to sign the return should consider information actually known to that CPA from the tax return of another client when preparing a tax return if the information is relevant to that tax return, its consideration is necessary to properly prepare that tax return, and use of such information does not violate any law or rule relating to confidentiality.

Explanation

.05 The preparer's declaration on the income tax return states that the information contained therein is true, correct, and complete to the best of the preparer's knowledge and belief "based on all information of which preparer has any knowledge." This reference should be understood to relate to information furnished by the client or by third parties to the CPA in connection with the preparation of the return.

.06 The preparer's declaration does not require the CPA to examine or verify supporting data. However, a distinction should be made between (1) the need to either determine by inquiry that a specifically required condition (such as maintaining books and records or substantiating documentation) has been satisfied, or to obtain information when the material furnished appears to be incorrect or incomplete, and (2) the need for the CPA to examine underlying information. In fulfilling his or her obligation to exercise due diligence in preparing a return, the CPA ordinarily may rely on information furnished by the client unless it appears to be incorrect, incomplete, or inconsistent. Although the CPA has certain responsibilities in exercising due diligence in preparing a return, the client has ultimate responsibility for the contents of the return. Thus, where the client presents unsupported data in the form of lists of tax information, such as dividends and interest received, charitable contributions, and medical expenses, such information may be used in the preparation of a tax return without verification unless it appears to be incorrect, incomplete, or inconsistent either on its face or on the basis of other facts known to the CPA.

.07   Even though there is no requirement to examine underlying documentation, the CPA should encourage the client to provide supporting data where appropriate. For example, the CPA should encourage the client to submit underlying documents for use in tax return preparation to permit full consideration of income and deductions arising from security transactions and from pass-through entities such as estates, trusts, partnerships, and S corporations. This should reduce the possibility of misunderstanding, inadvertent errors, and administrative problems in the examination of returns by the Internal Revenue Service.

.08   The source of information provided to the CPA by a client for use in preparing the return is often a pass-through entity, such as a limited partnership, in which the client has an interest but is not involved in management. In some instances, it may be appropriate for the CPA to advise the client to ascertain the nature and amount of possible exposures to tax deficiencies, interest, and penalties, by contact with management of the pass-through entity. However, the CPA need not require the client to do so and may accept the information provided by the pass-through entity without further inquiry, unless there is reason to believe it is incorrect, incomplete, or inconsistent either on its face or on the basis of other facts known to the CPA.

.09   The CPA should make use of the client's prior years' returns in preparing the current return whenever feasible. Reference to prior returns and discussion with the client of prior year tax determinations should provide information as to the client's general tax status, avoid the omission or duplication of items, and afford a basis for the treatment of similar or related transactions. As with the examination of information supplied for the current year's return, the extent of comparison of the details of income and deduction between years depends upon the particular circumstances.

Statement on Responsibilities in Tax Practice No. 4
Issued August 1988

USE OF ESTIMATES

Introduction

.01   This statement considers the CPA's responsibility in connection with the CPA's use of the taxpayer's estimates in the preparation of a tax return. The CPA may advise on estimates used in the preparation of a tax return, but responsibility for estimated data is that of the client, who should provide the estimated data. Appraisals or valuations are not considered estimates for purposes of this statement.

Statement

.02   A CPA may prepare tax returns involving the use of the taxpayer's estimates if it is impracticable to obtain exact data and the estimated amounts are reasonable under the facts and circumstances known to the CPA. When the taxpayer's estimates are used, they should be presented in such a manner as to avoid the implication of greater accuracy than exists.

Explanation

.03   Accounting requires the exercise of judgment and in many instances the use of approximations based on judgment. The application of such accounting judgments, as long as not in conflict with methods set forth in the Internal Revenue Code, is acceptable and expected. These judgments are not estimates within the purview of this statement. For example, the income tax regulations provide that if all other conditions for accrual are met, the exact amount of income or expense need not be known or ascertained at year end if the amount can be determined with reasonable accuracy.

.04   In the case of transactions involving small expenditures, accuracy in recording some data may be difficult to achieve. Therefore, the use of estimates by the taxpayer in determining the amount to be deducted for such items may be appropriate.

.05   In other cases where all of the facts relating to a transaction are not accurately known, either because records are missing or because precise information is not available at the time the return must be filed, estimates of the missing data may be made by the taxpayer.

.06   Estimated amounts should not be presented in a manner which provides a misleading impression as to the degree of factual accuracy.

.07   Although specific disclosure that an estimate is used for an item in the return is not required in most instances, there are unusual circumstances where such disclosure is needed to avoid misleading the Internal Revenue Service regarding the degree of accuracy of the return. Some examples of unusual circumstances include the following:

a.   The taxpayer has died or is ill at the time the return must be filed.

b.   The taxpayer has not received a K-1 for a flow-through entity at the time the tax return is to be filed.

c.   There is litigation pending (for example, a bankruptcy proceeding) which bears on the return.

d.   Fire or computer failure destroyed the relevant records.

Statement on Responsibilities in Tax Practice No. 5
Issued August 1988

DEPARTURE FROM A POSITION PREVIOUSLY CONCLUDED IN AN ADMINISTRATIVE PROCEEDING OR COURT DECISION

Introduction

.01   This statement discusses whether a CPA may recommend a tax return position that departs from the treatment of an item as concluded in an administrative proceeding or a court decision with respect to a prior return of the taxpayer. For this purpose, a "tax return position" is (1) a position reflected on the tax return as to which the client has been specifically advised by the CPA, or (2) a position about which the CPA has knowledge of all material facts and, on the basis of those facts, has concluded that the position is appropriate.

.02   For purposes of this statement, "administrative proceeding" includes an examination by the Internal Revenue Service or an appeals conference relating to a return or a claim for refund.

.03   For purposes of this statement, "court decision" means a decision by any federal court having jurisdiction over tax matters.

Statement

.04   The recommendation of a position to be taken concerning the tax treatment of an item in the preparation or signing of a tax return should be based upon the facts and the law as they are evaluated at the time the return is prepared or signed by the CPA. Unless the taxpayer is bound to a specified treatment in the later year, such as by a formal closing agreement, the treatment of an item as part of concluding an administrative proceeding or as part of a court decision does not restrict the CPA from recommending a different tax treatment in a later year's return. Therefore, if the CPA follows the standards in SRTP No. 1, the CPA may recommend a tax return position, prepare, or sign a tax return that departs from the treatment of an item as concluded in an administrative proceeding or a court decision with respect to a prior return of the taxpayer.

Explanation

.05   A CPA usually will recommend a position with respect to the tax treatment of an item that is the same as was consented to by the taxpayer for a similar item as a result of an administrative proceeding or that was subject to a court decision concerning a prior year's return of the taxpayer. The question is whether the CPA is required to do so. Considerations include the following:

a.   The Internal Revenue Service tends to act consistently with the manner in which an item was disposed of in a prior administrative proceeding, but is not bound to do so. Similarly, a taxpayer is not bound to follow the tax treatment of an item as consented to in an earlier administrative proceeding.

b. An unfavorable court decision does not prevent a taxpayer from taking a position contrary to the earlier court decision in a subsequent year.

c. The consent in an earlier administrative proceeding and the existence of an unfavorable court decision are factors that the CPA should consider in evaluating whether the standards in SRTP No. 1 are met.

d. The taxpayer's consent to the treatment in the administrative proceeding or the court's decision may have been caused by a lack of documentation, whereas supporting data for the later year is adequate.

e. The taxpayer may have yielded in the administrative proceeding for settlement purposes or not appealed the court decision even though the position met the standards in SRTP No. 1.

f. Court decisions, rulings, or other authorities that are more favorable to the taxpayer's current position may have developed since the prior administrative proceeding was concluded or the prior court decision was rendered.

Statement on Responsibilities in Tax Practice No. 6
Issued May 1991

KNOWLEDGE OF ERROR: RETURN PREPARATION

Introduction

.01 This statement considers the responsibility of a CPA who becomes aware of an error in a client's previously filed tax return or of the client's failure to file a required tax return. As used herein, the term "error" includes any position, omission, or method of accounting that, at the time the return is filed, fails to meet the standards set out in SRTP No. 1. The term "error" also includes a position taken on a prior year's return that no longer meets these standards due to legislation, judicial decisions, or administrative pronouncements having retroactive effect. However, an error does not include an item that has an insignificant effect on the client's tax liability.

.02 This statement applies whether or not the CPA prepared or signed the return that contains the error.

Statement

.03 The CPA should inform the client promptly upon becoming aware of an error in a previously filed return or upon becoming aware of a client's failure to file a required return. The CPA should recommend the measures to be taken. Such recommendation may be given orally. The CPA is not obligated to inform the Internal Revenue Service, and the CPA may not do so without the client's permission, except where required by law.

.04 If the CPA is requested to prepare the current year's return and the client has not taken appropriate action to correct an error in a prior year's return, the CPA should consider whether to withdraw from preparing the return and whether to continue a professional relationship with the client. If the CPA does prepare such current year's return, the CPA should take reasonable steps to ensure that the error is not repeated.

Explanation

.05 While performing services for a client, a CPA may become aware of an error in a previously filed return or may become aware that the client failed to file a required return. The CPA should advise the client of the error (as required by Treasury Department Circular 230) and the measures to be taken. It is the client's responsibility to decide whether to correct the error. In appropriate cases, particularly where it appears that the Internal Revenue Service might assert the charge of fraud or other criminal misconduct, the client should be advised to consult legal counsel before taking any action. In the event that the client does not correct an error, or agree to take the necessary steps to change from an erroneous method of accounting, the CPA should consider whether to continue a professional relationship with the client.[1]

.06   If the CPA decides to continue a professional relationship with the client and is requested to prepare a tax return for a year subsequent to that in which the error occurred, then the CPA should take reasonable steps to ensure that the error is not repeated. If a CPA learns the client is using an erroneous method of accounting, when it is past the due date to request IRS permission to change to a method meeting the standards of SRTP No. 1, the CPA may sign a return for the current year, providing the return includes appropriate disclosure of the use of the erroneous method.

.07   Whether an error has no more than an insignificant effect on the client's tax liability is left to the judgment of the individual CPA based on all the facts and circumstances known to the CPA. In judging whether an erroneous method of accounting has more than an insignificant effect, the CPA should consider the method's cumulative effect and its effect on the current year's return.

.08   Where the CPA becomes aware of the error during an engagement which does not involve tax return preparation, the responsibility of the CPA is to advise the client of the existence of the error and to recommend that the error be discussed with the client's tax return preparer.

---

1. The CPA should consider consulting his or her own legal counsel before deciding upon recommendations to the client and whether to continue a professional relationship with the client. The potential of violating Rule of Conduct 301 (relating to the CPA's confidential client relationship), the Internal Revenue Code and income tax regulations, or state laws on privileged communications and other considerations may create a conflict between the CPA's interests and those of the client.

Statement on Responsibilities in Tax Practice No. 7
Issued May 1991

KNOWLEDGE OF ERROR: ADMINISTRATIVE PROCEEDINGS

Introduction

.01   This statement considers the responsibility of a CPA who becomes aware of an error in a return that is the subject of an administrative proceeding, such as an examination by the IRS or an appeals conference relating to a return or a claim for refund. As used herein, the term "error" includes any position, omission, or method of accounting, which, at the time the return is filed, fails to meet the standards set out in SRTP No. 1. The term "error" also includes a position taken on a prior year's return that no longer meets these standards due to legislation, judicial decisions, or administrative pronouncements having retroactive effect. However, an error does not include an item that has an insignificant effect on the client's tax liability.

.02   This statement applies whether or not the CPA prepared or signed the return that contains the error; it does not apply where a CPA has been engaged by legal counsel to provide assistance in a matter relating to the counsel's client.

Statement

.03   When the CPA is representing a client in an administrative proceeding with respect to a return which contains an error of which the CPA is aware, the CPA should inform the client promptly upon becoming aware of the error. The CPA should recommend the measures to be taken. Such recommendation may be given orally. The CPA is neither obligated to inform the Internal Revenue Service nor may the CPA do so without the client's permission, except where required by law.

.04   The CPA should request the client's agreement to disclose the error to the Internal Revenue Service. Lacking such agreement, the CPA should consider whether to withdraw from representing the client in the administrative proceeding and whether to continue a professional relationship with the client.

Explanation

.05   When the CPA is engaged to represent the client before the Internal Revenue Service in an administrative proceeding with respect to a return containing an error of which the CPA is aware, the CPA should advise the client to disclose the error to the Internal Revenue Service. It is the client's responsibility to decide whether to disclose the error. In appropriate cases, particularly where it appears that the Internal Revenue Service might assert the charge of fraud or other criminal misconduct, the client should be advised to consult legal counsel before taking any action. If the client refuses to disclose or permit disclosure of an error, the CPA should consider whether to withdraw from representing the client in the administrative proceeding and whether to continue a professional relationship with the client.[1]

.06   Once disclosure is agreed upon, it should not be delayed to such a degree that the client or CPA might be considered to have failed to act in good faith or to have, in effect, provided misleading information. In any event, disclosure should be made before the conclusion of the administrative proceeding.

.07   Whether an error has an insignificant effect on the client's tax liability should be left to the judgment of the individual CPA based on all the facts and circumstances known to the CPA. In judging whether an erroneous method of accounting has more than an insignificant effect, the CPA should consider the method's cumulative effect and its effect on the return which is the subject of the administrative proceeding.

---

1. The CPA should consider consulting his or her own legal counsel before deciding upon recommendations to the client and whether to continue a professional relationship with the client. The potential of violating Rule of Conduct 301 (relating to the CPA's confidential client relationship), the Internal Revenue Code and income tax regulations, or state laws on privileged communications and other considerations may create a conflict between the CPA's interests and those of the client.

Statement on Responsibilities in Tax Practice No. 8
Issued August 1988

FORM AND CONTENT OF ADVICE TO CLIENTS

Introduction

.01   This statement discusses certain aspects of providing tax advice to a client and considers the circumstances in which the CPA has a responsibility to communicate with the client when subsequent developments affect advice previously provided. The statement does not, however, cover the CPA's responsibilities when it is expected that the advice rendered is likely to be relied upon by parties other than the CPA's client.[1]

Statement

.02   In providing tax advice to a client, the CPA should use judgment to ensure that the advice given reflects professional competence and appropriately serves the client's needs. The CPA is not required to follow a standard format or guidelines in communicating written or oral advice to a client.

.03   In advising or consulting with a client on tax matters, the CPA should assume that the advice will affect the manner in which the matters or transactions considered ultimately will be reported on the client's tax returns. Thus, for all tax advice the CPA gives to a client, the CPA should follow the standards in SRTP No. 1 relating to tax return positions.

.04   The CPA may choose to communicate with a client when subsequent developments affect advice previously provided with respect to significant matters. However, the CPA cannot be expected to have assumed responsibility for initiating such communication except while assisting a client in implementing procedures or plans associated with the advice provided or when the CPA undertakes this obligation by specific agreement with the client.

Explanation

.05   Tax advice is recognized as a valuable service provided by CPAs. The form of advice may be oral or written and the subject matter may range from routine to complex. Because the range of advice is so extensive and because advice should meet specific needs of a client, neither standard format nor guidelines for communicating advice to the client can be established to cover all situations.

.06   Although oral advice may serve a client's needs appropriately in routine matters or in well-defined areas, written communications are recommended in important, unusual, or complicated transactions. In the judgment of the CPA, oral advice may be followed by a written communication to the client.

---

1. The CPA's responsibilities when providing advice that will be relied upon by third parties will be addressed in a future statement.

.07   In deciding on the form of advice provided to a client, the CPA should exercise professional judgment and should consider such factors as the following:

a.   The importance of the transaction and amounts involved

b.   The specific or general nature of the client's inquiry

c.   The time available for development and submission of the advice

d.   The technical complications presented

e.   The existence of authorities and precedents

f.   The tax sophistication of the client and the client's staff

g.   The need to seek legal advice

.08   The CPA may assist a client in implementing procedures or plans associated with the advice offered. During this active participation, the CPA continues to advise and should review and revise such advise as warranted by new developments and factors affecting the transaction.

.09   Sometimes the CPA is requested to provide tax advice but does not assist in implementing the plans adopted. While developments such as legislative or administrative changes or further judicial interpretations may affect the advice previously provided, the CPA cannot be expected to communicate later developments that affect such advice unless the CPA undertakes this obligation by specific agreement with the client. Thus, the communication of significant developments affecting previous advice should be considered an additional service rather than an implied obligation in the normal CPA-client relationship.

.10   The client should be informed that advice reflects professional judgment based on an existing situation and that subsequent developments could affect previous professional advice. CPAs should use precautionary language to the effect that their advice is based on facts as stated and authorities that are subject to change.

The numbers in parentheses at the end of each definition refer to the chapters in which each term is discussed.

AOD. Action on decision. (15)

Abandoned spouse. See *filing status.* (8)

Ability-to-pay concept. A tax should be based on the amount that the taxpayer can afford to pay, relative to other taxpayers. (2)

Accelerated Cost Recovery System (ACRS). Applies to tangible property placed in service after 1980 and before 1987. ACRS was enacted to encourage investment that would lead to economic expansion by accelerating the capital recovery taxpayers received from depreciating property. (11)

Accountable plan. See *employee reimbursement plan.* (8)

Accounting method. The taxpayer must select an accounting method to determine the year(s) in which taxable transactions are to be reported. The two basic allowable methods are the *cash basis of accounting* and the *accrual basis of accounting.* Taxpayers using the cash basis are taxed on income as it is received and take deductions as they are paid. In contrast, accrual basis taxpayers report their income as it is earned and take deductions as they are incurred, without regard to the actual receipt or payment of cash. (2, 5, 14)

Accrual basis of accounting. See *accounting method.* (2)

Acquiescence. A pronouncement by the IRS that it will follow the decision of a regular Tax Court case to the extent that the decision favored the taxpayer. (15)

Acquisition debt. See *qualified home mortgage interest.* (8)

Active income. Income from a trade or business in which the taxpayer materially participates. This category includes wages and salaries, as well as income from a trade or business in which the taxpayer materially participates. Working interest in oil and gas deposits and certain low-income housing projects are always considered active income. Such activities may produce losses that are not subject to the passive loss rules. (7)

Active investor. See *securities dealer.* (5)

Active participant. See *active participation exception.* (7)

Active participation exception. *Active participants* in rental real estate may use passive activity losses amounting to as much as $25,000 per year to offset portfolio and active sources of income. An active participant must own at least a 10% interest in the activity and have significant and bonafide involvement in the activity, a standard less stringent than that for material participation. The $25,000 annual de-duction amount is phased out when the individual's AGI exceeds $100,000. (7)

Active trader. See *securities dealer.* (5)

Actual cost method. See *auto expense.* (6)

Adjusted basis. The original basis, plus or minus changes in the amount of unrecovered investment. It roughly corresponds to the book-value concept studied in financial accounting. At any point in time, the remaining capital investment to be recovered is represented by an asset's adjusted basis. An asset's adjusted basis may never be less than zero. (2, 10, 11)

Adjusted gross income (AGI). Deductions of individuals are broken into two classes—deductions for AGI and deductions from AGI. This difference in deductions results in an intermediate income number called the AGI. It is used to provide limitations on the deductions from AGI of an individual taxpayer. *Deductions for adjusted gross income* include trade or business expenses, rental and royalty expenses, capital losses, and certain other expenditures that the tax law specifically allows. Once the allowable amount of an expenditure has been determined, it is not subject to further reduction based on the income of the taxpayer. (1, 5, 8)

Adjusted sales price. Equal to the amount realized on the sale of a principal residence, less fixing up expenses. Fixing up expenses are noncapital expenditures that prepare the residence for sale, that are incurred within 90 days previous to the sale, and paid within 30 days after the sale. (13)

Administrative convenience concept. Items may be omitted from the tax base whenever the cost of compliance would exceed the revenue generated. The cost is generally the time and effort for taxpayers to accumulate the information necessary to implement the concept as well as the cost to the government of ensuring compliance. (2)

Ad valorem tax. Taxes that are based on the value of the property being taxed (e.g., property taxes). However, most property taxes are not based on the true fair market value of the property. Rather, the *assessed value* of the property is used to determine the tax. The assessed value of property is typically 50 to 75% of the estimated market value of the property. (1)

Alimony. In a divorce situation, one spouse often makes payments to a former spouse. The payments may be to provide for the support of children (called *child support pay-*

ments), they may be simply a sharing of income between the two parties (called *alimony*), or they may constitute a division of marital property *(property settlement)*. Payments that are a sharing of current income (alimony) are taxable to the recipient and deductible by the payer. (3)

All-events test. An accrual basis taxpayer may deduct expenses in the year in which two tests are met: the all-events and economic performance tests. The all-events test is met when all events have occurred that determine that a liability exists and the amount of the liability can be determined with reasonable accuracy. The *economic performance test* requires economic performance to have occurred with regard to the liability. Economic performance occurs when services or property are provided to the taxpayer or when the taxpayer uses property. (5)

All-inclusive income concept. All income received is taxable unless some specific provision can be found in the tax law that excludes the item in question from taxation or defers its recognition to a future tax year. The tax law always starts with the proposition that anything of value received is taxable. (2)

Alternate valuation date. See *inherited property.* (10)

Alternative Depreciation System (ADS). The ADS system must be used to calculate depreciation deductions for purposes of the alternative minimum tax. ADS depreciation is generally computed using the straight-line method during the specified longer alternative recovery period. An election to use ADS for regular tax purposes is made on a class-by-class, year-by-year basis for property other than real estate. For real estate, the ADS is elected on a property-by-property basis in the year of acquisition. (11)

Alternative minimum tax (AMT). An alternative calculation of the tax liability that results in the minimum amount of tax that the taxpayer must pay. The AMT is a separate, parallel tax system. Within this system, many preference items allowed in the calculation of the regular tax liability are either not allowed or the amount of tax relief provided is greatly diminished. (14)

AMT minimum tax credit. A problem can arise if accelerated income is taxed first under the AMT and later, when the timing difference reverses, for regular tax purposes. To avoid double taxation of reversal items, Congress enacted a minimum tax credit that can only be used to reduce the regular tax liability in later years when the regular tax exceeds the alternative minimum tax. The credit is calculated each year in which the AMT applies. (14)

Alternative minimum taxable income (AMTI). The tax base used to calculate the alternative minimum tax. AMTI is calculated by making modifications to regular taxable income for prescribed adjustment and preference items. (14)

Alternative minimum tax adjustment. Accounts for the effect of items that must be determined using either alter-

native calculations or alternative methods for AMT purposes. In general, the use of the AMT calculation or method results in either accelerating income items or deferring deduction items. The net effect of either is a higher taxable income in the initial period(s) of difference. However, most adjustment items are not disallowed for AMT purposes; they are merely spread out (in the case of deductions) or accelerated (in the case of income items). The difference in the two calculations is temporary, not permanent. (14)

Alternative minimum tax preferences. Preferences are different from adjustments in two distinct ways. First, the AMT preferences apply to all taxpayers. Second, preferences are always added in the computation of AMT income. Unlike adjustments, preference items will not reverse. (14)

Amortization. Amortization is a tax accounting method used to recover the investment in assets. This provides a reasonable allocation of bases to the annual accounting periods benefited by the use of the assets. Intangible property with definite useful lives, such as patents, copyrights, or agreements not to compete, may be amortized. (11)

Amount realized. Capital is recovered at disposition by offsetting the adjusted basis at the date of disposition with the amount realized from the *property disposition*. The amount realized from a disposition is the amount received from the disposition (generally the sales price of the property), less the expenses incurred to make the disposition. If the amount is greater than the adjusted basis, the taxpayer has a *realized gain* on the disposition. If the amount realized is less than the adjusted basis, capital investment is not fully recovered, resulting in a *realized loss.* (10, 12)

Annual accounting period concept. All entities must report the results of their operations on an annual basis (the tax year). Each tax year stands on its own, apart from other tax years. (2)

Annual loss. See *loss.* (1, 7)

Annual personal casualty loss limitation. See *personal casualty loss.* (7)

Annuity. An annuity is a string of payments received over equal time periods for a determinable period. The general formula for determining the amount of each payment that is a return of capital and therefore excluded from income is called the *annuity exclusion ratio.* The formula is the cost of the contract divided by the expected return (contract payment × expected number of payments) on the contract. (3)

Annuity exclusion ratio. See *annuity.* (3)

Arm's-length transaction concept. All parties to the transaction have bargained in good faith and for their individual benefit, not for the benefit of the transaction group. Transactions not made at arm's length are generally given no tax effect or are not given the intended tax effect. (2)

Assessed value. See *ad valorem tax.* (1)

Assessment for local benefits. Real estate taxes that are related to assessments for local benefits, such as sidewalks, streets, sewers, and other improvements, and are not deductible. The tax imposed for local benefits is deemed to increase the value of the taxpayer's property and is considered a capital expenditure. The tax is added to the improved asset's basis, which may be recoverable through depreciation, amortization, or upon its disposition. (6)

Assignment-of-income doctrine. The tax entity that owns the income produced is resposible for the tax on the income, regardless of which entity actually receives the income. Merely directing payment of income (assigning income) that has been earned by one entity to another, although legal, does not relieve the owner of the income from paying tax. (2)

Associated with. See *meal and entertainment expense.* (6)

At-risk rules. Taxpayers cannot deduct losses in excess of the amount they have at risk in an activity. The at-risk amount is equal to cash or other assets that have been contributed to the activity. In addition, any debts of the activity that the taxpayer would have to pay if the activity could not are also considered at risk. Thus, the amount at risk in an activity is the maximum amount of personal funds (assets) that could be lost if the activity failed. The amount at risk is also adjusted for the taxpayer's share of the income (loss) from the activity and reduced by withdrawals from the activity. Any current period losses that are not deductible beause they exceed the taxpayer's at-risk amount are carried forward and are deductible when the taxpayer has enough at risk to allow the deduction. (7)

Auto expense. A taxpayer can choose one of two methods of computing a deduction for using an auto for business purposes, the standard mileage rate method or the actual cost method. Using the *standard mileage rate method*, a taxpayer deducts a certain amount for each business mile the car was driven during the tax year. The standard mileage rate is designed to be an estimate of the cost of operating the car. Because these costs change over time, the standard rate is set each year to reflect changes in the cost of operating a car (30 cents per mile for 1995). In addition to the standard mileage rate, the taxpayer can deduct direct out-of-pocket expenses unrelated to the operating costs of the car that are incurred while attending to business. Using the *actual cost method*, a taxpayer can deduct depreciation, gas and oil, repairs, insurance, interest, license, and other expenses of driving the car. If the car is used for both business and personal purposes, the expenses must be allocated according to the miles driven for each purpose. (6)

Average tax rate. The average rate of tax on each dollar of income that is taxable. The total federal income tax divided by taxable income (tax base). See also *proportional rate structure.* (1)

Bargain purchase. A true bargain purchase is taxable to the buyer. Such a purchase occurs when the difference between the purchase price and the fair market value repre-sents an effort by the seller to confer an economic advantage to the buyer. Bargain purchases are typically found in employer/employee purchases and related party transactions. (3, 10)

Basis. The amount of unrecovered investment in an asset. As amounts are expended and/or recovered relative to an asset over time, the basis is adjusted in consideration of such changes. See also *adjusted basis.* (2)

Boot. When properties of different values are exchanged, the party with the property of lower value must equalize the value being exchanged by transferring cash, securities, services, assumptions of debt, or other property not of like kind. This nonqualifying property is called *boot.* (13)

Brother-sister relationship. See *controlled groups.* (9)

Business bad debt. To be deductible, a bad debt must be related to a transaction that has a business purpose. If the bad debt arose from a transction in the taxpayer's trade or business, the bad debt is allowed as a business deduction; otherwise, the bad debt is considered a nonbusiness bad debt. A *nonbusiness bad debt* cannot be deducted if the debt was voluntarily forgiven or the forgiveness of the debt was intended as a gift. Nonbusiness bad debts are deducted as a short-term capital loss, using the specific charge-off method. See also *specific charge-off method.* (6)

Business casualty loss. See *casualty.* (7)

Business gift. A taxpayer can deduct up to $25 per year per donee for gifts to business customers. Gifts are not subject to the 50% limitation that applies to meals and entertainment expenses. To apply the $25 limitation, direct and indirect gifts given to a person must be counted. An indirect gift is one made to a related party, such as a taxpayer's spouse or child. (6)

Business purpose concept. To be deductible, an expenditure or a loss must have a business or other economic purpose that exceeds any tax avoidance motive. The primary motive for the transaction must be to make a profit. Two general types of expense deductions in the tax law embody the profit motive requirement: expenses incurred in a trade or business and those related to the production of income (investment activity). These are commonly referred to as *trade or business expenses* and *investment expenses.* (2)

Business purpose tax year. See *natural business year.* (14)

Cafeteria plan. A menu of tax-free benefits that is offered at the employer's cost. Each employee is allowed to choose a certain dollar amount of benefits from the menu or may choose to take the cash cost of the benefit. Employees who choose the tax-free benefits are not taxed on the value of the benefit; however, those who elect to receive cash are taxed on the amount of cash received. The employer must make the benefits of the plan available to all employees on a nondiscriminatory basis. (4)

Capital asset.   Any asset that is *not* a receivable, inventory, real or depreciable property used in a trade or business, and certain intangible assets, such as copyrights. Common capital assets of individuals include stocks, bonds, and personal use assets. (2, 3, 7, 12)

Capital expenditure.   Taxpayers cannot deduct capital expenditures in total in the period in which they are paid. The main characteristic of a capital expenditure is that its usefulness extends substantially beyond the end of the tax year in which the expenditure is made. (2, 5)

Capital gain (loss).   The difference between the sales price of a capital asset and the adjusted basis of that asset. See also *net long-term capital gain* and *net capital loss.* (2, 6)

Capital recovery concept.   No income is realized until the taxpayer receives more than the amount invested to produce the income. The amount invested in an asset represents the maximum amount recoverable. (2)

Carryback.   See *net operating loss.* (7)

Carryforward.   See *net operating loss.* (7)

Carryover basis.   Indicates that all or part of an asset's basis transfers from one owner to another or from one asset to another. Transactions resulting in carryover basis are subject to special rules for determining holding period—an adding on of the holding period of the prior asset or of a prior owner. (10)

Cash basis of accounting.   See *accounting method.* (2)

Cash-equivalent approach.   Income does not have to be received in cash to be recognized. The receipt of anything with a fair market value triggers recognition of income. (3)

Casualty.   The result of some sudden, unexpected, and/or unusual event (i.e., fire, storms, earthquakes, and accidents). Thefts are treated as casualties. Actual physical damage to property must occur. When a business property is fully destroyed (or stolen), the measure of the *business casualty loss* for fully destroyed property is the property's basis. If the insurance proceeds received from a casualty exceed the adjusted basis of the property, the result would be a *casualty gain,* which is subject to a special election under which a casualty gain may be deferred. When a casualty occurs and property is not totally destroyed, an estmate must be made of the amount lost as a result of the casualty. In this case, a *casualty loss* is equal to the lower of the decline in the value of the property or the adjusted basis of the property. (7)

Casualty gain (loss).   See *casualty* and *involuntary conversion.* (7)

Centralized management.   See *corporation.* (9)

Charitable contribution.   Individuals are allowed an itemized deduction for donations to *charitable organizations*—those organized for religious, charitable, educational, scientific, or literary purposes. The deductible amount of charitable contributions has three major limitations. The overall amount of the deduction cannot exceed 50% of the taxpayer's AGI. Contributions of ordinary income property are limited to the lesser of the property's adjusted basis or its fair market value. Contributions of capital gain property that are deducted at fair market value cannot exceed 30% of AGI. But a taxpayer who is willing to give up the deduction related to the property's appreciation (i.e., use the adjusted basis as the deductible amount) is not subject to the 30% limit. Any contributions in excess of the limitations are carried forward for deduction for five years. (9)

Charitable organization.   See *charitable contribution.* (8)

Child and dependent care credit.   Taxpayers who incur expenses for child and dependent care that enable them to be employed are eligible for a nonrefundable credit based on the amount of their expenses and their earned income level. The taxpayer must incur employment-related expenses for the care of qualified individuals. A qualifying individual includes any dependent under the age of 13 or a dependent or a spouse of the taxpayer who is mentally or physically incapacitated. The expenditures qualifying for the credit cannot exceed the earned income of the taxpayer. (14)

Child support payment.   See *alimony.* (3)

Citator.   Primarily used to determine both the history of a judicial decision and how that decision has been criticized, approved, or otherwise commented upon in other court decisions. The most common citators are RIA's *Federal Tax Citator* and Commerce Clearing House's two-volume set, which is included in its tax service. (15)

Cited case.   Citators refer to the case being evaluated as the *cited case,* and any cases discussing that case are called the *citing cases.* Cited cases are listed alphabetically, followed by the citing cases and rulings. (15)

Citing case.   See *cited case.* (15)

Citizen or residency test.   See *dependent.* (8)

Claim-of-right doctrine.   A realization occurs whenever an amount is received without restriction as to its disposition. An item is received without restriction when the receiver has no definitive obligation to repay the amount received. (2)

Class life.   Both ACRS and MACRS require that assets be categorized in classes. The class life of an asset determines its cost-recovery period. In general, assets have longer class lives under MACRS than the same assets under ACRS. (11)

Closely held corporation.   For passive loss purposes, a corporation is closely held if five or fewer shareholders own 50% or more of the stock in the corporation during the last half of the tax year. Closely held corporations are allowed to use net passive losses to offset active income of the business. However, they cannot use passive losses to offset portfolio income. (7)

Complex trust.   See *trust.* (9)

Computer-assisted tax research (CATR).   Secondary source of tax information in which the computer is used to access a large database containing the full text of virtually all primary and secondary authorities. The major CATR systems are LEXIS and WESTLAW. (15)

Conduit entity. A nontaxable reporting entity, the tax attributes of which (income, deductions, losses, credits) flow through to its owner(s) for tax purposes. (2, 5, 9, 10)

Constructive ownership rules. These rules are related to the related party provisions. Some individuals might attempt to reduce their direct ownership in a corporation or a partnership by distributing ownership among family members, other corporations, or partnerships that they control. This effort is stymied by the constructive ownership rules, which state the relationships within which an individual is deemed to indirectly own an interest actually owned by another person or entity. (2)

Constructive receipt doctrine. Cash basis taxpayers are deemed to be in receipt of income when it is credited to their accounts or otherwise made unconditionally available to them. Physical possession of income is not required for it to be taxed. (2)

Continuity of life. See *corporation*. (9)

Controlled group. A controlled group is a group of two or more corporations that are owned directly or indirectly by the same shareholder(s). If a parent or subsidiary group in total owns 80% or more of the stock of another corporation, the other corporation is included in the *parent-subsidiary relationship*. Passing two tests creates a *brother-sister relationship*. The first test (the 80% test) requires that five or fewer persons own 80% or more of the stock of all corporations in the group. The second test (the 50% test) requires that five or fewer persons own more than 50% of the stock of two or more corporations (taking into account only the stock ownership that each person has that is identical with respect to each corporation). A shareholder's identical ownership is the percentage of stock the shareholder owns in common in each corporation. That percentage is the smallest amount owned in any single corporation. (9)

Corporate distribution. See *earnings and profits*. (9)

Corporation. An artificial entity created under the auspices of state law. As a separate legal entity, a corporation can enter into contracts in its name, own property, be sued for malfeasance, and is required to pay income tax based on its taxable income. Corporations provide limited liability to its owners such that the owner's liability extends only to the amount invested in the entity. The characteristics of free transferability of ownership, continuity of life, *limited liability,* and the characteristic of *centralized management* lend themselves to raising large amounts of money from many sources. *Free transferability of ownership* means that a corporate shareholder may sell or buy shares at any time without restriction. *Continuity of life* ensures that the business will not cease to exist, regardless of which shareholders trade their stock. The biggest disadvantage of a corporation is the double taxation of dividends. See *double taxation*. (9)

Cost depletion. One of two methods used to compute depletion of natural resources. The cost depletion computation allocates the unrecovered basis over the number of mineral units of the natural resource (useful life of the resource) to which the investment relates. Because an estimate of the remaining recoverable units at the end of each year is used to make the computation, the cost depletion per unit will probably change each tax year. See also *percentage depletion (statutory depletion)*. (11)

Courts. See entries under U.S.

Cumulative Bulletin (C.B.). An official publication of the IRS, consolidating material that first was published in the *Internal Revenue Bulletin* in a hard-cover volume (usually semiannual). (15)

DIF. *Discriminant Function System.* (15)

Damage payments. Damage payments for personal injury or sickness are excluded from taxation. The courts have interpreted *personal injury* to include any personal wrong committed against the taxpayer, such as libel, slander, breach of promise to marry, invasion of privacy, assault, and battery. The exclusion also applies to loss-of-income payments that result from the personal injury. In addition to payments for pain and suffering (which are excluded as damages), the courts often award punitive damages and/or *loss-of-income damages* in personal injury actions. Damage payments made to replace lost income are generally taxable as a replacement of taxable income unless they are related to a personal injury. *Punitive damages* are meant to punish the offender in a personal injury case for gross negligence or the intentional infliction of harm to the other party. Punitive damages are included in gross income unless they are the result of a claim for physical injury or physical sickness. (4)

Death benefit payment. The tax law allows one $5,000 exclusion for death benefits paid to a deceased employee's beneficiaries. In order to qualify for this exclusion, the payment must be made solely because of death and cannot represent payment for services performed before the employee died. If more than $5,000 is paid to more than one beneficiary, the $5,000 exclusion must be taken pro rata among the beneficiaries. (4)

Deductions. Amounts that the tax law specifically allows as subtractions from gross income. (1, 5)

Deductions for adjusted gross income. See *adjusted gross income*. (1, 5, 8)

Deductions from adjusted gross income. Certain personal expenditures and other specified nonpersonal expenditures are allowed to be deducted by individuals as deductions from AGI. These deductions are commonly referred to as *itemized deductions*. (1, 5, 8)

Deferral. An item that does not affect the current period's taxable income but will affect taxable income in some future tax year. (1)

Deferred (third-party) exchange. Allows a transaction to be structured as an exchange when the two parties to an exchange do not have property that they want to exchange directly. The property to be exchanged must be identified within 45 days of the date of the first property transfer. In addition, the exchange must be completed within 180 days of the first property transfer. (13)

De minimis fringe benefit. Those items that are too small to permit a reasonable accounting (i.e., free coffee in break room, employee parties, and small holiday gifts). The exclusion is based on administrative convenience. (4)

Dependency exemption. See *personal exemption.* (1, 8)

Dependent. In order to qualify as a dependent, five tests must be met. First, under the *gross income test,* the gross income of an individual must be less than the dependency exemption ($2,500 in 1995). The gross income test is waived for any child of the taxpayer who is either younger than 19 at the end of the tax year or a full-time student younger than 24 at the end of the tax year. Second, the *support test* requires that the taxpayer claiming the dependency exemption provide more than one-half of the support of the dependent. In the case of divorced parents, the custodial parent is entitled to the dependency exemption, regardless of actual support provided, unless the custodial parent agrees in writing to give up this right. Third, under the *relationship, or member of household, test,* a dependent must be either a relative of the taxpayer's or a member of the taxpayer's household for the entire year. Fourth, under the *citizen or residency test,* a dependent must be either a citizen of the United States or a resident of the United States, Canada, or Mexico. Fifth, under the *joint return test,* a dependent may not file a joint return with his or her spouse for the exemption year in question, unless they would not be required to file a tax return but file a return solely for the purpose of obtaining a refund. (8)

Depletion. A tax accounting method used to recover the investment in assets, such as oil or coal, that waste away through extraction. This provides a reasonable allocation of bases to the annual accounting periods benefited by the use of the assets. (11)

Depreciable basis. The amount of basis that is subject to depreciation and is the amount used to determine the annual depreciation deduction. The depreciable basis does not change during the asset's tax life unless additional capital expenditures are made in regard to the asset. (11)

Depreciation. A tax accounting method used to recover investment in long-lived assets. This provides a reasonable allocation of bases to the annual accounting periods benefited by the use of the assets. Tangible property, used in a trade or business or held for the purpose of investment, with definite useful lives, such as buildings and office equipment, are subject to depreciation. (11)

Depreciation convention. MACRS uses conventions to allocate depreciation to the first and last years. MACRS uses the mid-year, mid-quarter, and mid-month conventions to allocate depreciation in the first and last year of an asset's life. The *mid-year convention* assumes that all property is placed in service and disposed of in the middle of the year. The *mid-quarter convention* assumes that all property is placed in service and disposed of in the middle of the quarter year of acquisition and disposition. The *mid-month convention* also is based on the number of months in service, but the months of acquisition and disposition are counted only as half months. (11)

Depreciation recapture. Depreciation recapture rules reclassify gains from depreciation as ordinary income. Recapture can be considered as giving back the ordinary deduction that created the gain. Only the gain in excess of the recapture amount is accorded capital gain or Section 1231 treatment. The depreciation recapture rules apply only to gains caused by depreciation; losses are not subject to recapture. (12)

Direct construction costs. Costs that are actually incurred to physically construct an asset. Examples of direct costs include materials, labor, supplies, and payments to subcontractors. See also *indirect construction costs.* (10)

Directly related. See *meal and entertainment expense.* (6)

Disability payment. Amounts received as disability payments (sick pay or wage-continuation plans) from an employer-provided health and accident plan are included in gross income. However, the same payments made from a plan purchased by the individual taxpayer are excluded from gross income. (4)

Discharge of indebtedness. If a lender forgives all or a portion of the debt of the borrower, the borrower realizes an increase in wealth from the reduction of the liability. The borrower who is relieved of a debt has obtained a claim of right to the amount of debt forgiven. The increase in wealth is generally taxable to the borrower. The tax law provides an exception to the general rule of taxability of a discharge of indebtedness when the borrower is insolvent (liabilities exceed assets), both before and after the forgiveness of the debt, and for discharges of qualified real property indebtedness. (4)

Dividend. See *earnings and profits* and *stock dividends.* (9)

Dividends-received deduction (DRD). Because of the double taxation effect, if one corporation is a shareholder in another corporation, triple taxation results. The dividends-received deduction generally provides only partial relief from triple taxation. The actual amount of the DRD depends upon the percentage of ownership the recipient shareholder holds in the distributing corporation. See also *double taxation.* (9)

Dominant motive. An expense frequently is incurred for both business and personal reasons. To be deductible, the expense must bear a proximate relationship to the income-producing activity. In addition, the primary or dominant motivation for incurring the expense must be the business purpose. (5)

Double taxation. Obtaining cash distributions is generally the ultimate objective of corporate owners. Cash is distributed to shareholders via dividends. Dividends are payments of already-taxed earnings of corporations. When shareholders receive dividends, taxation occurs again. The double taxation effect results because the corporation is recognized as a separate taxpaying entity. See also *dividends-received deduction.* (9)

Earned income. Income derived from labor. The most common forms of earned income are wages, salaries, tips, bonuses, and commissions; income from the active conduct of a trade or business; income from the rendering of services; and income from the performance of illegal activities. (3)

Earned income credit (EIC). Provides tax relief to low-income taxpayers. The credit is refundable (paid even if no tax is due). The amount of the credit is dependent on the taxpayer's earned income and phases out after income reaches a predetermined level. Married taxpayers are required to file a joint return to take the EIC. (14)

Earnings and profits (E&P). Earnings and profits are a measure of a corporation's ability to pay dividends without impairing capital. The tax definition of a *dividend* is a distribution by a corporation from either its current-year or accumulated earnings and profits, referred to as a *corporate distribution.* If a corporate distribution exceeds both the current and accumulated earnings and profits, the capital recovery concept dictates that the excess distribution is tax free to shareholders. (9)

Economic performance test. See *all-events test.* (5)

Educational assistance program. Up to $5,250 in payments made by an employer to an employee for such costs as tuition and books are excludable if the payments are made from a nondiscriminatory educational assistance program. (4)

Education expense. A taxpayer may deduct education expenses if it meets either of the following requirements: The education is a requirement—either by law or the taxpayer's employer—for the taxpayer's continued employment, or the education maintains or improves the skills required in the taxpayer's trade or business. (6)

Effective tax rate. The total federal income tax divided by the taxpayer's economic income (the tax base plus nontaxable income). (1)

Employee discount. In order to exclude employee discounts from taxation, the discount must be made available to all employees on a nondiscriminatory basis and the goods and/or services provided must be in the same line of business. The excludable discount on goods is limited to the gross profit percentage on the goods purchased. Excludable service discounts are limited to 20%. (4)

Employer-provided lodging. In order for a taxpayer to exclude from taxable income the value of employer-provided lodging, the lodging must be on the employer's premises and must be for the convenience of the employer. In addition, the lodging must be a condition of employment—the employee has no choice but to live in the employer-provided housing. (4)

Employer reimbursement plan. An employer reimbursement plan is an *accountable plan* if employees are required to file an adequate accounting (documentation) of their expenses with their employer and to return excess reimbursements to the employer. If reimbursement equals actual expenses (any excess reimbursement is returned to the employer), the employee does not report the reimbursement. If reimbursement is less than actual expenses, the reimbursement must be included in the employee's gross income and the portion of the expenses reimbursed is deductible for AGI. The excess actual expenses are deductible as miscellaneous itemized deductions, subject to the 2% of adjusted gross income limitation. If the reimbursement is greater than actual expenses, the employee must include the excess reimbursement in gross income. If an employer reimbursement plan is *nonaccountable,* the employee must include the reimbursement (if any) in gross income. No deductions for AGI are allowed. The employee can deduct expenses only as miscellaneous itemized deductions. (8)

Employer's athletic facility. The value of the use of an employer's athletic facility may be excluded from taxation, provided that the facility is on the employer's premises and substantially all use of the facility is by employees and their families. (4)

Employment taxes. Businesses are liable for the payment of Social Security taxes *(FICA)* and federal and state unemployment taxes *(FUTA and SUTA)* for all employees. (9)

Entity concept. All items of income, deductions, and so on are traced to the tax unit responsible for the item. (2)

Estate. Created upon the death of an individual. Generally, the estate is merely a temporary, transitional entity. It holds the deceased person's property until the property is distributed to beneficiaries. After all property is transferred from the estate, its purpose has ended and it ceases to exist. During the estate's life, the property held by the fiduciary may earn income. That income is taxed to the estate and taxes are paid from estate assets. (9)

Estate tax. A tax that is paid on the fair market value of the assets of a deceased taxpayer. The tax is paid by the executor of the estate from the assets of the estate. (1)

Exclusions. Increases in a taxpayer's wealth and recoveries of the taxpayer's capital investment that Congress has decided should not be subject to income tax. Thus, income exclusions are not counted as gross income. Common income exclusions include inheritances, gifts, and interest on certain municipal bonds. (1)

Exemption. Individuals, trusts, and estates may subtract predetermined amounts to determine their taxable income.

Congress recognizes that people need a minimum amount of income to provide for their basic living expenses. This minimum amount of income is deducted as an exemption and is not subject to tax. See also *personal exemption.* (1)

Exemption deduction phase-out. High-income taxpayers must reduce their exemption deductions. The basic reduction is 2% of the allowable exemption amount for each $2,500 (or portion thereof) of AGI in excess of the threshold amount. The total exemption amount, not each individual exemption, is subject to the phase-out. (8)

Expense. A current period expenditure that is incurred in order to earn income. Deductions for expenses are limited to those incurred in a trade or business, in an income-producing activity (investment activity), and for certain specifically allowed personal expenses of individuals. (1)

F.2d. *Federal Reporter,* 2d series. (15)

FICA. Federal Insurance Contribution Act. See *Social Security* and *employment taxes.*

F. Supp. *Federal Supplement.* (15)

FUTA. Federal Unemployment Tax Act. See *employment taxes.*

Fiduciary. A person who occupies a position of special confidence, especially trustees, guardians, receivers, conservators, executors, and administrators. Such people have legal title to property, which they hold for the benefit of others, subject to strict duties under state law. Many, but not all, fiduciaries are required to file income tax returns on behalf of the entity (i.e., trust or estate) for which they are responsible. (9)

Filing requirements. Individuals are generally required to file a return when their gross income exceeds the sum of (1) their standard deduction amount (including the additional amount for age but not for blindness), and (2) their allowable personal (not dependency) exemptions. Three major exceptions are that individuals with net earnings from self-employment in excess of $400 must file a return, regardless of their gross income level; married taxpayers filing separate returns are required to file if their gross income exceeds $2,500, the personal exemption amount; and dependents with unearned income greater than $650. Taxpayers with gross income less than the required filing level will want to file a return when they are entitled to a refund. (8)

Filing status. All taxpayers must take deductions and pay taxes based on their filing status. Filing status indicates whether a taxpayer is married or unmarried. Married taxpayers may file jointly or separately. To qualify for *married, filing jointly* the taxpayers must be legally married on the last day of the tax year. In the case of a death of a spouse, a *surviving spouse* who has at least one dependent child or stepchild living at home may use the joint return tax rates to compute the tax for the two years after the year the spouse dies. Filing *married, filing separately* is primarily used when a husband and wife cannot agree to file together and

are not divorced or legally separated by year end. A *single* taxpayer is a person who is not married on the last day of the tax year and who does not have any dependents to support. In order to qualify as a *head of household,* the unmarried taxpayer must pay more than half of the cost of maintaining a home that is the principal residence for more than half of the year for a qualified dependent (children, parents, and other relatives). The taxpayer's parents do not have to live in the taxpayer's home if they meet the dependency tests. In addition, the principal residence may be for an unmarried child or other direct lineal descendent (i.e., parent, grandchild) who does not qualify as a dependent. The benefit of filing as a head of household is extended to an abandoned spouse. A married person is treated as an *abandoned spouse* if a dependent child lives in the taxpayer's home for more than half of the year and the taxpayer's spouse does not live in the home at any time during the last half of the year. (8)

Final regulation. The Treasury Department's official explanation of a related provision in the Internal Revenue Code. Also called a *Treasury regulation.* (15)

Fiscal year A period of 12 months ending on the last day of any month other than December, or a 52- to 53-week taxable year. The 52- to 53-week fiscal year ends on the same day of the week each year. The year must end either the last time a particular day occurs during the month or the day that occurs closest to the end of a particular month. (14).

Flexible benefits (salary reduction) plan. The employee has an annual amount withheld from his or her salary that is used to pay medical expenses or child-care expenses. Amounts paid into the account by the employee are not included in the employee's gross income, thus the term *salary reduction plan.* These plans allow employees to pay for medical costs and child care with before-tax dollars rather than after-tax dollars. (4)

Foreign earned income. To provide relief from double taxation for U.S. citizens working in foreign countries, the tax law allows individuals two options. First, taxpayers may include the foreign earned income in their taxable income, calculate the U.S. tax on the income, and take a tax credit for any foreign taxes paid. The amount of the allowable *foreign tax credit* is the lesser of the actual foreign taxes paid and the U.S. tax that would have been paid on the foreign earned income. Under the second option, individuals may exclude up to $70,000 in foreign earned income for each full year they work in a foreign country. An individual must be either a bonafide resident of the foreign country or must be present in the foreign country for 330 days in any 12 consecutive months to obtain the tax relief. (4)

Foreign tax credit. See *foreign earned income.*(14)

Free transferability of ownership. See *corporation.* (9)

GCM. General counsel's memorandum. (15)

Gain. The difference between the selling price of an asset and its basis; the result of disposing of the asset. Gains result in income. (1)

General asset class. See *like-kind property*. (13)

Gift. A gift in the statutory sense proceeds from a detached and disinterested generosity that originates from affection, respect, admiration, charity, or like impulses. What controls is the intention with which payment, however voluntary, has been made. A gift is a transfer of property from a donor to a donee that is not a profit-motivated arm's-length transaction. Neither the donor nor the donee recognizes any income or pays income tax on the transfer of gift property. A *gift tax* may be imposed on the donor for the fair market value of the gift at the date of transfer. (4, 7, 10)

Gift tax. See *gift*. (1)

Goodwill. In the purchase of a business, goodwill represents the difference between the purchase price and fair market value of the net assets acquired. If purchased after August 9, 1993, goodwill is amortized over 15 years. (10)

Grantor. See *trust*. (9)

Grantor trust. See *trust*. (9)

Gross income. Gross income is income broadly defined, minus income items that are excluded from taxation. Items of gross income are included in the computation of taxable income. Generally, gross income is the starting point for reporting income items on a tax return. (1, 5)

Gross income test. See *dependent*. (8)

Group term life insurance. Premiums paid by an employer on the first $50,000 face amount of group term life insurance are excluded from taxation. The exclusion is available only for term insurance that is provided to a group of employees on a nondiscriminatory basis. (4)

Guaranteed payment. See *partners*. (9)

Head of household. See *filing status*. (8)

Health and accident insurance. Premiums paid by an employer to purchase health and accident insurance coverage for employees (and their dependents) are excluded from the employee's income. (4)

Hobby. A taxpayer may engage in an income-earning activity primarily for personal reasons, such as recreation and personal enjoyment, which disqualify it as a trade or business or an investment activity; profitability is a secondary concern. Such an activity is classified as a hobby because it lacks a business purpose. A taxpayer's allowable hobby expenses cannot exceed the gross income from the hobby. Expenses in excess of hobby income are referred to as *hobby losses*, which are not deductible. Hobby expenses are reported as miscellaneous itemized deductions, which are subject to a limit of 2% of adjusted gross income. (6)

Hobby loss. See *hobby*. (6)

Holding period. The length of time an asset is owned. An asset's holding period normally begins on the day after it is acquired and ends on the day of its disposition. (3, 12)

Home equity debt. See *qualified home mortgage interest*. (8)

Home office deduction. Taxpayers who operate a trade or business out of their home can claim a deduction for expenses related to its business use. To claim a deduction, strict tests must be satisfied. The exclusive use test states that a specific part of the home must be used exclusively for carrying on a trade or business. The home office area must also be regularly used as the principal place to conduct a trade or business belonging to the taxpayer, or as a place to meet or deal with patients, clients, or customers in the normal course of the trade or business. Employee use must be for the convenience of the employer and required as a condition of employment before any deductions for a home office may be taken. The home office deduction is limited to the income earned from the home office activity after deducting all other business expenses that are unrelated to the use of the home office. (6)

Hybrid method of accounting. Allows the taxpayer to account for sales of merchandise and the related cost of goods sold on the accrual basis and to use the cash basis for all other items of income and expense; a mixture of the accrual and cash methods. (3)

Improvements by a lessee. A property owner does not have income when a lessee makes improvements to the owner's property or when such improvements revert to the property owner at the termination of the lease. This allows the property owner to defer the gain in value that results from the improvements until the property is sold, at which time the owner will have the wherewithal to pay the tax on the increased value. (4)

Imputed income. The three most common forms of imputed income subject to tax are below market-rate loans, payment of expenses by others, and bargain purchases. Most imputed income is not taxed. (3)

Indirect construction costs. General costs of a business not directly related to a construction project but that support the project. Examples include interest on funds to finance the construction, taxes, general administrative costs, and depreciation on equipment used in the project. See also *direct construction costs*. (10)

Individual accounting treatments. Individual treatments of specific items where the tax law allows the taxpayer options in the treatment of an item. Depreciation methods, accounting for inventories, installment sales accounting, and accounting for long-term contracts are all examples of individual accounting treatments. (14)

Individual retirement account (IRA). All taxpayers are allowed to contribute up to $2,000 per year of their earned income to an IRA. A husband and wife who both have earned sources of income may each contribute up to the $2,000 limit to separate IRA accounts. An IRA can also be established for a nonworking spouse. However, the total amount paid into the two IRAs cannot exceed $2,250, and no one account can receive more than $2,000. If an individual and spouse are not covered by an employer-sponsored retirement plan, all allowable contributions made to the plan are deductible for adjusted gross income. The IRA deduction is reduced if one taxpayer is covered by an employer-provided retirement plan. (8)

Inheritance.   The value of property received by inheritance is excluded from taxation. Property held in an estate is subject to the estate tax. Thus, the income tax exclusion for inheritances avoids a double taxation of the property of a deceased taxpayer. (4)

Inherited property.   Property passing from a dead person to an heir. The general rule for determining the initial basis is the fair market value of the property on the date of death, called the *primary valuation date*. The executor of the estate may elect to use the *alternate valuation date,* which is six months after the date of death. If assets are distributed before the six-month valuation date and the alternate valuation date has been elected, the asset's basis is the fair market value on the date it is distributed. (10)

Initial basis.   Represents the taxpayer's total investment in an asset on its acquisition date. It is equal to the purchase price of the asset plus any cost incurred to get the asset ready for its intended use (i.e., commissions, legal fees, surveys). (10)

Installment sale.   Occurs whenever property is sold and at least one payment is received in the tax year subsequent to the year of sale. Taxpayers who are not dealers in the particular type of property must recognize income from the casual sale of property by using the installment method, unless they elect to recognize the entire gain in the year of the sale. The installment method is based on the wherewithal-to-pay concept and recognizes income proportionally as the selling price is received. (3)

Intangible property.   Property that lacks any physical characteristics and exists only because of economic rights the property possesses. (10)

Internal Revenue Bulletin **(I.R.B.)**   An official weekly publication of the IRS that includes announcements, Treasury regulations, revenue rulings, revenue procedures, and other information that is of interest to a tax researcher. (15)

Interpretive regulation.   Issued under the general authority given to the Treasury Department to provide official interpretations of Internal Revenue Code provisions. (15)

Investment expense.   See *business purpose concept.* (2, 5, 8)

Investment interest.   Interest paid on debt used to purchase portfolio investments is deductible as an itemized deduction. The deduction for investment interest is limited to *net investment income* (investment income less investment expense other than interest) of the taxpayer for the year. Any interest not currently deductible because of the limitation may be carried forward indefinitely and applied to future years. (8)

Investment-related loss.   A loss on the sale or other disposition of an investment asset. (7)

Investment tax credit (ITC).   A credit for a percentage of the cost of qualifying property (generally, only personal property has been allowed the ITC) that is granted by Congress. The ITC was repealed in 1986 and has not been reinstated. (14)

Involuntary conversion.   Occurs whenever a gain or loss is realized from a transaction that occurs against the taxpayer's will (beyond the control of the taxpayer). Involuntary conversions result when property is destroyed or damaged in a casualty or theft, when a government unit condemns property under its power of eminent domain, or when a foreign government seizes or nationalizes property. Losses on involuntary conversions of business or investment property are always recognized in full. When an involuntary conversion results in a *casualty gain,* the taxpayer may elect to defer the gain if a qualified replacement property is purchased. (13)

Itemized deduction.   See *deductions from adjusted gross income.* (1, 5)

Itemized deduction phase-out.   High-income taxpayers must reduce the amount of their allowable itemized deductions. Allowable deductions for medical expenses, investment interest, gambling losses, and casualty and theft losses are not subject to reduction. In general, taxpayers with adjusted gross income in excess of $114,700 in 1995 must reduce their otherwise allowable itemized deductions by 3% of adjusted gross income in excess $114,700. In addition, itemized deductions may not be reduced by more than 80% of the otherwise allowable amount. (8)

Joint return test.   See *dependent.* (8)

Kiddie tax.   See *minor child.* (8)

Least aggregate deferral tax year.   See *partnership tax year.* (14)

Legislative grace concept.   Any tax relief provided to taxpayers is the result of specific acts of Congress that must be strictly applied and interpreted. All income received is taxable unless a specific provision can be found in the tax law that excludes the income from taxation. Deductions must be approached with the philosophy that nothing is deductible unless a provision in the tax law allows the deduction. (2)

Legislative regulation.   Issued when Congress specifically delegates authority to the Treasury Department to write specific rules for a designated Code section. Legislative regulations carry a higher level of authority than interpretative regulations. (15)

Letter rulings.   Private letter rulings and technical advice memoranda are generically referred to as *letter rulings* and, although they are not officially published by the government, they are unofficially made available to the public by many private publishers, such as Commerce Clearing House and Research Institute of America. (15)

Life insurance proceeds.   Payments from life insurance that are paid upon the death of the insured are generally excluded from income tax, although life insurance proceeds may be included in the dead person's gross estate, which is subject to estate tax. Life insurance proceeds are excluded even if the payments are received in installments, although any earnings included in the installment payments are taxable. (4)

Like-kind exchange rules. The exchange of like-kind property. The tax law requires the deferral of the recognition of gain or loss until the property is disposed of, providing cash (or other assets) with which to pay the tax. A gain on a like-kind exchange is recognized to the extent of any boot received (but never more than the realized gain on the exchange). Losses on like-kind exchanges are never recognized, even when boot is received. Nonrecognition of gains and losses on exchanges of like-kind property is mandatory. See also *boot*. (13)

Like-kind property. The like-kind exchange rules require that the property being transferred in an exchange be used in a trade or business or held as an investment. The property must be of like kind in the taxpayer's hands, not the prior owner's. Any real property may be exchanged for any other real property in a like-kind exchange. To qualify as like-kind property, personal property must be of like class—within the same *general asset class* as defined for cost-recovery purposes. If both properties being exchanged do not fall within one of the general asset classes, the properties are of like kind if they fall within the same product class. *Product class* is defined as the 4-digit product class of the *Standard Industrial Classification Manual (SIC Codes)*. (13)

Limited liability. See *corporation*. (9)

Limited liability company (LLC). Combines the corporate characteristic of limited liability with the conduit tax treatment of partnerships. Whereas corporations are created by filing articles of incorporation, LLCs file articles of organization. The entity must have two or more members, have an objective to carry on a business, and establish a specific method for dividing the profits and losses from the business. An LLC is not subject to corporate taxation, unless it has more corporate characteristics than noncorporate characteristics. (9)

Limited liability partnership (LLP). A general partnership with the added characteristic of limited liability for owners. An LLP permits the usual partnership conduit tax treatment but limits the liabilities of its owners (partners). (9)

Limited partnership. A partnership in which at least one partner's liability is limited to the amount of her or his investment in the partnership. This attribute provides a measure of protection for the limited partners' personal assets. To obtain the limited liability attribute, limited partners give up any right to participate in the management of the business. Management is left to at least one general partner whose liability is not limited and who is responsible for the ongoing activities of the business. (7)

Listed property. Listed property includes the following categories of property: passenger autos; other property used for transportation such as trucks, trains, buses or boats; property of a type that is generally used for purposes of entertainment, recreation, or amusement; any computer or peripheral equipment; any cellular telephone or similar communications equipment. The *listed property rules* require taxpayers to substantiate the extent of an asset's business use. If listed property is not used predominantly in a trade or business, the business use portion of the asset must be depreciated using the Alternative Depreciation System (ADS). If more than 50% of an asset's total use for each year of its tax life is related to the taxpayer's trade or business, the asset is treated the same as any other business asset. (11)

Listed property rules. See *listed property*. (11)

Long-term capital gain (loss). A gain (loss) on the sale of a capital asset that is held for more than one year. (3)

Lookback method. Pertains to the percentage-of-completed-contract method. To remove the incentive to overestimate costs, the taxpayer must use the lookback method at the completion of the contract to determine whether taxes have been underpaid or overpaid each year based on the actual total costs of the contract. If the taxpayer has underpaid (i.e., costs were overestimated) taxes, the taxpayer must pay interest on the income deferred by the underpayment. If an overpayment has been made, the taxpayer receives interest on the overpayment. See also *percentage-of-completed-contract method*. (14)

Lookback recapture rule. See *Section 1231 netting procedure*. (12)

Loss. Occurs when an asset is disposed of for a selling price that is less than its basis. Such a loss is referred to as a *transaction loss* and represents a loss of capital invested in the asset. An *annual loss* results from an excess of allowable deductions for a tax year over the reported income for the year. (1)

Loss-of-income damages. See *damage payments*. (4)

Lower of cost-or-market method. The lower of cost-or-market method requires a comparison of cost and market for each inventory item. Comparison of the total cost and total market value of dissimilar inventory items is not permitted. *Cost* refers to the amount determined under the cost method using the unicap rules. *Market for purchased merchandise* means the bid price for the particular inventory item in the volume in which it is normally purchased by the taxpayer. For manufactured goods, market is the total reproduction cost at current bid prices. (14)

Majority-interest tax year. See *partnership tax year*. (14)

Marginal tax rate. The rate of tax that will be paid on the next dollar of income or the rate of tax that will be saved by the next dollar of deduction. Used in tax planning to determine the effect of reporting additional income or deductions during a tax year. See also *proportional rate structure*. (1)

Married, filing jointly (separately). See *filing status.* (8)

Material participant. See *material participation* and *material participation exception.* (7)

Material participation. Requires that the taxpayer be involved in the operations of the activity on a regular, continuous, and substantial basis. The basic test for material participation is that the individual (including the individual's spouse) participates in the activity for more than 500 hours per year. Six other tests qualify a taxpayer as a material participant based on lower levels of participation. See also *passive activity.* (7)

Material participation exception. Rental activities of taxpayers meeting this exception are not passive activities. Losses from the rental activities are fully deductible against other active and portfolio income. To qualify for this exception, the taxpayer must materially participate in the rental activity, more than 50% of the taxpayer's total personal service time must be devoted to real property trades or businesses in which the taxpayer materially participates, and more than 750 hours of personal service time must be performed in real property trades or businesses in which the taxpayer materially participates. (7)

Meal and entertainment expense. A taxpayer can deduct 50% of the cost of meals and entertainment incurred for a business purpose. The expense must be an ordinary and necessary expense of the business and not be lavish or extravagant under the circumstances. Also, to be deductible, the expense must be either directly related to or associated with the active conduct of an activity for which the taxpayer has a business purpose. The expense is *directly related* to the active conduct of the taxpayer's business if it meets all four of the following conditions: there is more than a general expectation of deriving income or a business benefit from the meal or entertainment; a bonafide business activity takes place during the meal or entertainment; the principal reason for providing the meal or entertainment is to conduct business; and the expenses are related to the taxpayer and persons involved in the business activity. The *associated with* test has two conditions: the meal or entertainment has a clear business purpose and the meal or entertainment directly precedes or follows a substantial and bonafide business discussion. (6)

Meals provided by employer. The value of meals provided an employee free of charge may be excluded from the employee's income if the meals are provided on the employer's business premises and the provision of the meals is for the convenience of the employer. Cash meal allowances are generally taxable because they are not meals provided by the employer. (4)

Medical expense. Individuals are allowed an itemized deduction for their unreimbursed medical costs. To be deductible, medical expenses must be incurred for the diagnosis, cure, mitigation, treatment or prevention of disease, or they must be incurred for the purpose of affecting a structure or

function of the body. Unreimbursed medical costs are only deductible to the extent they exceed 7.5% of AGI. (8)

Mid-month convention. See *depreciation convention.* (11)

Mid-quarter convention. See *depreciation convention.* (11)

Mid-year convention. See *depreciation convention.* (11)

Minor child. Congress in 1986 enacted provisions that are designed to eliminate the tax rate advantage that could have been gained under prior law through shifting of unearned forms of income from parents to a minor child. The basic thrust is to tax the net unearned income of a child who has not attained the age of 14 (minor child) at the parent's marginal tax rate *(the kiddie tax). Net unearned income* is all unearned inome reduced by $650 and by the greater of the cost of producing the income or $650. (8)

Miscellaneous itemized deductions. Category of deductions that includes amounts expended for unreimbursed employee business expenses, investment expenses (other than investment interest), hobby-related deductions, and gambling losses to the extent of gambling winnings. Some expenditures are subject to an annual limitation of 2% of AGI. (8)

Mixed-use asset. See *mixed-use property.* (5)

Mixed-use expenditure (expense). Expenses that are incurred for both profit and personal reasons. These expenditures must be allocated between business and personal use and deducted according to the rules for each use. (5)

Mixed-use property. A single property may be used in more than one use category. Proper accounting for mixed-use property requires a reasonable allocation of costs between the uses of the property. Also called *mixed-use asset.* (10)

Modified Accelerated Cost Recovery System (MACRS). Applies to tangible property placed in service after 1986. Congress specified longer recovery periods for depreciable assets that would result in depreciation slower than allowed by ACRS. (11)

Moving expenses. Moving expenses are deductible for adjusted gross income if two tests are met. The distance test requires that the commuting distance from the old residence to the new job be 50 miles farther than the distance was to the old job. The time test requires the taxpayer to be employed at the new location for 39 weeks in the 12-month period following the move. Self-employed individuals must work in the new location for 78 weeks during the succeeding 2-year period. The time requirement is waived for death, disability, or discharge or transfer that is not the fault of the employee. (8)

Multiple asset purchase. When more than one asset is bought for a single price, the cost must be allocated to the individual assets in proportion to their fair market value on the date purchased. An appraisal of the individual assets usually provides a reasonable basis for allocating the purchase price. The buyer and seller can agree, at arm's length, on an allocation of the purchase price. The cost of real estate can also be allocated according to the values assessed for property tax purposes. (10)

Multiple support agreement. In the case of two or more individuals who collectively provide more than 50% of the support of an individual who meets all of the other tests for dependency, any member of the support group who contributes more than 10% of the total support may claim the dependency exemption through a multiple support agreement. All members of the support group must agree in writing which person in the group is entitled to receive the exemption. (8)

Municipal bond interest. The tax law provides an exclusion for interest earned on bonds issued by state and local governments (cities, counties, state agencies such as turnpike authorities) of the United States as well as those of U.S. possessions (Guam, Puerto Rico). (4)

Natural business year. The annual accounting period encompassing all related income and expenses. An S corporation must generally use a calendar year. However, an alternate year can be used under the ownership tax year or the business purpose tax year exceptions. To qualify, an S corporation must have peak and off-peak business periods. The natural business year is the end of the peak business period. An annual accounting period qualifies as a *business purpose tax year* if the gross receipts from sales or services for the final two months of the current year and each of the two preceding years equals or exceeds 25% of the gross receipts for the entire 12-month period. (14)

Necessary expense. To be deductible, an expense must be necessary—a reasonable and prudent businessperson would incur the expense in a similar situation. The expense need not be essential to the continued existence of the income-producing activity. (5)

Net capital losses. An excess of capital losses over capital gains for a tax year. Individuals are allowed to deduct up to $3,000 of net capital losses as a deduction for adjusted gross income. Any loss in excess of $3,000 is carried forward to the next tax year. (3, 7)

Net investment income. See *investment interest.* (8)

Net long-term capital gain. An excess of long-term capital gains over capital losses for a tax year. Net long-term capital gains of individuals are taxed at a maximum tax rate of 28%. (3)

Net operating loss (NOL). An annual loss incurred in a trade or business in which the taxpayer materially participates. It results from an excess of allowable deductions over income for the accounting period. For a taxable entity (i.e., individuals and corporations), a carryover system allows losses incurred in one year to be deducted against income in other years. A *carryback* means that the loss may be used to reduce income from prior years. A *carryforward* means that the loss is used to offset income in future periods. An NOL may be carried back three years. If taxable income in the three-year carryback period is not sufficient to fully absorb the NOL, any remaining loss may be carried forward for 15 years. A taxpayer may elect not to carry the loss back and only carry the loss forward for 15 years. (7)

Net unearned income. See *minor child.* (8)

No additional cost services. A service given to an employee by an employer free of charge. In order for a no additional cost service to be excluded from taxation, the service must be made available to employees on a nondiscriminatory basis and must also be in the same line of business in which the employee works. (4)

Nonaccountable plan. See *employee reimbursement plan.* (8)

Nonacquiescence. An announcement by the IRS that it will not follow the decision of a regular Tax Court decision that was adverse to the government. (15)

Nonbusiness bad debt. See *business bad debt.* (6)

Nonrecognition transaction. A transaction that is not given current effect. The initial realization is considered part of a continuing investment process. Under the substance-over-form doctrine, the new property acquired in the transaction (i.e., like-kind exchanges, involuntary conversions, and sale of principal residence) is viewed as a continuation of the original investment in the asset. Also, the taxpayer lacks the wherewithal to pay the tax on the realized gain, because the amount realized on the transaction is reinvested in the replacement asset. For total deferral of gain, any amounts realized from the disposition must be fully reinvested in a replacement asset. (13)

Nonrecourse debt. A liability that is secured only by the underlying property; the borrower is not personally liable for the debt. (7)

Nonrefundable tax credit. If the amount of the credit exceeds the tax liability, the taxpayer is not entitled to a refund of the excess. Although most business tax credits are nonrefundable, they generally provide that the amount of the credit not used in the current year may be carried forward and used in future years. (14)

One-year rule for prepaid expenses. A cash basis taxpayer may deduct prepaid expenses in the year paid if the prepayment does not create an asset that extends substantially beyond the end of the year of payment. The courts have held that a prepayment of an expense that will be used up before the end of the tax year following the year of prepayment can be deducted when paid. The taxpayer must show that the payment is required by the creditor and that the payment does not distort income. Prepaid taxes are deductible in the year paid, even if the prepayment results in a refund in a later year. Prepaid interest is not generally deductible under the one-year rule. (5)

One-year rule for services. Accrual basis taxpayers may continue to use the accrual method to account for prepaid service income, if the services will be performed before the end of the tax year following the year of receipt. (3)

Ordinary expense. To be deductible, an expenditure must qualify as an ordinary expense. The expense must be of a kind commonly incurred in the particular income-earning activity. The expense may be said to be customary or usual for the activity. The expenditure must also be assignable to the current accounting period. (5)

Ordinary income. Recurring income earned by a taxpayer for a tax year; the type of income that people and businesses expect to earn. Ordinary income typically includes business profits, rent from property, interest on investments, and wages. Ordinary income receives no special treatment under the tax laws. (1)

Organizational costs. Because a corporation is a legal entity formed under state law, various expenditures (i.e., legal services, accounting services, and fees paid to the state of incorporation) must be incurred to accomplish the corporate creation. Most of the expenses benefit future periods of the corporation's life. A corporation may elect to amortize qualified organizational expenses over a period of 60 months or more. If the election to amortize these expenses is not made on the tax return for the first taxable year, the costs are not deductible until the corporation ceases business and liquidates. (9)

Original issue discount security (OID). A debt instrument for which the interest is paid upon maturity of the debt rather than throughout the term of the debt. (3)

Overall accounting methods. The method or system by which taxpayers determine the amount of their income, gains, losses, deductions, and credits, as well as the proper time to recognize these items. The three acceptable overall methods are the cash method, the accrual method, and the hybrid method. The method must be used consistently from period to period and must clearly reflect the income of the taxpayer. (14)

Ownership tax year. The tax year of more than 50% of the owners of an S corporation. (14)

Parent-subsidiary relationship. See *controlled group.* (9)

Partners. Owners of a partnership. An employer/employee relationship cannot exist between a partnership and its partners. Compensation to a partner may be classified as a guaranteed payment or a compensatory payment. A partnership may offer a partner a *guaranteed payment*, which is determined without regard to the partnership's income. Such compensation is ordinary income for the partner and is a deductible compensation expense for the partnership. If a partner receives *compensatory payments* based in any way on the partnership's gross or net income, the payments are classified as the partner's share of partnership profits. The partnership records the payments as nondeductible withdrawals, and the partner recognizes the income in the year of receipt. (9)

Partnership. A general partnership is characterized as follows for tax purposes: a partner's liability is not limited; the life of the partnership depends on the life of the partner(s); all partners share in the partnership management; partnership interests are not freely transferable. Although partnerships are considered conduits for the purpose of income taxation, they are treated as separate entities under local law. Partnerships can transact business and own property in their own names, separate from the partners. (9)

Partnership debt. Initial basis in a partnership begins with a person's contribution of assets or services in exchange for a capital interest. Basis is increased by a partner's share of partnership liabilities. Partnership debt assumed by a partner and the partner's share of partnership debt are deemed to be additional cash contributions by the partner to the partnership. Decreases in partnership debt are deemed cash distributions to the partner and reduce the partner's basis in the partnership. (9)

Partnership distribution. A partner's receipt of a cash or property distribution from a partnership is generally tax free. No gain is recognized (capital recovery concept) until after the basis in the capital investment is recovered. Any excess of cash (or the basis of property) over the basis in a partner's interest is a recognizable gain for the partner who receives it. (9)

Partnership tax year. The selection of a taxable year for a partnership is done on a hierarchical basis that attempts to match the tax years of the partnership to the partners'. First, the partnership must use the same tax year as that used by those partners having a majority interest (more than 50%) in partnership profits and capital (*majority interest tax year*). If the majority interest partners do not have the same tax year, the partnership must use the tax year of its principal partners (a partner with at least a 5% interest), called the *principal partner tax year.* When the principal partners do not have the same tax year, the partnership must use the tax year that results in the least aggregate deferral of income of the partners. The deferral of each partner for each tax year is determined by the number of months from the end of the partnership's tax year forward to the end of the tax year of the partner. The aggregate deferral is determined by totaling the products of the number of months of deferral for each partner and multiplying the result by each partner's ownership interest. The tax year that produces the lowest deferral is the *least aggregate deferral tax year.* (14)

Passive activity. The conduct of any trade or business in which the taxpayer does not materially participate. Limited partnership interests are always passive. Rental activities are generally passive unless the material participation exception applies. Working interests in oil and gas deposits and certain low-income housing projects are always active and not subject to the passive loss rules. See also *material participation exception.* (7)

Passive activity loss rules. The purpose of the passive activity rules is to deny current loss deductions for tax shelter activities. The general rule is that passive losses may only be deducted to the extent of passive income, not against income from portfolio or active income. Any passive activity loss that is not deductible in the current year is suspended. A *suspended loss* is not permanently disallowed but is carried forward and may be deducted against passive income in subsequent years. Deductions of suspended losses are allowed when passive activities are disposed of by sale and because of death. Gifts of passive activities do not result in deduction of suspended losses from the activity. (7)

Pay-as-you-go concept. A tax should be collected as close as possible to the time in which the income is earned. (1, 2)

Percentage depletion (statutory depletion). One of two methods used to compute depletion of natural resources. Percentage depletion is calculated by multiplying gross income from the sale of the natural resource by a statutory percentage. The statutory percentage is the depletion rate specified by the tax law. The maximum allowable percentage depletion deduction for the tax year is 50 percent of the taxable income from the natural resource before subtracting the depletion deduction. See also *cost depletion*. (11)

Percentage-of-completed contract method. Most long-term construction contracts must be accounted for by using the percentage-of-completed contract method. Income is recognized according to the amount of work completed on the contract each year. The work completed must be based on costs incurred during the year in relation to the estimated total costs of the project. See also *lookback method*. (3, 14)

Personal casualty loss. The only personal use loss that the tax law allows as a deduction (itemized) is for losses from casualty and theft. Personal casualty and theft losses are always measured as the lower of the decline in the value of the property or the basis of the property. The amount of loss must be reduced by any insurance proceeds received. Personal use casualty losses are also reduced by a $100 *statutory floor* amount per occurrence. An *annual personal casualty loss limitation* is imposed that limits total personal casualty and theft loss deductions for the year to the extent that they exceed 10% of the taxpayer's adjusted gross income. (7)

Personal exemption. Individuals are allowed to deduct a predetermined amount for each qualifying exemption. The intention is to exempt from tax a minimum amount of income that is used to support the taxpayer and those who are dependent on that taxpayer. Because support costs increase with inflation, the exemption amounts are increased each year to account for the prior year's inflation. Personal exemptions are allowed for the taxpayer and the taxpayer's spouse. *Dependency exemptions* are granted for individuals who are dependent on the taxpayer for support. (1, 8)

Personal injury. See *damage payments*. (4)

Personal property (personalty). Any tangible property that is not real property. Personal property includes machines, equipment, furniture, computers, and autos. (1, 10)

Personal service corporation (PSC). A PSC is a corpora-

tion, the shareholder-employees of which provide personal services (e.g., medical, dental, legal, accounting, engineering, actuarial, consulting, or performing arts). PSCs do not enjoy the tax savings from the lower tax brackets assigned to regular corporations because they are taxed at a flat 35% on all income. (9)

Personalty. See *personal property*. (10)

Personal use property. Any property that is used by the taxpayer for purely personal purposes. *Personal use* applies to personal property, real property, and intangible property. (10)

Points. Points are prepaid interest amounts that are required in order to acquire financing. They are expressed as a percentage of the value of the loan and paid at loan acquisition. They represent prepaid interest, which usually is capitalized and amortized over the term of the loan. In the year the points are paid, the tax law allows a deduction for points paid to acquire an initial mortgage on a taxpayer's principal residence. Points paid to refinance an existing mortgage must be capitalized and amortized as interest expense over the term of the loan. (8)

Portfolio income. Consists of unearned income from dividends, interest, royalties, annuities, and other assets held as investments. In portfolio activities, the investor only receives income from the activity and does not share in the expenses related to the activity. Any losses on portfolio income generally occur at the point of sale of the asset producing the income. (7)

Primary authorities. The legislative, administrative, and/or judicial sources. The legislative authorities include the Constitution, tax treaties, and law enacted by Congress. The administrative authorities are the official interpretations of the law prepared by the Treasury Department and the Internal Revenue Service. Decisions by the various trial and appellate courts represent the judicial authorities. (15)

Primary valuation date. See *inherited property*. (10)

Principal partner tax year. See *partnership tax year*. (14)

Principal residence. To be eligible for gain deferral, both the old and new residences must be used as the principal residence (where the taxpayer lives most of the time) of the taxpayer. A taxpayer can have only one principal residence at a time. A principal residence can be a house, mobile home, cooperative apartment, condominium, or a houseboat. The old residence must be replaced by a new residence within a period beginning two years before the sale of the old residence and ending two years after the sale of the old residence. The taxpayer must occupy and use the new residence as a principal residence during this period. (13)

Private activity bond. A bond issued by a government unit, the proceeds from which are used by anyone other than a government unit. (14)

Private letter rulings (LTR). Issued by the National Office of the IRS in response to specific questions raised by taxpayers and typically deal with prospective transactions. An LTR applies only to the taxpayer requesting the ruling and does not bind the IRS to take the same position when dealing with a different taxpayer. (15)

Product class. See *like-kind property*. (13)

Progressive rate structure. A tax in which the average tax rate increases as the tax base increases. The marginal tax rate will be higher than the average tax rate as the tax base increases. The average tax rate, the marginal tax rate, and total tax all increase with increases in the tax base. (1)

Property. Any long-lived asset that is owned by a taxpayer. The terms *asset* and *property* are used interchangeably to mean anything owned or possessed by a taxpayer. Property is classified by both its use and its type for tax purposes. The use of property determines whether deductions are allowed for current-year expenditures made in relation to the property and for capital recovery deductions for depreciation, depletion, or amortization. In order to take any deductions relating to property, there must be a business purpose (used in a trade or business or held for the production of income) for the property. All property is either tangible or intangible property. The type of property does not change from taxpayer to taxpayer. (10)

Property disposition. See *amount realized*. (10)

Property settlement. See *alimony*. (3)

Proportional rate structure. A tax for which the average tax rate remains the same as the tax base increases (also referred to as a *flat tax*). The marginal tax rate and the average tax rate are the same at all levels of the tax base. As the tax base increases, the total tax paid will increase at a constant rate. Examples include sales taxes, real estate and personal property taxes, and certain excise taxes, such as the tax on gasoline. (1)

Proposed regulation. Issued to let the public know what the IRS believes is the proper interpretation of a related Code provision and to provide an opportunity for the public to comment before a regulation is issued in final form. (15)

Punitive damages. See *damage payments*. (4)

Qualified home mortgage interest. Only interest on debt that is secured by the taxpayer's principal residence and one other residence is deductible. Qualified home mortgage interest includes both acquisition debt and home equity debt. *Acquisition debt* is any debt incurred to acquire, construct, or substantially improve a qualified residence of the taxpayer. *Home equity debt* is any debt that is secured by a personal residence and that is not acquisition debt. The proceeds of home equity debt can be used for any purpose. Interest paid on up to $1,000,000 of acquisition debt is deductible. Interest on debt in excess of $1,000,000 is considered personal interest and is not deductible. Interest paid on home equity debt up to $100,000 is also deductible. (8)

Qualified pension plan. Payments made by an employer to an employee's account in a qualified pension plan are not

taxable in the period in which the payments are made. The tax on such payments is deferred until the employee actually withdraws the payments from the plan. Earnings on amounts paid into such plans are not taxed until they are withdrawn by the employee. (4)

Qualified real property business indebtedness. Debt that is incurred or assumed before 1993 in connection with real property used in a trade or business that is secured by that property. Debt that is a refinancing of previously incurred qualified debt or that is incurred after 1992 to acquire, construct, or substantially improve real property used in a trade or business is also qualified real property business indebtedness. (4)

RAR. Revenue agent's report. (15)

Real estate. See *real property*. (10)

Realization concept. No income or loss is recognized for tax purposes (is included in taxable income) until it has been realized by the taxpayer. In most cases, a realization occurs when an arm's-length transaction takes place. A realization involves a change in the form and/or the substance of a taxpayer's property rights that results from an arm's-length transaction. (2)

Realized gain (loss). See *amount realized*. (10)

Real property. In general, real property is land and any structures that are permanently attached to land, such as buildings. (1)

Real property trade or business. A trade or business involving the development, redevelopment, construction, acquisition, conversion, rental operation, management, leasing, or brokerage of real property. (7)

Reasonable compensation. Employee compensation is subject to two basic tests for deductibility. First, payments must be for services actually performed by the employee. Second, the total payment for services of the employee must be reasonable in amount. When the compensation paid to an employee is found to be excessive, only a reasonable salary deduction is allowed. Whether compensation paid an employee is reasonable is decided by considering several factors, including (1) the employee's duties, responsibilities, and pay history; (2) the volume and complexity of the business; (3) the time required to do the work; (4) the ability and accomplishments of the employee; (5) the general cost of living and the company pay policy; (6) the relationship of the compensation, the gross and net income of the business, and dividends paid to shareholders. Reasonable compensation issues generally arise in connection with related parties. (6)

Reasonable expense. To be deductible, an expense must be reasonable in amount. The reasonableness test most often becomes an issue in transactions involving related parties. (5)

Recognized gain (loss). To recognize a gain or loss means to include the amount of the gain or loss in the current year's taxable income calculation. (12)

Refundable tax credit. The taxpayer is entitled to a refund of any excess credit. This is a form of negative income tax. The taxpayer not only pays no tax but receives a payment from the government that is based on the taxpayer's income. (14)

Regressive rate structure. A tax in which the average tax rate decreases as the tax base increases. The marginal tax rate will be less than the average tax rate as the tax base increases. Although the average tax rate and the marginal tax rate both decrease as the tax base increases, the total tax paid will increase. (1)

Rehabilitation tax credit. In order to provide incentive for businesses to rehabilitate older buildings and certified historic structures, a 10% credit is allowed for the expenditures incurred in the rehabilitation of a building placed in service before 1936. Rehabilitation expenditures incurred on a certified historic structure are granted a 20% tax credit. The basis of the building or structure must be reduced by the amount of credit taken. In order to retain the full benefit of the tax credit, the property must be held for five full years. (14)

Related party. Family members and corporations that are owned by family members are considered related parties, as are certain other relationships between entities in which the power to control the substance of a transaction is evidenced through majority ownership. (2, 5, 7)

Relationship, or member of household, test. See *dependent*. (8)

Remainderman. See *trust*. (9)

Rental activity. A payment received primarily for the use of tangible property. Rental activities are generally considered passive activities, unless the material participation exception applies. Rental activities that also provide significant services (i.e., hotel rooms, car rentals, hospital rooms, and golf course fees) are exempt from the passive loss rules as long as the owner(s) of such activities meet the material participation standard. The most common forms of passive activity rentals involve the rental of real property (i.e., apartment buildings, rental houses, office building rentals, warehouse rentals, factory rentals, etc.). (7)

Reporter. A series of books published by the federal government or by a private publishing company that provides the full text of court decisions. Different reporters are cited for each court that renders a decision. (15)

Research and experimental (R&E) credit. Encourages research and development of new technologies and processes. The incremental credit is equal to 20% of the qualified research expenditures in the current year in excess of the base amount. The basic research credit is equal to 20% of qualified expenditures for research that is intended to advance scientific knowledge without a specific commercial objective. The payments must be made in cash under written agreement, and the research must be performed or controlled by a university, college, or other nonprofit scientific research organization. (14)

Revenue procedure. Issued to explain internal IRS administrative practices and procedures. (15)

Revenue ruling. Interpretation by the IRS of the Code and regulations as they apply to specific factual situations. A revenue ruling represents official policy of the IRS. (15)

Reversionary interest. See *trust*. (9)

S. Ct. *Supreme Court Reports.* (15)

SIC Codes. See *like-kind property.* (13)

SUTA. State Unemployment Tax Act. See *employment taxes.*

Salary reduction plan. See *flexible benefits plan.* (4)

Scholarship. A college student who is a candidate for a degree may exclude the value of the scholarship, provided that the award does not require the student to perform any future services such as teaching, grading papers, or tutoring. The scholarship must be gratuitous in nature and not merely a form of compensation for past, present, or future services. The amount of the exclusion is limited to the direct costs of the student's college education. Direct costs consist of the student's tuition, fees, books, supplies, and other equipment required in the course of instruction. Amounts received in excess of the direct costs of the education are taxable. (4)

Secondary authority. Serves primarily as a tool in locating the relevant primary authority and a source for better understanding, interpretation, and application of primary authorities. Secondary authorities include all statements, pronouncements, explanations, or interpretations of the law that are not primary and consist chiefly of tax services, citators, computer software systems that research tax databases, and tax journals and newsletters. (15)

Section 179. Under this provision, taxpayers are allowed to expense up to $17,500 (per year) of the cost of tangible personal property used in a trade or business. Amounts expensed under this provision reduce the depreciable basis of the property. The amount of the annual deduction limit is reduced when purchases of qualifying property exceed $200,000. In addition, the deductible amount cannot exceed the taxable income from the active conduct of all the taxpayer's trade or business activities. (11)

Section 1231 gain (loss). Results from the sale or other disposition of a Section 1231 property. (12)

Section 1231 netting procedure. Tax treatments accorded Section 1231 assets apply to the net gain or loss on all Section 1231 transactions occurring during a tax year. The Section 1231 netting procedure nets together all casualty (theft) gains and losses on Section 1231 assets to produce a single net casualty gain or loss for the year. If the result is a loss, all casualty gains and losses for the year are considered ordinary losses. If the result of the netting is a gain, the net casualty gain is netted together with all other Section 1231 gains and losses occurring during the year. If the result is a loss, all gains and losses for the year are considered ordinary. When the result is a gain, another netting must take place (*lookback recapture rule*). This nets the current year net

Section 1231 gain against any Section 1231 ordinary loss deductions taken in the previous five years. (12)

Section 1231 property. Property used in a trade or business, held for more than one year, that is used in a trade or business; timber, coal, and domestic iron ore; livestock that is held for more than one year and horses that are held for more than two years; and unharvested crops. (12)

Section 1245 property. All depreciable tangible personal property is Section 1245 property (i.e., autos, trucks, equipment, machinery, computers, patents, copyrights, leaseholds, and livestock). Certain real property depreciated using ACRS is also classified as Section 1245 property. (12)

Section 1245 recapture rule. Section 1245 assets are subject to a full recapture of all depreciation taken as ordinary income. No capital gain or Section 1231 treatment results from the sale of a Section 1245 asset unless it is sold for more than its original cost. (12)

Section 1250 property. In general, depreciable real property is Section 1250 property (i.e., office buildings, apartment buildings, warehouses, factory buildings, and low-income housing). However, certain real property depreciated using ACRS is also classified as Section 1245 property. (12)

Section 1250 recapture rule. Under Section 1250, only gains that are attributable to excess depreciation are recaptured as ordinary income. *Excess depreciation* is defined as the total depreciation taken to date, less the allowable straight-line depreciation on the asset. (12)

Securities dealer. A person who transacts in securities may be an active investor, an active trader, or a dealer in securities. Unlike active traders and dealers, active investors are not considered to be in a trade or business. A securities dealer purchases a security expecting to realize a profit from selling it to a customer for a fee or commission. An *active investor* is a person who continuously, regularly, and extensively manages his or her own portfolio with a view toward long-term appreciation in the portfolio's value and not short-term profit. An active investor's expenses are deductible only as miscellaneous itemized deductions. An *active trader* earns a livelihood buying and selling securities for personal profit. The active trader's expenses are deductible for adjusted gross income. (5)

Self-employment tax. Self-employed individuals pay a Social Security tax equal to the sum of the employer's and employee's payments (15.3%). Because employees are not taxed on the Social Security contribution made on their behalf by their employees, self-employed taxpayers are allowed to deduct one-half of their self-employment tax as a business expense to equalize the tax treatments of employees and the self-employed. (1, 8)

Self-insured medical plan. A plan established by a company that chooses to self-insure by making payments to a fund that is used to pay employees' medical expenses. The payments are excluded from employees' income. However, if a self-insured medical plan discriminates in favor of highly compensated employees, the amounts paid for medical expenses of a highly compensated employee covered by the plan are included in the individual's taxable income. (4)

Short sale. A technique for investing in a security that is expected to decline in value. Short sellers sell a security that they do not own and receive the net selling price from the buyer. Because short-sellers do not actually own the securities, they borrow them from their brokers, who give the actual shares of stock to the buyers. At a later date, the short seller purchases the shares previously sold on the open market and gives them back to the broker to repay the shares borrowed at the initial short-sale date (closing the short sale). The short seller's profit or loss is the net selling price of the shares in the first step minus the price that the short seller paid to purchase the shares back in the second step. Short sellers are betting that the shares sold short will decline in value and they will be able to buy them back for less than they initially sold for. (12)

Short sale against the box. The taxpayer closes a short sale by giving shares the taxpayer already owned (rather than buying them on the market) to the broker in the next tax year. This allows the taxpayer to lock in a gain on the shares owned in the current tax year while deferring recognition of the gain until the next tax year. (12)

Short-term capital gain (loss). A gain (loss) on the sale on a capital asset that is held for one year or less. (3)

Simple trust. See *trust*. (9)

Single. See *filing status*. (8)

Small business stock. LOSSES: The tax law provides an exception to the $3,000 annual capital loss deduction limitation on losses incurred on qualifying small business stock. This allows an individual taxpayer to deduct up to $50,000 in losses on small business stock per year or $100,000 for a married couple filing a joint return. The stock must be purchased directly from the corporation at original issue. The corporation must satisfy several other requirements, the most important of which is that the contributed capital of the corporation at the time the stock is issued must be less than $1,000,000. GAINS: The tax law provides that 50% of the gains from qualified small business stock held for more than 5 years are excluded from taxation. Qualifying stock is stock issued after August 10, 1993, by a corporation with gross assets under $50 million purchased from the entity or through its underwriter. (7)

Social Security taxes. Under the Federal Insurance Contribution Act *(FICA)*, a tax is levied on wages and salaries earned. Social Security taxes are matched by employers. Employees are not taxed on the Social Security contribution made on their behalf by their employers. In 1995, a tax of 6.2% is levied on the first $61,200 of wages for Old Age,

Survivors, and Disability Insurance (OASDI). A tax of 1.45% on all wages and salaries pays for Medical Health Insurance (MHI). (1)

Specific charge-off method. Bad debts are deductible when the taxpayer determines that a particular debt is no longer collectible. *Business bad debts* are deductible in the accounting period in which the facts known to the taxpayer indicate that the account is fully or partially uncollectible. Nonbusiness bad debts are not deductible until the accounting period in which the actual amount of worthlessness of the debt is known to the taxpayer. (6)

Split basis rule for gifts. If the fair market of the gift property at the date of the gift is less than the donor's basis, the property has one basis for determining gains and a separate basis for determining losses on dispositions (split basis). The basis for determining gains is the donor's adjusted basis. The basis for determining losses is the fair market value on the date of the gift. This effectively eliminates the transfer of unrealized losses from one taxpayer to another by gift. (10)

Split basis rules for business property. When property held for personal use is changed to property held for a business purpose, the split basis rules kick in. If the fair market value of personal use property is more than its adjusted basis on the date business use begins, the asset's adjusted basis is used to compute depreciation and gain or loss on its disposition. If the fair market value of personal use property is less than its adjusted basis on the date it is changed to a business use, the initial basis for gain is the property's adjusted basis on the conversion date and the initial basis for loss and depreciation is the property's fair market value on the conversion date. If the property is later sold for an amount that falls between the adjusted basis for gain and the adjusted basis for loss, the adjusted basis for the sale is the sales price. (10)

Standard deduction. An amount that Congress allows all taxpayers to deduct, regardless of their actual qualifying itemized deductions. Thus, taxpayers itemize their deductions only if their total allowable itemized deductions exceed the standard deduction. (1, 8)

Standard mileage rate method. See *auto expense.* (6)

Start-up costs. Start-up costs are related to investigating and creating a new active trade or business. Start-up costs are the expenses incurred before the new business begins its activities. Start-up costs include surveys and analyses of markets, facilities, and labor force; travel to develop the business and locate potential customers and suppliers; advertising the new business; salaries to train employees; salaries for executives and consultants; and various other expenses such as legal and accounting fees. (5)

Statute of limitations. The time period within which the IRS or the taxpayer must assert that a tax return is not correct. The general statute of limitations period is three years from the due date of the return. Several exceptions extend the statute of limitations beyond the general three-year period. (1)

Statutory depletion. See *percentage depletion.* (11)

Statutory floor. See *personal casualty loss.* (7)

Stock dividend. A dividend in cash or other property distributed to a shareholder generally is taxable as income to the shareholders. Also, the distributing corporation may not take a deduction for the amount of dividends distributed for tax purposes. But the receipt of a stock dividend does not constitute a realization of income. The value of a shareholder's interest does not change; it is merely spread over more ownership units. However, if the recipient of the stock dividend has the option to receive cash in lieu of stock, the dividend is taxed as if the cash option had been selected. In this case, the shares of the stock are deemed to have a cash equivalent and thus are taxable. (4, 10)

Substance-over-form doctrine. Transactions are to be taxed according to their true intention rather than some form that may have been contrived. (2)

Substantiation requirements. Entertainment, auto, travel, and gift expenses are subject to strict documentation requirements. The tax law requires the taxpayer to keep records that show the amount of the expense; the time and place of travel or entertainment or date and description of a gift; the business purpose of the travel, entertainment, or gift; and the business relationship to the person entertained or receiving the gift. Failure to keep the records necessary to substantiate an expense can result in loss of the deduction. (6)

Support test. See *dependent.* (8)

Surviving spouse. See *filing status.* (8)

Suspended loss. See *passive activity loss rules.* (7)

T.C. *Reports of the United States Tax Court.* (15)

TCM. *Tax Court Memorandum Decisions.* See also *tax court memorandum decision.*

TCMP. Taxpayer Compliance Measurement Program. (15)

TM. Technical memorandum. (15)

Tangible property. Any property that has a physical existence (form, shape, and substance). (10)

Taxable entity. Entities that are liable for the payment of tax. The four entities responsible for the payment of income tax are individuals, regular (or C) corporations, estates, and some trusts. (2)

Taxable income. The tax base for the federal income tax. The difference between the total income of a taxpayer and the deductions allowed that taxpayer. (1)

Taxable year. The period for which an entity reports its taxable income. (14)

Tax avoidance. The use of legal methods allowed by the tax law to minimize a tax liability. Tax avoidance generally involves planning an intended transaction to obtain a specific tax treatment. (1)

Tax base. The value that is subject to tax. See also *proportional rate structure*. (1)

Tax benefit rule. Any deduction taken in a prior year that is recovered in a subsequent year is reported as income in the year it is recovered, to the extent that a tax benefit is received from the deduction. The tax benefit received is the amount by which taxable income was actually reduced by the deduction recovered. (2)

Tax Court memorandum decision. All decisions that are not Tax Court regular decisions. They are only published by Research Institute of America (RIA) in *T.C. Memorandum Decisions* (T.C. Memo) and by Commerce Clearing House (CCH) under the title *Tax Court Memorandum Decisions* (TCM). (15)

Tax Court regular decision. Presumed to have value as precedents or involve issues that have not previously been considered. Regular decisions are generally regarded as having a stronger authority than memorandum decisions. Published by the government in a reporter called *Reports of the United States Tax Court* (T.C.). (15)

Tax credit. A direct reduction in the income tax liability. In effect, tax credits are treated like tax prepayments. (1)

Taxes. Itemized deductions are allowed for amounts paid in for state and local income taxes, real estate taxes, and other personal property taxes. In order to be deductible, personal property taxes must be ad valorem (based on the value of the property being taxed). (8)

Tax evasion. Occurs when a taxpayer uses fraudulent methods or deceptive behavior to hide the actual tax liability. Tax evasion usually involves three elements: a willfulness on the part of the taxpayer, an underpayment of tax, and an affirmative act by the taxpayer to evade the tax. (1)

Tax home. See *travel expenses*. (6)

Tax service. A type of secondary authority that principally serves as a tool in locating the primary authorities related to various factual circumstances. They generally consist of multivolume sets of loose-leaf binders that are constantly updated for new developments. One category of tax services consists of very limited editorial discussion and numerous brief interpretations and citations to the primary authorities other than the Code and regulations, which are provided in full text [i.e., *Standard Federal Tax Reporter* (CCH) and *United States Tax Reporter* (RIA)]. The other category of tax services contains extensive editorial discussion and interpretation of the law with citations to the primary authorities provided in footnotes [i.e., *Federal Tax Coordinator Second* (RIA), *Tax Management Portfolios* (Bureau of National Affairs), and *Mertens Law of Federal Income Taxation* (Callaghan and Co.)]. (15)

Tax shelter. Any investment activity that is designed to minimize the effect of the income tax on wealth accumulation. The term is generally applied to investments that produce significant tax losses as a result of the allowable deductions associated with the investment. The losses are then used to offset (shelter) taxable income from other income sources. Eventually, the taxpayer investing in such a shelter will have to pay a tax on the investment when it is sold. However, the deduction of losses from the shelter in tax years prior to the payment of tax on the gain presents a time value of money savings opportunity. (7)

Technical advice memorandum (TAM). A private letter ruling on a completed transaction. A TAM is a request for assistance by the local office of the IRS and typically arises during an ongoing audit. The TAM is issued by the National Office of the IRS and is not binding on the IRS. (15)

Temporary regulation. Issued to provide taxpayers with guidance until a final regulation is issued. All temporary regulations must be issued as proposed regulations; the regulation expires if not amended or issued as a final regulation within three years. (15)

Testamentary trust. See *trust*. (9)

Theft. Similar to a casualty in that it must be sudden and unexpected. A theft may occur as a result of a robbery, larceny, or an embezzlement. The damage caused by a theft is that the entire property is lost. A theft is treated as property fully destroyed (all value lost). (7)

Theft loss. See *theft*. (7)

Trade or business expense. See *business purpose concept*. (2, 5)

Trade or business loss. A general category that pertains to a transaction loss. These losses are treated as ordinary losses in the period they are incurred and deducted without limit against income from the trade or business. For an individual, a trade or business loss is deductible as a deduction for AGI. An exception to this rule is for losses on exchanges of business property that must be deferred to a future period. (7)

Transaction loss. Results from a single disposition of property. The loss must be categorized by the activity producing the loss to determine its deductibility: trade or business losses, investment-related losses, and personal use losses. In general, transaction losses must have a business purpose to be deductible. See *loss*. (1, 7)

Travel expenses. A taxpayer can deduct travel expenses (i.e., transportation, lodging, 50% of the cost of meals, and incidental expenses—telephone calls, laundry, etc.) incurred while pursuing a business purpose. For an expense to qualify as travel, the taxpayer must be away from her or his tax home overnight. A *tax home* is the general area where the taxpayer conducts her or his principal business activity. Overnight is substantially longer than a normal workday and can be less than 24 hours. The taxpayer cannot deduct any of the transportation costs if the purpose of the trip is primarily personal. If more than 50% of the total time is related to personal activities, the primary purpose will be deemed to be personal. (6)

Treasury regulation. The Treasury Department's official explanation of a related provision in the Internal Revenue Code. Also called a *final regulation.* (1)

Trial courts. Courts of original jurisdiction that are used to initiate litigation. Taxpayers willing to pay the tax in dispute and then sue for a refund have the option of taking their case to a *U.S. District Court* or the *U.S. Claims Court.* In order to have a jury trial, taxpayers must file in district court. Taxpayers may choose not to pay the additional tax and file a petition in U.S. Tax Court for relief. (15)

Trust. A legal entity created when a person transfers ownership of property to a *trustee* to be held for the benefit of another person. The person who transfers the corpus, or trust assets, to the trustee is called the *grantor.* The directions given the trustee by the grantor are included in the trust instrument, or indenture. The trustee's primary purpose is to preserve the trust assets for the benefit of the beneficiaries. If the trustee is required to distribute all annual income to the trust beneficiaries, the trust is called a *simple trust.* All other trusts are called *complex trusts.* In addition, there is a *remainderman,* the beneficiary who will receive the balance of the trust assets when the trust is terminated. For a trust to be recognized as a taxable entity, no more than 5% of the trust assets may revert to the grantor or spouse (*a reversionary interest*) upon the termination (if the trust was created or had additional assets transferred to it after March 1, 1986). If a trust does not meet this requirement, trust income is taxed to the grantor. This type of trust is called a *grantor trust.* A trust created at death and funded by the assets of an estate is called a *testamentary trust.* (9)

Trustee. See *trust.* (9)

U.S. *United States Reports.* (15)

U.S. Court of Federal Claims. A trial-level court in which the taxpayer typically sues the government for a refund of overpaid tax liability, although it also hears certain nontax claims against the federal government. Its decisions must be appealed to the U.S. Court of Appeals for the Federal Circuit in Washington, D.C. See *trial courts.* (15)

U.S. Courts of Appeals. Federal appellate courts that hear appeals from U.S. Tax Court, U.S. District Court, and U.S. Court of Federal Claims. The courts are organized as 12 geographic circuits, each of which hears appeals from taxpayers living within its geographic area. The U.S. Court of Appeals for the Federal Circuit hears all appeals from the U.S. Court of Federal Claims. (15)

U.S. Court of Appeals for the Federal Circuit. An appellate court that reviews decisions of the U.S. Court of Federal Claims. (15)

U.S. District Court. The trial-level federal court that hears cases only from taxpayers who live within the specific geographic area over which the court presides. (15)

U.S. Supreme Court. The ultimate appellate court of the United States. The Court limits its review of tax cases to those of major importance or to those in which the decisions of the circuit courts conflict. (15)

U.S. Tax Court. Often referred to as the "poor person's court" because taxpayers in dispute with the IRS may choose not to pay additional tax and file a petition for relief in Tax Court, which specializes in tax matters. (15)

Unearned income. Unearned income constitutes a return on an investment and does not require any labor by the owner of the investment in order to produce the income. The most common forms of unearned income are interest income, dividend income, income from rental and royalty-producing activities, income from annuities, income from conduit entities, and gains from the sale of investments producing any of the five forms of unearned income. (3)

Unified donative-transfers credit. A lifetime credit of $192,800 that taxpayers may use to reduce gift and estate taxes. The credit is equivalent to being able to exclude $600,000 in property from the gift and/or the estate tax. (1)

Uniform capitalization (unicap) rules. Manufacturers and certain retailers and wholesalers are required to determine the cost of their inventories using the uniform capitalization (unicap) rules. Retailers and wholesalers with average annual gross revenue of less than $10 million are exempt from the unicap rules. The unicap rules require a reasonable allocation of all direct and indirect costs to the cost of inventory. Indirect costs include all costs other than selling and administrative costs that are not related to production. (14)

Vacation home. A taxpayer who owns a vacation home that is used for family vacations and rented to unrelated persons during the remainder of the year is subject to special rules. The use of the vacation home for more than a minimal length of time as rental property and as a personal vacation home (i.e., personal use is more than 14 days) results in the deduction for expenses' being limited to the amount of the rental income. Vacation home expenses in excess of current income can be carried forward for use in a later year. (6)

Wash sale. Occurs when a security is sold at a loss and is replaced within 30 days before or after the sales date with a substantially identical security. A loss from a wash sale is deferred until the taxpayer's interest in the replacement stock is disposed of in a taxable transaction. The wash sale rule applies on a first-in, first-out basis only to the extent the loss stock is replaced. As a result, a loss on shares of stock not replaced is deductible. The wash sale provisions do not apply to dispositions at a gain, to securities that are sold at a loss but not replaced, or to dealers in securities. (7, 10)

Wherewithal-to-pay concept. Income is recognized in the period in which the taxpayer has the means to pay the tax on the income. (2)

Workers' compensation. Payments from a state workers' compensation fund are excluded from taxation. These payments are made to workers who become unable to work as a result of a work-related injury. (4)

Working-condition fringe benefit. Any item provided to an employee that would have been deductible by the employee as an employee business expense if the employee had paid for the item. This class of fringe benefits includes dues to professional organizations, professional journals, and uniforms. Free parking is specifically included as a working-condition fringe benefit. (4)

Working interest in oil and gas deposit. An outright ownership interest held by the operator of the property. A working interest has unlimited liability for all debts of the operation and is responsible for the costs of operating the property. A working interest in an oil and gas deposit is always considered an active business for purposes of the passive activity rules. (7)

Worthless security. When a security becomes worthless, a technical disposition does not take place. However, the tax law gives recognition to the loss of investment suffered by the taxpayer in such situations by allowing a realization of the loss on the last day of the tax year in which the security is determined to be worthless. The loss realized is the basis of the worthless security. Using the last day of the tax year as the date of realization determines the holding period of the security for classification as a short-term or long-term loss. (12)

A

Abandoned spouse, 333
Ability-to-pay concept, 50–51
Accelerated Cost Recovery System, 485
Accident policy payments, as income exclusion, 159–160
Accountable reimbursement plans, 335–336
Accounting concepts, 54–61
  annual accounting period concept, 58–61
  entity concept, 54–58
  summary of, 74
Accounting methods, 50, 58–59, 642–651. *See also* Accrual basis accounting method; Cash basis accounting method
  accrual basis, 58, 121–123
  bad debt and, 246
  basis in conduit entities, 442–443
  cash basis, 58, 119–121
    restrictions on, 643–644
  conduit entities, 407
  corporations and, 398–399
  defined, 208, 642
  effect of, on income, 119–124
  financial vs. tax income, 215–217
  for inventories, 647–651
  hybrid, 123
  individual accounting treatments, 642
  installment sales, 123–124
  long-term construction contracts, 124, 644–647
    lookback method, 645–647
    percentage-of-completed-contract method, 124, 644–645
  overall, 642
  timing of deductions, effect of, 208–217
Accounting periods, 637–642
  conduit entities and, 406–407
  corporations and, 398–399
  fiduciaries and, 404
  taxable year, 637–639
    limitations on choice of, 639–642
Accrual basis accounting method, 58, 121–123
  all-events test, 211–212
  bad debt and, 246
  economic performance test, 212–214
  exceptions to income recognition, 121–123
  one-year rule for services, 122
  related party accrued expenses, 215
  timing of deductions and, 211–214
Acquiescence, 692–693
Acquisition debt, 348
ACRS. *See* Accelerated Cost Recovery System
Actions on decisions (AOD), 693

Active income, 290–291
Active investor, 193–194
Active participant, defined, 298
Active participation exception, 298
Active trader, 194
Activity loss, 278
Actual cost method, automobile expense, 238–239
Add-on minimum tax, 661
Adjusted basis
  computation of, 443–440
  defined, 72, 439
Adjusted gross income (AGI), 104, 188
  deductions for, 26–27
  deductions from, 27
  defined, 26, 328
Adjusted sales price, 612
Administrative authority, 691–693
  acquiescence and nonacquiescence, 692–693
  other pronouncements, 693
  revenue rulings and procedures, 692
  treasury regulations, 691–692
Administrative convenience concept, 51–52
Ad valorem taxes, 15
Alimony, 61
  disguising child support payments as, 108
  recapture, 108
  requirements for, 107–108
  as taxable income, 107–108
All-events test, 211–212
All-inclusive income concept, 61–62
All the facts and circumstances test, rental activity, 195–196
Alternate valuation date, 455
Alternative Depreciation System (ADS), 486, 499–500, 504–505
  alternative minimum tax, 664
  recovery classes, 493
Alternative minimum tax, 504, 637, 660–671
  adjustment items, 662, 663–667
  basic computation of, 661–663
  credit against regular tax, 669–670
  exemptions, 668
  history of, 660–661
  minimum tax credit, 670
  net operating loss deduction, 666–667
  preference items, 662, 667–668
  private activity bond, 668
  purpose of, 660–661
  tax credits, 668–670
  tax planning, 670–671
  tentative minimum tax liability, 662
Alternative minimum taxable income (AMTI), 661
Alternative minimum tax rate, 661

Amended returns, 25
American Federal Tax Reports, 698
American Institute of Certified Public Accountants (AICPA), 36
  Statements on Responsibilities in Tax Practice, 36–38
Amortization, 482
  defined, 510
  intangible assets, 510–511
  exclusions from, 512
Amount realized, 444, 546–547
Annual accounting period concept, 50, 58–61
  accounting method and, 58–59
  substance-over-form doctrine, 60–61
  tax benefit rule, 59
Annual losses, 278
  defined, 21
  net operating losses, 280–283
  passive activity losses, 280, 287–298
  treatment of, 280
Annual personal casualty loss limitation, 308–309
Annuities
  miscellaneous deduction for unrecovered investment because of death, 352
  qualified plans, 101
  as unearned income, 99–101
Annuity exclusion ratio, 99–100
Appeal process, 19
Appellate courts, 695
Arm's-length transaction concept, 52–53
Assessments for local benefits, 250, 347
Asset Depreciation Range (ADR), 484–485
Assets. *See also* Property
  business expenses and, 202–203
  capital, 546
  classification of, 546
  defined, 435
  depreciable vs. nondepreciable, 491
  determining amount invested, 445–447
  goodwill and, 448–449
  improvements, 204
  intangible, 510–512
  mixed-use, 197–198, 437
  ordinary income, 546
  personal use, 546
  purchase of, 445–451
    bargain purchase, 447
    business, 448–450
    constructed assets, 451
    corporate stock, 450–451
    multiple assets, 447–448
  replacement, 204
  Section 1231, 546
  transfers of assets to controlled corporation, 462–463

Assignment-of-income doctrine, 57–58, 97
Associated with, meals and entertainment
    expenses, 234–235
At-risk rules, 285–287
    nonrecourse debt, 286
Audit process, 707–710
    administrative appeals, 709–710
    correspondence examination, 708
    discriminant function system, 708
    document perfection program, 708
    field examinations, 709
    information-matching program, 708
    office examinations, 708
    settlement procedures, 709
    special audit programs, 708
    taxpayer compliance measurement
        program, 708
    tax return selection processes, 708
Automobile expenses, 237–239
    actual cost method, 238–239
    adequate record keeping, 507
    business-related travel defined, 237
    depreciations deduction, 492
    limitations on, 506–507
    Section 179 and, 488, 506
    standard mileage rate method, 238
    substantiation requirement, 242
Average cost method, 650–651
Average tax rate, 7
    defined, 8
Awards, 103

B

Bad debts, 245–247
    accounting method and, 246
    business, 245–248
    nonbusiness, 245, 247, 248
    specific charge-off method, 246–247
    summary of, 248
Bankruptcy, 163
Bargain purchases
    basis of, 400, 447
    employee discounts, 154–155
    as imputed income, 113–114
Basis, 63, 71
    adjusted, 72, 439, 440, 492
    in bargain purchases, 447
    in conduit entities, 442–443
    decrease in, 440–442
    defined, 187
    depreciable, 492
    increases in, 439–440
    initial, 438, 445
    multiple asset purchase, 447–448
    in partnerships, 407–409, 412
    of property, 436
        acquired by gift, 452–454
        acquired by inheritance, 454–457
        acquired from spouse, 457–458
        personal use converted to business
            use, 458–460

in S corporations, 407–409, 417
in securities, 460–464
    stock dividends, 461–462
    taxable stock dividends, 462
    transfers of assets to controlled
        corporation, 462–463
    wash sale, 463–464
split basis rule
    for business property, 459–460
    for loss property, 453–454
subject to cost recovery, 492
summary of rules for, 466–467
Below market-rate loans, 109–113
Betterment, 204
Blue book, 691
Boot
    defined, 596
    effect of on like-kind exchanges, 601–604
Brother-sister relationship, 400–401
Business
    defined, 193
    purchase of, 448–450
        assets of, 448–450
        corporate stock of, 450–451
Business bad debt, 245–247
Business casualty gain, 301
Business casualty loss, 299–303
Business expenses, 68–69, 185–217, 232–258
    all-events test, 211–212
    automobile expenses, 237–239
    bad debts, 245–247
    business gifts, 241
    business purpose concept, 186
    compensation of employees, 243–245
    defined, 186, 193
    economic performance test, 212–214
    education expenses, 242–243
    insurance expense, 248
    legal fees, 251
    limited mixed-use expenses, 251–258
        hobby expenses, 252–253
        home office, 256–258
        vacation home, 254–256
    meal and entertainment, 233–237
    mixed-use assets, 197–198
    mixed-use expenditures, 198–199
    profit-motivated expenditures, 191–192
    reimbursed employee, 335–338
    rental activity, 195–196
    reporting deductions, 188–191
        conduit entities, 189–191
    substantiation requirements, 242
    taxes, 249–250
    tests for deductibility, 199–208
        expenditures must be for taxpayer's
            benefit, 208
        illegal business expenses, 206
        lobbying expenses and other political
            activities, 206–207
        necessary expense, 200–201
        not a capital expenditure, 202–205
        not a personal expense, 201–202

    not frustrate public policy, 205–207
    not related to tax-exempt income,
        207–208
    ordinary expense, 199–200
    reasonable in amount, 201
    repair-and-maintenance expense, 204
    start-up costs, 204–205
    timing of, effect of accounting method
        accrual method, 211–214
        cash method, 209–211
        financial and taxable income
            differences, 215–217
        related party accrued expenses, 215
        travel expenses, 239–241
Business gifts, 145
    substantiation requirements, 242
Business property
    fully destroyed, 299–301
    partially destroyed, 301–303
    personal use property converted to,
        458–460
        general rule for basis, 459
        split basis rule, 459–460
Business purpose concept, 68–71, 186
    dominant profit-motive requirement, 192
Business purpose tax year, 641
Business tax credits, 652–656
    foreign tax credit, 652–654
    investment tax credit, 652
    rehabilitation tax credit, 655–656
    research and experimental credit,
        654–655
    summary of, 653

C

Cafeteria plan, 156
Capital asset, 546
    defined, 62–63, 114, 303, 550
    holding period, 115
Capital expenditure, 202–205
    defined, 71, 202, 435
Capital gains, 63, 549–561
    conduit entities, 118–119
    exclusion on qualified small business
        stock, 555–556
    history of taxation of, 115, 549–550
    holding period, 115
    involuntary conversion, 608
    legislative grace concept and, 61
    long-term, 115
        vs. short-term, 550–551
    netting procedure for, 115–117, 551–556
    planning strategies, 556–557
    short-term, 115, 551–552
    tax treatment of, 117
    treatment of, 553–554
Capital losses, 63, 303–304, 549–561
    bad debt, 245
    conduit entities, 118–119
    corporations and, 304, 394–395
    history of taxation of, 115, 549–550

holding period, 115
of individuals, 303–304
legislative grace concept and, 61
long-term, 115
    vs. short-term, 550–551
netting procedure for, 115–117, 551–556
planning strategies, 557–561
    basis of securities sold, 560–561
    short sales, 557–559
    worthless securities, 559–560
rental real estate, 196
short-term, 115, 551–552
tax treatment of, 117–118
treatment of, 553–554
Capital recovery concept, 63, 71–73, 435–436, 442. See also Amortization; Depletion; Depreciation
Carryback, 281–282
Carryforward, 281–282
Carryover basis, 295, 445
    for divorce, 458
    received from spouse, 458
Cash basis accounting method, 58, 119–121
    bad debt and, 246
    exceptions to income recognition, 120–121
    original issue discount securities, 120–121
    related party accrued expenses, 215
    restrictions on use of, 643–644
    savings bonds, 121
    timing of deductions and, 219–221
Cash-equivalent approach, 97–98
Casualty, defined, 299
Casualty gain, 301
Casualty losses, 299
    annual personal casualty loss limitation, 308–309
C corporations, change from to S corporations to, 416
Centralized management, 385
Certainty, defined, 6
Charitable contributions, 28, 350–352
    corporations and, 395–396
    donated inventory, 396
    examples of, 351
    fiduciaries and, 404
    property and, 350
    summary of rules for, 351
Chief counsel's memoranda, 693
Child and dependent care credit, 155, 658–660
Children
    as employees, 390–391
    in sole proprietorship, 410
Child support payments, 61, 107
    disguising as alimony, 108
Citators, 699–700
Cited case, 699
Citing case, 699
Citizen or residency test, 330–331
Claim-of-right doctrine, 64–65

vs. constructive receipt doctrine, 66–67
Class lives, 492–493
    defined, 527
Closely-held corporations,
    defined, 292
    passive activity losses, 394
Code. See Internal Revenue Code
Commerce Clearing House (CCH), 697
Compensation of employees, 243–245
    covered employee, 244
    reasonable compensation, 243–244
    related parties and, 243–244
Compensation, unreasonable, 391
Complex trust, 402
Computer-assisted tax research, 700–701
Concepts
    accounting, 54–61
    constructs and, 50
    deduction, 68–74
    defined, 50
    doctrines and, 50
    general, 50–54
    income, 61–68
Conduit entities, 384, 405–419. See also Partnerships; S corporations; Sole proprietorship
    accounting methods, 407
    accounting periods, 406–407
    basis in, 442–443
        partnerships and S corporations, 407–409
    capital gains/losses of, 118–119
    comparison of characteristics, 418
    defined, 55
    income from, 102
    income splitting, 417–419
    losses and, 408–409
    partnerships, 410–415
    reporting deduction, 189–191
    S corporations, 415–417
    sole proprietorships, 409–410
Construct, defined, 50
Constructed assets, 451
    direct construction costs, 451
    indirect construction costs, 451
Construction, long-term contracts, 124, 644–647
    lookback method, 645–647
    percentage-of-completed-contract method, 124, 644–645
Constructive ownership rules, 53
Constructive receipt doctrine, 65–66
    vs. claim-of-right doctrine, 66–67
Continuity of life, 385
Controlled groups, 400–401
    brother-sister relationship, 400–401
    parent-subsidiary relationship, 400
Convenience, defined, 6–7
Copyright, 550
Corporate distributions, 399
Corporate tax rate, schedule for, 387
Corporation/shareholder loans, 111, 112

Corporations, 385–401
    accounting methods and, 398–399
        restrictions on, 643–644
    accounting periods and, 398–399
    advantages/disadvantages of, 419
    AMT adjustment items, 663
    articles of incorporation, 385
    calculation of taxable income, 397–398
    centralized management, 385
    closely-held, 292
    continuity of life, 385
    controlled groups, 400–401
    defined, 55–56, 385
    distributions to shareholders, 399–400
    free transferability of ownership, 385
    income tax considerations
        sole proprietorship vs. corporate tax rate, 386–389
        tax rate differentials, 386–389
    limited liability and, 385
    multiple corporations, 400–401
    net capital losses, 304
    owner-employee status, 389–391
        children as employees, 390–391
        double taxation, 391
        fringe benefits, 390
        unemployment taxes, 391
        unreasonable compensation, 391
    passive loss limitations, 291–292
    personal service corporations, 389, 393–394
    purchase of stock, 450–451
    special rules for
        capital loss limitations, 394–395
        charitable contribution limitations, 395–396
        dividends-received deduction, 392–393
        organizational costs, 397
        passive activity losses, 393–394
    transfers of assets to controlled corporation, 462–463
Correspondence examinations, 708
Cost depletion, 508–509
Cost recovery. See also Depreciation
    basis subject to, 492
    Modified Accelerated Cost Recovery, 490–507
Court decisions
    all other courts except U. S. Supreme court, 698
    Supreme Court, 698
    tax court, 697–698
    tax research and, 703–704
Covered employee, 244
Cumulative Bulletin (C.B.), 697

D

Damage payments, 158
Death benefit payments, as income exclusion, 148

Debt
  acquisition, 348
  assumption of, and realized gain/loss,
      548–549
  home equity, 348
  partnership, 412–413
Declining balance, method of depreciation,
    484
Deduction concepts, 68–74
  business purpose concept, 68–71
  capital recovery concept, 71–73
  legislative grace concept, 68
  summary of, 74
Deductions. See also Business expenses
  classification of business
      production of income, 194–195
      profit-motivated, 191–192
      trade or business, 192–194
  defined, 21
  exemptions, 21
  expenses, 21
  itemized, 27, 70, 189
  vs. losses, 21, 278
  mixed-use expenditures, 198–199
  personal expenditures, 197
  rental activity, 195–197
  reporting, 188–191
  restrictions on, 185
  standard, 27
  timing of, 30–33
      effect of accounting method and,
          208–214
Deductions for adjusted gross income, 188,
    334–342
  moving expenses, 341–342
  reimbursed employee business expenses,
      335–338
  rental activity, 196
  retirement plan contribution deductions,
      339–341
  for self-employed taxpayers, 338–339
Deductions from adjusted gross income,
    27–29, 188–189, 342–354
  itemized deductions, 343–354
      charitable contributions, 350–352
      interest expense, 347–349
      medical expenses, 344–346
      miscellaneous itemized deductions,
          352–354
      summary of, 345
      taxes, 346–347
  standard deduction, 342–343
Deferral, defined, 20
Deferred (third-party) exchange, 597–601
De minimis fringes, 155
Dependency exemption deduction, 29,
    328–329
  citizen or residency test, 330–331
  divorce and, 330
  gross income test, 329
  joint return test, 331
  relationship or membership household
      test, 330

  support test, 329–330
  standard deduction restrictions on,
      355–356
Depletion, 482, 507–510
  defined, 507
  methods, 508–510
      cost, 508–509
      percentage, 509–510
      statutory, 509–510
Depreciable basis, defined, 492
Depreciation, 203. See also Cost recovery
  defined, 482
  excess, 567
  introduction to, 482–484
  timing and, 482–484
Depreciation conventions, 495–499
  mid-month, 496–498
  mid-quarter, 496, 498–499
  mid-year, 495
Depreciation method
  Accelerated Cost Recovery System, 485
  Alterative Depreciation System, 486
  Asset Depreciation Range, 484
  declining balance, 484
  facts and circumstances, 484–485
  major changes in since 1980, 485
  Modified Accelerated Cost Recovery
      System (MACRS), 485–486, 490–507
  straight-line, 484, 499–500
  sum-of-the-years' digits, 484
Depreciation recapture
  defined, 566
  nonrecognition transaction, 595–596
  Section 1245 recapture rule, 567
  Section 1250 recapture rule, 567–570
Direct construction costs, 451
Directly related, meals and entertainment
    expenses, 234
Disability payments, 159
Discharge of indebtedness
  as income exclusion, 162–165
  qualified real property business
      indebtedness, 163–165
Discriminant function system, 708
Distribution date, 456
Dividend, defined, 399
Dividends-received deduction (DRD),
    392–393
Divorce
  alimony, 107–108
  carryover basis rule for property, 458
  child support payments, 107
  dependency exemption deduction, 330
  property settlements, 107, 108
Doctrine, defined, 50
Document perfection program, 708
Donated inventory, 396
Donative items, 143–148
  death-benefits, 148
  gifts, 144–145
  inheritances, 145
  life insurance proceeds, 145–147
  scholarships, 147–148

Double taxation, 391

E

Earned income, 96–98
  assignment-of-income doctrine, 97
  cash-equivalent approach, 97–98
Earned income credit, 657–658
Earnings and profits (E&P), defined,
    399–400
Economic income, 8
Economic performance test, 212–214
  recurring item exception, 213–214
  summary of, 212
Economic Recovery Tax Act of 1981, 485
Economy, defined, 7
Educational assistance program, 155
Education expenses, 242–243
Effective tax rate, 7
  defined, 8
Employee discounts, 154
Employer's athletic facility, 155
Employer benefit plans
  cafeteria plan, 156
  flexible benefits, 156
  as income exclusion, 155–157
  salary reduction plan, 156
Employer-provided lodging, as income
    exclusion, 153–154
Employer reimbursement plan
  accountable plan, 335–336
  nonaccountable plan, 336–338
Employment-related exclusion
  employer benefit plans, 155–157
  foreign earned income, 149
  fringe benefits, 154–155
  group term life insurance, 151–152
  health and accident insurance
      premiums, 152–153
  meals and lodging provided by
      employer, 153–154
  payments made on behalf of employee,
      149–157
  qualified pension plans, 150–151
Employment-related loans, 111, 112
Employment taxes, 12–15
  self-employment tax, 12, 14
  social security tax, 12–14
  unemployment, 14–15
Entertainment expense, 235
  reciprocal entertaining, 236
Entity concept, 54–58
  assignment-of-income doctrine, 57–58
  conduit entities, 55
  income shifting and, 57
  sole proprietorship, 56
  taxable entities, 55
Equity
  defined, 5
  horizontal, 5
  vertical, 5
Equity accounting method, 442
Estate tax, 16–18, 454

exclusions of, 17
rate for, 402
unified donative-transfers credit, 17
Estimated tax payment, pay-as-you-go
concept, 53–54
Ethics, in tax practice, 35–38
Excess depreciation, 567
Excise tax, 16
products subject to, 16
Exclusions. *See also* Income exclusions
defined, 20
Exemption deduction phase-out, 354–355
Exemptions
defined, 21
dependency, 29
personal, 29
Expenses. *See also* Business expense
defined, 21
investment, 68–69
personal, 68–69
trade or business, 68–69

F

Facts and circumstances method, 484–485
Farming business, accounting methods
and, 644
Federal estate tax, 17–18
Federal gift tax, exclusions of, 17
Federal Insurance Contribution Act
(FICA), 13
Federal Reporter, 698
Federal Supplement (F.Supp.), 698
Federal Tax Coordinator, 699
Federal Unemployment Tax (FUTA), rate
of, 14
Fiduciaries, 402–405
accounting periods, 404
AMT adjustment items, 663
charitable contributions, 404
defined, 402
estates, 402
exemption amounts, 404–405
income taxation, 403–404
calculation of, 404–405
tax rates for, 402
trusts, 402–403
Field examinations, 709
Filing requirements, 358
Filing status, 331–334
abandoned spouse, 333
head of household, 333–334
married, filing separately, 332
single, 332–333
surviving spouse, 332
Final regulations, 692
Financial accounting, vs. accounting
income, 215–217
Financial conformity rule, 651
Financial income, vs. taxable income,
215–217
First-in, first-out (FIFO) method, 560–561,
648

Fiscal year, defined, 637–638
Fixing-up expenses, 612
Flat tax, 8
Flexible benefits, 156
Foreign tax credit, 149, 652–654
Free transferability of ownership, 385
Fringe benefits
child and dependent care services, 155
de minimis fringes, 155
educational assistance program, 155
employee discounts, 154
employer's athletic facility, 155
no additional cost services, 154
owner-employee status and, 390
working-condition fringe benefit, 155
Full absorption costing method, 648
Functional use test, 609

G

Gains. *See also* Capital gains
character of from property disposition,
549
deferral of on principal residence sale,
612–614
defined, 20–21
involuntary conversion, 607–609
realized, 444, 545–549
recognized, 444, 544
Section 1231, 444, 561–565
General asset classes, 598–599
General concepts
ability-to-pay concept, 50–51
administrative convenience concept,
51–52
arm's-length transaction concept, 52–53
pay-as-you-go concept, 53–54
summary of, 74
General counsel's memoranda (GCM), 693
General Depreciation System, recovery
classes, 493
Generally accepted accounting principles
(GAAP), 20
Gift
business, 145, 241–242
defined, 144, 452
disposition by and passive activity rules,
295
as income exclusions, 144–145
property acquired by
basis of, 452–454
holding period, 454
split basis rule of loss property,
453–454
special sales price basis, 454
Gift loans, 111, 112
Gift taxes, 16–17, 452
exclusions of, 17
unified donative-transfers credit, 17
Golsen rule, 695
Goodwill, 448–449
amortization of, 510–511
Government revenues, source of, 11–12

Grantor, 402
Grantor trust, 403
Gross income, 19–20
defined, 20, 92–93
Gross income test, 329
Gross sales price, 546–547
effect of debt assumptions, 548–549
Group term life insurance, as income
exclusion, 151–152
Guaranteed payment, 411

H

Hand, Learned, 34
Hazards of litigation, 709
Head of household, 333–334
Health and accident insurance premiums,
as income exclusion, 152–153, 159–160
Hidden inflation tax, 23
Hobby expenses, 252–253
Hobby losses, 252
Holding period, 444
defined, 115
for gifts, 454
rule for determining, 551
Home equity debt, 348
Home mortgage interest, 348–349
Home office deduction, 196, 256–258
Horizontal equity, 5
H. R. 10 Plan, 339
Hybrid method of accounting, 123
restrictions on use of, 643

I

Illegal business expenses, 206
Improved real estate, 195
Improvements, 204
Improvements by lessee, as income
exclusion, 165
Imputed income, 108–114
bargain purchases, 113–114
below market-rate loans, 109–113
payment of expense by others, 113
Imputed interest rules, exceptions to,
112–113
Income. *See also* Adjusted gross income
active, 290–291
assignment-of-income doctrine, 97
cash-equivalent approach, 97–98
current view of, 95–96
defined, 19–21
derived from labor and capital, 93–94
earned income, 96–98, 121
economic, 8
foreign earned, 149
gross, 19–20, 92–93
historical view of, 92–94
imputed, 108–114
as increase in wealth, 92
ordinary, 20
passive, 291
portfolio, 290

realization of, 92, 95–96
sources of, 96–114
taxable, 20
vs. financial, 215–217
transfers from others, 102–108
unconditionally available, 65–66
unearned, 98–102
annuities, 99–101
rental and royalty, 98–99
Income concepts, 61–68
all-inclusive income concept, 61–62
capital recovery concept, 63
legislative grace concept, 62–63
realization concept, 63–67
summary of, 74
wherewithal-to-pay concept, 67–68
Income exclusions, 142–165
donative items
death-benefits, 148
gifts, 144–145
inheritances, 145
life insurance proceeds, 145–147
scholarships, 147–148
employment-related, 148–157
foreign earned income, 149
payments made on behalf of
employee, 149–157
investment-related exclusions
discharge of indebtedness, 162–165
improvement by lessee, 165
municipal bond interest, 160–161
stock dividends, 162
by IRS code section, 143
reasons for, 142
returns of human capital, 157–160
damage payments for personal injury
or sickness, 158
payment from health and accident
policies, 159–160
workers' compensation, 157
summary of, 166
Income shifting, 30, 33–34
entity concept and, 57
Income splitting, conduit entities, 417–419
Income tax
computational framework, 19
nature of, 11–12
revenues of, 11–12
Income tax credits. See Tax credits
Indirect construction costs, 451
Individual accounting treatments, 642
Individual retirement account (IRA), 150,
340–341
Individuals, taxation of, 327–358
AMT adjustment items, 663, 665
calculating tax liability, 25–29, 356–357
computational framework, 188
vs. corporate tax rate, 386–389
deductions for adjusted gross income,
26–27, 334–342
moving expenses, 341–342
reimbursed employee business
expenses, 335–338

retirement plan contribution
deductions, 339–341
for self-employed taxpayers, 338–339
deductions from adjusted gross income,
27–29, 342–354
itemized deductions, 343–354
standard deduction, 342–343
dependency exemption deduction,
328–329
restrictions on, 355–356
exemption deduction phase-out, 354–355
filing requirements, 358
filing status, 331–334
itemized deduction phase-out, 354
kiddie tax, 357
net capital losses, 303–304
personal exemption deduction, 328
summary of calculating, 328
Individual tax credits, 656–660
child and dependent care credit, 658–660
earned income credit, 657–658
purpose of, 656
summary of, 656
Information-matching program, 708
Inherited property, 145
alternate valuation date, 455
basis of, 454–457
distribution date, 456
estate tax, 454
as income exclusion, 145
other considerations, 456–457
primary valuation date, 455
In-house lobbying expenses, 207
Initial basis, 445
defined, 438
Installment sale, 123–124
of depreciable assets, 569–570
Insurance expense, as business expense,
248–249
Intangible property, 437, 510–512
amortization of, 510–511
defined, 510
excluded from, 512
Interest, 28
points, 211
prepaid, 211
Interest expense as itemized deduction,
347–349
home mortgage interest, 348–349
investment interest, 349
Interest-free loans, 109–110
exceptions to, 112–113
Interest income, 65
Internal Revenue Bulletin (I.R.B.), 697
Internal Revenue Code, 18, 687–691
citations to, 696
income exclusions by section, 143
legislative process and, 689–691
references to, 18
Revenue Procedure 87–56, 492–493
Section 61, 92
Section 162, 193
Section 170, 689

Section 179, 486–490
Section 197, 449
Section 212, 194
Section 280A, 705
Section 351 transfer, 462–463
Section 1202, 555
Section 1245, 567
Section 1250, 567–570
structure of, 687–689
subtitles of, 687
tax research and, 702–703
Internal Revenue Service
appeal to, 19, 709
tax defined by, 4–5
Interpretative regulation, 691–692
Inventories, 550
accounting methods for, 647–651
average cost method, 650–651
depreciation and, 491
determining inventory cost, 648–650
financial conformity rule, 651
first-in, first-out method, 648, 650–651
full absorption costing method, 648
inventory flow assumptions, 650–651
last-in, first-out method, 648, 650–651
lower of cost-or-market method, 649–650
specific indentification method, 650
uniform capitalization rules, 648–649
Investment expenses, 68–69, 194–195
capital gains/losses from, 101–102
defined, 349
Investment income, defined, 349
Investment interest, 349
Investment-related exclusions
discharge of indebtedness, 162–165
improvement by lessee, 165
municipal bond interest, 160–161
stock dividends, 162
Investment-related losses, 303–309
capital losses
of corporations, 304
of individuals, 303–304
personal casualty and theft losses,
307–309
on related party sales, 305–306
on small business stock, 304–305
wash sales, 306–307
Investment tax credit (ITC), 652
Involuntary conversions, 607–610
capital gain, 608
defined, 607
direct conversion, 608
functional use test, 609
gains/losses, 607–609
qualified replacement property, 609–610
replacement period, 610
Section 1231 gain, 608
Itemized deduction phase-out, 354
Itemized deductions, 27–29, 70, 189,
343–354
charitable contributions, 28, 350–352
interest, 28
interest expense, 347–349

medical expenses, 28, 344–346
miscellaneous itemized deductions, 28–29, 352–354
personal casualty and theft losses, 28
summary of, 345
taxes, 28, 346–347

J

Joint return test, 331
Judicial authority, 693–695
    appellate courts, 695
    Supreme Court, 695
    trial courts, 694

K

Keogh plan, 150, 339
Kiddie tax, 357

L

Last-in, first-out (LIFO) method, 648
Least aggregate deferral tax year, 640
Legal fees, business expense, 251
Legislative authority, 685–691
    IRS code, 687–691
    legislative process and, 689–691
    tax treaties, 691
    U. S. Constitution, 685–687
Legislative grace concept, 62–63
    deduction concepts, 68
Legislative regulation, 692
Letter rulings, 693
LEXIS, 700
Life insurance
    group term as income exclusion, 151–152
    proceeds as income exclusion, 145–147
Like class, defined, 598
Like-kind exchanges, 67, 596–606
    carryover of tax attributes, 606
    deferred (third-party) exchange, 597–601
    effect of boot, 601–604
    exchange requirement, 596
    losses and, 604
    related party exchanges, 605
Like-kind property
    defined, 598
    general asset classes, 598–599
    product class, 599
    requirements for, 598–601
    Standard Industrial Classification Manual, 599
Limited liability, 385
Limited liability companies (LLCs), 414
    characteristics of, 418
Limited liability partnerships (LLPs), 410–411, 414–415
    passive activity losses, 289
    tax shelters and, 284
Listed property
    adequate record keeping, 507
    defined, 505

limitations on, 505
    passenger autos, 506–507
Loans
    below-market rate, 109–113
    conventional, 110
    corporation/shareholder, 111, 112
    employment-related, 111, 112
    gift, 111, 112
    interest-free, 109–110
Lobbying expenses, in-house, 207
Lodging, employer-provided, 153–154
Long-term capital gains, 115, 550–551
Long-term capital losses, 115, 550–551
Long-term construction contracts, 644–647
    lookback method, 645–647
    percentage-of-completed-contract method, 644–645
        vs. completed contract methods, 645
    taxpayers exempt from, 647
Lookback method, 645–647
Lookback recapture rule, 563–564
Losses. *See also* Capital losses; specific losses
    annual, 21, 280
    at-risk rules, 285–287
    capital, 303–304
    casualty, 299
    character of from property disposition, 549
    conduit entities and, 408–409
    vs. deductions, 278
    defined, 21
    general scheme for treatment of, 279
    investment-related losses, 303–309
    involuntary conversion, 607–609
    like-kind exchanges, 604
    net operating, 280–283
    passive activity, 280, 287–289
    realized, 444, 545–549
    recognized, 444, 544
    Section 1231, 444, 561–565
    suspended, 292
    tax-shelter, 283–298
    theft, 299
    trade or business, 299–303
    transaction, 21, 279, 298–309
Loss-of-income damages, 158
Lower of cost-or-market method, 649–650
Low-income housing, 290
    as Section 1250 property, 570–571

M

MACRS. *See* Modified Accelerated Cost Recovery
Majority-interest tax year, 639
Marginal tax rate, 7
    defined, 8
Market for purchased merchandise, 649
Marriage penalty tax, 332–333
Married, filing jointly, 331–332
Married, filing separately, 332
Material participant

defined, 287
    exception, 295
    tests for, 287
Meals and entertainment expense, 233–237
    associated with, 234–235
    directly related, 234
    fully deductible, 236
    membership dues, 235
    reciprocal entertaining, 236
Meals and lodging provided by employer, as income exclusion, 153–154
Medical expenses, 28, 344–346
    for dependent, 208
Medicare Health Insurance (MHI), 339
    rate of, 13
Member of household test, 330
Mertens Law of Federal Income Taxation, 699
Mid-month convention, 496–498
Mid-quarter convention, 496, 498–499
Mid-year convention, 495
Miscellaneous itemized deductions, 28–29, 352–354
    fully deductible expenditures, 352, 353
    partially deductible expenditures, 352–354
Mixed-use assets, 197–198, 251, 437
Mixed-use expenditures, 198–199, 233, 251–258
Mixed-use property, 436–437
Modified Accelerated Cost Recovery (MACRS), 485–486, 490–507
    adequate record keeping, 507
    Alternative Depreciation System, 499–500, 504–505
    alternative minimum tax, 664
    basis subject to cost recovery, 492
    class lives, 492–494
    depreciation conventions, 495–499
    depreciation method alternatives, 499–501
    limitations on listed property, 505
    limitations on passenger autos, 506–507
    overview of, 514
    property subject to, 491–492
    recovery classes, 492–495
    recovery period, 492–495
    straight-line election, 503–504
    tables for
        classes, 493–494, 530–535
        depreciation for car placed in service after 1994, 541
        depreciation for nonresidential real property placed in service after May 1993, 497, 540
        depreciation for nonresidential real property placed in service before May 1993, 540
        depreciation for property other than real estate, 496, 536–538
        depreciation for residential rental property, 503, 539

optional straight-line MACRS
depreciation property other than
real estate, 541
using percentage tables, 501–503
Moving expenses, 341–342
distance test, 341
time test, 341–342
Multiple asset purchase, 447–448
Multiple support agreement, 330
Municipal bond interest, as income
exclusion, 160–161

N

Natural business year, 641
Natural resource
· depletion methods
cost, 508–509
percentage, 509–510
in place, 508
Net capital loss, 303
of corporations, 304
of individuals, 303–304
tax treatment of, 117–118
Net long-term capital gains, 63
tax treatment of, 117
Net operating losses (NOL), 280–283
carryback, 281–282
carryforward, 281–282
defined, 281
purchased, 283
Netting procedure, for capital gains/
losses, 551–556
90-day letter, 709
No additional cost services, 154
Nonaccountable reimbursement plans,
336–338
Nonacquiescence, 692–693
Nonbusiness bad debts, 245, 247
Nonrecognition transactions, 590–616
characteristics of, 617
commonalities of, 591–596
deferral of realized gain/loss, 591–595
depreciation recapture, 595–596
holding period, 595–596
replacement asset, 592
summary of, 592
tax attributes, 592–593
continuation of investment criteria, 591
defined, 590
involuntary conversions, 607–610
lack of wherewithal to pay, 591
like-kind exchanges, 596–606
rationale for, 591
sale of principal residence, 610–616
Nonrecourse debt, 286
Nonrefundable tax credits, 652

O

Office examinations, 708
Old Age, Survivors and Disability
Insurance (OASDI), 339
rate of, 13

Omnibus Budget Reconciliation Act
(OBRA)
lobbying expenses, 207
small business stock, 555
One-year rule for prepaid expenses, 210
One-year rule for services, 122
Ordinary expenses, 199–200
Ordinary income, defined, 20
Ordinary income assets, 546
Ordinary income loss, 62
Organizational costs of corporation, 397
Original issue discount (OID) securities,
120–121
Overall accounting methods, 642
Owner-employee status, 389–391
children as employees, 390–391
double taxation, 391
fringe benefits, 390
unemployment taxes, 391
unreasonable compensation, 391
Ownership tax year, 641

P

Parent-subsidiary relationship, 400
Partnerships, 410–415. *See also* Conduit
entities
accounting periods, 406–407
advantages/disadvantages of, 419
basis in, 407–409, 412, 442–443
characteristics of, 418
distributions, 413
guaranteed payment, 411
legal characteristics of, 410–411
limited liability companies, 414
limited liability partnerships, 414–415
partners are not employees, 411–412
partnership debt, 412–413
reporting deductions, 189–191
restrictions on accounting methods used,
643–644
Section 179 and, 487
taxable year
business purpose tax year, 641
least aggregate deferral tax year, 640
limitation on, 639–641
majority-interest tax year, 639
principal partner tax year, 640
terminations, 413–414
Passenger automobile limitation, 506–507
Passive activity, defined, 287
Passive activity loss (PAL) rules, 287
disposition of passive activities
active participation exception, 298
exceptions for rental real estate,
295–298
by gift, 295
material participation exception, 295
by sale, 293–294
upon death, 294–295
general rules for, 292
suspended loss, 292
taxpayers subject to limits, 291–292

types of income, 290–291
Passive activity losses, 280, 287–298
closely-held corporations, 394
limited partnership interests, 289
low-income housing projects, 290
personal service corporations, 393–394
rental activities and, 288–289
working interest in oil and gas, 290
Passive income, 291
Pay-as-you-go concept, 7
Payment of expenses by others, as
imputed income, 113
Pension plans, qualified, 150–151
Percentage depletion, 509–510
Percentage-of-completed contract method,
124, 644–645
Per-diem payments, 335
Personal casualty losses, 28, 307–309
limitations on, 308–309
measuring, 308
statutory floor, 308
Personal exemption deduction, 29, 328
Personal expenditures, 68–69, 197
vs. business expense, 201–202
Personal injury, 158
Personal itemized deductions, 197
Personal property, 15, 437
Personal service corporations, 389, 393–394
Personalty, 437
Personal use assets, 546
Personal use property, 436
converted to business use, 458–460
general rule for basis, 459
split basis rule, 459–460
Points, 211, 348
Portfolio income, 290
Prepaid expenses
one-year rule for, 210
recurring item exception, 214
Present value tables, 31
Primary authorities, 18
administrative authority, 691–693
citations to, 18, 695–698
code and regulation, 696
committee reports, 695–696
court decisions, 697–698
other IRS pronouncements, 697
defined, 685
judicial authority, 693–695
legislative authority, 685–691
Primary valuation date, 455
Principal partner tax year, 640
Principal residence
adjusted sales price, 612
deferral of gain, 612–614
defined, 610–611
gain exclusion requirement, 614–615
interaction of deferral and exclusion
provisions, 616–617
one-time exclusion of gain, 615–616
replacement period, 611–612
sale of, 610–616
taxpayers older than 55, 614–616

Private activity bond, 668
Private letter ruling (LTR), 693
Prizes, 103
Production of income expenses, 194–195
    defined, 194
Profit-motivated expenditures, 191–192
Progressive tax rate structure
    ability-to-pay concept, 51
    defined, 9–11
Pronouncement, tax research and, 703
Property. *See also* Assets; Business
        property
    assessed value of, 15
    basis of, 436
        acquired by gift, 452–454
        acquired by inheritance, 454–457
        acquired from spouse, 457–458
        adjusted, 439, 440
        decreases in, 440–442
        increases in, 439–440
        initial, 438, 445
        personal use property converted to
            business use, 458–460
    as charitable contribution, 350
    classes of, 436–437
        intangible, 437
        mixed-use, 436–437
        personalty, 437
        personal use, 436
        real estate, 437
        summary of, 438
        tangible, 437
    defined, 435
    improvements by lessee, 165
    intangible, 510–512
    investment cycle of, 437–445
    like-kind, 598–601
    listed, 505–507
    Modified Accelerated Cost Recovery
        and, 491–492
    personal, 15
    purchase of, 445–451
    real, 15
    real property tax year, 447
    Section 179 and, 486–487
    Section 1231, 561–565
    Section, 1245, 570–571
    Section 1250, 570–571
    with no class life, 528
Property disposition, 444–445, 543–571
    amount realized, 444, 546–547
    capital gains/losses, 101–102, 549–561
        long-term vs. short-term class, 550–551
        netting procedure, 551–556
        planning strategies, 556–561
        treatment of, 553–554
    carryover basis, 445
    character of gain/loss, 549
    depreciation recapture, 565–571
    effect of debt assumptions, 548–549
    gross sales price, 546–547
    holding period, 444
    introduction to, 543–545

passive activity loss (PAL) rules,
        292–295
    realized gain/loss, 444, 545–549
    of rental property, 565
    Section 1231 gain/losses, 444, 561–565
    steps in analysis of, 543–545
    summary of process, 572
Property settlements, 107, 108
Property taxes, 447
    as itemized deduction, 347
    nature of, 15–16
    personal property, 15
    real property, 15
Proportional rate structure, defined, 8–9
Proposed regulations, 692
Protest letter, 709
Publicly-held corporations, passive loss
        limitations, 291
Punitive damages, 158

Q

Qualified home mortgage interest, 348–349
Qualified pension plans, 101
    as income deferral, 150–151
Qualified real property business
        indebtedness, 163–165

R

Real estate, 437
    depreciation convention and, 498
    improved, 195–196
    MACRS
        recovery period, 501
        tables and, 502–503
    real property tax year, 447
    unimproved, 195–196
Real estate tax, as business expense, 250
Realistic possibility standard, 36
Realization concept, 63–67
    claim-of-right doctrine, 64–67
    constructive receipt doctrine, 65–67
    of income, 92, 95–96
Realized gain, 444, 545–549
    amount realized, 546–547
Realized loss, 444, 545–549
    effect of debt assumption, 548–549
Real property, 15, 437
Real property tax year, 447
Real property trade or business, defined,
        297
Reasonable compensation, 243–244
Reasonable expenses, 201
Reciprocal entertaining, 236
Recognized gain/loss, 444, 544
Recurring item exception, 213–214
Refundable tax credits, 652
Regressive tax rate structure, defined, 9–10
Rehabilitation tax credit, 655–656
Reimbursed employee business expenses,
        335–338

accountable reimbursement plans,
        335–336
    nonaccountable reimbursement plans,
        336–338
Related party
    accrued expenses, 215
    defined, 215
    investment-related losses and, 305–306
    like-kind exchange, 605
    provisions, 52–53
    reasonable compensation, 243–244
    relationships, 52–53
Relationship or member of household test,
        330
Remainderman, 402
Rental activity, 195–197
    all the facts and circumstances,
        195–196
    defined, 288
    passive activity losses, 288–289
Rental income, 98–99
Rental property, disposition of, 565
Rental real estate
    active participation exception, 298
    determining if active or passive, 296
    PAL rule exceptions for, 295–298
Repair-and-maintenance expense, 204
Replacement asset, 204, 592–593
Replacement period, of principal
        residence, 611–612
Replacement property
    functional use test, 609
    involuntary conversion, 609
Reporter, 697
Reports of the United States Tax Court,
        (T.C.), 697
Research and experimental credit, 203,
        654–655
Research Institute of America (RIA), 697
Residence, defined, 348
Residency test, 330–331
Retirement plan contribution deductions,
        339–341
Returns, tax
    amended, 25
    filing, 24–25
Returns of human capital, 157–160
    damage payments for personal injury or
        sickness, 158
    payment from health and accident
        policies, 159–160
    workers' compensation, 157
Revenue agent's report, 709
Revenue Procedure 83–35, 527–528
Revenue Procedure 87–56, 492–493
    class lives and recovery periods,
        528–529
    general rules of application, 527–528
    purpose, 527
Revenue procedures, 692
Revenue rulings, 692
Reversionary interest, 402–403
Royalty income, 98–99

S

Salary reduction plan, 156
Sale of principal residence, 610–616
　adjusted sales price, 612
　deferral of gain, 612–614
　defined, 610–611
　gain exclusion requirement, 614–615
　interaction of deferral and exclusion
　　provisions, 616–617
　one-time exclusion of gain, 615–616
　replacement period, 611–612
　taxpayers older than 55, 614–616
Sales tax
　business expense, 250
　nature of, 15
Savings bonds, 121
Scholarships, 147–148
S corporations, 415–417. See also Conduit
　entities
　accounting periods, 406–407
　advantages/disadvantages of, 419
　basis in, 407–409, 442–443
　change from C corporation to, 416
　characteristics of, 418
　defined, 55
　distributions and basis adjustment, 417
　employee status of stockholders, 416–417
　qualification requirements, 415
　reporting deductions, 189–191
　revocation of S election, 416
　Section 179 and, 487
　taxable year
　　limitations on, 641–642
　　natural business year, 641
　　ownership tax year, 641
Secondary authorities, 19, 698–701
　citators, 699–700
　computer-assisted tax research, 700–701
　defined, 685
　tax periodicals, 700
　tax services, 698–699
Section 61 of IRS code, 92
Section 162 of IRS code, 193
Section 170 of IRS code, subdivisions of,
　689
Section 179 of IRS code, 486–490
　automobile expenses and, 506
　limitations on deduction, 487–490
　　active trade or business income limit,
　　489–490
　　annual deduction limit, 487–489
　　annual investment limit, 489
　qualified property, 486–487
　qualified taxpayers, 486
Section 197 of IRS code, 449
　intangible assets, 510–511
Section 212 of IRS code, 194
Section 280A of IRS code, 705
Section 351 transfer of IRS code, 462–463
Section 1202 of IRS code, 555
Section 1231 of IRS code
　dispositions of rental activities, 565

　gains and losses, 561–565
　importance of, capital gain relief,
　　564–565
　involuntary conversion, 608
　lookback recapture rule, 563–564
　netting procedure, 561–565
　property defined, 561
Section 1231 property, 546, 549
Section 1245 property, 566, 570–571
　like-kind exchanges, 606
　recapture rules, 566
Section 1250 property, 566, 570–571
　installment sales of depreciable assets,
　　569–570
　like-kind exchanges, 606
　recapture rules, 566
Securities. See also Stocks
　active investor, 193–194
　active trader, 194
　basis in, 560–561
　　stock dividends, 461–462
　　taxable stock dividends, 462
　　transfers of assets to controlled
　　　corporation, 462–463
　　wash sale, 463–464
　commission paid, 203–204
　first-in, first-out order, 560–561
　purchase of corporate stock, 450–451
　short sales, 557–559
　worthless, 559–560
Securities dealer, 194
Self-dealing, related party provision and,
　52–53
Self-employed taxpayers, deductions for,
　338–339
Self-employment tax, 12, 14, 338–339
Self-insured medical plan, as income
　exclusion, 152–153
Settlement procedures, 709
Short sale, 557–559
　closing, 557
　defined, 557
Short sale against the box, 557–559
Short-term capital gain/loss, 115, 551–552
Sic codes. See Standard Industrial
　Classification Manual (SIC Code)
Simple trust, 402
Single, 332–333
Small business stock
　capital gain exclusion on, 555–556
　defined, 305
　losses on, 304–305
Smith, Adam, 5
Social Security benefits, as taxable income,
　103–107
Social Security taxes, nature of, 12–14
Soil and water conservation expenditures,
　203
Sole proprietors, characteristics of, 418
Sole proprietorships, 56, 409–410. See also
　Conduit entities
　compared to corporate tax rate, 386–389
　employment of children, 410

Special audit programs, 708
Specific charge-off method, bad debt
　deduction, 246–247
Specific identification method, 650
Split basis rules
　for gifts, 453–454
　for business property, 459–460
Standard deduction, 342–343
　administrative convenience concept, 51
　age and, 342–343
　amounts for, 343
　blindness and, 342–343
　defined, 27
Standard Federal Tax Reporter, 699
Standard Industrial Classification Manual
　(SIC Codes)
　2451 mobile homes, 632
　3523 farm machinery and equipment,
　　633–634
　3531 construction machinery and
　　equipment, 600, 621–622
　3537 industrial trucks, tractors, trailers
　　and stackers, 632
　3546 power-driven handtools, 632
　43553 woodworking machinery, 634
　43589 service industry mashinery, not
　　elsewhere classified, 632
　3711 motor vehicles and passenger car
　　bodies, 600, 621
　defined, 599
Standard mileage rate method, automobile
　expense, 238
Start-up costs, 204–205
Statements on Responsibilities in Tax
　Practices, 36–38
Statute of limitations, 24–25
Statutory authority. See Legislative
　authority
Statutory depletion, 509–510
Statutory floor, 308
Statutory notice of deficiency, 709
Stock dividends
　basis in, 461–462
　as income exclusion, 162
　taxable stock dividends, 462
Stocks See also Securities
　capital gain exclusion on qualified small
　　business stock, 555–556
　purchase of corporate stock, 450–451
　Section 351 transfer, 462–463
　transfers of assets to controlled
　　corporation, 462–463
　wash sale, 463–464
Straight-line method, 484, 499–501,
　503–504
Substance-over-form doctrine, 60–61
Substantiation requirements, 242
Sum-of-the-years' digits, method of
　depreciation, 484
Support test, 329–330
　multiple support agreement, 330
Supreme Court, 695
　decisions by, 698

Supreme Court Reports, 698
Surviving spouse, 332
Suspended loss, 292

T

Tangible property, 437
  Modified Accelerated Cost Recovery
    and, 491
Taxable entities, defined, 55
Taxable income, 20
  defined, 7
  vs. financial income, 215–217
Taxable year
  business purpose tax year, 641
  calendar year, 637
  defined, 637
  fiscal year, 637–638
  least aggregate deferral tax year, 640
  limitations on choice, 639–642
    partnership limitations, 639–641
    S corporation limitations, 641–642
  majority-interest tax year, 639
  natural business year, 641
  ownership tax year, 641
  principal partner tax year, 640
Tax accounting, vs. financial accounting
    income, 215–217
Tax avoidance, defined, 34
Tax base, 20
  defined, 7
Tax benefit rule, 59
Tax compliance, vs. tax planning, 701
Tax court, decisions of, 697–698
Tax Court Memorandum Decisions, 694, 697
Tax Court regular decisions, 694
Tax Court Reporter, 697
Tax credits
  alternative minimum tax, 668–670
  business tax credits, 652–656
    foreign tax credit, 652–654
    investment tax credit, 652
    rehabilitation tax credit, 655–656
    research and experimental credit,
      654–655
    summary of, 653
  defined, 24
  individuals tax credits, 656–660
    child and dependent care credit,
      658–660
    earned income credit, 657–658
    nonrefundable, 652
    refundable, 652
Taxes
  ad valorem, 15
  as business expense, 249–250
  computing, 7
  defined, 3–5
  employment, 12–15
  estate, 16–18
  evaluation of
    certainty, 6
    convenience, 6–7

economy, 7
  equity, 5–6
  excise, 16, 16
  flat, 8
  gift, 16–17
  income, 11–12
  as itemized deduction, 28, 346–347
  prepaid, 210
  property, 15–16
  purpose of, 3
  sales, 15
  self-employment, 12, 14
  social security, 12–14
  types of, 11–18
  unemployment, 14–15
  wealth transfer, 16–18
Tax evasion
  defined, 34
  elements of, 34–35
Tax guides, 699
Tax home, 239
Tax law
  legislative process for, 689–691
  primary sources of, 18
  secondary sources, 19
Tax management Portfolios, 699
Taxpayer compliance measurement
    program, 708
Tax periodicals, 700
Tax planning, 29–35
  alternative minimum tax, 670–671
  income shifting, 30, 33–34
  marginal tax rate considerations, 33
  mechanics of, 29–34
  vs. tax compliance, 701
  tax evasion vs. tax avoidance, 34–35
  time value of money, 32
  timing income and deductions, 30–33
  summary of, 33
Tax practice
  ethical considerations in, 35–38
  penalties for preparers, 36
  Statements on Responsibilities in Tax
    Practices, 36–38
Tax preference items, 660–661
Tax prepayments, 23–24
Tax rates
  average, 7–8
  defined, 7–8
  effective, 7–8
  individuals vs. corporations, 386–389
  marginal, 7–8
  1996 schedules, 21–22
Tax rate structures
  defined, 8–11
  progressive, 9–11
  proportional, 8–9
  regressive, 9–10
Tax research, 685–710
  comprehensive research example,
    704–707
  computer-assisted, 700–701
  court decisions, 703–704

defined, 685, 701
  IRS code and Treasury regulations,
    702–703
  primary authority, 685–698
  pronouncement, 703
  secondary authority, 685, 698–701
  step 1: establish facts and determine
    issues, 701–702
  step 2: locate relevant authorities, 702
  step 3: assess importance of authorities,
    702–704
  step 4: reach conclusions, make
    recommendations and communicate
    results, 704
  tax compliance vs. tax planning, 701
Tax return preparers
  I. R. C. violations with penalties for, 36
  Statements on Responsibilities in Tax
    Practices, 36–38
Tax revenue, sources of federal, 11–12
Tax services, 698–699
Tax shelter
  at-risk rules, 285–287
  defined, 283
  history of, 284
  limited partnership, 284, 289
  losses, 283–298
  passive activity losses, 287–298
  restrictions on accounting methods used,
    643–644
Tax treaties, 691
Technical advice memorandum (TAM),
    693
Technical memoranda (TM), 693
Temporary regulations, 692
10-percent luxury tax, 16
Testamentary trust, 402
Theft losses, 28, 299, 307–309
  annual personal casualty loss limitation,
    308–309
  measuring, 308
30-day letter, 709
Time value of money, 32
Trade or business expenses, 68–69. *See also*
    Business expenses
  defined, 193
Trade or business losses, 299–303
  business casualty, 299
  business property partially destroyed,
    301–303
  theft losses, 299
Transaction losses, 279, 298–309
  business property fully destroyed,
    299–301
  defined, 21
  investment-related losses, 303–309
  trade or business losses, 299–303
  treatment of, summary, 300
Transfer income
  alimony, 107–108
  prices and awards, 103
  Social Security benefits, 103–107
  unemployment compensation, 103

Travel expense, 239–241
  overnight test, 239
  substantiation requirement, 242
Treasury regulations, 18, 691–692
  citations to, 696
  final regulations, 692
  interpretative regulation, 691–692
  legislative regulation, 692
  proposed regulations, 692
  tax research and, 702–703
  temporary regulations, 692
Trial courts, 694
Trustee, 402
Trusts, 402–403
  complex, 402
  as conduit entity, 55
  grantor, 403
  revisionary interest, 402–403
  simple, 402
  tax rate for, 402–403

U

U. S. Constitution, 685–687

U. S. Court of Appeals for the Federal
    Circuit, 694, 695
U. S. Court of Federal Claims, 694
U. S. District Court, 694
U. S. Supreme Court, 695
U. S. Tax Court, 694
Unearned income
  annuities, 99–101
  calculation of gain/loss on sale of
    investment, 101–102
  conduit entities, 102
  rental and royalty income, 98–99
Unemployment compensation, 103
Unemployment tax, 14–15, 391
Uniform capitalization (unicap) rules,
    648–649
Unimproved real estate, 195–196
United States Reports, 698
United States Tax Reporter, 699
Unreasonable compensation, 391

V

Vacation home expenses, 254–256

  summary of tests for, 254
Vacation pay, 216
Vertical equity, 5

W

Waiver of restrictions on assessment (Form
    870), 709
Warranty repair allowances, 216
Wash sale, 306–307
  stock basis, 463–464
Wealth of Nations, The (Smith), 5
Wealth transfer tax, 16–18
WESTLAW, 700
Wherewithal-to-pay concept, 67–68
Withholding provisions, pay-as-you-go
    concept, 53–54
Workers' compensation, as income
    exclusion, 157
Working-condition fringe benefit, 155
Working interest in oil and gas, 290
Worthless securities, 559–560